D0203185

THE FACTS ON FILE
COMPANION TO

THE BRITISH NOVEL

VOLUME I
Beginnings through the 19th Century

THE FACTS ON FILE
COMPANION TO

THE BRITISH NOVEL

VOLUME I
Beginnings through the 19th Century

VIRGINIA BRACKETT

☑®
Facts On File, Inc.

The Facts On File Companion to the British Novel, Volume I: Beginnings through the 19th Century

Facts On File, Inc.
132 West 31st Street
New York NY 10001

Library of Congress Cataloging-in-Publication Data

Brackett, Virginia and Victoria Gaydosik
 The Facts On File Companion to the British Novel/Virginia Brackett and Victoria Gaydosik
  p. cm.
 v.1. Beginnings through the 19th Century/Virginia Brackett—v.2. 20th Century/Victoria Gaydosik
 Includes bibliographical references and indexes.
 ISBN 0-8160-6377-X (set: hardcover: alk. paper)—ISBN 0-8160-5133-X (v.1: alk. paper)—ISBN 0-8160-5254-9 (v.2: alk. paper)
 1. English fiction—18th century—History and criticism—Handbooks, manuals, etc. 2. English fiction—19th century—History and criticism—Handbooks, manuals, etc. I. Brackett, Virginia. II. Gaydosik, Victoria.
 PR821.F2 2005
 823'.509 22   2004020914

Facts On File books are available at special discounts when purchased in bulk quantities for businesses, associations, institutions, or sales promotions. Please call our Special Sales Department in New York at (212) 967-8800 or (800) 322-8755.

You can find Facts On File on the World Wide Web at http://www.factsonfile.com

Text design adapted by James Scotto-Lavino
Cover design by Cathy Rincon

Printed in the United States of America

VB FOF 10 9 8 7 6 5 4 3 2 1

This book is printed on acid-free paper.

CONTENTS

FOREWORD

The Facts On File Companion to the British Novel is a comprehensive reference for students, instructors, and aficionados of the novel. Tracing the development in English of the genre, this two-volume companion considers everything from the British works of the late 1600s that prefigured the novel to British novels published through the end of the 20th century. The wide scope of the companion allows the inclusion of all major writers of the English, Welsh, Irish, and Scottish traditions, in addition to important writers from countries of the British Commonwealth, as well as many minor, or "second tier," writers. Entries on all these writers' most important and interesting works are also included. Thematic entries help readers better grasp concepts connected to the novel, such as the narrative elements of fiction, as well as various critical approaches—from formalism to feminism—used to interpret and analyze fiction. Cross-references are indicated by SMALL CAPITAL LETTERS and can help readers easily locate additional information relating to specific works, authors, or concepts.

While the authors of each volume have followed a similar prescribed format, each remains solely responsible for her volume. The two volumes perfectly complement each other, with the second volume extending the discussion regarding the development of an art form that began more than 300 years ago. The thorough consideration of this magnificent genre allows readers to trace its evolution into the enduringly popular form that continues to capture the reader's imagination.

Virginia Brackett
Victoria Gaydosik

PREFACE

When approached with the idea of developing a study guide for the pre-1900 British novel, I enthusiastically embraced the idea, notwithstanding the enormity of the challenge such a two-year research and writing project would surely present. With my background and publication in 18th-century literature, women writers, children's literature, and the classical romance tradition, along with years of teaching the fiction I would write about, I felt I possessed at least the minimal knowledge and research skills to take on such a task. It has proven greatly satisfying. Not only could I spend all my hours outside my day job living in centuries past, immersed in fiction, I greatly benefited from the reminder that the novel remains a fairly new genre. It did not suddenly spring, fully formed, from the heads of poetry and drama, its unquestioned parents, but instead passed through a sometimes painful nascence, on to toddlerdom, and into awkward adolescence before finally standing on its own as a distinctive recognizable literary genre. Its development reflects, like all literature, vast influences, including those social, political, religious, ethnic, and nationalistic, as does the human nature on which it dwells.

As I considered the overall results likely to come from the project, I first of all did not judge that anyone could benefit much from one more summary of Henry Fielding's *Tom Jones, the History of a Foundling* (1749) or Jane Austen's *Emma* (1816) or Robert Louis Stevenson's *The Strange Case of Dr Jekyll and Mr Hyde* (1886).

Instead, I sought along with plot summaries to link each entry to at least one other in the collection, perhaps to a novel or novelist not nearly so well known, along the continuum that represents the novel's development. My hope was to demonstrate their unquestionable dependence upon one another, even if that dependence be represented in a countermovement, taking as an example George Meredith's work, which resulted in large part from his abhorrence of the sensation fiction produced by Mrs. Henry Wood, Charles Reade, Wilkie Collins, and others. Discovering what seminal novelists read as they wrote seemed of inestimable importance. A second factor I desired to work into entries were quotations from the works, especially those not enjoyed by a wide audience, in order to allow their authors to represent the novels with original wording. Finally, I planned to include more information on works often dismissed or perhaps only mentioned or alluded to in a brief paragraph by other encyclopedias, dictionaries, and guides I myself had used. In some instances, that proved impossible, due to difficulty in procuring the works themselves, but in others, such as Charlotte Smith's *Emmeline, or The Orphan of the Castle* (1788) or Thomas Trollope's admittedly forgettable *A Siren* (1870), the pleasure of enjoying and writing about such little-known works proved immense.

An additional pleasure derived from any project the size of this involves working with others who performed research for my entries, as did Lisa Meredith Lamb, or contributed to the writing of biographies on some of the euphemistically termed "lesser novelists," as did Shandra Meredith Chapman. Kay McAfee wrote entries on most of the periodicals, which proved so crucial to prepublication of early novels, and Ralph York Erwin wrote the entries on Daniel Defoe and his *Robinson Crusoe*. I am also grateful to my colleagues Victoria Gaydosik for her entries on George Eliot and her *Adam Bede, Daniel Deronda, Middlemarch,* and *The Mill on the Floss*; to Lynda Thompson for entries on Thomas Hardy and his *Tess of the d'Urbervilles* and Charlotte Brontë's *Jane Eyre*; to Michael Flaherty for the entries on Laurence Sterne and his *Tristram Shandy*; and to Shu-Dong Chen for the basis for my entries on Henry James and his *The Americans, The Europeans,* and *Daisy Miller.* I also owe a debt of gratitude to the librarians, specifically at Triton College, as well as all of those unseen librarians who so diligently support the intricate process of interlibrary loan at Triton's many sister institutions, for their inestimable contribution to this project; I literally could not have completed it without their efforts. Finally, as always I must thank my husband, Edmund, for his patience during my months of distraction; whatever may be his honest feelings toward my various writing projects, he has come to embrace them as an inevitable part of his world.

Virginia Brackett

INTRODUCTION

By necessity, any study of any literature of any culture produced over more than two centuries represents an overview of that culture's history. Nothing could be truer of a study of the 18th- and 19th-century British novel. Assign to that study the descriptive term "Companion," and one understands that it represents a challenging but pleasant walk, better accomplished with a bit of guidance, down a not-necessarily-linear historical path, eventually moving a reader from point A to point Z, albeit with various pauses and even back-steps along the journey. Because critics agree that the 18th century represented the age of definition for the English-language novel, and that most novels reflect social, political, ethnic, national, gender, and racial issues of the eras in which they are written, one must acknowledge the intimacy with which novels reflect their points of origin. A curious traveler need only step into the rare-books collection room of the British Library to note the celebration in literature of crucial stages of Great Britain's history. In a few steps, an onlooker moves past glass cases enshrining manu-scripts such as Charlotte Brontë's *Jane Eyre,* open to the page on which Mr. Rochester proposes to Jane; Jane Austen's *Persuasion,* along with her writing desk and eyeglasses; Charles Dickens's *David Copperfield;* Lewis Carroll's *Alice in Wonderland;* George Eliot's *Middlemarch;* Laurence Sterne's *A Sentimental Journey*— the collection represents a dizzying parade through 19th-century English fiction. A walk about historic

London finds visitors standing before buildings marked by uniformly fashioned medallions that declare important historic landmarks, many of them literary in nature, such as one of the houses in which Charles Dickens lived. Poet's Corner in Westminster Abbey memorializes within an edifice also honoring kings, queens, and princes, novelists, including George Eliot, Henry James, Lewis Carroll, Anthony Trollope, Samuel Johnson, Jane Austen, Sir Walter Scott, Thomas Hardy, Rudyard Kipling, Charles Dickens, and the Brontë sisters. Novelists remain as much a part of Great Britain's national identity as its long succession of monarchs. Both mythology and history, as we are taught from an early age, grew from an oral tradition that, after a time, conflated the two approaches to pro-duce fiction. Eventually, what had been brief, or short, stories expanded into book-length works.

Exactly what differentiates a novel from a short story is immediately evident—its length and physical bulk. But other characteristics are also important. A novel contains more action than a short story and may take its time working through that action, allowing greater development of characters and the conflict they face. But what of the unity of structure and illusion of reali-ty modern readers expect in the well-wrought novel? At what point did writers of book-length fiction under-stand those aspects as necessities? A consensus for what the novel required was not reached until well into the 18th century, and the discussion by those participating in writing often became part of their work. While Samuel Richardson in what was long touted as the first epistolary fiction, *Pamela* (1740), silently allowed its structure in correspondence to lend it form, Henry Fielding overtly and candidly discussed his development of form with his readers throughout *Tom Jones* (1749). But their concerns about format were not what brought readers to the novel. Rather, their offering readers characters with whom they could identify in familiar situations—characters that represented their own environment's increasing complexity, with its dawn of modern science, industry and technology; characters functioning in a medium built upon the practice of observation that foreshadowed scientific theory and formed the basis for 18th-century pragmatism and the structuring of society—that is what drew the public to the novel.

Works appearing previous to the 18th century that offered a foundation from which the novel would rise included most especially in the English language John Bunyan's *The Pilgrim's Progress from this World to that which is to Come* (1678). It contained all the ingredients desirable to an audience that appreciated entertainment along with instruction: an imperfect hero; conflict and spiritual struggle; monsters; characters, though allegorical, were still quite human; and a setting that represented the countryside readers knew. The printing of four editions in two years proved that the audience was ready for a well-told story containing aspects with which they could identify. Pamphleteering prior to the Restoration primed those readers to be accustomed to reading information written on their level.

Other individual writers followed Bunyan with seminal contributions to the novel's development. Aphra Behn would prove crucial in advancing the novel form as the first woman to earn her living from writing. Nicknamed "the incomparable Astrae" and agreeably known to an interested public, she moved from writing drama to recording the first epistolary narrative, titled *Love-letters between a Nobleman and his Sister*. Long ignored as serious writing due to gender discrimination in academe, Behn's work was promoted by feminist critics in the 20th century as a rival to *Pamela* for the first epistolary novel. Her later

Oroonoko, or The Royal Slave (1688) became a classic and made a crucial point in its introduction in which Behn explained how her novel and others differed from traditional romance. Unlike romance, the novel contained "a more familiar nature" for readers and dealt with events "not so distant from our belief." She summed up by writing that "Romances give more of wonder, novels more delight."

Following the development of that delight remains the purpose of this companion, and a quick summary, mentioning only a fraction of its entries, will be provided here. It surveys from the early 18th century works by Delarivière Manley, Daniel Defoe, and Eliza Haywood, and observes the movement from romance to realism, which would prove crucial to the novel. It takes care to note how one writer affected another, a prime example being Fielding's reaction against Richardson's *Pamela* to produce a satiric parody titled *Shamela*. More important was his second novel, *Joseph Andrews* (1742), which he intended to use as another parody. Instead, he developed an entirely new technique, identified in his first edition preface as "a comic epic poem in prose." When Fielding's sister Sarah wrote *Adventures of David Simple* (1744), her style was sentimental and the action episodic, but she incorporated a tone of sincerity and an examination of human nature that brought something new to the form.

As the century advanced, it produced the thesis novel, fiction of social conscience that proved the novel could be a political and social force. The philosophies of French writers Voltaire and Rousseau became important influences, and English writers including Samuel Johnson discovered fiction as a medium by which to express personal belief, as in his *Rasselas* (1759). Laurence Sterne would bring to the novel not only his own philosophy and many events from his own life, but a sense of humor and irony that marked nine volumes of *Tristram Shandy* (1760–67) as a different type of novel. Frances Sheridan introduced the complexity of the female mind into the novel with her *Memoirs of Miss Sidney Bidulph* (1761), while Horace Walpole almost single-handedly introduced the subgenre labeled Gothic in *The Castle of Otranto* (1764). Variations continued throughout the century, including Henry Goldsmith's use of the first-person point of view to great effect in *The Vicar of Wakefield* (1766). With the death of Tobias Smollett, who had gained a reputation for his savage satire based on personal experience, the first wave of novelists passed away, leaving behind a rich inheritance on which the next century might base its novel. But in the last decade or so of the 18th century, a group of women would rise to claim the genre with their novels of realistic terror and cautionary tales, including Mary Wollstonecraft, Charlotte Smith, and Fanny Burney, while William Godwin produced the radical *Caleb Williams, or Things as They Are* (1794), identified in its preface as a political work.

The 19th century saw a reaction against the heightened emotion of the Gothic and romance, prompting the redemption of the novel, which had earned in the preceding decades a poor reputation. Even solid authors, such as Godwin, felt for material reasons pressure to write the sensational novels demanded by the public. Soon after 1800, a community of women writers, including Amelia Opie, Maria Edgeworth, Sydney Owenson, and sisters Anna and Jane Porter, began to raise the novel's status. By the time Jane Austen began publishing her so-called novels of manners or domestic fiction that she had written as early as 1795, the intelligentsia was ready to read again. Mary Shelley proved a woman could write horror fiction, reflecting the public's new fascination and uneasy relationship with the promise of science and medicine, while Sir Walter Scott demonstrated through his seminal historical fiction that the reputation of an entire country, in this case Scotland, could be rescued through fiction. As the bourgeoisie flourished, the working class suffered, and novels made public their suffering and their movements to correct inequities, including the Chartist movement. Charles Dickens's rule as undisputed king of novelists included production of a series of novels that focused on social ills of the day. In later decades, the Gothic would return in a new form through the Brontë sisters to capture the public's imagination, as did novels of sentiment and sensation. They caused yet another later reaction against uncontrolled emotion in fiction to produce the problem novels of George Eliot and Joseph Henry Shorthouse; the novels that exposed the public to the unpleasant truths of everyday existence by Thomas Hardy and George Gissing; the adventure novels by Robert Louis Stevenson and his imitators; the psychological studies of Henry James; the detective and crime fiction of Wilkie Collins and Arthur Conan Doyle; the didacticism of Frances Trollope and the quiet novels of place by her son Anthony; George Meredith's novels investigating the travesty of legal marriage; and by the century's end, the sophistication of George Moore and celebration of the dilatory in Oscar Wilde's work.

Just as the above summary could not nearly include all the authors presented in this *companion*, the book could not possibly include every author that wrote novels over an astoundingly productive 200 years. Necessity dictated the inclusion of the traditional major authors and works read in high school and college, as well as entries featuring those additional individuals who contributed to the advance of the novel, in form or fashion. In addition, more women than one might find in previous guides and encyclopedias appear, as their contributions continue to receive increased attention thanks to the work of tireless feminist critics. At the same time, works not so well known and some even questionable as novels are included because of those very facts, for instance William Sharp's *Sport of Chance* and his works written as Fiona Macleod, *Washer of the Ford* and *The Sin-Eater and Other Tales*. Also, some novels of children's literature are included due to their dramatic increase in production during the 19th century, due to Lewis Carroll's inestimable influence on juvenile fiction as entertainment, not pure didacticism, and because of the manner by which they prepared young readers to later embrace adult-audience literature. Finally, some entries focus on terminology or literary movements important to a discussion of fiction, such as ones featuring the bildungsroman, the parody, various critical schools and subgenres including the Gothic and silver-fork fiction, or events or movements important to fiction of the era, including the Chartist movement, the kailyard school, the Industrial Revolution, and the Oxford movement. Within individual entries, careful connections between writers and writers, writers and works, works and works, and works and trends, in the vein of a New Historicist critical approach, reflect the close interweaving of all those elements and their reflection of the British world around them.

BIBLIOGRAPHY

Altick, Richard D. *The English Common Reader: A Social History of the Mass Reading Public, 1800–1900.* Chicago: University of Chicago Press, 1957.

Backsheider, Paula R., and John J. Richetti. *Popular Fiction by Women 1660–1730.* Oxford: Clarendon Press, 1996.

Beasley, Jerry C. *English Fiction, 1660–1800: A Guide to Information Sources.* Detroit: Gale, 1978.

Bowers, Toni. *The Columbia History of the British Novel.* New York: Columbia University Press, 1994.

Brantlinger, Patrick. *Rule of Darkness: British Literature and Imperialism, 1830–1914.* Ithaca: Cornell University Press, 1990.

Burke, Jerome H. *The Victorian Temper: A Study in Literary Culture.* New York: Vintage Books, 1964.

Coslet, Tess. *The "Scientific Movement" and Victorian Literature.* London: St. Martin's, 1982.

Cruse, Amy. *The Englishman and His Book in the Early Nineteenth Century.* New York: Benjamin Blom, 1968.

Demaria, Robert, Jr. *British Literature 1640–1789: An Anthology.* London: Blackwell, 2001.

Dyson, A. E. *The English Novel.* London: Oxford University Press, 1974.

Gilbert, Sandra M., and Susan Gubar, eds. *The Norton Anthology of Literature by Women: The Traditions in English.* 2nd ed. New York: W.W. Norton, 1996.

Phelps, Gilbert. *An Introduction to Fifty British Novels 1600–1900.* London: Pan Books, 1979.

Rogers, Katherine M., and William McCarthy, eds. *The Meridian Anthology of Early Women Writers: British Literary Women from Aphra Behn to Maria Edgeworth, 1660–1800.* New York: New American Library, 1987.

Stevenson, Lionel. *The English Novel: A Panorama.* Boston: Houghton Mifflin, 1960.

A

ABBOTT, THE SIR WALTER SCOTT (1820)

Sir Walter SCOTT's 11th novel, *The Abbott* represents his third prose fictional reconstruction of history. Whereas *IVANHOE* (1820) had focused on 12th-century medieval England, the next two historical novels took on 16th-century Scotland. Scott originally planned to write one lengthy work featuring the Reformation and the struggle for the Scottish throne between Queen Mary and her half-brother, James Stuart, to be titled *The MONASTERY* (1820). However, as he worked on the first part of this book, he realized that he had more than enough material to develop two three-volume novels. Ever aware of publishing advantages that might generate more income, he made the decision to release a three-volume novel, *The Monastery,* in 1820, and follow it the same year with a sequel, *The Abbott.* Featuring several of the same characters, *The Abbot* picks up where *The Monastery* left off. Labeled by some critics as part of Scott's Tales of My Landlord series, *The Abbott* focuses on the political and religious conflicts inherent to the period in which Scott placed it. While the novel characterizes and refers to many historical figures in addition to Mary and James Stuart, earl of Moray, including David Rizzio, Lord Patrick Ruthven, James Douglas, fourth earl of Morton, and Mary's husband Henry Stuart, Lord Darnley, it also introduces fictional characters who represent the common man caught up in the royal drama. Like some of Scott's other works, this one inspired at least one work of art, W. B. C. Fyfe's 1860 painting *The Abdication of Mary Queen of Scots at Lochleven Castle.*

Recurring characters from *The Monastery* include the Lady of Avenel, loved by both her Protestant husband, the knight Halbert Glendinning, and Halbert's brother, the Catholic clergyman Edward Glendinning. While the two brothers follow different faiths, they maintain a great love and respect for one another, allowing Scott to emphasize that religious differences may exist between people who care for one another. Halbert has earned his knighthood from James Stuart, earl of Moray, rather than inherited it, and thus must constantly prove he deserves his title. Left alone much of the time at the Castle of Avenel, her paternal mansion, while her husband patrols his lands, the Lady of Avenel mourns her lack of children and the lonely state in which she exists. One day, she observes some local children playing with a boat on a lake. When one 10-year-old child appears in danger of drowning, the castle's loyal hound rescues him, and the Lady decides to take him into her family as a page. His grandmother, the mysterious Madeline Graeme, agrees, and Halbert gives his wife his blessings. Young Roland Graeme matures among aristocrats, causing conflict with the castle servants and the commoners, once his fellows, who now must salute him as their lord. When the Lady eventually dismisses Roland due to his presumptuous and ill-tempered behavior, he welcomes the chance to prove that he is, in actuality, a noble by blood, something his grandmother has led him to believe. The Lady will reappear only briefly in the story and, like Halbert, remains a flat character.

Scott shapes Roland as something of an antihero during his character's early adventures. Roland cries when frightened and has a tendency to stab those with whom he disagrees. He wanders without direction, conveniently stumbling upon his grandmother, who had gone missing for seven years, when he visits an abbey where he has secretly received Catholic training from Edward Glendinning of St. Mary's. There he meets the novel's romantic interest, Catherine Seyton, who will reappear in ways that confound Roland with their seemingly mystical circumstances. Catherine and Roland become the novel's dynamic characters, with each experiencing an epiphany of sorts in this initiation story. Roland later witnesses the confirmation of Edward Glendinning as the new Abbott of Saint Mary's and comes back under the care of Sir Halbert Glendinning, who reveals that he has not ignored Roland as the youth thought, but has been biding his time to take part in Roland's training after his wife had completed her own efforts on his behalf.

Roland matures during his romantic QUEST and takes on the characteristics of the romantic hero Scott intends him to be. He retains and nurtures his passion for a rational justice, with little regard to circumstances, and his actions always support his motto, "That which is fairly won and freely given, is neither reft nor stolen." Of his own life he declares, "Let it be short, so it be honorable." In his position as knight's page, he brashly enters a street brawl that he judges an uneven dispute, without knowing the combatant that he supports. He then follows a figure that resembles Catherine and ends up in the aristocratic Catholic Seyton household, which has pledged support of Mary Stuart's claim to the Scottish throne. Confronted by the family's men-at-arms, he learns that he had protected Lord Seyton during the earlier street scuffle when the Lord himself presents Roland with a gold chain that acts as a token of the family's favoritism. Subsequently Roland is charged by the earl of Moray to travel with Lord Lindesey and Sir Robert Melville to act as page to the imprisoned Queen Mary, captive at Lochleven Castle. The party will meet Lord Patrick Ruthven, already at the castle as a guest of Mary, mother to the

earl of Moray and her son, Sir William Douglas, in an attempt to persuade Queen Mary to sign documents abdicating her throne to the earl of Moray.

As the intrigue develops along mostly historical lines, Roland meets up with Catherine, assigned as a lady to the queen, shaped by Scott as a graceful, courageous and captivating woman. Choosing loyalty to individuals over that to religion or political power, Roland totally commits to the protection of the queen and later participates in her famous escape from the Castle and her ensuing political defeat and self-exile to England.

Replete with characters of double and even triple identities, a journey, hand-to-hand combat, the winning of a fair lady, and the eventual revelation of its hero's true aristocratic identity as the only male heir of Julian of Avenel, the novel does not disappoint those who admire the historical-quest fiction that Scott quickly made popular in the 19th century. Scott offers, in addition to the expected elements, some additional touches that readers in all eras enjoy, including liberal quotations of, and references to, various writers to whom he obviously felt indebted and his strong characterizations that Virginia Woolf later compared to those of Shakespeare. One of those characters, Catherine Seyton, echoes Shakespeare's Beatrice, among other Shakespeare females, when she regrets not being a man, in order to take up arms in defense of her beliefs. Most interesting to those who know of Scott's own disgust over religious fanaticism is his honest look at the damage such radicalism can inflict on innocent bystanders.

BIBLIOGRAPHY

Fleishman, Avrom. *The English Historical Novel: Walter Scott to Virginia Woolf.* Baltimore: Johns Hopkins University Press, 1971.

Scott, Sir Walter. *The Abbot.* Edited by Christopher Johnson. Edinburgh: Edinburgh University Press, 2000.

Shaw, Harry E. *Narrating Reality: Austen, Scott, Eliot.* Ithaca, N.Y.: Cornell University Press, 1999.

***ADAM BEDE* GEORGE ELIOT (1859)** George ELIOT's first full-length novel, *Adam Bede* testifies to her skill in crafting a narrative of DOMESTIC REALISM. Although published in 1859, the story looks back nostalgically to the end of the previous century before railroads and factories had transformed the rhythms of rural English life. Both Eliot's contemporaries and later critics praised her realistic characters and settings. Few proved more skilled at shaping a purely innocent rustic character and the countryside that accommodated him. She captured the cyclic rhythms of country life, both in her narrative descriptions of planting and harvest, and in native speech patterns. The innocence of her novel's characters contrasts well with the sly Edenic setting that suggests sexual temptation. While the characters from her later works also proved realistic and well drawn, they could not match those in *Adam Bede* for human potential; like blank canvases, Adam and his fellow characters awaited the coloring of life. A popular novel into the 21st century, *Adam Bede* was adapted for television in 1991, and a movie version directed by Giles Foster was produced in the United Kingdom in 1992.

Eliot sets her story primarily in the idyllic village of Hayslope. The fictional lush England farming district, Loamshire, literally "soil province," is home to simple farmers and laborers who speak in a broad dialect, which the author captures in accurately rendered conversations. The farming community's surface simplicity, however, hides a complicated larger social order, from which conflict grows among various characters and between the characters and society itself. Adam's name symbolizes the first human, unblemished and naive, whose future depended not only on his own choices, but also on those of his mate. His occupation as a carpenter suggests a creative personality whose vision converts basic materials into symbols of domestic order, an order that eludes him when social conventions are shattered.

In Eliot's vision of social order, a particular community, such as a family or a group established by social custom, may set its own moral standards as a subset of civil law. It then holds individuals responsible for complying with those standards. Social responsibility directs a person's behavior. However, personal commitment to community ideals establishes that same individual's self-identity as part of a small group positioned within a larger CLASS STRUCTURE.

Eliot's subject came partially from the true case of a woman accused of child murder with whom Eliot's aunt, the Methodist minister Elizabeth Samuel, spent her final night before the execution. Historians later determined that the prisoner Samuel ministered to was one Mary Voce, executed in Nottingham in 1802. Critics point to other likely influences on Eliot, including Sir Walter SCOTT's child-murder novel, *THE HEART OF MIDLOTHIAN* (1818); one of Scott's probable inspirations, William Wordsworth's 1798 poem "The Thorn"; Charles DICKENS's *The Chimes* (1844), which focuses on the common belief that the 1834 Malthusian New Poor Law led to child murder and suicide among poverty-stricken mothers; and Elizabeth Barrett BROWNING's 1848 child-murder abolitionist poem, "The Runaway Slave at Pilgrim's Point."

In more than 55 titled chapters divided into six books, Eliot examines love's effects on five key characters and the disastrous consequences when that love is stymied by personal folly and class bias. Related by a third-person omniscient narrator, the novel begins at the leisurely walking pace of village life. Adam BEDE and his brother Seth are carpenters in a prosperous woodworking shop. Adam, the elder brother and shop foreman, is 25. Tall, handsome, and talented, he has a penetrating intelligence and has set his heart on beautiful 17-year-old Hetty Sorrel, the orphaned niece of a tenant farmer. In turn, Hetty falls prey to the attentions of Arthur Donnithorne, 20-year-old heir to the estate of which Hayslope is a part. Seth, meanwhile, attempts to court Hetty's cousin, Dinah Morris, a woman so moved by her Methodist faith that she begins preaching in Hayslope's village green. By the novel's end, each of these characters faces heartache, and some come to public shame and personal ruin.

The tragic drowning death of Adam's alcoholic father places the Bedes at the center of village attention and brings Dinah into their household for a day to comfort Adam's mother. Dinah soon makes clear that she cannot return Seth's love. She gently tells him that her service to God leaves no time or energy for marriage and family. She leaves Hayslope to continue her mission in the harsh upland factory town of Snowfield in rugged, forbidding, infertile Stonyshire.

In contrast to Dinah's cool avoidance of love, Hetty becomes enraptured with Arthur Donnithorne, imagining herself as his wealthy wife. She sees no reason why a fine gentleman should not marry the most beautiful girl in the district. She does not suspect that Arthur accepts class dictates not to marry a woman of a lower social status. He knows that he should not succumb to his attraction for Hetty, but his desire to possess her overmasters his will. Unfortunately, Arthur is unaware of Adam's intentions toward Hetty, because Adam remains too proud to declare himself until he feels sure of winning her love. Hetty allows Adam to cherish the hope of gaining her affection, but makes no commitment. Arthur respects and admires Adam, and longs to win approval from the villagers he will one day govern, but this very longing is his undoing. Arthur's rustic woodland lodge near the path Hetty takes every week to visit his aunt's maid for lace-making lessons soon becomes their secret trysting place.

In the book's midsection, as the summer crops ripen, Arthur celebrates his own coming-of-age with a grand party. Arthur leaves the village with the coming of the harvest season, joining his militia regiment in London. Hetty soon discovers she is pregnant but tells no one, suddenly accepting Adam's marriage proposal. She has never loved Adam, but he remains blind to her faults with no idea that his best friend, to the extent that friendship can cross class lines, has already unintentionally ruined all their hopes for happiness.

As plans for Adam and Hetty's marriage develop over the winter and Hetty's secret becomes harder to hide, she decides to find Arthur. Pretending to visit Dinah in Snowfield, she turns south toward London, unaware that Arthur's regiment has been ordered to Ireland. She considers suicide, but lacks the will to take her own life. When she arrives in London, Hetty learns that Arthur has departed and decides to go to Dinah as her second-best hope. She travels homeward, but gives birth one night along the way.

Two weeks after Hetty departs, Adam determines to go himself and bring both Hetty and Dinah home. He searches frantically for Hetty, but soon learns of her arrest on suspicion of murdering her newborn. Stunned by grief and rage, Adam immediately connects Arthur with Hetty. His great love for Hetty causes him to blame Arthur completely, because a gentleman should behave honorably. Hetty retreats into silence; her unwillingness to discuss events or name her child's father leads to her conviction and sentence to be hanged. As Hetty waits in jail, Dinah arrives to provide spiritual guidance. Her steadiness and deep faith soon move Hetty to a heart-wrenching confession of her affair, her journey, the baby's birth and abandonment, and her inability to leave the vicinity afterwards. Dinah vows to stay with Hetty, mounting the cart with her for the shameful journey to the gallows.

In contrast to the book's opening slow-paced narrative, the story races as Arthur is summoned home from Ireland upon his grandfather's death, and he learns of Hetty's impending execution. Deeply ashamed, Arthur realizes that he has squandered the villagers' respect and spoiled many lives. He makes an appeal in a higher court, galloping homeward with a commutation of Hetty's sentence from death to "transportation"— exile to the Australian penal colony. As the condemned girl stands on the gallows, he tears into the square waving the document and saves Hetty's life.

The final portion of the book sees Arthur beginning penance in form of a voluntary exile from Hayslope when he embarks on military service in distant lands. Adam will manage the estate, as Arthur had always intended. Dinah comes to help her aunt and uncle in the dairy and assists Lizbeth Bede, virtually becoming her daughter. Gradually Dinah realizes she has fallen in love with Adam, who has come to view her as a sister. He is slow to recognize her pain and to realize that she is the only woman who will understand his suffering. With Seth's blessing, he tries to court her. Knowing her devotion to a family would conflict with her divine mission, Dinah tries to stifle these emotions by again running away. This time, her passion cannot be cooled even in the symbolically named Snowfield; she at last joyously accepts Adam's suit.

In a tender epilogue set some eight years later, Adam and Dinah's son and daughter play under the eye of their devoted uncle Seth. Arthur will soon return to Hayslope, broken by wounds and illnesses; Hetty is also homeward bound, but dies at sea. Of the original five young people at the threshold of life and love in the novel's opening, only two achieve love, a happiness no less sweet for the bitterness they have tasted.

BIBLIOGRAPHY

Barrett, Dorothea. *Vocation and Desire: George Eliot's Heroines.* New York: Routledge, 1989.

Fulmer, Constance M. "Contrasting Pairs of Heroines in George Eliot's Fiction." *Studies in the Novel* 6.3 (Fall 1974): 288–294.

Hughes, Kathryn. *George Eliot: The Last Victorian.* London: Fourth Estate, 1998.

Karl, Fred. *George Eliot: Voice of a Century.* New York: Norton, 1995.

Marshall, Joanna Barszewska. "Shades of Innocence and Sympathy: The Intricate Narrative Syntax of Gossip, Metaphor, and Intimacy in Eliot's Treatment of Hetty Sorrel." *Dorothea's Window: The Individual and Community in George Eliot.* Edited by Patricia Gately, Dennis Leavens, and Cole Woodcox. Kirksville, Mo.: Thomas Jefferson Press, 1994.

McDonaugh, Josephine. "Child-Murder Narratives in George Eliot's *Adam Bede:* Embedded Histories and Fictional Representation." *Nineteenth-Century Literature* 56.2 (September 2001): 228–259.

Pangallo, Karen L., ed. *The Critical Response to George Eliot.* Westport, Conn.: Greenwood Press, 1994.

Rignall, John, ed. *Oxford Reader's Companion to George Eliot.* New York: Oxford University Press, 2000.

ADELINE MOWBRAY, OR THE MOTHER AND DAUGHTER AMELIA OPIE (1802)

When Amelia OPIE, the most popular novelist of her day, decided to write *Adeline Mowbray,* based loosely on the tumultuous public relationship of her acquaintances William GODWIN and Mary WOLLSTONECRAFT, she signaled readers with her subtitle that the female characters would receive by far most of her attention. It features three mother-daughter combinations, that of Mrs. Woodville and her daughter, Editha Mowbray, of Editha Mowbray and her daughter, Adeline Mowbray, and ultimately of Adeline and her own child, named Editha for her grandmother. Mrs. Woodville, of sensible and logical character, believed her daughter Editha to be a genius. She proved so concerned over her daughter's upbringing and schooling that she failed to school her at all. Preoccupied by abstracts such as romance, Editha married a man who captured her imagination but did not live long enough to help in the raising of her own daughter Adeline. Age 10 when her father died, Adeline would soon be "tormented by the experimental philosophy" of her genius mother. Still, she had her more practical grandmother as a model, and she loved her mother, despite her deficiencies. Those deficiencies were not in the area of affection, and Adeline often remembered her mother's constant care during a time of childhood illness.

As she matured, Adeline became an aficionado of a social philosophy that held man and woman could share a chaste love outside of the confines of marriage, an idea promoted by the writings of a has-been author named Frederic Glenmurray, intended to be a parallel to Godwin. Both Godwin and Wollstonecraft had eschewed the institution of marriage. When Woolstonecraft delivered her first child, Fanny, by her American lover, Gilbert Imlay, out of wedlock while living in Europe, she had well overstepped the boundaries of propriety set by her community. When she returned to England and took Godwin as her lover, the resultant pregnancy with him moved them both to decide to marry, although they did not live together. With a second pregnancy while unmarried, Woolstonecraft tempted society's ire. Thus they discovered what became a major theme of Opie's novel, that the conflict between life as the ideal and life as commonly accepted proved great. Adeline will also learn this truth and suffer for her independent attitudes. When her new stepfather, Sir Patrick O'Carrol, assumes he can rape her due to her revolutionary views, Adeline gains an idea of her precarious position. Her mother is so smitten with Sir Patrick that she feels Adeline has exaggerated his attentions, and eventually a gulf forms between the two women.

Almost every man Adeline meets becomes aroused when they learn she lives with Glenmurray, many taking liberties that include touching and embracing her. When pregnant with Glenmurray's child, she suffers rejection by her mother, who had served for so long as her touchstone. Like other members of society, Editha drew a sharp line separating theory from practice. Adeline loses that child but begins to realize that motherhood changes her ideas regarding marriage.

Adeline attracts a long string of admirers, beginning with Colonel Mordaunt, who pursues Adeline throughout her relationship with Glenmurray, once even rescuing her from the unwanted attentions of others. A libertine, he is nevertheless taken aback when he learns at one point that Adeline has at last married Glenmarry's cousin Berrendale, following Glenmurray's debt-ridden death, apologizing for his inappropriate actions while addressing a married woman. When Adeline has Berrendale's child, she names her daughter for her now-deceased mother, Editha, and will eventually take solace in the comfort of a supportive community, albeit a small one.

Adeline's group includes Mrs. Pemberton, Emma Douglas and the mulatto Savannah, and one supportive man, her lifelong physician and sentimental friend, Dr. Norberry. These individuals contrast with the more "respectable" Mrs. Norberry, Mrs. Beauclerc, Mrs. Wallington, and Miss Emily Maynard, all of Adeline's own social class and all too judgmental to associate with her. When such pillars of the community discover Adeline's past, she is removed from a teaching post where she had previously been widely praised, and only at that point marries Berrendale.

Autobiographical figures in addition to Godwin and Wollstonecraft likely inspired various Opie characters. The figure of Savannah may be based on a person with that name from Opie's background. Her mother, Amelia Briggs, was orphaned at age eight while in India and returned to England accompanied by a black nurse named Savannah who could not adjust to Europe and elected to return to Bengal. Opie spent a lifetime interested in issues involving blacks, and when she later became a member of the Society of Friends, worked for abolition of slavery, attending the famous London Convention of 1840, which would galvanize Americans, including Elizabeth Cady Stanton, to support suffrage for all. Rachael Pemberton represents many of the practical and peaceful ideas of the Quaker movement, most especially that of compassion. Emma Douglas represents a small number of women in Opie's own society who, due to a plain appearance, do not feel pressure to participate in the commodification of women, where

each trades on her beauty and charm in a patriarchal society. They could nurture their intellect and, if not wholly agreeing with revolutionary ideas such as sex outside of wedlock, could intelligently consider and discuss society's limits and their need for expansion.

Adeline Mowbray moved many who read it, with two interpretations arising from their reading—one camp saw Opie as legitimizing marriage in the end while others saw the opposite. The truth likely fell somewhere between those poles. Opie sought to problematize her community's simplistic view of the two genders as possessed by desires so different that they could never be satisfactorily resolved, certainly not in the name of morality. The book remains readily available and widely studied by FEMINIST CRITICS and other appreciators of women's literature.

BIBLIOGRAPHY

King, Shelley, and John B. Pierce. Introduction to *Adeline Mowbray,* by Amelia Opie. New York: Oxford University Press, 1999, vii–xxxii.

Spender, Dale. "Amelia Opie and the Novel of Ideas." In *Mothers of the Novel: 100 Good Women before Jane Austen.* New York: Pandora Books, 1986, 315–323.

ADVENTURES OF DAVID SIMPLE IN SEARCH OF A REAL FRIEND, THE SARAH FIELDING (1744–1747)

Sarah FIELDING described *David Simple* as a "moral romance." The episodic novel took a timely approach to the ROMANCE genre, moving away from the traditional chivalric tales to a story based on codes of middle-class ideology. Modern critics note that Fielding moved away from the Augustan objective approach to romance, which found meaning in political, social, and legal references. By Fielding's time, readers desired stories based on sensibility, or emotion and ideals, and thus dependent upon subjective references—personal, spiritual, and emotional. They valued the emotional over the logical.

The change to some extent reflected the conflict between the bourgeois, or landed, class and the novel's expanding working-class audience. When novels before the 1740s did focus on political ideology, it was one shared by individuals or small groups within the same political faction, that of the upper class. With the rise of the middle class, however, novels began to present political and social struggles between whole social classes. Thus Fielding's work took its place among novels of the 1740s that questioned the relationship of the novel to the reading public. With a middle-class set of readers expanding the consumer audience, novels had to undergo changes to satisfy their ideological, as well as intellectual, needs.

The title character's position as a romantic hero whose most pronounced characteristic is that of sensibility, rather than physical prowess in combat and love, requires a new definition of the term *hero*. Attempts to define him as a traditional QUEST hero are undermined by his choice simply to avoid confrontation, rather than to face and conquer challenges. He lacks traits traditionally connected to masculinity, displaying a sensitivity that Augustan audiences would have considered effeminate.

David Simple is an unremarkable middle-class male cheated from his inheritance by his younger brother, Daniel. He finds Daniel's actions so offensive that he launches into a quest, not with the traditional reward of wealth or romance in mind, but rather in search of friendship. His subsequent experiences with Mr. Orgueil, Mr. Splatter, and Mr. Varnish all confirm the presence of deceit and hypocrisy in the world. The characters are not meant to be well rounded, but rather to represent aspects of human nature to which David may react. No two characters are alike in their actions, nor is any one completely bad. However, each is revealed as a hypocrite, disloyal and unfaithful, and thus incapable of friendship. For example, Mr. Splatter performs good deeds but also spreads evil gossip about others.

David's quest is rewarded when he meets three other characters also cheated and mistreated by friends and family. They include Cynthia, swindled out of her father's fortune, and a sister-brother pair, Valentine and Camilla, whose stepmother has alienated their father's affections from them, partly by suggesting the two engage in incest. United by their like suffering and innocence, the friends form a happy community, with David eventually marrying Camilla, and Cynthia marrying Valentine. David regains his fortune and shares it with his friends. Valentine and Camilla also regain

their relationship with their father. Fielding resists a happily-ever-after denouement, however: The plot concludes with David's meeting late in his journey the one purely evil character of the novel, the Atheist. David is surprised to discover that the Atheist is actually his estranged brother, Daniel, who followed his shabby treatment of his brother with a brief but vice-filled life, stealing money from everyone he meets and corrupting their morals. Ironically, Daniel better represents the traditional active masculine hero than does David. However, masculinity does not equal heroism in Fielding's novel. Instead, Daniel fulfills his role in a cautionary tale by demonstrating the spiritual, mental, and physical destruction and debasement that awaits those who attempt to gain through the loss of others. Although still young, he dies the death of a decrepit old man, ravaged by alcoholism. As strong as David's goodness may be, it cannot rescue another human who resists the call to benevolence and generosity.

While David finds a seeming solution to his isolation, the novel's plot achieves no resolution. Instead of creating strategies to deal with the dilemma of human duplicity and treachery, David simply turns away from it to construct his own world, with the help of his friends. However, in the sequel, called the second volume, to the novel, *Volume the Last* (1753), Fielding sets a fatalistic tone as David's carefully constructed supportive world unravels over time, due to age, death, and financial setbacks.

Some NEW HISTORICIST critics have examined the novel in light of Fielding's own troubled youth in which her family circumstances produced multiple examples of personal betrayal, echoed as a theme in *David Simple*. The novelist Henry FIELDING, the author's older brother, wrote in the 1782 edition of his sister's novel that he tried to correct "some grammatical and other" mistakes in the first edition. He defends his earlier lack of involvement in his sister's work by his "absence from town" during its production. The errors are "small," and of such a nature that "no man of learning would think worth his censure in a romance; nor any gentleman in the writings of a young woman."

One group of FEMINIST CRITICS argues that the novel's heroine, Cynthia, represents gender stereotypes from which Fielding herself suffered, including the idea that women lack the imagination and intellect to pursue a traditionally male occupation and are suitable for little more than a sexual object/wife. Within the novel itself, Cynthia labels activities approved for a young lady, such as spending her day preparing her husband's dinner and her own appearance to please him, as those "a degree above a natural fool." Her experience on the road, following her dismissal from her father's house, includes suffering undignified demands from three male fellow travelers, one the Atheist, later identified as Daniel Simple. All ask her for sexual favors, emphasizing the traditional fictional characterization of foolish, vulnerable women. Other feminist critics evaluate Cynthia and Camilla as a rare set of double heroines, each possessing recognizable faults but representing positive characters. Camilla could, like Cynthia, be seen as a victim, beaten by her father and turned out of her house. Yet she also takes charge of her life and goes in search of happiness with her brother. Because David presents such a passive hero, what little action the females can take in their patriarchal surroundings are magnified, making them appear to be the more active figures. When Cynthia laughs in the face of a suitor, responding to his marriage proposal by declaring she will not spend a life serving him, her move proves unwise, and yet the female readers who made Fielding's novel so popular appreciated Cynthia's unconventional behavior. Feminist critics also point out that David's steadfast devotion to the fulfillment of duty through the practice of generosity, service, and benevolence, pursuits generally seen as feminine, marginalize him in the way that society marginalized women.

Samuel RICHARDSON praised Fielding's novel, as did the critic Arthur Murphy. Her book also pleased Lady Mary Wortley Montagu, an arts-patron cousin of Fielding renowned for her epistles from Turkey and her promotion of smallpox vaccination in England. A July 1757 comment in *The Monthly Review* said "It was superfluous to compliment the author of [David Simple] upon her merits as a writer." Although Sarah Fielding's works never received the attention that her brother's work did in the centuries just following their publication, 20th-century feminist criticism and a resurgence of interest in early women writers brought her novels and correspondence long-deserved attention from a scholarly readership. The original text of *David Simple* was reproduced for the first time in 1998 by Blackwell North America, Inc.

BIBLIOGRAPHY
Battestin, Martin C., and Clive T. Probyn, eds. *The Correspondence of Henry and Sarah Fielding*. Oxford: Clarendon Press, 1993.

Bree, Linda. *Sarah Fielding*. New York: Twayne Publishers, 1996.

Gautier, Gary. "Henry and Sarah Fielding on Romance and Sensibility." *Novel: A Forum on Fiction* 31.2 (Spring 98): 195–215.

Spender, Dale. *Mothers of the Novel: 100 Good Women Writers before Jane Austen*. New York: Pandora, 1986.

ADVENTURES OF HAJJI BABA OF ISPAHAN, THE JAMES MORIER (1824)

James MORIER based his SATIRE of Persian life on first-hand knowledge of the culture. Born in Smyrna (later Izmir), Turkey, Morier acted as attaché to two diplomats to Iran, Sir Harford Jones and Sir Gore Ouseley, from 1807 to 1814. As secretary to Jones, he traveled with a Persian envoy named Mirza Abul Hussan, on whom he based the *Adventures* character Mirza Firouz, the Persian ambassador to England.

A romantic first-person point-of-view PICARESQUE, the story moves with a skillful pace, remaining action-driven. It features a picaro, an adventurer, who enjoys various occupations, from water boy to executioner, in his steady climb toward pleasure and wealth. Morier mentions his debt to other writers of the picaresque in the epistle with which he opens his book. In the guise of one Peregrine Persic, he writes that a European might "give a correct idea of Oriental manners" to help his fellow countrymen understand "many facts and anecdotes of actual life as would illustrate the different stations and ranks which compose a Mussulman community, and then work them into one connected narrative, upon the plan of that excellent picture of European life, 'GilBlas' of LeSage." In the foreword to the 1937 Random House edition, Christopher Morley labels the "famous old book . . . droll," explaining that the term suggests "odd humor, unexpected and kindly, covertly facetious, mischievously wise."

Named Hajji, which means "the pilgrim," because of his birth during his parents' pilgrimage to the sacred tomb of Hosein (Husayn ibn Ali, a Muslim martyr), the protagonist begins the novel as a barber's apprentice to his father in Ispahan. Noticed by his village's holy man, he receives an education and states that, by age 16, it was difficult "to say whether I was most accomplished as a barber or a scholar." Later kidnapped by Turks while traveling with a merchant, he gains favor by practicing his barber skills and successfully plots to retrieve the merchant's lost fortune for himself. Forced to become an accomplice in the Mussulmen's nefarious activities, he returns to raid his own village and, in disguise, helps spare his father's life. After escaping his captors, Hajji travels through Iran and Afghanistan, apprenticing with various individuals to learn magic cures, poetry, and the ways of court and business. An unabashed liar, he even denies membership in the Shiite religious sect, masquerading as a Sunni to suit his purpose. Eventually, he succeeds in marrying the daughter of a wealthy man to gain court status of his own. Unfortunately, his own life stands at risk because of the changing whims of a shah not to be trusted.

Hajji endears himself to readers as a jovial profligate scoundrel, a consistent opportunist interested in money for money's sake. Endlessly resourceful, he treats all individuals with the same insolence, regardless of their social station. However, his life contains some tragedy. Early in his travels, he falls in love with the slave Zeenab, who eventually becomes a gift to the Shah. Excited about her future in the Shah's harem, Zeenab does not know she is pregnant with Hajji's baby. Seven months later, Hajji has become an officer to the chief executioner, assuming the post following the convenient death of his predecessor. In order to fulfill his duty, he must witness Zeenab's execution. Condemned by the shah, who cannot discover the identity of her unborn child's father, Zeenab is thrown from a high tower. Hajji suffers the horror of hearing her die and, as the executioner's officer, must help collect her body. Despite the danger of discovery, he dips his handkerchief in her blood. Morier follows this episode in his lightning-quick plot with one of the few

scenes that features a remorse-filled Hajji as he mourns alone by Zeenab's grave, describing his agony.

Morier's audience enjoyed Hajji's guileless hypocrisy, a stereotypical character trait often attributed to Persians. Readers also delighted in reading descriptions of Europeans visiting the Persian court: "who, with their unhidden legs, their coats cut to the quick, their unbearded chins, and unwhiskered lips, looked like birds moulting, or deceased apes, or anything but human creatures." In spite of the vast differences between English and Persian culture, readers could identify with Hajji's determination to return one day to his hometown a successful man.

Morier's careful portrayal of Persian life supposedly elicited an outcry from Abul Hassan, Persian minister to London, when its uncomplimentary portrait of the Persian adventurer appeared. The minister reportedly saw himself in the novel's slave-owning character, Mirza Farouz. According to Iraj Bashiri, his "protest" read:

> What for you write Hajji Baba, sir? King very angry, sir. I swear him you never write lies: but he say, yes—write. All people very angry with you, sir. That very bad book, sir. All lies, sir . . . Persian people very bad people, perhaps, but very good to you, sir. What for you abuse them so bad? I very angry . . . You call me Mirza Firouz, I know very well, and say I talk great deal nonsense. When I talk nonsense? Oh, you think yourself very clever man; but this Hajji Baba very foolish business.

That supposed "protest" did not come from Hassan, but rather from a practical joker, Dr. John McNeil. The novel proved so popular, despite its racist views, that Morier produced a 1828 sequel, *The Adventures of Hajji Baba of Ispahan in England,* which contained a copy of the "minister's protest" and a foreword written by Sir Walter SCOTT.

One of the first critical looks at Persia, the book joined the developing tradition of novels of social criticism. Through his colorful, but mainly accurate, presentation, Morier helped to demystify a country about which the public had little knowledge. Due to the astonishing detail in the novel, many believed that a

Persian aided in its writing. For decades, the novel served as the most accessible English-language book about Persia, and it eventually was translated into Persian. According to E. Cobham Brewster's *Dictionary of Phrase and Fable* (1898), Morier's novel introduced the Persian term *bosh,* meaning "nonsense," to English readers. Despite its appeal, the novel has yet to be converted into a high-quality screen presentation. Reviewers categorized a 1950s "B" movie, *The Adventures of Hajji Baba,* based loosely on the novel, as a "comedy of errors." Due to its easy-to-digest style and well-drawn adventures, the novel continues to be read by fans and students of the English picaresque.

BIBLIOGRAPHY

Bashiri, Iraj. "Introduction." *Writer's Corner.* Available online. URL: http://www.iles.umn.edu/faculty/bashiri/Writers%20 folder/WritersCorner.html. Downloaded December 2002.

Goad, Kathleen M. *Notes on Chosen English Texts: Hajji Baba of Ispahan.* London: James Brodie, 1962.

Morier, James. *The Adventures of Hajji Baba of Ispahan.* New York: Random House, 1937.

Wright, Denise. *The Persians Among the English.* London: L. B. Tauris, 1985, 69, fn.

AGE OF JOHNSON

A label often applied to the last half of the 18th century, the Age of Johnson takes its name from Samuel JOHNSON, lexicographer, critic, scholar, poet, and novelist most well known for his DICTIONARY OF THE ENGLISH LANGUAGE (1755). With little etymological background on which to draw, Johnson included definitions of more than 40,000 entries, relying on his voracious reading habits to help elucidate meanings. His essays on varied topics for *The Rambler, The Adventurer, The GENTLEMAN'S MAGAZINE,* and his *The Idler* series published in the *Universal Chronicle* made famous his attitudes defending reason. He also believed in the value of research into all subjects, once commenting, according to Leslie Stephen, father of Virginia Woolf, "Knowledge is of two kinds. We know a subject ourselves, or we know where we can find information upon it. When we inquire into any subject, the first thing we have to do is to know what books have treated of it." His critique of literature helped build a tradition of greater use of reality reflected in a series of 18th- and 19th-century novels by Tobias SMOLLETT, Charles DICKENS, George ELIOT, Thomas HARDY, and many others. While not a philosopher or a producer of original theory, he doggedly promoted the detrimental effects of idleness and offered a wide-ranging assessment of human behavior. His staunch attacks against poverty and suffering among the lower classes encouraged authors to use that and other socially conscious themes in their fiction, defying the early-18th-century "patina" of correctness with which many Augustan authors coated their writings. Johnson's literary criticism represented some of the earliest praise of honesty and originality in fiction that might lead to the discovery of general truths about human nature. His reputation for personal integrity helped legitimate the novel form when he published his only novel, RASSELAS, in 1759. Smollett referred to Johnson as The Great Cham, an archaic term meaning king, or leader. The "title" symbolized Johnson's position as an arbiter of artistic taste and criticism in support of morality and ethics within the arts.

The Age of Johnson connotes not so much the period in which Johnson lived, but instead his own defense of the use of logic and rational expression against the incorporation of overt sentimentality and uncontrolled imagination in writing. He voiced his belief in the responsibility of a writer to make a fair and balanced presentation to the reading audience and practiced that belief in his own writing. While some 19th-century critics considered Johnson merely an Augustan reactionary, his ideas excused by labels such as "eccentric" and "odd," he emerged over time as one of England's most celebrated thinkers and critics. The humanist values on which he based his commentaries would soon appear within much of British fiction.

BIBLIOGRAPHY

Lipking, Lawrence I. *Samuel Johnson: The Life of an Author.* Cambridge, Mass.: Harvard University Press, 1998.

Stephen, Leslie. *Samuel Johnson.* New York: Macmillan, 1900.

Waingrow, Marshall, ed. *James Boswell's Life of Johnson: An Edition of the Original Manuscript in Four Volumes.* New Haven, Conn.: Yale University Press, 1994.

AGNES GREY ANNE BRONTË (1847)

Anne BRONTË's autobiographical novel about a young woman governess features themes of social injustice, class consciousness, education, and isolation. Brontë's first-person narrative alerts readers in its opening sentence that, by presenting a "history," it intends to instruct and will be DIDACTIC. That instructive history concerns Agnes Grey, a 19-year old girl who describes two miserable experiences serving unlikable and overly demanding families as a governess. She makes clear that the unsatisfying nature of those positions result from support of an unfair CLASS STRUCTURE on the part of her employers, who treat her as something even less than a servant. Nothing subtle exists in the narration as Brontë shapes thoroughly unlikable characters to represent the wealthy class.

Like Anne Brontë, Agnes herself comes from a loving family in which the father is a poor clergyman. Because Agnes's once-wealthy mother had disobeyed her parents and married for love "below her station," she receives no parental financial support to help relieve the family's poverty. Her husband's dreams for his family cannot be realized because of his low income. Their poor situation is further exacerbated by the loss of what small investment he has to a scheme literally sunk by the unfortunate death of its manager, who plunges, along with his investment capital, to the bottom of a stormy sea. However poor the family may be, they are a loving and supportive group, and Brontë shows that, contrary to societal views, privilege does not automatically constitute morality or lead to happiness. Agnes demonstrates that misperception when she freely contrasts her family's devotion and unqualified love for one another with the loathing and recrimination evident in the two families she serves. Her character will come into conflict with her class-conscious environment, individuals who support that environment, and even herself during her struggle to fit into that environment.

When Agnes leaves her family in an attempt to contribute income by working as a governess, she sorely misses her parents and sister and finds no affection with her first family, the Bloomfields. With no help from parents who believe their children to be paragons of talent and virtue, Agnes must deal with overly indulged and recalcitrant charges she can hardly control, much less teach. She must depart after only a few months because she cannot instruct children who lack respect for others, an attitude they directly inherited from their snobby and disdainful parents. The reader understands that those adults have little cause for their feelings of superiority as Brontë illustrates the injustice in such attitudes. In one of the only roles available to "common" women, the governess must suffer the dual indignities of rejection and humiliation at the hands of mere children. Such disrespectful treatment far outweighs any physical suffering that results for Agnes from poverty.

In her second position with the Murray family at an estate called Horton Lodge, Agnes must teach, and serve as companion for, two young women. While more tolerable than her previous charges, the girls are spoiled and materialistic, and have little in common with Agnes. Although again unfulfilled by her governess position and stymied by the social and ideological barriers to close friendship with the Murray girls, Agnes finds her loneliness tolerable due to her occasional meetings with the local curate, Edward Weston. Like her author sisters, Charlotte BRONTË and Emily BRONTË, Anne Brontë emphasized the importance of nature in her writings, and in one scene, she equates the joy evoked in the governess by nature with that evoked by Weston's presence. When Agnes, walking with her charges that outdistance her, hears "the sweet song of the happy lark," her "misanthropy" dissolves, and she is reminded of her happy childhood. She longs for a plant to remind her of her early days on the moors, but knows she will not find any such thing in the area of the estate that serves as her temporary home. She discovers three primroses she wants to gather and carry away as a reminder of the world's beauty, but they sit out of reach on a high bank. Weston arrives on the scene and offers to pick the flowers for Agnes, a symbolic act that foreshadows their eventual union. As they discuss the flowers they prefer, Agnes remarks that her favorites are wildflowers, implying that she herself is an example of something wild and out-of-place among the more cultured women at Horton Lodge.

When the older Murray girl marries and Agnes's father dies, Agnes returns home to start a school with her mother. She fears she will never see Weston again, but he later appears and proposes marriage, which Agnes happily accepts. Brontë makes clear the admirable goals of the working class when she concludes her novel by writing, "[O]ur modest income is amply sufficient for our requirements: and by practicing the economy we learnt in harder times, and never attempting to imitate our richer neighbours, we manage not only to enjoy comfort and contentment, but to have every year something to lay by for our children, and something to give to those who need it."

Anne Brontë's first novel represents the movement away from the "social" or "aristocratic" novel, so popular in the 1830s, to the novel that focused on a "lower life," and the realistic heroism of work, in the 1840s. Based on her own unhappy experience as a governess for nearly five years, the novel illustrates Brontë's frustration over the limited vocations available to Victorian-era women and the attitudes of those who made unrealistic demands upon the working class. The novel did not prove as successful as Anne Brontë's second novel, *The TENANT OF WILDFELL HALL* (1848). The first publication, printed in London by T. C. Newby, contained several errors, which the 1850 edition would correct. Published by Smith, Elder & Company, the later edition appeared posthumously and was closely edited by Charlotte Brontë.

Agnes Grey is often considered the weakest of the seven novels produced by the three Brontë sisters. A lack of command over her materials is the most common criticism of Anne's writing, in addition to plot contrivances that seem too convenient. For a novel that purports to be realistic, this one allows its narrator frequent flights into a fancy that complicates her handling of her duties, and its conclusion with her "rescue" by Weston subverts Agnes's attainment of any true epiphany, undercutting a satisfying resolution to the conflict faced in the world of work by Agnes. Its greatest value may be that it provided Anne a complement to her sister Charlotte's *JANE EYRE* (1847), another governess tale, published in the same year.

BIBLIOGRAPHY

Bell, A. Craig. *The Novels of Anne Brontë: A Study and Reappraisal.* Braunton, Devlin, U.K.: Merlin Books, 1992.

Nash, Julie, and Barbara A. Suess, eds. *New Approaches to the Literary Art of Anne Brontë.* Aldershot, U.K.: Ashgate, 2001.

AINSWORTH, WILLIAM HARRISON (1805–1882)

A phenomenally successful author, editor, and publisher, William Harrison Ainsworth was born in 1805 in Manchester, England. Inspired by tales told by his father, he began his writing career at the age of 16 by publishing "a Serio-comic Tragedy" under a pseudonym in the *Pocket Magazine*. Planning to follow his father's profession and eventually take over his law practice, Ainsworth studied law and was admitted in 1826 as a qualified solicitor. He could not abandon writing, however, and became close friends with John Ebers, a publisher, whose daughter Fanny married Ainsworth in 1826. That same year Ebers published multiple works by Ainsworth, the most notable a piece of juvenilia called *Sir John Chiverton,* a work praised by Sir Walter SCOTT, who asked to meet the author. Ainsworth's focus on the mysterious Chiverton Hall prefigured his future success publishing GOTHIC NOVELS. Ebers convinced Ainsworth to write full time, which he did successfully for two years. He returned to the practice of law in 1830 and became friends with a literary group that founded *FRASER'S MAGAZINE* that year. He began work on a novel in 1831, published in 1834 by Richard Bentley in three volumes as *ROOKWOOD*. The novel popularized Ainsworth's most enduring character, the Gothic romantic highwayman-hero Dick Turpin. Its huge success gained Ainsworth immediate fame, and he settled into writing and publishing.

For unknown reasons, Fanny left Ainsworth in 1835 to live again with her father; she died in 1838. After Fanny's departure, Ainsworth first moved into Kensal Lodge on Harrow Road west of London, then into the adjoining Kensal Manor House in 1841, where he gained a reputation as the most notable author-host of the decade. Attendance at his gatherings became mandatory for aspiring as well as famous authors, such as William Makepeace THACKERAY and Benjamin DISRAELI. Ainsworth had a direct role in the success of several writers. He introduced Charles DICKENS, for example, then a young journalist, to Dickens's first publisher, his first illustrator, and his lifelong confidant and eventual biographer, John Forster.

Ainsworth published *Crichton,* another Gothic novel, in 1837, again enjoying huge sales. His next work, *Jack Sheppard,* appeared as a serial in BENTLEY'S MISCELLANY, then edited by Dickens, between January 1839 and February 1840; *Bentley's* also distributed the novel in three volumes later that year. Eight different dramas based on the novel were produced. Ainsworth took over the editorship of *Bentley's* in March 1839. He produced three popular novels between 1840 and 1841: *The Tower of London,* appearing in monthly installments between January and December 1840; *Guy Fawkes,* published in *Bentley's* from January 1840 through November 1841; and *Old Saint Paul's,* appearing as installments in the *Sunday Times* between January and December of 1841.

In 1841, Ainsworth sold *Bentley's Miscellany* and began his own periodical, *Ainsworth's Magazine,* in 1842, purchasing, in addition, the *New Monthly Magazine* in 1845. In 1853, Ainsworth moved from Kensal Manor Lodge to Brighton, marking the end of his great fame. Having spent most of his writing income on the extravagant entertaining he so enjoyed, he continued his editing but never again earned the income he had in the 1840s. His favorite styles of fiction—Gothic, HISTORICAL and rogue—had been replaced by the more realistic writing of Dickens and Thackeray, which prefigured the DOMESTIC REALISM novel that would catapult Anthony TROLLOPE and George ELIOT to success. In addition to continuing to write and publish more than a dozen additional novels, Ainsworth read thousands of pages of manuscripts, dozens of reviews and essays, and kept up an enormous correspondence.

Ainsworth decided to terminate *Ainsworth's Magazine* in 1854, but he re-purchased *Bentley's Miscellany* and continued editing the *New Monthly Magazine* as well. He sold *Bentley's* in 1868. In 1867, he had moved from Brighton to Tunbridge Wells and eventually helped support himself by selling his family property over time. In 1870 he sold the *New Monthly.* Copies of Ainsworth's final works became scarce in later decades, as they appeared in inexpensive paperback editions, easily destroyed. His publisher, John Dicks, also owned a penny weekly periodical named *Bow Bells* that carried the novels' first serializations. Ainsworth made his final move, to Reigate, in 1878, spending his last years with a second wife about whom practically nothing is known. His death in 1882 ended one of the most productive literary lives of the mid-19th century. By the 21st century, renewed interest in Ainsworth resulted in the publication of several of his books as electronic texts, available through the Internet.

BIBLIOGRAPHY

Ellis, S.M. *William Harrison Ainsworth and His Friends.* 2 vols. New York: John Lane Co, 1911.

Locke, Harold. *A Bibliographical Catalogue of the Published Novels and Ballads of William Harrison Ainsworth.* London: E. Mathews Ltd., 1925.

Worth, George J. *William Harrison Ainsworth.* New York: Twayne Publishers, 1972.

ALICE'S ADVENTURES IN WONDERLAND LEWIS CARROLL (1865)

Lewis CARROLL'S *Alice's Adventures Underground,* later published as *Alice's Adventures in Wonderland,* fascinated Victorian audiences from the moment of its appearance. Ostensibly classified as children's literature, focusing on the initiation/coming-of-age of its protagonist, seven-year old Alice, the book also caught the attention of adults. It revolutionized children's literature by moving beyond the usual didacticism of books for young readers popular during Carroll's time. The book succeeded in entertaining its readers while sharing a bit of implied instruction, adhering to Horace's doctrine to both teach and delight. It acts as SATIRE, poking good-natured fun at various Victorian practices, including manners, rituals, and CLASS STRUCTURE, emphasizing that Alice may successfully enter adulthood only when she has learned to follow rules. She must apply logic, intuition, and grace to all circumstances, no matter how outrageous. Although the Alice character is only seven, far too young to be on the verge of adulthood, the real-life Alice Liddell, for whom Carroll wrote the book and on whom he based his young heroine, was, at the time he wrote the book, 11 years old, an adolescent who would have begun questioning her self-identity.

With its beautiful illustrations by Sir John Tenniel, *Wonderland,* and its 1871 sequel, *THROUGH THE LOOKING-GLASS AND WHAT ALICE FOUND THERE,* remain enduring favorites. Converted into a number of television, film, and stage presentations, Carroll's books supplied some of the most well-recognized images and phrases in popular culture. Alice's comment on the events that she observes, "curiouser and curiouser," found its way into everyday speech, as did a phrase sung by the watch-toting white rabbit from the Walt Disney cartoon based on the classic, "I'm late! I'm late! For a very important date!" The phrase "grinning like a Cheshire cat," based on the cat that so startles Alice by disappearing, leaving behind only its smiling teeth suspended in air, came to connote a person with a sly or mysterious idea. These examples are only a small indication of the work's effect.

At its most basic, *Alice's Adventures in Wonderland* may be seen as an INITIATION/COMING-OF-AGE STORY in which Alice must make decisions regarding her behavior that will help determine her success in an adult environment. It also qualifies as a QUEST, containing hallmark plot elements from a call to adventure to a triumphant return home. Alice's adventures begin when she sees a white rabbit, symbolic of magic and transformations, then falls asleep, her head in her sister's lap. She follows the rabbit into a hole, through which she falls for quite some time. As she falls, Alice recounts lessons she has learned in school, allowing Carroll to reflect on the questionable value of children's schooling to the application of real life. Alice arrives in Wonderland when she finds herself in a house. She tries to enter a garden visible through a window, but she is the wrong size, beginning numerous conflicts with herself, other characters, and her new environment. The garden symbolizes childhood as well as reproduction, growth, and maturity. Alice alters her size in hopes of passing through a small door into the garden by ingesting the first of various magical foods and drink that she will encounter. Unfortunately, as she alternately grows and shrinks, she never reaches the proper size to fit through the door. Each of the several episodes in which she rapidly changes height emphasizes that mere physical size does not determine one's level of maturity. Not allowed into the garden, the land of childhood, Alice is forced to enter a much more adult world where all semblance of order seems to have disappeared. In the novel's second chapter, she chides herself, in the absence of any adult to do the scolding, for errors in logic and wonders aloud, "Who in the world am I?," concluding, "That's the great puzzle." Her confusion sets the scene for her ensuing self-identity struggle.

Some of Alice's adventures suggest traditional fairy/folktales containing figures that would have been familiar to young readers of Carroll's time, such as a young person with something to learn, talking animals, and enchanted forests and dwellings. However, while those tales move in a predictable fashion, Carroll's tale does not. Enchanted beasts that should act as guide figures simply confuse poor Alice, and normal symbols of order, such as a traditional English tea party, dissolve into chaos. At the party, Alice engages in confusing conversation with what would become extremely popular fictional figures: the Dormouse, the March Hare, and the Mad Hatter. According to NEW HISTORICIST critics, the Mad Hatter represents a working class that suffered terrible physical consequences from their labor, such as Victorian hatmakers who developed mental illness due to poisoning from the mercury used in fur processing, emphasizing the inequities of England's CLASS STRUCTURE.

After the tea party, Alice meets a puppy, one of the most common symbols of childhood delight, but his enormous size frustrates their interaction. Continued focus on physical size strongly carries through Carroll's emphasis on characteristics of maturity not equal to emotional or mental aspects. One of the novel's most striking figures, a hookah-smoking caterpillar, epitomizes the idea of metamorphosis that all children must face during maturity. The hookah, an accepted symbol of wisdom in its relationship to Eastern religions, introduces the idea of consciousness-altering drugs, still legal in England during the 19th century, that appear in other of its popular literature, such as Arthur Conan DOYLE's Sherlock Holmes stories. It is an adult pursuit that Alice must confront with grace and agility as she verbally spars with the caterpillar.

Conversations that engage Alice reflect Carroll's passion for mathematics, logic, linguistics, and riddles, as Alice is stymied in her attempts to carry on polite discussions in situations where the basic meaning of simple English terms, and their interrelationships, come into question. Alice's final confrontation of a queen in the garden she had hoped to visit when she entered Wonderland proves the success of her training. Important traditional symbols in this scene include its white and red roses. The white roses represent the process of aging and impending death, in this case, of the adult queen, while red roses represent youth, fertility, and passion, suggesting a juxtaposition of the Queen's maturity to Alice's youth. Playing-card men are dowsing the white roses with red paint in hopes of disguising the fact that they planted the wrong type of bush. With the red rose, Carroll again recalls fairy tales such as "Snow White and Rose Red." He also recalls the traditional, often fatal, female struggle between age and fading beauty with youth and dawning beauty in tales such as "Snow White" and "Sleeping Beauty."

As Alice attempts a polite conversation with the Queen, she finds herself "on trial" for supposedly rude and faulty behavior. Only when Alice realizes that a great part of that adult world is "Nonsense!" does she gain the ability to return to her own world. She awakens right back where she began, lying with her head in her sister's lap. She tells her sister of her dream; then the reader is privy to her sister's thoughts. As Alice's sister pictures her at some point in the future, sharing her adventures in Wonderland with her children, Carroll seems to be hoping that part of Alice Liddel's childhood memories will involve him. According to her later writings, she did recall Lewis Carroll, his stories and their many hours spent together with great fondness.

Carroll's tales continue to affect readers, from philosophers who examine his characters' statements about life, to mathematicians who study his chess moves and quadratic relationships, to authors like Joyce Carol Oates, who has stated that she views Alice's journey into the imagination as the collective destiny of all humans on their way to self-realization.

BIBLIOGRAPHY

Carroll, Lewis. *The Annotated Alice: Alice's Adventures in Wonderland & Through the Looking-glass.* Notes by Martin Gardner. New York: Norton, 2000.

Jones, Jo Elwyn, and J. Francis Gladstone. *The Alice Companion: A Guide to Lewis Carroll's Alice Books.* New York: New York University Press, 1998.

Oates, Joyce Carol. "Personal Best: Alice in Wonderland and Alice Through the Looking Glass." *Salon.* Available online. URL: http://www.salon.com/weekly/carroll960930.html. Downloaded July 12, 2002.

Phelps, Gilbert. "Lewis Carroll: Through the Looking-glass." *An Introduction to Fifty British Novels: 1600–1900.* London: Pan Books, 1979, 407–419.

Reichertz, Ronald. *The Making of the Alice Books: Lewis Carroll's Uses of Earlier Children's Literature.* Montreal: McGill-Queen's University Press, 1997.

ALLAN QUATERMAIN HENRY RIDER HAGGARD (1887)

Henry Rider HAGGARD wrote *Allan Quatermain* as a sequel to his popular first novel, *KING SOLOMON'S MINES* (1885). An instant best-seller, it appeared as a serial in *Longman's Magazine* between January and August of 1887. As a young fan, Winston Churchill wrote that he preferred "A.Q." to *King Solomon's Mines,* and many readers agreed.

Allan Quatermain features the three main characters from *King Solomon's Mines,* with its first-person point-of-view narrator Allan Quatermain, and compatriots, Sir Henry Curtis and Captain John Good. Readers recognized the three as stereotypes common to 19th-century QUEST/adventure stories. Sir Henry acts as the charming, self-courageous aristocrat who "gets the girl." The humorous Captain Good is an egotistical, comical, and skilled naval officer. Quatermain, however, varies from the quest's prototypical hero. He is neither young, handsome, nor dashing, and his voice of reason and emotional vulnerability, coupled with a lack of desire for fortune or fame, separate him from the norm. A two-year-old diary entry begins the novel, revealing his grief over his son's death. That loss underlies a sense of regret over a changing world in which society values material goods above human lives. A veteran Africa traveler, he considers similarities between the "civilized" English and the "uncivilized" Zulu natives, concluding, "civilization is only savagery silver-gilt." England cannot satisfy his longings, with its CLASS STRUCTURE, no longer focused on traditional ideals. When Curtis and Good agree to accompany him to South Africa, Quatermain seeks the wealth of self-understanding and self-acceptance. The group's goal is to determine the truth behind the legend of darkest Africa's hidden "great white race."

As the action rises, the trio and their servants meet a Zulu warrior from their past, Umslopogaas, who wields with deadly accuracy a battle-axe named *Inkosi-Kaas* (Chieftainess). He greets Quatermain using the Englishman's Zulu name, *Macumazahn,* or "he who keeps a bright look-out at night." Umslopogaas joins the group, which first visits a missionary outpost, based on a real-life station Haggard visited run by a Dr. Merensky. After proving themselves in battle against renegade natives to rescue the missionary's kidnapped daughter, the band moves on, encouraged by the missionary's tale of a visitor who claimed to have seen the lost civilization. Their entourage adds Alphonse, a clownish sidekick who introduces every possible Frenchman stereotype, including that of chef.

The four major characters and Alphonse discover their goal, "The Frowning City," only after surviving adventures that claim all the servants. A trip along a subterranean river suggests the traditional quest character's descent into Hades, including the adventurers' exposure to a pillar of fire. Produced by a volcano, the pillar offers stunning imagery and prototypical man-versus-environment conflict. The symbolism of water as a vehicle of rebirth signals the arrival of never-before-experienced situations in the characters' new lives as they emerge from the cavern.

Like all quest characters, this band faces many obstacles, some in the form of "monsters." The monsters include an impressively drawn group of giant foaming-at-the-mouth crabs that grimly suggest Charles DARWIN's theory of survival of the fittest, a topic of interest to Victorian readers. That suggestion would interest NEW HISTORICISM critics, as would the fear of the lost city's priests that foreigners might introduce a new religion to displace their sun worship. When the high priest questions Quatermain about religion, he almost swoons when Quatermain replies that his culture follows at least 95 different religions. FORMALISM critics would note the use of traditional literary symbols, such as the color white to represent purity and gold to note value or worth.

The adventure genre demands its heroes encounter and conquer beautiful women, fulfilled by the twin queens of the Zu-Vendi dynasty. The contrast between the twins, who first appear with right shoulders and breasts bared, would interest FEMINIST CRITICS. Queen Nyleptha, of "dazzling fairness," has a "sweet" smile and a "crown" of golden curls, with a mouth predictably "curved like Cupid's bow." Her sister and obvious foil, Sorais, has wavy black hair, darker skin, dark lustrous eyes, and a mouth that seems "cruel" to the observant Quatermain, suggesting the doppelgänger—an evil twin, from the German term that translates as "double walker." Victorian readers recognized similarities between Haggard's queens and females of fairy and folktales, where golden hair predicts goodness and passivity, characteristics preferable to those of the dark female, who typically embodies intelligence and activity, often challenging the gender role of the male hero. As the two queens battle, it is not over political or social disagreements, but rather disagreements of the heart; both desire Sir Henry, again suggesting tales in which two females battle for power or romance. Haggard's comments, through Quatermain, on the nature of women, delivered at times with a narrative wink, include reflection on the fact that "if ladies have a will," they will generally get their way; that they are, by nature "loquacious"; that women are weak and most often "actresses," not to be trusted. Haggard also questions traditional thought in a neat gender reversal when Nyleptha first accuses Quatermain of spinning "spiders' webs of words," and then remarks, "the poet has said that man is like a snake." Of additional interest are multiple uses of the traditional symbolic imagery of woman as a bird in a cage and Nyleptha's identification with the moon, while the civilization's male priests identify with the sun.

In a vicious battle, Nyleptha defeats her sister, or, more correctly, her forces, led not by herself but by the English visitors and Umslopogaas. By contrast, the more active Sorais, nicknamed "Queen of the Night," leads her own forces, but her defeat by her sister's male-led forces returns gender roles to their norm. When Sorais commits suicide by thrusting what amounts to a silver stake through her heart, Nyleptha reigns with her king consort, Sir Henry.

Sir Henry assumes much of the actual duties of royalty, making major decisions about the culture's future. However, contrary to what readers raised to believe in the benefits of IMPERIALISM expect, he refuses to force "civilized" activities from his own culture into that of the Zu-Vendis. Perhaps echoing Haggard's own doubts, Sir Henry expounds upon the fact that the "generous hearted" people of Zu-Vendi should continue to enjoy the "blessings" of their barbarism. He intends to save the culture being destroyed by tourists, politicians, and teachers who will bring "greed, drunkeness, new diseases, gunpowder, and general demoralization." In the end, Alphonse alone returns to the outside world to deliver Quatermain's account of all their adventures.

A superb example of the African adventure story, *Allan Quatermain* appealed to Victorian cultural sensibilities as much as to the desire for entertainment. In addition to offering thoughtful commentary on the pros and cons of imperialism, it also deals with class structure and questions of race, psychology, sexuality, and evolution, topics that greatly interested Victorians. The novel may be Haggard's comment on the threat to the British Empire that he saw everywhere evident, from the dissolution of the landed aristocracy to the threat against Christianity in Charles DARWIN's 1859 *On the Origin of Species*.

BIBLIOGRAPHY

Butts, Dennis. Introduction to *Allan Quatermain,* by Henry Rider Haggard. Oxford: Oxford University Press, 1995.

Campbell, Joseph. *The Hero with a Thousand Faces.* 1949. Princeton, N.J.: Princeton University Press, 1968.

Haggard, H. Rider. *Allan Quatermain.* Oxford: Oxford University Press, 1995.

ALLEGORY

Allegory is narration or description where elements including events, actions, characters, settings, and objects represent abstractions. Such elements may be interesting in themselves, but their importance lies in their implication, as with the character names Faith, Hope, or Charity. In an allegory, such names would not be symbolic, as the characters actually embody the abstraction. Readers derive meaning from associations made between fictional elements and the abstraction. The skill by which an author suggests such associations, and the success of their achievement in making a universal truth available to all readers, measures the success of the allegory. Allegories originally clarified divine mysteries in stories intended for a general audience, such as a church congregation, and were thus DIDACTIC, or meant to instruct.

Allegory may be figurative or narrative. An example of figurative allegory would be a character named Justice who carries a scale in order to weigh evidence; thus, a feature of justice is reproduced in the Justice figure. In narrative allegory, a sequence of events in the plot's rising action may correspond to a progression of historical or psychological events. An example would be *ROBINSON CRUSOE* (1719) by Daniel DEFOE, in which the main character's activities trace the events of civilization, as he must construct a livable environment for himself. Some Christian critics view J. R. R. Tolkien's *Lord of the Rings* trilogy as Christian allegory. Probably the best example of allegory in the English language is John Bunyan's *PILGRIM'S PROGRESS* (1678 and 1684) with its main character, Everyman. Children's fables, while not strictly allegory, may be labeled allegorical due to an inherent didactic theme.

Literary critics may employ allegory as a mode of interpretation of a work, not intended as allegory by its author. Such works may be seen as allegorical in relation to the author's culture.

BIBLIOGRAPHY

Byfield, Ted, and Virginia Byfield. "What Tolkien's Enduring Fables Can Teach Those Aiming to Captivate Today's Youth." *Newsmagazine* 29.17 (September 2, 2002): 49.

ALL THE YEAR ROUND

Founder and editor Charles DICKENS published the weekly magazine *All the Year Round* from its inception in 1859, when it superceded *HOUSEHOLD WORDS,* another publication edited by Dickens. As part of the announcement of the new publication, Dickens wrote,

> That fusion of the graces of the imagination with the realities of life, which is vital to the welfare of any community, and for which I have striven

from week to week as honestly as I could during the last nine years, will continue to be striven for "all the year round."

He held his position until his death in 1870, when his son, Charles Dickens the Younger, assumed editorship. He retained that post until its final issue appeared in 1895.

The size, format, and contributors were essentially the same as for *Household Words,* with an emphasis on a family audience. Thus, *All the Year Round* attracted a great deal of fiction that all ages could enjoy. Dickens published his own novels Great Expectations and *A* Tale of Two Cities in this magazine. Additional work included The Woman in White and The Moonstone by Wilkie Collins. Charles Lever, Edward Bulwer-Lytton, and Mrs. Elizabeth Gaskell were among the other contributors.

BIBLIOGRAPHY
Dickens, Charles. *Contributions to* All the Year Round. McLean, Va.: Indypublish.com, 2001.
Fader, Daniel, and George Bornstein. *British Periodicals of the 18th and 19th Centuries.* Ann Arbor: University Microfilms, 1972, 77–79.

ALTON LOCKE CHARLES KINGSLEY (1850)

Charles Kingsley's second novel, *Alton Locke,* guaranteed his fame as a writer about controversial topics. A clergyman, Kingsley regularly attacked social injustice and supported laborers' rights. Like other socially conscious writers including George Gissing, Kingsley publicized inexcusable conditions in which most workers toiled and lived. His writing added to the mid-1800's discussion broadly labeled the Condition of England, which focused on the quality of life following the Industrial Revolution. For his first novel, Yeast (1848), he became acquainted with Thomas Cooper, a shoemaker, poet, and self-educated member of the Chartist movement, whose life resembled that of the fictional Alton Locke. Two additional workers affecting the characterizations were Walter Cooper, Chartist and tailor, and Gerald Massey, a self-educated son of poor parents who wrote the working man's journal *Spirit of Freedom.* All three represented the fiercely independent, politically inclined, self-educated poet-laborer that fascinated Kingsley. A series of 1849 articles in the *Morning Chronicle* dealing with labor conditions endured by tailors and seamstresses inspired Kingsley to produce a pamphlet under the pen name Parson Lot titled *Cheap Clothes and Nasty.* It contained facts about the clothing trade he would feature in *Alton Locke.* A thesis novel with a didactic focus on social issues, *Alton Locke* doled out liberal doses of social consciousness to readers. The novel brims with references to classic and contemporary literature, philosophy and politics, and provides explanatory notes.

The novel opens with Locke's first-person pronouncement, "I am a Cockney among Cockneys. Italy and the Tropics, the Highlands and Devonshire, I know only in dreams." Kingsley shatters stereotypes of the workingman as unconcerned over self-identity with few dreams beyond fulfilling basic physical needs. The shattering continues as readers trace Locke's doomed efforts to attain a formal education and fame as a poet. Born to a shopkeeper who died when Locke is young, he matures in a household on the verge of penury with a fundamentalist religious mother and a frail sister. Mrs. Locke expects Alton will adopt her religious views. When he rebels against the ideas of religious election and the theory that some individuals are born to suffer, his mother evicts him. Experience later validates his belief that suffering is caused by "man's avarice and laziness and ignorance." He continues work in a tailor's shop until the owner dismisses all employees who protest lowered wages.

Locke meets a kindly Scottish bookstore owner named Saunders Mackaye, whose personality and philosophies resemble those of philosopher Thomas Carlyle. Mackaye represents moral authority, but takes no pleasure in punishment of lawbreakers. He encourages Locke's poetry, urging him to abandon imitation and discover his own voice. Locke declares, "if I had any poetic power, I must do my duty therewith in that station of life to which it had pleased God to call me, and look at everything simply and faithfully as a London artisan." He becomes interested in the Chartist movement and attends political meetings. Locke's friend Crossthwaite leads him to understanding by asking, "What interest or feeling of yours or mine, or any man's you ever spoke to [. . .] do Alderman A*** or Lord C***D*** represent? They represent property—and we have none."

Visiting a gallery with his wealthy cousin, George, Locke meets Lillian Staunton, her father, a university dean, and her cousin, Eleanor Staunton. He exchanges pleasantries, falls in love with Lillian, and departs inspired to write love poetry. At Mackaye's urging, he visits George at Cambridge, hoping to promote his poetry. He learns of George's attitude that life owes him happiness due to his wealth and station, and he becomes disenchanted with Cambridge, despite his ability to spend time with Lillian. Lillian is a delightful, but shallow, young woman, while Eleanor is the more intelligent, principled being. Her constant philosophical, religious, and intellectual challenges irritate Locke, who judges her "a proud, harsh and exclusive aristocrat."

The dean offers to help Locke publish his poetry, but he must first find subscribers. Desperate to publish in order to impress Lillian, Locke believes the dean's suggestion that "few great poets have been politicians." Ousted from tailoring, Locke writes for various publications. Disheartened by George's declaration of his intention to "win" Lillian, Locke considers suicide. He eventually complies with the dean and edits the socially conscious content from his poetry, failing his art and his fellow workers and Chartists. Guilt drives him to help conduct a Chartist protest, as he judges the workers dullards needing a "Londoner's" leadership. He loses control of the crowd, which riots, earning him a three-year prison sentence. He spends his time studying the Bible, Shakespeare, Hume, law, and philosophy, and learns French, then begins his autobiography. As he watches building progress on a Gothic cathedral and school through the window bars, he builds his own new life. After learning that his cousin George is a successful country rector and will soon be married to Lillian, he fears, Alton contemplates England's future, hoping George does not represent it.

When released, Locke returns to his friend Crossthwaite, who declares, "The towns shall win the Charter for England! And then for social reform, sanitary reform, [. . .] cheap food, interchange of free labour, liberty, equality, and brotherhood for ever!" But ruffians have infiltrated, and Locke fears his ideals will die. The death of his best friend, Mackaye, leaves him isolated until Eleanor appears. Locke struggles with the desire to trust, feeling "hers was the only intellect in the world to which I would have submitted mine," but he blames her for his loss of Lillian. Locke contracts typhus and has visions; upon regaining consciousness, he realizes Eleanor has nursed him back to health. At last prepared to listen, he chooses socialist Christianity to replace political ideology now tainted by violence and greed. Locke sails for America to join Crossthwaite in exile in Texas, but dies during the voyage.

Alton Locke shares stylistic aspects with other writings. Locke's visions closely resemble the drug-induced spectacles described by Thomas De Quincey in *Confessions of an English Opium Eater* (1821–22). Kingsley's introduction of politics and CLASS STRUCTURE into his novel helped answer some of his contemporaries' criticism that novels should not make only love and marriage the business of life. The novel's thoughtful approach to social rights and responsibility prefigured the social self-consciousness of books like George ELIOT's *MIDDLEMARCH* (1871–72). However, Kingsley later revised his novel to a charge of hypocrisy. He first wrote of Locke's stay at Cambridge lambasting a university system in which only young men who could afford private tutors were accepted. His own experience as a tutor to the Prince of Wales underlies Kingsley's description of frequent student drunkenness, rowdy behavior, and use of prostitutes on and near the university property. Later, however, when Kingsley accepted a position at Cambridge, he revised the novel's harshest scenes, earning criticism from fellow writers. Ironically, his own lines indicted him, as he had declared in one scene, "The masters of arts were humbugs . . . for 'they knew all the evils, and clamoured for reform till they became Dons themselves; and then, as soon as they found the old system pay, they settled down on their lees, and grew fat on port wine, like those before them.'"

BIBLIOGRAPHY

Cripps, Elizabeth. Introduction to *Alton Locke: Tailor and Poet, an Autobiography,* by Charles Kingsley. New York: Oxford University Press, 1983.

De Quincey, Thomas. *Confessions of an English Opium Eater and Other Writings.* Edited by Grevel Lindop. New York: Oxford University Press, 1992.

Tillotson, Kathleen. *Novels of the Eighteen-forties.* Oxford: Clarendon Press, 1954.

AMAZING MARRIAGE, THE GEORGE MEREDITH (1895)

The last of George MEREDITH's novels, *The Amazing Marriage* resembles his previous works in its defense of women against men's errors. In his fiction and real life, Meredith declared man to be in need of woman, who could educate and encourage him in combating adversity. He also believed man could learn from nature, such as the Austrian and German landscapes in *The Amazing Marriage.* He thus associates woman with nature, especially hills and mountains, suggesting she is a higher moral being. The novel's protagonist, Carinthia, whose very name echoes the city of Corinth, first comes to her future husband's attention through a written description that he believes succeeds in fusing "a woman's face and grand scenery, to make them inseparable." Later, she is described as "a noble daughter of the woods" and approaches her husband exhibiting "her rocky brows. They were not barren crags, and her shape was Nature's ripeness."

Critics note that *The Amazing Marriage* contains elements from each of Meredith's previous novels, in addition to reverence for nature, including themes of sibling and spousal love, respect, treachery and betrayal, and emphasis on the disaster resulting from actions based on passion, rather than logic. The various voices telling the story include those of a traditional narrator, anxious to distinguish his literary genre from romance, represented by another narrator identified as Dame Gossip. She acts as a chorus at the book's beginning, sharing mythology that grew up around the marriage of the novel's two main characters, including a popular ballad. The narrator declares his approach as based on intellect, not just on romantic emotions. A debate between the dame and the narrator shapes a self-conscious text that comments upon the growing popularity of the novel form. Meredith uses mythology to shape Carinthia, "a beautiful Gorgon—a haggard Venus," "something of Persephone rising to greet her mother," and "an Amazon schooled by Athene." In addition to the narrators, Meredith supplies characters' spoken aphorisms, written letters, and one "Note-book." The many voices emphasize his condemnation of society for allowing public opinion to influence a private relationship. Society forces a man and woman together to satisfy its requirements for gossip and intrigue, rather than supporting the couple in exploring their compatibility.

In Meredith's plot, the beautiful Carinthia and her brother, Chillon, lose their father, Captain Kirby, and depend on the largesse of their stingy English uncle, Levellier. Pulled from their Austrian mountain home, they demonstrate their close relationship to nature by following their father's tradition of walking outside to "call the morning." Carinthia meets Gower Woodseer, whose last name alludes to nature and his possession of insight that other characters lack. Woodseer, a philosopher entranced with Carinthia's beauty, writes of her in his Note-book. Meredith supposedly based Woodseer on Robert Louis STEVENSON, who had died the year before publication of the novel.

After Woodseer's friend, the wealthy, egotistical Lord Fleetwood, reads the notes, he wants to meet Carinthia. Fleetwood's name also connects him to nature, but suggests blind movement, rather than a communing. A womanizer, Fleetwood proposes to Carinthia at a ball after knowing her for only one day. While Fleetwood realizes his folly and wants to withdraw the offer, Levellier insists on his upholding it. Meredith emphasizes society's injustice and foreshadows the couple's disastrous future when one observer thinks, "very wealthy noblemen were commonly, perhaps necessarily, eccentric, for thus they proved themselves egregious, which the world expected them to be." As the carriage departs with the couple, Carinthia, ironically, feels grateful to be "in her husband's hands." She dreams of a fine future with Fleetwood, fancying herself "his comrade. . . . Now she had the joy of trusting her husband." Fleetwood quickly dashes that trust, making his new wife attend a prize fight before checking into an inn. When a friend who plans to accompany Fleetwood notices

Carinthia he asks with surprise, "Lady coming?" Fleetwood replies, "I fancy she sticks to the coach." The next morning, Fleetwood deserts Carinthia after impregnating her. Carinthia weeps with a maid who professes her loyalty, after which the narrator comments, "They were two women." He then describes Fleetwood and his companion in a coach, spouting "the lusty anecdote, relieved of the interdict of a tyrannical sex." Clearly, Fleetwood is the tyrant, not Carinthia.

The birth of his son further angers and frustrates Fleetwood, and Carinthia returns to the mountains. She stays at Whitechapel with Gower Woodseer and develops a relationship with his father, who cares for the poor. Gower thinks of his visitor as "Corinthia, Saint and Martyr," emphasizing her moral superiority to Fleetwood, but he tries to reunite the couple. He convinces Fleetwood of the merit of their marriage, but Carinthia has decided to serve as a nurse in Spain, where her brother lives. Carinthia tells Fleetwood, "I have my brother and my son. No more of husband for me!" In pursuit of Carinthia, Fleetwood encounters Owain Wythan and asks whether he knows Carinthia and her brother. Wythan replies, "They both come to the mind as faith comes—no saying how; one swears by them," making clear their spiritual nature. Fleetwood becomes a Roman Catholic monk, dying an unhappy and unfulfilled man. Following his death, Carinthia marries Wythan, a man of few words but worshipful eyes.

BIBLIOGRAPHY

Argyle, Gisela. "Meredith's 'Readable Marriage': a Polyphony of Texts." *Essays in Literature* 22 (Fall 1995): 244–52.

Bailey, Elmer James. *The Novels of George Meredith: A Study.* New York: Haskell House, 1971.

AMERICAN, THE HENRY JAMES (1877)

Henry JAMES published *The American* first as a serial in *The Atlantic Monthly* between June 1876 and May 1877, then as a volume in 1877. Born an American, James made his first extended visit to Europe at age 26, returned two years later, and would remain there for the next 25 years, returning intermittently to the United States. *The American* represented the first of his several quiet novels that examined Americans like himself, searching for an improved existence in new surroundings.

The narrator introduces the main character, Christopher Newman, an American who has traveled to France in 1868 and visits the Louvre. A confident businessman, he suffers self-doubt for the first time while deciding how to interpret art. That questioning of self-identity signals the reader of an approaching metamorphosis, as does the name Newman. The narrator clarifies that Newman does not represent the traditional romantic hero; instead, something "profoundly reassuring" exists in his manner and bearing. Newman becomes acquainted with Noemie Nioche, who sells her painted copies of the masters to tourists. Newman's question of her—"*Combien?*" or "How much?"—signals his approach to the world; he acquires through fair negotiation. After agreeing to take French lessons from Noemie's father, Newman meets an American acquaintance, Mr. Tristram. Newman adopts Tristram and his wife as touchstones, with Tristram considering himself integrated into the French culture. Newman likes Mrs. Tristram, who the narrator describes as a plain woman, unsatisfied with life and her husband, who she did not marry for love, but rather to validate her fine manners; his dullness complements her own spark. She introduces Newman to Parisian society; he feeds her gossip.

The narrator discusses Newman's military background, explaining that his killing experiences left him with "an angry, bitter sense of the waste of precious things." They also shaped his personality as a man in search of something to value, as society values the art in the Louvre. Before leaving the United States, he had discovered he needed a vacation when he did something very uncharacteristic; he passed up the chance to seek revenge against a business associate who had mistreated him in the past. Suddenly, the chance to make money off another's misfortunes did not appeal. That act foreshadows the novel's conclusion.

This character shaping lays the groundwork for Mrs. Tristram's matchmaking of Newman with Claire de Cintré, the 25-year-old widowed daughter of a deceased French aristocrat father named Bellegarde and an English mother. Her name suggests she possesses a clarity of self-vision, which Newman lacks.

Entranced by her beauty and grace, made all the more stunning in contrast to her formal and cold family, Newman does not question her loyalty to that family. Mrs. Tristram explained to Newman that in a family with a French head, "you must act, not for your own pleasure, but for the advantage of the family," a warning he ignores. Even when Madame Bellegarde, Claire's mother, admits, "I am on my knees to money," Newman feels he can overcome their influence with Claire. He later learns that from her brief, unhappy marriage to a much older gentleman, she should have inherited wealth. However, his family fought the young widow, and due to some unpleasant information, she gave up her suit, angering her mother, who expected to share in her fortune. All these facts foreshadow an unhappy future.

Befriended by Claire's brother, Valentin, whose name signals an affair of the heart, Newman succeeds in becoming engaged to Claire, accepted by family vote, including that of Claire's older brother, Urbain. She agrees to marry after Newman tells her she is the woman he always imagined marrying, except far more perfect. He is puzzled when his words seem to hurt her. Newman persists in the romance despite Valentin's warning regarding old established families like his: "[O]ld trees have crooked branches." The Bellegarde family, as suggested by its name, guards a dark secret. Newman assures Claire that she can trust him. When Mrs. Bread, another symbolically named character and an old Bellegarde servant, tells Newman to take Claire far away from the family, he begins at last to wonder about the household.

Through Newman, Valentin falls in love with Noemie, the artist from the Louvre. When Valentin learns Noemie has moved out of her father's house, he shares his concern with Newman that she has chosen some other man. After six months of romancing Claire, Newman wonders at her continued sadness. She declares, "I'm old, I'm cold, I'm a coward," but he protests her low self-assessment and rejoices over Madame Bellegarde's announcement that she will give a party to celebrate the couple's engagement. Shortly thereafter, Valentin passes along what he has learned of Noemie's lover, but she later contradicts Valentin, telling Newman she has not left her father. On the evening of the party, Urbaine's wife wears a crimson dress decorated with silver moon slivers, which Newman describes as "moonshine and bloodshed," echoed in her delighted cry of "murder by moonlight!" Their interchange foreshadows a tragic turn.

When Newman later visits Claire, Mrs. Bread takes him upstairs, where he discovers Claire is moving to the country, and she breaks their engagement, again declaring herself a terrible person. Despite his demand for an explanation, Madame Bellegarde declares only, "We are very proud." When he learns from Mrs. Tristram that the family wants Claire to marry Lord Deepmere, an English nobleman, he becomes incensed. As Deepmere's name suggests, he possesses no "deep" qualities, but only an outward appearance of value. As Newman becomes more upset, Valentin exchanges words with Noemie's escort to the theater, a duel transpires, and Valentin suffers a mortal wound. Just before dying, he shares with Newman the key to reclaim Claire. Something terrible happened to his father, and Mrs. Bread knows the story. Valentin tells Newman that he can blackmail the Bellegardes with the information, forcing the marriage.

Newman appeals to Claire, who again rejects him, claiming a curse on her family, "like a religion," forces her to leave Paris, but she will not marry Lord Deepmere. Instead, she will become a Carmelite nun. The news infuriates Newman, filling him with a "sorer sense of wrong than he had ever known." Newman speaks with Mrs. Bread, declaring of the Bellegardes, "I want to bring them down, down, down . . . to mortify them as they mortified me!" Mrs. Bread hesitates, and then tells Newman of the count's long illness, his rally toward health, then his sudden relapse, which ended in death. She suspected that Madame Bellegarde instigated the relapse, a fact the count verified. Mrs. Bread cautions Newman that Urbain alone knew of Madame Bellegarde's actions; Claire and Valentin only suspected them. Part of Madame's plot was to force Claire to marry a wealthy man she did not love, something that her husband had forbidden. Only with his death could Madame accomplish the match that she believed would bring her future wealth.

Mrs. Bread provides Newman with a piece of paper written in the old count's hand that states his wife had murdered him. Although Newman does not know the exact means she used, circumstances indicate that she administered an overdose of painkiller to the count. Newman understands that he can ruin the family that has caused him so much grief with the evidence. He also understands, however, that he can never reclaim Claire, who has committed herself to the convent, where she refuses to see her family. In the novel's conclusion, he elects to accept his fate and, true to his character, rejects the temptation for revenge. He has asked Mrs. Bread to join him as his housekeeper and makes plans to return to America. Before leaving, he visits Mrs. Tristram to explain that he could have ruined the Bellegardes but decided against it. This decision echoes the business decision made before he left the States and signals a permanent adoption of compassion. He burns the letter in the fireplace, with the fire symbolizing purification through destruction.

BIBLIOGRAPHY

Cargill, Oscar. *The Novels of Henry James.* New York: Macmillan, 1961.

Chen, Shudong. *Henry James: The Essayist Behind the Novelist.* Studies in American Literature, vol. 59. Lewiston, N.Y.: Edwin Mellen, 2003.

ANASTASIUS, OR MEMOIRS OF A GREEK THOMAS HOPE (1819)

Thomas HOPE's *Anastasius, or Memoirs of a Greek,* reached instant popularity. The anonymously published three-volume novel was at first credited to George Gordon, Lord Byron, who had written popular accounts of the Near East; Hope later claimed authorship in BLACKWOOD'S EDINBURGH MAGAZINE. According to a 1911 encyclopedia article, Byron was so impressed with the novel's depiction of Greece that he wept with regret that he had not written *Anastasius.*

Hope's vast travels allowed him to bring authenticity to the popular PICARESQUE form, focusing on an 18th-century Greek rogue who begins his first-person narration with a capsulated personal history: "My family came originally from Epirus: my father settled at Chio. His parentage was neither exalted nor yet low." The youngest of seven children, he states, "poor Anastasius brought up the rear with but indifferent prospects." Therefore, he must embark on wide travels and the great adventures common to a picaro to find his fortune. Barred by the Turks from becoming a soldier, and by his parents from becoming a sailor, he agrees early on to enter church service and gains a slight education, although study bores him. Attracted still by a militant lifestyle, he decides to lead a personal "crusade" with a band of "ruffians" as his followers. His father pays for the damage he inflicts, and Anastasius leaves the church and pretends an interest in learning a trade. While awaiting an appointment to an apprenticeship, Anastasius serves the local consul and falls in love with his daughter. He soon must escape her attentions and, when his merchant apprenticeship is denied, surrenders to the song of sailors on a Venetian brig, offering his services to its captain. Although terrified to leave home, Anastasius thrills to follow in the footsteps of his idol, Achilles, embarking on adventures of his own. As he moves about the country, he takes on various positions, learning "there is a danger in doing things too well. What was at first volunteered as an extraordinary feat, is soon assigned as a daily task." This becomes his credo, and the avoidance of routine prevents his settling down. He engages in varied adventures, including field battle; imprisonment; service to merchants, physicians, and wise men; encounters with pirates and with Jewish, Christian and Muslim leaders; numerous romances, and the gain and loss of fortunes along the way.

References to *Anastasius* prove that it was widely read. Thomas De Quincey mentions its lack of authenticity when dealing with the subject of opium usage in his own book *Confessions of an English Opium Eater* (1822). Although De Quincey declares the author of *Anastasius* "brilliant," he also writes that the author's "grievous misrepresentation" of the effects of opium clearly demonstrate he is not a user. The character of Anastasius was employed in a most uncomplimentary way by the writer of an 1860 review of *The Memoirs of William Beckford of Fonthill, author of "Vathek."* The North American Review noted that Beckford's life offered little to admire, as he was completely selfish and held his fellow man in utter disregard, his "pursuits" having less value than those of "Anastasius Hope, 'when he meditated on mutineers and planned pokers.'" Mary SHELLEY's journals indicated she owned the book in 1821.

Anastasius was highly autobiographical, as Hope filled it with his own travel experiences. Later critics found its style too elaborate and too heavy with narrative, seldom interrupted by dialogue. Ignoring the later commandment of fiction to "show, don't tell," Hope did little other than narrate the plot to the reader. When the narrator promises at the book's end to do away with the "eternal" I, he simply substitutes another narrator. While the novel remained of interest decades later as a specimen of picaresque, its heavy authorial intervention did not please audiences who appreciated realistic, dynamic characters and light narration. Copies of the book remain scarce, and few literature courses give it more than a cursory mention.

BIBLIOGRAPHY

"Hope, Thomas." *1911 Encyclopedia. Pagewise.* Available online URL: http://27.1911encyclopedia.org/H/HO/HOPE_SCOTT_JAMES_ROBERT.htm. Downloaded September 12, 2002.

Hope, Thomas. *Anastasius.* London: John Murray, 1820.

De Quincey, Thomas. *Confessions of an English Opium Eater and Other Writings.* Edited by Grevel Lindop. New York: Oxford University Press, 1992, 42.

"Mary Shelley's Reading: Chronological List." University of Pennsylvania. Available online. URL: http://www.english.upenn.edu/~jlynch/FrankenDemo/MShelley/bydates.html. Downloaded September 12, 2002.

ANTIQUARY, THE SIR WALTER SCOTT

(1816) Unlike Sir Walter SCOTT's heroic adventure novels, *The Antiquary,* third in his series of Waverley novels and his declared favorite, follows the foibles of a character named Jonathan Oldbuck who studies historic times. As his name symbolizes, and his title of antiquary implies, Oldbuck is enthralled with artifacts. He collects and dates them and evaluates their worth, emphasizing a theme of evaluation; while the value of objects may change, the worth of a man's integrity does not, a truth that Scott adopts as his theme. A second theme deals with man's attempts to understand the past in order to plan an enjoyable future.

In addition to Oldbuck, the novel's characters include a young man the reader first knows as William Lovel, who, as his name suggests, will provide half of the plot's romantic pair. Lovel and Oldbuck meet while traveling and form a bond. What Oldbuck later discovers is Lovel's purpose in visiting his Scottish village, Fairport. In his true identity as Major Neville, Lovel fell in love with Isabella Wardour, a recent transplant to Scotland who, along with her father, Sir Arthur Wardour, lives just outside the village. As suggested by his last name, Sir Arthur represents an aristocratic class that gained its fame and fortune by defending royalty. Sir Arthur had discouraged Isabella's relationship with Neville, believing him socially unsuitable. Neville will later be proven, thanks to the help of the antiquary's skills, heir of Glenallan and thus worthy of Isabella's hand. However, before that truth can be revealed, the reader enjoys the irony of Neville/Lovel existing under the nose of the irascible, egoistic Oldbuck, who fancies himself an expert in "sniffing out" objects of value.

Established as a complementary character to Oldbuck and somewhat of a foil, Edie Ochiltree, the local king's bedesman and type of privileged beggar, haunts the area and undercuts some of Oldbuck's claims regarding the historical value of certain sites. Scott adds an advertisement (foreword) to the novel explaining the unusual position of Scotland's bedesmen who, while to all outward appearances lacking any type of status, wear a badge that marks them as members of a select group originally put on stipend to pray for the king. Ochiltree increases the irony of the antiquary's claim to status when Oldbuck abuses the bedesman, one of the clearest symbols of tradition that exists in the Scotland of his day. This allows Scott to emphasize political themes, as the characters discuss their ancestors' loyalties to various rulers. W. M. Parker points out that in *The Antiquary,* Scott included the only example of a democratic viewpoint to be found in all his novels when giving an account of Mucklebackit, a fisherman who returns to work shortly after the death of his son. He defends his act by pointing out that he cannot afford to remain at home indulging his grief as a wealthy man might; he must feed his four remaining children.

Scott based his two main characters on real people. Oldbuck is somewhat autobiographical, as Scott was an antiquarian. However, Scott models him more definitely on George Constable, a lawyer Scott knew as a boy. Constable presented Scott with his first German dictionary, told him the tale behind Scott's later popular story "The Two Drovers," and introduced Scott to Shakespeare. Scott based Ochiltree on a resident of Ayrshire named Andrew Gemmels, a military man who had the greatest fame as a beggar in the area. Supposedly 106 years old at his death, Gemmels was immortalized in an 1849 memorial erected in Roxburgh-Newtown.

In the novel's early rising action, Lovel attends a dinner that includes Isabella and Sir Arthur Wardour and, with Ochiltree's help, rescues them from drowning at high tide as they return home. Isabella displays her tenacity when she asks, "Must we yield life . . . without a struggle?" The Wardours chose the potentially dangerous beach route home mainly to avoid further contact with Lovel. As Sir Arthur later explains to Oldbuck, Isabella had known Lovel as Major Neville while visiting her aunt in Yorkshire, but she had rejected his attentions because Neville was an apparent "illegitimate son of a man of fortune." Sir Arthur adds, "You know the opinions—prejudices, perhaps, you will call them—of our house concerning purity of birth." Oldbuck soon shows a sympathetic side that reveals he has also suffered wounds of his own due to failed relationships. He repeats a classical phrase to Lovel: "*Sed semel insanivimus omnes*—everybody has played the fool in their turn."

Sir Arthur will prove himself that fool as his family teeters on ruin due to his association with a dastardly German, Dousterswivel, whose name suggests changeability and a lack of trustworthiness. As one character remarks, Sir Arthur seems so "bewitched" by Dousterswivel, "he gars him e'en trow that chalk is cheese." Ochiltree makes clear his attitude toward the self-proclaimed philosopher by addressing him as "Maister Dustandsnivel." Ochiltree and Oldbuck both believe that Dousterswivel takes advantage of Sir Arthur's belief in spells and magic to extort money

from him. The novel's only clearly evil character, Dousterswivel uses a "spell" to detect buried treasure, luring Sir Arthur into risky investments. His incantations fit well with Scott's additional GOTHIC imagery of ancient structures, ghosts, dreams and visions, and family secrets.

Further increasing conflict, Lovel argues with Oldbuck's nephew, Hector M'Intyre, who fawns over Isabella. An egoistic hothead, M'Intyre is not favored by Oldbuck, who regards Lovel with more affection than his own family. When M'Intyre questions Lovel's military service, Lovel refuses to reveal his "identity as Major Neville, eliciting a challenge to a duel from M'Intyre. Lovel wounds M'Intyre and decides to hide in the woods, where Ochiltree takes him to a cave for shelter. A convenient secret passageway allows Lovel and Ochiltree to observe Dousterswivel convincing the naive Sir Arthur that buried treasure will solve all his problems. Additional rising action includes drownings, an accusation of murder against Ochiltree, and the realization by the earl of Glenallan, following the confession of an elderly former family servant, that Lovel is his legitimate son, the product of an early marriage for love with a woman of whom his family did not approve. As the plot reaches its climax, Neville/Lovel's identity, or true value, becomes clear, and he and Isabella are free to marry.

Scott displays his abundant knowledge of antiquities and classical literature, and a penchant for intellectual discussion that Oldbuck embodies. Scott's addition to Oldbuck's intelligence of a blustering, self-centered edge adds humor and enhances the novel with many comedic scenes. Scott's affection for his country is clear, as is his continuing fascination with its nonaristocratic population. The advertisement explains his focus on "the class of society who are the last to feel the influence of that general polish . . . because the lower orders are less restrained by the habit of suppressing their feelings." Well received by Scott's reading public, which immediate sales of 1,120 copies prove, the novel incorporated challenging colloquial Scottish expressions.

The novel influenced many, evident in various reactions by noted readers. Jane AUSTEN suggested to her rector brother James that they adopt Scott's approach of using text from actual documents in his novel by including sermons from their Uncle Henry in her novels. Maria EDGEWORTH, who became Scott's confidante, praised the book in a letter to Joanna Baille. Those who did not like the novel included poet John Keats (1795–1821), who compared it unfavorably to Henry FIELDING's *TOM JONES* (1749), and one *Edinburgh Review* critic found the character of Oldbuck disagreeable. However, a critique in the *Monthly Review* found Edie Ochiltree "sublime." Scott's friend, Daniel Terry, adapted the novel to the stage for a Covent Garden production on January 25, 1820, and the novel would be translated into seven languages. Twentieth-century author Virginia Woolf placed *The Antiquary* in the hands of her character, Mr. Ramsay, in her novel *To the Lighthouse* (1927).

Oldbuck's unconcealed misogyny interests modern FEMINIST CRITICS. He insults women regularly, labeling them "abominable" members of a "trolloping sex" and "sluts," and he calls one cleaning woman a "monkey." He also constantly berates his sister and niece with whom he lives, introducing them to Lovel as "my unlucky and good-for-nothing womankind." Scott reveals Oldbuck's hypocrisy, however, when the character explains that he keeps only women servants, as "the masculine sex was too noble to be employed in those acts of personal servitude, which in all early periods of society, were uniformly imposed on the female." He does, however, begrudgingly and fondly refer to Isabella Wardour as his worthy opponent and clearly depends upon her to help him retain the friendship of her father, just as he depends upon his waiting women to keep his life in order. Scott told friends that the novel lacked "the romance of Waverley & the adventure of G. M. & yet there is some salvation about it too for if a man will paint from nature he will be likely to amuse those who are daily looking at it." Readers in later centuries, who enjoy irony and strong character development, continue to find the book pleasurable.

BIBLIOGRAPHY

Parker, W. M. Introduction to *The Antiquary,* by Sir Walter Scott. Dutton: New York, 1966.

Grierson, Sir Herbert G. C., ed.. *Letters of Sir Walter Scott.* Vol. 4. London: Constable & Co., 1932, 238.

Wilt, Judith. *The Novels of Sir Walter Scott.* Chicago: University of Chicago Press, 1986.

ANTI-SLAVERY MOVEMENT

The anti-slavery movement in England began with 18th-century reformers determined to eliminate slavery in all English-speaking countries. While religious groups such as the Quakers had long declared themselves against slavery, abolitionists became a forceful movement when William Wilberforce and his Clapham religious sect of wealthy evangelical Anglicans began to protest enslavement of Africans in 1780. They succeeded in gaining the attention of the populace, and by 1807, abolition had become a political movement. It proved so successful that, by 1803, Parliament had abolished slavery in the West Indies, compensating slave owners who had to free their workers. In 1814, Britain purchased the Cape colony in South Africa from the Dutch, protected native workers with labor laws in 1828, and by 1833 had outlawed slavery there.

Fiction featured the anti-slavery theme, beginning with Apra BEHN's prose romance *OROONOKO* (1688), a story about an African prince who suffers enslavement and humility at the hands of English imperialists. In the 18th century, Daniel DEFOE provided a view of slavery as a moral question in his novels *ROBINSON CRUSOE* (1719) and *Colonel Jack* (1722). Mary SHELLEY filled her monster fiction, *FRANKENSTEIN* (1818), with the rhetoric of abolitionist ideals. In 1840, England held the first World Anti-Slavery Convention, a well-attended event, and in 1842 Charles DICKENS toured America, where his public speaking focused, in part, on abolition. The development of scientific theories, such as Charles DARWIN's theory of evolution made famous in *On the Origin of Species* (1859), helped convince people of the humanity of individuals, regardless of race. Joseph CONRAD's novel *The NIGGER OF THE NARCISSUS* (1897) takes this approach in featuring not simply the race of Wait, the title character, but a ship's crew split into factions that deal with the cost of sacrificing a single life to save that of several others. Adventure tales as such as those by Henry Rider HAGGARD, while racist in their emphasis on black characters as noble savages, remained clearly abolitionist in sentiment.

BIBLIOGRAPHY

Knox-Shaw, Peter. "Defoe and the Politics of Representing the African Interior." *Modern Language Review* 96, no. 4 (October 2001): 937–952.

Lee, Debbie. *Slavery and the Romantic Imagination.* Philadelphia: University of Pennsylvania Press, 2002.

Taylor, Gary. *Buying Whiteness: Race, Sex, and Slavery from the English Renaissance to African-American Literature.* Basingstoke, U.K.: Palgrave Macmillan, 2003.

AURORA LEIGH ELIZABETH BARRETT BROWNING (1856) Called by critics a confessional "novel in verse," Elizabeth Barrett BROWNING's *Aurora Leigh* represented a sustained cry for human intellectual and creative freedom, more specifically, for women's independence. A *Künstlerroman,* or story of the maturation of a young writer, the poem combines a range of forms and rhythms, including sonnet, verse drama, ballad, and blank verse, to produce what later critics termed a FEMINIST poetic. The novel form gave Browning a freer voice than her traditional genre of poetry as she attacked the lack of quality education and the civic freedom granted women in a patriarchal 19th-century Victorian society. Her targets include UTOPIAN socialism and poverty. While the poem assumes a first-person narration, it is not autobiographical. However, Aurora's name symbolizes new life, connected with the dawn of a new day and the early-morning baptismal dew, and Browning suggests that all poets should assume a new voice.

It begins with the death in Italy of Aurora's Florentine mother, symbolizing a fragmentation of the family and of Aurora's sense of self-identity. Her grieving English father pays an artist to capture his dead wife's essence in a painting that chills Aurora. She sees her mother in the portrait as "Ghost, fiend, and angel, fairy, witch, and sprite, / A dauntless Muse," suggesting the universal mother's positive and negative effects on her daughters, as she too often trains her daughter to take her place in an oppressive society. Aurora's British aunt does just

that, when the girl joins her in England at age 13, following her father's death. She literally enters her father's land, enduring a further separation from her mother by leaving Italy behind.

When Aurora observes her surrogate mother's orderly braids, wound tightly "As if for taming accidental thoughts," she sees her as "A sort of cage-bird" who had been taught that "to leap from perch to perch / Was act and joy enough for any bird." The discipline exerted on Aurora, mainly by organized religion, does not hobble her imagination, although her aunt "instructed piety" because "She misliked women who are frivolous." Aurora learns that "The works of women are symbolical" and many "pine / To a sick, inodorous light," but her soul endures. She "had relations in the Unseen, and drew / The elemental nutriment and heat / From nature, as earth feels the sun at nights," thus subverting the traditional symbol of the moon as woman who has no light of its own to the stronger female image of nature, that draws the sun's warmth and stores it as her own. Aurora's "inner life" sustains her as she exists in isolation to pursue the artist's life.

The plot contrasts Aurora with her cousin Romney Leigh, a philanthropist who supplies the physical needs of the poor but ignores their spiritual needs. Romney replaces Aurora's father as head of the family, thus causing more self-identity conflict for Aurora as he becomes her stepfather of sorts. He personifies the authority that England represents for the girl. The conflict between the two escalates as Romney proposes to Aurora in Book II, and she refuses. She answers Romney's dramatic proposal, "You misconceive the question like a man, / Who sees the woman as the complement / Of his sex merely." Romney feels Aurora's need to pursue her art is unseemly and unconventional. She explains that she aspires to the poet's life, and although Romney may be correct in suggesting her unworthy to be a poet, she will "try out your perhapses, sir, / And if I fail . . . why, burn me up my straw / Like other false works—I'll not ask for grace." Aurora will meet and interact with other women who act as potential wives for Romney, including the orphaned Marian Erle, beaten and abandoned by an alcoholic father and left with a mother who tries to prostitute her and the vicious, seductive Lady Waldemar. Themes of duplicitous motherhood continue, as Lady Waldemar evokes thoughts of maternity with her full breasts, tricking Marian into believing she will act as the girl's mother. However, her betrayal lands Marian in a French brothel to be drugged and raped, and as a result, she becomes an unwilling mother.

In Book V, Aurora shares her theories of poetry, emphasizing that poets must write about their own age: "I do distrust the poet who discerns / No character or glory in his times." She criticizes the popular romance genre as apolitical, sharing her belief that artists have an obligation to reflect on reform issues, when she writes in disgust of the poet who "trundles back his soul five hundred years . . . / To sing—oh, not of lizard of toad / Alive I' the ditch there . . . / But of some black chief, half knight, half sheep-lifter, / Some beauteous dame, half chattel and half queen." Some cite the fact that all characters end up reuniting in Italy as a weak plot convenience, but it is necessary for Aurora Leigh to return to her mother's land to resolve her issues of reproduction as an artist. Romney has been humbled, as many later BYRONIC HEROES, such as Charlotte BRONTË's Mr. Rochester, would be, through the purification of fire. Romney, like Rochester, is blinded in order to regain some inner vision.

In the end, Aurora recognizes her error in limiting her views only to those of the artist, causing her to reject all personal ties in order to pursue her ambitious vocation, while Romney agrees that his vision of care for the poor has also been too limited.

Aurora Leigh received mixed critical response, as its strong political bent offended some. However, it remained popular with the reading public, appearing in 20 editions before the century's end. Now widely anthologized in excerpts, it remains a popular work, reminding modern readers of Browning's importance to her age.

BIBLIOGRAPHY

Reynolds, Margaret, ed. *Aurora Leigh: Authoritative Text, Backgrounds and Contexts, Criticism.* New York: W.W. Norton, 1996.

Gilbert, Sandra M. "From *Patria* to *Matria:* Elizabeth Barrett Browning's Risorgimento." *Publication of the Modern Language Association* 99, no. 2 (March 1984): 194–211.

Mermin, Dorothy. "The Female Poet and the Embarrassed Reader: Elizabeth Barrett Browing's 'Sonnets from the Portuguese.'" *English Literary History* 48, no. 2 (Summer 1981): 351–67.

AUSTEN, JANE (1775–1817)

Born in England in 1775, Jane Austen was one of eight children of George Austen, a rector in Steventon, Hampshire, and his wife, Cassandra. She may have inherited her storytelling abilities from her mother, known for imaginative impromptu poetry and fiction sessions. Austen's closest companion was her sister Cassandra. While the girls obtained some formal schooling, their father actually educated them. Austen's voracious reading included works by Samuel RICHARDSON, Henry FIELDING, Alexander Pope, Oliver GOLDSMITH, David Hume, Samuel JOHNSON, Sir Walter SCOTT, William Cowper, and the romantic poet George Gordon, Lord Byron. Writings by contemporary women also interested her, including those by Fanny BURNEY, Mary BRUNTON, Ann RADCLIFFE, and Maria EDGEWORTH. Neither Jane nor Cassandra, an artist, married. However, Jane's large extended family of in-laws, nieces, nephews, and cousins gave her much domestic material on which to focus in her own writing. Her settings were informed by visits to the fashionable spa of Bath, one of her favorite places, and to London. She chose as subjects members of her own class, rather than the nobles favored by many of her female contemporary writers. She began writing seriously at age 12, and for the next six years produced plays, verse, prose works, and short novels. She collected them all into notebooks, labeled Volumes I, II, and III. Even in these early works her propensity for mild SATIRE was apparent, as she enjoyed writing PARODIES of the SENTIMENTAL FICTION so popular in her age.

Austen exhibited an antipathy toward female stereotypes and criticized through her selection of themes the lack of education and careers for women, an antiquated conception of love as idealized romance, society's view of all women as weak and incompetent, the exaggerated rivalry between women for the attention of men, and, perhaps most often, laws that forbade property inheritance by women. Her first manuscript, *Lady Susan,* written between 1793 and 1794, introduced what would become Austen's trademark character, a frustrated, independent female.

Austen may have received and refused a marriage proposal in 1802, and many critics believe she did experience a tragic love affair at some point, based on renderings of relationships in her novels. Little detail is known, because in a protective move, Cassandra later burned many letters and documents relating to her famous sister's private life. Austen's novels feature women who, while obviously passionate, conform to society's edict that they control their emotions, suggesting that she experienced that situation.

The novel that eventually became SENSE AND SENSIBILITY was begun in 1795. At first it was fashioned as an EPISTOLARY NOVEL, showing influence by Richardson, and titled *Marianne and Elinor* for its two main characters. In quick order, Austen also wrote PRIDE AND PREJUDICE, originally titled *First Impressions,* and NORTHANGER ABBEY, first titled *Susan.* She wrote *Northanger Abbey* to parody the GOTHIC romance, a subgenre out of favor with the public. Austen's father attempted unsuccessfully to sell *Pride and Prejudice.* Austen did sell *Susan* to publisher Richard Crosby; it was advertised but, for an unknown reason, was not published.

While Austen had enjoyed a peaceful existence as a single woman living with Cassandra and her parents, that ended in 1801 when George Austen retired to Bath at age 70. The family continued to move over the next eight years, sometimes living with relatives. Austen began a novel titled *The Watsons* in 1804 but could not complete it. A staggering double loss occurred when her best friend, Anne Lefroy, died in 1804, followed by her father's death in 1805. For the next four years, Austen lived with Cassandra and her mother in Bath, Clifton, and Southampton. When she later wrote of the uncertain lives of women living without a male to care for them, she was basing her writing on her own years of discomfort and insecu-

rity. Finally, in 1809, Austen's brother Edward provided a home for the three women in a cottage near his estate, close to the village of Chawton. Two years passed before Austen asked Thomas Egerton to consider publishing her novels. *Sense and Sensibility* at last appeared in 1811, when Austen was 36 years old. It was well received, with positive reviews in *The* CRITICAL REVIEW and *The* QUARTERLY REVIEW.

Egerton next published *Pride and Prejudice* (1813), followed by MANSFIELD PARK (1814). EMMA was published in 1815 by John Murray, Byron's publisher, who also brought out another edition of *Mansfield Park.* The first books appeared anonymously, but as their popularity grew, Austen revealed her identity. The Prince Regent, later King George IV, would keep a complete set of her writings at multiple residences and requested that Austen dedicate *Emma* to him. The reading public appreciated novels offering something other than the romantic melodrama and vulgarisms associated with the popular BYRONIC HERO figure. Austen's audience welcomed her domestic realism and in-depth character development.

Austen wrote up until her death, revising *Northanger Abbey (Susan)* and writing a new novel, PERSUASION (1818), both of which would be published posthumously. When she died, probably of Addison's disease, she was at work on SANDITON, a satire on invalidism and health resorts; later critics suggest she chose those topics as gentle self-mockery, because she was herself quite ill and living in Bath at the time. That remnant would later be completed by various authors who attempted to imitate Austen's style. Her brother Henry supervised publication of her final novels. They were enjoyed and praised by critics such as Scott, who reviewed *Emma,* writing that its unknown author proved important to the new movement toward realism. Scott's review, along with a later posthumous review in the January 1821 edition of the *Quarterly* by Richard Whaley, later formed the basis for most modern Austen criticism.

While Austen's work was included in the canon long before that of most other women, her true importance was realized in the 20th century with the rise of FEMINIST CRITICISM. Viewed as domestic literature emphasizing the quest by women for a partner who would allow them independence and the power to realize themselves fully, Austen's work retains a crucial place in literature studies. Her wit still delights readers as she takes to task foolish social conventions and her era's demands for proper decorum. Most of her novels have been converted to stage and to multiple cinema and television versions.

BIBLIOGRAPHY

Austen-Leigh, James Edward. *A Memoir of Jane Austen: and Other Family Recollections.* Edited by Kathryn Sutherland. New York: Oxford University Press, 2002.

Ross, Josephine. *Jane Austen: A Companion.* New Brunswick, N.J.: Rutgers University Press, 2003.

Shields, Carol. Jane Austen. New York: Viking, 2001.

B

BARCHESTER TOWERS ANTHONY TROLLOPE (1857) *Barchester Towers* was Anthony TROLLOPE's second in a group of novels, following *The WARDEN* (1855), later called the Barsetshire sequence. Published in 1857, it featured Trollope's trademark interest in religion as politics. In his focus on who would receive the reward of various religious appointments associated with the cathedral town of Barchester, Trollope features a clash between the high and low factions of the Church of England, supported by a charming love story, to produce a gently ironic tale that readers continued to find delightful more than a century later.

Set during the 1850s, the novel introduces characters concerned over who might be appointed archdeacon when the present archdeacon expired. The archdeacon's son, Dr. Grantly, held confident expectations of the appointment as his father's chosen successor, having served the church by managing diocesan affairs for years. However, Church powers appoint Dr. Proudie, whose transparent name foreshadows his character and the impression he makes as an outsider. Most damaging is his omnipresent wife, the first female ever to position herself as the power behind the deaconship. She offends Grantly and his father-in-law, Mr. Harding, choirmaster of the cathedral and the former warden, trying to impress them by making much of her set of London horses, which she will use to visit the locals. She gravely mistakes the effect of her bragging to Grantly, who, the narrator informs the readers, "could have bought every individual possession of the whole family of the Proudies, and have restored them as a gift without feeling much of the loss." Further offense is scored when Proudie appoints Mr. Slope, a supporter of low-church factions, as his public representative.

The disastrous first meeting between the old and new Barsetshire residents predicts their future combative relationships. Conflict escalates as a struggle begins between the two factions over the wardenship of the diocese-controlled charitable Hiram's Hospital, already vacant. Dr. Grantly's candidate, Mr. Harding, finds he will have to vie for the position with Mr. Slope. Seeking to exercise control over the wardenship, Slope offers it to Mr. Harding, but attaches conditions to the office that Harding rejects. With Mrs. Proudie's support, and that of some local women who enjoy Slope's sermons, Slope seems destined for success.

Mrs. Proudie's first visit to the bishop's palace to meet the Reverend Vesey Stanhope is unsuccessful, increasing her frustration with her husband's assignment. Stanhope returned from living abroad with two of his children, the charming La Signora Neroni, deserted by her Italian husband and left crippled by an accident, and her younger brother, Bertie Stanhope, an agreeable but crafty young man without income. Neither makes a positive impression on Mrs. Proudie, particularly the signora, who occupies a sofa seat intended for Mr. Slope. However, Slope falls immediately under the signora's trance, irritating Mrs. Proudie.

Mr. Slope pursues Eleanor Bold, widowed daughter of Mr. Harding, who has an admirable income, a relationship that causes Slope to regret his previous manipulation of Mr. Harding. As the action rises, Mrs. Proudie meets Mr. Quiverful, a poverty-stricken minister with a large family, and she wants him to receive the hospital wardenship; however, Mr. Slope manipulates Quiverful into claiming he does not want the appointment. Suddenly Slope finds Mrs. Proudie an indomitable force whose wishes he should not challenge.

In the romantic subplot, Eleanor visits the Grantlys at their Plumstead home, where she meets a favorite of Dr. Grantly to whom she is attracted, Mr. Arabin, minister of a nearby parish. His doctrine opposes that of Mr. Slope. A shy man without romantic experience, he cannot express his fondness for Eleanor. When Eleanor receives a letter from Slope, the Grantlys worry that she may accept his marriage proposal. She learns of their concerns and mistakenly believes that Arabin stated her intention to marry Slope. Feeling insulted by Arabin, she returns to Barchester. Meanwhile, Slope remains enthralled by La Signora Neroni but still wants to marry Eleanor. At a party, Eleanor receives and rejects marriage proposals from both Slope and Bertie Stanhope, who seeks to marry money. Trollope inserts yet another scene of crossed communication when Eleanor sees Arabin talking with the signora, and she mistakenly believes him to be attracted to her.

In the middle of all this conflict, the village receives news that the old dean of Barchester, Mr. Trefoil, is dying, meaning another vacancy would need filling, one that Slope wants to assume. He immediately visits the bishop and shares his wishes with political friends. However, he has forgotten his insult to Mrs. Proudie and underestimated her determination. As the true strength behind the bishop, she influences the move not only to retire Slope but also to have the dean position offered to Mr. Harding. In order to bring the story to its denouement, the signora refuses Slope's attentions while she shares the news of Arabin's love for Eleanor with Eleanor herself. The romance reaches a happy conclusion, and Mr. Quiverful becomes a warden. In addition, when Harding refuses the deanship offer, Arabin receives and accepts a nomination. Trollope's fictional village returns to the peace it craves, and the high-church sentiments have beaten the low.

Well received by Trollope's contemporaries, the novel was lightly criticized by some later scholars as being too "talky"; Trollope digresses into long narratives regarding women, the clerical scene, and various groups of workers. While his narratives never lack wit, their repetitive nature causes readers to skip ahead. Others have judged Trollope's handling of romance stilted and unimaginative. Nevertheless, his creation of the two antiheroes, Slope and Mrs. Proudie, mark a major accomplishment; both provide more entertainment than does Grantly. Readers may even admire Mrs. Proudie as a sharp woman who practices her ideals, desirable or not. Trollope admirably unfolds a political game before a skillfully detailed background, with his intimate knowledge of, and affection for, Barchester evident in his imagery. Moreover, while not in the comic novel category, *Barchester Towers* contains the type of humor arising from the absurdity produced by power struggles.

BIBLIOGRAPHY

Galbraith, John Kennet. Preface to *Barchester Towers,* by Anthony Trollope. London: Penguin Books, 1987.

Gilmour, Robin. Introduction to *Barchester Towers,* by Anthony Trollope. London: Penguin Books, 1987.

Glendinning, Victoria. *Anthony Trollope.* New York: Knopf, 1993.

BARRY LYNDON, THE LUCK OF

WILLIAM MAKEPEACE THACKERAY (1844 and 1852) William Makepeace THACKERAY's first novel, *The Luck of Barry Lyndon: A Romance of the Last Century by Fitz-Boodle [The Memoirs of Barry Lyndon, Esq.],* appeared in FRASER'S MAGAZINE as a monthly serial in 1844, then was revised and released in two volumes in 1852 as *The Memoirs of Barry Lyndon.* The delay of release in book form was due partially to the lack of critical response to the serial version, which discouraged Thackeray from publishing it as a novel. Because he kept a schedule of his writing and reading, much is known regarding his mental and emotional state, as well as his choice of sources.

Thackeray confessed in correspondence to not liking the work, having conceived the idea far more easily than he succeeded in executing it. He found concentration difficult while separated from his family without a permanent home. He was able to vent the frustration that supports the bitter tone of much of his early writings. His investigating the concept of "luck" no doubt reflected on his own continued lack of success. Uninterested in writing melodrama, Thackeray developed his main characters as fully formed individuals, although they are caught up in decidedly melodramatic circumstances. Thackeray's choice to position a protagonist/narrator bearing distinctly medieval mores, such as the subservience of women and the acceptance of capricious title adoption, in an unforgiving 18th-century Ireland accounts for the hyperbole that proves more ironic than comical. The first-person account delivered by Redmond Barry of Brady's Town was based mostly on a real-life figure, Andrew Robinson Bowes. Thackeray used as his source Jesse Foot's *The Lives of Andrew Robinson Bowes, Esq. and the Countess of Strathmore* (n.d., circa 1810).

Born Andrew Robinson Stoney of County Durham in King's County, Ireland, 1745, Stoney served as a lieutenant and received half pay at the age of 18. He physically and emotionally tortured his first wife, Hannah Newton, heir to a coal fortune, spending her inheritance, beating her, and, according to one account, pushing her down stairs in public. She died after a short marriage, and Stoney began to search for another means of support; he chose an heiress, Mary Eleanor Bowes, widow of the ninth earl of Strathmore. Through various schemes and seeming courageous acts, including sustaining a wound in a duel with a man who had publicly insulted the widow, Stoney won her heart, married her, and assumed the last name of Bowes. He quickly spent much of her fortune and began his pattern of abuse, but she bore him a son, strengthening their ties. His brutal affections, including whipping, beating, kicking, degrading, imprisoning, deceiving, starving, and lying, finally convinced his wife to file for a divorce. She produced an antenuptial deed of trust that freed her of Bowes's debts, and he lost all claim to their homes and income. Although he kidnapped and tortured her following

their separation, his efforts at forcing her to sign over any property to him failed, and she escaped. Bowes received a mere three-year prison sentence for his acts against his ex-wife, but his debt confined him to a cell for life. He died having earned the affection of various other women while imprisoned and produced five children with one.

Other rogue tales also influenced Thackeray, but he reproduced no details from them. Rather, his shaping Lyndon as a despicable yet fascinating man, mainly for his naiveté in believing himself always in the right, seemed to have been the outcome of various readings. He made Lyndon more appealing than Stoney when, following the death of his son, Lyndon genuinely grieves, the only instance in which his emotion seems unmotivated by potential self-gain. Thackeray's notes reveal accounts of certain events that also inspired some of the novel's scenes, one being the execution of Princess Caroline of Brunswick Wofenbuttel in 1788 by her husband, Frederic William of Wurtemberg, who beheaded her for infidelity. Thackeray may have drawn details from real-life inhabitants of Ireland, as discussed in *Burke's Landed Gentry of Ireland* (inception 1826). Thackeray also took inspiration from the fiction of some of his favorite writers, most notably Henry FIELDING's satire JONATHAN WILD THE GREAT (1743). He altered Fielding's third-person narration to first person, like that of Maria EDGEWORTH's Thady Quirk in CASTLE RACKRENT (1801), a likely influence due to the similar lack of guile in the totally untrustworthy first-hand reports. In addition, Thackeray's novel contains the same high degree of violence found in Tobias SMOLLETT's PEREGRINE PICKLE (1751).

From Redmond Barry's first sentence, "Since the days of Adam, there has been hardly a mischief done in this world but a woman has been at the bottom of it," the reader understands the narration as highly misogynistic, delivered by a man who lacks respect for all women, but cannot survive without them. The son of Roaring Harry Barry, a man "just on the verge" of making his fortune when he died, Barry lives with his mother's brother and his hated wife at Castle Brady. He becomes a self-confessed favorite with Uncle Cornelius and with some of his cousins who refer to him as "the English." Worming his way into the graces of one cousin by joining forces to hate another, he indulges in fistfights while romancing a female cousin, Honoria Brady. Eventually involved in a duel for her "honor," he must escape to Dublin where he alters his name to Barry Redmond. He joins the army and defends both sides in the Seven Years War. He openly confesses to later enjoying the title of Captain Barry, although he had never been more than a corporal, promised an ensigncy should he distinguish himself, "but Fate did not intend that I should remain long an English soldier." In an ironic scene, Barry deserts his post and masquerades as a British officer. His ruse is discovered when he claims to carry dispatches to a general who has been dead for 10 months. The truth revealed by a Prussian guard, Barry confesses to his audience, "[T]he game was up. I flung down a knife with which I had armed myself . . . 'I volunteer,' I said."

Barry eventually reunites with his uncle, Cornelius Barry. Now known as Chevalier de Blibari, Cornelius enlists Barry's company in cardsharp escapades that eventually lead to an "unfair" imprisonment. Barry later tricks the wealthy and widowed Countess of Lyndon into marriage and lives a life of debauchery and extravagance. As Barry Lyndon, he abuses his wife and stepson and spends the family fortune, actions his wife tolerates for the sake of their son, Bryan. Lyndon's luck disappears following Bryan's accidental death, when the countess's family helps her regain control of her estate. He moves to the Continent and, following the death of his wife, goes to Fleet prison for debtors, where he dies in his mother's care.

With a narrative approach appealing in its total lack of self-awareness, Lyndon presents a litany of his own achievements. Most involve some type of violence, which varies in its manner of delivery depending on the gender of Lyndon's enemies, which are legion. In his opinion born deserving all of wealth and status, Lyndon pursues his materialistic goals with enthusiasm, impervious to the moral or ethical guidelines employed by civilized humans. When he tells his readers of London's "merry" past, which he remembers fondly in his gout-ridden old age, he surmises "people have grown vastly more moral and matter-of-fact than they were at the close of the last century, when the world was young with me." That charming narrative

approach allowed the novel an enduring popularity, a later conversion to film and stage presentations, and its electronic availability on the Internet.

BIBLIOGRAPHY

Anisman, Martin J. Introduction. *The Luck of Barry Lyndon,* by William Makepeace Thackeray. New York: New York University Press, 1970.

McMasters, Juliet. *Thackeray: The Major Novels.* Toronto: University of Toronto Press, 1971.

Tillotson, Kathleen. *Novels of the Eighteen-Forties.* London: Oxford, 1965.

BEAUCHAMP'S CAREER GEORGE MEREDITH (1876)

George MEREDITH's 1876 novel, *Beauchamp's Career,* appeared serially in *The Fortnightly Review* between August 1874 and December 1875, becoming notable for its keen insight into the politics of England at the century's end. It features the life of a politician, Nevil Beauchamp, tracing the development of his interests from the Crimean War (1853–56). The narrator describes him as a youth "born with so extreme and passionate love for his country, that he thought all things else of mean importance." Meredith's trademark ironic humor appears in the first few paragraphs, as Beauchamp attempts to translate English idioms into French, in order that English naval forces might communicate with their allies against Russia: "How to be English and think French! The business was as laborious as if he had started on the rough sea of the Channel to get at them in an open boat." Beauchamp is popular with men and a favorite with women, a perfect English specimen. He develops concerns for England's political and social health, saddened that England showed "signs of decay. And signs how ignoble!" When the war ends, Beauchamp spends time in Italy, then returns to England, where patriotism inspires him to stand for Parliament.

In a romantic subplot, Beauchamp falls in love with a Frenchwoman named Renée de Croisnel. The sister of a "brother-at-arms" whose life Beauchamp once saved, the 17-year-old Renée enthralls Beauchamp when they first meet in Venice: "The air flashed like heaven descending for Nevil alone with Renée." However, Renée's father has engaged her to a wealthy marquis, whom she must marry. Beauchamp returns to England, thinking constantly of the French girl, but becomes caught up in politics and falls in love with Cecilia, daughter of Colonel Halkett. One of Beauchamp's friends explains that while "foreign women" are "capital to flirt with," English women are better for marriage. He describes Cecilia as a "Goddess," a "queen," a "charmer," and an "angel," and adds that a "man attached to a woman like that can never let himself look small."

Beauchamp's marriage to Cecilia seems certain until he hears from Renée and is tempted to renew their romance. Although Renée later leaves her husband, Beauchamp's sense of honor prevents his joining her, but in the process of making his decision, he also loses Cecilia's affections to his cousin. In the meantime, Beauchamp again finds himself caught between two additional opposing forces. One is represented by his aristocratic uncle Everard Romfrey, who holds the traditional materialistic, paternalistic views of England's landed class, and his long-time radical friend, Dr. Shrapnel, who envisions a more fair society with equally distributed wealth. The symbolically named Shrapnel foreshadows a future injury for Beauchamp.

In a reversal from the normal gender role, Beauchamp falls severely ill, with the suggestion that his illness results from scorned romance. Seemingly on his deathbed, he resembles a corpse, and his circle of friends grieves his impending death. He does serve to bring his uncle and Shrapnel together under terms of a mutually agreed upon truce. While Cecilia visits Beauchamp in his illness, Jenny Denham, Shrapnel's ward, nurses him back to health. He becomes engaged to Jenny, an act that symbolizes Beauchamp's commitment to those individuals included in the radical vision of a changing England. Long-lasting happiness threatens to elude Beauchamp, however, as Jenny does not return his love, but devotes herself to him out of a sense of duty. However, when they board a ship to leave England, she suddenly realizes her passion for Beauchamp, and they marry soon after, living together happily and enjoying the birth of a child. Meredith ends his novel tragically, drowning Beauchamp as he rescues an eight-year-old child from the ocean. He suggests the trade of a noble life for that of an ordinary worker's child to be deemed unfair through the

thoughts of Beauchamps' friends, who wait for his body to be found while staring at the child, "an insignificant bit of mudbank life." Meredith implies that the results of heroic actions are seldom logical. A true hero will act intuitively, not considering personal cost.

BIBLIOGRAPHY

Harris, Margaret. Introduction. *Beauchamp's Career* by George Meredith. New York: Oxford University Press, 1988.

BEHN, APHRA (ca. 1640–1689)   While the exact birth date of Aphra Behn remains unknown, it is generally recognized to fall between 1637 and 1643. Her baptism on December 14, 1640, makes 1640 the most likely year of birth. Problems also exist in the number of different spellings of her name: Ayfara, Aphara, as well as Aphra. Some accounts suggest her birthplace as the small town of Weye and her parents as John and Amy Amis, a barber and a wet-nurse, respectively, although they may have been her foster parents. While not wealthy, the Amises had decent professions. Through various contacts, Behn gained some education, picking up languages and knowledge of music. Behn commented in later years that the learning of classical languages was unimportant, as such learning led to a sense of superiority. In approximately 1663, Behn moved with the Amises to the West Indies, and John died en route. Amy settled there with her children, providing Behn with experiences vital to her later novel *OROONOKO, THE HISTORY OF THE ROYAL SLAVE* (1688).

The Amis family returned to England in 1664, when Aphra married a Mr. Behn, possibly an English merchant with a Dutch background. She may have spent time at the court of King Charles II, enjoying the licentious behavior reported to have occupied certain of the royals, for she was known to the king's cronies, who would give her employment. Behn needed that employment following her husband's death during the 1665 plague. She likely spent time as a professional spy in Holland for England, for which supporting evidence exists, found in references in her writings as well as in remarks by acquaintances. In her correspondence, she refers to herself by the code name Astrea, which would later become a pen name. Although she acquitted herself well in a number of dangerous missions, she had to beg the English court for payment. Upon her return to England in 1668, she could not pay her debts and ended up in debtor's prison, but not for long. A man named Tom Killigrew, with whom she had corresponded from Holland, likely paid her way out of prison, as she later spoke kindly of him. Historians cite her experience with espionage as a possible explanation for her fascination with the entanglement of sex and power. This "scandalous" topic led to Behn's reputation as a writer of late 17th-century smut.

Behn never remarried, though she did take lovers. Her main relationship was with a man named John Hoyle, whose attention to boys was well known. Perhaps bisexual herself, Behn was not concerned with John's affinity for the same sex but was frustrated by his reluctance to yield to her advances. While Behn remained obsessed, Hoyle proved cold, and the relationship eventually ended. Behn captured much of her experiences with Hoyle in her poetry.

Behn's first play, *The Forced Marriage* (1670), proved successful, running for six nights. She published and saw performed additional dramas, including *The Amourous Prince* (1671), *The Dutch Lover* (1673), and *The Town Fop, or Sir Timothy Tawdry* (1676), with varying degrees of success, over many years. Nel Gwyn, mistress to King Charles II, acted in Behn's most popular play, *The Rover* (1677), and in *Sir Patient Fancy* (1678). Although her dramas provided some social criticism of traditions such as forced marriage, overbearing parental authority, England's hypocritical moral hierarchy, and other aspects of gender inequity, many female members of the audience did not support her productions. Eventually, Behn concentrated on poetry, whose impassioned themes and stark sexual imagery raised several eyebrows.

Most important, Behn published the first part of LOVE LETTERS BETWEEN A NOBLEMAN AND HIS SISTER (1684–87), the first major epistolary novel in English, later labeled amatory fiction. Based on a sex scandal of her day, it featured characters modeled after public figures, such as the duke of Monmouth, illegitimate son of Charles II. At that time, prose fiction received little respect as serious literature, and for that reason could be undertaken by an uneducated woman such as Behn

without public criticism. Behn's amatory fiction offered more complex characters than those of her fellow writers, and her style in presenting plots heavy with sexual intrigue she distinguished with wit, irreverence, and intelligence. In her *The History of the Nun; or, The Fair Vow-breaker,* Behn emphasizes through the spouse murderer, Isabella, the dangers to beautiful women in a patriarchal society. Free from the influence of classics and traditional literature, she could produce innovative work, as seen in the realistic aspects of *Oronooko,* published successfully in 1688. This work, featuring a heroic African prince who engages in a slave rebellion, became her signature work with later generations. Behn died April 16, 1689, and was buried in Westminster Abbey.

Behn lived during the Restoration, which proved more accepting of sexual allusions in literature than the decades immediately following, which enjoyed an "improvement of the national delicacy and taste," according to Sir Walter SCOTT. Scott's aunt in 1821 declared *Oroonoko* shameful reading for a lady. The Marquis of Halifax actually blamed the oppression of women on Behn, remarking that, "The unjustifiable freedom of some of your sex have involved the rest in the penalty of being reduced." A Victorian critic judged Behn "a mere harlot." With the rise of feminism in the 1960s, Behn's works reemerged through FEMINIST CRITICISM to a more liberal generation of readers who explore them as legitimate and sensual examinations of gender, race, and class. A forward-looking Virginia Woolf commented that, "All women together ought to let flowers fall upon the tomb of Aphra Behn . . . for it was she who earned them the right to speak their minds."

BIBLIOGRAPHY

Backscheider, Paula R., and John J. Richetti, eds. *Popular Fiction by Women: 1660–1730, An Anthology.* Oxford: Clarendon Press, 1996.

Bowers, Toni. "Sex, Lies, and Invisibility: Amatory Fiction from the Restoration to Mid-Century." *The Columbia History of the British Novel.* New York: Columbia University Press, 1994, 50–72.

Day, Robert Adams. "Aphra Behn and the Works of the Intellect." *Fetter'd or Free: British Women Novelists,*

1670–1815. Edited by Mary Anne Schofield and Cecilia Macheski. Athens: Ohio University Press, 1986, 372–382.

Schofield, Mary Anne, and Cecilia Macheski. *Fetter'd or Free?: British Women Novelists, 1670–1815*. Athens: Ohio University Press, 1986.

Spencer, Jane. *The Rise of the Woman Novelist: From Aphra Behn to Jane Austen*. Oxford: Basil Blackwell, 1986.

BENTLEY'S MISCELLANY

Published by Richard Bentley from its founding in 1837, *Bentley's Miscellany* was edited by Charles DICKENS until 1839. Another well-known novelist, William Harrison AINSWORTH, edited the magazine until 1842. Its last issue appeared in 1868.

For four decades, a wide variety of stories and novels appeared in this popular magazine. Bentley risked publishing little-known writers such as Dickens and satirists such as Thomas Love Peacock. American works that appeared in its pages included Henry Wadsworth Longfellow's *Wreck of the Hesperus* and Edgar Allan Poe's *Fall of the House of Usher.* Early contributors were among the most famous wits of the period: Francis Sylvester Mahony, William Maginn, and Samuel Lover. Reviews of books were a mainstay, and in its later years, the magazine appealed well to the Victorian sense of empire and a civilized world with features on such far-flung places as India, Ceylon, South Africa, Egypt, Brazil, and America. Only William Makepeace THACKERAY's *CORNHILL MAGAZINE* challenged it in popularity.

Dickens's *OLIVER TWIST* appeared in *Bentley's* first edition in February 1837 and ran through April 1839 in 27 installments. Other novels that graced its pages included Ainsworth's *Jack Sheppard* and *Guy Fawkes,* and Robert Bell's *Ladder of Gold* in six installments. In June 1852, *Bentley's* published the only example known of a translation by Wilkie COLLINS, "The Midnight Mass," from a story by Honoré de Balzac. The magazine included additional work by Collins, such as his 1851 "The Exhibition of the Royal Academy," a review of the annual summer exhibit.

BIBLIOGRAPHY
Fader, Daniel, and George Bornstein: *British Periodicals of the 18th and 19th Centuries*. University Microfilms, Ann Arbor, Mich., 1972, 65–68.

BEVIS, THE STORY OF A BOY RICHARD JEFFERIES (1882)

Like most fiction written for boys in the late 19th century, Richard JEFFERIES's *Bevis, the Story of a Boy* is an adventure novel. Its main characters enjoy their own QUEST, as its plot mimics that of adult adventure novels in the style of Henry Rider HAGGARD. The adults in the novel remain conveniently absent, allowing the boys complete freedom. Jefferies's own unhappy childhood had offered little escape from harsh reality, and as an adult, he wanted to construct CHILDREN'S LITERATURE for 10- to 12-year-old boys that would allow them relief from everyday stress. He called on one of his few happy memories of the family farm, with its fields, stream, and large lake, to provide a setting for *Bevis.* An island in the middle of just such a lake provides endless pleasure for Bevis and his best friend, Mark.

During the first third of the book, Bevis, as one of several boys, fights Indians, sails the Suez Canal, seeks the Mississippi, and discovers Arabs in Africa. Not only do readers enjoy the boys' adventures, they review classical history through the exploits of Bevis and his "chums." Blessed with great imaginations, the boys re-create the Battle of Pharsalia, atop cliffs that jut out over the lake. They use wooden swords and spears as weapons, and Bevis, as Caesar, is on the verge of defeat by Pompey, portrayed by a boy named Ted. However, Mark arrives in the supportive guise of Mark Antony, called to the scene by little Charlie. Pompey's defeat sparks a fight between the boys, and when Bevis rolls over the cliff, the terrified Ted fears he has killed him. In reality, Bevis lies on a contrivance fashioned to catch sheep, a sheep-hurdle, just out of sight of the boys.

Bevis hides in a small boat, moored beside the white-capped lake, which drifts onto the waves, carrying him to the mostly unexplored island. In a moment of high tension, he pulls himself into a tree just before his boat sinks. The imagery of the battle and subsequent "journey" across water, with a "shipwreck" on a "foreign shore," all support the familiar quest plot. Meanwhile, Mark wants to hunt for Bevis but is locked in a cellar by the farm manager. While he can unscrew and remove the bars from the window, the opening is too small for escape. Instead, Mark uses a bar to pry open the door and returns to the lake with the devoted spaniel Pan, symbolically named for a nature deity.

Bevis explores the island, scaling its hill, where he lights a fire seen by Mark. Procuring a boat, Mark crosses to the island during a full moon, as "the raging waters rushed and foamed around him." The two friends reunite and thoroughly explore the mysterious island, building a hut and pretending to shoot kangaroos, taking aim at rabbits. They name their secret land New Formosa and make trips back and forth from the island to home, gathering supplies and clueing Charlie in on their game. Naming their boat the *Pinta,* they bring a gun to the island and hunt rabbits and squirrels, thus beginning multiple adventures that delighted several decades of boy readers.

Jefferies peppers the novel with exciting narrative and well-designed verbal exchanges between the best friends, reproducing dialogue that rang realistic to the young ear: "'We must go back,' said Mark. 'We can't turn round.' 'We can't paddle backwards. There, I'm in the weeds.' 'Turn round on the plank.' 'Perhaps I shall fall off.' 'Sit sideways first.' 'The plank tips.' 'Very well, I'll do it first,' said Bevis." When Bevis puts his confident plan into action, the plank pitches him into water, satisfying not only Mark, but readers as well.

As their adventures continue, something visits the hut and eats their bacon, and the boys speculate whether their visitors might have been lions, tigers, boas, or panthers. Before long their friends, Charlie, Val and Cecil, want to join them on the island, but Bevis and Mark remain determined to keep secret their exact location. One scene features the boys engaged in storytelling, while Bevis keeps a journal. Thus, Jefferies emphasizes the importance of the imagination and echoes the theme of tale swapping from the prototypical quest tale, Homer's *Odyssey.* The boys refer fancifully to areas of their island, naming a stream the Nile and a rise Kangaroo Hill. Deciding the invader is a panther, they set a trap, fitted with rabbits, bacon, and potatoes, but in a comic climax, succeed only in catching Loo, a girl who disgusts the boys, because a girl has discovered their hideout. They immediately make her a slave, and contentedly pass their days until they do at last make a big killing, not of the fabled panther, but of an otter. That exotic encounter marks the end of

their summer adventure, and upon their return home, they admire the night sky, something they have done repeatedly throughout the book. Jefferies again stresses mythological imagery, writing "Large Sirius flashed; vast Orion strode the sky, lording the heavens with his sword . . . 'We must go to the great sea,' said Bevis. 'Look at Orion!' The wind went seawards, and the stars are always over the ocean."

Bevis, and other books for young readers from the 19th century, mark a crucial change in juvenile literature, that of existence for pure entertainment's sake. Following in the steps of Lewis CARROLL, Jefferies and others produced stories without DIDACTIC intent. Jefferies's work remains available in hard print.

BIBLIOGRAPHY
Williamson, Henry. Introduction. *Bevis, the Story of a Boy* by Richard Jefferies. London: Dent, 1966, vii–x.

BILDUNGSROMAN   The bildungsroman novel features a young person who experiences an INITIATION through coming-of-age circumstances that move him/her closer to maturity. The term *bildungsroman* appeared with Goethe's *Wilhelm Meister's Lehjare* (1795–96) (*Wilhelm Meister's Apprenticeship*), translated by Thomas Carlyle into English in 1824. Traditionally, a series of trials confronts the bildungsroman's protagonist as he or she moves from childhood through adolescence and into adulthood. The early bildungsroman featured mostly males, but females became main characters in the later 19th century. Similarly, a *Künstlerroman* traces the development of a writer, as in Elizabeth Barrett BROWNING's verse novel, *AURORA LEIGH* (1856). While the specific terms look to German literary criticism for their origin, such stories existed for centuries and in many cultures. They have in common an epiphany, or realization, on the part of the protagonist, allowing the main character to become dynamic and rounded through change. Examples of novels classified as bildungsroman include Charles DICKENS's *DAVID COPPERFIELD* and *GREAT EXPECTATIONS;* Samuel BUTLER's *The Way of All Flesh;* Charlotte BRONTË's *JANE EYRE;* and Frances Hodgson BURNETT's *The Secret Garden.*

BIBLIOGRAPHY
Fuderer, Laura Sue. *The Female Bildungsroman in English: An Annotated Bibliography of Criticism.* New York: MLA, 1990.
Hardin, James, ed. *Reflection and Action: Essays on the Bildungsroman.* Columbia: University of South Carolina Press, 1991.

BLACK BEAUTY ANNA SEWELL (1877)

Just as writers before her sought to expose abuses against the working class, Anna SEWELL, in her enduring children's novel *Black Beauty,* exposed abuses against animals. Although ostensibly written for children ages nine through 12, adults also loved the book. Had it appeared decades earlier, it might not have attracted as much notice or had the reforming effect on animal treatment that resulted from its publication at the end of the 19th century, when audiences were more open to reformation in the area of animal rights. As some of the THESIS NOVELS of the mid-19th century hoped to elucidate harsh working conditions for humans, Sewell wanted to do the same for work animals. In one of the most celebrated juvenile novels ever published, she tracks the fate of Black Beauty, who is also the narrator in this anthropomorphological tale. While he begins well, in the care of a loving mother and an attentive owner, his life declines into a nightmare of overwork, beatings, and injuries inflicted by fashionable riding and driving equipment. In part due to Sewell's efforts, the painful "bearing rein" that forced horses' heads into an unnatural position, which curtailed their breathing and caused extreme neck discomfort, went out of use shortly after the novel's publication. It also inspired the founding of societies for the prevention of animal cruelty, and the enforcement of laws to curtail animal abuses.

The novel makes its grisly point by introducing readers to a mare named Ginger whose early mistreatment sours her disposition. She tells Beauty her story and becomes a tragic figure later in the book when she dies from abuse. Sewell fashions a memorable and wrenching final scene between Ginger and Beauty when he finds her near death on the streets of London. Her once-great spirit broken, she tells her old friend, "[M]en are strongest, and if they are cruel and have no feeling, there is nothing that we can do, but just bear it—bear it on and on to the end. I wish the end was come, I wish I was dead." Moments later, her wish is fulfilled as Beauty sees her lifeless body driven away in a cart. Beauty's story is only slightly better, although it does have the requisite happy conclusion for a children's book. He barely survives his overwork and lack of nourishment while pulling cabs in London; when he becomes too weak to pull a cab, he is placed in a sale of broken and ill horses. Fortunately, a young man from a kind family urges his grandfather to purchase Beauty, and the horse begins recovery. A former groom recognizes Beauty, and he is allowed to live out his life in a loving home, serving his masters with a ride or by occasionally pulling a cart. Another prominent animal character early in the book is Merrylegs, a pony that young readers find endearing, as do the children in the story who he looks upon as his charges.

Sewell uses her venue to attack additional forms of animal abuse and unethical behavior. Early in the novel, Beauty witnesses a rabbit hunt in which dogs are injured, a rabbit nearly torn to bits, and a man killed in a fall from a horse named Rob Roy, who Beauty later discovers to be his half brother. The horse must be shot, as his injuries cannot be treated. Later, a drunken driver loses control of his brewer's dray after urging his draft horses to move too quickly through a crowded street. The dray runs over a young girl, and a horse named Captain, pulling a nearby cab, is stabbed in the side with the dray's splintered shaft. Sewell, a Quaker, makes a stand against drunkenness, as Beauty tells his readers, "If there's one devil that I should like to see in the bottomless pit more than another, it's the drink devil." While these disagreeable scenes remain vivid and pointed, Sewell takes care not to demonize all humans, and she profiles the poverty among humans in London as one cause of animal abuse. The novel inspired various film versions and remains popular, more than a century after its first printing, in both book and electronic text form.

BIBLIOGRAPHY
Stevens, Gloria. *Anna Sewell and Black Beauty.* New York: Longmans, 1957.

BLACKMORE, R(ICHARD) D(OD-DRIDGE) (1825–1900)

R. D. Blackmore was born at Longworth in Oxfordshire in 1825. He attended Blundell's School in Tiverton, then matriculated at Exeter College, Oxford. Although called to the bar in 1852, ill health, in part, prompted him to pursue a career as a writer. He first published poetry and a few translations, gaining fame with his first novel, *LORNA DOONE* (1869), a historical novel featuring a 17th-century outlaw group of Exmoor, where he had spent much of his time as a child. This novel overshadowed additional works, including *Clara Vaughan* (1864), *Alice Lorraine* (1875), *Cripps the Carrier* (1877), *Christowell: A Dartmoor Tale* (1881), and *Springhaven: A Tale of the Great War* (1887), featuring southern England during Napolean's reign as setting. He produced 13 novels in addition to poetry collections. Only *Lorna Doone* endured as a staple of literature, enjoying multiple screen and stage adaptations.

BIBLIOGRAPHY

Dunn, Waldo Hilary. *R. D. Blackmore: The Author of* Lorna Doone. Westport, Conn.: Greenwood Press, 1974.

BLACKWOOD'S EDINBURGH MAGAZINE

Founded and published by William Blackwood, *Blackwood's Edinburgh Magazine* appeared monthly between April 1817 and December 1905. Edited in the beginning by James Pringle and Thomas Cleghorn, it was titled *Blackwood's Edinburgh Monthly* for its first six issues. Blackwood assumed all editing duties himself between October 1817 and 1834, after which his relatives and descendants took over. William Blackwood III would publish the final issue, the magazine's 1,022nd.

William Blackwood, known as patron to men of wit and amateurs of letters, targeted young Scotch Tories as readers when he founded his magazine to compete with the rival Whig *Edinburgh Review* and the QUARTERLY REVIEW. Through the privilege of anonymity, writers engaged in scandalous attacks on Whig institutions in essays and critiques, as well as against the "Cockney School" of writers that included Charles Lamb, William Hazlitt, Leigh Hunt, and John Keats. Blackwood often claimed he was not the editor, declaring that an "unknown editor" had had his way with notorious articles. J. G. Lockhart, son-in-law to, and later biographer of, Sir Walter SCOTT, lampooned the *Edinburgh Review* in pieces in early editions of *Blackwood's*.

Blackwood's team of seven writers, designated the Noctes Ambrosianae, adopted pseudonyms in discussing literature and politics. Among them Blackwood was known as Ebony, Thomas De Quincy as The Opium Eater, and James Hogg as The Ettrick Shepherd. By 1830, much of the magazine's savagery disappeared, but through the media of poetry, humor, and fiction, the championing of the Scotch Tory way of life continued. The articles upheld the privileged, landowning class, while the duties and responsibilities of such were acknowledged. Aimed at a conservative audience, it supported rural interests and espoused a romantic ideal of the rugged, independent farmer who worked the land. One of its innovations was the publishing of foreign literature, particularly translations from German. Goethe's *Dichtung und Wahreit (Life and Works)* appeared in 1839. The journal remained influential and consistent in its mission; an acceptance of work for publication brought considerable prestige to contributors. Its editors also used the journal to comment on the novel genre in general. One example from the September 1847 issue noted the increase in acceptability of the novel to the reader with refined tastes: "Novels are not objected to as they were; now that every sect in politics and religion have found their efficacy as a means, the form is adopted by all."

Additional essayists, including Scott, along with several short story writers such as Oscar WILDE, published their work in *Blackwood's*. Scott contributed several book reviews, including an April 1818 review of Mary SHELLEY's *FRANKENSTEIN*. George ELIOT first published three stories in *Blackwood's* in 1857, "The Sad Fortunes of the Reverend Amos Barton," "Mr. Gilfil's Love-Story," and "Janet's Repentance," which would be collected into *Scenes of Clerical Life* (1858). Several novelists also published their work as serials in *Blackwood's* before releasing the book versions. Anthony TROLLOPE's *Linda Tressel* appeared in eight installments between October 1867 and May 1868; his *John Caldigate* ran in 15 installments from April 1878 through June 1879; and his *Dr. Wortle's School* ran in seven parts between May and November 1880. Joseph CONRAD contributed *Heart of Darkness* in three parts between February and April of 1899, and *Lord Jim* ran between October 1899 and November 1900.

BIBLIOGRAPHY

Beach, Joseph Warren. *English Literature of the Nineteenth and the Early Twentieth Centuries.* New York: Collier Books, 1950.

Houghton, Walter E., Esther Rhoads Houghton, and Jean Slingerland, eds. "Blackwood's Edinburgh Magazine." *The Wellesley Index to Victorian Periodicals, 1824–1900.* Vol. I. Toronto: University of Toronto Press, 1989, 321–415.

Tillotson, Kathleen. *Novels of the Eighteen-forties.* Oxford: Clarendon Press, 1954.

BLEAK HOUSE CHARLES DICKENS (1853)

Offered first in installments between 1852 and 1853, Charles DICKENS's *Bleak House* provided its author the opportunity to add to his many attacks against Victorian social ills. He took the name for the novel and the home of the protagonist from his own residence on the cliffs of Broadstairs on the coast of Kent. Originally built in 1790 as a military fort and called Fort House, Bleak House provided a home for Dickens and his nine children, and a celebrated location for Dickens's many visitors. While a challenging and rather difficult novel with overlapping plots, *Bleak House* does reflect a unity and clear thematic structure that marked Dickens's mature writing, and it proved quite popular.

In *Bleak House,* Dickens launches what critics agree represents his most virulent attack against the debauched legal system. A proper symbol for that system is the Chancery, an edifice that should represent enlightenment, but instead represents its absence. His memorable dreary opening frames the narration with impenetrable fog, caused by both natural effects and soot, the product of an industrial age that reformists like Dickens saw as producing more evil than good. The first few paragraphs brim with imagery supporting the theme that knowledge has been extinguished by the system that should promote wisdom in phrases such as "the death of the sun," "no light of day in . . . the place," and "the Lord high Chancellor looks into the lantern that has no light in it." Dickens also inti-

mates that the system feeds upon itself, like the mud through which citizens of London must slosh, expanding a consistently ineffective entity; each individual was unwittingly "adding new deposits to the crust" and "adding layers upon layers to it." The narration soon familiarizes readers with the case of Jarndyce versus Jarndyce, one that has evolved into decades of conflict, involving and ruining many individuals. Dickens leaves no doubt as to the depressing truth about the case, which began when old Tom Jarndyce "blew out his brains at a coffee shop." The fact that the system perpetuates this endless case in order to sap the populace of resources results in a chilling indictment from Dickens as to its morally corrupt existence.

Like all Dickens novels, *Bleak House* shapes an enormous cast of characters while focusing on three main figures. The first is Esther Summerson, whose open and honest tone in a narration presented from her first-person point of view in chapters each titled "Esther's Narrative" greatly contrasts with the ironic, caustic tone of the third-person narrative. Critics agree that this contrast in tone represents a conscious choice on Dickens's part, where he establishes a more impersonal note when the narration deals with public matters, and a softer, gentler approach when Esther discusses the private sphere. She relates a tale of an unhappy childhood that begins with her godmother telling her, "Your mother, Esther, is your disgrace, and you were hers."

With this burden on her soul, Esther eventually moves in with the Misses Donny, twins who operate a boarding house, paid for by her mysterious guardian, Mr. Jarndyce, upon the death of her godmother. After six happy years there, she moves to Bleak House, the household of John Jarndyce, also guardian to his much younger cousins, Ada Clare and Richard Carstone, the additional two main characters. Jarndyce is deeply involved in the case that bears his name and that will supposedly settle an estate in which he has an interest. Esther becomes Jarndyce's protégée and develops a close relationship with Ada and Richard, who fall in love and eventually marry. However, the ever-evolving Jarndyce case consumes Richard, as it has many victims, and he dies of exhaustion close to the novel's end. His death accompanies that of the case, which at last concludes, having consumed all of the estate in question in legal costs.

In a subplot not relating directly to the Jarndyce case, Sir Leicester Dedlock and his wife become important to the plot when a scheming lawyer named Tulkinghorn learns Lady Dedlock's secret; she is Esther's mother through an early affair with the deceased Captain Hawdon, a fact that Tulkinghorn decides to expose. Esther learns her mother's identity, but makes the honorable choice not to share the news with Ada, as "it was not mine, and I did not feel I had a right to tell it." Before Tulkinghorn can carry out his plan, a serving woman to Lady Dedlock named Mademoiselle Hortense murders him.

Dickens introduces the forerunner to future protagonists of popular DETECTIVE FICTION with Inspector Bucket, who seeks to arrest Hortense. Bucket receives strong character shaping from Dickens, who gives him the specific eccentric personality that would endear future English detectives, including Sherlock Holmes, to the reading public. No matter how quickly he walks, Bucket still manages to "lurk and lounge," and "whenever he is going to turn to the right or left, he pretends to have a fixed purpose in his mind of going straight ahead, and wheels off, sharply, at the very last moment." Mortified by the fact that her secret may be made public, and despite the understanding of her situation by her husband, Lady Dedlock runs away and her disappearance involves another of the book's characters, Jo, the poverty-stricken and illiterate crossing-sweeper from whom she seeks help. She meets a terrible end, and Esther and Bucket later discover her body not far from the grave of her former lover.

Another important character, Alan Woodcourt, a physician, is a sunny figure in direct contrast to the novel's foggy, dark opening imagery and is credited for "brightening" the face of the novel's most pitiful and pitiable character, Jo. Woodcourt compares Jo to a loyal dog who follows him about, labeling him "this creature in human form," clarifying Jo's treatment by society as something less than human. He hopes to protect Jo until he can aid in solving a case and tells another character that the young man needs housing, although "decent people and Jo [. . .] have not been much acquainted." In one scene, Jo's hunger is so great that he paradoxically cannot eat. Dickens strengthens his indictment of the failed social system by comparing Jo to a cart used to bear the burdens of others. Following Jo's tortured death, Dickens makes clear his moral lesson, writing: "Dead, my lords and gentlemen. Dead, right reverends and wrong reverends of every order. Dead, men and women, born with heavenly compassion in your hearts. And dying thus around us everyday."

The novel does conclude on an uplifting note, as Jarndyce releases Esther from her promise of marriage to him when he recognizes how much she loves Woodcourt. Finally, she can relate that she is "the happiest of happy," married to Alan Woodcourt and still serving as the mistress of Bleak House.

BIBLIOGRAPHY

Collins, Philip. *A Critical Commentary on Dickens' 'Bleak House.'* London: Macmillan, 1971.

Harvey, W.J. "Chance and Design in Bleak House." In *Dickens and the Twentieth Century.* Edited by John J. Gross. Toronto: University of Toronto Press, 1962.

BLUESTOCKING   A term first used in English to refer to a mostly female intellectual circle that formed around Elizabeth Montagu in the 1750s, bluestocking later came to mean any educated woman with liberal and artistic ideas. Conversation reigned at Montagu's home, where she modeled her gatherings on the era's popular French coteries. Her guests discussed intellectual and aesthetic matters, often following presentations by notable males, including Samuel JOHNSON and David Garrick, rather than engaging in more traditional female activity, such as sewing or card playing. The nickname may have arisen due to the costume of Benjamin Stillingfleet, an English scientist, translator, and minor poet. Supposedly, upon receiving an invitation to the gathering, Stillingfleet confessed to being too poor to afford formal dress clothes, including the traditional black silk stockings worn by most male group members. When Montagu urged him to attend in everyday dress, he did so, wearing blue worsted hosiery that began a trend. Others trace bluestocking's etymology to the Italian expression *della calza,* or "of the stockings," the name of a 15th-century Venetian group whose members donned blue leg wear. Well-known members of Montagu's circle included Hannah More, Fanny BURNEY, Horace Walpole, who supposedly referred to the gatherings as "petticoteries," and Hester Chapone, moralist and minor fiction writer. Samuel Johnson referred to the bluestockings in his writing, as did his biographer, James Boswell. Bluestocking also became a label for women involved in social reforms.

BIBLIOGRAPHY

Myers, Sylvia Hartstark. *The Bluestocking: Women, Friendship, and the Life of the Mind in Eighteenth-century England.* New York: Oxford University Press, 1990.

Quinion, Michael. "Bluestocking." *World Wide Words.* Available online. URL: http://www.quinion.com/words/topical words/tw-blu1.htm. Downloaded October 16, 2002.

BRADDON, MARY ELIZABETH (1835–1915)

Author of more than 80 novels and nine plays, Mary Elizabeth Braddon was one of the most successful and popular Victorian writers of SENSATION FICTION. Born in London in 1835, Braddon had a sister, 11 years her senior, who lived with relatives until Mary was four, and a six-year-old brother who spent his time at preparatory school. Her parents separated in 1840, and Braddon lived with her mother, whom she would later support. She spent time at an expensive Brompton school but left to save money. Shortly thereafter, her mother moved her family to a poor suburb. In the 1850s, Braddon's father disappeared, leaving the family penniless, and she became a self-supporting actress. She toured the theaters of Britain with a repertory company, shocking friends and family with her scandalous career.

During her stage years, Braddon doggedly continued writing, and in 1860 received a commission to write a book-length poem. Writing the poem brought her little enjoyment, and she used her spare time to write *Three Times Dead,* an unsuccessful melodramatic thriller classified as a "penny dreadful" (of low cost and quality), published when she turned 19. The book was later condensed, rewritten, and republished successfully under the title *Trail of the Serpent.*

Braddon had a personal life worthy of her sensational novels. She lived with publisher John Maxwell for 14 years, waiting for his wife to die before she could marry Maxwell. Had Braddon not quickly given birth to three children, their relationship might have remained a secret. As it was, the pair became a public item amid much gossip, causing great disgruntlement on the part of Maxwell's in-laws. After producing five children (a sixth died at birth), Braddon and Maxwell finally married in 1874.

Braddon continued to write in the popular melodramatic style, producing serials under pseudonyms. While her hack work paid the bills, Braddon was free to spend time developing more serious fiction, and she finally caught the public's interest with LADY AUDLEY'S SECRET (1862), originally published in one of Maxwell's foundering journals. Braddon dedicated the book to Sir Edward BULWER-LYTTON "in grateful acknowledgement of literary advice most generously given to the author." Although not the focus of her novel, an investigation served as an important part of her plot, thereby contributing to the development of DETECTIVE FICTION.

Featuring bold, sexual heroines, Braddon's "serious" novels, reportedly read by Queen Victoria, were panned by shocked critics. Some critics believed her works would fill young readers with corrupting ideas. Still, she managed to keep her heroines safe from brazenly improper compromise. The ironic tone employed to feature virtue that always triumphed over scandal delighted readers and suggested that Braddon did not always agree with the highly moralistic positions of her protagonists. Regardless of critical condemnation, many of Braddon's novels proved immediate best-sellers.

Braddon continued to write about three novels each year, many centering on crime and women's discontent, although none eclipsed the popularity of *Lady Audley's Secret.* She competed with Mrs. Henry WOOD, a rival in sensationalist fiction whose EAST LYNNE (1861) was the only novel to outsell *Lady Audley's Secret* in 1862. She developed her skills according to her market and succeeded in entertaining readers for over 50 years, with 80 novels and nine dramas, in addition to short stories, to her credit. The *Daily Telegraph* hailed Braddon as "the queen of the living English novelists." Her works included HISTORICAL FICTION and SATIRE, with others, such as *Aurora Floyd* (1863), *John Marchmont's Legacy* (1863), and *Henry Dungar: The*

Story of an Outcast (1864), continuing the sensationalist vein. One book, *The Doctor's Wife* (1864), acted as an accompaniment of sorts to Flaubert's *Madame Bovary*. She also took over publication of the journal *Belgravia* and featured many of her own stories there, along with serving as editor of *Temple Bar*.

Braddon wrote an unpublished memoir shortly before her 1915 death, in which several passages indicate that at least a portion of her writing was autobiographical. Though her books endured lagging popularity after her death, they have enjoyed a revival since the late 20th century.

BRIDE OF LAMMERMOOR, THE SIR WALTER SCOTT (1818)

Sir Walter SCOTT based his novel *The Bride of Lammermoor*, second in his Tales of My Landlord series, on a true tragic love story about a Scottish family named Dalrymple, supported by fictional accounts, poetry, and popular ballad versions. He did not reveal his sources at its first printing, but included it in a later edition, explaining that he had not done so in the first edition for fear of causing offense to Dalrymple family members and others involved. However, upon later discovering through a friend's help the account in print in a publication titled "Notes to Law's Memorials," and also in a reprint of "the Reverend Mr. Symson's poems appended to the Large Description of Galloway," Scott felt he could relate the true story and identify its participants.

One James Dalrymple, from a Scottish family containing men of "talent, civil and military, and of literary, political, and professional eminence," married Margaret Ross, "an able, politic and high-minded woman." When she died, she ordered that her coffin stand erect at the head of her grave, promising that as long as it did so, her descendants would "continue to flourish." Such "necromancy" became an important aspect of the fable regarding the "unaccountable and melancholy" events that would befall a future elder daughter of the family, headed by Lord Stair and his wife. Janet Dalrymple engaged herself in secret to one Lord Rutherford, whom her parents found unacceptable due either to "his political principles or his want of fortune." To confirm their love pact, the couple shattered a gold coin, each keeping half. When another suitor accept-

able to her parents, named David Dunbar, proposed shortly thereafter to Janet, she rejected the proposal and confessed her secret engagement, infuriating her parents. Her mother insisted that she marry Dunbar, son and heir to David Dunbar of Baldoon, in Wigtonshire; her father feared contradicting his wife and agreed. When Rutherford mailed a letter protesting the new arrangement, Lady Stair answered that her daughter had decided to honor her duty to her parents, and that her marriage to Dunbar would proceed. Rutherford traveled to the Stair estate, at which point Janet told him that she was breaking their engagement, with Lady Stair as witness. When Rutherford protested, Lady Stair called upon Levitical law based on a passage from the biblical book of Numbers that declared that a father could break a vow on the part of his daughter, and that God would forgive the daughter the unfortunate vow. Despite Rutherford's pleading that Janet declare her own wishes, she remained mute, only holding out her half of the gold coin to restore to her lover. He left in a great passion, never to be heard from again, although according to Scott, his birth date supported the fact that he was the last Lord Rutherford, who died in 1685.

The marriage plans continued, with no protest from Janet Dalrymple. On the wedding night, "hideous shrieks" issued from the nuptial chamber. When the family investigated, they found the groom stabbed multiple times close to the door and Janet crouched near the fireplace, "mopping and mowing . . . in a word, absolutely insane." Scott reported that her only words were "Take up your bonny bridegroom." Two weeks later, Janet died. Dunbar recovered, but he would not share any details of the incident. The official record to which Scott referred stated that Stair's daughter, "being married, the night she was bride in, was taken from her bridegroom and harled through the house (by spirits, we are given to understand) and afterward died."

In Scott's novel, Lord Rutherford becomes Edgar, the master of Ravenswood, a young man who inherits the "pride and turbulence," but not the fortune of his house. Due to ill luck, Edgar's father, Alan Lord Ravenswood, had to dispose of Castle Ravenswood and his estate. Sir William Ashton and his wife, who hailed from a more distinguished family that that of her husband, demand certain conditions with the sale, causing a violent disagreement with Ravenswood; their dealings hasten his death. Ashton then insults Edgar Ravenswood by sending his agent with his legal claim to the land to Lord Alan's funeral. Edgar returns to the castle following the observance of rights for his father, and Scott sets the melancholy tone for the novel by writing of Alan's home, "But its space was peopled by phantoms which the imagination of the young heir conjured up before him—the tarnished honour and degraded fortunes of his house." The following day, Ashton declares Edgar's fate to be in his hands, and the young man shall either "bend or break." The statement provides ominous foreshadowing.

With the quarrel standing between the Ravenswoods and the Ashtons, the new Lord Ravenswood falls passionately in love with the story's Janet figure, the beautiful Lucy Ashton, his inherited enemy's daughter. Her description matches that of the prototypical romance heroine, with golden hair "divided on a brow of exquisite whiteness," which the narrator compares to sunshine on snow. The novel teems with such predictable romance imagery, enjoyable, nevertheless, for its skillful use by Scott.

The innocence and purity symbolized by the white imagery will soon be challenged. The love that Lucy returns to Edgar stands doomed by the ongoing feud between his family and hers. As with all star-crossed lovers caught up in an inherited feud, their relationship can only end disastrously. Lady Ashton opposes the marriage and tricks her daughter into marrying the Laird of Bucklaw. In typical romance fashion, incorporating mistaken identity and misunderstandings, Lady Ashton fabricates a story convincing Lucy that Ravenswood has rejected her. When Ravenswood reappears following the marriage and demands revenge on the groom, Lucy murders her husband. Declared insane, she dies shortly thereafter.

Scott includes topics additional to that of romance. He begins his story by expounding on the fate of artists, who become quite successful or die in poverty; there exists no "in between" state for the true artist. When the artist character of Dick Tinto tells the novel's first-person narrator, Peter Pattieson, that for the writer, "words were his colours, and, if properly employed, they could not fail to place the scene which he wished to conjure up as effectually before the mind's eye as the tablet or canvas presents it to the bodily organ," readers understand that Scott comments on his own occupation as an author. Dick proceeds to advise Peter that too much "conversation" in a scene will cause readers to lose interest and represents a lack of imagination, and Scott seems to advise his fellow writers in technique. When Dick produces a painting that represents the tale of Janet Dalrymple, along with a few notes regarding the story, Peter decides to record the history, using both the painting and the words on the notes. Scott's message regarding the importance of one art form to another remains clear.

Like many of Scott's works, the novel, and the introduction describing Scott's multiple sources, became available in electronic text in the 20th century.

BIBLIOGRAPHY

Project Guttenberg. Introduction to *The Bride of Lammermoor,* by Sir Walter Scott. Project Guttenberg. Available online. URL: http://ibiblio.org/gutenberg/etext96/brlam 10.txt. Posted March 1996.

Scott, Sir Walter. *The Bride of Lammermoor* Edited by Fiona Robertson. Oxford: Oxford University Press, 1998.

Wilt, Judith. *The Novels of Sir Walter Scott.* Chicago: University of Chicago Press, 1986.

BRONTË, CHARLOTTE (1816–1855), EMILY (1818–1848), and ANNE (1820–1849)

While no one denies the Brontë sisters merit individual consideration, joint consideration offers the advantage to the reader of a clearer grasp of the relationships between their works and publications. Born two years apart into a family with a clergyman father, Patrick, and his wife, Maria Branwell, Charlotte was the third daughter behind Maria and Elizabeth. Emily followed, then Anne, and finally the family's only boy, Branwell, was born. With a father poet, novelist, and sermon writer, and a mother essayist, the children came by their love of literature naturally. They lived in Thornton before relocating in 1820 to the Yorkshire-moors village of Haworth. The following year, Maria Branwell died, with her loss marking the first of many for the family. Patrick could not find a replacement for his wife and so asked the children's Aunt Branwell to move in as caretaker, a position she retained until her death in 1842. The children received free run of their father's library, learning to read on their own from the classics and John Milton's poetry.

Mr. Brontë's attempt to give the girls a formal education ended tragically when he sent the four older sisters to a charity school, Cowan Bridge. There Maria and Elizabeth both fell ill and returned home in 1825, where they died in short order of typhoid fever and consumption (tuberculosis) due in part to unsanitary school conditions. Charlotte and Emily returned home immediately to a much-saddened household.

The three remaining Brontë sisters and Branwell amused themselves on the isolated moors. Together they invented fantasy kingdoms based on Branwell's toy soldiers. Charlotte and Branwell developed the kingdom Angria, while Emily and Anne invented Gondal. They recorded in several small volumes the stories they wrote together in the popular style of Sir Walter SCOTT and George Gordon, Lord Byron. Byron's flamboyant lifestyle perpetuated the myth of the BYRONIC HERO, a dark, brooding mysterious character that would populate novels for decades, including the adult works by Charlotte and Emily Brontë.

Charlotte left home to attend Roe Head School for a year in 1831; she later served as an instructor there. While Emily and Anne participated in housekeeping chores with their aunt, they also cared for their distracted father and their moody brother. The tale telling continued, even with Charlotte away at school, and the fantasy tales grew. Charlotte found her position at Roe Head unchallenging, but understood that teaching was one of the few avenues for income available to women. She found various suitors lacking, including some who proposed marriage, and left Roe Head to care for and tutor her siblings from 1832–35. She eventually became a governess in several positions, while Anne and Branwell served as tutors to local children.

Shortly before her death, Aunt Branwell offered the girls a small amount of money to open their own school, and Emily and Charlotte departed for Brussels to study at a French school before founding their own. There, Charlotte's romantic ideals led her to become attracted to Constantine Heger, a married Catholic who operated the school the Brontës attended. Although Heger never encouraged Charlotte, her emotional attachment grew into a passionate unrequited love that she carried back home a few months later when Aunt Branwell died in 1842. Emily stayed at home, but Charlotte returned to Brussels to live a lonely existence that later inspired her to write VILLETTE (1853), in which the protagonist, Lucy Snow, experiences an overwhelming feeling of isolation while living far from home in Brussels.

With Anne, Branwell, and Charlotte out of the house, Emily lived with her father and wrote poetry. When Anne returned, she and Emily continued the fantasy-writing tradition. Charlotte returned home to England, and the girls advertised for students to enroll in the long-dreamed of school; unfortunately, they received no applications, and their dream never materialized. Charlotte nursed her own fantasies about Heger for a time but, by 1845, gave up on her love and turned to serious writing instead. Branwell's return home after being fired from his tutoring position for alcoholism and drug abuse interrupted his sisters' peaceful existence. He would never recover from his dependencies.

Charlotte discovered Emily's poetry and began to think seriously of writing for publication. She encouraged the sisters to pool their verses and publish them at their own expense in 1846 under the title *Poems by Curer, Ellis and Acton Bell*. Although the slim volume did not sell, it gave the sisters pseudonyms that would provide their anonymity for future publications and encouraged them to publish further. Each decided to try her hand at novel writing.

In Charlotte's first novel, *The PROFESSOR,* she produced a highly autobiographical work, written from a male view point and incorporating many of her own experiences in Brussels that would be published in 1857, after her death. For *SHIRLEY* (1849) and *VILLETTE,* Charlotte turned to elements of the GOTHIC NOVEL, including visions and romantic themes. Her second novel, *JANE EYRE* (1847), became her masterpiece. Many critics believe it reflects Charlotte's quiet frustration over contained passions and the low station that the governess position represented. Currer Bell gained immediate popularity with *Jane Eyre,* her novel appealing to a wide readership. No one suspected the true identity of the Bells; one rumor had it that the author of *Jane Eyre* was actually William Makepeace THACKERAY's ex-mistress.

In 1847, Anne published *AGNES GREY*, and Emily published *WUTHERING HEIGHTS*. Shortly after, all three women met their publisher, T. C. Newby, for the first time in London; Newby was stunned to discover their identities. Before long, all of England knew of the Brontë sisters. Most readers enjoyed *Jane Eyre,* but some critics attacked Gothic novels as unseemly women's fantasies that glorified female passion, particularly in relation to the arts, and wrongly celebrated the rebellious Byronic hero. Emily incorporated her own passionate personality, shaped by her wanderings on the moors, in her writing, and it was found inappropriate by some readers. Thus, *Wuthering Heights* would not enjoy complete popularity until after her death.

The Brontës did not celebrate their publishing victories for long. Branwell died from substance abuse in the fall of 1848, followed by Emily, whose cold caught during her brother's funeral led to a lung inflammation. The family buried Emily in December, and in May of 1849, Anne was laid to rest following an illness. In 1850, Charlotte added a biographical note for a reprinting of Emily's *Wuthering Heights* and included a few of her sister's poems.

Charlotte lived with Patrick Brontë during the next few years and continued writing. *Jane Eyre* was compared with Thackeray's *VANITY FAIR* (1847–48), and Thackeray publicly praised Brontë's novel, as did Elizabeth GASKELL, the woman who would write *The Life of Charlotte Brontë* in 1857. In 1852, Charlotte married Arthur Bell Nicholls, her father's curate. Evidence indicates the marriage lacked love, and that Charlotte married based on a sense of duty to Patrick Brontë. In 1855, pregnant with her first child, Charlotte Brontë died from tuberculosis, leaving Patrick Brontë the last surviving member of his once-large family. In 1893, admirers founded the Brontë Society, and the sisters' influence on women's writing remains almost unparalleled. Texts of all their books are widely available and read in private and academic surroundings, and *Jane Eyre* and *Wuthering Heights* have been dramatized in a number of screen and stage versions.

BIBLIOGRAPHY

Tillotson, Kathleen. *Novels of the Eighteen-forties.* Oxford: Clarendon Press, 1954.

Winnifrith, Tom. "Charlotte and Emily Brontë: A Study in the Rise and Fall of Literary Reputations." *Yearbook of English Studies* 26 (1996): 14–24.

BROWNING, ELIZABETH BARRETT (1806–1861)

Elizabeth Barrett was born March 6, 1806, at Coxhoe Hall in Durham, England, to Edward Moulton-Barrett and Mary Graham Clarke. Her father enjoyed a fortune through income from lands owned in Jamaica whose connection with slavery would contribute to Elizabeth's later abolitionist stand. Mary Clarke Barrett remained subservient to her husband in a markedly patriarchal household. Reports vary on whether Elizabeth was eldest in a family of 11 or 12 children, but she indisputably led a privileged childhood. Free to enjoy the life of the upper class, she spent her childhood mostly at the estate of Hope End. More important, she had the good luck to be born to a man who recognized the genius of his eldest child and encouraged her love of learning and her writing talent. Her readings before age 10 included Shakespeare and Homer. By the time she was a teen, she read Dante and had learned enough Hebrew to read the Old Testament. She also joined her brother Edward, whom she affectionately dubbed "Bro," in a serious study of Latin and Greek. Elizabeth's poetry was encouraged from the age of eight, when she wrote her first poems.

At 13, Elizabeth wrote the *Battle of Marathon* (1820), and her father printed 50 copies of the poem to distribute among friends. In 1821, she fell ill with a "nervous collapse," but recovered sufficiently to again participate in family activities, having long been known as the Poet Laureate of Hope End. While Mr. Barrett involved himself in his children's lives and learning, Elizabeth's mother appears as no more than a figure in the background. Seldom mentioned in the author's works, her death in 1828 at age 48 seemed to have little effect on her children's lives. Still, Elizabeth showed some affection for her mother in correspondence and journal entries that focused on her loss. When Edward Barrett lost Hope End to financial difficulties, he moved the family temporarily to Sidmouth before settling in London at 50 Wimpole Street. Elizabeth corresponded with contemporaries poet and essayist R. H. Horne and novelist and playwright Mary Russell MITFORD, eventually contributing to Horne's 1844 book of critical essays, *A New Spirit of the Age.*

As she matured, Barrett learned to critically assess her own work, noting the "flat" style of her 1833 poem, *Prometheus Bound,* which she later revised. *The Seraphim, and Other Poems,* the first volume of Barrett's mature poetry to appear under her own name, was published in the spring of 1838 to strong reviews. Henry Chorley, in the *Athenaeum,* mentioned that the work was "an evidence of female genius and accomplishment," although deficient in the feminine character of simplicity. Following the publication, Barrett suffered hemorrhaging of the lung and relocated for three years of recovery to Torquay. During her convalescence, she requested that "Bro" remain in residence, although her father protested. The accidental death of another brother, Samuel, while visiting Jamaica caused Elizabeth to relapse. When Edward also died in a sailing accident, Elizabeth's condition worsened, and she seemed destined to be a lifelong invalid. In her immeasurable grief over the loss of her brothers, she described herself as "dead before death."

Incapacitated for months, she returned to her family's London home and spent most of the next five years in her bedroom. Despite her physical condition, she began writing a series of essays on English literature and Greek Christian poets that appeared in the *Atheneum,* as well as in Horne's collection. Her volume titled *Poems* appeared in 1844 to a strong reception. Although described as "for most practical purposes, the first woman poet in English literature" by biographer Dorothy Mermin, Elizabeth's inspirations for emulation were limited to male-authored works. "I look everywhere for grandmothers," she wrote in 1845, "and see none."

In May 1845, friend Robert Kenyon arranged a meeting between Elizabeth Barrett and Robert Browning. She had praised his work in her poem "Lady Geraldine's Courtship," part of the *Poems* volume. The two wrote to one another often, and in 1845, Robert began visits to the bedridden Elizabeth. The author of work often considered too intellectual to be read by the common public, Robert struggled to achieve his aesthetic. He attempted writing drama, and its influence on his later use of dramatic narrative in his poetry is obvious. His admiration for Elizabeth's writing likely led to his imitation of her style as a way to develop his own. Robert declared his love, much to the surprise of Elizabeth, an invalid six years his senior. The two married in secret in 1846, despite Elizabeth's low opinion of marriage and the threat of disinheritance from a disapproving Edward Barrett, who had ordered all his children to remain single. Her father disinherited her when he learned of the marriage, but having money of her own, Elizabeth settled comfortably with Robert in Italy. There she enjoyed a vast improvement in her health through his support. They moved into Casa Guidi in Florence and, after several miscarriages, had a son, Robert Wiedemann Barrett Browning, in 1849. Her son, nicknamed "Pennini," reinspired his 43-year-old mother's poetry and appeared as a character in several of her important works.

At her husband's insistence, Barrett Browning included her love sonnets in the second edition of her *Poems* (1850). Her popularity increased with the publication of *Sonnets from the Portuguese,* written to Robert, and England seriously considered her a candidate for the Poet Laureateship in 1850, following Wordsworth's death. Critics and the reading public embraced her next publication, *Casa Guidi Windows* (1851), a reflection on Italy's nationalist movement, but her 1856 work, *AURORA LEIGH,* guaranteed her fame.

A verse novel, *Aurora Leigh* proved to be Barrett Browning's longest and most innovative work. Of epic size and scope, it depicted a woman-poet hero whose country's destiny hangs in the balance of her deeds. Promoting Barrett Browning's belief in the importance of reality to art, it also defended women's rights to education and the life of intellect that education allows. *Aurora Leigh* contained a variety of form and meter, including sonnet, verse drama, ballad, and blank verse, with highly dramatic dialogue and conflict between the speaker/protagonist and other characters, as well as between the speaker and her culture. Barrett Browning intended the shocking work to help change British society, specifically the subjugation of women to male domination. Social injustice provided a theme of many of Barrett Browning's poems, particularly *Poems Before Congress* (1860). The work celebrated a cause she had long supported, that of Italian unification. Many readers and critics disliked that highly polemic work, finding it unsuitable material for a woman, its tone described by some as "hysterical." Twentieth-century critics found it an excellent example of Barrett Browning's continued attacks on oppression, which she undertook regardless of which country, social class, or political group engaged in the exploitation of humans that she found intolerable. Those same critics felt that as a work of poetic quality, it remains lacking, although not in thought or feeling. Along with *Casa Guidi Windows, Poems Before Congress* would lose little, and might even gain, from conversion to prose.

Barrett Browning's health problems remain a mystery, but many historians agree that the opium repeatedly prescribed to make tolerable her symptoms worsened her condition. The death of her sister Henrietta in 1861, followed by that of the Italian leader, Cavour, contributed to a decline in her health, already complicated by bronchitis. Elizabeth Barrett Browning died in the arms of her husband on June 29, 1861. Many mourned her loss and visited her grave in Florence. Her final publication, *Last Poems,* appeared posthumously that same year.

In the early 20th century, Barrett Browning received more attention as a romantic figure than as the serious poet her own era celebrated. Her romance with Robert Browning inspired several movies and at least one stage performance, Rudolf Beisier's *The Barretts of Wimpole Street* (1930). But during her lifetime, her fame as a scholar and poet surpassed that of her husband, who later would be considered the more important of the pair. Not only did she gain the admiration of notable contemporaries such as William Makepeace THACKERAY, Alfred Lord Tennyson, and American writers Edgar Allan Poe, Harriet Beecher Stowe, and Margaret Fuller, her passionate support of social issues, including abolition, made her an important political figure. As FEMINIST CRITICS began to emphasize in the mid-20th century, focus on Barrett Browning as a romantic figure does not do her justice. A staunch feminist who abhorred war, child poverty, and slavery, subjects of her "The Runaway Slave at Pilgrim's Point," "The Cry of the Children," and "Ragged Schools of London," she inspired many female readers to emulate her "unfeminine" stands against social injustice.

BIBLIOGRAPHY

Bloom Harold, ed. *Elizabeth Barret Browing.* Philadelphia: Chelsea House, 2002.

Donaldson, Sandra, ed. *Critical Essays on Elizabeth Barret Browing.* New York: G. K. Hall, 1999.

Garrett, Martin. *Elizabeth Barret Browning and Robert Browning.* New York: Oxford University Press, 2001.

Gilbert, Sandra M., and Susan Gubar, eds. "Elizabeth Barrett Browning." *The Norton Anthology of Literature by Women: The Traditions in English.* 2nd ed. New York: W.W. Norton, 1996. 373–375.

BRUNTON, MARY (1778–1818)

Little is known about Mary Brunton. Born in the north of Scotland in 1778 to Captain Thomas Balfour, her mother undertook her education, and she became a proficient musician and learned French and Italian. At age 20 she married a Presbyterian minister named Alexander Brunton who later became a professor of languages at Edinburgh University. Reflecting her religious devotion, Brunton wrote sentimental melodrama with a highly moralistic tone, her career encouraged by a close friend, Mrs. Izett. Her emphasis on the importance of discipline is obvious in the title of her 1811 novel, SELF CONTROL, which she dedicated to her contemporary, poet and dramatist Joanna Baillie. The dedication laments the lax age in which they live, where good Christian girls often suffer temptation. Brunton shaped perfect heroines and monstrous villains in tales that often included violence. Modern readers easily dismiss *Self Control* as hyperbolic and unrealistic, although it received praise by Jane AUSTEN who called it a standard she hoped to reach. Not only does the virtuous main character, Laura, tutored by a minister's wife, fight off the evil Hargrave's rape attempts when he kidnaps her and transports her to America, she survives a dive over Canada's Montmorenci Falls in a canoe. Laura's training in virtue helps her win the day to return, triumphant, to Scotland. Brunton peoples the novel with type characters, including a profligate father and a kindly, virtuous surrogate mother figure, Lady Pelham, Laura's aunt. Her next work, DISCIPLINE (1814), receives kinder treatment by modern critics, likely due to Brunton's shaping of a more human protagonist, a young woman spoiled by overindulgence who matures due to her experiences. Later labeled a MANNERS NOVEL, *Discipline* joined Austen's works in advancing reality in fiction. Brunton's career was cut short when she died in childbirth with her first baby. Her novels proved quite popular in her own day, lapsed out of favor for a time, but attracted renewed interest during the latter 20th century from FEMINIST CRITICISM. Excerpts from both her works may be found in electronic texts, and both remain available in hard print copy.

BIBLIOGRAPHY

Brunton, Mary. *Self Control.* London: Pandora Press, 1986.

Spender, Dale. *Mothers of the Novel: 100 Good Women Writers before Jane Austen.* New York: Pandora, 1986.

Weldon, Fay. Introduction. *Discipline,* by Mary Brunton. London: Pandora Press, 1986, vii–viii.

BUCHANAN, ROBERT W. (1841–1901)

Robert Buchanan was born on August 18, 1841, at Caverswall in Lancashire and reared as an only child (one sister died in infancy). His doting parents appear in his works, by influence and direct reference. His adoration for his mother manifested in an idealization of womanhood extreme enough to warrant notice in a day when such idealization was commonplace. His father, though generous with attention when possible, had several jobs as well as many social activities that kept him from his family.

Robert's mother, like his father, believed in the Owenite philosophy of utopianism, and she took charge of her son's education. The founder of "Owenism," Englishman Robert Owen, held that circumstances molded the individual character. Manipulation of one's environment to achieve the optimum comfort, both physical and mental, would advance human development and, on a less grand scale, industrial profits. Instead of studying religion, Buchanan immersed himself in the theories of Owenite socialism. The struggle between his intellectual skepticism and

upbringing, and his desire to become a Christian, influenced his religious poetry. He attended high school and university classes in Edinburgh before moving to London to seek his fortune.

Buchanan arrived in London during 1860 with plans to become a playwright but, early on, focused on poetry instead. His 1863 volume, *Undertones,* he followed with *Idyls and Legends of Inverburn* (1865), *London Poems* (1866), *Ballad Stories of the Affections* (1866), and *North Coast and Other Poems* (1867). While most of his work focused on the Scottish peasantry and their difficult lives, he also focused on street life of the London poor. He personally attacked and offended Dante Rosetti and other Pre-Raphaelites in his 1872 pamphlet, *The Fleshly School of Poetry,* and was in turn attacked in Algernon Charles Swinburne's defense, *Under the Microscope* (1872). Additional poetry, including *Balder the Beautiful* (1877), reflected Buchanan's focus on the mystical and revealed his association with the group known as Spasmodics, due to its works' emotional extravagance and excessive length.

As a playwright, Buchanan entered an English theatre poised to embark on one of its most productive and stimulative periods. He is credited with more than 50 plays of varying quality produced over 37 years, including *The Rathboys* and *Two Little Maids from School.* Many of the plays, such as *Sophia* (based on Henry FIELDING's 1749 early novel, *TOM JONES*) and *Pied Piper of Hamelin* (first a well-known folktale and later the title of an 1842 children's poem by Robert Browning), were adaptations of well-known works, leaving only 10, according to biographer John Cassidy, made entirely of Buchanan's own work. He is credited, however, with bringing fresh inspiration to old works and even improving upon some of them.

Buchanan also proved a productive novelist. Between 1876 and 1900, he published 25 novels, including *The Shadow of the Sword* (1876), *God and the Man* (1881), *FOXGLOVE MANOR* (1885), and *Effie Hetherington* (1886). His ever-present need for money probably accounted for this surprising publication rate. His novels often expressed his strong opinions; some went unpublished due to their offensive nature. His Owenite upbringing and regular consultations with Owenite Victorians remains evident in his work.

While Robert Owen himself was a peaceful man, arguing for remedies to the wrongs of the world, Robert Buchanan preferred the aggressive print attack. His method remains in evidence not only in his creative works, but also in the many essays he published in various journals. Buchanan died on June 10, 1901.

BIBLIOGRAPHY

Cassidy, John A. *Robert W. Buchanan*. Boston: Twayne Publishers, 1974.

BULWER-LYTTON, EDWARD (GEORGE EARLE LYTTON), FIRST BARON LYTTON (1803–1873)

Born May 25, 1803, at 31 Baker Street in London, Sir Edward Bulwer-Lytton is probably most widely known, 200 years after his birth, for his prolific publications. Edward's father, Gen. William Earle Bulwer, had a fierce temper that caused his wife to seek legal custody of their three sons within a year of Edward's birth. William finally separated from his wife, losing guardianship of his three children; he was ordered by a court to pay child support, a relatively new idea in 19th-century England. The general died four years later, and Bulwer was enrolled in formal education.

Following problems at one school, Bulwer 's mother transferred him to Dr. Hooker's school at Rottingdean. Although he began a strong education at home, inheriting books from his eccentric grandfather and a love of poetry from his mother, he was not academically inclined, and his mother worried that he would not be accepted into university. Despite starting a weekly magazine, showing a zest for Byron's poetry, and exhibiting great energy and intellectual vigor, Bulwer left school in 1819 determined to avoid further education. Sent back to school by his mother, Bulwer finally reconciled himself to his education under the Reverend Charles Wallington at Ealing. There he fell in love with a girl known only as "Lucy D——" and developed a romantic idealism that would influence the rest of his life. Before a true love affair could blossom, the girl was forced into a quick marriage by her father, and Bulwer suffered a deep depression. A few years later, he received a deathbed letter from Lucy, whom he saw once more before her death.

In 1822, Bulwer entered Trinity College and Cambridge, where he won the chancellor's medal for a poem titled "Sculpture"; published a collection of poems, *Delmour; or, A Tale of a Sylphid and Other Poems*; finished a draft of his first novel, *Falkland* (1827), and the first chapter of *Pelham* (1828); and laid the ground for his historical book, *England and the English* (1833), a seminal sociological study. He began his publishing career as Edward Bulwer, but often referred to himself as Edward Lytton Bulwer, adopting Lytton from his mother's maiden name. In the early 1830's he edited *The New Monthly Magazine* while continuing his book writing.

After travel and a love affair broken off by his mother, Bulwer met Rosina Doyle Wheeler, a beautiful, witty Irish girl. World-weary, despondent, and always susceptible to romance, Bulwer fell in love with her. Despite his mother's protestations and a briefly broken engagement, the two married in August 1827 and had their first child, Edward Robert, within two years, followed later by a daughter, Emily, who would die at age 20 of typhus. The pair lived extravagantly, and, because his wife had little income and his mother had cut off his allowance, Bulwer became a prolific writer.

Falkland did not make much of a splash upon publication, but Bulwer's next effort, PELHAM; OR, THE ADVENTURES OF A GENTLEMAN, did. He continued producing novels by drawing on his own experiences, creating psychological thrillers, crime stories, attempting (for the first time, and unsuccessfully) the genre of the HISTORICAL NOVEL, and following a credo of writing novels "with a purpose." His work habits strained his marriage, and he separated from Rosina in 1836. He eventually published two dozen novels over 45 years and tried almost every genre popular in his day, including drama. Historical romances included The LAST DAYS OF POMPEII (1834), RIENZI (1835), *The Last of the Barons* (1843), and *Harold* (1848). He also wrote science fiction, such as ZANONI (1842), *A Strange Story* (1862), and *The COMING RACE* (1871), seen as a satire on the theories of Charles DARWIN. *Pelham* represented SILVER-FORK fiction, while other novels focused on the domestic scene, including *The Caxtons* (1849), *My Novel* (1853), and *What Will He Do With It?* (1858). His NEWGATE FICTION, *Paul Clifford* (1830) and *EUGENE ARAM*

(1832), caused outrage among those who viewed his work as glorifying common criminals. The public read everything he wrote, regardless of the style or subject matter. He also wrote 10 plays, three of which were performed throughout the 19th century; 11 volumes of poetry; and collections of essays, short stories, and history. Queen Victoria noted in one diary entry how much she enjoyed the performance of the five-act historical comedy *Not So Bad as We Seem; or, Many Sides to a Character.* He eventually enjoyed the reputation of the most widely read novelist during his time after Charles DICKENS, a close acquaintance with whom Bulwer often conferred regarding the purpose of the novel. Dickens named his 10th child for Bulwer, who served as godfather to the boy, despite the two authors' political differences.

Bulwer served twice in Parliament, first as a Liberal from 1831–41 and then as a Tory from 1852 until 1858. He received a knighthood in 1837 due to his commitment to political reform. His pamphlet entitled *Letter to a Late Cabinet Minister on the Present Crisis* (1834) enjoyed great success; it supported the immediate abolition of Negro apprenticeship in the West Indian colonies (1838). When his mother died in 1843, Sir Edward expanded his last name to Bulwer-Lytton. He resigned from the cabinet, due to poor health, in 1858.

Following his resignation, Bulwer-Lytton began writing again and produced some of his best novels. *A Strange Story* (1862) again challenged Darwinism; his *Caxtoniana* essays (1863) covered a great variety of topics; and he produced a rhymed comic play, *Walpole; or, Every Man Has His Price* (1869). He became a peer in 1866 and adopted the title Lord Lytton, enabling his son to become the first earl of Lytton in 1880; the two are sometimes confused in historical accounts. After suffering pains on the right side of his face and neck, losing his sight, and enduring a series of epileptic seizures and convulsions, all within a few weeks, Bulwer-Lytton died on January 17, 1873, from an inflammation of brain membranes.

Critics would later rank Bulwer-Lytton among the second tier of authors, below Dickens and the BRONTË sisters, but on par with Anthony TROLLOPE and Elizabeth GASKELL. He did not hold a long-lasting reader-ship, due to his mannered style, which included his fashioning almost of all his heroines after his forever lost Lucy D——, as well as a high sentimentality and archaic use of language, rendering his works unpleasant to later generations. The 20th century saw the introduction of an enduring competition to produce the worst possible line to open a novel, known as the Bulwer-Lytton Fiction Contest. However, his influence on contemporaries and later writers proved immense. *The Coming Race* likely influenced H. Rider HAGGARD's KING SOLOMON'S MINES (1885) and Samuel BUTLER's EREWHON (1872), while *Paul Clifford,* as the first Newgate novel, influenced the development of crime and detective fiction, including Harrison AINSWORTH's *Jack Shephard* (1839), Dickens's OLIVER TWIST (1838), and Wilkie COLLINS's The WOMAN IN WHITE (1860). His deep interests in the conjunction of things beautiful and evil remains part of his literary legacy.

BIBLIOGRAPHY

Allingham, Philip V. "Sir Edward G. D. Bulwer-Lytton: A Brief Biography." Victorian Web. Available online. URL: http://65.107.211.206/authors/bulwer/bio.html. Updated on December 12, 2000.

Campbell, James L., Sr. *Edward Bulwer-Lytton.* Boston: Twayne Publishers, 1986.

Shattuck, Charles H. *A Chronicle of the Early Victorian Theatre.* Urbana: University of Illinois Press, 1958.

BURLESQUE   Burlesque derives from the Italian term *burla,* meaning ridicule or joke. It refers to a mocking imitation of works within any of the arts. Henry FIELDING famously defined literary burlesque in his preface to JOSEPH ANDREWS (1742) as that which readers find "monstrous and unnatural," with any "delight" arising "from the surprising absurdity, as in appropriating the manners of the highest to the lowest." He took great care to distinguish the hyperbole of burlesque from the reality of comedy. In Fielding's opinion, burlesque required little skill to write and preserved "the ludicrous instead of the sublime." Divisions into low and high burlesque are useful in order to distinguish between the literary mock-heroic (high) and travesty or just burlesque (low). In mock-heroic, a low theme is presented in high style, while travesty presents a high theme in low style. Jonathan SWIFT'S *The Battle of the Books* (1697) represents mock-heroic, in which Swift mocked in a classic style the raging argument over the comparative merits of the study of the classics to the study of contemporary writing. Humor derives from the contrast between subject matter and its treatment by the author. Closely related is PARODY, which focuses on specific works.

BIBLIOGRAPHY

Battestin, Marin C. Introduction. *Joseph Andrews.* Boston: Houghton Mifflin, 1961.

Lewis, Peter Elfed. *Fielding's Burlesque Drama: Its Place in the Tradition.* Edinburgh: Edinburgh University Press, 1987.

Shepperson, Archibald Bolling. *The Novel in Motley: A History of the Burlesque Novel in English.* Cambridge, Mass.: Harvard University Press, 1936.

BURNETT, FRANCES HODGSON (1849–1924)

Frances (Eliza) Hodgson was born on November 24,1849, on the edge of Manchester, the eldest daughter of loving and successful parents. Her beloved father died from stroke and illness when Frances was only three, and Mrs. Hodgson attempted briefly to keep up her husband's business. A dismal economy closed the business, and Mrs. Hodgson moved the family to Salford. At her Salford school, Frances was popular and gained a reputation as a great storyteller. As a child she displayed the imagination and love for books that would lead her later to write several of her own.

In 1865, at the age of 15, Frances, her mother, two sisters, and two brothers immigrated to Knoxville, Tennessee, where the impoverished group depended on the two boys to support them. At 16, Frances opened a school that eight pupils attended daily, paying their teacher in vegetables and eggs. Two years later she earned enough money picking grapes to buy paper and stamps for her first short story submission, which was sold to *Godey's Lady's Book.* Just four years after submitting her first short story, Hodgson published her first widely read short story in *Scribner's Magazine.* The following year, 1873, she married Dr. L. M. Burnett, whom she would divorce in 1898. In 1877, Hodgson Burnett applied the knowledge she had gained in Sal- ford about the lives of the poor to the sentimental novel that began her career, *That Lass o'Lowrie's.* While the novel earned a respectable readership, her children's books would establish her fame.

Hodgson Burnett continued to write, earning substantial sums of money as the public gained as increasing respect for her work. Though her children's books would carry her fame into the following centuries, her romance novels were very popular during her lifetime. Her notable works included *Through One Administration* and *A Lady of Quality,* published between 1877 and 1886.

In 1886, Hodgson Burnett published LITTLE LORD FAUNTLEROY, a novel about a character based on her son, Vivian. The novel not only brought greater recognition to its author, it influenced the culture of her time, causing fascinated mothers to dress their sons in velvet suits with lace collars like the book's main character. In 1888, she published *Editha's Burglar* and an autobiography titled *The One I Knew Best of All* in 1917. *Little Lord Fautleroy's* popularity endures, and it has been dramatized and reproduced in several media, as have two of Hodgson Burnett's other novels, *The Secret Garden* (1911) and *Sara Crewe,* later rewritten as *The Little Princess* (1905). Hodgson Burnett's life was often found in her books, though they were not autobiographical. Of *Little Lord Fauntleroy,* she said, "It is not a portrait; but certainly, if there had not been a Vivian there would not have been Fauntleroy." She once described a favorite childhood memory of a garden with high brick walls and a door that had long been unopened, and her love of gardening endured throughout her life. She continued publishing, producing a novel about the supernatural, *The White People* (1917). Having published the *Head of the House of Coombe* and *Robin,* in 1922, Hodgson Burnett died at her home in Long Island on October 29, 1924.

BIBLIOGRAPHY

Burnett, Vivan. *The Romantick Lady.* Charles Scribner's Sons: New York, 1927.

Laski, Marghanita. *Mrs. Ewing, Mrs. Molesworth, and Mrs. Hodgson Burnett.* New York: Oxford University Press, 1951.

Overton, Grant. *The Women Who Make Our Novels.* Dodd, Mead & Company: New York, 1928.

BURNEY, FANNY (1752–1840)

Frances Burney was born June 13, 1752, in King's Lynn, England, into a family described by critic and journalist William Hazlitt as a group of "wits, scholars, novelists, musicians, artists, in numbers numberless." Her birth mother died before Fanny turned 10 years old, and her father later married a woman who did not support her stepdaughter's writing. Disapproving of novels, as many of her day did, Mrs. Burney forced Fanny to burn her first effort at fiction, *The History of Caroline Evelyn.* Fanny often hinted at the tension between daughter and stepmother in her extensive journals, where she developed much of her work. By contrast, Fanny's father kindly encouraged her, although he liked to joke about her seriousness and did not believe her writing would come to anything. A member of Samuel JOHNSON's intellectual circle and a musician, Dr. Charles Burney approved of his daughter's pursuits and did not deny her the self-education that she sought. He once found a page of her journal left behind on a parlor table and teased that he would never return it. Responding to his daughter's desperate pleas, he finally returned the page, claiming that any other papers he found lying around he would post at the market square. Later, Burney's work would show great influence by her father's sense of style and writing skills. The young Fanny also found a mentor in "Daddy Crisp," a friend of her father. Mr. Crisp filled a void left in Fanny's life following her mother's death, and he became the driving force behind the writing, revising, and publishing of her work.

Burney's propensity for memorizing, and then recounting in detail and storytelling style, the conversations of others stood her in good stead when she began to write seriously. In recording these conversations, she reproduced people's characters down to their speech patterns and phrase usage. Her first novel, *EVELINA, OR THE HISTORY OF A YOUNG LADY'S ENTRANCE INTO THE WORLD* (1778), provided a mix of social comedy, realism, and wit. She based her anonymous novel on *The History of Caroline Evelyn,* burned many years earlier by Mrs. Burney. *Evelina* proved a great success, and readers assumed its author to be male. When the truth about Burney's authorship was revealed, she became a celebrity.

Burney's second novel, *Cecilia, or Memoirs of an Heiress* (1782), brought additional fame and made Burney the first woman to earn respectability as a female novelist. Her novels influenced the development of the novel by featuring domestic comedy, which she practiced in imitation of Samuel RICHARDSON and Henry FIELDING. Jane AUSTEN would later reflect Burney's influence in *PRIDE AND PREJUDICE.* Burney's third novel, *CAMILLA, OR A PICTURE OF YOUTH,* appeared in 1796.

Burney produced work mirroring her own social and economic problems and later extended her writing to drama. Although she wrote several theatrical comedies, her father wholly disapproved of theatrical writing for women and suppressed most of her efforts. Only one of her eight plays, a tragedy named *Edwy and Elgiva,* would be produced during her lifetime. The rest of her plays would wait until the late 20th century for critical assessment; six did not achieve publication until 1995.

Burney's diaries outline a life more exciting than any novel's heroine. She served as a member of the Royal Household in 1786, becoming Second Keeper of the Robes for Queen Charlotte, a position she hated and gained release from in 1791. She married a refugee French general, Alexandre Gabriel Jean-Baptiste d'Arblay, an adjutant general to Lafayette, and waited anxiously near Waterloo for the results of the battle. After first residing in England, the couple returned to France from 1802 until 1812, when they moved back to England. She published her final novel, *The Wanderer,* in 1814 and spent time in Bath and London. Following her husband's death, she devoted much energy to editing *The Memoirs of Dr. Burney.* Burney continued writing throughout most of her 87 years, although in her last year she suffered some mental confusion. She died on January 6, 1840, in London and was buried in Bath near her husband and son.

In addition to her contributions to fiction, Burney's *Early Diary 1768–78* remains important for its accounts of Johnson as well as actor and prolific dramatist David Garrick (1717–79). *Her Diary and Letters* (1778–1840) features important accounts of court life. By the end of the 20th century, much of her work could be accessed in electronic text.

BIBLIOGRAPHY

Adelstein, Michael E. *Fanny Burney.* New York: Twayne Publishers, 1968.

"Frances Burney d'Arblay." The Burney Society. Available online. URL: http://dc37.dawsoncollege.qc.ca/burney/biofb.html. Downloaded February 8, 2004.

Hemlow, Joyce. *Fanny Burney, Selected Letter and Journals.* Oxford: Clarendon Press, 1986.

Schrank, Barbara G., and David J. Supina. *The Famous Miss Burney.* New York: The John Day Company, 1976.

Spender, Dale. *Mothers of the Novel: 100 Good Women Writers before Jane Austen.* New York: Pandora, 1986.

BUTLER, SAMUEL (1835–1902)

The son of a clergyman and grandson of a bishop, Samuel Butler received religious instruction early on. His strict father contributed to a rather unhappy childhood. Butler was educated at Shrewsbury and St. John's College in Cambridge, but after graduation, his religious doubts led to a strong career disagreement with his father. As a result, in 1859 he left England for New Zealand, where he found success in sheep farming and began to recover from childhood disappointments.

A First Year in a Canterbury Settlement, which contained the core of the later novel EREWHON (1872), was compiled from Butler's letters home and published in a New Zealand journal in 1863. In 1864, Butler returned to England, where he settled at Clifford's Inn. For the next 10 years he pursued painting, becoming successful enough to exhibit occasionally at the Royal Academy. By undertaking an activity of which his father had earlier expressed disapproval, Butler proclaimed his independence. His family problems led him to be critical of family connections in general, which may have contributed to his own lack of close, personal relationships; he remained a lifelong bachelor. His 1865 publication, *The Evidence for the Resurrection of Jesus Christ as Given by the Four Evangelists Critically Examined* summarized his doubts regarding Christian tenets; it also provided the basis for his later satire, *Fair Haven* (1873). As he seriously pursued an ultimately successful painting career that resulted in the display of his work at Royal Academy exhibitions, he wrote little between 1865 and 1870.

In 1872 Butler anonymously published *Erewhon,* a book that some critics regard as UTOPIAN FICTION, while others do not classify it as a novel due to the secondary importance of plot and characterization to that of SATIRE. Butler later wrote, in a preface to the 1901 revision, that he had once complained to a friend that, compared to the great popularity of *Erewhon,* his other works had seemed "still born." His friend reminded him there existed "one charm" *Erewhon* had that his other works could never share: "The sound of a new voice, and of an unknown voice." Virginia Woolf, a great fan of Butler's work, later disagreed with that friend, noting that Butler's many artistic pursuits, while not all successful, exposed his "mind to the light," keeping him "amazingly fresh to the end of life."

In 1873 Butler published *Fair Haven,* an ironic attack on the Resurrection so subtly presented that many readers did not recognize its defense of miracles as satiric. From 1877 through 1890, he wrote a series of works attacking contemporary scientific ideas, particularly Charles DARWIN's theory of natural selection, and in support of Lemarck and creative evolution. His theories supported the idea of a specific "Life Force," rather than chance, as responsible for reproductive variations that Darwin attributed to survival of the fittest organism. In 1881, Butler published *Alps and Sanctuaries of Piedmont and the Canton Ticino,* the first of several illustrated works on travel and art. Butler's interest in music and experiments with musical composition led to an 1888 collaboration with his friend H. Festing Jones to produce the comic cantata *Narcissus.* His eclectic interests also included photography, and many of his photographs, capturing a wide diversity of subjects, from beggars to priests, treat each with a marked dignity. Thousands of his photos found a home at Cambridge College.

Pursuing an interest in the works of Homer, Butler published *The Authoress of the Odyssey,* in which he argued that a woman wrote Homer's work. He followed this with English prose translations of *The Iliad* and *The Odyssey* in 1898 and 1900. In 1899 he also published *Shakespeare's Sonnets Reconsidered,* speculating that

Shakespeare wrote the sonnets to a lover he took from the lower social class.

In 1901, Butler published *Erewhon Revisited. The Way of All Flesh,* an autobiographical BILDUNGSROMAN and Butler's only novel according to some critics, was published posthumously in 1903, the year after he died. It satirizes Victorian family, religion, and education through a tale of four generations of the Pontifex family. The book supported, if not precipitated, an early-20th-century revolt against Victorian ideals, promoting the value of individual intellect in the face of the failure of convention. One popular line from the novel sums up that thought: "All animals, except man, know that the principal business of life is to enjoy it." Heavy with the author's opinion, the work gained high praise. George Bernard Shaw called it one of the great books of the world, while Woolf added it to the works by Butler that kept him "busy planting his darts in the flanks of his age," describing his novel as differing from others in its originality and liveliness. In 1915, Butler's works enjoyed larger total sales than in any year since their publication, proof of the enduring appeal his writings held. Twentieth-century critics characterized Butler as one of the previous century's most original, and belligerent, thinkers. Twenty-first-century readers would agree, with the continued popularity of Butler's works promoting electronic text versions, available on the Internet.

BIBLIOGRAPHY

Furbank, P. N. Introduction to *The Way of All Flesh,* by Samuel Butler. New York: Alfred A. Knopf, 1992.

Drabble, Margaret E. "Samuel Butler." *The Oxford Companion to English Literature.* Oxford: Oxford University Press, 1985.

Jeffers, Thomas L. *Samuel Butler Revalued.* University Park: Pennsylvania State University Press, 1981.

Mudford, Peter. Introduction to *Erewhon,* by Samuel Butler. London: Penguin Classics, 1970.

Raby, Peter. *Samuel Butler: A Biography.* Iowa City: Iowa University Press, 1991.

Woolf, Virginia. "A Man with a View." *Contemporary Writers.* New York: Harcourt, Brace & World, 1965. 28–32.

———. "The Way of All Flesh." *Contemporary Writers.* New York: Harcourt, Brace & World, 1965. 33–35.

BYRONIC HERO   This type of character, named for romantic poet George Gordon, Lord Byron (1788–1824), became a favorite of GOTHIC NOVEL authors, including Emily and Charlotte BRONTË. Based on Byron's character Don Juan, from the epic poem of the same name, the Byronic hero often did not adhere to the mores of his society. Generally a rake or scoundrel, he was a womanizer and adventurer who sought revenge for what he perceived as others' wrongful treatment of him. He could soften for those he loved, revealing a tender side, but for the most part remained a formidable force with which to deal. Fellow characters found themselves both attracted to, and repelled by, the Byronic hero's enigmatic nature. Surprisingly, the reader forgave the hero his loose morals, focusing instead on the development of his strength of character as he bravely encountered conflicts within himself, with others, and with his environment. While he did not always achieve victory over those forces, he inevitably gained the admiration of readers who appreciated his attempts to follow his own code. Dark, brooding, often with a mysterious background and a physicality bordering on the brute, the Byronic hero appeared a highly passionate and intelligent character. Figures such as Mr. Rochester, from Charlotte Brontë's *JANE EYRE* (1847), and Heathcliff, from Emily Brontë's *WUTHERING HEIGHTS* (1847), both qualify as Byronic heroes. In many plots, the Byronic hero must metaphorically die in order to enjoy symbolic "rebirth," often suffering a physical maiming, such as Mr. Rochester's baptism by fire in *Jane Eyre,* or a literal death and rebirth as a spirit being, such as that enjoyed by Heathcliff.

C

CAIRD, MONA (1854–1932) Mona Caird, considered one of the first feminist journalists and novelists, was born Alice Mona Alison on May 24, 1854, on the Isle of Wight. Mona's mother, Matilda Ann Jane Hector, came from a well-to-do family and married John Alison at age 19. Her family lived in what was then Denmark but later became northern Germany. Mona's father, a landowner, engineer and inventor, was 22 years his wife's senior and also enjoyed wealth. The Alison family later relocated to Kensington in London, where a photo of Mona reflects a confident nine-year-old, perhaps an only child. Few facts were recorded regarding her childhood, but her relationship with her mother may have been contentious, the type of relationship reflected in daughter/mother pairs in her later writing.

At 23, Mona wed James Alexander Henryson-Caird. Eight years Mona's senior, Caird came from a distinguished landed Scottish family and owned an estate, Cassencary (later Castle Cary, near Galloway), a location on which Mona modeled the settings for later writings. Its 14th-century Gothic mansion excited Caird's romantic imagination. The mansion had already been featured as the "Woodbourne" of Sir Walter SCOTT's novel GUY MANNERING (1815).

Caird's affection for the country was obvious in her writing, although she eschewed the lifestyle that accompanied country living, which she found stifling. Caird joined her husband at Cassencary for only two months each year, choosing to spend most of her time as part of the London social scene. Highly independent and opinionated, she often traveled without her husband, searching for the intellectual stimulation that marked her life. Whether she found her marriage sustaining is undetermined, but friends agreed that James's lack of assertiveness made their relationship acceptable. Perhaps tellingly, Caird's fiction depicted simple incompatibility as the most common reason for a marriage dissolution.

Caird's first novel, *Whom Nature Leadeth,* appeared in three volumes in 1883 under the pseudonym G. Noel Hatton. Her second novel, titled *One That Wins* (1887), was credited simply to the author of *Whom Nature Leadeth.* Another three-volume work, *The Wings of Azrael,* followed in 1889. Caird's most famous novel, DAUGHTERS OF DANAUS (1894), chronicled an artistic woman's struggle to express herself, while smothered by family members that insist she follow a more traditional lifestyle. Although she eventually adopts a daughter and finds a surrogate mother to replace her birth mother, who she feels has betrayed her, her moves are shaped by a patriarchal society that overpowers her desires. Caird not only analyzed the complexity of the mother/daughter relationship, but, according to Ann Heilmann, "constructed a feminist theory of the female self and its development."

Caird's theme directly reflects the beliefs she expressed in her famous 1888 article titled simply

"Marriage" that appeared in the *Westminster Review.* In an attack against male-centered culture, she claimed that marriage and prostitution provided the framework of a religious, economic, and political system designed to leave all power in the hands of men. Until society acknowledged every woman's right to power over her own body, marriage equated to "united degeneration" in its most positive aspect and "the degradation of womanhood" in its most negative. Another publication, the *Daily Telegraph,* called for an open debate on Caird's ideas and ultimately received about 27,000 letters. The letters would later be published as a book titled *Is Marriage a Failure?* Her attack against prostitution and marriage as, according to Heilmann, "institutionalized violence against women," may have excited such public passion due in part to its publication at the same time that Jack the Ripper terrorized London. Caird served to demystify motherhood, exploding the myth that every woman was predisposed to motherhood. Thus, she opened the door to other feminists to perform closer examination of the tradition that had acted to define women's roles for centuries. By the time she published her collection *The Morality of Marriage and Other Essays* (1897), Caird had added her voice to the heated debate over Victorian feminism.

Caird had given birth to her only child, Alister James, in 1884. Her critique of motherhood suggests the maternal life brought her much conflict and little satisfaction. A nervous breakdown she suffered in the early 1890s may have been the result of her feelings of guilt over her desire to be free of the confining domestic scene. No photographs exist of Caird with young James, although pictures survived of James and his father. Such facts have encouraged the belief that Caird was not a particularly good mother. She even located her son's bedroom in the guest quarters, at the opposite end of the mansion to her own. Family mythology held that Caird presented young James with a vial of poison when he left to fight in World War I to take in case of captivity. He chose to survive various injuries and returned home having earned the rank of major following the war.

Once frail, James matured into a man who commonly stood in direct idealistic opposition to his mother. While he seemed only interested in shooting, she forbid the caretaker to place traps and snares. He never read the books in which she advocated a world without war and guns and patriarchal control. When James married, predictably Caird had little in common with her new daughter-in-law and chose not to spend much time with the couple. As she aged, Caird's focus on mother/daughter relationships shifted from the rebellious daughter to the disappointed mother.

In 1898, Caird published another novel, *Pathway of the Gods,* followed in the early 1900s by the three shorter pieces, "For Money or for Love," "A Romance of the Moors," and "The Yellow Drawing Room." Before her death, she published two additional novels, *The Stones of Sacrifice* (1915) and *The Great Wave,* published in 1932, the year of her death.

Mona Caird left a legacy to all feminist fiction writers of protagonists reluctant to make choices. Their exaggerated feelings of familial duty and emotional insecurity represented their imprisonment within a system detrimental to women and perpetuated by a patriarchal society, which supported a marriage system Caird viewed as barbaric. She held that men needed to adopt an ethical responsibility toward women who, in their turn, should embrace the revolutionary ideal of individual rights for the female. While her works would not become important as literature until late in the 20th century, they had a strong political effect on her own society. *Daughters of Danaus* remains available in hard copy and electronic text.

BIBLIOGRAPHY

Gullette, Margaret Morganroth. Afterword. *The Daughter of Danaus* by Mona Caird. New York: The Feminist Press, 1989, 493–534.

Heilmann, Ann. "Mona Caird: Wild Woman, New Woman, and Early Radical Feminist Critic of Marriage and Motherhood." *Women's History Review* 5, no. 1 (1996): 67–95.

CALEB WILLIAMS, OR THINGS AS THEY ARE, THE ADVENTURES OF WILLIAM GODWIN (1794)

William GODWIN's first novel, *Caleb Williams* reflects its author's anarchist belief that social conflicts could be resolved only through face-to-face discussion by offended parties; governmental bodies accomplished nothing. An important voice during the Age of Reason, Godwin and his works were forgotten in later decades until Percy Bysshe Shelley (his son-in-law) took an interest in them. *Caleb Williams* provided an excellent vehicle for Godwin's philosophy, when his opposition not only to institutions but also to movements against them gained an audience. In addition, his use of the GOTHIC style, an approach later perfected by his daughter, Mary SHELLEY, in her novel *FRANKENSTEIN, OR THE MODERN PROMETHEUS* (1818), made for an exciting read.

The title character narrates the story, opening with the chilling line, "My life has for several years been a theater of calamity." He recounts a childhood of poverty and the self-education that qualified him as a secretary to Squire Falkland. A self-proclaimed "natural philosopher," Williams remarks, "I could not rest until I had acquainted myself with the solutions that had been invented for the phenomena of the universe." The compassionate Williams becomes concerned regarding Falkland's chronic melancholy and decides to delve into his master's past, hoping to help alleviate the "hasty, peevish and tyrannical" Falkland's "distemper." Williams believes these "paroxysms" are due to mental torment, rather than physical illness. Additional characters populate the early chapters, including the exotic Italian Marquis Pisani, his daughter Lucretia, and her lover, Count Malvesi. Rather than having a positive effect, Williams's discoveries turn his master against him.

Williams learns that a violent neighbor, Squire Barnabas Tyrrel, had terrorized the countryside before Falkland's arrival. Falkland's developing friendship with the district's intellectual, Mr. Clare, infuriates Tyrrel, who insults Falkland repeatedly. Clare's symbolic last name, suggesting clarity of vision, establishes him as a wise man.

Jealous of the challenge by Falkland to his "reign," Tyrrel eventually humiliates Falkland's poetry publicly, sparking a visit from Falkland to his home. Falkland hopes for peace, but Tyrrel remains disagreeable. When Clare dies from a contagious disease, he removes the only person who might have mitigated the enmity between the two squires. Falkland rescues Tyrrel's young cousin, Emily, from a fire, causing Tyrrel's bad feelings toward Falkland to escalate. Insults continue; then Tyrrel turns up dead.

Williams learns that two of Tyrrel's tenants, a man named Hawkins and his son, were convicted of murder and hanged. Although without hard proof, Williams reveals Falkland as the murderer. Afraid that Williams will reveal his secret, Falkland falsely accuses him of theft and has him imprisoned. Falkland's guilt and fear drive him to confess to the crime, which leads to his immediate collapse and death. While Williams gains freedom, he suffers guilt over having caused Falkland's death.

Godwin commented on November 20, 1832, about his writing of *Caleb Williams* on the occasion of the reprinting of *Fleetwood,* his later novel (1805), in Bentley's "Standard Novels" (No. XXII). He reveals that he first sent the manuscript to a friend for assessment, and the friend returned it with a note reading, "I return you your manuscript, because I promised to do so. If I had obeyed the impulse of my own mind, I should have thrust it in the fire. If you persist, the book will infallibly prove the grave of your literary fame." Godwin persisted in revising it anyway. He had begun the novel with a third-person point of view but decided the tale's hero should "be his own historian." He tells of reading several works about pursuit and terror as he searched for models, noting with humor that he always fancied some similarity between Falkland and Blue Beard: Both had committed horrible crimes, and Caleb Williams assumes the role of Blue Beard's wives in discovering Falkland's atrocity.

Later interest in Godwin's works led to electronic publication of *Caleb Williams.*

BIBLIOGRAPHY

The Adventures of Caleb Williams: Or, Things As They Are by William Godwin. Homepage of the International Society of Political Psychology. Available online. URL: http://dwardmac.pitzer.edu/anarchist_archives/godwin/caleb/toc.html. Downloaded on January 25, 2003.

CAMILLA, OR A PICTURE OF YOUTH

FANNY BURNEY (1796) As Fanny BURNEY planned her 1796 novel, *Camilla, or a Picture of Youth,* she determined to imitate the popular style of SENTIMENTAL FICTION, focusing on highly dramatic incidents. She intentionally shaped it as "a crying volume" from the first words of *Ariella,* her initial title for the novel. The scenes dripped with "tender sympathy," accumulating to form the "picture of youth" referenced in her title. That phrase appears as well in the novel's final paragraph, when Dr. Marchmont thinks of Camilla's "pure innocence, open frankness" and the "spotless humor of her heart" as overriding youthful transgressions, such as past "errors" and "desperation" that occurred as products of her youth. This observation advances the happy conclusion to her novel, planned by Burney to promote its popularity. The lengthy novel features Camilla and her suitor Edgar Mandlebert, supported by numerous characters including her sisters Eugenia and Lavinia and her brother, Lionel, who mature in the modest and respectable Tyrold family. Their family extends to cousins Indiana and Clermont Lymere. They all circulate among a cast of social figures, such as General Kinsale, Miss Margland, Mrs. Arlbery, Miss Dennel, Lord Newford, and others. All promote a theme of sentimentality, based on contrived social interactions and mistaken conjecture that manipulate personal feelings and often lead to misperception, all of which are correctable by the operations of romance.

Burney planned for the marketability of *Camilla* in a way she had not with her previous works. Observing how well works of Ann RADCLIFFE captivated her public, Burney elected to incorporate the GOTHIC elements she had previously eschewed, as she wrote what she labeled her "Udolphish" volumes, referring to Radcliffe's most famous work, *The MYSTERIES OF UDOLPHO* (1794). After consulting with her husband, she determined to sell the novel in subscription form, and an advertisement for the novel appeared in *The Morning Chronicle* on July 7, 1795, seeking proposals from parties interested in its printing. Ironically, she sold its rights at the urging of her family for £1,000, and received little to nothing for reprints and later American sales. Critical reaction proved mixed; Jane AUSTEN liked it, while Horace Walpole, a noted proponent of aestheticism, found it sickening. Others praised its "highly animated scenes of life and manners," its "rich and varied characters," and general structure, but criticized its inordinate length, redundancies, and errors in grammar. While it sold out in three months, publishers hesitated to undertake a lengthy revision printing, but one appeared in 1801. It was quickly withdrawn, however, due to questionable actions on the part of booksellers. Burney waited for a decade to be able to retain the copyright herself and produce a third edition. By 1836, at the age of 84, Burney prepared to produce a new edition in hopes of helping to support her hopelessly ill son. However, he died in 1837, and by the time the new edition appeared in 1840, the year of Burney's death, she no longer cared much about the project. Later critics labeled that a blessing, as the new edition printed in three cheap volumes, was a "shabby replica" of the original, with no incorporation of Burney's years of laborious revisions.

It revived in the 20th century with the interest of FEMINIST CRITICS and exists in print and electronic versions.

BIBLIOGRAPHY

Bloom, Harold. Introduction to *Camilla, or a Picture of Youth,* by Fanny Burney. Oxford: Oxford University Press, 1983, ix–xxvi.

CAN YOU FORGIVE HER? ANTHONY TROLLOPE (1865) Serialized between January 1864 and August 1865, Anthony TROLLOPE's first in his Palliser series, *Can You Forgive Her?* proved instantly popular. Based on reworked material from his failed comedy *The Noble Jilt,* its plot focuses on Victorian discontent with social attitudes toward courtship and marriage. The system forced women too often to choose between love and security, leading to the self-questioning emphasized by the novel. Although that might have proved true, Trollope's premise in the novel, that once a woman had agreed to marry a certain man she could never change her mine, did not. In a preface to a 1948 edition, Sir Edward Marsh stated he felt Trollope erred in believing that even the strictest of Victorians would expect a woman to keep her promise of love, no matter how "unworthy its object might be."

For balance and variety, Trollope features three different love triangles, one comedic and the remaining two serious. Of all its characters, Lady Glencora Palliser dominates the novel and becomes a character for which devoted readers would return to every book in the series of six Palliser tales. Trollope's skill in developing Glencora as a woman of spirit and wit compensated for the flat treatment he affords to her aristocratic husband, Plantagenet Palliser, declared by the author to be one of his favorite characters, although readers did not share his opinion. They first met the Pallisers in Trollope's fifth Barsetshire sequence novel, *The SMALL HOUSE AT ALLINGTON* (1864). Trollope may have later regretted his introduction of Palliser as a misguided hero involved in a momentary flirtation with a married woman.

Each of the novel's love triangles involves a woman who cannot choose between two men, one representing a wild and sometimes evil personality, the other a stodgy and trustworthy one. The triangle involving the Widow Greenlow and her two suitors, Mr. Cheesacre and Captain Bellfield, serves purely for comic effect, and not a very skillful one. Most critics agree that readers may skip that narrative and miss little. It does serve to balance the other two triangles, as the widow runs away with the ne'er-do-well, while the two young women choose more wisely. Her connection to two other main characters, Alice and George Vavasor, should provide a link to the main body of the novel, but even that relation appears doubtful as the Vavasors' reputation as gentlefolk does not accommodate the widow's foolish behavior.

In the more serious and enjoyable portion of the novel, Alice Vavasor breaks her engagement to a country gentleman named John Grey, described by both Alice and the title of the third chapter as a "Worthy Man." She longs for the past excitement shared with her rascal cousin, George Vavasor, and she develops a scheme to invite him to travel with her and his sister Kate to the Continent. Grey proves his commendable nature when he "approves" of Alice's plan, even though she had been engaged to marry George in the past. The letter he writes to her on the subject contains a passage of interest to FEMINIST CRITICS:

It's a very fine theory, that of women being able to get along without men as well as with them; but, like other fine theories, it will be found very troublesome by those who first put it in practice. Gloved hands, petticoats, feminine softness, and the general homage paid to beauty, all stand in the way of success.

Alice remains enthralled with George's false charm, as he pursues her fortune, which he plans to use to obtain a position in Parliament. This appeals to Alice's desire to be a political wife, and she breaks her engagement to the devoted Grey. Her blindness to George's failings can be explained in part by the fact that she knew him originally as a brilliant, courageous, and respectable man. However, pressure from peers and his family, including the self-centered Alice, drives him to sacrifice his honor and converts him into an evil, manipulative personality. He stoops to emotional blackmail of those closest to him for money to support his "career." He embarrasses Kate by demanding that she request money on his behalf from Alice. At first taking "immense pride in the renewal of the match between her brother and her cousin," Kate knows she can no longer speak to Alice "of George as one who was to be their joint hero." He falls so far from being a hero that he even considers murdering John Grey.

While readers understand George's callow self-centeredness, they still feel little sympathy for Alice, due to her egoistic attitude and her continual insistence that others allow her to take charge of her own affairs when she obviously lacks the self-confidence to do so. Readers also find her an unrealistic character, almost as much so as the comic widow, as she makes and breaks engagements to both men twice, despite Grey's obvious superiority. Alice eventually regrets leaving Grey, particularly when she learns that he stands for election representing the borough of Silverbridge. By the novel's conclusion, the two reunite, much to the relief of readers who care for Grey, and Alice somewhat redeems herself as she considers the sacrifice that Grey makes for her: "She had no right to such happiness after the evil that she had done. She had been driven by a frenzy to do that which she herself could not pardon." Grey answers the book's title question affirmatively, and Alice gets her happy future.

The final triangle involves another of Alice's cousins, Lady Glencora, who has already married prudently to Palliser, a promising politician and heir to a dukedom. The independent Glencora, unlike Alice, becomes an instant favorite with readers. A woman of imagination, she desires a passionate mate. However, Palliser knows little of how to charm a woman, and Glencora begins to long for Burgo Fitzgerald, the beautiful cad she had rejected in favor of Plantagenet in *The Small House at Allington*. As the narrator tells readers, "I think that she might have learned to forget her early lover, or to look back upon him with a soft melancholy hardly amounting to regret, had her new lord been more tender in his ways with her."

Burgo, a charming, egoistic womanizer, convinces Glencora to run away with him. Palliser learns of the plan and arrives just in time to rescue Glencora. He understands he must sacrifice to retain his wife's devotion, and he chooses not to run for Chancellor of the Exchequer. Instead, he takes Glencora on a tour of the Continent. There they enjoy the birth of their first child, Lord Silverbridge, who ensures inheritance of the Duke of Omnium title. Palliser proves himself compassionate when he advances the destitute Fitzgerald's landlord three months' rent, preventing Burgo's ending up on the street. He also counsels John Grey regarding problems with the Vavasors.

As in all of Trollope's novels, these characters operate with clear motivations. Although readers may not agree with choices the characters make, they find the plot realistic and believable. Sir Edward Marsh wrote that when he first read Trollope's works at the close of the century, his portrayal of English life remained true. When he returned to it, the culture had changed, but the novel offered new readers the opportunity to live fully in another era, due to Trollope's accomplished attention to exquisite detail and his devotion to capturing correctly human nature.

BIBLIOGRAPHY

Glendinning, Victoria. *Anthony Trollope.* New York: Knopf, 1993.
Marsh, Edward, Sir. Preface to *Can You Forgive Her?,* by Anthony Trollope. Oxford: Oxford University Press, 1977.
Skilton, David. *Anthony Trollope and His Contemporaries: A Study in the Theory and Conventions of Mid-Victorian Fiction.* New York: Pallgrave McMillan, 1996.

CAPTAINS COURAGEOUS RUDYARD KIPLING (1896)

A predictable INITIATION/COMING-OF-AGE STORY, Rudyard KIPLING's *Captains Courageous* was long a favorite among young readers, especially boys. It features as protagonist a wealthy and spoiled American teenage boy named Harvey Cheyne. Sent away to boarding school in May by his parents and on a steamer traveling to England, Harvey becomes seasick after showing off in front of the adult male passengers by trying to smoke a small cigar. He falls overboard to be picked up by a fishing crew on the *We're Here* from Gloucester, captained by Disko Troop. The outraged Harvey accuses Troop of having stolen his pocketful of money and is disbelieving when told he must remain on the fishing ship until it docks in September. No amount of arguing and claiming his father will pay handsomely for his return can change Troop's mind. Harvey will spend the remainder of the voyage with Dan, Troop's son, learning to be a man by tackling difficult tasks at sea. The ship becomes his classroom, and Penn, Uncle Salters, Manuel, Tom Platt, and Long Jack his teachers. Some of the lessons are sobering, including his witnessing the sinking of the *Jennie Cushman* and the grief of its captain, Jason Olley, who loses his son and all his crew in the wreck. By the novel's conclusion, Harvey reunites with his family, learns the history of his father's past, which represented, according to the narrator, a history of America's settling of the West, and Dan earns a position on a ship belonging to Cheyne. In the final scene, Dan and Harvey meet several years after the adventure, when Dan has become a second mate and Harvey is attending school at Stanford.

BIBLIOGRAPHY

Amis, Kingsley. *Rudyard Kipling and his World.* New York: Scribner, 1975.

CARROLL, LEWIS (PSEUDONYM OF CHARLES LUTWIDGE DODGSON) (1832–1898)

Born in 1832 at Daresbury in Cheshire to a scholarly country Anglican parson, Charles Dodgson, and his wife, Frances Lutwidge Dodgson, Charles Lutwidge Dodgson was the third child of 11 and the first son. He attended a Yorkshire grammar school and matriculated to Rugby for three years. In his youth, he often entertained family gatherings and produced his own magazine of comic verse, stories, and illustrations. At Christ Church, Oxford, from 1850 to 1855, he exercised a lifelong love of equations and relationships in a study of mathematics. His studies earned him a lectureship, but his shy nature and tendency to stutter made classroom lectures difficult and embarrassing. Although ordained in 1861, Dodgson's stutter caused him to preach rarely, and he concentrated his efforts on the production of mathematics textbooks. He also contributed humorous writing to the magazine *The Train,* signing his work "B.B.," as he did not want to reveal his identity. When the editor requested a full pseudonym, Dodgson allowed him to select from several alternatives, and the editor chose Lewis Carroll. According to Cameron Newham, Dodgson developed the name by Latinising and reversing his own Christian names: Lutwidge = Ludovicus = Lewis; Charles = Carolus = Carroll.

Dodgson loved little girls and formed a close friendship with Alice Liddell, daughter of Henry Liddell, who had assumed duties as dean of Christ Church in 1855. Entranced by her and her siblings, he took multiple photographs of the Liddell children, and in 1856 Mrs. Liddell requested that he limit his visits. However, the Liddells soon departed on a lengthy trip, and the caretaker for the children in their absence allowed Dodgson to spend as much time as he wished with them. His relationship with Alice led him to write possibly the most famous work in CHILDREN'S LITERATURE *Alice's Adventures Under Ground* (1865). Later more commonly known by the title *ALICE IN WONDERLAND,* the book revolutionized juvenile literature, acting to entertain more than to instruct, as riddles, nonsense terms, and puzzles pepper the story. The popularity and tremendous influence of the book surprised Dodgson and his acquaintances, and he followed it with a sequel, *THROUGH THE LOOKING-GLASS AND WHAT ALICE FOUND THERE* (1871), indulging his love for games by plotting the book as a chess match. A lengthy nonsense poem titled *The Hunting of the Snark* (1876) completed Dodgson's major body of work, although he also produced additional textbooks and the *Sylvie and Bruno* stories.

As a photographer, Dodgson specialized in photos of young girls. Always with the supervision and approval of their parents, the girls often appeared in various forms of undress, causing later scholars to speculate as to Dodgson's psychological makeup. By 1880, he had stopped his photography, perhaps aware of the negative impression it sparked. However, no evidence exists to indicate any tendency toward impropriety on Dodgson's part.

As a testimony to the author's enduring popularity, a Lewis Carroll Society later emerged, and numerous Web sites are devoted to the author and his works. The books featuring Alice remain a staple of children's literature, as well as subjects for study in Victorian literature and humor. They have also been adapted repeatedly to various film and theater formats.

BIBLIOGRAPHY

Clark, Beverly Lyon. *Lewis Carroll.* Mercer Island, Wash.: Starmont House, 1990.

Leach, Caroline. *In the Shadow of the Dreamchild: A New Understanding of Lewis Carroll.* Chester Springs, Pa.: Peter Owen, 1999.

Newham, Cameron. The Lewis Carroll Page. Available online. URL: http://www.lewiscarroll.org/cam/lewis.html. Downloaded April 6, 2003.

CASTLE OF OTRANTO, THE: A GOTHIC STORY HORACE WALPOLE (1764)

Horace Walpole's *Castle of Otranto* proved crucial to the development of GOTHIC FICTION. As indicated by the book's subtitle, Walpole (1717–97) designed it to provide readers with a ROMANCE incorporating a dark moody villain, an endangered heroine, a hero with a mysterious past/identity, mysticism, and adventures set in a forbidding and mysterious structure. In his first edition, Walpole's preface claimed he based the book on an Italian tale. By the next edition, he admitted that the story was his own, and his preface's opening claim that

The following work was found in the library of an ancient Catholic family in the north of England. It was printed at Naples, in the black letter, in the year 1529. How much sooner it was written does not appear. The principal incidents are such as were believed in the darkest ages of Christianity; but the language and conduct have nothing that savours of barbarism. The style is the purest Italian.

had been part of a playful ruse. He continues his fun with the later claim that, "Yet I am not blind to my author's defects. I could wish he had grounded his plan on a more useful moral than this: that 'the sins of fathers are visited on their children to the third and fourth generation.'" Walpole praises the "author's" fashioning of secondary characters who prove so crucial to the plot, singling out in particular Bianca, whose "womanish terror and foibles" remain essential to the novel's final "catastrophe." When he claims that the English language does not provide a good vehicle for such "simple tales," because its narrative either falls too low or rises too high, he good-humoredly makes excuses for the melodrama necessary to the Gothic romance. Finally, he claims that the story "is undoubtedly laid in some real castle, proven by the author's frequent descriptions of the edifice's 'particular parts.'" Walpole's serious tone as he urges readers to accept as at least half true the hyperbolic effects reflects his understanding of the writer's ability to manipulate his audience.

During the 13th century, Manfred, Prince of Otranto, has assumed his rule from his grandfather, who poisoned the true prince, Alfonso. Based on prophecy, Manfred believes he must produce a male heir in order to perpetuate his family's false claim to title and property. Others are not so sure that Manfred has correctly interpreted the confusing prophecy that "the Castle and Lordship of Otranto 'shall pass from the present family, whenever the real owner shall be grown too large to inhabit it.'"

Manfred dotes upon his two children, the beautiful Matilda and the sickly Conrad. Anxious to fulfill what he believes to be the point of the prophecy, Manfred rushes Conrad into marriage to Isabella, daughter of the Marquis of Vicenza, at what his mother, Hippolita, believes to be too early an age. As the bride awaits the groom's arrival, screams echo outside the chapel, and cries including "The prince!" and "The helmet!" disturb those waiting within the church. To Manfred's horror, his son has been crushed to death by an enormous helmet covered in black feathers, "a hundred times larger" than any made for a human. Unaccountably, Manfred appears more concerned for Isabella than for his mangled son, whom the peasants carry

into the castle. When one bystander comments that the helmet resembles that worn by a black marble statue representing Alfonso the Good, a former prince, in the church of St. Nicholas, Manfred becomes incensed. Another group of peasants reveals that the helmet is now missing from the statue, and Manfred accuses the bystander of necromancy. In a move appropriate to Gothic fiction, onlookers simply accept the odd occurrence, and Manfred declares that the "magician" be imprisoned in the helmet, commanding his men to lift the edge and push him under. The crowd agrees with the verdict, convinced that the man will not die in his prison, as he can conjure up sustenance for himself. In a fury, Manfred refuses to speak with Matilda, who fears, but does not love, her father, or with Hippolita. He commands Matilda to bring him Isabella instead.

Because Hippolita remains barren after having produced Conrad, Manfred decides to marry Isabella and produce another heir. He horrifies the young princess by declaring that Conrad had not been worthy of her and that he will divorce Hippolita and take Isabella that night to his bed. Suddenly, the giant black helmet's plumes outside the window begin to wave, and Manfred hears the portrait of his grandfather, who had usurped Alfonso's rightful position, release a long sigh. When the figure in the portrait steps to the ground and beckons Manfred to follow, he understands that his castle is haunted. A door slams in Manfred's face, blocking him from contact with the ghost, and Isabella uses the opportunity to escape her pursuer.

All this action occurs in the first few pages of the novel, alerting readers to the fact that the plot will incorporate a tremendous amount of rising action. When the narrator states "Words cannot paint the horror of Isabella's situation," the audience accepts that declaration as irony, because the narration immediately does what it claims it cannot. Isabella subsequently flees the castle with the help of the young peasant Theodore, the imprisoned bystander who had escaped from beneath the helmet by squeezing through a casement shattered by the helmet's fall. Matilda loves Theodore, and she sets him free after Manfred catches and imprisons him.

Isabella's father, Frederick, also contributes to the action. Frederick's tale involves his having had a vision while fighting "the infidels" that his daughter needed his aid. Following his arrival, Hippolita proposes that Matilda marry Frederick to relieve the pain and torment at the castle. Matilda can hardly contain her distress, as she still loves Theodore, and he returns her passion, despite the fact that Isabella also loves him. The two young women discuss the love triangle, and Isabella yields Theodore to Matilda. Meanwhile, Hippolita learns of Manfred's plan to divorce her. Instead of the anger the two young women expected, Hippolita meekly accepts the plan for the good of her prince. Frederick cancels the marriage to Matilda, however, when he learns from the servant Bianca that the castle is haunted due to Manfred's past crimes and guilt. When Frederick is later overcome by passion for Matilda and returns to find her, a skeleton advises him to depart.

Manfred, rightly believing Isabella to be in love with Theodore, learns that Theodore intends to meet his love at Alfonso's tomb. He stabs the woman he believes to be Isabella, then discovers he has murdered his own daughter. Theodore, distraught at her death, reveals himself as the descendant of Alfonso. The ghost of Alfonso then grows so enormous that he destroys the castle, and in his terror, Manfred admits he has no claim to the realm. The ghost declares that Theodore is the rightful heir, and Manfred and Hippolita both depart to live in nearby convents. The newly crowned prince finally agrees to marry Isabella, as only she can understand and indulge forever "the melancholy that had taken possession of his soul."

Walpole's work remained popular within the Gothic genre and by the 20th century became available in electronic text.

BIBLIOGRAPHY
Clery, E. J. Introduction to *The Castle of Otranto: A Gothic Story,* by Horace Walpole. Oxford: Oxford University Press, 1998.
Project Guttenberg. Preface to *The Castle of Otranto,* by Horace Walpole. Project Guttenberg. Available online. URL: http://ibiblio.org/gutenberg/etext96/cotrt10.txt. Posted October 1996.

CASTLE RACKRENT MARIA EDGEWORTH (1800)

Maria EDGEWORTH broke new narrative ground with her 1800 novel, *Castle Rackrent*. While her methodology of developing an imaginary hero who writes a memoir "edited" by an author had been popular since *ROBINSON CRUSOE* (1719), she developed a new approach to setting. *Castle Rackrent* represents the first regional novel focusing on a definite identifiable place. That place was Ireland, where Edgeworth, an Oxfordshire native, lived for decades with her father. Sir Walter SCOTT praised the novel as a springboard into one of his favorite forms, HISTORICAL FICTION, a form representing large societies made up of distinct individuals, rather than stereotypical figures. Scott claimed in 1814 in "A Postscript" to his novel *WAVERLEY* that he hoped "in some distant degree to emulate the admirable Irish portraits drawn by Miss Edgeworth." William Makepeace THACKERAY declared himself in debt to Edgeworth's use of a first-person narrator blind to truth for the development of his own narrator in *BARRY LYNDON* (1844).

When Edgeworth arrived in Ireland in 1782, Constitutional Independency had been established by an Irish Parliament determined to work with England to become self-governing. The optimism supporting the wish for independence is obvious in *Castle Rackrent,* as the aging subject of its memoir, Thady Quirk, represents a past that chooses to make way for a bright new future. According to Edgeworth, she based Thady on her father's elderly steward, with whom she had spent much time. She enjoyed listening to him tell stories of the history of the family estate and the surrounding area and credited him with the natural voice she was able to project through Thady when, some time between 1797 and 1799, she composed her novel as a secret gift for her father. Retaining the area's natural dialect through Thady, Edgeworth created a lively, affectionate, and accurate picture of a happy, although dying, system of aristocratic control of Irish land. She wrote what she observed and what she heard from an older generation; her novel did not represent ancient history but rather a contemporary report that offered a sociological study of a culture long before academia found that approach of interest. Its focus on the domestic scene, and the importance of individuals as members of defined communities, make it an early version of DOMESTIC REALISM, a form that George ELIOT would bring to maturity several decades later.

Thady Quirk is a simple man whose naiveté allows others to victimize him, but which also permits him to report his surroundings without guile. Thady has no reason to lie, and his untainted, compassionate honesty makes him a trustworthy narrator. The reader meets four different masters of the estate that Thady stewards for decades. He appreciates each master in different ways, despite the fact that each suffers from a glaring weakness that causes the eventual dissolution of the estate. The first lord, Sir Patrick O'Shaughlin, took the title Rackrent through an act of Parliament. Thady's grandfather drove Sir Patrick's carriage, and Thady never recognized Sir Patrick as the drunk he was. Instead, he describes how everyone flocked to the funeral of the beloved man, rumored "to be the inventor of raspberry whiskey." Thady also remains respectful of Sir Patrick's successor, Sir Murtaugh, who accumulated 49 lawsuits and enjoyed fighting each of them. He died ostensibly of a stroke while "sparring and jarring" with his wife, and Thady diplomatically declares himself glad to see the wife depart, suggesting she bore the guilt for her husband's problems. Murtaugh's younger brother, Sir Kit, inherits the estate, and Thady loved him as a generous individual, but unfortunately, he accrues gambling debts. Eventually, he marries a wealthy Jewish woman who, despite his hopes, does little to alleviate his debt. Although a victim of circumstances, Sir Kit's wife does not endear herself to the servants, even when the master takes a mistress and dies in a duel with the mistress's brother. Again, Thady excuses a master, blaming the wife for his death. The final master of the estate, Sir Conolly, called Sir Condy and Thady's favorite, gets much more page space than his predecessors. Like them, Sir Condy dies a sad death following attempts to bear the great costs of a political career, the indignity of having the ownership of his land challenged by others, and a great quantity of drink that set his gut on fire.

Edgeworth shapes Thady's son, Jason, as a sly attorney whose manipulative personality balances Thady's forthright one. Jason begins to benefit from Sir Kit's debts, accumulating titles to the estate where his father

works, and later tries unsuccessfully to take the estate from Sir Condy's wife. Thady, who has excused every weakness in four men undeserving of his respect, cannot excuse the greed exhibited by his son. He seems to envision their problems as honest ones in which they alone stand victimized, while Jason knowingly uses others to his own benefit. In the end, Thady remains far more loyal to his masters and the estate family than to his own son.

Edgeworth completes the novel with a comment from the "Editor" about the "truth" of the story: "He lays it before the English reader as a specimen of manners and characters, which are perhaps unknown in England." As for Edgeworth's contribution to the development of the novel, George Watson writes in his introduction that without *Castle Rackrent* and the larger novels that followed, each of which told the stories of societies, both living and dying, "the novel of the nineteenth century could not have been made."

BIBLIOGRAPHY

Watson, George. Introduction to *Castle Rackrent,* by Maria Edgeworth. New York: Oxford University Press, 1981.

Weinstein, Mark A., ed. *The Prefaces to the Waverley Novels by Sir Walter Scott.* Lincoln, Neb.: University of Nebraska Press, 1978.

CATHERINE FURZE WILLIAM HALE WHITE (1893)

William Hale WHITE first fictionalized his attempts to escape his childhood's Calvinistic training by writing an autobiography under the name of Mark Rutherford. He later used his own name when he published another serious exploration of the conflict caused by organized religion in *Catherine Furze* (1893), a novel that appeared in two volumes. While critics found little to praise in White's colorless style and rigid characters, they had to appreciate his complete sincerity, as through his narrator he warned readers against the "professionally religious" who rush to judge others with a self-important energy lacking adherence to any Christian tenet. His own tendency to depression appears in his protagonist, as does his fluid attitude toward the nature of religious affiliation through the conflicts suffered by several additional characters.

Ostensibly, the novel considers the passions of 19-year-old Catherine Furze, daughter during the 1840s to the largest ironmonger in Eastthorpe, "in the eastern Midlands." However, Catherine will realize her love only as a future impediment, one that she eventually accepts as too large to overcome, resigning herself to a fatalism that literally kills her. Her unrequited love for a married preacher, Mr. Cardew, is balanced by the unrequited love felt for her by her father's workman, Tom Catchpole. In an overlapping plot, Catherine must parry her social-climbing mother's desire for a "good" marriage for her while struggling to continue her relationship with an upright country family, the Bellamys, who her mother finds too "simple" for her daughter's interests. White uses the Bellamy family to symbolize a clearer-headed approach to day-to-day life contrasted with the social status so important to townspeople like the Furzes (or Mrs. Furze, to be exact). When fire destroys Mr. Furze's iron shop and home, his wife pressures him to leave the neighborhood of shop residences and move to "The Terrace," a group of new houses built at the north end of town. He does so with concerns about leaving behind loyal customers and fellow Dissenters with whom he attends chapel. A weak-willed man, he cannot stand up to his wife's badgering, so the move takes place.

Soon after relocating, Mrs. Furze sends Catherine to the Ponsonby School to learn to behave in a manner more suitable to the elevated life she foresees for her daughter. While there, Catherine falls in love with Mr. Cardew, simultaneously developing a fondness for his wife. In the meantime, Tom has fallen in love with Catherine, much to the dismay of Mrs. Furze, who deems him an unsuitable match. When Catherine returns home and is seen with Tom, she could honestly deny the romantic connection her mother assumes to be the case. She does not, believing her protest will be seen as a lie. She is also so confused regarding her feelings for Mr. Cardew that she refuses to return to school. During Catherine's visit to the Bellamys, Mrs. Furze concocts a plan with Jim, a disgruntled Furze employer jealous of Tom's value to Mr. Furze, to help get rid of Tom. Jim frames Tom for theft, forcing Mr. Furze, who remains completely dependent on Tom's help, to reluctantly fire him.

In the middle of all this turmoil, the novel's narrator remarks on the main characters' approaches to faith, taking Mr. Cardew to task for intellectualizing religion. That prevents his understanding the need for compassion while dealing with his congregation: "Evangelicalism, however, to Mr. Cardew was dangerous. He was always prone to self-absorption, and the tendency was much increased by his religion." He had felt an attraction to Catherine and encouraged her, although not intentionally, to respond to him, causing her immeasurable harm, as he tended to base his judgments "on his own imagination," when in actuality they "were not in the least apposite to what was actually before him." His intellectualism proves especially harmful for Catherine, who is at her most vulnerable, having "suddenly opened" to new experiences. She asked herself "strange questions," and needed help answering those questions from Cardew. As for Tom, he recognizes his own ignorance as a simple worker, desperately wishing himself able to share Catherine's passions in questions of faith, and not understanding why she cannot return his love. After he is fired, he finds Catherine to explain that he had been framed, and she plainly tells him that she can never love him. However, she gives him her ring to wear, explaining to him that she plans never to marry, and Tom must take solace from that fact. After Tom departs, "terrors vague and misty possessed her . . . she could not put into words what ailed her, and she wrestled with shapeless, clinging forms which she could hardly discern." White describes his own former despair when he adds that her doubts "wound themselves about her, and, although they were but shadows, they made her shriek."

Catherine falls physically ill due to the conflict she feels over Cardew, and the realization "that her life would be spent without love, or, at least, without a love which could be acknowledged." Cardew, however, suddenly realizes love for his long-suffering wife when "something came to him—the same Something which had so often restrained Catherine. It smote him as the light from heaven smote Saul of Tarsus . . . his eyes were opened." White demonstrates one way that people may redeem themselves, simply through a sudden epiphany, but they must be ready to receive it.

Mr. Furze pays for his foolish dismissal of Tom and for allowing his wife's manipulation. Following a huge flood, which symbolizes a washing clean of past sins, his business collapses and his creditors must agree not to foreclose. He and his proud wife are forced to return to the lowly group of shop homes, having lost all they had, including their daughter.

As Catherine grows more ill, her alarmed mother calls in Dr. Turnbull, allowing the introduction of another attitude toward faith, probably that closest to White's own. Because Dr. Turnbull does not attend church, those who do consign him to a future hell, yet hypocritically summon him when their medical problems are serious. Although a materialist, the narrator explains, Turnbull represented the most spiritual of all the town's inhabitants, taking "the keenest interest in science . . . a believer in a spiritualism infinitely beyond that of most of his neighbours, for they had not a single spiritual interest." His attempts to pull Catherine's energies outside herself fail, however, and she becomes progressively more ill until she dies, but not until she asks to see Cardew, who had been away for a time with his wife. In his newfound wisdom, Cardew tells Catherine that she had saved him; she tells him the same, and the narrator declares, "By their love for each other they were both saved. The disguises are manifold which the Immortal Son assumes in the work of our redemption."

The novel concludes with Tom's name cleared of all wrongdoing and Mr. Cardew remaining devoted to his wife. The final note from the narrator reinforces the fact that the supposedly upright Cardew learned more from the experience of death than from his study of theology and ethics. White himself had tried various religions, agnosticism, and finally settled on a resignation to absorb experiences and allow them to mold him. *Catherine Furze* echoes that philosophy of resignation.

CHARTIST MOVEMENT/CHARTISM

The Chartist movement, or Chartism, refers to an English social-reform movement from 1838 to 1848, based on the belief that Parliamentary legislation could correct economic and social exploitation. In 1837, the London Working Men's Association submitted a program titled the People's Charter to Parliament, and the reform group derived its name. Chartism developed due to working-class discontent with the Reform Bill of 1832 and the Poor Law of 1834. Many saw the bills as discriminatory against workers who faced multiple abuses in the new industrialized society. Novels of the day, termed THESIS NOVELS, including books by Charles DICKENS, Charles KINGSLEY, Frances TROLLOPE, Benjamin DISRAELI, and Mrs. GASKELL, reflected the working-class concerns championed by the Chartists. Newspapers supporting the movement included the *The Charter, The Champion,* and *The Weekly Police Gazette.*

The Charter presented six demands that included voting rights for all males over 21 years of age, all of which the House of Commons rejected. That led to a petition bearing 1.25 million signatures presented to Parliament, which again rejected all demands. Over the next 10 years, organization continued, including that of a Chartist branch supporting violence, led by Feargus O'Connor, an Irish radical. The group donned red caps symbolizing liberty, carried arms and waved banners with slogans such as "He that hath no sword, let him sell his garment and bear one." Talk of organization among the Chartists alarmed the government, which organized paramilitary forces led by the Duke of Wellington to be used in case of attacks against Parliament. The Chartists then attempted a strike (which failed), and riots in 1839 resulted in many arrests. Following years of inactivity, the Chartists presented another petition to Parliament in 1848, but rather than the 6 million signatures Chartists had declared they would collect, it contained fewer than 2 million. The movement failed because of forged signatures and the discovery of Chartist armaments concealed around London, which contributed to the movement's loss of credibility.

Built on poverty, the movement was doomed to fail due to little material support. Although Chartism as such disappeared, all the reforms demanded eventually became law, thanks to continued efforts by political and social leaders. Charles KINGSLEY, among others, began in 1849 to sponsor workmen's cooperative associations, and such organization strengthened the reform drive originally begun by the Chartist movement.

BIBLIOGRAPHY

Cripps, Elizabeth. Introduction to *Alton Locke: Tailor and Poet, An Autobiography,* by Charles Kingsley. New York: Oxford University Press, 1983.

Haywood, Ian. *Working-class Fiction: From Chartism to Trainspotting*. London: Northcote House, 1998.

CHILD OF THE JAGO, A ARTHUR MORRISON (1896)

Arthur MORRISON's *A Child of the Jago* focused on the shameful physical and emotional environment that provided a backdrop for the many children living in London's slums. Morrison not only highlighted the abject poverty of the district, but also the violence it spawned. He renamed the "Nichol" neighborhood in London's Behnal Green the "Jago" to provide a setting for the novel that disturbed many readers. It tells the story of Dicky Perrott, a boy of the slums whose talent and motivation is stifled by his subculture. After the hanging of his father, an amateur boxer, for murder, Dicky inherits the neighborhood's violent lifestyle, with fatal results.

In his preface to the novel's third edition, Morrison notes his gratification that the kind reception to the novel did not prove unanimous. While he received "many gratifying assurances" that his goal to write a novel reflective of London's failed social system had succeeded, he also heard from some opposition. In his opinion, even the opposition signaled success, in that "there is no truth worth telling that will not interfere with some hearer's comfort." Much of the criticism came in the form of his categorization as a "realist," a label he felt detracted from his reputation as a fiction writer when applied by reproachful critics. Referring to himself as neither a statesman nor a rich man, but "a mere writer of fiction," he discharged the duty he felt toward the poor of London by bringing "the conditions of this place within the apprehension of others." He took the opportunity to lambaste his critics by grouping them as those who did nothing "by way of discharging their responsibility toward the Jago and the people in it." Clearly Morrison intended his novel, supplied with a glossary explaining "Slang and Criminal Terms," as a social statement.

Scenes intended to upset readers included those of Dicky's mother Hannah, pleading with her husband Josh not to keep an appointed fight, as she sat, baby in her lap, "wretched and helpless, sometimes putting her face in her hands." Dicky's innocence as he is drawn into the later scene, watching the fight from his window and relaying regular reports of Josh's blows to his mother, remains poignant while driving home the nature of training he receives from his earliest years. The imagery of "the foul Jago mob, swaying and bellowing" at the fight illustrates the environment that Dicky will not escape, as does the brutal detail with which Morrison imagines the hand-to-hand combat that provides entertainment to a brutal crowd. Following the fight, Hannah leaves the baby with a neighbor named Pigeony Poll in order to attend to her injured husband. When Pigeony summons Hannah home, the narrator makes clear that Hannah lacked the instincts for such a life: "The ghost of Hannah Perrott's respectability rose in resentment." When Hannah finds the infant dead, she sits in clueless wonder with his body, as voices outside the window issue "the Jago chant": "Six bloomin' long months in a prison, / Six more bloomin' months I must stay, / For meetin' a bloke in our alley, / An takin' 'is uxter [money] away!" The sad verse foreshadows the impending deaths of both Josh and Dicky, with the literal prison symbolizing the imprisonment of the slums.

Even the ever-present figure of Father Sturt, based on the real-life Arthur Osborne Jay, vicar of Holy Trinity, Shoreditch, to whom Morrison dedicated the novel, acts as an ironic judgment against a supposedly modern social system in which the only relief comes in the form of religion. One character in the novel does succeed in escaping the slums, as Kiddo Cook prospers by setting up a stall where he acts as an informal banker. Dicky's escape at age 17 will be of another type. On the day of Kiddo's wedding to Pigeony, Dicky thinks "it would be a comfortable thing for himself if he could die quietly then and there." A short time later, his enemy, the hunchback, stabs Dicky, but he will not identify his murderer. He answers Sturt's inquiry as to the killer's identity with the phrase, "Dunno, Fa'er." The narrator terms that response, "the staunch Jago lie. Thou shalt not nark [inform]."

Morrison may have modeled his straightforward, unbending prose on that of George MOORE, as he also anticipated the social realism of later writers. His narration distinguishes itself from that of many other Victorian novels, as it does nothing to pass judgment on the novel's characters. Along with *Tales of Mean Streets* (1894) and *The Hole in the Wall* (1902), *A Child of the Jago* represents one of Morrison's most popular works.

BIBLIOGRAPHY

Brome, Vincent. *Four Realist Novelists: Arthur Morrison, Edwin Pugh, Richard Whiteing and William Pett Ridge.* London: Longmans Green, 1965.

Miller, Anita. Introduction to *A Child of the Jago,* by Arthur Morrison. Chicago: Academy Chicago Publishers, 1995.

CHILDREN'S LITERATURE

Despite John Locke's admonition in his 1693 *Some Thoughts Concerning Education* that children needed different reading materials than adults, stories created for sheer entertainment's sake did not appear regularly in England until the late 19th century. Before then, children might read John Bunyon's PILGRIM'S PROGRESS (1676) or *Aesop's Fables* (published by Caxton in 1485) as cautionary and morality tales. Later, they read adaptations of their parents' reading, including Daniel DEFOE's ROBINSON CRUSOE (1719) and Jonathan SWIFT's *Gulliver's Travels* (1726). French renditions of fairy tales, and *The Arabian Nights,* translated in 1708, captured children's imagination with their fantasy aspects, but their sexual implications caused most English parents to ban them from their decorous homes. With few exceptions, 18th-century children's literature existed to instruct and moralize.

John Newbery became highly successful selling six-pence volumes for children in London at St. Paul's Cathedral, each volume consisting of "pretty rhymes" or tales of "Nurse Truelove," in addition to books with instruction in mathematics, history, and science. He sold the famous *The History of Little Goody Two-Shoes* in 1766, a book that taught moral actions to juveniles. His great effect could be measured when many later authors wrote of reading Newbery's works as children. Several famous pious women writers followed Newbery, all intent on developing a generation of highly self-disciplined and moral children. Mrs. Barbauld (1743–1825) worked with her brother, John Aiken, who edited the *Monthly Review,* to publish poetry and prose for her own adopted son. Their collaboration resulted in *Easy Lessons for Children* (1760), *Hymns in Prose for Children* (1781), and *Evening at Home* (1792), all featuring instructional conversations between a mother and child. Mrs. Sarah Trimmer (1741–1810), a highly religious mother of 12 children who supported the Sunday-school movement, wrote six volumes of *Sacred History for Children* (1782–84) and founded the first periodicals for children, designed for home reading. Her most famous book, *Fabulous Histories Designed for the Instruction of Children Respecting their Treatment of Animals* (1786), contained talking characters, including Dicksy, Flopsy, and Pecksy. In 1803, she began publication of *The Guardian of Education,* aimed at a middle-class family and its servants as its audience. It advised families to resist the corrupting influence of fantasies, attacking stories from "Cinderella" to *Robinson Crusoe.* Mary WOLLSTONECRAFT's children's book, *Original Stories from Real Life with Conversations Calculated to Regulate the Affections and Form the Mind to Truth and Goodness* (1788), included beautiful illustrations by William Blake of its heroine, an unattractive tyrant assigned to control two children and assure their discipline.

With the arrival of Jean-Jacques Rousseau (1712–78), the anti-intellectualism in English children's literature broadened to include aspects of his philosophy. An orphan himself, Rousseau struggled to develop a self-identity, and his adult writings emphasized the importance of the individual who could look to nature for examples of harmony and to his own feelings as a guide to virtuous behavior. One important precept in his approach was the restriction of reading, which appeared in Rousseau's popular book *Emile* (trans. 1763). Emile discovers all necessary knowledge by following his own innate reasoning and is allowed to read one work, after the age of 12—*Robinson Crusoe.* The woman judged by many to be the most talented children's writer of her era, Maria EDGEWORTH (1767–1849), was the child of Richard Lovell Edgeworth, who raised his children by adhering to Rousseau's theories. His approach resulted in disaster for one son, but Maria survived a bizarre childhood and spent her life helping her father educate his 20 additional children from his four marriages. She cowrote with her father, then produced her own books based on the philosophy that pleasure, rather than fear, motivated children to learn. Her series of fiction included *The Parent's Assistant* (three volumes in 1798, six volumes in 1800), *Early Lessons* (10 volumes in 1801) and *Moral Tales* (1810). While she upheld a moralistic approach, Edgeworth included more imaginative juvenile characters, all based on her siblings, than had been seen in previous works for children. Her lessons included "virtue is its own reward" and stressed that most individuals sinned due to poor judgment, rather than inherent weakness. Foolish behavior led to humiliation, punishment enough for children. Her ideas sparked an educational revolution. Edgeworth also became an acknowledged writer of adult fiction, equaling her effect on children's education with her effect on literature when she wrote the first regional novel, CASTLE RACKRENT (1800). Developments in education, both public and private, affected the development of children's literature, and vice versa.

William GODWIN (1756–1836), husband to Mary WOLLSTONECRAFT and father of Mary SHELLEY, seemed an unlikely individual to stress the value of fantasy in works for children. Described as a philosophical anarchist and a radical, he revived classics, such as works by Homer and Shakespeare, for children, all of which incorporated magic and the supernatural. They appeared as a series of chapbooks, acceptable to parents. In *Political Justice, II,* he wrote, "The imagination . . . if cultivated at all, must be begun with in youth." He opened a juvenile library in 1805 that revolutionized reading for children, offering Aesop's fables, Mother Goose tales, "Beauty and the Beast," and the ubiquitous *Robinson Crusoe.* Mary Wollstonecraft Godwin encouraged brother and sister Charles (1775–1834) and Mary (1764–1847) Lamb to write *Lamb's Tales from Shakespeare, Designed for Young Persons* (1807). Lamb also transformed *The Adventures of Ulysses* (1808), the George Chapman (1559–1634) translation, for children. Lamb argued against Godwin's protest of the inclusion of realistic details, such as the Cyclops's devouring of Ulysses's men, the description of vomit, and the graphic depiction of the blinding of the Cyclops, but Lamb held firm, claiming that he could not present such a gruesome tale without featuring its more sensationalized passages. Lamb firmly believed that children raised without such images would conjure even more terrifying ones of their own. The Lambs produced additional children's literature, capturing the childlike aspects of adult stories.

When poet Robert Southey (1774–1843) published "The Three Bears" in 1831, as part of his seven-volume work *The Doctor,* his sobering version of the popular oral tale became a classic in its own right. Although grim, with a demonized Goldilocks who fell from the bears' second-story window, the story caught the imagination of the reading public. By October 1853, Charles DICKENS defended fairy tales, calling on his readers to "respect" them in an essay in HOUSEHOLD WORDS. He need not have worried. A stream of writers challenged the sensible children's literature of the early 19th century. Edward Lear's *Book of Nonsense* (1846), William Makepeace THACKERAY's *The Rose and the Ring* (1855), and Charles KINGSLEY's *The WATER BABIES* (1863) all continued the revolution to emphasize the importance of imagination in children's literature. They prepared the way for Lewis CARROLL's *ALICE'S ADVENTURES IN WONDERLAND* (1865), considered the first English novel for juveniles intended solely to entertain. An industry in literature for very young children blossomed as well, with works contributed by writers such as Charlotte YONGE (1823–1901). Anna SEWELL's (1820–78) *BLACK BEAUTY* (1877) prompted the founding of the first society to prevent cruelty to animals, and Francis Hodgson BURNETT produced her first children's classic, LITTLE LORD FAUNTLEROY in 1886. Adventure stories of the late 19th century for boys grew popular, thanks to the efforts of Richard JEFFERIES, whose novel BEVIS, THE STORY OF A BOY (1882), among works of others, captivated young male readers for decades.

BIBLIOGRAPHY

Demers, Patricia, and Gordon Moyles, ed. *From Instruction to Delight: An Anthology of Children's Literature to 1850.* Toronto: Oxford University Press, 1982.

Gaull, Marilyn. *English Romanticism: The Human Context.* New York: W.W. Norton, 1988.

Sutherland, Zena. *Children and Books.* 9th ed. Reading, Mass.: Addison-Wesley, 1996.

CHIVALRY The word *chivalry* derives from the French term *cheval,* or horse, and those practicing chivalry in medieval times possessed highly developed horseback-riding skills. Dressed in armor during times of battle and known as knights, from a term that originally meant "boy" or "youth," these chivalric young men came to represent a local form of justice. At the fall of the Roman Empire, many chiefs assumed power in a northern Europe bereft of central leadership. Such chiefs felt hostility toward one another, as each coveted the others' land and the power that land and loyal citizens brought them. As the feudal system developed, and lords grew more powerful, they kept a careful watch on each other to retain a peaceful balance in their regions. The knights worked for their lords to help in that control. Simultaneously, the church impressed upon the feudal leaders and their knights the importance of protecting the weak, a crucial aspect of right living. Thus, the ideals of chivalry emerged. The chivalric knight practiced fair play, exhibited extreme valor, served a spiritual leader represented by the church, and an earthly master represented by his feudal lord. He practiced forbearance and modesty, extending courtesy and compassion to all. His service to a man of rank resulted in his also achieving rank, but to be worthy of honor, he had to bear up well under the demands of chivalry's lofty ideals. Often from a moneyed background, in order to practice humility a knight ignored his material possessions or the status of his family name to depend instead on others for his sustenance, choosing sometimes to eschew comfortable lodging to sleep on the ground under the stars as evidence of devotion to the pure and simple life.

The knight served as a warrior when called upon, but in peacetime often embarked on QUESTS suitable to his stature. His adventures might emerge from a pledge of love or religion, result in actions meant to right injustices, and occasionally win rewards of treasure, although most often the honors and titles resulting from completing a quest sufficed. Called knights-errant, such individuals traveled about the country seeking justice for others. All castles and households routinely extended generous hospitality to knights in recognition of their importance to society.

In some instances, even feudal lords might be seduced to commit evil in the name of greed or power. In that condition, castles that once protected their inhabitants and kept them secure became prisons, sometimes of torture and horror. A knight errant from outside the castle keep would then have to free the prisoners, usually after confronting and defeating the castle's leader.

In some quests, knights served aristocratic women, often the wives of their leaders, and declared a chaste, or courtly, love for such ladies, to whom they pledged lifelong loyalty. They represented their ladies during contests called jousts in which knights could display their skills as horsemen, charging one another on horseback in an attempt to dismount their competitor with a weapon; long poles called lances often served as weapons of choice. Strict rules controlled such contests. For instance, horses could not be stabbed, nor could a knight who had raised his visor, the drop-down face cover on his helmet, be struck. Jousts generally drew a large attendance and often resulted, despite the safety rules, in cruel maimings of man or beast and even death. Sir Walter SCOTT featured jousts in some of his historical novels, most notably, *IVANHOE* (1819), the first of his novels to use England as a setting, even though Scott himself found jousts repugnant. Such adventures were labeled ROMANCES, originally denoting a composition written in a Romance language, those evolving from western Europe, where a blend of Latin with native languages was called Langue Romaine.

Stories of chivalry often grew from INITIATION plots, where a young man experienced training, usually by an aged, skilled knight retired from the field. A task would draw the trainee into duty, and in some plots, the older teacher-knight would fall to the evil that the young hero then pledged himself to defeat. Many chivalric tales grew from the British legend of King Arthur, a figure who was a blend of fact and fantasy, perhaps based on a fifth-century warrior chieftain named Riothamus. Arthur supposedly established a round table that hosted a gathering of the noblest knights. Many tales evolved that focused on the Knights of the Round Table, some involving mystical creatures, monsters, and disguises, such as *Gawain and the Green Knight*. While that story focused on an individual who had to pass a test, a second type of romantic quest featured conflict between duty and passion, such as the German *Tristan und Isolde*. A third type of romance, represented by Chretien de Troyes's *Perceval*, focused on a search for the Holy Grail and reflected aspects of the Arthurian legend.

Eventually the term *chivalry* became associated with manners rather than actions. Chivalry still connoted loyalty, skill, generosity, and devotion, without the added dimensions of warfare and horseback skills. While fiction of the 20th and 21st centuries did not feature the high sentimentality of the earlier romance genre, and readers might find the high ideals of traditional chivalry laughable, even harmful to the development of gender and self-identity, aspects of chivalry and the romantic quest continued to shape plot and characters in literature and film media.

BIBLIOGRAPHY

Campbell, Joseph. *The Hero with a Thousand Faces.* 1949. Princeton, N.J.: Princeton University Press, 1968.

De Rougemont, Denis. *Love in the Western World.* 1940. Princeton, N.J.: Princeton University Press, 1983.

Gleckner, Robert F., and Gerald E. Enscoe, eds. *Romanticism: Points of View.* 2nd ed. Detroit: Wayne State University Press, 1974.

CHRISTIE JOHNSTONE CHARLES READE

(1853)   While not considered among Charles READE's major works, *Christie Johnstone* provides a delightful insight into his sense of humor. Not only does the novel's subject matter entertain, but its format also proves of interest, as Reade designed some chapters as dramatic scripts, complete with dialogue. The format grew from one of his dozen plays, titled "Masks and Faces." A writer celebrated equally as novelist and playwright, he found a way to combine his talents.

Generally described simply as a novel about a Scottish fishing village, the story focuses on Viscount Ipsden, a wealthy, effete, but unhappy young aristocrat. Reade opens conceding that some might be surprised by Ipsden's state of mind, then explaining "[T]here are certain blessings the non-possession of which makes more people discontented than their possession renders happy." Those aware that Reade was born at Ipsden House, Oxfordshire, where he matured as the spoiled seventh son and 10th child of a Tory squire, will appreciate the irony and Reade's self-deprecatory rendition of the viscount. Additional autobiographical elements exist in Reade's knowledge of the fishing life through his own Scottish herring business, as well as

in a possible love affair between Reade and one of the local fisherwomen.

Ipsden is bored; pleasure has ceased to please and amusement to amuse. He is trapped in unrequited love for Lady Barbara Sinclair, a woman with a mind "somewhat original, full of fire and faith, and empty of experience," greatly affected by writers of romance and on the lookout for a hero of sorts. She informs Ipsden, "[T]he man I marry must have two things, virtues and vices—you have neither; you do nothing, and never will do anything but sketch and hum tunes, and dance and dangle." Her pronouncement throws Ipsden into despair.

When Ipsden's butler, Saunders, becomes concerned about his master's ennui, he contacts a physician who informs Ipsden, "You have the maladies of idle minds," and he prescribes "acquaintance with all the people of low estate," directing his patient to "learn their ways, their minds, and above all, their troubles." Ipsden fears such an occupation will bore him, but he perseveres, and Saunders brings two female members of the lower class to meet him. One of the women is Christie Johnstone, and the fun of the novel begins.

Reade's description of the two unfortunates spares no detail, including each item of clothing and concluding with a description that would interest FEMINIST CRITICS: "These women had a grand corporeal tract; they had never known a corset! so they were straight as javelins; they could lift their hands above their heads!—actually!" Reade establishes the lower class, probably too romantically, as refreshingly natural and free from the concerns that burden their wealthy counterparts. A healthy dose of their various philosophies and several adventures in a world Ipsden had never known fill the prescription to return him to health.

Reade enjoys playing off stereotypes. In addition to those of the upper and lower classes, he also takes on nationalities, writing, "The Scotch are icebergs, with volcanoes underneath; thaw the Scotch ice, which is very cold, and you shall get to the Scotch fire, warmer than any sun of Italy or Spain." Johnstone represents that fire. Her passion, and that of her community, will help arouse Ipsden's own. When Lady Barbara arrives on the scene, she learns of Ipsden's good deed in offering his entire fortune to bribe fishermen to save an endangered ship. She deems it "a noble action," deciding that her lover is "browner and charitabler" than he had previously been. She also observes the "perilous adventure" she had longed to see, as Christie effects a dramatic rescue of her love, Charles, and Ipsden tells Barbara, "You have seen something great done at last; and by a woman, too!" Ipsden marries Barbara, as Christie does Charles, and both couples enjoy long happy lives, but it is Christie upon whom Reade expounds in his last several pages.

Reade may have attempted a comic parody that dissolved too often into melodrama, but *Christie Johnstone* contains enough humor to entertain those who appreciate his style and intelligence.

BIBLIOGRAPHY

Vitanza, Diana. *Charles Reade: A Revaluation.* Dekalb, Ill.:
    Northern Illinois University Press, 1977.

CLARISSA, OR THE HISTORY OF A YOUNG LADY SAMUEL RICHARDSON (1747–1748)

Samuel RICHARDSON published his second novel in seven volumes, the first two in 1747, and the remaining five the next year. Like his first work, PAMELA (1740), *Clarissa* is an EPISTOLARY NOVEL, made up of letters written between characters. While *Pamela* focused on the letters of only three characters, the protagonist and her parents, Richardson expanded his approach in *Clarissa* to focus on two sets of correspondents, Clarissa Harlowe to Miss Howe, and Robert Lovelace to John Belford, with occasional letters from additional characters. Thus, he avoided the first novel's restricted point of view, which forced the narrator to step into the novel to explain certain circumstances to the reader. In *Clarissa,* that need no longer existed, as the two pairs commented upon each other. In the longest novel in the English language at more than 1 million words, Richardson did have to take care to avoid repetition and overlapping. While he still occasionally intervened as the "editor" to provide explanation, his voice did not prove as intrusive as in the first novel. One problem caused by the epistolary form was slow movement in the rising action, as time needed to pass between the delivery of letters.

Clarissa seemed in other ways an attempt by Richardson to improve on *Pamela*. He had expressed concern that *Pamela* may have carried the false message that "a reformed rake makes the best husband," and he reacted to critics' claims that Pamela's speech and expressions were too vulgar, although that merely reflected her station as a servant. As a member of the upper class, Clarissa Harlowe was not vulgar.

A beautiful and musically inclined young lady, Clarissa is pressured by her family to marry well. When she falls in love with the misogynist Robert Lovelace, family members discourage her flirtation, as they prefer she marry Mr. Solmes. Spending about 500 pages of the novel locked in her room, Clarissa considers her situation and attempts to make a decision, although she lacks the power to act. While willing to agree not to see Lovelace, Clarissa protests her planned marriage to the elderly, mean, but quite wealthy Solmes.

Clarissa's brother fights and loses a duel to Lovelace, who declares revenge on the Harlowes, prompting Clarissa to write and beg him to change his mind. He will comply only if Clarissa agrees to move in with the women of his family. On the verge of having to marry Solmes, she agrees to Lovelace's plan, then backs out, but he abducts her. Clarissa assumes they will marry, but Lovelace delights in humiliating her first, trying many tactics to seduce her, all of which she repels. Clarissa shares all these events through correspondence with her best friend, Anna Howe, while Lovelace writes to fellow rake, John Belford, to assure him that he retains his reputation as a womanizer.

When Lovelace carries her away to London to what he claims will be a respectable boarding house, Clarissa hopes they will finally marry. Their destination turns out to be a brothel where, under the watch of the bawdy Mrs. Sinclair, Clarissa remains in captivity. Lovelace at last drugs Clarissa and rapes her. Before Lovelace's attack, Clarissa had vacillated between love and revulsion for him, but after the rape, she refuses his offers of marriage. Lovelace grows desperate, as he did all along plan to marry Clarissa, but she continues to reject him.

The strain of the events causes Clarissa to fall ill and then escape from Lovelace, and the final part of the novel focuses on her vindication. Through many pages, those important to Clarissa discover the truth, as does the only family member who believes her, a cousin, Colonel Morden. Some of her friends urge Clarissa to accept Lovelace's frantic proposals, but she stands firm. She will die from her shame, killed by her era's moral code, but her death before an audience of ardent admirers frees her to represent a shining example of virtue to others. When the Harlowes discover Lovelace's dastardly actions, Morden kills him in a duel. Others who betrayed and mistreated the innocent young woman receive their just deserts, while Clarissa lives on in her admirers' memories as a martyr. Belford, the one-time rake, reforms, becomes Clarissa's executor, and provides an edited version of her letters as an example to others.

Richardson's abundant imagery of reflection, or the gaze, locked upon Clarissa objectifies but also liberates her from the confines of self-expression. When readers see her dressed in white, they confirm her innocence; when framed by a keyhole, Clarissa's imprisonment behind close doors becomes clear; when caught kneeling in prayer, her devout attitude cannot be faked.

The massive rising action, climax, and denouement take place over less than a year, during which times the correspondents produce hundreds of letters. Richardson appreciated the epistolary approach for its immediacy and inherent sense of the urgent, spoken by his characters through their own writing. Richardson confessed to shocking himself with the development of Lovelace's evil character. His talent at building tension was so great that many readers admitted to pleading aloud with Clarissa not to give in to Lovelace. Henry FIELDING, a jovial critic and satirist of Richardson, reviewed the first two volumes of *Clarissa* and wrote to Richardson, requesting that he not kill his heroine. Samuel JOHNSON labeled the novel as "the first book in the world for the knowledge it displays of the human heart."

For all of Richardson's sermonizing in his novels regarding high moral behavior, he revealed his fascination with the prurient details involved in seduction. He converts readers into voyeurs, as well, in the rape scene, for instance. The door to Clarissa's room remains open, and the women who live in the brothel walk back and forth in front of it, watching the act in progress and inviting readers to do the same. Accord-

ing to Lionel Stevenson, the English poet Samuel Coleridge later expressed a view that many shared. He supposedly admitted vexation when forced to admire Richardson's works, while at the same time declaring Richardson's mind "so very vile . . . so oozy, so hypocritical, praise-mad, canting, envious, concupiscent." Although not vulgar on the surface, Richardson's works gave way to the next stage of novel writing, led by Tobias SMOLLETT, in which vulgarity would reign. However critics judge Richardson's motives, they continue to admit to the popularity of his writing, readily available into the 21st century in print version as well as electronic text.

BIBLIOGRAPHY

Phelps, Gilbert. "Samuel Richardson: Clarissa, or The History of a Young Lady." *An Introduction to Fifty British Novels: 1600–1900.* London: Pan Books, 1979. 81–88.

Stephenson, Lionel. *The English Novel: A Panorama.* Boston: Houghton Mifflin, 1960.

Van Ghent, Dorothy. *The English Novel: Form and Function.* New York: Harper Torchbooks, 1953.

CLASS STRUCTURE/SYSTEM

England's marked class system, a subject of much of British fiction, has a long history. It began under the reign of England's first Norman king, William I "the Conqueror." William ruled from 1066–87, inheriting the task of beneficially mixing Norman elements with those of the Saxon culture, the group in power since the Romans departed England in the sixth century. William introduced the feudal system in which certain elements held power over others based on the ownership of land. He also introduced the French language to the upper classes, and it became a staple at court, while Latin became the language of choice for literature.

The order that dictated the power of the landed over their workers became a positive aspect when England faced threats of invasion by other countries. However, its inherent internal divisions further developed between classes of England's peerage, those who inherited aristocratic titles along with their land, and the workers. The system's influence marked England's parliamentary government through the 20th century. Parliament contained two separate bodies, the House of Lords and the House of Commons, based on the ancient definitions of class. The former represented the interests of the aristocracy and consisted of inherited seats; the latter, those of the nonaristocratic "commoner," with elected seats. The highest political office holder, the prime minister, always came from the House of Commons because of party affiliation. Radical change did not occur until 1999 when the House of Lords became, with the exception of two seats, an elected body, and a move to greatly reduce its judiciary power began in 2004.

The decline of feudalism in the 14th century led to the rising of a middle class, workers who became business owners employing other workers, most in trading goods and other maritime-determined activities. As sea trade increased, England distributed its growing wealth throughout the middle class. A national language emerged, its use distinguishing educated classes. Speech marked by "uncouth" dialect distinguished the noneducated citizen.

Fiction of the 17th and 18th centuries often focused on scandals among the upper classes, in which a person born to a lofty social station failed through seduction, slander, betrayal, or personal greed. Samuel RICHARDSON was among those writers whose fiction focused on the seduction of young innocent women by "distinguished" males. Much early fiction appealed primarily to the upper classes that enjoyed an education and could read well. Comic fiction in the form of BURLESQUE and SATIRE grew in popularity, along with the availability of education to all classes. Examples include novels by Henry and Sarah FIELDING, and later Tobias SMOLLETT, who vulgarized the adventure novel. Others introduced the exotic appeal of the Orient, one of the best known being Samuel JOHNSON, who wrote mainly from his imagination. As the English civil-service system grew, those employed in ambassadorial or military duties, such as James MORIER, wrote of their experiences. English readers envisioned the cultures of India and other areas of the Orient as less civilized than their own, adding further striation to social class divisions. The appeal of realism grew, and crime, politics, and social reform became acceptable subjects for fiction among all classes.

At the turn of the century, workers relocated to city factories following the INDUSTRIAL REVOLUTION, during which time distinctions between the rich and the poor grew more pronounced. A quiet, yet firm, emphasis on class separation arose in the fiction of Mary BRUNTON, who prefigured anticipated fiction by Jane AUSTEN. Austen abandoned the old-fashioned romance, with its stereotypical view of women, to introduce a thinking woman protagonist from the upper middle class, well aware of her stigmatization by society. Her social satire emphasized the hypocrisy of the upper classes and their social exploits. She featured the marginalization of women due to a misogynistic class structure that blocked women from inheriting property and forced them into marriage as a business venture.

As realistic fiction flourished, novelists exercised their social consciences by focusing on the crippling results of poverty, particularly in London. Abuse of city workers included abysmally low pay, resulting in slums where crime thrived and inhabitants suffered scant medical care and social support. Novelists from the 1840s, their literature later labeled "problem fiction," featured the poor to attract public concern over that segment of society's shameful living conditions. THESIS NOVELS that preached against abuses proliferated, often focusing on worker movements such as the CHARTIST MOVEMENT. Contributors of often DIDACTIC literature included Charles DICKENS, Frances TROLLOPE, Benjamin DISRAELI, Elizabeth GASKELL, and Charles KINGSLEY. By "putting a face" on the ravaged poor through their fictional characters, these authors, and many others, advanced the causes of the lower classes.

Romances, SILVER-FORK FICTION, and DOMESTIC REALISM focused on class divisions separating lovers from different financial backgrounds. Attitudes varied over the propriety of intermarriage between social classes. For instance, a man might marry a woman of a lower class, thus elevating her to his own, but rarely would society approve a marriage between an upper-class woman and a lower-class man. The children of such "mixed marriages" also faced challenges by an unforgiving culture, featured in fiction. The authors mentioned above included romantic emphases in their novels, as did Edward BULWER-LYTTON and Mrs. Catherine Grace GORE. Victorian fiction, in addition to taking an interest in proper social interaction between the classes, focused on the social effects of division in the church, with authors such as Anthony TROLLOPE excelling in use of that theme. Joseph CONRAD questioned England's IMPERIALISM, and its instinct for taking advantage of cultures less developed than its own. Samuel BUTLER, among others, also satirized the English colonial instinct and the assumption that science, particularly the theories of Charles DARWIN, advanced man's self-knowledge. Henry Rider HAGGARD, on the other hand, produced wildly popular adventure fiction that highlighted the idea of the noble savage, popularizing imperialistic and racist views as necessary to the world's civilization.

As the 19th century closed, writers had developed a strong heritage that focused on class divisions, social customs, and civic laws, all designed to separate and classify individuals into lesser and more desirable groups. While some authors attracted attention to such divisions in order to alleviate the resultant suffering of those considered "subhuman," others featured the class system to advance their own success as popular writers or their approval of exclusivity based on materialism and/or genetics.

BIBLIOGRAPHY

Beach, Joseph Warren. *English Literature of the Nineteenth and the Early Twentieth Centuries: 1798 to the First World War.* New York: Collier Books, 1966.

Joyce, Patrick. *Work, Society, and Politics: The Culture of the Factory in Later Victorian England.* New Brunswick, N.J.: Rutgers University Press, 1980.

Thompson, E. P. *The Making of the English Working Class.* Gloucester, Mass.: Peter Smith, 1999.

Tillotson, Kathleen. *Novels of the Eighteen-forties.* Oxford: Clarendon Press, 1954.

CLOISTER AND THE HEARTH, THE

CHARLES READE (1861)   Charles READE's popular historical romance, *The Cloister and the Hearth: A Tale of the Middle Ages,* represented the labor of two years. Reade was hired in 1859 by the publishers of *Once a Week* to help that periodical compete with Charles DICKENS's ALL THE YEAR ROUND. Dickens had deserted those same publishers when he abruptly discontinued HOUSEHOLD WORDS in 1859, having led the publication to success by publishing his own work in serial form. The publishers would have preferred to hire work from Anthony TROLLOPE, at that time engaged by *The* CORNHILL MAGAZINE. Because Reade had enjoyed recent success with IT IS NEVER TOO LATE TO MEND: A MATTER OF FACT ROMANCE (1856), the publishers turned to him to contribute to *Once a Week*. Reade began a serial titled *A Good Fight,* which he based on the early life of Gerard Eliason, Dutch father to Erasmus. However, an argument with the publication's editor over changes made to Reade's manuscript prompted the author to conclude the series abruptly. He decided to continue with the plot and advance his interest in 15th-century history, so, secluded at Oxford until 1861, he produced *The Cloister and the Hearth,* an extension of his previous serial at five times its length.

Reade's background in SENSATION FICTION allowed him to exploit the dramatic aspects of the many adventures of Gerard, and he structured the novel much like the old PICARESQUE. With heightened emotion, he produced a book that embodied the spirit of pre-Renaissance times, emphasizing the human desire to move forward, both intellectually and artistically. Reade's scholarly efforts are obvious in his attention to authentic detail of the era, but those details never become tedious. An example is the description of a confectionery "on a Titanic scale," served by Philip "the Good," Earl of Holland, at a celebratory feast: "cathedrals of sugar, all gilt and painted in the interstices of the bas-reliefs; castles with their moats, and ditches, imitated to the life; elephants, camels, toads; knights on horseback, jousting; kings and princesses looking on; trumpeters blowing; and all these personages delicious eating." *The Cambridge History of English and American Literature* comments that "the documentary method" proves triumphant in Reade's novel, adding that Reade rises above his morass of research "to view as from a peak the dawn of the renascence over medieval Europe." Critics found his book most appealing in reflecting the curiosity of Reade's own age, the excitement over new discoveries and inventions, even though set centuries earlier. At the time of its publication, Walter Besant stated in an introduction to the novel that the book was Reade's greatest work. He declares it better than HISTORICAL FICTION by Sir Walter SCOTT, noting that the reader of *The Cloister and the*

Hearth "breathes the air just before the Great Dawn of Learning and Religion; it is still twilight, but the birds are twittering already on the boughs; it is a time when men are weary of the past; there is no freshness or vigour in the poetry; all the tunes are old tunes."

As with Reade's other books, this one reflected autobiographical elements. In the rising action, Gerard loses touch with Margaret, the woman he loves, due to the plotting of his own family and the local burgomaster, Van Swikten, guilty of defrauding Margaret and her father of their fortune. Forced to flee Holland, he goes to Rome and, as an artist, meets with an honored reception and gains a certificate to marry Margaret. When he returns home, Van Swikten has him arrested, and his plans for marriage to the pregnant Margaret are ruined. He escapes and returns to Italy with documents that prove Van Swikten's guilt.

As he wanders through Europe, he joins a soldier, Denys, and after several adventures, Denys returns to Rotterdam with a letter for Margaret. She and Gerard's parents are reconciled and summon Gerard home, but Van Swikten prepares a forged letter to Gerard, informing him that Margaret has died. Inconsolable, Gerard indulges in wide-ranging debauchery, blaming the church for his problems. Rescued from a suicide attempt at drowning, Gerard comes into the care of Father Jerome and eventually becomes a Dominican monk, a position that prohibits his marriage. Reade himself had become a Fellow of Magdalene College, Oxford, an appointment that carried with it a requirement that he remain unmarried. He condemned adherence to such severe rules in the novel, suggesting the same condemnation of such controls still exercised centuries later.

Known as Brother Clement, Gerard gains a reputation for his art and language skills and eventually returns to his homeland. He sees Margaret and confronts those who had deceived him, after which the dying burgomaster returns Margaret's fortunes. Brother Clement explains they can never marry, but Margaret leaves their son in his cell. Not knowing the child's identity, Brother Clement shows him affection, after which Margaret reveals the child is his. She swears never to interfere with Brother Clement's brilliant career and dies of the plague when Little Gerard is school age. Brother Clement also dies in the Dominican convent, and their orphaned son matures into the great Erasmus.

In early printings, Reade engaged in creating a format suggesting his background in drama. He inserted various typographical techniques for emphasis, including tiny type when characters whispered and all capital letters for important passages. That technique also reflected on the protagonist's talents for manuscript calligraphy and illustration featured in the novel. The chapter structure depended heavily on dramatic scenes, and most ended abruptly, imitating the fall of a theater curtain. Such a format may put off modern readers, as might Reade's complicated dialogue with abundant anachronisms, as when Gerard tells his QUEST guide, Denys, "So prithee call me at the first blush of rosy-fingered morn, and let's away ere the woman with the hands be stirring." They may also chafe at the coincidence that dooms the lovers, as Reade shapes his fiction to suit history. The rendition does provide ready material for application of MARXIST, FEMINIST and NEW HISTORICAL criticism, with its obvious power structures, strict gender roles, and reflection of Reade's own era and interests.

Although Reade's works no longer enjoy the popularity afforded them in the 19th century, *The Cloister and the Hearth* remains easily available in both print and as electronic text. Of all Reade's works, it is the most read in the 21st century. *The Cambridge History of English and American Literature* states that it escapes true classification, suggesting the novel's whole far outweighs the sum of its parts. It concludes its entry on the novel by stating that "the age must be rich indeed" which can consider Charles Reade a minor novelist. By the time of the 1944 edition, the introduction ranked Reade "not among the great novelists," noting his characters as "picturesque rather than psychological" and pointing to the novel's sensationalism as a weakness.

BIBLIOGRAPHY

Besant, Walter. Introduction to *The Cloister and the Hearth*, by Charles Reade. Available online. URL: http://www.black mask.com/jrusk/ch/ch01.htm. Downloaded on February 25, 2003.

"Cloister and the Hearth, The." *The Cambridge History of English and American Literature in 18 Volumes (1907–21)*.

Volume 13. *The Victorian Age,* Part One. Available online. URL: http://www.bartleby.com/223/1311.html. Downloaded on February 25, 2003.

COLLINS, WILKIE (1824–1889) Considered crucial to the development of modern DETECTIVE FICTION, Wilkie Collins was the eldest son of landscape painter William Collins. He was named for his father's friend and Wilkie's godfather, the painter David Wilkie. Collins had a conventional early education in English private schools, but gained an artistic education while touring Italy with his family from 1836 until 1838. Upon his return, he continued his education at Mr. Cole's boarding school until he apprenticed to a tea merchant in 1841. To help pass the time during monotonous work, Collins wrote an erotic novel set in Tahiti that was never published. When he showed his father a section of an historical romance based on the fall of the Roman Empire, William Collins agreed to let Wilkie abandon the tea business.

In 1846, Collins began law study at Lincoln's Inn. Although he never practiced, his legal knowledge proved a valuable resource for his later novels. A year after his father's death, he published *Memoirs of the Life of William Collins, Esq., RA* (1848); the biography was in response to his father's request, and the Collins family paid publishing expenses. After that project, Collins became one of the first writers to consciously and rationally choose writing as his vocation. He studied writing as he would any trade and gave as much attention to the logistic and financial details of publishing as he did to creating his material. He understood his goal as entertainment, not art.

Living with his mother, Collins used his ample inheritance to support a full-time writing career. He published his first historical novel, *Antonina; or the Fall of Rome* (1850), at 26 years of age. His second novel, *Basil: A Story of Modern Life,* published in 1852, was a melodramatic suspense novel in which he began to develop his distinctive style. To enhance authenticity, he traveled by bus around London, listening to conversations and later recording parts he thought he might use. With its roots in Collins's admiration of sensational French drama, the novel's plot proved unrealistic, but its first-person narrative added plausibility. In *Basil's* preface, Collins explained that extraordinary events and people provided just as valid writing material as did the everyday events of common individuals. This theory became the basis for his development of SENSATION FICTION. His third novel, *Hide and Seek, or The Mystery of Mary Grice,* published in 1854, is considered his first true mystery novel.

During the early 1850s, Collins met Charles DICKENS. The two may have affected one another's work, as both employed gloom and horror in GOTHIC settings. In addition, for *Hide and Seek* Collins borrowed from Dickens his BLEAK HOUSE plot point of the questionable parentage of an illegitimate girl. Dickens later used Collins's plot line of two men with similar appearance serving as substitutes for one another in his *A TALE OF TWO CITIES* (1859), but Dickens's treatment of the historical scene and the plot's tragic conclusion elevated it above sensation fiction. They often collaborated, and Collins frequently published short fiction, including *The Dead Secret* (1857), in Dickens's periodicals, HOUSEHOLD WORDS and ALL THE YEAR ROUND. The two were close friends personally and professionally, often traveling together, and Dickens served as mentor to the younger author. They collaborated on at least two melodramas, *The Lighthouse* (1855) and *The Frozen Deep* (1857), in which they occasionally performed. The two remained close friends until Dickens's death in 1870, and some consider the loss of his mentor one cause of the decreased quality of Collins's late works.

Collins is best remembered for the series of popular mystery novels he wrote in the 1860s. The first, *The WOMAN IN WHITE* (1860), the first of the Victorian sensation novels, exhibits the detailed and meticulous plot for which Collins became known. It appeared as a magazine serial in London in *All the Year Round,* simultaneously published in Paris and New York, catapulting Collins to fame. *The Woman in White* was followed by *No Name* (1862), *Armadale* (1866), and *The MOONSTONE* (1868), considered the first modern detective novel. T. S. Eliot, for one, described *The Moonstone* as "the first, the largest, and the best of modern English detective novels." In it Collins uses constantly shifting perspectives to reveal the intricate details of the plot, involving an editor/narrator who turns out to be intimately involved in the novel's key events. Some modern readers also see in it issues of social and gender class and status.

Some identify the real "woman in white" as Caroline Graves, a woman who Collins apparently met in circumstances similar to those recounted in the novel. Except for a period from 1868 until 1871, the two lived together from 1858 until Collins's death. They never married, and Collins referred to Graves as his housekeeper, although the relationship clearly exceeded what that title implied. Collins also had a long-term relationship with Martha Rudd, with whom he fathered three children. Although he maintained households with both women for years, and they may have all lived together at some point, details of the relationships remain unclear.

Collins produced an additional 15 novels after 1870 to a lukewarm reception. He suffered considerably in later years from ill health, especially gout. He also maintained an opium addiction for the last 27 years of his life.

Today's readers best remember Collins for his contributions to the mystery novel and sensation fiction, especially his clever and detailed plots and his experimentation with different narrative techniques. Later novelists such as Robert Louis STEVENSON would adopt the sensationalist approach but apply a more graceful style, rejecting its crude sadistic and horror elements, while Sir Arthur Conan DOYLE, a devotee of Stevenson, combined Collins's mystery technique with a more energetic style. Collins also contributed the witty advice to novelists: "Make 'em laugh, make 'em cry, make 'em wait." *The Moonstone* and *The Woman in White* are available in electronic text; both have been dramatized for stage and screen.

BIBLIOGRAPHY

Donaldson, Norman. Introduction. *Hide and Seek, or, The Mystery of Mary Grice.* New York: Dover Publications, Inc., 1981.

Kemp, Sandra. Introduction to *The Moonstone,* by Wilkie Collins. London: Penguin Classics, 1998.

Page, Norman, ed. *Wilkie Collins: The Critical Heritage.* New York: Routledge, 1974.

Sweet, Matthew. Introduction to *The Woman in White,* by Wilkie Collins. London: Penguin Classics, 1999.

COMING-OF-AGE   See INITIATION/COMING-OF-AGE STORY.

COMING RACE, THE EDWARD BULWER-LYTTON (1871)   In Edward BULWER-LYTTON's 1871 novel, *The Coming Race,* later classified as SCIENCE FICTION, the author writes a futuristic novel that complemented his HISTORICAL FICTION. In this plot, often considered a SATIRE on Charles DARWIN's evolutionary theory, an American mining engineer travels to Earth's center after a miner acquaintance tells him of descending into a crevice and spotting a mysterious light, which appeared to come from within the depths of the Earth. The narrator/protagonist agrees to accompany the miner back into the "abyss" to investigate, but after arriving, the miner dies in a fall, and the narrator immediately encounters "a vast and terrible head, with open jaws and dull, ghastly, hungry eyes" belonging to a monstrous reptile, "infinitely larger" than a crocodile or alligator. Thus begins his QUEST, which includes encounters with winged creatures that have human characteristics, such as the power to learn English. They control a mysterious energy, called "vril," which Zee, a female member of the College of Sages, attempts to define for the narrator. No English term equates to vril, but the narrator explains it as electricity that also "comprehends in its manifold branches other forces of nature," such as "magnetism, galvanism, etc." Vril gives the creatures incredible powers, including the ability to influence the weather and to "exercise influence over minds, and bodies animal and vegetable, to an extent not surpassed in the romances of our mystics." Following the novel's publication, the term *vril* became associated with strength and was incorporated into names of elixirs, such as Bovril, a beef broth with additives believed to benefit humans.

In addition to monsters, the narrator encounters all the elements expected of science fiction, such as altered natural forces, futuristic domiciles and machines, including "automatons," or robots, and utopian conditions, including a lack of poverty and illness. All this is achieved, however, by conformation to certain rules that prove restrictive of personal freedom. The narrator pronounces that the social system governing "the Vril-ya prohibits their development of individual greatness, such as that observed in Hannibal, Washington, Demosthenes, Webster, Wendel Holmes, Shakespeare and Moliere."

The protagonist offers a lengthy discussion of the culture's language and relays several myths relating to philosophy and the origin of the species, which grew from the "Wrangling Period of History," during which time some believed the frog race preceded the human. The theories that follow form the basis for analysis of the novel as a satire against evolution; one learned figure informs the narrator that two schools rage "against each other, one asserting the An (man) to be the perfected type of the Frog; the other that the Frog was the highest development of the An." In addition, "moralists were divided in opinion with the naturalists, but the bulk of them sided with the Frog-preference school," because in moral conduct there was "no doubt as to the superiority of the Frog." Eventually romance with one of the foreign beings tempts the protagonist, but he predictably rejects that opportunity in order to return home.

While its detail may prove tedious to some readers, the novel offers an entertaining look at early science fiction with an editorial bent that concludes with the narrator longing to depart Utopia and return to his own flawed culture. MARXIST CRITICS find interesting the lack of financial structure in the perfect world and perhaps even the ironic setting, where a civilization has literally moved underground in order to reach perfect equitable order. FEMINIST CRITICS note that primarily female professors make up the College of Sages, specializing in "philosophy, the history of remote periods, and such sciences as entomology, conchology, etc." The female's better-perfected "nervous organization" renders her especially perceptive to the powers of vril, a trait supporting the traditional engendered attribution of intuition to women. PSYCHOANALYTIC critics note the descent into space intellectually controlled by women with the masculine intrusion into the space by a human man.

BIBLIOGRAPHY

Christiansen, Allan Conrad. *Edward Bullwer-Lytton: The Fiction of New Regions.* Athens: University of Georgia Press, 1976.

CONRAD, JOSEPH (1857–1924)

Joseph Conrad, highly acclaimed writer of late-19th- and early-20th-century English literature, greatly influenced future generations. His innovative style, most notably his use of an intermediate narrator and of changing points of view, and his focus on the psychological and moral state of his principal characters, proved distinctive and comparatively unusual. Perhaps the most surprising aspect of his writing was that Conrad composed in English, a language he did not learn until in his 20s.

Joseph Conrad was born Jozef Teodor Konrad Nalecz Korzeniowski in 1857 to Polish parents living in the Ukraine. His parents, Apollo and Ewa, were descended from Polish nobility who lost their lands due to their opposition to Russian rule. His parents were educated and politically active, and Apollo provided his son reading material that included fiction by Charles DICKENS and James Fenimore Cooper, in either French or Polish. While Conrad was still quite young, Russian authorities arrested and imprisoned his father for opposition activities. After seven months in prison, in 1862 Apollo gained release and exile with his family to a remote Russian province.

Conrad and his mother soon fell ill, and authorities permitted the family to relocate to a warmer southern climate in a small village near Kiev. His mother died there of tuberculosis in 1865. His father's health also deteriorated, and Apollo and Conrad returned to Poland in 1867, where Apollo died of tuberculosis in 1869. Conrad's elder brother, Tadeusz Bobrowski, assumed responsibility for Conrad. However, he spent most of his remaining adolescence with his grandmother in Poland, because his uncle's estate was in the politically repressed area near Kiev.

Conrad's primary language was Polish, although he learned sufficient French to read voraciously in both languages from a young age. While his physically and politically difficult childhood left problematic wounds, it also produced in Conrad an awareness of, and an interest in, the difficulties of a moral life and the struggles necessary to maintain ethical values in the face of authority. These themes of ethical struggle, of doomed resistance, and of fidelity and loyalty he later stressed in his writing.

By the age of 14, Conrad decided he wanted to go to sea. Despite his uncle's objections, he left home at 17 and made his way to France. He spent the next four years either at sea or ashore in Marseilles. During this time he met the man on whom he would base several romantic characters, a Corsican named Dominic Cervoni, and the two engaged in daring adventures that included gun running, some of which proved disastrous. According to his uncle, the author attempted suicide in 1878 due to what he viewed as a waste of his previous years, but that same year began working on English ships and learning English. Between 1878 and 1886, he sailed in the South Pacific, the Indian Ocean, and the Mediterranean, experiences he later drew from extensively in his novels. In 1886, he received his master's certificate and became a naturalized British citizen.

Conrad's first command came in 1888, and on May 6, 1890, he left France on a sailboat for the coast of the Congo. His Aunt Marguerite Poradowska had used her influence to obtain a captain's commission for Conrad on a steamer. During a lengthy journey down the African coast, he worked on the ship *Almayer's Folly* and eventually met Roger Casement, a man who hoped to combat the Arabian slave trade and develop a railway from the coast to the inner Congo. Promised a command position on a steamer that never materialized, Conrad served as mate on a small steamboat that moved down the Congo River. The excursion fulfilled a desire Conrad first felt at age nine, according to his later memoir, *Some Reminiscences* (1912): "while looking at a map of Africa of the time and putting my finger on the blank space then representing the unsolved mystery of the continent, I said to myself with absolute assurance . . . When I grow up I shall go there." However, the trip discouraged Conrad as he discovered the abuse of native workers by colonialists.

Conrad's dislike of the area increased after he met a dissipated agent named Klein, who died shortly thereafter, and the steamboat carried his corpse for the next four weeks during its return trip. Conrad wrote to his aunt in a letter later included in *The Collected Letters of Joseph Conrad,* "Everything here is repellent to me . . . Men and things, but above all men." Ill with dysentery, Conrad returned to England. His Congo experiences proved crucial to the later writing of *Heart of Darkness* (1902), considered his signature work.

In 1892, Conrad became first mate on a ship that made two long voyages to Australia. He finally ended his sea career in 1894, in large part for lack of work, but also because he had completed his first novel, *Almayer's Folly,* published in 1895. In addition, in 1895 Conrad married Jessie George, with whom he had two sons, Borys and John.

Almayer's Folly proved reasonably successful, in part because it provided an exotic adventure and a love story with a happy conclusion. The novel also introduced many of the traits that would become distinctive of Conrad's work. In his vivid description of Sambir, Conrad creates an atmosphere of stagnation, decay, and doom that conveys the violent and threatening state of nature and life. Conrad followed *Almayer's Folly* with *An Outcast of the Islands* (1896), in which he continued to develop his distinctive writing style and technique.

In 1897, Conrad published *The NIGGER OF THE NAR-CISSUS,* inspired by his experience sailing on the ship the *Narcissus* in 1884; it was widely regarded as his first significant work. Henry JAMES described it as "the very finest and strongest picture of the sea and sea life that our language possesses." The novel presents a striking and troubling look at ideological conflict and class conflict. He then began his busiest writing years, a period extending to 1911.

In 1900, Conrad published *Lord Jim,* firmly establishing his reputation as a significant writer. In this complicated novel, Conrad introduces Marlowe, an observer, as an intermediate sometime-narrator. The book follows the story of Jim, a former seaman seeking to redeem himself for an apparent act of cowardice performed years earlier. Its narrative employs multiple reflective perspectives and can be read as a reflection on honor, integrity, bravery, shame, and redemption, as well as a commentary on colonialism. It later became a staple of English literature classes.

Conrad continued writing a number of significant novels, publishing both *Typhoon* and *The Heart of Darkness* in 1902. The latter again used the character Marlowe and drew on Conrad's experiences in the Congo almost a dozen years earlier. A major work, *Nostromo* (1904), explored man's corruptibility. Conrad followed that work with the politically themed novels *The Secret Agent* (1907) and *Under Western Eyes* (1911). While Conrad's novels received some critical acclaim and the praise of other writers such as James and John Galsworthy, they did not sell well, and Conrad struggled financially. However, in 1913 he published *Chance,* a love story involving a romantic sea setting that brought popular and financial success. In 1914, he visited his birth nation of Poland with his sons, but had long before declared himself loyal to his adopted country and its language. Other significant works included *Youth* (1902), the biographical *The Mirror of the Sea* (1906), *The Secret Sharer* (1909), *Victory* (1915), *The Rescue* (1920), and *The Rover* (1923).

By the time of his death in 1924, Conrad had achieved popularity and adulation as a leader in the modernist school of literature. He made a successful and highly popular tour of the United States in 1923, was offered, but declined, knighthood in 1924, and was buried at Canterbury when he died later that same year. His work suffered some decline of interest in the 1930s but has received ever-increasing critical attention since then. Authors such as James Joyce, T. S. Eliot, Graham Greene, Virginia Woolf, and Ernest Hemingway all proclaimed their debt to Conrad. Critics now consider him one of the great modern writers of English literature, and his works remain standard fare in most high school and college English curricula; several exist in electronic text format.

BIBLIOGRAPHY

Conrad, Joseph. *Some Reminiscences.* London: Eveleigh Nash, 1912.

Ford, Maddox F. *Joseph Conrad: A Personal Remembrance: 1873–1939.* 1924. Reprint, New York: Octagon Books, 1965.

Guerard, Albert J. *Conrad the Novelist.* Cambridge, Mass.: Harvard University Press, 1958.

Karl, Frederick, and Laurence Davies, eds. *The Collected Letters of Joseph Conrad.* Cambridge: Cambridge University Press, 1983.

Murfin, Ross C. Introduction to *Heart of Darkness,* by Joseph Conrad. New York: St. Martin's Press, 1989, 3–16.

Thorburn, David. *Conrad's Romanticism.* New Haven, Conn.: Yale University Press, 1974.

Tucker, Martin. *Joseph Conrad.* New York: Frederick Ungar Publishing Co., 1976.

Watt, Ian. *Conrad in the Nineteenth Century.* Berkeley: University of California Press, 1979.

COPYRIGHT ACT OF 1710

Until the 16th century and the appearance of the printing press, printed documents required no particular protection. When printing became popular and its use spread, England feared the publication of inflammatory materials by the enemies of the king. The Licensing Act of 1662 authorized the Stationer's Company, an exclusive guild whose members consisted of printing companies appointed by royal decree. Part of the agreement between members allowed one to print material and remain competition-free; no other printer would duplicate that publication. Only those select members could print books, and the content of those books remained under close review and control by the royal court. The Stationer's Company established a register of licensed books, along with the requirement to deposit a copy of the book to be licensed. This arrangement changed when Parliament passed the Copyright Act of 1710, sponsored by Queen Anne, who ruled 1702–14. The Act allowed authors to control the publication of their own works for a set number of years. The first copyright law to resemble those that later became commonplace, it liberated printers from strict censorship and left the rights to their works with authors. Known as the Statute of Anne, it read in part:

> every such Offender . . . shall Forfeit One Peny [sic] for every sheet which shall be found in his, her, or their Custody, either Printed or Printing, Published or Exposed to Sale, contrary to the true intent and meaning of this Act, the one Moiety thereof to the Queens [sic] most Excellent Majesty, Her Heirs and Successors, and the other Moiety thereof to any Person or Persons that shall Sue for the same.

BIBLIOGRAPHY

Loewenstein, Joseph. *The Author's Due: Printing and the Prehistory of Copyright.* Chicago: University of Chicago Press, 2002.

CORNHILL MAGAZINE, THE

CORNHILL MAGAZINE, THE In 1860, founder and publisher George Smith hired William Makepeace THACKERAY as the first editor to write and critique material for *The Cornhill Magazine*. Eight other men worked as editors until the last issue appeared in 1900. Thackeray devoted issues to polite, family-oriented entertainment. He once censored a poem by Elizabeth Barrett BROWNING and terminated a John Ruskin series, both because of content he believed too strong for his family audience. In the two years that Thackeray served as editor, he published his own first serial novel, *Lovel the Widower,* as well as his two novels, *Denis Duval* and *The Adventures of Philip.* Thackeray also requested that Anthony TROLLOPE provide the magazine's first serial. Trollope felt so honored by the request that he wrote the fourth Barsetshire novel, *FRAMLEY PARSONAGE,* for *The Cornhill Magazine.* Trollope's novel received a great deal of credit for the magazine's popularity.

By 1870, competition from other publications reduced circulation from 100,000 to 20,000. After 1871, the magazine's focus altered, and it enjoyed a reputation for high-class literary criticism under the editorial leadership of Sir Leslie Stephen (father of Virginia Stephen Woolf) until 1882. During that time, publication included the early work of Henry JAMES (*WASHINGTON SQUARE* in five parts and his *The Siege of London* in two parts), in addition to writing by Thomas HARDY (*FAR FROM THE MADDING CROWD* in seven parts and *The HAND OF ETHELBERTA* in 10 parts). After Stephen retired in 1882, the magazine carried primarily light fiction, eliminating classical and literary essays. It became an unprofitable venture, but in its last years expanded its focus to include military and nationalistic memoirs, autobiographies, diaries, anniversary studies, and commentary on famous criminal trials. The magazine's final editor, Reginald Smith, continued to publish serialized novels and returned the form of the literary essay to the publication.

Over its lifetime, *The Cornhill Magazine* received contributions from many well-known writers. Matthew Arnold published essays, and John Ruskin's *Unto This Last* appeared in four parts. Harriet Beecher Stowe's *Agnes of Sorrento* appeared in 13 parts, while Arthur Conan DOYLE's popular DETECTIVE FICTION, *The White Company,* appeared in 12 installments. Additional publications included Joseph CONRAD's *The Lagoon;* Stephen Crane's *A Self-made Man* and *God Rest Ye, Merry Gentlemen;* and Bret Harte's *The Rise of the Short Story.*

BIBLIOGRAPHY

Wellesley Index to Victorian Periodicals, Vol. 1. Edited by Walter E. Houghton, Esther Rhoads Houghton, and Jean Slingerland. Toronto: University of Toronto Press, 1989, 321–415.

CORN LAWS

CORN LAWS Corn laws instituted in Great Britain in the 15th century regulated the trade of various grains, such as wheat, and corn, referred to collectively as "corn" for legal purposes. The laws strove to keep grain prices at a reasonable level while ensuring the availability of corn domestically. This they accomplished by price controls on imports and exports. Eventually controlled wages and inflated wheat prices increased the cost of bread, negatively affecting mostly low-income people, thus widening the economic gap between upper and lower classes. Ongoing protests over the laws, fluctuations in corn supply and demand, and economic shifts caused revision of the Corn Laws over the next 300 years, with none of the changes appreciably benefiting England's working class and its farmers.

The Corn Laws of 1815, enacted during the economic depression following the Napoleonic Wars, excluded almost entirely the import of wheat, causing an increase in bread prices that led to mass demonstrations on the part of the working class. Parliament reacted by passing severe laws that suspended the right of habeas corpus, the right to public gatherings, and made legal some arbitrary property searches. An 1828 Corn Law renewed grain imports but leveled import duties that resulted in maintaining the high price of corn.

With the INDUSTRIAL REVOLUTION, a new manufacturing class that needed grain imports demanded the repeal of the Corn Laws. Five Manchester merchants joined John Bright and Richard Cobden in 1839 to form the anti–Corn Law League, a coalition that organized workers and farmers against their landlords and demanded more reasonably priced grains, a demand that increased when Ireland's 1845 potato famine eliminated the availability of potatoes. The Corn Laws lasted only a few additional years, with Prime Minister Robert Peel leading Parliament to establish free trade in 1845. By 1846, Corn Laws had been repealed, although a small tax was leveled on imported wheat. Even that tax disappeared by 1869, and the term *Corn Law* disappeared along with it.

Such restrictive regulations became a focus of protest novels, some labeled THESIS NOVELS, of the 19th century, including those by Charles DICKENS, Benjamin DISRAELI, and Elizabeth GASKELL, which featured the suffering of the lower and middle classes.

BIBLIOGRAPHY

Adams, Leonard Palmer. *Agricultural Depression and Farm Relief in England, 1813–1852.* New York: A. M. Kelley, 1965.

Barnes, Donald Grove. *A History of the English Corn Laws, from 1660–1846.* New York: A. M. Kelley, 1965.

CRANFORD ELIZABETH GASKELL (1853)

One of Elizabeth GASKELL's best-known novels, *Cranford* focuses on an English community of mature women, to which men seldom gain admittance. It first appeared in series form (1851–53) in Charles DICKENS's periodical *HOUSEHOLD WORDS* and was meant only as a short sketch in the form of its first two chapters. However, it grew into a novel, well received by Gaskell's contemporaries. Her affection for, and trust of, the country values she enjoyed as a child remain obvious in her rendering of Cranford and its inhabitants.

Although the narrator introduces Cranford as a community of "Amazons," imagery of strong warrior women does not follow. Instead, Gaskell shapes a group of elderly, gentle women who arm themselves with custom and wear ritual like a mantle. Mary Smith, the first-person narrator, does not live in Cranford, instead visiting frequently. Thus, her point of view may be more trustworthy and objective than were she an inhabitant of Cranford. She also becomes an actor in the novel, contributing to the generous amount of dialogue that overpowers action in this character-driven story. While it depends on the pathos generated by the seemingly isolated existence of its main characters, *Cranford* succeeds due to the positive tone underlying Gaskell's portrayal of a sense of community among these sisters-in-circumstance.

Gaskell introduces several figures the reader believes will be her main characters, chief among those being Deborah Jenkyns. However, Deborah dies before long, leaving her meek and admirable sister Miss Matty, or Mathilda Jenkyns, as the novel's protagonist. Most other characters, including the narrator, reveal their personalities in relationship to Miss Matty, and the series of chapter-length vignettes rotate around her. But it is Gaskell's affectionate, ironic tone that so effectively frames and colors each action, transforming what many might regard as the mundane existence of a group of spinsters and widows into a consistently humorous portrayal that evokes reader admiration for the women.

The narrator emphasizes from the first page that the ladies of Cranford have little money and must practice "elegant economy," allowing the introduction of small telling details that help shape personalities. For instance, despite their sober dress, the women go to great ends to wear nice hats, always in the latest style. Headdress becomes an ongoing theme throughout the novel, used in both serious and humorous ways. Miss Matty's only love, Mr. Holbrook, a respectful farmer rejected during Matty's youth by her family as not worthy of the rector's daughter, re-enters her life, only to die shortly thereafter. Here, Gaskell uses the theme of hats, not only to add a somber note to the scene, but also to advance her rounding of Miss Matty's character. The narrator notes that Miss Matty requested of the local milliner a cap "something like the Honourable Mrs. Jamieson's." When the milliner replies that Mrs. Jamieson "wears widows' caps," Matty answers absently, "Oh? I only meant something in that style." Too proud to speak of her lifelong love for Holbrook, Miss Matty will silently mourn his passing, just as for years she keeps private her recurring dream about the child she never had.

However, Gaskell executes a neat reversal by using the same hat for comic effect, making quiet sport of the social conventions to which the community so closely adheres. In a subsequent scene, Betty Barker, former owner of a millinery, which "would not sell their caps and ribbons to anyone without a pedigree," arrives at Miss Matty's house to invite her to a social gathering. Miss Matty is so flustered by the early morning visit that she places her new faux-mourning cap on top of the yellow-ribboned stay-at-home cap already on her head. When Matty questions whether Miss Pole will attend Betty Barker's social event, Betty Barker replies, "I am going to ask Miss Pole. Of course, I could not think of asking her until I had asked you, madam—the rector's daughter, madam." Matty next inquires about a Mrs. Forrester, and Betty Barker replies that she thought of asking her before Miss Pole, because, "although her circumstances are changed, madam, she was born at Tyrerell, and we can never forget her alliance to the Bigges, of Bigelow Hall." Gaskell follows this remark with "Miss Matty cared much more for the little circumstance of her being a very good card-player." Throughout the interchange, Miss Matty represents the essence of correct conduct, although she remained "double hatted."

While many characters move in and out of Miss Matty's circle, only a few are male. In addition to Mr. Holbrook, Captain Brown becomes a temporary community favorite, although he irritates Deborah Jenkyns, by reading "Boz," or Charles DICKENS, in favor of "Mr.[Samuel] Johnson." Although his lack of subtlety at first alienates the women, his good heart eventually wins them all over, and they mourn his passing when he dies a hero while rescuing a toddler from an oncoming train. Cranford seems to prove unhealthy for most males, but a few do survive to enjoy and challenge its rigid social structure, and all have clear effects on the community. Captain Brown's younger daughter, Miss Jessie, who long remained single to help her father care for her invalid sister, eventually marries Major Gordon, her former love, and brings a joy to the community that it had not experienced for some time. Mr. Holbrook's death brings Miss Matty to soften and reconsider her injunction against "followers," or male admirers for her maid, Martha, as she recalls her heartbreak as a young woman prevented from seeing her only love. The memory of one particular male, Miss Matty's

long-lost brother, Peter, haunts her more than any other does. Due to a family dispute, Peter disappeared decades earlier, joining the service. Following a set of realistic occurrences, Mary begins to wonder whether Peter is not still living and sets about launching a search, with the help of her father, for a man living in India whose reputation has reached her in England. The book's climax reunites brother and sister, and the highly deserving Miss Matty finds relief from the loneliness she has suffered since her sister's death. The novel ends with the satisfying pronouncement by Mary, the narrator, "We all love Miss Matty, and I somehow think we are all of us better when she is near us." The overriding theme could be stated as "Virtue is rewarded," but that would simplify the rich texture from which Miss Matty's portrait emerges. In one of Gaskell's many letters, she makes clear that she had never intended to stretch the Cranford story into a novel: "I never meant to write more, so I killed Capt. Brown very much against my will."

Gaskell's presentation in *Cranford* stood in stark contrast to the activist approach she took in her first work, MARY BARTON (1848). Surrounded by the tragic conditions of unemployment in the Manchester of the 1830s, including sickness, poverty, hunger and crime, Gaskell struck out in the only way available to her, by producing protest literature. In *Cranford,* she revealed a more positive side and a delicate style that some found dull, particularly when comparing her work to that by Jane AUSTEN, whose sharp wit delivered heavy blows to the social system against which none of Gaskell's characters rebelled. Neither did it bear any resemblance to the passionate, action-centered fiction by Emily and Charlotte BRONTË. Although Gaskell shared with George ELIOT a focus on locality and the quotidian, she lacked Eliot's force and demanding philosophical approach. She herself admitted to a friend that she might as well not write while books such as Eliot's ADAM BEDE were available. And yet the seductive charm of *Cranford,* its insistence on the importance of self-respect and acceptance of one's station in life as respectable, cause it to remain a highly popular work, readily available in electronic-text versions. Lionel Stevenson describes *Cranford* as "the most placid book in English fiction," in which Gaskell pays homage to her own childhood village of Knutsford, still extant in Cheshire; Knutsford later became a tourist attraction for Gaskell's fans. All critics emphasize setting as the thread that brings continuity to *Cranford*'s series of domestic vignettes, which together evince a tranquility that proved fiction could successfully adopt serenity as a tone. The sense of a community made up of members that remain fiercely loyal to one another, through grief and joy, remains pronounced and seductively attractive in *Cranford*.

BIBLIOGRAPHY

French, Yvonne. "Elizabeth Cleghorn Gaskell." *From Jane Austen to Joseph Conrad.* Edited by Robert C. Rathburn and Martin Steinmann, Jr. Minneapolis: University of Minnesota Press, 1958, 133–145.

Stevenson, Lionel. *The English Novel: a Panorama.* Boston: Houghton Mifflin, 1960.

Watson, Elizabeth Porges. Introduction to *Cranford,* by Elizabeth Gaskell. New York: Oxford, 1998.

DAILY NEWS, THE *The Daily News,* a radical newspaper founded and edited by Charles DICKENS from January to October 1846, allowed him an outlet for his later well-known focus on social causes. William Henry Wills, whose work Dickens had accepted while editor of BENTLEY'S MISCELLANY, became chief of the sub-editorial staff and an informal secretary to Dickens. Dickens's friend and later biographer, John Forster, eventually took over editorial duties. The paper was much later (1930) absorbed into *The Daily Chronicle,* which became *The News Chronicle* and remained in publication until 1960.

BIBLIOGRAPHY

Graham, Walter. *English Literary Periodicals.* New York: Octagon Books, 1966.

DAISY MILLER HENRY JAMES (1879) *Daisy Miller* is a simple story about a young American girl's experience in Europe and her premature death following incidents of her brief romance and her costly defiance of an unfriendly European community, which is bewildered by her American way of conducting herself. The title character represents a type that would appear again in Henry JAMES's fiction, in the mature and more dynamic figure of the independent Isabel Archer in the novel, *The PORTRAIT OF A LADY* (1881), who learns through her experiences to be a survivor. Annie P. "Daisy" Miller, however, does not learn or change as a result of her family's visit to Europe or her friendship with Frederick Forsythe Winterbourne, whose symbolic last name predicts his failure to understand and nurture a flower such as Daisy. The novella may be read simply as a story of Daisy, whose American innocence bewilders the unruffled European mind and community, or it may be read as a story of Winterbourne, a more complicated character, particularly regarding his reflective mind that enlivens and enriches the story when his point of view takes over the narration from the initial unseen narrator. One can also read the novella as a fictional praise of American innocence opposed to European hypocrisy or as an implicit criticism of American innocence that causes the tension—being unable or unwilling to mend its ways regarding respect for different cultures. As a critical thinker, one highly sensitive and responsive to cultural differences, James does not offer any "right" answers.

Daisy attracts the displeasure of Winterbourne's judgmental aunt, Mrs. Costello, who embodies the repressed mores of the Victorian Age. Her voice represents those of many who judge Daisy inferior and undesirable because she differs from them. Daisy eventually travels to Rome, as do Mrs. Costello and Winterbourne, where she keeps company with a local boy named Giovanelli, a relationship that "good" society frowns upon. She brings him to a social gathering, despite the warning of one of Mrs. Costello's friends, Mrs. Walker. She even insists that Giovanelli be allowed to sing, and she openly resists Winterbourne's explanation that her flirting is not seen as innocent in Rome, the way it might be in America. When she replies that at least her new friend does not try to tell her what to do, Winterbourne understands the rebuff and realizes he will be unable to win Daisy's heart. Her subsequent death from malaria, or "Roman fever," following a nighttime venture into the Colosseum with Giovanelli, appears to her critics as simple poetic justice.

Daisy Miller stresses the moral issue regarding whether, how, and why one should treat fellow humans with respect and dignity regardless of intricate differences in gender, age, and culture. At first, the novella reads like praise of American innocence that falls prey to European prejudice, as Daisy is apparently misunderstood and mistreated not for who she is but who she represents. Shunned or ostracized by the particular European society due to her American way of behavior, Daisy is undoubtedly the victim of prejudice. However, James implies that Daisy's innocence also contributes to her own victimization, because that innocence suggests her inability, if not her unwillingness, to adapt herself to the new environment or show her respect accordingly.

Meanwhile, Winterbourne demonstrates not only his great interest in Daisy but also his desire to understand and appreciate her. Unfortunately, he will not achieve those goals, because he has been de-Americanized, having "lived too long in foreign parts." He either underestimates her as "a little American flirt" or overestimates her as "a clever little reprobate [. . .] smartly playing an injured innocence." As Winterbourne cannot stop questioning "whether Daisy's defiance came from the consciousness of innocence or from her being, essentially, a young person of the reckless class," he can never really approach Daisy without distorting her in his mind.

Infuriated and inexperienced as she is, Daisy indiscreetly defies not part but all the social taboos that the community holds in awe, from its regular code of social behavior to its superstition about the Colosseum. Such defiance proves to be too costly for Daisy, who remains too innocent or ignorant to know how to consciously accommodate herself to a different world. Winterbourne finally realizes, much too late, that Daisy

demands and defends, even at the cost of her life, nothing more than the basic human respect or "esteem" that the prejudiced community denies her.

BIBLIOGRAPHY
Chen, Shudong. *Henry James: The Essayist Behind the Novelist.* Studies in American Literature, vol. 59. Lewiston, N.Y.: Edwin Mellens, 2003.

DANIEL DERONDA GEORGE ELIOT (1876)

The last of George ELIOT's seven novels, published in eight parts between February and September 1876, *Daniel Deronda* has a double structure that follows two protagonists, Daniel Deronda and Gwendolyn Harleth, in their intertwined search for self-fulfillment. Eliot breaks new ground both in content and narrative style. She creates a hero who is an English gentleman by his rearing and education, but is by birth a member of a despised ethnic group, the Jews. In doing so, she deliberately and subtly places English anti-Semitism on trial without having to display it, a move of interest to NEW HISTORICIST CRITICS. She also comments on the limited lives that women lead as dependents on the goodwill and good fortune of the men to whom they have ties by birth or marriage, an approach of interest to FEMINIST CRITICS. Both of her protagonists are problematic: Deronda is at times stiff and sanctimonious, while Gwendolen is mostly scheming and self-serving.

Contrasting with the slow unfolding panorama of Eliot's first novel, *ADAM BEDE* (1859), *Daniel Deronda* opens *in medias res* at a German spa and casino, narrated through omniscient third-person point of view. The coldly beautiful young woman who is the focal point of the opening scene wins and loses a large sum of money. Although she remains seemingly indifferent to her changing luck, she suffers anxiety beneath her cool demeanor; she fears seeming to be concerned about money in front of the glittering roulette-table throng more than she fears losing it. Only a strong will controls her emotions. She notices a darkly handsome man watching in apparent fascination, but he is unknown to her. The gambler turns out to be Gwendolen Harleth; the man watching her, Daniel Deronda.

As the action rises, Gwendolen's mother summons her home. Hoping to recover some losses before leaving, Gwendolen sells her turquoise necklace. Almost immediately, before she can return to the gaming tables, an anonymous benefactor purchases the necklace and returns it to her. She suspects that the unknown young man has redeemed the necklace and feels too embarrassed to gamble with the money acquired from the sale of her jewelry. Her reticence foreshadows Deronda's later effect on her future.

When she arrives home at Offendene, her mother informs her that the family fortune has been lost through risky investments, calling to mind Gwendolen's own recent gambling. Gwendolen, her widowed mother, and four homely stepsisters will be obligated to move into a humble cottage and Gwendolen will have to work as a governess. Desperate to find a means of support, Gwendolen searches for a simple and quick way to income.

Then begins a lengthy flashback, relating events that led Gwendolen to the gambling tables of Leubronn. Readers learn that her mother had relocated to Offendene a year earlier in order to place her daughters within the social sphere of her wealthy, respectable sister and brother-in-law, the Gascoignes. Gwendolen had rejected her cousin's offer of love in order to pursue the newly arrived Mallinger Grandcourt. The symbolically named Mallinger is the n'er-do-well heir of Sir Hugo Mallinger, a wealthy man who lacks sons but has a male ward—Daniel Deronda. Although Deronda believes himself Sir Hugo's illegitimate son, reared by him to the exacting standards of an English gentleman, he has no certain knowledge of his origins, and the family inheritance has been settled on Grandcourt, whose surname correctly suggests a man of high ambition but little substance. Then begins a pursuit of self-identity by the two main characters that will lead each to find an unexpected destiny.

Gwendolen eventually marries Grandcourt for his money, although she had promised Mrs. Lydia Glasher, with whom Grandcourt had fathered four children, that she would abandon her pursuit of him, as Lydia confided she hoped to marry Grandcourt and legitimize their children. That Gwendolen breaks her promise and marries for money, trading her honor for material goods, proves her lack of self-value and highlights her desperation, egoism, and manipulative

nature. Her view of herself as a commodity interests MARXIST, as well as feminist, critics.

The exposition also provides insight into Deronda's history. A successful student at Cambridge, he had befriended the poverty-stricken Hans Meyrick and helped him earn a scholarship. However, Deronda is dissatisfied with his life at university, feeling undirected. While reared as a member of the English upper class, he lacks a sense of identity and goals. He leaves school and travels to expand his practical education. While rowing on the Thames one day, he rescues the beautiful Jewish woman, Mirah Lapidoth, from drowning, then lodges her with the Meyrick family. He later discovers Mirah has run away from a brutal father and become separated from a beloved mother and brother. The Meyricks provide her a secure home while Deronda undertakes locating her family as his personal QUEST. In his pursuits, he develops a strong interest in Judaism, thus making strides toward discovering his self-identity, in contrast to Gwendolen, who has nearly destroyed hers.

Grandcourt turns out to be a good match for Gwendolen. Dictatorial, cold, and cruel, he makes her miserable despite the wealth and prestige the marriage brings her. Deronda's connection to Sir Hugo places him in the same social sphere, so that Gwendolen sees him frequently at parties and dinners. She eventually confesses her guilt to Deronda, who advises Gwendolen to atone by devoting herself to the welfare of those oppressed by misfortune. She promises to follow his advice but does not at first succeed.

Searching for Mirah's lost family, Deronda locates and reunites them with Mirah. Their unification foreshadows his own personal identification with the Jews, as well the suggestion that the Jews as a race must unite. He also meets a Jewish intellectual named Mordecai and learns to share his political ideas, which include the dream of a Jewish nation-state. Unexpectedly, Deronda receives a letter from Sir Hugo telling him the identity of his mother, who wishes to meet her son before expiring of a fatal illness. He learns from her of his Jewish descent and how she had placed him with her friend, Sir Hugo, so he might escape common prejudice against the Jews.

As Deronda develops a Jewish identity, Gwendolen further alienates herself from family when she allows

Grandcourt to drown through her inaction following a boating accident. She later shares her suffering over Grandcourt's death with Deronda, and readers understand that she loves him. However, Deronda hopes to marry Mirah and not only physically join a Jewish family but also share their racial struggle, serving the Jews by helping to establish a homeland. Deronda meets Gwendolen one last time to tell her of his plans, and she does not receive the news well. Later, however, she at last masters her feelings and sends Deronda a letter, ironically on his wedding day, informing him that his presence in her life has made her a better person.

Gwendolen and Deronda represent mimetic inverses of each other. He repudiates life among the upper classes, embracing his exile heritage, and she begins an exile from self-fulfillment, repudiating her most basic human instincts in order to secure her place in the upper classes. Gwendolen manages to remain a sympathetic character, however; victimized due to her gender, she must accommodate herself to limited options. Such limitations cause her great suffering but also promote her final heroic epiphany as she moves beyond her bitterness to accept Deronda's rejection, yet still acknowledge his value. Deronda, on the other hand, possesses a sacrificial nature that many critics find part of a too-perfect character. The events of the plot prepare him to accept and embrace his Jewish identity, so he exhibits little heroism in that act. He could reject his identity and hide the evidence to secure his elevated position in the English CLASS STRUCTURE, but he never shows any inclination to do so.

Some critics also indict the novel as too intellectually based. Unlike with her previous novels, Eliot had no memories or experiences on which to base her plot and characters, resulting in what some declare a colorless novel. Those who appreciate the novel, however, note that Eliot unifies her dissimilar stories through carefully crafted parallels, inversions, recurring images, character motivations, and plot developments; Eliot herself proclaimed that themes, images and symbols interconnected the "Jewish story" and the traditional tale of marital machinations. The novel's supporters also claim that Eliot executed a superb interrogation of 19th-century English assumptions about nation, class, race, religion, and gender. As part of that era, they write, she automatically identifies with those assumptions and can invest more than her intellect in plot development. While perhaps her least critically successful novel, *Daniel Deronda* remains popular. Modern readers find of special interest the prophetic nature of the story, as the novel predates the rise of Zionism by some two decades.

BIBLIOGRAPHY

Caron, James. "The Rhetoric of Magic in *Daniel Deronda*." *Studies in the Novel* 15, no. 1 (1983): 1–9.

Gray, Beryl. *George Eliot and Music*. New York: St. Martin's Press, 1989.

Irwin, Jane, ed. *George Eliot's* Daniel Deronda *Notebooks*. New York: Cambridge University Press, 1996.

Nurbhai, Saleel, and K. M. Newton. *George Eliot, Judaism, and the Novels: Jewish Myth and Mysticism*. New York: Palgrave, 2002.

Perkin, J. Russell. *A Reception-History of George Eliot's Fiction*. Rochester, N.Y.: University of Rochester Press, 1990.

Semmel, Bernard. *George Eliot and the Politics of National Inheritance*. New York: Oxford University Press, 1994.

Shalvi, Alice, ed. *Daniel Deronda: A Centenary Symposium*. Jerusalem: Jerusalem Academic Press, 1976.

DARWIN, CHARLES (1809–1882)

Charles Darwin was born on February 12, 1809, at Shrewsbury, England, into an intellectual environment that greatly affected his childhood. His father, Robert Darwin, was an accomplished physician famous for his powers of observation, while Darwin's grandfather, Erasmus Darwin, had written the well-known *Zoonomia, or, the Laws of Organic Life* (1794–96). However, Darwin did not prove to be an exceptional student. He showed interests in many areas, including botany, zoology, and geology, and had inherited his father's acute powers of observation, but seemed unable to focus in any one area as his education required.

The classical tract of study at Shrewsbury and Darwin's later medical training at Edinburgh University did not rouse his interests. In 1827, he registered at Christ's College to take a B.A. degree preparing him for church service and became a friend of James Henslow, a professor of botany. Henslow recognized Darwin's intellectual potential, as others had not. Encouraged by Henslow to expand his general scientific knowledge, Darwin decided to join the crew of the *Beagle* (1831–36) as its naturalist. That experience would prove vital to his intellectual life and to the development of theories of evolution.

The published result of Darwin's five-year observation of nature, *Journal of Researches into the Geology and Natural History of the Various Countries Visited by HMS Beagle* (1839), revolutionized ideas regarding natural science. In a readable form, he presented theories regarding the interconnected nature of all living organisms, an idea that threatened a public long content to view humans as the only important entity on earth. He wrote that after reading "for amusement 'Malthus on Population,'" he formulated the idea for which his study and reading had prepared him, that under favorable circumstances, "variations would tend to be preserved, and unfavorable ones to be destroyed."

Darwin did not publish his invaluable *On the Origin of Species* until 1859, fully knowledgeable of the disturbing effect of its cultural and religious implications. He assembled his theories and evidence quickly after receiving a manuscript from A. R. Wallace that contained a statement regarding a theory of the origin of species that matched Darwin's own. He included voluminous support of his claims, which displaced man as the center of natural order, undermining the creationist view of humanity as it directly contradicted the Genesis story of God's creation of Adam and Eve. His book also contributed to the ongoing conflict over slavery in its discussion of the conflicts between indigenous Indians and the Spaniards who sought to colonize them. ANTI-SLAVERY factions chose him as a champion, while others saw his theories as critical of England's own imperialistic activities. Response against his theories included Charles KINGSLEY's novel *The WATER BABIES* (1863). His later works would continue his focus on the interconnectedness of all living organisms, including *The Descent of Man and Selection in Relation to Sex* (1871) and *The Expression of the Emotions in Man and Animals* (1872). One offshoot of Darwin's theories was "Social Darwinism," which also focused on theories of Herbert Spencer. It postulated the survival capabilities

of an organism as related more to moral concepts of fitness, powered by mental acuities, than environmental causes. This idea contributed to a hierarchical order in society resulting from conflict in which the strong would eagerly sacrifice the weak to their desire for power. Many writers responded to the various concepts of Darwin's theories, including George ELIOT, Samuel BUTLER, Thomas HARDY, and Joseph CONRAD. An introductory note to the 1909 edition, celebrating the centennial anniversary of Darwin's birth and the 50th birthday of *Origin of Species*, described Darwin's "disinterestedness," "modesty," and "absolute fairness" as "proof of the importance of character in intellectual labor." Virginia Woolf, George Bernard Shaw, H. G. WELLS, and others later analyzed Darwin's writings as literature. In addition to its profound effect on scientific and social theory, Darwin's work also affected the genre of SCIENCE FICTION, evident in work by Isaac Asimov, Stanislaw Lem, and others.

BIBLIOGRAPHY

Bowler, Peter J. *Charles Darwin: The Man and His Influence.* New York: Cambridge University Press, 1996.

Eliot Charles. W., LL.D. Introduction to *The Origin of Species by Charles Darwin.* New York: P. F. Collier & Son, 1909.

Howard, Jonathan. *Darwin: A Very Short Introduction.* New York: Oxford University Press, 2001.

Nardo, Don, ed. *Charles Darwin.* San Diego, Calif.: Greenhaven Press, 2000.

DAUGHTERS OF DANAUS MONA CAIRD (1894)

Mona CAIRD revealed her strong feminist leanings in all her writings, both fiction and nonfiction. Her 1894 novel, *Daughters of Danaus*, contained all the themes she stressed in her essays, including a need for female independence, both physical and emotional, and the related idea that not all women possess a natural desire to produce and raise children. She bases her revealing title on a Greek myth in which 50 daughters of Danaus marry simultaneously, and 49 of the wives slaughter their husbands on their wedding night to regain their freedom. Through her protagonist, Hadria Fullerton/Temperley, Caird also demonstrates the ways women contribute to their own oppression, as well as to that of other women. FEMINIST

CRITICS find of great interest Caird's understanding of the true tragedy underlying her novel and society, that women internalized society's dictates and so proved their own worst enemies.

Born to a bitter mother who likely should never have had children, Hadria bears the brunt of her mother's disappointments and expectations. At first Hadria shares her conflict with her mother with an older sister, Algitha. Mrs. Fullerton demands that both young women lead conventional lives, taking husbands and producing children. Caird emphasizes that her brothers are not challenged in the same way, but instead allowed to live as they choose. Algitha rebels and moves out to work with London's poor, leaving Hadria to shoulder the mother/daughter conflict. Although she longs to develop her musical talents, Hadria instead bows to her mother's pressure and marries a man she does not love. She produces two sons and lives a depressed existence, with several attempts at escape failing. Gaining little satisfaction from her sons, she adopts the orphaned daughter of a single mother named Martha and moves with the girl to Paris.

Far from living an idyllic life, Hadria feels guilt over her relationship with her mother and uses Martha as a pawn in a game to "prove" her independence. Therefore, she undercuts efforts at self-sufficiency and hurts Martha as much as Mrs. Fullerton has hurt her. In addition, a surrogate mother figure, a writer named Valeria du Prel, at first inspires Hadria, representing the free artistic personality Hadria longs to be. However, Valeria eventually confuses Hadria when she expresses regrets over never having married and had a family. She also insults Hadria by writing a story about a protagonist named Caterina, modeled on Hadria, who leaves her husband to live independently of men, but then allows herself to be seduced. Valeria confuses Hadria with the fictional Caterina and only feels true sympathy for Hadria when she begins having an affair, as Caterina had.

When Mrs. Fullerton becomes ill, Hadria returns home, ending her bid for freedom. Bored with country living and caring for her mother, Hadria has her affair, then tries to end the relationship, enraging her lover. For the sake of revenge, the lover declares his paternal rights for Martha. Rather than escape her mother's

influence, Hadria mirrors her mother's miserable failure at life, even manipulating her own daughter. Her hopes that a "chosen" child, in contrast to her natural children, would help her find her motherly instincts represents a big part of her failure. Even Algitha, the single female symbolizing independence, cannot escape her guilt regarding her mother. Algitha appears to balance Hadria's submission to duty through her own resistance, but only escapes her mother's tyranny due to Hadria's self-sacrifice. Thus, Algitha completes the circle of women using women, not better to understand one another and themselves, but to support society's gender expectations. The "ethic of responsibility" traps Hadria a second time as she stays on to care for her mother.

Caird prefigured many later feminists and psychologists by suggesting that a woman cannot properly care for another unless she can value herself. *Daughters of Danaus* makes the clear claim that self-sacrifice generally results in the sacrifice of mental and emotional health to duty. Hadria at one point thinks how much better off she would have been had her mother simply left the family. Instead, Mrs. Fullerton endured an unendurable situation, taking advantage of her daughter in the process.

The novel remains resonant with feminist critics who resuscitated Caird's works in the late 20th century. *Daughters of Danaus* is available in print as well as in electronic text form.

BIBLIOGRAPHY

Gullette, Margaret Morganroth. Afterword to *The Daughter of Danaus,* by Mona Caird. New York: The Feminist Press, 1989, 493–534.

Heilmann, Ann. "Mona Caird: wild woman, new woman, and early radical feminist critic of marriage and motherhood," *Women's History Review* 5, no. 1 (1996): 67–95.

DAVID COPPERFIELD CHARLES DICKENS (1850)

In his novel *David Copperfield,* Charles DICKENS produced his own favorite work and the favorite of many of his readers. He had honed his style through previous novels, and *David Copperfield* reflects his mature skill, partially accounting for the novel's enduring popularity. In addition, the main character breathes a special life into the novel through first-person point-of-view narration, thanks to a suggestion by Dickens's friend and biographer John Forster. David's perspective delivers naive honesty to the novel's early narrative, something lacking in Dickens's previous books. The novel's autobiographical aspects also add a sincerity and emotional strength to the narrative, which endears its main character to readers. Dickens based Mr. and Mrs. Micawber on his own parents, with Micawber's stint in debtors' prison mirroring that of John Dickens. The Micawbers are generally considered the epitome of Dickens's comic characters by virtue of their vitality, seen in Mr. Micawber's imagination and Mrs. Micawber's awareness of her life's tragic-comedic dimensions. Through the novel, Dickens adopts an ironic attitude toward his parents, who, although unable to make a stable life for their family, remained interesting figures for whom he had more compassion as he matured. David's experience in the wine warehouse exactly matches Dickens's in a blacking warehouse pasting labels on bottles, in an attempt to support his family. David works as a court reporter for a time, as did Dickens, who, like David, also served as a clerk in a law office. Dickens's first love has been described as a frivolous girl, much like David's first wife, the beautiful but simple Dora Spenlow.

The story appeared in installments between May of 1849 and November of 1850 as *The Personal History, Experience and Observations of David Copperfield the Younger, of Blunderstone Rookery, Which He Never Meant to Be Published on Any Account.* It received immediate positive criticism. William Makepeace THACKERAY famously declared on May 4, 1849, after reading the first installment, "Bravo, Dickens," and a piece in the June 1870 edition of *BLACKWOOD'S EDINBURGH MAGAZINE* declared *David Copperfield* the Dickens novel in which readers would take the most satisfaction. The novel never lost its popular status both as a novel read for pleasure and studied academically, and in multiple theatrical and screen versions. In the 20th century, it became available in electronic text.

The story begins with David's statement, "Whether I shall turn out to be the hero of my own life [. . .] these pages must show." His desire to tell the truth and reflect the life he considers lived in accordance with an ethical code immediately commends him to the reader. What follows is the typical parade of Dickensian characters, all of whom have an effect on the narrator/protagonist. Prior to David's birth, his mother was visited by his eccentric Great Aunt Betsey Trotwood, who had loved David's father but refused to see him following his marriage to David's mother, a woman she labeled "a wax doll." She declares that she expects the baby will be a girl, and when David is born, she becomes disgusted and stomps out of the house, "like a discontented fairy," never to return.

Raised for his first few years by his widowed mother with the help of his loving nurse, Peggotty, David enjoys a happy childhood. One important episode in that early contentment involves David's visit to the home of Peggotty and her brother, Mr. Peggotty, who live in the hulk of an old ship near the ocean. The family also includes Ham and Little Em'ly, both orphans and relatives that the Peggottys take in to raise. David falls in love with Em'ly, although it soon becomes clear that Ham intends to marry her. When Em'ly plays a risky stunt, balancing on a timber over the ocean and commenting on the death of her family members at sea, Dickens warns the reader through foreshadowing that death at sea for someone looms in Em'ly's future.

David's brief period of happiness concludes when his mother marries his cruel stepfather, Mr. Murdstone, his symbolic name suggesting a combination of murder and stone, who brings his equally cruel sister to live at David's house. After abusing David, Murdstone decides to send him to Salem House Academy, operated by another bully, headmaster Creakle. David's experiences there are not all negative, as he becomes friends with the older James Steerforth, a young man whose spirit David finds alluring. He also finds a friend in the less colorful but steady student, Tommy Traddles. David's mother dies, her spirit murdered by her husband and sister-in-law, causing David profound grief when he receives the news on his 10th birthday. Murdstone has him dismissed from school and sent to work in a wine warehouse. The Micawber family with whom he boards provides the only light in his dark existence. Profligate to a fault, Mr. Wilkins Micawber nevertheless cheers David with his kind nature, and

David becomes a favorite. Micawber's financial situation becomes so grave that he faces debtors' prison.

Even the cheer of the Micawbers cannot improve the horrible work conditions of the warehouse, and in desperation, David sets out to Dover to find his Aunt Betsey. After several adventures, he arrives at Betsey's house and soon convinces her to allow him to stay. She contacts Mr. Murdstone against David's wishes, and he arrives to testify against David's character, but angers Aunt Betsey by driving his donkey across her front yard. She astounds him by delivering a sermon against his mistreatment of David's mother, and then asks David whether he wants to return home. He chooses to remain with her, and she fondly refers to him as "Trot," short for her own surname, and his life greatly improves as his aunt formally adopts him. He enjoys school at Dr. Strong's in Canterbury, living there with his aunt's lawyer, Mr. Wickfield, who consumes what seems to David an excess of wine. He meets Wickfield's daughter, Agnes, and one of the most famous fictional villains, Wickfield's sickly, pale law clerk, Uriah Heep. Ingratiating and pandering, Uriah constantly declares himself "too umble" (meaning "humble") to participate in activities with those better than he, a declaration that serves as part of his manipulating front. He horrifies David with a clammy handshake David describes as "as ghostly to the touch as to the sight," adding that he had to rub his hand "to warm it, *and to rub his off.*" The scene foreshadows Uriah's "touching" all those important to David with financial and emotional ruin.

David develops an easy friendship with Agnes, admitting to himself that although he loves Em'ly, Agnes provides a peace for which he longs. Wickfield gradually seems to lose control of his law practice and his life, and Agnes eventually turns to David for help. Steerforth resurfaces and joins David in a visit to the Pegottys, where he meets and decides he must possess Em'ly, although she has officially become engaged to Ham. David also learns that a mysterious man has been bothering Aunt Betsey, and that Micawber had made the acquaintance of Heep, who favorably impressed Micawber.

David decides to serve as a proctor in Doctor's Commons for the law firm of Spenlow and Jorkins. He enjoys the post, but is lonely and wants to see Steer-forth again. He enjoys a night out with friends, but embarrasses himself before Agnes by making a drunken public appearance. This humorous scene helps to round David's character, exposing a weakness, but making light of an incident that caused no one any damage. Embarrassed the next day, David wonders how to repair his reputation with Agnes. He understands that she does not bear a grudge when he receives her note, asking him to visit. Grateful for her forgiveness, David refers to Agnes as his "good angel." That imagery promotes Agnes as a figure who will always serve David in a protective manner, regardless of his actions.

Agnes expresses concern about her father and Heep's manipulative ways, and the news that he will soon become a partner in the firm shocks David. However, even more shocking to him is Agnes's warning that Steerforth is David's "bad angel." She knows of his reputation for promoting a false sense of goodwill. David does not believe her, but remains troubled by the warning. Dickens increases foreshadowing of a dark end for Steerforth when his image in David's mind "darkens." When David attends a party the next day, Heep haunts the room. Dickens's choice of terms, such as "writhe" and "snaky undulations" to describe Heep's movements, leave no doubt as to his suspicious character. However, David is distracted when he meets his old classmate, Traddles. Traddles becomes the focus of one of the many subplots that Dickens weaves into the main story. His engagement to marry delights David, as does David's discovery that he works at a publishing firm and boards with Micawber, who is at work in the "corn business" while waiting for something to "turn up." David also continues contact with Steerforth, whose mysterious behavior heightens David's suspicions about his one-time mentor. David learns that Steerforth has been secretly courting Em'ly, and when they run away, devastating the Peggottys and especially breaking the kind Ham's heart, David feels guilty for having introduced Steerforth to the family.

As David continues to work hard, he falls in love with Spenlow's pretty but nonintellectual daughter Dora. Agnes tries gently to reveal Dora's shortcomings to David, as does his Aunt Betsey, who, due to the loss of her income, which she blames on Wickfield, has moved in with David. David also discovers from Traddles that Micawber has changed his name to Mortimer and assumed a disguise in order to escape his creditors. In the middle of trying to help others with their problems, David marries Dora following her father's death. Too late, he discovers he has a child bride, one incapable of caring for either herself or her household. Despite her helplessness and tendency to overspend David's small income, David remains devoted to Dora, who seems to hold her dog Jip in higher esteem than her husband. Aunt Betsey refuses to explain housekeeping responsibilities to Dora, gently explaining to David that she lacks the capacity to understand. David embarks on a writing career, with which Dora helps by holding the pen for him. During this time, Wickfield appears to sink into madness, as Heep begins to take control of his practice and makes clear his intention to marry Agnes, who has become close friends with Aunt Betsey.

As the rising action advances, Aunt Betsey stuns David by revealing her mysterious visitor is her husband, a man she has not lived with for some years due to his gambling. Even Aunt Betsey has her faults, as she continues to support her immoral husband. A year and a half after his marriage, David enjoys the positive reception of his first novel, and delights in the news of Dora's pregnancy. He hopes the child will bring stability to a marriage that has remained rocky, not due to a lack of love, but to the constant household disorganization. David thinks of Dora and her nickname, used even by Aunt Betsey, of "Blossom," and admits that his blossom seems to have "withered in its bloom upon the tree!" This foreshadows the deaths of both the baby and Dora. David takes comfort in his love for his aunt and his friendship with Agnes. He becomes immediately involved with Micawber, who now works for Heep and has discovered his villainous qualities; he feels that he can reveal Heep's fraudulent activity and asks for David's and Tommy Traddle's help. In addition, Em'ly is discovered in London and reunited with her aunt and uncle. A comic scene follows in Wickfield's office, now Heep's, when Micawber reveals the truth about him. He will go to prison, and his victims, including Aunt Betsey, will receive refunds of a portion of their losses, and Agnes no longer has to worry about marrying the despicable Heep. Micawber sees an opportunity to begin a new life in Australia, where Mr. Peggotty intends to move with the disgraced Em'ly, and Aunt Betsey's wayward husband dies, freeing her of that burden.

More tragedy must strike before Dickens can conclude his plot. In a storm at seaside, Ham dies in an effort to rescue Steerforth, and David realizes he still loved his friend, despite his weaknesses. He decides to go abroad in an attempt to begin a new life. Gone for several years as he works through his guilt, he publishes and becomes a well-known fiction writer. Agnes continues a correspondence with David, and the two at last marry. In a final statement 10 years following his marriage, David fills in details of the surviving characters for readers and declares himself nothing without the presence of Agnes, whom he compares to "a heavenly light."

David Copperfield did not crusade against as many issues or with the ferocity that Dickens's previous novels had. Rather, Dickens focuses on social prejudice and opportunism, two factors that his own family had confronted, mirrored particularly in the situation of Micawber, whose able mind, crippled by a lack of practicality, dooms him. Dickens writes in his preface to later editions of *David Copperfield* that the novel so interested him that he regretted at its conclusion "separation from many companions." When he confesses his sorrow at having to lay down his pen "at the close of a two-years' imaginative task," and describes his feeling of "dismissing some portion of himself into the shadowy world," readers centuries later can relate to the regret of concluding the reading of a near-perfect novel, which likely represented Dickens's own life history.

BIBLIOGRAPHY
Bush, Douglas. "A Note on Dickens' Humor." *From Jane Austen to Joseph Conrad.* Edited by Robert C. Rathburn and Martin Steinmann, Jr. Minneapolis: University of Minnesota Press, 1958, 82–91.

DEFOE, DANIEL (ca. 1660–1731)

Considered by many the father of the English novel, Daniel Defoe was undoubtedly one of the most important novelists of the early 18th century. As a product of the Age of Reason, he supported empirical thought, such as that proposed by Isaac Newton in the sciences and John Locke in economics. He rejected all fanaticism and extremes in religion and politics, a fact reflected in his voluminous writings. With a record of more than 500 published works, Defoe claims title to the most prolific English-language writer.

Born to James and Alice Foe, Daniel adopted Defoe as a last name for unknown reasons, sometime between the late 1690s and the early 1700s. His father was a butcher who made clear his position as a Dissenter, one who protested religious intolerance on the part of the Anglican Church. Apparently involved in local political activities, James Foe enrolled his son in Stoke Newington Academy, a Dissenters' school where he eventually studied for the ministry. Although he decided against the calling, Defoe remained a lifelong Presbyterian. He became a small merchant and trader, traveling widely on the Continent. He married Mary Tuffley in 1683 and settled with her at Cornhill near London, where he worked as a wholesale hosiery merchant.

Defoe took part in the Monmouth rebellion in 1685, but briefly served in the army for William of Orange (William II) in 1688, all the while trying to maintain his business activities. Such switching of allegiance gained him the reputation of a political expedient. He went bankrupt in 1692 with debts of the then extraordinary sum of £17,000 and spent a short period in debtor's prison. Defoe developed a number of business schemes, but he lacked planning and follow-through skills. However, his first writings reflected his mercantile theories and experiences. He published *Essay on Projects* in 1697 but earned little money from it. In 1700, he attempted to start a tile factory in Tilbury and then found success with *The True Born Englishman* (1701), a work of verse SATIRE supporting William of Orange. With a style marked by irony and a deft impersonation of others, Defoe gained a staunch readership; by 1750 *Englishman* enjoyed its 50th printing.

In 1702, Defoe published *The Shortest Way with the Dissenter,* which ironically defended Anglican oppression, pretending to support the execution of all Dissenters. His work resembled the approach of that of his contemporary, Jonathan SWIFT, whose *Modest Proposal* suggesting the slaughter for meat of Irish children would stand as the epitome of political satire.

Shortest Way led to Defoe's arrest and conviction for sedition; as punishment, he stood in pillory three times and spent five months in Newgate Prison, becoming a hero to the common working man. He used his time in prison to write a mock ode titled *Hymn to the Pillory* (1703). Robert Harley, earl of Oxford, helped secure his release.

While Defoe's sympathies remained largely Whig, his release through the aid of the Tory Harley led him to spend the next decade in Harley's employ as a political spy and an agent in Scotland. A speaker of six languages, Defoe represented the ultimate in the self-educated man. During this time he founded, published, and wrote *The Review,* a thrice-weekly paper published until 1713 that supported Harley's interests. One of the first to recognize the value of propaganda, Harley also recognized Defoe's talent. Defoe expressed his anti-Jacobite sentiments in his 1712 *Reasons against the Succession of the House of Hanover,* which landed him in prison again, this time for treasonable publication. Following the demise of *The Review,* Defoe wrote for a trade journal, *Mercator,* and supported free trade in his *A General History of Trade* (1714). That same year Queen Anne died, and the Whigs ascended to power. Due to his shifting Whig-Tory support and opinions, Defoe found himself without a party. By 1715, he found employment as an agent for Lord Townshend, Whig secretary of state, a position that protected him against libel charges leveled by various political figures.

By 1720, Defoe no longer wrote political controversy. He published several works of historical interest and was almost 60 years old when he began the prolific novel-writing career for which he would become the most famous. ROBINSON CRUSOE, the first of a series of important novels, appeared in 1719. *Crusoe* sold reasonably well, enjoying several editions. Some see the book as an ALLEGORY of Defoe's life, because Robinson Crusoe represents the ultimate Age of Reason product, focused on money and life's practical aspects, even at the moment of his shipwreck. Much of the novel's early charm involves Crusoe's categorization of the goods he recovers from the wreck. The book draws on Defoe's knowledge of the bourgeoisie, commerce, rogues and villains, as well as his experiences with solitude and captivity.

Defoe also published the sequel to *Crusoe, Further Adventures of Robinson Crusoe,* in 1719. He continued producing astounding work with the *Life, Adventures and Piracies of Captain Singleton* (1720), *The Fortunes and Misfortunes of the Famous MOLL FLANDERS* (1722), *Colonel Jack* (1722), *A JOURNAL OF THE PLAGUE YEAR* (1722), and *ROXANA* (1724), among others. Defoe also produced essays and treatises such as *The Great Law of Subordination Considered* (1724), which examined the treatment of servants, and *The Complete English Tradesman* (1726), which considered the movement of the merchant class into honorable society.

When Defoe died on April 26, 1731, he left a written legacy that changed the way readers viewed the English word. His plain-style approach, in contrast with the more elaborate expressions of his contemporaries, may account for his popularity with the 18th-century reading public. Defoe did not sign many of his works, and his name is hardly mentioned by the two most immediately important writers in the novel's development, Henry FIELDING and Samuel RICHARDSON. He did not focus on or discuss the novel genre, as Fielding would, nor did he acknowledge his work as related to novels, which may account for a lack of focus by his readers on his position in its development. While collected editions of works by Fielding, Richardson, and Tobias SMOLLETT all appeared in the 18th century, no such collections or any biographical work on Defoe would be issued until the 19th century.

Nevertheless, Defoe's production of more than 200 pamphlets at a time when such printings actually had an effect on their audience caused 18th-century lay readers to embrace him in a way not enjoyed by more formal satirists, such as Swift. His themes of man's survival in a structured society, self-sufficiency, and material endeavors support Defoe's emphasis on the concrete and all things observable, a crucial step in the novel's development. With *Robinson Crusoe,* readers enjoyed the first fiction that had nothing in mind other than creating a realistic picture of everyday life, the quotidian. Like many later 18th-century novels, Defoe's first important work bore the name of its main character, suggesting a true account of an individual, and thus a departure from the fantastic romances previously labeled novels. Whether he puzzled over his place in the developing novel tradition, and incorporated what would come to be known as REALISM into fiction in a conscious attempt to advance the genre, is unknown. While many critics support Defoe's position as the first English novelist, others counter by noting that his rational work lacks the character exploration necessary to the fully developed novel.

BIBLIOGRAPHY

Backscheider, Paula. *Daniel Defoe: His Life.* Baltimore: Johns Hopkins University Press, 1989.

Bloom, Harold, ed. *Daniel Defoe.* New York: Chelsea House, 1987.

Brown, Homer. "The Institution of the English Novel: Defoe's Contribution." *Novel: A Forum on Fiction* 29.3 (Spring 1996): 299–319.

Daniel Defoe: A Collection of Critical Essays. Edited by Max Byrd. Englewood Cliffs, N.J.: Prentice Hall, 1976.

Novak, Maximillian E. *Daniel Defoe, Master of Fictions: His Life and Ideas.* Oxford: Oxford University Press, 2001.

Rogers, Pat. *Defoe: The Critical Heritage.* Boston: Routledge and Kegan Paul, 1972.

DEMOS: A STORY OF ENGLISH SOCIALISM GEORGE GISSING (1886)

Reflective of his general focus on hard work as an anecdote to failure and poverty, George GISSING's *Demos: A Story of English Socialism* blasts socialism as an ideal never to be realized, due to the greed of its leaders. He ennobles his working-class characters, particularly females, who resign themselves to physical labor for their support. One character remarks, "when women are educated, they will take the world as it is and decline to live on illusions," a direct reference to socialistic idealism. For organizers of political movements supposedly meant to relieve abuses against workers, Gissing shows marked contempt. Examples, like his characters Richard Mutimer and Daniel Dabbs, abandon their ideals to embrace capitalism, and thus "sell out" fellow workers. Mutimer establishes a so-called model community, a worker's UTOPIA based on the precepts of Robert Owen, a socialist and philanthropist who, at the age of 19, became the wealthy owner of cotton-spinning mills in Manchester. Owen had himself established such a model community in Manchester and another in the United States, both of which eventually failed. The factual background foreshadows the failure of the novel's community as well.

Set in an idyllic valley below the scenic Stanbury Hill, the community honors the Eldons, original owners of Wanley Manor, which sits at the top of the hill over the town. Although the manor has been purchased by Mr. Mutimer, as a relative of the family, he allows the widow Eldon and her two children, now reduced to near-poverty, to remain in the mansion, where the son, Hubert, matures. The respectable Walthams live in a smaller house on the side of the hill, and Adela Waltham eventually falls in love with Hubert, four years older than her, although others, including her brother, think him presumptuous and assuming. As the presumed heir to Mr. Mutimer's fortune, he travels to London for a time, and rumors of his ruthless spending and womanizing reach the town. Gissing's plot involves the loss and recovery of Mutimer's will, suspected to pass on his fortune to Hubert Eldon. The loss renders Hubert penniless, something his mother does not regret, as she believes Hubert corrupt and urges him to follow the example of old Mr. Mutimer: "He was without education; his ideas of truth and goodness he had to find in his own heart." Her comment promotes Gissing's view of the common worker who can, as he did, increase his lot in life through hard work. The complicated plot develops with other of Mutimer's relatives taking control of the ironworks. Richard Mutimer, the socialist who opens the ironworks with great plans for the local workers, abandons his wife to marry Adela. In the remaining plot, Mutimer loses his investment, the workers lose their jobs, they attack Mutimer, and he dies. The elder Mr. Mutimer's will is restored, allowing Hubert to inherit the Mutimer fortune. Adela, now a widow, loves Hubert but will not express her passion, feeling he only cares about her due to the business matters caused by his inheritance; he settles some of the Mutimer fortune on her. The two do unite by the end of the story, supporting Gissing's suggestion that the hard-work philosophy often skips a generation in a family, settling upon the third generation. Although

the ironworks is gone, a beautiful valley setting is symbolically restored, and a love affair realized.

Gissing published his bitter portrayal of socialism during a time of socialist agitation in 1886, when proletarian rioters supposedly looted London's West End. The fortunate timing resulted in excellent sales for Gissing, as *Demos* earned more than his previous works.

BIBLIOGRAPHY
Poole, Adrian. *Gissing in Context*. Totowa, N.J.: Rowman and Littlefield, 1975.

DETECTIVE FICTION

English detective fiction developed over decades, with the modern version, emphasizing the application of deductive logic to a crime as the reader's major focus, appearing during the second half of the 19th century. It resulted partly from the momentum toward realistic fiction (REALISM) seen in the mid-1800s. In other languages, stories in which most of the narrative focused on the logical investigation of clues leading to a revelation had appeared as early as the 17th century. In 1719, the chevalier de Mailly translated a popular Italian tale as his *Les voyage et adventures des trois princes de Sarendip*, in which three princes discuss how they determined through deductive reasoning that a camel they never directly observed is blind, lame, and missing a tooth. The story appeared in England as *The Travels and Adventures of Three Princes of Sarendip* (1722). Additional French writers, including Voltaire (François-Marie Arouet), Honoré Balzac, and Alexandre Dumas wrote tales featuring mysteries solved through deduction. In England, GOTHIC novels by such authors as Ann RADCLIFFE, as well as William GODWIN's *The Adventures of CALEB WILLIAMS* (1794), include characters that operate as amateur detectives, but the works do not focus exclusively on crimes. A vital step in the development of detective fiction occurred with the publication of *Memoirs* (1828) by the French ex-criminal François-Eugène Vidocq. He described his investigative methods as the head of Paris's detective bureau, Sûreté. In the 1840s, American writer Edgar Allan Poe introduced the first famous detective, C. Auguste Dupin, into his short stories, and the subgenre gelled into its present form. Charles DICKENS introduced mystery aspects into his novel BLEAK HOUSE (1853), which featured Inspector Bucket, the first English fictional detective.

Wilkie COLLINS's *The MOONSTONE* (1868) became the first English novel to feature an investigator, modeled after a real inspector of Collins's acquaintance, as a main character. Celebrated as the first true English detective novel, it nevertheless contained the crime investigation within a larger narrative. Collins was likely influenced by the supernatural mystery fiction of Irish author Joseph Sheridan LE FANU, who published a series of stories for the *Dublin University Magazine.* Just as Le Fanu exhibited some psychopathic symptoms that influenced his writing, Collins's immersion into the opium and laudanum cultures gave *The Moonstone* an unearthly, mystical quality, supported by its mysterious East Indian characters. Among Collins's readers was Sir Arthur Conan DOYLE, whose detective, Sherlock Holmes, became the most famous detective of short fiction. First introduced in "A Study in Scarlet" for *Breton's Christmas Annual* (1887), Holmes took on a life of his own that would continue beyond Doyle's death.

Detective stories lent themselves to a shortened form in which the reader's attention could be easily held by the protagonist's step-by-step deductive investigation. Many authors followed Doyle's lead, including Arthur Morrison with his Investigator Hewitt and Baroness Orczy, who introduced Sir Percy Blakeney in his exploits as *The Scarlet Pimpernel,* first featured in 1902. After detective fiction gained popularity, novel-length versions became more popular, leading to the guaranteed propagation of the form by prolific detective novelists such as Agatha Christie in the 20th century.

BIBLIOGRAPHY

Eames, Hugh. *Sleuths, Inc.: Studies of Problem Solvers, Doyle, Simenon, Hammett, Ambler, Chandler.* Philadelphia: Lippincott, 1978.

Stevenson, Lionel. *The English Novel: A Panorama.* Boston: Houghton Mifflin, 1960.

Thoms, Peter. *Detection and Its Designs: Narrative and Power in Nineteenth-Century Detective Fiction.* Athens: Ohio University Press, 1998.

DIANA OF THE CROSSWAYS GEORGE MEREDITH (1885)

When George MEREDITH published his 1885 novel, *Diana of the Crossways,* women readers welcomed his heroine as representative of recent social reforms. The novel reflects its era's obsessive interest in the breakdown of standards, which had been part of a now waning traditional religious practice. Religious dogma had given way to new legal, economic, and educational opportunities for women. The Marriage Act of 1858 introduced the possibility of divorce, while the Married Women's Property Act of 1882 granted women crucial financial rights. Decades of female SUFFRAGE efforts kept women and their social needs before the public, with voting rights for women almost included in the Reform Bill of 1884, following compulsory education for females instituted in 1870. New careers opened to women included medicine, which admitted females into practice in 1876. These events changed the traditional heroines of fiction. Whereas heroines of the past required males to rescue them through marriage, the more modern heroine achieved a modicum of fiscal and emotional independence on her own. Even the inconsistencies in Meredith's protagonist, Diana Merion, delighted critics, particularly later FEMINIST CRITICS, who viewed her as a more complete portrait of a heroine than Meredith had formerly produced.

The novel became Meredith's most popular to date, as he used a new approach to SILVER-FORK FICTION, combining it with a ROMAN À CLEF. Meredith adopted high society's true stories of Lord Melbourne, Sidney Herbert, John Delane, and other well-known early Victorians as his plot. In a notorious political scandal from the 1860s, the Honorable Mrs. Norton took blame for revealing a crucial Cabinet secret told her by her lover to a *Times* editor, an action similar to Diana's well-intentioned error. Meredith's tale demonstrated that blunders committed by an otherwise clever woman resulted, not from inherent weakness, but due to the lack of a responsible educational system and instruction in social responsibility for females. While the facts of Meredith's novel are obviously drawn from real life, when Mrs. Norton's relations complained that Meredith had slandered her, he inserted a disclaimer in later editions, telling his audience the novel should be read as fiction.

The novel opens in Dublin, where the charming Diana Merion gains admirers at a ball to honor an Irish soldier, Lord Larrian. Much is made of her Irish background, reflected in her stunning beauty, although she has not yet reached the age of 20. As clever and witty as she is beautiful, Diana captivates everyone present, including the guest of honor, who becomes a devoted friend. Her older best friend, Lady Emma Dunstane, a semi-invalid, receives much of Diana's attentions. Thomas Redworth, a young Englishman neighbor to Crossways, Diana's home, also loves her, providing her with intellectual stimulation. A low-level government official, Redworth wants to propose marriage to Diana, but feels of insufficient financial means to support her. He successfully invests in the railroads, but when Diana reacts coolly to that news, praising the life of a soldier instead, Redworth still does not propose.

When Diana visits Emmy, Emmy's husband, Sir Lukin, is overcome by her beauty and makes advances, which Diana resists, and he instantly regrets. Disgusted by high society, she decides to marry her cousin, Augustus Warwick, a cold gentleman of leisure and 15 years her elder. Emmy is shocked by the match, but Diana explains that Warwick has agreed to allow her to keep Crossways forever. As foreshadowed, the marriage dissolves into disaster; Warwick accuses Diana of having an affair with her politician friend, Lord Dannisurgh, and then sues for divorce. Friends help Diana clear her name, but in the meantime, she becomes depressed and leaves society. With attentions from Emmy, Tom Redworth, Lord Larrian, and her faithful maid, Danvers, Diana works her way back into society, following a declaration of her innocence. Stuck in an unhappy marriage to Warwick, she lives separately from him in London, where she becomes a popular novelist.

Diana travels abroad, and in Italy meets Percy Dacier, a handsome and brilliant man of influence in Parliament. Although engaged to Miss Constance Asper, Dacier finds Diana intriguing, and his admiration grows when she fulfills the final request of Lord Dannisburgh and sits with his body. Their passion grows, and although Diana at first rejects him, she later consents to run away with Dacier. When she is called away to care for the suddenly ill Emmy and does not keep a rendezvous with Dacier, he gives up hope for their union. When they later meet, their passions have cooled, and a year passes with no interaction. However, when Dacier accepts an invitation to Diana's home, their friendship grows, and Diana's social salon helps further Dacier's career, to Diana's financial detriment. Facing ruin, she sells political information Dacier had confided to her to a journalist, not realizing its importance. Dacier reacts by deserting Diana to marry Constance Asper.

When Warwick dies in an accident, even the promise of her freedom cannot lift Diana's spirits. Determined to die, she refuses food, but Emmy rescues her, persuading her of the value of life. Diana recovers and at last agrees to marry the faithful Redworth.

Young female readers conceived in Diana a representative of their newly emancipated group, due to the spirit that allowed her to separate from an intolerable mate, take up a man's profession of writing, and flourish. Although they protested her selling her lover's confidence, Meredith again emphasized that society's marginalization of women left Diana's position unstable, despite her seeming triumphs.

BIBLIOGRAPHY

Bedford, Herbert. *The Heroines of George Meredith*. Port Washington, N.Y.: Kennicat Press, 1972.

Manos, Nikki Lee. Introduction to *Diana of the Crossways,* by George Meredith. Detroit: Wayne State University Press, 2001.

Roberts, Neil. *Meredith and the Novel*. New York: St. Martin's Press, 1997.

DICKENS, CHARLES (JOHN HUFFAM) (1812–1870)

The best-known novelist of his era, Charles Dickens was born at Portsmouth, England, to John Dickens and his wife, Elizabeth. Due to John's profligate lifestyle and irresponsible attitude toward his position as clerk in the Naval Office, procured for him by his mother, the family led a troubled existence, at first in London. When Dickens was five years old, the family moved to the shabby dockyard town of Chatham. From 1817 to 1821, a schoolmaster named William Giles encouraged the boy's obvious talent.

Dickens fed his voracious appetite for books with works by Tobias SMOLLETT and Henry FIELDING, along with tales by the Spanish writer Miguel Cervantes. When his father was transferred back to London, Dickens no longer had a mentor to encourage him and, while never physically abused by his self-absorbed parents, suffered from neglect. When John finally went to debtors' prison, Dickens, at age 12, had to work to support his parents and five siblings. He took a position in a boot-blacking factory under horrendous conditions, not fully known to his family and acquaintances until after his death, when his friend, John Forster, wrote his biography. The factory experience materialized in later novels, as did much of Dickens's early painful life.

Following his father's release from prison, Dickens attended school at Wellington House Academy. While hardly a top-ranked academic institution, it provided a welcome relief from physical labor and allowed Dickens to again stretch his imagination. After leaving Wellington in 1827, he served as office boy in a law firm where he mastered shorthand and assumed the duties of court reporter. Although he had hoped to act on the stage, Dickens pursued his writing duties, and in 1829, he fell in love with Maria Beadnell. Her family's low opinion of Dickens's position doomed the relationship.

By 1832, Dickens wrote for his uncle's publication, *The Mirror of Parliament,* and served as reporter for *The True Sun.* The following year, he wrote for the Liberal publication *The Morning Chronicle,* reporting on various political gatherings. He also produced short sketches for a number of journals, notably *The Monthly Magazine,* published by his friend George Hogarth. He attracted wide public attention with the publication of his first book, *Sketches by Boz* (1836–37), assuming a nickname he had given himself as a child. The novel CRANFORD (1853) by Elizabeth GASKELL later featured works by Boz as a favorite of one of its early characters, evidence of Dickens's influence on future readers and writers. His interest in drama had honed his skill for dialogue and helped him produce scenes of remarkable clarity, particularly as his style matured.

Dickens fell in love with Hogarth's attractive daughter Catherine and married her in April 1836. That same month, he began publication of *The Posthumous Papers of the Pickwick Club,* later better known as *The* PICKWICK PAPERS. At first an uncertain political SATIRE that produced only type characters, the fourth of the papers introduced a cockney handyman named Sam Weller who caught the reading public's fancy. Sales soared, and Dickens found permanent wealth and fame, as he produced more fully realized and sympathetic characters. He marked some characters with the absurd touches that would become a trademark of his fiction, influenced by his early reading of Cervantes's *Don Quixote* (1605 and 1615). Circulation of the papers exceeded 40,000, and people from all social levels began to quote their characters.

Dickens advanced his career with the publication of his first book-length works. Two wildly popular novels appeared first as serials, OLIVER TWIST (1837–39) and NICHOLAS NICKLEBY (1838–39). A periodical planned by Dickens, *Master Humphrey's Clock,* did not fare nearly as well as his books; it faced too much competition from other weekly publications and soon failed. However, Dickens did expand a story intended for *Master Humphrey's Clock* into another popular novel, *The* OLD CURIOSITY SHOP (1840–41). It introduced one of several famous Dickens child characters, Little Nell, who represented the patient heroism and kindliness of the poor. *Barnaby Rudge* (1841), a first venture into historical fiction, followed, and with those several novels, Dickens had barely begun his career.

Dickens had also served as editor of BENTLEY'S MISCELLANY since its conception in 1837, but by 1839 he ended his duties following a quarrel with the publishers. He moved his growing family to various residences, finally inhabiting a mansion on Devonshire Terrace, where he entertained budding authors, politicians, and spent his energies writing and rescuing his parents from several financial disasters. He traveled to Boston in 1842 and on to New York, Philadelphia, Baltimore, Washington, D.C., and Virginia, along with many other towns, all of which received him with great enthusiasm. Although he professed to enjoy America, his subsequent negative portrayal of Americans in *American Notes* (1842) and the novel MARTIN CHUZZLEWIT (1843–44) insulted many Americans. He produced one of many gems with *A Christmas Carol* in 1843, destined to become a classic in multiple languages. He lived the following year for a time in Italy, but returned to England in 1845, where he wrote and published *Pictures from Italy.* His rendition of Italians was far more positive than that of Americans.

During the 1840s, Dickens wrote a series of stories, including *The Chimes, The Cricket on the Hearth, The Battle of Life,* and *The Haunted Man,* which appeared in a single volume, along with *A Christmas Carol,* titled *Christmas Books* (1852). Further editing duties focused for a short time in 1846 on his own DAILY NEWS, which he left to found HOUSEHOLD WORDS and ALL THE YEAR ROUND. As a mature writer, Dickens wrote his next novel, DOMBEY AND SON (1846–48), followed by the beloved DAVID COPPERFIELD (1849–50), whose protagonist he claimed to be his favorite of all his characters. Additional publications in the 1850s included *A Child's History of England* (1851–53), BLEAK HOUSE (1852–53), HARD TIMES (1854), LITTLE DORRIT (1855–57), and *A TALE OF TWO CITIES* (1859). Much of his fiction focused on social injustices, such as the abuse of workers, overcrowded prisons, the abuse of children, and the general shameful effects of POVERTY, adding a reputation as a producer of THESIS FICTION to that of a realistic-fiction author. In addition to his book-length works, he continued to write short stories and plays.

In the middle of all this activity, Dickens indulged his affection for the theater and helped mount productions at Knebworth House and Rockingham Castle, where he occasionally acted and organized benefit performances for friends and acquaintances suffering financial problems. Always involved with various social-reform movements, he remained busy highlighting capital punishment, poverty, prostitution, and work-house laws. In the 1850s, Dickens fell in love with a young actress named Ellen Ternan, who influenced some of his later character development, and his relationship with Catherine, which had been turbulent for some time, worsened. He moved again, first to Tavistock and later, in 1857, to Gad's Hill in Kent, an area that he loved. He continued traveling by touring Switzerland and returning to Italy with novelist Wilkie COLLINS (1824–89), and by visiting France. His marriage ended, famously announced in an 1858 edition of *Household Words,* but his domestic problems did not

curtail his writing and speaking energies. He continued to travel, visiting the United States again in 1867, and presented many public readings upon his return to England. During the 1860s, Dickens continued to produce astounding novels, including GREAT EXPECTATIONS (1860–61), OUR MUTUAL FRIEND (1864–65), and an incomplete mystery, *The MYSTERY OF EDWIN DROOD,* left unfinished at his death in 1870.

Charles Dickens's influence on readers and writers from his own era, including William Makepeace THACKERAY (1811–63), Elizabeth GASKELL, and Benjamin DISRAELI (1804–81), and into the 21st century cannot be overestimated. All his works remain in constant production, have been translated for stage, television, and cinema, and appear as electronic texts.

BIBLIOGRAPHY
Schlicke, Paul. *The Oxford Reader's Companion to Dickens.* Oxford: Oxford University Press, 2000.

Smiley, Jane. *Charles Dickens.* New York: Viking, 2002.

Tillotson, Kathleen. *Novels of the Eighteen-Forties.* Oxford: London, 1965.

DICTIONARY OF THE ENGLISH LANGUAGE, A (1755)

Written by Samuel JOHNSON over a span of eight years and published in 1755, *The Dictionary of the English Language: In Which the Words are Deduced from Their Originals, and Illustrated in Their Different Significations by Examples from the Best Writers, To Which are Prefixed a History of the Language and an English Grammar* represented an enormous undertaking. Johnson approached potential patrons, including Lord Chesterfield, with whom he later feuded, for financial support, but Chesterfield gave him only £10. Johnson had little in the way of etymology to guide his choices; rather, he turned to the writings of Edmund Spenser and Sir Philip Sydney, both excellent examples of wordsmiths from the period Johnson considered the golden era of the use of English, the Renaissance. He used many quotations from classic works to illustrate the dictionary usage and support his own definitions. Johnson adopted as one goal the rejection of what he saw as the French encroachment on English, "Gallick structure and phraseology." He faithfully included colloquialisms and dialect, and attacked his task applying his own wide knowledge gained through voracious reading. His limitations produced a non-definitive work, but one crucial in the development of English-language dictionaries. Determined to produce a work equal to those comprehensive ones already produced in Italy and France, which introduced standardized spellings, Johnson worked on his project even as he produced several other works in order to support himself. While not the first English-language dictionary, his two volumes proved the most complete and established a standard. In the preface to the dictionary, he wrote, "I am not so lost in lexicography as to forget that words are the daughters of earth, and that things are the sons of heaven."

BIBLIOGRAPHY

Bate, Walter Jackson. *Samuel Johnson*. Boulder, Colo.: Counterpoint Press, 1998.

Boswell, James. *The Life of Samuel Johnson*. New York: Knopf, 1993.

DIDACTIC LITERATURE

Didactic literature, from the Greek *didakitkos,* or skillful in teaching, refers to literature that overtly demonstrates a truth or offers a lesson to readers. Not a subtle approach, didacticism delivers a specific and pointed message and was present in the earliest stories developed to teach moral behavior, such as fables and parables. Medieval ALLEGORY proved didactic in its forceful presentation of commentary on religious and ethical doctrine and became refined in Renaissance works such as Edmund Spenser's *The Fairie Queene* (1590 and 1596), a commentary on social conditions in 16th-century England, and John Bunyan's PILGRIM'S PROGRESS (1678 and 1684), in which an allegorical character named Everyman searched for spiritual fulfillment. Authors also might insert themselves into their own novels in a method termed authorial intervention, interrupting their narrative to speak directly to the reader for instructional purposes.

Didacticism remained long entrenched in stories for children, particularly with the rise of Puritanism and attempts to reform the Church of England from the 16th through the 17th centuries. Until the 18th century, all children's literature served to instruct. Following the French Revolution (1789–99), egalitarian principles spread to England, and children's literature grew less preachy, although writers still strove to teach a lesson. The French philosopher Jean-Jacques Rousseau (1712–78) theorized that children were not merely small adults but thinking beings whose mental and emotional needs should be considered separate and apart from those of adults. Through the end of the 18th century, English children's literature tended to feature all-knowing adult characters, which often interrupted action to deliver sermons to readers. Maria EDGEWORTH followed this format in her two story collections for children, *The Parent's Assistant* (1796) and *Moral Tales* (1801). Decades would pass before literature devoid of didacticism, such as Lewis CARROLL's ALICE'S ADVENTURES IN WONDERLAND (1865) and THROUGH THE LOOKING-GLASS (1872), offered children entertainment, and CHILDREN'S LITERATURE could be read for its own sake.

THESIS NOVELS offered strongly didactic messages to adults during the first half of the 19th century. Authors whose fiction overtly highlighted the disgrace of depressed social and economic conditions for the working classes and emphasized the inequities of CLASS STRUCTURE included Charles DICKENS, Frances TROLLOPE, Benjamin DISRAELI, Elizabeth GASKELL, and Charles GISSING. Elizabeth Barrett BROWNING's novel-poem AURORA LEIGH (1856) features didacticism in her defense of the intellectual and creative rights of women. By the 20th century, a more sophisticated reading audience demanded more subtlety in its fiction. Authorial intervention proved unacceptable, and didacticism became a narrative technique of the past.

BIBLIOGRAPHY

Demers, Patricia, and Gordon Moyles, ed. *From Instruction to Delight: An Anthology of Children's Literature to 1850.* Toronto: Oxford University Press, 1982.

Morse, David. *The Age of Virtue: British Culture from the Restoration to Romanticism.* New York: St. Martin's Press, 2000.

DISCIPLINE MARY BRUNTON (1815)

Like her first novel, SELF CONTROL (1810), Mary BRUNTON's second novel, *Discipline,* remains most important for its contribution to the development of SILVER-FORK FICTION and the manners novel, later made most famous by Jane AUSTEN. DIDACTIC in nature, the novel offered a blueprint of behavior to readers by elevating the value of religious piety. Its message held that, if one avoided seduction, whether of a carnal or a materialistic nature, one received reward. Shrewdly voiced and drawn with minute detail, the plot remains filled with erotic intrigue. Couched in a style that marks its author as intelligent and imaginative, with an ear for realistic dialogue and an eye for the motivation behind human action, *Discipline* tempers its preachiness with an appealing first-person narrator in the form of Ellen Percy. Her humanity becomes immediately evident as she confesses herself once willful and egotistical, a storyteller who will attempt to avoid the very "professions of humility" that often mark a narrator as "glorifying" in the "candour" of her "confession." She foreshadows her tale of a failed attempt to join the historically aristocratic English community by noting her father's lack of "illustrious descent," and his own frequent statement that those who flaunt their social stature engage in the worst of vices. Those who have read Austen's *EMMA* (1816) will note definite similarities between the two novels' young heroines, despite their differences in social status.

Young Ellen has a high opinion of herself, encouraged by her mother's reticence to correct her misbehavior—actions her mother feels grow more from an admirable spirit than a wicked nature. She describes herself by age eight as perverse, importune, obstinate, combative, all traits that her father deems desirable for a boy but not for Ellen. In a statement that supports the novel's interest for FEMINIST CRITICS, he tells his wife, Fanny, of his daughter's intelligence and keen sense of analysis: "It is a confounded pity she is a girl. If she had been of the right sort, she might have got into Parliament . . . but what use is her sense of?" When Fanny replies, "I hope it will contribute to her happiness," she foreshadows Ellen's eventual emotional state, but one that will be reached only after much suffering.

Almost immediately, Ellen suffers the grief of her mother's death and the simultaneous loss of her father in an emotional sense, developments that endear her to readers before they can judge her too harshly. She takes solace in trying her leadership capabilities at boarding school, where she lives until age 16 and adopts as an enemy the well-born Lady Maria de Burgh, simultaneously making a lifelong friend of Juliet Arnold. These individuals remain important to the novel's rising action, and both will reappear in various capacities. When Ellen returns home, her father asks his dead wife's faithful friend, Miss Elizabeth Mortimer, to oversee Ellen's care. From Miss Mortimer, Ellen eventually learns piety and faith but, most important, will meet Miss Mortimer's acquaintance, Mr. Maitland, whose language is that of a gentleman, "always correct, often forcible, and sometimes elegant." When he rescues the ladies from a potential disaster caused by Ellen's poor judgment, she shows little gratitude and judges him too quiet, which she believes marks his lack of passion. Time will teach her that it actually marks his grace and strength. Maitland and Miss Mortimer become models for Ellen, although she at first rejects their guidance.

Ellen experiences a number of temptations, including those exercised by Lord Frederick, who pretends to love her but has only evil thoughts in mind. She discovers that Mr. Maitland holds her in high esteem, despite her self-centered behavior. A masquerade ball adds imagery of a lively social scene, but a damaging rumor about Ellen threatens to discredit her, even in the eyes of Juliet. Too late, she learns that Juliet has helped construct her fall, out of jealousy of Ellen's relationship with Miss Mortimer. A lengthy letter from Miss Mortimer, who has left the Percys due to Ellen's actions, makes Ellen realize for the first time her folly. She notes that "the darkness of midnight" surrounded her, as she confesses, "I could not disguise from myself the uselessness of my past life; and I shrunk under a confused dread of vengeance." Brunton extends the imagery of dark and light to emphasize a moment of near-epiphany for Ellen.

When Maitland appears to explain he is leaving, Ellen learns that he has loved her, but he explains he also "perceived, pardon my plainness, that your habits and inclinations were such as must be fatal to every plan of domestic comfort." Stating she had no ambition to become his wife, Ellen dismisses Maitland, an act she later regrets. In short order, her father loses his fortune and commits suicide, leaving Ellen completely isolated.

Ellen's transformation into a woman of character still moves slowly until threatened by the loss of Miss Mortimer, with whom she lives following her father's death, to illness. Only then can Ellen realize how much she depends on her caretaker. Even Juliet Arnold's transfer of affections to Lady Maria and her abandonment of Ellen fail to arouse Ellen's famous temper in light of Miss Mortimer's death. Before dying, her friend charges Ellen to know her own religious faith and piety, but warns her that will be impossible until Ellen is forced to turn to faith due to a lack of support from family, friends, and material goods. Ultimately her prophecy is fulfilled as Ellen loses everything. Destitute, she finds the faith and humility that return her chaotic life to order through several near-melodramatic turns of fate, including a reuniting with Juliet Arnold and her subsequent death; a meeting of Charlotte Graham and her family, among whom Maitland is a part; and the restoration of a portion of her inheritance. Maitland's return is advanced through a subplot common to romance, that of mistaken identity, and through that contrivance the novel concludes on a happy note.

Discipline remains available in print and electronic texts due to the efforts of feminist critics who recovered Brunton's works in the mid-20th century. Even those who object to Brunton's overt Christian dogma find much to enjoy in her work.

BIBLIOGRAPHY

Spender, Dale. *Mothers of the Novel: 100 Good Women Writers Before Jane Austen.* New York: Pandora, 1988.

DISRAELI, BENJAMIN, FIRST EARL OF BEACONSFIELD (1804–1881)

Benjamin Disraeli was born on December 21, 1804, in London, first son to Isaac, author of several works on literature and a history book, *The Life and Reign of Charles I* (1828), and Maria D'Israeli. Although of Jewish heritage, Disraeli was baptized into the Church of England at the age of 13. Initially interested in law, in 1821 he began a three-year stint with a firm of solicitors, but the promised rewards of stock market speculation soon seduced him. After losing a good sum of money, he decided in 1825 to found a daily paper called *The Representative,* a project that quickly failed.

Heavily in debt, Disraeli published his first novel, *Vivian Grey,* in 1826. The successful novel proved autobiographical, as Disraeli attributed to his protagonist his own egotistical wit. He also portrayed important members of contemporary London society in thin disguise, a style that followed in many of his works. In 1827, he traveled to Italy and, later that year, published a satire titled *The Voyage of Captain Popanilla.*

Despite his writing success, Disraeli entered a period of depression, fueled by his remaining debts and his failure to read for the bar as planned. His depression lifted in 1831 when he published *The Young Duke.* He ran twice for a seat in the Parliament in 1832, first as a radical and then an independent, but was defeated. Disraeli traveled throughout Spain, Greece, Albania, and Egypt, and his experiences would influence his later fiction. His interest turned to full-time politics but not before he published two additional novels, *Contarini Fleming* (1832) and *Alroy* (1833).

In 1835, Disraeli switched political allegiance, joining the Tories and suffering two more defeats for Parliament. Despite his repeated failures, he gained a reputation as a political pamphleteer while also writing letters published in *The Times* and a political satire, *The Infernal Marriage.* In 1837, Disraeli finally triumphed in his bid for Parliament, becoming a Conservative representing Maidstone Borough of Kent County in the House of Commons, just as Queen Victoria took the throne. That same year, he published two additional novels, *Henrietta Temple* and *Venetia,* the latter a supposed look at the lives of Percy Bysshe Shelley and George Gordon, Lord Byron, a pair attracting much attention for their scandalous activities. In 1839, Disraeli married the wealthy widow Mrs. Mary Anne Wyndham Lewis. He often joked that he had married for money, to which his wife supposedly once replied, "Ah! but if you had to do it again, you would do it for love." Following the election in 1841, he asked Robert Peel to make him a minister, but Peel refused his request, alienating Disraeli.

Disraeli showed reformist concern for the working class and in 1843 led the Young England party in Parliament. The group supported the view that the middle class needed to be contained through the unity of the working class with the aristocracy, a move that would also protect the poor. The following year, Disraeli published the first in a trilogy of novels for which he became most famous. The novels, *Coningsby: or, The New Generation,* followed by SYBIL OR, THE TWO NATIONS (1845) and TANCRED, OR THE NEW CRUSADE (1847), were labeled THESIS NOVELS. They attacked regulations oppressive to the poor, including Poor Laws, Factory Reform Law, the CORN LAWS, and Jewish Disabilities Law. Disraeli's opposition to Peel's repeal of the Corn Laws split the Conservative Party, leading to Peel's ouster.

In 1848, both Disraeli's parents died, and he continued his political career, publishing his next book, *Lord George Bentinck: A Political Biography* (1851). In 1852, under Edward Stanley, the 14th earl of Derby's administration, he became Chancellor of the Exchequer. He lost the post a short time later with Lord Derby's defeat but regained it with Lord Derby's 1858 victory. In 1859, with the election of Henry John Temple, Lord Palmerston, as prime minister, Disraeli again lost his post. Following seven years of British political control by the Liberal Party, Disraeli returned to the Cabinet as Exchequer for Lord Derby. In order to preempt action on the part of William Gladstone and the Liberal Party, he pushed through an 1867 Reform Act extending the vote to every male householder within a borough constituency, as well as to males paying at least £10 in rent, which totaled about 1.5 million males. In 1868, with Lord Derby's resignation, Disraeli became prime minister. However, in the general election that followed that same year, William Gladstone and the Liberals returned to power.

The Conservatives reclaimed power in 1874, and Disraeli again became prime minister. He acted on his social conscience to pass legislation including the Factory Act (1874) and the Public Health Act (1875), protecting workers against abuses. His 1875 Conspiracy and Protection Act allowed workers to stage peaceful demonstrations, and the Employers and Workmen Act of 1878 allowed workers to sue employers for unfulfilled promises. A staunch defender of IMPERIALISM, he pushed to make Britain a world power, a move Queen Victoria approved. She took the title empress of India partly due to Disraeli's urging. The queen granted his request to become the first earl of Beaconsfield in 1876, and he assumed a title he had used for a character in *Vivian Grey,* his first novel.

Although consumed by politics, Disraeli continued to write, publishing *Lothair,* a novel focusing on religious dissent in 1870. One of his best-known works, ENDYMION appeared in 1880, in which he featured a foreign secretary named Lord Rochampton, a character based on Lord Palmerston. It also featured a caricature of William Makepeace THACKERAY as St. Barbe. That year, the Conservatives suffered defeat, and Disraeli conceded the ministry. He had hoped to continue a long writing career but died on April 19, 1881. He left nine chapters of an unfinished novel titled *Falconet.*

BIBLIOGRAPHY

Levine, Richard A. *Benjamin Disraeli.* Boston: Twayne Publishers, 1968.

Smith, Paul. *Disraeli: A Brief Life.* New York: Cambridge University Press, 1996.

Weintraub, Stanley. *Disraeli: A Biography.* New York: Dutton, 1993.

DOCTOR THORNE ANTHONY TROLLOPE

(1858)   Anthony TROLLOPE produced the best-selling novel of its time in this the third book in his Barsetshire sequence, *Doctor Thorne,* published in three volumes. He departed from his normal village setting in this novel to consider county characters, focusing on members of high society and their desire for wealth and the status it promised. While the characters resemble those of his other stories, the plot somewhat differs, the reason for which Trollope himself explained in his autobiography. After completing *The* THREE CLERKS (1858), he traveled to Florence, where he asked his brother to help him develop a plot for a new story, the only instance of his ever asking for help with his writing. He adopted his brother's plot, which offered the potential for creating the typical Victorian SENSATION FICTION, complete with aspects of mistaken or hidden identity and reader titillation leading up to an enormous character revelation. Trollope later seemed bothered by the fact that readers may have begun his novel in anticipation of reading a suspenseful plot, rather than concentrating on the character development that to Trollope remained all important.

The protagonist, Dr. Thomas Thorne, practices medicine in Greshamsbury, where he raises his niece

Mary. He protects the secret of her illegitimate birth, but because Trollope particularly hated sensationalism, he avoided keeping his readers in suspense regarding her heritage. Readers learn by the second chapter that the doctor's brother, Henry, fathered the girl with Mary, the sister of a stonemason named Roger Scatcherd. When Scatcherd took revenge for his sister's embarrassment by murdering Henry Thorne, he served time in prison but emerged to become a successful railway contractor, known by the locals as Sir Roger. He lives with his sickly son, Louis, and both have a reputation for occasional drunkenness. Thus, Trollope avoids another aspect of sensationalism, the emotionally charged reunion between rediscovered family members. Sir Roger's repugnant personality would devalue for the reader any reunion between himself and Mary.

In the rising action, Mary falls in love with Frank Gresham, son to the local squire, whose family she has known all her life. Although the Greshams like Mary well enough, they want Frank to wed a wealthy woman to relieve the debt leveled against the Gresham estate. Lady Arabella Gresham had long felt she married beneath herself, and she spends her energies trying to pull her family up to her social level. However, the hard times that hit many aristocrats had also visited the Greshams, a fact that Trollope makes clear through ironic dialogue. At one point, Lady Arabella demands that her husband cut off Frank "without a shilling," to which Gresham replies, "I haven't a shilling to cut him off with." The Greshams's aristocratic relatives, the DeCourcys, attempt to railroad Frank into marriage with an older spinster, Miss Dunstable, a clever, but kind, heiress to a fortune.

Trollope's focus on social differences and CLASS STRUCTURE gives the novel its excellence. His rendition of the incomes and possessions of the landed gentry reflect his usual superbly detailed REALISM, allowing readers a look inside the life of those who aspired to aristocratic life. As a self-described conservative liberal, Trollope supported England's aristocracy, believing it would alleviate social ills suffered by lower classes. His narrative reveals the pressures on the landed populace by the newly wealthy, who could buy lands that old families might have mortgaged to support the costs of estates and family businesses long allowed to run themselves. This precarious situation also allows Trollope to incorporate humor as he affectionately pokes fun at the attitudes of those who take wealth and status for granted. Retaining the best aspects of an approach made popular in the 18th century by EPISTOLARY NOVELS such as Samuel RICHARDSON's *PAMELA* (1740), Trollope introduces correspondence between the vainly ambitious Augusta Gresham, Frank's sister, who wants to marry a lawyer, Mr. Mortimer Gazebee, and her hypocritical and presumptuous cousin, Lady Amelia De Courcy. Gazebee desires to marry into Augusta's social status, but she is betrayed by Lady Amelia, who forces Augusta to adopt her view of Gazebee as unworthy. The two women discuss their responsibilities toward their "blood" and social position, creating a comic effect in their stance outside the boundaries of life's realities experienced by the majority of the population. Lady Amelia convinces Augusta that Gazebee is beneath her, writing, "It is not permitted us, my dear Augusta, to think of ourselves in such matters. As you truly say, if we were to act in that way, what would the world come to?" All the while, Lady Amelia schemes to win Gazebee for herself. The two women provide excellent contrast to Thorne's unpretentious prosperity. While Mary and Frank occupy the novel's romantic center, Dr. Thorne serves as its moral center. A conservative who values rank and stability, he nevertheless raises his illegitimate niece and projects no false gentility.

Mary and Frank despair until both Sir Roger and Louis die, leaving the Scatcherd fortune to Mary, who learns of her heritage. Her sudden wealth causes the Greshams to accept her. In spite of the facts of Mary's birth, she becomes engaged to Frank. The old way of life triumphs over the new as Mary's inherited old money shores up the lands of the Greshams.

One critic writing for the *Saturday Review* expressed concern over the author's flaunting of moral convention through Mary's illegitimacy. He felt that Trollope featured only the delights of romance and none of its pitfalls, encouraging young readers to marry without prudence. His was one of few critical voices.

BIBLIOGRAPHY
Glendinning, Victoria. *Anthony Trollope.* New York: Alfred A. Knopf, 1993.

Skilton, David. Introduction to *Doctor Thorne,* by Anthony Trollope. New York: Oxford University Press, 1987.

DODGSON, CHARLES LUTWIDGE   See CARROLL, LEWIS.

DOMBEY AND SON CHARLES DICKENS (1848)

Charles DICKENS's seventh novel, first published in 20 serial parts between October 1846 and April 1848 with the complete title *Dealings with the Firm of Dombey and Son, Retail, Wholesale, and for Exploration,* marked what many critics agree to be the author's mature writing period. Dickens moves from the use of poverty-stricken characters to concentrating instead on members of the monied class. Many contrast *Dombey and Son* with Dickens's previous novel, MARTIN CHUZZLEWIT (1844), to make this point. While *Martin Chuzzlewit* clearly represents the trend in 1840 novels to highlight a character weakness indicative of problems within English society, its emphasis on self-ishness through the figure of Pecksniff is delivered with little narrative planning. That approach marked much of Dickens's early fiction, in which improvisation played a crucial part in plotting. However, by adding the foil character of Martin to balance Pecksniff's overwhelming negativity, Dickens divides his stage. In *Dombey and Son,* the focus remains firmly on one character and his moral weakness of pride. That focus gives the novel a center, adding strength to the character and allowing Dickens to avoid the caricature that Dombey might have become. Dickens succeeds in attaining the goal for *Dombey and Son* "to do with Pride what its predecessor [*Martin Chuzzlewit*] had done with Selfishness." Dickens outlined the entire novel before writing it, and that intent and planning are obvious in its execution, supporting an elaborate plot with balance and theme.

Mr. Dombey invests overwhelming pride in his business. He represents a product of his era, one who plans his life according to rules of logic. Intent upon producing a male heir, Dombey ignores his loving daughter and first-born child, Florence. Following Mrs. Dombey's death during the birth of his son, Paul, Dombey focuses all of his ambitions on the boy. A sickly child devoted not to Dombey but to Florence, Paul dies, further alienating father and daughter. In Dickens's letter of July 25, 1846, he describes the hoped-for effect of Paul's death on Dombey:

> I purpose changing his feeling of indifference and uneasiness towards his daughter into a positive hatred. For he will always remember how the boy had his arm round her neck when he was dying, and whispered to her, and would take things only from her hand, and never thought of him.

Dombey's crippling pride will not allow him to admit his approach to life is wrong. Dickens allows Dombey to retain his pride by not directly revealing much of his inner turmoil. He illuminates Dombey's thoughts and emotions in only one section of the novel, an incident that falls between Paul's death and Dombey's second marriage. The title of Chapter 20, "Mr. Dombey Goes upon a Journey," evokes in readers thoughts of the traditional QUEST protagonist, who experiences a journey, physical, emotional, and spiritual, that leads to a positive change and a new life, allowing Dickens to emphasize that this journey will have the opposite effect on Mr. Dombey. During a train ride, Dombey contemplates the general meaning of life, with the background of the landscape rushing by, as seen through the passenger car window. This technique allows imagery to imitate, but not fully reveal, the character's specific thoughts: Dombey hurries "headlong, not through a rich and varied country, but a wilderness of blighted plans and knowing jealousies." According to Kathleen Tillotson, Dickens analyzes his character by employing the tool of the dream, allowing readers to apply their own imagination and sense of identification to perceive Dombey's "lonely thoughts, bred late at night in the sullen despondency and gloom of his retirement." However, he gains nothing from his journey, other than a deep sense of doom, inspired by "the track of the indomitable monster, Death."

Dombey marries again, seeking yet another heir. The marriage proves childless and loveless on Dombey's part. His second wife, Edith Grainger, is a passionate woman with no outlet for that passion within her marriage, although she can express her fondness for Florence. In a long narrative explanation, Dickens compares Edith's early affection for Dombey to a plant expected to grow in polluted poisoned air. Dombey's sins breed "infancy that knows no innocence" and "maturity that is mature in nothing but in suffering and guilt." The narrator refers not only to Dombey, but also to Edith and her mother, and the interactions of those characters, trapped in an abusive relationship, aids in developing an edginess in Edith that helps temper her position as a predictable melodramatic character.

Edith leaves Dombey for his manipulative business manager, Carker, who represents a pride that differs from that of Dombey. Carker's pride remains hidden in a false subservience that covers his desire to gain success through Dombey's efforts. Edith's motive equates to simple revenge against her husband's cruelty. When Edith dies in a train accident, Dickens creates a deeply ironic situation. The fortune-teller who had urged Carker to pursue Edith earlier in the novel by remarking, "One child dead, and one child living; one wife dead, and one wife coming. Go and meet her!" had made clear that Dombey would make Edith one more sacrifice to his pride.

Dombey descends further into distress, his pride preventing his asking for help, even when he discovers feelings for Florence. The conflicts he encounters at work parallel his emotional and spiritual suffering, and only through threat to his material possessions can he realize the superior value of human relationships. By the novel's conclusion, he decides to accept Florence's attentions.

Dombey's hypocrisy regarding values challenged Dickens as he worked to develop a dynamic and rounded protagonist, a goal he achieved partly by making clear the presence of a certain dignity within Dombey's humiliation. Positive minor characters, such as Cook and Perkins, supply moral commentary on Mr. Dombey. They add comedy to the plot but hold the focus on Dombey as the most important character and one deeply flawed. In the 1846 letter, Dickens states, "Dombey and Son . . . is a Daughter after all." This vision guided Dickens's effort, succeeding in his development of characters both appealing and interesting.

Some contemporaries and later critics point to the character of Florence as a weakness, due to her seeming perfection. Like all Victorian writers, Dickens had to deal with creating a heroine that could possess only the limited character facets allowed females in that era's fiction. In other Victorian fiction, the virtue of such heroines made them boring, one-dimensional, and lacking any individuality. However, by allowing the reader to meet Florence as a young child, Dickens engenders sympathy for her, and her retention of a purity and naiveté becomes more acceptable. She remains crucial in allowing the reader to recognize the depths of Dombey's parental confusion as the child who had been "unwelcome to him from the first" . . . "her patience, goodness, youth, devotion, love, were as so many atoms in the ashes upon which he set his heel." As Tillotson writes, Florence must be approached "differently from Mr. Dombey," as the reader should see her "as a character drawn wholly within the bounds of her situation; to an extent that she, and the pathos of that situation, are one and the same."

Like much of Dickens's work, the novel remained popular into the 21st century, when it, along with multiple sources important to understanding its development, appeared in electronic format, accessible online.

BIBLIOGRAPHY

Forster, John, ed. *The Life of Charles Dickens.* London: Cecil Palmer, 1872–74.

The Life of Charles Dickens. Dickens Fellowship, Japan Branch. Available online. URL: http://www.lang.nagoya-u.ac.jp/~matsuoka/CD-Forster.html. Downloaded on May 1, 2003.

Tillotson, Kathleen. *Novels of the Eighteen-Forties.* Oxford: London, 1965.

DOMESTIC REALISM   A fiction subgenre of a realistic nature that focuses on the home scene, domestic realism evolved from the reaction against romanticism that occurred in the mid-19th century. Following the preoccupation of the romantic writers (1789–1837) with the superiority of intuition and passion over intellect, the value of nature as a mirror for literature, and the prioritization of the individual's needs over that of the group, Victorian Age (1837–1901) writers moved from a focus on mysticism and spirituality to dwell on the particulars of everyday life, or the quotidian. The rise of a preoccupation with materialism that grew from the appearance of a new working middle class, the problem of educating that class, and the challenge to religion by science gave realism momentum. Written generally by middle-class women for middle-class women, like all realism, domestic realism dwelled on the immediate, the "here and now," and represented concerns of the middle class, especially its members' failure to obtain fulfillment within a strict social class structure. Character always remained more important than plot. Domestic realism should not be confused with domestic fiction, or women's fiction/SENTIMENTAL FICTION, also popular during the mid-19th century.

Jane AUSTEN provided forerunners to domestic realism through her novels of minute observation of social and familial transactions on the home scene. Charles DICKENS and William Makepeace THACKERAY further advanced realism with their focus on the family unit as a reflection of society. Ironically, Thackeray refused to publish Elizabeth Barrett BROWNING's ballad "Lord Water's Wife" in CORNHILL MAGAZINE in 1861, as he felt its stark realism might dismay his middle-class readers, who would find it insulting to their moral code. Browning reacted by declaring that issues such as the abuse of women needed to be acknowledged by the very audience Thackeray sought to protect.

When George ELIOT, probably the best-known writer of domestic realism, arrived on the scene, she advanced the subgenre through novels that included ADAM BEDE (1859), which received critical praise for its presentation of rural life and focus on the responsibility of the individual to conform to mores of his or her community. The MILL ON THE FLOSS (1860) offered another example of Eliot's skill in the evocation of rural domesticity, and MIDDLEMARCH (1871–2), subtitled A Study of Provincial Life, gave birth to a large cast of characters who represented the economic, social, and religious scene in England at a time when the individual was devalued apart from his/her place in a hierarchical social order. Notable contemporaries of Eliot who also wrote domestic realism included Charlotte YONGE, whose numerous novels for adults and juveniles excelled in the presentation of authentic Victorian middle-class life, and Maria EDGEWORTH, whose CASTLE RACKRENT (1800) is acknowledged as the first regional novel in English and a forerunner of domestic realism.

BIBLIOGRAPHY

Barrett, Dorothea. *Vocation and Desire: George Eliot's Heroines.* London: Routledge, 1989.

Colby, Vineta. *Yesterday's Woman: Domestic Realism in the English Novel.* Princeton, N.J.: Princeton University Press, 1974.

Pollack, Mary S. "The Anti-canonical Realism of Elizabeth Barrett Browning's 'Lord Walter's Wife.'" *Studies in the Literary Imagination* 29, no. 1 (Spring 1996): 43–54.

DOYLE, SIR ARTHUR CONAN (1859–1930)

Arthur Conan Doyle was born in Edinburgh on May 22, 1859. His mother, Mary, was of Irish extraction and traced her ancestry to the Plantagenet line, while his father, Charles Altamont Doyle, traced his to the D'oel or D'Ouilly family, nobles of 12th-century France. The pride that the Doyles took in their lineage partially accounted for Doyle's emersion in history, even as a child. One of 10 children, Arthur, along with six siblings, survived to adulthood as part of a troubled household. Charles earned the inadequate salary of £240 year in his position as a low-level civil servant. The son of a successful caricaturist and sibling to three successful brothers, one an author, one an artist, and one a manager of the National Gallery in Dublin, Charles never developed his own artistic skills. His lack of ambition led to the loss of his post in the Office of Works in Edinburgh, and he slid into alcoholism. Afflicted with epilepsy, Charles needed to be institutionalized during his final years. One effect of Arthur Conan Doyle's early experience with his father was his later severe dealing with alcoholic characters in his writing.

Doyle's education consisted of a mix of home schooling with attendance until age nine at public school in Edinburgh. He then transferred to a Jesuit preparatory school called Hodder, located in Lancashire, England. Two years later, he moved to the associated school of Stonyhurst. Although he performed well as a student, the strict Jesuit discipline did not appeal to Doyle, who often suffered punishment at the hands of the priests. Mary Doyle took in boarders and worked hard to pay the tuition for her favorite child rather than trade her son's education for induction into preparation for the priesthood. Doyle seemed to understand well her sacrifices and remained a devoted son. By 1875, when he graduated, he had rejected formal religion in favor of agnosticism, another autobiographical aspect that would surface in his writing.

After leaving Stonyhurst, Doyle spent one additional year in Jesuit education at Feldkirch, Austria, and then returned to Edinburgh to study medicine at the University from 1876 to 1881, where he received his bachelor of medicine and master of surgery degrees. In 1879, he published his first story, "The Mystery of Sarassa Valley," and served as a ship's surgeon during the Arctic voyage to Greenland of the *Hope* in 1880. While in medical training, he formed relationships with two individuals who would provide models for later crucial characters. Professor Rutherford would later be immortalized in the character of Professor George Edward Challenger of *The Lost World* (1912), while Dr. Joseph Bell's amazing deductions concerning the history of his patients would provide the basis for the deductive skills of Sherlock Holmes.

From 1881 to 1882, Doyle served as a doctor on the ship *Mayumba* and visited the west coast of Africa. After moving to Portsmouth in 1882 to establish a medical practice with a friend from school, Dr. George Turnavine Budd, they disagreed so often that he decided to move to Southsea to establish his own practice. With his practice slow to develop, he had time to write as well as for romance. He met Louise "Touie" Hawkens, daughter of his landlord, whom he married on August 6, 1885. Touie's health problems would later lead to great personal turmoil for Doyle. He began to develop an interest in psychic studies following a meeting of believers in Southsea.

In 1887, Doyle published his first important work, A STUDY IN SCARLET, a story that introduced the character of Sherlock Holmes in *Beton's Christmas Annual;* he received payment of £25. Following the birth of his first child, Mary Louise, in 1889, he published his first major novel, a historical fiction titled *Micah Clarke.* The novel formed the basis for conversation with Doyle's contemporary Oscar WILDE during a dinner in 1889. The two dined with the editor of *Lippincot's Magazine,* J. M. Stoddart, and Doyle received a commission to write a second novel, *The* SIGN OF FOUR, featuring Sherlock Holmes. Its appearance in 1890 added immeasurably to the development of the DETECTIVE FICTION genre. Also in that year, he published a second historical novel, *The White Company,* and moved his family with him to study ophthalmology in Vienna.

In 1891, his attempt to establish practice as an eye specialist failed, but he published the first of six Sherlock Holmes stories, beginning with "A Scandal in Bohemia" in *The* STRAND MAGAZINE. However, he expressed a wish for immortality through his historical fiction, rather than popular stories, in a letter to his mother when he wrote, "I think of slaying Holmes [. . .] and winding him up for good and all. He takes my mind from better things." The enthusiastic reception of his fiction did convince him to focus on a writing career, and in 1892 he began to publish a large series of Holmes stories. During that same year, he celebrated the birth of his first son, Alleyne Kingsley. In 1893, the year of his father's death, Doyle killed Holmes in his story "The Final Problem" and moved to Davos, Switzerland, for the sake of Touie's health in hopes of helping cure her recently diagnosed tuberculosis. He toured the United States, delivering lectures in 1894, and visited Egypt with Touie in 1895. He thought that the arid climate would lessen the severity of Touie's illness, and, secondarily, Doyle hoped to witness a battle in the Sudan War. By 1896, the Doyles had returned to England, and Arthur's experiences provided inspiration for the desert drama *The Tragedy of the Korosko,* which would appear two years later. Doyle moved his family into the Surrey mansion called Undershaw, whose construction he had directed, but as the family settled in, he had a fateful introduction on March 15, 1896, to a woman named Jean Lekie, with whom he fell completely in love. However, he determined to remain faithful to Touie and maintain a platonic relationship with Jean. His public wanted more mystery stories, resulting in Doyle's writing a series of 12 unconnected stories under the title *Round the Fire,* which ran in *The Strand* from 1898 to 1899.

In 1900, Doyle served for seven months as head of a South African hospital during the Boer War. A short time later, he wrote a defense of Britain's activities in Africa, a pamphlet titled *The Great Boer War,* for which he would be knighted in 1902. Later in 1900, he unsuccessfully ran for a seat in Parliament as a representative of the Unionist Party. Such an outcry had continued over his having killed Sherlock Holmes that Doyle resurrected him in the wildly popular 1901 novel, *The Hound of the Baskervilles.* He continued to publish Holmes stories and care for Touie, although his love for Jean Lekie grew. In 1903, he again exercised his social consciousness on behalf of George Edalji, son of an East Indian Christian vicar and his English wife. Edalji was accused of writing threatening letters to his own family, raising suspicion regarding his character. When a series of livestock attacks took place in 1903, anonymous letters to the authorities accused George Edalji. Scant evidence produced during a search of the Edalji home led to a seven-year prison sentence for Edalji. Doyle investigated the case and produced several articles that annoyed some but drove other citizens to demand an investigation. Money raised for George's defense led to his eventual release. Long after he left the area, the livestock killings continued.

Touie died in 1906, freeing Doyle to marry Jean the following year after his second defeat for a seat in Parliament. In 1909, he welcomed a second son, Denis Percy Stewart, and joined a reform movement for the Belgian Congo. His family continued to expand with the 1910 birth of a son, Adrian Malcolm, and he worked for the second time to help liberate a high-profile prisoner, Oscar Slater, a German Jew accused of murder. Like many others, Doyle believed the accusation to be false, and he continued working in Slater's behalf over the next 18 years of his imprisonment.

In 1912, the character Professor Challenger first appeared in *The Lost World,* and the Doyles celebrated the birth of his second daughter, Lena Jean. Doyle continued acting on his political interests, attempting to enlist to fight in World War I in 1914; following his rejection, he established a Civilian Reserve Corps. That year he also published the final Sherlock Holmes novel, *The Valley of Fear.*

For decades, Doyle had coped with religious uncertainty, having at last become interested in the occult and mysticism. He formally converted to spiritualism during 1915 after an experience in communication with the dead. He spent the next few years delving further into the mystical and called upon his faith when his eldest son, Alleyne Kingsley, died in 1918. The official cause of death was influenza, but Alleyne had been weakened by wounds sustained during military service.

With the death of one of his brothers the following year, Doyle began a serious pursuit of spiritualism, becoming a champion of the mystical who traveled to Australia, America, Canada, and South Africa publicly supporting various metaphysical claims. His reputation suffered in 1922 when he declared the famous Cottingley Fairy photographs genuine and they were later proved fakes. Doyle's final Sherlock Holmes story appeared in 1927, but the most important event of the year occurred when Oscar Slater finally gained release from prison and received £6,000 compensation, mostly due to Doyle's efforts on his behalf. Doyle died from a heart attack on July 7, 1930.

While Sir Arthur Conan Doyle hoped to gain his reputation through his major historical novels, *The White Company, Sir Nigel, Micah Clarke, Uncle Bernac, The Refugees,* and *The Great Shadow,* the public instead became enthralled with the remarkable number of short stories he published. His detective fiction, the most influential of any 19th-century popular fiction writer, succeeded in establishing Doyle as crucial to the development of English literature. His major characters lived far beyond their creator, appearing repeatedly in new novels and spawning consideration of Holmes's youth, the early development of his relationship with his famed sidekick, Dr. John Watson, and fictionalized stories based on Doyle's relationship with his mentor and inspiration for Holmes, Dr. Joseph Bell, into the 21st century. His works have been seen in many dramatic productions, for both the stage and the screen, as have the works inspired by his characters.

BIBLIOGRAPHY
Haining, Peter. Introduction. *The Final Adventures of Sherlock Holmes: Completing the Canon by Sir Arthur Conan Doyle.* Seacaucus, N.J.: Castle Books, 1981, 8–26.

Pascal, Janet B. *Arthur Conan Doyle: Beyond Baker Street.* New York: Oxford University Press, 2000.

Patterson, Robert O. Introduction to *The Original Illustrated Arthur Conan Doyle.* Seacaucus, N.J.: Castle Books, 1980, v–vi.

DRACULA BRAM STOKER (1897)

Bram STOKER followed the lead set by Robert Louis STEVENSON in *The Strange Case of Dr. Jekyll and Mr. Hyde* (1886) to write HORROR FICTION. Such stories were enjoying a renewed prestige among the French, and Stevenson proved that modern readers welcomed frightening tales, as long as they preserved a vestige of reality. An author named Minnie Mackay who assumed the pseudonym Marie Corelli had advanced flamboyant tales such as *A Romance of Two Worlds* (1887), which presented readers with a theory called The Electric Origin of the Universe, advanced by a character who used the occult and claimed relation to the Magi. Some adopted the themes of her books as a weak philosophy, proving that minds like those of Queen Victoria and Oscar WILDE could be captivated by what most critics deemed nonsense. Stoker's *Dracula* sold well enough to support him, its acceptability due mainly to his adaptation of Wilkie COLLINS's use of documentary devices, including letters, news reports, and journals, to present his tale. It sold even better in America than in England, but due to copyright problems, Stoker received little to nothing from foreign sales. His scenes in Romania, a country Stoker never actually visited, were powerful and memorable in their horrifying detail. By basing his monster on a historical figure, Vlad the Impaler, a fierce, loathsome, and inhumanly cruel combatant of medieval times, Stoker further imbues his tale with authenticity and the figure of Count Dracula with validity.

The novel introduces Jonathan Harker, a London solicitor who agrees to meet the vampire Count Dracula in his Transylvanian castle for the assumed purpose of drafting documents. He describes the count, in part, as possessing "a very strong, aquiline" face, with "peculiarly arched nostrils" and "lofty domed forehead" with little hair around the temples, but growing "profusely" elsewhere," including "massive" eyebrows that almost "met over the nose." The mouth, under a thick mustache, "was fixed and rather cruel-looking, with peculiarly sharp white teeth. These protruded over the lips, whose remarkable ruddiness showed astonishing vitality in a man of his years. For the rest, his ears were pale, and at the tops extremely pointed. The chin was broad and strong, and the cheeks firm though thin. The general effect was one of extraordinary pallor." Legend has it that Stoker based the creepy description on the appearance of his employer, Sir Henry Irving.

Readers will recognize themselves in Harker's comment that he is naively "deceived" by his own fears. Those fears are aroused by the stories the count tells of his own family history, peppered with warriors who laid waste to entire cultures. When Harker compares his own tales to those of the *Arabian Nights,* Stoker makes clear the power of the imagination to extend life or extinguish it. Harker describes unspeakable horrors, including the sacrifice of infants to the count's blood lust and the visitation of three brides of Dracula who resemble succubae. Audiences excused the seduction by the brides of the morally upright Harker due to the magic spells cast by their feminine enchantments. Stoker includes effective descriptive passages, such as one in which Harker describes seeing the count scaling walls in the form of a bat. Harker's fiancée, Mina Murray, awaits him in Whitby, England, where the count goes to pursue her entrapment. Harker eventually escapes to spend six weeks in a Budapest hospital where his "brain fever" eventually subsides, allowing him to return home.

During Harker's absence, Mina's diary entries describe experiences shared with her friend Lucy Westenra, described as a "New Woman," who will do her own proposing of marriage to one of her several suitors, which include Mr. Holmwood, Quincey Morris, and Dr. John Seward. However, the count will soon upset the plans of the two friends. Mina follows Lucy outside one night and sees "undoubtedly something, long and black, bending over the half-reclining white figure" of Lucy. When she calls to her friend, "something raised a head, and from where I was I could see a white face and red, gleaming eyes." Later Mina discovers what appears to be "a good sized bird" at Lucy's side, hinting at the bat form Dracula can assume. Dr. John Seward attempts to care for Lucy as she shows symptoms of some mysterious "disease" following her encounter with Dracula, and he summons Van Helsing, a Dutch physician with expertise in vampirism, for consultation. In addition, Stoker introduces Renfield, a lunatic who imitates various animals while housed in Seward's private asylum. Renfield falls under Dracula's spell, fantasizing he is the count's servant, destined to help supply him victims. Stoker reflects negatively on religious fundamentalism as he writes, "a strong man with homicidal and religious mania at once might be dangerous. The combination is a dreadful one."

Thus, Stoker juxtaposes two figures considered mad according to convention, although Van Helsing, the "mad scientist," is acceptable because he can defend against the greater madness of vampirism, whereas Renfield's madness, dedicated to the service of the occult, is not.

As with Harker, Mina and Lucy succumb to occult sexual overtures due to the strength of dark powers. A victim of Dracula's bite-kiss, Lucy becomes a vampire, dying from her affliction and then suffering a living death as she rises from her grave to search for victims who may supply her with the blood she craves. She is "rescued" from "eternal damnation" by Van Helsing and the others, thanks to the magical effects of a stake driven through her heart that releases her from vampirism. Other weapons against vampires included the Christian cross and garlic, which ward off their powers, and exposing them to deadly sunlight. Enraged by his failure to retain Lucy, the count pursues Mina, but she is spared, thanks to the efforts of Harker, Lucy's lovers, and Van Helsing.

Mina and Harker marry and then help pursue the count to Transylvania. Although in love with Harker, Mina still feels the effects of Dracula. As the group travels to his castle, she lapses in and out of various trances, telling the men of one vision, "'Something is going out. I can feel it pass me like a cold wind. I can hear, far off, confused sounds, as of men talking in strange tongues, fierce falling water, and the howling of wolves.'" In a gruesome scene, Van Helsing helps release the three brides of Dracula by decapitating their beautiful bodies in the count's castle. In the meantime, Harker and Morris overtake gypsies transporting the box with the count's "undead" body toward the castle, fight them in order to remove the coffin lid before the sun goes down, and dispatch Dracula with some well-placed knife stabs in the setting sun. Morris dies from a mortal knife wound, but Mina and Jonathan are freed from the Count's curse to enjoy happy lives.

The book concludes with a note from Harker, seven years following the trial by fire on his son's seventh birthday, the anniversary of Morris's death. As the child sits on Van Helsing's lap, the doctor comments, "We want no proofs. We ask none to believe us! This boy will some day know what a brave and gallant woman his mother is. Already he knows her sweetness and loving care. Later on he will understand how some men so loved her, that they did dare much for her sake."

The novel remained popular long past its era, absorbed into mythology and reappearing in popular culture into the 21st century. Its focus on religion, sexual powers, hypnotic tendencies, political and social ALLEGORY, and powers of the female offer literary critics of all interests much to analyze. The count's supernatural figure resonates with audiences who have viewed him as a type of antihero, admiring his cunning and transformative abilities.

BIBLIOGRAPHY
Florescu, Radu. *The Complete Dracula.* Acton, Mass.: Copley Publishing Group, 1993.

DUKE'S CHILDREN, THE ANTHONY TROLLOPE (1880)

Anthony TROLLOPE published the final of six books in his Palliser sequence, *The Duke's Children,* as a serial from October 1879 to July 1880 in ALL THE YEAR ROUND and later in 1880 in a three-volume book set. It represented his final work featuring his favorite character, Plantagenet Palliser, later titled the Duke of Omnium. The previous volumes featured the duke in various political battles, along with his independent-minded wife, Glencora, Duchess of Omnium. A one-time prime minister in the series, Palliser loses his seat and in the final book has lost his beloved wife, a popular figure with the reading public. Trollope decided to expose a new side of his character, that of single father to adult-age children who had, for the most part, inherited their mother's independent streak. Trollope may have hoped by revealing more of the personal side of Palliser to endear him to the public who, up to that point, had not received him particularly well. That chilly reception may have been due to readers' attempts to identify Palliser too closely with a particular real-life politician. By offering his readers the opportunity to identify instead with the character as family man, Trollope helped Palliser break into his readers' circle of favored figures. Those figures were one reason readers returned to Trollope's novels. His habit of bringing characters from past books into present ones delighted an audience who looked for those familiar faces in new stories.

The original intention for the *The Duke's Children* was to match its length to that of its predecessor, *The Prime Minister* (1876). At 320,000 words and four volumes, *The Prime Minister* was to be the final addition to the series. However, Trollope must have thought better of his decision to leave Palliser as the retiring prime minister with no office and many regrets, and his publisher agreed to an addition to the series. Nevertheless, when Trollope completed another enormous manuscript, for reasons unknown, he revised it, shortening it a great deal. Whether by order of the publisher or not, the manuscript was cut down; the original, never published manuscript resides in the Yale University Trollope collection. Despite the tremendous amount of revision, critics agree the novel remains seamless, a tribute to Trollope's narrative skill.

As a retired politician and a widower, Palliser must assume a role he had not anticipated. The narrator makes clear the effect of Glencora's death in the first chapter, writing of the duke's "utter prostration" due to a heart "torn to pieces" and a feeling that he had suddenly been called upon to live "without hands or even arms." Forced finally to proceed with life and look up from his grief, he does not like what he sees in his offspring, as the next generation exercises its right to new cultural mores. At first thinking his children will act as links to his departed wife, he welcomes the opportunity to spend more time with them. He had always been a loving father, but his many duties had kept him away from home, leaving the children in Glencora's capable hands. He looks forward to knowing them again.

Unfortunately, neither his older son nor his daughter please him. The older son, Lord Silverbridge, having been expelled from Oxford, has taken up company with men of whom Palliser does not approve. Major Tifto's reputation for betting on the horses dismays Palliser while it seems magnetic to his son, for whom Palliser had hoped to garner a seat in the House of Commons. His son will stand to represent Silverbridge, but offends and disappoints his father by rejecting Palliser's Liberal Party for the Conservative. Tifto's inclination for sports does allow Trollope to indulge in his normal penchant for hunting and shooting scenes.

The middle child, Lady Mary, who Palliser presumed would make a good marriage, disappoints her father in her choice of Francis (Frank) Oliphant Tregear, a nice enough man educated at Eton and a friend of Silverbridge, but one lacking fortune and social rank. Unknown to Palliser, Mary had met Tregear during a visit to Rome the previous year, and Glencora had admired his outgoing charm and his intelligence, evidenced by the fact that he could speak French and immediately learned Italian. She had gone so far as to share her hope with Palliser while on her death bed that her inherited fortune would be divided in such a way that Mary would be well taken care of, even if she were to marry a poor man, indicating her belief that Tregear would remain a part of Mary's life. Although Palliser dislikes Tregear on general principles, he does not realize that Tregear shares the duke's negative attitude toward Tifto. When Tregear advises Silverbridge against socializing with Tifto, he is rebuffed. Thus, Trollope hints that the younger and older man may share some values after all.

Lord Gerald, the youngest child in school at Trinity, does not prove much of a bother. Although he chafes when his father forbids him to see his brother's horse race, Silverbridge advises him to be cautious and do nothing that would cause a school expulsion. In that manner, Trollope shows that Silverbridge can prove a help to his father, although, as with Tregear, Palliser remains unaware of any shared views.

As the action rises, Lord Silverbridge builds up gambling debts, which his father indulgently pays, and Palliser suggests that his son marry in order to find stability in life. He feels he is at last making some headway with his eldest when Silverbridge is attracted to Lady Mabel Grex. While Lady Mabel does not have much money, she has excellent social connections that will help Lord Silverbridge's career. However, he turns to a new love, the American Isabel Boncassen. The granddaughter of a Dutch immigrant, her lack of aristocratic background insults Palliser. He firmly believes in the value of an aristocracy, one that will stand as the "most faithful bulwarks of the constitution," and he doubts that an American girl can produce heirs to that system.

Palliser stands his ground, refusing to sanction the marriage. Isabel is clever enough not to marry without the duke's approval and gradually wins over her future father-in-law with her intelligence and wit. Critics agree that Isabel becomes the heroine of the story in a way that Mary never could. Mary's resentment against her elders and lack of originality as a character does not recommend her to readers, whereas Isabel's charm does. She likely appeals to readers who know the series, because she resembles Glencora Palliser in her tenacity and retains enough humility to be acceptable to an English audience who anticipates her assuming Glencora's position as Duchess of Omnium. While previous American characters had received harsh treatment by Trollope, he softens his approach for Isabel. He also characterizes her father, a senator and possible future presidential candidate, as intelligent and open-minded, loving and attentive to Isabel, and sensitive to his position as a guest in a foreign culture.

Meanwhile, the fact that his wife had encouraged Lady Mary's relationship with Tregear causes Palliser conflict, particularly when he realizes that Lady Mabel, a woman he has long admired, also loves Tregear. He will eventually gain an admiration for both of his children's spirits, in which he recognizes his wife, realizing that they do act as the link to Glencora's memory he had desired. That spirit and independence make amends for what seems to Palliser a decided lack of principles, particularly when he realizes those principles are of his generation, not theirs. The happiness he had shared with his own wife causes him to reevaluate his priorities for his children, and he approves of the marriages. The wedding of Silverbridge and Isabel proves one of the "most brilliant remembered in the metropolis." He also finds contentment in answering an invitation to help form a new Liberal government as the Conservatives lose power in Parliament. He struggles briefly over whether he could serve under another man, having once been prime minister himself, but realizes how much he desires "immediate work." By the time Palliser appears at Mary's wedding, guests remark on his jovial appearance, even though he has not forgotten what disappointments he has suffered in his acceptance of his children's decisions. Trollope will not let the novel conclude on a falsely happy note, however, as he makes clear the pain caused to the worthy Mabel Grex by her rejection by both Palliser's son and Tregear; she is left with neither love nor money.

Some critics claim that to enjoy fully this novel, readers need familiarity with those earlier in the series. For instance, Lady Mary's affair with the commoner Frank Tregear calls to mind her mother's affair with Burgo Fitzgerald, featured years earlier in the first work of the Palliser sequence, CAN YOU FORGIVE HER? (1865). What readers familiar with Trollope's work will not find in this volume is his trademark conclusion that looks to the future. He had written such a conclusion in the original lengthy manuscript, in which the younger Palliser generation muses on their futures, but it did not appear in the published version. At the age of 66, Trollope likely decided he should not promise his readers yet another volume in his lengthy and honored Palliser series. He concludes his novel with Palliser's abrupt comment to Silverbridge regarding Tregear, "I will accept that as courage which I before regarded as arrogance."

BIBLIOGRAPHY

Glendinning, Victoria. Anthony Trollope. New York: Alfred A. Knopf, 1993.

Tinker, Chauncey B. Preface to The Duke's Children, by Anthony Trollope. Oxford: Oxford University Press, 1977.

E

EAST LYNNE MRS. HENRY WOOD (1861)

East Lynne represents prototypical 19th-century SENSA-
TION FICTION, extremely popular with English readers.
The novel was the second for Mrs. Henry (Ellen Price)
WOOD, who had begun publishing highly moralistic
fiction at the age of 41. It became an immediate hit
when it appeared first as a serial in the *New Monthly
Magazine*, edited by novelist Harrison AINSWORTH.
Though it was rejected for publication in novel form
by several publishers with readers that included novelist George MEREDITH, Richard Bentley published it in
three volumes in the fall of 1861. *East Lynne* contained
all the ingredients that appealed to aficionados of this
genre: drama heightened by characters' greatly exaggerated emotional expressions; an aristocratic female
protagonist who suffers a fall from grace and must
redeem herself; a stalwart romantic male lead; a subplot involving a murder mystery; and the death of
innocent children. It also offers constant authorial
intervention as the narrator preaches to her audience.
In one scene, the narrator admonishes, "We never
know the full value of the thing until we lose it. Health,
prosperity, happiness, a peaceful conscience—what
think we of these blessings while they are ours?" Rather
unpalatable to later readers, such fiction sold well to
Victorian readers accustomed to DIDACTIC LITERATURE.

The aristocratic Lady Isabel Vane, daughter of the
earl of Mt. Severn, enjoys a childhood of excess at the
estate of East Lynne. Her profligate father, encumbered
with debts, can leave her nothing at his death but feels
confident that her legendary beauty will result in her
marrying wealth. At his death, she marries the novel's
epitome of moral living, Archibald Carlyle, a lawyer
from the nearby village of West Lynne, who purchases
East Lynne prior to the earl's death. While Mr. Carlyle's
behavior remains impeccable, Mrs. Wood takes care not
to paint him as a prude, offering his maiden sister in
that role to serve as a foil to Carlyle and remind her
readers that virtue leading to severity is not virtue at all.
In the rising action, Mr. Carlyle attempts to help his
longtime friends and neighbors, the Hares, in clearing
their son Richard of the accusation of murder. Barbara
Hare has been in love with Archibald for some time, but
he views their relationship as one of friendship only.

With all these basic elements in place, the characters
encounter the coincidence and mysterious identities
expected by readers of sensation fiction. Isabel misinterprets Archibald's attentions to Barbara, and in a fit of
jealousy and suspicion, abandons her husband and
children, lured to Europe by the evil attentions of a rake
who impregnates her with no intention of marriage.
Isabel learns a difficult lesson about trust through his
ignoble actions and commands him to leave her to raise
their son alone. Archibald, now divorced from Isabel,
would like to marry Barbara, but as a staunch Christian
cannot do so. He quotes the verse with which he must
comply: "Whosoever putteth away his wife, and marri-
eth another, committeth adultery." As Isabel mulls her

past mistakes, the narration continues its moralistic tone: "A conviction of her sin ever oppressed her; not only of the one act of it, patent to the scandal-mongers, but of the long, sinful life she had led from childhood."

A convenient train accident leaves Isabel disfigured and kills her infant. Because she is reported dead, Archibald may marry Barbara, who becomes step-mother to Isabel's children. Readers voyeuristically view Isabel's suffering as the narrator states, "I do not know how to describe the vain yearning, the inward fever, the restless longing for what might not be." As with classical tragic aristocratic characters, whose falls allowed catharsis for their audience, Isabel stands as cautionary tale to her viewers. Circumstance evolves, and she becomes governess to her own children in the home of Archibald and Barbara, where she suffers detailed daily remorse over her haughty misjudgment of her devoted ex-husband. She endures the death of another child, while the murder mystery, in which her ex-lover is discovered to be the murderer, is resolved. In an emotionally hyperbolic death scene, Isabel reveals her identity to Archibald and dies knowing he has forgiven her foolish actions and the implied fact that she made him a bigamist. The audience may take comfort in the fact that she will join her two dead children in repose. Additional melodramatic factors in the novel include various invalid women, one of whom has prophetic dreams; devoted servants, one of whom discovers Isabel's identity but does not reveal it; a falsely accused man who shadows his home in various disguises; the passing of a great deal of time; and multiple mini morality plays involving servants and masters, fathers and offspring.

The novel became one of the biggest best-sellers in fiction history and evolved into a successful stage production. It offered its readers taboo subjects such as adultery and bigamy made acceptable through its highly moralistic narrative. Although it lapsed in popularity for a time, with the increased interest in women writers that surged in the 20th century, new editions of *East Lynne* became available, as did an electronic text version.

EDGEWORTH, MARIA (1767–1849)

Maria Edgeworth arrived at a propitious moment in the development of the novel. Born probably in January 1767, at Black Bourton, Oxfordshire, about 14 miles from Oxford, she grew especially close to her father, Richard Lovell Edgeworth, who was 19 years old at the time of her birth. Maria was six years old when her mother, Anna Maria Elers Edgeworth, died in 1773. Richard Edgeworth passed his famous energy and reformist mindset to Maria, who observed his participation as a Fellow of the Royal Society with notables including Thomas Day, Sir Humphry Davy, and Erasmus Darwin. He encouraged his daughter's intellectual endeavors, inviting her involvement in his business managing his Irish estate. Her exposure to Ireland's working class and to political matters involving both Ireland and England led her to later write the first regional novel, CASTLE RACKRENT (1800), emphasizing setting as integral to plot.

Maria first visited Ireland the year of her mother's death, 1773. She shared a normal childhood with her original four siblings, as well as rapidly accumulating half-siblings, with her father's second wife, Honora, and attended school at Derby until age 13. She enjoyed letter writing, and her father encouraged her to write stories. After Honora's death in 1780, Mr. Edgeworth married her sister, Elizabeth, and Maria attended school in Upper Wimpole Street in London. In 1782, the family settled into life at Edgeworthstown in County Longford, Ireland. Maria had a good relationship with Elizabeth and enjoyed life on her father's estate, assuming gardening and baby-sitting duties for the expanding family. Although she would never marry, she also never suffered isolation, surrounded by her family, the servants, and farm workers, and she accompanied her father on business visits, serving as scribe, bookkeeper, and confidante. According to Maria's biographer, Emily LAWLESS, Mr. Edgeworth wrote to Dr. Darwin, "I do not think one tear in a month is shed in this house." However, in 1791, "consumption," a disease common to 18th-century Ireland, struck the household, killing the child Honora, named for Maria's first stepmother, and causing Elizabeth's only child, a son named Lovell, to fall dangerously ill. The family eventually recovered, and Maria could enjoy exciting times. As a young, impressionable girl, she witnessed the establishment of Irish independence. Optimism ran high that Ireland would develop into a strong, free society, an attitude supported by Richard Edgeworth and others who noted that by 1792, Ireland's population had more than tripled, to 4 million, ironically the level at which it would remain for centuries.

At age 20, Edgeworth began writing *The Freeman Family,* later to be renamed *Patronage,* and visited Clifton for a year. In 1795, she finished her first book, *Letters for Literary Ladies.* In 1795, she published her first work for children, a short story collection titled *The Parent's Assistant,* to a good reception. Sometime within the next 20 months, Edgeworth likely began work on *Castle Rackrent.* She worked on the novel in private, possibly wanting to surprise her father with the book as a gift. Tragedy again struck when Elizabeth Edgeworth died in 1797. Within one year, Richard Edgeworth wedded his fourth wife, Frances Beaufort, in the middle of the Irish rebellion; Lawless includes an anecdote claiming that the newlyweds observed a man hanged in a wagon by rebels as they traveled from Dublin to Edgeworthstown. Although Maria did not immediately warm to her latest stepmother, before much time passed, a lifelong friendship developed between the two.

In 1798, Edgeworth and her father published a text for children titled *Practical Education,* to which other family members had also contributed. That same year, the French attacked Ireland by way of County Mayo, and the Edgeworths hid in September in Longford. Maria wrote to an aunt of the "two most fortunate escapes from rebels, and from the explosion of an ammunition cart." The Irish defeated the French in short order, and Richard Edgeworth was elected to Parliament.

In January 1800, Edgeworth published *Castle Rackrent* anonymously to great acclaim. Sir Walter SCOTT modeled his first historical novel, *WAVERLEY* (1814), on Edgeworth's work, which identified a set geographical location and era, a new approach to novels. Supposedly, he guessed the author's identity before it became public. Edgeworth first learned of her influence on Scott when her stepmother Frances read a postscript fastened to *Waverley* that identified *Castle Rackrent* as its inspiration, "so as in some distant degree to emulate the admirable Irish portraits drawn by Miss Edgeworth." Supposedly Edgeworth was writing a complimentary note of her own to Scott at that time. Following his receipt of her letter, a great friendship began between

the two. Lawless would later describe the relationship as "unflecked by even a passing cloud." The social concerns made prominent in *Castle Rackrent* acted as impetus for the later more formal economic and political studies of communities by social scientists. However, as the critic George Watson later pointed out, despite Scott's confidence, before the 20th century, few later critics of historical fiction even mentioned Edgeworth's name. Scott labeled her "the least feminine of female novelists," explaining that her father's business tutoring proved most unusual for a woman of her time.

In August 1800, Great Britain and Ireland formed a union, dashing hopes of Irish independence. That same year, when Maria turned 33 years of age, Frances Beaufort Edgeworth gave birth to her first child, the 17th born to Richard Edgeworth. Maria published a book of stories for older children, *Moral Tales,* in June 1801, and her society novel, *Belinda,* followed. The following year, her father again contributed to a book she wrote discussing Irish humor, titled *Essay on Irish Bulls.* When Maria joined Richard and Frances on a vacation to Brussels and Paris in October, she became involved in what may have been her only love affair as she enjoyed the attentions of a Swedish courtier identified as Edelcrantz. She wrote to her aunt that he possessed "superior understanding and mild manners," offering her "his Hand and Heart! My heart, you may suppose, cannot return the attachment," she explains, as she does not know him well. She adds, "I think nothing would tempt me to leave my own dear friends, and my own country, to live in Sweden." According to Frances, turning down a marriage bid hurt Maria more than she allowed others to believe.

In 1803, the Edgeworths landed at Dover just as the Napoleanic Wars resumed, traveling on to Edinburgh a short time later. Maria advanced her publishing career with *Popular Tales* (1804) and *Lenora* (1806), a romantic epistolary novel for which she may have employed Edelcrantz as inspiration. In 1807, she suffered the loss of another sister to consumption, and the family worried they might be attacked by roving groups of "Thrashers," who raided private homes, searching for weapons. Episodes i–iii of *Tales of Fashionable Life,* which included an Irish novel titled *Ennui,* appeared in 1809. Maria continued work on *Patronage,* producing other material as well. Episodes iv–vi of *Tales of Fashionable Life* appeared in 1812 and, like the first episodes, contained an Irish novel, *The Absentee.*

Maria visited London in April 1813 and met George Gordon, Lord Byron. Lawless quotes from one of Byron's letters about Maria and Richard Edgeworth, "Her conversation was as quiet as herself; no one would have guessed she could write her name. Whereas her father talked, not as if he could write nothing else, but as if nothing else were worth writing." In December, Maria published *Patronage,* which had long been in development; it proved a public disappointment, with few sales. However, 1814 proved a crucial year for Edgeworth; her correspondence with Scott began. That relationship would prove some comfort when her father died in June 1817. Despite her loss, Edgeworth published two short novels, *Harrington* and *Ormond.* Her father had helped her write *Ormond* and had, although terminally ill, provided prefaces for both books.

In 1820, *Memoirs of Richard Lovell Edgeworth, Begun by Himself and Concluded by His Daughter* appeared, and Maria enjoyed her second Paris visit in the company of her sisters. She visited Scotland to meet Scott for the first time in Edinburgh in August 1823, and spent two weeks at Abbotsford. Her first collected edition, made up of 14 volumes, was issued in 1832 with Maria as editor, and her final novel, *Helen,* appeared in 1834. Maria Edgeworth died in May 1849, in the arms of her stepmother.

A prominent public figure and later highly valued as an early woman author, Edgeworth became the subject of Lawless's popular biography in 1904. Lawless stated as part of her goal in writing about Edgeworth that she hoped to enlighten readers concerning the Edgeworth family's extreme affinity for Ireland, a fact not stressed by her former biographers. Containing not only Edgeworth's life story but also her correspondence, much of which focused on *Castle Rackrent,* the biography, along with the novel and various excerpts from Edgeworth's writing, appeared by the late 20th century in electronic format. Lawless offers amusing opinions on many topics, including Richard Edgeworth's rumored influence on his daughter's life and works: "The author of Miss Edgeworth's being was also too frequently the author of the least satisfactory portions of her books."

BIBLIOGRAPHY

Harden, Oleta Elizabeth McWhorter. *Maria Edgeworth.* New York: Twayne Publishers, 1984.

Hollingworth, Brian. *Maria Edgeworth's Irish Writing: Language, History, Politics.* New York: Palgrave McMillan, 1997.

Lawless, Hon. Emily. "Maria Edgeworth." *A Celebration of Women Writers.* Available online. http://digital.library.upenn.edu/women/lawless/edgeworth/edgeworth.html. Downloaded October 23, 2002.

Spender, Dale. *Mothers of the Novel: 100 Good Women Writers before Jane Austen.* New York: Pandora, 1986.

Watson, George. Introduction to *Castle Rackrent* by Maria Edgeworth. New York: Oxford University Press, 1981.

EGAN, PIERCE (1772–1849)

Pierce Egan was born in London and gained a reputation as a vigorous and undignified newspaper sportswriter. Like many during the early stages of the novel, when standards of writing remained loose, he decided to write novels. His first book, *The Mistress of Royalty* (1814), exposed the Prince Regent's love life. In 1818 he published the first in a series of biographies, titled *Boxiana, or Sketches of Modern Pugilism,* that continued through 1824, appearing monthly at the cost of a single shilling. A comic by choice, Egan is best remembered for his amusing portrait of Regency manners, the popular novel *Life in London, or the Day and Night Scenes of Jerry Hawthorn Esq. and His Elegant Friend Corinthian Tom, Accompanied by Bob Logic, the Oxonian, in Their Rambles and Sprees through the Metropolis.* Dedicated to George IV, it contained outrageous wordplay and sometimes-crude comic illustrations by George Cruikshank. It appeared in monthly installments, was produced on the stage, and influenced writers including William Makepeace THACKERAY (1811–63), who read it as a youth. Egan followed his success with the publication in 1824 of a periodical titled *Life in London and Sporting Guide,* which later merged into *Bell's Life in London.* He published an additional novel, *The Life of an Actor* (1824–25), and then published further adventures of Tom and Jerry. The second book proved unpopular, as Egan attempted to cast it in a serious tone.

Egan's son, also named Pierce, published several historical novels and edited *Home Circle* in 1849–51. He produced several serial novels that gained him the reputation as a pioneer in cheap literature. The two authors should not be confused.

BIBLIOGRAPHY
Reid, J. C. *Bucks and Bruisers: Pierce Egan and Regency England.* London: Routledge and Kegan Paul, 1971.

EGOIST, THE GEORGE MEREDITH (1879)

George MEREDITH indulged himself with a comedic presentation in his 1879 novel, *The Egoist: A Comedy in Narrative.* It allowed him to engage in his favored approach of satirizing bourgeois stupidity. In doing so, he satirized himself. He felt he was among the group that practiced such ignorance and that his self-interest led to the failure of his marriage, blinding him to his wife's needs and the realities of life. Rather than adopt a realistic view toward their relationship, he had remained blinded by a romantic attitude that prevented his making sensible decisions that might have relieved marital stress. He first featured a character of enormous ego in *The Ordeal of Richard Feveral* (1849). By the time he returned to this approach in *The Egoist,* he had reached full maturity as a writer. In addition, he had time to absorb the ideas of Darwin, which invaded fiction by casting the spotlight on character motives and actions. This led naturally into studies of relationships. Meredith supplies an essay on comedy to open what critics term his most intellectual novel. He may have hoped the challenging foreword would discourage non-serious readers.

The novel's protagonist, Sir Willoughby Patterne, is so self-centered that he cannot fathom anyone or anything not holding him as the center of the universe. His apt epitaph reads, "Through very love of self himself he slew," and he is described as one who possessed "without obligation to the object possessed." His tendencies appeared at a young age, as one character recalls, when he climbed onto a chair in the middle of a room where he demanded that all gaze at him, declaring, "I am the sun of the house." His admirable estate serves as the setting for events that take place over about six weeks.

Wealthy, handsome, and vacuous, Patterne, as his name suggests, engages repeatedly in attempts to snare a wife, never varying his approach, regardless of his failures. This represents Meredith's definition of a failed man, one deserving of the harshest judgment by society, a man so closed-minded that he refuses to learn and change. While engaged to Constantia Durham, he encourages the love of Laetitia Dale, who he wants to "move" without "exposing himself." Contrary to her name's suggestion of constancy, Constantia deserts Patterne as soon as she recognizes him as a selfish fatuous individual who needs others only as an audience. She abandons her one-time fiancé to elope with an officer of the Hussars, completely shaming Patterne. Victorian mores viewed a broken engagement to be almost as serious as a broken marriage. More serious still is Patterne's failure to meet the test of his character, in contrast to Constantia, who seeks independence and self-development.

Due to his boundless ego, Patterne does not suffer long from chagrin, and he begins the pursuit of a new victim, Clara Middleton. Despite her name, which suggests clarity of thought, Clara gives in to Patterne's attentions but will not plan a wedding after learning about the former engagement to Constantia. Her father, Dr. Middleton, based on Thomas Love PEACOCK, Meredith's father-in-law, sides with Patterne, swayed by his attentions and impressive wealth. An additional major character is a handsome scholar named Vernon Whitford, based on Meredith's good friend, Leslie Stephen, father to Virginia Woolf. One final character that proves important to the man-versus-man conflict is Crossjay, a young, poor relation of Patterne. To gain revenge on Patterne for once having insulted his father, Crossjay shares with Clara the fact that he overheard Patterne proposing to Laeititia Dale. Clara has already transferred her affection to Whitford, meaning that Patterne finds himself again rejected. Daunted only momentarily, he proposes in earnest to Laetitia. When she also has the intelligence to reject him, Patterne becomes persistent, at last convincing her to marry. Unfortunately, he never undergoes any epiphany to help change his behavior and overblown sense of self. However, Meredith takes care not to villainize Patterne. Instead, readers likely feel sympathy for him as they recognize that his unacceptable behavior has its basis in universal human traits.

FEMINIST CRITICS find interesting Meredith's theme of female self-repression of intelligence in response to male aggressiveness, while MARXIST CRITICS will find abundant reference to the social classes and the noticeable gap separating the wealthy from the poor. Replete with simple yet admirable dialogue, the novel resembles a play filled with verbal irony. *The Egoist* sold the best of any of Meredith's many novels and remained among his most popular into the 21st century.

BIBLIOGRAPHY

Stevenson, Lionel. *The English Novel.* Boston: Houghton Mifflin, 1960.

Van Ghent, Dorothy. *The English Novel: Form and Function.* New York: Harper Torchbooks, 1953.

ELIOT, GEORGE (PSEUDONYM OF MARY ANN [MARIAN] EVANS) (1819–1880)

Born Mary Ann Evans, and adopting a pen name inspired by the French novelist George Sand, George Eliot is widely regarded as one of the world's finest novelists. She was reared in a rural Midlands environment in Warwickshire where her father, Robert Evans, managed the 7,000-acre Newdigate family estate. When Mary Ann was 16, she lost her mother, Christina Pearson Evans, to breast cancer. She had to leave her star-pupil position at school to help her older sister, Chrissey, manage the household. About a year later, Chrissey married, leaving Mary Ann housekeeper for her father and older brother Isaac until Isaac married in 1841. Her father retired, handing over his duties to Isaac, who established his new family in the Evans house. Evans moved with her father to Coventry, an act that proved a significant turning point in her intellectual development.

During her youth, Evans's belief in evangelical Christianity greatly strengthened, and she devoted herself to pious thoughts and work. In Coventry, however, she entered the social circle of the Bray family. Intellectuals, writers, and freethinkers frequented the Bray home, exposing Evans to bracing new ideas. Although her formal schooling had ended, she had continued to educate herself by reading widely and studying European languages. Through the Brays, she learned ideas of German philosophers, including Feuerbach (whom she translated). By 22 years of age, Evans had essentially lost her faith in Christianity. This change caused a split with her father. However, she continued as his housekeeper and nursed him in the long terminal illness that ended his life in 1849. Soon after began a long estrangement from her family.

Evans's modest inheritance provided a small annual income, but she had to supplement it or live with one of her sibling's families. A plain-featured 30-year-old woman of strong intellect and unconventional opinions, she found few respectable employment options available to unmarried women. She traveled to the Continent with the Brays and lived on her own in Geneva for a time, pondering what to do next. When she chose work in London as a journalist, she changed the spelling of her name to Marian. She lived with the Chapman family, whom she had met through the Brays. John Chapman published *The WESTMINSTER REVIEW,* and Evans was soon the de facto editor of this liberal periodical. She wrote reviews and managed most aspects of the publication. Through contributors, she knew the work of leading writers and thinkers of her day.

One new acquaintance was George Henry Lewes, an unhappily married writer. His wife had borne children to another man, and by acknowledging the children as his own, Lewes had lost his legal right to sue for divorce. He and Evans eloped to Germany in 1854, beginning a relationship that would last for 24 years. Because their union was not a legal marriage, Isaac Evans cut off relations with his sister, and Marian Evans became a social outcast. During this period, with Lewes's encouragement, she began writing fiction. Although she had written essays, reviews, translations, and criticism for years, she had not attempted fiction until she began *Scenes from Clerical Life*, consisting of three short stories with related themes and published in 1857. Because of the notoriety caused by her liaison with Lewes, she chose the masculine pen name of George Eliot. Her identity remained unknown until 1859, after the publication of her first full-length novel, *ADAM BEDE*. Her stories and her novel were immediate successes, producing financial security for herself and Lewes. *The MILL ON THE FLOSS* (1860) was followed by *SILAS MARNER* (1861). Eliot and Lewes traveled more frequently and found better accommodations, purchasing The Priory in 1863, the year that her only historical novel, *Romola,* was published. With success, she received a warmer welcome in the society; she and Lewes began hosting a salon at their home on Sunday afternoons. In 1866, she published *Felix Holt, the Radical;* neither it nor *Romola* were as successful as her earlier works. In 1871–72, however, she published her masterpiece, *MIDDLE-MARCH.* This study of small-town life, love, and politics captures the rise and enfranchisement of the middle class in mid-19th-century England with an unprecedented fullness and psychological depth in the presentation of its many characters. In 1876, Eliot published her last novel, *DANIEL DERONDA,* controversial for its sympathetic portrayal of Jewish life.

Lewes was in declining health after 1866, although the couple continued to travel and write. In 1876, with *Daniel Deronda* completed, they purchased a country house but enjoyed it for only two years. Lewes died of cancer in 1878 at the age of 61, devastating Eliot. She withdrew from society, seeing only Lewes's son from his legal marriage, and a banker friend, John Cross, also suffering grief from the loss of his mother.

At 40, Cross was 20 years younger than Eliot, and although somewhat mismatched, they decided to marry in 1880. They formalized their union in church, and Eliot's brother Isaac broke years of silence to congratulate his sister. Cross and Eliot honeymooned in Italy and then returned to her country house. In December, they moved into a new London house, but Eliot died three weeks later of kidney infection. She was one month past her 61st birthday. Because of her unconventional life, George Eliot was not immediately welcomed into Poet's Corner in Westminster Abbey; instead, she was buried beside Lewes at Highgate Cemetery. In 1980, a commemorative stone for her was finally placed in Poet's Corner.

As a writer, George Eliot advocated REALISM. In chapter 17 of *Adam Bede,* her first novel, she had halted her narrative to discuss narrative in the abstract. There, she articulated a doctrine of realism, and particularly PSYCHOLOGICAL REALISM, in calling for believable characters and events to be fictional subjects. Her stories frequently highlight characters grappling with a personal or moral dilemma or a discontinuity between duty and desire. Although Eliot had abandoned Christianity and lived an unconventional life, she did not abandon morality—even Christian morality—as a framework for merciful and compassionate interactions among characters (and by extension among real people). She created characters who had opportunities to make good decisions and frequently used mentoring figures to help provide guidance though complex situations; those who made selfish, vain, or foolish decisions, however, were punished with disappointment, disaster, or even death. Combined with the fullness, charm, and believability of her characterizations, George Eliot's fiction thus fulfills the dictate of Horace that requires literature to be both *"dulce et utile,"* delightful and usefully instructive.

BIBLIOGRAPHY

Ashton, Rosemary. *George Eliot: A Life.* New York: The Penguin Press, 1996.

Bodenheimer, Rosemarie. *The Real Life of Mary Ann Evans: George Eliot, Her Letters and Fiction.* Ithaca, N.Y.: Cornell University Press, 1994.

Hughes, Kathryn. *George Eliot: The Last Victorian.* London: Fourth Estate, 1998.

Hutchinson, Stuart, ed. *George Eliot: Critical Evaluations.* 4 vols. East Sussex: Helm Information, 1996.

Karl, Frederick. *George Eliot: Voice of a Century.* New York: W.W. Norton, 1995.

Laski, Marghanita. *George Eliot and Her World.* London: Thames and Hudson, 1973.

Leavis, F. R. *The Great Tradition: George Eliot, Henry James, Joseph Conrad.* London: Chatto & Windus, 1948.

Pangallo, Karen L., ed. *The Critical Response to George Eliot.* Westport, Conn.: Greenwood Press, 1994.

Rignall, John, ed. *Oxford Reader's Companion to George Eliot.* Oxford: Oxford University Press, 2000.

Taylor, Ina. *A Woman of Contradictions: The Life of George Eliot.* New York: Morrow, 1989.

EMILIA IN ENGLAND   See *SANDRA BELLONI.*

EMMA JANE AUSTEN (1815)   *Emma* is not Jane AUSTEN's most popular work; that distinction belongs to *PRIDE AND PREJUDICE* (1813). However, critics invariably agree that *Emma* is Austen's greatest

work, for a number of reasons, including its satiric humor, and its likely reflection on the author herself as a woman who may seem, at first glance, simple and uncomplicated, but who remains in reality a complex individual. Thus, Emma, who perceives herself as a matchmaker extraordinaire, and who may be perceived by readers as a simple egoist, surprises those same readers by revealing herself to lack the narrow-mindedness of other Austen egoistic characters. She reveals this fact by demonstrating her ability to change, thus endearing herself to readers who can identify with a well-meaning, but gently flawed, individual who at last awakens to a truth that she has, in essence, taught herself. Austen also achieves an enduring comic effect by satirizing her culture's privileging of innuendo and suggestion above clarity in communication. Because readers remain privy to the truth of circumstances, they can observe how foolish the characters become as they simply mystify themselves through what they perceive as skilled verbal sparring.

Emma Woodhouse has lost her mother when the novel opens. She lives alone with her wealthy and well-regarded father in Highbury, her sister Isabella having married John Knightley. Undoubtedly spoiled, Emma has recently lost her governess, Anne Taylor, who has married the Woodhouses's neighbor, Mr. Weston, a match for which Emma claims full credit. As her next project, she attempts to match Harriet Smith, a young girl whose parentage is unknown and who Emma has chosen as beneficiary of her friendship, to Mr. Elton, the local vicar. Elton is actually enamored of Emma, a fact that allows much humor to enter the story when Emma, who believes that Elton desires Harriet, eventually discovers the truth. Sadly, before discovering that Elton has no interest in Harriet, Emma discourages Harriet from her pursuit of a local farmer, Robert Martin, a good man who proposes to Harriet. Although marriage for Harriet had supposedly been Emma's intention, part of that intention is that Harriet marries the man that Emma chooses for her. Emma insists that Harriet reject Martin's marriage proposal, deeming him unworthy of Harriet.

Readers could misunderstand this action as cruel and thoughtless meddling on Emma's part, but Austen makes clear Emma's good-hearted nature and only slightly skewed motivations. She clarifies for the reader Emma's self-centeredness, which makes her matchmaking more a power game than an attempt to find happiness for others. However, because the novel clearly operates as a comedy, not a tragedy, such power moves may be seen in their proper role, as character shaping that prepares Emma for a later epiphany that will allow her to escape such self-centeredness when she recognizes the importance of true love. One method by which Austen helps readers understand Emma's desire for control as innocent is her creation of a truly manipulative character in Mrs. Elton, the eventual wife of the vicar. Emma's culture values subtle wittiness as a mark of distinction, but Mrs. Elton's wit is anything but subtle, often transgressing into painful vocal barbs. In one scene, Emma muses that Mrs. Elton desires "to be wiser and wittier than all the world." While Mrs. Elton would inflict her own order upon the universe through control of others, Emma desires simply to help establish the social order that her culture seeks for itself. Austen also develops a masterful scene of situational irony in which Harriet burns in Emma's fireplace certain tokens by which she remembers Mr. Elton—a symbolic destruction of her misguided feelings toward him. Emma feels smug watching her friend conduct this ceremony, considering herself far above such simplistic foibles. As the reader well understands, Emma is at least as foolish as Harriet in her attempt to advance rational control over the emotion of love.

Austen takes her time in allowing Emma recognition of her weakness, unfolding a witty narrative that contains a healthy dose of SATIRE regarding the social mores and CLASS STRUCTURE of English society. She shapes a voice of reason in the character of George Knightley, Emma's brother-in-law, who at first annoys Emma but later becomes the object of her affection. While Emma finds Knightley at times a trial, she appreciates his noble character, clearly demonstrated at a party where Mr. Elton snubs Harriet, refusing to dance with her. Knightley fulfills the symbolism of his name by rescuing Harriet from an embarrassing scene in asking her to dance with him. The scene becomes a crucial one, as Knightley later dances with Emma, and the two show they can make a perfect match, with the movements of each complementing those of the other. In strong foreshadowing of their future romance, they both agree their dancing with one another is proper, as they are not related by blood. This emphasizes the opportunity for their development of a relationship outside that of the already established in-law order.

However, that romance will be delayed as the rising action adds further delightful romantic confusion. Knightley peeves Emma with his attempts to warn her away from the charming Frank Churchill, stepson of her former governess, who seems to bring out all Emma's character flaws. Churchill encourages Emma's already strong penchant for gossip, as he pretends to make fun of Jane Fairfax, a woman Emma dislikes, when all the time he is engaged to Jane. Before discovering that fact, Emma schemes to match Harriet with Churchill and then decides she herself has designs on him. She fears clarifying her attraction for Churchill, and what she perceives to be his attraction for her, to Harriet. When Churchill rescues Emma and Harriet from the unwanted attention of local Gypsies, Emma believes Harriet to be impressed by his heroism, a belief strengthened by Harriet's declaration of love for a gentleman who had at one time rescued her. More comedic confusion follows as Emma gently tries to disengage what she supposes are Harriet's strong feelings for Churchill, only to discover that Harriet has designs on Mr. Knightley; it was his rescue of her at the dance that Harriet had in mind as the mark of one romantically inclined toward her.

Emma's epiphany occurs not through realization of her miscalculations regarding Mr. Churchill but rather due to Mr. Knightley's severe criticism of her flippant treatment of poor Miss Bates. Emma takes witticism too far when she injures the helpless Miss Bates through a barbed comment that would have seemed natural from the mouth of Mrs. Elton but contrasts greatly with Emma's normal remarks. It is the reaction of a child who does not consider the effects of her actions on those around her, and Knightley's private shaming of Emma over her actions leads Emma to realize she lacks the very social graces she believed extended her a status above those around her. While at first deeply offended by Knightley's remarks, she later respects him for having shared so obvious a truth with her. She also realizes that she loves Knightley, a revelation that, when shared with Harriet, sends Harriet into

despair, as that totals three marriage prospects she seems to have lost. However, the gallant Robert Martin later reappears and again declares his feelings for Harriet, who, now much wiser thanks to the foibles of Emma Woodhouse, joyously accepts his marriage proposal. Emma also finds happiness with Knightley, although Austen allows a bit more confusion, just for the fun of it, before concluding the novel with all its single characters having made admirable matches, none of which Emma had planned.

Emma represents masterful writing by an author adept at shaping satirical figures, such as Mrs. Elton, while simultaneously easing the lash of satire with her warm and scrupulously honest development of Emma's character. Emma's own narrative assures the reader that her self-centeredness remains unperfected, and thus open to change.

BIBLIOGRAPHY

Copeland, Edward, and Juliet McMaster, eds. *The Cambridge Companion to Jane Austen.* Cambridge: Cambridge University Press, 1997.

Fraiman, Susan. *Unbecoming Women: British Women Writers and the Novel of Development.* New York: Columbia University Press, 1993.

Lerner, Laurence. *The Truth Tellers: Jane Austen, George Eliot, D. H. Lawrence.* New York: Schocken Books, 1967.

Trilling, Lionel. Introduction to *Emma*, by Jane Austen. Boston: Houghton Mifflin, 1957.

EMMELINE, OR THE ORPHAN OF THE CASTLE CHARLOTTE SMITH (1788)

Like all Charlotte SMITH's novels, her first, *Emmeline*, contained strong autobiographical elements. Through fiction, Smith found a way to protest her situation as mother to a large brood of children with a profligate husband who had abandoned the family. According to Anne Henry Ehrenpreis, one reader remarked that she hoped the novel would bring badly needed "benefit" to Smith, who had to "purchase her freedom from a vile husband." Smith modeled the protagonist of her first novel after herself, shaping a highborn sensitive young woman forced to live beneath her deserved social status. Smith also incorporated her own poetry into the novel, having first gained notice from publishing her sonnets. While not all her readers appreciated her public airing of personal circumstances, most enthusiastically received the novel. Influenced by contemporary writer Fanny BURNEY's *Cecilia, or The Memoirs of an Heiress* (1782), *Emmeline* continued the development of the novel of sensitivity, one focused on domestic issues that affected a vulnerable young woman. Smith added to the conventional plot a new focus on detail, creating settings more clearly drawn than those of her predecessors, reflecting her poetic bent. Her addition of elements such as a gloomy castle surrounded by dense woods and fog reflect the influence of the GOTHIC NOVEL as well.

Emmeline received praise from Sir Walter SCOTT, among other notables, and immediately sold out its first printing of 1,500 volumes. A second edition of about 500 copies was published before year's end, and a third followed in June 1789. Author Henry James Pye, selected England's Poet Laureate a year later, devoted almost 40 pages to discussing the morality of the novel in his own epistolary novel, *The Spectre* (1789), and Jane AUSTEN would refer to the novel both in and out of her fiction. Pye enjoyed the novel but complained that the author placed characters whom readers wished to admire in situations where they could only behave immorally. However, he praised Smith's attempt at promoting virtue, even though some of the book's scandalous action might result in dangerous emotional arousal of female readers. Austen found Smith's heroine much too perfect for her realistic tastes, and her Catherine Morland, protagonist of the novel that satirized the Gothic style, *NORTHANGER ABBEY* (1818), appears to be a complete inversion of Emmeline.

The novel's Emmeline Mowbray had been born to an elder brother in the ancient family of Mowbray. Her father died when only 30 years old, and Emmeline, whose mother had already died, remained at Mowbray Castle, an orphaned infant. Her care passed into the hands of her father's younger brother, who had married into the wealthy family of Lady Eleonore Delamere, with whom he had a son and two daughters. Because the Delamere name would die due to lack of male "issue," he assumed her family's name and later, upon her father's death, became Viscount Montreville. He rarely visited Mowbray Castle, where Emmeline was raised by the kindly housekeeper, Mrs. Carey, who provided her little education. However, Emmeline's "intuitive knowledge" and facility for comprehension stood her in good stead, and she matured bright and happy, despite her perilous situation in a castle falling into disrepair with a surrogate parent she would soon lose. Emmeline discovered on her own in the dilapidated library copies of works by Pope, Shakespeare, and other sources that would help her mind develop along with her body.

When Mrs. Carey dies, Emmeline fears the attentions of the steward Maloney, who becomes enthralled with the 16-year-old beauty. When the viscount learns of his niece's situation, he visits the castle, bringing his son, the spirited Frederic Delamere, to enjoy a hunting vacation. Delamere immediately falls in love with his cousin, much to his father's dismay. The viscount had far greater plans for his son, as had his mother, as the only male heir to his title and fortune. Blind to any of her son's imperfections, Lady Montreville also rendered him incapable of sound judgment.

When Maloney makes clear his intentions toward Emmeline, who has remained too distressed to discuss her situation with her uncle, the viscount assumes she has agreed to a future as Maloney's wife. Emmeline at last finds a voice to speak with her uncle and makes clear her horror over the prospect of marriage to Maloney. He relents and agrees to her plan to go live with Mrs. Carey's sister. That night Delamere stages a scandalous entry into Emmeline's room at 2 A.M., begging her not to depart. She resists his charms, and asks the viscount to protect her from his son. The following day, she begins the first of many adventures as she departs the castle. Delamere does not give up his pursuit, rejecting the prospective matches his mother contrives, deeming them "rather pretty women" but not possessing the "native elegance of person and mind" possessed by the Orphan of Mowbray Castle.

At her new home, Emmeline forms a fast friendship with the polished and mannered Mrs. Stafford, who will become her role model. She staunchly waits the appearance of a man she feels worthy of her, withstanding pressure by the conniving Lady Montreville, who hopes to discourage Delamere by forcing Emmeline to marry a wealthy suitor she does not love. Emmeline endures many tribulations as Delamere's pursuit continues, including kidnapping. Delamere and his soldier friend, Fitz-Edward, force her into a carriage by applying a "gentle violence," a phrase that would interest FEMINIST CRITICS.

Emmeline eventually accepts Delamere as her fiancé, although she later breaks her pledge. She rejects him, much to the dismay of many readers, for Captain William Godolphin, brother to the ever-ill and appealing Lady Adelina, neither of whom appear until half way through the novel. Although not nearly as interesting as Delamere, Godolphin possesses a far superior character and does his best to rescue the young man from the fatal passions that lead him into a duel. When Delamere dies, the viscount realizes his error in allowing his wife to turn him against Emmeline, who had always behaved with the utmost propriety. The book concludes with a return to Castle Mowbray for Emmeline and Godolphin, "the tenderest of husbands, the best, the most generous and most amiable of men," along with Lady Adelina and her son. Well-drawn type characters brighten the novel. They include the wicked schemer, Lady Montreville, and Fitz-Edward, described as possessing an "inveterate and cowardly malignity" of heart.

BIBLIOGRAPHY

Ehrenpreis, Anne Henry. Introduction to *Emmeline, or the Orphan of the Castle,* by Charlotte Smith. London: Oxford University Press, 1971, vii–xv.

EPISTOLARY NOVEL   In an epistolary novel, the story unfolds through letters written by, and exchanged among, the main characters, often with an anonymous "editor." In English, the earliest example is likely a lengthy anonymous work titled *The Image of Idleness* (1555). However, Aphra BEHN produced the first broadly popular example in 1683 with LOVE LETTERS BETWEEN A NOBLEMAN AND HIS SISTER, although for centuries, Samuel RICHARDSON received that credit. Richardson's extraordinarily popular PAMELA, OR VIRTUE REWARDED (1740) is recognized as the prototype in English. It grew from Richardson's work on a letter-writer instruction booklet that contained 173 letter models, at least 100 of which dealt with concerns of women. Part of his style in demonstrating the proper way to write letters involved his extension of subject matter from one letter to another, or structuring one type of letter as a reply to a previous one. Thus, *Pamela* developed from Richardson's interest in women's letter writing. While *Pamela* remained simple, with one major correspondent, Richardson's later epistolary novel, CLARISSA (1747), complicated its narrative by a crossover of letters among several correspondents, none of whom knew what the others had written.

Pamela offered the first extended-length book unified in terms of character, as well as a target for mimicry by other writers who despised its melodramatic tone and overly sentimentalized characterizations. Henry FIELDING produced a mock epistolary novel based on *Pamela* titled *An Apology for the Life of Mrs. Shamela Andrews* (1741). When Fielding attempted a second burlesque featuring Pamela's brother and named for its main character, JOSEPH ANDREWS (1742), he advanced the novel far beyond the epistolary stage. His having used the epistolary novel as his springboard testifies to its vital importance in the development of the more familiar novel form that included multiple characters operating in a broad social and geographic range within a unified plot structure. The epistolary novel remained popular for more than two centuries, with examples written by Tobias SMOLLETT, Fanny BURNEY, Jane AUSTEN, Maria EGEWORTH, and Henry JAMES. Although not used much during the 20th century and beyond, some notable examples at least partially employing the form exist, including C.S. Lewis's *The Screwtape Letters* (1942), William Golding's *Rights of Passage* (1980), and Alice Walker's *The Color Purple* (1982).

BIBLIOGRAPHY

Flachmann, Michael. "The First English Epistolary Novel: *The Image of Idleness.* (1555). Text, Introduction and Notes." *Studies in Philology* 87, no. 1 (Winter 1990): 1–75.

Sale, William M., Jr. Introduction. *Pamela, or Virtue Rewarded* by Samuel Richardson. New York: W.W. Norton, 1958, v–xiv.

Thomas, O. Beebee. *Epistolary Fiction in Europe: 1500–1850.* New York: Cambridge University Press, 1999.

EREWHON SAMUEL BUTLER (1872)

Samuel BUTLER'S *Erewhon* took its place in an honored tradition as SATIRE against what Butler perceived as the intellectual, emotional, and moral stagnation of English society and human nature in general. Revolting against the Victorian values that negatively affected English education, politics, and family life, Butler produced a philosophical novel that took those elements of his culture to task. Through the application of paradox, he made clear in this example of ironic UTOPIAN FICTION, or a dystopia, his belief that his culture had failed its members in every way.

Erewhon, an anagram for *nowhere,* consisted of irreverent satire on Victorian society, religion, and morality, made up, in part, of articles by Butler that included "A First Year" and "Darwin Among the Machines" (1863); an 1865 revision and extension of "Darwin Among the Machines"; "The World of the Unborn" (1865); and "The Musical Banks" (1869). He had, in his words, "strung" those essays together, along with some additional material, at the suggestion of a friend. In the novel, set in 1868 in an unidentified country whose geography resembles that of England, the protagonist, Higgs, discovers a country ruled by philosophers and prophets where morality equates to health and beauty while crime equates to illness. One Erewhonian court declares that the infliction of pain and suffering upon those who suffer represents the only way to control their disease. The new territory offers Higgs a skewed reflection of his own society. For instance, machines exist, but they are isolated in a museum, declared evil for their negative effects on human nature. Higgs enjoys a narrow escape from persecution for his possession of a watch; only his plea of ignorance regarding the cultural edict prohibiting machines saves him. A latter section of the work, "The Book of the Machines," explains the philosophy. He remains imprisoned as an encroacher, rescued from harsh punishment due to his healthy appearance.

Higgs describes a socially unjust but civically acceptable attitude that clearly parodies the socially acceptable attitude of his own Victorian culture: Self-respecting individuals would never relate to those less fortunate. Those of lower birth, with little money, good looks, and health, are to be disliked and viewed as objects of disgust, an approach "not only natural, but desirable for any society, whether of man or brute." Misfortunes of birth or health receive much greater punishment than crime, as Butler illustrates through Higgs's experiences. His adventures include a house-arrest arrangement in which he lives with a family named Nosnibor, the reverse spelling of Robinson, suggestive, perhaps of Daniel DEFOE'S *ROBINSON CRUSOE* (1719). The Nosnibor patriarch had committed fraud. Rather than imprison the man for criminal behavior, the court severely restricts his diet and sentences him to weekly visits from a "straightener" who administers beatings. No one bears a grudge against Nosnibor for his misdeeds. Likewise, no respectable citizen will admit to enjoying anything less than perfect health. When a neighbor woman visits the Nosnibors without her husband, she does not say he could not accompany her due to ill health. Instead, she claims he had stolen a pair of socks in the town square. Higgs has learned the proper reaction, sympathy, and confesses his own recent temptation to steal a clothes brush. The Victorian banking industry does not escape Butler's attack, as he parodies its control of Victorian society by characterizing the banks, in which people make deposits that result in a worthless currency, as churches symbolic of organized religion. The grandiose structures contain enormous gardens filled with birds, stained-glass windows, and even a choir, although the music produced is intolerable "to a European ear." When Higgs draws back a curtain to spy on the inner workings of the establishment, he is roundly corrected by a menacing guard dressed in black. Higgs explained the saving grace of the Musical Bank was, "while it bore witness to a kingdom that is not of this world, it made no attempt to pierce the veil that hides it from human eyes," an approach other religions might do well to imitate. Higgs engages in various discussions with Professors of Unreason, faculty from the local educational institution, that allow Butler to also attack Victorian philosophy. After Higgs contracts measles, he learns he will be prosecuted ostensibly for that illness, but in reality for his attempts to reintroduce machines into the society through his watch. He escapes in a hot-air balloon with an Erewhonian native, Arowhena, to avoid prosecution.

The public received *Erewhon* well, with the first edition selling out in three weeks. Many readers believed the novel to be anti-Darwinian, critical of the idea of "thinking" machines. However, later critics countered that claim, declaring Butler an accurate predictor of the future and a man who believed in the advancement of civilization through proper use of technology. Considered a forerunner of Aldous Huxley's *Brave New World* (1932) and George Orwell's *1984* (1949), Erewhon occupies an important position in SCIENCE FICTION literature. In 1901, Butler published, with the help of George Bernard Shaw, *Erewhon Revisited,* in which the son of Higgs and Arowhena tells of Higgs's further adventures in Erewhon 20 years following his escape. *Erewhon* remains available in electronic text versions.

BIBLIOGRAPHY

Beach, Joseph Warren. *English Literature of the Nineteenth and the Early Twentieth Centuries: 1798 to the First World War.* New York: Collier Books, 1966.

ESTHER WATERS GEORGE MOORE (1894)

George MOORE's novel *Esther Waters* proved his most successful work. The novel's realistic portrayal of the hardships of a servant girl departed from the over-sentimentality by which much Victorian fiction, and some of Moore's earlier works, were marked. According to an essay about *Esther Waters* by Virginia Woolf, the novel succeeds due to its lack of authorial passion; Moore does not intervene to express his outrage in an attempt to influence audience reaction. Therefore, readers may feel their own passions in a more natural way. For Woolf, that fact made *Esther Waters* an excellent reading experience. Moore succeeded in his portrayal not only of the working class but also of the landed class. The influence of French writers such as Gustave Flaubert becomes obvious in Moore's portrayal of the lack of control humans have over circumstances. However, he had also read much Ivan Turgenev, Fyodor Dostoevsky, and Henrik Ibsen, all of whom emphasized the power of character, instinct, and human will to help battle circumstance. As Helmut E. Gerber points out in his introduction, the philosophy that environment or heredity propels the main character on a road to disaster, so prevalent through the first portion of the novel, disappears midway through when Esther's strong character takes over, reversing her fortunes.

The novel opens with the phrase, "She stood on the platform watching the receding train." Like the railway to which it refers, the novel itself will come full circle in its story about 17-year-old Esther Waters, a member of the Plymouth Brethren who enters the serving life to escape her alcoholic and abusive father. The highly symbolic imagery in the opening scene includes a "white vapour" that evaporates and "white gates" that swing forward slowly to close behind Esther. Their color and suggestion of semi-blindness and imprisonment clue readers that the protagonist's innocence and naivety that will soon disappear. The physical setting also becomes important, as Esther walks among trees, including laurels, elms and fruit trees, all symbolic of the clear, unblemished wisdom imparted by nature, which, while at times cruel, at least does not attempt to cloak reality. This imagery contrasts with that of the ironically named Woodview mansion, home to the Barfield family, where almost everything is contrived, from iron gates to "the angles and turns of an Italian house" with "gables and ornamental arches." Esther has entered the world of temptation and betrayal. She learns that the estate's major endeavor is the breeding and racing of horses for money. Moore puts to excellent use his knowledge of his father's racing stables, and his detailed descriptions in chapters 31–33 of Derby Day are some of the best in English literature.

For a young woman like Esther, unfamiliar with the greater world's cruelty, the mansion stands as a threat, ready to deceive. Even the racehorses masquerade in hoods, "clothed" in gray cloth, with only their questioning black eyes visible, foreshadowing the mansion's culture, which is based on half-truths and leaves much unrevealed. That scene also aligns the servants, similarly clothed in serving garb, with the working animals. The first time Esther sees the horses, "small, ugly boys" sit in the saddles. Esther learns later they are jockeys, unnaturally small men, who must starve themselves to participate in racing's fantasy world, with its promises of fortune that few will enjoy. A romance filled with similar false promise will soon devastate Esther.

Gossip also figures importantly in the story from the first few pages, when the footman, William Latch, tells Esther of a man fired because after drinking "he'd tell every blessed thing that was done in the stables." Moore foreshadows the fact that Esther's reputation will tarnish in this unclean place. Latch's symbolic name signals that he will unlock both mysteries and miseries for Esther in another clear example of foreshadowing. She immediately experiences a conflict with William's mother, the cook, when she refuses to obey an order after the cook makes fun of her. Moore will later sketch a more complete picture of the cook when, through exposition, the reader learns she had to return to the Barfields from a year's savings the money embezzled by her husband, a former employee at Woodview who handled bets. As with the other characters in his novel, the author makes clear her motivations and thus shapes personalities that ring true. Moore took a great interest in what he termed in the original version "the fight between circumstance and character . . . A hair would turn the scale either way."

William Latch, whom even his mother calls a worthless scoundrel, impregnates the gullible Esther and then abandons her. As is custom, the family must dismiss Esther, and only Mrs. Barfield acts kindly. Turned out of her home, Esther first stays with her mother, who dies just after Esther's baby, Jack, is born. Esther eventually comes under the care of Miss Rice. She attempts to raise her son "right," despite the constant humiliation as a single mother that she experiences from others. A respectable man named Fred Parsons, aptly named as a member of the Salvationist sect, and described by the narrator as "a meager little man about thirty-five," wants to marry Esther, but when Latch returns, she feels that she must marry him for the sake of their child, despite the problems he faces in divorcing his first wife.

Latch becomes a surprisingly decent family man, making a good enough living to send Jack to school. However, his bookmaking eventually ruins his health, and the pub he used to take bets in is closed. On his death bed, he tells Jack, "Your mother [. . .] is the best woman that ever lived." When he dies, he leaves no resources for his family. Esther's son eventually comes of age to make his own way as a soldier, and the novel closes with Esther's return to Woodview, 20 years after her arrival there.

Esther moves in with Mrs. Barfield, whom she has always remembered for her kind actions. Now a poor widow allowed only a corner of the mansion, Mrs. Barfield needs Esther's help, and both women enjoy happiness in one another's company. Moore makes clear the arbitrary nature of social differences, writing that the two became "more like friends and less like mistress and maid," their "slight social distinctions" causing "no check on the intimacy of their companionship." When Esther's son visits her at Woodview on the final page of the novel, the narrator writes, "She was only conscious that she had accomplished her woman's work—she had brought him up to man's estate and that was sufficient reward." Moore's use of the term "estate" signals that Esther has built a non-material mansion and established spiritual and emotional ground of her own.

Critics contrast Esther Waters with Thomas HARDY's TESS OF THE D'URBERVILLES (1891) (a book that Moore claimed to hate) and George ELIOT's ADAM BEDE (1859), which depended on theories of determinism to bring their female characters to a bitter fate. Despite their differences, critics proclaim all three novels to have been essential in the development of modernist fiction.

Esther Waters has long been honored as Moore's finest work. Made into a 1948 movie, it became available in electronic text in the late 20th century.

BIBLIOGRAPHY

Gerber, Helmut. Introduction to Esther Waters, by George Moore. Chicago: Pandora Books, 1977.

Phelps, Gilbert. "George Moore: Esther Waters." An Introduction to Fifty British Novels: 1600–1900. London: Pan Books, 1979, 513–518.

Woolf, Virginia. "A Born Writer." The Times Literary Supplement. July 7, 1920. Available online. URL: http://xroads. virginia.edu/~CLASS/workshop97/Gribbin/bornwriter.html. Downloaded on February 3, 2003.

EUGENE ARAM EDWARD BULWER-LYTTON (1832)   An example of NEWGATE FICTION, in which writers based novels on true criminal accounts, Edward BULWER-LYTTON's Eugene Aram established him as the most popular novelist of England during the same year Sir Walter SCOTT, to whom Bulwer-Lytton dedicated the book's first edition, died. Although some protested Newgate fiction as overly sensational and even immoral, it enjoyed a wide readership. It derived its name from the Newgate Calendar, a collection of 18th- and 19th-century descriptions of the careers of notorious criminals, providing popular reading material, especially for the semi-literate. Protesters claimed that Bulwer-Lytton's novel lionized a common murderer and actually encouraged crime.

In fact, Aram was anything but common. An English philologist who lived from 1704 to 1759, Aram was the first to identify the relationship between the Celtic languages and other European languages. The Newgate Calendar account gives a biography that emphasizes his propensity for books and study, and notes that at age 16, he "found in polite literature much greater charms than in mathematics; which occasioned him now to apply himself chiefly to poetry, history and antiquities." Caught in an "unhappy" marriage, Aram would blame his later "misfortunes" on the "misconduct" of his wife. Those writing the report note a great inconsistency between Aram's scholarly pursuits and the motivation of gaining mere wealth that "induced" him to commit a crime. The report explains that Aram convinced his friend, the shoemaker Daniel Clark, to convert his worldly goods to cash, of which Aram and a partner, Richard Houseman, planned to rob him; Houseman would later testify that he saw Aram murder Clark. When a body discovered 14 years later was identified as Clark's, Mrs. Aram testified that she believed her husband had murdered his friend. Authorities arrested Aram and charged him with murder in 1758 as he worked on an Anglo-Celtic lexicon. He was hanged on August 6, 1759, as indicated in *The Complete Newgate Calendar*, Volume III. Thomas Hood also based a ballad, titled "The Dream of Eugene Aram," on the popular story, and the cave where Aram supposedly hid Clark's body became a popular tourist site.

The novel relates in detail the story of Aram's poverty-stricken childhood, which supposedly drove him to participate in the murder of his friend. The friend is reported missing, but no body is found. Self-educated, with an insatiable drive for knowledge, Aram distinguishes himself in studies. He matures into a scholar attempting to live a normal life, despite the terrible guilt he feels. His crime returns to claim him 14 years following the murder on his wedding day, adding to the sensationalism of the story, and he is tried and sentenced to death. True to the facts of Aram's real crime, the novel emphasizes the emotional and mental effects of a crime on its perpetrator, in the vein of William GODWIN's *CALEB WILLIAMS* (1794). Bulwer-Lytton used the GOTHIC style to sensationalize not only the horrors of the crime but also those that followed for Aram. Enhanced by Bulwer-Lytton's research and literary elevation, the criminal subject matter gained a wide audience.

Bulwer-Lytton was not the first to feature a criminal sympathetically. He drew on a tradition that glamorized those outside the law, including that of Scott, who showed sympathy in his novels for smugglers, Gypsies, and the famous Robin Hood. Some criticism of the novel came from unsuccessful writers, annoyed that a social "dandy" politician like Bulwer-Lytton had transformed himself into a successful writer. However, the legitimate concern reflected the growing power of fiction to affect its readers, as well as a critical call for authors to develop a social consciousness.

BIBLIOGRAPHY

Tarlton Law Library, University of Texas Law School. "Eugene Aram." *The Complete Newgate Calendar,* Vol. 3. Available online. URL: http://www.law.utexas.edu/lpop/etext/newgate3/aram.htm. Downloaded on February 8, 2002.

EUROPEANS, THE HENRY JAMES (1878)

Published serially in *The Atlantic Monthly* between July and October 1878, Henry JAMES's *The Europeans* appeared later that year as a slightly revised single volume. The plot reflects James's fascination with the misplaced individual who tries to take root in a foreign land. An artist named Felix Young brings his sister, Eugenia, about to be renounced by her German nobleman husband due to political reasons, from Europe to Massachusetts. There they visit with relatives, the Wentworths. With reservations, Mr. Wentworth establishes them in a neighboring house, but before long, he begins to enjoy the siblings' company.

Wentworth's daughter Gertrude falls in love with Felix, while his son Clifford finds Eugenia enthralling. Fortunately, Felix returns Gertrude's affections, but Eugenia has no desire to form a relationship with Clifford as she searches for a wealthy husband. Flattered by Clifford's attentions, however, she permits him to continue his pursuit. Gertrude cannot commit to Felix, due to a previous "understanding" to marry a Unitarian minister named Mr. Brand, whom she does not love, although her sister Charlotte does.

Two characters from outside the family who increase tension in the rising action are Robert and Lizzie Acton. Robert is attracted to Eugenia, although he has some reservations regarding her marriage and past relationships, and Lizzie has set her sights on Clifford. The novel concludes with Mr. Wentworth's approval of Felix and Gertrude's engagement; Clifford's recovering from his infatuation with Eugenia to marry Lizzie; and Mr. Brand realizing and acting upon his love for Charlotte. However, Robert Acton cannot conquer his prejudice against Eugenia's past marriage, and she ends up returning to Europe alone.

James supposedly wrote *The Europeans* as a response to a request by William Dean Howells that he submit a story to the *Atlantic Monthly* that was more cheerful than *The AMERICAN* (1877). James complied, but *The Europeans* still reflects his interests in the complexities or incongruities of human pride and prejudice that separate people, often despite their best endeavors for mutual understanding and acceptance. There are no deep minds in the book, but rather incongruities of life for readers to enjoy, seen in lines like "'The men in this country,' said the Baroness, 'are evidently very obliging.' Her declaration that she was looking for rest and retirement had been by no means wholly untrue; nothing that the Baroness said was wholly untrue. It was but fair to add, perhaps, that nothing that she said was wholly true." Similarly, there are humorous depictions of Acton as a man of the world in the eyes of the local community, when he is actually rather provincial. Such descriptions also suggest that Acton retains a significant self-consciousness, despite how the village folk perceive him: "Acton had seen the world, as he said to himself; he had been to China and had knocked about among men. He had learned the essential difference

between a nice young fellow and mean young fellow." What James offers is a comic sketch, bordering on cartooning, rather than in-depth character depiction, even though Eugenia (and Acton to a lesser degree) often appears close to a full and dynamic character. James reveals not the thing itself, but its façade, which generates a good-hearted laugh. He pokes fun *at* the façade of manners that makes the fun possible.

Nevertheless, despite the lighthearted touches, there are occasions of inconsistency when James seems to go beneath and beyond what he intends for the story as a comedy of manners. After some mild conflicts and comic cases of misunderstanding, resolved through good intention and in good faith, it should culminate in uplifting harmony, as demonstrated by such good matching between Charlotte and Brand, Clifford and Lizzie, and Gertrude and Felix. Yet, Eugenia is not matched up to Acton. Those two characters seem to be comically, but also tragically, depicted as the puppets of their own manners and mentality.

The novel reveals, for instance, a very serious topic that suggests James's constant concern over the impossibility of cross-cultural dialogue for mutual understanding. As a result, Eugenia often emerges as a significantly developed dynamic character *against* or *from within* a pool of comic sketches of innocent girls, clever women, and simple men. All her intricate and dynamic emotions enrich not only herself but also the entire story. Eugenia obviously wants to love the country but cannot because she is overburdened with the cultural heritage lavished upon her, and she cannot change to be part of the life that initially moves her. Like Winterbourne in James's *DAISY MILLER* (1879), she is too de-Americanized or Europeanized to assume a simple life in the native land of her parent: "she appears to feel justified in generalizing—in deciding that the conditions of action on this provincial continent were not favorable to really superior women. The elder world was after all their natural field." No matter how hard she tries, she is always the artful European, reflected even in the most innocent compliments that she receives. In addition, between Eugenia and Acton there are essential communication barriers. Eugenia fails to understand, or at least feels it hard to accept and appreciate, silence or reticence that characterize the community. As in *Daisy Miller* and *The American,* James raises questions regarding how much humans can control the manners that make them who they are.

BIBLIOGRAPHY

Chen, Shudong. *Henry James: The Essayist Behind the Novelist.* Studies in American Literature, vol 59. Lewiston, N.Y.: Edwin Mellen, 2003.

Leon Edel. *Henry James.* Minneapolis: University of Minnesota Press, 1963.

EUSTACE DIAMONDS, THE ANTHONY TROLLOPE (1873)

The third in his sequence of Paliser novels, *The Eustace Diamonds* represents one of Anthony TROLLOPE's darkest tales. He departs from his gently ironic presentations of everyday human relationships with their small but important emotional battles. This novel focuses on the unscrupulous newly widowed Lizzie Eustace, who insists on retaining family diamonds she claims her husband gave her before his death. Aspects of the story resemble Wilkie COLLINS's popular 1868 work, *The MOONSTONE,* in which stolen jewels seduce several characters with their near-mystical charm. The novel appeared as a serial in *The FORTNIGHTLY REVIEW* between July 1871 and February 1873, and was published in three volumes later in 1873.

After the death of Sir Florian Eustace, the beautiful Lizzie is left a wealthy widow following only a few months of marriage. The narrator suggests Lizzie might have "hurried him to the grave" due to "a positive falsehood" in her character. She lied to Florian about purchases she had made, although she had no reason to do so, foreshadowing future lies that will indict her when the truth is known. Florian's family claims the Eustace diamonds, which had been in the family for ages, their claim supported by the family lawyer, Mr. Camperdown. Trollope suggests that traditional values of family are superior to contemporary values that are purely material. Lizzie's delivery of a son within months of Florian's death complicates matters, as the family worries what might happen to the Eustace heir. The child also stresses the difference between Lizzie, who views this new member of her family as a means for manipulation of others, and the older generation, who view the child as an extension of themselves.

Always on the outlook for a champion, Lizzie appeals to Lord Fawn, an aptly named falsely attentive and dull politician who covets her fortune. They become engaged, as Lizzie loves the idea of being in love, even though she finds actually loving another impossible. The narrator clarifies this by describing her as a "hard-fisted little woman who could not bring herself to abandon the plunder on which she had laid her hand." For Lizzie, human relationships are important only for the material goods they might yield. Even Lord Fawn, despite his need for funds, values family more than Lizzie, insisting she give up the diamonds. A prolonged recurring argument over the point infuriates Lizzie, who decides to look elsewhere for support.

Unbeknownst to Fawn, she abandons him for her poor cousin, Frank Greystock, who also holds political ambitions. Her uncle Eustace had asked Frank, a friend of Florian, to propose to Lizzie earlier, but Frank had declined, declaring Fawn would be a better husband for her. As a teenager, Lizzie had ignored Frank's family, as she "had higher ideas for herself" than spending time with her female cousins at the deanery in their native Bobsborough. The irony of that thought is not lost on the reader. Now in need of an ally, she pursues Frank, who gives in to her charms while visiting at her Scottish castle. Tension rises, as Frank is supposedly engaged to Lucy Morris, described as "a treasure though no heroine." Trollope uses a materialistic term to describe Lucy, marking her as a foil to Lizzie. Lucy serves the Fawn family as governess, complicating Lizzie's plans to abandon Fawn.

As Lizzie travels south from her castle, her hotel room at Carlisle is robbed. Seeing her chance to secret the diamonds away, she claims they were stolen. When they actually are stolen a short time later from her London home, she must confess the truth to the police. Finally caught in her own trap, Lizzie can do little to defend her actions. Finding those actions abhorrent, Fawn officially breaks their engagement, while a horrified Frank returns to Lucy, following the counsel of an aunt who refers to Lizzie as "that little limb of the devil." The diamonds are traced to Hamburg, then Vienna, and finally to an "enormously rich Russian princess" where they will apparently remain.

Lizzie so infuriates the court officers who hope to bring her to trial that one thinks "she ought to be dragged up to London by cart ropes." Rejected by all, Lizzie marries her match in the larcenous Mr. Emilius, a Jew who has converted and become a popular preacher. Lizzie convinces herself she had been ill-treated by the other men in her life, and that Mr. Emilius intends to treat her in the way she deserves, which ironically proves true; she will receive her just desserts. The narrator assures readers that the new husband will have his way and "be no whit afraid" of his new wife "when she is about to die in an agony of tears before his eyes." That sparkling tears rather than diamonds should grace Lizzie's form provides a satisfactory conclusion to her self-serving actions.

BIBLIOGRAPHY

Glendinning, Victoria. *Anthony Trollope.* New York: Knopf, 1993.

EVANS, MARY ANN (MARIAN)   See ELIOT, GEORGE.

EVELINA, OR THE HISTORY OF A YOUNG LADY'S FIRST ENTRANCE INTO THE WORLD FANNY BURNEY (1778)

Fanny BURNEY published her first work, *Evelina,* anonymously, basing it on a piece of juvenilia titled *The History of Caroline Evelyn,* which she had destroyed on the advice of her stepmother. As an account of the unhappy life of Evelina's mother, it served as a prequel of sorts to Burney's later first novel. Due to her father's reputation as a musicologist, Burney matured surrounded by artists who gathered in their home. Because her stepmother believed novel writing too frivolous an activity for a well-bred young woman, Burney began a journal that extended into multiple volumes. Her prolific practice of dialogue and description nurtured her strength as a fiction writer, as did her ardent attendance of plays. Still bowing to her stepmother's opinion regarding novelists, she took elaborate steps to guarantee that no reader could identify her as the author of *Evelina* (1778).

The novel's instant popularity assured her she had found her calling, as did positive critical reception, including that of Samuel JOHNSON (1709–84), who remarked that the book contained passages that "might do honour to [Samuel] Richardson." The celebrity she enjoyed after revealing herself as the author earned Burney a Keeper of the Robes position to Queen Caroline. In the later *The Memoirs of Dr. Burney,* she wrote that she had written the book for her "private recreation" as "a frolic." She acknowledges in her preface a debt to Johnson, along with Jacques Rousseau, Samuel RICHARDSON, Henry FIELDING, and Tobias SMOLLETT.

Burney adopted the EPISTOLARY NOVEL technique made famous by Richardson to tell her story, opening the novel with an exchange between Lady Howard and her friend, the Reverend Mr. Villars. Those letters supply exposition to the plot and summarize *The History of Caroline Evelyn.* Mr. Villars had once tutored and grown close to Mr. Evelyn, a wealthy young man who married beneath himself to a barmaid, their union producing one daughter, Caroline. Just before Mr. Evelyn's death and two years into his marriage, he requested that Villars look after Caroline. He expected that his wife would pass on his fortune to the girl. However, conflict later arose between the girl and her mother when, remarried to a Frenchman named Duval, the then Madame Duval tried to force Caroline to marry a man she rejected. Caroline escaped the arranged marriage by secretly marrying Sir John Belmont, a fortune seeker. When he learned that Caroline had no money of her own, he subsequently burned their marriage license and declared himself single, although Caroline carried their child. She returned to Villar's care, gave birth to Evelina, and died. Villars raised Evelina, educating her as he had her grandfather and her mother.

Madame Duval enters their lives, enquiring about her granddaughter, and Villars maintains Evelina's secrecy in the country, hoping to protect her from her grandmother's negative influence and the influence of society. After a time, however, he permits Evelina to see London in the company of Lady Howard and her married daughter. At 17, the naive Evelina becomes enraptured with the city's swirling society life. She falls in love with Lord Orville while fending off the attentions of Sir Clement Willoughby. She innocently offends the social fop Mr. Lovel, inadvertently gaining an enemy.

Tensions rise as Madame Duval locates her granddaughter in London and argues for Evelina to return with her to France. Evelina takes offense at her grandmother's nephew, Mr. Branghton, and his family of tradespeople, whom she finds vulgar, emphasizing the theme of CLASS STRUCTURE. Their continuous intrusion into her life, along with problems caused by Sir Clement and Mr. Lovel, leave Evelina "pained" and no longer enthralled with London's social scene. She comments on one member of the group, Mr. Smith, that "his vivacity is so low-bred, and his whole behaviour so forward and disagreeable, that I should prefer the company of dullness itself, even as that goddess is described by Pope, to that of this sprightly young man." He stands in contrast to Lord Orville, about whom Evelina states, "the politeness, the sweetness, with which he speaks to me, restore all my natural cheerfulness." Lord Orville subsequently neutralizes Mr. Lovel so he no longer bothers her. Evelina's grandmother further complicates conditions by planning to force Sir John Belmont to recognize Evelina as his daughter and heir. Villars counters by suggesting that Lady Howard contact Sir John. When she does, Sir John responds that he wants to meet with her in England.

While Villars agrees to Evelina spending time with Madame Duval in London, he forbids travel to France. He hopes that Evelina may inherit some of the fortune due to her from her grandfather. The Branghtons, who hope to inherit Madame Duval's fortune themselves, force Evelina into embarrassing situations that she finds herself having to explain to Lord Orville in a letter. Having returned home to Villars, she receives a curt reply from Orville that shocks her into illness. As she recuperates at a Bristol spa, she meets Orville, who shows no signs of the hostile attitude evident in his letter. Evelina eventually discovers that Lord Orville did not receive her letter, which had been intercepted by Sir Clement Willoughby, who had written the nasty reply. His ruse discovered, Willoughby departs, and Lord Orville declares his love for Evelina.

Before any plans for a wedding can develop, Sir John Belmont arrives in London declaring a young woman with him his daughter and Evelina a fraud. This further complication is explained by the fact that Caroline's nurse had swapped her own child with Evelina, hoping for a better life for her daughter. Sir John must then recognize Evelina as his daughter and heir, and her happy union with Sir Clement proceeds. She writes to Villars of Lord Orville's declaration, "and, pressing my hand affectionately to his heart, 'you are now,' said he, in a low voice, 'all my own! Oh, my Evelina, how will my soul find room for its happiness?—it seems already bursting!' I could make no reply, indeed I hardly spoke another word the rest of the evening; so little talkative is the fullness of contentment."

Critics remark on Burney's narrative skill in preserving the excitement of her lengthy plot. The narration through Evelina's point of view rings true, as Burney draws on her own experiences. Some compare Villars to Oliver GOLDSMITH's (ca. 1730–74) protagonist from The VICAR OF WAKEFIELD (1766), while Burney bases Lord Orville on one of Richardson's characters. In addition, her comic social scenes reflect influence by Fielding, and the combination of influences results in what some labeled the first novel of manners, anticipating the work of Jane AUSTEN (1775–1817). The book remains available in print as well as electronic text.

BIBLIOGRAPHY

Phelps, Gilbert. "Frances Burney: *Evelina, or the History of a Young Lady's First Entrance into the World.*" *An Introduction to Fifty British Novels: 1600–1900.* London: Pan Books, 1979, 145–150.

EVELYN INNES GEORGE MOORE (1898)

George MOORE's melodramatic ROMANCE novel *Evelyn Innes* is replete with characters based on real people. The author fashioned Evelyn's father after the French-born musician Arnold Dolmetsch (1858–1940), who studied Renaissance music, and the instruments that produced it, in London. A celebrated musician and musicologist, Dolmetsch attracted people from all over the world interested in purchasing his instruments, which included lutes and viols. Irish poet William Butler Yeats, with whom Moore and Edward Martyn formed the Irish Theatre, is said to have bought a Dolmetsch instrument to accompany his poetry readings; James Joyce remarked that he would travel to south England playing his Dolmetsch lute, although he was unable to obtain one; George Bernard

Shaw enthusiastically attended and reported on Dolmetsch's concerts; and Ezra Pound immortalized him in his poetry. Moore also shaped Evelyn's young Celtic lover, Ulick Dean, on Yeats and featured his own great admiration of Honoré Balzac, which earned Moore the nickname the Irish Balzac, through literary comments by Evelyn's older lover, Sir Owen Asher. Asher was modeled on Sir William Eden, whose reputation for aestheticism was emphasized through Asher's love of art and music. Finally, Moore likely based Evelyn on novelist Pearl Mary Teresa Craigie, who wrote under the pen name John Oliver Hobbes. Moore shared a probable sexual relationship with Craigie, one that she severed. After divorcing her husband, she became devoted to the Catholic Church in 1892, a plot line echoed in *Evelyn Innes.*

The novel opens in Mr. Innes's home, where his exasperated thoughts reveal his love of Renaissance music and the instruments that best produced it. Although his own era tends to ignore that music, he perseveres in its support and gains a reputation restoring old instruments such as viols and virginals while acting as organist for the Jesuits in his village of Southwark, England. As he longs for the return of the popularity of 16th-century composers, he also longs for his wife, a singer who died many years before. Innes's daughter Evelyn aspires to be a singer like her mother. While occupying herself singing her father's music, she dreams of becoming a Wagnerian diva, a plan that will be promoted by Sir Owen Asher, a wealthy, womanizing aristocrat who has become enthralled with Evelyn. Evelyn views Owen as a sophisticated aesthete who stands in exotic contrast to the provincials of her village. Thinking to keep Evelyn as one of his many mistresses, he convinces her to leave her father and accompany him to Paris for operatic training, where he will undertake her education and manage her career. She believes she will one day marry Owen but not until her career has developed.

A voracious reader of DARWIN, Huxley, and Herbert Spencer, Owen revels in quoting Balzac. Owen pronounces Paris Balzac's town, the writer's work and its sexual imagery providing a backdrop for Evelyn's own artistic and sexual awakening. While ardently supporting Evelyn's development into a world-renowned performer, Owen falls completely in love and asks her to marry him. Ironically, Evelyn is the one who chooses to delay the marriage during their 10-year relationship. She remains faithful to Owen, despite many temptations by other men, until in Italy she meets the young musician, Ulick Dean. Evelyn's struggle between her loyalty to the devoted Owen and the passion she feels for Ulick fills many subsequent pages. She finally escapes by supporting a Catholic convent concertizing for charity, rejecting her public music career and both of her lovers.

Moore provides an overview of Victorian mores through his shaping of their mixed effect on Evelyn. Religion and morality remain important to Evelyn, but not in a strictly traditional manner. She views fidelity to one man, even outside of the marriage bond, as adhering to religious edict prohibiting adultery. While Owen views religion as repressive and lacks belief in an afterlife, opting for art as his religion, Evelyn views her faith as expressive and even liberating, closely linked to her art. Moore sketches Evelyn as an amazingly independent and sensual woman. While dedicated to her music and self-indulgent with her two lovers, she retains a healthy sense of ethics that will not allow her to leave Owen for Ulick. Moore recounts in detail her struggles between loyalty to Owen and passion for Ulick, resulting in her choice of the freedom from sexual entanglement provided by a Catholic convent and its community of women. He creates a lengthy conversation between Evelyn and a monsignor that allows readers to see her work through her confusion to arrive at a conviction that relieves her conflict. This conveniently allows Evelyn to abandon, or at least delay, her choice between marriage and the single life and provides an opportunity for Moore to write the novel's sequel, *Sister Theresa* (1901). Both novels are thought to have been part of one original manuscript in excess of 300,000 words. Moore would later revise the second novel, producing two versions; in the first, Evelyn becomes a nun, while in the second she leaves the convent, dissatisfied with its spiritual offerings.

Extremely popular when published, the novel eventually went out of print for decades. Its melodramatic plot contributed to its eventual decrease in popularity, but its importance as a step toward the development of the realistic novel revived it. Many aspects of *Evelyn Innes* prove of interest to FEMINIST CRITICS, including multiple scenes with birds, creatures traditionally symbolic of women. These birds are not caged, but fly freely and sing with abandon, as does Evelyn. When Ulick observes her performance as Isolde, he feels he observes "a soul's transfiguration," complete with a sound like wings and a rising "like a lark's flight." Later, as Evelyn reads St. Teresa's *Book of Her Life,* she feels she stands on a hill watching a wild bird soar with heaven's light on its back. In addition, Evelyn's primary interest in her career, rather than in the domestic sphere, contrasts to that of the "typical" woman of her era. In struggling over whether she should leave her father, she thinks that only "study" and "seriousness and fidelity to an idea; fidelity to Owen above all things" proves essential. Her placement of her "idea" above "Owen" proves predictive of her eventual choice of artistic ideals over physical passion.

Issues of power remain important, as evidenced in a later scene that reveals Owen's premature confidence in Evelyn's enjoyment of "the gentle imposition of his will," which "never galled the back that bore it, but lay upon it soft as a silken gown." Slowly a gender role reversal occurs, as Evelyn clearly takes charge of herself and of the relationship, earning an admirable income and controlling Owen's will. He engages in reflection on his image in mirrors, an activity usually reserved for female characters, and he worries that Evelyn will consider herself living in sin, oppressed by a guilt that she never feels. Ironically, she comes simply to accept that she had sinned, with no fear other than that of perhaps losing those she loves. As she comes to doubt her passion for Owen, he declares his more fervently, comparing her to "a marvelous jewel" he had found, emphasizing the traditional male view of females as objects to collect. Additional traditional symbolism of woman as an ocean, the mother of all life, appears within the same scene. Such words suffocate Evelyn, as she matures beyond her need for Owen's support and then for Ulick as well. Of additional interest to feminist critics is the declaration by Owen's friend that some type of madness must possess Evelyn to cause her to ask for a separation from Owen after their 10-year relationship. The idea that a woman must suffer from insanity if she rejects the company of men is another tradition of romantic fiction.

By the time Moore wrote *Evelyn Innes,* he had moved beyond his fascination with Émile Zola, an early influence on his writing that led him to focus on minute physiological details, resulting in a clumsy style. In this novel, his style remained somewhat burdened by a partially successful attempt at a sophisticated tone. Moore believed his focus on art and music would result in a narrative elegance, but he knew too little about both topics. His insertion of technical terminology and attempts at witty flippant remarks on the part of his characters appears forced and mars his narrative. However, the three years spent in revisions on *Evelyn Innes* is evident in the novel's gentle humor and consistent compassion toward its characters. Lionel Stevenson compares Moore to Henry JAMES, as *Evelyn Innes* deftly shapes a woman in three stages of emotional development: early conflict, self-deception, and eventual graceful acceptance of personal failure.

BIBLIOGRAPHY

Blood, Brian. "The Dolmetsch Story." *Dolmetsch.com.* Available online. 2002. http://www.dolmetsch.com/Dolworks. htm. Downloaded December 20, 2002.

Stevenson, Lionel. *The English Novel.* Boston: Houghton Mifflin, 1960.

Sutherland, John. *The Longman Companion to Victorian Fiction.* Essex, U.K.: Longmans, 1988.

EWING, JULIANA (HORATIA) (1841–1885)

A crucial figure in the development of CHILDREN'S LITERATURE, Juliana Gatty was born in 1841, oldest daughter to a Yorkshire vicar. As a young woman, she entertained her siblings with stories, and by the age of 20 had published in *The Monthly Packet,* Charlotte M. YONGE's periodical. She married army captain Alexander Ewing in 1867. Her mother, Margaret, published her own children's journal in 1866 titled *Aunt Judy's Magazine,* in which Juliana later published a book in serial installments, *Mrs. Overtheway's Remembrances* (1869). A popular work, it received critical praise for its detailed and well-rendered scenes of family life.

Ewing published many stories, some featuring animals, such as a pink-nosed bulldog in "Amelia." Other well-known stories included "Timothy's Shoes" and "A Flat Iron for a Farthing." She married Major Alexander

Ewing on June 1, 1867. A sympathetic woman, she generally elicited positive reactions from others, including one male admirer, quoted in the biography of Ewing written by her sister, Horatia K. F. Gatty, who supposedly told Ewing, "'It's the trust that such women as you repose in us men, which makes us desire to become more like what you believe us to be.'" Ewing's next novel, *Jan of the Windmill* (1876), featured a foundling who would mature into a famous painter. The title of her *The Brownies and Other Tales* (1870) prompted Sir Robert Baden-Powell to adopt the name "Brownies" for the youngest members of the Girl Guide movement. Later posted with her husband overseas, she suffered a long illness and died at age 44. Although her works lost favor in the 20th century, they proved influential in the continuing development of reading for juveniles.

BIBLIOGRAPHY

Avery, Gillian. *Mrs. Ewing.* New York: H. Z. Walck, 1961.

Gatty, Horatia Katherine Frances. *Juliana Horatia Ewing and Her Books.* London: Society for Promoting Christian Knowledge, 1885. A Celebration of Women Writers. Available online. URL: http://digital.library.upenn.edu/women/ewing/gatty/part-i.html. 2001. Downloaded March 15, 2002.

Laski, Marghanita. *Mrs. Ewing, Mrs. Molesworth, and Mrs. Hodgson Burnett.* New York: Oxford University Press, 1951.

F

FALCON FAMILY, THE MARMION SAVAGE (1845) Marmion SAVAGE's first novel, *The Falcon Family, or Young Ireland*, satirized parasitic socialites, traditionalists within the Church of England, and the Young Ireland Party, a group of extremists who campaigned for Ireland's independence. Published anonymously, the novel proved popular, although its heavy-handed, relentless, and sometimes strained humor worked against that popularity in later generations.

Savage focuses on the English Falcon family of the novel's title for its plot framework. That family includes Mr. Peregrine Falcon, nicknamed "Red Rover" for his red nose and mobile lifestyle; his wife, Mrs. Falcon, nicknamed "The Gypsy," for transient ways equal to those of her husband; their three daughters, one of whom adds to the novel's romantic-interest subplot, and a son. The Falcons have a reputation for moving into the homes of acquaintances under the ruse of a temporary visit and commandeering, long-term, all resources. They so traumatize their reluctant "hosts" that members of high society tremble when they heard the family's name. Savage satirizes the Falcons' victims as much as he does the Falcons themselves. Too embarrassed to shirk their perceived social duty by turning away a family they all clearly detest and recognize as opportunists, the entire upper echelon of Marylebone allows itself to be held hostage by the hard and fast rules of hospitality. Specifically, "the Puddicomes, of Wimpole-street quaked; the Jenkinsens of Portland Place were fluttered; a family of Duckworths retreated to Norwood; and the Bompases, of Byanston-square, were divided between burning their house and starting upon a continental tour" when they heard that the Falcon family was on the move. The Freemans agree to let them move in, but abandon their house to the unwanted guests, despite the fact that they describe Mrs. Falcon as having "peculiarities," including "vagrant habits, and the loose morality: she's Egyptian all over; a handsome strolling beggar," because, as Mrs. Freeman points out, the Falcons are "such friends of the Bompases." Mr. Falcon was "living proof that a man may be shallow, without being indebted to Cambridge, or under the slightest obligation to Oxford." These two caricatures provide much of the novel's comedy.

As Savage maps the Falcon family's strategy for survival, he transports them to Ireland, where Falcon takes one of dozens of various positions he has held, becoming "Secretary to the Irish Branch Society for the Conversion of the Polish Jews." Savage also traces the activities of additional characters, including the Irish students Mr. Tigernach Mac Morris and Mr. Dominick Moore, who agree that in Ireland "your poets are politicians and your politicians poets." They decide that when classes dismiss, they will briefly suspend their poet lifestyle and join the Young Ireland Club, Savage's send-up of the Young Ireland Party, simply as a hobby. They are joined by Virus Verdaunt, the Brehon; Myrald O'Harper, the Bard; Shane Mac Ever-boy, and his brother Vincent, all of whom attend meetings at the Hall of Clamour. Savage makes fun of every aspect of the political group, including their yellow-shirted uniforms. In one memorable scene, Shane pulls out an enormous stretch of saffron colored material, a shirt that Vincent mistakes as a curtain. The conversation includes mention of a statute by Henry VIII prohibiting the use of saffron dye, and of the English poet Edmund Spenser's criticism in his essay "State of Ireland" of the "glybbe, the mantle, and the saffron shirt." In further SATIRE of Ireland itself, when Falcon questions why it is called the Green Isle, one native replies that he yearns for "less babbling of green fields" and "more tilling of them."

Jibes against the ritualization of the church include one scene in which two pages of detail describe the ornate fixtures in one chapel. It holds a special reliquary box that contains a tooth of St. Munchin, with altars tended by lovely young virgins. As the plot evolves, a romance develops between Emily Falcon and Tigernach Mac Morris, with class expectations causing conflict. All conflict resolves, however, when Tigernach is recognized as possessing sufficient funds and social standing to meet Mrs. Falcon's demands for her daughter. The book concludes with "the Norman falcon" swooping "up the Celtic eaglet" or, as Moore sums up, "This is the Norman invasion all over again— a new chapter for Thierry."

Some critics view Savage's gentle satire as an expression of his affection for both England and Ireland, with the young people's marriage symbolizing essential political arbitration. He believed moderation was the key to solving the England/Ireland problems of the 1840s.

BIBLIOGRAPHY

Paralee, Norman. *Marmion Wilme Savage: Dublin's Victorian Satirist.* Lewiston, N.Y.: Edwin Mellen, 2000.

FANTASY FICTION   Fantasy fiction incorporates aspects that demand a suspension of expectations of reality on the part of the reader. The plot depends on any of a number of fantastical elements to succeed. These might include travel through time; a suspension of adherence to normal physical rules, such as that of gravity; the changing of physical shape and or format on the part of living beings; the creation of life by means other than physical conception and birth; the existence of organisms much smaller, larger, or monstrous than the norm; the existence of beings from another universe; the ability of animals to speak and behave with human intelligence, known as anthropomorphism; and the presence of magic or mysticism. Much fantasy fiction is fashioned for children, such as Lewis CARROLL's ALICE IN WONDERLAND and THROUGH THE LOOKING-GLASS, which contain many of the above elements, or Anna SEWELL's BLACK BEAUTY, in which horses speak to one another. However, adult fiction may also contain fantasy elements, an example being Emily BRONTË's WUTHERING HEIGHTS, in which the character of Cathy appears in ghost form on the moors following her death. Fantasy elements may be simply suggested in GOTHIC FICTION, which depends greatly on visions and ghosts, or injected into the plot as a reality. In Horace Walpole's CASTLE OF OTRANTO, for example, an ancient prophecy proves true when a statue comes to life and grows to extraordinary size, eventually growing larger than a castle. Adventure novels, such as Henry Rider HAGGARD's KING SOLOMON's MINES and ALLAN QUATERMAIN, incorporate many of the fantastic elements present in the QUEST plot on which they are based. One type of fantasy fiction called SCIENCE FICTION was represented in the 19th century in works such as Edward BULWER-LYTTON's satirical utopian novel The COMING RACE, based on the existence of a race of humans living at the center of the Earth. Science fiction may involve all the elements of fantasy, but almost always includes time travel, suspension of natural laws, and a setting that includes aliens from another world that differs in geography and/or dimension from that of Earth. Two of the best-known products of fantasy/science fiction are the novels DRACULA and FRANKENSTEIN, featuring monsters of the same names, by Bram STOKER and Mary SHELLEY, respectively. Early fantasy novels enjoyed by both children and adults were Daniel DEFOE's ROBINSON CRUSOE and Robert Louis STEVENSON's TREASURE ISLAND and The STRANGE CASE OF DR. JEKYLL AND MR. HYDE.

Popular in the earliest of fiction, the fantasy genre remains extraordinarily popular in the present as well.

BIBLIOGRAPHY

Kelleghan, Fiona, ed. *Classics of Science Fiction and Fantasy Literature.* Pasadena, Calif.: Salem Press, 2002.

Westfahl, Gary, and George Slusser, and David Leiby, eds. *Worlds Enough and Time: Explorations of Time in Science Fiction and Fantasy.* Westport, Conn.: Greenwood Press, 2002.

FAR FROM THE MADDING CROWD

THOMAS HARDY (1874) Thomas HARDY's fourth novel, *Far from the Madding Crowd,* became his first commercially successful venture, allowing him to leave his vocation of architecture and write full time. First published as a serial in *The CORNHILL MAGAZINE* from January through December 1874, it would appear later that year in book form. The novel introduced "Wessex," a fictional geographical location that Hardy would also include in future works as his setting. He drew the title from poet Thomas Gray's famous "Elegy Written in a Country Churchyard." The novel bears its episodic imprint in "cliff-hanger" conclusions to various chapters that entice the reader to anticipate what follows. The novel reflects Hardy's turn from traditional religion, based on tenets of blind faith, to scientific ideas of natural chance, such as that expressed in Charles DARWIN's evolutionary theory, to explain the fate that seems to govern humans. As he did in other novels, Hardy focuses on the country and nature as relief from what he shaped as the negative consequences of industrialization, his title reflecting the idea that one must substitute the rural for the urban to find a modicum of peace. In a plot populated by characters with highly symbolic names, Hardy uses the themes of uncontrollable fate and misunderstanding to weave his tale of betrayal, death, and eventual partial redemption. Often compared to George ELIOT in his emphasis on the sadly predictable illogic of human nature, Hardy was never accused of framing an optimistic or lighthearted novel.

The aptly named temptress protagonist, Bathsheba Everdene, charms several males, including 28-year-old Gabriel Oak. Owner of a sheep flock, Oak's surname and his flute playing identify him with tales of sylvan fields, a mythological and antiquated force. The narrator describes his first sighting of Bathsheba in terms that strongly foreshadow their cursed future, seemingly determined in typical Hardy approach by uncontrollable universal forces: "He saw her in a bird's-eye view, as Milton's Satan first saw Paradise." Oak faces not only romantic disappointment when Bathsheba rejects him but also financial ruin as his sheepdog goes berserk and herds his entire flock of 200 sheep, many of them pregnant ewes symbolically and literally filled with promise, off a cliff to their deaths. That action foreshadows the later "driving to death" by human forces of the deceived Fanny Robin and her infant. When Oak then loses his property, he takes up residence as a worker on Bathsheba's farm, which she has recently inherited. Once penniless, she becomes financially independent, an unusual state for a single woman.

Oak heroically stops a destructive fire on the farm, gaining Bathsheba's gratitude. In an interesting turn on the use of traditional symbolism, Hardy does not allow the fire to complete its normal purification through destruction, foreshadowing a later more serious destruction of human life. Oak does well, moving from his original shepherd duties to become a bailiff. Meanwhile, Bathsheba, true to her capricious nature, sends a Valentine greeting to her neighbor, Farmer Boldwood, who guesses the anonymous note is from Bathsheba. A weak-willed man, Boldwood misinterprets Bathsheba's gesture and falls in love with his teasing neighbor solely on the basis of the Valentine. A third male character, the unlikable Sergeant Troy, has impregnated Fanny Robin, then refused to marry her after she mistakenly goes to the wrong church for the wedding ceremony. The abandoned Fanny is left to bear her child alone, suffering through a lonely pregnancy while working to support herself at the dreaded Casterbridge workhouse. Simultaneously, Troy romances Bathsheba. They marry in a secret ceremony, resulting in a miserable marriage haunted by Troy's concerns about Fanny Robin. When Fanny and her infant die, Troy grieves at the coffin in Bathsheba's presence, then, overcome with remorse, disappears. He is thought to have drowned, a mistaken impression that will later be corrected with tragic results. Again Hardy employs a traditional symbol of cleansing, rebirth, and new life, that of water, in an ironic way. Troy indeed moves on to a new life, but not one of a spiritual nature. He joins a traveling circus in the West Country.

Never able to exist long without a love interest, and believing herself a widow, Bathsheba accepts Farmer Boldwood's frantic attentions, and they become engaged, marking her turn to more practical thinking. When Troy resurfaces at their engagement party, the enraged Boldwood murders him and then attempts an unsuccessful suicide. Bathsheba reacts with newly developed strength, cradling the murdered Troy's head in her lap. The narrator comments that she astonished "all around her now, for her philosophy was her conduct, and she seldom thought practicable what she did not practice. She was of the stuff of which great men's mothers are made."

Boldwood turns himself over to the police, is tried, convicted of murdered and sentenced to execution, but his sentence is eventually commuted to life in prison. Capital punishment would remain a focus for Hardy, reappearing as a theme in several additional novels, all of which condemn the practice. The commutation of such sentences signals a redemption for those convicted, who generally murder rashly as a result of romantic passion. The object of the passion seldom deserves the sacrifice. In the novel's conclusion, Oak, now manager of both Bathsheba's and Boldwood's farms, plans to depart the area, feeling he can never win Bathsheba's hand. But after the passing of "one legal year" of widowhood for Bathsheba, the two do agree to marry. Their marriage, her second, and the result of his second request, also mark a redemptive second chance for both. As the closing narrative states, their relationship held that "substantial affection" that grows from two people first knowing "the rougher sides of each other's character, and not the best till further on, the romance growing up in the interstices of a mass of hard prosaic reality."

FEMINIST CRITICS will find of interest roles occupied by women characters. Hardy falls back on traditional caricatures. He labels Bathsheba a temptress, simply by giving her the name of one of the Bible's most famous temptresses. However, he also reminds readers that Bathsheba played an innocent part in her biblical temptation of King David, who spied on her and accomplished the death of her husband, his loyal soldier, in order to possess her as his own. In Fanny Robin, Hardy invokes images of a harbinger of spring and new life who does engage in the sin of premarital sex and is symbolically rejected by the church, which should support all those in peril, when she goes to the wrong chapel. However, rather than imitating the typical whore figure, Hardy shapes Fanny as a sympathetic character, wronged not only by the male sex drive and refusal of responsibility but also by religion and society. She pays the ultimate price for her sins in death, taking her innocent child with her, and Hardy clearly suggests that fate is better for her than would be her fate had she married the undependable and shallow Troy. Freudian/PSYCHOANALYTIC critics focus on the multiple emphases on sexual alliances and, along with feminist critics, on women as sex objects. Traditional FORMALIST critics focus on the symbolism of the characters' names, including that of Gabriel Oak. Bearing the first name of an avenging angel, he will obviously play a part in rescuing the novel's heroine. His surname of Oak suggests strength and wisdom and aligns him with nature and the pastoral scene, a frequent emphasis in Hardy novels. By associating Oak so closely with nature, and vice versa, Hardy promotes a vision common to his best poetry, soon to follow publication of this novel. The irony inherent to the novel's title, which falsely suggests that humans can escape their own destructive natures by relocating from an urban to a rural scene, is also helpful in understanding the story.

The novel remains extremely popular and has been transformed into multiple dramatic versions for stage and screen.

BIBLIOGRAPHY
Schweik, Robert C., ed. *Far from the Madding Crowd: An Authoritative Text, Backgrounds, and Criticisms.* New York: Norton, 1986.

FEMINIST CRITICS/CRITICISM/FEMINISM

Feminist criticism, born of a political and social movement to claim material, social, and civic rights for women, became important in the mid-20th century. The feminist agenda is basically fourfold: to recover works written by women but not originally credited to them, and to include known women writers in the literary canon; to revise the approach to reading female-written works, searching for a subtext that works against stereotypes of women in literature; to investigate whether naturally engendered differences exist between writing by women and writing by men; and to study stereotypes of women created in literature by male writers and observe how such characterizations changed over time, as well as how women read about women. Like all literary critics, feminist critics use the tools of FORMALISM to arrive at the meaning of fiction. Those tools include the ELEMENTS OF FICTION, or narrative elements of fiction, such as plot, character, theme, setting, style, and point of view. However, they consider additional elements, including the historical era in which authors write, and how fiction depicts that era and its social mores, particularly those pertaining to women's rights, and the biographies of the authors, especially if the author's background seems to be responsible for that author's inclusion of certain subjects and themes.

Particularly important to feminist critics are power relationships in fiction. While the male traditionally holds material power over the female, especially in works before the mid-20th century, she may succeed in subverting that power. One way to do so is by using her talents or sexuality to bargain for her own power, as does Lady Lyndon in William Makepeace THACKERAY's highly misogynistic *BARRY LYNDON* (1844) and the aptly named Becky Sharp in Thackeray's *VANITY FAIR* (1848). She may also subvert power relationships by turning what may at first be a disadvantage to her advantage. For example, males might demand silence of females as a culturally approved point of control, but the female character might, by failing to reveal crucial knowledge, use her silence to her benefit. Examples include Isabella Wardour from Sir Walter SCOTT's *The ANTIQUARY* (1816), who remains at first silent regarding her knowledge of the secret identity of William Lovel, or Claire de Cintre in Henry JAMES's *The AMERICAN* (1877), who takes her silence and isolation so far as to move into a convent, a female bastion free of male sexual and materialistic demands. Others claim power bestowed by their particular talents, such as the title heroine of Charlotte BRONTE's *JANE EYRE* (1847), whose art fills her with a most unladylike passion, which she freely expresses in her narration. In a few cases, female characters claim male power, such as Jane AUSTEN's title character in *EMMA* (1816), who, secure in her inheritance of her father's fortune, a circumstance other Austen female characters lack, states that she will not marry as she wields her considerable social power in an attempt at love matches. Rowena, of Scott's *IVANHOE* (1819), proves herself an able match in nobility and courage to the novel's male title character. In still other cases, the female protagonist may meet tragedy as punishment for her independence, a characteristic that would have been admired and rewarded in a male, a good example being the title character of James's *DAISY MILLER* (1879). However, James would later fashion a more mature Daisy in the character of Isabel Archer, protagonist of *The PORTRAIT OF A LADY* (1881), a woman punished by her husband for her spirit but who remains victorious due to the self-understanding she acquires.

Feminist critics also focus on the importance of traditional symbols in fiction, such as the caged bird, long symbolic of a woman admired for her appearance and her talent, yet restrained and imprisoned, physically, emotionally, or spiritually. Other traditional symbols include all types of flowers, but especially the rose; a rosebud generally symbolizes a young virginal woman, while a fully bloomed rose symbolizes a woman of sexual maturity. Certain colors relate symbolically to women, such as white, which in the Western tradition represents purity or naiveté. Thus, women who wear white may be innocent young girls, or white may be used ironically, to indicate women who have lost their innocence. The moon traditionally represents woman, who lacks her own importance, and thus reflects the light of the sun, symbolic of man. Mirrors are symbolic of self-reflection and indicate questions of self-identity for both male and female characters, but they are even more important for females, who traditionally had to worry constantly about their appearance. In writing about literature, feminist critics have also noted how women themselves have been used as mirrors for men, who desired their praise and support in such a way that the women served as reflections for the men. In literature, women of great beauty may also be compared to statuary or other collectible works of art, often important to men only for their acquisitive value. Equally important to feminist critics is the presence of any type of domestic creative endeavor on the part of women characters, as women had for centuries to suppress their artistic bent; painting, writing and sculpting were viewed as imprudent and impractical for women. They engaged instead in "approved" activities, such as needlework, cooking, and gardening to express their artistic talents.

Feminist critics find interesting three traditional roles for women in early fiction, including that of the angel in the house, an idea especially associated with Victorian women. In the late 1850s, British poet Coventry Patmore wrote a series of poems titled *The Angel in the House* that praised women who could manage large families, serve others, and remain pure and "angelic." This image led writer Virginia Woolf to later declare that she had to kill the angel in the house in order to liberate her imagination to write as she should. A second stereotype, also promoted by Victorian fiction, was the invalid. Many women did suffer physical disability following multiple unrestricted childbirths, and the prone position was quite an acceptable one for a wife and mother. The third stereotype, that of the whore, appeared in various versions. The whore might appear as a temptress, stealing an unwitting male from his wife and family. In another version, she might be the "whore with a heart of gold," who sacrificed not only her body to support herself financially but also her emotional and spiritual needs, falling in love with men who, lacking the stigma attached to the women whose sexual services they used, rejected whores as potential wives or serious lovers.

By the time that feminist criticism arrived in the mid-20th century, those critics also had as a focus changing the traditional literary canon studied in education. Long filled mainly with works by white male writers, the canon slowly altered over several decades to include not only white women writers but also women of color and of various ethnic backgrounds.

BIBLIOGRAPHY

Backscheider, Paula R., and John J. Richetti. Introduction. *Popular Fiction by Women 1660–1730. Oxford: Clarendon Press*, 1996.

Buikema, Rosemaire, and Anneke Smelik, eds. *Women's Studies and Culture: A Feminist Introduction.* Atlantic Highlands, N.J.: Zed Books, 1995.

Felski, Rita. *Literature after Feminism.* Chicago: University of Chicago Press, 2003.

Gilbert, Sandra M., and Susan Gubar, eds. *The Norton Anthology of Literature by Women: The Traditions in English.* 2nd ed. W.W. Norton: New York, 1996.

Heilbrun, Carolyn G. *Writing a Woman's Life.* New York: Ballantine, 1988.

FERRIER, SUSAN (EDMONSTONE) (1782–1854)

Susan Edmonstone was born in Edinburgh on September 7, 1782, daughter to Helen Coutts and James Ferrier. Her father served as Writer to the Signet and advised the fifth duke of Argyll in legal matters. Ferrier was a friend and colleague of Sir Walter SCOTT, a novelist who had a strong effect on her later writings. She often accompanied her father on visits to the duke's estate, Inverary Castle, and those journeys supplied details later included in the settings of her novels. Ferrier lived with her father and managed their household affairs following her mother's death in 1797. Never married, she left Edinburgh only for a four-year period from 1800 to 1804 to live with her sister in London. She returned to live with her father, becoming an active member of the Edinburgh literary scene. Scott enjoyed her three novels that focused on Scottish life, and he described her as "simple, full of humour, and exceedingly ready at repartee, and all this without the least affectation of the BLUESTOCKING."

Ferrier's first novel, MARRIAGE (1818), reflected the influence of Jane AUSTEN, an author also praised by Scott, and appeared in the same year as Austen's posthumous novel, PERSUASION (1818). Like *Marriage*, The INHERITANCE (1824) was published anonymously by William Blackwood. Praised by Scott and others, the novel attracted the manager of Covent Garden Theatre, and he petitioned the novelist Catherine Grace GORE to write a dramatic version for the stage. Apparently the novel's well-developed plot and acutely derived characters made it a prime topic for dramatization. However, Mrs. Gore declined the assignment, and it was produced under different authorship, quickly closing. According to Sir George

Douglas, the famous English poet Alfred Lord Tennyson used the plot of *The Inheritance* as an outline for his ballad *Lady Clare*. Ferrier published *Destiny* in 1831 and, as in her two previous novels, sketched a comedy of manners. She dedicated that novel to Scott, who had helped her negotiate the large advance of £1,700 from her publisher. Even critics who had previously praised Ferrier's efforts agreed that *Destiny's* effect was dulled by her heavy-handed didacticism, representing the author's decline. Her strong moral vision led her to join the Free Church in later years, prompting the end of her writing career. Suffering from poor eyesight in later years, she lived a quiet existence until her death on November 5, 1854. Ferrier offered cautionary tales to young women who make imprudent decisions regarding marriage, warning against the selection of a mate based on romantic illusions. While not widely read in later centuries, Ferrier's novels remain of interest to FEMINIST CRITICS and NEW HISTORICIST CRITICS with interest in the development of the female novelist's voice and literary influences on 19th-century women writers.

BIBLIOGRAPHY

Cullinan, Mary. *Susan Ferrier.* Boston: Twayne, 1984.

Douglas, Sir George Brisbane. *The Blackwood Group.* Edinburgh: Oliphant Anderson & Ferrier, 1897.

Grant, Aline. *Susan Ferrier of Edinburgh, a Biography.* Denver: A. Swallow, 1957.

FIELDING, HENRY (1707–1754)

Henry Fielding was born into an aristocratic family that managed always to need money. He spent his childhood at Sharpham Park, Somerset, with his father, Edmund, a profligate who would marry four times, the last time as a convicted debtor under arrest in the Old Bailey. Henry's mother died when he was an adolescent, and he matured under the care of an aunt and his maternal grandmother. Educated at Eton, he went later to London to study law during the later 1720s. His disputed inheritance left him short of funds. Even so, he desired to become a playwright and enjoyed a modicum of success, particularly with his 1730 drama, *Tom Thumb: A Tragedy,* produced at the Haymarket Theater. He wrote more than two dozen plays before political forces imposed censorship on play productions. At that point, he decided to turn to fiction in order to support himself and his wife, Charlotte Cradock, whom he married in 1734.

Fielding returned to legal studies and was called to the bar in 1740; soon after, he engaged in writing political articles, editing *The Champion* from late 1739 to mid-1741. Adopting the pseudonym of Captain Hercules Vinegar, Fielding continued his opposition to Walpole. When Walpole lost his post as prime minister, Fielding began to edit *The True Patriot* and later the burlesque *Jacobite's Journal* through 1748. He reacted to the popularity of Samuel RICHARDSON's epistolary sentimental work, PAMELA, OR VIRTUE REWARDED (1740), labeled by many as the first English novel, by making clear his disdain in his PARODY titled *Shamela* (1741). Thinking to write an additional parody, he began work on JOSEPH ANDREWS (1742), a tale of Pamela's brother. However, the book became something quite more than a parody, advancing Fielding as a prominent name in the continuum of the development of the novel. A popular, humorous work, it followed the adventures and mishaps of the naive Joseph and his friend Parson Adams. He followed that work with the three-volume *Miscellanies* (1743), Part 3 comprised The LIFE OF JONATHAN WILD THE GREAT, an ironic fable that considered the life and execution of real-life criminal Wilde, much to the chagrin of some critics who considered such works, later labeled NEWGATE FICTION, damaging to readers through their focus on unsavory characters.

After Fielding's wife died in 1744, he was criticized for marrying her maid, Mary Daniel, three years later. The match proved a solid one, however, supporting the work he had begun on one of the 18th century's most important works, *The History of* TOM JONES, A FOUNDLING (1749). In 1748, Fielding enjoyed an appointment as Justice of the Peace for Westminister and for Middlesex. He produced several essays reflecting the concerns that preoccupied him during office, social injustice and abuses and judicial corruption. Along with his brother John, he organized Britain's first detective police force, called the Bow Street Runners. He also occupied himself helping his sister Sarah FIELDING in her writing career. Sarah had, ironically, become close friends with Richardson, the target of her brother's disgust, and she developed a literary circle of her own. Henry maintained a positive relationship with the unmarried Sarah, the last surviving of his four sisters, helping her financially throughout her life.

Tom Jones became a comic classic, considered Fielding's finest achievement. The adventures of its hero, a man of everyday appetites and weaknesses, is related by a narrator who also proved a crucial character to the novel, not only in sharing the plot with readers but also commenting on the art of fiction and the development of the novel. His final novel, *Amelia* (1751), proved less popular, likely due in part to its grim tone as Fielding developed a plot based on his own experience of social hardships, shared by many in the city. In 1752, Fielding took up journalism again, editing *The Covent Garden Journal,* adopting the pseudonym Sir Alexander Drawcansir. Just as he had expressed his negative assessment of Richardson, he engaged in a written quarrel with Tobias SMOLLETT, a well-known novelist. However, deteriorating health somewhat curbed his ability to participate in many such jousts. Hoping to improve his asthma and gout, he sailed for Lisbon in 1754 with his wife and daughter. He would die there in 1754, leaving one work, the rather depressing record of his final travels, *The Journal of a Voyage,* to be published the following year.

Fielding was remembered by his contemporaries as a witty, intelligent man with a generous nature and a great sympathy for the human condition, delighting in, as he wrote in *The Champion,* "the happiness of mankind." While his plays are no longer popular, his fiction remains widely read, acknowledged as some of the first to embrace an interest in what would later be termed PSYCHOLOGICAL REALISM, formulated through linear narrative.

BIBLIOGRAPHY

Battestin, Martin C., and Clive T. Probyn, eds. *The Correspondence of Henry and Sarah Fielding.* Oxford: Clarendon Press, 1993.

Paulson, Ronald. *The Life of Henry Fielding: A Critical Biography.* Oxford: Blackwell, 2000.

FIELDING, SARAH (1710–1768)

Long known most commonly as younger sister to playwright, novelist, and essayist Henry FIELDING, Sarah Fielding was born in Dorset on November 10, 1710, fourth child and third daughter of Edmund Fielding, the third son of William, fifth earl of Denbigh, and Sarah Gould, daughter to a judge of the Queen's Bench. The rise of an increased interest in women's writing in the mid-20th century, spurred by FEMINIST CRITICS, gained a modicum of fame for Sarah as an author in her own right. When Sarah was almost eight years old, her mother died, and her father would remarry, bringing an additional six stepbrothers into the family. Sarah and her siblings lived with their maternal aunt in between their father's marriages. Their grandmother, Lady Sarah Davidge Gould, aided their aunt in attempts to alienate the children from their father and new stepmother, a task made simpler by Edmund's appointment as colonel of a new Regiment of Invalids, a job that kept him away from his family. Lady Gould kept Sarah's brother Edmund, while Henry left home to board at Eton and all the girls were enrolled in a boarding school. Lady Gould sued their father for the children's inheritance, fearing it would be lost to their stepmother, whose Catholic influence she also feared. She proved successful, and the children were appointed to her care during vacations from school. While in school at Salisbury, Sarah made several important acquaintances, including Arthur Collier, Henry's contemporary, who acted as a tutor for Sarah and introduced her to his sister, Jane, later to become her closest companion and literary collaborator. If Sarah's later novel, *The Governess, or the Little Female Academy* (1749), was based on fact, her years at the school proved happy ones.

Many gaps exist in her biography following her departure from school, but in 1744, she became a celebrity with the publication of *The ADVENTURES OF DAVID SIMPLE* (1744), which would become her most famous work; she signed all subsequent works "by the author of *David Simple.*" In 1747, she published *Familiar Letters between the Principal Characters in David Simple,* and a second edition of *The Adventures* came out that same year. By that time her brother was quite famous, and he contributed prefaces to both her works. Feminist critics note that he implies in his preface to *The Adventures* that the original might have been of higher quality had he not been absent during Sarah's writing of it and unable to advise her in literary manners. She became close friends with Samuel RICHARDSON, whose crucial work PAMELA (1740) her brother satirized.

Edmund Fielding continued to run the family into debt, and following the death of Sarah's grandmother, Sarah received little guidance from any family authority figure. Edmund married for the third time in 1729 to a well-to-do widow, but with her death 10 years later came more debt. Eventually taken to court and committed to lodge in the Old Bailey, he married a fourth time but died penniless in 1741. Sarah's novels reflect the family dilemmas, emphasizing the dire straits single women could find themselves in with lack of financial support. They also featured fierce bonds between siblings who felt themselves often at war with the adult world. While she was entitled to one sixth of the inheritance from her grandmother, she never married and possessed only reading and writing skills with which to support herself. She experienced what critics term a "genteel poverty," never suffering from abject poverty or from the total dependence on a significant male that other female writers of her age did. She always enjoyed the company of lively and intelligent women, including Mrs. Frances SHERIDAN, a novelist in her own right. While financial support came from her writing income and the generosity of her brothers and various friends, she gained lifelong emotional support from a circle of faithful women companions. The theme of female companionship and the dangers of men became a great concern of her novels.

Henry helped his sister in her literary career, and she produced *The Cry: A New Dramatic Fable* in 1754, in collaboration with Jane Collier; *The Lives of Cleopatra and Octavia* (1757); *The History of the Countess of Dellwyn* (1759); and *The History of Ophelia* (1760). She produced many pages of text, as well as a collection of letters, mostly to her famous brother. At her death on April 9, 1768, she left behind a rich inheritance for later women writers. Her monument in Bath Abbey notes that she provided "incentives to virtue and honour to her sex" and that her learning in the classics taught "Athens' Wisdom to her Sex."

Fielding's works remain popular and are readily available in traditional form, as well as in electronic format, some in excerpt version.

BIBLIOGRAPHY

Battestin, Martin C., and Clive T. Probyn, eds. *The Correspondence of Henry and Sarah Fielding*. Oxford: Clarendon Press, 1993.

Bree, Linda. *Sarah Fielding*. New York: Twayne, 1996.

FOREST LOVERS, THE MAURICE HEWLETT (1898)

The Forest Lovers was the first of several ROMANCE novels by Maurice HEWLETT, who began writing of knights in medieval settings at a time when such books were at the height of popularity. He prepared readers for all the hallmarks of such fiction as he began Chapter I, titled "Prosper Le Gai Rides Out." Inserting himself into the tale in an example of authorial intervention, Hewlett announces of his story, "Blood will be spilt, virgins suffer distresses; the horn will sound through woodland glades; dogs, wolves, deer and men, Beauty and the Beasts, will tumble each other, seeking life or death with their proper tools. There should be mad work, not devoid of entertainment." He holds true to his promise, offering much in the way of enjoyable, if predictable, reading.

As the title of the first chapter indicates, the novel's protagonist, Prosper Le Gai, hears the call of destiny and leaves home to seek adventure. Son of the dead Baron Jocelyn, and turned out of his own home by his brother, Malise, Baron of Starning and Parrox, Prosper departs during the month of September, with the time of harvest serving as a symbol of an important stage in the young knight's life. Readers will gather from the novel's title and also from his symbolic name that Prosper will find romance, of both the spiritual and romantic types. In a paradox, Hewlett couples images of the forest, long a symbol of hidden danger, with that of love, suggesting the love will be gained with difficulty. Prosper sets off toward Morgraunt, a country "spoken of in a whisper," "deep . . . dark as night, haunted with the waving of perpetual woods [. . .] a mystery." There he will encounter early on the requisite resistance to his presence by bandits, allowing him to vanquish them in an easy victory.

His adventures with women, whom he claims to pay little notice, prove more difficult. First he meets a mysterious tall lady who asks his aid in burying a man she claims attacked her, then died in the middle of their struggle. Later, Prosper will encounter the equally mysterious Isoult, of unknown parentage, called La Desirous. While her name indeed suggests an object of fleshly desire, as a character points out to La Desirous, it actually means that she desires, not that others should desire her. However, her beauty and association with woodspeople cause the local authorities to label her a witch, and her life is in danger from the scheming Abbey of Saint Giles of Holy Thorn. He convinces the twice-widowed Countess Isabel, Lady of Morgraunt, to allow him to execute local undesirables, including Isoult. Readers learn early on that the so-called witch is actually Isabel's only child, removed from her shortly after her birth in a first secret marriage to a man later killed by Isabel's second husband-to-be. When Prosper rescues a female snow-white pigeon from attack by birds of prey, then learns from a local seer named Alice that she had a dream featuring a similar scene, Hewlett clearly signals the reader that Prosper will be called upon to save at least one fair damsel in distress. Because Prosper has made clear his lack of interest in women, readers also understand that he will have to learn to love the woman he rescues. That woman is Isoult.

In order to rescue Isoult from a fate even worse than execution, marriage to a despicable abbott, Prosper marries her himself. Because he considers her only a child, he leaves her in a convent to be raised by nuns. However, secret identities will later be revealed and, as the opening promised, blood spilled in the name of religious corruption and aristocratic deceit. Isoult is kidnapped and Prosper will encounter various conflicts as he honors God in "fair works," eventually battling the bully Galors in a detailed knightly combat on horseback. An unplanned revenge of his father's death and a realization by Lady Isabel, the woman Prosper had aided in the woods, all contribute to a satisfying conclusion. Reunited with Isoult, whom Galors would have claimed as his own, Prosper discovers they had met before, when, as a youth, he accompanied his father on a hunt and one of their birds of prey had attacked Isoult, then a small child, whom he rescued. Thus, he understands that destiny had reunited the two, as the seer's vision predicted, and that he is fated to reunite Isoult with her mother.

A satisfying example of the romance genre, *The Forest Lovers* is not widely read. However, it should be reintroduced to aficionados of medieval tales of knights and their lovers.

FORMALISM   Within the disciplined activity of literary analysis several different critical approaches have arisen from the most basic approach to literary analysis, which is formalism. Most recently labeled New Criticism in the 1940s, formalism has also been called modernism, aesthetic criticism, textual criticism, and ontological criticism.

Formalist criticism is a traditional way of gaining meaning from literature through the application of tools known as the ELEMENTS OF FICTION, or narrative elements of fiction. Those elements include plot, character, theme, setting, style, and point of view. They look to symbolism, both traditional and literary, imagery, vocabulary choices, author tone, foreshadowing, and irony to deduce the meaning of a story. Formalists believe only these elements are necessary to meaning in fiction. Information such as that about the historical era during which an author lived, or details relating to an author's life, or details relating to a reader's perception of the work remain unimportant to understanding literature. In the extreme, they might pronounce the author dead as soon as the words hit the page and the reader completely unimportant to a work of literature. For instance, a formalist critic would ignore the fact that Sir Walter SCOTT abhorred jousts when reading *IVANHOE* or that he loved his homeland of Scotland while enjoying *The ABBOTT* and *The ANTIQUARY*. That Charles KINGSLEY supported workers' rights and actually lived during the CHARTIST revolution would not distract a formalist critic reading *ALTON LOCKE*. They could ignore the gender of Jane AUSTEN while reading her novels that reflected on the pretentious social scene of her age, such as *SENSE AND SENSIBILITY*, and on the lack of inheritance guarantees for female children, such as *PRIDE AND PREJUDICE*. The homosexuality of Oscar WILDE would not influence their view of his male characters; Emily BRONTË's life on the moors would not color their view of the setting in *WUTHERING HEIGHTS*; they would disregard the fact that many early women authors such as Austen and the

Brontë sisters at first published anonymously due to a low view of writing women; and they would not focus on the social views and mores in Victorian novels such as those published by Elizabeth GASKELL, Charles DICKENS, Anthony TROLLOPE and many others as growing from the cultural atmosphere in which those writers lived. While all other types of literary criticism incorporate formalism, it does not return that favor, choosing to approach works as if they were created in a total vacuum. This type of criticism, while popular in the early 20th century, particularly among those practicing New Criticism, lost its popularity in light of the advances of other approaches, such as FEMINISM, MARXISM, NEW HISTORICISM, Freudianism/PSYCHOANALYTIC CRITICISM, and READER-RESPONSE CRITICISM.

BIBLIOGRAPHY

Bressler, Charles E. *Literary Criticism: An Introduction to Theory and Practice.* Prentice Hall. Englewood Cliffs, N.J., 1994.

FORTNIGHTLY REVIEW

George Henry Lewes edited the first edition of *Fortnightly Review,* founded by Anthony TROLLOPE and Frederic Chapman in 1865. Its founders hoped to offer a venue for serious liberal discussions and at first offered the magazine weekly. Because it did not prove particularly successful, publication was changed to biweekly. Editors included John Morley, who published work by George MEREDITH, John Mill, Aldolus Huxley, Algernon Swinburne, and Sir Leslie Stephen. T. H. S. Escott, Frank Harris, and W. L. Courtney also edited the magazine, which continued publication for almost 100 years. Harris took over in 1886 during a decline and, by attracting more literary work, rescued the magazine. When Courtney took the helm in 1894, he added an academic dimension to the magazine, supporting an urbane tone.

Influenced by French journalistic invention, the publication featured criticism, fiction, and plays. One of the first magazines to forego shrouding its contributors in secrecy through the use of pseudonyms, its writers who critiqued new work wanted to claim the attention of a fiction-reading public. The editors boldly dispensed with the notion that proper judgment was somehow more influential when offered by a group instead of one individual. Other magazines followed suit, using *Fortnightly Review* as a model.

Contents included serial novels, criticism, announcements of new books, articles on public affairs, and biographies. Editor Morley, an agnostic, made the magazine a mouthpiece of the positivists in the battle of rationalism against religious orthodoxy. W. L. Courtney later secured articles about World War One, giving the magazine prestige and authority.

The *Fortnightly Review* published prose by George ELIOT, Matthew Arnold, Walter Pater, Trollope, Rudyard KIPLING, and H. G. WELLS, while Thomas HARDY, Alfred Noyes, and John Basefield all contributed poetry. Sir J. M. Barrie's first serious play, *The Wedding Guest,* was published as a supplement.

BIBLIOGRAPHY

Graham, Walter. *English Literary Periodicals.* New York: Octagon Books, Inc., 1966, 258–262.

FOXGLOVE MANOR ROBERT BUCHANAN (1884)

When Robert BUCHANAN wrote *Foxglove Manor,* he had experienced years of poverty, worsened by the illness of his wife. Her death in 1881 followed the failure of his journal, *Light,* leaving him penniless and desperate for funds. In order to produce quick money, he began to produce two novels per year, some falling into the "potboiler" category. They provided shallow entertainment through sensational love stories. The first few honestly dealt with social and moral conflicts, and with *Foxglove Manor,* Buchanan focused on the corruption of the English clergy, emphasizing the devastating effects men in such positions of leadership can have on naive female congregational members. As Buchanan wrote in a "self interview" later of his poem "Wandering Jew," "Christianity had been a cloak to cover an infinity of human wickedness." He wanted to emphasize, "how Churchmen had juggled and cheated and lied in the name of Christ, and forgotten the real sweetness of [their] humanity."

Buchanan's plot pits religion against science with no subtlety. Its protagonist, a clergy of the English church, bears the surname Santley, significant in its ironic suggestion of a saintly nature. Santley is vicar to the village of Omberley, where the also significantly named Edith Dove loves him. Her surname acts as foreshadowing of her later sacrifice upon the altar of Santley's passion. The narrator makes clear Santley's devotion to ritual, which he incorporates in his worship services to combat his "age of spiritual disquiet and unbelief," in which man's natural yielding to the physical was necessary in order to combat the loss of souls to indifference or to Catholicism. This statement will prove essential to reader comprehension of the novel's conclusion.

A hypocrite in every way, Santley rekindles an immoral passion for Ellen Haldane, a previous student of his, now wife of the master of the local Foxglove Manor. When Ellen attends his service, she means only to rekindle a platonic relationship, but Santley has other plans. Throughout the novel, he vigorously pursues Ellen, who retains her spiritual strength and consistently denies him the physical love he craves. Edith understands from the first meeting of the two ex-lovers that Santley has changed his attitude toward her. Buchanan does not shape her as a foolish, blind devotee victim, but rather as a religious woman who remains open-eyed in her consideration of Santley. After witnessing his forcing an unwanted kiss on Mrs. Haldane, Edith accuses Santley of being unfaithful to his promise to marry her. With high rhetoric and the infliction of guilt, he convinces her to forgive him. Her trust is rewarded when he eventually impregnates and then abandons her. In the meantime, Haldane acts as Buchanan's mouthpiece regarding scientific theories, including evolution, as he works in his laboratory, an avowed atheist. Ellen's attempts to convert her husband to her religion continue to fail, as he remains convinced that religion is folly and only appropriate for women. Long before his wife recognizes Santley's evil hypocrisy, Haldane observes his mistreatment of Edith and labels Santley a satyr.

Haldane travels to the Continent for a scientific meeting, leaving behind his Spanish servant, Buchanan's attempt to add an exotic touch to the novel, to watch over his wife and household. His absence renders Ellen vulnerable to Santley's visits. Santley convinces himself in a melodramatic scene

that his desire for Ellen is acceptable as he asks of himself, "What is sin? Surely it is better than moral stagnation, which is death. There are certain deflections from duty which, like the side stroke of a bird's wing, may waft us higher." He actually convinces himself that his immoral passion for Ellen will lift him closer to God.

When Haldane returns, he shares with his servant his discovery of a mysterious potion that places the body in a state resembling death. He experiments by giving his servant the potion and calling the horrified Ellen to observe his deathlike state. As Santley's unwanted attentions to Ellen escalate, Haldane decides to interfere so as to discourage Santley while teaching him a lesson in faith as well. Before the lesson begins, the pregnant Edith, driven to near-madness by Santley's desertion and her pregnancy, runs away into the woods, feeling the stream there had called her. In midwinter, she lies down in the stream in a suicide attempt. She is rescued by the local Gypsy prostitute, Sal, a figure who allows Buchanan to emphasize that even the inherent goodness in the lowest socially placed human remains preferable to Santley's treacherous hypocrisy.

Haldane executes his plan by administering the mysterious potion to the unknowing Ellen, placing her in a coma. He then convinces Santley, who almost swoons at the sight of her "dead" body, that he has murdered his wife, due to her involvement with a clergyman. He accuses Santley as the true murderer through his duplicitous deceit, with Haldane acting only as the instrument. Santley contracts a "brain fever" and runs mad, accusing Haldane of murdering his wife in the presence of several villagers. When he recovers after a protracted delirium, he learns that Ellen Haldane is in perfect health and has moved to Spain for a time with her husband. Edith, following her recovery with Sal's aid, has contacted her aunt, and they too have moved away. When Santley frantically sends Edith a letter asking her to return and declaring his newly realized love for her, she replies, "I, too, have had an illness, in which, also, God has been pleased to open my eyes." She will never return to Omberley; her aunt, having realized all she suffered, "approves an eternal separation." In an obvious, although ironic, pro-Protestant reflection, Buchanan concludes the novel by stating that Santley left his parish to enter the Church of Rome.

In addition to obvious aspects of interest to FEMINIST CRITICS in the treatment of women, the story will appeal to FORMALIST critics as well, with its abundant use of symbolism, not only in character names but also in the traditional application of the seasons to signal the state of human existence. The heavy-handed symbolism and irony apparent in the conversion of Foxglove Manor's chapel to a scientific laboratory seems humorous to 21st-century readers. However, Buchanan's use of quotations from Shakespeare's *Macbeth* and allusions to Jonathan Swift, Charles Swinburne, and various "natural" philosophers trusts the reader's knowledge of cultural references for understanding, suggesting that Buchanan considered his readers neither dull nor naive, but approached his subject matter with a suitable seriousness. His "Prefatory Note" to the 1889 edition reflects that concern, as he states, in part, "I have simply pictured, in the Reverend Charles Santley, a type of man which exists, and of which I have had personal experience. Fortunately, such men are uncommon." He adds in what may or may not have been an ironic pronouncement, "fortunately, the clergymen of the English Establishment are for the most part sane and healthy men, too unimaginative for morbid deviations."

BIBLIOGRAPHY

Cassidy, John A. *Robert W. Buchanan.* New York: Twayne Publishers, 1973.

Harriett, Jay. *Robert Buchanan; some account of his life, his life's work, and his literary friendships.* 1903. Reprint, New York, AMS Press, 1970.

FRAMLEY PARSONAGE ANTHONY TROLLOPE (1861)

First published in *The CORNHILL MAGAZINE* from January 1860 through April 1861, Anthony TROLLOPE's *Framley Parsonage* was the fourth in his Barsetshire novels sequence. That sequence had opened in 1855 with *The WARDEN* and would conclude with *The LAST CHRONICLE OF BARSET* in 1867. Trollope had never intended to write the series. While the third in the series, *DOCTOR THORNE* (1859), garnered a

measure of success, he had not planned a fourth. Fortunately, circumstances dictated that he do so.

At the end of 1859, Trollope returned from the West Indies and began work on an Irish novel titled *Castle Richmond.* He offered the work for serial publication to George Smith, who operated the newly founded *Cornhill Magazine.* Smith liked the idea of publishing a Trollope work, but he wanted another English novel, and Trollope obligingly produced *Framley Parsonage* in a matter of weeks. Despite a weak critical reception, readers immensely enjoyed encountering again some of their favorite characters from previous novels in the sequence. They recognized the Grantlys and their foolish daughter Griselda, who in this sequence marries Lord Dumbello, a perfectly named match for her. They also knew well Bishop Proudie and his wife, the grasping, selfish, and decidedly un-Christian Mrs. Proudie. In addition, this novel continued the character development of Reverend Josiah Crawley, Trollope's saddest and most pitiable character. Despite the novel's popularity, *The Examiner*'s critic found Trollope without "a touch of original fancy," adding that he shaped his characters with lack of insight, while the *SATURDAY REVIEW* deemed the work of a quality fit only for "circulating libraries." Later critics redeemed *Framley Parsonage,* as in Graham Handley's evaluation of the work as "carefully constructed" and "artistically coherent."

In addition to familiar characters, the plot introduces a large cast of newcomers to Trollope's quiet setting. The living at Framley Parsonage is presented by the widowed aristocrat Lady Lufton to Mark Robarts, a friend of her son, Lord Ludovic Lufton. While Robart seems ostensibly the book's protagonist, much of the novel's attention will focus on two romantic subplots, one involving Robart's sister, Lucy, and her foil, the pretty but intellectually unchallenged Griselda Grantly. Robart meets Mr. Sowerby, whose profligate ways will affect Robarts, and the Duke of Omnium, whose lack of discretion will pull Robarts into further difficulty. Both badly influence the naive Robarts, who offends Lady Lufton by agreeing to sign for Sowerby's debts, despite his hesitation to do so. When he tells Sowerby, "As a clergyman it would be wrong of me," Sowerby responds, "If there be one class of men whose names would be found more frequent on the backs of bills in the provincial banks than another, clergymen are that class." Robarts loses sleep worrying about the £400 debt, although he is promised a prebendary, or special endowment at Barchester, for his action. His devoted wife, Fanny, warns him against overindulgence, but, enthralled with high society, Robarts accumulates additional debt.

In the meantime, Lord Lufton falls madly in love with Lucy Robarts, but she resists his advances, because she knows that Lady Lufton does not approve of the relationship due to Lucy's middle-class standing. Lucy lies, telling Ludovic that she does not love him, as she cannot bear the thought of Lady Lufton spreading rumors that she had trapped her son. Her insistence that Ludovic's mother approve of their marriage eventually influences Lady Lufton to admire her integrity and eventually agree to the match. Critics tout Lucy and Lady Lufton as two of Trollope's best female characterizations.

For a novel that centers on the clergy, *Framley Parsonage* produces few church characters that act in a Christian way. Mrs. Proudie behaves in the most hypocritical manner, instigating a plan to break up the engagement of Griselda and Lord Dumbello, due to her jealousy. The self-centered Harold Smith declares himself a Christian, yet proves in reality to be a grasping and selfish politician. Mark Robarts allows himself to be led astray by the promise of social status. Even Archbishop Grantly displays little Christian behavior. Instead, Lucy represents the only true practicing Christian through her self-sacrifice. However, she does not become a stereotypical blameless sacrificial female lamb to her culture's social mores. She clearly regrets the loss of the fine life she might have led as Lord Lufton's wife, even though the narrator prefaces her thought by stating, "that girls should not marry for money we are all agreed." He goes on to compare such a marriage to the sale of sheep and oxen. Instead, she struggles with a lack of self-confidence that she must overcome in order to convince Lady Lufton that she will make a good match for her son, and even when she succeeds in developing that inner strength, Lady Lufton cannot fully participate without first experiencing her own conversion. Lucy places herself in physical danger by nursing the long-suffering Mrs. Crawley, and this dis-

play of raw humanity does influence Lady Lufton. But only when Lady Lufton also experiences self-conflict, understanding that she may lose her son in an attempt to force him to marry the undesirable Griselda Grantly for all the wrong reasons, does she capitulate. In one of Trollope's strongest scenes, Lady Lufton actually proposes to Lucy on behalf of her own son.

Lucy also allows Trollope to emphasize the sad character of Reverend Crawley, whose mania he may have based on the mad melancholy that often gripped Trollope's father. Forced to live in the poverty inherent to his assignment at Hogglestock, caring for an impossibly large family, Crawley becomes a tyrant, inflicting his pain on his wife, who is in no way strong enough to bear up under the assault. Misplaced pride denies his family relief in the way of charity and leads to the reverend's emotional disintegration. His painful existence is exacerbated by the necessary comparisons to his one-time good friend Dr. Arabin, the Dean of Barchester, whom he cannot forgive for having paid his debts. Crawley likely exists to demonstrate that suffering may not always prove ennobling.

Eventually Ludovic must rescue the overly ambitious Robarts, who has managed to accumulate debts living beyond his income. Robarts then vows to return to the business of the parsonage, foregoing the idle life of the high social class. However, Sowerby's debts are too enormous for rescue, and the duke has a lien on all his property. He hopes to alleviate his problems by marrying the wealthy Miss Dunstable. She, however, refuses, choosing instead to marry the sensible Dr. Thorne, the one man she knows does not love her for her money.

Trollope demonstrates through Griselda, Lucy, and Miss Dunstable that material goods should not dictate marriage. While he does not create a purely happy ending for all involved in his novel, it does end happily for the characters that deserve such a conclusion. While Lucy is filled with pride as the plot resolves itself, her pride is the type "in no way disgraceful to either man or woman."

BIBLIOGRAPHY
Handley, Graham. Introduction to *Framley Parsonage,* by
   Anthony Trollope. New York: Knopf, 1994, ix–xxi.

FRANKENSTEIN, OR THE MODERN PROMETHEUS MARY SHELLEY (1818)

The story of the events that led Mary SHELLEY to write her Frankenstein story is now almost as well known as the plot itself. The tale began to take shape in 1816 as a result of ghost-story-telling sessions held among Mary; her husband, British poet Percy Bysshe Shelley; and the self-exiled British poet George Gordon, Lord Byron, when the Shelleys lived in Switzerland. After several days lacking inspiration, Shelley had her now famous "waking dream," which she described in a preface to the novel's third edition in 1831. In part, she wrote, "What terrified me will terrify others, and I need only describe the spectre which had haunted my midnight pillow." The work and its monster-hero became such a popular subject for film and stage, in serious, comedic, and parodic productions, that many acquaint themselves with Victor Frankenstein's monster long before encountering it in Shelley's book. Many first-time readers discover with a shock that the monster remains unnamed, with his creator bearing the Frankenstein moniker. A second, stronger shock may occur when readers realize that the monster, in great contrast to the bumbling, murderous, wild-eyed, grunting, crazy-stitched object of film, proves the most rational and also the most eloquent of any of the novel's characters.

The basic plot of the novel remains powerful in its simplicity. Most of it appears in flashback, as a defeated, guilt-ridden Victor Frankenstein relates on his deathbed his tale of horror to a ship's captain, Robert Walton, the first of the novel's three narrators. He writes letters that relate his contact with Frankenstein, who hunted his human creation in the Arctic, where Walton and his crew found him. The letters advance the novel's strongest theme, that of the conflict between science and poetry, or art. While Frankenstein, once a young Swiss premedical student studying in Geneva, represents science, his beloved cousin Elizabeth Lavenza, who loves poetry, and best friend Henry Clerval, an aficionado of romance and chivalry whose surname describes his clarity of vision, represent art. As the story unfolds, readers learn that Frankenstein sought to create a composite human being from dead body parts. He reasons that those who have died might be restored if the secret to life can be found. Thus his focus is not at first on the generation of life but rather on regeneration. In what becomes a madness to reach his goal, he isolates himself from Elizabeth and Henry, ignoring their pleas that he abandon the ungodly project that comes to obsess him. Dismayed by the creature, Frankenstein allows him to escape and eventually pursues him after the monster murders several members of Frankenstein's family, including his beloved younger brother William, which leads to the execution of the Frankenstein family's maid, an innocent unjustly accused of William's murder. Frankenstein himself acts as the second narrator, his tale appearing within Walton's own, while the monster's third narration appears within Frankenstein's own.

Shelley's sophisticated structure emphasized the close connection of points of view and touched on many concerns of her era. At a time when the theory of evolution added to an ongoing debate over the nature and center of life, as well as to a prevailing argument regarding the value of science over religion, the monster's existence personified the public's greatest fears. Not only were his physical acts of violence frightening but also the cause of those acts, his rejection due to his "difference" by all humans he comes into contact with except for a blind man, leading astute readers to question in which being the true monstrous nature lurked. The monster was not "born" hating others; his hate was taught him by people who refused to see beyond his external appearance to the brilliant warm nature existing just below its surface. While science might be expected to lack compassion, the same could not be said of religion, which should have prepared the public to be more accepting. That the monster possesses a quick intellect and a natural warmth and goodness that is corrupted only by his exposure to humans remains an indictment of shallow social values and a rigid class structure. Timely political concerns surface as the monster hears lessons from Volney's *Ruins of Empire* that relate to the correct division of property and the inherent conflict between the rich and the poor.

The ironic death of Frankenstein, indirectly caused by the life he created, remains part of a cautionary tale that bears just as strong a message against humans acting outside rational boundaries two centuries after

Shelley wrote her novel. At its simplest, it is a rebuke of fathers who refuse to take responsibility for their children. At its most complicated, it represents all the ideals of romanticism and the conflicts inherent to everyday life that continue to haunt the human condition.

Because Mary Shelley became one of the few women of her age to gain eventual fame from her publication, originally published anonymously, FEMINIST CRITICS and others who study women's literature have continued to study *Frankenstein* with great interest. Although Shelley's mother, Mary WOLLSTONECRAFT, wrote the most important feminist work prior to the 19th century, *A Vindication of the Rights of Woman* (1792), and strongly advocated women's independence, Shelley did not create well-rounded female characters in her book. Critics explain this by noting she shaped the women surrounding Victor Frankenstein realistically in order to demonstrate the lack of power for women of her age. They also see the monster himself as representative of women, with his marginalization and control by the book's male protagonist. That he achieves a modicum of intellectual and physical independence, and must move beyond civic law to do so, may represent the fate of women who refused to conform to patriarchy's strict control. Shelley's emphasis of freedom of the imagination through art, while strongly romanticist in nature, also relates to one of the few types of freedom available to women, who often had to participate in the arts secretly. Like the monster that had no name, Mary Shelley herself remained officially nameless as the author of her classic for five years, until her name appeared in the 1823 second edition. Believing that Percy Bysshe Shelley had written the novel, Sir Walter SCOTT wrote of it in a review for *BLACKWOOD'S EDINBURGH MAGAZINE*, 20 March/1 April, 1818 edition:

> Upon the whole, the work impresses us with a high idea of the author's original genius and happy power of expression. We shall be delighted to hear that he has aspired to the *paullo majorica;* and, in the meantime, congratulate our readers upon a novel which excites new reflections and untried sources of emotion. If Gray's definition of Paradise, to lie on a couch, namely, and read new novels, come any thing near truth, no small praise is due to him, who, like the author of Frankenstein, has enlarged the sphere of that fascinating enjoyment.

BIBLIOGRAPHY

Jump, Harriet Devine, ed. *Women's Writing of the Romantic Period, 1789–1836: An Anthology.* Edinburgh: Edinburgh University Press, 1997.

Mellor, Anne K. *Mary Shelley: Her Life, Her Fiction, Her Monsters.* New York: Routledge, 1988.

Stillinger, Jack. Introduction to *Frankenstein,* by Mary Shelley. New York: W.W. Norton, 1996, vii–xi.

FRASER'S MAGAZINE   A publication that published reviews, serials, SATIRES, comic sketches, parodies, and BURLESQUES by novelists such as William Makepeace THACKERAY, John GALT, and Charles KINGSLEY, *Fraser's Magazine* was founded in February 1830 by William Maginn and Hugh Fraser. A longtime voice for novel criticism, it contained editorial comments such as that from the November 1850 edition: "Whoever has anything to say, or thinks he has [. . .] puts it forthwith into the shape of a novel or a tale." It reached its heights in popularity and literary influence during its management by Maginn, but continued as an important publication throughout the Victorian Age. Additional contributors included historian and philosopher Thomas Carlyle, whose immortal *Sartor Resartus* was published in *Fraser's* between November 1833 and August 1834.

BIBLIOGRAPHY

Thrall, Miriam. *Rebellious Fraser's: Nol Yorke's Magazine in the Days of Maginn, Carlyle and Thackeray.* New York: Columbia University Press, 1934.

Wellesley Index to Victorian Periodicals. Vol. 1. Edited by Walter E. Houghton, Esther Rhoads Houghton, and Jean Slingerland. Toronto: University of Toronto Press, 1989.

FREUDIANISM   See PSYCHOANALYTIC CRITICISM.

G

GALT, JOHN (1779–1839) John Galt was born in Irvine, Ayrshire, and spent his youth in Greencock. His father was a sea captain of ordinary skill, and the young Galt engaged in what his mother believed were effeminate activities, including lounging on the bed reading. In 1804, Galt moved to London to earn his living as a merchant. He wrote in his spare time and published poetry and prose. Following the failure of his business in 1808, he sailed to the Continent in hopes of avoiding wartime restrictions to trade during the Napoleonic period. He became friends with George Gordon, Lord Byron, as Byron undertook his Childe Harold pilgrimage at the Mediterranean. Galt later wrote Byron's biography, but it did not sell well. In addition to such nonfiction, he attempted poetry, plays, and journalism, none of which was successful. He returned to London following 1813 and there published his first mildly successful work, an account of his travels titled *Voyages and Travels in the Years 1809, 1810 and 1811* in BLACKWOOD'S EDINBURGH MAGAZINE in 1820. He modeled that piece on Tobias SMOLLETT'S HUMPHRY CLINKER (1771), using as a narrative vehicle letters exchanged within a Scottish family visiting London. He featured interesting current events, such as the succession of George IV, incorporating humor through the foreigners' reactions to English events.

Galt's first two novels proved failures as he attempted to write in the GOTHIC style, for which he had little tal-ent, producing incoherent and unintentionally humorous results. He at last hit his publishing stride with three successful novels. *The Annals of the Parish* (1821) had been conceived years earlier, based on *The VICAR OF WAKEFIELD* (1766) by Oliver GOLDSMITH. Narrated by a Scottish country minister who records life in a quiet neighborhood over a 50-year span, the book earned a negative evaluation by one publisher in 1813 who said the public would not find it entertaining. Although the book deals with no single topic, it was the first in English to focus on an entire community, producing a semblance of real life in its disperse events. While Maria EDGEWORTH'S CASTLE RACKRENT (1801), set in Ireland, had featured an estate community, its form was not as unified as that of Galt's works. His next books retained the humor of the Scottish atmosphere but offered centralized plots with clearer action. In *Sir Andrew Wylie* (1822), Galt's young Scottish protagonist rises to wealth and fame in London, while *The PROVOST* (1822) was intended to be "a companion" to *The Annals of the Parish,* showing the effects of improvement in an industrial, rather than a rural, area. *The Entail* (1823) features Galt's most complex plot, covering three generations, and was the first English novel to center on the history of a family. He relocated to Canada in 1826, working as secretary in a development company. He lost the post after three years, returned to England, and was imprisoned for debt. King William IV finally provided financial relief, and Galt lived out his years quietly, doing little additional writing. His final two novels, *Laurie Todd* (1830) and *Bogle Corbet* (1831), focus on his Canadian experiences.

John Galt is best remembered for his contribution to the development of the novel of local color. Some time would pass before anyone in England would try such a novel, as English life seemed far more ordinary when contrasted with that of the eccentric Scots and Irish.

BIBLIOGRAPHY
Douglas, Sir George Brisbane. *The Blackwood Group.* Edinburgh: Oliphant Anderson & Ferrier, 1897.

GASKELL, ELIZABETH (CLEGHORN) (1810–1865)
Born in Chelsea, London, Elizabeth Cleghorn was daughter of William Stevenson, a civil servant who also practiced as a Unitarian minister. She grew up in Cheshire, raised by an aunt, and attended the Avonbank School in Stratford-upon-Avon. Following her schooling, she lived for two years with a cousin, the Reverend William Turner, at Newcastle upon Tyne. She married a Unitarian parson named William Gaskell in August of 1832. He had authored various tracts and pamphlets related to his religion while holding an English history and literature chair at Manchester New College.

Gaskell wrote several short stories but found fame with her first novel, MARY BARTON (1848). Its subtitle, *A Tale of Manchester Life,* indicated its theme of the abuse and worker unrest connected with the CHARTIST MOVEMENT. While critics found the writing supported by an amateurish optimism and confidence in the goodwill of individuals, Gaskell's talent for sketching sympathetic and enduring characters made it a lasting favorite with readers. The death of her son, William, apparently motivated her to find a distraction from her grief in writing. Charles DICKENS, who also wrote THESIS NOVELS, or books protesting social inequities, publicly admired Gaskell's novel and invited her to publish in his magazine, HOUSEHOLD WORDS. She produced probably her most famous work, CRANFORD, first as a serial that ran from December 1851 until May 1853 in Dickens's publication. That novel's scenes of domestic and village life mimicked those of Knutsford, focusing on a compassionate spinster and bringing to life the quotidian for delighted readers. In RUTH (1853), Gaskell used an unwed mother as her protagonist, a bold move for her era, and again oversimplified the novel's social and moral issues. Notable is her lack of knowledge of the passions needed to shape a convincing seduction scene. However, her sympathies remain firmly with Ruth, shaped as a victim of society's ruthlessness toward women pregnant out of wedlock and the social inequities suffered by most women in the patriarchal culture. *North and South* (1855) also dealt with social confrontations.

Gaskell also wrote lengthy short stories, which she collected into several volumes, including *Life in Manchester* (1848) and *Lizzie Leigh and Other Tales* (1855). She met and became friends with Charlotte BRONTË in August 1850, and after her death in 1855 wrote the still well-received *The Life of Charlotte Brontë,* a biography that supplied a sympathetic overview of Brontë's life. The openness with which she confronted Branwell Brontë's alcoholism and behavior caused strong criticism and even questions of legal action against Gaskell, who removed the questionable passages. The final novel published during her lifetime was *Sylvia's Lovers* (1863), followed by *Wives and Daughters,* published posthumously in 1866, a novel said to be fashioned in the tradition of Jane AUSTEN's works.

Gaskell is remembered for her compassion and honesty and her style's development from melodrama to the more balanced and better-structured later novels. Horrified by the poverty in her husband's slum parish, she launched a campaign through her fiction to bring such deplorable conditions to the public's attention. Her works, especially *Cranford,* remain popular and have found a permanent place in the canon of women's fiction.

BIBLIOGRAPHY
Foster, Shirley. *Elizabeth Gaskell: A Literary Life.* New York : Palgrave Macmillan, 2002.
Nestor, Pauline. *Female Friendships and Communities: Charlotte Brontë, George Eliot, Elizabeth Gaskell.* New York: Oxford University Press, 1985.

GENTLEMAN'S MAGAZINE, THE   Founded

and edited by Edward Cave in 1731, *The Gentlemen's Magazine* was published monthly across three centuries until 1907. Cave, who died in 1754, was succeeded by his nephew Richard and others, including John Nichols, who wrote for the magazine until 1826. Samuel JOHNSON was a contributing editor.

Paving the way for the format of many modern magazines, *The Gentleman's Magazine* was a storehouse of information on many subjects. It included summaries and reprints of work from dailies and weeklies, biographies of scientists such as Hermann Boerhaave, admirals such as Francis Drake, and essays on writers such as John Milton and William Shakespeare. Reporting on parliamentary debates gained the magazine fame, since the debates were touchy subjects for journalistic reporting. Johnson used anagrams and adaptations to hide the real names of politicians, as "Castroflet," "Pulnub," and "Gibnob" participated in "Debates in the Senate of Magna Lilliputia." The writing on these debates is among the classics of English literature. The last was written in 1743.

One feature, "Dissertations and Essays from Correspondents," included original contributions on theology, literary criticism, popular science, history, and miscellaneous topics. Under this heading, Benjamin Franklin's writings introduced him to the British public. Cave established a poetry contest in the 1730s. John Nichols (writing as Sylvanus Urban) praised romantic writer William Wordsworth early on but condemned him later. Other targets included Percy Bysshe Shelley, Lord Byron, and Leigh Hunt.

BIBLIOGRAPHY
Fader, Daniel, and George Bornstein: *British Periodicals of the 18th and 19th Centuries.* University Microfilms, Ann Arbor, Michigan 48106. 1972, 98–104.

GISSING, GEORGE (1857–1903)   Born

into a Wakefield, England, Quaker family with a chemist father, George Gissing was educated at a Quaker school, Owens College, Manchester, where he received a scholarship. However, he was expelled for theft of money to buy a prostitute a sewing machine, a crime for which he received a year's imprisonment.

Upon his release at age 19, he spent a year wandering about America in hope of outliving his soiled reputation. While in the United States, he taught at the high school level and contributed occasional stories to the *Chicago Tribune.* Depressed over his dire straights to the point of being suicidal, he returned to London, where he gained a reputation as a classical scholar. He tutored for a time, earning poverty wages, and married two girls beneath his own social class, expecting, but not receiving, gratitude for his attempts to "raise" them to his own level. The first, a prostitute, left him, but he continued to supply her alcohol until her death from alcoholism. A man of obsessive personality, Gissing focused most in his writing on themes of poverty and inequality and made few friends, one being the novelist H. G. WELLS, who also suffered deprivation. Gissing gained respect, if not a great deal of money, from his novels, which included WORKERS IN THE DAWN (1880), *The Unclassed* (1884), *Eve's Ransom* (1885), *Isabel Clarendon* (1886), and DEMOS (1886). While embracing identical subject matter to that of the wildly popular author Charles DICKENS, Gissing imbued his works with a gloomy fatalism not present in the ever-optimistic Dickens's work. Though a realist who refused to compromise, he did investigate the psychology of his characters and spoke to his readers from the pages, establishing a relationship that many received enthusiastically.

Gissing wrote an additional 10 novels, including NEW GRUB STREET (1891), often considered his best work and focusing on the challenges to professional authors, and *The ODD WOMEN* (1893), which focused on a lack of opportunities for even well-educated women in a patriarchal society. He also published short stories, a critical life of Dickens, and biographical works. One historical romance with its setting in sixth-century Italy, *Veranilda* (1904), appeared posthumously. While his works languished for a time, they regained attention in the 1960s due to a resurgence of interest in social and political protest fiction, supported by efforts of MARXIST and FEMINIST CRITICS. They found important his themes of material inequality resulting from social class division and the power of the ruling class. While not considering his works to be in the "highest tier" of Victorian fiction, critics accord

Gissing an important place among reform writers, and his works remain popular, available in print and electronic text versions.

BIBLIOGRAPHY

Halperin, John. *Gissing, a Life in Books.* New York: Oxford University Press, 1982.

Korg, Jacob. *George Gissing: A Critical Biography.* Seattle: University of Washington Press, 1979.

GODWIN, WILLIAM (1756–1836)

Born to a highly religious family in 1756, William Godwin would turn to a study of philosophy that undermined his Calvinistic background. Although he became a minister in 1778, he turned to atheism in 1783 and gave up his ministry, instead steeping himself in the ideas of French philosophers such as Jacques Rousseau, d'Holbach, and Helvétius. Ironically, his religious youth had focused his sympathies toward social reform, which he would pursue following his association with organized religion. He spent most of his life in London, contributing at first multiple essays to various journals and following his interest in political philosophy. When the French Revolution threatened, he attended radical political group meetings, including the famous pro-revolutionary sermon delivered on November 4, 1789, by Dissenting minister Richard Price. He worked for two years developing his *Enquiry Concerning Political Justice* (1793), which found instant success with its condemnation of all organized control over humans, including, in part, taxation, marriage, and all contractual agreements, as well as legal punishment of crimes.

Godwin's most popular novel, CALEB WILLIAMS (1794), highlighted his elaborate ideas regarding the inner psychological workings of the mind. Rather than presenting a murder as a mystery in which readers must determine the perpetrator, Godwin presents his story as an analysis of the murderer and his detective, suggesting that the social conventions of pride and honor lead to the crime. Godwin turned to fiction to reach a popular reading audience not adept at following abstract reasoning. His preface, which clearly labels his book in the vein of a political tract, so worried his publishers, who feared accusations of treason, that it would not appear until later editions. Critics consider *Caleb Williams,* subtitled *or Things as They Are,* the best-written radical doctrine novel of its age. The work contributed to the development of the novel with its highly planned structure in an era when novels often proved rambling and disjointed. Godwin's method was to determine his climax, then plan the plot backward, resulting in a tightly knit series of events. The only weakness is one shared with many novels of his age: characters shaped as mere mouthpieces for an author's political and social opinions, or as stock GOTHIC figures with stereotypical attitudes and reactions.

A major anarchist of the Age of Reason, he opposed what he saw as the tyranny of institutions as well as organized resistance to them, insisting men could settle their differences only through one-on-one interaction and negotiations. His ideas earned an accusation of simplistic optimism, as they contradicted his own rationality. Although concerned by the opinion of the London Corresponding Society that social agitation was the best choice for change, he anonymously published *Cursory Strictures on the Charge Delivered by Lord Chief Justice Eyre to the Grand Jury.* That work helped convince a jury to declare several members of the society innocent in their trial for treason in 1794. *The Enquirer,* a long political philosophical thesis, appeared in 1797, the same year that he married early campaigner for women's rights Mary WOLLSTONECRAFT, author of *A Vindication of the Rights of Women* (1792), her most famous publication. She died shortly after the birth of Mary Wollstonecraft Godwin, later Mary SHELLEY, author of the novel FRANKENSTEIN (1818), which reflected on much of her father's philosophy. Shelley's poet husband, Percy Bysshe Shelley, helped bring attention back to Godwin's writings. However, because Shelley eloped with Godwin's daughter, in Godwin's view "stealing" her from the Godwin household, the two men had strained relations until Shelley's early death by drowning by 1822.

Godwin would later repudiate many of his most famous early ideas, at least their radical aspects. In the 1820s he spoke against the suffrage movement. He produced an important work in reply to Thomas Robert Malthus's *Essay on the Principle of Population* titled *Of Population* (1820). He proposed that rational humans would limit procreation through voluntary restraint of sexual desire for the good of the race. Following Percy Shelley's death, Mary Shelley moved back to England and spent much time with her father in his later years. His prolific works also include *Thoughts on Man* (1831), a life of Chaucer (1803–04), and the novels *Fleetwood* (1805), *Mandeville* (1817), *Cloudesly* (1830), and *Doloraine* (1833). He became Usher of the Exchequer with a pension in 1833 and died three years later at age 80.

BIBLIOGRAPHY

Clemit, Pamela, Harriet Jump, and Betty T. Bennett, eds. *Lives of the Great Romantics III: Godwin, Wollstonecraft & Mary Shelley by their Contemporaries.* London: Pickering & Chatto, 1999.

Marshall, Peter H. *William Godwin.* New Haven, Conn.: Yale University Press, 1984.

GOLDSMITH, OLIVER (1728–1774)   Oliver

Goldsmith was born in 1728 in West Meath, Ireland. His father, a man of English ancestry, served as a clergyman in the Church of Ireland. Goldsmith spent his early childhood near a village called Lissoy, but later left the village school to take an education at several grammar schools. Due to his small stature and a face disfigured by smallpox, he suffered much bullying as a child. When he entered Trinity College in Dublin, he had little enthusiasm for education, but graduated, barely obtaining a bachelor of arts degree. After failing at several professions, he engaged in a halfhearted attempt to pass medical school at Edinburgh and then in Holland but failed in both places. He wandered about Flanders, France, Switzerland, and into Italy, earning a living by playing his flute. When he arrived in London in 1756 and applied for medical-related jobs, he lacked the competence to pursue any of them. Following miserable service assisting a schoolmaster, he lived in poverty resulting from his poor attempt to make a living as a freelance journalist.

Goldsmith at last published his first important work in 1759, *An Enquiry into the Present State of Polite Leaning in Europe,* while also writing for various publications, including Tobias SMOLLETT's *Critical Review, The Busy Body, The Weekly Magazine, The Royal Magazine,* and *The Lady's Magazine.* He found some success when he copied an approach made popular by Voltaire and assumed the persona of a Chinese mandarin visiting England, sending reports regarding his experiences home to Peking. Published in 1762, his work was titled *The Citizen of the World,* having appeared first as "Chinese Letters" in John Newbery's *The Public Ledger.* Goldsmith's astute description of London's local color gained a readership, and the public warmed to the adventures, some of which he set in Persia and Russia.

Goldsmith's works prior to the 1760s appeared anonymously and included essays, histories, anthologies of poems, and biographies. His rise in success gained him entry into the select coterie dominated by Dr. Samuel JOHNSON, called The Club. Although always in need of money, Goldsmith favored expensive attire and enjoyed gambling. He also enjoyed giving his money away to those he felt less fortunate than himself, attributes which annoyed friends, who knew of his constant indebtedness. In order to support his activities, he sold a manuscript in 1764 at a pittance to pay his rent, and the bookseller who purchased it ignored it for a time. As the story goes, he stood on the verge of debtors' prison, called his friend Johnson to peruse his manuscripts, and Johnson selected a novel-length work, which he deemed of high enough quality to sell. The novel did not particularly impress its purchaser, because it was short and devoid of the currently popular melodrama, lacking characters who suffered endless agony. In addition, it offered a much gentler humor than the SATIRE and obscene BURLESQUE that seemed to hold public attention. However, following Goldsmith's successful publication of "The Traveller" (1764), a lengthy poem and the first work published under his own name, the seller decided to market the manuscript. Thus, *The VICAR OF WAKEFIELD* (1766) found an enthusiastic audience, becoming one of the most enduring 18th-century novels. Its tale of a simple, good man forced to bear up under worldly challenges struck a chord with the reading public, despite its variance from the normal reading fare. It would be Goldsmith's only novel but would gain the reputation of one of his century's most important works.

The novel's great success inspired Goldsmith to publish his best poem in 1770, *The Deserted Village,* followed three years later by the performance of his wildly popular and successful play *She Stoops to Conquer*. His poetry achieved its popularity through his departure from the stiff rule of the heroic couplet and his presentation of the seemingly simple and pleasurable themes of childhood, based on memories of his travels and his childhood home. His monetary success proved brief, as his gambling habits depleted his support. Due to a kidney infection rumored to have been badly treated by himself, Goldsmith died in London in 1774 and was buried in the Temple churchyard. His cohorts in "The Club" felt moved to recognize properly Goldsmith's genius by erecting a monument in Westminster Abbey bearing an epitaph composed in Latin by the great Johnson. His works remain popular centuries later, and many are available in both print copy and electronic format.

BIBLIOGRAPHY

Lucy, Sean. *Goldsmith: The Gentle Master.* Cork: Cork University Press, 1984.

Phelps, Gilbert. "Oliver Goldsmith: The Vicar of Wakefield." *An Introduction to Fifty British Novels: 1600–1900.* London: Pan Books, 1979, 134–136.

GORE, CATHERINE GRACE (1799–1861)

Catherine Moody was born in East Retford, Nottingham, the daughter of a wine merchant, and married Captain Charles Arthur Gore at the age of 23. She later supported her family by writing fashionable novels, also known as SILVER-FORK FICTION. Considered by traditional critics to be a genre written by mediocre aristocrats, such fiction had its heyday in the 1820s, but Gore continued publishing fashionable novels for two more decades. Jane AUSTEN's influence may be seen in Gore's absolute devotion to precise detail and her unity of form, although Gore did not consider the nonaristocratic character as did Austen. Gore's prolific output included 70 works of fiction, drama, and songs produced in 40 years. Her career may have been helped in its early stages by her husband's connection to publishers who had printed his travel narratives. Deemed a hack-level writer by contemporaries such as William Makepeace THACKERAY, who included her work in his PARODY of popular fiction, *PUNCH'S PRIZE*

NOVELISTS (1847), Gore would be redeemed by later evaluations that characterized her as a sharp and witty satirist.

Like her contemporary Susan FERRIER, whose character Lady Juliana Douglas in MARRIAGE (1818) is a cold, egotistical woman who should never have had children, Gore created Lady Maria Willingham in *Mothers and Daughters* (1831), a heartless society type, but one more finely developed. Despite its didactic tone, the novel proved popular, along with *Women as They Are, or Manners of the Day* (1830), MRS. ARMYTAGE, OR, FEMALE DOMINATION (1836), *Cecil, or, The Adventures of a Coxcomb* (1841), and *The Banker's Wife* (1843). She lived for a time in Paris, where her husband took a diplomatic post, and upon returning to England contributed to the periodical BENTLEY'S MISCELLANY, adopting the name Albany Poyntz. She and Charles had 10 children before his death in 1843; she survived all but two of their offspring. Only blindness in 1859 ended her writing career; she died two years later.

BIBLIOGRAPHY

Jump, Harriet Divine. *Silver Fork Novels: 1826–1841.* Vol. 6. London: Pickering & Chatto, 2005.

GOTHIC FICTION/NOVEL

The term *Gothic* derived literally from the word *Goth,* a label for a Germanic people who invaded the Roman Empire early during the Christian era. The Goths were judged crude, uncultured, and barbaric, and their name later became associated with medieval art. When a certain style of fiction popular during the 18th and 19th centuries assumed the label Gothic, it emphasized the grotesque and depended heavily on mystery, mysticism, coincidence, and secret identity as plot aspects. Gothic novels choose as setting a past era and ancient, mysterious structures, often with secret passages and unexplained noises and movement. Such castles/mansions may have existed in medieval times under the control of powerful and mysterious rulers. Writers appropriated the association of the term Gothic with untamed, brooding, often crude elements to produce fiction in reaction against the 18th century's cultivated neoclassicism. In many instances of early Gothic fiction, evil men with dark secretive pasts wreaked havoc on communities until salvation appeared in the form of a younger warrior/knight figure, whose true identity remained disguised, either by accident or purposefully, an early example being Tobias SMOLLETT's *Ferdinand, Count Fathom* (1753). However, the novel recognized as the true first Gothic is Horace Walpole's *The CASTLE OF OTRANTO* (1764), in which a helmet leaves its statue and grows to enormous proportions, as does the statue itself, eventually overwhelming the castle, shattering its walls. Ann RADCLIFFE made the Gothic form famous and introduced persecuted, helpless heroines in imminent danger of death; the most widely read of her novels was *The MYSTERIES OF UDOLPHO* (1794). Jane AUSTEN parodied *Udolpho* and the Gothic form in general, which for a short time lost favor with its readers, in her superb, posthumously published *NORTHANGER ABBEY* (1818). The same year, Mary SHELLEY single-handedly resuscitated the Gothic with her *FRANKENSTEIN*, a story of murder, mayhem, and miscreants in which she used her romantic idealism to frame questions of her day regarding the value of science and the worth of individual imagination. While Sir Walter SCOTT did not write Gothic novels in a pure sense, many of his works contained Gothic elements, including ghosts. Both Charlotte and Emily BRONTË employed the Gothic in their mid-19th century novels. In *JANE EYRE* (1847), Charlotte Brontë set her diminutive protagonist in a mysterious estate mansion, complete with ghostly attic forms, fires, a brooding BYRONIC HERO, and extrasensory contact, and aligned Jane's creativity with her animal passions, revolting the more conservative of her readers. Emily Brontë chose the wild surroundings of the British moors for her ghostly tale of revenge and love beyond the grave, *WUTHERING HEIGHTS* (1847). Gothic romances continued their popularity into the 21st century, both through the continued reading of classic Gothics and the production of new novels, which adopt old formats but may add new emphases, including sexual relations and the occult.

BIBLIOGRAPHY

Hogle, Jerrold E. *The Cambridge Companion to Gothic Fiction.* New York: Cambridge University Press, 2002.

Le Tellier, Robert Ignatius. *Sir Walter Scott and the Gothic Novel.* Lewiston, N.Y.: E. Mellen Press, 1995.

GRANIA: THE STORY OF AN ISLAND
EMILY LAWLESS (1892)   Emily LAWLESS's fourth novel, *Grania: The Story of An Island,* published in two volumes, was eagerly awaited by her readership. Like her third novel, *HURRISH* (1886), *Grania* focused on a poor Irish family and was intent on leading its readers to a new sympathy and understanding of major Irish problems, many of which resulted from neglect by the English. The isolated setting of Inishmann, the middle island of the three islands in Galway Bay, reflected metaphorically the isolation felt by the novel's three main characters, Grania, her half sister Honor, and her fiancé, Murdough Blake. With infertile ground often wrapped in storms, the island symbolizes Grania herself, whose healthy physique and indomitable spirit is not enough to save her from a tragic fate. Like the island, she remains vulnerable to the seasonal elements, with the changeable atmosphere paralleling her own emotional conflict and upheaval. The opening description of the "whole expanse of sky" over Galway Bay as "everywhere a broad indefinable wash of greyness, a grey so dim, uniform, and all-pervasive, that it defied observation," foreshadows Grania's own colorless life. Lawless titles the novel's sections with names of seasons and months, literally marking the time of the islanders' existence.

When Grania's father, twice disappointed by wives who deserted him through death, dies himself, Grania's sister raises her. As her symbolic name indicates, Honor retains the purest of characters. However, she lacks Grania's strength, and falls ill of consumption, dying a slow death. Her religious bent is not shared by Grania, and represents some of society's many rules to which Grania is forced to conform. The island world is one of sacrifice. Men give their hopeless existence to liquor, and their women either die birthing children who will also likely die, or live to become the shrewish flock that constantly criticizes Grania for her masculine strength and desire for a love match, rather than the formal planned marriages that most of the older women endure.

FEMINIST CRITICS find of interest Grania's masculine characteristics, as well as the passages regarding abuse of women that is accepted as tradition by the Irish community. As she does in *Hurrish*, Lawless suggests in this novel through an anti-marriage speech by Honor that a convent and the life of a nun may be the better choice for many women. When Grania asks whether Honor ever "cared" for a man, Honor cries, "men is a terrible trouble, Grania, first and last. What with the drink and the fighting and one thing and another, a woman's life is no better than an old garron's down by the seashore. . . . there's nothing for a woman like being a nun—nothing, nothing!" However, Lawless also characterizes priests as equally abusive as husbands. When Honor expresses horror over Grania's attitude toward a priest who unjustly punished a small girl, declaring that priests cannot be compared to men, Grania mutters to herself, "I'd think him a man if he hit me, let him be what he would!"

Lawless subverts traditional symbols as she maps out Grania's future. Spring, a traditional symbol of rebirth and new life, brings death to the potato crops with too much rain. Even light takes on a negative meaning in superb descriptive passages, such as "It was growing dark, but there was a pale splinter of white light far away, almost lost on the horizon—a sinister light, like a broken war-arrow. Everywhere else the plain was one mass of leaden-coloured waves, solid and unillumined."

Better weather at last arrives, freeing Grania from what had felt like entombment, but only temporarily. When she agrees to travel to the mainland with Murdough to visit the Galway Fair, she anticipates adventure. Instead, Murdough deserts her, her dignity is threatened by the pressing crowds, and she experiences an epiphany after witnessing abject poverty. Suddenly, she recognizes "a new impression upon the intolerableness of life, its unspeakable hopelessness, its misery, its dread, unfathomable dismalness. Why *should* people go on living so?" When Murdough finally reappears, she barely hears the explanation for his delay and separates from the group immediately upon their return to the island. She convinces herself that Murdough only wants to marry her for her property. However, Grania later decides she prefers his misuse to living without him. But when he continues to visit the mainland, returning only to borrow money from Grania, she ends their engagement. She will again regret that decision and shame herself with a plea to

Murdough that he ignores. In allowing Murdough to shake her self-trust, Grania relinquishes her special strength, her remarkable spirit.

In the novel's conclusion, Grania sacrifices herself to Honor's religious beliefs, although she has never shared her sister's vision. She agrees to go by boat in a storm to the mainland to pick up a priest for Honor's last rites, but the boat sinks. She boosts the young boy who has accompanied her to safety, but she cannot escape. Grania calls for Murdough as the sea lifts her up on a symbolic natural raft of seaweed, the substance she had depended on for her livelihood. As Grania accepts her fate, Lawless constructs a scene of last rites every bit as spiritual as the Catholic ritual craved by Honor. The sea builds a funeral bier for Grania, its own child, and "Sea, sky, land, water, everything seemed alike to be lapped in the drowsiest, the most complete and immovable repose. Sleep seemed everywhere to be the order of the hour, to have taken possession of all things." PSYCHOANALYTIC CRITICS find of interest Grania's sleep of death, and the return to the dreamy state she has previously experienced. Reality dissolves into fantasy, suggesting the human condition is more a matter of one's private perception than of material existence.

Lawless's imminently readable works remain available in both hard print and electronic text. Their timeless themes strike a chord with modern readers.

BIBLIOGRAPHY
Wolff, Robert Lee. Introduction to *Grania, the Story of an Island,* by Emily Lawless. Vol. I. New York: Garland Publishing, 1979, vi–xv.

GRAVES, RICHARD (1715–1804)
Not much is known of novelist Richard Graves's early life, other than his birthplace in Mickleton, Gloucestershire, and that he attended Pembroke College, Oxford. He later became a fellow of All Souls, served as rector of Claverton, near Bath, and gained popularity in Bath high society. He enjoyed corresponding with people who distinguished themselves through politics and the arts, including poet and landscaper William Shenstone. Shenstone served as the basis for at least two of Graves's fictional characters and was prominent in Graves's *Recollections* (1788). Some felt Graves

represented the pleasure-loving, social-climbing clergyman against whom the Methodists moved for social reform of activities considered irresponsible on the part of Church of England clergy. Others, however, testified as to his dedication, using as evidence the fact that he was never absent from his duties for more than one month at a time during his more than 50 years of service. He became famous for his social-condition novels, including *Columella, or the Distressed Anchoret* (1779), *Eugenius, or, Anecdotes of the Golden Vale* (1785), and *Plexippus, or the Aspiring Plebeian* (1790). Some judged him adept at writing unemotional natural fiction, in contrast to SENSATION FICTION by Samuel RICHARDSON and Tobias SMOLLETT. In his best-known novel, *The SPIRITUAL QUIXOTE* (1773), Graves satirized Methodism and a preacher named George Whitfield, one of his acquaintances at Pembroke. Later critics described the novel as hackneyed in its reliance on an imitation of Miguel Cervantes, using as its protagonist Geoffrey Wildgoose, an Oxford-educated country squire, with a village cobbler as attendant. Although the writing itself was acceptable, the taste of the reading public had moved beyond such SATIRE to crave the more pointedly DIDACTIC fiction.

BIBLIOGRAPHY

"Letter Writers: Richard Graves and His Literary Work." *The Cambridge History of English and American Literature in 18 Volumes.* Vol 10. Bartleby.com. Available online. URL: http://www.bartleby.com/220/1122.html. Downloaded on July 8, 2003.

GREAT EXPECTATIONS CHARLES DICKENS (1861)

Appearing first as a serial in the author's periodical *ALL THE YEAR ROUND* (1860–61), Charles DICKENS's *Great Expectations* advanced his traditional focus on parent/child relationships. This novel in particular contains autobiographical elements, such as the protagonist/narrator Philip Pirrip (Pip) spending his youth in poverty. Just like Dickens, Pip spends later years attempting to deal with the stamp of shame and guilt his childhood homelessness had caused. Unlike Dickens, Pip had no parents and was abandoned to grow up in a system of foster parenthood. Similarly, Dickens felt abandoned by his parents, as his father's debt landed the entire family in debtors' prison. Young Dickens's income from his work in a boot-blacking factory acted as their sole income for a time, and his memories of the abuse he suffered there influenced the characterization of most of the children populating his novels who overcome adversity, most directly that of David Copperfield, title character of the novel Dickens claimed to be his favorite.

In the first of Pip's three developmental stages, as an orphan he lives in Kent with his unkind sister, Mrs. Joe, and her compassionate husband, Joe Gargery. They live close to the marshes where Joe works as a blacksmith. In a graveyard scene containing nightmare imagery, Pip is accosted by a common criminal named Abel Magwitch. When Magwitch holds the boy aloft by his heels, he literally inverts Pip's world, signaling a change in Pip's emotional environment. The description of Magwitch—soaked through, torn by briars, covered with mud, and ravaged by hunger—symbolized his haunting of a society that refused to protect its most needy. The convict fits perfectly into Pip's dream-state life, touched with crime both real, as when Mrs. Joe is attacked, and imagined, as when Wopsle reads a play in which one character wants to murder his nearest relative.

Frightened for his life, Pip aids the convict by bringing him food and promising not to reveal Magwitch's hiding place. Adding to Pip's horror is the fact that Magwitch's chain, removed by a file that Pip supplies, becomes the weapon in the attack on Mrs. Joe. Eventually Magwitch is recaptured and sent to a nearby prison ship, but Pip continues to think about him, conflicted over whether to pity or despise Magwitch. Critics agree that Magwitch himself represents a type of mistreated foster child, cast off by a cruel society that punishes him by withholding life-sustaining love and compassion. At the same time, he represents another stand-in parent for Pip, due to the strong impression he makes on the boy.

Pip next meets Miss Havisham, an eccentric wealthy local who has existed in isolation since being jilted by her lover. She hires Pip to perform chores at her home and introduces him to her ward, another foster-child figure, named Estella. The coldhearted Miss Havisham trains Estella to hold men in low esteem, wreaking her revenge on the opposite sex through the lovely young woman. Pip falls deeply in love with Estella, despite her lack of warmth and affection for him. He understands that he needs education and polish in order to become Estella's social equal. This becomes possible through a generous allowance he begins to receive from an anonymous benefactor, through a lawyer, Jaggers.

Pip travels to London in order to improve himself. He rooms with the good-natured Herbert Pocket who helps him gain some education. However, rather than broadening his mind, the smattering of knowledge leads Pip to vanity. He becomes so taken with himself in his new polished stage of life that he wounds his kindest foster parent, Joe Gargery, who in his lowly station as a blacksmith is not good enough for Pip.

Pip is emotionally awakened by the return of Magwitch, who had been deported to Australia, and by the discovery that Magwitch has served as his benefactor. While in exile, Magwitch mailed money from the fortune he earned to Jaggers to give to the Pip in repayment for his childhood kindness. Thus begins the third stage of Pip's life, in which he will at last find true enlightenment. Conflicted once again as to whether he should feel positively or negatively toward Magwitch, who is clearly recognizable as a foster father by this point in the novel, Pip plans to help him leave England to which he has returned illegally. His plans are foiled with Magwitch's capture, conviction, and subsequent death while a prisoner. In a typical Dickensian plot twist, Magwitch is revealed as Estella's father. Estella has left Miss Havisham and married a wealthy high-society ne'er-do-well who abuses her, then suffers an early death. Pip, sobered by his experiences, turns from his extravagant ways, developing humility and a sense of decency toward his fellow man. The two young people meet again, and in Dickens's original version, separate to go their different ways. At the urging of contemporary novelist Edward BULWER-LYTTON, Dickens changed the ending to unite the two in the book version of his novel.

Dickens uses his traditional enormous cast of characters, many serving a comic purpose to lighten the melodrama. The weight proved necessary in a story calculated to highlight the social and moral crimes he observed parents, and parent figures, commit against their children, as well as the social abuses against children inflicted by his culture. As in most of his plots, this one finds no solution for those criminal acts; it instead offers redemption of the public crime through a private character. Magwitch offers himself up to Pip, his death purchasing a freedom from ego for Pip, who may then overcome his childhood abuses. In the original version, Magwitch's death did not serve as redemption for Estella, even though he was proven her father. Instead, she sacrifices herself to a controlling misogynist, achieving exactly the opposite effect on men that Miss Havisham, a completely perverted character, intended. Through her own symbolic death within that relationship, Estella may be seen as redeeming herself. Pip symbolizes the expectations to which all children should be entitled but few realize. His own survival and success he owes more to his strength of character than to any role model.

Great Expectations remains one of Dickens's most popular works, readily available in print form and in electronic and media versions; it also inspired multiple stage and film productions.

BIBLIOGRAPHY

Schlicke, Paul, ed. *The Oxford Reader's Companion to Dickens.* Oxford: Oxford University Press, 2000.

Van Ghent, Dorothy. *The English Novel: Form and Function.* New York: Harper & Row, 1953.

GREEN CARNATION, THE ROBERT S. HICHENS (1894)

When Robert S. HICHENS published his ROMAN À CLEF, or novel with a key, *The Green Carnation*, he joined others in mimicking the famous style of Oscar WILDE, arguably England's best-known writer at the end of the 19th century. Wilde, a gay novelist, playwright, poet, essayist, and epigrammatist, had charmed some members of high society, while infuriating others, with his outlandish dress and outspoken irreverence for anything not supportive of his aesthetic lifestyle. Most critics agree that of all the pastiches in the style of Wilde, Hichens's holds up the best, but his attitude toward Wilde is never made clear in the novel. Published anonymously, the novel elicited expressions of gratitude to Hichens from both Wilde and his lover, Alfred Douglas.

As with any *roman à clef, The Green Carnation* contains a key to the identity of the real people its characters represent. Wilde is represented by Esmie Amarinth; his lover, Lord Alfred Douglas, by Lord Reginald Hastings; Lord Douglas's father, the Marquess of Queensberry, is labeled simply "elderly gentleman"; and several other minor characters correspond to members of London's society easily recognizable by readers. Hichens even includes Wilde's famous novel, *The* PICTURE OF DORIAN GRAY (1890), renaming it *The Soul of Bertie Brown*. In a simple plot, Esmie romances Reggie, who romances Lady Locke. Most of the action takes place at the country home of Lady Locke's cousin, Mrs. Windsor, who invites several friends to her manor to practice being rustic. Lady Locke is described as "sensible," with "calm observant eyes, and a steady and simple manner." That observant and sensible personality causes her to reject Esmie Amarinth and all of his followers, including Reggie, as unnatural men who will never understand women. The green carnation with its fake, loud color, worn by Esmie and his faithful followers, symbolizes what seems to Lady Locke a pretentious, contrived approach to life. After attending an opera, she tells her cousin that she noticed "about a dozen" green carnations, worn by men who all looked alike with "the same walk, or rather waggle, the same coyly conscious expression, the same wavy motion of the head . . . Is it a badge of some club or some society, and is Mr. Amarinth their high priest? They . . . all seemed to revolve round him like satellites around the sun." Clearly, Lady Locke represents that aspect of society who perceived Wilde as an influence that constricted men's minds rather than broadening them.

During the country retreat, readers enjoy a deluge of the type of epigrams for which Wilde was famous, including "That is really the secret of my pre-eminence. I never develop. I was born epigrammatic, and my dying remark will be a paradox"; and "thank Heaven! there [sic] are no nightingales to ruin the music of the stillness with their well-meant but ill-produced voices. Nature's songster is the worst sort of songster I know." But when he speaks with Lady Locke regarding what he calls the "value of doubt," she remains unconvinced. In her response to his remarks about Reggie being unlike anyone else, living "for sensations, while other people live for faiths, or for convictions, or for prejudices," she questions whether simply "being what others are not" is a sign of intelligence.

Reggie's actions convince Lady Locke that he should not marry her when she sees how easily he gains her son's attentions. In the rejection scene, Lady Locke tells Reggie that he interests her, but she is convinced he does not love her; he does not love anything. When she adds, "I can never love an echo, and you are an echo," he defends his imitation of Esmie's style, adding "expression is my life." It is that very expression that Lady Locke regrets.

Hichens leaves readers unsure of his attitude toward Esme/Wilde. While Esme seems to cause Reggie's failure at loving a woman, it is Reggie, not Esme, who is rejected. Esme also appears sympathetic at one point in the novel when, as he listens to young choirboys sing, he mourns the loss of his youth that had "left him alone with his intellect and his epigrams. Sometimes he shivered with cold among those epigrams. He was tired of them." Readers at the century's end would see no such regret or weariness in Oscar Wilde, however, and might have wondered whether the novel represented Esme's regret correctly as he gazed at the young boys. Whatever Hichens's true attitude, events leading up to Wilde's imprisonment for homosexual acts in 1895 would change society's acceptance of all things Wildean. Following his conviction, *The Green Carnation* was withdrawn for a time. In the later 1948 edition, Hichens explained that he met Wilde through Douglas and found him to be a kind person.

BIBLIOGRAPHY

Pritchard, David. *Oscar Wilde.* New Lanark, Scotland: Geddes & Grossett, 2001.

GRIFFITH GAUNT, OR JEALOUSY

CHARLES READE (1866) Charles READE, a playwright as well as a novelist, became well known for his attacks against human injustice and his pleas for compassion through his fiction, of which *Griffith Gaunt* became a strong example. Reade's fiction proved melodramatic and dealt in what the public considered daring themes. *Griffith Gaunt,* much to the chagrin of some critics, dealt with the topics of bigamy and religious intolerance, but offers redemption through the improbable reform of one wife by another. Incorporating duels, a murder trial and a "female Iago," a reference to Shakespeare's treacherous character from his play *Othello,* the book looked forward to its later dramatic production on a New York stage. When Reade compares his character to Shakespeare's, echoes of the phrase "green-eyed monster" from *Othello* support the novel's focus on jealousy.

The story opens with an argument between a married couple based on religious differences. Moving into a lengthy flashback, the plot reviews the romance of Catherine "Kate" Peyton, a high-minded independent socialite, with two male characters, the immature and passionate Griffith Gaunt and the more logical George Neville. Additional conflict develops due to Gaunt's selection as heir to Catherine's cousin, Mr. Charlton of Hernshaw Castle and Bolton Hall. Unfortunately, Charlton had offered Catherine's only hope of inheritance, her father having promised his property to his son. But when Charlton "took a fancy" to Gaunt, his late wife's relation, hope of her inheritance was lost. Further complicating matters, Catherine's profligate father was becoming desperate for funds. When Griffith proposes to Catherine, she refuses him mainly because, as a staunch Catholic, she cannot agree to marry a Protestant. When she shares the news that she will never marry but instead enter a convent, the incensed Gaunt, suspecting that she loves another, threatens to depart England for the United States. Simultaneously, Neville visits Mr. Peyton, who accepts money from him in exchange for permission to ask Catherine to marry. Peyton believes that by assuring his daughter of the title Lady Neville, he has fulfilled his responsibility as her parent. This tension escalates when both men bequeath all they own, should they die, to Catherine, then stage a duel in which wounds are inflicted, but which Kate ends before anyone dies. In a surprising turn of events, Catherine does inherit her cousin's property, while Griffith inherits nothing, leading Mr. Peyton to deny his request to marry Catherine. Neville rejoices over that news, but Catherine eventually marries Gaunt anyway, following a plea from her as she looks down upon him from a high turret, recalling similar scenes from fairy tales.

They have a daughter, Rose, but the tale does not end with marital bliss. It proceeds through traditional melodramatic complications, such as Griffith's seeming death and long illness and recovery, away from home, miscommunications, and mistaken identity. In the confusion, and due to treachery by a trusted acquaintance, Griffith marries his nurse, Mercy Vint. A pregnant Kate eventually stands accused of Griffith's murder and receives the support of Neville, who had remained loyal to her. Aptly named, Mercy will later find redemption from bigamy through Catherine's guidance and reform. She testifies that the man whom Kate supposedly murders is not Griffith Gaunt, and the dead man is shown to have drowned of natural causes. During Kate's childbirth, doctors transfuse the remorseful Griffith's blood directly into the veins of his wife, rescuing her and giving them a spiritual tie. The novel concludes happily with that relationship mended, and a new one begun between Neville and Mercy.

Readers will immediately find many descriptive passages marked by Reade's trademark melodrama, particularly in his character descriptions. In an early fox hunt scene, Catherine is described: "one glossy, golden curl streamed back in the rushing air, her gray eyes glowed with earthly fire, and two red spots on the upper part of her cheeks showed she was much excited without a grain of fear." When Reade first introduces his theme of jealousy, it is in connection with Gaunt. Having caught a glimpse of Neville approaching Catherine's house, Gaunt reacts, as Catherine observes "the livid passion of jealousy writing in every lineament of a human face. That terrible passion had transfigured its victim in a moment: the ruddy, genial, kindly Griffith, with his soft brown eye, was gone; and in his place lowered a face older and discolored and convulsed, almost demoniacal." When Kate, dressed in red, interferes with a duel between her two lovers by riding between them on her grey gelding, she is referred to as a "crimson Amazon." She later demands the bullet that had wounded Griffith and finds he has had it engraved with the phrase "I love Kate." Reade describes her reaction: "her face, glorified by the light, assumed a celestial tenderness he had never seen it wear before." Such dialogue is of interest to FORMALIST critics, who look to the elements of fiction alone to gain meaning from a story. Also of interest is Reade's design of portions of the courtroom scene as dramatic dialogue, formatted like that of a play.

FEMINIST CRITICS would find of interest the dependent positions of several women in the plot, but most of all Catherine Peyton's male qualities. She stands six feet tall and is a woman of strength and intelligence, yet can strategically faint on a whim to benefit herself socially, like all well-trained young women of her era. At one point she echoes Shakespeare's heroines, such as Beatrice in the comedy *Much Ado About Nothing,* when she cries, "Oh that I were a man!" wishing to fight her own duel over insulted honor. Feminist critics will also note the passage in which an imprisoned Kate requests that Neville interview the deceived second wife of her husband, instructing "All I beg of him is to [. . .] see women with a woman's eyes and not a man's; see them *as they are.*" When Mercy clears Kate's name, the judge tells her, "You have shown us the beauty of the female character," helping balance Reade's consistent authorial intrusions to comment in the broadest terms and usually with negative connotations on the nature of women.

Some critics found the story so outrageous and so likely to cause harm to female readers that they publicly attacked Reade's morals, accusing him of inciting readers to an unhealthy passion and even lending his name to a writer of low reputation who actually wrote the novel. Most of the early accusations came from American publishers who Reade accused of cowardice, as they published their comments anonymously. When a British periodical, *The Globe,* printed the statement that "'Griffith Gaunt' was declined by some of the lowest sensational weekly papers of New York," Reade responded angrily. He wrote a public letter that accused the editors of not having read his novel, adding, in part, "But even assuming that you really had not the brains to read 'Griffith Gaunt' for pleasure, nor yet the self-respect and prudence to wade through it before lending your columns to its defamation, at least you have read my letter to the American press; and, having read that, you cannot but *suspect* this charge of

immorality and indecency to be a libel and a lie. Yet you have circulated the calumny all the same, and suppressed the refutation."

Both the novel and the two letters are readily available in electronic format on the World Wide Web.

BIBLIOGRAPHY

Rusk, J. "Letters by Charles Read concerning *Griffith Gaunt.*" Blackmask.com. June 1, 2003. Available online. URL: http://www.blackmask.com/jrusk/gg/readletters.html. Downloaded July 30, 2003.

GROSSMITH, GEORGE (1847–1912) and WEEDON (1854–1919)

George and Weedon Grossmith worked together to produce one of Victorian England's most memorable comic characters, Charles Pooter, in their wildly popular *The Diary of a Nobody* (1892). Vain, insufferable, accident-prone, and judgmental, with firm middle-class values, Pooter's unfounded snobbism delighted readers who adopted his "Pooterisms," repeating them at social gatherings.

The Weedon brothers' father, also named George, was a journalist who enjoyed attending the theater. Weedon began his career as an artist, later illustrating *Diary,* while George began his writing career as a court reporter at *The Times.* In the 1870s, George appeared in a performance of *Trial by Jury,* witnessed by the famous musical team of Gilbert and Sullivan. They asked him to audition for a part in their opera *The Sorcerer,* a move the directors of the Comedy Opera Theater objected to, due to his lack of experience. Despite such qualms, George made an enormous hit with audiences and critics. He subsequently helped make the Gilbert and Sullivan opera *The Mikado* a huge success. His son, George Grossmith, Jr., would enjoy a singing and acting career equal to his father's.

Weedon also enjoyed a successful acting career while continuing to write. Weedon's additional novel, *A Woman with a History* (1896), and several dramas, while popular, did not match the star quality of *Diary.* The same proved true of George's memoirs, *Reminiscences of a Clown* (1888) and *Piano and I* (1910). *Diary of a Nobody* remains popular and may be found in hard print and electronic versions.

BIBLIOGRAPHY

Orel, Harold. *The World of Victorian Humor.* New York: Appleton-Century-Crofts, 1961.

Stanford, Derek, ed. *Writing of the Nineties: From Wilde to Beerbohm.* New York: Dutton, 1971.

GULLIVER'S TRAVELS JONATHAN SWIFT

(1726) Jonathan Swift likely began writing *Travels into Several Remote Nations of the World. In Four Parts. By Lemuel Gulliver, First a Surgeon, and then a Captain of Several Ships* five years before its publication. Later known simply as *Gulliver's Travels,* it became one of the most often reprinted books in English. With a hero to which few readers could relate, a lack of structural unity, and a purpose in its SATIRE lost on many later readers, it lacked elements crucial to classification as a novel. It did, however, help advance progress toward the production of that genre, which would gain popularity in its nascent form a few decades later, thanks to the contributions of writers including Samuel RICHARDSON and Daniel DEFOE.

Swift adopted a familiar convention when he fabricated the persona of Gulliver, a man who supposedly related his adventures to another, with that second party, in this case Gulliver's cousin, being responsible for its publication. A letter attached as a foreword to the tale from Gulliver to his Cousin Sympson added realism to the fantasy through Gulliver's defense of his original version and his satiric attack against the version that appeared in print. Swift wrote his four-part fantasy as an indictment against a government that had mostly ignored his many political contributions and that did not serve the populace well. First a member of the Whig party, Swift changed his allegiance to the Torys due to ill treatment by the Whigs. Often too narrowly characterized as a misanthrope bearing an unhealthy fascination with bodily functions, Swift was in reality an active member of his community who served for a time as dean of St. Paul's in London and staunchly defended his country of Ireland. His many works in addition to *Gulliver's Travels* reflect a thoughtful humor and depth of experience too often later dismissed, particularly by PSYCHOANALYTIC CRITICS, who focused on his misogyny and bitterness, both of which were common attributes found in works published in the early 18th century. Due to the vulgarity of *Gulliver's Travels,* it is often reproduced in abridged form and has been paraphrased to preserve its popularity with a young audience who finds its fantasy aspects fascinating.

In Book I, Gulliver shipwrecks off the island of Lilliput, where he awakens to find himself bound to the earth by the island's tiny inhabitants. Swift used their size to suggest the small-minded attitudes of many humans. They argue over ridiculous matters, such as which end of an egg to break, with Big-Endians protesting to the death against the emperor's order that all shall break the egg at its small end. The emperor also holds a ceremony testing the dexterity of his subjects who must navigate over or under a stick that the emperor holds. The disputes and competition for the emperor's attention suggest Swift's low opinion of the religious and political disputes of his era, often settled by favoritism. In Book II, Gulliver travels by sea to Brobdingnag, and in a reversal from the first book, he is tiny by comparison to that culture's enormous inhabitants. Gulliver expounds on the pretentious ideas of his hosts, which he finds as exaggerated as their bodies. However, when he feels moved to join the bragging and tries to impress the ruler with an account of England's history, the monarch is appalled: "He was perfectly astonished with the historical account I gave him of our affairs during the last century, protesting it was only an heap of conspiracies, rebellions, murders, massacres, revolutions, banishments, the very worst effects that avarice, faction, hypocrisy, perfidiousness, cruelty, rage, madness, hatred, envy, lust, malice, and ambition could produce." When Gulliver wonders over the "strange effect of narrow principles and short views" practiced by the Brobdinagians, Swift reflects that criticism onto his audience. Book Three features Laputa, an island on a cloud that floats about the sky, its imagery suggesting the fantastic ideas of its inhabitants who function in an unrealistic manner. Swift criticizes in that tale the so-called scientific advances of his time and especially satirizes the Royal Academy in a depiction of an academy at nearby Lagado where members attempt absurd acts, such as the extraction of sunbeams from vegetables. Gulliver also meets the sorcerers of Glubbdubrib, who can summon famous persons from the past into the present with disappointing results, and the inhabitants of Struldbruggs, who have gained immortality but lose their physical prowess and earn the enmity of their fellow beings. Finally in Book IV, Gulliver's journeys take him to the land of the Houyhnhnms, coldly rational horselike creatures of a superior bent who keep as slaves the filthy Yahoos, beings with an uncomfortable resemblance to humans. Most impressed by the morality and intellectual capacity of his hosts, Gulliver will gravitate toward the stable when he eventually returns home, rejecting the company of his own family and his friends. Swift emphasizes two unsavory possibilities in human nature in the last portion of *Gulliver's Travels*. One is that humans may choose to embrace their uncivilized animalistic nature, as did the Yahoos, and the other that they might reject all emotion to function only with logic, as did the Houyhnhnms.

Swift's tale remains extremely popular and has been converted to various media forms. While it continues to be studied academically, its abridged versions are appreciated as entertainment by a broad popular audience.

BIBLIOGRAPHY

Cline, Kelly Ann. *Jonathan Swift and Popular Culture: Myth, Media, and the Man.* New York: Palgrave, 2002.

Probyn, Clive T. *Jonathan Swift, Gulliver's Travels.* London: Penguin, 1989.

GUY LIVINGSTONE, OR THOROUGH
GEORGE ALFRED LAWRENCE (1857)   G. A. LAWRENCE's *Guy Livingstone* represents a briefly popular trend toward "manly" fiction. Its protagonist, as full of life and as hard as his surname suggests, embodies the masculine idea of strength unmitigated by any subtlety, particularly not in the area of intellect. Lawrence placed his protagonists in situations that could only be handled with brute strength and reckless bravado. Like many best-sellers of its time, *Guy Livingstone* depended on exaggeration and sensationalism for its appeal to both women and men; military men contributed greatly to its popularity. Not meant to teach any particular moral lesson, the book basically offers male-oriented entertainment with its violent male camaraderie. Lawrence used his novel as he did his others, to express contempt for the clergy, and others of the professional classes, particularly those engaged in private trade. His admiration for the military reflected his own brief experience in service with the Northampton Militia as a lieutenant.

Blessed with patrician courage, Livingstone remains ready to defend the weak against threat. He protects a schoolmate from a bully, frees him from the police following his innocent presence at a fight at Oxford, and combats a professional boxer, his grit and spirit bringing him, although an amateur, victory. In other parts of the novel, Livingstone crushes a silver cup with his bare hands, rides wild and unruly horses, and engages in various forms of combat, including the use of dueling pistols at 15 paces, proving himself truly a man's man. Lawrence reflects his own passionate and combative nature, having been part of a duel with the duke of Wellington, whom he accused of "introduction of popery into every department of the state."

Livingstone finds the promise of love with Constance Brandon, who represents the typical Victorian heroine in remaining helpless in the face of challenges to her well-being. Constance acts as foil for the decidedly more interesting and wicked adventurous Flora Bellasys. Constance's very name suggests a dull stagnation, while Flora's brings to mind color and vibrancy. Constance exemplifies the female virtue of chastity, while Flora exists to tempt men who readily fall victim to her beauty and charms. Guy gives in to that charm as "the fiery Livingstone blood, heated seven-fold by wine and passion, was surging through his veins like molten iron." When Guy kisses Flora, Constance observes his betrayal, emitting a low "plaintive cry, such as might be wrung from the bravest of delicate women, in her extremity of pain, when stricken by a heavy brutal hand." Like his contemporary Benjamin DISRAELI did in his novel *HENRIETTA TEMPLE* (1837), Lawrence has his hero fall in love with two women. However, while Disraeli took the opportunity to moralize on the damaging effects of such involvement, Lawrence portrays Livingstone as troubled by no moral or civil laws.

Guy will reunite with Constance but only as she is dying from an attack of consumption that follows close upon their separation. A first letter she wrote to him mysteriously never arrives into his hands, and the second warns of her impending death. Colonel Mohun blames Flora, thinking "that handsome tiger-cat has laid her claw on it, I am certain."

Guy rushes to London to Constance's side, his journey filled with foreshadowing imagery of dark skies and "foul weather." After a soulful reunion, the "two parted, to meet again—upon earth, never any more," allowing Guy to bear up under tremendous challenge and tragedy. As he travels home "the brain fever was coming on fast," and he takes to "the sick-bed of delirium." His mother nurses him back to health, withholding the news of Constance's death until he recovers. After his recovery, he resists Flora's attentions and travels to Italy, but takes a fall from a horse while in mid-hunt, loses the use of his legs, and after being robbed of his virility, succumbs to life's challenges in a melodramatic death scene in the company of Frank, his best friend.

FEMINIST CRITICS find the female characters of interest for their portrayal of types, not only Constance and Flora, but also Lady Caroline Desborough, mentioned in a story within the main story as part of a cautionary tale, and Cornelia, who verbally attacks members of her own gender. Lady Caroline falls in love outside her loveless marriage with Colonel Mohun, runs away with him, then conveniently dies, to be remarked upon by another female character, Cornelia, as "rightly served . . . such women ought to be miserable." While not read in later decades, book such as *Guy Livingstone* acted as prototypes of the later pure adventure novel that would introduce romance and, eventually, allow their masculine protagonists a weakness or two to make them more realistic. It proved so popular that Lawrence's additional works generally bore the subtitle "by the author of *Guy Livingstone*." Not until the 1880s did the Aesthetic Movement challenge the popular portrait of the aristocratic militaristic athlete, introducing more cultured, mature, and intellectual heroes. The novel produced several "literary descendants," according to Anthony Powell, including works by English writers Louise de la Ramé, popularly known as OUIDA, and Rudyard KIPLING, as well as the American novelist Ernest Hemingway, all of whom focused on "hard" men.

BIBLIOGRAPHY

Fleming, Gordon H. *George Alfred Lawrence and the Victorian Sensational Novel.* Tucson: University of Arizona, 1952.

Kaye-Smith, Sheila. Introduction to *Guy Livingstone,* by George Lawrence. London: Elkin Mathews & Marrot, 1928, vii–ix.

Powell, Anthony. Introduction to *Novels of High Society from the Victorian Age.* London: Pilot Press, 1947, vii–xv.

GUY MANNERING SIR WALTER SCOTT (1816)

Sir Walter SCOTT's *Guy Mannering* makes the most of coincidence and mistaken identity to shape an 18th-century Scottish adventure based on a Scottish ballad. Early in his career, Scott heard that a Galloway excise officer named Joseph Train had begun collecting local history in order to write a book. Train so admired Scott that after the author contacted him, he decided not to use any of his information for his own publication, but instead to turn it over to Scott. He made frequent visits to the famous author to relay stories he had learned, and the two became good friends. Scott credited Train in the prefaces to all of his Waverley novels and found his anecdotes concerning Galloway Gypsies fascinating. He decided to incorporate aspects of those stories into his own novels, along with one told by a local character named John MacKinlay. That tale begins with an astrologer knocking on the door of a farmhouse at the moment of birth of the farmer's son. The astrologer writes out the son's horoscope, predicting his fortune, and Scott repeats the tale in its entirety in the introduction to the 1829 edition of *Guy Mannering*. According to Scott, he wrote the novel, the second in his Waverley series, over a six-week period around the 1815 Christmas holiday.

The novel's plot turns on the kidnapping of the child Harry Bertram, heir to Ellangowan, by a dastardly lawyer named Gilbert Glossin. The kidnapping brings an early death to Harry's mother, just after she delivers a daughter named Lucy. Glossin assumed that, by ridding the estate of Harry, he could purchase it himself. Involved with the plot and the original tale on which it is based is Meg Merrilies, a Gypsy woman believed by the locals to be a witch but who is quite dedicated to the Bertrams. She takes part in the mysticism with which Scott enjoyed imbuing many of his novels, indulging his fondness for local lore. He inserts a retelling of a version of the "true" tale of the kidnapped child within the novel.

The title character, Guy Mannering, had been shown kindness by Lewis Bertram, laird of Ellangowan, when, as a young man, he accepted Bertram's overnight hospitality. His night's stay coincided with the birth of Harry, and Guy prophesied to his host that his son would one day be in peril. Mannering's presence at the estate foreshadows his lifelong association with Bertram, who, in the manner of romance plots, matures with the name of Vanbeest Brown, joins the army in India, and ends up coincidentally serving under Colonel Mannering. Mannering likes the young man whom he knows as Brown but, when returning after six weeks absence on business, finds that Brown has become quite familiar with his wife and daughter. As Mannering later relates the story to his longtime friend, Mervyn, he compares himself to Shakespeare's jealous character Othello, because he listened to a so-called friend's gossip regarding Brown's flirtation with his beloved wife. Mannering challenges Brown to a duel and delivers what he believes to be a mortal wound to the young man, which brings on the death of Mrs. Mannering. Leaving his daughter Julia in the care of Mervyn, Mannering returns to England and Ellangowan, which he discovers is up for purchase. At age 17, Lucy Bertram helps care for her infirm father, who in his weak mental capacity does not recognize Mannering. The strain of the sale of his ancestor's property proves too taxing for Lewis Bertram, and he dies, leaving Lucy to deal with the delayed estate sale. Mannering bids to buy the estate to prevent Glossin's purchase, but the drunken carrier of his bid arrives too late, and Glossin wins the estate for himself.

In the meantime, Brown has recovered from his wound and returned to England. When he discovers that Julia lives in Dumfries with the Mervyns, he sets out to find her, alerting her first to his presence in the country. He befriends a farmer named Dandy Dinmont, helping him fight a gang of thieves, and then travels to Ellangowan, where he is recognized by Meg. As the plot's true heroine, Meg conceals Brown from her rowdy sons and their fellow "ruffians." As Brown makes his way across Scotland, Julia and Lucy have become close friends. While Julia thinks often of Brown, she develops a romance with a young man named Hazlewood who intends to marry her. When Hazlewood challenges Brown, sticking a gun in his ribs, Brown begins a scuffle, resulting in Hazlewood's wounding of himself.

Brown returns to Ellangowan, hoping to hide from Hazlewood. There Glossin recognizes him and engages him in discussion, agonized over the prospect that Brown/Bertram might remember his former home and identity. While Glossin remains "eager to learn what local recollections young Bertram had retained of the scenes of his infancy," he is also "compelled to be extremely cautious in his replies, lest he should awaken or assist, by some name, phrase or anecdote, the slumbering train of association." Glossin fears the loss of Ellangowan and takes Brown prisoner, escorting him to Baron Hazlewood's estate in order that revenge may be extracted for the wounding of young Hazlewood. Although Hazlewood has told his father that his wounding was accidental, Glossin convinces the Baron that he must serve justice on Brown. Through his interrogation, the Baron discovers Brown's connection with Colonel Guy Mannering and insists that he be contacted. Glossin does not want any information about Brown discussed in court, as his true identity might be revealed. Using a building fire as cover, Brown/Bertram escapes his trial, and Meg, in another heroic act, foils the conniving Glossin's plan with Dandy's help.

Glossin meets a grisly death by his henchman, Dirk Hatteraick. Bertram's true identity is recognized, and he regains not only the estate but also Mannering's favor and approval of his romance of Julia. In a happy ending, even Hazlewood becomes enamored of Bertram's friendship, and Mannering himself finds the guilt he felt for his wife's loss balanced by the forgiveness he receives from Bertram.

Guy Mannering offers no surprises to readers familiar with Scott's works. All the expected cast of characters are present—the nobleman forced to regain a lost fortune, the older/wiser confidant figure who also suffers conflict, the various sidekicks, damsels in need of rescue, and the introduction of mysticism.

While a traditional figure for Scott, Meg proves the most interesting, particularly to FEMINIST CRITICS. Her independence, courage, and special empowerment through a "magic" that results from her sharp wit and a honed intuition she has the wisdom to consult highlights her contrast with the lovely, dependent, and rather helpless young beauties.

BIBLIOGRAPHY

Bradley, Phillip. *An Index to the Waverley Novels.* Metuchen, N.J.: Scarecrow Press, 1975.

Gordon, Robert C. *Under Which King? A Study of the Scottish Waverley Novels.* New York: Barnes & Noble, 1969.

Rhys, Ernest. Preface to *Guy Mannering,* by Sir Walter Scott. New York: E. P. Dutton, 1954.

HAGGARD, SIR HENRY RIDER (1856–1925)

Henry Rider Haggard was born on June 22, 1856, in Bradenham, Norfolk. The sixth son of William Haggard's 10 children, Henry went at age one to Garsington Rectory, Oxford, to the care of the Reverend H. J. Graham. He later attended Ipswich Grammar School, where he was a mediocre student. He loved to read, particularly romances, and produced competition-winning essays. When Haggard failed an army entrance exam in 1873, his barrister father sent him to London in hopes that he might pass the entrance examination for the Foreign Office. While studying for his exam, Haggard fell in love with Lilly Jackson (the relationship would never develop) and engaged in spiritualist pursuits, including séances. When his father procured Haggard a staff position with Sir Henry Bulwer, lieutenant-governor of Natal, a province on the coast of South Africa, Haggard traveled to South Africa in 1875. When Britain annexed the Boer Transvaal in 1877, Haggard accompanied Sir Theophilus Shepstone to that area and began to write articles about the area, which were published in London periodicals. His firsthand knowledge of Britain's IMPERIALISM would later add much realism to his adventure stories set in Africa. These earlier experiences convinced him of the value of colonization and he would remain a lifelong supporter of Britain's imperialistic actions. He enjoyed his appointment as Master and Registrar of the High Court of Justice of the Transvaal but suffered devastation at the news of Lilly Jackson's marriage.

Following the 1879 Zulu defeat of the British at Isandhlwana, Haggard served for a time in the Pretoria Horse. Attracted more to the agrarian possibilities in South Africa than to militaristic endeavors, he left the service to establish an ostrich farm. He visited England that same year and fell in love with Louisa Margitson, orphaned heir to a Ditchingham estate, and married her in 1880. A few months later, the couple traveled to South Africa at the beginning of the First Boer War. In 1881, their son Arthur John "Jock" Rider was born, and the family returned to England, where Haggard studied law. In 1882, he published *Cetywayo and His White Neighbours, or Remarks on Recent Events in Zululand, Natal and Transvaal,* and gained notice as an expert in South African politics.

After the 1883 birth of the couple's daughter, Agnes Angela Rider, the family moved to the Ditchingham estate, and Haggard began writing a novel. Haggard published two novels in 1884, *Dawn* and *The Witch's Head,* and a third child, Sybil Dorothy Rider, joined the family. In 1885, Haggard received his call to the bar, but the publication of his third novel, *KING SOLOMON'S MINES,* brought him such success that he considered becoming a full-time writer. He followed one success with another when he published *ALLAN QUATERMAIN,* the sequel to *King Solomon,* also in 1885. His editor wrote to tell Haggard he had broken all records, with the publisher receiving 10,000 orders for copies. He continued his law practice, writing two additional novels, *Jess* and *She,* in 1886, then quit his practice in 1887. In 1887, he published SHE, A HISTORY OF ADVENTURE, a work that received great praise, and vacationed in Europe. When another Allan Quatermain story, *Maiwa's Revenge,* appeared in 1888, it sold 20,000 copies on its first day of release. He visited Iceland and returned to England, barely avoiding a shipwreck off Scotland. By 1889, Haggard enjoyed a huge popularity, published another novel, *Cleopatra,* and became friends with Rudyard KIPLING.

Haggard joined with friend Andrew Lang to publish *The World's Desire* (1890). The following year during his and Louisa's treasure-hunting expedition to Mexico, tragedy struck Haggard, shattering what had seemed to be his charmed life. They received word that their son, Jock, had died. Despite his grief, Haggard continued to write and in 1891 published *Eric Brighteyes,* a novel supported by his experiences in Iceland. He followed that novel with another, *Nada the Lily,* in 1892 and also celebrated the birth of another daughter, Lilias. His bid for parliamentary election in 1895 failed by a close vote, but in 1896, Haggard was elected chairman of the Society of Authors. He published *A Farmer's Year* in 1898 and in 1901 made a tour of 26 countries, writing articles on the state of agriculture that were collected and published as *Rural England* in 1902.

Haggard traveled to America in 1905 to examine and report on labor colonies established by the Salvation Army and met President Theodore Roosevelt. Later that year he saw publication of his 13th novel, *Ayesha—The Return of She.* In 1906, Haggard joined the Royal Commission on Coast Erosion and Aforestation and in 1912 was honored for his public service with the title Knight Bachelor, receiving an invitation to join the Royal Commission on the Dominions. His trilogy of Zulu tales began with the publication of *Marie* (1912) and continued with *Child of Storm* (1913) and *Finished* (1917). During the years of work on that trilogy, Haggard returned to South Africa, visiting the Zimbabwe excavations, where he reunited with Mazooku, a Zulu servant from his early service there. He also visited Australia, New Zealand, and Canada to discuss the possible settlement of members of the British armed forces following World War I and published *Moon of Israel* in 1918. Due to a shift in public reading tastes toward stronger characterization in fiction following the devastation of the war, Haggard's adventure writings no longer enjoyed the popularity they once had. After being made a Knight Commander of the British Empire in 1919, he published one additional novel, in 1921, *She and Allan.* Following a 1924 visit to Egypt, Haggard became ill and died on May 14, 1925.

Haggard's novels remain exceptional in several regards. His detailed descriptions, based on his own vast knowledge of South Africa and its peoples, fascinated his readers. Also, Haggard used time-tested plot devices, such as the QUEST, but added his own twists, such as making his hero an aged, grieving British gentleman (Allan Quatermain), and ignoring the traditional QUEST element of the triumphant return home on the part of the hero. In addition, several of Haggard's novels embodied Victorian preoccupation with evolution, suggested by the Charles DARWIN's *On the Origin of the Species* (1850); racially predicated social structures; psychological theories promoted by Sigmund Freud during the century's second half; and sexuality and its definition. Haggard also surprises readers by questioning his own imperialistic attitudes. Generally, inherent within imperialism is the idea that "lesser" civilizations can be improved by "superior" ones. But during an era when Haggard observed his own "superior" British culture distressingly evolving from an ordered land-centered society to a chaotic industrial one, he clearly recognized the possibility of an impending collapse of his society. Having studied the collapse of once-thriving civilizations on the East African coast, he well understood that Britain, too, could decline. And even with his racist attitudes that denied "inferior" races could support great civilizations alone (his novels proposed a long-lost race of "superior whites" in the middle of "the Dark Continent"), he characterized the Zulus as a dignified race and emphasized the rich culture of Africa, prefiguring 20th-century fiction by writers such as Chinua Achebe.

Even with his vast popularity, Haggard came under criticism of plagiarism, suffering accusations that he did not give credit to important sources. He also was criticized for the use of unnecessary violence; as a writer for the *British Weekly* in 1887, J. M. Barrie, under the name Gavin Ogilvy, noted that Haggard had presented more than 50,000 deaths in his various novels. Haggard responded by appealing to the need for realism in his work, but by the time he wrote *Allan Quatermain,* he had become sensitive to such accusations. He added a note on his use of sources at the novel's conclusion, mentioning, among others, Thomas HARDY's *FAR FROM THE MADDING CROWD* (1874). While Haggard states he never read that novel, nor does he mention Hardy by name, he does note that friends had pointed out similarities in scenes from the two novels. He also began accepting editorial advice for cutting some heavier violence. Some critics also disliked his style, noting his use of archaic language in the attempt to establish native speech, and his overuse of clichés and chauvinistic expressions. Known to be a rapid writer sometimes given to making careless errors (he wrote *Allan Quatermain* in 10 weeks), Haggard's revisions often weakened his stories, and he later worked hard at revisions.

Despite various complaints about his work, Haggard's publications proved enormously successful. That success, producing 68 published books of fiction and nonfiction, grew from Haggard's enormous store of firsthand adventures, memories, and legends of exotic lands that endlessly piqued his readers' imaginations.

BIBLIOGRAPHY

Butts, Dennis. Introduction to *Allan Quatermain,* by Henry Rider Haggard. Oxford: Oxford University Press, 1995.

———. Introduction to *King Solomon's Mines,* by Henry Rider Haggard. Oxford: Oxford University Press, 1991.

Etherington, Norman. *Rider Haggard.* Boston: Twayne, 1984.

Katz, Wendy R. *Rider Haggard and the Fiction of Empire: A Critical Study of British Imperial Fiction.* Cambridge: Cambridge University Press, 1987.

Phelps, Gilbert. *A Short History of English Literature.* London: The Folio Society, 1962.

HAMILTON, THOMAS (1789–1842)

Thomas Hamilton came from a distinguished Scottish family. His father, William, served as professor of anatomy and botany at the University of Glasgow, while his brother, Sir William Hamilton, became what George Douglas describes as an "intellectual luminary of Edinburgh." Thomas Hamilton attended school in southern England, transferring to Glasgow University in 1803. During his three years there, he completed an unremarkable education and decided on a commercial career. However, in 1810, he purchased a commission in the 29th Regiment and was almost immediately engaged in the Napoleonic Wars, ordered first to the Continent, where he sustained a musket bullet wound to the thigh. He later served in Nova Scotia and New Brunswick and retired on half-pay in about 1818. Moving to Edinburgh, he studied literature and published in *BLACKWOOD'S EDINBURGH MAGAZINE.* He married in 1820 and lived during the summer near Melrose, where he became friends with his neighbor, Sir Walter SCOTT.

Neither the Napoleonic Wars nor the INDUSTRIAL REVOLUTION had been used as novel topics in the 1820s, despite their importance. In the case of the war, none of the popular novelists had taken part in it. Finally, in 1825, George Robert Gleig published *The Subaltern,* a novel that traced his own military career. In 1827, Hamilton, who had been wounded in the war, followed suit, publishing *The YOUTH AND MANHOOD OF CYRIL THORNTON,* a novel following the exploits of a young man who has the misfortune early on of accidentally killing his brother. The public eagerly consumed his account of university and military life. While popular enough to see three printings, it would be his only novel.

BIBLIOGRAPHY

Douglas, George Brisbane. *The "Blackwood" Group.* Edinburgh: O. Anderson & Ferrier, 1897.

HANDLEY CROSS   R. S. SURTEES (1843)

R. S. SURTEES creates a SATIRE of the hunting set in his novel *Handley Cross.* Surtees, an avid hunter, sportsman, and sportswriter, knew his topic well and adds to reader enjoyment by openly making fun of his own passion. He reintroduces readers to Mr. John Jorrocks, a character first made popular in *Jorrock's Jaunts and Jollities.* While some of his contemporaries felt his stories to largely lack an orderly construction, even his critics admitted to enjoying the tales, despite their uncomfortable style. Surtee's disjointed approach might reflect his background in journalism writing. Even negative critics agree that his accurate reproduction of humorous speech patterns, an essential aspect of his close character observation, makes his novels engaging.

Before Surtees introduces Jorrocks, readers encounter a number of individuals whose names reveal their importance as type characters: the leader of the hunt, Michael Hardey; a "roistering, red-faced, round-about apothecary," Roger Swizzle; Swizzle's competitor with "pale and sentimental countenance," Dr. Sebastian Mello; and a roster of local high-society hunter types that include Alfred Boltem, Simon Hookem, Walter Fleeceall, Judas Turnbill, Michael Grasper, and, most important, Captain Doleful. In the opening chapters, Surtees also satirizes health spas through the characters of Swizzle and Mello, giving an account of how they "create" a health business that promotes growth of Handley Cross, allowing it to support a hunt team. Swizzle, an acknowledged swindler, pedals so-called healing properties of his leased spring and specializes in treatment of "languid hypochondriacs." One treatment involves his carrying a woman who claims she cannot walk to the top of his house and screaming, "Fire!" causing her to come "spinning down stairs in a way that astonished herself." Surtees establishes the foolishness of the hunting group that forms in the area by presenting a detailed report of the group's first meeting and the bylaws it draws up. They include detailed instructions for dress, the evening "or dress uniform" being "a sky-blue coat, lined with pink silk, canary-coloured shorts, and white silk stockings."

When the longtime huntsman, Michael, dies and the dog "whipper-in," Peter, abandons the hunting group following a hilariously described initial disastrous jaunt, the Handley Cross club requires a new leader. They solicit Jorrocks, described as a sports grocer, to his great satisfaction. He accepts the position of master of the hunt and establishes himself at Handley Cross with the expectation of royal treatment. Surtees makes much of Jorrocks's fondness for marmalade, a habit that apparently qualifies him for high society. Jorrocks's aristocratic expectations are shared by his silly, egotistical wife, and the couple moves to Handley Cross, accompanied by their lovely niece Belinda. Jor-

rocks's lazy cockney servant, Benjamin, always pronounced "Binjimin" by Jorrocks, becomes whipper-in, and the drunken, yet skillful, James Pigg of Newcastle becomes huntsman. Following numerous boondoggles involving well-detailed hunts and social activities, Mrs. Jorrocks attempts to arrange a marriage for Belinda with Captain Doleful, although Belinda prefers another of Jorrocks's recruits, Charlie Stubbs. Adding high-society conflict is the desire of Mrs. Brantinghame that her own daughter, Louisa Letitia Carolina Jemima, referred to simply as "Miss," capture the affections of Captain Doleful.

Send-ups of high society life, led by the indomitable Barningtons and the interchangeable Romeo Simpkins, Miss Trollope, Miss Mordecai, and Miss Somebodyelse, add humor to the patently ridiculous situation. In one satiric scene, Mrs. Brantinghame, taxed to the limit by bills for entertainment, "gradually lowered the standard." Rather than serve the traditional expensive fowls and roast game, "she jobbed a joint from Saveloy's beef and sausage shop in Grudgington Street." Miss does become Mrs. Doleful, but soon after declares her husband a "'orrid man,'" at which point her mother repeats Mr. Jorrocks's advice. Although Jorrocks had applied the advice to a horse, Mrs. Brantinghame feels it applies also to husbands, toward which a wife should be, "to his faults a little blind, and to his virtues ever kind." A large cast of additional characters peppers the novel, including Mr. Prettyfat, Mr. Bowker, Sir Archy, Partridge, Mr. Moonface, Mr. Cowmeadow, Catherine Christian Clementina Constance, and others. Eventually Mrs. Jorrocks moves to have her husband certified as insane, but he delivers one of his well-known speeches and regains his liberty, causing Mrs. Jorrocks to faint dead away upon his return home. All ends happily with Belinda marrying Charley Stobbs and Jorrocks taking the position of grand protector to Mr. Prettyfat's poultry.

While the novel may be at times too dense for modern readers, the depiction of the pomposity of the upper and sporting classes remains amusing. In a preface to the 1854 edition, the author cautions, "The reader will have the kindness to bear in mind, that the work merely professes to be a tale, and does not aspire to the dignity of a novel."

BIBLIOGRAPHY

Collison, Robert Lewis. *A Jorrocks handbook; a centenary dictionary of the characters, places, situations, and allusions which occur in the Jorrocks novels and in the short stories by Robert Smith Surtees.* London: Coole Book Service, 1964.

Welcome, John. *The Sporting World of R. S. Surtees.* New York: Oxford University Press, 1982.

HAND OF ETHELBERTA, THE: A COMEDY IN CHAPTERS THOMAS HARDY (1876)

First published as a serial in *The CORNHILL MAGAZINE* between July 1875 and May 1876, *The Hand of Ethelberta* represents Thomas HARDY's sole published attempt at humor. Whether because his reading public did not expect him to write humor, or whether, as he states in his preface to the 1912 edition, the book simply arrived before its time, it was not popular and has been seldom read since. Although its subtitle indicates it is a dramatic comedy converted to novel form, critically it reads like a comedy in search of humor. Little of the exaggeration or incongruity from which humor grows is present in the book. It purports to be a romance, focused on its poet/storyteller protagonist, Ethelberta Chickerel, yet offers at least one serious purpose, if not two. Hardy notes that his work "undertook a delicate task: to excite interest in a drama . . . wherein servants were as important as, or more important than, their masters." Because this idea challenged the norm of his age regarding the importance of class distinctions, Hardy seems more intent on producing a social statement than humor. In addition, much energy is spent in commenting on the life of a writer/artist and how that life can be manipulated by public expectation and reward, or the lack thereof. Hardy contends that circumstances which in his novel first struck readers as "eccentric and almost impossible," were, as he wrote 35 years later, common on the stage and in novels, "and accepted as reasonable and interesting pictures of life; which suggests that the comedy (or, more accurately, satire)" appeared too soon. His struggle to categorize the piece as either SATIRE, a biting, often-ruthless subgenre that never tries to pass off sarcasm for humor, or comedy, suggests his own ambivalence about the piece.

Ethelberta, born into a large family of 10 children headed by a butler and his kind wife, has moved up the social ladder to marry as a teenager the son and heir of Sir Ralph Petherwin and his widow. However, the son dies during their honeymoon, and she lives with her mother-in-law for the next three years. Opening the novel with the death of a beloved husband may be the first obstacle for readers in seeing the plot as comic.

Lady Petherwin becomes upset over poetry published anonymously by Ethelberta but later known as her own, because she feels Ethelberta has betrayed the memory of her son. The two women quarrel. Ethelberta foolishly states that she could not continue to love a memory, particularly one from her youth, and Lady Petherwin responds that extended love was exactly the expectation she had of Ethelberta. She then destroys her will, which left to her daughter-in-law a great deal of money, in a fit of passion. Although she later repents of her action and mails her brother a letter noting that Ethelberta is to receive a portion of his cash inheritance at her death, the brother declares the document not legal, and Ethelberta inherits only furniture and the lease on the home she had shared with her mother-in-law.

From the opening pages, she has been pursued by an ex-boyfriend named Christopher Julian, a musician who falls in love with her younger sister, Picotee, but does not realize it for a time. Ethelberta returns to live with her family, where she does not lack for romance. Three men court her, a painter named Eustace Lovell, a wealthy socialite named Alfred Neigh, and the older, wealthy Lord Mountclere. To earn a better living, she abandons her successful poetry career and turns instead to public storytelling. She eventually chooses to marry Lord Mountclere, over the protestations of all, despite his doubtful reputation with women, in what seems to be a reaction against her earlier marriage to such a young man. Hardy offers no explanation to counter Mountclere's reputation and adds little humor to the situation. Some sympathy for Mountclere is aroused in readers when he reacts with compassion and understanding following Ethelberta's telling of her own story one night in a public place. He lets her know that he understands the "girl of the poorest and meanest parentage" with "strange dreams and ambitious longings" is actually Ethelberta. The fact that he excuses her lack of social connection is admirable, and one can perhaps understand why this simple act moves Ethelberta to feel it a "great honour" to be his wife. However, no humor lightens the sorrow and shame felt by Ethelberta, or the pity felt by Mountclere. While Julian happily ends up with Picotee, neither character has personalities that permit any lighthearted banter. Their final discussion focuses on their unpromising financial state, eased by the knowledge that Ethelberta will provide for them.

In order to emphasize his desire to incorporate dramatic form into his work, Hardy titles each chapter with the name of a place, moving readers from one "set" to another. The detailed scenes and use of popular-culture references hold reader interest, as do the situations of the characters. What readers remember from the book are not humorous moments, however, but ones such as Julian's performance as a hired musician at a social gathering and his bittersweet recollection of "when he had mingled in similar scenes, not as servant but as guest." And when Ethelberta explains to Julian that she decided to become a storyteller following her fall from the protection of Lady Petherwin, and he responds, "There is a way for everybody to live if they can only find it out," little joy exists in her discovery of a new talent. Readers also may find it difficult to celebrate her later marriage when they recall she first mentioned marriage to Mountclere in order to "have some groundwork to enable me to keep up to the mark in my profession." FEMINIST CRITICS and Hardy scholars find interesting the fact that Ethelberta is the only Hardy heroine who does not sacrifice herself to society's expectations. Her unemotional pragmatic choice in marriage works in her material favor. The book is readily available in print.

BIBLIOGRAPHY

Hardy, Thomas. Foreword to *The Hand of Ethelberta: A Comedy in Chapters* by Thomas Hardy. London: Macmillan, 1966, vii–ix.

HANDY ANDY: A TALE OF IRISH LIFE
SAMUEL LOVER (1842)   Samuel LOVER was best known as a miniaturist painter and a dramatist, often performing his own written sketches and stories. *Handy Andy* remains his best-known novel, probably his only work to have remained palatable to later audiences. Lover writes ironically in the novel's "Address" of having been "accused, in certain quarters, of giving flattering portraits of my countrymen." His punning reference to both his painting and his writing prepares the reader for the type of humor to follow. Openly shaping stereotypes, he notes that "the hero is a blundering servant" who no respectable Englishman would hire, and that his minor characters include two "Squires," one good, one evil, meant to represent those universal types. He adds, "As a tale cannot get on without villains, I have given some touches of villainy, quite sufficient to prove my belief in Irish villains, though I do not wish it to be believed the Irish are *all villains.*"

The handy figure referred to in the title is Andy Rooney, a servant who does not know how to serve that works for Squire Egan. Much of the novel's action focuses on Egan's conflict with his rival, the bad Squire O'Grady. Andy mostly interferes with his own squire, due to his hopelessly inept actions, but in the novel's conclusion is proved, in a PARODY of 18th-century novels of men of fortune, to be heir to the estate of Lord Scatterbrain. From the opening page, Andy is a problem to everyone, including his mother, whose hair he pulls and whom he scratches until she bleeds. Nevertheless, she deems him "a darlin'," and Andy himself seems unaware of his shortcomings. When he claims ability to ride a wild horse for his neighbor, the horse ends up falling through a bridge so that "half the saws, hatchets, ropes and poles in the parish" are required to free him. Still, Andy becomes a stable worker, then whipper of the hounds for Squire Egan. He must face the ire of Dick Dawson, later Andy's staunch supporter, from whom he hides under the bed of his mother, falling asleep there and later making her believe he is an Irish spirit come to murder her when he awakes and accidentally grabs her hand as she sleeps. His ineptness is so blatant that he tricks many into believing he pretends inefficiency as part of some intelligent plan. When the local magistrate, Squire O'Grady, questions him about one mishap, Andy responds to his "string of questions" in such an "entangled" way that O'Grady was "as much puzzled as before, whether Andy was stupid and innocent, or too knowing to let himself be caught." He decides the latter is true and hires Andy himself. Squire O'Grady desires to marry his daughter to the present Lord Scatterbrain, and thus the association with that family begins. This allows the action, including Andy's being implicated in a murder, to develop into the good fortune of Andy's inheritance, his assuming the apt title of Lord Scatterbrain, and his marriage to the faithful and devoted Oonah. The novel's slapstick humor is continually showcased in scenes of mishap, such as one in which Andy is disguised as a girl by the local women for protection, then kidnapped in place of Oonah and almost "seduced" by the "blackguard" Shan Mor, a circumstance, along with Andy's arrested emotional development and attachment to his mother, of interest to PSYCHOANALYTIC CRITICS. With audience demand for such bawdy and simplistic humor extended into the 21st century, many readers continue to appreciate *Handy Andy*.

BIBLIOGRAPHY

Burke, Jerome H. *The Victorian Temper: A Study in Literary Culture.* New York: Vintage Books, 1964.

Orel, Harold, ed. *The World of Victorian Humor.* New York: Appleton, Century, Crofts, 1961.

Symington, Andrew. *Samuel Lover, a Biographical Sketch with Selections from His Writings and Correspondence.* New York: Harper & Brothers, 1880.

HARD CASH CHARLES READE (1863)

Upon beginning Charles READE's sequel to his novel *Love Me Little, Love Me Long* (1850), a reader might believe the book is purely ROMANCE. Mrs. Dodd and her children, Edward and Julia, keep one another company in the absence of David Dodd, a seaman who is in India. The three seem not only a close family but also close friends. They prepare for Edward to enroll at Oxford, Julia feeling jealous not to be able to continue her education in the same manner, while Mrs. Dodd worries over their use of slang, her concerns helping produce a lighthearted tone.

That tone continues as Mrs. Dodd and Julia travel to Oxford to watch Edward compete in a rowing contest and encounter Edward's new schoolmates. One of the young men, Alfred Hardie, falls in love with Julia, their romance develops, and he asks Mrs. Dodd for Julia's hand. In another plot aspect, Julia is treated for a mysterious illness, allowing Reade to confront the restrictions placed on women in his society. Julia requests to see a "doctress" or a "she-doctor," to which her mother responds, "There is no such thing. No; assurance is becoming a characteristic of our sex; but we have not yet intruded ourselves into the learned professions, thank Heaven!" Reade also ironically foreshadows the family's later battle with just such "learned" professionals who decidedly act against the better good of their so-called patients.

Because Mr. Dodd remains absent, Mrs. Dodd dutifully suggests that Alfred write to his own father, the banker Richard Hardie, to ask his permission for the marriage. At this point, the novel's tone darkens, as Hardie responds with a decided no, thanking Mrs. Dodd for her "delicacy," but informing her "this match is out of the question." The young people are heartbroken and Alfred perplexed, as he cannot persuade his father to explain why he is against the marriage. When Mrs. Dodd awakens in the middle of the night, crying out for her husband, Reade foreshadows a far more sober emotional awakening in the Dodds's future.

As the action rises, the Dodd family learns that Richard Hardie has swindled David Dodd out of his family's support, the "hard cash" he worked diligently to earn. Driven to distraction by the loss, Dodd is confined to a private mental institution, with the persuasion of authorities by Hardie. His surname well earned, Hardie goes so far as to commit his own son, Alfred, to the same institution, to ensure that Alfred will not reveal the secret he discovers of his father's theft. While the situation eventually works out well, the horrors of the institution are revealed, including physical and emotional abuses of the patients. Alfred remains sedated much of the time to prevent any protest, the presumed treatments only exacerbate most patients' problems, and Dodd cannot make anyone listen to his explanations. The appointed attorneys are even less help, not taking any of the patients' pleas seriously. Eventually, Dodd escapes and is able to return to the sea, and Alfred is aided by sympathetic attendants and rescued by the persistent Edward and other supporters, with Richard Hardie exposed.

Reade intended his novel to alert the public to the abuse of mental patients, one of his many social causes. Just as interesting as the novel are the letters it generated, printed in later editions. Reade comments in a preface that his book does represent a "matter-of-fact romance; that is, a fiction built on truths," which he gathered from many sources, including firsthand interviews. However, the authenticity of the facts of abuse were questioned. As Reade writes, "The madhouse scenes have been picked out by certain disinterested gentlemen who keep private asylums" who indulged in "a little easy cant about Sensation Novelists." That particular correspondence to the editor of the *Daily News,* signed by J. S. Bushnan, M.D., of Laverstock House Asylum, Salisbury, hints at Reade's "terrible slander" of a group of professionals of which he is proud to be a part. Bushnan challenges Reade to "quote his case, and openly and fearlessly declare when and where such atrocities occurred." Reade provides just such details in a chilling relation of not only facts he researched but also of information gleaned from his own recent challenge. With the help of the press, Reade gained release of a sane man "falsely imprisoned," housing and supporting that man during his legal appeals, in which a "functionary . . . did all he could to defeat justice, and break the poor suitor's back and perpetuate the stigma." He quotes another case, "Mathew v. Harty," that furnished details for his novel. Additional gruesome information regarding physical abuse of a specific patient leading to his death concludes with Reade's comments as to the shocking situation that "brute force and traditional cunning" is used against those of "weak understanding." More shocking is "that they should be so often massacred, so seldom avenged."

Hard Cash retains its interest for 21st-century readers as an example of well-written protest fiction, in its day ranked with the best of Charles DICKENS's "novels with a purpose."

BIBLIOGRAPHY

Reade, Charles. Preface to *The Complete Works of Charles Reade: Hard Cash.* New York: Kelmscott Society, n.d.

"Correspondence Elicited by the First Edition of 'Hard Cash.'" *The Complete Works of Charles Reade: Hard Cash.* New York: Kelmscott Society, n.d.

HARD TIMES CHARLES DICKENS (1854)

First published as a serial between April and August 1854, Charles DICKENS's *Hard Times* deals with the traditional battle between reason (logic or, later, science) and the imagination (the arts). He labels logic "fact" in his novel and sets out to demonstrate that fact alone cannot lead to a positive life. The book clearly offers a harsh critique of the utilitarianism movement, in which logic reigns supreme. The utilitarian philosophy allowed little room for what it considered the superfluous aspects of the imagination. Dickens had attacked the same system in *DOMBEY AND SON* (1848), in which Mr. Dombey represented the product of a system that found its roots in rationality and valued only material gain. Both that novel and *BLEAK HOUSE* (1853) had eased into his anti-utilitarian message through the development of characters into representatives of that system. However, in *Hard Times,* Dickens immediately reveals the harsh contrast between the undesirable, although necessary, world of "fact" versus that of "fancy." While common sense predicts that neither world could exist on its own in pure form, Dickens emphasizes that only disaster can result when "fact" is allowed to do so.

Dickens cleverly chooses the mysterious and exotic world of Sleary's circus to represent the imagination. It offers color, excitement, and a figurative escape from the real world for its audience. The escape proves a literal one for Dickens's protagonist, Sissy, a purposely universal name establishing her as representative of all, who is born into the wonderfully imaginative life. However, Sissy Jupe becomes an orphan when deserted by her father, leaving her to be adopted by the symbolically named Thomas Gradgrind, whose household is a literal "grind," void of all humor, love, or imagination. Gradgrind ignores his own children, to their great disadvantage, and does the same to Sissy. She pities Gradgrind's daughter, Louisa, and his son, Tom, both of whom have been raised without affection or encouragement to find and exercise their creative selves. Dickens emphasizes the terrible results that arise from such treatment, much as he would do again with the character Estella in GREAT EXPECTATIONS (1861). He typically offered cautionary tales to his audience, many of which focused on children; their abuses generally represented those of the author's own Victorian society toward its less-fortunate members, day laborers and the poor. Dickens himself suffered under such a system as a child who endured the abuses of work in a factory to support his family imprisoned due to his father's debt. However, he did have loving, if often misguided and unrealistic, parents. A message shared by all his novels that focus on young children remains the strength a child may gain from a firm belief in their own capacity to achieve, a belief that must build on the bedrock of nurture from parental figures.

The lack of such nurture for Louisa and Tom leads to disastrous decisions. Louisa marries an abusive, wealthy cad, Josiah Bounderby, whose name represents his approach to life; he uses others for personal gain. Tom turns to a life of crime, but is rescued by Sissy and her original circus family, a direct comment from Dickens that individual creativity helps any person imagine more than one choice for their life. In Dickens's traditional approach, the novel contains several plotlines, and a secondary line in Hard Times follows another individual who suffers due to "fact," represented, again, by Gradgrind. Gradgrind frames for his own crime one of his factory workers, Stephen Blackpool, who does honest work to support his alcoholic wife, although he loves his fellow factory worker, Rachel. Blackpool is ostracized by his peers for his love and loses his job; it is his absence that allows Gradgrind to accuse him of his own actions. Blackpool is found innocent of his supposed crime only after dying. Blackpool's fate reflects Dickens's dislike of any organization and his promotion of the value of individual responsibility in its purist form. The character of the worthless union organizer, Slackbridge, judged by his critics to be the least realistic of Hard Times's characters, represents an organization that does little to support the individual in need. The too idealistically drawn Blackpool suffers due to conflict between the union and the factory owner, a fate that Dickens feared for all workers. He saw labor unions as denying their members' basic rights, such as personal choice of work.

Notable in Hard Times is the lack of comic relief normally provided by Dickens through humorous characters that populate even his harshest cultural attacks. While dozens of characters extraneous to those absorbing most of the reader's attention exist, none supply any escape from the harsh reality that frames the plot's action. Judged by modern critic Lionel Stevenson as Dickens's only "openly revolutionary" novel in its "implications," it received praise by Victorian reformer and essayist John Ruskin and Socialist promoter and playwright George Bernard Shaw. While judged by critics to be well conceived and tightly executed, the novel never shared the popularity of his other works. Most critics agree that is due to the fact that Dickens offers no characters about whom the reader may care. The book remains readily available.

BIBLIOGRAPHY

Kaplan, Fred, and Sylvère Monod. Hard Times: An Authoritative Text, Contexts, Criticism. New York: W.W. Norton, 2001.

Simpson, Margaret. The Companion to Hard Times. Westport, Conn.: Greenwood Press, 1997.

Stevenson, Lionel. The English Novel: A Panorama. Boston: Houghton Mifflin, 1960.

HARDY, THOMAS (1840–1928)

HARDY, THOMAS (1840–1928)   Novelist and poet Thomas Hardy was the son of a master mason and builder, born in Dorsetshire, the region that he later fictionalized as Wessex in his novels. As a child, Hardy immersed himself in country life, legend, and folklore. His early acquaintance with the harshness of rural living contributed to the sympathy for country workers and animals that appears throughout his works. A naturalist, Hardy wrote forceful studies of life in which characters continually face defeat in conflict with their physical and social environments, their own impulses, and the malevolent caprices of chance. Hardy fixated on the changing English countryside in Dorset, where he saw nothing of comfort. His prose voice served to criticize Victorian mores and beliefs, expressing doubt as to their value.

Hardy's life and career can be organized into three recognizable phases. During phase one, his early life and young adulthood (1840–72), he worked as an architect and made an unsuccessful attempt at writing poetry. His inability to sell the poetry not withstanding, he considered himself first and foremost a poet, even converting some verses into prose, just so they might be read. In phase two, middle adulthood (1873–97), he engaged in writing the most ambitious and success-ful of his 14 novels. In his third and final phase (1897–1928), he gave up novel writing and devoted his energies primarily to writing poetry.

From 1856 to 1862 Hardy apprenticed himself to a local architect and met the poet William Barnes and the intellectual Horace Moule. Both encouraged his intellectual aspirations and later introduced him to the theories of Charles DARWIN. Hardy claimed that after reading Darwin's *On the Origin of Species* (1859), he gave up his plan to become a country parson and spent the rest of his life trying to reconcile the ortho-dox notion of a benevolent God with Darwin's theory of evolution through natural selection. At the same time, he witnessed the growing impoverishment of southwest England.

Between 1871 and 1898, Hardy wrote 14 novels, three volumes of short stories, and a volume of poetry. Hardy divided his prose into three groups. The first focused on character and environment and included the best known of his novels, such as UNDER THE GREENWOOD TREE (1871), FAR FROM THE MADDING CROWD (1871), The RETURN OF THE NATIVE (1878), The MAYOR OF CASTERBRIDGE (1886), The WOODLANDERS (1887), TESS OF THE D'URBERVILLES (1891), and JUDE THE OBSCURE (1896). The second group included romances and fantasies, such as *A Pair of Blue Eyes* (1873), The TRUMPET-MAJOR (1880), TWO ON A TOWER (1882), and *The Well Beloved* (1897). The third group has been labeled novels of ingenuity and includes *Desperate Remedies* (1871), The HAND OF ETHELBERTA (1876), and *A Laodicean* (1882). Hardy's writing career spanned almost six decades. He wrote for a broad audience composed of people from various classes and education levels. He was not university edu-cated but became a novelist, and later a poet, of the first rank, although his poetry continues to be less widely read and appreciated than his novels. The quality and

quantity of his fiction put Hardy in the company of the most highly regarded 19th- and 20th-century novelists. Hardy's abundant, technically accomplished poetry makes him unusual among these or any other group of English and American novelists. We know little of the intimate details of Hardy's life. A reticent man, he destroyed many personal papers before he died. Reports indicate that his first marriage was extremely troubled, yet after his wife's death Hardy wrote a number of poems in expiation of her death, collected in *Satires of Circum-stance, Lyrics and Reveries* (1914); they remain among Hardy's finest literary works.

Tess of the D'Urbervilles and *Jude the Obscure* are gen-erally considered the more accomplished and memo-rable of his novels. All Hardy's longer works rely on a strong realistic element. They concern characters and events that might have existed in a social and natural world that are recognizable. Hardy's narratives focus on relations of power in society, particularly the rela-tions between men and women and between individu-als and the larger controlling, often cruel, limiting tendencies of their society. His characters face over-whelming odds in a world that does not satisfy their needs. He combines in his work issues of aesthetic form with questions of value, both political and ethi-cal. Not a romantic, Hardy set his fiction in the gloomy and isolated moors of Dorset, reflecting a pessimistic view in which men are the insignificant and ineffectual playthings of an often ironic fate. Hardy said of his early novels that the bleak natural setting seems an active character, participating in the plot of his fiction.

The second phase of his career began to reach its cul-mination and to develop into the third phase when in 1887 he started *Tess of the D'Urbervilles,* published in 1891, first serially in the *Graphic,* then in three volumes. The decade from 1887 to 1897 is the period of Hardy's transition from fiction to poetry, even though none of his poetry was published during these years. *Tess,* the most poetic of Hardy's novels, is premonitory of his shift in artistic interests. It contains much repetition of word and phrase and many other instances of echoic language (language that contains a repetition of sounds).

Hardy's poetry is as distinguished as his novels. While much is made of his ending his fiction career, following negative criticism of *Jude the Obscure,* to take up poetry, he had always regarded himself primarily as a poet. He chose fiction writing as a career only after determining that he could not earn a living writing poetry. Unlike many of his contemporaries, he never claimed to express his own views through his characters, and his materialistic goals seemed to some to diminish the importance of his writing. He was criticized for allowing various editions to be excerpted and carved to fit the format of periodical publication and other forms of distribution, but he had never hidden the fact that, as stated in *Jude,* he envisioned himself as nothing more than "a chronicler of moods and deeds." Due to his reputation as a fiction writer, Hardy could, unlike in his early attempts at poetry, enjoy a comfortable career as a poet. His diction is distinctive, and he experimented constantly with form and stress, the singing rhythms subtly respond to the movement of his intense feelings. His lyrics nearly always center on incident in a way that give them dramatic sharpness. Hardy's death was an occasion for national mourning. His ashes were buried in Westminster Abbey, but in accordance with his last wish, his heart was returned to his own parish churchyard in the little Dorsetshire village of Stinsford.

Hardy's work remains under the constant scrutiny of FEMINIST CRITICS, some of the more discerning of whom have interrogated the crude simplification of his works as fatalist or pessimistic and exposed the criticism of social institutions that underpins his remarkable portrayals of women. MARXIST CRITICS find the power and material issues of interest, while PSYCHOANALYTIC CRITICS examine the seeming acceptance of fate, as well as sexual conflict, in Hardy's characters. His works continue to be the most widely read and studied of any English author, with, perhaps, the exception of Charles DICKENS, and remain readily available in print form and in various media, having been frequently dramatized.

BIBLIOGRAPHY

Beach, Joseph Warren. *The Technique of Thomas Hardy.* Chicago: University of Chicago Press, 1922.

Carpenter, Richard C. *Thomas Hardy.* Twayne Publishers: New York. 1964.

Child, Harold. *Thomas Hardy.* Haskell House Publishers: New York. 1972.

Heilman, Robert B. Introduction to *Tess of the d'Urbervilles,* by Thomas Hardy. New York: Bantam Books, 1992.

HARRADEN, BEATRICE   (1864–1936)

Beatrice Harraden was born in Hampstead and attended school first in Dresden, then at Cheltenham College, Queen's College, and Bedford College, London. After her 1883 graduation, she began her career as a devoted and vocal suffrage worker. She worked closely with the famed Emmeline Pankhurst and her daughters, taking a leadership position in the Women's Social and Political Union, a controversial and militant branch of the women's movement. She also participated in London literary circles. She sold to fiction to BLACKWOOD'S EDINBURGH MAGAZINE as well as to the Suffragette paper *Votes for Women,* and she worked tirelessly for women's rights, making speeches and distributing printed materials. Adept at using fiction to promote the goals of suffrage, she first visited the Continent on behalf of suffrage and then moved on to the United States to campaign in 1894–95. She once refused to pay tax on her belongings, which were sold at auction. The auction and gathering protest against it caused a reverse protest, and anti-suffragettes threw objects at the women, injuring Harraden's eye. She wrote in part to explain her actions, "It is obviously unfair and increasingly intolerable that a woman who earns her own living by direct use of her brain should be called upon to pay tax on her earnings, and yet be denied any voice whatsoever in the choice of representatives to Parliament." She would also contribute to the growing endeavor for Oxford University that would become famous as the *Oxford English Dictionary.* Like hundreds of private individuals around the world, Harraden mailed to the dictionary's editors research on individual words later incorporated into the publication.

Harraden's first novel, *Things Will Take a Turn* (1891), preceded her second effort, the hugely successful *SHIPS THAT PASS IN THE NIGHT* (1893), which garnered more than a million sales. Its story of a doomed affair between tuberculosis patients captured the imagination of the public, many of whom thought of Harraden as a ROMANCE writer. That novel focused on her feminist beliefs, as did her short story collection, *In Varying Moods* (1894), and her novels *Hilda Stafford*

(1897), *The Fowler* (1899), *Katharine Frensham* (1903), *Interplay* (1908), *Youth Calling* (1924), and *Search Will Find It Out* (1928). *Youth Calling* supposedly fictionalized her working relationship with journalist Eliza Lynn Linton, who held strict anti-feminist views but agreed with the theory of fiction as a powerful conduit for political ideas. Harraden retired in the 1930s, living partially on a pension earned for service to the cause of literature. Her works are available in print as well as in electronic text. The University of London has several of her manuscripts in a special collection donated by her family in the years 1938 and 1939.

BIBLIOGRAPHY

Jorgensen-Earp, Cheryl R. *Speeches and Trials of the Militant Suffragettes: The Women's Social and Political Union 1903–1918.* Madison, N.J.: Farleigh Dickinson University Press, 1999.

Pankhurst, Estelle, and Sylvia Pankhurst. *The Suffragette Movement: An Intimate Account of Persons and Ideals.* London: Chatto & Windus: 1987.

Willis, Chris. "Beatrice Harraden." *Crime, Gender and Victorian Popular Culture.* Available online. URL: http://www.chriswillis.freeserve.co.uk/index.html. Downloaded on July 18, 2003.

Winchester, Simon. *The Meaning of Everything: The Story of the Oxford English Dictionary.* New York: Oxford University Press, 2003.

HARRISON, MARY ST. LEGER KINGSLEY See MALET, LUCAS.

HAYWOOD, ELIZA (1693–1756)

Judged a "hack" writer by later generations, Eliza Haywood produced an enormous amount of popular work. Practically nothing is known of her childhood and youth, other than that her father was a London shopkeeper and that she married early a clergyman many years her elder. She initially gained notice while acting in Dublin around 1715, then moved to London and wrote unsuccessfully for the stage. Between 1719 and 1725, she produced several short "exemplary novels," intended as cautionary tales, in an attempt to imitate England's first woman writer to earn a living with her craft, Aphra BEHN. Her written comments

indicate that by 1719, she was no longer in the marriage she described as "unfortunate." In later letters, she indicated that her husband and father had both died prior to 1730 and she referred to two children, neither of whom were fathered by her husband. The older child may have been fathered by Richard Savage, a writer friend of Samuel JOHNSON, and the other by William Hatchett, with whom she cohabitated for about 20 years.

Haywood focused on her career, enjoying multiple reprintings of her books, released in a collected edition in 1725 that included the popular *Fantomina: Or, Love in a Maze.* In 1733 she collaborated with Hatchett on a comic opera version of Henry FIELDING's popular drama, *Tragedy of Tragedies,* renamed *Tom Thumb the Great,* which was well received. She edited the periodical *The Female Spectator* for two years in the mid 1740s, and published literally dozens of novels, some of which fell into the category of ROMAN À CLEF. Judged a "scandal monger" by many, she imitated Mary de la Rivière MANLEY, especially in two of her popular revelations, *Memoirs of a Certain Island Adjacent to the Kingdom of Utopia* and *The Secret History of the Present Intrigues of the Court of Caramania.* Despite later low judgments of her work, she collaborated with arguably the 18th-century writer most important in the development of the novel, Daniel DEFOE, to publish *The Life of Mr. Duncan Campbell* (1720). Perhaps because of her didacticism, the great essayists and critics Alexander Pope and Jonathan SWIFT both insulted her in print, with Pope terming her in his *Dunciad* "the libelous Novelist" and Swift labeling her a "stupid, infamous, scribbling woman." Sir Walter SCOTT later referenced her book *The History of Jemmy and Jenny Jessamy* (1753) in his novel OLD MORTALITY (1816) by having one of his characters praise its "pathos." His reference was satirical, as he wrote in his *Memoirs,* "The whole Jemmy and Jenny Jessamy tribe I abhorred."

Despite critical opinion, Haywood published more than 80 works, including drama, poetry, fiction, essays, and conduct books. FEMINIST CRITICS of the 20th century treated her more kindly as she was rediscovered as one of the early women writers in the English language. Her engagement in activities such as a PARODY of Samuel RICHARDSON's PAMELA, titled *Anti-Pamela, or Feigned*

Innocence Detected, in a Series of Syrena's Adventures, aligned her with Henry FIELDING, whose *Shamela* (1741), also a parody of *Pamela,* marked the beginning of his novel-writing career. Traditional criticism of her preachy approach as merely a mask to allow inclusion of highly erotic written material was later characterized as a patriarchal judgment, one seldom applied to male writers using the same approach. The fact that Haywood had to defend herself against criticism by both female and male readers for writing approaches accepted in works by men, helps to neutralize criticism of her subject matter and approach. Paula R. Backscheider writes that both of her "anthologized fictions contain the explicitly erotic writing that earned Haywood the title 'Great Arbitress of Passion, or, less flattering, 'purveyor of' the luscious style.'" Both, however, also demonstrate Haywood's creative strengths and her serious treatment of the sex-gender and the class systems." That critic goes so far as to claim that Haywood may have done more to "set the course of the English novel" than anyone else writing in the early 1700s. Her works again became available in print and electronic format in the latter half of the 20th century.

BIBLIOGRAPHY

Backsheider, Paula R., and John J. Richetti. *Popular Fiction by Women 1660–1730.* Oxford: Clarendon Press, 1996.

Bowers, Toni. "Sex, Lies, and Invisibility: Amatory Fiction." *The Columbia History of the British Novel.* New York: Columbia University Press, 1994. 50–72.

Hewlitt, David, ed. *Scott on Himself.* Edinburgh: Edinburgh University Press, 1981.

Scott, Sir Walter. *The Tale of Old Mortality.* Edinburgh: Edinburgh University Press, 1993.

HEADLONG HALL THOMAS LOVE PEA-COCK (1816)

Thomas Love PEACOCK published his first novel, *Headlong Hall,* anonymously, reflecting in it his dislike of progress and all of its "new-fangled" ideas. In what would become a regular approach for Peacock, *Headlong Hall* presents a SATIRIC discussion in Platonic symposium form among a group of guests, each symbolic of a particular personality or character type. Their host, Squire Headlong, invites his acquaintances to pay him a Christmas visit for good food and good conversation, which varies in emphasis from cultural to philosophical to scientific. The debate, ironic in its detachment from reality, reflects Peacock's stronger affinity for books than for people. He seems to satirize his own self-imposed isolation, in which he preferred interacting with the written word to interacting with his fellow humans. Peacock likely understood the dangers in such a life, which could lead to devotion to abstract ideals. Such ideals could prove useless when one was forced to embrace the reality of everyday living and the cultural expectations that colored real-world activities.

Peacock's belief in free intellect undercuts the dogma voiced by his major characters. They include Mr. Foster, the perfectionist; Mr. Escot, who believes in the deterioration of life, as he knows it; Mr. Jenkison, who supports the norm, or status quo; and Reverend Doctor Gaster, who, as his name suggests, appreciates gastronomics more than economics, evidenced by the fact that he presents a treatise on the proper approach to turkey stuffing. The "ice is broken," the narrator states, by a discussion of "the various knotty points of meteorology." Mr. Escot voices some of Peacock's own beliefs when he states that the improvements to society noted by his colleagues "appear to me so many links in the great chain of corruption, which will soon fetter the whole human race."

The aptly named Dr. Cranium, a phrenologist, and his daughter Cephalis join the group later, as does a landscape gardener named Mr. Milestone and Mr. Panscope, the polymath. Escot's affection for Cephalis is obvious to all, and the narrator remarks that Escot could imagine "one change for the better." His love for her lifts him above the gloom "even in this terrestrial theatre of universal deterioration." While he had previously attempted to romance Cephalis, he made the grave error of laughing at one of her father's "craniological dissertation[s]," incurring his wrath.

Peacock does not support any of these characters' individual philosophical approaches in isolation, but rather demonstrates the irrationality that often accompanied support of pure doctrine. He inserts an absurd comparison of the dancing of "savage" Indians to that of the "magnificent beau," in an attempt to determine which activity is more justifiable as a survival act.

Eventually an assortment of musicians, poets, and single young daughters are added to the mix, orbiting around the debate over civilization and its need for progress. Peacock peppers the discussion with allusions to classical ideals, supported by occasional Greek phrases, a reflection of his leisurely training in the classics. The characters also support philosophies of more contemporary figures, including English philosopher, essayist, critic, and novelist William GODWIN, French philosopher and essayist Rousseau, English economist Thomas Malthus, and English poet Percy Bysshe Shelley. They mostly frame Foster's arguments, and his rational optimism generally wins the debate. A close friend of Shelley, Peacock gives a nod to his great poetic talent, a talent that Peacock himself admitted he lacked. The esoteric character conversation is enlivened by explosions and comic near-death experiences and concludes with Headlong bargaining marriage agreements for four different gentlemen, including him. That conclusion reminds readers that the demands of reality can be counted upon to shatter the façade of idealistic dogma.

Peacock's approach echoes that of Tobias SMOLLETT, who constructed characters representing the various "humours" that marked individuals as having particular types of personalities. *Headlong Hall* prefigures Peacock's future works, which not only continued the debate premise but also included characters based on real-life figures in the ROMAN Á CLEF style. As his intellectual works regained an audience at the end of the 20th century, *Headlong Hall* became available as an electronic text.

BIBLIOGRAPHY

Dawson, Carl. *His Fine Wit: A Study of Thomas Love Peacock.* Berkeley: University of California Press, 1960.

Freeman, Alexander Martin. *Thomas Love Peacock: A Critical Study.* Folcroft, Pa.: Folcroft Press, 1969.

HEART OF MIDLOTHIAN, THE SIR WALTER SCOTT (1818)

The second series in Sir Walter SCOTT's Tales of My Landlord was to consist of one short tale and one novel, *The Heart of Midlothian.* The final product consisted only of the novel and was issued in four volumes, for which Scott's publisher,

Constable, agreed to pay him £5,000 and publish 10,000 copies. It has been judged the best of all Scott's books, due to his fine characterization of its protagonist, Jeanie Deans. Scott based Deans on the real-life Helen Walker, a Dumfries-shire woman who in 1738 walked to London to petition for her sister's release from prison. Scott had received correspondence from a Mrs. Goldie, wife of the Commissary of Dumfries; she described having met Walker. Then in her 70s or 80s, she still supported herself by knitting feet into stockings. Mrs. Goldie died before Scott could talk with her about the experience, but her daughter supplied additional information. Scott printed their letters in later editions of the book. Heart of Midlothian was the nickname for the Tolbooth, an infamous Edinburgh prison; during its demolition, Scott had brought some of its stones and fittings to be used in the construction of his country house, Abbotsford. Scott follows his usual pattern in basing the novel on a historic event, opening it in 1736 with the Porteous Riots.

Prison guard captain John Porteous had fired into a Scottish crowd gathered to watch the hanging of a robber named Wilson. Porteous was convicted of murder and sentenced to hang, but on the day scheduled for his execution received a pardon, so angering the populace that they revolted. Led by an associate of Wilson named George Robertson, who dressed in women's clothing as a disguise, a crowd stormed the Tolbooth, kidnapping Porteous and demanding revenge. Unbeknownst to the crowd, Robertson had little interest in Porteous. He had only wanted their help to break through the prison gates to rescue his love, Effie Deans, accused of killing her illegitimate baby. His personal rescue attempt fails and, despite his disguise, Robertson is recognized by a prison informer, the aptly named Ratcliffe. He is forced to hide from authorities.

In the meantime, the crowd hangs Porteous in the Grass-market, the center of many public executions. A young minister named Reuben Butler, forced by the crowd to attend Porteous just prior to his death, witnesses the violence. The frail Butler had grown up a part of the Deans family and loved them dearly. Both the Butlers and the Deans had been tenants on land belonging to the Laird of Dumbiedikes. Because of the support of David Deans and his daughter, Jeannie,

Reuben had decided to attend the university and study for the ministry. Reuben hoped to marry the sturdy, dependable, and religious Presbyterian Jeannie. Jeannie's half-sister Effie had always been a shy and sweet girl, and David was horrified by her imprisonment. While her hardworking widowed father had at last made a comfortable life for his family, Effie's situation saddened him to the point of immobility. The local magistrate, sketched as a fair and reasonable man by Scott, detains Butler for a time for questioning but eventually frees him.

Butler receives a message from a stranger who asks him to give it to Jeannie. The message requests her to meet with Robertson, now in hiding for his crime. He asks Jeannie to swear that Effie had confided in her regarding the pregnancy before the baby's birth, explaining that would mitigate the charges of infanticide. In reality, Effie had never shared information about the pregnancy, and Jeannie's code of ethics will not allow her to commit perjury in court, even to save her beloved sister's life. She remarks to her father, "We are cruelly sted between God's laws and man's laws—What will we do?—What can we do?"

The child's body had never been discovered, and Effie seems doomed to die. The night before the trial, Jeannie visits the Heart of Midlothian to comfort Effie, who adamantly refuses to testify as to Robertson's paternity of the infant. She preferred to sacrifice herself, especially when she heard of Robertson's gallant attempt to rescue her. She faints when she learns her child's body has never been discovered and begs Jeannie to testify in her favor, but Jeannie again refuses.

During the trial, Effie calls out to Jeannie to testify, but Jeannie will not bear false witness, causing their father to faint in the courtroom. Even though Effie is condemned to death, Jeannie remains determined to find an honest way to free her. Learning that a criminal could be granted a pardon by the king, Jeannie decides to travel to London to make her request. She leaves her ill father with a relative and explains her plan to Effie, who forgives Jeannie for not testifying. Jeannie takes her leave of Butler, who, already ill and anxious, pleads with her to marry him, vowing to protect her on her mission. She asks him instead to remain behind to care for her father. He reluctantly agrees and gives her a letter to the duke

of Argyle, a powerful figure who owed an obligation to his grandfather. Jeannie walked barefoot for miles through Scotland but bought some shoes in England to avoid curious stares. As she came closer to London, she was offered rides in various wagons and carts.

When Jeannie reached London, the letter gained her admission to see the duke. Supporting Scott's emphasis on the conflict between justice and morality of his era, the duke tells Jeannie, "It seems contrary to the genius of British law [. . .] to take that for granted which is not proved, or to punish with death for a crime, which, for aught the prosecutor has been able to show, may not have been committed at all." Following their audience, the duke took measures to help Jeannie, including gaining her a meeting with Queen Caroline. The queen hesitates to help a Scot due to the country's history of rebellion against England but at last agrees as she recognizes Jeannie's high moral character. Effie receives her royal pardon but is banished for 14 years from Scotland. Jeannie accepts transport in the duke of Argyle's carriage to the Isle of Roseneath, where her ill father waits to see her. Her father explains he had added his personal banishment of Effie to the royal order and sent her away with her outlaw lover, vowing never to think of her again.

The devoted Butler marries Jeannie as he receives a parish appointment at Roseneath by the duke. They learn that Gypsies had stolen Effie's baby, who everyone believed was dead. When Jeannie meets later with Effie and Robertson, now recognized correctly as the wealthy George Staunton, she cannot conceal her feelings for him, shrinking away "with a feeling of internal abhorrence." Scott demonstrates that while Jeannie remains devoted to her sister, her actions had not been intended to help Staunton in any way. She is dismayed that Effie has married Staunton following his reform. George Staunton proves an upright member of society, and the sisters reunite. The novel concludes on a melodramatic tone, with the death of Staunton and with Effie, now Lady Staunton, being driven almost mad. Jeanie again cares for her sister, and some of her acquaintances at last learn of her relationship to the Stauntons, and the truth behind their past.

The novel retains a serious tone, with little comic relief. Critics believe it could have been further strengthened had it concluded with the pardoning of Effie. One of its most distinctive features for its era was the focus on a lower-class woman as protagonist. However, unsatisfied with his noble portrait of Jeannie, Scott felt he had to add the more melodramatic ending. In his third series he would include *The Bride of Lammermoor* (1819), taking readers deeper into a more pure and unrelieved tragedy. His darker tone during those two works may have been due to chronic pain he experienced or to his having exhausted the Scottish historical topics he wanted to research and convert to fiction. Scott's production of his series earned him universal popularity as well as respectability for the novel, a genre despised as low literature only a few years previously. *The Heart of Midlothian* thus played a crucial role in the development of the novel as literature.

BIBLIOGRAPHY

Inglis, Tony. Introduction to *The Heart of Midlothian,* by Sir Walter Scott. New York: Penguin, 1994.

Scott, Paul Henderson. *Walter Scott and Scotland.* Edinburgh: Saltire Society, 1994.

HEIR OF REDCLYFFE, THE CHARLOTTE M. YONGE (1853)

Supposedly, Charlotte M. Yonge was challenged by a friend to write a story about a hero with a flaw requiring reform who does not triumph through strength or talent, but rather proves his heroism through forbearance and forgiveness. She accepted her friend's idea and produced in *The Heir of Redclyffe* one of her era's most popular novels, enjoying 17 editions in 15 years, easily rivaling works by Charles Dickens and William Makepeace Thackeray. Rather than adopting the traditional approach to romance and shaping a plot around a protagonist less privileged than his antagonist, Yonge created equally well-placed cousins in her main characters, Guy Morville, an orphan since infancy, and his cousin Philip Morville. Philip is the son of Archdeacon Morville, who is brother to Mrs. Edmonstone, wife of Guy's guardian. Guy is destined to inherit Redclyffe before Philip, and both represent feuding branches of the Morville family. Both have dark aspects to their personalities, but only Guy battles to overcome his, a temptation to gamble. Guy's grandfather "had such a dread of his going wrong" that he controlled Guy with strict discipline and isolation from others.

Additional characters populate the novel, including Charles, crippled due to a hip problem; Laura, Charlotte, and Amabel, or Amy, Edmonstone; Mr. and Mrs. Edmonstone; and Guy's ne'er-do-well but lovable uncle. Guy loves Amy but will be separated from her due to an unjust accusation by Philip. In an early scene, that disaster is foreshadowed as Philip accidentally breaks the stem from a camellia that Amy brings to the house. She has bragged of its perfect white blossom, and readers understand the flower and its suggestion of purity and innocence represents Amy herself. While Philip does not destroy the bloom, he does damage its support system, predicting his future effect on Amy and Guy. In the opening scene, the young characters discuss the fact that Mr. Edmonstone has agreed to serve as guardian to Sir Guy Morville's grandson upon the old man's death. They provide plot exposition, remarking on the presence of a Redclyffe ghost that was purportedly a murder victim at the mansion. Mrs. Edmonstone states the Redclyffes were always feared, considered a fiery violent group, with the enmity between brothers perpetuated through many generations.

When Edmonstone first met Guy as a child, he annoyed him by perpetual activity and a continuous whistle, reflecting "buoyant spirits" that his grandfather felt needed checking to avoid his maturing into a hothead as his father had been. Guy and Edmonstone later discuss Philip, who remains quite friendly toward Guy, despite the mythology of family enmity. Edmonstone explains to Guy that Philip, now Captain Morville, gave up his inheritance, including the family estate of Stylehurst, to his two sisters, forgoing an Oxford education to take a military commission instead. His statements help to establish Philip's high moral character. Guy also elicits favor when he asks Mrs. Edmonstone to treat him as she would her own son, correcting his wrongs. Despite Philip's open goodwill toward his cousin, he insinuates that he believes young Guy will one day "go wrong," laying the framework for his later betrayal. Only Charles eventually can discern Philip's true manipulative character. As the action builds to Guy's conflict, Mrs. Edmonstone admonishes him to always face temptation, battling it from within and upholding his moral duty to himself and others, as she encourages him to continue his reading and education. She also supports Philip as a fine young man whose books have helped him tolerate the loneliness caused by his older sisters' marriages. Guy's continued flashes of temper bother the young Edmonstones.

The narrator reveals that in telling Guy of his father's sins, old Sir Guy all but set him on the path of wickedness, as if he suffered from the need to fulfill his grandfather's prophecy of tragedy despite his sunny disposition. The Edmonstones continue to like Guy and all encourage him when he departs for Oxford. Guy makes a friend in young Wellwood, whose seafaring father had been killed in a duel with Old Sir Guy. Mrs. Edmonstone continues to champion her husband's ward, telling her family, "Never had anyone a greater capacity for happiness than Guy." In further action, Philip declares his love for Laura in fear that Guy might do so first. Her genuine attachment to Philip allays his fear that her family might not accept him, despite their friendliness, due to his low financial station. The romantic themes are advanced as Edmonstone's friend, Lady Eveleen, has designs on Captain Morville, but quickly the plot turns with the appearance of Guy's uncle, Sebastian Bach Dixon. Dixon, a musician, has lived in America for some time and returns with debts to pay. He convinces Guy to loan him money, and chaos follows.

When Edmonstone questions Guy's lack of money, Philip, seeing his chance to get rid of Guy, accuses his cousin of gambling. Edmonstone assumes the wicked family ways have gripped Guy, and he sends him away, leaving a heartbroken Amy. During a protracted absence, Guy again gains the favor of his adopted family and marries Amy. His patience and good character seem rewarded, but the novel does not conclude at that point. When the young couple travel to Italy, they find Philip on the verge of death due to illness. Guy determines to nurse him back to health, despite Philip's past treachery, and the family curse is broken, with redemption offered all around. However, in a bittersweet conclusion, Guy dies, ironically having contracted Philip's fever, as if the emotional disease the two had shared has materialized. He leaves behind a pregnant Amy, who gives birth to a girl; as a female,

she cannot inherit Redclyffe before any male progeny. Thus, Philip becomes the heir to Redclyffe after all.

Amy finds comfort in the memory of her bright, happy husband, such a contrast to the constantly worried Philip as he adopts his title and responsibilities. Charles also celebrates Guy's contribution to his own life, one much more fulfilled for Guy's positive influence. Philip and Laura marry, and to all onlookers appear the happy couple. Philip is seen as prosperous and honored, but in reality, lives a "harassed anxious" existence with "little repose or relief." The fact that the spoils that have fallen to Philip are "nothing but a burden" to him stands as a cautionary tale to readers. While Philip experiences redemption, it comes with a price for both himself and his loved ones.

BIBLIOGRAPHY
Mare, Margaret Laura. *Victorian Best-seller: The World of Charlotte M. Yonge.* London: G. G. Harrap, 1948.
Sturrock, June. *"Heaven and Home": Charlotte M. Yonge's Domestic Fiction and the Victorian Debate over Women.* Victoria, B.C., Canada: University of Victoria, 1995.

HE KNEW HE WAS RIGHT ANTHONY TROLLOPE (1869)

Anthony TROLLOPE first began work on *He Knew He Was Right* at the end of 1867, following in that same year the publication of *The LAST CHRONICLE OF BARSET,* the final entry in the series that had won him fame and critical acclaim. Also in 1867 Trollope published what later critics judged his best short novel, *The Claverings.* In the 12 years since introducing readers to the world of Barsetshire, Trollope had published 19 novels along with numerous short stories, sketches, essays, and travel pieces. He had become an institution in the world of fiction.

At that point in his career, feeling assured of success, he at last left the post office where he had worked for over 30 years and became editor of *St. Paul's Magazine.* Its owner, James Virtue, purchased Trollope's novel *PHINEAS FINN* to serialize in the magazine, then paid Trollope the most money he had ever received in advance for his next novel. The lengthy *He Knew He Was Right* was serialized from October 1868 through May 1869. Virtue and Company publishers had planned a 32-weekly-part issue but went bankrupt in early 1869, necessitating that a different company print the final three parts, still under the Virtue name. That misfortune was compounded by the lukewarm critical reception of the book.

Later critics suggested the lack of popular and critical success may have in part been due to Trollope's prodigious output; critics had grown tired of dealing with his multiple books per year, and the public missed the Barset crowd with which they had grown so familiar. It disappointed his faithful readers by varying from his traditional output but did not vary enough to attract new readers. Only novelist and critic Henry JAMES recognized the quality in the novel that later critics emphasized.

Like all Trollope's works, the plot of *He Knew He Was Right* moves at a snail's pace. That proved crucial to framing the gradual decline into a paralyzing insanity of its protagonist, Louis Trevelyan. Educated and from a privileged background, Trevelyan marries Emily Rowley, who comes from a large family of eight daughters headed by a colonial administrator, Sir Marmaduke Rowley. In one of several subplots, Emily's sister, Nora, will fall in love with Trevelyan's friend Hugh Stanbury, although she is courted by the wealthy and well-placed Mr. Charles Glascock. At first a seemingly traditional Victorian woman, Nora cautions Emily against refusing to "obey" Trevelyan, who makes demands that Emily defines as a "gross insult." As her sister, Nora knows Emily is truly upset: "As she spoke the fire flashed from her eye, and the bright red colour of her cheek told a tale of her anger." However, Trollope allows Nora to undergo a change in attitude. While Emily is doomed to suffer a terrible marriage, Nora will eventually throw over convention and make a solid love match.

As part of Trollope's focus on "the woman question," the debate over women's proper social roles, Nora intellectually chooses first what promises to be a loveless but ambitious union. Additional characters drawing attention to a woman's place in Victorian society include Aunt Stanbury and Wallachia Petrie, both spinsters enjoying the power and freedom that lack of a spouse affords them. Although they share the basic single lifestyle, the two women represent foils. While Aunt Stanbury retains control over an inherited fortune

against threats of other family members, she does not support militant feminism. She finds suffragettes offensive in their demand that women vote and enter traditionally male vocations, and she judges increasingly open female interaction with males as a sign that women "are very far gone on the road to the devil." However, her own independent lifestyle makes difficult her judgment of other women who desire the same. Wallachia contrasts with Aunt Stanbury in her outspoken and overt feminism. In Trollope's hands, she becomes a strident caricature, one of several he would include in his fiction. Supposedly she is based on the real American feminist Kate Field, whom Trollope met in Italy in 1860 while visiting his brother Adolphus, a popular person in a Florentine social circle that included Robert and Elizabeth Barrett BROWNING, also supporters of women's rights. Field and Trollope developed an affection, despite their differences. When Field later playfully accused Trollope of injecting her as a buffoon into his novel, he responded that he had never said Kate resembled Wallachia. He had merely said that their attitudes were the same and that Wallachia was "only absurd in her mode of expressing them." Despite his negative attitudes toward feminists, Trollope reveals his sympathy for women held hostage by an obviously patriarchal system. Both Emily and Nora mention that women are little better socially situated than dogs.

Raised in the Mandarin Islands, Emily is somewhat more independent than her English sisters. While Emily conducts herself with integrity, Trevelyan becomes suspicious of her interactions with members of their high society circle, in particular one Colonel Osborne. A longtime friend of Sir Marmaduke, Osborne has a reputation as a womanizer, and Trevelyan forbids Emily to receive him in their home. After making his demand, he recalled someone telling him "that no man should look for a wife from among the tropics, the women educated amidst the languors of those sunny climes rarely came to possess those high ideas of conjugal duty and feminine truth which a man should regard as the first requisites of a good wife." His Othello-like descent is clearly one lacking motivation, the suggestion being that for all of Trevelyan's distinction and privilege, his character proves weak.

Emily dotes on their son and decides the family is worth preserving, so she agrees to what seems a ridiculous demand, even though it embarrasses her with an old family friend. Seemingly convinced by Emily's good faith, Trevelyan at first relents, allowing Osborne back into their home, then becomes more possessive than before, again forbidding Emily's reception of him. As his obsession increases, Emily confronts him, declaring that she cannot promise to never see Osborne. Trollope emphasizes women's victimization by society, suggesting the great harm that will be done to Emily's reputation should Trevelyan persist in his accusations. Emily's upright character allows her to adhere to the law's demand that she obey her husband, but she cannot submit to his spiritual abuse. Unbending, Trevelyan succeeds in driving her to a separation.

The next portion of the novel reveals just how far Trevelyan's jealousy has transported him. Convinced of Emily's adultery, he hires a private detective and places his wife under constant surveillance. In a move both pitiful and chilling, Trevelyan eventually kidnaps his son and takes him to Italy. There, ironically framed by some of the most beautiful scenery in the world and surrounded by warmth and the sun's healing light, Trevelyan's moods darken as he is gripped by a cold madness. The ever-faithful Emily rescues him, locating Trevelyan and her son and bringing them back to England. Almost too far gone for redemption, Trevelyan lies dying when Emily begs him for a sign that he did acknowledge her innocence. She places two fingers on his lips and asks him to kiss them. For a moment she fears he will not comply: "She had time to think that were she once to withdraw her hand, she would be condemned for ever;—and that it must be withdrawn. But at length the lips moved, and with struggling ear she could hear the sound of the tongue within, and the verdict of the dying man had been in her favour." In an ironic turn, Trollope adopts the act of the kiss, often planted on a hero's cheek as an accusation of guilt, to indicate innocence. The narrator does not equivocate over the results of Trevelyan's misguided act, referring to "the evil that he had done" to a "woman whom he had so cruelly misused." The novel concludes not on a happy note, but at least looks toward the future for several of its many characters, most especially Nora and Hugh, who decide to marry.

P. D. Edwards suggests that Trollope may have found inspiration for his plot in an 1866 *Spectator* article titled "Madness in Novels." Its writer mourned "the inability of a novelist such as Mrs. Henry WOOD to 'paint jealousy in its extreme forms' without resorting to sensationalism," adding that she lacked "the power to create Othello, or the art to paint, as [William Makepeace] THACKERAY or Trollope might have done, the morbid passion in its naturalistic nineteenth-century dress." For whatever reason, Trollope accepted that challenge. He fashioned Trevelyan's mental dissolution with a psychological perspective that avoids suggestions of imbecility. In addition, by making so much at stake for Emily based on her husband's insanity, Trollope assured acceptance on his reader's part of the mental illness. He also avoids placing the traditional marriage relationship at risk as a popular institution by guiding additional couples in the novel to embrace marriage, despite its clearly damaging effects to Emily. While not Trollope's most popular novel, *He Knew He Was Right* remains a ready topic for study in academia and in demand by Trollope aficionados.

BIBLIOGRAPHY

Edwards, P. D., ed. Introduction to *He Knew He Was Right* by Anthony Trollope. St. Lucia, Queensland: Queensland University Press, 1974.

Mullen, Richard. *Anthony Trollope: A Victorian in his World.* London: Duckworth, 1990.

Mullen, Richard, and James Munson, ed. *The Penguin Companion to Trollope.* New York: Penguin, 1996.

HENRIETTA TEMPLE BENJAMIN DISRAELI

(1837) Later to become famous for his THESIS NOVELS, Benjamin DISRAELI used the popularity of SILVER-FORK FICTION to produce a ROMANCE in *Henrietta Temple*. While the plot did emphasize the pressures placed on individuals by society to marry well, that is not its major focus. Instead, it produces a bittersweet tale of romantic confusion where all comes out well in the end. The novel moved beyond Disraeli's melodramatic excesses first displayed in the anonymously published

Vivian Grey (1826), but it did not come close to the quality of his later works. He based the novel on his own affair with Lady Henrietta Sykes, important to literature historians, with Ferdinand's poverty and ambition reflecting his own.

The poor Henrietta Temple is engaged to Ferdinand Armine, also from a poverty-stricken, although noble, family. While Ferdinand sincerely loves Henrietta, he has felt driven also to engage himself to a wealthy cousin, Katherine Grandison. The situation produces an often-quoted phrase from the novel, in connection with Disraeli: "Debt is the prolific mother of folly and crime." When Henrietta discovers Ferdinand's double engagement, she abandons him to move from England to Italy. While Ferdinand is not without scruples, Disraeli yet moralizes on his portrait. However, he basically presents the situation as a problem needing a solution. The simple story proves successful, as Disraeli makes no demand on society to "fix" the relationships but leaves that to his characters. His novel, like most society plots, accepts the world as a place where love may be seen as one more commodity, where people want simply to advance their lives through material and emotional gain. It represents more of an 18th-century portrayal, incorporating a real character, Lady Bellair, who had actually had her portrait painted by Sir Joshua Reynolds and knew Dr. Samuel JOHNSON. Disraeli offered a detached approach concealed by an enthusiastic and attractive style, never allowing his tone to become overly serious and shaping his male protagonist as a good-natured, if completely self-centered, man. He disregards what other writers of his day termed nature to create an artificial dialogue and improbable plot meant only to entertain.

Her heart broken, Henrietta bows to her father's pressure and becomes engaged to the wealthy Lord Monfort. Katherine, in the meantime, has released Ferdinand from his commitment to her and works with Count Mirabel to help Ferdinand mend his relationship with Henrietta, actions supported by the novel's line, "Time is the Great Physician." When Ferdinand encounters Henrietta again, his passion for her is renewed, while Katherine feels drawn to Lord Monfort, whom she marries. Henrietta conveniently inherits a fortune and chooses to help Ferdinand financially.

Disraeli's novel came during a decade that lacked superior fiction. However, it helped the future politician and novelist hone his craft, something silver-fork fiction also did for Disraeli's contemporary Edward BULWER-LYTTON. The novel remains important only in moving Disraeli's fiction closer to the important contributions to the development of the novel that it would make in the next decade.

BIBLIOGRAPHY

Jump, Harriet Divine. *Silver Fork Novels: 1826–1841*. London: Pickering & Chatto, 2005.

Ridley, Jane, ed. *The Early Novels of Benjamin Disraeli*. Vol. 5. London: Pickering & Chatto, 2004.

Powell, Anthony. Introduction to *Novels of High Society from the Victorian Age*. London: Pilot Press, 1947, vii–xv.

HENTY, G(EORGE) A(LFRED) (1832–1902)

Born near Cambridge, with a father who was a stockbroker, G. A. Henty finished Westminster School to attend Cambridge University and participate in sports, serve in the Crimean War, and become a war correspondent during later conflicts. He observed Garibaldi in Italy and the Franco-Prussian War from the vantage point of Paris. Additional adventures included his attending the opening of the Suez Canal and travels with the Prince of Wales, later to be crowned Edward VII. Henty's military and journalistic backgrounds figured prominently in most of more than 100 stories and novels he wrote for boys as CHILDREN'S LITERATURE. Supposedly, he began his career telling stories to his children and was urged by a friend to commit them to paper. His heroes participated in various types of adventures, sailing the seven seas, prospecting for gold, and fighting wars against evil dictatorial regimes. Nicknamed the "Prince of Story Tellers" and "The Boy's Own Historian," he published as many as three novels per year, all of which focused on some aspect of British history, and all popular in the United States as well as England. His best-known work included *The Young Bugler* (1880), *UNDER DRAKE'S FLAG* (1883), *The Lion of the North* (1885), *With Clive in India* (1884), and *With the Allies in Pekin* (1904). Like most Victorian literature for young male readers, Henty's novels emphasized male camaraderie and virtue. Although scrupulously accurate in detail, the novels seemed too "Christian" for some critics. Highly idealistic in their portrayal of Great Britain, they caused journalists, including H. G. WELLS, to question the validity of such jingoistic patriotism. While later popular mainly as artifacts of their time, a number of the novels remain available as electronic text.

BIBLIOGRAPHY

"George Alfred Henty, the Prince of Story Tellers." Preston Speed Publications. Available online. URL: http://www.prestonspeed.com/About%20Henty.html. Downloaded on August 7, 2003.

HEWLETT, MAURICE (HENRY) (1861–1923)

Born in Weybridge, Surrey, in 1861, Maurice Hewlett was the oldest in the family of Henry G. Hewlett, keeper of the royal land-revenue records. As a child, he attended the Sevenoaks grammar school, the Palace School, and matriculated to the International College in Spring Grove, Isleworth. He studied law and received a call to the bar, but elected never to practice, although he did join his cousin's law office in 1878. He delayed marriage until 1888, and he and his wife, Hilda Beatrice Herbert, had two children. In 1896, he assumed his father's post and remained keeper of the royal land-revenue records until 1900, while also lecturing on medieval art at South Kensington University. His first novel, a medieval romance titled *The FOREST LOVERS* (1898), secured his reputation as an author, and he decided to continue a lifelong love of writing. He published two additional romances, *Richard Yea and Nay* (1900) and *The Queen's Quair* (1904). T. E. Lawrence (Lawrence of Arabia) especially enjoyed *Richard Yea and Nay,* which featured "Richard Couer de Lion" (Richard the Lion-Hearted); Lawrence told his family that he read the book nine times.

Hewlett diverged from his historical fiction to publish a trilogy of his own times, *Halfway House* (1908), *Open Country* (1909), and *Rest Harrow* (1910), featuring a homeless scholar named John Maxwell Senhouse as protagonist. He followed his novels with the lengthy narrative poem *The Song of the Plow* (1916), a socially conscious work focused on the abuses of the agricultural worker. He also published several essay volumes and died in 1923. His works are available in hard copy and in original form in several rare book collections, including the Beinecke Rare Book and Manuscript Library, Yale University, and at Cornell University. Some also exist in electronic format.

BIBLIOGRAPHY

Catalogue to the T. E. Lawrence Centenary Exhibition. London: National Portrait Gallery, 1988. Available online. URL: http://www.lawrenceofarabia.info/NPG/part1/049.htm. Updated 1998.

n.a. *Maurice Hewlett, author of "The forest lovers." "Little novels of Italy," "The life and death of Richard Yea and Nay," etc. A sketch of his career and some reviews of his books.* New York: Macmillan, 190?.

HICHENS, ROBERT (SMYTHE) (1864–1950)

Best known for his novel *The GREEN CARNATION* (1895), Robert Hitchens was the eldest child of a rector father who served near Canterbury. His early music studies led him to consider a career in piano and organ. He decided to enroll in studies at Bristol and the Royal College, London, to help determine whether he had the necessary talent. After deciding that he did not, Hitchens became a journalist, describing his experiences in his later novel, *Felix* (1902). His writing of music and lyrics supplied a steady lifelong income, and he eventually succeeded George Bernard Shaw as music critic for *The World.* Toward the end of his life, Hitchins lived for a time in Sicily, moving into a Trappist monastery for several weeks. Of his 66 books, none would surpass *The Green Carnation* in popularity. A SATIRE based on the relationship of famous writer and wit Oscar WILDE and his partner, Lord Alfred Douglas, the novel was published anonymously, but when Wilde and Douglas discovered the author's identity, they congratulated him on a fine satire. Publishers withdrew the book during Wilde's later sex scandal and trial, but it regained popularity in later decades. It remains readily available as an excellent example of a ROMAN À CLEF, or novel with a key.

HILLINGDON HALL R. S. SURTEES (1845)

Robert Smith SURTEES became the most popular of the "squire novelists" with his series featuring the inexpert fox-hunting enthusiast and London grocer John Jorrocks. Made famous first in *Jorrocks's Jaunts and Jollities* and later in its sequel, HANDLEY CROSS (1843), Jorrocks made his final appearance in HILLINGDON HALL (1845), published first as a series, which focuses on his life after retirement. Totally inept, Jorrock indulges in experimentation with scientific applications in this novel, which strengthens the humor in Jorrocks' trademark struggles to succeed in an unfair world. Once committed to an asylum, certified insane by his social-climbing wife, but then released due to the confusion of the legal system, Jorrocks represents the ultimate survivor, a user of systems who pays little attention to law when dealing in horse trading and other methods of commerce. Surtees' use of the horse-trading theme throughout the Jorrocks series supports his cynical tone toward human dealings with one another in what amounts to a type of social barter system. That the undeserving Jorrocks consistently profits by corrupt activities should not be funny, but it is, due to what Tim Congdon terms the "audacity of the fraud." Readers end up admiring in Jorrocks what they would attack in a real person who dealt with them as Jorrocks does with his fellow humans.

In *Hillingdon Hall,* Jorrocks moves from master of the hunt into politics, absurdly becoming a justice of the peace. Readers of the previous novel will recall James Pigg, Jorrocks's former huntsman, who is delighted to return to Jorrocks's household, where he consistently counters Jorrocks's schemes. The normal Jorrocks hijinks occur, leading not to disaster, but rather to the promise of election to Parliament. The novel proves autobiographical for Surtees, a politician who features the push for CORN LAWS in the novel, criticizing the Anti–Corn Law League. As a prosperous landowner and investor, Surtees' satirizing the Corn Laws remains understandable, but in doing so, he also masterfully satirizes Parliament. Jorrocks must campaign against one Marquis of Bray, who represents the dukes of Donkeytown in a pitting of the faux gentleman farmer against the aristocracy. Some feel Surtees overextended the satire, attacking the belief in an industrial age that country living was somehow more pure than that of the city. This occurs when Jorrocks's own estate manager, Joshua Sneakington, defrauds him. Jorrocks understands then that the country harbors "as big thieves" as London.

Surtees also emphasizes the need for protection of land rights, although he remains skeptical about the lawyers appointed to do so. However, he softens in his approach to his culture by including a marriage between a landowner and a commoner, emphasizing that barter can successfully occur in the abstract as well as in the material. During an era marked by the ideology of laissez-faire, Surtees produces self-reliant characters always alert to the possibility of fraud, unafraid to perpetrate it themselves in what generally amounts to an innocent manner. Such soft fraud proves equivalent to the ubiquitous white lie, perceived by readers who practice that usage themselves as necessary for character survival in the Jorrocks tales.

BIBLIOGRAPHY

Congdon, Tim. "Surtees and Money." *The New Criterion.* Available online. URL: http://www.newcriterion.com/archive/20/jun02/surtees.htm. Downloaded on August 12, 2003.

HISTORICAL FICTION   As with other categorizations of fiction, historical fiction may be difficult to define. While everyone agrees it exists, not everyone can agree on its aspects. Simply stating that historical fiction tells a story set in the past can cause confusion over whose past is indicated, that of the author, the reader, or the narrator. Some choose an arbitrary number of years that must have passed since the era during which an historical is set, such as 50 years. Others qualify it according to its author, who must not have lived during the period that is the novel's subject, so that one must gain the necessary knowledge of the era through research, rather than experience. But how much of that research should be included before it overshadows the fictional plot? Still others focus on the style of the novel, including alternative histories, pseudo histories, and fantasy histories, the last categorization begging the question of how much fiction may a book contain before it is considered FANTASY. One clear quality of successful historical fiction is that it shapes characters in plots set in the past that transcend time to offer readers a knowledge or awareness applicable to their own time and situation.

While not all readers and critics may agree to the definition of historical fiction, most will agree that it remains an enduring approach to novel writing, one that continues to remain popular with the reading public. An early example includes Daniel DEFOE's *A JOURNAL OF THE PLAGUE YEAR* (1722), an account of the Great Plague of 1664–65, as reported by a supposed eyewitness. Nineteenth-century examples of historical fiction include several novels by Sir Walter SCOTT, said to have more or less invented the modern historical novel. His most popular was *IVANHOE* (1819), set in medieval times, an era also appreciated by Maurice HEWLETT, as evidenced in his ROMANCE *The Forest Lovers* (1898). Edward BULWER-LYTTON, a historian as well as novelist, applied his fascination with Roman times to his novels *The Last Days of Pompeii* (1834) and *RIENZI: THE LAST OF THE TRIBUNES* (1835). Wars and insurgence supplied settings for novelist Anna Maria Porter, whose *The Hungarian Brothers* (1807) occurred during the French Revolution, a war that also acted as setting for Charles DICKENS's *A Tale of Two Cities* (1859), while Henry KINGSLEY's *RAVENSHOE* (1861) is set during the Crimean War, and Robert Louis STEVENSON chose the period following the 1745 Scottish Rebellion for *The Master of Ballantrae* (1889). CHILDREN'S LITERATURE also produced historical fiction, such as Kingsley's *WESTWARD HO!* (1855), which features England's victory over Spain during the time of the Inquisition.

BIBLIOGRAPHY

Brown, David. *Walter Scott and the Historical Imagination.* London: Routledge and Kegan Paul, 1979.

Buckley, J. H. *The Triumph of Time: A Study of the Victorian Concepts of Time, History, Progress and Decadence.* Cambridge: Cambridge University Press, 1967.

The Historical Novel Society. Available online. URL: http://www.historicalnovelsociety.com/. Updated 2003.

Rance, Nicholas. *The Historical Novel and Popular Politics in Nineteenth-Century England.* London: Vision Press, 1975.

HISTORY OF HENRY ESMOND, THE
WILLIAM MAKEPEACE THACKERAY (1852)

William Makepeace THACKERAY achieved his goal of making history familiar to his readers in *The History of Henry Esmond*. He established a model for HISTORICAL FICTION, using true occurrence as the basis of his novel in a way never done before. While others had incorporated historical events into their fiction, Thackeray constructed his novel in such a way that it depended on the events. Framed by the final days of Stuart rule, the plot introduces a young intelligent boy named Henry Esmond, maturing in Castlewood House, a structure symbolically filled with secret passageways. But this is no GOTHIC NOVEL, as Henry is familiar with each mysterious corner of the house, representing the self-knowledge and realization that will become crucial to his development. A supposed orphan, his search for self-identity can represent that of every human unsure of his or her place in the world. His ability to shape his own identity independent of outside forces allows Thackeray to suggest that individuals can find fulfillment on their own.

Henry Esmond is supposedly the illegitimate son of the third viscount Castlewood. His early years prove lonely as he matures in a household headed by Lady Castlewood, once famous for her great beauty but now pitifully using makeup to recover that beauty. Her sad grasping after past glory symbolizes the Stuart rule. Henry, also called Harry, spends part of his time studying Latin and training in swordplay with the Jesuit Father Holt. Henry's loneliness is relieved when his cousin Francis Esmond inherits the title and moves into Castlewood, along with his lovely young wife, Rachel. Henry becomes fond of their children, Frank and Beatrix, and soon is devoted to the entire family, who treat him with a kindness he has never experienced. Henry is especially fond of Rachel, and he develops a lifelong loyalty to her. He admires her worship of the viscount, but Francis finds it oppressive and relieves his passions with other women in London. Ironically, Henry mars Rachel's beauty when he unwittingly introduces smallpox to the household. Despite the dulling of her appearance, Rachel is still attractive, and the viscount becomes jealous of the attentions of Lord Mohun to his wife. He foolishly challenges Mohun to a duel and is mortally wounded. Henry, who had tried to stand in for Francis, is heartbroken. On his deathbed, Francis confesses that Henry was actually the legitimate son of Viscount Thomas and should have inherited the title and the estate. Francis supplies a paper that proves him a usurper, but Henry burns the paper; he wants young Frank to become the next viscount. Henry's move represents an incredible sacrifice. While he gives up his title, he demonstrates honorable behavior that an aristocratic title alone cannot give an individual.

Because Henry took part in the duel, he is imprisoned, dangerously ill from a wound. Blaming Henry for the death of her husband, Rachel forbids him to ever visit her family. Despair sets in, but then Henry receives a request for him to visit Lady Castlewood, his father's widow, where she now lives in Chelsey. She establishes a stronger relationship with Henry, divining that he knows his true parentage. Admiring his strength of character, she uses her influence to help "Son Esmond," as she refers to him, procure an ensign's commission. Henry distinguishes himself in service and advances to Colonel, serving General Webb, to whom he devotes himself as an aide. In this section of the book, critics note Henry's prioritizing devotion to Webb over that to the duke of Marlborough is likely based on Thackeray's own family history, as one of his ancestors served Webb, who reportedly quarreled with the duke.

Henry encounters the teacher of his youth, Father Holt, who explains that Viscount Castlewood had an affair with his mother, a Flemish daughter of a weaver, then deserted her to a convent, where she died, leaving Henry to be raised by his father. He visits her grave, gaining further ground in his QUEST for self-identity.

Henry again encounters Rachel in Winchester Cathedral, and they resume their former relationship. Despite their eight-year age difference, Henry could love Rachel, but then he meets the now beautiful 16-year-old Beatrix, whom he had protected as a youth. Henry spends 10 years attempting to convince her to marry him, but she finds him too common as a soldier and too serious. Her brother Frank, now the viscount as Henry had planned, remains a fine young sportsman and swordsman. He falls in love with a Catholic Dutch woman while on campaign with Henry and converts to the religion his family had abandoned long ago for political reasons. Henry occupies himself in a new literary relationship with true-life figure English essayist

Joseph Addison (1672–1719), supposedly helping him compose his famous poem "The Campaign" (1704), which celebrates England's victory at Blenheim.

After a number of engagements, Beatrix accepts betrothal to the much older and honorable duke of Hamilton, with Henry faithfully continuing to support her. Henry chooses from the inheritance of Lady Castlewood a lovely diamond necklace to present to Beatrix as a wedding gift. It represents a sacrifice, as his inheritance proved modest, although sufficient to his nonmaterialistic lifestyle. It also symbolizes the value in which he holds Beatrix as a symbol of an ideal to which he aspires. When the duke protests a gift of such value from a bastard false aristocrat, Rachel angrily explains Henry's legitimacy. Startled by that fact, Beatrix wishes she had accepted Henry's marriage proposal.

Beatrix's future is shattered when Henry's old nemesis, Lord Mohun, kills the duke on the evening of the wedding. Mohun also dies, removing one threat from Henry's life. Perceiving a final opportunity to gain Beatrix's hand, Henry decides to join a restoration plot in an attempt to restore James Edward Stuart, the "Pretender," to the throne in place of Queen Anne. Frank also served the Pretender, or Prince, and allowed him to return to Lady Castlewood's London home, where the pretender impersonates Viscount Castlewood. He gains an interview with his sister the queen, which all hope will lead to her naming him her successor as she lies ill and dying. Henry is devastated when the prince becomes enthralled with Beatrix and orders her to Castlewood. Henry's fascination with Beatrix ends, and he destroys before the prince the papers that prove his birth. In a dramatic gesture that at last ends his conflict over identity, he breaks his sword, denounces the Stuart line, and is joined by the equally disillusioned Frank. As the two devoted friends return to London, they hear that George of Hanover has been named king, following Anne's death. Beatrix follows the Pretender to France, and Henry at last acts on his lifelong devotion to Rachel and marries her. Sadly taking leave of Frank, the couple sails for America, both literally and symbolically beginning a new life there at the Castlewood they build in Virginia. Henry Esmond at last makes his own identity, free from false titles and concerns.

The novel established Thackeray's reputation as one of the finest historical fiction writers, as he had to sustain an 18th-century style throughout his pseudo-autobiography. He not only faithfully represents the facts of the era that acts as his focus, he also shapes a fascinating psychological tale, one of the first to look at the internal hauntings of memory, favored over outward Gothic hauntings. Thackeray's own experience of a lack of identity as a child influences his character shaping of Esmond. He obtained his goal of creating a true man, in the style of Henry FIELDING, that had frustrated him in The HISTORY OF PENDENNIS (1850). Autobiographical aspects contained in the novel's romance strengthen Thackeray's resolve in contrasting his two heroines, the lively clever Beatrix with the compliant Rachel, as were his own true-life loves, his wife and Mrs. Brookfield. However, he does not give Henry a wife to reject, and he avoids the cloying expected conclusion of Henry marrying Beatrix. Instead, he chooses the older widow, a fact that bothered some contemporary readers, likely due to its taint of incest, as Rachel had helped to raise Henry when he was a youth. Such contrast with the romantic tradition of historical fiction helped bolster his bid for reality in fiction.

BIBLIOGRAPHY

Gilbert, E. L. William Makepeace Thackeray's Vanity Fair, and Henry Esmond. New York: Monarch Press, 1965.

Ray, Gordon. The Buried Life: A Study of the Relation Between Thackeray's Fiction and His Personal History. Darby, Pa.: Arden Library, 1979.

HISTORY OF PENDENNIS, THE WILLIAM MAKEPEACE THACKERAY (1850)

William Makepeace THACKERAY published his second novel, The History of Pendennis, as a serial between November 1848 and December 1850. It ran at the same time as Charles DICKENS's DAVID COPPERFIELD, a novel to which it is often compared. The two are similar in presenting BILDUNGSROMANS, both with autobiographical elements. However, the two contrast in many ways. While Dickens devotes the first third of his novel to David's childhood, the section in which details most resemble the author's life, Thackeray begins with Arthur Pendennis preparing to enter university. Thackeray also spends many pages developing a SATIRE of London's literary life, including characters representing those who had assisted, or blocked, his own career, such as critic and writer Edward HOOK, the model for Thackeray's Mr. Wagg. Thackeray had received much criticism of his first novel, VANITY FAIR (1848), due to his unrealistic division of humans into two groups—wily types who take advantage of others, and the fools who allow themselves to be taken advantage of. He also hoped to change his reputation as a misanthropist, a charge sparked by Vanity Fair's cynical tone.

When Arthur "Pen" Pendennis's physician/country squire father dies, his loving but unsophisticated mother raises him at Fair Oaks with his adopted sister, Laura Bell. Pendennis depends on his uncle, Major Pendennis, to rescue him from an improvident love affair with an actress, Miss Fotheringay. The Major appeals to her father, the foolish and drunken Captain Costigan, through their shared military connections, to break the young people's ill-founded engagement. Pen takes off for Oxbridge, where he performs horribly, fails his course work, and enjoys an extravagant and idle existence. In a second major rescue, his mother and Laura make good his debts, and, shamed into reform, he returns to classes, improves his performance, and earns a degree.

All is not well in his romantic life, however, when he returns home and becomes enthralled with the silly and vacuous Blanche Amory, daughter of the second wife of baronet Francis Clavering. Out of duty, he proposes to Laura, but she rejects him, having little desire to marry one with little ambition and much ill judgment. When he returns to London to attend law school, he instead begins to write for a publication called the Pall Mall Gazette, through the influence of his friend, George Warrington. He achieves success with his first novel, Walter Lorraine, and enjoys London society.

Pen reunites with Blanche, but does not seek to court her. Instead, he introduces her to his friend Harry Foker, who immediately becomes enthralled. As for Pen, he develops feelings for Fanny Bolton, daughter of a porter, and struggles with his desire to seduce her. When Fanny nurses him through an illness, Mrs. Pendennis suspects her as Pen's mistress and sends her away. Fanny writes to Penn, with whom she has fallen in love, but his mother hides her letters. Pen at last discovers and reads the letters, which prove Fanny's innocence to his mother. Pen forgives his mother, who dies soon after.

Pen's uncle feels the boy should marry, and he sets about to arrange a socially convenient marriage between Pen and Blanche. However, he does so by blackmailing Blanche's father, Sir Francis, with information regarding a scandal. Sir Francis agrees to the marriage and also gives up his Parliament seat to Pen. The plot becomes complicated when Pen discovers Blanche's real father is a still-living criminal. He struggles with his commitment to marry Blanche, deciding he must honor it. All ends well when Blanche breaks the engagement to marry Foker, now a wealthy man, leaving Pen to realize his love for Laura. She accepts his wiser, more compassionate character, and the two plan to marry.

Thackeray felt he had ultimately failed in his quest to produce a realistic portrayal of a contemporary man. He had hoped to paint a portrait similar to that of Henry FIELDING's Tom Jones, to which he refers in a preface appended to the final serial issue. He states, in part, "Since the author of 'Tom Jones' was buried, no writer of fiction among us has been permitted to depict to his utmost power a MAN. We must drape him, and give him a certain conventional simper. Society will not tolerate the Natural in our Art." However, most critics feel Thackeray succeeded in his stated goal to shape in Pen a character with "the passions to feel, and the manliness and generosity to overcome them." In presenting Pen as an autobiographical figure, Thackeray avoided Dickens's rendition of David Copperfield as exposed in his youth to mainly abominable, selfish influences. Instead, Thackeray frames the fictionalization of his own youth in irony, reflecting both positive and negative forces.

Some critics feel Thackeray's own near-death illness just prior to writing the novel corrected the misanthropy present in *Vanity Fair*. Thus, he frames Pen's early foolish involvement with Emily Costigan with nonjudgmental affection, creating a comic rendering of the innocence of youth yet to be tried by the world. And although he does include the scandal affecting the Clavering family, he sketches it as part of a broader worldview. Thackeray illustrated the novel himself, drawing on the cover Pen tempted on the one side by a mermaid and flanked on the other by a conventional looking woman with children. He makes clear that the fantasy world, while always a temptation, remains idealistic and unachievable, characterizing the more traditional lifestyle as a viable and attractive option.

BIBLIOGRAPHY
Lund, Michael. *Reading Thackeray*. Detroit: Wayne State University Press, 1988.

HISTORY OF SIR CHARLES GRANDISON, THE SAMUEL RICHARDSON (1753–1754)

When Samuel RICHARDSON began *The History of Sir Charles Grandison,* he had no plan other than to present a moral tale to counter the bawdy tone and content of Henry FIELDING's wildly popular *The History of TOM JONES, A FOUNDLING* (1753). His own cautionary tales, *PAMELA* (1740) and *CLARISSA* (1747–48), had been satirized by Fielding and others, but Richardson, whose nicknames as a youth were "Serious" and "Gravity," remained unashamed by jibes regarding his style and high subject matter. In *Grandison* he asked for equal time from the reading community for a novel that would engage their interest while reaching a high ethical purpose. Released in seven volumes over a year's time, the novel's lack of unity continues to receive critical comments by readers who must be reminded to consider the time in which it was produced and also Richardson's particular method of writing. As he produced each volume, he printed copies on his own press, distributing them to friends for comments and suggestions before proceeding to the next volume. The letters regarding the novel prove as interesting as the work itself, as various correspondents plead that Grandison choose the beautiful product of nobility, Clementina della Porretta, over the novel's supposed heroine, the lovely young Harriet Byron. At one point, Richardson writes of his frustration in having spent so much energy developing Clementina, who threatens to take over the female protagonist role from his intended heroine. When he finally decides to marry Grandison and Harriet, Clementina's fate offers a conundrum, leading a Mrs. Donnellan to write that she could not tolerate Richardson's possible marriage of "the angel Clementina to the hair-brained Count de Belvidere." Such participation by readers/reviewers in the development of a 21st-century novel would be unheard of. It contributed to what critics label an inorganic presentation.

As with Richardson's other tales, *Grandison* is presented as an EPISTOLARY NOVEL, producing a satisfying irony in light of the important part that Richardson's own epistolary activity played in the novel's development. Harriet Byron unsettles London's social scene, arousing the passion of Sir Hargrave Pollenxfen, representative of one of Richardson's favorite character types, the dishonorable male who uses his aristocratic position to excuse dastardly behavior. When Harriet rebuffs him, he predictably kidnaps her, fails to frighten her into marriage, and sends her as a prisoner to his country estate. This allows the gallant Sir Charles Grandison to interrupt Pollexfen's design, rescuing the fair heroine who falls in love with her knight, as he does with her. However, Sir Charles is already promised to the magnificent Clementina della Poretta, whose noble Italian family owes him a favor. The two never married due to religious differences, a fact that allows Richardson to emphasize his moral themes. In Grandison's absence, the delicate Clementina suffers an emotional breakdown, prompting her parents to beg Grandison's return to Italy. He answers their summons, his presence allows Clementina a full recovery, and Richardson settles the dilemma of the two loves by having Clementina release Grandison from his promise.

This proved a far more satisfying solution to his reviewers than one possibility he had considered, which was to allow another character, Greville, to assassinate Sir Charles. Richardson still foreshadows this possibility, increasing the anticipation of readers. He was writing his sixth volume with no decision having been made on his conclusion. Other possible endings he considered included a marriage of Grandison to Harriett, who would later die in childbirth, freeing Grandison as a romantic widower to then unite with Clementina. He had even considered polygamy, as he could not bear the thought of leaving Clementina single and alone. However, his reviewers made clear that Grandison must not continue to toy with the affections of both women, as that countered his clearly noble character.

Later critics would challenge the interminable extension of virtue evidenced by all characters, except for the clearly distinguished villains. This, however, was a part of Richardson's distinct style. His releasing of the novel in slow volumes, later to be condensed to only three, enticed readers to near-frenzy in expectation of the all-important final seventh volume. Richardson carefully controlled that printing by doing it himself. The earlier volumes had been printed by hired publishers, with some pirated by an Irish publisher. Such publishing behavior strikes modern readers as odd, but in the 18th century, when printing remained fairly uncommon and the novel form was still in the developmental stage, approaches to distribution were not well controlled. Commentary from the period and during subsequent years by notables, including the aesthete Lady Mary Wortley Montagu; critic, essayist and novelist Samuel JOHNSON, who found the novel particularly satisfying; critic William Hazlitt; novelist Jane AUSTEN; essayist and critic Thomas Babington Macaulay; and novelist George ELIOT shows just how widely the novel was read and used as a model. While Montagu wrote a note in her copy describing the novel as "Mean sentiments meanly expressed," that proved the attraction for contemporary middle-class readers who enjoyed its colloquial, or more common, style, a new development in "polite literature," according to Jocelyn Harris.

Along with Richardson's additional work, *The History of Charles Grandison* remains readily available, representing an important step in the history of the development of the novel itself. Because its form was not yet firmly in place, Richardson could incorporate various literary approaches, including corrections of "oversights" in early volumes printed in later volumes. He uses the memoir approach in assigning only initials as last names to certain characters, suggesting they really exist. He also incorporates the letter form, sermonettes, news bits, what appear to be legal memoranda, popular "commonplace book" forms, and historical events from his own day. At one point he remarked that he could not continue the novel, because its events had not yet happened. Such an approach remains worthy of study and enjoyment apart from the reading of the novel itself. As Harris explains, the novel proved popular due to its use of traditional character shaping based in "philosophical and religious convictions," but also due to a new approach incorporating "knowledge of the human heart," involving the novel in "radical social questions."

BIBLIOGRAPHY

Harris, Jocelyn. Introduction to *The History of Sir Charles Grandison,* by Samuel Richardson. New York: Oxford University Press, 1972, vii–xxiv.

HISTORY OF THE FAIRCHILD FAMILY, PART I, THE MARY MARTHA SHERWOOD

(1818) Mary SHERWOOD's example of highly DIDACTIC LITERATURE, *The History of the Fairchild Family,* eventually appeared in three parts, with the first and most popular published in 1818. Sherwood's deeply religious background as an English clergyman's daughter led her to write more than 400 works in various genres, all with a religious bent. Almost every middle- and upper-class British family had a copy of the story of two parents devoted to the stern Christian upbringing of their three children, Emily, Henry and Lucy. While the format varies from the typical novel, in that each fictional cautionary tale concludes with a related prayer and hymn, the series of stories hangs together well. Later readers find fascinating the stilted interactions between parents set on teaching their children that their hearts remain filled with sin and "vileness" that only God and Christ the Saviour can relieve. To read that Henry, a child of "between five and six," tells his father, "I wish I could love the Lord Jesus Christ more than I do; but my wicked heart will not let me," assures readers that each story represents a parable. Eight-year-old Lucy's jealousy over Emily's doll is handled by a lecture from pious Mamma regarding "corrupt hearts" full of "adultery, fornication, uncleanness, lasciviousness, idolatry, witchcraft, hatred, variance, emulations, wrath, strife, seditions, heresies, envyings, murders, drunkenness, revelings, and such like." British parents found it simple to adopt the words of the symbolically named Fairchilds as they read and simultaneously instructed their children.

More shocking to later readers are the harsh punishments of the children, including hand switchings, long periods standing in corners, hours of being locked in rooms, some of them dark, and doing without multiple meals. These punishments are doled out for misbehavior that includes running inside, dirtying clothes, not learning Latin lessons, quarreling with one another, and eating a forbidden apple, an act that suggests Adam's original sin. Even more shocking is Mr. Fairchild's taking the children, following their transgressions, to view a dead body in a symbolically overgrown garden reminiscent of the once-idyllic Eden, later transposed by original sin. They must first traipse through a thick dark wood, creating a scene to rival any child's nightmare. Clinging to their reassuring father, they encounter "a gibbet, on which the body of a man hung in chains: it had not yet fallen to pieces, although it had hung there some years. The body had on a blue coat, a silk handkerchief round the neck, with shoes and stockings, and every other part of the dress still entire: but the face of the corpse was so shocking, that the children could not look at it." As the children cry, Papa explains, "When people are found guilty of stealing, they are hanged upon a gallows, and taken down as soon as they are dead; but when a man commits a murder, he is hanged in iron chains upon a gibbet, till his body falls to pieces." Also grotesque to modern tastes are the discussions of death, most particularly the "happy death" of children like the symbolically named servant Charles Trueman, who tells "Master Henry" shortly before he dies, "I never was so happy before in all my life, as since I have been ill, and have thought of going to my Saviour." Following his death scene, the book concludes with a long sermon by Mr. Somers, the local clergyman, who offers multiple Bible verses designed to comfort any bereaved family.

BIBLIOGRAPHY

Westburg, Barry. Preface to *The History of the Fairchild Family,* by Mary Sherwood. New York: Garland Publishing, 1977.

HOGARTH, GEORGE (1783–1870) George

Hogarth remains important as a 19th-century music critic and writer, but is most famous for his relationship with Charles DICKENS. One of many critics and editors who helped advance the careers of rising 19th-century novelists through periodic publication of their works, he was educated in law and once served as adviser to Sir Walter SCOTT. Hogarth became friends with Dickens and subsequently helped get published some of the author's earliest sketches in the periodical for which he served as music critic, *The Monthly Magazine,* founded in 1825. In 1835, he worked at the *Evening Chronicle,* for which Dickens did some court reporting. In January of that year, Dickens wrote to Hogarth, asking if he might contribute some "light sketches" to the publication for additional pay. Hogarth agreed, and 20 contributions by Dickens followed. Hogarth liked the young writer so well that he invited him to visit at the Hogarth home, which included several children and his wife, Georgina. The editor informally adopted Dickens into his family, and Dickens began to give Robert Hogarth, the eldest son, shorthand lessons. He also courted Hogarth's eldest daughter, 19-year-old Caroline, marrying her in April 1836. Dickens's observations became famous under the signature of "Boz" and later were published in *Sketches by Boz* (1836–37), the author's first published book. Hogarth released excellent reviews of the work, promoting its sales. He also introduced his son-in-law to Richard Bentley, who hired Dickens four months later to edit his new periodical, BENTLEY'S MISCELLANY. He began that position in 1837, and Hogarth contributed some of the periodical's first articles. Their relationship remained warm and social during the first, successful years of Dickens's marriage. By 1850, when Dickens's relationship to Catherine soured and he found another love interest, Hogarth joined other family members in ostracizing and criticizing Dickens.

Books written by Hogarth included *Musical History, Biography and Criticism* (1835); *Memoirs of the Opera* (1851); and a history of the Philharmonic Society, of which he served as secretary (1862).

BIBLIOGRAPHY

"A Charles Dickens Journal." *Charles Dickens LIVE!* Available online. URL: http://www.dickenslive.com/journal/index. htm#yearindx. Last updated 2001. Downloaded July 28, 2003.

Graham, Walter. *English Literary Periodicals.* New York: Octagon Books, 1966.

"Hogarth, George." *Michael R. Thompson Bookseller Bibliopoly.* Available online. URL: http://www.polybiblio.com/. Downloaded on July 28, 2003.

Perdue, David. "Family and Friends." *The Charles Dickens Page.* Available online. URL: http://www.fidnet.com/~dap 1955/dickens/index.html. Downloaded on July 28, 2003.

HOLCROFT, THOMAS (1745–1809)

Thomas Holcroft was born in London. His father was a shoemaker, and young Thomas educated himself in the evenings after working all day as a stable boy at a Newmarket racetrack. Before beginning his writing career, he followed his father in becoming a shoemaker for a time and worked as a tutor before becoming a strolling actor and then a writer. His first novel, *Alwyn, or the Gentleman Comedian* (1780), contained autobiographical aspects of his unremarkable acting career. His knowledge of poverty and discrimination added REALISM and contributed to the novel's radical tone. His proletarian approach later earned Holcroft the reputation as the first English radical to become a novelist. At a time when the novel remained in early development, Holcroft contributed to the definition of the term ROMANCE, at that time still used to describe all prose fiction. In *Alwyn's* introduction, Holcroft proposed using the term to describe all episodic stories, from the picaresque "real-life" accounts to those that were completely fictional, which focused on exotic locations and previous time periods. The term *novel* he proposed to apply only to stories with "unity of design," such as Henry FIELDING'S *TOM JONES* (1744).

Holcroft wrote some successful plays, including *Duplicity* (1781), a cautionary comedy about the evils of gambling. In 1784, he produced a highly successful adaptation of French dramatist Beaumarchais's *The Marriage of Figaro,* naming his version *The Follies of a Day.* Additional well-received works included *The School for Arrogance* (1791), *The Road to Ruin* (1792), and *Love's Families* (1794). He followed his reformist instincts to write his second novel, *Anna St. Ives* (1792), which reflects his dramatic background in its use of strong dialogue and melodramatic scenes, although later critics felt his use of the traditional epistolary format weakened the story of a radical couple who share a passion for the improvement of society. The male protagonist, Frank Henley, a bailiff's son, was the first working-class hero in English fiction. Other heroes who began plots as "common men" would later be discovered to be of aristocratic background, in typical GOTHIC romance fashion.

Holcroft's participation in a post–French Revolution propaganda group that supported social and political reform led to his arrest for high treason in 1794, resulting in two months' imprisonment. His treatment left him furious and led to his writing HUGH TREVOR (1797), in which he sought to sketch a history "of the progress of mind" on the part of his hero. Abused by the educational and social system, Trevor forgoes violence to work for peaceful revolution. Authorities never vindicated Trevor of the treason charges and continued to observe him for any signs of "free thinking" for the rest of his life. His beliefs helped develop friendships with other social reformers, including Thomas Paine and William GODWIN, whose *CALEB WILLIAMS* (1794) shares much in common with *Hugh Trevor.* In 1802, he wrote the first English play to be formally labeled a "melodrama," *A Tale of Mystery,* an adaptation from French writer Pixérécourt's *Coelina.* His final novel, *The Memoirs of Bryan Perdue* (1805), was judged forgettable.

Holcroft remained important for his influences on the development of the novel and on later writers, including Mrs. Amelia OPIE, who attended the treason trials of his associates. The famous essayist and critic William Hazlitt considered him important enough to publish *Memoirs of the Late Thomas Holcroft* in three volumes (1816). He based the book on Holcroft's autobiographical writings, later reprinted as part of larger works on Holcraft and his peers. While Holcroft's writing remained too stilted to be widely enjoyed in later centuries, his works are readily available in print.

BIBLIOGRAPHY
Baine, Rodney M. *Thomas Holcroft and the Revolutionary Novel.* Athens, University of Georgia Press, 1965.

Colby, Elbridge. *The Life of Thomas Holcroft.* 1925. B. Blom: New York, 1968.

Deane, Seamus. Introduction to *The Adventures of Hugh Trevor,* by Thomas Holcroft. Edited by Seamus Deane. London: Oxford University Press, 1973, vii–xiii.

HONORIA SOMMERVILLE: A NOVEL
ELIZABETH AND JANE PURBECK (1789)
Written by sister writers Elizabeth and Jane Purbeck, *Honoria Sommerville* falls squarely into the category of ROMANCE of the popular type, considered tasteless by most. However, this first novel published in four volumes received the most positive reviews of their several romances. *Town and Country Magazine's* reviewer wrote, "If all novels were written with the propriety and knowledge which distinguishes these volumes, circulating libraries would no longer be declared nuisances." *The Critical Review* in 1789 and 1791 pronounced its "heroine well drawn and apparently sketched from nature"; that same publication also admired the novel's "moral." However, it, along with other periodicals, pronounced the Purbecks' novels too dependent upon coincidence, a staple of the romance genre.

That coincidence is immediately evident. The well-to-do Mr. and Mrs. Fortescue, traveling in Northern Ireland, find an overturned carriage whose driver is injured and whose adult passenger, an obviously poor woman, has been killed. The infant traveling with the woman is unhurt, and Mrs. Fortescue decides to adopt her. Fearing her in-laws' disdain for an impoverished creature and one not of family blood, she decides to tell them the child is her niece, as her sister lost a child about the same age as the infant. Her parents, the Sommervilles, also die in short order, securing the child's secret, and she is raised along with the Fortescues' daughter, Henrietta, two years the baby's elder. They ask the local clergy, Mr. Richardson, to baptize her and name her Honoria Sommerville, charging him to discover anything he can about the child's mother. The only clues they have to the baby's true identity are a gold seal in her pocket bearing the cipher "EB," a crown piece, and a silver cross.

Mrs. Fortescue's quick thinking is praised by the narrator, who notes that her "understanding and strength of mind" prove "superior to most of her sex," making "her capable of directing" her husband "in all affairs of consequence." Such an active and intelligent 18th-century female romance character would interest FEMINIST CRITICS, as it works against traditional characterization of the dependent, helpless heroine. Within a few paragraphs, the young Honoria blossoms into a beautiful 17-year-old of refined wit, "the wonder of all who knew her." She remains best friends with the gracious Henrietta, who bears her adopted cousin no ill will.

To celebrate Honoria's birthday, a local regiment is invited to the estate, and everyone notices Miss Fortescue and Miss Sommerville. The young women eagerly await a chance to meet the dashing Captain Effingham, the topic of many discussions. When Mr. Fortescue falls ill, each girl insists the other go to the celebration, and finally Henrietta elects to stay with her father, while Honoria accompanies Mrs. Fortescue into town. Honoria admires the captain, who, she learns, lost both his parents as an infant, as did she. The excesses of style expected of a romance are evident in the passage where the captain fears he has offended Honoria: "'Pardon you!—Oh! Captain Effingham!'—She could add no more; the tears were forcing their passage down her cheeks, and she feared to trust her voice, lest it should betray the sentiments of her soul. Love in a young mind is ever inclined to hope: he seized her hand in a transport of gratitude."

As winter arrives, Sir James Eustace, a baronet, marries Henrietta, and Honoria pines for the captain, who has traveled to America. He continues to contact the family through Mr. Fitzosborn. Following the general lines of a foundling plot, Honoria learns of her lack of relation to the Fortescues when Mrs. Fortescue becomes ill and, fearing her death, realizes that she must tell Honoria the story of her discovery. Mortified, Honoria later reads a statement of her origin signed by Mr. Richardson, kept with the seal, the crown, and the cross. Mrs. Fortescue dies, and Lady Henrietta and Sir James must depart Ireland for India to investigate a fortune owed to Sir James. The unhappy Honoria feels relieved after receiving a mysterious locket, thinking it came from the captain.

Conflict escalates as the home is invaded by the supposedly sympathetic Kilmoreys and their guests, Miss and Mr. O'Carrol. Miss O'Carrol has designs on Mr.

Fortescue and his fortune, while she hopes that Honoria will allow her brother Patrick to court her, although both disgust Honoria, who recognizes their manipulation. She retires to her room when the O'Carrols appear, her only relief in the form of visits from a local favorite named Cleveland. He escorts her to visit her friend, Sophia Meriton, although she feels a presentiment of disaster as she leaves Mr. Fortescue in the daily company of Miss O'Carrol and later must refuse Cleveland's offer of romance. Her fears prove legitimate, as Miss O'Carrol convinces Mr. Fortescue to marry her in Honoria's absence. Naturally, he tells his new wife of Honoria's secret, and troubles begin for her in earnest. She is unable to alert Henrietta in Bengal as to the new Mrs. Fortescue, who begins to alienate Mr. Fortescue against his adopted "niece."

As Honoria's history becomes public, Cleveland again appeals to Honoria to marry him, and she again refuses. She decides to move to England and adopt the name Miss Wentworth, hoping to obtain some type of low position that will prevent her beloved captain from ever discovering the shame of her foundling status. As she travels to Dublin with the help of Mrs. Connor, who had served as nurse for her and Henrietta, she meets a Major Southmore, who is struck by the beauty and grace of the 19-year-old Honoria and also by the fact that she travels alone. Other passengers exchange gossip about the ungrateful foundling that lived with the Fortescues that upsets Honoria. The major expresses compassion for "this Miss Sommerville," arousing Honoria's gratitude. Upon their arrival in London, the major escorts her to the home of the Middletons, where plans had been made to receive her, and the major tells her to contact him, should she need help.

Within a few pages, Honoria's new position as companion to Lady Mortimer brings her back into contact with Captain Effingham, now a major, who has apparent plans to marry Miss Mortimer, following his ill uncle's death. Feeling betrayed by Effingham and not wanting to leave her position with Miss Mortimer, Honoria declares she must leave for health reasons. The wise Miss Mortimer shares with Honoria that she had discerned that the young woman was of a better background than she pretended and refers her to new employment with a Mrs. Campbell. Honoria encounters Major Southmore and his son Charles and learns they are related to Mrs. Campbell. Before she can move into her new life, all her belongings, stored in a trunk at Mrs. Middleton's, are destroyed in a fire, and she despairs of ever learning her true origins.

In her newest position, Honoria meets the Wintertons and Mr. Hunter, whose names symbolize their personalities. Honoria's intelligence and education are emphasized when Mrs. Campbell asks her to translate a work into Latin and allow Mrs. Campbell to receive credit. Mr. Audley, supposedly a paramour for Miss Winterton, turns his attention to Honoria, to her dismay. Her dismay grows as she encounters one of Effingham's friends previously known to her, Mr. Burnthwaite, who recognizes her as Miss Sommerville.

All the expected challenges occur over the remaining three volumes of the novel, including Effingham's wild search for Honoria. By the time of her 21st birthday, Honoria has confirmed her identity as daughter to Lady Clarendon, although the revelation brings consternation as well as joy, due to various social misunderstandings. However, in the novel's conclusion, the wicked, as well as the good, receive their due. The O'Carrols are caught in a forgery scheme, Sir James receives his inheritance, and he and Henrietta take up residence comfortably close to Honoria, who claims double fortune, that of the Clarendon estate as well as the eternal love and devotion of Colonel Effingham, her husband. She enjoys a reunion with her old devoted nurse, Mrs. Connor, as does Henrietta. Mr. Fortescue is rescued from his grasping wife, and additional deserving characters end up happily married or, as in the case of the helpful Major Southmore, in possession of resources that allow them to do good for the world. Those who married unwisely must live with the results, while those who made well-informed decisions "live in that perfect harmony with each other, which is ever the result of a choice, built on a well-grounded opinion, and secured by encreasing [sic] affection and confirmed esteem."

A solid representative of popular fiction, *Honoria Sommerville* also gained kudos for its high moral intentions. Its heroine acts nobly, befitting her heritage, and is always vindicated for any offense she causes. All four volumes of the book remain available in electronic text.

BIBLIOGRAPHY

Gibbs, Samantha. "Critical Reception of the Works of Elizabeth and Jane Purbeck." *The Corvey Project at Sheffield Hallam University*. Available online. URL: http://www.shu.ac.uk/schools/cs/corvey/corinne/1purbeck/.htm. Downloaded on July 18, 2003.

Watson, Nicola J. *Revolution and the Form of the British Novel 1790–1825: Interrupted Letters, Interrupted Sermons.* Oxford: Clarendon, 1994.

HOOK, THEODORE EDWARD (1788–1841)

Although Theodore Hook wrote several novels, his importance was as an editor who encouraged publications by top authors, including William Makepeace THACKERAY, for whom he is said to have been a model for Mr. Wagg, a character in Thackeray's *The HISTORY OF PENDENNIS* (1848–50). He moved in high literary circles, as evidenced by letters auctioned to pay debts later in his life. His correspondents included England's poet laureate, Robert Southey, poet William Wordsworth, and English politician and writer Benjamin DISRAELI.

Hook was born into a well-connected family and grew up especially close to his older brother, James, despite the 17 years that separated them. James took holy orders following graduation from Oxford and became chaplain to the Prince of Wales, whom he attended until his death. When the prince was crowned King George IV, James obtained an appointment as dean of Worcester. However, Theodore lacked the self-control and commitment of James and, following his education at Harrow, enjoyed high society. He later detailed many of his early adventures in his novel *Gilbert Gurney*, in which the protagonist has a wiser brother, 17 years older. That brother admonishes Gurney that he could not have achieved his success had he continued his imprudent behavior. Gurney ignores him, comparing himself to Lord Byron and his infamous exploits. Hook's biographer blames the early death of Hook's mother, the only individual who could restrain him, for the writer's lack of perseverance in his studies. His father's reportedly easygoing personality proved no match for the wild son. He became known for his practical jokes and for employing his acting talents to stage hoaxes, convincing his victims he was someone else. His prodigious memory stood him in good stead in his later editing duties. He became engaged, but broke the engagement after a short time.

In 1813 Hook became accountant general in Mauritius, although he lacked the skills required. He was recalled after several years due to a shortfall of £12,000 from his accounts, about which he claimed ignorance. He served prison time, but was never regarded as a criminal. His crime was seen as one of omission, rather than commission. Even while in jail, he had been writing steadily, producing poetry and some drama along with essays.

Following Hook's release, he became a sought-after editor, first for the Tory-sympathizing *John Bull,* with which Sir Walter SCOTT was early on incorrectly rumored to have been connected, and later for the *New Monthly Magazine and Literary Journal* (1820). In early 1820, he attempted with a friend to start up a periodical titled *The Arcadian,* but it soon failed. That same year, George IV was crowned king and shocked his Whig supporters when he embraced the Tory Party. His estranged wife, Queen Caroline, returned to England in hopes of claiming her place. A Whig sympathizer, she was perceived as a threat to the Tory Party, and the *John Bull* adamantly opposed her. However, when the queen died suddenly in 1821, the *John Bull* faced a challenge in the need to alter its tone; England had no perceived threats to the Tory Party. Because Hook collected about £2,000 annually from his work with that publication, he determined to continue to challenge Whigs and Radicals.

In the meantime, the chief editor of the *New Monthly,* Thomas Campbell, previously a journalist for the political-leaning *Morning Chronicle, Star,* and *Courier,* determined to make the *New Monthly* into more of a literary vehicle. A focus on poetry was added, and the editorship passed to novelist Edward BULWER-LYTTON, also a contributor, and then to Hook from 1836 to 1841. Thanks in part to Hook's fame as a popular novelist, and from his own publications in journals including *Sharpe's London Magazine,* the *New Monthly* gained status that passed to those who published in its pages. It contained some of the first signed contributions by writers and was considered

quite progressive, with a respectable circulation of 5,000 at the height of its popularity. Hook continued his writing career with publication under the editorship of Charles DICKENS in BENTLEY'S MISCELLANY. His books included a collection of short stories, *Sayings and Doings* (1824); the novels *Maxwell* (1830); *Gilbert Gurney* (1836), judged by his biographer, R. H. Dalton, "the most mirth-provoking and remarkable" of Hook's works; and *Jack Brag* (1837).

BIBLIOGRAPHY

Barham, R. H. Dalton. *The Life and Remains of Theodore Edward Hook.* London: R. Bentley, 1877.

Graham, Walter. *English Literary Periodicals.* New York: Octagon Books, 1966.

HOPE, ANTHONY (1863–1933)

Born Anthony Hope Hawkins to an upper-class family, Hope wrote using his first two names as a pseudonym. His father, the Reverend E. C. Hawkins, served for 10 years as assistant master at Brighton College and for more than 20 years as headmaster of S. John's Foundation School for the Sons of Poor Clergy. Interested in liberal politics and theology, he enjoyed sports of all types. Anthony's mother was Jane Isabella Grahame, aunt to the famous Scottish children's author Kenneth Grahame, who would write *The Wind in the Willows* (1908). A spoiled child who attended his father's school, Anthony nevertheless charmed his teachers and most adults. As he progressed through school, he excelled in debate and attended Balliol College, Oxford, later practicing as a lawyer until 1894.

While practicing law, Hope published some short fiction and one unsuccessful self-published novel, *A Man of Mark* (1890). That project cost him £50, and its sales brought in only £13, but it inspired him to write more, despite the mainly negative reviews. In October 1891, after readings by several publishers, Hope's second novel, *Father Stafford,* was published, again to little attention. Several works followed, including *Mr. Witt's Widow* (1892), which gained more positive notice; one reviewer wrote of it, "the frivolity was extremely clever." *A Change of Air* (1893) and *Sport Royal* (1893), a volume of short stories, followed.

Hope's *The Dolly Dialogues* (1893) at last received the positive attention for which he had long hoped. Published first as a series in the *Westminster Gazette,* the stories delighted readers with their sketches of London high society. A proponent of the romance adventure story popularized by Robert Louis STEVENSON, Hope achieved his greatest success with *The PRISONER OF ZENDA* (1894), praised by Stevenson himself. Hope told of mulling over the idea for his novel and wanting to place it in some undiscoverable country, like Aureataland or Glottenberg. As he was thinking, he saw two men on the street that looked amazingly like, and the idea for *Zenda* was born. His publisher wrote to Hope that he would definitely accept the manuscript. However, according to Hope's rather hagiographic biographer, Anthony Mallet, the publisher expressed concern that the "earthenware pipe in the Castle of Zenda, which was to carry a body from a cell into a moat, would surely find some difficulty in discharging its burden if it emerged three feet below the level of the water." *Zenda* became a great success in England and America, where a dramatic version enjoyed a profitable run. It received praise from Hope's contemporaries, including novelist and historian Edward BULWER-LYTTON and playwright J. M. Barrie, who wrote *Peter Pan* (1904).

The novel's sequel, *Rupert of Hentzau* (1898), also proved popular and was adapted to the stage. While Hope published several additional novels, including *Tristram of Blent* (1901), *Sophy of Kravonis* (1906), and *Lucinda* (1920), he never matched his previous success. He earned a knighthood due to service in the First World War and in later years became a popular social figure, serving as the president of the literary Omar Khayyam Club. His final publication was a memoir, *Memories and Notes* (1927). Following his death, J. M. Barrie wrote of Hope and his works, "that first adventure into Ruritania, *The Prisoner of Zenda,* may be the most inspired, the one in which he first danced on that wig. He made more people happy than any other author of our time."

BIBLIOGRAPHY
Mallet, Sir Charles. *Anthony Hope and his Books.* Port Washington, N.Y.: Kennikat Press, 1968.

HOPE, THOMAS (1769–1831) Born to a wealthy family in Amsterdam, Thomas Hope traveled widely before he settled in England in 1795. Independently wealthy due to his descendence from Scots who had earned a fortune in banking and trade after settling in Amsterdam, he could easily support his extensive trips to Asia and Africa, which began when he was 18 years old. In 1796, he settled in Cavendish Square in a house decorated by his own design. A devotee of neoclassicism, an artistic movement reflecting the values of nature, a concern for social reality, and fearful of the individual's threat to the status quo, Hope patronized many artists, becoming a widely known aesthete. In his travels he assembled a notable art collection, and he trained furniture makers as craftsmen who produced his own Greek and Egyptian designs. In 1806 he married Louisa Beresford and published nonfiction that focused on his pasttime, including *Household Furniture and Interior Decoration* (1807), and the anonymous novel *ANASTASIUS, OR MEMOIRS OF A GREEK,* a SATIRE. The book achieved instant popularity, its REALISM rooted in Hope's experiences. Its hero's brooding introspection and indulgence resembled that of characters produced by the poet George Gordon, Lord Byron, and the novel was at first attributed to Byron.

BIBLIOGRAPHY
Watkin, David. *Thomas Hope 1769–1831 and the Neo-Classical Idea.* London: Murray, 1968.

HORROR FICTION PSYCHOANALYTIC CRITICS agree that horror fiction remains popular because it allows readers to confront their own interior "evil" in a safe, socially acceptable manner. Horror fiction has long confronted the "other," however current social mores might define that other. It includes tales of the occult, of ghosts, of subhuman crimes committed against other humans, the demonic, witchcraft—all acts of an antisocial nature that erupt from the nightmare world. The "monstrous" featured in horror fiction goes beyond the idea of the unworldly to include simply foreign racial or ethnic makeup; the physically, emotionally, or mentally disabled; and other marginalized groups. Many horror stories find their basis in ancient myths, designed as morality tales. Whatever its specific topic, horror fiction uses suspense to frighten and repulse, playing upon human fears, the most common one being isolation leading to death. They may contain aspects of FANTASY, as long as they maintain some REALISM. While many novels may contain scenes of horror, they may not actually constitute horror fiction. Examples include Emily BRONTË's WUTHERING HEIGHTS (1847), which portrays an unpleasant ghostly haunting of loved ones by the dead character Catherine Earnshaw Linton. Spirits in true horror stories go beyond mere haunting, or making mortals miserable. Their actions lead to a mortal threat.

An example of a deadly ghost is found in Horace Walpole's The CASTLE OF OTRONTO: A GOTHIC STORY (1764). A helmet from a statue representing the usurped ruler of a territory disconnects from the statue, grows enormous, and falls onto the usurper's son, killing him. Later the statue itself grows so huge that it literally bursts the castle walls, taking several human lives before the usurper abdicates his undeserved position. As indicated by that novel's subtitle, the GOTHIC genre often incorporates horror, through its use of ghosts, visions, violence, threat, mystery, and a setting usually dark and foreboding, as in the case of writing by the BRONTË sisters.

Horror fiction need not involve graphic physical detail but may prove successful simply through its suggestion of transgression through antisocial behavior. The most common crime is that of murder, but, as in the case of vampirism, the murder of an earthly body does not preclude the spirit's continued existence. Tradition tells of dead beings that can only move about at night in various forms to suck blood from humans. Such creatures require the blood of live victims to support their "undeath," and their bite transforms their victims also into "undead." The intimacy of the puncture and the drinking of blood added erotic tones to the act, increasing its taboo value. The most famous story of vampirism is Bram STOKER's DRACULA (1897), in which a group of men are required to battle and defeat a single vampire. Stoker's novel goes beyond heterosexuality connections in its suggestion of homosexuality in the relationship between Mina and Lucy, highlighting an additional taboo aspect of the "other." FEMINIST CRITICS, among others, surmise that the suggested lesbianism relates to the 19th century's attitude toward female sexuality. Commonly viewed as a source of evil, it required neutralization by a male, in Bram Stoker's story represented by the phallic wooden stake plunged through the undead Lucy's heart.

Another type of horror reflects on a scientific experiment gone wrong, as in Mary SHELLEY's FRANKENSTEIN, OR THE MODERN PROMETHEUS (1818). Shelley intended her novel not only to shock but also to teach the moral lesson that man should not assume control over the creation of life or he will be punished. In her novel, a man-created being has a monstrous appearance and superhuman strength. He fails at an attempt to interact with humans, who are repulsed by his appearance, and ends up a murderer, not of his own volition. Rather, his evil aspects are due to human rejection. Another famous science-run-amok tale is The STRANGE CASE OF DR. JEKYLL AND MR. HYDE (1886) by Robert Louis STEVENSON. Dr. Jekyll, a respected physician, attempts to separate human personality aspects of good from evil. His experiments result in his transformation at times into the purely evil murderer Mr. Hyde through the use of a chemical formula he developed. When he depletes, and cannot duplicate, the transformative formula, Dr. Jekyll commits suicide in order to kill the evil within. His suicide note reveals the two men were actually one person, playing on the famous doppelgänger myth, which claims that each human may have an evil twin. This work suggests that all readers need to explore their own evil tendencies in order to rid themselves of them.

Playing on the Faustian myth that tells of a human exchanging his soul for immortality, Oscar WILDE's The PICTURE OF DORIAN GRAY (1890) features a protagonist who exchanges his soul for eternal beauty. Wilde also suggests homosexuality through the relationship of Gray with Basil Hallward, representative of Gray's conscience, and the amoral Lord Henry Wotton, thus incorporating a second taboo into his novel. Additionally, out-of-control passion may lead to horrific "other" behavior on the part of fictional characters. Sheridan Le FANU's UNCLE SILAS: A TALE OF BARTRAM-HAUGH (1864) focuses on the sinister Silas, a suspected murderer who seeks to kill his ward in order to inherit her fortune. To heighten horror, Le Fanu introduces the grotesque character Madame De La

Rougierre. By suggesting legitimacy through Madame's traditionally trustworthy vocation of governess, Le Fanu brilliantly plays on the betrayed trust of the ward, and by extension that of his readers, to shape suspense, danger, and dismay.

BIBLIOGRAPHY

Barron, Neil, ed. *Horror Literature: A Reader's Guide.* New York: Garland, 1990.

Bleiler, E. F., ed. *Supernatural Fiction Writers: Fantasy and Horror.* 2 vols. New York: Scribner, 1985.

Tymn, Marshall B. *Horror Literature: A Core Collection and Reference Guide.* New York: Bowker, 1981.

HOUSEHOLD WORDS

In 1850 Charles DICKENS founded and edited *Household Words,* a periodical he designed to provide family entertainment by publishing high-quality fiction. He worked with his subeditor William Henry Wills to produce the periodical for nine years before it became part of another Dickens publication, ALL THE YEAR ROUND. The 479 issues offered readers complete stories, novel serializations, poems, biographies, social and political essays, and humor, earning it a reputation as a weekly journal for instruction and entertainment. Dickens held absolute control as he emphasized the instructional aspect of addressing the preoccupations of his era. His novel HARD TIMES appeared as a serial in the magazine from April to August of 1854. Scientist Michael Farraday's lecture notes were published with titles such as "The Chemistry of a Candle," "The Laboratory in the Chest," and "The Mysteries of a Tea Kettle." Other contributors included the journalist and literary expert Henry Morley, poet and critic Leigh Hunt, poet and verse novelist Elizabeth Barrett BROWNING, and novelists Wilkie COLLINS and Elizabeth GASKELL.

BIBLIOGRAPHY

Fader, Daniel, and George Bornstein: *British Periodicals of the 18th and 19th Centuries.* University Microfilms, Ann Arbor, Michigan 48106. 1972, 65–68

HUGHES, THOMAS (1822–1896)

Thomas Hughes, the son of a gentleman, was born in Uffington in Berkshire and later gained an education at Rugby, where he studied with the famous Dr. Thomas Arnold, and later at Oriel College, Oxford. Called to the bar in 1848, he served in the Liberal Party, becoming a circuit judge in Chester. He supported ideals of Christian socialism and workmen's education, campaigning to support representatives of his ideals, F. D. Maurice and Charles KINGSLEY. He acted on his beliefs to help found London's Working Men's College and served for a time as its principal.

Hughes's most famous book, TOM BROWN'S SCHOOL-DAYS (1857), provided an autobiographical account of his own schooling under Arnold. An idealized picture of school life, it stressed loyalty, generosity, and friendship as uncomplicated, pure, and desirable attributes for young men. In the spirit of DOMESTIC REALISM, it characterized school chums as brothers who engaged in largely innocent bullying, wrestling, sports, and pranks. Counted as CHILDREN'S LITERATURE, the book did little to challenge or offend its readers. Falling under the critical label "muscular Christianity," the book stresses ethics over academics with a humor that led Kingsley to label it "the jolliest book ever written." The sequel, *Tom Brown at Oxford* (1861), provided a more accurate view of life at the college level, although it did not gain nearly the popularity of the first book. It complemented other school-day books, such as Kingsley's YEAST: A PROBLEM (1850). Hughes's *The Scouring of the White Horse* (1861) compiled tales from Berkshire, while *Alfred the Great* (1869) and *David Livingstone* (1889) were biographies reflecting his interest in famous individuals. He also published *The Manliness of Christ* (1870), which focused on his religious ideals, and a tribute to his brother George, *Memoir of a Brother* (1873). He visited the United States twice to observe educational institutions. While readily available, his time-bound works are seldom read other than as topics of study.

BIBLIOGRAPHY

Goodwin, Daniel. *Thomas Hughes of England and His Visits to Chicago in 1870 and 1880.* Chicago: Chicago Literary Club, 1896.

Worth, George J. *Thomas Hughes.* Boston: Twayne Publishers, 1984.

HUGH TREVOR THOMAS HOLCROFT (1794–1797)

The first three volumes of Thomas HOLCROFT's *Hugh Trevor* appeared in 1794. In October of that year, before he could add the final three volumes to his novel, Holcroft went to Newgate Prison on a charge of high treason, due to his participation in the Society for Constitutional Information. Released after eight weeks, he completed his book in 1797, publishing an exposure of societal moral decay in the form of a BILDUNGSROMAN. His plot features the maturation of Hugh Trevor from the impoverished child of a widowed mother disowned by her wealthy parson father into a man who learns through multiple negative experiences that the institutions he initially reveres, including university education, Parliament, the aristocracy, religion, and law, are all corrupt. He finds redemption from society only through the individual friendships he secures. One of many reformist novels that appeared at the close of the 18th century, *Hugh Trevor* offers liberal doses of Holcroft's strident rhetoric. Critics like Seamus Deane note that the work's contribution to the development of the radical novel proves more important than its questionable literary value.

Young Hugh at first experiences a pampered life with loving parents. When his father loses his money, enlists in the military, then dies on board a ship to India, the family's destitution will not be relieved by Hugh's angry grandfather, who had protested his daughter's marriage to a "rake." The family's only benefactor, Hugh's uncle Mr. Elford, has left his mother's sister for self-exile. Mr. Elford had been fond of Hugh, following the boy's rescue of a family servant, Mary, from death at the hands of a mysterious man who had impregnated her.

Hugh becomes a farm worker, suffers terrible abuse, coincidentally saves his rector grandfather's life, and thus is reunited with that gentleman. Following the rector's most unclergymanlike protracted litigation with his neighbor, Squire Mowbray, much of his fortune is exhausted. However, Hugh retains an allowance that will support him through education at Oxford and a trust of £1,000 he will receive after earning his degree. He becomes immediately disenchanted with Oxford, learning that each student has a tutor and all engage in debauchery. His one saving grace is meeting an old schoolmate who had been an enemy in his youth, Hector, son of Squire Mowbray. Hugh retains no fondness for the young man, but he has long loved his sister, Olivia Mowbray, and sees her again through his connection with Hector. He also reunites with Turl, a student who had proved a voice of reason during their undergraduate years, the only student who could best Hugh in English lessons.

Due to his outspoken opinions, Hugh is not allowed to graduate from Oxford. He leaves for a time to try his hand at various types of writing, planning to return to Oxford after the time set for him by the dean. He falls first under the influence of a bishop who hires him to write defenses of doctrines that the bishop publishes under the pen name, Themistocles, quickly attributed to the bishop himself. All goes well for a time, and Hugh meets the bishop's "niece," Miss Olivia Wilmot, who he discovers is sister to his one-time favorite teacher. Hugh also dabbles in politics, writing tracts and statements for an earl. He asks Turl's opinion on his work, but ignores his friend's judgment that it lacks substance, making points based on emotion. Hugh recognizes that he possesses a temper and a great capacity for revenge. Before long, Hugh is dismissed by both of his false benefactors and feels betrayed by the institutions of education, religion, and politics. Furthermore, his role model, Wilmot, attempts suicide, due to the rejection of his writing by society, but is rescued by Turl.

Through a series of misfortunes, Hugh loses his money along with his faith in society, partly due to his mother's remarriage to their attorney's nephew, Wakefield. He fears his destitution and behavior will cause him to lose Olivia's favor. Despite that concern, his desperation leads him to gamble, a harmful activity spurred on by the mysterious and charismatic Belmont. In the meantime, Miss Wilmot is badly used by the same Wakefield who, coincidentally, had promised to marry her as well. Hugh discovers that the servant whose life he once saved, Mary, lives with and cares for Miss Wilmot.

Hugh encounters and fights with a carpenter named Clarke, who later becomes his devoted companion on several additional adventures. As they travel to London, they meet a wealthy physician named Mr. Evelyn, who has concocted a scheme to try to convince all wealthy people to share their good fortune with the working classes. He explains to Hugh, "It is the moral system of society that wants reform. This cannot be suddenly produced, nor by the efforts of any individual; but it may be progressive, and every individual may contribute . . . The rich, in proposition as they shall understand this power and these duties, will become peculiarly instrumental." In the most stridently DIDACTIC portion of the novel, Evelyn launches into a long speech about his ideas, telling the mesmerized Hugh, "Let the rich therefore awake: let them encourage each other to quit their pernicious frivolities, and to enquire, without fear or prejudice, how they may secure tranquility and promote happiness." Again Hugh enters into the emotion of the moment, and again he will be disappointed.

Only when Hugh is able to separate reason (represented by Turl) from passion (represented by himself and most additional characters) will he attain happiness. He reclaims Olivia's love and admiration and discovers that Belmont is actually the despicable Wakefield. Through his own guilty conscience, Wakefield is driven to repent and develop integrity through Hugh's influence, confirming the trust Hugh had placed in him. Hugh's wealthy uncle Mr. Elford reappears, discovers Hugh, makes him his beneficiary, and thus inserts Hugh into the high society he has so disdained. The plot concludes with the marriage of the reformed Wakefield to his original love, Miss Wilmot.

Critics have castigated the novel's conclusion as an unexplainable "sellout" on the part of Holcroft that reduces the entire plot to melodrama or farce. Problems in characterization include Hugh's unexplainable attraction to Belmont/Wakefield, a scoundrel cheater who represents everything the protagonist supposedly detests. That Miss Wilmot also will accept her former lover after his misuse of her rings false, although most female fictional characters in the 18th century proved little more than strategically placed backdrops to male drama. The novel remains important, however, as a type also represented by *CALEB WILLIAMS* (1794), written by Holcroft's friend William GODWIN. Both offer an insight into the moral issues and political energies that

occupied the thinking person at the close of the 18th century. In his preface to his work, Holcroft wrote, "all written books, that discuss the actions of men, are in reality so many histories of the progress of mind; and, if what I now suppose be truth, it is highly advantageous to the reader to be aware of this truth."

BIBLIOGRAPHY

Baine, Rodney M. *Thomas Holcroft and the Revolutionary Novel.* Athens, University of Georgia Press, 1965.

Deane, Seamus. Introduction to *Hugh Trevor,* by Thomas Holcroft. London: Oxford University Press, 1973, vii–xii.

HUMPHRY CLINKER, THE EXPEDITION OF TOBIAS SMOLLETT (1771)

When Tobias SMOLLETT published the last of his novels, *The Expedition of Humphry Clinker,* he used the familiar EPISTOLARY NOVEL form first made famous by Samuel RICHARDSON. Five of his flat, predictable characters wrote letters that differed in their points of view on the many episodes comprising the novel's plot. Marked by his trademark heavy-handed caricature, the book also contained some factual information based on his travels. This resulted in an unusual blend of fact with comic fiction and resulted in removing much of the violence that had marked Smollett's previous works. While violent acts exist, their sadistic aspects have been softened, resulting in characters somewhat more broadly shaped than his earlier ones. Matthew Bramble, the main letter writer, cranky but full of heart, resembles Smollett himself. Although only 50 years old, Smollett suffered from overwork and bitterness that eventually translated into an illness that would take his life by the end of 1771. The irascible Bramble mirrors his creator in old age, as the heroes of *RODERICK RANDOM* (1748) and *PEREGRINE PICKLE* (1751) had mirrored the younger Smollett.

Bramble sets out on a journey through England and Scotland along with several family members. They include his strong-willed, spouse-hungry sister, Tabitha; her maid, Winifred Jenkins; a congenial nephew who is an Oxford student, Jerry; and a teenage niece, Lydia. Humphry Clinker serves the group as its ostler, or hostler, a keeper of their horses. He soon becomes their postilion, riding the near horse of those leading to guide the horses as they pull a coach. His position comes to symbolize his importance as leader and guide to the group, who, while holding higher social positions than his own, all fall into his debt by the story's end. A devoted servant, Clinker guides the family through Bristol, Bath, Harrogate, York, Scarborough, and Durham. As the group visits various "spa" towns, Smollett uses his characters to comment on 1760s manners, with Matthew Bramble criticizing much of what he observes. Fashionable society disgusts him, but his negativity translates into a more gentle humor than that produced by Smollett in earlier novels. Smollett delights in the language and applies SATIRE to what he considered pretentious ideas of the so-called educated. In one passage, a doctor expounds upon the positive aspects of a "stink," educating his fellow travelers by explaining that "in the Dutch language, *stinken* signified the most agreeable perfume, as well as the most fetid odour, as appears in Van Vloudel's translation of Horace, in that beautiful ode, *Quis multa gracilis,* &c." He also provides connections to an earlier work, reintroducing some characters from previous novels. Readers discover a chink in the aptly named Bramble's armored exterior by chapter two, through Jerry's letter to a friend. After commenting that he and his uncle seemed as little suited as oil and water, he adds that although he had believed his uncle a "complete Cynic; and that nothing but the necessity of his occasions could compel him to get within the pale of society," he is "now of another opinion. I think his peevishness arises partly from bodily pain, and partly from a natural excess of mental sensibility; for, I suppose, the mind as well as the body, is in some cases endued with a morbid excess of sensation." That comment may reveal much about Smollett's self view just before his death.

In Durham, Lieutenant Obadiah Lismahago joins the group. An eccentric Scot, Lismahago masks under his grotesque behavior good sense that eventually leads him to marry the love-starved Tabitha following her conversion to Methodism by Clinker. Bramble remarks of the Scot that many would misjudge him by his startling exterior. He explains Lismahago's appeal by using a comparison: "I have often met with a crab-apple in a hedge, which I have been tempted to eat for its flavour, even while I was disgusted by its austerity." Another

member of the group, Lydia, also falls in love with a handsome actor from a good family whom she eventually will marry. Along the way, Clinker is falsely accused of a crime, convicted, and imprisoned. The novel's tone remains light in part due to Winifred's muddled impressions. Smollett humorously distorts her vocabulary, as in a letter toward the close of the novel when she attempts to explain her feelings to a confidante: "But then I have such vapours, Molly. I sit and cry by myself, and take ass of etida, and smill to burnt fathers, and kindal-snuffs; and I pray constantly for grease, that I may have a glimpse of the new light, to show me the way through this wretched veil of tares." She declares her love for Clinker, who over several chapters is proven to be Matthew Bramble's long-lost bastard son.

With the unlikely plot twist of a discovered son, Smollett parodied the famous plot of Henry FIELDING's *TOM JONES* (1749), helping maintain what critic Lionel Stevenson describes as "the anti-sentimental ferocity of the Fielding school." Such an approach to fiction would soon disappear, and although Smollett's novel is considered his best PICARESQUE, it also stood as somewhat of an anachronism in an age of growing sensibility that Smollet's natural misanthropy caused him to abhor. The novel remains popular and may be accessed as an electronic text on the Internet.

BIBLIOGRAPHY

Adamson, William Robert. *Cadences of Unreason: A Study of Pride and Madness in the Novels of Tobias Smollett.* New York: Peter Lang, 1990.

Gassman, Byron. "The Briton and Humphry Clinker." *Studies in English Literature* 3 (1963): 397–414.

Stevenson, Lionel. *The English Novel: A Panorama.* Boston: Houghton Mifflin, 1960.

HUNGARIAN BROTHERS, THE ANNA MARIE PORTER (1807)

Anna Marie Porter's novel of the French Revolutionary War, *The Hungarian Brothers,* proved her most popular ROMANCE. It either delighted or repulsed readers in later centuries, depending on their fondness for the genre. One contemporary review of the novel read, "In the invention of the incidents, and in the management and general conduct of the tale in which their characters are delineated, or developed, the fair authors [sic] has displayed very considerable ingenuity, and an intimate acquaintance with those cords of the heart, which can be touched with the liveliest interest and pleasure."

Filled with traditionally stereotyped figures, the novel proves entertaining, if only as a perfect example of type. Set in Germany and Austria, it features the two brothers, Charles and Demetrius, both sons of the Hungarian count Leopolstat, who deserted the family, leaving the boys to be raised by their mother. The family fortune has been looted and/or dissipated by the time Charles reaches adulthood, when he is left by their mother's death to care for Demetrius. Thus, one plot line involves the brothers regaining the fortune to support their titles, another focuses on their romantic entanglements, and another reveals details regarding important military and political campaigns.

The aristocratic characters include an assortment of predictable counts, countesses, princes, princesses, barons, and baronesses, all involved in either various love triangles or present as supportive authority figures. Charles proves the perfect and devoted role model for Demetrius, surviving an excruciating punishment following an undeserved charge of desertion during battle. In truth, he had not deserted, but was tending to his first love, Leonora Berghi, at her deathbed. After her death, he immediately returned to the field. His accuser, the villainous Saxon officer Joseph Wurtzburg, is jealous of Charles's relationship with Signora Berghi, allowing "envy, like a canker worm," to eat into his heart. However, Charles rises above his brief period of deranking to distinguish himself as a volunteer battlefield hero. He saves the life of Archduke Charles and, after regaining his previous rank, is presented a major's commission by the prince. He also safely removes Baron Ingersdorf's wife and niece from danger, for which he earns the lifelong friendship of that family.

Demetrius, an impassioned and handsome 19-year-old, remains devoted to his brother but does exercise his independence, acting against advice to become involved with the duplicitous, married Madame de Fontainville, a lookalike for another scandalous female, the "melodious wonder of Europe," Signora

Albertina. She is eventually revealed as the mysterious "incognita" who sends Charles secret messages for months prior to identifying herself as his devotee. Both women are described traditionally, the madame first appearing with only white roses, an ironic, symbolic blend of innocence and sexuality, and described as having incredibly white skin and the type of appearance that dazzles but will fade. When Signora Albertina is compared to the madame, her beauty also lacks permanence. FEMINIST CRITICS will find these the most interesting of the female characters, due to their strength and independence. The madame leaves her husband when he acts against her political ideals, while the signora takes the unusual action of communicating with a man, considered a trait of an aggressive female. When Charles finally meets with her and "awkwardly" thanks her for "her intended kindness," professes his "inability to return so sudden a passion," and attempts to leave, she actually bars his path and "acted for two hours . . . a most pathetic scene of despair, tenderness, and entreaty," using her talents and assets to bargain for her future.

These two "bad" women are balanced by the lovelies with whom the brothers will finally find bliss, the symbolically named Princess Constantia and the irrepressible Adelaide, whom Charles had rescued months earlier. Adelaide contrasts with the madame in her "olive complexion," which, "though warm with native bloom, was less dazzling than if it had been fair." She has "uncommonly brilliant eyes," but keeps them chastely lowered, her lips closed with "a gentle confusion." "Her charms," the reader learns, "were the touching charms of twilight; Madame de Fontainville's the blaze of day." Constantia's attributes are more of the personality, which reflects "little girlish simplicity," always charming and "possessing an instinct . . . of whatever would be most consonant to the tastes or feelings of her associates." She proves "playful, but never excessively lively . . . it was her happy destiny to endear, even while she entertained." In romance fashion, both young women, virginal and pure, remain inactive and objectified by the male gaze, desirable for their appearance and the way by which they will complement their male partners. The men sing, strum and paint their way through high society, adopting female attributes. However, their gender role reversals are viewed as evidence of refinement, safely balanced by their strength in the most male of arenas, the battlefield.

Neither brother is informed regarding his own emotions. Charles at first denies his love for Adelaide, not recognizing his feelings until the baron she has been appointed to marry by her father appears. Then he cannot speak of his love, as that would constitute loutish behavior. Like his brother, Demetrius remains ignorant of his love for Constantia. When he realizes it, he has unwisely pledged himself to the madame. At his epiphany, "he muttered now and then to himself, as if in delirium; and frequently he smiled, but it was a smile of despair." He attempts to carry on, having "studied the self-command and graceful restraint of Charles."

Through convoluted plot twists and turns, misrepresentations, disguises, battles of the heart and battles of war, both the male and female protagonists will faint, become ill with brain fever, and suffer the traditional vicissitudes of romance. They include, most dramatically, the unjust charge of treason against Demetrius, supported by fabricated documents and charges by Wurtzburgh and the dastardly Nuremberg, with the help of his servant Pierre. Demetrius subsequently disappears, is "brought to the verge of the grave," and rescued by his devoted brother. As demanded by the genre, all ends well. Pierre dies of wounds, while Wurtzburgh is "arraigned, tried, condemned, and executed as a traitor." The narrator adds that while his death proved "shocking . . . it excited no pity." In the final sentence, Charles looks first at his infant son, then at Demetrius, and then turns his eyes, "floating in tears," to Heaven.

In her introduction to the 1831 edition, Porter noted that she found "much to smile at" in this work of her youth. She discovered "much lacking" and felt burdened to "remedy the deficiencies." She did not apologize, however, for the accuracy of her "military statements" summarizing "five campaigns." Her details had been praised by a "great general," and she explains that accuracy by mentioning an entire winter when, away from her own home, she read the many books in the strange house, all of which considered military history. Her great admiration of "martial glory" led her to believe that her "humble romance" might achieve her goal of "exalting the military character in public opinion."

BIBLIOGRAPHY

"Review: *The Hungarian Brothers.*" *Sheffield Hallam University: Corvey Women Writers 1796–1834 on the Web.* Available online. URL: http://www2.shu.ac.uk/corvey/cw3/ ContribPage.cfm?Contrib=218. Updated November, 1999. Downloaded February 15, 2003.

HURRISH: A STUDY EMILY LAWLESS (1886)

As indicated by its subtitle, *Hurrish: A Study* was intended by Emily LAWLESS to reflect as much about Ireland's general masses as about any one person. Thus, her characters serve as basic types or symbols. They scratch out a living in post-famine Ireland and are, for the most part, bitter and torn apart by land squabbles and emigration.

The novel's protagonist stands in contrast to those conflicted individuals, happy with his life as a widower with beloved children. The enormous black-Irish Hurrish O'Brien is the gentle giant, out of place in an era and setting that demands violence from everyone. The thinly drawn Mat Brady represents the "land grabber" of the day, a foolish individual who moves in on land foreclosed on and taken from honest working folk, with sure retribution from the locals to follow. Mat's brother, Maurice, fondly referred to as Morry by the fatherly Hurrish, also remains two-dimensional, serving as the object of retribution for his wicked brother's murder. He represents the unspoken Irish code of his district, much stronger than any civic law, which demands an eye for an eye when one's blood kin is killed.

Hurrish's self-defense killing of Mat is the catalyst that prompts Maurice's act of violence against a man he admittedly loves like a father. When he shoots the justly acquitted Hurrish, he basically kills himself as well, fulfilling the local code but marking himself as an outcast following the court ruling of Hurrish's actions against Mat as self-defense. Alley Sheehan, Hurrish's niece by marriage and love object for Maurice Brady, lives with the O'Briens and adores Hurrish. Her virginal, angelic personality types her immediately, and readers anticipate her eventual move into a convent long before the plot's conclusion. The landlord, Pierce O'Brien, acts somewhat against type in his fair dealings with his tenants, his rejection of the offer by the English law structure for bodyguard protection, and his refusal to testify against Hurrish during his trial for the murder of Mat Brady. However, he hardly had a choice in that matter, knowing Hurrish's neighbors would kill him should he take the stand.

More interesting is Hurrish's mother, the violent Bridget O'Brien, a type often present in drama as the mother who lives vicariously through her offspring. She has urged Hurrish to kill the loutish Mat, goading her son to act totally against character in order to satisfy her own blood lust. When Sal Connor, who has decided the widowed Hurrish will be her own, is accosted by Mat, Bridget exclaims to Sal and her son about the evil man, "Trath an' he won't be 'bout it long, I tell yis all that! . . . There's boys that, for the wink ov an eyelid, wud put him out of that,—yis an' proud to do it too." Although Hurrish laughs off his mother's thinly veiled demand with "'Tis an iligant Christsheen yer makin' me out, mother, anyhow!" readers understand the grim foreshadowing. Bridget also represents the highly politicized Irish figure with an inborn hatred for all outsiders, particularly the English, but also those of her own people who, like Mat, become outsiders due to their actions. She exults in the stoning death by local residents of Buggle, "the little black villin that was servin' writs," and, upon the death of Hurrish's wife, Mary, "would willingly have turned Alley out upon the cold high-road to beg." She interests FEMINIST CRITICS as a powerful character, one with more traditionally male characteristics than female. Bridget O'Brady is nothing like the traditional nourishing mother figure; however, her love for her son is stronger than her desire to live, leading her to die soon after Maurice murders Hurrish.

Another interesting character is the mentally diminished Thady-na-Taggart, described as "the idiot or 'natural' of Tubbamina." The author comments that "Village idiots, once common institutions in England, are now scarce," blaming that fact on increased civilization. Readers are told that "The 'natural' only does rather better what every one else does more or less—namely as little as possible." But when Thady does act,

his actions prove crucial. In an early confrontation between Hurrish and Mat, Mat dangles his enemy's dog, the well-drawn terrier Lep, over cliffs above the ocean. Hurrish knows he can never rescue his beloved pet, but then suddenly "a wild tatterdemalion figure, with white vacant face, starting eyes, and long lank hair streaming in the wind" grabs Mat around the legs and rescues little Lep. Thady remains reminiscent of Shakespeare's fools, who often prove his dramas' wisest characters. In his rescue of the freely loved Lep, who returns affection without judgment, Thady seems to tell his fellow Irish that love must be given freely, without expectations, if it is to prove of any value. Following Hurrish's death, Thady adopts Lep, and the two characters symbolic of a sane loyalty and affection live their patient lives out together.

As Hurrish lies dying, the narrator labels him a "martyr to a not very glorious cause," one certainly not worth his life. He was "dying because Hate of the Law is the birthright and the dearest possession of every native son of Ireland." This statement continued to ring true, as "the Irish question" remained unanswered into the 21st century. While to modern readers, Lawless's superb descriptions and relentless conflict development prove her novel's most attractive aspects, her confused English readers in 1887 received the book as news from a battlefield whose bloodshed they grappled to understand. Lawless's attempts to elucidate the life of the Irish linked her with other regional writers of the day, most notably Margaret Oliphant, who did the same with the Scottish, and to whom Lawless dedicated *Hurrish.*

BIBLIOGRAPHY

Mulkerns, Val. Introduction to *Hurrish,* by Emily Lawless.
  Belfast: Apple Tree Press, 1992, vii–x.

HYPATIA, OR NEW FOES WITH AN OLD FACE CHARLES KINGSLEY (1853)

In his third novel, Charles KINGSLEY seemingly departed from his previous focus on his own era to produce a historical ROMANCE in *Hypatia, or New Foes with an Old Face.* However, as the title indicates, he still dealt with contemporary issues. The book first appeared in serial form in *FRASER'S MAGAZINE* from January 1852 to April

1853. As a radical Christian, Kingsley hoped to villainize Catholicism through historical fact. He suggested certain Catholic leaders of his own time through characters such as Cyril, the Bishop of Alexandria, who proved far more interested in political expediency than humanitarianism. For contrast, he borrowed an additional real-life character in Synesius, Bishop of Cyrene, a figure who more closely shared Kingsley's own ideology, an affinity for sports, and the belief that priests should be allowed to have families.

Set in fifth-century Alexandria, the novel features a pagan prefect who governs his city with ineptitude. The novel's heroine, Hypatia, daughter to the learned mathematician Theon, represents the teachings of Neoplatonists and comes in conflict with the strong forces of developing Christianity, led by Cyril. The lovely Hypatia struggles to maintain a philosophical academy devoted to the old Greek model, representing the transcendentalism that Kingsley so despised in his own age. Kingsley implies that the freedom afforded women by an education and the right to withhold sex will always conflict with the male need for power over females. Hypatia struggles to pit wisdom against passion, while Kingsley calls readers' attention to the similarity between her ideals and those of ascetic Christians, whose denial of the human need for love disgusted Kingsley.

When a Christian monk, Philemon, arrives, he finds his fellow Christians' fanaticism repugnant and campaigns against their mindless devotion. He falls in love with Hypatia's humanitarian approach and her desire for moderation in all things. While he appeals to his fellow Christians to be more reasonable, he finds the extreme skeptical intellectualism of Raphael Aben-Ezra unpalatable. Kingsley modeled Raphael, the most interesting character, on a Jewish friend who had left his own beliefs to join the Church of England. He manages to create brilliant parallels between Alexandria and his own Victorian London, picturing both cities as commercial centers with all the cultural advantages such centers offer, including the theater and halls of learning, shadowed by decrepit slums filled with violence and turmoil. Forces get out of control when Hypatia is falsely accused of turning the prefect against the Christians. A mob captures her and literally rips her to pieces, after which Philemon leaves the city in total disillusionment.

Critics find brilliant Kingsley's representation of the many cults of classic times, as well as his mob scenes, but his plot becomes difficult to follow with the myriad of unnecessary characters and their convoluted esoteric arguments. Philemon seems to be the male protagonist but remains an observer, too uninvolved to be heroic. Kingsley hoped to reveal Christianity as superior to transcendentalism but managed to avoid characterizing either one as purely good or evil. In order to remain true to history, he had to acknowledge that any philosophical or religious movement, however humanitarian, could fail its followers if it had a poor or corrupt leader and followers too blind by irrational passions to question those leaders. Many Christians felt Kingsley should have villainized all creeds other than Christianity, a failure which ironically lost him the very readers he sought to vindicate. Charges of immorality resulting from his description of sexual excesses marked him so strongly that Kingsley was denied an honorary Oxford degree a decade later. The book moved John Henry Newman, a lifelong adversary of Kingsley, to interrupt his theological studies and write a novel in response, *Callista* (1856).

While not widely read in later generations, *Hypatia* stands as an excellent example of fiction written for a specific purpose, as well as an impeccably researched novel that remains true to history.

BIBLIOGRAPHY
Stubbs, Charles William. *Charles Kingsley and the Christian Social Movement.* 1899. Reprint. New York: AMS Press, 1974.

I

IMPERIALISM   Imperialism may be defined as one nation or political entity's power, influence, or control over another for economic, political, and/or ideological purposes. While similar to colonialism, imperialism may appear in a more informal manner, where colonialism implies the exercise of formal and strict political control. One of the earliest English novels to reflect negatively on colonialism and imperialism was titled OROONOKO: OR, THE ROYAL SLAVE (1688) by English writer Aphra BEHN. Nineteenth-century Great Britain, particularly after 1870, extended imperialism into the Near East and later Africa, prompting various novelists, such as Rudyard KIPLING and Edward BULWER-LYTTON, to urge white men to bear the "burden" of uplifting more "savage" cultures. Others, including Sir Henry Rider HAGGARD and Joseph CONRAD, wrote works countering imperialism and colonialism, noting the destructive effects of overpowering a foreign culture and forcing its inhabitants to adopt ideology not their own. They also emphasized the injustice in Great Britain profiting from the natural resources and manpower of other countries without sharing the profit with its source. German philosopher Karl Marx linked such economic imperialism with capitalism in his theories shared in the three volumes of *Das Kapital,* published from 1867 to 1894.

BIBLIOGRAPHY

Ingram, Edward. *The British Empire as a World Power.* Portland: Frank Cass, 2001.

Laffey, John F. *Imperialism and Ideology: An Historical Perspective.* London: Black Rose, 2000.

INCHBALD, ELIZABETH (1753–1821)
Born near Bury St. Edmunds in Suffolk into a staunchly Catholic family, Elizabeth Simpson learned early to deal with a speech impediment. Maturing on a farm as one of nine children of John Simpson and Mary Rushbrook, she received little encouragement of her love for acting. That did not prevent her running away in 1772 to seek the life of an actress. A beautiful woman, she was romanced by many men but settled on a fellow minor actor named Joseph Inchbald, whom she married in 1772 despite his being much older than her. He died in 1779 after Elizabeth had worked for two years on her most famous novel, *A SIMPLE STORY* (1791). It included in Dorriforth a characterization of her real love, the great actor John Philip Kemble. In her preface, she adopted the approach used by many early women writers in excusing her presumption to write, by feigning a type of helplessness that begged kindness from critics. She lied, stating she was a destitute invalid who wrote in spite of her "utmost detestation to the fatigue of inventing." When she could not find a publisher, she turned her attention to playwriting. *A Mogul Tale* (1784), her first drama, focused on hot-air balloons, all the craze at that time, and enjoyed a successful run at the Haymarket. Inchbald acted until 1789, then became a full-time writer, producing at least 20

additional plays as well as fiction. While later considered a minor writer, many of her works were well received in her own age. She produced several successful comedies, including *I'll Tell You What* (1785), *Everyone Has His Fault* (1793), *Wives as They Were, and Maids as They Are* (1797), and *To Marry, or Not to Marry* (1805). Her ambitious *The Child of Nature* (1788) she adapted from Kotzbue's *Lovers' Vows* (1798), later mentioned in Jane AUSTEN's *MANSFIELD PARK* (1814). Her friendship with philosopher and novelist William GODWIN influenced her second novel, *Nature and Art* (1796). She lived a thrifty life, and at her death left behind a fortune of £5,000.

BIBLIOGRAPHY

Sage, Lorna, ed. *The Cambridge Guide to Women's Writing in English.* Cambridge: Cambridge University Press, 1999.

Showalter, Elaine. *A Literature of Their Own: British Women Novelists from Brontë to Lessing.* Princeton, N.J.: Princeton University Press, 1999.

INDUSTRIAL REVOLUTION   The Industrial Revolution was the label applied to a worldwide movement to replace man with machines that began in 18th-century England and remains ongoing. Great Britain led the world in industrialization, due in part to its introduction of property laws, protecting individual rights to inventions with patents. British law also protected citizenry against the seizure of property by royalty or aristocrats. Such factors encouraged risk and resulted in iron and steel manufacture, the building of steam engines, and the ready production of textiles from natural materials. The mining of iron and coal led to an increase in transportation and railroad operations. Industrialization's immediate results included improved production of goods, expanding trade options, and a conversion of an agrarian society into an industrial one, as people moved off farms and into growing cities in search of work. A rapid growth in efficiency led to an increase in production, as men applied new scientific knowledge to the manufacturing process, thereby revolutionizing the world.

Economic changes led to social changes, including the development of a new social/political/economic class composed of workers. Increasingly wealthy members of the middle class, along with the upper class, benefited at the expense of the new factory worker and further exacerbated the inequities of the CLASS STRUCTURE. While access to goods, wealth, and opportunity increased, so did poverty and crime among these poor. Widespread abuse of factory workers included long workdays with no or few breaks, low pay, and child labor. Those producing the goods often could not afford to enjoy them. The first large slum areas appeared, as people used any type of structure for shelter. Lack of income led to a lack of medical care, resulting in increased infant mortality and early adult deaths from illnesses spread in the close quarters of "sweatshops" and the loss of limbs and life to the machinery. The division of labor into boring repetitive tasks provided little in the way of intellectual stimulation. Labor movements, including the CHARTIST MOVEMENT, were organized to protect workers, focusing on factory abuses and including the push to reform CORN LAWS and the poor laws. Fiction, especially in the 1840s, began to reflect the era, with authors supporting various reform causes, including the abolition of capital punishment. Authors of such THESIS NOVELS, also popularly called novels with a purpose, included Charles DICKENS, Charles KINGSLEY, Frances TROLLOPE, Benjamin DISRAELI, and Elizabeth GASKELL, all of whom called for reform of shameful and exploitive working conditions.

BIBLIOGRAPHY

More, Charles. *Understanding the Industrial Revolution.* New York: Routledge, 2000.

Polak, Ben, and Jeffrey G. Williamson. *Poverty, Policy, and Industrialization: Lessons from the Distant Past.* Washington D.C.: World Bank, 1991.

Stearns, Peter N. *The Industrial Revolution in World History.* Boulder, Colo.: Westview Press, 1998.

INHERITANCE   SUSAN FERRIER (1824)   Susan FERRIER allowed six years to pass between the release of her well-liked novel of manners, *MARRIAGE,* and *Inheritance,* another anonymously published story that focused on the romantic choices of young women. She had worked on the novel at Morningside House, outside of Edinburgh, where her father spent

the summer season. Her desire to conceal her activity was made difficult by the closeness of her surroundings, but her skill at characterization triumphed, causing BLACKWOOD'S EDINBURGH MAGAZINE to proclaim the novel "a hundred miles above *Marriage*." Marked by what critic George Douglas labeled "an interesting and admirably compact plot, and a vigorous literary style," the novel proved just as popular, if not more, than its predecessor. Containing references to works by Shakespeare and classical Greek writers, its emphasis on the importance of the wisdom of literature reflects Ferrier's own beliefs. She also uses the drama format of those writers to structure her highly dramatic romance, interchanging the tragic with the farcical.

The plot premise is based on the sacrifice, in the name of love, of the Honourable Thomas St. Clair, the youngest of the earl of Rossville's five sons, described as a man of "weak intellects and indolent habits." Because he married below his rank to "the humble Miss Sarah Black, a beautiful girl of obscure origin and no fortune," he sacrifices his inheritance, which, upon his father's death, was directed to pass to St. Clair's children, should he have any. The eldest brother assumes the earl's title and estate. St. Clair and his wife spend some time in France, and eventually, due to three brothers' deaths, he stands next in line to inherit his brother's estate and title. Neither he nor his remaining brother have produced any children, when suddenly Mrs. St. Clair announces her pregnancy. St. Clair decides to take her to Scotland, his brother having agreed to meet with him. However, she goes into premature labor during the journey and delivers a daughter, Gertrude, which "although born in the seventh month . . . was a remarkably fine thriving baby, which Mrs. St. Clair, contrary to the common practice of mothers, ascribed entirely to the excellence of its nurse." Those accustomed to reading romances note the signal that something is not quite right in this situation, which foreshadows later disaster. Thus, the family never returns to Scotland.

The novel's second chapter opens with Mrs. St. Clair widowed and Gertrude having blossomed into a beautiful girl. Through the coincidence shared by ROMANCE novels of the day, they end up sharing housing with the aging and now single Lord Rossville. Members of the earl's household recognize a strong resemblance of Gertrude to Lizzie Lundie, a beauty of low birth who once sat for a painting that hangs in the Castle. Comments regarding the resemblance upset Mrs. St. Clair, who seemingly interprets them as slurs on her husband's character. In actuality, she knows something of Gertrude's birth that she declines to share with her daughter and is revealed as an ambitious, even violent and bitter character.

Two cousins to Gertrude pursue a romance with her. As required by romance tradition, they serve as foils. Young Colonel Delmour is handsome, elegant, and sophisticated, a traveled man of the world, while his competitor Edward Lyndsay is serious with a sensitive nature. A mysterious visitor to Mrs. St. Clair named Mr. Lewiston apparently exercises some negative power over the widow. His identity is later revealed as a husband to one of Gertrude's childhood nurses, a man believed to be dead. Mrs. St. Clair agrees to meet with Lewiston and bring Gertrude with her, but he attempts to molest sexually the young woman. Lyndsay rescues her, eliciting gratitude, but Delmour declares his passion, and Gertrude agrees to marry him.

In the meantime the earl has made marriage plans of his own for his granddaughter. For political and economic reasons, he desires Gertrude to marry the colonel's older brother, a passionless man but one powerful in political intrigues. Gertrude protests, angering the earl, who considers disinheriting Gertrude as Lyndsay intervenes to declare his love. The earl's sudden death before any change is made to his will, however, leaves Gertrude free to follow her heart. Gertrude again attempts to speak with Lewiston, and again must be rescued by Lyndsay. In the meantime, Delmour engages in activities causing Gertrude and others to doubt his sincerity and his character. Gertrude remains devoted to Delmour and, while she recognizes and appreciates Lyndsay's obvious commitment to her well-being, chooses to wed Delmour; he stands to enjoy her estate that accompanies her title, Countess of Rossville.

Delmour connives to involve Gertrude in a series of financial schemes, all meant to defraud her of her money. Even so, in London she becomes the talk of the social scene and allows herself to be involved in its various pleasures, to the dismay of Lyndsay, who counsels wisdom and discretion. She ignores his pleas and falls to the temptations of fashionable life. When she later returns to Rossville, she has another visit from the dastardly Lewiston, who was mistakenly believed to have drowned. He at last breaks the news that she is not even related to the Rossville family but instead is the daughter of Mrs. St. Clair's nurse, thus having no true claim to her title. That nurse, named Marian La Motte, had been the daughter of Lizzie Lundie, whose portrait Gertrude had been said to resemble. The St. Clairs met her as they traveled to Scotland, while she was pregnant, separated from her husband, Jacob Lewiston, and fearful of dying and leaving her baby an orphan. The St. Clairs agreed to adopt the child, as with the only heir, they would surely inherit the family fortune. Their plan was ruined by a letter that Marian wrote to a priest who promised, upon her death, to send the letter to Lewiston, then living in America. The priest served as a missionary in the United States years later and met up with Lewiston, who immediately traveled to Britain to claim his daughter. During Gertrude's dismay at the discovery of her origin, she accuses Mrs. St. Clair of treachery, and her real mother of not loving her. Attempting to placate her daughter, Mrs. St. Clair explains, "You could bring nothing but additional care and poverty to her; to me you would ensure riches and honour. Do not condemn us."

When in trust Gertrude shares this news with Delmour, who had already expected something was amiss, he considers breaking their engagement, not out of a lack of love for her, but rather because he needs her fortune, having lost his own. Brokenhearted when she discovers his motivation, she gives up her profligate lifestyle and turns to the stalwart love of Lyndsay. Impressed by her behavior, he tells her, "You have been the victim of imposture; but your own name is pure and spotless; it is more. To those who can appreciate virtue, it will carry a nobler sound along with it than any that heraldry could have bestowed."

Lyndsay discovers the truth from Lewiston, that he is not actually Gertrude's father after all, but his cousin. Lyndsay promises to give him money in exchange for the priest's letter and for his leaving Britain forever. After Lyndsay receives a letter from Delmour, releasing Gertrude from their engagement, he marries Gertrude. She reconciles with her mother and regains not only a title but, more important, also a true inheritance of love.

As does her idol Sir Walter SCOTT, Ferrier includes literally dozens of characters who add interest to the plot. They include the comical Miss Pratt, a busybody type who, in one of the novel's funniest scenes, scandalizes the old earl by arriving at his castle in a hearse, driven by Mr. McVitae, a known radical. Miss Pratt's continual quotation of the questionably nonexistent Anthony Whyte add extreme situational humor. The misanthropic Indian uncle, Adam Ramsay, annoys everyone by his constant references to the lost romance of his youth, yet in actuality offers Gertrude a cautionary tale, which she ignores to her own later detriment. His kind consideration of her in the novel's concluding scenes help round his type character. The ridiculous Mrs. Major Waddell, neé Bell Black, portrays the fool character so popular to tragic drama. The required poor relation, also symbolic of Gertrude's future, Miss Becky Duguid, joins the poetess, Miss Lilly, and various representatives of the peasant class to remind readers that few members of society enjoy the fortune that the aristocratic earl's family simply take for granted. All the characters' names, such as Vitae (life), Whyte (innocence and wisdom), Bell (an harbinger of caution), Black (danger), and Lilly (flower of funerals), traditionally symbolize important aspects that add pleasure to the narration, while the more unusual Duguid, whose name is phonetically "Do Good," provides a literary symbol, its meaning peculiar to this specific novel, supporting Ferrier's reputation as an imaginative writer, meticulous in regards to her craft.

BIBLIOGRAPHY
Douglas, Sir George Brisbane. *The Blackwood Group.* Edinburgh: Oliphant Anderson & Ferrier, 1897.

INITIATION/COMING-OF-AGE STORY

Closely related to the BILDUNGSROMAN, an initiation story, also termed a coming-of-age-story, expanded and augmented the bildungsroman concept. While the bildungsroman is a label appropriate to novels that feature young people who mature into adults, the initiation plot generally features a child or teen that does not mature. Indicated by the name, the plot incorporates an important experience that "initiates" the protagonist into the world of adults. While the character moves closer to adulthood emotionally and mentally, she/he does not immediately become an adult. As in real life, many experiences are necessary to advance an individual into adulthood. The character may experience romantic love, an adult emotion, but remain immature, or be challenged by a situation demanding the application of adult logic, as in Lewis CARROLL's ALICE'S ADVENTURES IN WONDERLAND (1865). In the early novels, because young people matured later than those of subsequent generations, books such as *The History of* TOM JONES, A FOUNDLING (1749) by Henry FIELDING, particularly with its shaping of Tom as an innocent scoundrel, despite his propensity for sex, might be classified as coming-of-age. Many novels by Charles DICKENS published in the 1830s to 1860s involved children, often victims of an uncaring society, who come of age. In Frances Hodgson BURNETT's LITTLE LORD FAUNTELROY (1886), the protagonist, Cedric Errol, learns respect and care for the poor, and in BEVIS, THE STORY OF A BOY (1882), Richard JEFFERIES' boy characters enjoy summer adventures that try their imaginations and logic. Some initiation tales, such as Arthur MORRISON's A CHILD OF THE JAGO (1896), are cautionary tales in which children lose their lives through initiations rising from social inequities, a fate often reserved as well for young minor characters in Dickens's novels. DAISY MILLER (1879), by Henry JAMES, also introduces a young female, barely past her teens, who meets her death, mostly due to the cruelty of social conventions.

INVISIBLE MAN, THE H. G. WELLS (1897)

H. G. WELLS often used his SCIENCE FICTION tales to teach a moral lesson. In *The Invisible Man,* he warns against the abuse of scientific capability and the misuse of power it encourages. The protagonist, Griffin, was driven to find a potion that would make flesh and bone invisible. He tried it on himself, and it proved successful.

When the novel opens, the Invisible Man enters an inn as a mysterious stranger, swaddled in clothing with bandages around his face and wearing glasses to hide his condition. The fact that the season is winter signals the reader that death will become important to the story. As the stranger mutters to himself, the reader understands the isolation he suffers, but he is in no way a sympathetic character, frightening the other visitors at the inn and behaving rudely toward the landlady. He moves his scientific equipment into the room he rents in order to continue experimenting, but soon becomes focused on his newfound power as a manner by which to wreak havoc and injury on others. Individuals hear noises, but can find no cause; they close a door, then walk back to find it open again. This trickery proves harmless enough, but it whets Griffin's appetite for power. Soon he is a hunted man and is wounded by a group of pursuers. He takes refuge in the home of Doctor Kemp, identifying himself by name for the first time in the story, reminding Kemp they had been in school together. The Invisible Man jolts Kemp's memory by describing himself as "a younger student, almost an albino, six feet high, and broad, with a pink and white face and red eyes,—who won the medal for chemistry." Griffin's appearance would have marked him as aberrant, one who would never fit into a group due to his odd appearance. Ironically, his disappearance into invisibility, like the ghost form he already resembled, does not change his role as an "other" in society. The winning of the medal suggests his mental acuity and creative vision, but his lack of humanity mitigates against such natural talents to render him undeserving of admiration. He represents the classic mad-scientist character that Wells used repeatedly in stories to make clear that a desire for metaphysical powers equates to a madness born in a lack of self-control. Wells suggests Griffin's monstrosity through his strange appearance, and the character seems almost destined to complete his transformation into something inhuman.

Kemp allows Griffin to stay in his house, then reads an article describing the manner in which a village had been terrorized and recognizes that Griffin is losing his faculty of reason. As the action rises, Griffin becomes more agitated and further loses a grip on reality, assuming that Kemp will join his scheme to terrorize the world. When he discovers that Kemp has betrayed his whereabouts, he rushes from the house in "a blind fury," bumping into a child and breaking the child's ankle. Furious with Kemp, he writes a letter stating that "the Epoch of the Invisible Man" has begun, and his first official act will be to execute Kemp. Now a complete homicidal maniac, Griffin does attempt to kill Kemp and in the process injures several additional people. At last tackled to the ground by a crowd who comes to Kemp's aid, his chest is crushed, and his body loses its invisibility, revealing his sickly white skin and "garnet" eyes.

Like other of Wells's novels, *The Invisible Man* was converted to multiple film versions, with critics pronouncing the 1933 movie starring Claude Rains as the superior presentation.

BIBLIOGRAPHY

Gill, Stephen. *Scientific Romances of H. G. Wells: A Critical Study.* Cornwall, Ontario: Vesta, 1975.
West, Anthony. Introduction to *The Invisible Man,* by H. G. Wells. New York: Bantam Books, 1987, vii–xvi.

ISLAND OF DR. MOREAU, THE H. G. WELLS (1896)

Described by some critics as gruesome and by others as grim, H. G. WELLS's *The Island of Dr. Moreau* depends on the mad scientist characterization that would continue to be popular into the 20th century. Intent on transmitting a moral in his tale, Wells conjures up a surgeon named Moreau who seeks to develop a civilization of animals converted into humans. His experiments go amiss, and in an echo of Mary SHELLEY's *FRANKENSTEIN* (1818), the results of his efforts prove monstrous.

The novel's format adopts the familiar journal narrative, as it opens with a statement by Charles Edward Prendick explaining that his uncle had been lost for 11 months. Following the sinking of the vessel on which he traveled, the *Lady Vain,* he was presumed drowned until rescued from a small open boat believed to have belonged to another shipwreck named the *Ipecacuanha.* Suffering from memory loss attributed to trauma, Prendick did have among his possessions a written account of his time spent on what the nephew presumed was Noble's Isle, a small uninhabited island. When his nephew later discovered the account, he verified that the *Ipecacuanha* disappeared while carrying various

animals toward the South Pacific at about the time of his uncle's supposed adventure, a fact that supported the truth of his story.

As Prendick's tale unfolds, Wells inserts much foreshadowing of the horrors to come. While floating in a small boat with two companions from the shipwreck, Prendick writes that one "gave voice to the thing we had all been thinking" after their store of fresh water had been exhausted. He never states what that horrible thing is, but adds that if the proposal were accepted, "we should have drink," suggesting that they discussed drinking their own blood, or perhaps even cannibalism. The two men grapple with one another and fall from the boat, leaving the narrator to write that he remembered laughing and later wondered at his own reaction: "The laugh caught me suddenly like a thing from without." The blood imagery and suggestion of some inhuman force clues readers that a bizarre fate awaits Prendick. At last rescued and taken aboard a ship, Prendick is kept inside a room where he hears various animal sounds and is given some "scarlet stuff, iced" to drink. He notes that "it tasted like blood, and made me feel stronger," and then observes a "misshapen man," with hairy neck and sunken head between his shoulders who turns at the sounds of dog growls "with animal swiftness." The blood elixir, mysterious noises, and inhuman characteristics of the ship's servant further intensify reader anticipation.

When Prendick arrives on the island, he comes to know its two human inhabitants, the assistant Montgomery and Dr. Moreau, well. He spends some time there before discerning Moreau's purpose. The odd creatures he sees on the island bother him for an unknown reason, striking him as strange, yet familiar. Suddenly, he perceives why they cause offense; all resemble both animals and humans. He learns that Moreau has created creatures from parts of dogs, pigs, pumas, rats, hyenas and other animals, then imbued them with human characteristics, such as speech. When Prendick expresses his outrage, Moreau explains his "grafting" experiments will prove a boon to mankind, allowing weaknesses to be corrected and new civilizations to form. Prendick recoils, labeling the work "monsters manufactured." Moreau excuses the seeming immorality of his act by claiming, "it all lay in the surface of practical anatomy years ago, but no one had the temerity to touch it."

Prendick establishes an uneasy relationship with the humans/animals, demanding they address him as master and obey his commands. Predictably, the creatures revolt and overpower and kill first Moreau and then Montgomery in horrifying fashion. Prendick is left to battle a hyena-swine, but enjoys the loyalty of a Saint Bernard–man who remains by his side.

He observes the "Beast Folk" over the next weeks as they slowly regress, their animal natures taking over. What speech they had learned disappears, and they stop wearing clothes. FEMINIST CRITICS would find interesting the fact that "the pioneers in this, I noticed with some surprise, were all females," and that the narrator labels their acts a "disregard" for "the injunction of decency." Monogamy was disregarded and "the tradition of the Law was clearly losing its force." The Beast People kill Prendick's dog protector, and then he spots a schooner sail. He signals the boat on which he sees two men facing one another, but it drifts aimlessly, eventually coming to shore and revealing that the men are dead. He climbs in and pushes from shore, observed by wolf-beasts and "the horrible nondescript of bear and bull." Upon returning to London he becomes a recluse, as men begin to remind him of the Beast People.

Wells succeeds in suggesting that man's animalistic nature can prove detrimental to culture, but his prose somewhat sacrifices subtlety to sensationalism, partially due to its format as an emotional first-person account. He clearly emphasizes the fact that scientific developments do not always promote progress and that an ungoverned pursuit of scientific power may lead to the ultimate sacrifice, as it did for Moreau. The novel caught the public's imagination and was converted to film three times, in 1933, 1977, and 1996. In reviewing the 1996 version, critics claimed it translated well to that time period, with the Prendick character a plane crash survivor and Dr. Moreau a Nobel Prize in medicine winner. The addition of a romantic plot between Prendick and Moreau's daughter offended some purists, but technology makes the premise of the animal conversion more plausible, and special effects blend men and beasts more satisfactorily than had previous versions.

BIBLIOGRAPHY

Barclay, Dolores. "Brando's Dr. Moreau Portrayal a Mockery." *Jam Movies Review.* Available online. URL: http//www. canoe.ca/JamMoviesReviewsI/drmoreau_ap.html. Downloaded on September 1, 2004.

Gill, Stephen. *Scientific Romances of H.G. Wells: A Critical Study.* Cornwall, Ontario: Vesta, 1975.

Lightman, Alan. Introduction to *The Island of Dr. Moreau,* by H. G. Wells. New York: Bantam Books, 1994, vii–xiv.

IT IS NEVER TOO LATE TO MEND: A MATTER OF FACT ROMANCE CHARLES READE (1856)

Already known as a writer with a social conscience, Charles READE published *It Is Never Too Late to Mend* specifically to stimulate public interest in social revolution. He proved successful, spurring his reading public to lead a movement to reform the prison system. Like THESIS NOVELS of the previous decade, *It Is Never Too Late to Mend* showed readers the disaster that existed within their society, as well as the fact that they had the power to salvage corrupt systems. Spurred to investigate published findings regarding the cruel treatment by prisoners at the hands of the governor of Birmingham jail, Reade studied facts about the Durham, Oxford, and Reading jails, incorporating his findings into this first novel. The setting in part reflects the English prison in New South Wales, characterizing the Australian colony's attempt to rebuff the effects of early convict settlers.

The novel focuses on two stories. One incorporates the news regarding the Australian colony's gold-rush fever in 1851, describing the dangers of the miner's life. The details Reade supplies regarding the camp caused critics to first recognize him as a powerful realistic and dramatic novelist. Reade's narrative first points out the seeming incongruity in an earl's son, the Honorable Frank Winchester, leaving England to seek his fortune in a distant colony. Despite his title, however, Frank is without fortune or prospects, and loves a woman he cannot formally court until he procures that fortune. In the opening scene, he tries to convince George Fielding, a farmer who had saved Winchester's life, to accompany him to become a bailiff or agricultural manager. George is also in love with a woman beyond his reach, his cousin, Susan Merton, a woman who had "a host of lovers." Conflict arises as George's brother, William, quietly loves Susan as well, but the two farmer brothers lack cash. When they approach their uncle, called old Merton, for a loan, he disapproves of their lack of resources and declares that Susan will not marry a penniless man. Reade also introduces John Meadows, a man with "a cool head, and iron will," and "an eye never diverted from [. . .] wealth and money." Meadows is missing some money, part of which is recovered by a merchant who accepted it from a Mr. Robinson, a stranger from California who the authorities look to arrest. He has "pestered" George to travel to California to make his fortune in gold there. In addition, "an oriental Jew" named Isaac Levi requests that Meadows not turn him out of his home. When an argument arises and Meadows prepares to strike Levi with his whip, Fielding blocks the blow, reflecting the contrast between his and Meadows's personalities.

A short time later, the Fieldings learn that a lien has been placed on their farm; they do not realize Meadows has pushed the lien. At that moment, a letter arrives for George from Frank Winchester, advising George he has booked two berths to Australia. When George accepts the offer to travel with Frank, Susan blames her father for driving him away. As George leaves to pack his belongings, the police arrive to arrest Robinson, who, the onlookers learn, has several aliases. When told he will be shipped to Australia, Robinson makes light of the sentence, saying, "I would rather have gone to California; but any place is better than England." However, Robinson will remain in England to serve his torturous sentence, while George attempts to survive his miner's camp. Meadows celebrates George's imminent departure, hoping to convince Susan to marry him. When the narrator explains, "a respectable man can do a deal of mischief; more than a rogue could," the reader understands more than one type of criminal exists within this plot.

The plot then branches into two tales, one focusing on the prison, and the other on the camp. Horrors revealed at the hand of Governor Hawes at the English prison include prisoner torture through starvation; their being tied to various machinery they were required to operate upon ridiculous demands; the use

of "the jacket," described as a crucifixion without nails, using a constricting collar instead—all in the name of turning the prisoners into honorable citizens. While their suffering is somewhat relieved through the attentions of a chaplain named Evans, Robinson and the others seem doomed to die. When Evans requests a copy of the prison rules from Hawes, Hawes determines to rid the prison of the effects of the chaplain.

A reformer aptly named Mr. Francis Edens, known to Susan through the school where she teaches, tries to discover evidence against Hawes, even urging the inmates to publish a paper telling their stories. Susan participates in attempts to reveal to the public the deplorable prison conditions. Reade makes these clear, including calls to the reader such as "Imagine yourself cramped in a vice, no part of you movable a hair's breadth, except your hair and your eyelids. Imagine a fierce cramp growing and growing, and rising like a tide of agony higher and higher above nature's endurance, and you will cease to wonder that a man always sunk under Hawes's man-press." Deaths in the prison bring the dismissal of Hawes, and Robinson's story figures prominently. While that relation could have served as a novel of its own, Reade returns to George's departure, starting a new plotline that incorporates many of the already-known characters. It will allow George to fulfill his predictable role as a romantic hero and Robinson to become a more nontraditional type of hero.

George's story begins with Chapter 36, as he joins Winchester for the journey, sunk in misery over leaving Susan. George works for Winchester for several months, then leaves to find his own fortune; Winchester basically disappears from the tale at this point. Within a year, George doubles his investment in his sheep farm and learns that he must be patient. However, disaster strikes, and he loses the herd slowly to disease, constantly regretting having left Susan. George then falls ill, nursed for a time by his hired man, Jacky, whom he sends away when he suspects he will die. In a switch to England, readers observe Mr. Edens helping to operate the prison from which Robinson will soon depart to travel to exile in Australia. Edens urges Robinson to find George on his farm as soon as possible. After several harrowing experiences, Robinson realizes that he needs the company of a good man to help him "walk straight." He retrieves a letter to George written by Susan, and sets out to find George. He discovers the cabin where George lies ill and nurses him back to health.

George finds a five-pound note meant for Robinson in Susan's letter and presents it to him. It is meant for Thomas Sinclair, one of Robinson's alternative identities. Robinson is puzzled that someone knows his real name. He and George travel to a mining camp to attempt earning their fortune, earning deadly enemies as well, accompanied by George's devoted dog, Carlo. When Carlo is shot by one of the competing miners and dies, Robinson urges George to go back home, saying, "Gold can't pay for what we go through in this hellish place." George is determined to remain until he earns an additional £500 and can return to Susan.

Robinson decides to set traps for the men who killed Carlo, assuming they will also want to kill George and himself. He catches Black Will, who manages to untangle himself and almost kills George and Robinson, but they are saved by a patrol. Levi rejoins the characters, having sailed to Australia, where he operates a gold-dust-weighing facility, and Robinson, in an ironic turn, becomes a judge for the mining group. Robinson and George engage in a frightening hunt for Black Will and the evil Crawley, actually employed by Meadows to murder George. They discover the gold that had long eluded them, prompting George to kiss a large nugget and say, "Oh, you beauty! . . . not because you are gold, but because you take me to Susan." Robinson tempers his joy, reminding him they must act carefully and keep their secret, as "the very honest ones would turn villains at sight of it. It is the wonder of the world." The two return to England with an enormous fortune, but Meadows constructs a lie, telling Susan that George made his fortune and has already married. She falls ill, but recovers, although deeply hurt by George's perceived betrayal. George appears to rescue Susan from marriage to Meadows, and virtue proves worthy of reward.

At a time when fiction was taken seriously, Reade's work was enough to move popular sentiment toward prison reform, while also providing them a satisfying romance. In George they had their traditional romance

hero, while Robinson's heroism lies in his admission of weakness and the necessity of the company of decent men to keep himself decent. The book remains readily available in both hard and electronic print.

BIBLIOGRAPHY

Phillips, Walter Clark. *Dickens, Reade, and Collins: Sensation Novelists: a Study in the Conditions and Theories of Novel Writing in Victorian England.* New York: Russell & Russell, 1962.

IVANHOE SIR WALTER SCOTT (1819)   Sir Walter SCOTT's most popular novel, *Ivanhoe,* takes place during the 12th-century reign of Richard I. While historians took him to task for incorrectly extending the Saxon-Norman conflict into that century, the public enthusiastically received his tale of knights, displaced inheritance, what was later labeled anti-Semitism, deeds of derring-do and medieval jousts, romance, and the triumph of good over evil.

Scott begins his novel with a well-used premise as readers learn that Wilfred of Ivanhoe, heir apparent to the estate of his father, Cedric, has invoked Cedric's disapproval by expressing his love for his father's ward, Rowena, a descendant of King Alfred. Cedric's displeasure in the desired union of his son and ward is due to his plans that Rowena marry Athelstane of Conningsburgh, also a descendant of Saxon royalty, and has resulted in Ivanhoe's banishment. Ivanhoe has served with King Richard in the Crusades, but while Richard has been out of the country, his brother, John, attempts to usurp his position as monarch, gathering the Norman barons as his support. Ivanhoe has returned to England in disguise and begins the book as a mysterious pilgrim who practices good deeds. He joins a Jewish traveler named Isaac and his daughter Rebecca, along with the Norman knight, Brian de Bois-Guilbert, in his own home. Cedric has unwillingly offered shelter to Bois-Guilbert, as the rules of chivalry and hospitality demand. Ivanhoe overhears Bois-Guilbert planning to ambush the wealthy Isaac, and he warns Isaac and Rebecca to depart the castle early, which they do.

John has celebrated his brother's capture by Leopold of Austria, but, unbeknownst to John, Richard escapes and arrives in England in disguise as a black knight called the Black Sluggard, just in time to aid Ivanhoe during sporting games in the defeat of John's knights, including the dastardly Templar, Bois-Guilbert. As victor, Ivanhoe must remove his helmet to accept the prize, awarded by Rowena, and she recognizes him just before he faints due to blood loss. Isaac and Rebecca decide to travel with Ivanhoe to nurse his wounds, and they join Cedric's entourage, Ivanhoe's father remaining unaware of his presence in England.

Bois-Guilbert has designs on the lovely Rebecca and kidnaps her, Isaac, Rowena, and the wounded Ivanhoe, spiriting them away to imprison them in his castle. All except Rebecca, who has fallen in love with Ivanhoe, are eventually liberated by the Black Sluggard, now revealed as Richard the Lion-Hearted, his Saxon force, and Locksley, better known by the locals as Robin Hood. Bois-Guilbert moves Rebecca to a high tower, where she vows to stand by her religious creed to the death, spurning the knight's insistence that she convert to Christianity and marry him. He must check his desires when the Grand Master of the Order arrives. Accused of witchcraft, Rebecca chooses Ivanhoe as her champion to fight Bois-Guilbert, who has been forced into accusing Rebecca. During the battle, Bois-Guilbert mysteriously falls dead on the field, supposedly due to the conflict between his romantic feelings and his loyalty to his political cause. Richard arrives to replace the Templar flag with his own royal standard, to which Robin Hood pledges allegiance. Rebecca observes Ivanhoe's love for Rowena and decides to depart England for Spain with her father, hoping for a better reception than that received in England. Athelstane agrees to drop his claim of Rowena, and Cedric recognizes his son as a great knight, agreeing to Ivanhoe's union with Rowena.

Critics have noted that the two symbols of England's rule, Richard and John, along with their supporters, Ivanhoe and Bois-Guilbert, represent nobility and debasement. The nobility derives from a love of God and loyalty to Saxon ideals, while the debasement grows from greed and a desire for self-aggrandizement. Scott indulged his love of medieval times in forming his tale, although he made known his hatred for the violence inherent to jousts and other forms of knight-testing games. He makes clear his negative attitude by having John and Bois-Guilbert begin each armed conflict, forcing Richard and Ivanhoe into combat.

Feminist critics find of interest the contrasts between Rowena and Rebecca. Rowena exhibits many stereotypes assigned to women not only during medieval times but also during Scott's own era. Their fragility, their positions as objects of desire to be won or purchased, and their requisite stunning physical appearance are a few of those well-worn ideas. Rowena allows Scott to emphasize a common thought during medieval and Renaissance times, that the noble nature of an aristocratic female might inspire ennobled behavior among men. Interestingly, however, Rebecca becomes the female protagonist in the view of many readers. In a mock trial for her supposed sins through witchcraft, she refuses to unveil her face before strangers, defending her modesty and her faith. Eventually she must drop the veil, in order to prevent the touch of strangers, and she delivers an accusatory invective, unusual for women normally forced to remain silent. She scathingly maintains her innocence and correctly predicts that God will send a champion to stand for her honor. She also makes the heroic choice to leave England and sacrifice herself for Ivanhoe's happiness.

BIBLIOGRAPHY

Duncan, Ian. *Modern Romance and Transformations of the Novel: The Gothic, Scott and Dickens.* Boston: Cambridge University Press, 1992.

J

JAMES, GEORGE PAYNE RAINSFORD
(1799–1860) George James established his reputation as a prolific writer with over 100 HISTORICAL FICTION novels to his credit. He learned Sir Walter SCOTT's approach to such fiction early on, reducing it to a formula that marked his work as ordinary. His grandfather had made a fortune from his medical practice and moved in circles that included Dr. Samuel JOHNSON and Oliver GOLDSMITH; his connections allowed the young James to meet George Gordon, Lord Byron. A man of leisure, James had few financial demands on his energies. His years of experience as a British consul in both Europe and the United States supported his interest in the political history of England and the Continent. Well-known novels, marked by foreign settings, included his first, *Richlieu* (1829), supposedly encouraged for publication by Scott, and *Darnley* and *De L'Orme* (1830), *Philip Augustus* (1831), *Henry Masterton* (1832), *Mary of Burgundy* (1833), *The Man-at-Arms* (1840), *Arabella Stuart* (1844), and *The Man in Black* (1860). He published two to three stereotyped novels per year, competing with his rival in historical fiction, William Harrison AINSWORTH, who favored English settings. He also produced nonfiction, including *Memoirs of Great Commanders* (1832) and *Life of the Black Prince* (1836). For all his writing, he was later probably best known as one of the authors parodied by William Makepeace THACKERAY in *PUNCH'S PRIZE NOVELISTS*, a work that helped that far more important author hone his critical style.

BIBLIOGRAPHY

Ellis, Stuart Marsh. *The Solitary Horseman: The Life and Adventures of G.P.R. James*. London: Kensington, 1927.

JAMES, HENRY (1843–1916)
Although born in New York City in 1843, Henry James spent much of his life in England, where he wrote in the English tradition. A member of an erudite family in which everyone held an innate curiosity regarding human behavior, during his childhood James was exposed to multiple influences on his later writing. His brother William became the most famous American psychologist ever, founding the American Center for Psychic Research, while his sister, Alice James, published her diaries. James recognized early on the close relationship between fiction and psychology, insisting in some of his famous essays that a writer must focus on the inner workings of his or her characters and not inflict their own interpretations into their books. The characters must be left free to behave in the way their personalities dictate.

James enjoyed a private-tutor education, not entering school until age 12, when his family enrolled him in a series of European schools, including institutions in Boulogne, Paris, Geneva, and Bonn. His familiarity with French literature, and his experiences beyond his own confines, allowed him later to avoid the provinciality in much of English writing. While other authors also had foreign experiences, most reproduced them in fiction encumbered with a distinctly English point of view. When the Jameses returned to the United States, he enrolled at Newport, Rhode Island, entered Harvard Law School in 1862, but left school after a year. Encouraged by individuals including American novelist, journalist, and critic William Dean Howells, James withdrew from classes to concentrate on writing and publishing.

Over the next few years, James's criticism and essays appeared in *The North American Review* and *The Atlantic Monthly*. He published a farce titled *Pyramus and Thisbe* in 1869, the year of his first lengthy visit while an adult to Europe. A novel titled *Watch and Ward* followed in 1871, appearing in serial form in *The Atlantic Monthly;* it would not be published in book form until 1878. During his next visit to Europe in 1872, traveling with his sister Alice and his Aunt Kate, he remained for two years, basing his works *A Passionate Pilgrim and Other Tales* and *Transatlantic Sketches,* both published in 1875, on those experiences. Preferring Italy to France, he settled in Rome, enjoying the company of a group of Americans there, and began work on a novel. James struggled over the next two years as to whether to return to the United States, as his brother William urged him to do, telling James that he believed the quality of his writing would be much higher at home. James spent a few months at home, then realized his mistake in returning from Europe in 1874, sailing for Boston from Italy along with the great American writer and politician Oliver Wendell Holmes.

At age 32, James wrote that "the best thing I could imagine" was "to take up residence in Paris." His opportunity arose a few months later, and in 1875 James lived in Paris, spending time with famous authors such as Turgenev, Daudet, Flaubert, and Zola. That exposure helped convince him that fiction could be shaped into serious art. This continental idea clashed with that of the majority of English writers, who continued to view fiction simply as entertainment. His voice joined that of a minority, including Walter Pater, who believed in "art for art's sake." Pater's doctrine complemented James's ideas well, and James set out to design fiction that offered its readers beauty and pleasure with little accompanying moral dicta.

The following year James began a 20-year residence in London, publishing the novel he had begun while in Rome, *Roderick Hudson* (1876), followed by two of his soon-to-become famous works, *The AMERICAN* (1877) and *The EUROPEANS* (1878). He continued his critical work with the essay "French Poets and Novelists" (1878) and published the novella *DAISY MILLER* in 1879, which introduced a prototype in its protagonist of later female characters, most notably Isabel Archer in *The PORTRAIT OF A LADY* (1881). He continued his insistence that authors not project their own views into fiction, an approach still practiced by some writers who continued to believe in didacticism and authorial intervention. In 1879, James also wrote for the English Men of Letters Series on American author Nathaniel Hawthorne; a brief novel, *An International Episode;* and a story collection titled *The Madonna of the Future and Other Tales.* An additional two novels, *Confidence* and *WASHINGTON SQUARE,* were published in 1880. His visit that same year to Florence inspired the main setting for *Lady,* while an 1882 visit to France inspired the 1884 publication of *A Little Tour in France.*

Continuing an amazingly prolific career, James published additional short stories as *The Siege of London* and another travel book, *Portraits of Places,* in 1883. The following year he published his celebrated essay "The Art of Fiction," a work that would be studied in the classroom into the 21st century. He stated in his essay, "The air of reality (solidity of specification) seems to me to be the supreme virtue of a novel." Not everyone agreed. James's contemporary Robert Louis STEVENSON challenged that idea in "A Humble Remonstrance," writing that art does not "compete with life," but rather it allows man to "half-shut his eyes against the dazzle and confusion of reality." James would soon prove the world of fiction could accommodate both of those views. However, his own theory would guide the fiction produced in the 20th century. James believed in the writer's "power to guess the unseen from the seen, to trace the implication of things, to judge the whole piece by the pattern."

In short order, James produced *The Bostonians* (1886); *The Princess Casamassima* (1886), judged by critics to be his best example of judging "the whole piece by the pattern"; *The Reverberator* (1888); *The Aspern Papers* (1888); and *The Tragic Muse* (1890); as well as an essay collection, *Parial Portraits* (1888). In the early 1890s, he produced drama, including a dramatic version of *The American,* and published additional short story collections. One play, *Guy Domville,* opened in London but quickly closed following negative critical reviews. More short story collections appeared in the late 1890s, as well as novels including *The Spoils of Poynton* (1897), WHAT MAISIE KNEW (1897), and *In the Cage* (1898). He moved in the best of literary circles that included a who's who of contemporary authors, such as Joseph CONRAD, Stephen Crane, H.G. WELLS, George GISSING, Ford Madox Ford, William Dean Howells, Oliver Wendell Holmes, and Sarah Orne Jewett. He continued to produce exemplary work at an incredible pace, publishing *The TURN OF THE SCREW,* one of the most famous horror stories, first in *Collier's Weekly* as a serial in 1898, and *The Awkward Age* in 1899. Of the story, critic F. W. Dupee notes it is "notoriously a tale of which it is hard to say whether the pathological or the supernatural predominates in it."

During the first years of the new century, James published much additional work, some of it reflecting on struggles of the artist. In contrast to his earlier works, where America's lack of culture proves the challenge, in his later works it is often the universal public that presents challenges to an artist's development. His collection of short stories, *The Soft Side* (1900), included the story "The Coxon Fund," based on the life of English poet, Samuel Taylor Coleridge. Published work included the novel *The Sacred Fount* (1901), as well as his last more famous novels, *The Wings of the Dove* (1902), *The Ambassadors* (1903), and *The Golden Bowl* (1904), demonstrating the height of his power to produce psychologically complex, sophisticated fiction. Critics see *The Ambassadors* as beginning his final writing period, in which he returned to his earlier international theme, the particular plot having grown from a visit by his friend Howells to his son in Paris, who was enrolled in the École des Beaux Arts. James observed that Howells seemed to rebel against the passing of time and his lack of worldly experience, admonishing James, "It doesn't matter what you do—but live."

James's philosophy of writing touched many of his contemporaries, including Joseph Conrad and E. M. Forster. In his later novels, James focused on the reactions of a sole individual to everyday experience, a model later adopted by Irish author James Joyce, whose use of the stream-of-consciousness approach owes much to James's theory. James published his celebrated short story "The Beast in the Jungle" in another collection, *The Better Sort* (1903). In 1903, he also began a devoted friendship with American author Edith Wharton and, in 1904, at last returned to the United States following a 20-year absence. He enjoyed lecturing and meeting President Theodore Roosevelt.

Between 1907 and 1909 James worked on revisions of his novels and wrote 18 new prefaces for their release as the "New York Edition." A work based on his experience in America, *The American Scene,* appeared in 1907, the year he also visited Italy and then France for several months. His account of those travels appeared in *Italian Hours* (1909), and in 1910, back in America, he released another collection of short stories titled *The Finer Grain,* followed in 1911 by his final novel, *The Outcry.* He moved back to England after receiving an honorary degree from Harvard, where he also received an honorary degree from Oxford in 1912. Before his death, James published two volumes of autobiography, *A Small Boy and Others* (1913) and *Notes of a Son and Brother* (1914), and *Notes on a Novel* (1914). A third volume of autobiography appeared after his death, *The Middle Years* (1917). When World War I broke out, he served as chairman of the American Volunteer Motor Ambulance Corps and at last became a British citizen in 1915, a year in which he would suffer two strokes. Still a force in English fiction, James influenced H. G. Wells to attempt what no other author would, incorporating the confusion of the war into fiction, producing a burlesque of Jamesian psychological subtleties that attacked English detachment titled *Boon.* Wells's reaction against James made famous his portrayals of individuals whose own actions seem to have no effect on their own lives; rather, they are completely controlled by outside forces. On New Year's Day 1916, King George V presented Henry James with the Order of Merit. At his death in February, he was still at work on two novels, *The Ivory Tower* and *The Sense of the Past.*

Henry James's contribution to all of fiction cannot be overestimated. His advocacy of psychological realism introduced a new brand of fiction that would later dominate high literature. His thousands of essay pages contain carefully theorized critical ideas that continue to guide readers and writers in their approach to fiction. His passionate theory held that a writer's most important action, according to Greg W. Zacharias, Center for Henry James Studies at Creighton University, was "engaging issues of representation, rather than solving them." He accepted contradictions in life as part of its psychological richness: "Grappling with aspects of his subject rather than resolving its (his) contradictions, moves James to think, to write, to live."

BIBLIOGRAPHY

Bell, Milicent. *Meaning in Henry James.* Cambridge: Harvard University Press, 1991.

Chen, Shudong. *Henry James: The Essayist Behind the Novelist.* Studies in American Literature. Vol 59. Lewist, N.Y.: Edwin Mellens, 2003.

Daugherty, Sarah B. *The Literary Criticism of Henry James.* Ohio University Press, 1981.

Dupee, F. W. *Henry James.* New York: William Morrow & Company, 1974.

Edel, Leon. *Henry James: A Life.* New York: Harper, 1977.

Gard, Roger. Introduction. *Henry James: The Critical Muse: Selected Library Criticism.* London: Penguin, 1987.

Graham, Kenneth. *Henry James: A Literary Life.* New York: St. Martin's Press, 1995.

Kaplan, Fred. *Henry James: The Imagination of Genius.* Baltimore: Johns Hopkins University Press, 1999.

Page, Norman, ed. *Henry James: Interviews and Recollections.* New York: St. Martin's Press, 1984.

Veeder, William. *Henry James: The Lessons of the Master: Popular Fiction and Personal Style in the Nineteenth Century.* Chicago: University of Chicago Press, 1975.

JANE EYRE CHARLOTTE BRONTË (1847)

Charlotte BRONTË's *Jane Eyre* is the story of the protagonist's QUEST, not for material treasure, but rather for equality and selfhood. Equally important, Jane seeks the proper manner to rebel against men who seek to dominate and control her, eventually appropriating power by means of her creative spirit and her artistic passion. A BILDUNGSROMAN, the novel contains several autobiographical aspects, most specifically the attendance by Jane at a girls' school where abuse of the students leads to rampant disease and death; a similar situation killed two of Brontë's sisters. Brontë also worked for a time as a governess, one of the few acceptable wage-earning positions for a young, single woman in her era. Like Jane, Brontë discovered the loneliness of that position. Although the family viewed her as a servant, other household servants often shunned the governess, considering her a snob, due to her education. Brontë makes a statement against such social mistreatment through her focus on Jane. She also appalled many readers with her focus on female passion, inspired by art, at a time when such emotions were considered improper in a woman character.

GOTHIC and classic ROMANCE elements appear throughout the novel in the form of symbolic colors; names, evident in naming the plain and unattractive heroine Jane; characters, including the mysterious and brooding Mr. Rochester; and frightening, threatening, suspenseful events and settings. The orphan Jane begins her journey at Gateshead, household of her judgmental aunt, Mrs. Reed, and her hateful, bullying cousins. In Gothic tradition, while imprisoned in Gateshead's "red room" as punishment, the 10-year-old Jane becomes terrified when she senses the presence of her deceased Uncle Reed's ghost. Jane's reaction to this fiery "red room" while "imprisoned" there foreshadows the importance of fire later in the novel.

Aunt Reed sends Jane to Lowood Asylum, a charitable school, based on Cowan Bridge School, which Brontë and her sisters attended. Students at Lowood suffer harsh treatment under the control of schoolmaster Mr. Brocklehurst, who is described as a "black pillar," symbolizing the deadly conditions at Lowood School, where girls are "starved and frozen" and where there is "neither food nor warmth." Jane also meets Miss Temple, whose name symbolizes the Victorian ideal and who serves as a sanctuary for Jane. Jane's friend Helen possesses a surname, Burns, that metaphorically suggests fire or flame. She dies from fever's fire and also "burns" with a spiritual passion and with anger evident in her comments to Jane—"by dying young I shall escape great sufferings," and

"Where is God? What is God?"—as she is dying. Helen, a martyr, creates a conflict for Jane between her Christian faith and the laws of nature—a conflict Jane carries into adulthood. In time, conditions at Lowood improve; Jane excels as a student and eventually becomes a teacher for the school. While at Gateshead and at Lowood, Jane considers whether she will ever live happily.

From Lowood Jane goes to Thornfield to become a governess. The Gothic mansion contains secrets, strange noises, dark passages, and mysteries, and as the name suggests, Thornfield ensnares its inhabitants. Jane's first encounter with her master features Gothic influences; Mr. Rochester must lean on her for support to walk, because he has fallen from his horse, who slipped on ice, foreshadowing danger and his dependence on her at the novel's conclusion. At Thornfield Jane meets Grace Poole and attempts to understand what some feminist critics call the "dark pool" of the woman's behavior. The elusive Poole only spends "1 hour in 24 with fellow servants below." The remainder of the time, the ironically named Grace, whose drinking problem frequently causes calamity, remains out of sight in a mysterious upper room at Thornfield, supposedly sewing. Grace Poole presents a great enigma for Jane, who tries to understand the woman's relationship with Mr. Rochester. Brontë portrays Mr. Rochester as a BYRONIC HERO with his questionable past, suggested by Jane's charge, little Adele, and his commanding and gruff outward presence. Not until Jane stands at the altar to marry Mr. Rochester does she discover that he is married to a madwoman "entrapped" in the attic of Thornfield. Prior to the planned wedding, Brontë employs the Gothic image of lightning striking a large tree, splitting it in half to foreshadow the tragic events that follow, including the foiled wedding, Jane's flight from Thornfield and Mr. Rochester, and the impending catastrophe at Thornfield.

Jane wanders on the road from Thornfield to Marsh End. There the Rivers family takes her in, their surname suggesting a cleansing or a new birth. While with them, Jane does become more independent and confident. Jane discovers, in a recognizable romantic coincidence, her relation to the Rivers family. Jane is tormented by the cold St. John Rivers, whose total devotion to Christianity, symbolized by his given name, remains his only passion. He proposes a marriage of convenience to Jane. In the midst of suffering conflict between her love for Rochester and the proposal of St. John, Jane senses a telepathic communication from Rochester. His spiritual call for her to return represents another element common in romance novels.

While St. John represents the icy side of Jane's nature, Rochester represents the fiery side. She chooses to follow the fire in her heart, and upon her return to Thornfield, Brontë offers the culminating Gothic element with the fire, set by Rochester's mad wife, Bertha. In the fire Bertha falls to her death, Rochester is left maimed in his attempts to save her, and Thornfield is destroyed. In line with Victorian beliefs, he pays for his past sins and is offered a second chance at life with Jane. The fire that purifies Rochester appears in other Gothic novels, particularly in Daphne du Maurier's *Rebecca* (1938), where a fire destroys the presence of the previous wife of the novel's Byronic hero and purifies him of his past. The cleansing power of the fire provides the means of a new beginning for the romantic couple in that novel, as it does in *Jane Eyre*.

Brontë's novel proved seminal, as it introduced characters new to English fiction. Jane, a shy yet strong-willed orphan, never, either in her unhappy days at Lowood or in her career as a governess, displays the superficial beauty and charm common to typical Victorian heroines. She is instead intelligent and creative and seeks solace throughout her life from her reading material and painting. Brontë's inclusion of Jane's readings reveal her intellect and the development of her character's thoughts and insights concerning history. References include Oliver GOLDSMITH's 18th-century historical work *History of Rome,* Samuel RICHARDSON's romance *PAMELA* (1740), and Jonathan SWIFT's *GULLIVER'S TRAVELS* (1726), as well as the popular *Arabian Nights;* the latter two works suggest mystical elements.

At the novel's conclusion, Rochester at last views Jane as his equal and once again leans on her for support, literally as well as figuratively, as foreshadowed by their first encounter. Those visiting the British Library may see in the rare books room the manuscript opened to the page on which Rochester proposes marriage.

Throughout the novel, Jane displays extraordinarily self-assertive acts, not characteristic of Victorian women. She was a woman of passion at a time when women were considered passionless. *Jane Eyre* was popular when it was originally published, and it remains widely read, both for enjoyment and for study by FEMINIST and PSYCHOANALYTIC CRITICS. It remains readily available in print and electronic form and has been converted to film and stage multiple times.

BIBLIOGRAPHY

Benet's Reader's Encyclopedia, Third Ed. Katherine Baker Siep-
    mann, ed. New York: Harper Perennial, 1987
The Bloomsbury Guide to English Literature. 2nd Edited by
    Marion Wynne-Davies. London: Bloomsbury, 1995.
Brontë, Charlotte. *Jane Eyre. Case Studies in Contemporary
    Criticism.* Edited by Beth Newman. New York: Bedford
    Books, 1996.
Green, Sally. "Apocalypse When? Shirley's Vision and Politics
    of Reading." *Studies in the Novel* 26, no. 4 (1994): 350–372.
    Academic Search File. Ebsco Host. East Central University
    Lib., Ada, Oklahoma. Downloaded on April 23, 2002.
Lawson, Kate. "Madness and Grace: Grace Poole's Name and
    Her Role in *Jane Eyre.*" *English Language Notes* 30, no. 1
    (1992): 46–51.
Moers, Ellen. *Literary Women: The Great Writers.* New York:
    Doubleday, 1976.

JEFFERIES, (JOHN) RICHARD (1848–1887)

Born at Coate Farm, Liddington, in 1848, Richard Jefferies was a journalist and novelist, gaining a reputation for knowledge of farm life. His approach to detailing country life resulted in an honest and affectionate rendition reflecting his own experience. He began writing for *The North Wiltshire Herald* in 1864, and in 1873, for *Reporting, Editing and Authorship.* His articles about nature gained attention following publication in *The Pall Mall Gazette,* and Jefferies received attention for a letter published in the *Times* championing the Wiltshire agricultural laborer. He married in 1874 and began work on novels, most of which failed due to heightened melodrama. Critics noted a lack of realistic details of aristocratic life in *The Scarlet Shawl* (1874), *Restless Human Hearts* (1875), and *The World's End* (1877). Jefferies hit his artistic stride in the autobiographical *BEVIS, THE STORY OF A BOY* (1882), *Amaryllis at the Fair* (1887), and an autobiography, *The Story of My Heart* (1883). He gained more exposure through nonfiction than fiction, with essayistic works such as *The Gamekeeper at Home* (1880), *Greene Ferne Farm* (1880), and *The Open Air* (1885). Each elevated outdoor writing to an art form through minute detail. While somewhat cynical, Jefferies produced prose that city dwellers found pleasantly naive and romantic. Toward the end of his life, as he suffered from tuberculosis, Jefferies published another novel, titled *After London* (1885), a disaster scheme with a stronger tone than previous works. When Jefferies died, a monument was erected in Salisbury Cathedral and a bust placed in Taunton Shire Hall to honor his memory.

BIBLIOGRAPHY

Taylor, Brian. *Richard Jefferies.* Boston: Twayne Publishers,
    1982.

JEWSBURY, GERALDINE ENDSOR (1812–1820)

Born in Derbyshire to a cotton merchant, Geraldine Jewsbury lost her mother when she was six years old. Raised by her Aunt Maria, she hoped to write as a journalist, but poor health confined her at home. She eventually became a professional writer, writing in the 1840s for *Shilling Magazine* and contributing reviews to *Athenaeum.* She published several novels that were well received in her own time but mostly ignored in later generations. *ZOE: THE HISTORY OF TWO LIVES* (1845), probably her best-known work, was followed by a visit to Paris and the publishing of *The Half-Sisters* (1848). An "industrial novel," *Marian Withers* appeared in 1851, first serialized in the *Manchester Examiner and Times. Constance Herbert* (1855), *The Sorrows of Gentility* (1856), and *Right or Wrong* (1859) followed, all of which focused on the "woman question," or woman's proper place in society. She also acted as a reader for the House of Bentley publishers.

Jewsbury's friendship with the great English essayist Thomas Carlyle and his wife, Jane, initiated a flood of correspondence, and she dedicated *Constance Herbert* to Carlyle. Unfortunately, most of the letters were destroyed, but those that do exist allow insight not only into Jewsbury's life, but also into that of the professional woman writer of the mid-19th century. As cited by feminist critic Elaine Showalter, Jewsbury once lamented to Jane Carlyle that when women gain their own writing reputations, they must live in the world as businessmen, causing them to "use" people. While she regretted that fact, she also understood that inexperienced women suddenly exposed to the real world must quickly learn to survive. In another letter, she referred to herself and other women writers as "indications of a development of womanhood which is not yet recognized," one that had tried society's rules, which could not block them from reaching their goals. Women who followed would be better able to reach full stature. She also expressed sympathy for female writers' husbands, referring at one point to contemporary writer Elizabeth GASKELL's husband as "Mr. Mary Barton," after Gaskell's well-known novel MARY BARTON, and mentioning the attitude of some that "authoresses" should never marry. She even placed dialogue in her characters' mouths voicing her concerns. In The Half Sisters, one character expresses dismay over the loss of a woman's "bloom and charm of her innocence" when she begins to work "out of her own sphere," where that work is deemed of little value, and the woman seen as "dogmatic" and "harsh." She admitted to the paradox of holding her own deep-seated prejudice against women's novels, which caused her to publish her first anonymously. Showalter notes Jewsbury was all that the Victorian imagination believed of that era's female authors—nontraditional, passionate about her work, keenly focused, and fearless in the face of opportunity.

BIBLIOGRAPHY

Showalter, Elaine. A Literature of Their Own: Women Novelists from Brontë to Lessing. Princeton, N.J.: Princeton University Press, 1999.

JOHN HALIFAX, GENTLEMAN DINAH MULOCK (1856)

Dinah MULOCK (CRAIK) emphasized noncomformist ideals in her popular fifth novel, John Halifax, Gentleman. Noncomformist churches believed that each member should freely respond to the Gospel and take responsibility for their own membership, while the church should maintain its congregation's purity by considering only potential members of strong character. Raised in a family stressing evangelistic piety, Mulock valued hard work as benefiting one's spiritual life. When her protagonist, John Halifax, begins with nothing of material value and manages to work his way up the social chain to wealth and comfort, he realizes the lower-class dream. As some of her contemporaries made light of old-fashioned values of self-respect and hard work as narrow-minded and too materialistic, she vindicated those values, reflecting through her protagonist the strong character that can be built through work.

John Halifax begins the book as a destitute orphan. When Halifax first meets the Quaker family that will rescue him from the streets, Mulock carefully describes him as bedraggled but clean. Simply by looking into his eyes, the tanner of Norton Bury, aptly named Abel Fletcher, can discern the boy's high character. Contrasted to Abel's weak, disabled son and first-person point-of-view narrator Phineas, Halifax is a near-perfect physical specimen. Phineas notes his desire for such a vigorous body but does not become jealous of Halifax. Instead, he declares strong feelings for the boy almost his age, comparing his reaction to Halifax to that of the biblical Jonathan for David, an immediate love and devotion. That reference allows Mulock to stress the importance of a strong character to spiritual matters.

When Halifax is hired by Abel Fletcher to escort Phineas home and carries the helpless boy into his house, he symbolically offers through his physical support the emotional support that the lonely Phineas has long needed. Another character introduced in the first scene is Ursula March, daughter of the wealthy mayor, who can discern Halifax's hunger when she sees him standing with Phineas under an eave to escape the rain. The rain signals a cleansing of the past and a new beginning for all involved. Moved to offer the boy "wheaten" bread, which the narrator notes as a luxury for the poor, who normally consume rye, she leaves the comfort of her house to do so, only to be pulled back inside with a sharp cry by a family servant. That retraction symbolizes the hesitancy Mulock observed in her culture of the middle and upper classes to aid those in need. Halifax picks the bread up off the ground and, rather than ravenously attack it, consumes it thoughtfully and slowly, as if the bread represents more than mere physical nourishment. Phineas learns later from his father that Ursula had an accident with a knife, and had to be sent away from home. Readers understand that her injury occurred following her slicing the bread for Halifax. Mulock later adds a bread riot scene to emphasize the often-dire straights of the poor.

Early on, Halifax requests that Phineas note his mother's death in the family Bible, a blunt reference to his illiteracy, but also a clear recognition of his spiritual values. Only one of many references Mulock uses to emphasize the gulf separating the lower classes from the middle and upper, it emphasizes the importance of education for all children, regardless of social rank, a social leveller. An independent individual possessing great integrity, Halifax goes to work for Fletcher. When Fletcher offers him a position driving a cart carrying the carcasses of dead animals to his tannery, Phineas is appalled, but Halifax willingly accepts, demonstrating that no honest work should be rejected, regardless of its nature. Perhaps because Mulock understood that readers might feel Halifax's high character to be inflated, she adds a narrative comment from Phineas: "Perhaps I may be supposed imaginative, or, at least, premature in discovering all these characteristics in a boy of fourteen; and possibly in thus writing of him I may unwittingly be drawing a little from after-experience; however, being the truth, let it stand." This allows readers to accept instances in which Halifax rejects the offer of money from Abel Fletcher, commenting, in one instance, "It is quite enough reward that I have been useful to my master, and that he acknowledges it." When Fletcher thoughtfully agrees with him, signaling he has become the pupil and Halifax the teacher, readers understand that Halifax's transformation has begun.

Mulock takes care that the station of "gentleman" is understood as one possible to earn. Halifax will be helped along the way by characters such as Mr. Charles, an orator who quotes Shakespeare, and those who help him gain literacy. When Halifax later comments to Phineas, "You have a bad habit of jumping at conclusions," he reveals a new stage in his intellectual development that makes him somewhat superior to his benefactor. He meets up with Ursula March again through the help of Mrs. Tod and deems her fresh, healthy, youthful and pleasant "as a breeze in spring."

Halifax eventually marries Ursula and has fine children, symbolizing his rise in society, but more important, that his fine character reaps emotional as well as material rewards. However, the novel does not end with those circumstances. It incorporates all of the CLASS STRUCTURE conflicts that do not disappear simply due to marriage and work, using as a negative example an aristocrat of questionable character, Ursula's cousin, Lady Caroline Brithwood. She does not learn from her "wickedness" that brings her to divorce and a bedridden dementia, followed by an early death, allowing her to stand as a cautionary tale to her own community and to readers. Ursula and Halifax must also face problems with their eldest son, Guy, in which Phineas sympathetically shares. Guy's separation for years from the family becomes Halifax's greatest burden. The novel concludes with a reunion of the family and Guy as Halifax dies peacefully. Ursula lies beside him in the bed, and is found there dead as well, with the two joined in the predicted heavenly reward awaiting them both.

Interesting to FEMINIST CRITICS will be the feminine characteristics of Phineas Fletcher. Not only is he physically weak, he longs for tenderness in treatment by others, indicating what contemporaries would have considered a weak personality. Due to his semi-useless legs, he also must spend much time in the prone position, as female characters traditionally did, investing his energy in such luxuries as reading; several literature references, from Dick Whittington, hero of adventure books, to the classics, have prominent places in the narration. Feminists also will note that a woman, Caroline Brithwood, provides the strongest target of criticism. FORMALIST critics point out that, while Phineas's voice adds strength and interest as a narrator recalling events with the perspective of 50 years' experience, his character rarely appears in the action of the novel's second half. That weakens the narrative, which supported action that hints of the melodramatic without the strong realistic voice. But Mulock makes her point regarding the value of work. She would continue her reformist approach in her next book, *A Life for a Life*, attacking capital punishment and prison life, as had Charles READE, another prominent member of the movement. *John Halifax, Gentleman,* while little read or studied in later decades, well represents mild DIDACTIC LITERATURE, important to the mid-19th century's reformist movement through literature. It remains readily available in book form.

BIBLIOGRAPHY
Mitchell, Sally. *Dinah Mulock Craik.* Boston: Twayne, 1983.
Showalter, Elaine. "Dinah Mulock Craik and the Tactics of Sentiment: A Case Study in Victorian Female Authorship." *Feminist Studies* 2 (1975): 5–23.

JOHN INGLESANT JOSEPH HENRY SHORTHOUSE (1881)

John Inglesant by J. H. SHORTHOUSE found popularity as a problem novel, the type made famous by George ELIOT in the decline of domestic and SENSATION FICTION. Focusing on the religious and political conflicts of early 17th-century England, it reflected some autobiographical aspects. Shorthouse had undergone religious conflict in his late 20s when he left the Quaker faith to join the Church of England. He printed the book privately in 1880 following 10 years of work, publishing it in 1881 through Macmillan and Company.

The novel recounts the experience of John Inglesant, a young aristocrat during the age of Charles I, trained by the Jesuits. As he remains a loyal royalist, he slowly learns how to forgive. Chosen due to his high passion, Inglesant is trained by the Jesuits to serve the king and is influenced by Nicholas Ferrar's community at an estate near Huntingdon. Called Little Gidding, the group of about 30 adhered to the precepts of the Church of England, practicing good works and a life of prayer. Because the king supports the community, Inglesant decides to devote himself to the king's cause, accepting dangerous assignments in the negotiations to secretly introduce an Irish military faction into England. Although the king must repudiate Inglesant and other supporters, the young man remains dedicated to the royalists, refusing to expose Charles.

In a plot developed in the second portion of the novel, following Charles's execution, Inglesant searches for an Italian who killed his brother. Shorthouse focuses on political intrigue in Rome, as a successor for Pope Innocent X is sought. Through association with Molinos, a Spanish mystic who practiced Quietism,

Inglesant accepts that all human activity pales in comparison to the practice of religious faith. His newfound faith permits him to forgive the murderer he sought, and he refuses to carry out his initial plan.

Prime Minister Gladstone praised the novel, helping it reach immense popularity. A scrupulously researched work, compared with William Makepeace THACKERAY's *The HISTORY OF HENRY ESMOND* (1852) for REALISM and historical accuracy, critics valued the novel due to its focus on spiritualism. It continues to be studied academically, and its ready availability centuries later speaks to its enduring quality.

BIBLIOGRAPHY
Wagner, F. J. *J.H. Shorthouse.* Boston: Twayne Publishers, 1979.

JOHNSON, SAMUEL (1709–1784)

Samuel Johnson, a sickly child whose father was a bookseller, was born in Lichfield. In 1728, he entered Pembroke College, Oxford, and began his literary life with a translation of a collection of religious writings by Alexander Pope (1731). He could not afford to complete his education, and would later be awarded an honorary "Dr." title. Following his father's death in 1731, Johnson taught grammar school to ease his family's debt during 1732, then spent three years in Birmingham, where he published his first essays in the *Birmingham Journal.* His first book, a translation from a French account of a Portuguese missionary, appeared in 1735 under the title *A Voyage to Abyssinia.* That same year he married a widow many years his elder, Mrs. Elizabeth Porter, beginning a lifelong romance. The couple's efforts at starting a school failed, so they moved to London in 1737. One of their students, David Garrick, later to become one of England's most celebrated actors, accompanied the Johnsons.

Johnson at last earned a stable living, contributing an enormous number of pieces to Edward Cave's journal, *The GENTLEMAN'S MAGAZINE.* His famous poem, "London," appeared in 1738, offering commentary on Johnson's favorite themes, social degeneracy, the self-importance of the wealthy, and economic abuses against the poor. Next, he published biographical commentary on Richard Savage, a friend who died in 1744.

A series of such biographies later were published in a volume titled *The Lives of the Poets*. Urged by a publisher named Robert Dodsley to help codify the ever-shifting English language by writing a dictionary, Johnson applied for financial support to Lord Chesterfield in 1747 but received none. He decided to undertake the project anyway and worked on it for eight years. In 1749, he published his longest and most accomplished poem, *The Vanity of Human Wishes,* showcasing subject matter he would consider again a decade later in his only novel, *The History of RASSELAS, PRINCE OF ABYSSINIA* (1759). Also in 1749, Garrick staged Johnson's forgettable play *Irene.* While not his most accomplished work, *Irene* earned £300 for Johnson, who always needed funds.

In 1750 Johnson began publication of *The Rambler,* a twice-weekly periodical that he almost single-handedly wrote. His *A DICTIONARY OF THE ENGLISH LANGUAGE,* a momentous and vitally important work, at last was published in 1755. When Chesterfield stepped forward to "support" the project, Johnson blasted him by including in the work the definition for "patron" as "Commonly a wretch who supports with insolence, and is paid with flattery." Despite the work's popularity, Johnson barely stayed ahead of his debts. Finally, after 1762, Johnson received a state pension and some measure of financial security. He became known famously as an arbiter of taste, labeled "The Great Cham" by Tobias SMOLLETT, and led an artistic group called simply "The Club." Its membership included painter Sir Joshua Reynolds, politician and writer Edmund Burke, novelist Oliver GOLDSMITH, and David Garrick, as well as James Boswell, who would later write the most famous biography in English, *Life of Samuel Johnson* L.L.D. (1791). Johnson continued his voluminous writing, which included an eight-volume edition of *The Plays of William Shakespeare* (1765). A deservedly famous figure, he toured Scotland with Boswell and published his observations in 1775 as *A Journey to the Western Islands of Scotland* (1775). *The Lives of the Poets* appeared in 1782, offering 52 studies that featured his literary criticism.

Continuing to suffer ill health, Johnson fought bouts of depression in his later years. He died in 1784 and was buried, a celebrated hero of letters, in Westminster Abbey. For the most part due to Boswell's detailed and imminently readable biography, Johnson enjoyed more fame following his death than he had during his life. The rational practicality he brought to his critiques of literature and philosophy guaranteed Johnson a solid place in the continuum of the development of fiction and the novel.

BIBLIOGRAPHY

Boswell, James. *Life of Johnson.* Edited by R. W. Chapman. New York: Oxford University Press, 1998.

Phelps, Gilbert. "Samuel Johnson: The History of Rasselas, Prince of Abissinia." *An Introduction to Fifty British Novels: 1600–1900.* London: Pan Books, 1979, 107–109.

Redford, Bruce. *Designing the Life of Johnson.* New York: Oxford University Press, 2002.

JONATHAN WILD THE GREAT, THE HISTORY OF THE LIFE OF THE LATE HENRY FIELDING (1743)

Henry FIELDING received some criticism for romanticizing a common criminal in his novel *The History of the Life of the Late Jonathan Wild the Great.* Based on the career of a well-known criminal executed earlier in the 18th century, the novel is meant to be a SATIRE, although some readers, including Sir Walter SCOTT, did not see it as such. Fielding's shaping of Wild, with his wonderfully ironic name, as protagonist took to task society's penchant for characterizing actions out of control as "great" or heroic, particularly those of government officials.

The real Wild, born about 1682 and executed in 1725, was not a robber in the common sense but rather a receiver of stolen goods. He would return the stolen property to its rightful owners, charging them the "ransom" he had paid. His habit of sacrificing his underlings whenever he felt in danger of the law marked him as especially despised, even by his own followers. His execution for theft came under a law providing that those who received stolen goods were equally guilty as those who originally stole them. Fielding decried the acceptance of influence regardless of motive prevalent among society, particularly in its elected officials, with Sir Robert Walpole his real-life target. Although the title prime minister did not yet exist, Walpole was later commonly considered the first prime minister of England. He solidified the Whig Party, influencing domestic and foreign policy of England through his persuasive power with Parliament, which approved of his low-taxation approach. However, his policy led to a war with Spain over trade in 1742, disgusting many of his devotees, who expressed indignation over Walpole's own profiting through war.

Adding his usual commentary to his tale, Fielding notes that his novel is not meant to be a true history of Wild, but rather that he presents actions Wild might have taken. Almost from the moment of his baptism by Titus Oates, Wild lives up to his surname, behaving in an unacceptable manner. He goes to work in a sponging house run by its warden, Snap, where debtors were interrogated and detained before their imprisonment. There he learns extortion as if from a schoolbook, accepting graft and exploitation as a creed. Later, as a gang leader, Wild demands the majority of the gang's profits, exposing any disagreeing members to the law. His unquestioned leadership leads to the gain of enormous wealth and power. Wild puts that power to use to ruin a good man, his one time schoolmate, now a jeweler named Heartfree, characterized in contrast to Wild as foolish and "low." Heartfree's name symbolizes his personality, as does his employment as a jeweler, dealing with goods whose value never vacillates. After robbing Heartfree, Wild manipulates his arrest and imprisonment as a debtor, forcing him to declare bankruptcy. He also tricks his wife into leaving the country, and then accuses Heartfree of her supposed murder when she turns up "missing."

Wild also marries Snap's daughter Laetitia, whose hypocrisy well matches his own. Theirs will not be a happy marriage, and they soon separate, as Wild, predictably becomes unfaithful. The novel concludes with Wild's exposure as a criminal and Heartfree's release, allowing Fielding's emphasis on the difference between the eventual rewards of fabricated "greatness" versus those of true "goodness." As Wild is escorted to his execution, the populace declares him a "great man" and their "hero," ignoring the harm his actions have inflicted on scores of innocents. His hanging becomes the highpoint of a great career, martyring Wild as a man of the people.

Daniel DEFOE had also written about Jonathan Wild, but not in Fielding's satirical manner. Fielding succeeded in exposing the misconception of hypocrisy and greed as aspects of greatness. Compared to works by reknowned satirist Jonathan SWIFT for its grave and engaging tone, the novel succeeds in demonstrating how truth can be tainted in the service of so-called great men. Fielding not only aimed his barbs at well-known political figures of the Whig Party, for whom he had developed a deep disgust, but also at the public's interest in books passing as pseudo-biographies about criminals, which would later be labeled NEWGATE FICTION, after an infamous prison. More important, he targeted society's tendency to find success admirable, regardless of the immorality of the individual considered successful.

Fielding detested aggrandizement and self-inflation in any individual, but especially in politicians who he felt owed their constituency a measure of honest effort. He skillfully projects this attitude in his development of the parallel between a common criminal and a popular politician. Published as part of Fielding's *Miscellanies, Jonathan Wild* predicted his extraordinary talent and brilliant writing career. Celebrated centuries later as a magnificent example of sustained irony, the novel is readily available in electronic as well as printed text.

BIBLIOGRAPHY

Maynadier, G. H. Introduction to *The History of the Life of the Late Mr. Jonathan Wild the Great,* by Henry Fielding. Project Gutenberg. Available online. URL: http://ibiblio. org/gutenberg/ etext04/thllm10.txt. Downloaded on August 31, 2003.

JOURNAL OF THE PLAGUE YEAR, A
DANIEL DEFOE (1722)   While it purports to be a journal, Daniel DEFOE's novel, *A Journal of the Plague Year,* is an imaginatively drawn "history" of the Great Plague that seized England from 1664 to 1665. Defoe likely based his narrator, a Whitechapel saddler identified only as "H. F.," on his uncle, Henry Foe, who survived the plague while working as a saddler in St. Botolph. The book details survival tactics assumed by various individuals as London, and then most of their country, comes under siege. H. F. chooses to remain in London, feeling that is God's will for him, chronicling the progression of the plague and its effects on the citizenry,

from disbelief to terror. In engaging detail H. F. describes the changes in the city so acutely that the city almost becomes a character. Infected inhabitants remained literally imprisoned in their houses with little access to any relief, while those unaffected fled the city for the country, in some cases unwittingly carrying the plague with them. Small towns began to place constables and guards at their borders, preventing weary travelers from settling in. Defoe's rendition of the dialogue in dramatic fashion helps build a realistic tension. The city remains so long deserted that nature begins to take over, as grass sprouts in the unused streets.

Defoe continues to receive high critical praise for his approach. He skillfully interconnects factual reports, including city statistics and mortality reports, historical reports, and anecdotal information. He focuses on human fortitude, or lack thereof, in the face of disaster, supposedly spurred to write this book following an outbreak of the plague in France. His subjects include not only everyday London citizens, but also its civic leaders, with round criticism for their hesitancy to act. In the opening paragraphs, the narrator relates that although the government "had a true account" of the spreading plague, that information was not released in time to help many citizens. They first suspected the truth when weekly bills, or announcements, showed an increase in burials beyond the normal in a local parish. Defoe inserts what appear to be columned journal entries as H. F. begins to keep a tally of the dead. When the flight from the city begins, H. F. describes it as "very terrible and melancholy."

Reaction to the work in his own era proved strong, with Sir Walter SCOTT's voice of praise joining that of others in the 1821 *Memoir of Daniel De Foe, Miscellaneous Works.* First noting the "hideous almost to disgust" subject, Scott adds, "even had he not been the author of 'Robinson Crusoe,' De Foe would have deserved immortality for the genius which he has displayed in this work." The 1720s saw several novels in which all the elements of fiction were not required: some plots, like Defoe's, supplied a strong setting but no specific strong characters.

Defoe exhibited his skill at confusing fact and fiction in *MOLL FLANDERS* (1722), a popular novel in which he convinced many readers, through his inclusion of realistic detail, that his protagonist actually existed. About *A Journal of the Plague Year,* a reviewer named H. Southern wrote in an 1822 review, "Such is the veri-similitude of all the writings of Defoe, that unless we have had some other means of refuting their authenticity than internal evidence, it would be a very difficult task to dispute their claims." The book remains popular and may be accessed as electronic text as well as found in published print form.

BIBLIOGRAPHY

Moulton, Charles Wells, ed. "Daniel Defoe." *The Library of Literary Criticism of English and American Authors.* Gloucester, Mass.: Peter Smith, 1959, 42.

Novak, Maximillian. *Daniel Defoe: Master of Fictions, His Life and Ideas.* New York: Oxford University Press, 2001.

JUDE THE OBSCURE THOMAS HARDY (1895)

Like other novels by Thomas HARDY, *Jude the Obscure* offers a bleak picture of choices available to the working man. First published as a serial in *Harper's New Monthly Magazine* between December 1894 and November 1895, the novel upset many. They found Hardy's overt protest against poverty depressing; in his previous novels, characters had accepted their poverty and not struggled against it, as does Jude, an intelligent and creative individual who will never realize his gifts due to social stigma. Readers also found unacceptably vulgar the novel's focus on the everyday and indecent in its characterization of sexual relations between unmarried men and women. Hardy found indecent the fact that sexual mores could be used to manipulate couples, forcing them into disastrous relationships with little concern for the destructive results. He was accustomed to negative reaction; George MEREDITH had reviewed his first manuscript, *A Pair of Blue Eyes,* and pronounced it too revolutionary to publish. However, the public outcry by readers and critics alike to *Jude* proved too much even for Hardy to tolerate. He found the reaction against his novel so distasteful that he ceased writing fiction altogether, turning to poetry and introducing a second change into his writing career. He would likely have been amazed by the intense popularity of his novel with later generations.

The novel's protagonist, the stonemason Jude Fawley, emulates the journey of his beloved schoolmaster, Mr. Phillotson, from his small village of Maygreen to Christminster in an attempt to gain an education. He also escapes an unbearable marriage to a seductress, Arabella Donn, who lied to Jude about being pregnant just so he would marry her. When she leaves him to travel to Australia with her parents, Jude also decides to escape his miserable life. He searches for Phillotson and discovers him managing a small school, having failed to reach his goal of attending university. Jude intends to work as a stonemason until he can enter university, fantasizing in the meantime over a photograph of his beautiful distant cousin, Sue Bridehead. He eventually meets Sue and falls in love with her, helping her to get work with Phillotson as his assistant. His love for Sue intensifies the more he is exposed to her intellectual, creative nature, contrasting her refined personality with the crude opportunist, Arabella. Although the young people try to deny their love, they eventually admit what they feel for one another.

Sue enrolls in an all-female school, studying to become certified as a teacher. Despite her love for Jude, she becomes engaged to Phillotson, and they plan to marry following her completion of school. Sue vacillates in this arrangement, as at times she finds the thought of marriage to the much-older man repulsive. As she nears graduation, Sue visits Jude and is unjustly condemned for improper behavior by her imaginative schoolmistress, who moves to expel her. She turns to Jude for comfort, but discovers only then that he is a married man. Distraught, she marries Phillotson. Heightening the conflict of an already dark plot, Arabella reappears, telling Jude that she married in Australia and begging him not to reveal her secret bigamy, to which he agrees. He continues to see the desperately unhappy Sue, begging her to leave Phillotson. Aware of the situation, Phillotson tells her to go to Jude, which she does.

Blocked from entering university by financial problems and his low social status, Jude accepts his position as a stonemason. Sue's arrival buoys his spirits, but he is dismayed to learn that she does not want to have sex. He agrees to abide by her rule in order to keep her with him, and they live together. Arabella requests a divorce in order to legally marry her Australian husband who has relocated to England. When he agrees, Phillotson learns of the divorce and decides to divorce Sue, legally freeing her. By this time, however, despite her new liberty, Sue will not marry Jude. Hardy condemns the institution of marriage, not only through his multiple examples of failed unions, but also through Sue's belief that marriage will ruin her relationship with Jude.

Again Arabella enters the scene to make misery for Jude. She brings him a young boy nicknamed Father Time, due to his incurable melancholy, that she claims is Jude's. Jude and Sue take him in. Condemned by society due to their divorces and their early cohabitation, they remain miserable, driven from one village to another and not allowed to enjoy any happiness. Their only lasting friendship is with Mrs. Edlin, who does not judge them. They do consummate their union, eventually having two children of their own. In the most tragic of many tragic scenes in the novel, Father Time eventually murders the two younger children and then commits suicide, unable to face the family's poverty any longer and mistakenly considering the children the source of their problems. Readers found coping with the grotesque scene almost impossible.

Sue's reaction is to become fundamentally religious, constantly condemning herself for the children's deaths, believing her suffering to be punishment by God. She urges Jude to return to his true wife, Arabella. Jude vigorously objects, protesting that he and Sue obviously belong together, as evidenced by their true love for one another. Sue will not listen. She returns to Phillotson, begging him to take her back. He agrees, but extracts her promise to always obey him. Weary of having to make what seem consistently disastrous decisions on her own, Sue agrees, and they wed, although they do not sleep together.

Sue's action devastates Jude, at that point broken in spirit and ill. The widowed Arabella takes advantage of him, tricking Jude into marriage for the second time. Distraught and inconsolable, Jude makes a final journey to beg Sue to renew their relationship. She acts on her passion to kiss him and declare her love, and then pulls back, remembering her pledge to a higher moral purpose. After that incident, she joins Phillotson in bed as a type of punishment. Jude travels home in the rain, which signals a cleansing of the past and a time of change. He dies miserable and alone, while the reader observes Arabella laying a trap for her next victim. To add to the reader's heavy burden of pity for the characters, Mrs. Edlin tells Arabella at Jude's funeral that Sue has at last found peace. The irony of the statement undercuts any redemption such declarations of peace normally bring. The novel concludes with Jude's needs having been ignored not only by Sue and Arabella but also by society in general. Critic Lionel Stevenson describes the novel as "repulsively black," a comment with which many agree. However, the novel remains popular as a study subject in higher education and is readily available. Hardy's own description of the novel as "a series of seemings, or personal impressions, the question of their consistency or their discordance, of their permanence or their transitoriness, being regarded as not of the first moment" indicates he might be surprised by its longevity.

BIBLIOGRAPHY

Adelman, Gary. *Jude the Obscure: A Paradise of Despair.* New York: Twayne, 1992.

Buckler, William E. Introduction to *Jude the Obscure,* by Thomas Hardy. New York: Dell, 1959.

Page, Norman, ed. *Jude the Obscure: An Authoritative Text: Backgrounds and Contexts and Criticism.* 2nd ed. New York: Norton, 1999.

Stevenson, Lionel. *The English Novel: a Panorama.* Boston: Houghton Mifflin, 1960.

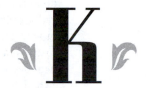

KAILYARD SCHOOL The kailyard school grew from the term *Kailyard,* meaning "cabbage patch," an expression used by Ian Maclaren (real name John Watson, 1850–1907) in connection with his story collection *Beside the Bonnie Briar Bush* (1894). The label was adopted by a group of Scottish writers who published at the end of the 19th century. They included J. M. Barrie, whose additions to the school's work included *The Little Minister* (1891), although he is best known as the author of *Peter Pan* (1904), a play that grew from his earlier kailyard-school novel, *Sentimental Tommy* (1896), about a Scottish boy who does not want to grow up. Another member, S. R. Crockett, wrote *The Stickit Minister* (1893). Their books focused on quotidian Scotland, adopted a homey narrative approach, and focused on sentimentality and small-town values, an approach that developed as a manifestation of Robert Louis STEVENSON'S ROMANCE adventures. While the group might have focused on the grim poverty often present in Scottish peasant life, they instead filled their writings with charm, emphasizing family values and local color within a humble lifestyle.

KAVANAGH, JULIA (1824–1877) An Irish novelist, Julia Kavanagh was born in Tharles, County Tipperary, where she was homeschooled. Her parents, Morgan Peter and Bridget Kavanagh, took her on a tour of France and London as a child, inspiring her long-lasting love of France and leading her eventually to settle in London in 1844 to write. She would spend much additional time in France and later used her experiences in her novels, with France supplying several of her settings. She traveled with her mother again in 1854, to Switzerland, France, and Italy. The two lived together following Bridget Kavanagh's separation from her husband, with Julia supporting her mother. They settled in Paris, where Kavanagh contributed to *Irish Monthly Magazine.* At the outbreak of the Franco-Prussian War, they moved to Rouen, then to Nice, where the author died following a fall from her bed. Her mother contributed a portrait of Kavanagh by Henri Chanet to the National Gallery of Ireland and was buried next to her daughter upon her own death in 1888.

Kavanagh produced in excess of 20 novels and short stories, as well as the collection of biographical sketches *Women of Letters* (1862–1863), featuring English and French writers, and *Woman in France in the Eighteenth Century* (1850). Novels included *Madeleine* (1848), which focused on an Auvergne peasant; *Nathalie* (1850); *Daisy Burns* (1853), in the genre of DOMESTIC REALISM; *Adéle* (1858); and *Bessie* (1872). She offered to contribute to the *Nation* representing Irish topics, claiming that although she had not lived in Ireland for some time, she remained loyal to its interests. While a popular writer of her day, with her works translated into French, Kavanagh held little interest for later readers. Her lack of originality caused her typically hyperbolic Victorian writing to be an unrewarding reading experience.

BIBLIOGRAPHY

Read, Charles, ed. *A Cabinet of Irish Literature*. Vol. 4. Dublin: Blackie & Sons, 1880.

Showalter, Elaine. *A Literature of Their Own: British Women Novelists from Brontë to Lessing*. Princeton, N.J.: Princeton University Press, 1998.

Sutherland, John. *The Longman Companion to Victorian Fiction*. New York: Longman, 1988.

KEARY, ANNIE (1825–1879)

Born on March 3, 1825, in Yorkshire to an Irish Anglican rector named William Keary and his wife, Lucy, Ann Marie Keary listened to her father's stories as a child and, according to her sister, she took "her first lesson in novel-writing at her father's knee." The youngest in the family, she had two brothers, Arthur and Henry, and a sister Eliza, later her biographer, with whom she played many games. Those activities often began with a favorite line, later spoken by a character in her tale *Father Phim,* "This house is a story house." Never thought particularly bright by her teachers, she had many friends and gained a reputation for talking during lessons. At boarding school, she was exposed to the religious fervor of her instructors but had no interest in spiritual matters until later in life. When her father became ill and had to quit work, the family moved to Clifton, and Keary quickly made new friends. Never one to appreciate much change, "she was in no hurry to begin her experience of life," according to her sister. Her reading included works by Charles DICKENS and Charles KINGSLEY.

Despite her happy childhood, Keary found her surroundings dull, and as an adult, was purported to have rejected all attachments to things Irish. A frail woman who from childhood had seemed unfit for life's conflicts, she experienced a religious awakening in her 20s, which involved correspondence with Charles KINGSLEY on the matter of "eternal punishment." She became a part of a movement adopting the "doctrine of eternal hope," which Keary viewed as "a bridge of light across the darkness." She needed her newfound spiritual strength almost immediately to help her accept the death of her brother Arthur, followed by that of her father. The 15 years following her father's death were her "intellectually active years" when she began to write, often at her ill mother's bedside. She lived at first with Eliza and her mother in the family home and later cared for Henry's children, following the death of his first wife. She suffered a nervous breakdown when he remarried, followed by a religious crisis, partly precipitated by her travel to Egypt. Her sister published much of her correspondence from Egypt in the biography, and Keary's novel *Janet's Home* (1863) later reflected her experience in its religious theme.

Keary lived on the Riviera, where she remained bedridden for much of the second half of her life. While known also as an adult novelist, she gained most fame for her CHILDREN'S LITERATURE. Her works included *Mia and Charles* (1856); *The Heroes of Asgard* (1857), written in conjunction with Eliza; *Sidney Grey* (1857), a story that focused on school experiences; and *The Rival Kings* (1858). For adults, she published *Oldbury* (1869), a fictionalized portrayal of her hometown, and *Castle Daly* (1875), regarding an Irish uprising and first published in *MacMillan's Magazine*. She left *A Doubting Heart* (1879) uncompleted at her death.

BIBLIOGRAPHY

Keary, Eliza. *Memoir of Annie Keary, by Her Sister*. London: Macmillan, 1883.

KENILWORTH SIR WALTER SCOTT (1821)

In his novel *Kenilworth,* Sir Walter SCOTT tells his romanticized version of the death of Amy Robsart, wife to Robert Dudley, the earl of Leicester, favored by Queen Elizabeth I. Set in 1560, the novel seeks to, as Scott writes in his introduction, equal the "delineation of Queen Mary" by providing a similar story "respecting 'her sister and her foe,' the celebrated Elizabeth." He provides the caveat that, as a Scot naturally more sympathetic to Mary, he will hope that prejudice, as natural to the author "as his native air," will not greatly affect his "sketch."

As in all his novels, Scott provides information regarding his sources. The main source used as the basis for this story is "Ashmore's Antiquities of Berkshire," and he includes a lengthy quoted passage that outlines the earl's supposed murder of his wife, a crime he committed with the hope that Queen Elizabeth would marry him. The description of Dudley reports that he was "singularly well featured, being a great favorite to Queen Elizabeth," whose wife feared for her life, and for good reason. A "professor of physic" at New College, Oxford, stated that when he refused to participate in poisoning the "poor, innocent lady," the earl "endeavored to displace him in the court." The description of Amy Robsart, as a woman persuaded that "her present disease was abundance of melancholy," would arouse sympathy in the coldest of readers.

Robsart's murder proved vicious. Men "first stifling her, or else strangling her . . . afterward flung her down a pair of stairs and broke her neck." Bribed by the earl, the local coroner ruled the death accidental when Robsart's father demanded an investigation. In an act portraying great grief, the earl later exhumed the body of "so virtuous a lady," dear "to his tender heart," and had her reburied in St. Mary's church in Oxford "with great pomp and solemnity." Several men supposedly involved in the deed later confessed, as each died miserable, guilt-ridden deaths. As for the earl, he died from poisoning, with the location of his murder disputed; some claim it occurred at one Cornbury Lodge, while others placed it at the ironically named Killingworth in 1588. The famous Renaissance poet and playwright Ben Jonson wrote that Leicester, apparently intent on another in a string of murders, had given poison to "his lady," telling her it was a treatment for her fainting. He departed and then returned to court, at which point his lady, not knowing the liquid was poison, gave it to Leicester. Not recognizing its source, he drank it and died.

The story eventually influenced many ballads and plays, one drama named the "Yorkshire Tragedy" containing the lines, "The only way to charm a woman's tongue / Is, break her neck—a politician did it." Scott borrows incidents and names from Ashmole but also cites a favorite poem by Mickle, published in "Evan's Ancient Ballads." He readily admits his easy influence by all things romantic, as one verse from the poem named for the setting of the murder, "Cumnor Hall,"

demonstrates, its speaker using flowers as symbols for both Amy and Elizabeth: "Yes! now neglected and despised, / The rose is pale, the lily's dead; / But he that once their charms so prized, / Is sure the cause those charms are fled."

Scott's version does adhere to many facts regarding the murder, although they are inserted within a romance format. Amy Robsart is persuaded to marry the earl of Leicester in secret; because Queen Elizabeth considers him a favorite, the earl does not want her to learn of the marriage. Robsart is hidden away at Cumnor Place, outside Oxford, by the dastardly "moral monster" Richard Varney. Because of his attentions to Robsart, Varney appears to be her lover to outsiders. One of those men is Robsart's ex-lover, Edmund Tressilian, who remains bitter over his rejection. When his attempts to convince her to return to her home fail, Tressilian charges Varney at court with abduction of Robsart. Varney declares to the queen that Robsart is his wife in order to protect the earl, and Elizabeth summons Robsart to Kenilworth, one stop on the queen's royal progress around England. Varney and Leicester fail in their plea to Robsart that she claim she is wife to Varney, and she rebelliously declares her true identity to the queen after an adventurous escape from Cumnor Place to Kenilworth. Leicester believes her to be involved in an affair with Tressilian, particularly when she is discovered hiding in his room at Kenilworth. However, she has no ulterior motive but only wants to be reunited with her husband. Leicester's anger toward Robsart causes him to send her home to Cumnor Place and charge Varney to murder her. He cries in the highly charged dialogue that marks the story as romance, "she shall die the death of a traitress and adulteress, well merited both by the laws of God and man!" Varney willingly agrees to the murder plan, having already been spurned by Robsart, who fought off Varney's attention with the help of the monster guard, Laurence Staples, as Varney attempted to rape her.

When the earl realizes Robsart's innocence, he repents his action and confesses his marriage to an outraged Elizabeth. Despite efforts to resist her fate, Robsart dies in an "accidental fall," when Tressilian is unable to rescue her. In an especially cruel act, Varney imitates the earl's voice, to which Robsart responds, leading to her death. As Varney's partner in crime, Foster, passionately notes, "Thou hast destroyed her by means of her best affections. It is a seething of the kid in the mother's milk!"

Peopled with romantic characters, such as the artist, Wayland, the ne'er-do-well Michael Lambourne, and Staples, in addition to interestingly imagined historical figures, including the queen, Robsart's father, and Sir Walter Raleigh, the plot manages to retain tension, even though readers already know its outcome. Scott adds liberal doses of detailed imagery to enhance his scenes. For instance, Elizabeth is described as wearing a "sylvan dress, which was of a pale-blue silk, with silver lace . . . approached in form to that of the ancient Amazons," a look well suited "to the dignity of her mien," which "long habits of authority had rendered in some degree too masculine to be seen to the best advantage in ordinary female weeds." Such gender-linked description interests FEMINIST CRITICS as well as NEW HISTORICIST CRITICS. The scenes of pomp and outrageous drama framing Elizabeth during her visit to Kenilworth provide additional engaging imagery. Based on real reports of the pageantry produced for the queen, specifically a reenactment of the tale of the Lady of the Lake, the woman portraying that Lady "amid her long silky black hair [. . .] wore a crown or chaplet of artificial mistletoe and bore in her hand a rod of ebony tipped with silver. Two nymphs attended on her, dressed in the same antiques and mystical guise." Finally, Scott imbues his tale with a surprising irony that casts doubt over the earl's motivation for the killing of his wife.

Throughout the fictional version of what history purports to be a true story, Robsart carries with her a letter of great import. Her husband believes the letter will implicate her as an adulterer with Tressilian. When he finally procures the letter, he discovers it simply explained his wife's flight from Cumnor Place to Kenilworth, and her need for the protection of Tressilian upon her arrival there. She had come to Kenilworth seeking only Leicester's protection and care. He allowed the covetous Varney to convince him that she possessed motives that never existed. This understanding moves him to confess his marriage to the queen and to send, too late, Tressilian to rescue Amy Robsart.

He also dies a gentler death, although still by poison, than in real-life accounts, a proper ending for a ROMANCE character.

BIBLIOGRAPHY
Kerr, James. *Fiction Against History: Scott as Storyteller.* New York: Cambridge University Press, 1989.
Scott, Sir Walter. Introduction to *Kenilworth.* New York: Wm. L. Allison, n.d.
Shaw, Harry E. *The Forms of Historical Fiction: Sir Walter Scott and His Successors.* Ithaca, N.Y.: Cornell University Press, 1983.

KICKHAM, CHARLES J(OSEPH) (1828–1882)

Born in County Tipperary, Charles Kickham matured on his father's prosperous farm, observing his father at work in his shop. His mother, Anne O'Mahony, was kinswoman of the leader of the Irish revolutionary group the Fenians. An explosion of a cask of damp gunpowder disfigured Kickham and left him partially deaf and blind, requiring him to have private tutors. Like many other young Irishmen, he felt passionately in favor of the cause of the Young Ireland movement, joining the Fenians in 1860. An editor of the Fenian paper, *The Irish People,* Kickham was jailed following a police raid on the newspaper's Dublin offices in 1865 and tried for treason felony. Although sentenced to 14 years in an English prison, thanks to the efforts of John McGuire, member of Parliament. for Cork, he gained release after only four. Those four years deeply affected his health, but he returned to a political life, leading the Irish Republican Brotherhood. He wrote for a variety of periodicals, including two titled *The Irishman,* as well as *The Nation, The Celt,* and *The Shamrock.* The novel he wrote in prison lovingly depicting his mother, *Sally Cavanagh* (1869), did not prove very popular. However, in 1879 he published the wildly popular KNOCKNAGOW, OR THE HOMES OF TIPPERARY (1879), which would become one of the best-known Irish novels ever. A master portrait of country life in Ireland, the novel revolves around the greed of landlords and the suffering of those actually working the farms. Led to write by his nationalist interests, Kickham succeeded in producing a detailed account of the suffering of the Irish people, with an emphasis on Catholicism as their solace. Matthew Russell described Kickham as "earnest, thoughtful, rather sad, and so good," with "keen piercing eyes" that could read one's thoughts.

BIBLIOGRAPHY

Comerford, Richard Vincent. *Charles J. Kickham: A Study in Irish Nationalism and Literature.* Dublin: Wolfhound Press, 1979.

Murphy, William. *Charles J. Kickham: Patriot, Novelist and Poet.* 1903. Blackrock, Ireland: Carraig Books, 1976.

Russell, Matthew, S.J. Introduction to *Knocknagow, or, the Homes of Tipperary,* by Charles Krickham. Available online. URL:http://www.exclassics.com/knockngw/kn2.htm. Downloaded on September 1, 2003.

KIDNAPPED ROBERT LOUIS STEVENSON (1866)

Robert Louis STEVENSON continued in the vein of writing adventure stories for boys when he published *Kidnapped,* first as a serial in a boy's magazine. However, adults had taken notice of his accomplished style in earlier novels, such as *TREASURE ISLAND* (1883), which seemed to elevate his work beyond CHILDREN'S LITERATURE. In *Kidnapped,* Stevenson supplies a psychological study of his protagonist and adds realistic detail appreciated by discriminating readers of his own and later eras. In addition, he approached the subject matter of the Jacobite rebellion undertaken by Partisans of the Stuart claimant to the British throne with the enthusiasm that only Scottish writers, beginning with Sir Walter SCOTT, seemed singularly to supply. The resultant enthusiastic tone caught and held his readers' attention, and they hardly noticed they were reading HISTORICAL FICTION.

Stevenson's main character, David Balfour, is orphaned by his father's death and forced to approach his irascible Uncle Ebenezer for help, unaware that Ebenezer had swindled him out of his rightful inheritance. When a plot to murder David fails, Ebenezer hires kidnappers, reflecting the novel's title, to smuggle David aboard the brig *Covenant* bound for America. On the way to the Carolinas, the crewmen rescue Alan Breck from his damaged boat. David learns that Alan is a Jacobite rebel who longs to return to Scotland. While David is a fictional creation, Alan Breck Stewart was a supporter of the Stuart monarchy, an admirer of "the Pretender," Prince Charles (Bonnie Prince Charlie).

Their own ship wrecks and the young men strike out together on the coast of Mull in Scotland. Unintentional witnesses to the murder of the king's favorite and a man Alan hates, Colin Campbell, known as the Red Fox, the young men become suspects and must flee, climbing into the hills. In the Highlands they find escape and eventually unmask Uncle Ebenezer's fraud, and David regains his fortune. Stevenson provides a typical QUEST tale, complete with a sea voyage, loss on the part of the hero, monsters in human form, a guide, and a victorious return home.

Stevenson later wrote a sequel titled *Catriona* (1893), in which David falls in love with the title character and finds himself again embroiled in false accusation for the murder of Campbell, this time against a man named James Stewart. While both novels proved popular, *Kidnapped* endures into the 21st century and has been converted to various movie and television versions. It translates beautifully to film, primarily due to Stevenson's talent in detailing the terrain through which his characters pass so that it helps to determine the real characters' actions. He accomplishes that not with painstaking descriptions but with acute, well-placed details. Such details give the Stevenson novel a physicality of setting that not only frames but echoes the physically exacting journeys followed by his protagonists.

That Stevenson's popularity has barely diminished is evident not only in the continued publication of his body of work, including *Kidnapped,* but also in the continued reaction to his novel. As an example, a group that calls itself "The Stevenson Way" today seeks to establish a special walk across Scotland that would follow the apparent path taken by David and Alan. Its representatives have traced the *Covenant*'s wreck to rocks near Erraid Island, which sits off the western edge of Mull. The direction of the walk would be west to east, determined by Stevenson's description, which happily, as the group's Web site notes, "places your back to the prevailing weather." If walkers begin at the more inhabitable point of Iona, an isle close to the tidal Erraid Island, the walk should stretch some 230 miles, its end point still undecided.

BIBLIOGRAPHY

Livesey, Margot. Introduction to *Kidnapped,* by Robert Louis
Stevenson. New York: Modern Library, 2001. xiii–xxvi.

"The Stevenson Way." Undiscovered Scotland. Available
online. URL: http://www.undiscoveredscotland.co.uk/.
Downloaded on September 1, 2004.

KINGSLEY, CHARLES (1819–1875)

Born in Devonshire on June 12, 1819, to a father who would later become vicar of St. Luke's, at Chelsea, Charles Kingsley attended school in Bristol, where, as a youth, he saw the Bristol riots. This early exposure to the consequences of CLASS STRUCTURE and social inequities may have sparked the lifelong devotion to social consciousness that Kingsley would practice. He later attended King's College in London and went on to Magdalene College, Cambridge, from 1838 to 1841. Following ordination in 1842, he became curate of Eversley, Hampshire, and in 1844 married Frances Eliza Grenfell, after which he was appointed rector. The year 1848 would prove an important one. In addition to publishing *The Saint's Tragedy* that year, Kingsley traveled to London for the presentation of the CHARTIST petition to Parliament. He returned to Eversley to preach on April 16 about the Chartist riots, declaring his dedication to social equality. His radical activity may have precipitated his rejection by King's College, London, as a lecturer. His first THESIS NOVEL, focusing on social concerns, *YEAST: A PROBLEM* (1850), appeared as a serial in 1848 in *FRASER'S MAGAZINE.*

In 1849, Kingsley published *Twenty-five Village Sermons* at year's end and helped fight a cholera epidemic in London. By 1850, his interest in the scandalous abuses faced by clothing trade workers led him to release a pamphlet, under the name Parson Lot, attacking those conditions. He titled it *Cheap Clothes and Nasty,* a work that he followed up that year with his second novel, *ALTON LOCKE,* published in two anonymous volumes. That novel, based on friendships with real tailors, took its place in the group of social-consciousness novels that became prominent in the second third of the century. In November 1850, he helped found a periodical called *Christian Socialist, A Journal of Association,* supporting the working class. In 1851, *Yeast* appeared anonymously in novel form, and

in June Kingsley preached at St. John's, Fitzroy Square, on the church's responsibility toward laborers. He received orders not to preach in that diocese again from the bishop of London. He visited Germany and in January of 1852 published *HYPATIA, OR NEW FOES WITH AN OLD FACE* in *Fraser's Magazine,* considered by many of his contemporaries and later critics to be his finest work. He followed that with *Phaethon: Or, Loose Thoughts for Loose Thinkers* and *Sermons on National Subjects, 1st Series. Hypatia* was released in two volumes in the spring of 1853, and Kingsley served as part of a group appointed by Lord Palmerston to study sanitary reform.

Kingsley continued to use both publishing and the church pulpit to preach social reform, releasing several works in addition to his second series of *Sermons.* Two years later in 1855, *WESTWARD HO! Or, the Voyage and Adventures of Sir Mayas Leigh,* set in Elizabethan times, appeared in three volumes, followed by *Glaucus; or the Wonders of the Shore,* along with *Sermons for the Times.* In January of 1856, Kingsley added CHILDREN'S LITERATURE to his credits with *The Heroes: Or Greek Fairy Tales for My Children.* Over the next 20 years, Kingsley published an additional 23 works, including *The WATER BABIES: A FAIRY TALE FOR A LAND-BABY* (1863). Public reaction to its tale of an unfortunate chimney sweep was responsible, in part, for the passing of the 1864 Chimney Sweepers' Act.

In 1860, Kingsley received an appointment as Regius Professor of Modern History, Cambridge, and tutored the Prince of Wales during 1861. Following his Cambridge appointment, he revised for a new edition some of the material in *Alton Locke* that criticized Cambridge, eliciting charges of hypocrisy from critics. Never shy of controversy, Kingsley took on John Henry Newman himself, publishing *What, Then Does Dr. Newman Mean?* (1864) in response to Newman's pamphlet, *Mr. Kingsley and Dr. Newman; a Correspondence on the question whether Dr. Newman teaches that truth is no Virtue.* Kingsley's review of James Anthony Froude's *History of England,* which claimed that Roman Catholicism was indifferent to truth, prompted Newman's famous *Apologia pro Vita Sua* (Apology for his life).

By 1869, Kingsley left Cambridge and accepted appointment as Canon of Chester in April. He visited the West Indies that same year, following up on an interest in Jamaica that had led him in 1866 to support Edward John Eyre, an ex-governor of Jamaica who crushed a rebellion there. In March 1873, Kingsley moved into the position of Canon of Westminster, continuing his writing career to produce *Prose Idylls, New and Old,* a collection of essays distinguished by their clarity and skill. He visited North America in 1874, and the year of his death, 1875, *Lectures Delivered in America* was published.

Kingsley's importance lies in his tremendous contribution to socially conscious British literature that began to appear with Charles DICKENS's works in the 1830s. While much of Kingsley's fiction was viewed by later readers as too DIDACTIC, it exposed social injustices with a passionate REALISM. In applying to England's social problems the Christian ethics he so fervently believed, he frequently found himself embroiled in controversy.

BIBLIOGRAPHY
Cripps, Elizabeth. Introduction. *Alton Locke.* New York: Oxford University Press, 1983.

KINGSLEY, HENRY (1830–1876)
Henry Kingsley, younger brother to famed novelist Charles KINGSLEY, spent his undergraduate years at Oxford. He did not graduate, however, due to some vaguely referenced "instabilities" and left the university to relocate to Australia. At first a fortune hunter in search of gold, he remained there from 1853 until 1858, where he served temporarily in Sydney's mounted police. His move may have been in reaction against the strong political leanings of his brother, who compulsively engaged anti-socialist political forces. His experience helped him shape the setting for his first novel, *Geoffrey Hamlyn* (1859), which he published following his return to England. While well received, that novel was far outpaced in popularity by *RAVENSHOE* (1862), the romance work set during the Crimean War for which Kingsley is best remembered. His later works made clear his position as a leading writer for the school of "muscular Christianity," along with Thomas HUGHES, who joined Kingsley's brother, Charles, in campaigning for socialist ideals. He published more than a dozen additional novels, including *Austin Elliott* (1863); another novel set in Australia called *The Hillyars and the Burtons* (1865); *Leighton Court* (1866); *The Boy in Grey* (1871), and *Reginald Hetherege* (1874). For a time he edited *The Edinburgh Daily Review,* then became a reporter during the Franco-Prussian War, for the German side. Later critics found his novels secondary in quality to those of his brother, due to their weak structure. However, they continue to engage readers due to their action and the inclusion of sympathetic characters, and remain readily available in print.

BIBLIOGRAPHY
Scheuerle, William H. Introduction to *Ravenshoe* by Henry Kingsley. Lincoln, Neb.: University of Nebraska Press, 1967, vii–xxv.

KING SOLOMON'S MINES   HENRY RIDER HAGGARD (1885)
While Henry Rider HAGGARD had written several works prior to *King Solomon's Mines,* that novel assured his fame. It reached instant success, being labeled by the *Atheneum* "one of the best books for boys—old or young—which we remember to have read." This was precisely the effect for which Haggard wished, made clear in the novel's dedication. Supposedly written by the book's protagonist Alan Quatermain, it dedicates the "faithful but unpretending record of a remarkable adventure . . . to all the big and little boys who read it." A quintessential QUEST story, it opens with Quatermain as the narrator aboard a boat where he meets his future fellow adventurers, Sir Henry Curtis, aristocrat, and John Good, English naval officer. The characters will return for further activities in the sequel, *ALLAN QUATERMAIN* (1885).

Readers of the quest will expect the call to adventure; Curtis's desire to find his long-lost brother in South Africa; the hero's initial resistance, as Quatermain only agrees to participate in the quest after Curtis guarantees lifetime financial support of Quatermain's son; and the many life-and-death adventures experienced by the travelers as they cross a deadly desert, scale threatening mountains, battle wild animals and South African natives, and deal with witchcraft, disguises, and mistaken identities. The fortune in diamonds the travelers eventually find acts as the quest reward, and Quatermain's promise to return home on the novel's final page concludes the prototypical quest. However, Haggard manages to handle the expected plot and character devices in ingenious ways while speaking to Victorian ideology, such as the prohibition of interracial marriage, the heroic nature of the male, and the inherent weak, and sometimes evil, nature of females.

For instance, the quest disguise is not one of dress but rather of heritage, as the group's native member, Umbopa, is discovered to be the rightful ruler, Ignosi, of the hidden civilization of Kukuanas. In addition, at one point the Englishmen symbolically assume South African identities by wearing the war clothing of the Kukuanas, rather than the natives taking on English dress, offering a neat reversal of the norm. While Haggard uses the familiar plot contrivance of an eclipse to "prove" the white man's special powers, he adopts a more unusual approach to the sacrifice of their fellow tribe members by the natives. He clearly mimics England's own early witch-hunts in the brutal manner by which the natives seek out and destroy supposed "wicked ones" who plan evil against their king and their neighbors. Haggard also uses Good as a comic character when he is surprised in partial dress, literally without his pants, by the natives and must retain that appearance due to the natives' fascination with his beautiful white legs as well as his half-shaven face.

Haggard's support of Victorian ideals is obvious. When the native king offers the adventurers their pick of the tribe's beautiful brown-skinned girls, Quatermain explains, "We white men wed only with white women like ourselves." In another scene, the superiority of white values is expressed when Ignosi states, "The ways of black people are not as the ways of white men . . . nor do we hold life so high as ye." And when the lovely native maiden, Foulata, later dies, unable to marry Good, she says, "I am glad to die because I know that he cannot cumber his life with such as me, for the sun cannot mate with the dark." The scene illustrates racism and also emphasizes that the male, symbolized by the sun, is light, or knowledge, and all things good, while the female is dark, or threatening, ideas of interest to FEMINIST CRITICS. This scene echoes an earlier one in which Quatermain assures the reader that "women

bring trouble as surely as the night follows the day." The book's blood-curdling villain is a hideous old wise-woman, religious-leader miscreant named Gagool, a name that suggests "gargoyle," a mythical monster, which in various hideous faces and shapes decorated Europe's houses of worship and wisdom. Gagool also fulfills the role of older women in traditional fairy tales, by seeking to destroy younger, beautiful women. By contrast, all the males in the novel are to be admired for their strength and/or agility and wisdom, even the villainous pretender to the throne, Twala.

Haggard also examines the Victorian questioning of man's relationship to nature and the tenants of evolution in an imaginative scene within King Solomon's mines. Quest fans will recognize the adventurers' descent into darkness, whereby they will survive a threat and emerge somewhat wiser. As they reach the depths of the outer cave, they notice ghastly forms that resemble humans but reach enormous heights, one especially frightening form holding "a great white spear" and looking like "*Death* himself, shaped in the form of a colossal human skeleton." As they peer more closely, they discover the corpses placed in the cave are actually becoming part of it, covered in slow drips from the cave roof that seal the human bodies into stalactites. While the form of Death remains a human creation, the stalactites that preserve the bodies are products of nature.

King Solomon's Mines offers a rousing example of the adventure story that so appealed to Victorians. It has retained that appeal for decades and has never been out of print.

BIBLIOGRAPHY

Butts, Dennis. Introduction to *King Solomon's Mines,* by Henry Rider Haggard. New York: Oxford University Press, 1989, vii–xx.

KIPLING, RUDYARD (1868–1936)   Rudyard Kipling was born in Bombay, India, where his father taught art before becoming director of the Lahore museum. His mother's family connections, particular that of her sister's marriage to the painter Edward Burne-Jones, were to provide social promotion for the young Rudyard. In 1871 he and his sister moved to

Southsea, England, where Rudyard spent several unhappy years due to feelings of isolation. He would later capture his discontent in the story "Baa, Baa Black Sheep" (1888). The only bright moments he recalled as an adult were those spent with the Burne-Jones family. His exposure to the world of art, philosophy, and political thought through his uncle and visitors to the home, which included artist, writer, and socialist William Morris, greatly influenced Kipling's development. Mainly due to such influences, he enrolled in 1878 in the United Services College, Westward Ho! in Devon, but poor eyesight would prevent service in the military. His pleasant days there influenced the subject matter of his later work *Stalky & Co.* (1899), although that work contrasted with the popular depiction of boyhood school days as idyllic. It emphasized the more brutal aspects of English school life and introduced the popular characters Corkran, M'Turk, and Beetle.

Kipling entered the world of journalism with a return to India in 1882. He wrote in Lahore for *The Civil and Military Gazette;* his insight into the Anglo-Indian community made his poems and tales, also published by the *Gazette,* popular. They would later appear as collections titled *Departmental Ditties* (1886) and *Plain Tales from the Hills* (1888). Kipling's popularity continued to grow, with the publication of additional stories by the Indian Railway Library. His observation of the great contrasts between the European and native approaches to life led to his cynical judgments regarding the need by the unwashed masses of the civilizing effects of British IMPERIALISM.

In 1889, Kipling returned to England, where his writings brought him into a critical circle that included Henry JAMES and Henry Rider HAGGARD. While his early attempts at novel writing with plots containing a strong misogynistic bent were unsuccessful, *The Light That Failed* proved of interest in its depiction of a journalist who suffers blindness, reflecting on Kipling's own situation. His popularity as both a poet and short story writer grew with *Barrack-Room Ballads and Other Verses* (1892), *Life's Handicap* (1891), and *Many Inventions* (1893). He collaborated on a second failed novel, *The Naulakha,* in 1890 with his friend Wolcott Balestier, whose sister, Caroline, Kipling married in 1892.

The couple moved to the United States to join Caroline's family in Vermont from 1892 to 1896, years that proved happy for them with the arrival of their children. During this period, Kipling wrote the short story collection *The Jungle Book* (1894), one of his most enduring works and an exceedingly popular addition to CHILDREN'S LITERATURE, and *The Second Jungle Book* (1895). Mainly through the characters of Mowgli the man-cub, Baloo the bear, Bagheera the panther, and the deliciously wicked tiger, Shere Khan, Kipling's popularity would survive into the 21st century. He became the most accomplished of his era's romantic storytellers, thanks in part to the exotic settings of his tales. Along with other popular romantic writers of his period, including Robert Louis STEVENSON and Scottish playwright and novelist J. M. Barrie, Kipling departed from the traditional depiction of perfect heroes overcoming impossible odds. He imbued his protagonists with flaws, such as alcoholism and vengeful personalities, described with precise detail.

In 1896, the Kiplings returned to England, where Rudyard continued his writing and enjoyed the birth of his son, John, in 1897. That same year he published CAPTAINS COURAGEOUS, a novel featuring a Mowgli-type boy protagonist who must survive in an alien environment. Spurred by his continuing military and imperialistic sympathies, he began several visits to South Africa after 1898, where he took a great interest in the Boer War. The family suffered the loss of one daughter during her visit to the United States in 1899.

Kipling moved the family to Sussex in 1902 after publishing the work most popular during his lifetime, *Kim* (1901). He followed that novel with a collection of tales for children, *Just So Stories* (1902), begun during the Boer War period. His obvious sympathy for the young was again evident in further story collections, including *Puck of Pook's Hill* (1906) and *Rewards and Fairies* (1910). The crowning achievement of his career occurred in 1907, when he became the first English writer to win the Nobel Prize for Literature. While his final story collections, including *Traffics and Discoveries* (1904), *Actions and Reactions* (1909), *A Diversity of Creatures* (1917), *Debits and Credits* (1926), and *Limits and Renewals* (1932), never reached the popularity of his earlier work, Kipling remained an important contributor to the literary scene. His fragments, *Of Myself:*

And Other Autobiographical Writings, appeared posthumously in 1937.

Kipling's work fell out of favor, largely due to its sentimental tone and themes of British imperialism, during the middle of the 20th century. Later his children's stories returned to popularity, due to their interesting and rousing adventure subjects, always supported by a sharp authorial eye for detail and fondness for children. Several became popular through movie and stage versions, particularly the *Jungle Book* stories, and all of Kipling's works remain readily available in print and electronic form.

BIBLIOGRAPHY

Kipling, Rudyard. *Something of Myself: And Other Autobiographical Writings.* Edited by Harry Pinney. New York: Cambridge University Press, 1991.

Ricketts, Harry. *Rudyard Kipling: A Life.* New York: Carroll & Graf, 2001.

KNOCKNAGOW, OR THE HOMES OF TIPPERARY   CHARLES J. KICKHAM (1879)

Charles J. KICKHAM's novel *Knocknagow, or the Homes of Tipperary* is still considered the most popular Irish novel ever written. Shortly after its release, it could be found in almost every Irish home. Although more important for its political content than for the superiority of its writing, it appealed to every class of reader. The poet William Butler Yeats pronounced it the most honest of any Irish novel. Although described as overly sentimental with a lumbering, disjointed plot, it does paint a true picture of the rural Ireland of Kickham's day, due to the author's personal experience on an Irish farm and as a member of an Irish protest society, the Fenian movement.

The novel is told from the point of view of Mr. Henry Lowe, a young man from Ireland's "sister country," who admittedly knows little of Ireland. Arrived at the home of his uncle's main tenant, Mr. Maurice Kearney, Lowe wakes on Christmas Day and decides to accompany the family to early Mass to learn more about the inhabitants, the sounds of the holiday procession led by the famous Knocknagow drums ringing in the distance. Once inside the ornate Catholic Church and into the service, Mr. Lowe feels a respect for that faith above that of any other religion. The sermon provides comfort to the poor, and a reminder to the wealthy that they need to relieve the suffering of their poor brethren. As Kickham exposes his readers to other scenes of daily life, he inserts metaphorical messages, such as the scene in which a robin flies inside a house and crashes into a window. When the beautiful Miss Kearney gently removes the bird outside, she remarks that while ready to come into the house, the bird always struggles for his independence, adding, "I believe no bird loves liberty so well." When Kickham responds "If you could set all your captives free as easily, it would be well," he speaks as an Englishman about the Irish. Further captivity imagery includes that of a wren, the traditional symbol of Christmas, the "king of the birds," symbolic of Christ, caught and killed on Christmas Day in various Irish mythology. The tone remains even, as does the action, which never actually peaks. Not at all DIDACTIC, *Knocknagow* will not entertain everyone who reads it. Its popularity in its own age related to its readers, most of whom could strongly identify with the locale. Out of print for decades, the novel now can be found in many libraries and in electronic form.

BIBLIOGRAPHY

Russell, Matthew, S.J. Introduction to *Knocknagow, or, the Homes of Tipperary,* by Charles Kickham. Available online. URL:http://www. exclassics.com/knockngw/kn2.htm. Downloaded on September 1, 2003.

L

LADY AUDLEY'S SECRET MARY ELIZA-
BETH BRADDON (1862)   First serialized in *Robin
Goodfellow* and then in *The Sixpenny Magazine,* Mary
BRADDON's most famous novel, *Lady Audley's Secret,*
became an instant hit with the reading public, if not
with critics. In its year of publication in volume form,
1862, it was second only to Mrs. Henry WOOD's EAST
LYNNE in sales. A typically melodramatic Braddon
tale, the novel featured a beautiful title character who,
although a murderer of her illegitimate child's father,
captured the sympathy of readers. Later critics viewed
Braddon's use of irony as salvation for her SENSATION
FICTION, as she suggested something hypocritical in
those who would eagerly read her work then criticize
its nature.

George Talboys deserts his wife, living for a time in
Australia chasing a fortune in gold, a circumstance that
guarantees his characterization as a ne'er-do-well.
When he returns to England, he finds his wife has
died, and he renews social contacts. In reality, the
clever heroine has left her child with her father, faked
her death, and adopted a new identity by switching
with a girl suffering consumption. She becomes a governess, adopting the alias Lucy Graham, transforming
herself into a young woman others believe to be "the
sweetest girl that ever lived." She counts on leaving her
hard life behind and suffering "no more humiliations"
when she accepts a marriage proposal from the elderly
Sir Michael Audley.

The conflict escalates as Talboys accompanies his
friend Robert Audley to Audley Court on holiday,
where Talboys meets Uncle Sir Michael Audley and his
lovely young bride. Lady Audley fears her ex-husband
will discover her identity and reveal her bigamy. Talboys's immediate mysterious disappearance allows
Robert Audley to suddenly transform from an idle rich
boy into a serious detective, one of fiction's first, as he
seeks to find his friend. Lady Audley proves to be a formidable foe, attempting to halt Audley's inquiries by
burning down the inn where he stays. He escapes
harm and confronts Lady Audley, eventually extracting
a confession of murder. She mesmerizes her audience
as she explains that she pushed Talboys down an Audley Court well when he recognized her, and she had
also considered poisoning her second husband. Rather
than facing the gallows, Lady Audley spends her
remaining years in a private asylum, suffering from a
self-confessed hereditary insanity. However, Braddon
leaves open the question as to whether her heroine is
actually mad. As her doctor states, she presents no true
evidence of madness. Her escape from an abusive
home life to find a better one proved quite logical. She
broke the law in committing bigamy, but doing so
gained her wealth and high social stature, and thus was
certainly not an act of madness. In plotting her first
husband's demise and that of Robert Audley to protect
her new life, she "employed intelligent means . . .

which required coolness and deliberation in its execution. There is no madness in that."

Braddon's contemporaries, including Edward BULWER-LYTTON, with whom she corresponded, recommended that she "deepen" her fiction, displaying the talent they knew she possessed. She replied in part to one suggestion, "I am such weary miles away from you now in the wide realms of thought," adding, "I have begun to question the expediency of very deep emotion." Having suffered through life with a father who regularly engaged in affairs, then abandoned her family; having then bore the weight of supporting her family through acting; and being forced to live unmarried with John Maxwell, caring for his children and bearing him an additional six children while his wife lived in a mental hospital, Braddon had reason for what others characterized as her "flippancy of tone." As she explained, "I can't help looking down upon my heroes when they suffer, because I always have in my mind the memory of wasted suffering of my own."

Modern critics such as Elaine Showalter find Lady Audley a brilliantly fashioned protagonist in the vein of the BYRONIC HERO. Shaped in "a witty inversion of Victorian sentimental and domestic convention," Lady Audley is not the typical dark villain, like Charlotte BRONTË's Bertha Rochester in JANE EYRE (1847). Instead, she is the blond delicate creature generally celebrated as the "angel" of domestic fiction. Not a BLUESTOCKING, but a romantic, Lady Audley proves a special danger, due to her deceivingly innocent demeanor. Braddon may have quite consciously intended to convert Wilkie COLLINS's victim in his popular detective mystery The WOMAN IN WHITE (1860) into a villain to be reckoned with. Perhaps Lady Audley's biggest secret is not her new identity or her indulging in bigamy but that she remains completely sane, yet escapes a deserved death sentence by convincing others she is mad. FEMINIST CRITICS suggest that Braddon may have employed the trite sensationalist tactic of blaming a character's illegal or unsocial acts on heredity in an ironic subversion.

BIBLIOGRAPHY

Showalter, Elaine. *A Literature of Their Own: British Women Novelists from Brontë to Lessing.* Princeton, N.J.: Princeton University Press, 1999.

LANDON, LETITIA ELIZABETH (1802–1838)

Letitia Elizabeth Landon was both a poet and novelist, known by her use of only her initials, L.E.L. She first published in 1821 as a teenager, when the *Literary Gazette* included her "Poetical Sketches." They appeared as a highly successful collection, *The Improvisatrice and Other Poems* (1824). A wildly successful writer, her works included her first publication, *The Fate of Adelaide* (1821), and *The Troubadour, Catalogue of Pictures, and Historical Sketches* (1825), which she followed with a sequel titled *The Golden Violet* (1826). Her family's sole source of support, Landon worked as editor of *Fisher's Drawing Room Scrap-book* from 1831 to 1838, publishing as well two novels, *Romance and Reality* (1831) and *Francesca Carrara* (1834). *The Vow of the Peacock* (1835) offered readers a glimpse of the well-known author in an engraved portrait. She also published a children's book titled *Traits and Trials of Early Life* (1836), which contained some autobiographical materials. *Ethel Churchill: Or, the Two Brides* (1837) proved her most famous and final novel. While rumors linked Landon with various sexual partners, she secretly married George Maclean, governor of Cape Coast Castle in West Africa, in 1838 but died almost immediately. Her colorful career prompted speculation as to the cause of the mysterious death, which included suicide, drug overdose, and murder. She also wrote for various periodicals, and her poetry collections appeared posthumously in 1850 and 1873. Despite her popularity, Landon was among those early professional women writers who, according to critic Elaine Showalter, "did not see their writing as an aspect of their female experience, or as an expression of it." Showalter quotes a statement by Landon from *A Book of Memories of Great Men and Women of the Age* (1877): "What is my role? . . . One day of drudgery after another; difficulties incurred for others, which have ever pressed upon me beyond health, which every year, in one severe illness after another, is taxed beyond its strength; envy, malice, and all uncharitableness—these are the fruits of a successful literary career for a woman." Her works faded from popularity later in the 19th century but remain readily available and studied in academics, particularly by FEMINIST CRITICS who have turned their attention to works by women often overlooked by the traditional canon.

BIBLIOGRAPHY

Sage, Lorna, ed. *The Cambridge Guide to Women's Writing in English*. "Landon, Letitia Elizabeth." Cambridge: Cambridge University Press, 1999, 376.

Showalter, Elaine. *A Literature of their Own: Women Novelists from Brontë to Lessing*. Princeton, N.J.: Princeton University Press, 1999.

LAST CHRONICLE OF BARSET, THE
ANTHONY TROLLOPE (1867)   Victorian readers enjoyed reunions with familiar characters in Anthony TROLLOPE's final entry into his Barsetshire series, *The Last Chronicle of Barset*, claimed by Trollope to be his favorite of all his novels. He approaches his topic of everyday people living everyday lives not with the melodrama of contemporary Charles DICKENS, nor with the judgmental tone of another contemporary, William Makepeace THACKERAY. Instead, he simply tells their stories, capturing his readers' intellectual curiosity at first as casual observers, and later as an involved and invested audience.

As the title suggests, the novel aimed to bring to a literal close the stories of families and couples by then well-known to Trollope fans, particularly that of the poverty-stricken but always pious Josiah Crawley, curate of Hogglestock. He is accused of theft when he cashes a £20 check left in a wallet lost in his house by Lord Lufton's agent, Mr. Soames. He claims the money was a gift from another familiar character, Dean Arabin, but he is arraigned for trial. Mrs. Proudie, appropriately named and long familiar to readers as the egotistical power behind her husband's bishopric, leads the attack against Crawley in her normal tenacious manner. While other wives in the novel, including Archdeacon Grantly's spouse, take their husbands to task, they do it privately. Mrs. Proudie does not care who witnesses her regular attacks on her husband, and he seems to have at last had enough of her inappropriate remarks. In one notable scene, he actually wonders what life might be like should she die, assuming that because she is younger, he will never know. When she dies soon after of a heart attack, readers sympathize with his feelings of guilt but also feel some relief for him. Trollope's third-person narrator does not judge Proudie but rather allows readers to observe him in a prayer that God might forgive him for being glad that his wife is gone.

As the action both inside and outside the courtroom rises, romantic subplots unfold. Readers once again hope that Lily Dale, the spinster heroine of *THE SMALL HOUSE AT ALLINGTON* (1864), fifth in the series, will at last return the attentions of the ever-faithful Johnny Eames. However, Trollope disappoints them but pleases critics by allowing Lily to remain true to her character. Having previously chosen over Johnny's attentions those of a lover who abandons her for a titled woman, Lily cannot envision herself as anything other than independent and single. For Trollope, her maintaining this self-perception remains a heroic act, falling into the category of heroism "painted from nature" that he referenced in *The Claverings* (1867) as difficult for readers to accept. She explains it beautifully when Eames begs her to marry him, and she replies with an emphatic "No!" Eames asks why she will not marry when she no longer loves the jilter, and she replies, "I cannot tell, dear. It is so. If you take a young tree and split it, it still lives, perhaps. But it isn't a tree. It is only a fragment." He asks her to be his fragment, to which she agrees, as long as he relegates her to "some corner of your garden. But I will not have myself planted out in the middle, for people to look at."

While this couple does not unite in marriage, and the Proudie's unhappy marriage is undone, Trollope continues to characterize the Crawley marriage as a strong one, mainly due to Mrs. Crawley's unquestioning love of her husband. At one point he feels he must give up his appointment, despite the threat of loss of income to his family. Filled with self-pity, he thinks only of his own suffering, romanticizing it through comparisons to biblical characters. Where Mrs. Proudie might have castigated such presumption, Mrs. Crawley only heaps more love and respect on her husband. Other relationships include that of the nouveaux riches Dobbs Broughtons and the pretentious Mrs. Van Siever, whose false front hair and curls symbolize her shallow existence. Their marriage remains a purely commercial venture. However, the uplifting romance by Archdeacon Grantly's son, Major Henry Grantly, with Crawley's daughter, Grace, proves satisfying to the romantic reader. Although Grantly protests the union,

Henry perseveres and Grace eventually wins the day with the archbishop, allowing one healthy marriage to proceed.

During the disagreement of Grantly with his son, Crawley naturally feels alienated from his mentor, and conflict escalates. However, Mrs. Arabin, formerly known to readers as Eleanor Harding, steps in, claiming she had included the check in a letter to Crawley sent by her husband. Once proven innocent, Crawley moves from poverty to comfort, proving the rewards of virtue, through an appointment to the parish of Eleanor's late father, Mr. Septmius Harding. Trollope includes a touching funeral scene, a celebration of the life of the most beloved of all Barset characters. Harding had influenced every individual's life as the former warden of Hiram's Hospital in the city of Barchester. He reminds readers of the series' beginnings when he had followed in the footsteps of his mentor Bishop Grantly, as unworldly and devoutly just a man as his son, the present archdeacon, is worldly and moved by convenience. Trollope's reminder that virtues from the past can help shape the future proves a vital theme of the novel.

The Last Chronicle of Barset remains one of Trollope's most widely read and enjoyed works. Many readers would agree with his closing comments that include the pronouncement, "to me Barset has been a real county, and its city a real city, and the spires and towers have been before my eyes, and the voices of the people are known to my ears, and the pavements of the city ways are familiar to my footsteps."

BIBLIOGRAPHY

Gill, Stephen. Introduction to *The Last Chronicle of Barset* by Anthony Trollope. New York: Oxford University Press, 2001, ix–xxii.

Glendinning, Victoria. *Anthony Trollope.* New York: Alfred A. Knopf, 1993.

LAST DAYS OF POMPEII, THE EDWARD BULWER-LYTTON (1834)

Edward BULWER-LYTTON found an opportunity to capitalize on his interest in the past and wrote the HISTORICAL FICTION *The Last Days of Pompeii*. While he had looked to the past for novel plots before, his choice of ancient Italy as a setting offered more of a challenge. In the preface to the first edition, he wrote of the problem in framing a society on the page of a culture to which his own era had "no household and familiar associations." He had ample materials from which to choose, but felt the burden to select historical materials of great interest to his readers. He fell upon the idea of writing about a natural disaster, feeling that anyone could relate to the stress and challenge to the human condition of such an occurrence. Thus, he selected as a specific setting the ancient city of Pompeii, just prior to and during the eruption of Vesuvius. The event was familiar enough to readers to pique the interest required to follow various characters through their reactions to the event. Critics find most interesting Bulwer-Lytton's villain, Arbaces, the priest of Isis. When the reader first meets Arbaces, he approaches a group of young men who all salute him but make a sign against his "fatal gift of the evil eye."

As for the author, he enjoyed developing all his characters, placing them within the struggles inherent to a first-century Christian group fighting for a place among the pagan religions. In his preface he describes his characters as "natural offspring" of the era he shapes. He confesses to readers that the "first art" of any poet "is to breathe the breath of life into his creatures," after which he must make them authentic to their age. He drew on the rituals associated with the worship of Isis to shape false oracles and "heathens" including the Egyptian Arbaces, the "base" Calenus, and the "fervent Apaecides." But of all the characters, he seems to most favor the blind girl, Nydia. Her benefactor, Glaucous, pities his servant, thinking, "Thine is a hard doom! Thou seest not the earth, nor the sun, nor the ocean, nor the stars." However, Nydia will ironically become the most fortunate of the group of characters. She grew from a conversation Bulwer-Lytton had with a man at Naples known for his knowledge regarding the history of his area and also of human nature. He remarked to Bulwer-Lytton that a blind person would have an easier time of escape during an eruption, due to the complete and utter darkness described as part of its aftermath. A blind person would not find that situation disconcerting.

Bulwer-Lytton explains his careful avoidance of the use of any type of cold and stilted dialect, choosing instead to feature common Romans speaking in the expected vernacular. He closes with hopes that, despite any imperfections related to verisimilitude, his novel will truthfully represent "human passions" and "the human heart." He succeeded as he described Nydia's jealous love of Glaucous as "what a man of imagination, youth, fortune, and talents readily becomes when you deprive him of the inspiration of glory." Glaucous naturally cannot return a slave's affection and desires instead the lovely Jone. Unfortunately, the dangerous Arbaces also longs to possess Jone, producing love intrigues on multiple levels.

Regarded as Bulwer-Lytton's best work, the novel was praised by contemporaries and later critics as an impressive attempt at reconstructing classical times. It remains readily available in print and electronic form, as well as in a 1913 silent Italian movie version and a 1984 television miniseries.

BIBLIOGRAPHY

Christensen, Allan Conrad. *Edward Bulwer-Lytton: The Fiction of New Regions*. Athens: University of Georgia Press, 1976.

LAWLESS, EMILY (1845–1930)

Little is known of Emily Lawless's private life and youth, although the existing facts prove interesting. Born during the years of the Great Famine, she was daughter of Lord Cloncurry of Lyons House, County Kildare, in Ireland. Her grandfather, Valentine Lawless, had been of the second peer, and was an ardent sympathizer with the Irish worker. He opposed union with England and was twice imprisoned for his political views. His father had withdrawn from the Catholic Church to join the Church of England and received his Peerage in 1789. Emily's mother, described as beautiful, had nine children, of which Emily was the second and eldest daughter. Her father's aristocratic position allowed her great insight into the social and political issues of Ireland that she would later make famous in her regional novels. Her childhood reading included Elizabethan plays, from which she memorized lengthy sections. She developed an interest in wildlife, particularly bugs of all kinds, and later wrote in *Traits and Confidences*

(1897) of her hunt for a rare moth at age 10. Although her father died when Emily was 14, she had by then developed a firm interest in Irish history.

Educated privately, Emily Lawless rode to hounds, spending childhood summers with the Kirwans of Castlehacket, Tuam, members of her mother's family. She was presented at court and had another politically connected relative, General Lawless, who helped interview Napoleon with requests for French aid to the Society of United Irishmen; the French forces arrived too late to be of much help in the Irish peasantry rebellion of 1798. Her father befriended Daniel O'Connell, a politician active in the move to repeal English laws that forbade Catholics from serving in Parliament. He also later sent £100 to the widow of John Mitchel. Mitchel was a revolutionary convicted of high treason, sent to Australia in 1848, who escaped to the United States, then returned to Ireland, where he was elected to Parliament, despite his status as a convicted felon, but died before he could take office. Such family sympathies likely helped develop an open attitude toward Ireland's working class, often absent in individuals of Lawless's social stature. Her interests varied from the normal interests of the aristocracy, and she spent much time in study of Irish folklore and history.

Although she never attempted to learn the language, she does imitate it well in the dialogue in her novels. Her writing was prompted by the prolific Scottish novelist Margaret Oliphant, and she published her first novel, *A Millionaire's Cousin,* in 1885. Her second and most important and popular novel, HURRISH (1886), contains a landlord character said to be based on her father. She followed a single-volume of Irish history (1887) with a fictionalized "firsthand account" of the Earl of Essex's expedition to Ireland in 1599, where he represented Queen Elizabeth as her Lord Lieutenant. Then-three-time English prime minister William Gladstone was so impressed with the work, he visited Lawless in person, at her hotel room in Cannes. One story tells of her answering the door in her stocking feet, assuming it was a clerk delivering her tea, much to her later embarrassment.

Lawless published a third novel, GRANIA: *The Story of an Island* (1892), followed in 1894 by *Malecho,* a grim historical novel set in 16th-century Ireland.

Her final novel about Ireland, *Traits and Confidences* (1897), included some autobiographical material along with a short medieval romance, two different stories about assassination, and other selections. She also published a well-received book of verse, *With the Wild Geese* (1902), and a children's book, *Gilly* (1906), as well as *The Point of View* (1909), a book privately published with all proceeds going to Galway fishermen. All her books are available in print, and some are available online, including a biography of one the first female British regional writers, Maria EDGEWORTH (1904).

BIBLIOGRAPHY
Kirkpatrick, Kathryn, ed. *Border Crossings: Irish Women Writers and National Identities.* Tuscaloosa, Ala.: University of Alabama Press, 1999.
Mulkerns, Val. Introduction to *Hurrish,* by Emily Lawless. Belfast: Apple Tree Press, 1992, vii–x.
Wolff, Robert Lee. Introduction to *Grania, the Story of an Island,* by Emily Lawless. Vol. I. New York: Garland Publishing, 1979, vi–xv.

LAWRENCE, GEORGE ALFRED (1827–1876)

George Alfred Lawrence wrote novels at a time when his contemporaries produced books for boys featuring virtuous heroes, fashioned to teach proper conduct. Unlike his old Rugby classmate Thomas HUGHES, whose TOM BROWN'S SCHOOL DAYS (1857) glorified academic trials meant to mold model citizens, Lawrence focused on heroes of great strength and reckless attitude. Their daring deeds depended on brawn, rather than brains, for success. Though he was called to the bar in 1852 following his graduation from Oxford, he chose instead to focus on producing novels. His first novel, GUY LIVINGSTONE, OR THOROUGH (1857), proved his most famous SENSATION FICTION, offering a title hero the antithesis of Charles KINGSLEY's "muscular Christian" types. Guy Livingstone embodied an unprincipled courage and died unfulfilled. Lawrence published *Guy Livingstone* anonymously but followed it with *Sword and Gown* (1859), *Barren Honour* (1862), *Breaking a Butterfly* (1869), and *Hagarene* (1874), which bore his name. While Lawrence's individual works fell out of favor, his emphasis on pure masculinity to the detriment of intellectualism became crucial to the development of the action novel.

BIBLIOGRAPHY
Fleming, Gordon. *George Alfred Lawrence and the Victorian Sensation Novel.* Tucson: University of Arizona, 1952.

LE FANU, (JOSEPH) SHERIDAN (1814–1873)

Born in Dublin and named for his famous relative, the Irish playwright Richard Brinsley Sheridan, Joseph Sheridan Le Fanu enjoyed a pleasant childhood in an attentive family. After attending Trinity College, he was called to the bar in 1839 but chose not to practice. Instead, he became a writer, contributing to the *Dublin University Magazine* several "uncanny" tales of the supernatural. A scholarly personality, he studied the occult throughout his life. Early in his career, he was best known for his Irish ballads, including "Shamus O'Brien" (1837), but gained additional fame with the appearance of his first novel, *The Cock and Anchor* (1845). While owner and editor of the *Dublin University Magazine* after 1869, Le Fanu published an additional 20 books, novels as well as story and ballad collections and an occasional drama. He gained wide renown with his terrifying mystery tales, becoming the master of supernatural fiction. His penchant for fashioning exquisitely tense suspense made his *The House by the Churchyard* (1863), UNCLE SILAS (1864), and the short story collection *In a Glass Darkly* (1872), some of the best ghost stories written in the English language. He indulged so frequently in horrific speculation that toward his life's end he became literally haunted by his own demons and visions, rarely leaving his house.

BIBLIOGRAPHY
McCormack, W. J. *Sheridan Le Fanu.* Stroud, Gloucester, U.K.: Sutton, 1997.

LEGEND OF MONTROSE, THE SIR WALTER SCOTT (1819)

The Legend of Montrose became the third in Sir Walter SCOTT's Tales of My Landlord series. As with most of Scott's novels, this one is actually based on a "tale" popular in his day, explained by Scott in his introduction. It centers on the 1644 rising of the Scots Highland clans in support of

Charles I against the Covenanters, fighting that was an offshoot of the English Civil War. Scott refers to it as a story of "deadly feuds," featuring that between John Lord Kilpont, the eldest son of William Earl of Airth and Monteith and James Stuart of Ardvoirlich.

Scott based his plot on a legendary feud between the families of Drummond and Murray. Supposedly the Drummonds trapped "eight score" of Murrays in the kirk of Monivaird and set it on fire. Only one boy escaped, aided by a Drummond. While several Drummonds were executed, the one aiding the boy fled to Ireland, recalled to Scotland later in payment for his rescue of the boy. He resettled in Scotland and became a forester for King James in an area known for its group of raiders. They belonged to an outlawed clan, the MacGregors, who called themselves Children of the Mist because they lived in the forest, considering it their domain. Angered at Drummond for "trespassing" in their woods, they murdered and beheaded him, then visited his sister. When she offered hospitality, serving them bread and cheese, they placed their grisly trophy on her table, filling the mouth with food and so horrifying their pregnant hostess that she fled to the woods and went mad. Her husband later managed to bring her home, where she delivered a son.

As the tale goes, the MacGregors retained their gory trophy, using it as a center of various celebrations and ceremonies, their actions recorded in a local popular ballad "Clan-Alpin's Vow." The baby born to the murdered man's sister, James Stewart of Ardvoirlich, matured "moody, fierce and irascible" and joined with Montrose's forces in 1644, becoming a favorite of Lord Kilpont, earl of Airth and Menteith. One account told that before a week passed, Stewart stabbed the earl in the heart, apparently believing himself to be extracting vengeance for his refusal to help murder Montrose, although that theory was never confirmed. Stewart escaped, was pardoned for killing Lord Kilpont, verified by Parliament, and taken into the forces of the Covenanters, Montrose's adversaries. In an interesting footnote, Scott tells that the "present Robert Stewart of Ardvoirlich" wrote to give the "true account" of Kilpont's murder. He explained that while marching across James Stewart's lands, Montrose's troops, joined then by Irish forces commanded by Alexander Mac-

Donald, "committed excess." Stewart demanded redress from MacDonald, who refused a one-on-one combat. Montrose attempted to smooth over the quarrel, and Kilpont supported him, thus making an enemy of young Stewart, who later, "heated with drink," came to "high words" with Kilpont, stabbing him.

Scott admits that he "enlivened" his own tale by not following the facts closely. In Scott's version, young Allan M'Aulay's uncle has been killed by the group named Children of the Mist. Filled with a desire for revenge, M'Aulay has enough passion left over to fall in love with Annot Lyle. Also a victim of the raiders, Annot was saved by M'Aulay following her kidnapping. Unfortunately she does not return M'Aulay's love but instead fancies the earl of Menteith. Although the earl loves her in turn, Annot's mysterious background prevents their marriage. Stronger characterizations and interactions occur in the meantime between other characters, such as the Royalist Montrose and his opposition, Argyle, with the strongest character being that of the Falstaff-like Dugald Dalgetty, overshadowing the romantic subplot. Dalgetty proves a humorous character in the vein of creations by Tobias SMOLLETT. Scott quotes a statement from the BLACKWOOD'S EDINBURGH REVIEW, no. 55, praising Dalgetty as a character who can appear in scene after scene of "unbounded loquacity" and never exhaust his eloquent humor. Modern critics, however, feel he lacks the sympathetic portrayal of most of Scott's comic characters. In what should lead to a happy conclusion, Annot discovers her heritage as the daughter of Sir Duncan Campbell. Her aristocratic connection makes possible her wedding to Menteith, but M'Aulay savagely attacks and stabs the groom, then disappears.

Many critics find the characterization secondary to the strong historic depiction. While Scott handled this work with a lighter tone than most of his others, readers familiar with his nine-book *Landlord* series may find it lacking. Its lesser quality could be due to the fact that Scott admittedly was coming to the end of his historical "stock" of local legends and traditional tales. While the creation of such a large group of novels in only five years proved a phenomenal task, Scott was ready to move on. However, his innate storytelling abilities prove evident in *Montrose,* as his fluent style holds his reader's attention. It remains a popular novel, available in book form and also electronic text.

BIBLIOGRAPHY
Hart, Francis Russell. *Scott's Novels: The Plotting of Historic Survival.* Charlottesville: University Press of Virginia, 1966.

LEVER, CHARLES JAMES (1806–1872)

Charles James Lever was born and raised in Dublin. An Irishman descended from English settlers, he attended Trinity College in Dublin and gained a reputation as a prankster. His sense of humor and bon vivant would flavor most of his future published works. He wandered America for a time and then studied medicine in Germany, collecting stories in each new location. By the time he received his medical degree, he was more interested in writing stories than practicing. However, he settled into his role as country physician for a time in Northern Ireland, beginning in 1837 a serial printed at irregular intervals titled *The Confessions of Harry Lorrequer.* Printed in the *Dublin University Magazine,* the serial became a popular success, mainly due to its lively, humorous first-person narrative voice. It would be reissued in monthly parts in 1839, and Lever's career as a writer was fully launched. As a military officer, Lorrequer roams about Ireland on leave, his trials all converted to audience entertainment value. His works focused on the sport-loving, careless, and sometimes foolish landed Irish gentry, but without the judgmental tone marking works about the same topic by his contemporary Maria EDGEWORTH. Lever celebrated the lifestyle, obviously enjoying telling tales of duels, hunts, and races, lacing his narrative with multiple practical jokes, silly prejudices and imprudent decisions on the part of his characters for entertainment of his audience.

By the time of his next publication, *Charles O'Malley, the Irish Dragoon,* Lever had moved to practice in Brussels. Surrounded by survivors of the Napoleonic War, he dealt again with military life but added liberal doses of Galway sports and practical jokes at Trinity College. As the plot advanced to scenes on the battlefield, Lever rendered them in such detail that even the old Duke of Wellington approved. However, Lever's trademark humorous tone carried the novel to another success. Edgar Allan Poe, offering a negative review, had to admit that in popularity, Lever challenged Charles DICKENS.

Lever followed his success with two additional novels, jointly titled *Our Mess. Jack Hinton, the Guardsman* (1842) followed the pattern of his initial novels, while *Tom Burke of Ours* (1843–44) became a companion to *Charles O'Malley,* fashioning the Napoleonic conflict from a French point of view. At the same time, he published a group of stories titled *The Wanderings and Pondering of Arthur O'Leary,* which grew from his experiences abroad. No longer practicing medicine, Lever turned his full attention to publishing and became editor of the *Dublin University Magazine.* That experience convinced him to take politics more seriously and to show more than the lighthearted side of Irish life. He familiarized himself with the life of the Celtic poor and the function of Irish priests in community life. *The O'Donohue* (1845) greatly contrasted with his previous publications in its serious tone and greater plot unity. His focus on the dying way of life of an Irish aristocrat clarified sociopolitical factors leading up to the 1798 Irish revolt. William Makepeace THACKERAY chose Lever's style as one to PARODY in his *PUNCH'S PRIZE NOVELISTS* (1847).

Lever left Ireland to tour the Continent in 1845, accepting two consulships in Italy, first at Spezzia (1865) and later at Trieste (1867). He continued writing, but developed an even more somber tone in his later works, as his attitudes became more sophisticated regarding the elitism of his own countrymen. They included *Roland Cashel* (1850), *The Daltons, or Three Roads in Life* (1851–52), *Sir Jasper Carew* (1855), *The Fortunes of Glencore* (1857), *A Day's Ride* (1863), *Luttrell of Arran* (1865), and *Lord Kilgobbin* (1872).

BIBLIOGRAPHY
Haddelson, Stephen. *Charles Lever: The Lost Victorian.* New York: Colin Smythe, 2000.

LEWIS, M(ATTHEW) G(REGORY) (1775–1818)

Enjoying a privileged childhood in a monied family, M. G. Lewis was the son of a wealthy West Indian proprietor, schooled at Westminster and Christ

Church, Oxford. While an undergraduate at Oxford, he vacationed on the Continent. He studied languages and became attracted to contemporary German literature, particularly its more grotesque and sensational details. Favorite books included the seminal BILDUNGSROMAN Goethe's *Werther;* Schiller's "gloom and doom" *Robbers,* and the terrifying *Schauersromane* (shudder-novels). Following graduation at age 19, he became a member of the diplomatic service as an attaché in Holland and read Anne RADCLIFFE'S immensely popular GOTHIC novel *MYSTERIES OF UDOLPHO* (1794). His gloomy interests earned him the nickname "Monk."

Lewis set out to imitate Radcliffe's work but produced a novel that varied widely in style from her high moral and delicate tone. He incorporated grossly sensational details and did not use Radcliffe's technique of rational explanation for uncanny events. Instead he incorporated a crude approach, using the grotesque conclusion of *Dr. Faustus* on which to base his own. His novel, *Ambrosio, or The Monk,* simply known as *The MONK* (1796), so offended readers at first that it was banned as immoral. Its climax focused on a demon rescuing the protagonist and then flying through the air to drop him to rocks below. The novel is credited for introducing English readers to German Romantic literature and contained enduring characters such as the "Wandering Jew" and a bleeding nun. Abundant atrocious details from the tortures of the Inquisition reportedly nauseated many readers. Lewis revised its grotesque sensationalism, issuing another edition, which was better received.

Although he produced additional works, Lewis is best remembered for *The Monk.* It had an immediate influence on Mrs. Radcliffe, who was likely offended. Yet her next novel, *The Italian* (1797), also employed aspects of the Inquisition and focused on a heroine imprisoned in a convent, although it retained her high moral tone. Lewis also wrote *The Bravo of Venice* (1804), *Feudal Tyrants* (1806), and some dramas, *The Castle Spectre* (1796), *The East Indian* (1799), *Alphonso, King of Castille* (1801), and *The Wood Demon* (1807), as well as verse. His best-known poem, "Alonzo the Brave and the Fair Imogine," he included within *The Monk.* An acquaintance of some of the most famous writers of

the day, Lewis visited Lord Byron, who declared him a fine fellow but boring, and Sir Walter SCOTT, who held Lewis in some favor. Elected to the House of Commons in 1796–1802, he continued writing but, after his father's death, directed his energies to improve conditions on West Indian sugar plantations. He died of yellow fever, contracted during his second of two visits to Jamaica in 1818, leaving an unfinished work, *Journal of a West Indian Proprietor,* published in 1834. Its importance regained his strong reputation, which had waned since publication of *The Monk.* That novel remains popular and is readily available.

BIBLIOGRAPHY

Irwin, Joseph James. *M.G. "Monk" Lewis.* Boston: Twayne, 1976.

Macdonald, David Lorne. *Monk Lewis: A Critical Biography.* Toronto: Toronto Press, 2000.

LIFE AND ADVENTURES OF PETER WILKINS, THE ROBERT PALTOCK (1751)

The sole novel written by Robert PALTOCK, *The Life and Adventures of Peter Wilkins* is one of the earliest written examples of SCIENCE FICTION in English, enjoyed as children by notables including the poet Robert Southey; critic, poet, and journalist Leigh Hunt; and novelist Sir Walter SCOTT. Wilkins serves as the first-person narrator, telling his life's story to the author, in a common narrative device of the day.

Wilkins's life had proved an adventure since his childhood, when his father was executed for his part in Monmouth's rebellion against James II. While his early years proved happy enough, when his mother remarried, her new husband, the squire, shuffled Wilkins off to boarding school at age 14. While there he seduces, then marries, his tutor's lovely servant Patty, and a few years later returns home a young man. To his dismay, his mother has died and his stepfather has claimed his inheritance. He leaves to clerk on a ship, enjoys many adventures, and ends up an unhappy laborer in Angola. The courageous African slave and fellow laborer Glanlapze helps Wilkins escape. They travel through Africa, with Glanlapze repeatedly proving his heroism in encounters with wild animals and people. They return to Glanlapze's home for his joyful reunion with his wife and children, then Wilkins joins a gang of homeless youths like himself to steal a ship. Untrained in navigation skills, the group wrecks the ship, with Wilkins, the only survivor, swept onto an island. There he lives a life similar to that of Daniel DEFOE's protagonist in ROBINSON CRUSOE (1719), the likely model for Paltock's work. Unable to return to his ship for any supplies, Wilkins must live wholly off the land's offering of plant and animal life. He explains the mysterious voices he hears that seem to come from above as unusual bird noises.

In the next plot turn, Wilkins discovers a lovely injured girl outside his hut, whom he revives and nurses back to health. He learns that she and her fellow islanders can fly, details about which Paltock remains vague, simply depending on readers' willingness to suspend their disbelief. Wilkins believes the "news" of Patty's death that comes to him in a vision and decides to marry the girl, Youwarkee. Many of her moves are batlike, and Wilkins must fashion a pair of dark glasses for her to wear to protect her sensitive eyes from offensive sunlight. He learns more about her, and the "graundee" that allows her to fly, including the fact that she worships a God who, although his name is Collwar, Wilkins accepts as the same spirit as his own Jehovah. He convinces her that she should not worship idols, and she adopts Christianity. After hearing about his ship, she flies to it one day and returns with supplies, later fashioning waterproof containers in which to float more articles to the island. Several years later, Youwarkee visits her family and returns with several members, whom Wilkins impresses with various belongings, including his gun. Before long, Wilkins ingratiates himself with the king by discovering a plot against his life. As the king's favorite, he continues to help him defeat adversaries, introducing the use of several handy English weapons, including a cannon that breaks apart the flying formation of the enemy.

Wilkins proceeds to civilize the culture, leading a move to abolish slavery, which he openly detests, teaching the populace to read, and improving their international relations by helping arrange a marriage for the king with a foreign princess. He lives many years with his new family and eventually, following his wife's death, considers returning to England. A relay of flyers seeks to return him, but a ship fires on them as strange objects in the sky, causing them to drop Wilkins into the sea, where he is rescued and can tell of his QUEST.

FEMINIST CRITICS would find of interest Paltock's depiction of women as intelligent, self-sufficient beings, while NEW HISTORICIST CRITICS would notice Paltock's pre-Victorian anti-slavery attitude and his fashioning of the slave Glanlapze as brave, loyal, and resourceful. The book remains available in print form.

BIBLIOGRAPHY

Hugh, David. "Guest Reviews: *The Life and Adventures of Peter Wilkins*." *Lost Books*. Available online. URL: http://www.lostbooks.org/guestreviews/2002-04-01-2.html. Downloaded on September 10, 2003.

LINTON, MRS. ELIZA (ELIZABETH) LYNN (1822–1898)

The daughter of a Keswick clergyman, Eliza Lynn lost her mother at age five and left home at age 23 determined to be a writer. Later considered to be part of what critics would later call the "second tier" of women writers, she published her first novel, *Azeth the Egyptian,* in 1846. While not a popular success, the novel did for Lynn what publishing even a mediocre novel did for other women, earning her with copyright sale the equivalent of a year's wages for a governess. It also afforded her a staff position with periodicals including *The Morning Chronicle* and later *The SATURDAY REVIEW* and *ALL THE YEAR ROUND,* as she became one of the first women to support herself as a journalist and researcher. Neither of her next novels, *Amymone* (1848) and *Realities* (1851), proved successes.

Lynn lived in Paris for a time and then, in 1858, married William James Linton, engraver, poet, Chartist Republican, and father to seven children although they amicably separated a short time later. Lynn took in Beatrice Harraden, noted suffragette and writer, as her ward. Lynn passed along her independent attitudes to Harraden, although Lynn detested women's causes. She reacted to criticism of her inferiority to "normal" women by displaying embroidered cushions, fire screens, and chair seats when interviewers visited her home, stressing her domesticity. She also commented that women writers could never realistically shape male characters. Elaine Showalter cites from Linton's letters the statement that women could never "understand the loftier side of a man's nature," as they know "nothing, subjectively, of the political aims, the love for abstract truth, the desire for human progress," all of which remove him from the female "narrow domestic sphere, and make him comparatively indifferent to the life of sense and emotion." She later published *The True History of Joshua Davidson, Christian and Communist* (1872), featuring a Christ figure; *Patricia Kemball* (1874); *The Atonement of Leam Dundas* (1876); *Under Which Lord?* (1879); and *The Autobiography of Christopher Kirkland* (1885), an obvious story of her own life. She revealed anti-feminist attitudes in her collection of prose *The Girl of the Period and Other Essays* (1883). She also attacked "athletic" women and those with professional aspirations in an article titled "The Shrieking Sisterhood." While her writing is little read, due to its reactionary propagandistic bent, historians remain fascinated with the contradiction between that work and her many accomplishments that helped advance women's rights.

BIBLIOGRAPHY

Sage, Lorna. "Linton, Eliza Lynn." *The Cambridge Guide to Women's Writing in English*. Cambridge: Cambridge University Press, 1999, 393.

Showalter, Elaine. *A Literature of Their Own: British Women Novelists from Brontë to Lessing*. Princeton, N.J.: Princeton University Press, 1999.

LITTLE DORRIT CHARLES DICKENS (1857)

First published as a 20-part serial between December 1855 and June 1857, Charles DICKENS's *Little Dorrit* served to expose several social abuses of interest to its author, including rampant financial corruption and an incompetent civil service members were appointed through favoritism. At first Dickens intended to explore the theme that such conditions were claimed to be "Nobody's fault," and he considered that phrase as the novel's title. He rendered a discouraging view of the effects of Britain's economic and social system on its citizens. The Circumlocution Office is composed of self-satisfied figures who block all promotion of good for the common man.

The main plot in this dark novel involves a family named Dorrit and centers on Amy Dorrit, nicknamed "Little Dorrit." Amy was born in the prison Marshalsea, where her father, William, has spent so much time as a debtor, he is known as "the father of Marshalsea." Like Dickens's BLEAK HOUSE (1853), *Little Dorrit* incorporates aspects of the Gothic to bring an air of horror to the tale. Dickens also similarly offers several plot lines that appear unrelated at first, set in London, Marseille, and also Italy. The characters eventually connect with one another in a plot that Jane Smiley has labeled "overelaborate and creaky," filled with many uninteresting figures.

Amy's bright disposition keeps hopes alive for a happy future, as she and her father find a friend in Arthur Clennam, newly returned to England after having lived abroad. He tries to care for his mother, a bitter, gloomy paralyzed figure whose dark and foreboding house symbolizes her bigotry and misanthropy. Clennam helps Amy take a job sewing for Mrs. Clennam, who becomes involved with the French villain, Rigaud/Blandois, and his partner in crime, Jeremiah Flintwich. Dickens depicts Mrs. Flintwich as a victim of her husband's and Mrs. Clennam's abuse, with her visions that become reality adding a touch of mysticism to the novel. The collapse of Mrs. Clennam's frightening house symbolizes the eventual decay of her own life, which lacks foundation in any faith in her fellow man. An additional wicked figure meant to represent hypocrisy is Mr. Casby, a supposed humanitarian who spouts morality while supporting himself with income from slum houses that he rents at exorbitant fees to the poor.

William and Amy eventually leave the prison, and through an inheritance, the family becomes wealthy, traveling to Italy. William dies there a broken man, remembering only his experiences in prison, representing the inability of money to heal deep wounds. Meanwhile, Clennam struggles with the Circumlocution Office in London, where Merdle, a millionaire speculator praised by church and state alike, draws Clennam and others into a fraud that lands Clennam in the Marshalsea. Merdle's eventual suicide acts as a heavy-handed caution by Dickens to those who prey on others, while he incorporates his era's attitude toward the Circumlocution Office as representing the worst of government's meaningless activities. Little Dorrit returns to the Marshalsea and finds Clennam. In contrast to her siblings, who have assumed the pretensions expected of the wealthy, Amy remains untouched by money's evils. Generous and without guile, she lacks her sibling's social aspirations, valuing her love for Clennam more. He eventually recognizes that love and, after the Dorrits lose their fortune, the two are able to make a life together.

Dickens incorporates some real-life and autobiographical aspects into his novel. The imprisonment for debt of his own family during his childhood had already been used in DAVID COPPERFIELD (1850), but it is explored in more depth in *Little Dorrit*. The Micawber figure in *David Copperfield* was a comic representation of Dickens's father, while William Dorrit is much more serious and realistic. Disgusted by what he viewed as governmental blunders during the Crimean War, Dickens sketched most government offices as nothing more than bureaucratic boondoggles. He based Merdle on the real figure of John Sadleir, a financial promoter who killed himself in 1856.

Dickens also includes his trademark humorous characters, such as Mrs. General, a venerable lady who lives up to her name. Mr. Dorrit hires her to be a traveling companion for Amy following their social elevation due to his inheritance. A woman of "high style" and "composure," others testify as to her "piety, learning, virtue and gentility," one archdeacon even weeping at the thought of her perfection. She accepts the offer to accompany the Dorrits to the Alps, thinking she might help to "form the mind" of Amy Dorrit. Her absurd moralizing and philosophizing help to lighten an otherwise often dark tone. In a like turn, Mrs. Winter, at first annoyingly repugnant as a drinker and a silly flirt, proves that she possesses compassion, a quality highly valued in Dickens's characters. She understands her faults, making her a strong foil for Mrs. General, who deems herself perfect in every way.

Little Dorrit proved popular with Dickens's readers. It was converted to various media versions and remains readily available in both print and electronic form.

BIBLIOGRAPHY

Schlicke, Paul, ed. *The Oxford Reader's Companion to Dickens.* Oxford: Oxford University Press, 2000.

Smiley, Jane. *Charles Dickens.* New York: Viking, 2002.

LITTLE LORD FAUNTLEROY FRANCES HODGSON BURNETT (1886)

In one of history's best-beloved novels for children, *Little Lord Fauntleroy,* Frances Hodgson BURNETT emphasizes the importance of love over material wealth. Before the birth of the little lord, Cedric Errol, his aristocratic father, Captain Cedric, marries beneath himself, angering his father, the earl of Dorincourt. He has little hope of inheriting the family fortune, as his two elder brothers stand to receive the title and property first. When Cedric's wife proposes that they move to America, the lord becomes enraged and refuses to acknowledge his daughter-in-law. The captain sells his commission, using the funds to depart England. All that action is revealed through exposition, taking place before the plot begins, soon after Cedric's death.

Little Cedric, a favorite in his New York neighborhood, has notable blond curls and blue eyes, along with a beautiful disposition. He has inherited his parents' "always loving and considerate and tender" ways in a household where he never "heard an unkind or uncourteous word spoken." The boy is especially close to Mr. Hobbs, the grocer, and Dick, a bootblack. Following a discussion with Mr. Hobbs in which he says some "very severe things" about aristocrats, including that one day "those they've trod on" will "rise and blow 'em up sky-high," a representative of the earl visits Mrs. Errol. He informs her that both of Cedric's uncles have died, and the boy has inherited the title. When Cedric reluctantly informs Mr. Hobbs of his new title, fearing a violent reaction, Mr. Hobbs recognizes that the boy remains "just a handsome, cheerful, brave little fellow in a blue suit and red neck-ribbon," foreshadowing what will follow.

Cedric moves to England to live with his grandfather, "John Arthur Molyneux Errol, Earl of Dorincourt," as he explains to Hobbs. The irascible old man persists in his refusal to receive Mrs. Errol, who lives nearby, but he comes to love Cedric. Cedric's strong character allows him to remain untouched by the class-consciousness and snobbery of others of his group, as predicted by Hobbs's earlier impression. His influence is so strong that he convinces his grandfather to end abuses of his own tenants and to come to respect the poor inhabitants of the land around his estate. Conflict develops, however, when another woman appears, claiming to be the true Mrs. Errol, with a son she insists was fathered by Cedric's Uncle Bevis and is the heir to the earl's title and fortune. Cedric writes to Mr. Hobbs explaining the situation in a breathless line: "It is all a mistake and i am not a lord and i shall not have to be an earl." Burnett retains the light tone of the story in the boy's signature, "Cedric Errol (Not Lord Fauntleroy)."

Their sense of justice wounded, Hobbs and Dick join forces to prove the woman an impostor. In a touching scene, the earl tells Cedric, "You'll be my boy as long as I live; and, by George, sometimes I feel as if you were the only boy I ever had." He mends his own break with Mrs. Errol and declares Cedric will always be cared for. As the adversity brings those three closer, in America Dick recognizes a picture of the interloper as a New York commoner. He and Hobbs engage an attorney, and they reveal her true identity as Minna Tipton. They travel to England along with Ben, father to the fake Little Lord, whose real name is Tom Tipton. Ben takes the boy home with him, and Cedric and Mrs. Errol move in with the earl. The earl graciously invests in a California cattle ranch and hires Ben to manage it, in order to support the boy "who might have turned out to be Lord Fauntleroy," exercising the grace he learned from his grandson. Dick and Hobbs linger in England, enjoying a grand celebration with Cedric and his family, particularly the earl, who is the happiest of the group. Burnett tempers her statement of his happiness with the realistic revelation that the earl "had not, indeed, suddenly become as good as Fauntleroy thought him; but, at least, he had begun to love something." That clear-headed view of her characters prevents the novel's dissolving into a wholly sentimental presentation.

The book remains a classic, cherished more for its representation of a certain innocence of an era than as a realistic everyday story often read in the classroom.

BIBLIOGRAPHY

Bixler, Phyllis. *Frances Hodgson Burnett.* Boston: Twayne, 1984.

Carpenter, Angelica Shirley. *Frances Hodgson Burnett: Beyond the Secret Garden.* Minneapolis: Lerner, 1990.

LONDON MAGAZINE, THE

The *London Magazine* was founded in 1732 and run for a time by the distinguished James Boswell, biographer of Samuel JOHNSON, with a promise to serve all tastes, political, social, economic, and literary. It was often parodied by other periodicals, including the *Grub Street Journal,* which viciously attacked all publications that did not defend Augustan ideals as it did. It was also satirized by Bonnell Thornton's important early periodical, *Have at You All, or Drury Lane Journal.* Such volleys may have resulted due to *The London Magazine*'s tendency to imitate the *Gentleman's Magazine,* founded by Edward Cave and considered an important literary clearing house for essays of the day, news, and parliamentary proceedings. Cave subtitled his magazine "Monthly Intelligencer," and the *London*'s subtitle read "Gentleman's Monthly Intelligencer." It contained a "View of Weekly Essays and Disputes this Month," quoting from other magazines, and also contained "poetical essays," which featured current news and columns of births, deaths, stocks, and book catalogs. Whenever *Gentleman's* added a new column, *London*'s would follow suit. London's did gain a reputation as decent fare in its own right, featuring pieces by distinguished writers such as Boswell, who contributed 70 "Hypochondirack" essays between 1777 and 1783. It also had its imitators, including *The Magazine of Magazines* (1750) and the *Newcastle General Magazine* (1747), which used specifically *London*'s "Debates of the Political Club." A provincial periodical titled *Exshaw's Magazine* was simply *The London Magazine* reprinted. Printing lapsed for a time, then enjoyed a revival in 1820, after which it was closely affiliated with the liberal "Cockney school" of romantic poetry, particularly that of Wordsworth and Keats.

John Scott, a well-known romantic critic, took the editorial chair and promised to give London a periodical of "sound principles in questions of taste, morals, and politics." Its first issue at 188 pages included Thomas De Quincey's "Confessions of an Opium Eater," William Hazlitt's "Table Talk," and Charles Lamb's "Essays of Elia." John Scott's remarkable appraisals of work by Sir Walter SCOTT, along with the romantic poets, put the editorial work of contemporary periodicals to shame. He eventually attacked in print what he viewed as *BLACKWOOD'S MAGAZINE*'s lack of editorial integrity and rigor, leading to a duel between Scott and the second to John Gibson Lockhart, J. H. Christies. Scott died, and the periodical began to slide into desperate straights, due to mismanagement. It ended publication in 1825, having surpassed all other contemporary periodicals in literary quality. It established benchmarks for literary criticism, which stood throughout the 19th century.

BIBLIOGRAPHY
Graham, Walter. *English Literary Periodicals.* New York: Octagon Books, 1966.

LORD ORMONT AND HIS AMINTA
GEORGE MEREDITH (1894) When George MEREDITH wrote *Lord Ormont and His Aminta,* he focused on a theme he would use again: incompatibility in marriage. Many critics considered it a slight work; some felt Meredith wrote it during a break after the far more demanding *ONE OF OUR CONQUERORS* (1891). The novel appeared first as a serial in *The Pall Mall* and focused on the failure of a one-time military hero, also a member of aristocracy, to move beyond the past and develop relationships with others; he wastes his prospects while playing at revolt against the expectations of the upper class to which he clearly belongs. The novel opens with two of its main characters in childhood. Aminta and Matthew "Matie" Weyburn both admire Lord Ormont as a champion for England in adventures in India. The aging Lord Ormont later marries the romantic and lovely but "common" Aminta at the embassy in Madrid, then refuses to introduce her to London high society. His refusal is based mostly on what he perceives as a slight, when his culture seems to ignore his due as a military star. Meredith supposedly based Ormont on a melding of two real-life ex-military men, the earl of Peterborough, dubbed the last of the knights errant, and the earl of Cardigan, who led the light brigade at Balaclava. Ormont's staged revolt appears ludicrous, emphasizing his class position rather than marginalizing it, and symbolizing the frustration of those caught within the mores of the class to which they so badly want to belong.

Lonely, embarrassed, and disillusioned with Ormont, Aminta finds her own friends among a scandalous group, which includes Morsfield, a particularly hateful individual. Ormont does nothing to "validate" the marriage that many, including his sister, Lady Constance Eglett, doubt ever took place; they view Aminta as no more than a mistress to Ormont. When Matie Weyburn turns up to work on putting Ormont's library in order, he renews his relationship with Aminta, taking steps to separate her from Morsfield's harmful influence. When Ormont recognizes Weyburn's efforts on behalf of his wife, he acknowledges her value and decides to return to his social circles with his wife on his arm. However, she has fallen in love with Weyburn, returning his affections.

Not only does Aminta find Weyburn's romantic passion desirable, she also finds attractive the partnership, based on his consideration of her as an equal. Matie's respect for Aminta helps her regain her dignity and leave a farewell note for Ormont untinged by bitterness. The couple departs London and its judgmental social scene for Switzerland, where they decide to conduct a school, living outside accepted social convention by not marrying. Ormont offers them forgiveness prior to his death, which also offers them the freedom to marry. Meredith indicts society through Ormont, chastising its failure to develop a social awareness in a more modern age. He suggests the doom of individuals dehumanized by materialism and the values of the bourgeoisie. While not one of Meredith's most popular works, the book remains readily available.

BIBLIOGRAPHY
Jones, Mervyn. *The Amazing Victorian: A Life of George Meredith.* Constable: London, 1999.

Lindsay, Jack. *George Meredith: His Life and Work*. London: The Bodley Head, 1980.

LORNA DOONE: A ROMANCE OF EXMOOR R. D. BLACKMORE (1869)

When R. D. BLACKMORE wrote *Lorna Doone*, REALISM had begun to infiltrate the English novel. However, Blackmore makes clear in his preface that his work is a traditional ROMANCE, because all its elements "are alike romantic." He had no desire to "claim for it the dignity or cumber it with the difficulty of an historic novel." Having himself matured in the West Country, he sought to capture its picturesque quality for readers in describing the Doone valley. He wrote that "any son of Exmoor" would recognize in the story his own childhood "nurse-tales." When he notes the "Herculean power" of John Ridd, he refers to the story's narrator and protagonist who, most critics agree, gives the book a special attraction. Blackmore bestows on Ridd a colloquial speech pattern, produced in such an honest tone that readers cannot resist.

Set in the 17th-century days of Kings Charles II and James II, the plot focuses on Ridd, who has lost his father to the violence of the clan of Doone. That group lives in the Doone Valley and gains a reputation for murder and theft. While John seeks vengeance for his father's death, he also loves a member of the Doone clan, the innocent Lorna, daughter to the clan's leader and his father's murderer. He first met her when he ventured into the valley a year after his father's death, carrying bullets that his sister Lizzie helped him shape from molten lead to use against the Doones. He happens upon Lorna by accident and, as the two talk, is almost discovered by the Doones, who are searching for Lorna, their "queen," fearing she has drowned. Lorna helps John escape, but he plots to return someday to carry out his plan and continue romancing the young woman who has enchanted him. Eventually John does return, and he steals her from the clan. In typical romance fashion, Lorna's true identity as the kidnapped daughter of a nobleman is revealed. This causes conflict for John, due to his lowly position as a yeoman. However, Lorna's love remains unshaken, and she feels confident in their relationship. John later serves the king and one of Lorna's relations in the Monmouth rebellion of 1865, earning not only their respect, but also his own self-respect. Freed from his previous concerns, he can marry Lorna.

The novel became one of the most popular ROMANCES of the 19th century. In addition to its main characters, the novel's serving woman, Betty Muxworthy, offers some comic relief and complements other positive characterizations of women. In addition, Tom Faggus, an outlaw with a good heart and one of John's relations, allows the protagonist's character to be fleshed out. At one point, John confesses that he never knew whether to claim relation to Faggus or not. To "the boys at Brendon," he was "exceeding proud to talk of him," but with "rich parsons of the neighborhood," and justices and tradesmen, "in a word, any settled power, which was afraid of losing things," he would claim no kinship to the infamous outlaw. Such consistent honesty and lack of guile on John's part greatly endeared him to readers. The novel appeared in various media forms in later decades and continues to be read in the 21st century.

BIBLIOGRAPHY
Budd, Kenneth George. *The Last Victorian: R. D. Blackmore and His Novels*. London: Centaur Press, 1960.
Dunn, Waldo Hilary. *R.D. Blackmore: The Author of Lorna Doone: A Biography*. London: Robert Hale, 1956.

LOTHAIR BENJAMIN DISRAELI (1870)

Benjamin DISRAELI wrote *Lothair* 23 years after his last novel, *TANCRED* (1847). His political career had prevented his pursuit of fiction, but when the general election of 1868 propelled Gladstone to power in Disraeli's place, he decided to return to writing. The prospects of the new novel caused tremendous anticipation. The public wondered whether he would produce another work of social-consciousness, like *SYBIL* (1845), or whether the novel might focus on the political world. Even his secretary knew no details, and when the novel appeared, it proved everyone wrong in their guesses regarding its plot. While Disraeli did base his novel on real-life events that featured political favoritism, it was not set in Parliament. Rather, he chose the Vatican as the power seeking to procure the favor of a wealthy nobleman. In 1868, one Monsignor Capel had influenced the enormously wealthy Third

Marquess of Bute to convert to Catholicism, in hopes of manipulating his political influence on behalf of the church, offering Disraeli the seed of his plot.

The fact that the machinations of Cardinal Manning, Catholic archbishop of Westminster, had probably cost Disraeli the 1868 election likely added fuel to his literary fire. *Lothair* became highly successful, allowing Disraeli revenge through his characterization of the despicable Cardinal Grandison. The first English edition of the novel sold out in 48 hours, and eight more editions were issued in 1870. When the novel appeared in the United States, 15,000 copies sold in a single day, rivaling in popularity Harriet Beecher Stowe's *Uncle Tom's Cabin*. While critics did not blast the novel, they also withheld praise for a story they found to be of little substance, containing no hint at what they termed the "author's principles" or "convictions." Disraeli's political cronies did not appreciate his efforts as the first prime minister ever to publish a novel; it did not seem a suitable activity. Modern readers find the novel melodramatic in a way less acceptable than the same type of hyperbolic excess characteristic of Charles DICKENS. Vernon Bogdanor suggests that is because Dickens used preposterous plot twists as a "vehicle" for crucial "revelation," whereas Disraeli employed them simply to advance an otherwise fairly realistic plot. Later readers also did not enjoy the novel as SATIRE, due to its gentle nature.

The novel features an orphaned nobleman of immense wealth named Lothair. He is raised by Lord Culloden and by Cardinal Grandison, at first a mere clergyman who manipulates his way to high office. Lothair matures as a Scots Protestant, taking part in Garibaldi's Italian campaign as an adult. Clare Arundel joins forces with Grandison and Monsignor Catesby to lure Lothair into conversion. On the other side of the private battle are Lord Culloden, the admirable Lady Corisande, and the highly dramatized Italian Garibaldi champion, Theodora, whom Lothair finds fascinating. While his thoughts focused regularly "on religion, the Churches, the solar system, the cosmical order, the purpose of creation, and the destiny of man," he was so enthralled with Theodora that they always returned to her, although she married an American. The Catholic forces felt her influence on Lothair, but, as the narrator notes, "Jesuits are wise men; they never lose

their temper. They know when to avoid scenes as well as when to make them." When Lothair presents her with an anonymous gift of priceless pearls, she returns them to him, explaining that an unknown admirer did not realize that she did not wear jewelry. She asks him to take charge of them for one year, and the astounded Lothair departs "with his own gift."

Disraeli makes abundantly clear Theodora's position as an ideal when, like the Virgin Mary, she rides a beautiful mule during a military campaign through the Appenines. The setting adds to the fantasy atmosphere, as the group halts "in a green nook, near a beautiful cascade that descended in a mist down a sylvan cleft, and poured its pellucid stream, for their delightful use, into a natural basin of water." The mist and water foreshadow an as yet unclear change in Lothair's future. A short time later, Theodora suffers a "theatrical" death, killed by papal supporters. As she dies, Lothair pledges he will never convert to Catholicism, "the scarlet lady," and he suddenly matures into a determined man. Despite his own later wounding and the cardinal's attempts to sway him, Lothair returns to England still a Protestant, where he marries Lady Corisande.

While Disraeli appreciated the historic significance of the Catholic Church and even admired its ideology, he also realized that it could usurp individual independence and creativity, encouraging instead conformity. He had written in various political works of the importance of religious ideology to politics. In an article that appeared in *BLACKWOOD'S EDINBURGH MAGAZINE* in 1868, he wrote that religion "instills some sense of responsibility even into the depositories of absolute power"; however, he recognized the danger to civil rights that religious edict posed. Although by the time he wrote *Lothair* he no longer championed the liberal ideals expressed in his earlier novels, he handled the characterizations of the politically idealistic Theodora and Clare Arundel with respect. Whether their motives proved "right" or "wrong," they remained pure. However, Clare proves unrealistically saintly and Theodora becomes a martyr, leaving Lady Corisande as the practical female voice, that of an English woman proud to represent her country. Lothair offers her the box of pearls one year after Theodora's death, and she presents him with a rose.

Readers then understand he has at last found the treasure he sought in his religious and military QUEST. Upon opening the case, they find on the jewels a slip of paper written by Theodora, which prophetically reads, "The Offering of Theodora to Lothair's Bride." When Lothair fastens the pearl ropes around her neck, Corisande tells him, "I will wear them as your chains," symbolizing that the past will not be forgotten.

BIBLIOGRAPHY

Bogdanor, Vernon. Introduction to *Lothair,* by Benjamin Disraeli. New York: Oxford University Press, 1975, vii–xvii.
Masefield, Muriel Agnes. *Peacocks and Primroses: A Survey of Disraeli's Novels.* 1953. Reprint, Millwood, N.Y.: Krause Reprints, 1973.

LOVE LETTERS BETWEEN A NOBLEMAN AND HIS SISTER APHRA BEHN (1684)

While Aphra BEHN's *Love Letters Between a Nobleman and His Sister* is not a well-known work, it remains crucial to the development of the novel. Many sources, including Ian Watt in his landmark work *The Rise of the Novel* (1957), credit Daniel DEFOE as writing the first successful English novel with ROBINSON CRUSOE (1719). Not discussed in nearly so grand an arena is the fact that Defoe found his models for early narrative fiction in 17th-century works by women, such as those by Behn. Her erotic *Love Letters* offered arguably the first ROMAN À CLEF and the first EPISTOLARY NOVEL a half century before Samuel RICHARDSON's PAMELA (1740), generally credited as the first epistolary novel. Based on a contemporary sex scandal, the novel appeared in three parts and proved extremely popular. While not historical fiction in the strictest sense of the term, it also featured her era's famous political figures, including the Protestant duke of Monmouth, son to Charles II, who was executed in 1685 for an attempted overthrow of his Catholic uncle, James II. Like Behn's other works, *Love Letters* features an elegant and witty fashioning of a sex-centered aristocratic world.

The plot mirrored the real-life scandal between Ford Lord Grey and his sister-in-law, Lady Henrietta. His wife, Lady Mary, daughter of the house of Berkeley, fell in love with James Scott, duke of Monmouth and the eldest illegitimate son of the deposed Charles II. While news items freely referenced the affair, Grey chose to ignore it in public. He may have gained his forbearance due to his own fixation on his wife's younger sister, Henrietta. While legally his in-law, Henrietta was known as his sister in the custom of the times, and the suggestion of incest fueled gossip regarding the entire affair. Not only did Grey seduce Henrietta, he "eloped" with her in the middle of political turmoil in which he was a major player, mesmerizing the public. The aristocratic Berkeley family had to advertise in the September edition of the 1682 *London Gazette* in order to locate and reclaim their daughter, an indignity for which they would not soon forgive Grey. They demanded a trial in which five accomplices were tried with Grey, four being found guilty. During the trial, Henrietta, although forbidden to speak in the patriarchal proceedings, declared that her family could not force her return, as she had married. Her husband proved to be one Mr. Turner, a servant to Lord Grey, who offered his master a convenient excuse for remaining close to Henrietta. A published transcript titled *The Trial of Ford Lord Grey* provided an excellent source for Behn's book. The court may have encouraged the publication, knowing of Grey's close involvement with Monmouth, who would soon rebel and attempt to wrest power from his uncle.

Although dedicated to King James, Behn closely followed Monmouth's career, finding him fascinating. Handsome and emotional, he inherited his father's strong physical presence and sexual appetites. She created the character Cesario based on Monmouth, who, in the end, presented a pitiful figure, led to his execution speaking of his mistress rather than of the legitimate Stuart power he represented. Other of Behn's characters represent composites of real people. Her Tomaso had attributes of Thomas Armstrong, a famous rebel, as well as Anthony Ashley Cooper, the first earl of Shaftesbury, recently dead, who was Monmouth's major supporter in his bid for the throne. Her Philander character represented Lord Grey, who retained his life following the rebellion only because he was able to pay a £40,000 ransom. Turner became the character Brilljard, and Henrietta became Silvia.

Behn produced the novel anonymously for reasons of personal safety, and it was never recognized publicly as hers during her lifetime. Two years following her 1689 death, Gerard Langbaine ascribed the work to Behn, based on some of her later works that bore similar passages to those of the novel. She introduces the work with a letter to Thomas Condon, a royalist and supporter of James II, in which she urges him not to be out of sorts with the dedication of the "Letters of a Whigg" to him, as Silvia proves a true Tory who only loves a "Whigg." The novel proved so erotic that one character in an Eliza HAYWOOD novel fainted upon reading from it. In Behn's version, adultery on the part of the two aristocratic lovers commodifies Silvia to the subject of an advertisement, reducing her to common status. As Behn writes to Condon, "youth and beauty" prove a "commodity" whose "value" is "rated by opinion and is at best a curious picture."

The book quickly fell out of favor with the stricter moral codes that emerged in the 18th century and during the Victorian era. More important, 20th-century critics who turned to Richardson and Defoe for the origins of the novel ignored it. Deserving the charge of dramatic and narrative excess, the book does not appeal to modern tastes. Hyperbole haunts every page. For example, one letter from Silvia to Philander begins:

> Oh, where shall I find repose, where seek a silent quiet, but in my last retreat the Grave! I say not this, my dearest *Philander,* that I do, or ever can repent my love, though the fatal source of all: For already we are betray'd, our race of joys, our course of stoln [sic] delight is ended e're begun.

It became important to feminist and women's studies in the mid-20th century and remains available in print.

BIBLIOGRAPHY

Todd, Janet. Introduction to *Love Letters Between a Nobleman and His Sister,* by Aphra Behn. Edited by Janet Todd. New York: Penguin Books, 1996, ix–xxxii.

LOVER, SAMUEL (ca. 1796/97–1868)

Born in Dublin, Samuel Lover worked for a time as a teenager in his father's stockbroking office and became a member of that rare group, the Protestant Irish. By 17, he had left that work to become a painter of miniatures and seaside scenes. Also an accomplished musician, he sang at age 21 for Sir Thomas Moore and, by 1818, had become secretary to the Royal Hibernian Society of Arts. As his reputation as an artist grew, he wrote songs, brief sketches, and short fiction, published in Dublin magazines. An early story, "The Gridiron," later became a basis for an oral recitation and was included in his first book, *Legends and Stories of Ireland* (1831). His miniatures were so celebrated that a Lover painting appeared at the London Royal Academy each year from 1833 to 1844. In 1834, he moved to London, where he enjoyed an active social life. Along with Charles DICKENS, he helped found BENTLEY'S MISCELLANY, where a portion of his most famous book, HANDY ANDY (1842), appeared as a serial. He also contributed dramas, performed at Haymarket and Adelphi, and composed music and lyrics for a popular BURLESQUE opera, *Il Paddy Whack in Italia.*

Lover continued his painting until 1844, when failing eyesight forced him to cease that part of his career. He began to appear on the stage, singing his own songs and telling stories, and developed a repertoire presented in what he called "Lover's Irish Evenings." When he toured the United States and Canada in 1846, he continued writing while presenting his Irish Evening performances. He revised his presentation upon his return to England, adding reflections on his experiences abroad, and suffered the death of his wife in 1847. Additional dramas included *Sentinels of the Alma and MacCarthy More,* well as two libretti. Lover remarried in 1852, and in 1856 received a pension for his service to literature and art. In his remaining years, he continued writing and editing poetry and nurturing his many relationships with performers and artists. A decline in health left him a semi-invalid in 1864. He relocated to the Isle of Wight and then to Jersey in search of a better climate and died at St. Helier in 1868.

Noted for his writings about the Irish peasantry, Samuel Lover excelled in caricatures, resulting in collections of loutish, lovable figures. His memorial tablet at Dublin's St. Patrick's Cathedral reads: "In memory of Samuel Lover, poet, painter, novelist, and composer, who in the exercise of a genius as distinguished in its versatility as in its power, by his pen and pencil illustrated so happily the character of the peasantry of his country that his name will ever be honourably identified with Ireland." While modern readers do not generally appreciate Lover's shorter pieces, *Handy Andy* remains a popular representative of slightly bawdy 19th-century Irish humor.

BIBLIOGRAPHY

Bayle, Bernard. *Life of Samuel Lover.* New York: D. Appleton, 1874.

Sheridan, John D. Introduction to *Handy Andy,* by Samuel Lover. London: J. M. Dent & Sons, 1961, v–vii.

Symington, Andrew. *Samuel Lover, a Biographical Sketch with Selections from His Writings and Correspondence.* New York: Harper & Brothers, 1880.

M

MACDONALD, GEORGE (1824–1905)

Born at Huntley, West Aberdeenshire, George Mac-Donald was the son of Scottish weaver George Mac-Donald and Helen MacKay. He spent his early years in rural schools and, in 1840, moved to Aberdeen University, where he studied for a year, returning again to study between 1844 and 1845. An able student, he took prizes in both chemistry and natural philosophy. He next enjoyed three years of tutoring before studying to become a Congregationalist minister, which he did in 1850. As pastor at Arudel, he lacked the dogmatism his congregation required, due to his support of individualism, and left the post after only three years. He relocated to Manchester, and then lived for a time in Algiers for health reasons before returning to England to settle down to serious writing. He converted to the Church of England and formally was a layman, although he occasionally preached.

MacDonald's writing offered an intriguing blend of myth, Christian symbolism, and mysticism, which resulted in popular children's stories. His novel *At the Back of the North Wind* (1871) gained him true fame and was followed by classics including a moral allegory titled *The Princess and the Goblin* (1872) and *The Princess and Curdie* (1883). All his books for juveniles featured admirable protagonists who faced and defeated evil. Works for adults include the allegory *Phantastes* (1858), *Lilith* (1895), and *David Elginbrod* (1863). Unable to support his family of 11 children by writing alone, he received a pension in 1877, requested by Queen Victoria. Never of a strong constitution, MacDonald moved his family to Italy for the sake of an equally weak daughter. Although she subsequently died, he decided to remain in the milder climate and lived there until 1902. His wife served as a local organist, and they lived pleasantly until her death, one year short of their 50th wedding anniversary. He died within a few years, and one son, the writer Greville MacDonald, later wrote a biography of his father.

George MacDonald's large number of publications included more than 50 fiction volumes, stories for juveniles, poetry, and sermons. His works for children are still considered classics, and critics agree that his prodigious imagination influenced works of G. K. Chesterton, C. S. Lewis and J. R. R. Tolkein.

BIBLIOGRAPHY

Hein, Rolland. *George MacDonald: Victorian Mythmaker.* Nashville: Star Song Publications Group, 1993.

Lynch, Michael, ed. "Culture." *The Oxford Companion to Scottish History.* Oxford: Oxford University Press, 2001, 137–150.

Raeper, William. *The Gold Thread: Essays on George MacDonald.* Edinburgh: Edinburgh University Press, 1990.

MACKENZIE, HENRY (1745–1831)

Henry Mackenzie was born in Edinburgh, where his father Joshua was a prominent physician and his mother Margaret was distinguished as the eldest daughter of an old Nairnshire family. He attended the Edinburgh high school and later the University of Edinburgh. An intelligent boy, he often served at literary tea parties hosted by members of Edinburgh's fashionable society. In 1765 he studied in London to become an exchequer, later returning to Scotland to join George Inglis as partner, finally replacing him as attorney for the crown in Scotland.

Influenced by Laurence STERNE, he produced a highly sentimental novel titled *A MAN OF FEELING* with a protagonist so sensitive that he could barely exist in man's harsh world. His publishers did not release the novel until 1771, and then it appeared anonymously. A Mr. Eccles who supposedly produced its manuscript form, complete with notes and editing changings, claimed its authorship. While the publishers disputed that claim, identifying Mackenzie as the novel's author, according to James Boswell's *The Life of Samuel Johnson* (1791), Eccles was buried with an epitaph that begins "Beneath this stone the Man of Feeling lies." Despite that remarkable state of affairs, the novel was credited to Mackenzie, and Sir Walter SCOTT ranked him Sterne's equal. He followed his novel with a balancing work titled *The Man of the World* (1773), which did not prove popular. Several critics judged its plot too complicated and tedious. Many also criticized his next book, *Julia de Roubigné,* as a morosely sentimental EPISTOLARY NOVEL, although others found it "delightful." One reviewer judged it too melancholy for readers.

In addition to fiction, Mackenzie produced several dramas, including the tragedies *The Spanish Father* and *The Prince of Tunis* and a comedy *The White Hypocrite,* some of which enjoyed brief stage engagements. He enjoyed the company of other young men interested in literature and led them to found a periodical titled *The Mirror* (1779–80). He based it on Joseph Addison's famous *The Spectator,* whose format and ideas Mackenzie followed so closely that he suffered accusations of plagiarism. It was later reissued in volume form and of its 110 papers, Mackenzie wrote 42 of them. Supporters of *The Mirror* again supported a Mackenzie endeavor in *The Lounger,* a periodical issued between February 1785 and January 1787, in which Mackenzie authored more than half of the entries. One of the earliest members of the Royal Society of Edinburgh,

Mackenzie became enthralled with German drama, although he could not read German. Sir Walter Scott praised Mackenzie's exposure of German literature to the public. He also produced anti-revolution tracts and in 1793 published *The Life of Dr. Blacklock,* about a popular poet and essayist.

Mackenzie wrote several political works, all published anonymously, including *An Account of the Proceedings of the Parliament of 1784,* and for his support of the constitutional cause received an appointment to the office, comptroller of taxes for Scotland, a position he held until he died. In 1807, an unauthorized collection appeared in Edinburgh as *The Works of Henry Mackenzie,* prompting the author himself to publish the following year his own *Miscellaneous Works,* eight volumes containing almost every piece he had written. Several portraits and a bust of Mackenzie remain on display in various museums, including the National Portrait Galleries of London and Edinburgh. Although many people assumed him to be a soft and sentimental individual, suggested by his fiction, his entry in *The Dictionary of National Biography* pronounced him "far better—a hard-headed, practical man, as full of practical wisdom as most of his fictitious characters are devoid of it."

BIBLIOGRAPHY

Barker, Gerard A. *Henry Mackenzie.* Boston: Twayne Publishers, 1975.

Lynch, Michael, ed. "Culture." *The Oxford Companion to Scottish History.* Oxford: Oxford University Press, 2001, 137–150.

Stephen, Leslie, Sir, and Sir Sidney Lee. "Henry Mackenzie." *The Dictionary of National Biography.* Vol. 12. 1882. Reprint, Oxford: Oxford University Press, 1968, 594–596.

MACMILLAN'S MAGAZINE

Founded in November of 1859 by the Macmillan publishing firm, *Macmillan's Magazine* joined a total of 115 London periodicals founded that year. It would continue through 1907, existing long after the production of many of its fellow periodicals halted. Its initial 80-page issues offered the reading public articles, stories, and poetry bearing the bylines of celebrated writers including W. E. Forster, F. D. Maurice, David Masson, Richard Monckton Milnes, and Alfred, Lord Tennyson. While its focus included not just literature but also travel, history, politics, and miscellaneous topics, *Macmillan's* remained important as one of the first periodicals to contain signed work. Its editors included the cream of the editorial crop: David Masson, George Grove, John Morley, and Mowbray Morris. In 1864, it was cited in an article by the high-brow *The London Review and Weekly Journal of Politics, Literature, Art and Society,* featuring the best "miscellanies" of the time.

BIBLIOGRAPHY

Graham, Walter. *English Literary Periodicals.* New York: Octagon Books, 1966.

MALET, LUCAS (PSEUDONYM OF MARY ST. LEGER KINGSLEY HARRISON) (1852–1931)

Mary Kingsley was the second daughter of Charles KINGSLEY, the Anglican novelist and poet, and niece of novelist Henry KINGSLEY. She married the Rector William Harrison in 1876, one year following her famous father's death. She began writing and publishing in 1879, and over a prodigious career would produce 17 novels, complete one of her father's novels, publish two short fiction volumes, and write a large number of essays and poems. In her first novel, *Mrs Lorimer: A Sketch in Black and White* (1882), she fashioned a protagonist who renounced her lonely childhood in a vicarage and escaped through marriage, a plotline that may have been autobiographical. She later left her husband, scandalizing acquaintances who accused her of sullying her father's memory. The charges against her increased when she rejected her Anglican heritage to embody precepts of the "New Woman," produce Amazonian female characters, embrace Catholicism in 1902, and write a "Catholic" novel, *The Far Horizon* (1906).

Her best-known works were the novels *The Wages of Sin* (1891) and *The History of Sir Richard Calmady* (1901), the second of which featured a protagonist who, like Malet, was emotionally crippled by his family connections. In her day, she proved far more popular than any of the writing Kingsleys. Recent critical studies even suggest that Thomas HARDY may have lifted the plot and its female protagonist in his enduring *JUDE THE OBSCURE* (1885) from *The Wages of Sin,* which offers what the fin-de-siècle public knew as a "New Woman" figure. Such a woman was likely to involve herself in social and/or political movements, challenging traditional gender roles for females. Malet presents an intellectual artist who, like Hardy's Sue Bridehead, dies at the novel's close. However, unlike the figure that Hardy describes in his preface as a "bachelor girl" who ends up a "cluster of nerves," Malet's protagonist is unhappy, disillusioned by a lover who fathers a child with another woman, but not hysterical or broken. Where Hardy seems to embrace the familiar Victorian characterization of his protagonist as a conflicted Madonna/whore, Malet rejects that opposition. That distinct approach marks her as a writer of extreme importance in the development of the female author and has revived interest in her works on the part of FEMINIST and NEW HISTORICAL CRITICS. Hardy did write a letter to Malet in 1891 thanking her for a copy of the novel.

A writer who, according to Patricia Lorimer Lundberg, "detested the intellectually squelching effects of marriage, especially for creative artists, and feared having children, who praised celibacy in others," Malet featured themes considered unsuitable for women writers, such as disabilities, lesbianism, and sexuality from the woman's point of view. Her disruption of middle-class views and social restrictions against discussion of sadism, seduction, licit and illicit love affairs also interest PSYCHOANALYTIC CRITICS.

Although, due to financial strain, Malet produced slighter work in her later years, damaging her hard-earned reputation as a courageous Modernist, her books received few negative critical reviews. The only negativity focused on their unseemly themes, and gave more attention to the author's gender than her artistry. Much energy continues to be poured into efforts to revive her popularity, which waned after the 1930s. Several of her works are available in electronic text, as well as print.

BIBLIOGRAPHY

Lundberg, Patricia Lorimer. *"An Inward Necessity": The Writer's Life of Lucas Malet.* New York: Peter Lang, 2003.

Schaffer, Ralia. "Malet the Obscure: Thomas Hardy, 'Lucas Malet' and the Literary Politics of Early Modernism." *Women's Writing* 3, no. 3 (1996). Triangle Journals. Available online. URL:http://www.triangle.co.uk/wow/content/pdfs/3/issue3_3.asp. Downloaded on 4 April 2004.

MANLEY, MARY DELARIVIÈRE (1672–1724)

Mary Delarivière Manley, likely born at Portsmouth, was daughter to the lieutenant governor of the isle of Jersey, the Channel Islands, Sir Robert Manley, who died in 1687. His death caused his daughters to move in with a cousin, John Manley, who supposedly seduced Mary into marriage, despite the fact that he was already married. He refused to support their child and, according to Mary, he abandoned her, leaving her in the care of the duchess of Cleveland. She remained in Jersey for several years and wrote two dramas before moving to London in 1696, a comedy titled *The Lost Lover: or The Jealous Husband* and a tragedy, *The Royal Mischief*. While her plays were produced, they proved unsuccessful.

Manley became lover to John Tilly, the married warden of Fleet Prison. She continued writing, scoring a success with her 1705 work, *The SECRET HISTORY OF QUEEN ZARAH AND THE ZARAZIANS*, which she followed with an immediate sequel. Its popularity lay in its titillating ROMAN À CLEF approach, the first written in English, to the political scandal of the day, involving the supposed manipulation of Queen Anne by the duke and duchess of Marlborough. Another work of Tory SATIRE followed and became her most famous, *Secret Memoirs and Manners of Several Persons of Quality, of Both Sexes. From the NEW ATALANTIS, an Island in the Mediterranean* (1709). Less political than *Queen Zarah,* it emphasized various sexual themes, including adultery and the more scandalizing topics of incest and homosexuality. Her insistence that the book was fiction freed her from imprisonment by the Whig government, which attempted to prevent the book's release to the public. She followed the same themes and patterns in its two-volume sequel published the following year. Her political prowess and popularity as an author led to her succession of Jonathan SWIFT as editor of the Tory publication *The Examiner.* Supposedly she became mistress to her publisher, John Barber, and in 1714 published an autobiographical novel titled *The Adventures of Rivella.* It proved useful later in a study of her life, when factual evidence was lacking. A final play, *Lucius, the First Christian King of Britain,* was produced in 1717, and Manley died in 1724. Manley proved crucial to the FEMINIST CRITIC movement in the mid-20th century as a "lost" woman author rediscovered by many academic programs as an important topic of study.

BIBLIOGRAPHY

Anonymous. *The Female Wits.* Introduction by Lucyle Hook. Los Angeles: William Andrews Clark Memorial Library, 1967.

Backscheider, Paula R., and John J. Richetti. *Popular Fiction by Women 1660–1730.* Oxford: Clarenden Press, 1996.

MANNERS NOVEL

See SILVER-FORK FICTION.

MAN OF FEELING, A HENRY MACKENZIE (1771)

Henry MACKENZIE's *A Man of Feeling* owed a debt to Tobias SMOLLETT's *RODERICK RANDOM* (1748). Like Smollett's protagonist, the good-hearted Harley of Mackenzie's tale is a naive traveler in a too-sophisticated world, sacrificed to professional cardsharps. A narrator that readers meet in the book's introduction tells his tale secondhand. Hunting with a parson, the narrator spies a young woman walking with a book who the clergyman identifies as the daughter of a gentleman named Walton, once a friend of Harley. The clergyman took charge of some papers Harley left behind, which he describes as erratically written, with not "one strain for two chapters together," explaining, "I don't believe there's a single syllogism from beginning to end." The narrator takes the papers, which the parson is using as wadding for his weapon, exchanging his own wadding, one of the "German Illustrissimi." The narrator comments on Harley's writing that if only the pages had born the name of a Marmontel, Richardson, or Rousseau, "tis odds that I should have wept; But One is ashamed to be pleased with the works of one does not know whom." In this pronouncement, Mackenzie ironically winks at the reader, as he published the work anonymously.

Only when a clergyman tried to claim credit for *A Man of Feeling* did Mackenzie admit to its authorship.

As a student of the teachings of Francis Hutcheson at Edinburgh University, Mackenzie encountered the beliefs of the earl of Shaftesbury. The earl proposed that man possesses an innate sense of morality that will lead him to approve moral acts and disapprove immoral ones. He further believed that that sensibility should not simply be enjoyed but must result in actions supporting the humanity of all individuals.

As the narrator recounts, after Harley's fleecing at the hand of confidence men, he continues his quixotic journey to London in hopes of practicing humanitarianism. In one such act, he befriends a luckless prostitute by returning her to her father and interacts with other characters from the lower class. They present their moral views, supplying many of the "syllogisms" the clergyman had claimed did not exist in the writing.

Harley visits Bedlam, the asylum for the insane, as part of his investigation of the human condition, where he meets a girl destined for the pages of SENTIMENTAL FICTION, as she has been driven to madness by lost love. He also meets a one-time celebrated mathematician, driven mad when he could not prove Newton's theories, and a gentleman once worth £50,000 who suffered "an unlucky fluctuation of stock." Their encounters lead Harley to pronounce, "the passions of men are temporary madnesses; and sometime; very fatal in their effects." Another character, the misanthrope, says about Truth, "your very nurseries are seminaries of falsehood; and what is called Fashion in manhood completes the system of avowed insincerity. Mankind, in the gross, is a gaping monster, that loves to be deceived, and has seldom been disappointed." His statement that females are not "trained to any more useful purpose; they are taught . . . that a young woman is a creature to be married" and expect an income, would be of interest to FEMINIST CRITICS.

Regardless of his cruel treatment by others, Harley remains steadfastly dedicated to relieving their suffering. He falls in love with a Miss Walton, but does not express his feelings, possibly due to the belief clear in his earlier statement that equated passion to madness. She attends him at his deathbed, along with the physician who writes the final two chapters of the account. As he contemplates death, Harley pronounces the world "a scene of dissimulation, of restraint, of disappointment," one he is not sad to leave. In an intriguing gender role reversal, Harley's health declines due to unrequited love for Miss Walton, a member of a class beyond his reach.

The book brims with a sincerity and dignity that Mackenzie felt any inclusion of humor might undercut. Although the tale begins with the promise of comedy suggested by the use of its pages for gun wads, Mackenzie never intended the slightest hint of hilarity. That absence makes the book a difficult read for modern aficionados of the sentimental novel.

BIBLIOGRAPHY

Thompson, Harold William. *A Scottish Man of Feeling: Some Account of Henry Mackenzie, Esq., and of the Golden Age of Burns and Scott.* New York: Oxford University Press, 1931.

MANSFIELD PARK JANE AUSTEN (1814)

Jane AUSTEN began writing *Mansfield Park* in 1811 but did not publish it until 1814. With this, the penultimate novel published during her lifetime, she focused on financially comfortable small communities of individuals, raising the quotidian to a level of importance. Focusing on everyday matters, she shaped a "comedy of manners," a phrase that would later become synonymous with her name. While this novel, like her next work, *EMMA* (1816), carried a moral message, Austen edged her tone with less irony than usual.

Not a particularly popular novel when published, *Mansfield Park* focuses on Sir Thomas and Lady Bertram of Mansfield Park, along with their adult offspring, Maria, Julia, Tom, and Edmund. The younger generation has been raised to follow proper social behavior but knows little of morality. Austen chose to represent the regrettable Regency support of capitalist enterprise through the descent into chaos of the Bertram family, so focused on materialism that they lose the order dictated by traditional ethical behavior. Lady Bertram's not-so-wealthy niece, Fanny Price, lives with the family for a time, suffering patronizing treatment from all except Edmund. Her quiet demeanor at first marks her as merely dull, but her later refusal to join the ensuing chaos allows readers to reinterpret her seeming passivity as quiet strength. FEMINIST CRITICS interpret the traditional enforced silence of Fanny as her method of coopting power from her judgmental surroundings.

When Sir Thomas must leave the country for a time, his children turn completely self-indulgent, a turn resisted by the teenage Fanny, who, despite her lesser financial status, has been raised with far more grace and sense of value than her cousins. Although engaged to Mr. Rushworth, Maria flirts with Henry Crawford, whose sister Mary enthralls Edmund. When the fickle Maria decides to end her flirtation and return to Rushworth, Henry Crawford expresses his attraction for Fanny. Sir Thomas returns in time to note Fanny's rejection of Crawford; he upbraids her for throwing away a chance at a secure financial future. Fanny returns home to Portsmouth, but almost immediately wants to return to Mansfield Park to Edmund, whom she comes to understand she loves. She arrives to find that Maria Bertram Rushworth has scandalized the family by running away with Henry Crawford, while Julia elopes with another ne'er-do-well named Mr. Yates. Edmund has hoped to escape his home by taking orders, but he sacrifices the affections of Mary Crawford, who has no desire to marry a preacher. Fanny suffers no such qualms, however, and she and Edmund realize their love and plan their wedding. They develop the only relationship among the several in the novel that promises any happiness.

BIBLIOGRAPHY

Ross, Josephine. *Jane Austen: A Companion.* New Brunswick: Rutgers University Press, 2002.

Southam, B. C., ed. *Jane Austen, Sense and Sensibility, Pride and Prejudice and Mansfield Park: A Casebook.* London: Macmillan, 1976.

MARRIAGE SUSAN FERRIER (1818)

Susan FERRIER's first novel, *Marriage,* has been labeled "shrewdly observant" by one critic and a novel "justified by its painting of Scottish manners" by another. Compared to her contemporaries Maria EDGEWORTH and Jane AUSTEN, Ferrier develops her plot mostly within the domestic scene. As the title suggests, the book does focus on the institution of marriage, framed within two generations of the same family. That double

focus is handled with much humor and acute detail, but its format flaws the plot. Readers reach the middle of a very long novel and suddenly find that almost 18 years have passed, the male protagonist from the first portion of the novel has disappeared to India, two Scottish aunts allowed ample page space have also been removed, and the twin teenage daughters of the original female protagonist occupy the spotlight. The transition proves jarring, as does Ferrier's attitude toward her female characters. Many are caricatures, which exist easily in a SATIRE, but need softening for a ROMANCE. While they add humor to the presentation, they also jar the reader's sensibility, their idiosyncrasies proving more annoying than entertaining.

The novel opens with the introduction of Lady Juliana, the egoistic sole daughter of the earl of Courtland, who has been schooled in the demands of high society and its rewards. An uneducated woman, ignorant of life beyond her social circle, her life's goal is a suitable husband. She is engaged by arrangement to an elderly aristocratic for whom she has no feelings. Desperate for love and attention, she elopes to Scotland with Harry Douglas, a handsome military officer, born in Scotland but raised in England by a wealthy patron. Predictably, as the honeymoon period ends, Douglas learns his expected prospects have evaporated due to his absence from military duty, while Juliana has been disinherited by the earl. The near-destitute couple must live in Scotland with Douglas's father, a group of eccentric aunts, and slightly less-eccentric cousins.

Juliana, who has no concept of poverty and cares more for her dogs than humans, expects to be entertained in a great Scottish estate, at her father-in-law's Highland home, the castle of Glenfern. When she discovers the frontierlike appointments of the so-called "castle," she is dismayed. She treats the aunts like servants, making her needs the primary concerns of the castle, much to the chagrin of the laird, who recognizes her as a weak and silly woman. She acts condescendingly toward everyone except her sister-in-law, Mrs. Douglas, who eventually tells her tale of turning away from the love of her life to make a steady union with Harry's older brother.

Conditions disintegrate, as Juliana understands they will spend months, if not years, taking advantage of old Mr. Douglas's hospitality. She celebrates Harry's taking control of a nearby farm until she discovers its poor condition, although she is heartened when she sees the cheerful and attractive results of the years of work that Mrs. Douglas and her husband have achieved at their home. Eventually she gives birth to twins, rejects both of them as too demanding, and gives the weaker twin, Mary, to Mrs. Douglas.

When Juliana and Harry return to England, she gives birth to a son, Edward, and moves in with her brother, Frederick Lindore, Lord Courtland, who has inherited their father's estate, and he basically raises her daughter, Adelaide, with his own son and daughter, Emily Lindore. At this point in the story, Harry, who has regained his patron's good favor, washes his hands of his difficult and haughty wife and leaves the country in service, terminating his relationship with his wife "in an eternal farewell." Within a few pages, about eighteen years have passed, during which time a number of events have occurred. Lady Emily has, at age six, declared plans to marry her cousin, Edward Douglas, and later matured into a young woman "as insupportably natural and sincere as she was beautiful and *piquante*"; Adelaide has become "as heartless and ambitious as she was beautiful and accomplished"; and the lovely and wise Mary has become depressed and ill. When her doctor prescribes time in the English air, Mary joins her twin and her cousins in England, received coldly by her own mother.

During the remainder of the novel, all three young women pursue husbands, their experiences differing as widely as their personalities. Adelaide marries at first the Duke of Altamont for his wealth, despite his stodginess and old age. Juliana encourages that union and simultaneously discourages Mary in her pursuit of the not-so-wealthy, but far more congenial and loving, Colonel Charles Lennox. Emily follows through on her plans to marry Edward Douglas, cousin to Mary and Adelaide and judged "a perfect model of youthful beauty . . . handsome, brave, good-hearted, and good-humoured," but not clever. Emily enjoys the only marriage not edged with melodrama and protest, a fact that disappoints her romantic nature in some ways, as she explains to Mary: "Here am I, languishing for a little opposition to my love. My marriage will be quite an insipid, every-day affair; I yawn already to think of it." Adelaide survives only a year with the duke, and ends up running away with Lord Lindore, Emily's brother, "vainly hoping to find peace and joy amid guilt and infamy." Juliana concludes the novel by moving to the South of France, having never shown Mary any affection, where she is joined by the likewise vain Adelaide, an outcast of society, and an "object of indifference even to him for whom she had abandoned all." Mary will never see her mother again but enjoys the love of her Scottish family and her husband.

As George Douglas notes, Ferrier's tone may be the novel's greatest weakness. It lacks compassion or sympathy for her own characters, which suffer through an unrealistically uncompromising world. While everyone meets their challenges in life, most humans may take comfort from fellow sufferers, or find redemption in some small aspect of the human condition. This is not true in the case of Lady Juliana, who, while a victim herself, never garners ready sympathy. She is received by the reader in exactly the manner Ferrier draws her, as a nasty, contemptible, vacuous, and spoiled Englishwoman, whom no reader would want to encounter in the flesh.

BIBLIOGRAPHY
Kirkpatrick, Kathryn. Introduction to *Marriage* by Susan Ferrier. New York: Oxford University Press, 2002.

MARRYAT, CAPTAIN FREDERICK (1792–1848)   Frederick Marryat was born in London. His father, a Member of Parliament, was a Huguenot, or Norman, who had escaped the 1572 St. Bartholomew's Massacre, while his mother was part of a family of American loyalists. He was educated at a boarding school run by a schoolmaster who flogged unruly students like Frederick, who proved rebellious. He ran away three times, hoping to go to sea, a fantasy he had nurtured since a very young child.

Marryat's famous navy career began shortly after his 14th birthday, when he joined the crew of the frigate *Imperieuse* as a midshipman. He received commendation at age 16 for his part in a military skirmish and later risked his life to go overboard and save a fellow seaman; by age 23 he assumed duties as a commander.

He eventually accepted the Royal Humane Society's Gold Medal for bravery and the French Legion of Honor. He married Catherine Shairp, daughter to England's consul general of Russia, with whom he would father seven daughters and four sons. In 1822, a pamphlet written by Marryat titled *Suggestions for the Abolition of the Present System of Impressment for the Naval Service* was published. Although some naval officials viewed its suggestions to reform the navy's method of boarding ships in disguise, then pressing the crew into service, as worthy, the Lord High Admiral, the duke of Clarence, asked that the pamphlet be recalled. He had no desire to inflict a reform program on the navy at that time.

Resigning his commission in 1830, Marryat began a prolific writing life. He first published *The Naval Officer, or Scenes and Adventures in the Life of Frank Mildmay* in 1829, following this with *Jacob Faithful* and *Peter Simple* (1834) and MR. MIDSHIPMAN EASY (1836). Each novel drew on his considerable naval experience and reflected his conservative views. While others had attempted to write fiction based on military experience, Marryat was the first to do so with talent characterized by a lively writing style and a broad comic approach that made his books successful. In 1836, he relocated to Brussels, where he enjoyed himself immensely and proved quite popular, his fluent French helping him feel at home. He continued publishing for adults with *Japhet in Search of a Father* (1836) and *Snarleyyow, or The Dog Fiend* (1837), considered by some critics his best novel with its mix of GOTHIC grotesque and farce. Marryat then turned to children's literature after traveling through Canada and the United States for a two-year period. There he urged the abolition of publishing piracy, from which his own works had suffered, researching American politics and economics, and visiting with Martin Van Buren, eighth president of the United States. He also pursued his interest in the state of black Americans, commenting on their lack of equality to whites.

Marryat next wrote and published for a younger audience. He sought to counter Johann Wyss's romantic view of a marooned family in *The Swiss Family Robinson* with his juvenile novel MASTERMAN READY (1841), in which he made clear the desperation and hardships that would accompany such a situation. Although qualifying as DIDACTIC literature, the novel's sense of adventure and realistic detail continues to delight young readers.

Marryat relocated to a small Norfolk farm where, although in poor health, he continued writing. Another popular book for young readers, *The Children of the New Forest* (1847), focuses on the Civil War, featuring Royalist main characters that must evade their Roundhead foes, resourcefully living in the wild until they receive their proper inheritance with the Restoration. Marryat's work for children affected later juvenile novels, as many contained his conservative political prejudices. The loss of Frederick, his eldest son, who died in a frigate off the north coast of Africa in December of 1847, compounded his condition, already weakened by the death of two other sons. He died soon after, leaving a legacy of adventure writing imitated by others who sought to profit from seafaring experience, including Michael Scott, Frederick Chamier, and William J. Neale. Many of his works may be found in print and electronic form.

BIBLIOGRAPHY

Pocock, Tom. *Captain Marryat: Seaman, Writer and Adventurer.* Mechanicsburg, Pa.: Stackpole Books, 2000.

MARTIN CHUZZLEWIT CHARLES DICKENS (1844) Charles DICKENS first published his sixth novel, *Martin Chuzzlewit,* as a 10-part serial between January 1843 and July 1844. He later stated that he thought the lengthy tale of a young man's emotional and ethical maturation the "best" of his stories. In young Martin Chuzzlewit, Dickens creates a prototype of the overly ambitious gentleman who bases his actions in self-interest. Such egoism will be tempered by experience leading to a better understanding of the human condition. However, when Martin goes to work for his grandfather, the elder Chuzzlewit despairs that his namesake will ever be worthy of that family name. He does not care for Martin's interest in his companion and ward, Mary Graham. He puts Martin to work with a hypocritical architect, one of Dickens's most popular villains, Pecksniff, but becomes so annoyed with the young man that he instructs Pecksniff to fire him. Martin decides to depart England with his loyal servant, Mark Tapley, and they travel to America. Basing many events in this section on his own experience in America, Dickens could not see what critics later found as a serious weakness. The America diversion becomes an annoyance, introducing too many superfluous characters who will later be dropped, and fracturing the novel's continuity. However, it works well to emphasize Dickens's theme of greed, personified in the grasping materialistic characters necessary to Martin's eventual redemption.

Meanwhile, Chuzzlewit's wicked nephew Jonas Chuzzlewit murders his father and carries out a plan to marry Mercy Pecksniff, even though the elderly Chuzzlewit had warned her against Jonas. Mercy ignores Chuzzlewit's advice, inviting grief and abuse at the hands of Jonas. Jonas also joins the schemer Montague Tigg and draws his father-in-law into their nefarious activities. The dedicated and naive Tom Pinch, a loyal assistant to Pecksniff and a devotee of Mary Graham, loses his position, and circumstances grow grim in the Chuzzlewit household. Again, the somber tone remains necessary to Dickens's study of selfishness, as circumstances must darken before Martin's epiphany helps return the Chuzzlewit world to order.

In America, Martin invests in the Eden Land Corporation, which defrauds him. He becomes ill and nearly dies, but recovers in time to care for the dedicated but also ill Mark Tapley, a character sometimes criticized as too cheerful to prove realistic. That first act of mercy on Martin's part teaches him the value of selflessness, and his character begins to change for the better. He decides to return to England, hoping to become close to his estranged grandfather, but he finds Chuzzlewit in Pecksniff's house, seemingly under his complete control. Alarmed, Martin proves his new devotion to his family by remaining staunchly loyal to his grandfather and defending him against Pecksniff. Eventually he learns that the elder Chuzzlewit had been testing both him and Pecksniff, having actually retained control of his life and his fortune. While Martin passes the test famously, Pecksniff's true nature is revealed.

Chuzzlewit celebrates Martin's devotion to Mary and agrees the two shall marry. Not only is Pecksniff exposed as a scoundrel, Jonas Chuzzlewit is arrested for murdering Montague Tigg; the crook had threatened to blackmail Jonas over his killing of his father. Tom Pinch, almost destroyed by his faith in Pecksniff, is hired to work for Chuzzlewit and celebrates the marriage of his beloved sister Ruth to Martin's friend and confidant, John Westlock. Having resigned his love for Mary Graham, Tom find happiness living with the newly married couple.

Dickens's clear message is that virtue will be rewarded, and although he shapes a novel containing some of his best villains, its comic highlights prevent the tragedy that often haunted his later youthful protagonists. The critical view of America is now understood through Dickens's problems in retaining rights to his own works. Unscrupulous American publishers often stole his works, publishing and selling them and paying Dickens and his publisher nothing. The novel remains available in print version, as well as in electronic text.

BIBLIOGRAPHY

"Locution and Authority in *Martin Chuzzlewit*." *English Studies* 74, no. 2 (April 1993): 143–154.

Matz, Nancy. *The Companion to Martin Chuzzlewit*. Westport, Conn.: Greenwood, 2001.

Selby, Keith. *How to Study a Charles Dickens Novel*. Basingstoke, U.K.: Macmillan Education, 1989.

MARXIST CRITICISM

Marxist criticism grew directly from a sociopolitical movement, as did the later related FEMINIST CRITICISM approach. Growing from ideas perpetuated by Karl Marx and Friederich Engels in *The Communist Manifesto* (1848), Marxist criticism examines the power structures within fiction, particularly those powers that control wealth under direction of the bourgeoisie, thus oppressing the working class, or proletariat. It also takes an interest in aspects of revolution against such control, whether on the part of individual characters or groups of characters. Marxist critics believe that no text exists apart from the cultural situation of its author, whose ideology remains crucial to textual development. Text reveals the class struggles inherent to the author's culture, and criticism allows denunciation of anti-proletariat sentiment. THESIS NOVELS from the 1840s by authors including

Charles DICKENS, Elizabeth GASKELL, and Benjamin DISRAELI offer Marxist critics an abundance of material to understand the class values of that era. A pragmatic approach to literary criticism, Marxism assumes that a culture's understanding of its citizens is determined by the pragmatics of economics, that the dominant class employs materialism to define the subservient class, and that spiritual health cannot exist in such an environment. Thus, an era's literature reflects its class-consciousness and its culture's superstructure composed of social and legal edicts, religious views, and educational systems. In one Marxist approach, critics examine literature to determine how art produced by the dominant powers contributes to the intellectual enslavement of the working class. Authors may contribute to that control without being aware they are doing so.

BIBLIOGRAPHY

Bressler, Charles E. *Literary Criticism: An Introduction to Theory and Practice.* Englewood Cliffs, N.J.: Prentice Hall, 1994.

MARY: A FICTION MARY WOLLSTONECRAFT (1788)

Mary WOLLSTONECRAFT wrote her first novel, *Mary: A Fiction,* to express her most personal beliefs. An autobiographical work, *Mary* has been evaluated by later critics as too sentimental an expression to represent high-quality writing, and that inferiority in expression results in a work that contributes little toward an understanding of its author. Twenty-first-century critics, however, differ in their approach to the novel, evaluating it based on its value, to borrow a phrase from critic Dale Spender, as a "consciousness raising activity." In writing a fictional character based on herself, Wollstonecraft could investigate the events in her own life and attempt to answer a question that constantly plagued her: Why did her society consider women to possess weak characters? The traditional answer to that question attributed their weakness and, therefore, lesser value than that of men, to their innate natures. Wollstonecraft sought a different answer, one supported by her belief in the tenets of romanticism. Those tenets grew from Rousseau's philosophy and stressed the possibility that one could change through experience in a continual re-creation of self. Such an idea proved especially attractive to writers who, in fiction, refashioned their experiences to achieve a new self-realization.

In *Mary,* Wollstonecraft focused on her own sensibilities through her protagonist. She remained fully aware of the prevailing attitude, which suggested that the female manner of interacting with the world using instincts or intuition marked them as incapable of intellectual activity. Even so, she chose to allow her protagonist's emotions to play a prominent role in order to highlight important social issues in the novel in a nonpolemical way. When Mary is forced into an arranged marriage that will result in improved economic conditions for her father, she "stood like a statue of Despair, and pronounced the awful vow without thinking of it; and then ran to support her mother, who expired the same night in her arms." Without becoming essayistic, Wollstonecraft reflects on the terrors of such unions for women; her emotional description allows her emphasis.

To balance Mary's emotional bent, Wollstonecraft stressed throughout her novel the critical importance of education for women and their intellectual capacity to learn. Mary realizes that she lacks the learning she saw in others and seeks to correct that problem, hoping to escape her oppressive life. Thus, it is Mary's emotion, her "anxiety," that leads her to study physic, "this knowledge, literally speaking," ending "in vanity and vexation of spirit, as it enabled her to foresee what she could not prevent." Wollstonecraft continues to tie intellect to emotion in a cause-and-effect relationship, continuing, "As her mind expanded, her marriage appeared a dreadful misfortune; she was sometimes reminded of the heavy yoke, and bitter was the recollection." Mary does not find the escape she sought but will be disappointed not only by her loveless marriage but also by the deaths of her best friend and her lover. Even so, Mary's experiences and studies allow her to metamorphose into a complex being well aware of her environment and its dangers, instead of remaining a simple organism that merely reacts to stimulus. That awareness allowed her ultimately to choose life over the suicide that might have concluded a more melodramatic and clichéd presentation.

Many critics feel Wollstonecraft's attempts to write fiction failed. They accuse Wollstonecraft of filling

Mary with too much emotion, while her second novel, *The Wrongs of Women* (1798) (left incomplete by Wollstonecraft's death following the birth of her daughter, the future Mary SHELLEY), would be declared too polemic. A later readership would find her style in both novels unacceptable. The fault may have been due to her extreme autobiographical approach. While conventional wisdom holds that a reader should not confuse an author with the author's protagonist, in the case of Wollstonecraft, the author actually invited the reader to do so. She remained so true to the details of her own life, with, for instance, the death of Mary's best friend imitating that of Fanny Blood, the author's own soul mate, that she did not create the imaginative supportive framework of narrative and transition that readers centuries later desired. Still, *Mary* allowed Wollstonecraft to depict the personal sphere as political realm, permitting the reader to understand the distressing effects of the oppression inflicted on women by a patriarchal society.

As critic Janet Todd suggests, the value of Mary Wollstonecraft's novel may lay in its interest as a work illustrating the "literary beauties" of writing marked by sensibility. More likely, she adds, it should be appreciated for its depiction of the "alienated intellectual woman" in early form, a characterization that would reappear in the more refined "substantial heroines" created by Charlotte BRONTË in *JANE EYRE* (1847) and *VILLETTE* (1853).

BIBLIOGRAPHY

Kelly, Gary. Introduction to *Mary and The Wrongs of Woman,* by Mary Wollstonecraft. New York: Oxford University Press, 1976, vii–xxi.

Poovery, Mary. *The Proper Lady and the Woman Writer: Ideology as Style in the Works of Mary Wollstonecraft, Mary Shelley and Jane Austen.* Chicago: University of Chicago Press, 1984.

Spender, Dale. "Mary Wollstonecraft, Mary Hays, and Autobiographical Fiction." *Mothers of the Novel: 100 Good Women Writers before Jane Austen.* New York: Pandora, 1986, 246–269.

Todd, Janet. Introduction to *Mary Wollstonecraft, Mary, Maria, Mary Shelley, Matilda.* New York: New York University Press, vii–xxviii.

MARY BARTON: A TALE OF MANCHESTER LIFE ELIZABETH GASKELL (1848)

Elizabeth GASKELL's novel of social injustice, *Mary Barton,* would be banned in 1907 by the London County Council, which deemed the novel unfit for children 14 and under. That action supports the power of Gaskell's prose to influence readers in judging their own society corrupt and tainted by inequality and abuses of members of the working class. Of one character, Gaskell writes, "In his days of childhood and youth, Mr. Carson had been accustomed to poverty; but it was honest decent poverty; not the grinding squalid misery he had remarked in every part of John Barton's house, and which had contrasted strangely with the pompous sumptuousness of the room in which he now sat." Through the Barton family, readers become acquainted with a privation stunning in its ability to reduce even a highly moral individual to despicable acts for the sake of his family. Gaskell titled the novel after her female protagonist at her editors' insistence. They may have thought sales would be stronger with a woman's name in the title, ironic in light of the fact that the book was published anonymously, due to fears that Gaskell's identity as a woman might discourage sales.

Most critics agree that what separates *Mary Barton* from other so-called THESIS NOVELS is its male protagonist, John Barton. While the novel's quality may not meet that of Gaskell's contemporaries, such as Charles DICKENS and Charles KINGSLEY, her first book shows the promise of her later signature treatment of subjects. She remains a humane writer, not so steeped in theory that she sacrifices her characters to the symbolic needs of moralistic fiction. John Barton, despite his poverty and suffering, despite his membership in the CHARTIST movement, despite his eventual crime, is no stereotype. Rather, Gaskell shapes him with such compassion that his humanity remains obvious. Gaskell wants to shine the light of public awareness on the disgraceful treatment of England's working classes in the mid-19th century, but she also wants to illuminate details that result from minute examination of her subject. While she may not have been steeped in the knowledge of politics and economics of Benjamin DISRAELI, she did have something that Disraeli, Dickens, and Kingsley all lacked—an intimate knowledge of her characters and setting. As the wife of a Unitarian minister, she had firsthand experience with the suffering of the working class and wrote of that suffering without the condescension or distance of those who knew only the group, and not the individual. She had also lost a child of her own to illness, allowing further identification with destitute parents whose children died in droves, often due to the effects of crippling poverty. Gaskell had lived within the Manchester setting for 12 years, and she reproduced scenes designed to haunt her readers, inhabited by figures like John Barton. He so represents the novel's emotional center that many agree it should have borne his name as a title, rather than that of his daughter, Mary.

When readers first meet John, he is a loving father and husband attending a picnic. The narrator describes him as a man whose face told others that as a child, "he had suffered from the scanty living consequent upon bad times," wearing an expression of "extreme earnestness" with a "sort of latent, stern, enthusiasm," in which "the good predominated over the bad." Barton is dynamic and opinionated, dedicated to his family's support. Almost immediately he loses his wife, Mary, in childbirth with her daughter, Mary, and readers learn that his wife had influenced John as "one of the ties which bound him down to the gentle humanities of earth." The loss affects his spiritual equilibrium, allowing difficult circumstances eventually to drive him to murder. He engages in violence but only after having been its victim. Barton and others like him are at the mercy of the ignorance of employers who neglect workers' needs, the ambivalence of a public intent on owning goods produced at the cost of human lives, and the waste of precious resources by the wealthy class. In one scene John feels defeated by the isolation caused by a class structure separating human from human. He understands that separation is an unnatural situation inflicted by man upon man, not by God upon man. One character says of John, "He were sadly put about to make great riches and great poverty square with Christ's Gospel."

Wracked by remorse following his murder of his employer's son, John remains at all times human; his faults recommend, rather than condemn, him. By the novel's conclusion, Barton is "a wan, feeble figure" who carries a water cask "with evident and painful labour," his head bowed into a "sinking and shrunk body."

Gaskell produces a somewhat contradictory character in Mary Barton, who, while a member of the decidedly oppressed working class, speaks without a hint of the dialect of her peers and, as one point in a love triangle, seems at first to have more in common with traditional romance heroines rather than the female characters populating 1840s novels. Mary enjoys the devotion of both Jem Wilson, a worker of her own class, and Harry Carson, from a propertied family whose father owns the mill where many in Mary's community are employed, including her father. Gaskell uses Mary to personalize class conflict, borrowing from a modified Romeo-and-Juliet plot. Mary is "ambitious," one who "did not favour Mr. Carson the less because he was rich and a gentleman." However, her ambitions will be thwarted when her own father murders Harry Carson and Jem Wilson stands accused of the murder. For characters like Mary Barton, the world of romance remains illusion, blurred by subsistence conditions.

However, as something more than a traditional ROMANCE character, Mary may be more active, and she assumes a crucial role in helping to acquit Jem of murder charges. She also acts a focus for several scenes in which Gaskell reveals important details regarding abuses against the working class and gender issues within the tightly knit community. As Mary sews mourning garments with a seamstress friend, their discussion hints at the abuses of the funereal business and its inflicted guilt on the poor, causing them to spend precious funds on burial rites. In the same scene, Mary's friend reveals her terror of losing her vision, crucial to her craft and the only means of income for her poverty-laden family. The women view the burning of Carsons's mill with two men trapped inside and witness a dramatic rescue of the men, not by any emergency personnel, but by Jem, the son of one of the men. The fire will result in a loss of their only income for many workers, while the Carsons delay its rebuilding, enjoying their insurance income, all of which serves to interest MARXIST CRITICS.

FEMINIST CRITICS will be interested in the conversation that follows Jem's show of heroism between Mary and her father, in which her father declares that Jem "should have her tomorrow, if he had not a penny to keep her." While John Barton departs from the convention of trading his daughter for titles or money, he believes himself in full control of her fate. When he prepares to travel to London to represent his group in the presentation of the Chartist petition to Parliament, Mary cleans his shirts, a role Gaskell compares to that of Beau Tibbs's wife, referring to Oliver GOLDSMITH's SATIRE of English life, *Citizen of the World* (1762), in which Tibbs adopts "the role of the man of society without having the means." In the novel's conclusion, following Mary's display of intelligence and courage in Jem's defense, she assumes the prone position through illness so common to romance females and reverts to a childlike state as others prepare her father for his funeral.

Mary's character remains interesting, if not fully developed. She symbolizes the restricted choices available to women of her class who had slim chances to marry into a higher class; could marry into their own class, lose children to poverty and disease and likely die as young women; could become street walkers, as did her Aunt Esther; or could escape England altogether. She selects the final option to escape her surroundings, although only with Jem's help, as they decide to marry and relocate to Toronto.

Gaskell's overwhelming message appears clearly in the scene in which John not only receives forgiveness from his victim's father but dies in his arms. Legislation will not accomplish reconciliation, nor will theoretical church sermons. Only recognition of each individual's humanity and the willingness to practice compassion on an individual basis will solve England's social ills. John Barton, more than any fictional character from the troubled period of the 1840s, best personalizes that message.

BIBLIOGRAPHY

Tillotson, Kathleen. *Novels of the Eighteen-forties*. Oxford: Clarendon Press, 1954.

MASTER HUMPHREY'S CLOCK   See *OLD CURIOSITY SHOP, THE*.

MASTERMAN READY, OR THE WRECK OF THE PACIFIC CAPTAIN FREDERICK MARRYAT (1841)

Already a proven author for adults with several naval adventure novels to his credit, Captain Frederick MARRYAT published *Masterman Ready* as CHILDREN'S LITERATURE. He hoped to add a voice of reason that he found missing in Johann Wyss's *The Swiss Family Robinson,* a book that made being shipwrecked on an island sound more like a romantic adventure than the hazard Marryat knew it to be. Maryatt maroons his Seagrave family, fashioning much conflict for them to overcome, beginning with a horrific storm and then wreck of the ship *Pacific* at sea, with injuries suffered by the crew. The family's son William references Daniel DEFOE's *ROBINSON CRUSOE,* a tale of survival following a ship's destruction, to Masterman Ready, a 50-year-old sailor on the sea since age 10. He will join the family, composed of Mr. Seagrave, a bright man who had held government office in Australia; an ill Mrs. Seagrave; their sons, William, Thomas and baby Albert, cared for by a "black girl who had come from the Cape of Good Hope" named Juno; and their daughter, Caroline. The group at first faces the elements with little more than a magnifying glass, tea, coffee, and a few potatoes. The worst threat comes from marauders on the island, whose attacks against the Seagraves have fatal and sobering consequences when Ready dies in a melodramatic scene, giving his life for the family. William, with "tears rolling down his cheeks," calls the family to attend to Ready who "called them all by name, one after another," as they kneel to kiss him. He told each "farewell in a faint voice, which at last was changed to a mere whisper. They still remained, in silence and in tears, standing round him, William only kneeling and holding his hand, when the old man's head fell back, and he was no more!" He dies just as rescue arrives in the form of Captain Osborn, the *Pacific*'s leader, believed to have died in the storm.

An example of DIDACTIC literature, *Masterman Ready* yet provided tremendous pleasure for a young generation of readers captivated by Marryat's accurate and stirring details. Having served as a midshipman at age 14, Marryat also brought an acute ability to see the tribulations faced on the sea through the eyes of his young readers. They did not care that critics found Marryat short of technical abilities; he could tell a great story. It remains available in both book and electronic form.

BIBLIOGRAPHY

Pocock, Tom. *Captain Marryat: Seaman, Writer and Adventurer.* Mechanicsburg, Pa.: Stackpole Books, 2000.

MASTER OF BALLANTRAE, THE: A WINTER'S TALE ROBERT LOUIS STEVENSON (1889)

Robert Louis STEVENSON found himself attracted to the subject matter of his novel, *The Master of Ballantrae: a Winter's Tale,* due to his interest in the years following Jacobite Scotland's 1745 rebellion. He also drew inspiration from Captain MARRYAT commenting, according to critic J. R. Hammond in a letter to a friend, "Let us make a tale, a story of many years and countries, of the sea and the land, savagery and civilization." He based the tale on the factual life of the Marquis of Tullibardine, choosing as his first-person point-of-view narrator one Ephraim Mackellar. Mackellar proved a favorite of readers and critics, who found him one of the author's best-realized narrator characters.

Although a gloomy man, Mackellar appreciates the value of human life, and imbues his dour comments with a touch of humor readers found engaging and realistic. His working-class credibility tempers the mystic aspects surrounding the novel's aristocratic characters. Stevenson tells of shaping his narrator while abroad, signing his dedication to Sir Percy Florence and Lady Shelley from Waikiki in May 1880. He writes that "the problem of Mackellar's homespun and how to shape it" gave him "superior flights" of fancy and were his "company on deck in many star-reflecting harbors."

Mackellar traces the feud between James Durie, Master of Ballantrae, and Henry, his younger brother. The two prove excellent foils, with James a hotheaded but charming individual, and Henry a dull but dependable fellow. Mackellar writes of James resembling his father in his love of serious reading and perhaps "some of his tact . . . but that which was only policy in the father became black dissimulation in the son." Mackellar's master, Henry, later Lord Durrisdeer,

"was neither very bad, nor yet very able, but an honest, solid sort . . . little heard." In the face of the revolution, James urges Henry, a cadet, to enter the fray, but he refuses and urges James to take part. The two flip a coin, and James loses. James foreshadows the brothers' future when he asks whether Henry intends to "trip up my heels—Jacob?" His allusion to the enmity between the biblical brothers of Jacob and Isaac portend future conflict over birthright. His love, Alison Grame, expresses her anger, telling him, "If you loved me as well as I love you, you would have stayed." James replies that he could not love her if he did not "love honor more," prompting Alison to cry, "you have no heart—I hope you may be killed!" She will become a part of the conflict that will destroy the family. The story turns profoundly pessimistic, dealing with the evil aspects of human nature in a way that Stevenson would never replicate.

James leaves to fight for the Young Pretender and is later reported killed in battle, allowing Henry to claim title and property, including Alison. However, James survived the fight and returns a vindictive man, determined to ruin his brother. MacKellar's devotion to Henry causes him to distort James's character into that of a duplicitous devil. Although Henry could prove just as vindictive as James, MacKellar's prejudice in favor of his master blinds him to that fact. The resultant "good" and "evil" brothers mirror Stevenson's most famous creation of duality, Dr. Jekyll and Mr. Hyde, of his 1886 work.

James launches a plan to bankrupt Henry by expending all of Ballantrae's assets. The two brothers eventually duel, and Henry appears to defeat James, leaving him for dead. The irrepressible James survives, this time frightening Henry and his family into moving to America. James pursues his brother, who eventually loses his grip on reality due to his brother's persistent heckling. When James himself starts the rumor that he is to regain the title and estate, Henry's sanity completely gives way. He orders James's murder during a hunting trip, but James is privy to the plan, and he arranges for his faithful East Indian servant Secundra to bury him, claiming his death. The servant teaches James a technique to appear to be dead. The plan goes awry, and Secundra begs Henry and his search party to dig up the body. They can't understand the servant's repeated rant, "Buried and not dead," until Secundra explains, "The Sahib and I alone with murderers; try all way to escape, . . . Then try this way: good way in warm climate, good way in India; here in this damn cold place, who can tell? . . . light a fire, help run . . . I bury him alive . . . I teach him to swallow his tongue." The men dig up the body and prove James at last dead. But as Secundra continues to dig and James's face becomes more distinct, his eyes appear to open and his mouth to grin, causing Henry to die from the shock of fright. The seeming rising from the dead of James is blamed on his "black spirit." The two brothers share a grave at the novel's conclusion, as they share reader empathy.

Stevenson does not set out to convince readers that either brother is in the right. Rather, he wants to prove the dramatic potential of true-life conflict and the importance of sharing such stories. The tale continues to fascinate readers and has appeared in various media forms. It is also available in electronic text.

BIBLIOGRAPHY

Calder, Jenni, ed. *Robert Louis Stevenson: A Critical Celebration*. Totowa, N.J.: Barnes & Noble, 1980.

Hammond, J. R. *A Robert Louis Stevenson Companion: A Guide to the Novels, Essays, and Short Stories*. New York: Macmillan, 1984.

MAYOR OF CASTERBRIDGE, THE: A MAN OF CHARACTER THOMAS HARDY (1886)

Thomas HARDY first published *The Life and Death of the Mayor of Casterbridge: A Man of Character* in serial parts; it appeared in *The Graphic* between January and May 1886, to be published in book form later that year. It tells the story of a man who first loses his luck, then gains a new identity, but eventually suffers for his past actions.

Michael Henchard is a field hand out of work who gets drunk at a fair and, for the measly sum of five guineas, sells his wife, Susan, and their daughter, Elizabeth-Jane, to a sailor named Newson who takes Susan as his own wife. When morning and sobriety arrive, Henchard realizes the magnitude of his act and swears not to touch liquor again for 21 years. Years later, Susan Newson believes her sailor husband dead and sets out to search for Henchard, who has reformed and become a model citizen. In the town of Casterbridge, he has made a life as a successful grain merchant and has become the mayor. When Susan and Elizabeth-Jane arrive, Henchard generously promises them aid, although he wants to keep their identities secret in order not to threaten his status. He meets with Susan and promises to marry her, although he is engaged to marry Lucetta Le Sueur. Lucetta is told of the circumstances and breaks with Henchard, although she still moves to Casterbridge. She keeps quiet her past relationship with Henchard, not wanting everyone to understand that she has been jilted.

Henchard hires a bright and enterprising Scots manager new to Casterbridge named Donald Farfrae. He also carries out his promise to marry Susan, but she dies a short time later, shocking Henchard with the revelation that Elizabeth-Jane is actually Newson's daughter. Henchard alienates himself from the young woman, unable to bear her any longer, and he becomes daily more bitter. The same energy and defiance that in the past had brought him success now afford only loneliness and disappointment. Eventually Elizabeth-Jane feels she must leave, and she moves in with Lucetta, becoming her housekeeper. Farfrae had appeared interested in courting Elizabeth-Jane, but marries Lucetta instead. He also becomes estranged from Henchard over a misunderstanding.

As Henchard indulges in hardheaded isolation from his daughter and friend, Farfrae opens his own business. He gains success as Henchard nears bankruptcy. The old relationship between Henchard and Lucetta, including his having already been married when he became engaged to her, comes to light and she literally dies from the shame. Newson suddenly appears, not lost at sea after all, and joins the happy couple Farfrae and Elizabeth-Jane, who marry. Henchard cannot reconcile himself to his fate. He becomes even more bitter and less employable and eventually must be cared for by a long-time friend, Able Whittle. The two live on Egdon Heath for a time until Henchard dies a broken and lonely man.

As Hardy himself remarked in the preface to his second edition, the novel "is more particularly a study of one man's deeds and characters," than any of the other stories in his "Exhibition of Wessex Life." Therefore, only Henchard is completely drawn, and his frailties made glaringly apparent. Early critics took issue with Farfrae's speech as not being appropriately Scottish, to which Hardy replied that Farfrae "is represented not as he would appear to other Scotsmen, but as he would appear to people of outer regions." As for Susan, Elizabeth-Jane, and Lucetta, they are sketched as other of Hardy's female characters, with respectful attention to both strengths and weaknesses, but necessarily secondary to the male characters.

The setting of Casterbridge represents Dorchester, to which Hardy had returned in 1883 and where he lived until his death. The setting grants unity to the novel, representing the process of life and its tragedy, as well as its delights. Surrounded by farmland, the town owes its character to the country and is indelibly marked by rural life. It has lovely gardens in which one cannot dig very deeply before unearthing skeletons of the ancient Romans, symbolic of the intimate juxtaposition of life and death of the spirit, a major theme of the book. Past and present exist together, affecting one another forever, as Henchard's past will strongly affect his present. In a curious embracing of his destiny, Henchard compares himself to the ultimate outcast, Cain, who committed murder as his sin. While Henchard's sins may be something less, he notes his isolation is "as I deserve" and comments his "punishment is *not* greater than I can bear!" His strength tested and found sound, he lives alone in the misery and sorrow that he concocted. The dizzying height of his expectations remains responsible for the nauseating depths of his later despair. Still regularly read and studied, the novel remains readily available and has been converted to various media forms.

BIBLIOGRAPHY

Allen, Walter. Afterword to *The Life and Death of the Mayor of Casterbridge: A Story of a Man of Character,* by Thomas Hardy. New York: Signet Classics, 1962, 328–334.

Mallet, Phillip V., and Ronald P. Draper, ed. *A Spacious Vision: Essays on Hardy.* Newmill: Patten, 1994.

Turner, Paul. *The Life of Thomas Hardy: A Critical Biography.* Oxford: Blackwell, 1998.

MELINCOURT, OR SIR ORAN HAUT-TON THOMAS LOVE PEACOCK (1817)

Thomas Love PEACOCK wrote his second novel, *Melincourt, or Sir Oran Haut-ton,* with the goal of lambasting various political and literary figures. The book proved more ambitious, particularly in its length, than its predecessor, *HEADLONG HALL* (1816). Some critics found its satirical excesses equal to that of its length, and its lack of a clear narrative voice an additional weakness. Its SATIRE proved sharper in reaction to the period following the Battle of Waterloo, with Peacock targeting varied ideas regarding progress. However, he focused his attacks on specific individuals, rather than just ideologies, resulting in undeserved and unfair caricatures of some of the most important figures of the day.

It opens following the fortunes of Anthelia Melincourt, a 21-year-old heiress, and efforts on the part of her various suitors to woo her into marriage. Early on, the narrator explains that Anthelia's father was of the group who "maintained the heretical notion that women are . . . rational beings; though, from the great pains usually taken in what is called education to make them otherwise, there are unfortunately very few examples to warrant the truth of the theory." Peacock later lampoons such lack of education for females and the poor when the wealthy character Mr. Sylvan Forester takes great pains to educate the charming, flute-playing orangutan, of the book's title, which will also court Anthelia. That the ape is able to gain a seat in Parliament reflects obvious disdain for the political system. Peacock satirizes the rotten borough phenomenon, in which boroughs with zero or very low population gained government seats, controlled basically by political machines or aristocracy, proving blatantly problematic during the "One vote" election.

Peacock's additional characters include Mr. Anyside Antijack, representing George Canning, a Tory supporter of government reform and relief for the poor, and Mr. Killthedead, assumed to represent Sir John Barrow, secretary to the Admiralty. As public figures, they invited such lampooning. However, his characterizations of poets Samuel Taylor Coleridge as Mr. Mystic; William Wordsworth as Mr. Paperstamp; and Robert Southey, also a historian, critic, and England's poet laureate, as Mr. Feathernest are deemed unfair by critic George Saintsbury. Saintsbury agrees that Coleridge and Southey opened themselves to satire due to certain erratic changes in their opinions, but that the attacks on the always modest and unassuming Wordsworth as the self-indulgent, materialistic Paper-stamp are absurd. He also contends that Southey in no way "sold his soul" for the poet laureateship, nor did he "feather his nest" with nothing but books, and that the lack of humor in that characterization remains unpardonable. Notable features are the novel's poems and songs, with Anthelia's ballad, "The Tomb of Love," labeled as "first class." It also describes a dance based on the game of chess, which grew from Peacock's devotion to pageantry, materialized in the "revels" he held for his grandchildren.

Peacock wrote a new preface to the 1856 edition, in which he recognized that certain reforms of political and social inequities had occurred since the novel's original printing, one of the most notable being the forced freeing of slaves by British colonists. He also notes that, because the "Court is more moral," the "public is more moral; more decorous, at least in external semblance." However, he adds that "the progress of intellect" has not kept stride with the "progress of mechanics," and "the 'reading public' has increased its capacity of swallow, in a proportion far exceeding that of its digestion." Peacock obviously felt that England's civic structure still merited lampooning, with the hopes that satire would, as expected in its classical origins, lead to change. The book remains readily available.

BIBLIOGRAPHY

Dawson, Carl. *His Fine Wit: A Study of Thomas Love Peacock.* London: Routledge & Kegan Paul, 1970.

Saintsbury, George. Introduction to *Melincourt, or Sir Oran Haut-ton,* by Thomas Love Peacock. London: Macmillan, 1927, vii–xiii.

MELMOTH THE WANDERER CHARLES ROBERT MATURIN (1820)

In Charles Robert Maturin's GOTHIC FICTION, *Melmoth the Wanderer,* the protagonist strikes a deal with Satan that lengthens his life, but he will eventually owe his soul to Satan. The traditional theme of dealing with the devil supported Maturin's eccentric interests in terror. As a clergyman,

he surprised others by expressing his belief that terror transcended even love as the most universal emotion. In *Melmoth,* he produced what some critics believe to be the best English HORROR novel. While his Faustian plot is hardly original, Maturin framed it in a contemporary setting and shaped a character who did not realize the full disaster caused by his greed until well into the story, strengthening suspense.

Satan promises to release Melmoth, doomed to wander the earth, from his debt only if he can find another human to assume it. Melmoth sets out to accomplish that mission, assuming if he finds humans desperate enough, they will agree. However, a descendant and Dublin college student discovers the ghastly truth, leaving readers to observe Melmoth travel across not only continents but also time, in a living death state. He works to persuade a lunatic, a tortured victim of the Inquisition, and a parent forced to watch his own children die from starvation, but none agrees to substitute for Melmoth. He remains doomed to meet the debt himself. A famous descendant of Maturin, Oscar WILDE, adopted the name of Sebastian Melmoth when he moved to Paris following his imprisonment.

BIBLIOGRAPHY

Scholten, Willem. *Charles William Maturin, the Terror-Novelist.* New York: Garland, 1980.

Smith, Amy Elizabeth. "Experimentation and 'Horrid Curiosity' in Maturin's *Melmoth the Wanderer.*" *English Studies* 74.6 (December 1993): 524–536.

MEMOIRS OF MISS SIDNEY BIDULPH: EXTRACTED FROM HER OWN JOURNAL FRANCES SHERIDAN (1761)

When Frances SHERIDAN wrote *The Memoirs of Miss Sidney Bidulph,* she dedicated it to Samuel RICHARDSON, whose PAMELA (1740) she greatly admired. Both share a focus on morality, and both use a heavy hand in stressing that theme for their readers in their faithful imitation of French SENTIMENTAL FICTION. While *Pamela* appeared in epistolary format, *Memoirs* uses that of a journal; both employ the first-person narrative for immediacy's sake. However, Richardson explores the challenges of men to women's purity, while Sheridan explores the manner by which women challenge other women, revealing their helplessness in the face of the double standard that favored men where the act of sex was concerned. Even with such a serious topic, Sheridan imbues Sidney with a sense of humor in meeting the many challenges to her well-being. The traditional story behind the novel holds that Mrs. Sheridan had to steal moments to work on the project from her many household duties, including caring for a busy house that hosted visitors such as James Boswell and Samuel JOHNSON. They visited her actor husband, Thomas Sheridan, a moody spouse whose various speculations reduced the family to poverty. As an adult, she had to care for her father, who had originally forbidden her to learn to read and write. She did so with the help of her brothers and worked for years on her novel, which was published anonymously.

Young Sidney gives into her mother's wishes not to marry her love, Faulkland, when they discover he has impregnated another woman. She marries Arnold instead, a man for whom she has little feeling or trust, although, with the birth of their two daughters, she develops an affection for her husband. Her trust is shattered when she discovers in a most melodramatic but entertaining manner he has committed adultery. Having recently seen Faulkland again, Sidney attends a musical performance with friends where the playhouse catches on fire; the flames foreshadow the destruction of her marriage. Faulkland is present and rescues Sidney, who, while recovering nearby, overhears her husband romancing his companion, Mrs. Gerrarde. Adding to her grief over losing what she believed was her husband's loyalty, she learns that Faulkland was trapped into marrying a woman who is also an adulterer.

Following heightened suffering and indignity on Sidney's part, Arnold at last dies, and Sidney marries Faulkland, who believes his wife to be dead. She reappears, however, wrecking Sidney's chance for happiness. Following Faulkland's death, Sidney seems to her childhood friend Cecilia at peace with her children, but an addendum by Cecilia hints that the comfortable circumstances which Sidney had wished for her children later caused them great grief. Cecilia writes that Sidney so often warned her children of the dangers brought by wealth that "she seemed to have a presentiment of those evils, which were now ready to pour in like a torrent upon her." Her noble suffering predicted, but not detailed, it remains pointless, as she gains nothing from it, allowing Sheridan to construct a social SATIRE on the consequences of women's actions.

Some critics pronounced the novel better than others like it of the era, with Sidney at least expressing her emotion instead of suffering dumbly at the hands of unscrupulous males. They praise especially the engaging tone of Sidney's correspondence with Cecilia, who, although living away from England, remains faithfully supportive of Sidney, balancing the female-versus-female theme of the story. While little read later due to a change of taste that found sentimental hyperbole unpalatable, the novel proved so popular in its own day that Sheridan published a sequel titled *Conclusion of the Memoirs* (1767). Sheridan's famous playwright son, Richard, later appropriated scenes from his mother's book into his play, *School for Scandal,* although without apparent recognition of their source.

BIBLIOGRAPHY
Sage, Lorna, ed. *Women's Writing in English.* Cambridge: Cambridge University Press, 1999, 430.
Townsend, Sue. Introduction to *Memoirs of Miss Sidney Bidulph,* by Frances Sheridan. New York: Pandora, 1987, ix–xi.

MEREDITH, GEORGE (1828–1909)

Although George Meredith hesitated in supplying details of his youth, many of them apparently appeared in his novel *Evan Harrington* (1861), in which the protagonist, like Meredith himself, is the son of a tailor who lives and works in Portsmouth. The novel also supplies information regarding Meredith's family, particularly the patriarchal grandfather, Melchizedec, spelled Melchisedec in the novel. Although Meredith never knew him, "the Great Mel" was often mentioned in family mythology as an adventurer and affected Meredith's vision of himself. In the autobiographical novel, Evan fantasizes he is actually the son of aristocracy, something that Meredith apparently also did, believing his origins to be Welsh. He later viewed his childhood with a pain that prevented his discussing it. His mother, whom he described as "handsome" and "witty," died when he was five years old, and he was left with a father he later labeled a "fool." A frightened and only child, Meredith detested being alone. Due to funds from his maternal relatives, he was able to attend a school in Southsea believed to be superior to the local institution, a fact that Meredith's heightened sensitivity appreciated. At age 10, Meredith's father, Augustus, lost his position to a competitor. Burdened not only with supporting his son but also the care of a "housekeeper," Matilda Buckett, he moved the family and married Matilda six months later. That permanently alienated Meredith, and he separated from his father a year later, using the income left by his mother to attend a boarding school.

Meredith became a ward of the Chancery, and his father renounced his parenthood, freeing Meredith from the confinement he had always felt. One year later, Meredith moved to Germany with the approval of his official lawyer guardian and, at the age of 14, felt himself mature. He attended the Moravian School at Neuwied, a school based on a community theory that emphasized tolerance, where Meredith became fluent in both French and German over the next two years. He left the school to work with a London solicitor at age 17 but never pursued the career in law he had anticipated. Instead, he turned to writing.

Meredith first wrote and published poetry when he returned to England, becoming a friend of novelist Thomas Love PEACOCK, with whom he shared the theory that ideas and philosophy had a place in fiction. He married Mary Ellen Nicholls, Peacock's widowed daughter in 1849, and the two wrote together, often borrowing themes from one another. The handsome couple were popular in London society, but their family life suffered from the death of two infants. At last, in 1853, one infant son, Arthur, survived, joining Mary's daughter from her first marriage, Edith Nicolls, to complete the Meredith family. Meredith soon made the acquaintance of literary luminaries Charles DICKENS, editor of HOUSEHOLD WORDS, and G. H. Lewes. Lewes edited *The Leader* and engaged in a discreet relationship with Mary Ann Evans, later to publish under the pen name George ELIOT. Both publications published some of Meredith's poetry.

Just as Meredith's writing career began to blossom, Mary left him in 1852 for a liaison with the painter Henry Wallis. His first published book, *Poems,* appeared in 1851, followed by the fantasies *The Shaving of Shagpat* (1856), based on a tale told by the mysterious Herr von Haxthausen at a friend's house, and *Farina* (1857). Working as a journalist on the *Ipswich Journal,* he published his first of several novels in 1859, *The Ordeal of Richard Feveral,* followed in 1861 by *Evan Harrington.* Both introduced a variety of complex themes, including conflict between fathers and sons, social class relationships and conflicts, English education, misogyny, morality, and sexuality. Meredith felt the age was ready to confront serious themes in fiction, as it was the era of Charles DARWIN, Karl Marx, and Frederick Engels. However, it was not until the 20th century that his approach would receive the credit it deserved by critics, among them Virginia Woolf.

The critical failure of *Richard Feveral* proved painful, and sympathy for Meredith may partly explain Edward Chapman's offering him a position reviewing manuscripts for the publisher Chapman and Hall. As a reader, he played an important role in encouraging novelist and poet Thomas HARDY and novelist George GISSING. He gained a reputation for exhorting both male and female authors to produce better work. One of his greatest errors was in the rejection of Mrs. Henry WOOD's *EAST LYNNE* (1861). Even when novelist Harrison AINSWORTH later championed the novel, Meredith would not accept it for Chapman and Hall; it would later sell a million copies, become a famous drama and movie, and remain in print in perpetuity. He did recommend publication of Olive SCHREINER's *The STORY OF AN AFRICAN FARM* (1883), although he asked for revision. His rejection of Samuel BUTLER's *EREWHON* (1872) was later considered his most egregious mistake.

Meredith's publication in 1862 of a volume of poetry titled *Modern Love* (1862) secured his fame as a poet. His personal fortunes also turned when, in 1863, he met Marie Vulliamy, 24-year-old daughter of a Frenchman, and fell in love. When he petitioned her father for her hand, he was required, based on the failure of his first marriage, to supply personal references. Her father also required Meredith to produce written replies to eight questions that varied in topic from the mode of his separation from Mary to his income. They were satisfactory, and the couple married in September. Their family grew with the addition of Will (1865) and Marie Eveleen, also called Mariette and Riette (1871). Meredith and Marie never became intimate with his son Arthur, although the group remained cordial, and Meredith supported Arthur's education.

Encouraged by renewed critical praise, Meredith again turned to fiction and published multiple novels over the next two decades, including SANDRA BELLONI (originally titled Emilia in England, 1864), RHODA FLEMING (1865), Vittoria (1867), The Adventures of Harry Richmond (1871), BEAUCHAMP'S CAREER (1876), The EGOIST (1879), and The TRAGIC COMEDIANS (1880), with several affected by John Stuart Mill's The Subjection of Women. He next published another volume of poetry, Poems and Lyrics of the Joy of Earth (1883), then an additional novel during that decade, DIANA OF THE CROSSWAYS (1885). His later novels are considered some of his best, including ONE OF OUR CONQUERORS (1891), LORD ORMONT AND HIS AMINTA (1894), and The AMAZING MARRIAGE (1895), all focusing on the relationships between men and women, some offering criticism of the marriage contract often forced upon young couples. Marie died of throat cancer in 1885, and Meredith became more ill and frail over the remaining years. After he died, the Society of Authors, for which he had served as president, wanted him buried in Poet's Corner in Westminster Abbey, but the dean of Westminster objected on the grounds that Meredith was not a practicing Christian. He was cremated and buried with Marie in the cemetery at Dorking.

Meredith's understanding of women is often cited as his most remarkable quality, particularly in his projection of the gender inequalities involved in relationships. He especially attacked the Victorian prototype of the tyrannical, self-indulgent husband, although he offered balance in accompanying characterizations of more liberated understanding males. He was also known for designating narrow-minded English middle class characters as anti-Semites and xenophobes, while his aristocrats were not burdened by such narrow views. In the realm of prose, his essay "On Comedy and the Uses of the Comic Spirit" (1897) continues to be studied, in addition to short stories

and further volumes of poetry, noted for their emphasis not only on the beauty of nature but on its destructive aspects as well.

Meredith's innovations in using his novels as vehicles for personal philosophy greatly affected the development of the novel, as seen in works by Robert Louis STEVENSON and others.

BIBLIOGRAPHY

Jones, Mervyn. The Amazing Victorian: A Life of George Meredith. London: Constable, 1999.

Lindsay, Jack. George Meredith: His Life and Work. Reprint, 1956, Millwood, N.Y.: Kraus, 1980.

MIDDLEMARCH: A STUDY OF PROVINCIAL LIFE GEORGE ELIOT (1871–1872)

Often identified as the greatest English novel ever written, Middlemarch by George ELIOT examines the lives of several members of the rising middle class in the early to middle 19th century in a midsized town in the Midlands of England. The title refers to the name of the town that serves as the novel's setting, but it also suggests the story's focus.

The plot follows the life changes of a large cast of characters divided into four interconnecting story lines centered on Miss Dorothea Brooke, Dr. Tertius Lydgate, the banker Mr. Bulstrode, and Fred Vincy. Each stands at the center of a group of family members, friends, and acquaintances, some of whom interact with more than one of the main characters, giving the story its complex texture and increasing its social and PSYCHOLOGICAL REALISM. Each protagonist seeks fulfillment in both ambition and love. Repeatedly, the fulfillment of one goal affects the fulfilling of the other, but the wide range of characters allows the author to explore numerous variations on these double themes.

A young woman of marriageable age, Dorothea Brooke belongs to the gentry. Her behavior and choices, however, derive from her desire to improve conditions of the world rather than to charm the town's young men. She makes elaborate plans and creates designs for better workers' cottages on her uncle's estate; however, since raising the living standards of the workers costs money resulting in no increase of income from labor, her uncle resists her efforts. Dorothea looks for a way to contribute something to the larger world when she meets Mr. Casaubon, a wealthy older scholar who is working on a key to all mythologies—an ambitious undertaking that has occupied him for years. She sees assisting Casaubon as a way to fulfill her ambition within the narrow range of options open to women, a theme of interest to FEMINIST CRITICS. By marrying and helping Casaubon, she will find satisfaction. Dorothea sacrifices romantic love to her ambition, but soon after her marriage meets Casaubon's impoverished but talented young cousin Will Ladislaw. Although Dorothea does not at first realize the strength of his effect on her, Casaubon does and amends his will to disinherit her if she marries Ladislaw; soon after, he dies. Dorothea must choose between the wealth and status she possesses as Mr. Casaubon's widow and the fulfillment of both love and ambition in a union with Will Ladislaw.

In contrast to Dorothea's devotion to ambition at the cost of love, Dr. Lydgate begins as an ambitious young physician hoping to discover the cause of fever, then thought to be a disease rather than a symptom. When he begins to court beautiful Rosamund Vincy, the daughter of a newly wealthy manufacturer, he thinks that he will find love and continue to pursue his scientific ambitions, even though they do not bring him a lucrative practice. What he finds, however, is that a beautiful wife from a wealthy family cannot be denied the comforts and the status to which she has been accustomed. Dr. Lydgate must relinquish his ambitions to satisfy his wife's financial needs, and he finds himself increasingly devoted to the gouty feet of clients in fashionable London and Paris who can afford to pay well for his ministrations.

Mr. Bulstrode serves as the novel's antagonist, both in his business connection to Fred Vincy and in his hidden crime. When his misdeeds stand to be revealed, he makes choices that lead to his life being completely disrupted. Having already fulfilled his ambitions and established a stable emotional bond with his wife, he loses his wealth and status but discovers something valuable in her devotion. While Dorothea and Lydgate place ambition above love but keep it within the bounds of law and morality, Mr. Bulstrode is revealed as a man who would violate laws to pursue ambition. He becomes a social outcast, departing Middlemarch in disgrace.

Only Fred Vincy fulfills his goals in Middlemarch. His expectation of a large inheritance from a wealthy old uncle nearly leads to his destruction. Confident of a financially secure future, he lacks ambition to exert himself and shape a future. His false sense of security sets him on a self-destructive path, and when his hopes of the inheritance are dashed, only the love of his sweetheart Mary Garth draws him back to a realistic understanding of what he can hope for in life. He must curtail the ambitions of a wealthy future and learn to be happy as a man who pursues a profession to earn his way. Mary's love compensates for his acceptance of reduced ambitions.

Running throughout the story is the historical impact of the political reforms of 1832, which extended the voting franchise to a much wider spectrum of the male population. Dorothea's uncle finds himself unable to navigate the complex waters of democratic elections and unwilling to make the compromises required of a successful politician. Other characters also are drawn into the redefined political realm, including Will Ladislaw. The class-based elitism that had dominated English social arrangements for centuries begins to erode once the middle class is enfranchised to vote. The march to power of the middle class has begun by the novel's end, heralding the impending arrival of a more egalitarian order. Eliot's third-person omniscient narrator allows readers to relive the mid-Victorian era through an understanding of the underlying attitudes that drive the realistic behaviors of the diverse characters. Demonstrating a keen insight into human nature and using a sensitive awareness of narrative pacing, Eliot draws the four story lines to a satisfying resolution.

BIBLIOGRAPHY

Hutchinson, Stuart, ed. *George Eliot: Critical Assessments.* 4 vols. East Sussex: Helm Information, 1996.

Pangallo, Karen L., ed. *The Critical Response to George Eliot.* Westport, Conn.: Greenwood Press, 1994.

Rignall, John, ed. *Oxford Reader's Companion to George Eliot.* Oxford: Oxford University Press, 2000.

MILL ON THE FLOSS, THE   GEORGE ELIOT (1860)

The most tragic novel by George ELIOT, this story is also her most autobiographical. It was published after her highly successful first novel, *ADAM BEDE* (1859), and it proved to be another great success, helping to establish Eliot's reputation as an important novelist.

The protagonist of the novel, Maggie Tulliver, combines paradoxical aspects of the two main female characters from *Adam Bede,* Hetty Sorrel and Dinah Morris: like Hetty, Maggie can be self-indulgent and impetuous, but like Dinah, she does not shrink from self-sacrifice and is a deeply compassionate individual quickly touched by the suffering of others. Maggie's brother Tom is also her closest friend, but Tom has a mean streak that comes out when he teases her or takes it upon himself to command her obedience. Although Maggie is a bright and talented girl, she has been born into a world that offers only marriage and childrearing as a profession for her in adulthood; even as a child, she demonstrates her need for a larger sphere of activity and achievement. In contrast, Tom proves to be a reluctant learner when he is sent to study under the clergyman, Mr. Stelling.

Tom's education indicates the ambition of the Tullivers to move up in the world, but Mr. Tulliver's temper soon lands him in a dispute over water rights: His mill must have water if it is to function, but landowners upstream want to irrigate their property by diverting some of water from the Floss. Ironically, Tom's fellow-pupil is Philip Wakem, the son of the lawyer representing Mr. Tulliver's opponents. Philip is crippled, and when Maggie meets him while on a visit to her brother, she befriends him. By the time Maggie's father is ruined in the lawsuit, Philip is in love with her. After Mr. Tulliver swears an oath never to forgive or forget Mr. Wakem and his clients, Maggie and Philip must meet secretly. Tom had been coerced into joining in his father's oath, and so in addition to bringing about the family's financial ruin, Mr. Tulliver's pride also contributes to the contortion of Tom's emotions and to the duplicity of Maggie's meetings with Philip. Tom in turn takes out his anger on Maggie, forbidding her to meet Philip any longer after he discovers their connection. Tom comes home to work and earns enough money to pay off his father's legal debts, but Mr. Tulliver dies after an enraged but ineffectual assault on Mr. Wakem.

By the time the mortgage on Dorlcote Mill is lifted, Maggie has become a marriageable young woman. On a visit to her friend and cousin Lucy, she meets Stephen Guest, the young man expected to become Lucy's fiancée; Stephen and Maggie are attracted to each other in spite of his courtship of Lucy. Philip is also still in love with Maggie against his father's outraged prohibitions. Maggie is in a quandary: encouraging Philip will alienate her from Tom, who is carrying his father's hostile oath to the next generation, but encouraging Stephen, a man who would be acceptable to Tom, will hurt Lucy. A careless afternoon boating on the Floss with Stephen leads to Maggie's unmerited disgrace in the local village. She refuses Stephen's offer of marriage, and Tom shuts the door of the family home on her, forcing her and Mrs. Tulliver to lodge in the village. When the Floss breaks its banks and rises in a flood, Maggie takes a rowboat to the Mill to rescue Tom, hoping that he will accept reconciliation. She misjudges the power of the flood and disaster brings them together in a watery death.

The autobiographical elements in this novel relate to George Eliot's estrangement from her family upon becoming the common-law wife of writer Henry Lewes, a married man separated from his wife but unable to attain a divorce. Eliot's father, Robert Evans, and her brother, Isaac Evans, repudiated her as an adulteress and cut off all contact with her. Just as the character of Adam Bede is a portrait inspired by Eliot's father, so too is the character of Tom Tulliver a portrait inspired by her brother Isaac. The impossibility of Maggie making a love-match that is acceptable to her brother reflects Eliot's own personal life. The tragedy that befalls Maggie and Tom suggests that perhaps only death can resolve the differences between George Eliot and her brother.

Critics have questioned whether the tragic ending suits the warm portrayal of family life and especially of childhood that Eliot develops in detail in the novel's early chapters. The tragic end comes on suddenly and does not grow out of the novel's structure: Instead of resolving the conflicts that have developed in the plot, the ending terminates any possibility of resolution.

Nonetheless, the richness of Eliot's portrayal of a large and diverse cast of characters and the PSYCHOLOGICAL REALISM with which she develops the personalities of her characters as they encounter the conflicts of the plot make the novel a satisfying and rewarding reading experience.

BIBLIOGRAPHY

Hutchinson, Stuart, ed. *George Eliot: Critical Assessments.* 4 vols. East Sussex: Helm Information, 1996.

Pangallo, Karen L., ed. *The Critical Response to George Eliot.* Westport, Conn.: Greenwood Press, 1994.

Rignall, John, ed. *Oxford Reader's Companion to George Eliot.* Oxford: Oxford University Press, 2000.

MISFORTUNES OF ELPHIN, THE THOMAS LOVE PEACOCK (1829)

Thomas Love PEACOCK published his *The Misfortunes of Elphin* in an attempt to satirize what he viewed as affectations employed by his contemporary fiction writers, also taking aim at his traditional targets, including theories regarding universal education, the removal from public usage of land by the gentry, and irresponsible politics. He chose a legend dear to the Englishman's heart, that of King Arthur and his fabled knights. Welsh mythology was especially interesting to Peacock, who had married a Welsh wife. He departed from his usual approach of gathering a group of characters together to engage in Socratic dialogue with little semblance of plot, instead presenting a traditional adventure narrative. While he drew his ideas for plotlines from historical works such as Bishop Percy's *Reliques of Ancient English Poetry* (1765), the embellishments were his own.

Containing familiar aspects of various legends, the novel follows the fortune of one Elphin, a king who comes to the throne of Ceredigion, inheriting many problems, including a loss of territory, the loyalty of his people, and material support. The losses were incurred by Seithenyn, a drunken member of foreign royalty, described early on as "Prince Seithenyn ap Seithyn Saidi, who held the office of Arglwyd Gorwarcheidwad yr Argae Breninawl, which signifies, in English, Lord High Commissioner of Royal Embankment; and he executed it as a personage so denominated might be expected to do: he drank the profits,

and left the embankment to his deputies, who left it to their assistants, who left it to itself." Peacock characterizes the typical politico as one who, once elected, did as he pleased with little regard for the needs of those who elected him, but in Seithenyn he also supplied one of literature's distinctive comic figures. A drunk who spouts nonsense logic in the vein of Shakespeare's Falstaff, he also proves important to Peacock's SATIRE. In justifying neglecting his duties and allowing the floods to overflow the embankment, he represents the Tory opposition to constitutional reform that Peacock's readers would have easily recognized. Foreshadowing his later injection of various drinking songs, and ballads, some traditionally Welsh, others written by Peacock, the narrator reveals that Elphin's father, King Gwythno, had been warned of the perils of Gwynhidwy, a white mermaid, symbolic of the power of the sea. A happy but foolish ruler, he appointed the incompetent Seithenyn to a crucial task, likely a statement by Peacock against failed foreign policies.

Elphin receives the same warning against the dangers of the sea, but he pays more attention to it than did his father. When he attempts to urge Seithenyn to repair the embankment, the inebriated prince replies, "Our ancestors were wiser than we: they built it in their wisdom; and, if we should be so rash as to try to mend it, we should only mar it." Again Peacock parodies politicians who lack innovation, imagination, and initiative. Readers understand the sarcasm in the narrator's remark that he and his audience are "happy that our own public guardians are too virtuous to act or talk like Seithenyn, and that we ourselves are too wise not to perceive, and too free not to prevent it, if they should be so disposed." Many such remarks utilize the 16th century to reflect on shortcomings of the 19th century.

Romance blooms as Elphin falls in love with and marries Seithenyn's daughter, Angharad, just before the embankment gives way. They later come upon the foundling, Taliesin, a child abandoned in the flooded ruin of the country, and Angharad delightedly adopts him. Two years later the couple produces a daughter, Melanghel, and Elphin being an expert fisherman, they found a fishery that becomes successful and pleases the old king, who spends time playing with his grand-daughter. Taliesin becomes a member of the bards, the "general motto of their order" being "Y GWIR YN ERBYN Y BYD: the Truth against the World." Peacock quickly adds that, while this was the ideal, "many of them, instead of acting up to this splendid profession, chose to advance their personal fortunes by appealing to the selfishness, the passions, and the prejudices of kings, factions, and the rabble." His attitude regarding artists who misuse their talents is clear. In short order, he also lambastes the press and the outrageous claims of political and physical science, medicine in particular.

Dramatic speeches enrich the narrative fabric of Elphin's struggles, including his imprisonment many years later by his evil neighbor and competitor, Maelgon, in the Stone Tower of Dignawy. The songs and poetry retain focus firmly on the society's bards, Taliesin in particular, who heroically rescues Elphin through the aid of Arthur. The tale concludes on a strong romantic note, as Taliesin is given the hand of Elphin's daughter.

Throughout, Peacock emphasizes the importance of the arts, through music, poetry, and storytelling, to enrich man's humanity and to spur him to great acts. However, he makes clear that art should be produced for art's sake, not in order to win critical or political favor. He begins one chapter lampooning pride among poets by writing, "amongst the Christmas amusements of Caer Lleon, a grand Bardic Congress was held in the Roman theatre, when the principal bards of Britain contended for the pre-eminence in the art of poetry, and in its appropriate moral and mystical knowledge."

The Misfortunes of Elphin represents classic Peacock, displaying a sharp irony in the dissection and study of his culture. He ridicules all dogma by not propagating any particular personal theory. The novel did not prove popular in its day, likely due to its mix of ROMANCE and satire, which made readers uncomfortable. However, later readers found its celebration of the ridiculous in human nature most entertaining; it is available in print and electronic texts.

BIBLIOGRAPHY

Dawson, Carl. *His Fine Wit: A Study of Thomas Love Peacock.* Berkeley: University of California Press, 1960.

Dodson, Charles B. Introduction to *Thomas Love Peacock: Nightmare Abbey, The Misfortunes of Elphin, Crotchet Castle.* Holt, Rhinehart, and Winston, 1971, vii–xxviii.

MITFORD, MARY RUSSELL (1787–1866)

A writer of short stories, novels, and plays, Mary Russell Mitford was born in Alresford, Hampshire. Her father, a physician, did not practice, choosing rather to gamble, depending on the fortune from his heiress wife. An only child, Mitford attended a London school of reputation, later finishing her education on her own; the circulating library records at Reading indicate Mitford checked out 55 books during one month's time. By the age of 26, she had published two poetry collections. Her physician father's extravagant lifestyle bankrupted the family in 1820, and they relocated to a village cottage at Three Miles Cross, between Reading and Basingstoke. Forced to support her family, she focused on writing verse tragedies. Her remarkable success in a patriarchal field included the acceptance of her play *Julian* by the dramatist Talfourd. Its performance in Covent Garden in 1823 proved so successful that she immediately followed up with *Foscari,* produced in 1826, and *Rienzi,* in 1828. *Rienzi* exceeded a 20-night run, earning the most that any play was allowed, £400.

For further income, Mitford turned her energies to short tales, which reflected a mixture of essay and fiction writing elements. Her "Our Village" was published in *The Lady's Magazine* in 1819 as a series of extremely popular sketches, based on her own life at Three Mile Cross. Elizabeth Barrett BROWNING praised Mitford's work, which was later compared, although not positively, to that of Elizabeth GASKELL. While Mitford's detail in describing setting and scene received praise, her characterizations were described as shallow and insipid. However, her series remained important for ushering in a new pastoral approach based upon a keen observation of detail of a real place and loyalty in presenting that detail. The series appeared in five published volumes between 1824 and 1832. Mitford also published the novels *Belford Regis, or Sketches of a Country Town* (1837) and *Atherton and Other Tales* (1854), neither of which found the success of her earlier works, although the famous critic John Ruskin praised *Atherton*. Following her father's death in 1852, Mitford resided in Swallowfield, a village close to Reading, where she published *Recollections of a Literary Life: Or Books, Places, and People,* an autobiographical work (1852). Mitford remains crucial as the earliest female fiction writer to make distinctive use of locale. Virginia Woolf included Mitford's picture in her 1933 biography of Elizabeth Barrett Browning, *Flush: A Biography* (1933). Her writing is important as some of the last to feature a pre–Industrial Age Britain.

BIBLIOGRAPHY

Broomfield, Andrea, and Sally Mitchell, eds. *Prose by Victorian Women: an Anthology.* New York: Garland Publishing, 1996.

Edwards, P. D. *Idyllic Realism from Mary Russell Mitford to Hardy.* New York: St. Martin's Press, 1998.

Horn, Pamela, ed. *Life in a Country Town: Reading and Mary Russell Mitford.* Abingdon: Beacon Publications, 1984.

Sage, Lorna. "Mitford, Mary Russell." *The Cambridge Guide to Women's Writing in English.* Cambridge: Cambridge University Press, 1999, 437–38.

MOIR, DAVID MACBETH (1798–1851)

Born at Musselburgh in Scotland, David Macbeth Moir was the second of four children. He studied Latin, Greek, French, and mathematics after a basic grammar school education, and then began an apprenticeship with Dr. Stewart, a medical practitioner, at the age of 13. Even at such a young age, Moir developed a devotion to the healing profession that remained with him until his death in 1851.

The 15-year-old Moir published his first poetry in a periodical called the *Cheap Magazine*. By all reports his mother, herself a talented writer, helped him develop taste and style by encouraging and listening to his writings. Three years later, his mother's widow status prompted Moir to become a partner of Dr. Brown of Musselburgh in 1817. Although he had just received his surgeon's diploma, he dove headlong into grueling hours of medical practice in order to provide for his mother. His immediate dedication to his profession, along with a growing love for literature that kept him writing and studying by candlelight in the evenings after work, held him in Musselburgh from 1817 to 1828; he never slept a night elsewhere. Known by his pen name, "Delta," to the readers of BLACKWOOD'S EDINBURGH MAGAZINE, Moir also published both prose and verse in *Constable's Edinburgh Magazine* and became the chief contributor to the *Edinburgh Literary Gazette,* publishing anonymously.

In 1828, Moir married Catherine Lee Bell; the couple had a total of 11 children. Following the abatement of the cholera epidemic in Europe, the couple lost three of their children in the space of two years, two dying in 1838. The death of Charles Bell at age two years prompted Moir's most movingly written elegy for "Casa Wappy," young Charles's name for himself. Moir's contemporaries, including Wordsworth, Tennyson, Charles DICKENS, and Ferrier, urged Moir to publish his privately circulated expressions of grief, which he did in the collection *Domestic Verses* in 1843.

Though the opportunity arose time and again for Moir to move to Edinburgh and practice medicine, he never left his hometown of Musselburgh. This prolific author and dedicated physician averaged 220 miles per week in attending the sick, even after being sickened at a patient's bedside in 1844, an illness from which he never fully recovered. He was lame for life after a carriage wreck in 1846 that injured his hip joint, yet continued his duties on horseback and on foot. In 1851 he managed to give several lectures at the Philosophical Institution of Edinburgh in addition to his busy patient schedule. Later that year, Moir badly wrenched himself dismounting a horse, an injury that ceased his labors and prompted him finally to leave home to travel to Dumfries in hopes of restoring his vigor. This was not to be, and his health continued to worsen until his death July 6, 1851. At his death, Catherine was still living, as well as eight of his children.

Moir's literary work became a fixture in northern Scottish literature. Today his reputation rests mainly on his FANTASY FICTION: the *Autobiography of Mansie Wauch: Tailor in Dalkeith* (1828) first appeared in serial form in *Blackwood's* and was dedicated to his good friend John GALT. It featured a flying tailor popular for his personality—merry and wise, yet sly and with a dry humor—that seemed to mirror the national character of Scotland. Moir was a frequent contributor and co-editor of *The*

Edinburgh Gazette, in which he pushed romanticism in publishing frequent reviews and other notices of such writers as Samuel Coleridge; George Gordon, Lord Byron; and Mary SHELLEY. In his time Moir was probably most famous as Delta (Δ), his signature to thoughtful ballads in *Blackwood's* that numbered almost 400. Moir published several highly comic caricatures of figures including Sir Walter SCOTT (*Eve of St. Jerry*) and, despite his promotion of romanticism in official circles, William Wordsworth (*Billy Routing*) and Samuel Coleridge (*Auncient Waggonere*), they were never connected to an unknown small-town doctor because they carried no signature.

David Moir published more than enough prose and verse to be a well-respected writer, but he enhanced his reputation with additional professional publications. Although his *Outlines of Ancient History of Medicine, Being a View of the Progress of the Healing Arte Among the Egyptians, Greeks, Romans and Arabians* never saw the publishing of the planned second and third volumes, his *Practical Observations of Malignant Cholera* and *Proofs of the Contagion of Malignant Cholera* sold well in several editions.

BIBLIOGRAPHY

Significant Scots: David Macbeth Moir. ElectricScotland.com. Available online. URL: http://www.electricscotland.com/ history/other/moir_david.htm. Downloaded on April 15, 2004.

Stephen, Sir Leslie, and Sir Sidney Lee, eds. *The Dictionary of National Biography.* 66 vols. Oxford: Oxford University Press, 1921.

Lynch, Michael, ed. "Culture." *The Oxford Companion to Scottish History.* Oxford: Oxford University Press, 2001, 137–150.

MOLESWORTH, MARY LOUISA (1839–1921)

A writer of CHILDREN'S LITERATURE, Mary Louisa Molesworth was born Mary Louisa Stewart in Rotterdam. Educated in Switzerland, she published her first novel, *Lover and Husband,* in 1869. Adopting the male alias of Ennis Graham in hopes of being taken more seriously by the public, she wrote additional novels that did not sell well. When she turned to children's works, she found the success that previously eluded her.

Through the publisher Macmillan, a new Molesworth book appeared every Christmas, with the well-known Walter Crane illustrating some of them. Her staunchly Victorian outlook on the proper behavior of children accounted for her popularity. Her moral tales were approved by parents who appreciated DIDACTIC LITERATURE aimed at teaching their daughters proper behavior. While boys enjoyed adventure tales, girls still read instructional manuals disguised as fiction, later a subject of FEMINIST CRITICISM. Although often entertaining, the stories aimed at producing future wives and mothers well immersed in lessons of self-sacrifice and self-exclusion. The formulaic ROMANCE plots of her books invariably featured middle-class girls learning the importance of helping those of lower social classes. Some of her characters lisped, a characteristic reproduced in many stories for girls, designed to signal innocence and an appropriate lack of education. Highly prolific, Molesworth published more than 100 novels, including the most popular *The Cuckoo Clock* (1877), *The TAPESTRY ROOM* (1879), *The Adventures of Herr Baby* (1881), *The Carved Lions* (1895), and *The Story of a Year* (1910). Some of her works are available as electronic texts and have been studied by feminist critics as promoting proper female behavior within a patriarchal society. However, works such as *The Tapestry Room* have also been viewed as producing a subtext that encouraged escape by women to an inner sanctum where they might be themselves, away from the public gaze. Such spaces are seen by some to represent the cells in which many suffragettes were imprisoned for demanding rights for women, including protection under law for physical abuse by men. Molesworth was one of several women writers, including Frances Hodgson BURNETT and Elizabeth Lynn LINTON, who would divorce.

BIBLIOGRAPHY

Green, Roger Lancelyn. *Mrs. Molesworth.* New York: H. Z. Walck, 1964.

Laski, Marghanita. *Mrs. Ewing, Mrs. Molesworth, and Mrs. Hodgson Burnett.* New York: Oxford University Press, 1951.

Showalter, Elaine. *A Literature of Their Own: British Women Novelists from Brontë to Lessing.* Princeton, N.J.: Princeton University Press, 1999.

MOLL FLANDERS, THE FORTUNES AND MISFORTUNES OF THE FAMOUS

DANIEL DEFOE (1722) While Daniel DEFOE's most loved book is still ROBINSON CRUSOE (1719) due to its appeal to young readers, *Moll Flanders* is considered by critics his most artful. Although it features the same hyperbole used in *Robinson Crusoe,* with Moll taking almost two dozen lovers and five husbands and birthing multiple children, it boasts an admirable narrative unity produced by the strong characterization of its protagonist. Defoe relates Moll's adventures in a series of episodes lacking smooth transition, and at times covers years in a single sentence, but readers overlook such distractions, enjoying the realism Defoe's knowledge of the criminal class gives his novel. They also find his familiar theme of survival by a poverty-stricken heroic figure inspiring, despite the facts of Moll's crude existence. That existence is made clear in the complete title, which continues, *Who was born in Newgate, and during a Life of continu'd Variety for Three-score Years, besides her Childhood, was Twelve Year a Whore, five times a Wife (whereof once to her own Brother), Twelve Year a Thief, Eight Year a Transported Felon in Virginia, at last grew Rich, liv'd Honest, and died a Penitent, Written from her own Memorandums.*

Moll's entrance into the world proves a blessing for her mother, who had been convicted of theft and sentenced to execution. However, her pregnancy gains her a delay of execution, and following Moll's birth in Newgate, she is ordered to Virginia in the United States. Her deportation leaves Moll to be raised by various caretakers, including the mayoress of Colchester. While with one gentlewoman she gains an education, she is also educated in sex when the son of the house seduces her. This begins a long series of sexual adventures for Moll, who eventually marries and has children. When she sails with her family to Virginia to find her mother, she makes the horrifying discovery that she has married her brother, who she leaves in the states with his offspring. He protests her plans, and Moll does not dispute his reasoning. She wrote of his reaction as "horror" when he understands that she plans to leave her children. She tells her audience, "as to the charge of unnatural, I could easily answer it to myself, while I knew that the whole relationship was unnatural in the highest degree."

Upon her return to England, she continues her adventures, marrying multiple men, and eventually ending up homeless and penniless. She turns to crime to survive, honing her skills as a thief. Even operating outside the law, she is a sympathetic character, explaining why she does not want to give up her illegitimate child in order to marry: "I wish all those women who consent to the disposing their children out of the way, as it is called for decency sake, would consider that 'tis only a contrived method for murder, that is, killing their children with safety."

Moll is eventually caught and exported to Virginia, following her mother's example. All is not lost, however, as on the ship she encounters an ex-husband, deported as a highwayman, and the two reunite. Moll finds a new life in the States as a landowner when she inherits her mother's estate. At last materially blessed, she becomes successful and eventually returns to England with her husband, enjoying a happy middle life into old age. At age 70, she reflects on her past, one that would be judged wicked by any reader. Defoe avoided accusations of immorality in his subject matter by claiming, "The best use is made of even the worst story" and by stating that Moll repented of her earlier life. He explained that "to give the history of a wicked life repented of, necessarily requires that the wicked part should be made as wicked as the real history of it will bear."

Defoe focuses reader attention firmly on his protagonist, not depending on an adventure plot to carry the novel, although many of Moll's adventures are reported. He cleverly circumvented criticism regarding the unrealistic nature of Moll's refined manner and speech, considering her low social status, by claiming in a preface that the "editor" worked with an earlier version, written in a "language more like one still in Newgate." Supposedly the editor chose "modester words than she told it at first" in a tone "grown penitent and humble."

A wildly popular work, *Moll Flanders* remains readily available in print and has been transformed to multiple media versions.

BIBLIOGRAPHY

West, Richard. *Daniel Defoe: The Life and Strange, Surprising Adventures.* New York: Carroll & Graf Publishers, Inc., 1998.

Zhang, John C. "Defoe's Moll Flanders." *The Explicator* 47, no. 3 (Spring 1989): 13–15.

MONASTERY, THE SIR WALTER SCOTT (1820)

Sir Walter SCOTT introduced the modern novel to the Western world with his publication of WAVERLEY (1814) and invented the subgenre of HISTORICAL FICTION known as the historical novel, which, in the words of David Daiches, would "show history and society in motion: old ways of life being challenged by new; traditions being assailed by counter-statements." Scott did so by focusing on place to bring unity to action, and often that place was his beloved Scotland. Eventually concluding that certain historical truths belonged in fiction, Scott adopted true events and people to frame fiction that delivered a message contemporary to his own times. He would use characters from *The Monastery* in a later sequel of sorts, *The ABBOTT,* both published in 1820, to make clear his message regarding the importance, not only of power, but also of how one goes about gaining that power.

Scott chose a monastery of Kennaquhair for the setting of *The Monastery,* basing that edifice on the real-life Montrose Abbey, supposedly existent during the reign of Queen Elizabeth I. The locale offered a GOTHIC backdrop to his tale, allowing him to incorporate mysterious elements without offering a purely Gothic novel. The story begins with the egoistic English aristocrat Sir Percie Shafton's escape to Scotland due to his Catholic sympathies. There he stays with the abbot of Kennaquhair's tenant, Simon Glendinning. Simon also hosts an orphan named Mary Avenel, and a love triangle develops as both of his sons fall in love with her. The young men represent foils, with Edward being quiet and bookish, while Halbert remains the more active gallant, attracting Mary with his high spirits. Halbert duels with Sir Percie following what he feels to have been an insult and believes he has killed Percie. At that point, Scott introduces the White Lady of Avenel, a ghost character later readers felt weakened his plot. She magically "heals" Percie, restoring him to

life. The novel ends on a divisive note, with Edward choosing life at the monastery, a fate predicted by the White Lady. Halbert serves the Earl of Murray and becomes successful and wealthy, enabling him to marry Mary.

Scott bases the pretentious Sir Percie on John Lyly's *Euphues: The Anatomy of Wit* (1578) and *Euphues and His England* (1580), as well as on works by Shakespeare and Ben Jonson. For the White Lady, he turned to a German tale featuring a water nymph named Undine, written by Freidrich de La Motte Fonqué, adding details from various Celtic myths. Neither of those two characters proved popular with readers, perhaps because the audience sought a more promising conclusion than either characters allowed to the novel. As it closes, Edward has reluctantly accepted his fate in the monastery, thanks to the help of the able and kindly Abbot, and he seeks the spirit for a final meeting. He finds her singing a sorrowful song of farewell. She "seemed to weep while she sung; and the words impressed on Edward a melancholy belief, that the alliance of Mary with his brother might be fatal to them both." His words predict the weakening relationship between Halbert Glendenning, who must defend his title against those who believe he received it unjustly, and Mary Avenel, featured in Scott's next novel.

BIBLIOGRAPHY

Daiches, David. Foreword. *The Monastery* by Sir Walter Scott. Edinburgh: Edinburgh University Press, 2000.

Scott, Paul Henderson. *Walter Scott and Scotland.* Edinburgh: Saltire Society, 1994.

MONK, THE M. G. LEWIS (1796)

Following Anne RADCLIFFE in creating fiction of the GOTHIC genre, M. G. LEWIS published his SENSATION FICTION, *The Monk,* for a public eager to indulge in entertainment highly dependent on horror elements. Unlike Radcliffe's more sophisticated *The MYSTERIES OF UDOLFO* (1794), Lewis attempted no rational explanation of the crude supernatural elements present in his novel. Only 20 years old when he published *Ambrosio, or The Monk,* Lewis had nevertheless invested great effort in study of the literature produced by the decidedly more melancholy Germans. Upon reading *Udolpho,* he so admired it that he immediately wrote an imitation piece. When *The Monk* appeared, the immorality inherent in Lewis's theme of sexual repression on the part of religious devotees proved so great that it was banned. Reissued following Lewis's revision, in which he eliminated some of Ambrosio's physical abnormalities, the book proved popular. Although Mrs. Radcliffe may have found Lewis's blood-curdling imitation less than complimentary, its effect proved clear in her next novel, *The Italian, or the Confessional of the Black Penitents* (1797), which contained a cast of familiar characters, including a monk and a young woman held prisoner in a convent.

In the early chapters of the novel, readers meet the chaste Antonia, who becomes the love of the dashing Lorenzo, and they plan to marry. They meet in a Spanish cathedral where the crowds wait to hear from the popular young monk, Ambrosio. Ambrosio soon finds himself tempted by the beauty of the model for his favorite portrait of the Virgin Mary, Matilda. PSYCHOAN-ALYTIC and FEMINIST CRITICS take note of Matilda's appearance when she dresses as a boy. Her garb empowered her to enter the monastery, territory strictly forbidden to women. Her masquerade does not last long as she transforms into the stereotypical temptress, luring the aptly named Ambrosio into depravity and the discovery of his own enormous sexual capacity. Eventually he tires of her, and she "redoubled her efforts to revive those sentiments which he once had felt." Although "disgusted" with Matilda, Ambrosio continues their "illicit commerce," led not by love but by "the cravings of brutal appetite."

Matilda then decides to help Ambrosio seduce Antonia. He drives Antonia's mother to her death and kidnaps Antonia, whom he imprisons in the monastery's lower levels. Lewis constructs a shocking rape scene, which culminates in Ambrosio making "himself master of her person," attacking "his prey, till he had accomplished his crime and the dishonour of Antonia." Ambrosio eventually stabs Antonia to death, and then discovers that the women he destroyed were his own mother and sister, and thus, his acts prove also self-destructive. Lewis reflects his influence by Goethe's work when Ambrosio believes he will be rescued by the devil in return for his mortal soul. He

appears before the Grand Inquisitor, who condemns the monk to die in an auto da fé. As he approaches death, he discovers that Matilda is a lesser devil herself, and he plunges into eternal damnation in a grisly scene. The demon carries Ambrosio aloft, then dashes him onto rocks where his broken body is attacked by "myriads of insects" who drink his blood, followed by eagles that tear his flesh, digging his eyeballs from their sockets.

The Monk is still enjoyed as a prototype, although most modern readers judge it a silly one, of various genres, including HORROR and SCIENCE FICTION.

MONTHLY REVIEW Published from the 1740s through 1845, the *Monthly Review* gained a reputation as the earliest important reviewer of English literature. It began publishing abstracts of new publications, as had its competitors, but its editor Ralph Griffith was advised by Samuel Babcock in 1783 to publish more than mere abstracts. Griffith followed Babcock's advice, improving the *Review*'s articles so that for 100 years, it would be considered the standard in periodical criticism. Letters exchanged between Griffiths and Babcock were later preserved in the Bodleian Library. Griffiths and his son conducted the enterprise for more than 50 years, originally publishing in St. Paul's Chuchyard, moving later to Paternoster Row and finally to the Strand. The master of an academy in Chiswick, Dr. William Rose, wrote its first article. Griffiths understood that a periodical was judged by its contributors, and he worked to attract the best. They included William Taylor of Norwich; Alexander Hamilton from Edinburgh; Richard Porson, classical editor; and Thomas Holcrosft, who wrote reviews that helped build the *Monthly*'s reputation as hostile toward the state and church. Additional contributors included A. L. Geddes, John Wolcot, Richard Brindsley Sheridan, William Gilpin, Charles Burney, and writer Oliver GOLDSMITH, who contributed 20 reviews. By 1790, it ran to 120 pages, filled by a dozen lengthy articles and a section titled "Monthly Catalogue" composed of shorter pieces. Critic William Hazlitt commented that the style of philosophical criticism made popular by the later *BLACKWOOD'S EDINBURGH REVIEW* was an inheritance from the *Monthly*

Review. It remains a crucial source of information for those who study the 18th century.

BIBLIOGRAPHY

Graham, Walter. *English Literary Periodicals.* New York: Octagon Books, 1966.

MOONSTONE, THE WILKIE COLLINS (1868)

Wilkie COLLINS is best known for his works *The WOMAN IN WHITE* (1860) and *The Moonstone,* both of which reflected aspects of Collins's own experience. By the time *The Moonstone* appeared serially between January and August 1868, in the periodical *ALL THE YEAR ROUND,* Collins had become a regular user of laudanum and had begun experimenting with opium. The use of drugs by one character in *The Moonstone* was one of several components that captured readers' imagination, along with murder, theft of an incredibly expensive jewel, suicide, a love affair, the exoticism of East Indian priests, superstition, an admirable detective, and even humor. Collins made an enormous contribution to DETECTIVE FICTION with the novel.

One of the first English fiction writers to use a detective as a main character, Collins focused his novel on the moonstone, an incredible diamond stolen from a Hindu holy place by British colonel John Herncastle, with a murder involved. Narrated by a number of witnesses, the story follows the fate of the gem and those who would possess it. The numerous references to Daniel DEFOE's *ROBINSON CRUSOE* in the first chapters prepare readers for an adventure tale, but what follows is nothing like the stranded Crusoe's tale of survival. The good-natured narrator Mr. Betteredge constantly seeks wisdom from the novel, feeling a kinship with another man treading a threatening and strange path, totally unfamiliar to him.

Mr. Betteredge, a servant in the Verinder family, highlights the challenges of telling a good story straight through, without diversion, as if Collins himself were remarking on the challenges to writing. According to the account, when the colonel bequeaths the moonstone to Rachel Verinder, his niece, Franklin Blake, his nephew, travels with it to Yorkshire, planning a presentation for Rachel's 18th birthday. Blake tells Betteredge that he believes the colonel had sent the diamond on purpose to curse the Verinder household, where his sister had refused to see him in the past. As might be predicted, the stone disappears before it can reach its destination. The first investigator on the scene is dull-witted enough to provide sharp contrast to the clever but sad Sergeant Cuff, brought into the case from London. Investigators suspect three Hindus sighted in the locale, their presence allowing Collins to emphasize the exotic and to play on reader prejudices regarding the mysterious Orient and its inhabitants. Those prejudices had been earlier revealed, hidden in Betteredge's claim that "Now I am not a sour old man. I am generally all for amusement, and the last person in the world to distrust another person because he happens to be a few shades darker than myself."

Betteredge continues the humor foreshadowed by his name when he asks the reader, regarding the possibility that the family might be the focus of a vendetta by East Indians, "Who ever heard the like of it—in the nineteenth century, mind; in an age of progress, and in a country which rejoices in the blessings of the British constitution?" Also suspected are Rachel and her servant, Rosanna Spearman, a former thief who eventually commits suicide. During Blake's visit, he meets another houseguest named Godfrey Ablewhite, a verse-writing philanthropist to whom Rachel becomes engaged. Betteredge describes him as, "a barrister by profession; a ladies' man by temperament; and a Good Samaritan by choice. Female benevolence and female destitution could do nothing without him. Maternal societies for confining poor women; Magdalen societies for rescuing poor women; strong-minded societies for putting poor women into poor men's places, and leaving the men to shift for themselves—he was vice-president, manager, referee to them all."

Although Cuff has done his best, Franklin Blake must assume the investigation in order to make progress on the case. In a twist suggesting Collins's self-consciousness regarding his drug usage, Blake, an opium user, discovers through a local doctor assistant, Ezra Jennings that he himself had absconded with the jewel while under the influence of opium. That lead proves a red herring, and Cuff returns to the scene, establishing that Ablewhite is the actual thief. However, he never makes an arrest, as Ablewhite receives his just dessert, killed by a group of Hindus who reclaim the moonstone.

Collins's book enjoyed a wild popularity and established a trend in detective stories, influencing works to follow. His good friend Charles DICKENS wrote *The MYSTERY OF EDWIN DROOD* (1870), left uncompleted at his death, adopting Collins's method and including gruesome opium dreams and an investigator of murder. *The Moonstone* remains available in print and electronic form.

BIBLIOGRAPHY

Grinstein, Alexander. *Wilkie Collins: Man of Mystery and Imagination.* Madison, Conn.: International Universities Press, 2003.

Phillips, Walter Clark. *Dickens, Reade, and Collins: Sensation Novelists; a Study in the Conditions and Theories of Novel Writing in Victorian England.* 1919. Reprint, New York: Russell & Russell, 1967.

MOORE, GEORGE (1852–1933)

George Moore was born at Ballyglass in Mayo, Ireland, son of a member of Parliament. His father also operated a racing stable and owned several estates on which he owed debts. Young George took no interest in his father's pursuits. He attended a Jesuit school at Oscott College in Birmingham but completed his rebellion against his parents' social and religious values, later spending a decade in Paris pursuing his artistic passions, painting and writing. Seven years there convinced him of the value of the erotic poets, and his first two publications were collections of poetry, *Flowers of Passion* (1878) and *Pagan Poems* (1881). By 1880, he had returned to Great Britain, taking up residence in London, where he continued his publishing career determined to follow French literary styles. Like his contemporary Henry JAMES, he represented a foreign force within the English tradition, under the control of theory rather than innate passion. Releasing additional poetry, drama, and essays, Moore published novels written in the REALISM mode, reflecting the influence of the French writer Émile Zola. Zola's support of the scientific theory that

humans were motivated by base needs, such as survival and sexual reproduction, provided a foundation for Moore's own support. His first novel, *A Modern Lover* (1883), shocked his readers with its explicit story of a painter who used and disposed of three women, all from different social classes; the book was banned by circulating libraries. It also reflected Moore's lack of skills in the use of English; his abbreviated and reluctant academic career, combined with a life dominated by Irish and French, resulted in a shoddy awkwardness.

A Mummer's Wife (1885) showed improvement in basic mechanics and usage, but revolted readers with its overabundance of physiological description of his setting of Hanley, one of England's least attractive towns. The descent of his alcoholic protagonist into depression and death found little appeal with his audience. Its cheap, single-volume production, where a smart three-volume issue was still the norm, caused it also to be eschewed by libraries, although, ironically, Moore's move set a precedent, and by the 1890s the expensive multivolume novel had all but disappeared. *A Drama on Muslim* (1886) dealt explicitly with female sexual frustrations, taking its place among a group known as "problem novels," usually focused on women and their new roles in an era that saw a decrease in rigid morality and a new legal and economic status due to legal rulings that included Married Women's Property Act of 1882 and the Reform Bill of 1884. The novels of writers such as George ELIOT had served as precursors to plots missing the innocent female requiring male protection and reaching a goal of marriage in the book's final chapters.

Moore followed with *A Mere Accident* (1887) and *Spring Days* (1888), and in 1888 published a memoir, *Confessions of a Young Man*, which showcased his improved writing skills. Additional novels included *Mike Fletcher* (1889) and *Vain Fortune* (1891). But it was his 1894 novel *ESTHER WATERS* that would gain him fame. He had by that time rejected Zola's harsh realism to write a more sympathetic novel about a young, illiterate, crude servant girl who suffers the same indignity as Thomas HARDY's Tess d'Urberville, but engages in none of that character's histrionics and certainly does not stoop to the murder of her seducer.

According to Lionel Stevenson, Moore found Hardy's treatment of the subject ridiculous and illogical, and his protagonist found meaning in the love for her child, eventually married her seducer in preference to a more traditional suitor, and then supported him as his wife. Circulating libraries at last accepted a Moore novel, despite its casual treatment of sex, and he felt that his work had much to do with the prosecution of those operating the types of "baby farms" that his novel featured.

Moore later became a modern art critic, writing for *The Speaker* and publishing a book on the topic, *Modern Painting* (1893). Opposing the Boer War, in 1899 he returned to Ireland, where he converted to Protestantism and helped promote the Irish cultural revival. He invested much energy in developing the Irish National Theater, and later based three volumes of memoirs on his experiences, *Ave* (1911), *Salve* (1912), and *Vale* (1914), later collected as *Hail and Farewell*. In addition, he published the short story collections *Celibates* (1895) and *The Untilled Field* (1903) with the novel EVELYN INNES (1898) and a sequel, *Sister Theresa* (1901), not quite as well received as *Evelyn Innes*. He also published another book about art, *Reminiscences of the Impressionist Painters* (1906). Returning to London, Moore would remain there, becoming a valued literary figure. He produced a religious novel, *The Brook Kerith* (1916), additional short stories, dramas and essays, and the novels *Heloise and Abelard* (1921) and *Aphrodite in Aulis* (1930).

Most critics agree that Moore retains most importance as a phenomenon, rather than as a strong literary writer. His attitudes served the development of the novel well, as he helped destroy what Stevenson terms the "bourgeois monopoly" in the novel. Not widely read in later centuries, his books are studied as representative of a social movement in fiction.

BIBLIOGRAPHY

Dunleavy, Janet Egleson. *George Moore in Perspective.* Totowa, N.J.: Barnes & Noble Books, 1983.

Frazer, Adrian Woods. *George Moore, 1852–1933.* New Haven, Conn.: Yale University Press, 2000.

Stevenson, Lionel. *The English Novel: A Panorama.* Boston: Houghton Miflin, 1960.

MORGAN, LADY SYDNEY   See OWENSON, SYDNEY, LADY MORGAN.

MORIER, JAMES JUSTINIAN (1780–1849)

Born one of seven children of the Swiss-born consul general of the Levant Company in Smyrna and his Dutch wife, James Morier would apply his knowledge of foreign countries to his later fiction. After serving overseas for a time, Isaac Morier moved his wife, Clara, and their children to England. Later concerned that his partner in Smyrna was cheating him, he returned to his business, leaving the family behind until the newest baby could mature enough to travel. When the French Revolution prevented the family's travel to Smyrna, Isaac, a devoted father and husband, returned to England to reunite with his wife and children. James gained an education at Harrow, later working in his father's London office and gaining a reputation for his sense of humor and delight in classical and biblical history. He returned to Turkey to enter the diplomatic service in 1807, following his brothers Jack and David. His other brother, William, became an admiral, proving the family's belief in the importance of service to one's country.

After accompanying Sir Hartford Jones to Persia and then traveling in Egypt, James published *Journey Through Persia, Armenia and Asia Minor* (1812), followed by the more popular *Second Journey through Persia* (1818). In 1824, he traveled to Mexico to take part in negotiations on behalf of Britain. Retiring later that year, Morier captured the public's imagination when he turned to novel writing with *The* ADVENTURES OF HAJJI BABA OF ISPAHAN (1824). Offering a PICARESQUE in the style of the French work *Gil Blas,* Morier used his experience to bring a REALISM to his work that made it the seminal English-language fiction about Persia. Only the poet Lord Byron had featured the exotic Near East in a manner accessible to the public. Morier's sequel, *The Adventures of Hajji Baba in England* (1828), proved less successful. Following his death, Morier was praised for his work by notables including William Makepeace THACKERAY.

BIBLIOGRAPHY

Johnston, Henry McKenzie. *Ottoman and Persian Odysseys: James Morier, Creator of Haji Baba of Ispahan and His Brothers.* London: British Academic Press, 1998.

MORLEY, HENRY (1822–1894)

Henry Morley was one of a group of editors writing and working during what some consider the golden age of English periodicals. His name is intimately linked with that of Charles DICKENS, as he edited and contributed to that author's journals, *HOUSEHOLD WORDS* and *ALL THE YEAR ROUND*. Although he had studied medicine at King's College in London and had a medical practice for a time, journalism excited Morley more than his profession. He would edit *The Examiner* and publish various works, including some important biographies, *Palissy the Potter* (1852), *Jerome Cardan* (1854), and *Cornelius Agrippa* (1856). He established a school in Manchester in 1848, publishing a volume of poetry titled *Sunrise in Italy* later that year. After moving the school to Liverpool, he continued with it for two additional years, publishing a series of papers, ironically titled "How to Make Home Unhealthy" in the *Journal of Public Health.* Those articles attracted the attention of Dickens.

A respected voice in journalism, Morley's approval of a newly created periodical, Richard Steele's *Tatler,* proved deserved. While the *Tatler* at first did not justify Morley's positive prediction, it eventually became one of the highest quality English periodicals ever produced, fulfilling Steele's prophecy that it would be widely read and discussed in coffeehouses. Morley also published in the *Review,* in the company of such notables as poet Alfred Tennyson and philosopher Matthew Arnold. In his later position at University College, London, as professor of English, Morley became known for his work in adult education and his contribution to the production of English literary classics in affordable volumes, Cassell's Library of English Literature (1875–81); Morley's Universal Library (1883–88), publishing 63 volumes; and Cassell's National Library (1886–90), which produced 214 volumes. He died having produced 11 of 20 planned volumes of a collection titled *English Writers.*

BIBLIOGRAPHY

Graham, Walter. *English Literary Periodicals.* New York: Octagon Books, 1966.

MORRISON, ARTHUR (1863–1945)

Arthur Morrison was a child of the London slums who by the late 19th century was regarded by his contemporaries as a pioneer of the new REALISM. Born in London, the son of a steamfitter, Morrison was so private a man that little biographical information survives beyond the name of his wife, Elizabeth Adelaide Thatcher (married in 1892), and that the couple had one son.

What is known about Arthur Morrison is that beyond his gritty, unsentimental portrayals of life and crime in London slums with his novel *A CHILD OF THE JAGO* (1896) and a collection of short stories, *Tales of the Mean Streets* (1894), he was second only to Arthur Conan DOYLE in his craft of DETECTIVE FICTION. Martin Hewitt, a detective modeled on Sherlock Holmes, is the subject of 18 short stories published in *The STRAND MAGAZINE* and *The Windsor Magazine.*

Although it is believed that the poverty and crime that surrounded Morrison as a child informed much of the rest of his life, it might have been that those early experiences enabled him to "take the detective story out of 221B Baker Street." *The Hole in the Wall* (1902), regarded by some as his best work, is the best example of this marriage of experience and detective story. Morrison's sole attempt to embed slum naturalism within a detective story can be found in the last adventure of a criminal that occasionally moonlights as a detective in *The Dorrington Deed-Box.*

After the turn of the century, Arthur Morrison wrote less and less as his interest in Oriental paintings developed into a passion. He eventually became a leading authority on the subject; the British Museum acquired his collection of Oriental paintings in 1913. Although he published only three works as the sole author after 1905, one of which was *The Painters of Japan* (1911), he was a fellow of the Royal Society of Literature in 1924 and a member of the council of that same body in 1935. Arthur Morrison died in December of 1945, just after his 75th birthday.

BIBLIOGRAPHY

A Treasury of Victorian Detective Stories. Edited by Everett F. Bleiler. New York: Charles Scribner's Sons, 1979.

Twentieth-Century Crime and Mystery Writers. Edited by John M. Reilly. 2nd ed. New York: St. James Press, 1985.

MOTHS OUIDA (1880) OUIDA practices her typical effusive style in the 1880 novel *Moths,* so named for one character's pronouncement that the "fashionable," or high society, world damages a woman. Moths, half of which immolate themselves "in feverish frailty," and half of which "are corroding and consuming all that they touch," constitute that world. For a time, moths and their self-destructive acts also seem a metaphor for the naive and untouchable Vere Herbert, who sacrifices herself to rescue the honor of her foolish mother, Lady Dolly Vanderdecken. Her husband, the wealthy and unfaithful Russian Sergius Zouroff, proves himself insufferable, objectifying Vere and treating her with such lack of sympathy that after three years of marriage, "all her youth had been burnt up in her; all hope was as dead in her heart as if she were already old." In the predictable plot, Vere becomes enamored of the opera singer Corréze, rumored to have been based on a handsome young man named Mario who captured Ouida's own passions. Her love for him both liberates and imprisons her.

Vere endures untold agonies during her marriage, which is rumored as a failure among society types. Eager for gossip, they spread the false rumor that Vere has been unfaithful to Zouroff, and she disappears into exile. Zouroff challenges Corréze to a duel and shoots him through the throat, a desperate wound for a singer. The act had been foreshadowed by Zouroff's often-repeated phrase, "I will slit the throat of that nightingale." Corréze's wounding brings Vere out of hiding as she declares that she will be courageous and help care for him.

The book proves of interest to FORMALIST critics, who recognize many traditional symbols, such as the moon, cherries, and roses, representing women in general, and the lark's song, representing Corréze, a type of woman figure himself, with his female sensibilities and sympathies. Within Ouida's florid style lurks admirable metaphors, such as when Vere ponders her imprisonment within marriage: "Never to escape from the world grew as wearisome and as terrible to Vere as the dust of the factory to the tired worker, as the roar of the city streets to the heart-sick temptress." Such comparisons illustrate Ouida's own naivete, as she believes the condition of a lovelorn woman comparable to the tortures suffered by members of the ill-used working class and prostitutes.

However, in a later scene noted by FEMINIST CRITICS, the comparison tries to prove itself as Vere seeks to "work" at her art of painting and despairs over the fact that her husband wants her just to hire someone to paint. She understands that "it is the only mission we have, to spend money," then the narrator explains, "It is a mission that most women think the highest and most blest on earth, but it did not satisfy Vere. She seemed to herself so useless, so stupidly, vapidly, frivolously useless; and her nature was one to want work, and noble work." In a later scene, she comments to Corréze that "a woman's courage" is to remain "mute" if struck by a man. In many feminist works, that silence is subverted into power by the heroine, but not in this novel. Ironically, Corréze becomes metaphorically a mute but ends his days devoted to his hard-won wife when he and Vere at last marry.

The moth persists as a crucial symbol throughout the novel. When Corréze gives Vere a necklace bearing a medallion of a moth and a star, Zouroff becomes incensed, demands the medallion, and crushes "the delicate workmanship and the exquisite jewels out of all shape and into glittering dust." Readers understand that Vere will not find an easy happiness. Zouroff annuls his marriage, based on testimony by his servants, and society rejects Vere, even though it knows of her innocence. In marriage to Corréze, she must live apart from society but welcomes "the gracious silence of the everlasting hills." The narrative makes clear those hills' decided superiority to the vacuous existence enjoyed by such individuals as Vere's mother, who "mourns" her daughter's absence, giving it equal weight to her regret over the "dreadful" conditions: "to have to wear one's hair flat, and the bonnets are not becoming . . . and the season is so stupid." The novel concludes with the line, "So the moths eat the ermine; and the world kisses the leper on both cheeks." The popular novel was later dramatized, enjoying a solid run.

Ouida's effect on fiction proved profound. Writers including George Bernard Shaw, John Galwsorthy, and D. H. Lawrence used her character prototypes. She remains a favorite in feminist literature courses, and her works are easy to locate.

BIBLIOGRAPHY
Powell, Anthony. Introduction. *Novels of High Society from the Victorian Age.* London: Pilot Press, 1947, vii–xv.
Sage, Lorna, ed. "Moths." *Women's Writing in English.* Cambridge: Cambridge University Press, 1999, 450.

MR. MIDSHIPMAN EASY CAPTAIN FREDERICK MARRYAT (1836)

Captain Frederick MARRYAT's *Mr. Midshipman Easy* proved extremely popular. Informed by Marryat's own naval experience, all his work allowed a gifted writer the opportunity to shape realistic adventure tales in which he expressed himself in a vigorous style undergirded by slapstick comedy. Like all Marryat's heroes, the protagonist Mr. Midshipman Easy, named Jack Easy, is a mischievous, willing, and brave practical joker, able to take a joke as well as administer one. Raised by a father who deals in rigid democratic notions that rarely prove demonstrable in real life, Jack must learn through multiple adventures at sea that most of his father's beliefs are absurd. A spoiled boy, he experiences his first dose of reality at the hands of a stern schoolmaster, Mr. Bonnycastle. Marryat exercises a wry wit in the scene when Bonnycastle explains to Jack's physician that he has "no opinion of flogging, and therefore I do not resort to it," only to later explain, "I can produce more effect by one caning than twenty floggings." He manages to teach his unruly pupil a small modicum of self-control. However, Jack finds ways to do whatever he desires, basing his actions on the ridiculous logic taught him by his father, who found Jack's "loquacity" pleasing. In one scene, when Jack attempts to convince the owner of a pond where he fishes that he is not trespassing, he explains, "the world and its contents are made for all." As the gentleman asks how he then accounts for some individuals having more material goods than others,

Jack explains that, according to his father, that "only proves that the strongest will take advantage of the weak, which is very natural." The gentleman bids Jack thank his father for making an important point, as he and his two companions, being stronger than Jack, may take Jack's fish and his rod and throw him into the pond. While Jack's interest in fair play remains focused on himself in such early scenes, he eventually broadens his views, developing true-life skills that replace his useless rhetorical skills.

Marryat's female characters generally remain flat and, in the case of Jack's mother, Mrs. Easy, easily manipulated. Marryat often included romance in his adventures, but only to attract a certain readership. Love relationships provided seldom more than a backdrop for more masculine pursuits. In this novel, the hero faces shipwreck and mutiny on the vessel *Harpy,* at times with the aid of only a "wily negro," an "excellent" slave named Mesty, an aristocrat in his own Ashantee homeland who refers to Jack as "Massa Easy." Mesty's characterization must be understood in the context of Marryat's era, providing interest for NEW HISTORICIST CRITICS and colonial critics interested in racism and the closely related ideology of IMPERIALISM.

Mesty offers Jack comfort when some of the sailors die due to Jack's "example of disobedience," having abandoned the ship to an island. Jack warns them not to try to swim back to the ship in shark-infested waters, but they believe he exercises his normal predilection for practical jokes. In a scene typical of Marryat's attention to gruesome detail, reflecting his debt to Tobias SMOLLETT, Jack looks up in time "to see the coxswain raise himself with a loud yell out of the sea, and then disappear in a vortex, which was crimsoned with his blood," a shark having attacked him. Jack never forgets the horror of the scene, sobering thoughts that help him mature into a strong leader. When he later becomes involved in a foolish duel with the purser's steward, he understands that he has demeaned himself and promises Captain Wilson to learn from the experience and never commit the "mad pranks" that make the captain anxious.

Jack conducts himself well in the face of later danger, and the novel concludes on a happy note. The narrator tells readers, "Our hero, who was now of age, invited all within twenty miles of home to balls and dinners; became a great favourite, kept a pack of hounds, rode with the foremost, received a deputation to stand for the county in the Conservative interest, was elected without much expense, which was very wonderful, and took his seat in Parliament," becoming an excellent husband for his sweetheart, Agnes, eventually fathering three boys and a girl. A satisfying conclusion to a thrilling adventure tale is one aspect that continues to attract readers to Marryat's works, which are readily available in print.

BIBLIOGRAPHY

Pocock, Tom. *Captain Marryat: Seaman, Writer and Adventurer.* Mechanicsburg, Pa.: Stackpole Books, 2000.

MRS. ARMYTAGE, OR FEMALE DOMINATION CATHERINE GRACE GORE (1836)

Despite criticism of Catherine Grace GORE's work by notables such as William Makepeace THACKERAY, it proved highly popular in its day and included some novels decided superior to others. One of her best works, *Mrs. Armytage, or, Female Domination,* excels in its characterization. Always a strong point for Gore, her female protagonists exhibited independence and spirit, and Mrs. Armytage, the Lady of Holywell, provides a clear example. However, her independent mind also proves a closed one, leading to conflict with her son and daughter and great personal loss. Described early on as pretending to encourage her daughter, Sophia, and son, Arthur, in "freedom of thought and action," in truth she exercised over them "the utmost rigour or petty despotism." This personality flaw leads to her alienating her children when Arthur decides to marry Marian Baltimore, a commoner his mother feels is undeserving of her son. As the only daughter of "a wealthy, high-principled, high-tempered English squire," she is judgmental and contrary, all the while preserving a reserved demeanor. Ungovernable as the young Caroline Maudsley, she defied her own father's wish for her to marry a distant relative, Sir John Maudsley, choosing instead Arthur Armytage, far more attractive but far less suitable. With little wealth, his subservient nature mostly recommended him, and he died at age 28, leaving Caroline Armytage to raise her children alone as a young widow. Now mature and understanding of the importance of decisions, she has forgotten the value of love and insists on making a desirable match for her children.

Cold and dignified, Mrs. Armytage stands in contrast to her neighbor, the earl of Rotherham, an aristocrat blessed with a good nature shared by his family. His daughter Laura becomes good friends to Sophy, and Lady and Lord Rotherham hope that Arthur would one day marry her. However, his mother felt Laura not on a par with Arthur, a sentiment she regretted when she discovered his attraction to the commoner Marian. They marry despite her protests and have a baby, as Arthur contracts a number of debts from which his mother must help release him. Arthur struggles with his feelings of gratitude. Due to his mother's temper, he "dared not exhibit half so warmly as he could have wished the tenderness of a son." Exposure to her mother's continued disagreeable demands affects Sophy's constitution, and she begins to grow weak. When Arthur becomes alarmed over her condition, Mrs. Armytage insists it is only due to the weather. He would like to remove the despondent Sophy from Holywell but at his income cannot afford it. The plot includes many additional characters, many enjoying the high social positions that abound in SILVER-FORK FICTION.

Predictably, Sophy suffers acute disappointment in life due to her mother, becomes an invalid, and dies. This, among other circumstances, moves Mrs. Armytage to repent and recognize the goodness in her son and daughter-in-law in time to enjoy a position in their home with her grandchild. Arthur undergoes a transformation of sorts, gaining strength following Sophy's death to confront his mother, releasing his emotions in a manner that would have proved impossible a short time before. The novel ends on a note of justice for Mrs. Armytage, who suffers loss due to her actions. However, her family is restored to her, supporting her position as a dictatorial, but not hateful, woman.

Highly DIDACTIC, but entertaining and offering a magnificent characterization of its protagonist, *Mrs. Armytage* reveals its debt to Jane AUSTEN's DOMESTIC REALISM in its detailed rendering of a family's everyday life. Its sober tone, however, owes nothing to Austen's often wickedly ironic presentations. A fine representation of the matters of the wealthy, Gore's novel depicts the leveling power of grief and loss, resulting from a powerful woman whose world proves of interest to FEMINIST CRITICS.

BIBLIOGRAPHY
Jump, Harriet Divine, ed. *Silver Fork Novels: 1826–1841*. Vol. 6. London: Pickering & Chatto, 2005.

MULOCK (CRAIK), DINAH (1826–1887)

Dinah Mulock was born near Stoke-on-Trent. Her father, Thomas, hailed from Irish gentry and was a Liverpool merchant before becoming an evangelical preacher who once tried to "convert" Lord Byron, according to the poet's own report. He married Dinah Mellard in 1825, and Dinah's birth a year later was followed by that of two brothers. Thomas became more insistent in his evangelicalism and was committed to a mental institution briefly when Dinah was six. The family later moved to Newcastle, where her mother taught school, aided by Dinah as a young woman. Mulock later wrote of her childhood as a happy and independent one, with her two parents too busy to devote much time to overseeing their children. She enjoyed an education at a school near home, Brampton House Academy, and enjoyed reading books, particularly Daniel DEFOE's *ROBINSON CRUSOE* (1719). During a long spell of illness she became a voracious reader, consuming works by Jane AUSTEN, Charles DICKENS, Edward BULWER-LYTTON, and Sir Walter SCOTT, among others. The elder Dinah inherited money following her mother's death, and in 1839 the family moved to London, where the younger Dinah was allowed to study languages. As her father wrote religious pamphlets, she met several writers and began to hope for a writing career. Her mother fell ill, and Mulock began to care for her family at age 16. Following her mother's death three years later, Thomas completely deserted his family, leaving Mulock to arrange for some means of support, as she would not receive a trust fund left by her mother until she became 21. Her youngest brother, Ben, at age 16 was capable of working, and the siblings had various aunts and uncles they could depend on for some support. Mulock turned to writing and publishing children's stories, then novels, as writing proved

one career, she would later comment in her famous essay "A Woman's Thoughts About Women," where women could better men.

Following the tragedy of her brother Tom's death in 1847, Mulock published *The Ogilvies* (1849), followed quickly by *Olive* (1850), and dedicated her 1852 work, *The Head of the Family,* to Elizabeth Barrett BROWNING. In 1850, Ben departed for Australia, and Mulock shared lodgings with Frances Martin, who later helped found a school for the blind. The two women were mentioned by novelist Elizabeth GASKELL as "two handsome girls,[. . .] writing books, and going about society in the most independent manner." Elaine Showalter tells of her plea to the publisher of her first three novels for additional pay above and beyond the original sale of her copyrights, as *The Head of the Family* went into its sixth printing. In 1856 she changed to a new publisher, Hurst & Blackett, to produce her most popular work, *JOHN HALIFAX, GENTLEMAN* (1857), for which she received more generous pay. She was one of the few women who learned to demand firmly more pay for her work, and her businesslike demeanor supposedly caused her publisher to "pale."

In 1865, Mulock married George Lillie Craik, a partner at Macmillan's, and was able to cease worrying about her contracts. She published her personal-favorite novel in 1859, *A Life for a Life,* formatted as a dual narrative in which the narrators question gender roles. She continued her fruitful career with *Christian's Mistake* (1865), *The Woman's Kingdom* (1869), and *Young Mrs. Jardine* (1879), as well as with several volumes of poetry and various essays. She supported her father in his later years, as he was arrested on more than one occasion. Craik even purchased one of Thomas Mulock's manuscripts, although he never intended for Macmillan's to publish it. Mulock doted on her daughter, Dorothy, and was helping prepare for her wedding when she died suddenly from heart failure. Her life was celebrated with a memorial in Tewkesbury Abbey.

BIBLIOGRAPHY
Mitchell, Sally. *Dinah Mulock Craik*. Boston: Twayne, 1983.
Showalter, Elaine. *A Literature of Their Own: British Women Novelists from Brontë to Lessing.* Princeton, N.J.: Princeton University Press, 1999.

MYSTERIES OF UDOLPHO, THE ANN RADCLIFFE (1794)

In her fourth novel, Ann RADCLIFFE explores the machinery of the GOTHIC NOVEL but reveals the mysteries referenced in her most popular work's title. Its popularity validated her publisher's interest in the work, which had gained an unprecedented support by the established London publisher G. G. and J. Robinson. Previously all Gothics, including Horace Walpole's *The CASTLE OF OTRANTO* (1764) and Charlotte SMITH's *EMMELINE* (1788), had been issued by circulating publishers. Radcliffe's *Mysteries* earned an unheard-of copyright payment of £500.

As do many Gothics, Radcliffe's novel introduces a damsel in peril, Emily St. Aubert of Gascon, who feels her life threatened, as she remains captive in the 16th-century Italian Castle Udolpho in the Apennines. However, Radcliffe departs from the typical in allowing readers to enter Emily's mind through third-person narration, allowing readers a glimpse into her perceptions of illusion and reality missing from previous first-person-narration epistolary novels. The distinction between the real and the imagined also separate Radcliffe's plot from that of the more traditional writings of Walpole, whose use of unabashed mysticism drew criticism. Radcliffe positions her Gothic in the time period acknowledged as a transition between the superstitions that grew from the feudal tyrannical order and those of the more modern era preceding the 18th-century Enlightenment. Her characters reflect those differences, with some representing a Machiavellian sense of design and religious superstition and others representing a new order of sensibility.

The setting provides the traditional trappings of mysterious noises, gloomy recesses, hidden passages, and ancient mythology, causing conflict for the orphaned protagonist. However, Emily's virtue eventually leads to her escape, unharmed and still innocent, in the company of two sympathetic castle servants. Despite Emily's despair, she escapes the control of her guardian aunt, Madame Cheron, and her wicked step-uncle, Montoni, who separate her from her true love, Chevalier de Valancourt, a man of whose moderate means her aunt does not approve. She retains control of her emotions to outwit Montoni, whose evil ways kill her aunt, allowing him to develop designs on Emily. She must suppress her imagination to control the horror that threatens to overcome her senses during her hours alone in the moldering darkness of the castle and seeks to avoid the unwanted attentions of Count Morano. She reunites with Valancourt following further adventures in France and understands the superiority of her rational nature over that of high emotion. The novel concludes with the capture and punishment of Montoni, who has begun to wreak havoc in the countryside.

Radcliffe is careful to offer rational explanations for mysterious phenomena, not depending upon coincidence and magic for her plot developments. Emily becomes a rounded character, maturing both emotionally and intellectually, not losing her virtue. She learns to trust her intellect over her imagination and to accept evil as the result of corrupted human nature, not supernatural sources. FEMINIST CRITICS and NEW HISTORICIST CRITICS find this novel of interest in its divergence from the Gothic demand that readers simply accept its mystical aspects and from the stereotype of hysterical helpless women who depend on BYRONIC HEROES for rescue. The novel enormously affected later writers, including Sir Walter SCOTT, the romantic poets, Jane AUSTEN, William Makepeace THACKERAY, Charles DICKENS, and Wilkie COLLINS. Still appealing and continuously in print since its original publication, *The Mysteries of Udolpho* has proved one of the most enduring representatives of the Gothic genre.

BIBLIOGRAPHY

Howard, Jacqueline. Introduction to *The Mysteries of Udolpho,* by Ann Radcliffe. New York: Penguin Putnam, 2001, vii–xxv.

Norton, Rictor. *Mistress of Udolpho: The Life of Ann Radcliffe.* New York: Leicester University Press, 1999.

Sage, Lorna. "Mysteries of Udolpho, The." *The Cambridge Guide to Women's Writing in English.* Cambridge: Cambridge University Press, 1999, 458.

MYSTERY OF EDWIN DROOD, THE CHARLES DICKENS (1870)

Charles DICKENS's final novel, *The Mystery of Edwin Drood,* was left unfinished at his death, sparking much controversy over how the plot might have reached resolution. Six of the planned 12 monthly installments reached publication, enough to reveal that Dickens had planned a much more action-centered story than in his other novels, suitable to the mystery genre made popular by his contemporaries, including his friend Wilkie COLLINS. The setting of Cloisterham resembles that of a GOTHIC NOVEL, with its focus on a graveyard and supported by what most critics label a dark tone. That darkness continues in the characterization of John Jasper, known publicly as a choirmaster but leading a secret life as an opium addict. The title character is Jasper's nephew, and the mystery alluded to in the title is Edwin's disappearance.

Additional characters include Rosa Bud, whose symbolic name confirms her innocence and naiveté, betrothed to Edwin as a girl but no longer in love with him. The couple end their engagement, and then Edwin goes missing on Christmas Eve following a symbolic thunderstorm that foreshadows great conflict. Part of that conflict is Jasper's openly lustful pursuit of Rosa. Other characters, barely developed, include twin orphans named Neville and Helena Landless who have moved to Cloisterham to live with Mr. Crisparkle, and Dick Datchery, an investigator arrived to determine Edwin's fate. Other characters represent traditional Dickensian themes, such as Honeythunder, a philanthropist obviously intended to be revealed as a hypocrite, and Mr. Sapsea, a civil servant who does anything but serve.

Jane Smiley notes that the Gothic label often applied to the story does not bear up under scrutiny—the dead in the cemetery enjoy a peaceful and unaroused rest, while Jasper represents the chaos normally attributed to mystical causes in the Gothic genre. She finds value more in the novel's representation of Dickens's eternal investigation in fiction of gender relationships that reflects his own lifelong pursuit of a happy relationship with a woman.

BIBLIOGRAPHY

Jacobson, Wendy S. *The Companion to The Mystery of Edwin Drood.* Boston: Allen & Unwin, 1986.

Jordan, John O., ed. *The Cambridge Companion to Charles Dickens.* Cambridge: Cambridge University Press, 2001.

Smiley, Jane. *Charles Dickens.* New York: Penguin Putnam, 2002.

NEW ATALANTIS, THE MARY DELARI-VIÈRE MANLEY (1709)

When Mary Delarivière MANLEY published her ROMAN À CLEF that bore the complete title *Secret Memoirs and Manners of Several Persons of Quality, of Both Sexes. From The New Atalantis, an Island in the Mediterranean. Written Originally in Italian,* it immediately sparked a public furor. The Whig-powerful peers and politicians suppressed it from publication during England's Stuart reign. A devoted Tory, Manley intended to unmask machinations at court that directly affected English citizens. She opened her piece with a reference to a well-known work by the Roman writer Juvenal, a misogynistic SATIRE titled "On Women." It included two sisters named Astrea (Justice) and Charity who abandoned earth. In Manley's work, Astrea returns to earth and meets her mother, Virtue, tours the island of Atalantis guided by Lady Intelligence, and unveils various corruptive influences in order to later teach her future student, prince of the moon, about the ways of man. The material was actually used by various court forces to strengthen charges of abuse of power. One Arthur Maynwaring served as secretary to Sarah, duchess of Marlborough, and he urged her to glean the story to use against Queen Anne. Sarah and other Whig loyalists feared a loss of influence with the queen, due to interference by the newly arrived Tory Abigail Masham and her brother-in-law Robert Harley. Manley took aim at the duke and duchess of Marlborough, insulting the duchess by exposing her to public scrutiny. She considered Manley's work slanderous and had Manley and her printer arrested in October 1709, nine days following the publication of the second volume of *New Atalantis*. The charges against the book were later dismissed, and it avoided the charge of *scandalum magnatum,* as did other pieces of political propaganda, because it used fictional names and published the key to the true identities of its characters separately.

Themes in Manley's book included polygamy and, of interest to FEMINIST CRITICS, the independence granted to women by money. However, the women Louisa and Zara meet tragic ends in an attempt to satisfy both material and sexual needs. Literary critics suggest that Manley may be drawing on her own experiences of exploitation in a male-dominated profession in which men promising to act as her advocate instead caused her to suffer abuse and abandonment. She suggests through her narrative that Anne herself could benefit from Manley's cautionary tale, in light of the politicians and favorites constantly vying for her favors. History reveals her likely court informants for the basis of her plot as Barbara Villiers, duchess of Cleveland and Charles II's mistress, and John Manley, the husband she left in 1694, both irrevocably alienated from her later in life.

Manley's loyalty to the reactionary politics of the Tory Party often caused conflict with her ideology regarding independence for those women who wished to seek a career, especially in writing, and her obvious recognition of their oppression by a patriarchal society. Still, as noted by critic Ros Ballaster, her "peculiar brand of proto-feminism, despite the obscurity of some of her references to contemporary political history, seems remarkably 'modern.'" This important work remains readily available in print and electronic form.

BIBLIOGRAPHY

Ballaster, Ros. Introduction to *The New Atalantis* by Delariv-iere Manley. Washington Square, N.Y.: New York University Press, 1992, v–xxi.

Gilbert, Sandra M., and Susan Gubar, eds. "Delariviere Manley." *The Norton Anthology of Literature by Women: The Traditions in English.* 2nd ed. New York: W.W. Norton, 1996. 180.

NEWCOMES, THE: MEMOIRS OF A MOST RESPECTABLE FAMILY WILLIAM MAKEPEACE THACKERAY (1855)

William Makepeace THACKERAY issued in 24 installments what would become his most popular novel, first published between October 1853 and August 1855. In *The Newcomes,* Thackeray offered an uncomplimentary view of Victorian ideas of respectable marriages; hence, the meaningful subtitle for the novel. While not so pointedly critical of arranged unions as later novels, such as those by George MEREDITH, would be, Thackeray nevertheless gives readers pause as they consider the sometimes-tragic outcomes resulting from society's harsh treatment of those short of money and pedigree, attacking CLASS STRUCTURE.

The novel opens with a fable of sorts that challenges readers to compare human existence to that of creatures common to cautionary tales, such as those presented by Aesop. Narrated by Arthur Pendennis, the "Overture" features an owl, ox, fox, frog, lambkin, wolf, crow, and donkey, all symbolizing villainies of human nature: "The fox is a flatterer; the frog is an emblem of impotence and envy; the wolf in sheep's clothing, a bloodthirsty hypocrite, wearing the garb of innocence; the ass in the lion's skin, a quack trying to terrify, by assuming the appearance of a forest monarch . . . the ox, a stupid commonplace; the only innocent being in the writer's (stolen) apologue is a fool—the idiotic lamb, who does not know his own mother!"

Thackeray's fable does double duty, attacking literary critics as well as human nature, and readers understand that the humor in the tale disguises sobering lessons. When the novel's plot opens with the lament that "there was once a time when the sun used to shine brighter than it appears to do in this later half of the nineteenth century; when the zest of life was certainly keener," they also understand that the author intends to find their era wanting.

Colonel Thomas Newcome represents all honorable gentlemen who come by their modest family fortunes honestly and who possess the best intentions for their children. They are also vulnerable, targets for certain members of their culture with a tendency to take advantage of the innocent. The colonel's son Clive, the novel's protagonist, loves Ethel, a cousin whose father is the well-placed wealthy banker, Sir Brian Newcome. However, as indicated by the young lovers' surnames, they are new to what becomes a game of high-society romance, and they soon find that love does not suffice for a match. Many family members illogically oppose the union, led by Ethel's egoistic brother, Barnes, and her narrow-minded grandmother, the matriarch Countess of Kew. While her love is strong, her constitution at that point is not, and Ethel capitulates to the family's demand for a "good" marriage, engaging herself first to another cousin, Lord Kew, and then to the repulsive and cowardly Lord Farintosh. Before a marriage can occur, Ethel's sense and strong character succeed in her canceling a union. Unfortunately, in his grief over losing Ethel, Clive has allowed himself to be manipulated into an unfortunate, but culturally approved, union with Rosey Mackenzie, the vacuous daughter of the greedy widow Mackenzie, who dominates not only her daughter but all in her immediate circle. Her lust for the suffering and humiliation of others becomes frightfully clear when the colonel appears to lose the family fortune. She drives him into his grave with her infliction of guilt. His melodramatic death scene greatly appealed to Thackeray's contemporary readers, who saw it as honor bested by false pride. Thackeray chooses not to conclude his novel on such a sad note, and Clive's fortunes gain miraculous restoration through the convenient discovery of a will. Rosey subsequently dies, in another plot twist of convenience, but one that proves satisfactory to readers still mourning the colonel's demise. An independently wealthy widower, Clive is freed to pursue again his first love, Ethel.

Critics take issue with the second third of the novel, noting Thackeray's obvious attempts to achieve the number of issues desired by his publishers by inserting unnecessary scenes. They also site the characters of Mr. Honeyman, Lady Ann, and Mrs. Hobson Newsome as needlessly showcased, noting that the odious Barnes Newcome does not need further vilification to make Thackeray's point. According to M. R. Ridley, plot contrivances such as having the colonel pitted against Clive in a political race remain just that, contrivances that distract from Thackeray's "marriage market" theme. And modern readers may find the conclusion that depends on wealth to achieve its happy end somewhat disheartening. Still, the novel remains popular with readers. In 1996, the University of Michigan Press continued its plans to produce the first scholarly edition of all Thackeray's work by publishing *The Newcomes* in a new version. They touted its important position to FEMINIST CRITICS as representative of Thackeray's overall sensitivity to the Victorian woman's plight. Thackeray also used this novel to characterize his own abuses, including caning, as a young man in Britain's educational institutions. Like many novelists, he viewed fiction as a vehicle for social change. *The Newcomes* remains readily accessible in print and electronic versions.

BIBLIOGRAPHY

Peters, Catherine. *Thackeray's Universe: Shifting Worlds of Imagination and Reality.* Boston: Faber and Faber, 1987.
Ridley, M. R. Introduction to *The Newcomes* by William Makepeace Thackeray. New York: Dutton, 1965, vii–xii.
Shillingsburg, Peter. *William Makepeace Thackeray: A Literary Life.* New York: Palgrave, 2001.

NEW CRITICISM   See FORMALISM.

NEWGATE FICTION

The label "Newgate fiction" applied to novels mainly of the 1830s depicting low-life characters and settings distinguished by a focus on crime. The authors Edward BULWER-LYTTON and William Harrison AINSWORTH wrote the majority of Newgate fiction. The name for the subgenre grew from the fact that most of the crime stories found basis in real crimes, highlighted in the prison publication *The Newgate Calendar.* Critics of Newgate fiction claimed the authors presented their protagonists in too positive a light, turning them into sympathetic figures. The title character in Bulwer-Lytton's *Paul Clifford* (1830) is softened as a victim of society, while the title character of *EUGENE ARAM* (1832) has a fully developed conscience. Ainsworth's *ROOKWOOD* (1834) and *Jack Sheppard* (1839) fashioned charismatic criminals. In its September 1845 edition, *BLACKWOOD'S EDINBURGH MAGAZINE* declared that such novels "deviate . . . from the standard of real excellence" by showing "low and humble life" to be just as "sophisticated . . . as elevated and fashionable." Newgate fiction receives credit for creating notable reactions from writers such as William Makepeace THACKERAY and Charles DICKENS. In his 1841 introduction to *OLIVER TWIST,* Dickens emphasized his new form of novel by remarking he had read about many "seductive" thieves, "bold," "fortunate," and "fit companions for the bravest. But I had never met with the miserable reality," which he then proceeds to depict in graphic, for his era, imagery. Thackeray, however, charged even Dickens with making his scoundrels too sentimental, accusing parts of *Oliver Twist* of "something a great deal worse than bad taste" in its making the public familiar with crime. The passing of the Newgate novel ushered in a new type of low-level novel focused on introducing the reading public to social problems resulting from poverty. Dickens would participate, as would Charles KINGSLEY in *YEAST: A PROBLEM* (1848) and Benjamin DISRAELI in *SYBIL, OR THE TWO NATIONS* (1845). All revealed the deplorable conditions in which large segments of society had to exist.

BIBLIOGRAPHY

Tillotson, Kathleen. *Novels of the Eighteen-forties.* Oxford: Clarendon Press, 1954.

NEW GRUB STREET GEORGE GISSING (1891)

George GISSING's tendency to see life as castastrophe is apparent in his most popular and critically acclaimed novel, *New Grub Street.* Gissing's personal experience, marked by brief imprisonment, two disastrous marriages, and a lifelong struggle to embody the ideals he projected onto the writing life, are mirrored in the partially autobiographical figure of Edwin Reardon, his novel's protagonist. Reardon's belief in writing as an art contrasts with that of other characters, including his nemesis and antagonist, Jasper Milvain, a journalist whose ambition and greed cause him to view writing and publication as simple business. Milvain considers audience and market and shapes a product to match those considerations, representing the "new" approach to literature. The gentle but hopeless Reardon stands for what he views as literary tradition, considering writing an artistic endeavor based on inspiration. Gissing's title came from the actual Grub Street, which, Gissing explained in a letter to his friend Eduard Bertz, had existed in London 150 years prior to his writing the novel. English essayist Alexander Pope and others of his era utilized the name to represent "wretched-authordom." In his contrast between Reardon and Milvain, Gissing suggested a larger contrast between modern society and that of an older, simpler, and perhaps more idealistic age. However, critic Bernard Borgonzi explains that Gissing, like others, exaggerated the purity of literary pursuits; Daniel DEFOE had written more than a century earlier of writing as a "very considerable branch of English commerce."

While Gissing finds the state of writing deplorable, he does not preach reform for this or any other social ill. Consistent with the seemingly fatalistic attitude that prevented his taking advantage of offers of aid throughout his career, he simply accepted societal ills as immutable forces not to be challenged. He views Reardon, Milvain, Reardon's wife, Amy, and other characters, including Alfred Yule and his daughter Marian, with nonjudgmental irony. Milvain must support his sisters, Maud and Dora, and his idea that they write children's stories, rather than work as governesses, is both logical and consistent with society's demands. Marian's ghostwriting for her father emphasizes the impurity of his endeavors, but the reader retains sympathy for Marian, who is inhumanly pressured by Yule to use her legacy to peg on his scheme to support a periodical he wants to edit. While Rear-

don and his friend Biffen, who blends realism with idealism by selling popular journal pieces and teaching fiction writing while working on his own great novel, could become pitiful characters, Gissing respects them both, emphasizing the mechanical approach most writers had to assume toward their work. Publishers demanded three-volume works, due to their commercial superiority to single- or two-volume forms, a truth in 19th-century England. He also tempers Reardon's rejection of writing as commodity with his weakness and the doubts he harbors, which no true idealist would. Reardon admits to a certain relativity in life and echoes Gissing's idea that labels such as "good" and "bad" are fallacies. While Reardon accepts that he will never achieve greatness, he continues to work toward a modicum of success. That may have also been Gissing's hope.

While his characterizations and sense of place are often compared with those of Charles DICKENS, Gissing remained a second-tier writer. Thus, he knew well the character of Reardon and injects no bitterness into the rendition of his protagonist's death, or the fact that his widow, Amy, marries Milvain following the journalist's publication of a complimentary article regarding Reardon's writing. When Gissing has Mr. Whelpdale tell Reardon, "I've been reading your new book. Uncommonly good things in it here and there—uncommonly good," he allows Reardon the intelligence to understand both the speaker and his comment. He writes "Whelpdale had the weakness of being unable to tell a disagreeable truth, and a tendency to flattery which had always made Reardon rather uncomfortable." The remarks irritate Reardon, who easily recognizes insincerity. Even when Reardon later confronts Milvain for his role in Reardon's failure, it is without true bitterness: "Your old way of talk isn't much to my taste, Milvain. It has cost me too much." He goes on to explain to the surprised Milvain that he has always "glorified success" in a public manner, not to Reardon alone, but always in the presence of others as well, stressing it "as the one end a man ought to keep in view." Reardon claims, "It's very much owing to you that I am deserted, not that there's no hope of my ever succeeding." Milvain does not pity Reardon but rather feels compassion for a man whose tone "revealed such profound misery." Reardon does not blame Milvain for turning his own wife against him but rather assumes it is simply his "misfortune."

To impress the reader on just how practical Milvain can be, Gissing writes a later scene in which Milvain and Marian mention the famous bankruptcy of the successful novelist Sir Walter SCOTT, who set about to pay his debts in a manner that Milvain explains would be "quite unbusinesslike" in that era. When Marian, who Milvain well knows is the true creative power behind her father, explains that she must use her legacy to support her parents, rather than give it to Milvain, he protests, asking whether she is "content to lead a simple, unambitious life [. . .] Or should you prefer your husband to be a man of some distinction?" Milvain's brand of ambition precludes love and dedication to anything other than income, yet he hardly proves an evil character. When he and Amy conclude the novel in his comparison of Amy to Marian—"you are a perfect woman, and poor Marian was only a clever school-girl"—the reader understands that in Gissing's view, the Milvains of the world will seek "the glorious privilege of being independent," a privilege afforded only by wealth.

Gissing's novel continues to attract readers who seek to understand better the author and his society. Bergonzi notes that Reardon is recognizable as the too sensitive and conscientious driven protagonist of 20th-century novels, but with an important difference. As part of a "social context," Reardon seeks an independence from his types; he is destined to fail, lacking the strength to reach that freedom. Readers may admire both Reardon and Milvain, realizing that Gissing had to reconcile Reardon with his fate by allowing him to die, and allow Milvain achievement of a victory that might prove hollow to others but is everything that Milvain desires.

BIBLIOGRAPHY

Bergonzi, Bernard. Introduction to *New Grub Street* by George Gissing. New York: Penguin Books, 1985. 9–26.
Michaux, Jean Pierre, ed. *George Gissing: Critical Essays.* Totowa, N.J.: Barnes & Noble, 1981.
Young, Arthur C., ed. *The Letters of George Gissing to Eduard Bertz 1887–1903.* New Brunswick, N.J., Rutgers University Press, 1961.

NEW HISTORICISM   As indicated by its name, New Historicism became popular later than other forms of literary criticism. While practiced informally for quite some time, not until the late 1970s and early 1980 did the approach come into its own. New Historicists believe that in order to understand a work of literature, the reader must apply any knowledge regarding the author, that author's culture, including social attitudes, historical events during the author's era, and any additional information outside the work itself that relates to its traditional narrative elements, including theme, characters, plot, setting and point of view. It contrasts with old or traditional historicism, which believed only an accurate objective view of history can allow proper analysis of literature. New Historicism challenges that idea, holding that history is only one of many useful analysis tools. It considers that all aspects of human nature and activities are interrelated, and that literary analysis has prejudices. Acceptance of those ideas promotes a more complete understanding of a text.

The beginnings of New Historicism may be traced to the period 1979–80, during which several critics produced works projecting a similar concern that historical methods of analysis were in error. No amount of historical knowledge can lead a person to reproduce any era in exact accuracy. Stephen Greenblatt named the new approach in the introduction to a 1982 collection of essays discussing the Renaissance. His book, *Renaissance Self-Fashioning,* demonstrated how historical figures created their own realities, proving that "truth" in history is a paradox. At first believed to be subversive in its challenge to tradition and its revisionist nature, the approach later became accepted as one more tool of literary criticism. Its interests have been advanced by writers such as philosopher and historian Michel Foucault, who believed history to be composed of a complex set of discourses, or discussions, that people adopt to discuss themselves and their environment. That discussion depends on each group's *episteme,* or unifying principle, determining how that group regards reality. Each group establishes its own standards for morality, its own criteria for what actions and values are acceptable. No one discourse is superior to another, history being itself a narrative discourse. It can never be fully understood or proven. New Historicists applied his ideas to the act of "unlocking" a work of literature for meaning. All art, including the written word, is a product of a particular society. To understand art, one must investigate the author's life, the rules for social behavior reflected by a text, and that text's historical situation.

BIBLIOGRAPHY

Colebrook, Claire. *New Literary Histories: New Historicism and Contemporary Criticism.* New York: St. Martin's Press, 1997.

Bressler, Charles E. *Literary Criticism: An Introduction to Theory and Practice.* Englewood Cliffs, N.J.: Prentice Hall, 1994.

Gallagher, Catharine, and Stephen Greenblatt. *Practicing New Historicism.* Chicago: University of Chicago Press, 2000.

Veeser, H. Aram, ed. *The New Historicism Reader.* New York: Routledge, 1994.

NICHOLAS NICKLEBY CHARLES DICKENS (1839)

In the third novel by Charles DICKENS, *Nicholas Nickleby,* readers for the first time glimpsed what would become the traditional Dickens novel, uniting several of the author's private social concerns as themes and offering myriad characters representative of the cultural ills of his day. First serialized in 20 parts between April 1838 and October 1839, the novel focused attention on what Dickens believed to be the cause of much of the poverty and crime haunting British culture, the neglect of education for children. While not the novel's total focus, much emphasis is on the "Yorkshire schools" that had proliferated in England, educational institutions where "inconvenient" children were deposited and often terribly abused. When the novel's protagonist suffers the death of his father from grief over lost property, he turns to an uncle for aid for himself, his mother, and his younger sister, Kate. The prosperous and successful, greedy and heartless Ralph Nickleby is the greatest of the novel's several villains, as his evil grows from jealousy over his dead brother's success in finding love and happiness with his family. Ralph will help his brother's family only if Nicholas agrees to work in one of the hateful educational institutions representative of those Dickens hoped to expose for gross mistreatment of students.

Told in episodes, the plot lacks the unity granted by a strong central figure, as both Nicholas and Ralph are so stereotypically drawn as to be near-caricatures of good and evil. However, the characters Nicholas must deal with as he is forced to make important choices in life add depth to the novel. Unlike Dickens's previous heroes, such as the orphaned boy in *OLIVER TWIST* (1838) who need only escape his surroundings to find success and happiness, Nicholas must learn to dwell in his world, choosing a vocation and finding maturity through the exercise of responsible action. When he rebels against the horrible Wackford Squeers, schoolmaster of Dotheboys Hall, Nicholas must accept the responsibility of his actions. By beating Squeers for his mistreatment of the half-wit boy Smike, Nicholas must become Smike's caretaker. As it happens, they end up in the company of an acting troupe, led by the agreeable Vincent Crummles and later in London in the business of the Cheeryble brothers, who live up to the gaiety suggested by their surname. There he can oversee Kate's treatment, and he eventually ends up thrashing another evil figure, Sir Mulberry Hawke, when he overhears a disrespectful comment regarding his sister.

His choices are also of a moral tenor. Dickens supplies several "dirty old men" that Nicholas must reject as role models, including the slimy and appropriately named Sir Mulberry Hawke, who act as predators in pursuit of Kate's virginity. An additional figure of female innocence, Madeline Bray, also suffers the desires of the stingy old Gride. She ends up sacrificed to marriage in a clear statement by Dickens on the tenuous position of unprotected women in British culture. Additionally, Dickens creates another type of sexual predator in Mr. Mantalini, husband of the dressmaker to whom Kate apprentices. He uses overt but patently false romantic ploys to distract his wife from the fact that he is leading the family into financial ruin.

The plot runs to an inevitable conclusion as a plan on the part of Ralph and Squeers to use Smike against Nicholas fails, the sickly boy dies, and Ralph discovers that Smike was his own illegitimate child and subsequently commits suicide. While flawed by its overuse of melodrama, the novel retains a happy liveliness that mimics that of youth, one readers may eventually celebrate along with the characters. Unlike most of Dickens's other novels, *Nicholas Nickleby* is no longer much read, despite its early success. However, critics credit it with advancing Dickens's trademark style, later to make his works some of history's most enduring.

BIBLIOGRAPHY
Smiley, Jane. *Charles Dickens.* New York: Penguin Putnam, 2002.

NIGGER OF THE NARCISSUS, THE
JOSEPH CONRAD (1897)   In what critics label Joseph CONRAD's first accomplished work, he produces a text at once revered and criticized. Conrad asked W. E. Henley, poet and editor of *The New Review,* to publish the novel in his magazine. Conrad hoped that its inclusion in a publication that had showcased work by American author Stephen Crane, Henry JAMES, Arthur MORRISON, and poet W. B. Yeats would legitimize his work.

The novel's plot appears deceptively simple. Aboard a craft named the *Narcissus,* an intelligent black man named James Wait becomes an invalid, creating tension between two different generations of accomplished seamen, Captain Alistoun and veteran sailor Singleton, and their crew. While the crew remains dedicated to saving Wait's life, Alistoun and Singleton are reticent to endanger the ship to do so. Although Wait survives the voyage, at one point rescued by five crewmen who risk their own lives to save him from drowning in his bunk, he dies before the ship reaches its destination.

Conrad sought to feature, as did one of his models, Rudyard KIPLING, the tensions that grow in organized purposeful groups between those in charge and the workingmen they supervise. The two groups often do not share motivations or ideology, and the "good" leader must determine a way to cross the social gulf that divides him from his crew. When one crewmember named Donkin confronts Alistoun over whether Wait may return to duty, their argument escalates, and

Donkin hurls a belaying pin at the captain. Alistoun knows his reactions will prove crucial, as the entire crew is looking on, and he responds with a calm that allows him to again command authority. Conrad, like Kipling, celebrates the importance of unity among patriots and the value of everyday labor to build character and advance a cause. It is that hands-on labor that qualifies the common man to know more regarding the reality of his cause than his remote leader.

Another inspiration for Conrad's tale was American author Stephen Crane, an impressionist writer who also wrote of a community of men united in battle in his novel *The Red Badge of Courage,* published in England in 1895. Their shared theme, what the reviewer W. L. Courtney labeled "the psychology of the mass" in the December 8, 1897, edition of *The Daily Telegraph,* was solidified by Conrad in an acute, intense, sometimes inconsistent narrative, which occasionally played on racial stereotypes. Critics sometimes question his unusual narrative structure, whereby the first-person narrator seems at one point a part of the crew, at another point a simple onlooker standing apart from the action. Other questionable aspects include what some view as an overabundance of detailed description that occasionally burdens the plot, and what Cedric Watts terms "marked tensions within its thematic structure." He points out that many readers accept the detail as Conrad's inheritance from previous sea novels, such as those by Captain MARRYAT, and enjoy the tensions as paradoxes imitating those encountered by all humans as they tend to the business of life. Whatever their complaints, most critics agree that Conrad did accomplish the famous objective that he states in his preface to the novel as "to make you *see.*" Readers accept his wish for them as one of insight, as well as an understanding of Conrad's own vision for his novel.

BIBLIOGRAPHY
Kimbrough, Robert, ed. "Racism, or Realism? Literary Apartheid, or Poetic License? Conrad's Burden in *The Nigger of the Narcissus.*" *The Nigger of the Narcissus.* New York: Norton, 1979, 358–68.
Watts, Cedric. Introduction to *The Nigger of the Narcissus,* by Joseph Conrad. New York: Penguin Books, 1988, xi–xxx.

NIGHTMARE ABBEY THOMAS LOVE PEACOCK (1818)

In his third and most popular novel, *Nightmare Abbey*, Thomas Love PEACOCK supplied a PARODY of contemporary literature and authors that greatly resembled in format his previous satires, *HEADLONG HALL* (1816) and *MELINCOURT* (1817). All three contain little by way of plot, depending instead upon energetic Socratic dialogue among their diverse characters to advance a purposely thin story. The characters themselves bore the greatest importance, all representing persons and/or various ideologies of Peacock's era. Peacock expects readers of *Nightmare Abbey* to be informed regarding British political, social and intellectual controversy in order to understand its points. As indicated by the novel's title, he takes on the GOTHIC NOVEL, as well as the romantically idealized theme of melancholy. In his caricatures of romantic poets Percy Bysshe Shelley, Samuel Coleridge, George Gordon, Lord Byron, and novelist William GODWIN, author of the Gothic work *Mandeville* and father of HORROR writer Mary Godwin SHELLEY, he seeks to, as he explained to Shelley in a letter, "bring to a sort of philosophical focus a few of the morbidities of modern literature." He hoped to mount an attack against the "black bile" represented in works like Byron's lengthy *Childe Harold's Pilgrimage,* which included the horror of cannibalism, and he footnotes all references in the novel to that morbid work. Peacock thus ridicules what he conceived of as excess found in the romantic melancholy marking much of the popular poetry and fiction of the early 19th century.

The novel's setting contains the predictable machinery of Gothic fiction, including secret passages and dark mysterious towers, but Peacock's major focus remains on the abbey's inhabitants, and the anticipated contrived dialogue of the genre is conspicuously absent. In its place appears the animated interchange between the abbey's master, Mr. Glowry, and fellow misanthropes Mr. Toobad, Mr. Flosky (Coleridge), Mr. Cypress (Byron), and Mr. Listless (the consumer of popular literature), in addition to Scythrop Glowry (Shelley), Glowry's son. Scythrop is a foppish, weak-willed ineffectual romantic who parodies the traditional devilish Gothic villain. Once hurt by misplaced love for Miss Emily Girouette,

Scythrop "was a burnt child, and dreaded the fire of female eyes," as did all Gothic figures that suffered for love. Dour servants with suggestive surnames, like Raven, Crow, and Graves, surround the men. Another character, Mr. Hilary, may be the closest to a caricature of Peacock himself, as he roundly criticizes the Gothic and romantic literature valued by the other members of the party.

Rounding out the cast are Scythrop's cousin Marionetta and Toobad's daughter, Celinda, nicknamed Stella, both of whom form love interests for Scythrop. He discusses with the philosophical Celinda his idea to make life imitate art, and acts on that instinct when he proposes to Marionetta that they imbibe one another's blood as testimony to their devotion. The drinking of blood was a favorite Gothic device, found in the German novel *Horrid Mysteries,* which Scythrop keeps under his pillow. When Glowry asks Scythrop whom he loves, he replies "Celinda—Marionetta—either—both." Glowry protests, "that may do very well in a German tragedy," but that it will not due in Lincolnshire, and Scythrop declares he will shoot himself. Scythrop never does decide which woman to romance seriously, and so he loses both, drowning his sorrow in Madeira wine.

Peacock cloaks Flosky's remarks in a metaphysical terminology that satirizes Byron's melancholy approach to poetry, while Cypress's rejoinders represent Coleridge's position as the foremost authority on the German romantics and his ideas regarding organic form. In one discussion, Cypress remarks, as Peacock quotes from the fourth canto of *Childe Harold,* "The mind is diseased of its own beauty, and fevers into false creation. The forms which the sculptor's soul has seized exist only in himself." Flosky replies, "Permit me to discept. They are the mediums of common forms combined and arranged into a common standard." While Peacock developed multiple characters in his various works to represent Coleridge, Flosky is considered his most skillful. As noted by critic Charles Dodson, Flosky symbolizes "the excesses of Byronism" joined "with the obscurity of transcendental philosophy."

Peacock played off the public conception of the poets to fashion his characters, who were never intended to reflect biographical fact. This was especially true with the character Scythrop, who, as a seeming alcoholic and parasitic only child, differed vastly from Shelley. The poet took no offense at the characterization, writing to Peacock of his delight with the novel.

Accessible and entertaining for fans of both Gothic fiction and romantic poetry, *Nightmare Abbey* continues to be read and studied as a strong work of satire, and as its author's best novel.

BIBLIOGRAPHY

Dodson, Charles B. Introduction to *Thomas Love Peacock: Nightmare Abbey, The Misfortunes of Elphin, Crotchet Castle.* New York: Holt, Rinehart and Winston, 1971, vii–xxviii.

NORTHANGER ABBEY JANE AUSTEN (1818)

Jane AUSTEN had begun writing her final book, *Northanger Abbey,* in 1798. It was accepted by a publisher in 1803 but would not be published until 1818, one year following her death. The book was a SATIRE on the wildly popular GOTHIC genre, particularly works by Ann RADCLIFFE. However, by the time it appeared, others written with the same purpose in mind had already been published, including *Romance Readers and Romance Writers* (1810) by Sarah Green and *The Heroine, or Adventures of Cherubina* (1813) by Eaton Stannard Barrett.

In Austen's novel, the protagonist, Catherine Morland, travels to Bath, an area Austen knew well, to spend the social season with Mr. and Mrs. Allen as their houseguest. She meets General Tilney and falls in love with his son, Henry, while becoming friends with his daughter, Eleanor. They invite Catherine to visit their home, Northanger Abbey. A fan of the Gothic genre, Catherine's imagination runs wild, envisioning what she'll discover in the abbey. However, she's disappointed, finding large windowpanes, "so clear, so light! To an imagination which had hoped for the smallest divisions and the heaviest stone work, for painted glass, dirt, and cobwebs, the difference was very distressing."

She projects her fears on to the general, whom she comes to believe is engaged in many secret activities, including having murdered his wife, who died nine years previously. When she sees the general pacing the room at night, she thinks, "What could more plainly speak the gloomy workings of a mind not wholly dead to every sense of humanity, in its fearful review of past scenes of guilt! Unhappy man!" In an embarrassing scene, Catherine is proven wrong by Henry who asks, "What have you been judging from? Remember the country and the age in which we live. Remember that we are English: that we are Christians. Consult your own understanding . . . Dearest Miss Morland, what ideas have you been admitting?" Catherine leaves at the suggestion of the general, who believes her to be a fortune hunter. When Henry catches up with Catherine, he explains that his father had made a faulty assumption about her, as she had him, believing her to be poor. Once the general understood that not to be true, he agrees to their romance. Then "the event which it authorized soon followed: Henry and Catherine were married, the bells rang and everybody smiled; and . . . it will not appear, after all the dreadful delays occasioned by the general's cruelty, that they were essentially hurt by it."

Critics comment on the novel's skillful narrative, but also on its lack of subtlety, a necessary component in an imitative style, and its vulgar caricatures, in the vein of novels by Fanny BURNEY. While not as popular as Austen's earlier works, *Northanger Abbey* is studied as part of her oeuvre and as a reaction to the 19th-century craze over the Gothic novel. A movie version, directed by Giles Foster, was produced in 1986.

BIBLIOGRAPHY

Mansell, Darrell. *The Novels of Jane Austen: An Interpretation.* London: Macmillan, 1974.
Ross, Josephine. *Jane Austen: A Companion.* New Brunswick, N.J.: Rutger University Press, 2003.

O

**ODD WOMEN, THE GEORGE GISSING
(1893)** As did most novels by George GISSING, *The Odd Women* focused on working-class poor in an uncaring society. The novel opens with six happy sisters, living with their widower physician father. He believes that women should not have to worry about finances and counsels his daughter Alice, "I should grieve indeed if I thought my girls would ever have to distress themselves about money." Shortly, he dies in an accident, never acting on his plans to purchase life insurance. Suddenly the daughters must focus on money, or the lack thereof. While the atmosphere of their home had been "intellectual," and they had studied partly at school, "it never occurred to Dr. Madden that his daughters would do well to study with a professional object." Thus, they have few skills. Few family members exist to offer help, and among their friends, including Rhoda Nunn, none can care for six young women.

Sixteen years later, in the spring of 1888, two of the sisters have died, leaving four to fend for themselves. At 33, Virginia is unhealthy, but not as unhealthy as her older sister Alice, corpulent and prone to headaches. Isabel at 22 is so plain, she would never attract a suitor. She develops a melancholia that advances into brain fever and drowns herself in a bathtub. Only Monica, the youngest of the group, seems to have a chance at happiness, although her job working long hours in a store threatens her health. The two older sisters move in together when both lose their jobs, Virginia as a lady's companion and Alice as governess in a demanding household where she earned little. Gissing emphasizes the limited choices available to such women.

When Virginia and Alice meet again with their friend Rhoda Nunn, she speaks of the "half a million more women than men" in their "happy country" who constitute "odd women—no making a pair with them. The pessimists call them useless, lost, futile lives." Rhoda refuses to join that camp, however, viewing women with some education as a resource, a "reserve" to be trained. Teaming with a Miss Barfoot, she teaches women to type and earn a living. While it is too late for Alice or Virginia, they push Monica to join Miss Barfoot's training program.

Gissing does not give readers much hope for this sad group. Monica will meet and marry Edmund Widdowson, who can easily support her, but he is much older than she, and she marries him from semi-desperation. Virginia and Alice descend deeper into their own desperate attempts to keep up the charade of respectability, but their loneliness remains acute, and Virginia becomes addicted to gin. Monica eventually has an affair with a man called Bevis and leaves Edmund, giving birth to a daughter and then dying. Rhoda Nunn enjoys an ill-fated passion for Miss Barfoot's cousin, Everard. She proves of too strong a character for him, refusing to bend to his will. As she wonders how she might destroy her love for him, she considers taking poison. However, she recovers her good sense, understanding that such an act would "feed his vanity" and "give him the lifelong reflection that, for love of him, a woman excelled by few in qualities of brain and heart, had died like a rat."

Early in the novel, Monica thinks of her sisters "their loneliness was for life [. . .] they would grow older, sadder, perpetually struggling to supplement that dividend from the precious capital—merely that they might keep alive. Oh! . . . how much better if the poor girls had never been born." Yet Gissing does not seem to support that bleak a view. Through Rhoda Nunn he offers a feminist figure that finds value in work. While the ideal would allow her to note value in herself as an individual, that would prove unrealistic in her era. Instead, she has her freedom, whether as a simple product of her rationalizing her situation or as a true commodity. In the end, it proves more valuable than the false love that led to Monica's demise and that which had threatened Rhoda's own well-being. In realizing her intellectual superiority to Everard, she can live with the knowledge that he chose to marry a socialite. She exclaims to Virginia at the book's conclusion that her work training women to be productive members of society flourishes "like the green bay-tree." She and Miss Barfoot plan to expand to bigger premises and free even more women, because "The world is moving!"

But Gissing concludes with a caution that while signs of progress exist, much needs to be done. When Virginia goes into the house, leaving Rhoda to hold Monica's baby, Rhoda looks into the child's sleeping face. Both her literal and figurative vision grow "dim," as she murmurs, "'Poor little child!'"

BIBLIOGRAPHY
Colon, Susan. "Professionalism and Domesticity in George Gissing's *The Odd Women*." *English Literature in Translation: 1880–1920* 44, no. 4 (Fall 2001): 441–59.

Comitini, Patricia. "A Feminist Fantasy: Conflicting Ideologies in *The Odd Women*." *Studies in the Novel* 27, no. 4 (Winter 1995): 529–543.

Michaux, Jean Pierre, ed. *George Gissing: Critical Essays.* Totowa, N.J.: Barnes & Noble, 1981.

OLD CURIOSITY SHOP, THE CHARLES DICKENS (1841)

As one of Charles DICKENS's early works, *The Old Curiosity Shop,* first published in the periodical MASTER HUMPHREY'S CLOCK from April 1840 to February 1841, was a favorite among his contemporary readers. That favorable reception changed over time, as readers no longer could accept the drawn-out melodramatic death of Little Nell, the novel's protagonist, in the way that Victorian-age audiences could. Their craving of pathos in fiction gave way to disgust in later readers, trained to read with a more developed sense of irony. Scenes judged powerful in the past appear unintentionally comic or even silly to 21st-century readers. Thus, the novel elicits extreme reactions; readers either embrace or reject it, based on their tolerance for melodrama and sad sentimentality. As did his earlier OLIVER TWIST (1838), the novel features a child victim who long suffers the cruelty of adult predators, representative of the many ills of commerce, a constant target of Dickens's social consciousness. In their mechanical acts of violence, greed, and calumny, the villains suggest the inhumanity that Dickens perceived as inherent to the industrial revolution.

Nell Trent, nicknamed Little Nell, lives with her grandfather in the Old Curiosity Shop that he manages. The reader meets her along with the first-person narrator, who emphasizes the fantasylike setting of London's dark evening streets when he references the destruction of "air-built castles" that foreshadows destruction for all Nell's childish dreams. The narrator takes exception to Nell's wandering the streets alone, and he confronts her grandfather upon reaching the shop; his description of its exotic contents adds to the nightmarish landscape, which Dickens emphasizes using adjectives such as *strange, distorted,* and *haggard.* While filled with signs of future disaster, that scene assures the readers as well as the narrator of the grandfather's passionate devotion to Nell. It also emphasizes Nell's role as victim of society, when the narrator tells the grandfather, "It always grieves me . . . to contemplate the initiation of children into the ways of life, when they are scarcely more than infants. It checks their confidence and simplicity—two of the best qualities that Heaven gives them—and demands that they share our sorrows before they are capable of entering into our enjoyments."

Although the grandfather clearly treasures Nell, he is also foolish and frustrated, contracting with the evil swindler, Daniel Quilp, to finance repayment of many debts, some forced upon him by grasping relatives, through gambling. Quilp's initial description as "so low in stature as to be quite a dwarf," "grotesque," and sporting a "ghastly smile" that gave him the appearance of a "panting dog," signal his predatory position, although his wife loves Nell. The grandfather predictably loses through betting all Quilp's money and flees to the English countryside with Nell, pursued by Quilp, who believes him to be a wealthy miser. Quilp takes over the shop and launches a revenge scheme. Also in pursuit is Kit Nubbles, a devoted employ of the Curiosity Shop and beloved by Nell. He also falls victim to Quilp, nearly framed by the villain's false accusations, just escaping a dire fate. As Nell and her grandfather become more pitiful, reduced to begging, she begins her prolonged death process. The narrator increasingly includes readers, insinuating their responsibility for the conflict, by adopting inclusive terms such as *we* and *our*.

Critics find a problem in Dickens's juxtaposition of Nell's nightmarelike suffering with the more comedic and realistic presentation of the problems of the character Dick Swiveller, a friend to Nell's worthless brother Fred. Swiveller is introduced in the second chapter of the novel in one of Dickens's trademark subplots containing dozens of characters. While Dick's problems are not as serious as Nell's, he must grapple with the ill intent of others. However their pairing may succeed or fail, their complete separation from the totally inhumane Quilp results in the contrast that Dickens desired between good and evil.

Nell, however, is so good and so innocent that no human can possibly rescue her. Although her greatuncle seeks and eventually finds the castoffs, he is too late to salvage the situation, and Nell's grandfather dies soon after she does. Just as no one can save Nell, Dickens develops no character strong enough to revenge the evil that Quilp has committed. Instead, he must snuff his own life, drowning in the Thames as he seeks to escape pursuing law enforcers. Dick and Kit represent differing blends of good and bad, and both

enjoy redemption. For extremes Nell and Quilp, such redemption remains unavailable. They do allow Dickens to advance his theme of the importance of storytelling, both through the first-person spectator narrator and through the emphasis of the adult Kit, who shares "that story of good Miss Nell who died" with his own children.

The Old Curiosity Shop is probably the least read of Dickens's many novels, due to changing tastes among even the most devoted of his followers, although it is available in both print and electronic text. It remains of interest as a study of Victorian readers, eliciting overt emotional reactions from males who would soon, according to social critics, suffer a demand to curtail displays of public emotion. It has been dramatized in various versions, including a 1975 musical titled *Quilp*.

BIBLIOGRAPHY

Horne, Lewis. "*The Old Curiosity Shop* and the Limits of Melodrama." *The Dalhousie Review* 72, no. 4 (Winter 1992): 494–508.

Smiley, Jane. *Charles Dickens*. New York: Penguin Putnam, 2002.

OLD MORTALITY SIR WALTER SCOTT (1816)

When Sir Walter SCOTT published the second in his Tales of My Landlord series in 1816, *Old Mortality* quickly became a favorite of his reading public. The novel focuses on the month of June 1679, with Scott compressing time to describe events on that day that led to the later historical Glorious Revolution of 1688. He imported some historical figures into his tale, but it represents a study of revolution, not history. Scott creates the protagonist Henry Morton, a completely fictional being, as a protector of the true historical figure John Balfour of Burley. Morton does not know that Burley took part in an assassination of the archbishop of Andrews as a member of the Covenanters, militant Presbyterians who hoped to recall the days of religious freedom, which existed before the Restoration of Charles II in 1660 and his Stuart policy of interference in Scotland's church polity and ritual.

In the novel, Burley is not a Covenanter, but he joined their cause in angry response to English suppression of his fellow Scots. While the historical Burley did help murder James Sharp, the archbishop, on May 3, 1779, he did not undertake the additional action that Scott gives him in the novel. And neither Morton nor Burley as sketched by Scott resembles in any way the historical Robert Hamilton, leader of the real Covenanter uprising. The novel's title derives from a nickname of the true Robert Paterson, who cared for the graves of the Covenanters at the close of the 18th century. His stories form the basis for Scott's novel, and the author would return often to Scottish mythology in that same manner for future novels.

Scott uses the historical revolt as framework for a ROMANCE plot in which Morton loves Edith Bellenden, whose family proves loyal to the English crown. Edith returns Morton's love. However, a love triangle involves Lord Evandale, also in love with Edith, who in true heroic style rescues, at Edith's request, Morton from execution when he is discovered to harbor the fugitive Burley. Following the Covenanter's historic defeat at Bothwell Bridge, a historical reality on June 22, 1679, Morton is banished. When he returns following William III's ascendance to the throne, Edith is ready to marry Evandale, having given up hope that Morton will ever return. When she learns that Morton lives, Edith cancels the wedding plans, a happy event for Morton. The novel ends on a gloomy note, however, as Evandale is murdered by religious fanatics, a devoted core of remaining Covenanters, despite Morton's desperate attempts to protect and rescue him.

Scott focuses on themes other than simply revolution, investigating problems occurring when revolutionaries, despite impressive numbers and raging devotion, band together without leadership or resources in a disorganized attempt to support religious ideology. Secondarily, he scrutinizes exactly what constitutes a "good" leader, examining the fictional Burley. Clearly motivated by a desire for power rather than by religious fervor, Burley controls his ruthless nature only through an equally forceful will. Simultaneously he exhibits a fearless rhetoric, supported by courageous actions that combine to shape a charismatic leader. When the lesser revolutionary leaders falter, Burley simply lies to each one and succeeds in

retaining their faith in him and, ironically, their cause. As a foil to Burley, Ephraim Macbriar possesses all the courage exhibited by Burley but is also devoutly religious and scrupulously honest. Scott suggests that Burley's willing use of deceit is necessary to revolution, bothering some critics. They feel that Scott should have stressed opposition to revolution and to power-crazed political leaders like Burley. Scott did the opposite, allowing Morton's involvement, even though Morton knows Burley can't be trusted. In the opinion of critic Alexander Welsh, Scott makes clear that "the release of energy implicit in revolution is analogous . . . to the release of passion from the restraint of reason." An intelligent people cannot be restrained or controlled, and they will find leadership where needed.

Old Mortality offers, in addition to a story of love and revolution, an admirable comic characterization in the figure of Goose Gibbie. Although drawing the scorn of other characters and perhaps of readers as well, Goose is crucial to the plot. Through Goose, Scott reminds his readers of the huge part fate can play in determining the fortunes and futures of the most powerful humans.

BIBLIOGRAPHY

Welsh, Alexander. Introduction to *Old Mortality,* by Sir
    Walter Scott. Boston: Houghton Mifflin, 1966, vii–xviii.

OLIVER TWIST, OR THE PARISH BOY'S PROGRESS CHARLES DICKENS (1838)

Likely Charles DICKENS's best-known novel, *Oliver Twist, or the Parish Boy's Progress* first appeared in serial form in BENTLEY'S MISCELLANY between February 1837 and April 1839. The author's third novel, it would later become the most dramatized of any fictional work, appearing as movie, television, and stage productions, both in musical form and as straight drama. The appeal of the story lies in the characterization of the victimized protagonist, Oliver Twist. As his surname indicates, the young boy will experience many turns of fate during childhood as he seeks the security of a family. An appealing orphan who survives as part of the London underworld, although not very successfully, Oliver interacts with one of fiction's most famous "light" villains, Fagin, as well as one of its most evil, Bill Sikes. The first English novel with a child as main character, *Oliver Twist* offered a view of the lower depths of Victorian society through a child's innocent viewpoint. Dickens based the setting, the underbelly of London, on his observations. His disgust and anger over the conditions of the poor supports an outrage present in many of his later novels.

Oliver's mother dies in the poorhouse after giving birth, and he grows until age nine in the care of Mrs. Mann at a branch workhouse. He moves from there to a true workhouse, run by the hypocritical Mr. Bumble, a parish beadle. In one famous scene, Oliver dares to demand a second helping of food under feeding regulations of the New Poor Law, an 1834 edict that, among other things, resulted in family members being separated according to gender. Dickens joined enlightened society in opposing that law, which resulted in inhumane treatment of those who most needed aid. Even so, Dickens's liberal use of humor and irony lightened what could have resulted in a too tragic tone. The novel's melodrama remains tolerable in view of its skillful SATIRE and rich dialogue.

Oliver moves on to work with an undertaker, then runs away and meets the Artful Dodger, a fellow orphan named Jack Dawkins. Dodger is part of a children's gang trained by Fagin in petty theft and burglary. While readers may have tolerated Fagin, even while recognizing themselves in the boys' victims, they could not tolerate the dastardly Bill Sikes, to whom Fagin must account. Fagin became a more positive character in later dramatic presentations of the novel, benefiting by comparison to Sikes. Sikes's villainy is heightened through his cruel treatment of the children and his brutalizing of Nancy, a sympathetic prostitute who becomes attached to Oliver, the child she never had. Dickens succeeds in retaining the humanity of all the characters. Even Sikes proves interesting, as details regarding the orphans and their poor treatment must be assumed as a story of Sikes's own background, adding to reader understanding of his lack of humanity. Sikes is not one-dimensional, like Dickens's other villains.

Also involved in Oliver's life is the kindly Mr. Brownlow. He rescues Oliver from street life, but the gang kidnaps him, hoping to use him in barter after learning something of his origin from the outlaw Monks. Oliver accompanies Sikes on a burglary that goes wrong and is shot, horrifying the owner of the house, Mrs. Maylie. Her adopted daughter Rose joins her in nursing Oliver through his illness. They help balance the cruelty previously inflicted upon the child but also foreshadow the coincidence so common to Dickens's stories.

While Oliver remains with the Maylies, Nancy prods Monks for information. She visits the Maylie house to warn Rose that Fagin will corrupt Oliver and to alert Rose that she may be related to the boy. Mr. Brownlow helps trace Oliver's background, and Nancy is seen as a traitor, leading Sikes to murder her. Sikes later accidentally hangs himself, while members of the gang and Fagin are arrested. Fagin is tried and hanged, although critics have pointed out that he would not actually have suffered death under the laws of Dickens's times. Dickens may have destroyed both criminals to counteract the glamorization of outlaws in the popular NEWGATE FICTION of the day.

When Brownlow investigates Monks, he discovers Monks is Oliver's half-brother; had Oliver died, Monks would have been alone to enjoy an inheritance. Facts reveal that Rose is the boy's aunt, and Oliver gains a family at last when he is adopted by Mr. Brownlow.

As with other of Dickens's THESIS NOVELS, *Oliver Twist* presents a cast of exaggerated characters, representing good, evil, and additional aspects such as hypocrisy, greed, benevolence, cunning, and charity. While some critics cite a lack of realism in the novel, it remains a favorite among readers. It satisfyingly validates the power of society's good elements to overcome the bad and encourages its readers to take part in reforms necessary to redeem the lives of innocent victims of social CLASS STRUCTURE.

BIBLIOGRAPHY

Paroissien, David. *The Companion to Oliver Twist.* Edinburgh: Edinburgh University Press, 1992.

Smiley, Jane. *Charles Dickens.* New York: Penguin Putnam, 2002.

Thompson, Corey Evan. "Dickens's *Oliver Twist.*" *The Explicator* 61, no. 3 (Spring 2003): 147–149.

ONCE A WEEK   Begun by former publishers of Charles DICKENS's defunct periodical *HOUSEHOLD WORDS, Once a Week* was developed during an age of strict competition over the printing of serial versions of novels by popular writers. Dickens had begun a new venture himself, titled *ALL THE YEAR ROUND,* which naturally introduced his latest work, and *The CORNHILL MAGAZINE* featured work by Anthony TROLLOPE. In order to compete, the publishers of *Once A Week* asked Charles READE, author of the recently popular *IT IS NEVER TOO LATE TO MEND* (1856), to write for their publication. Reade based a serial named *A Good Fight* on the early life of Erasmus but, like Dickens, became so aggravated trying to work with the publishers that he ended the series after only three months. Two years later he published *The CLOISTER AND THE HEARTH* (1861), arguably his most popular work, based on that initial effort for *Once a Week.* Such developments were not uncommon, thus demonstrating an unintentional manner by which periodicals helped novelists' careers. Later that year, it published George MEREDITH's second and autobiographical novel, *Evan Harrington* (1861).

ONE OF OUR CONQUERORS GEORGE MEREDITH (1891)   In George MEREDITH's *One of Our Conquerors,* the author employs his favored theme of marriages forced by society to the detriment of all involved, particularly females. His protagonist, 21-year-old Victor Radnor, is trapped in a pressured marriage to a rich widow, Mrs. Burman Radnor. Victor alludes to an aristocratic Welsh ancestry that cannot be proven, something Meredith also did. Victor falls in love with his wife's companion, Nataly Dreighton. As the novel opens, he has lived with her for 20 years. Their relationship produced a daughter named Nesta Victoria, and the truth about Victor's real marriage is known only to good friends, including Simeon Fenellan and Colney Durance. For all the affection he feels for Nataly and Nesta, Victor represents the conventional Victorian male, who cannot help drawing on nature metaphors for the women they see as static ornaments, decorating the male life. He refers to women as "stationary [. . .] flowers" destined to be visited by men,

the "bees" who may seem volatile in their activity, but remain "faithful to the hive."

As an investment broker, Victor has become a millionaire and acquired two country houses, enhancing his credentials in the eyes of society, while ever fearful that his wife may appear and expose his secret. Rumors have already caused him to move from two previous estates, and he hopes the present sumptuous residence under construction in Surrey will at last afford the peace and acceptance for which he longs, primarily for the sake of Nesta. Nataly feels the investment to be unwise and likely to call more attention to Victor, and its construction has indeed been revealed to Mrs. Burman by her butler/spy, Jarniman. Nesta does not know of her illegitimacy, as she happily enjoys romance with two suitors, the Honorable Dudley Sowerby, who stands to inherit an earldom, and the Reverend Septimus Barmby, a lowly clergyman. Their relationships allow Meredith to emphasize the Victorian ideal of the suitable mate.

Victor's hopes grow as the loyal Fenellan learns that Mrs. Burman might be willing to grant him a divorce, but that rumor is never substantiated, leading to growing internal conflict for Victor. His hope again mounts when he learns of her illness and perhaps imminent death. Time grows short for Nesta to marry, and Victor gives his approval for proposals from either of her young men. Victor decides to host a party at his new estate, Lakelands, and Fenellan's half-brother, Dartrey, now in England after having left the army in Africa, appears. Nesta finds Dartrey, recently widowed and happily divested of a miserable marriage, charming. The party goes well until Jarniman surfaces, signaling Mrs. Burman's knowledge and disapproval of Lakelands.

Because the secret seems sure to be out soon, Nataly visits Sowerby to explain Nesta's origins while the girl spends a month with the Duvidneys, elderly relatives of Victor and the few comic touches to the novel. Sowerby is dismayed by the news; while he loves Nesta, his social standing might suffer from their union. Nataly, already secretly ill, leaves his estate dispirited and abject. Nesta runs into Dartrey when the sisters escort her to Brighton, where she makes friends with a Mrs. Marsett, strongly disliked by Sowerby and others because she cohabitates out of wedlock with Captain

Marsett. Nesta learns that story from Mrs. Marsett and also suffers the unwanted attentions of Worrell, one of the Marsett's acquaintances. Dartrey must reject the brazen advances of the married Mrs. Blathenoy. Tension rises as Mrs. Marsett asks Dartrey to warn Nesta away from her, lest the girl injure her own reputation. Dartrey also learns of Worrell's attempt to force himself on Nesta, while she comes to understand that Sowerby has no further interest in her. When Barmby proposes to marry Nesta despite her past, he does not supply details. However, Nesta begins to suspect Barmby knows some secret about her past. The odious nature of his clearly purposed "slip" of the tongue to reveal Nesta's origin symbolizes Meredith's total disdain for the clergy, an attitude that runs throughout his novels.

When Nesta returns to London, she confronts her parents, having guessed their secret, sharing that she still loves them. Though more individuals in their social set have heard rumors of the illegitimacy, and some refuse to attend Victor's gatherings, he hosts another musical group, having decided to run for a seat in Parliament. Sowerby resurfaces to meet with Nataly, confessing his love for Nesta, but explaining her interactions with undersirables such as Worrell and Mrs. Marsett make marriage impossible. Nataly assumes that Nesta's unhappiness, coupled with her own terminal illness, is God's punishment for her life with Victor. She takes solace in Dartrey's version of what actually happened at Brighton, in which Nesta remains completely innocent. He adds that Nesta has actually had an influence on Mrs. Marsett, who has benefited from their acquaintance. Dartrey loves Nesta and makes that clear the next time they meet, although Nataly remains reserved about that relationship. Her concern that the two will always be ostracized by society for their rebellious ways dampens her joy over Nesta's happiness, especially when Nesta takes Sowerby to task for his attitude, telling him she would never marry him. Nataly's reaction is crucial to the development of her character as a woman who has lived outside of marriage only because convinced by Victor to do so. Not rebellious herself by nature, she has suffered a torment of conscience that may even have hastened her death. Her relationship to Victor is as a "slave," rather than a "helper," their relationship

dependent upon traditional gender roles while not being a traditional marriage. The contradiction proves unbearable for Nataly, and her debilitating terminal illness may symbolize her all-consuming guilt.

Once again shattering the tenuous happiness at Lakelands, Mrs. Burman summons Victor, and Nataly accompanies him. They receive her forgiveness as she is on her deathbed, although Meredith does not develop her as a sympathetic character. Any reader viewing her in light of her age must feel some compassion for her, however, as she is just as imprisoned by societal expectations as Victor and Nataly, fearful of granting a divorce in such an unforgiving age. As critic Mervyn Jones suggests, Meredith's attitude may be based on his view of her inflexibility as contradicting the natural law of love supporting Victor and Nataly's relationship.

Victor feels at last triumphant as he leaves to continue his campaign. He represents the pursuit of a Victorian ideal that could not be achieved. Nataly cannot accompany him, and he leaves her at home where she dies, shattering Victor. Mrs. Burman's death immediately follows Nataly's, an ironic sequence that leaves Victor, grieving for his beloved Nataly, in a tenuous mental state. The only bright spot is Nesta's marriage to the devoted Dartrey. The couple visits the Continent for a year and returns to find that Victor has died from his sorrow.

BIBLIOGRAPHY

Jones, Mervyn. *The Amazing Victorian: A Life of George Meredith*. London: Constable, 1999.

OPIE, AMELIA (1769–1853)

An only child of Amelia and James Alderson, Amelia Alderson Opie inherited her radical humanist views from her father, a respected physician and devoted member of the Unitarian Church. Born in Norwich, she later met and admired William GODWIN and Mary WOLLSTONECRAFT, parents to later author Mary Godwin SHELLEY. Her writing career began with her contributions to periodicals such as the *London Magazine*. She published her first novel, *The Dangers of Coquetry*, anonymously in 1790. After marrying the artist John Opie in 1798, she wrote and published popular fiction, including *The*

Father and Daughter (1801), her best-known work during her own lifetime; its 10 separate editions made her famous. The book for which later generations best knew Opie was ADELINE MOWBRAY (1802), which she based on the life of Mary Wollstonecraft. A great admirer of Wollstonecraft and a supporter of social causes, Opie nevertheless found the treatment of intellectual revolutionaries like Wollstonecraft shocking and shameful, discouraging her from loudly voicing her own opinions apart from the traditional domestic scene. Along with poetry, she printed additional fiction, including Simple Tales (1806). Her fiction focused on domesticity shaped in a didactic and sentimental voice, although her plots countered oppression and supported a type of subversive revolution.

Her husband died in 1807 and Opie returned to Norwich, where she published Valentine's Eve (1816) and Madeline (1822). After adopting the Quaker religion she ended her career in 1825 but remained active in readers circles. She devoted much time to the Bible Society and the Anti-Slavery Society. Her anti-slavery views are expressed in The Black Man's Lament (1826). Her final work, a book of poetry titled Lays for the Dead, appeared in 1833. The popularity of her works varies according to critical attention.

BIBLIOGRAPHY

Brightwell, Cecilia Lucille. Memoir of Amelia Opie. London: Religious Tract Society, 1855.

Memorials of the Life of Amelia Opie: Selected and Arranged from Her Letters, Diaries and other Manuscripts by Cecilia Lucille Brightwell. New York: AMS Press, 1975.

OROONOKO, OR THE ROYAL SLAVE

APHRA BEHN (1678) Written by Aphra BEHN, Oroonoko or the Royal Slave was the first English novel offering a sympathetic view of the suffering of slaves. While little is known of Behn's younger life, she claimed to have lived in Surinam, the setting for her story. First published in 1678, it appeared a decade later as part of her Three Histories. Behn was one of the first to mix what had been considered separate elements from the ROMANCE and the novel. She designed a tale she hoped would appeal to logic, set within exotic surroundings and featuring as a protagonist an individual representing what Renaissance readers would recognize as a "noble savage." His innocent nature, reminiscent of humans prior to the Edenic fall from grace through sin, appealed to them. Oroonoko's physical prowess contributes to the aforementioned "miraculous contingencies and impossible performances," as in one scene when he kills a tiger that multiple bullets could not stop. However, it is his ethical and moral fiber that Behn designs to most impress her readers, as her narrator writes of the Indians, "the People represented to me an absolute Idea of the first State of Innocence, before Man knew how to sin: And 'tis most evident and plain, that simple Nature is the most harmless, inoffensive and virtuous Mistress."

Oroonoko belongs to a tribe of Indians called Caribs who proved themselves superior to supposedly more sophisticated Europeans because they lack vice. They stand ready to be corrupted by the white practitioners of IMPERIALISM. Furthermore, Oroonoko represents royalty as the grandson of an African king. He loves the beautiful Imoinda, daughter of his grandfather's general, but unfortunately, so does his grandfather. When the king recognizes that he shares his love of Imoinda with his grandson, he sells her into slavery. Oroonoko is captured by white slavers and finds Imoinda, who soon becomes pregnant with his child. Renamed Caesar, he helps unite and inspire the black slaves to escape with an impassioned speech in which he questions the actions of the enslavers who did not honorably defeat those they enslaved, but rather have "bought and sold" the captives "like Apes or Monkeys, to be the sport of Women, Fools and Cowards." Behn carefully distinguishes the Indians, whom she views as noble and possessing innate value, from the blacks, who are simple brutes. Her first-person narration from the position of a white woman allows her to express the desire to separate herself from the barbarian acts of the whites, whose lack of a moral code repulses her. However, she realistically remains a powerless female who can do nothing to help rescue Oroonoko from her culture's self interest.

The slaves are hunted down and surrender to Byam, a deputy governor, who promises to pardon them. Byam does not keep his word and publicly whips Oroonoko, committing an act the tribesmen cannot understand. Their honorable culture lacks language to describe the results of a man breaking his promise. As the narrator states, the deputy-governor, "who was the most fawning fair-tongu'd Fellow in the World and one that pretended the most Friendship to *Caesar,* was now the only violent Man against him." Oroonoko desires revenge but understands he will be executed if he kills Byam. He also understands that once the men take possession of Imoinda, she will suffer an intolerable fate. She agrees to place her life in his hands, and he slits her throat as her eyes smiled "with Joy she should die by so noble a Hand." When the murder is discovered, Oroonoko suffers execution by dismemberment for that crime, and his "quarters" are dispatched to "several of the Chief Plantations." The narrator idealizes Oroonoko, imbuing him with courage, honor, and intelligence. Behn's clear message is that the imperialists are the savages, while members of the native tribes are not yet perverted by self-interest.

BIBLIOGRAPHY

Metzger, Lore. Introduction to *Oroonoko or, The Royal Slave,* by Aphra Behn. New York: W.W. Norton, 1973, ix–xv.

Todd, Janet. *The Secret Life of Aphra Behn.* New York: Pandora, 2000.

OUIDA (PSEUDONYM OF MARIE LOUISE DE LA RAMÉE) (1839–1908)

Marie Louise de la Ramée was born at Bury St. Edmunds. Her nickname, Ouida, which she later adopted as a pen name, derived from Louise. Ouida's father taught French and was rumored to have involved himself with Prince Louis Napoleon during his exile to England. Rarely present in the home he shared with his daughter and an English wife who had a small independent income, Ramée eventually left the family in 1871, never to return. As a child, Ouida was encouraged by novelist William Harrison AINSWORTH to use her writing talents, and she first published in 1859, while in London, in the periodical Ainsworth edited for a time, BENTLEY'S MISCELLANY. By age 26 she had published frequently; some even suspected George ELIOT had written her books. She stayed at London's Langham Hotel in 1867 and became friends with its manager, an American Confederate Army ex-colonel.

Ouida and her mother often entertained at all-male parties held in the hotel, frequented by many Americans, including the poet Henry Wadsworth Longfellow. Most of the guests had military connections, or were authors or journalists. Her notoriety grew, and Ouida attempted to move into more elevated social circles. She published her first novel, *Held in Bondage,* in 1863 and followed it with *Strathmore* (1865) and *Chandos* (1866). Her most famous work, *Under Two Flags* (1867), was based on the Foreign Legion. She had begun a prolific career that would include more than 40 novels, with *Tricotin* published in 1869 and *Puck* in 1870. Ouida relocated to Florence in 1871, succeeding at finding her desired social niche, and remained there until her death in 1908.

While a highly successful author, Ouida's extravagance left her in constant financial embarrassment. Sometimes having to beg money, she became a caricature of her own ROMANCE NOVEL protagonists, an ill-tempered and unattractive snob with a shrill voice that often alienated others. Lacking much sense of plot, Ouida nevertheless injected a noted vitality into her fictional narrative. Critics offer her 1880 novel, MOTHS, as an example, remarking on the marathonlike pace that draws readers through a plot they feel might fall apart. Mystified by human nature, she never explores motivations behind her characters' conduct, but the crude manipulation of their actions gave them a force that fascinated readers. Her manner proved aggressive, and her florid style kept her novels popular until the end of the 19th century. After 1890, her debts overcame her, and she lived in poverty for several years until receiving a Civil List pension during the final decade of her life.

BIBLIOGRAPHY

Bigland, Eileen. *Ouida, the Passionate Victorian.* New York: Jarrolds, 1950.

Powell, Anthony. Introduction to *Novels of High Society from the Victorian Age.* London: Pilot Press, 1947, vii–xv.

OUR MUTUAL FRIEND CHARLES DICKENS (1865)

Published like Charles DICKENS's other works, first as a serial from May 1864 through November 1865, *Our Mutual Friend* reflects the author's traditional multiple plots. It would be Dickens's final completed work, and some critics see it as the culmination of the author's dark vision of his own culture, corrupted by greed and materialism. Others disagree, noting that those of questionable character who are redeemed by love in the novel are allowed a chance to enjoy a new life, unlike other Dickens characters, such as Sydney Carton in Dickens's previous novel, *A TALE OF TWO CITIES* (1859). Additional disagreement focuses on the lack of any grand scheme to the story, or any overriding theme. That criticism is countered by Jane Smiley's observation that the book represents "one of the greatest examples of sustained perfection of style in the English language."

The novel focuses on John Harmon, heir to an English family fortune made in "dust" trade, an English euphemism for the sale of bat guano, but believed suspiciously drowned. Harmon returns to England following a long absence, doing nothing to discredit the story of his demise, as he wishes to observe incognito Bella Wilfer, the woman his father's will demands that he marry before he may take possession of his inheritance. He uses two aliases, Julius Handford and John Rokesmith, and as Rokesmith is secretary for Mr. Boffin. The well-to-do Boffin also possesses aliases, including Noddy and the Golden Dustman, as he also is a dust merchant. Rokesmith will inherit Harmon's property should the young heir choose not to wed Bella. Boffin and his wife serve as Bella's guardians of sorts, as Boffin orders a lawyer named Mortimer Lightwood to sponsor a reward for information regarding Harmon's supposed death. As Boffin's employee, Harmon/Rokesmith falls in love with Bella, but she refuses his proposal of marriage. Hoping to change her mind, Boffin implicates Harmon as untrustworthy and discharges him, upsetting Bella, who decides to return to her parents' home and accept her common lot in life. She eventually also accepts Harmon's bid for marriage and quickly learns his true identity as heir to a fortune.

In a subplot allowing Dickens to present his usual moral tale, Lizzie Hexam is loved by Bradley Headstone, who serves as master of the school attended by her brother Charley. Their father, Gaffer Hexam, supports his family by pulling dead bodies from the Thames, and he is accused of murdering Harmon. Lizzie does not love Headstone, instead fixing her affections on the unethical barrister Eugene Wrayburn, an undesirable friend of Mortimer Lightwood. Headstone lives up to the symbolism of his surname when he attempts to kill Wrayburn in order to remove competition for Lizzie's affection. Lizzie cares for Wrayburn, curing his evil with her kindness, and she wins his love. They are married, while the would-be murderer Headstone is blackmailed by a villain appropriately named Rogue Riderhood. The two engage in physical combat that leads to both of their deaths, while Hexam is cleared of murder charges and Harmon's identity is revealed.

BIBLIOGRAPHY

Cotsell, Michael. *Companion to Our Mutual Friend*. Boston: Allen & Unwin, 1986.

Fulweiler, Howard W. "'A dismal swamp': Darwin, Design, and Evolution in *Our Mutual Friend*." *Nineteenth-Century Literature* 49, no. 1 (June 1994): 50–73.

Smiley, Jane. *Charles Dickens*. New York: Penguin Putnam, 2002.

OWENSON, SYDNEY, LADY MORGAN (1776–1859)

Sydney Owenson was reportedly born on a ship while her English mother and Irish father crossed the Irish Sea. She later used that questionable circumstance as symbolic of her attempts to help the English better understand the Irish. Known as an idiosyncratic, she often romanticized facts in her favor, but her dedication to Irish nationalism was never questioned. Probably because her mother died when Owenson was a child, her father's Irish heritage most influenced her. Like her sister, she enjoyed a decent education in a loving and attentive home.

Raised behind the scenes at her father's Irish theater, the young Owenson matured immersed in Dublin life with a love for dramatic portrayals. She accompanied her father around the countryside for performances, developing an intimate knowledge of Irish country life that she later incorporated into her writing. Known for her early ROMANCE NOVELS, *St. Clair* (1803) and *The Novice of St. Dominick* (1805), she found true popularity with *The WILD IRISH GIRL* (1806). Criticized for political intentions, she ignored attacks by the Tory press and continued her approach with *O'Donnel* (1811),

Florence Macarthy (1811), and *The O'Briens and the O'Flahertys* (1827). All supported Irish independence from England. In addition to novels, she wrote travel books about France (1817) and Italy (1821), resulting from her journeys with her physician husband, Sir Charles Morgan.

According to critic Lorna Sage, the poet George Gordon, Lord Byron, wrote that Lady Morgan's travel accounts were both "fearless" and "excellent." She also produced feminist works in *Ida of Athens* (1809) and *Woman and Her Master* (1840), in addition to publishing poetry and versions of Irish songs that she had learned at her father's theater. A charismatic literary figure, she established a coterie attracting many renowned literary individuals. Lady Morgan was the first female to be pensioned for her "services to the world of letters" and was celebrated in the 1862 book edited by W. Hepworth Dixon, *Lady Morgan's Memoirs: Autobiography, Diaries, and Correspondence.*

BIBLIOGRAPHY

Campbell, Mary. *Lady Morgan: The Life and Times of Sydney Owenson.* New York: Pandora Press, 1988.

Newcomer, James. *Lady Morgan the Novelist.* Lewisburg, Pa.: Bucknell University Press, 1990.

Sage, Lorna. "Owenson, Sidney." *The Cambridge Guide to Women's Writing in English.* Cambridge: Cambridge University Press, 1999, 486.

Spender, Dale. *Mothers of the Novel: 100 Good Women Writers Before Jane Austen.* New York: Pandora, 1986.

Stevenson, Lionel. *The Wild Irish Girl: The Life of Sydney Owenson, Lady Morgan (1776–1859).* New York: Russell & Russell, 1936.

OXFORD MOVEMENT

The 19th-century Oxford Movement sought to reform the English church, reconstituting it on High Church principles. The movement formally began in July 1833 with a sermon by Oxford professor of poetry John Keble on national apostasy. Keble attacked threats to the church, including erastianism (subordination to the government), and latitudinarianism, the formal name for the laxness with which his contemporaries approached church ritual and dogma. Three additional Oxford dons joined Keble's lead: Edward Bouverie Pusey,

Hebrew professor; John Henry Newman; and Richard Hurrell Froude. Over the next 12 years following the presentation of Keble's ideas, a crucial period for reform occurred that proved seminal to all aspects—religious, political, and social—of Britain's 19th-century development. These four men launched a crusade to counter what they viewed as the liberal spirit of their era. They were also known as Tractarians, based on their publication of *Tracts for the Times,* a document that attacked Parliament's passing of the Irish Church Bill in 1833 as a threat to the sovereignty of the sacred church. The bill resulted from the fears of the duke of Wellington, then prime minister, and some members of his Tory Party that the Irish might revolt if they did not pass a bill repealing the Corporation Acts of 1661 that prevented Roman Catholics from holding an elected seat in Parliament. Representatives of the Church of England at Oxford saw the act as a betrayal and sacrilege.

As the movement expanded, it sought to reinstitute High Church doctrine, supported by the belief in the divine nature of the Church of England and the importance of the Book of Common Prayer, a service book in use since the 16th century. As part of the rituals, accompanying vestments were donned and incense used. Influenced by Methodism, the movement urged "earnestness" on the part of young men and led to an Evangelical approach. Anglo-Catholic practices had their roots in medieval times, dictating appropriate food for certain days.

Keble later moved to Hursley to serve as a clergyman, partly because as a reserved individual, he did not like the type of intellectualism and lack of humility practiced by some of Oxford's dons. He saw little place for logic in matters of faith. The lively and outspoken Froude, conversely, thrived in such an atmosphere, while the scholarly Pusey used his authority to establish six features, comprising "Puseyism." They included high regard for two sacraments, for ordinances, and for "the visible part of devotion," which included the "decorations" of the church.

Keble's departure pushed the movement into a new stage. More liberal church members protested the movement, charging its leaders with an attempt to return to Roman Catholicism, a charge Pusey countered by expressing a desire for a blend of the English and Roman churches. While the four dons did not agree on every issue, their common goal led to a near-unshakable unity. It was broken by Newman's famous conversion to Catholicism in 1845, a consequence of the call to a return to medieval ritual that Keble had foreseen as a possible result and hoped to avoid. While that conversion signaled the movement's formal conclusion, it simply moved the center of activity from Oxford to London and into the country.

The Oxford Movement eventually touched all areas of English life, including education and the social challenges that arose with industrialization, art, and architecture. Tractarian missions were founded and operated by nuns, usually from nursing orders. They offered health and education services to the poor and helped train young women in nursing. The English landscape reflected the religious revolution, adding schools and orphanages, as well as in the new churches, almost always of a Gothic design to emphasize the ideals of an earlier age.

Novels of the time, including Charlotte BRONTË'S *SHIRLEY* (1849), alluded to the movement, while others, including everything published by Charlotte YONGE, a neighbor of John Keble, built entire plots and designed themes around the doctrines. In the country, his ideals slowly became a part of rural life, and Yonge determined that her novels would imaginatively reflect the stages of the movement. She discussed many of the plots with Keble, whom she referred to as "my vicar," listening as he cautioned her not to specifically mention doctrines but to emphasize the movement's code of conduct. Her popular *HEIR OF REDCLYFFE* (1853), for example, promoted the idea that redemption may only be achieved through self-sacrifice. As her popularity grew in the 1850s and 1860s, she included among her friends individuals representing the various phases and influences on the religious revival. Her two-volume *Pillars of the House, or, Under Wode Under Rode* (1873) brought all the church themes together, treating what were innovations as commonplace; society had accepted the reforms and the marks of the movement were everywhere evident.

BIBLIOGRAPHY

Dennis, Barbara. *Charlotte Yonge: Novelist of the Oxford Movement: A Literature of Victorian Culture and Society.* Lewiston, N.Y.: E. Mellen Press, 1992.

Fought, C. Brad. *The Oxford Movement: A Thematic History of the Tractarians and Their Times.* University Park, Pa.: Pennsylvania State University Press, 2003.

P

PALTOCK, ROBERT (1696–1767)

Robert Paltock was born in Westminster, the only son of Thomas and Anne Paltock; he would lose his father at age five. He received an inheritance of £150 from his grandmother and a house when he came of age. His mother died in 1712, and little is known of his life until 1747, when his financial problems became public. Educated as an attorney, he married Anna Skinner, daughter of an Italian merchant, and they had two sons and two daughters. Paltock earned brief fame with the publication of his ROMANCE NOVEL *The LIFE AND ADVENTURES OF PETER WILKINS* (1751). Paltock assigned rights to the novel to Jacob Robinson and Robert Dodsley in January 1749 for £21 and 12 printed copies. At first published only under the initials R. P., the book's true authorship was revealed in the *British Register* in 1802, and in 1835 the original document noting the sale agreement and bearing Paltock's full name and address were discovered.

Translated into both French and German, the work gained praise from Samuel Coleridge, Robert Southey, Charles Lamb, and Sir Walter SCOTT. It represents an early example of SCIENCE FICTION, in which the protagonist travels to a world populated by flying humanoids. Paltock comments in his fiction against slavery and supports the value of independence to intelligent women, facts of interest to FEMINIST and NEW HISTORICIST CRITICS. While he owed some debt to Daniel DEFOE'S *ROBINSON CRUSOE* (1719) and Jonathan SWIFT'S *GULLIVER'S TRAVELS* and their depiction of an imagined voyage, critics such as Christopher Bentley note Paltock's original use of flight as a human power. He also finds the relationship between Paltock's hero and heroine wittier than those in Defoe, and the culture Paltock invents far more sophisticated and challenging than that of Defoe's single island.

Paltock moved to Back Lane, St. Mary, Lambeth, in 1759, and his financial affairs apparently improved, as a 1764 *London Gazette* notice called for all creditors to present their claims. He died at his home in Back Lane, his novel fading into obscurity for a time. The 18th century's penchant for SATIRE caused it to judge the imaginative, but not highly ironic, work a bit dull. With the surge in popularity of romance and the GOTHIC NOVEL in the 19th century, the book returned to popularity. It exists in both print and electronic form.

BIBLIOGRAPHY

Bentley, Christopher. Introduction to *The Life and Adventures of Peter Wilkins,* by Robert Paltock. New York: Oxford University Press, 1973, ix–xviii.

PAMELA, OR VIRTUE REWARDED SAMUEL RICHARDSON (1740)

Long touted as the first English novel, or at the least the first EPISTOLARY NOVEL, Samuel RICHARDSON'S *Pamela* has since had both those positions questioned in light of work by earlier writers, most notably Aphra BEHN. It remains of extreme importance, however, in the novel's development and proved a wildly popular work in its day.

The novel consists entirely of correspondence on the part of its title character, Pamela Andrews, a young servant prey to the sexual advances by her new master Mr. B., son to her recently deceased mistress. Unceasingly objectified by Mr. B. and his helpful servants Mrs. Jewkes and Monsieur Calbrand, Pamela eventually is driven from her home by their lusty pursuits. Under a type of house arrest in her new location, and separated from family and friends, Pamela struggles to retain her high moral purpose. In a relationship interesting to FEMINIST CRITICS as evidence of the stereotypical competition between females for male approval, Mrs. Jewkes gains Pamela's trust and steals her journals. Mr. B. reads the journals, becomes privy to Pamela's ideology, and enacts the role of one in complete agreement with her high morality, eventually proposing marriage.

However, Richardson extends the conflict as an unknown correspondent warns Pamela of her master's duplicity. She despairs to her parents, "What shall we say of this truly diabolical master! O, how shall I find words to paint my griefs, and his deceit! I have as good as confessed I love him; but, indeed, it was on supposing him good.—this, however, has given him too much advantage. But now I will break this wicked forward heart of mine, if it will not be taught to hate him! O, what a black dismal heart must *he* have!" Mr. B. eventually "does right" by his one-time intended victim, and the two marry. The delighted Pamela transforms in the novel's second portion into a suspicious wife who doubts her husband's fidelity and the loyalty of his disapproving family and servants. She retains her moral beliefs, however, acting with a dignity that proves less engaging than did her emotionally expressed conflict over Mr. B.'s scandalous behavior in the novel's first section. While Richardson seems to suggest that a partially reformed rake can make a fine husband, critics later pointed out that he can not resolve the compromise of human values such a stance represents.

The novel's domestic tension is credited with its success. A dominant appeal, according to William Sale, Jr., was Pamela's representing the change in values evident in the 18th century. While society insisted that Pamela's position as a servant meant she must conform to her master's wishes, new forces supporting the development of a middle class urged an independence that made Pamela a new woman type. Her position as such should not be overemphasized, however, a point clearly made at the altar when Mr. B. presents her with a ring, and she replies, "Thank you, sir." At the least, she served as a prototype for later, more fully realized heroines developed by novelists including George MEREDITH. Society's attempts to keep the real-life figures represented by Pamela "in their place" spawned entire fields of literary criticism that focused, in part, on such power structures in fiction, including not only feminist critics, but also MARXIST and NEW HISTORICAL critics. The obvious sexual thrust of the novel also attracted the interest of later PSYCHOANALYTIC CRITICS.

Richardson came upon the idea for the novel from an instructional book he composed about proper letter-writing format. While such books were common, he included many more examples than had his predecessors, including several lengthy letters offering models to corresponding women. He offered 173 different epistle approaches, more than 100 of which focused on women's interests and needs. Having no previous writing experience, Richardson confounded critics of later generations seeking to understand how he came to produce such an important work. Its plotline may have been inspired by the letter example numbered 138, based on a true case Richardson knew involving a 12-year-old girl put to service who, when her mistress died three years later, drew the attention of the household's young master, a man of "free principles." With no particular model to follow, Richardson presented himself on the title page not as author but as "editor" of Pamela's letters, thus suggesting reality in fiction, a remarkable and sustainable approach, also to be later imitated and refined into a movement in writing labeled REALISM. *Pamela* proved crucial due to its narrative and characterization unity, a format that subsequent novels would imitate. Richardson himself continued the epistolary format in *CLARISSA* (1747), but expanded his speakers to include multiple correspondents.

Furthermore, the value of a piece of literature may often be judged by the reaction it provokes, particularly from other writers, and *Pamela's* inspiring the fledgling novelist Henry FIELDING's parody of *Pamela,* titled *Shamela* (1741), is a case in point. While modern readers may resent or find amusing *Pamela's* stilted DIDACTIC style, marked by a high moral tone, melodrama, and sexism, critics agree on its unquestioned importance to the development of the novel. It retains a seminal position in academic literature programs and still appeals to aficionados of mid-18th-century fiction.

BIBLIOGRAPHY

Sade, William, Jr. Introduction to *Pamela, or, Virtue Rewarded,* by Samuel Richardson. New York: W.W. Norton, 1958, v–xiv.

PARODY

Parody represents mockery by one author of another author's style and often of specific works. Generally good-natured in tone, a parody closely follows the original and has as its goal to caution the author and that author's readers as to the low style of the work. Structure may also be mimicked when elements of the original are well known, as with DETECTIVE and ROMANCE FICTION. Parody may also contain caricature, an exaggeration of the qualities of certain individuals to produce an absurd effect. While moral, social, or political themes may be present in parody, those appear more commonly in another type of mockery called SATIRE. One of English literature's best-known parodies is Henry FIELDING's *Shamela* (1741), which presents Samuel RICHARDSON's *PAMELA, OR VIRTUE REWARDED* (1740) in a ridiculous light. Dismayed by the public's embracing of *Pamela,* an absurd and pretentious work in Fielding's opinion, Fielding used *Shamela* to present a devastating, near scene-by-scene mimicry of Richardson's EPISTOLARY NOVEL about a young servant's endless defense of her virginity against the deflowering schemes of her master.

BIBLIOGRAPHY

Battestin, Marin C. Introduction to *Joseph Andrews,* by Henry Fielding. Boston: Houghton Mifflin, 1961.

Rose, Margaret A. *Parody: Ancient, Modern and Post-modern.* New York: Cambridge University Press, 1993.

PAUL FERROLL CAROLINE CLIVE (1855)

Caroline Clive's popular novel *Paul Ferroll* was likely published at Clive's expense, first advertised for sale in *Publisher's Circular.* While Clive (1801–73) had published poetry, the novel was her first, and ultimately most successful, attempt at fiction. By March 1856 *Paul Ferroll* had gone into a fourth edition, and by 1859 had been translated into both French and Russian. It continued repeat editions through 1929 in the United States, then lost favor until its revival by certain academic courses and publishers in the late 20th century. A precursor of the 1860s wildly popular SENSATION FICTION, it remains of interest in that respect, but also for its own merits, which include Clive's unique dealings with the topic of murder and her inclusion of erotic male imagery.

The plot proves simple. A man named Paul Ferroll murders his first wife, Anne, lives a free and happy existence as a fine citizen for years, and only confesses his crime when another is accused of it. Even then, he escapes imprisonment and disappears into self-exile, never suffering punishment for his crime. Clive's style is what proves of special interest, in that her narrative never moralizes about the murder, nor does Ferroll ever suffer any of the remorse or guilt that Victorian readers expected. Nor did he suffer the consequences his crime demanded. Other murderers in fiction of the day did suffer, leading readers to expect the same of Ferroll. According to critic Charlotte Mitchell, William Makepeace THACKERAY confessed to Clive that Becky Sharp, the notorious female protagonist of his novel *VANITY FAIR* (1848), did murder Jos Sedley, although that fact was not expressed in overt terms for readers. However, they could surmise she had added murder to her long list of crimes against her fellow man, and they saw her ultimate fall from wealth and power as a fitting result. Other murder novels featuring punishment for murder that may have influenced Clive included William GODWIN's *CALEB WILLIAMS* (1749) and Edward BULWER-LYTTON's *EUGENE ARAM* (1832). Like the protagonists of those novels, Ferroll commits a vicious murder that remains long concealed, but Clive includes no discussion about ethics, retribution, justice, remorse, or guilt as do Godwin and Bulwer-Lytton. Another big difference, as Mitchell notes, is that the victims in the other novels proved detestable and, if not deserving of murder, at least were undesirables who would not be missed. But Ferroll's victim remains not only an innocent but also one trusted to his care and protection.

Many reviewers expressed outrage over the novel, which seemed not only to excuse murder but also invite readers to admire the criminal. He did, after all, not profit from the murder, signing over his dead wife's considerable fortune to her brother. Naysayers chastised Clive for apparently arguing that a man may plan and execute a ghastly murder but later live an exemplary and virtuous life. Some may have wondered at the degree of irony intended by Clive when she fashions Ferroll for a short time a writer, and also why she gave him a name she herself adopted in her early writing. Also of interest to PSYCHOANALYTIC CRITICS is that Ferroll expresses an extreme male erotic energy with some sexual transference. He remains extremely possessive of Elinor, his second wife, a woman he had loved previous to his first marriage. He engages in bizarre fantasies, wondering, for instance, if his wife's excessive kissing was on purpose to try to transmit cholera, something the two might share. Elinor understands that Ferroll craves danger "for stimulation," and while waiting for his trial, he engages in extreme amounts of physical exercise. He enjoys contrasting his wife's beauty and allure with the physical attributes of the ill, cannot stand children, ignoring even his own daughter, Janet, and during Elinor's absence, once plunges his horse under a waterfall to help relieve his tensions. While he does not abuse Janet, he neglects her: "the whole tenderness" of his "nature was centred on his wife; and anything that interfered with that passion he put aside." He demands that Elinor devote herself entirely to him to the total exclusion of Janet: "He would have no nursing, no teaching, no summer day's expedition. The nursery was Janet's Place, a governess her teacher; she came to her mother when her mother was alone."

Clive's diaries and collections of various newspaper articles reflect her interest in the macabre. She also took a great interest in letters her husband collected as governor of a lunatic asylum. The outburst against *Paul Ferroll* put Clive on the defensive, and she felt inclined to try to defend her character, later publishing a not-nearly-so-successful sequel titled *Why Paul Ferroll Killed His Wife* (1860). Readers of later generations would find nothing unusual in Clive's interests or in a book not reflecting the Victorian belief that loss of one's reputation equaled a loss of social status, a dev-astating effect of transgressions in that age. The late 20th century observed a phenomenon in which much of English-speaking society began to celebrate fraud and even some types of violence if they led to monetary success. This change in moral outlook may make Paul Ferroll easier to accept as a representative human being today, particularly in a century that celebrates the antihero, a perfect fictional example being the cannibalistic serial killer Hannibal Lecter created by Thomas Harris.

BIBLIOGRAPHY
Mitchell, Charlotte. Introduction to *Paul Ferroll,* by Caroline Clive. New York: Oxford University Press, 1997, ix–xx.

PEACOCK, THOMAS LOVE (1785–1866)
Often considered one of the most undeservingly neglected of the writers publishing in the early 19th century, Thomas Love Peacock was born at Weymouth, an only child. His glassmaker father died while Peacock was still a child, and the boy received formal schooling through age 13 at a private school in Englefield Green. He did not have to work until age 30, due to an inheritance from his father, and he developed a love for books, which he preferred to the company of other people. He met Percy Bysshe Shelley in 1812 and formed a lasting close friendship. While the two men seemed to have little in common, they shared a revolutionary spirit, along with their great interest in literature. Peacock served as an informal tutor in literary matters to Shelley, who encouraged Peacock's poetic talents. His published the first of many satiric novels with HEADLONG HALL (1816), followed closely by MELINCOURT (1817) and NIGHTMARE ABBEY (1818). An erudite and sophisticated intellectual, he assumed his readers would be the same, thus appealing to a small but extremely culturally aware audience. He repeatedly attacked all types of dogma, whether social, political, economical, or artistic, criticizing narrow-mindedness with his fiction. His trademark format included a thin PLOT NARRATIVE framing strong dialogue among characters representing theories recognizable by his audience. While some could be recognized as based on real persons, such as Shelley and other romantic poets, others symbolized universal types.

After entering the East India Company in a senior position in 1819, he met and married Jane Gryffydh, whose Welsh heritage influenced several of his novels through their setting or Welsh characters. In addition to poetry and songs, many of which he included in his fiction, he published several more novels, including *Maid Marian* (1822) and *The* MISFORTUNES OF ELPHIN (1829), which offered his traditional SATIRE but also acted as parodies of romantic literature and the affectations practiced by some contemporary writers. After he published *Crochet Castle* (1831), he took a hiatus from novel writing, not publishing his only additional novel, *Gryll Grange*, until 1861. Through the 1830s, when other novelists of his age focused on writing SILVER FORK or fashionable fiction, Peacock doggedly pursued the intellectual novel. *Crochet Castle* parodied new theories of education and economy, attacking those who spoke in slogans, but it would act as his final attack on what he viewed as the vulgarity of social experimentation that worshipped all things new, without discretion.

During Peacock's early years, his poetry gained attention, as did his critical writings, with the *Essay on Fashionable Literature* (1818) and *The Four Ages of Poetry* (1820) being his most famous. His skeptical stance on art's usefulness during an era in which science was growing more popular so bothered Shelley that he responded in his much more famous and enduring work *A Defence of Poetry;* critics point out that Shelley may have taken Peacock more seriously than Peacock had intended.

Peacock also enjoyed a successful personal life in a happy marriage that produced three children. In 1837, he became examiner at India House, a position he would retain until retirement in 1856. His domestic peace was shattered by the death of his youngest child at age three, driving Jane into a depression and mental collapse from which she would not recover. He lost both his wife and a daughter, also named Jane, in 1851. His other daughter, Mary Ellen, married contemporary novelist George MEREDITH, a union that proved desperately unhappy, and she died in 1861. Meredith supposedly based the character of Clara Middleton's father in his *The* EGOIST (1879) on Peacock. Peacock's last publication was *Memoirs of Shelley* (1858–60), and he died six years later.

BIBLIOGRAPHY

Dawson, Carl. *His Fine Wit: A Study of Thomas Love Peacock.* Berkeley: University of California Press, 1960.

Fenton, Felix. *Thomas Love Peacock.* London: Allen and Unwin, 1973.

Freeman, Alexander Martin. *Thomas Love Peacock: A Critical Study.* Folcroft, Pa.: Folcroft Press, 1969.

PELHAM, OR THE ADVENTURES OF A GENTLEMAN EDWARD BULWER-LYTTON (1828)

In his first novel, *Pelham, or the Adventures of a Gentleman,* Edward BULWER-LYTTON shaped a character named Henry Pelham who introduced an enduring ritual into English society. A dandy known for his pretentious behavior, Pelham dressed in black for dinner, a trend that would spread in England and remain popular. After Pelham's mother remarked on his distinguished appearance in black, colored coats were rarely seen in London high society, and black remained the acceptable evening wear for men for decades. An unlikely hero, Pelham nevertheless proves the innocence of a friend accused of murder by launching an investigation, and acts as a foil to his fellow character Richard Glanville, a criminal. He expresses his own intellectual development, opening chapter 44 in the fourth volume: "Beneath all the carelessness of my exterior, my mind was close, keen, and inquiring; and under the affectations of foppery, and the levity of a manner almost unique, for the effeminacy of its tone, I veiled an ambition the most extensive in its object, and a resolution the most daring in the accomplishment of its means." Although some critics label Pelham a BYRONIC HERO, others feel he stands in direct contrast to that popular characterization.

More important than Pelham's effect on the styles of the day was the novel's effect on the popular BILDUNGSROMAN. While the book contained some inconsistencies, it varied the genre's traditional German intensity, offering instead an upbeat tone laced with humor and common sense. Along with Benjamin DISRAELI's *VIVIAN GREY* (1826), *Pelham* introduced English readers to what would later be labeled the intellectual novel, one that focused on ideas rather than promotion of a specific political point of view. Building on Laurence STERNE's momentum, Bulwer-Lytton and Disraeli urged independent thought among their readers, employing SATIRE and scandal as plot elements.

Based on the true Thurtell case of 1824, the novel owed an additional debt to William GODWIN's *CALEB WILLIAMS* (1794), a psychological novel with a GOTHIC narrative frame. *Pelham* also served as SILVER-FORK FICTION, an extremely popular subgenre of social fiction. Bulwer-Lytton remains sensitive to all the current patterns of his society, skillfully capturing scenes representative of the early 19th century. The witty novel was blasted by many of the author's contemporaries as insubstantial and contemptuous of English society. But Bulwer-Lytton sought through irony, rather than mean-spiritedness, to undercut the criticism of such moralists who failed to recognize in Pelham a dispassionate honesty sorely missing from many relationships. It remains available in print and electronic form.

BIBLIOGRAPHY

McGann, Jerome J. Introduction to *Pelham,* by Edward George Bulwer-Lytton. Lincoln: University of Nebraska Press, 1972.

Mitchell, L. G. *Bulwer-Lytton: The Rise and Fall of a Victorian Man of Letters.* New York: Hambledon and London, 2003.

PERSUASION JANE AUSTEN (1818)

Jane AUSTEN composed *Persuasion,* her final completed novel, between 1815 and 1816; it would be published posthumously in 1818. Unwell and forced to return to Bath, a location she had celebrated in her younger years, Austen produced a story with marked autobiographical aspects, as often remarked by 19th-century critics. Their attitudes proved common regarding women's fiction, as many believed women lacked the intelligence to write about topics outside their own personal environment. This work is celebrated in the 21st century through the display of its original manuscript on Austen's writing desk in the British Library rare collection room.

Austen's last novel supplied an unusual focus on social and political conditions, supported by the change in land ownership taking place around her. That alteration in the landscape, noticed by *Persuasion's* protagonist Anne Elliot, was one reason that Austen did not enjoy her return to Bath as much as she had her visit decades before. Her novel took the gentry to task for problems caused small farmers by the change in land division, as conglomerates began to consume property. Long a fan of clergyman and amateur artist William Gilpin, whose ideas she borrowed for her novels, she embraced his idea that country scenes should be viewed as a picture, with appreciation for foreground, background, and framing by natural formations and plant life. She SATIRIZED her own culture for sacrificing natural beauty to the artificial tastes that claimed aesthetics of her era and criticized the aristocratic class for judgments based on materialistic, rather than spiritual or ethical, values. Most important to reviewers of the day, *Persuasion* was marked by a passion and romance not previously present in Austen's work. For later critics, the power and skill involved with her rhetoric, resulting in skilled understatement, proved her creative intellect.

The plot focuses on one of three daughters of the foolish and egotistical Sir Walter Elliot of Kellynch Hall, 27-year-old Anne Elliot. Raised by a father who delights in reading his own entry in *The Baronage* with equally vacuous sisters Elizabeth and Mary, Anne was the neglected daughter. Elizabeth's ego matched that of her father, thus giving them common ground, while Mary's condescension even toward her own husband, Charles Musgrove, son of a neighboring squire, unites her with her opinionated father and sister. Although more sensible, sensitive, and intelligent than the other members of her family, Anne is excluded from all decisions and adheres to the others' wishes.

Due to financial embarrassments, Anne's father must rent his estate to Admiral and Mrs. Croft, allowing Anne to again meet Mrs. Croft's brother, Captain Frederick Wentworth, a previous suitor. Anne loved and would have married Wentworth, but yielded to her godmother's wishes and refused his offer eight years earlier. Her godmother, the honorable but biased Lady Russell, felt Wentworth to be beneath Anne's aristocratic station. Anne still loves Wentworth, now worth a solid £20,000 per year, but must keep her feelings secret. Anne likes and admires the Crofts, feeling their marriage to be one of the few sound unions she has observed. Anne's sister Mary enjoys Wentworth's company as does her husband Charles, and they ensure the presence of Charles's sisters Louisa and Henrietta whenever possible, in hopes that Charles might be drawn to one. He seems to choose Louisa, made clear by his concern over a head wound she suffers in a fall. Anne loses hope of regaining his affections.

Anne travels to Bath to reunite with Sir Elliot and Elizabeth and meets a cousin, William Elliot. Austen incorporates one of her favorite themes, that of the inheritance through the male line; William is Sir Elliot's heir, rather than any of his offspring. A heartless schemer, William pretends to romance Anne, who learns of his true character from a widowed invalid and Anne's friend, Mrs. Smith, enabling Anne to avoid his attentions.

Suddenly the Elliots learn that Louisa will marry Captain Benwick, not Captain Wentworth, who travels to Bath in hopes of reuniting with Anne. Through the coincidence so common to romance, Wentworth overhears Anne speak of a woman's love. She characterizes it by adopting a wayfaring metaphor as "capable of bearing most rough usage, and riding out the heaviest weather." He is filled with hope that her love has survived their separation, confesses his feelings for her, and the two at last reunite with plans for marriage. While Anne previously allowed herself to be persuaded to reject her passions, neither she nor Wentworth, both wiser and more mature, can be dissuaded to abandon their love.

Critics have long held that Austen created Admiral and Mrs. Croft as predictors of Wentworth and Anne's future positions, with FEMINIST CRITICS paying special attention to the Croft's childlessness, as well as to Mrs. Croft's role in the "guidance" of their movements. She even accompanies her husband aboard ship. However, Austen never indicates that Anne will do the same, choosing instead to emphasize the separate natures of the younger couple's interests and activities.

Austen's nephew, J. E. Austen-Leigh, published a now famous biography of his aunt in 1871 in which he supplied canceled chapters from *Persuasion* that she had removed due to its weak contrivance. Critics felt this helped prove Austen a witty and intelligent writer. The chapters, which Austen pulled from her text, represent the sole manuscript containing all editing marks still existing today, housed in the British Museum. Like Austen's other novels, *Persuasion* remains readily available in print and electronic forms, and has spawned Web sites of its own. A movie version was made in 1995.

BIBLIOGRAPHY

Ross, Josephine. *Jane Austen: A Companion.* New Brunswick: Rutgers University Press, 2003.

Rzepka, Charles. "Making It in a Brave New World: Marriage, Profession, and Anti-romantic Ekstasis in Austen's *Persuasion.*" *Studies in the Novel* 26, no. 2 (Summer 1994). Expanded Academic ASAP. Infotrac. Triton Col. Lib. Available online. URL: http://web3.infotrac.galegroup.com/. Downloaded April 12, 2004.

Wilkes, Joanne. "Song of the Dying Swan?: The Nineteenth Century Response to *Persuasion.*" *Studies in the Novel* 28, no. 1 (Spring 1996). Expanded Academic ASAP. Infotrac. Triton Col. Lib. Available online. URL: http://web3.infotrac.galegroup.com/. Downloaded April 13, 2004.

PHINEAS FINN: THE IRISH MEMBER ANTHONY TROLLOPE (1869)

Anthony TROLLOPE continued throughout his career to focus his novels on everyday life. As the trend of SENSATION FICTION faded in the late 1860s, Trollope began a new trend of his own, adding the theme of politics to his writing. Intensely interested in politics, as evidenced by his own defeat as a parliamentary candidate in 1867, the novelist added as the second book in his second major series, the Palliser sequence, *Phineas Finn: The Irish Member.* As the title indicates, it followed the fortunes of its protagonist, Phineas Finn, during his political career. It also contains Trollope's trademark multiple overlapping subplots, all of which turn on romance, but of the sensible, rather than sensational, type. The first book in the series, *CAN YOU FORGIVE HER?* (1864) focused on romance between Lady Glencora and her husband, Plantagenet Palliser, destined eventually to become prime minister in a later book. Some of the characters from that novel reappear in *Phineas Finn,* which emphasizes political machinations far more strongly than did the first. Trollope developed his characters first in serial form in *St. Paul's Magazine,* which he edited, between October 1867 and May 1869.

Phineas Finn is an appealing character, son of a doctor, a Roman Catholic, charismatic and handsome, and an immediate attraction for females. While supposedly promised to his Irish sweetheart, Mary Jones, when Finn moves to London following his election for the borough of Loughshane, he attracts Lady Laura Standish. She starkly contrasts with the provincial Mary in her ambition to marry a politically connected man. He boards with Mr. and Mrs. Bunce, emphasizing his lack of a home, a persistent theme throughout the novel noted by critic W. J. McCormack. The emphasis on homelessness and alienation represented a deviation for Trollope, whose novels had always emphasized the importance of home and family. He suggests Mary's connection to home in both a symbolic and literal sense for Finn, who remains ever aware of her presence, even while living away and romancing other women. Finn will vacillate throughout the novel in matters romantic and political, but will remain grounded by his love for Mary and Ireland, as well as through the influence of his highly principled mentor, Joshua Monk.

Intelligent and persuasive, Lady Standish has knowledge of, and interest in, politics that lead her to support Finn, although she is forced by financial circumstances to marry the wealthy Scots laird Robert Kennedy, particularly following Finn's rescue of Kennedy from a dangerous situation in the streets of London. Attacked by a gang who attempt to choke him, Kennedy escapes only due to Finn's interference. As Finn's personal life is revealed, his political life takes shape with the new reform bill supported by Finn's Liberal Party. Finn eventually succeeds to a junior minister post, then resigns when he chooses to support Irish tenant-rights, a factor in the Home Rule demanded by Ireland. He learns through that harsh lesson that he must sometimes support his party even when he did not agree with its policies. Again, Trollope asks readers to consider the meaning of home, in both a political and personal sense, as he asks them to consider Finn as both a public and private figure.

Unable to resist temptation, Finn begins to romance Violet Effingham, who lives with the judgmental Lady Baldock. Her situation as an orphan supports the continued emphasis on homelessness in the novel. Threatened by Finn, Violet's suitor Lord Chiltern, brother to Lady Laura, challenges him to a duel while the two are away from England. During that conflict, they regain a respect for one another that leads Finn to break the love triangle, and Lord Chiltern wins Violet as his bride. Trollope interestingly makes Lord Chiltern, the male, experience the higher passion. When he proposes to Violet and she does not answer him, "he rushed at her, and, seizing her in his arms, kissed her all over,—her forehead, her lips, her cheeks, then both her hands, and then her lips again. 'By G—, she is my own!' he said." She reacts by quietly taking a seat on a sofa and deciding she would accept and at least "be gracious to him."

Finn's romances continue as he next begins a relationship with a rich widow, Madame Max Goesler, who has been the companion of the elder duke of Omnium and whom he meets at the dining table of the Pallisers. Although Madame Goesler proposes to Finn, offering to become his wife and make him wealthy, he has become discouraged with politics as well as foreign romance. At the novel's conclusion, he returns to Ireland to marry Mary, even though "she had not the spirit of Lady Laura, or the bright wit of Violet Effingham, or the beauty of Madame Goesler," but she loved him with a most "satisfying devotion." He does fear he may not find employment, believing that "men were afraid of him, thinking that he was unsteady, arrogant, and prone to failure." After two months in Dublin, he receives his reprieve from his former political friends, an appointment as Inspector of Poor Houses in the County of Cork.

While the novel is political, it continually emphasizes domestic issues, both in the small arena of individual homes, and in the broader geographic sense. The issue of violence exists not only in the street for Kennedy, but also in his home, as Trollope strongly intimates that he abuses Lady Laura. She will later exit the home to go into a self-appointed exile, living apart from her husband who will actually attempt to kill Finn in the sequel to the novel, *PHINEAS REDUX* (1873). Chiltern's horse, Bonebreaker, suffers a violent death after breaking his own bones. As McCormack notes, an early zoo scene suggests that potential violence causes the necessity for cages separating the animals. The appearance at the zoo of another character, Aspasia Fitzgibbon, known for the "violence of her jokes," further emphasizes the potential for violence that finds parallel in human interaction. When Miss Fitzgibbon invites comparison of Kennedy to a monkey, she touches on another topic of great concern to Trollope's era, that of evolution. While Trollope felt unqualified even to edit papers concerning the theories of Charles DARWIN during his stint at *Saint Paul's Magazine,* he includes oblique references to the theories throughout the novel.

Many critics have searched for real-life figures that might have inspired Phineas Finn, and politicians have been suggested. Some suggest that Trollope may be the incarnation of Finn. Finn's insecurity regarding his family's poverty, his public shyness, and lack of social success represent characteristics shared by Trollope. The author had served Ireland through his post office job, quitting at about the same time Finn would have assumed his political post. As for women, Trollope developed a lifelong relationship with the American feminist Kate Field, whom he enjoyed teasing. Mirroring Finn's loyalty to Mary, however reluctant, Trollope would likely never have considered committing the slightest impropriety outside his marriage.

Like all works of fiction, however, *Phineas Finn* does not claim to be a historical or factual account regarding either individuals or politics. As proof, Trollope fictionalizes the results of a crucial reform movement in Parliament, in which England's Liberal government of 1866 suffered defeat due to a revolt by radicals who wanted secrecy in balloting as part of parliamentary reform. Their move ushered in a new Conservative government, led partially by Benjamin DISRAELI, which would introduce reform that included secret balloting. In the novel, the reform fails, and the Liberals return to power, introducing a movement of their own. This countered claims by Trollope's critics that he based Mr. Turnbull, a character supporting the secret ballot, tenant rights, defense cuts, and the disestablishment of the Church of England, on the real politician Radical leader John Bright. As noted by Trollope's biographer, Gloria Glendinning, to claim any Trollope character literally "is" a true figure "is to misunderstand the high art of Trollope's castle-building fantasies, and the low cunning with which he judged how close to draw his parallels—which by definition can never meet." The novel, while never rated among Trollope's best work, continues to be widely read and enjoyed.

BIBLIOGRAPHY

Glendinning, Victoria. *Anthony Trollope.* New York: Knopf, 1993.

McCormack, W. J. Introduction to *Phineas Finn* by Anthony Trollope. London: J. M. Dent, 1997, xvii–xxxv.

PHINEAS REDUX ANTHONY TROLLOPE (1874)

Anthony TROLLOPE published the fourth entry in his Palliser series, *Phineas Redux,* first as a serial in *The Graphic* between July 1873 and January 1874. It appeared seven years after its predecessor, PHINEAS FINN, which introduced the adventurous protagonist named in the novel's title. At the conclusion of that novel, Phineas had left behind a political career in London to return to Ireland, having become discouraged with the political scene. He married his childhood sweetheart, Mary Jones, and took the post of Inspector of the Cork Poor Houses.

In *Phineas Redux,* Mary has died in childbirth, leaving Phineas a grieving widower. Surprised by a call from his former Liberal peers to reenter the political fray, he accepts the offer. Upon his arrival in London, readers recognize many of the characters with whom he interacts, as Trollope continues his previous story line. He enjoys the hospitality of a former love interest, Violet Effingham, who in the previous novel married Lord Chiltern, with whom Phineas had fought a duel, although the two men later became great friends. Lady Laura Standish, who also once loved Phineas but was forced by family to marry the depressing Robert Kennedy, has left her husband to travel abroad with her father. Another of Phineas's previous admirers, wealthy widow Madame Max Goesler, renews her interest in the young Irish barrister. She continues as companion to the elderly duke of Omnium, despite gossip regarding their relationship.

Believing Phineas to have caused his separation from Lady Laura, Kennedy attempts to shoot Phineas, missing his mark. The event threatens to grow into a scandal, thanks to Phineas's previous nemesis, the radical journalist Quintus Slide, but an injunction prevents publication of a letter from Kennedy in Slide's possession. With the help of friends, Phineas manages to hide the facts of the events, but Kennedy descends into depression, then madness, eventually committing suicide. However, Phineas cannot cover up the scandal of a public argument with the cabinet minister Mr. Bonteen, who is jealous of Phineas's rise to power. After a visit to his Club, Bonteen is murdered. When suspicions fall on Phineas, his arrest and trial leave him exhausted. His friends surround and support him, helping him retain a "manly dignity," although he wonders whether Mary is looking down at his plight from heaven. Thanks to his lawyer, Chaffanbrass, and the efforts of Madame Max Goesler in finding crucial evidence, Phineas is acquitted. The husband of Lady Eustace, Mr. Emilius, is suspected as the murderer, but his guilt cannot be proved.

Phineas continues his political career with reelection as Tankerville's representative. He subsequently refuses an important post, once again disillusioned with the political and legal systems. While he once fantasized about public service, "during the last few months a change had crept across his dream—which he recognized but could hardly analyse. He had seen a man whom he despised promoted, and the place to which the man had been exalted had at once become contemptible in his eyes. And there had been quarrels and jangling, and the speaking of evil words between men who should have been quiet and dignified." When the duke of Omnium dies, Madame Max Goesler will accept none of the inheritance he designated for her, proving her innocent motivation in their relationship. Because of her refusal, Adelaide, a cousin of Plantagenet Palliser, the title character for Trollope's series, may marry the poor but honorable Gerard Maule. Phineas again finds happiness in marriage to Madame Max Goesler, although he decides to leave politics permanently.

Trollope focuses on traditional themes, those that often held his interest. In addition to politics, in which he, like Phineas, had become increasingly disillusioned, Trollope regularly examined the plight of women in high-society Victorian England, of interest to FEMINIST and NEW HISTORICISM CRITICS. In one early discussion,

Lady Chiltern tells Phineas that men seldom have sympathy for women: "What man thinks of changing himself so as to suit his wife? And yet men expect that women shall put on altogether new characters when they are married, and girls think that they can do so. Look at this Mr. Maule, who is really over head and ears in love with Adelaide Palliser. She is full of hope and energy. He has none. And yet he has the effrontery to suppose that she will adapt herself to his way of living if he marries her." The book remains popular, available in electronic and print versions.

BIBLIOGRAPHY
Glendinning, Victoria. *Anthony Trollope*. New York: Knopf, 1993.
Halperin, John. *Trollope and Politics: A Study of the Pallisers and Others*. Totowa, N.J.: Barnes & Noble, 1977.

PICARESQUE

The term *picaresque* derives from the Spanish word *pícaro,* meaning "a rogue." The original Spanish works focused on an adventurer who often lacked virtue, exulting in cheating people less sharp-witted as they traveled about a prescribed countryside. A light writing style encouraged the reader to find such novels of character and the swindles and insults meted out by the protagonist humorous and entertaining, rather than events requiring moral judgment. Miguel de Cervantes Saavedra's *Don Quixote de la Mancha* (1605) offered the first well-known example of a picaro in its windmill-adverse protagonist and adventurer. The most famous, and oft-imitated in English, example of the form appeared in a 1724 French work title *Gil Blas of Santillane* by Alain Ren Le Sage; it became a model on which others, such as Daniel DEFOE, Henry FIELDING, Tobias SMOLLETT and Charles DICKENS, based their stories. The picaresque, also known as rogue fiction, in its purest form remained popular in England only into the early 1800s, with works such as The ADVENTURES OF HAJJI BABA OF ISPAHAN (1824) by James MORIER supporting the tradition.

BIBLIOGRAPHY
Castillo, David. R. *(A)wry Views: Anamorphosis, Cervantes, and the Early Picaresque*. West Lafayette: Purdue UP, 2001.
Goad, Kathleen M. *Notes on Chosen English Texts: Hajji Baba of Ispahan*. London: James Brodie, 1962.

PICKWICK PAPERS, THE CHARLES DICKENS (1837)

Like most novels by Charles DICKENS, his first, with the formal title *The Posthumous Papers of the Pickwick Club,* appeared in installments, running from April 1836 through November 1837, before appearing in volume form as *The Pickwick Papers.* The novel represented an amazingly productive time in Dickens's life. As he wrote the last 10 episodes on Pickwick, he produced just as many installments of what would be his second novel, OLIVER TWIST (1838), representing, as estimated by critic Jane Smiley, around 90 pages per month, while also producing essays, speeches, and other creative work. Both works appeared first in BENTLEY'S MISCELLANY, a periodical edited by Dickens, which involved his reviewing and preparing 80 manuscripts each month for publication.

A travel novel with loose plot structure, it follows the on-the-road adventures of the Pickwick Club, compared of Samuel Pickwick and three friends, Tracy Tupman, Augustus Snodgrass, and Nathaniel Winkle. Because Pickwick is a trusting soul, he often provides the focus for various comic situations, simplistic, yet humorous and engaging, as they represent awkward and challenging moments with which readers can identify. He displays his lack of grace on horseback and on ice, his inability to hold his liquor, his lack of orientation by ending up in a stranger's lodging room, and innocently leading his landlady to incorrectly believe he wants to marry her. Most episodes advance a moral, and their melodramatic tone reveals the author's lack of maturity as a writer. However, one future trademark is present—Dickens's traditional enormous number of characters. Those included in these stories represent all social levels and various employment, from medical students to actors, musicians to coachmen, poets to watermen, lawyers to soldiers, lovely women to plain, and most remain memorable. Some speak with accents represented by Dickens's drop of a letter or insertion of an apostrophe, as with the servant Sam Weller's Cockney speech, allowing Dickens to develop a rhythm through dialogue. Weller is probably the favorite character of the novel, balancing Pickwick's innocence with street smarts, and acting as an effective foil.

While not as strongly representative of Dickens's social causes as would be his later characters, several figures in *Pickwick Papers* ask readers to consider the perceived differences in the quality of individuals based on arbitrary social standards. Pickwick does not escape the author's trademark dark side, as one of his experiences involves imprisonment, hinting at Dickens's own boyhood experience when his honest, but foolish, father landed in a debtor's prison. This first novel does not contain the sharp irony for which Dickens would became famous, but it does offer some sharply satiric moments, such as with the Eatanswill election.

BIBLIOGRAPHY
Smiley, Jane. *Charles Dickens.* New York: Penguin Putnam, 2002.

PICTURE OF DORIAN GRAY, THE OSCAR WILDE (1890)

Oscar WILDE's version of the Faust temptation tale, *The Picture of Dorian Gray,* proved so popular that it was later converted to drama and opera and imitated by other writers in subsequent novels. It first appeared in 1890 in *Lippincott's Magazine* and was lengthened later that year for publication as Wilde's only novel. The magazine and book versions vary in ways that, while not substantially altering the story's theme of the perils of temptation, do alter some metaphors and cultural inferences. Students of the work should read both versions to observe how Wilde simultaneously fashioned a traditional GOTHIC tale and one particularly suited to fin de siècle interests, including that of modern art.

A naive orphan, Dorian Gray wishes that he might remain young while his portrait ages, proclaiming that his 18-year-old form will mock him as he grows old. But when the portrait painter, Basil Hallward, picks up a knife to destroy the picture, Dorian stops him, saying that would be like murder. That scene foreshadows an ironic later turn of events when Dorian, grown callous and desperate, murders Hallward. Hallward's friend, Lord Henry Wotton, plays the part of the devil in Wilde's tale, granting Dorian his wish for eternal beauty and youth in exchange for his soul. Lord Henry's evil, destructive personality is balanced by

Hallward's good and generous nature, his artistic bent rendering him a positive and creative character.

By making Gray a high-society figure, Wilde suggests the duplicity and hypocrisy inherent to the London social scene in which he immersed himself. He also inserts his trademark ironic humor, evident, for example, in a discussion between Lord Henry and Hallward of Gray's plan to marry the actress Sibyl Vane. When Hallward exclaims over the foolishness of such an idea, Henry responds, "Dorian is far too wise not to do foolish things now and then, my dear Basil." Hallward rejoins that one can hardly marry "now and then," to which Henry answers, "Except in America." Wilde's light tone indicates a less-than-serious attitude toward his dark story, which he enlivens with his trademark witty repartee between characters. Following Sibyl's suicide, Gray sinks into low-class activities while remaining active on the social scene. The physical weight of the aging portrait, borne at one point by the doomed Hallward as he struggles upstairs under its load, metaphorically suggests the weight of Gray's sin. As Gray dies at the book's conclusion, the portrait is magically restored to its original quality, suggesting a rebirth of creativity.

In the novel's preface, Wilde anticipated criticism of his book by famously writing, "There is no such thing as a moral or immoral book. Books are well written or badly written. That is all." *The Picture of Dorian Gray* remains popular and is available in print and electronic text.

BIBLIOGRAPHY

Haslam, Richard. "Wilde's *The Picture of Dorian Gray*." *The Explicator* 61, no. 2 (Winter 2003): 96–98.

McCormack, Jerusha Hull. *The Man Who Was Dorian Gray*. New York: St. Martin's Press, 2000.

PILGRIM'S PROGRESS, THE: FROM THIS WORLD TO THAT WHICH IS TO COME JOHN BUNYAN (1678–1684)

The son of a village tinker with little schooling, John Bunyan experienced a tremendous religious conflict that led him to write a book in two parts that would become one of the most popular of all times, translated into dozens of languages. In composing his ALLEGORY, *The Pilgrim's Progress*, he ironically achieved what those far more steeped in the literary tradition of classical romance could not. Eschewing romantic couplets, idealized figures, and fantasized landscapes, he adopted a colloquial prose to produce a tale containing a brilliant illusion of reality, an absolute requirement of the genre later to be called the novel. Thus, his work proved seminal to the development of the British novel.

Writers of Bunyan's 17th-century era remained caught between the challenge of producing a new genre and their adherence to a tradition that refused to characterize humans engaging in acts clearly inherent to a lower more animalistic nature than the romance tradition allowed. Because Bunyan remained ignorant of that conflict, he could write undistracted. While burdened with a DIDACTIC message and distinct moral goal, *The Pilgrim's Progress* also depicted a flawed hero who encouraged the reader identification later inherent to the novel. A second crucial component aligning Bunyan's work with the novel was its convincing suggestion of reality. Finally, Bunyan's use of characters and events to suggest moral qualities resulted in the production of a consistently unified body, prefiguring the unity that would prove so important to defining the novel.

It was partially the absence of artifice that allowed Bunyan's Part I of *Pilgrim's Progress* (1678) to be so accessible. He had proved the value of his natural style in his 1666 autobiography, *Grace Abounding to the Chief of Sinners*, where he claimed in his preface that he could have "steeped" his writing "into a style much higher" and "adorned all things more than here I have seemed to do," but resisted a type of "play" in order to "be plain and simple, and lay down the thing as it was." He continued that approach in *Pilgrim's Progress*, allowing readers to enjoy as well as learn from that book. In his description of a man on a journey toward truth, Bunyan adopted a classical plot format familiar from Homer's *The Odyssey*. His protagonist Christian undergoes all of the challenges present in the classical QUEST, including personal loss, a call to adventure, the use of various guides, a descent into darkness, emergence from darkness to continue his quest, the encountering of monsters, and even a return home, although home is redefined as the heavenly home available to those who best life's temptations, experience conversion, and cross the river, long a symbol of new life.

Advancing reader identification, Bunyan adopts the element most essential to the quest, that of the vision/dream world. His entire story takes place as a dream, suggesting to readers that the dream may directly relate to the dreamer himself, as had their own cultural mythology long before psychologists such as Carl Jung expressed it as theory. Not only then might they identify with Christian, but they also could, by extension, identify with Bunyan himself. In addition, Christian's lack of a name in the opening of Part I advances reader identification through its characterization of the protagonist as any man. Even when his name is made clear, it places Christian within a group, that of the followers of Christ, failing to individualize him. Furthermore, when the story opens Christian is engaged in the act of reading, yet another suggestion that Bunyan's audience will find much in the tale to which they may relate.

Christian's book tells him he presently lives in the City of Destruction, where he is condemned not only to death but also to judgment. Both literally and figuratively bearing a burden, he leaves his home and family, who refuse to join him, to embark on a lengthy journey, helped by the figures Faithful and Hopeful. They encounter many other figures, both bad and good, including the monstrous Apollyon, killed by Christian; Lord Hategood, responsible for Faithful's execution; Giant Despair; Mr. Worldly Wiseman; Ignorance; Talkative; and By-ends. In Part II, published in 1684, Christian's family joins him, bringing their neighbor Mercy. During the continued journey they meet additional allegorical characters, including Mr. Ready-to-halt, Mr. Honest, Mr. Stand-fast, and Mr. Despondency with his daughter Much-afraid.

In arguing that *The Pilgrim's Progress* influenced the novel's development, critics suggest it moves beyond the traditional Christian allegory familiar to audiences through morality plays to introduce a strong sense of reality in its setting as well as in the symbolic characters themselves. Critic Dorothy Van Ghent explains that Bunyan uses "physical topography," such as his muddy Slough, the Hill Difficulty, the well-used highway that acts as a gathering place for verbal exchange, valleys, mountains, and bog to bring a note of recognition to readers. She extends her point to argue that without such sharp evocation of physical setting, Bunyan could not have suggested its psychological effect on the travelers. Scene and "atmosphere" exist not only outside the pilgrims but also inside, evoking a "spiritual topography." Readers make their own connections between physical circumstances and morality, without Bunyan's needing to insert an explanation, prefiguring the use of more subtle and suggestive symbolism that would become a crucial element in fiction. His artistry in creating familiar imagery evoked a spontaneous multiple reading for multiple meanings, based on audience instinct and "stored experience." Van Ghent also discusses the manner by which Bunyan shapes characters, his clear and unadorned language allowing him to create a tone that immediately identifies character types; they divulge their own personalities through syntax and idiom. For instance, Obstinate's series of exclamatories, complete with exclamation marks, helps readers perceive him as rushing toward opinions without thinking about his statements.

To be sure, *The Pilgrim's Progress* contains passages of debate about doctrine that may dull a modern reader's senses, and Bunyan's didactic intentions are never deep beneath the surface of his tale, told in sometimes jarring episodes rather than as a smooth, uninterrupted plot. However, literary critics agree that its unrivaled popularity had much more to do with its entertainment value than its moral guidance. It would advance development of the novel and have an enduring effect on later fiction, as evidenced by William Makepeace THACKERAY's reference to it in the title of his own popular work VANITY FAIR (1848).

BIBLIOGRAPHY

Batson, E. Beatrice. *John Bunyan's Grace Abounding and the Pilgrim's Progress: an Overview of Literary Studies, 1960–1987.* New York: Garland, 1988.

Mullett, Michael A. *John Bunyan in Context.* Pittsburgh: Duquesne University Press, 1997.

Van Ghent, Dorothy. *The English Novel: Form and Function.* New York: Harper and Row, 1959.

PORTER, JANE (1776–1850)

Older sister to Anne Maria Porter, a ROMANCE writer, Jane Porter produced one of the earliest historical romances. History proved important to her, evidenced by the fact that she often discussed her famous ancestor, the Elizabethan poet Endymion Porter. While she was famous for her HISTORICAL FICTION, she also served as an editor, specifically of sayings by 17th-century Protestant martyr and poet Sir Philip Sidney. Her novel *Thaddeus of Warsaw* (1804) focused on the Polish member of the Sobieski family as he joins the Polish patriots to march against the Russians. Following their defeat, Thaddeus sees his estate destroyed, and he moves to England, where he is later discovered to be the lost son of minor English nobility. Her hero arouses the admiration of the protagonist in Mary BRUNTON's novel, *SELF CONTROL* (1810). Porter's *Thaddeus of Warsaw* and *The SCOTTISH CHIEFS* (1810) influenced others as well, including the famous novelist and Porter's childhood friend, Sir Walter SCOTT. In *The Scottish Chiefs,* she portrays Wallace and other warriors of his time as heroes deserving praise, beginning with the murder of Wallace's wife by the English governor of Lanark. Porter enjoyed the company of royals, and George IV's request that she write a book focusing on his ancestor resulted in the publication of *Christian of Luneburg* (1824). She also published novellas with her sister, Anna. Her works continue to be studied and remain available in book form and electronic text.

BIBLIOGRAPHY

Dennis, Ian. *Nationalism and Desire in Early Historical Fiction.* New York: St. Martin's Press, 1997.

Sage, Lorna. "Porter, Jane." *The Cambridge Guide to Women's Writing in English.* Cambridge: Cambridge University Press, 1999, 505.

PORTRAIT OF A LADY, THE HENRY JAMES (1881)

Henry JAMES's *The Portrait of a Lady* appeared first as installments in *The Atlantic Monthly* (1880–81) where readers recognized in its protagonist, Isabel Archer, a more mature version of the title character from his earlier novella, *DAISY MILLER* (1879). Like Daisy, Isabel is an American on tour in Europe, searching for adventure. A poor orphan, she becomes a ward of her wealthy aunt, Lydia Touchett, and travels to England to live with her for a time. She becomes fond of her aunt and her uncle, a retired American banker, and grows close to their sickly son Ralph, who suffers from tuberculosis. Dynamic, bright, and desirous of independence, Isabel captures the attentions of several would-be lovers, hitting the romantic mark suggested by her surname. She is made all the more desirable when, following his father's death, Ralph gives a portion of his vast wealth to Isabel. She refuses marriage offers from a wealthy American named Casper Goodwood, as well as from the older Touchett neighbor and English aristocrat, Lord Warburton.

When Isabel travels to the continent with her aunt and her aunt's friend, Madame Merle, she meets Gilbert Osmond in Florence. She remains unaware of Madame Merle's previous relationship with Osmond, with whom she had a daughter named Pansy. Impressed by Osmond's erudite manner, Isabel falls in love with and marries him, despite her previous determination to remain independent. Although she believes Osmond will encourage her independence and spiritual growth, his true cruel nature is revealed following their marriage. He takes on Isabel as a private project, working to break her spirit as he spends her money. When she learns that Ralph is on his deathbed, she plans a return to England, which Osmond refuses. He threatens to place Pansy in a monastery, and Isabel at last learns of Osmond's relationship with Merle, whom he doomed to suffer existence as his mistress.

Isabel could remain in England, but she shows her strength and determination by deciding to return to her horrible husband in order to protect Pansy, an innocent victim of her parents' excess. In that decision, she achieves some measure of redemption from her former error in judgment that led to marriage with the shallow, evil Osmond. Her determination strengthens her to refuse a second offer from Casper Goodwood, who, as suggested by his name, proves of far better character than Isabel's husband. She returns to the very servitude she had always abhorred, embracing self-denunciation and the acceptance of responsibility as a form of freedom.

An avid observer of human nature, James chose to deal with the ethics of choice in his novel, allowing his plot to unfold based on the inner workings of his characters' minds as they discovered the painful difference between their naive American approach to life and that of the more sophisticated Europeans. In suggesting that the novel offers a portrait of Isabel, he invites readers to observe his artful reproduction of human nature and its reaction to its surroundings. He presents the age-old tension between the power of the individual will and that of circumstance, where the will's vision becomes blurred by wealth and refinement. His works are continuously read and studied; *The Portrait of a Lady* has also been converted to various media forms.

BIBLIOGRAPHY

Chen, Shudong. *Henry James: The Essayist Behind the Novelist.* Studies in American Literature, vol. 59. Lewiston, N.Y.: Edwin Mellen, 2003.

Van Ghent, Dorothy. *The English Novel: Form and Function.* New York: Harper & Row, 1953.

PRIDE AND PREJUDICE JANE AUSTEN (1813)

The main character of Jane AUSTEN's *Pride and Prejudice,* Elizabeth (Lizzy) Bennett, has the unenviable position of the second child in a family of five daughters and represents one of the sister-pair characters for which Austen became famous. Her older sister, Jane, also her closest confidante, was likely based on Austen's own sister, Cassandra, with whom she shared a bond as close as any of her fictional characters. This support system proved crucial in Austen's first novel, *SENSE AND SENSIBILITY* (1811), and she turns to it again through the sisterly relationship in *Pride and Prejudice* as an important defense against the fickle attacks of society's demand for order based on arbitrary and often cruel social conventions.

Due to an entailment of Mr. Bennett's property, it must pass to the closest male relative, which will leave the Bennett daughters with no place to live following their father's death. Therefore, they must each pursue husbands, a challenge better accepted by her sisters than by Elizabeth, who is by far the family's most independent female character. Through her, Austen could express her indignation over the limited rights held by women, particularly property rights, which were almost nonexistent for females. Lizzy also

acts as a mouthpiece for Austen in revealing her contempt for the confining social structure that directed marriageable women through a round of activities that placed them on display for men seeking wives. Situational irony proves ripe when Mr. Bennett clearly favors Elizabeth as his most intelligent daughter, yet still regards her as a liability, a woman whose wit and mental acuity may prove burdensome in a man's world.

While some FEMINIST CRITICS see Elizabeth as an early feminist, others question her supposed separation from social convention when, in fact, it actually consumes her, as it does the other female characters. However, her obsession reflects itself in constant criticism of the system, enabling her to later break her bonds through self-realization. She represents the "prejudice" in the novel's title but eventually acknowledges that she herself is guilty of stereotyping the opposite sex, a charge she often lays at the feet of the novel's male characters. That epiphany leads to her reward of true love with a man who is her intellectual equal, Fitzwilliam Darcy, and whose quiet emotion will well support her own more public passions.

Darcy, although he represents the "pride" in the novel's title, remains worthy of consideration as representative of a new type of hero, promulgated through Austen's series of novels that considered society from her realistic view, based on her own experience. Darcy contrasts with the heroes of Austen's contemporary women authors of SENSATION FICTION, whose exaggerated and hyper-emotional accounts of romantic situations Austen found detestable. In Darcy, Austen portrays a person much like herself, an individual who analyzed what she observed with wit and common sense. Darcy did not represent the brooding BYRONIC HERO of Gothic fiction any more than he did the hyperbolic hero of sensation fiction. Austen does not even waste much page space in the physical description of her hero so common to those other forms of popular fiction. Darcy reveals himself through action and sparse dialogue, forcing the reader to observe his character as closely as Austen herself observed her society. He embodies the character flaw of pride from the novel's title. But the reader remains open to deciding whether his pride has some basis in wisdom, rather than in an empty claim to money and title. His own best friend, Charles Bingley, describes Darcy as "clever," "haughty," and "reserved," but due to Bingley's trustworthy character, readers understand those adjectives compose only a partial description of Darcy. Bingley also makes it clear that Darcy possesses intelligence, a factor that will allow him to change his views should he be convinced to do so.

Austen avoids the plot weakness common to the traditional romance, which demands that the heroine be consumed by love at first sight. Elizabeth Bennett develops affection for Fitzwilliam Darcy over time, a more realistic rendering of romantic involvement. Thus, readers watch her enjoy the self-reinvention common to Austen's heroines, who, never simplistic, must suffer assorted challenges to their beliefs in order to reach an epiphany and act upon their realization. Lizzy neither gushes nor swoons, but instead, when Darcy at last becomes her fiancée, informs him that she intends to continue her teasing and baiting of him, a challenge that he willingly accepts from this woman, his equal in wit. Due in part to her fashioning of female protagonists like Elizabeth Bennett, Jane Austen became known for framing her novels in a satisfying REALISM that served to PARODY British social mores and gender stereotypes.

BIBLIOGRAPHY

Austen, Jane. *Pride and Prejudice.* 1813. Reprint, New York: Viking Penguin, 1997.

Watt, Ian. Introduction. *Jane Austen: A Collection of Critical Essays.* Englewood Cliffs, N.J.: Prentice Hall, 1963.

Wolfe, Jessee. "Jane Austen and the Sin of Pride." *Renascence* 51, no. 2 (Winter 1999): 110–132.

PRIME MINISTER, THE ANTHONY TROLLOPE (1876)

The Prime Minister took its place as Anthony TROLLOPE's fifth book in the Palliser sequence. It first appeared as a serial between November 1875 and June 1876, before its issue in four volumes. While many of Trollope's contemporaries, including Henry JAMES, labeled it a political novel (one so dull, by James's account, that he could not read it), it offers readers much more in the way of rich character interaction than an ideological treatise. As do all Trollope's novels, *The Prime Minister* places British society under a microscope, revealing its blemishes as well as its luster through themes including family and romance. Several of the characters were familiar to Trollope's wide readership as they appeared in earlier novels, although readers would not necessarily have read the novels in order.

Trollope begins with the traditional conflict inherent to the love triangle. Emily Wharton is desired by two men, one a man of action but doubtful family background named Ferdinand Lopez, and the other his foil in every way, the well-to-do barrister Arthur Fletcher, who has been in love with Emily since she was a child. Emily's father naturally prefers Fletcher to Lopez, but Emily marries for love, taking Lopez as her husband. Her choice proves disastrous, as Lopez wastes little time in convincing her to help him borrow money from her father to invest in his questionable schemes.

As Emily's fortunes seem both literally and figuratively to fade, readers simultaneously observe Plantagenet Palliser, duke of Omnium, ascend to become prime minister. With the help of his beautiful wife, Glencora, he entertains various members of the government at the posh Gatherum Castle, "giving dinners, balls and garden parties," hoping to hold together a shaky coalition. The impetuous and strong-willed Glencora decides to promote the political fortunes of Lopez, not realizing his true nature. She urges him to take part in the Silverbridge by-election, despite the fact that the duke separates himself from her plans. Although a battle occurs in the political arena, the most noticeable conflict remains between Lopez and Palliser, and Trollope offers little by way of a satisfying political framework. Additional themes, including the social system, demand more attention than do the workings of the government. The fair-haired Fletcher defeats Lopez, whose inept characterization as a stereotyped Jew in the vein of Shylock has surprised Trollope aficionados. While Lopez begins the novel as rather questionable, he maintains an air of breeding and formality. When the duchess asks whether he would not like to try politics, he replies that he is "into another groove," having become "essentially a city man—one of those who take up the trade of making money generally." He goes on to comment that his vocation "disgusts" him, and that, although he likes money well enough, it seems an "insufficient use of one's life." That he would even reflect aloud about wealth sets him apart from Trollope's other well-bred characters, and would have been enough to stamp him an undesirable by Trollope's readership.

Lopez's political loss reflects badly on the duke, who turns on his wife, accusing her of betrayal. The duke is caught up in one of Lopez's schemes to increase his wealth when Lopez demands that he pay all his bills in order to protect Glencora's reputation. While Palliser may not be the best politician, his integrity remains admirable and proves a more valuable commodity, in Trollope's view, than political astuteness. Only when Phineas Finn, the subject of two previous novels by Trollope, speaks to the House of Commons are its members distracted from what looms as a possible scandal for the duke. Trollope allows fate to reach its usual balance, as Lopez ruins himself, then commits suicide in a leap from a train. Emily at first feels responsible for her husband's death and is ill for several weeks. Eventually she recovers and notes some feeling for Fletcher, whom she had allowed at one point to "caress" her before Lopez's death. For that reason, she feels ashamed, even though her husband "had ill-used" and "betrayed her [. . .] sought to drag her down to his own depth of debasement." However, after a respectable amount of time, the faithfully patient Fletcher convinces Emily to marry him, despite his family's early protest over his selection of the shamed widow. They begin a happy life together, but the prime minister's party loses its support.

The Pallisers first appeared before their marriage in Trollope's THE SMALL HOUSE IN ALLINGTON (1862–64), and then in CAN YOU FORGIVE HER? (1864–65), again in PHINEAS FINN (1867–69), and PHINEAS REDUX (1873–74), and would make their final appearance in *The Duke's Children* (1879–80). Trollope's accomplishment in retaining a coherent story line through literally thousands of pages (*The Prime Minister* alone is more than 280,000 words) remains remarkable. Some critics believe he stumbled in making Lopez Jewish, then abandoning him to a flat stereotype about whom Fletcher remarks, "I wish I could have the pleasure of shooting him as a man might a few years ago." Unlike George ELIOT, whose *DANIEL DERONDA* (1876) offered a more balanced study of what it meant to be a Jew in England, Trollope ignores the broader significance of Lopez's Jewishness. However, that flaw does not negate the value of his novel. The perfectly executed dialogue and detailed view of high-society life and strain remain eminently readable, and his exploration of women's rights is of interest to FEMINIST CRITICS. Emily is little more than chattel to Lopez, while the duchess contrasts through her independent nature.

BIBLIOGRAPHY

Glendinning, Victoria. *Anthony Trollope.* New York: Knopf, 1993.

McCormick, John. Introduction to *The Prime Minister* by Anthony Trollope. New York: Oxford University Press, 1983, vii–xviii.

PRINCESS CASAMASSIMA, THE HENRY JAMES (1886)

Henry JAMES first published *The Princess Casamassima* as a serial in *The Atlantic Monthly* between September 1885 and October 1886. He reintroduces the princess as a character from a previous novel, *RODERICK HUDSON* (1875), in which the sculptor Hudson dies in a thunderstorm following rejection by the fascinating Christina Light, who marries Prince Cassamassima. In James's later novel, Christina has divorced the prince, but remains a princess, interacting with the novel's protagonist, Hyacinth Robinson, a young boy whose mother died in prison. James offers his traditional view of social CLASS STRUCTURE relationships, which lead to a proletarian revolution and the ultimate destruction of Hyacinth, whose lack of a firm self-identity leads to tragedy. Jamesian scholar Shudong Chen writes of James's attraction to the British tradition as one "that encourages people to *feel* the clashes and impacts of perspectives, perceptions, and prejudices in relation to place, people, and personality as an inevitable part of life." That tradition is reflected in Hyacinth's experiences, imagined, James wrote in the preface to his novel, as he walked once through London and mused what impact the city's great promise of social and intellectual fulfillment might have on an individual allowed only to observe it as an outsider.

In 1880s London, Hyacinth lives with a dressmaker named Miss Pynsent in a lower-class neighborhood. He regrets having seen his mother, proclaimed murderer of his father Lord Frederick, only one time. Taking an apprenticeship with the bookbinder Eustache Poupin, Hyacinth learns of communism from the exiled Frenchman. He also meets Paul Muniment, a revolutionary who convinces Hyacinth to join a secret society dedicated to the rights of the workingman. James begins his traditional investigation of the psychological truth by examining the fragile mental makeup of the symbolically named Hyacinth. Torn between his desire to relate to the proletarian movement and his perceived connection to his aristocrat father, his sense of self begins to disintegrate.

Participating in the revolutionary proletariat group, Hyacinth meets Princess Casamassima. No longer wealthy, and an aristocrat mainly by title, she wants to know more about the seamier side of London. The princess represents James's interest in bourgeois guilt in the face of poverty and the exploitation of the working class. Miss Pynsent dies and her death foreshadows the death of Hyacinth's never independently formed vision of the revolution held by Muniment and his supporters. They function within James's idea of the British tradition that views social clash as an inevitable part of their lives. But when Hyacinth disconnects with England and its prejudices to visit Europe, his ideas about social revolution change, leading him to no longer want to be a part of the society. When its members assign him the duty of assassinating a duke, he resists and is visited by the princess, who plans to assume the duty herself. However, she arrives too late and finds Hyacinth dead from suicide. Hyacinth serves as an example of James's belief that individual lives cannot be determined by politics or social movements but, rather, are dependent on personal and individual reactions to life's challenges.

The Princess Cassmassima did not prove nearly as popular as James's early novels. His focus on the slow development of self-awareness on the part of Hyacinth could not hold readers' attention as some of his more fanciful romantic novels had. James's total and complete devotion to realism remains evident in this story of a young boy who is an orphan in the most literal sense, as well as in the figurative sense of his possess-ing no political vision or social inspiration he could claim as his own.

BIBLIOGRAPHY

Bell, Milicent. *Meaning in Henry James.* Cambridge: Harvard University Press, 1991.

Chen, Shudong. *Henry James: The Essayist Behind the Novelist.* Studies in American Literature. Vol 59. Lewiston, N.Y.: Edwin Mellen, 2003.

Daugherty, Sarah B. *The Literary Criticism of Henry James.* Ohio University Press, 1981.

King, Jeannette. *Tragedy in the Victorian Novel: Theory and Practice in the Novels of George Eliot, Thomas Hardy, and Henry James.* New York: Cambridge University Press, 1978.

PRINCESS OF THULE, A WILLIAM BLACK (1873)

During a decade when readers and critics were beginning to view fiction and the novel as a source of subtle intellectual exercise, they also continued to enjoy novels for sheer entertainment's sake. *A Princess of Thule,* by William Black (1841–98), fell into this category. Like works by Black's contemporaries OUIDA and R. D. BLACKMORE, his books featured local color, raising the setting to such an obviously important position as to make it a character adding conflict to plot. Black's picturesque Scottish scenery featured virtuous heroines no reader could fail to love, including the protagonist of *A Princess of Thule,* Sheila Mackenzie. Readers are assured of both Sheila's wholesome character and the novel's sentimentality when they read in the first scene of her departure. She waves a white handkerchief from the deck of a vessel to her father on land, where "he knew that a pair of eyes that had many a time looked into his own—as if with a faith that such intercommunion could never be broken—were now trying, through overflowing and blinding tears, to send him a last look of farewell."

While later generations of readers found Sheila's QUEST story predictable, though still enjoyable, they appreciated more the splendid description of the rugged Scottish coast at which Black excelled. Its symbol as the life force of the Scottish community is obvious to practitioners of NEW CRITICISM, while NEW HISTORICIST critics can easily observe the effect of

Black's nationalism on his art. No doubt is left in readers' minds that the sea ruled the area when they read descriptions such as, "Everywhere around were the traces of the glacier-drift—great gray boulder of gneiss fixed fast into the black peat-moss, or set amid the browns and greens of the heather," and "There was not much moon now, but a clear and lambent twilight showed all the familiar features of Loch Roag and the southern hills; and down in the bay, you could vaguely make out *Maighdean-mhara* rocking in the tiny waves that washed in on the white shore." A FEMINIST CRITICAL reading notes the efforts of Sheila as she struggles to understand her own "notions of wifely duty," while characters such as Mrs. Lavendar emphasize the place of mature women in society.

The novel inspired American writer L. Frank Baum, best known for his *Wizard of Oz* series, to write a successful musical titled *The Maid of Arran*. Black's novel remains in print.

BIBLIOGRAPHY

McGovern, Linda. "The Man Behind the Curtain: L. Frank Baum and the Wizard of Oz." Literary Traveler. Available online. URL: http://www.literarytraveler.com/spring/west/baum.htm. Downloaded on March 7, 2004.

PRISONER OF ZENDA, THE ANTHONY HOPE (1894)

Of Anthony HOPE's many short stories and various novels, *The Prisoner of Zenda* remains his best known and enjoyed, praised by contemporaries such as Robert Louis STEVENSON, followed by its less successful sequel, *Rupert of Hentzau* (1898). The novel offers a fairy-tale-like quality, replete with princes and princesses, kings, chivalry and castles, but it adopts as a setting an area of Europe that would disappear after 1918. Hope supposedly got the idea for his novel while walking down the street one day when the name Ruritania popped into his head, followed by his sighting two men on the street who, although unrelated, bore a startling resemblance to one another. He later placed his English protagonist, Rudolf Rassendyll, in the fictional setting of Ruritania, where his resemblance to the king would lead to many adventures. While the novel could have dissolved into so much fantastic fluff, Hope anticipates and holds at bay readers' skepticism with his inclusion of such realistic detail that his audience recognizes the era as their own and the setting as eastern Europe.

Rassendyll reflects Hope's own youthful self, a young well-to-do man about town who can wield a sword, shoot a gun, and sit a horse well. Always ready to travel, he decides to journey to Ruritania to view the coronation of Rudolph the Fifth. He has more than a passing interest in the country, due to an 18th-century affair between Rudolf the Third of Ruritania and the wife of a Rassendyll ancestor. Rassendyll has inherited that ancestor's remarkable red hair, long nose, and captivating blue eyes, physical aspects immediately recognized upon his arrival in the foreign country. Rudolph is away much of the time, earning a reputation as a playboy drinker and remaining unfamiliar to his countrymen. They prefer his illegitimate half-brother, Duke Michael. Also known as Black Michael, the duke rules Elphberg Castle and has invited Rudolph to enjoy a few days of hunting at his lodge. Two hunters who exclaim over his resemblance to Rudolph discover Rassendyll in the duke's forests. The king greets him jovially and drinks all night long with his newfound "cousin," ignoring his aides' pleas that he sleep before a journey the next morning to Zenda to meet with his guard and ride on to Streslau to his coronation. Black Michael's steward presents a special bottle to the king, who passes out after drinking it.

The following morning, the king is too drunk to complete his coronation, and his men fear that Black Michael will take the throne. They convince Rassendyll to play the king's role temporarily, and the predictable occurs when he must continue in the role for some time following Black Michael's kidnapping of the real king. He falls in love with Princess Flavia, who also possesses flaming hair and who pays him homage following his coronation, as she is actually the next in line to the throne as the king's cousin. They fall in love, to Flavia's surprise, as she has never enjoyed the king's company. Eventually the king is restored to the throne after being rescued from Black Michael and his adventuresome band, one of whom is the raucous Rupert of Hentzau, subject of Hope's sequel. Flavia remains faithful to her duty, marrying Rudolf, although she adores Rassendyll. He writes at the book's conclusion that he sees her as noble for her act: "She has followed where her duty to her country and her House led her, and is the wife of the King, uniting his subjects to him by the love they bear to her, giving peace and quiet days to thousands by her self-sacrifice." His knowing her has ennobled him, as he vows to live as "becomes the man whom she loves."

The popular novel appeared in a 1937 screen version with a star-studded cast, including Mary Astor, Ronald Colman, Douglas Fairbanks, Jr., Raymond Massey, and David Niven. Twenty-first-century readers continue to enjoy the ever-popular plot of mistaken identity, while FEMINIST CRITICS enjoy Flavia's position as far more heroic in her sacrifice than any of her male counterparts. The book is readily available in electronic as well as print version.

BIBLIOGRAPHY

Household, Geoffrey. Introduction to *The Prisoner of Zenda,* by Anthony Hope. London: J. M. Dent & Sons, 1984, vii–xiii.

PRIVATE MEMOIRS AND CONFESSIONS OF A JUSTIFIED SINNER JAMES HOGG (1824)

Private Memoirs and Confessions of a Justified Sinner, long acknowledged as the best of the many works by James Hogg (1770–1835), focuses on the religious and political conflict in Scotland at the end of the 18th century. The first portion, labeled "a Detail of Curious Traditionary Facts, and Other Evidence by the Editor," assumes a threatening, yet morbidly comic, tone to relate details of Colwan, Lord of Dalcastle's, stormy marriage to a woman described as "the most severe and gloomy of all bigots to the principles of the Reformation." When the laird enters her bedchamber on their wedding night, he finds her reading evangelical materials, demure and resistant of his attentions. As the laird abandons all hope of a joyous union, and falls asleep while his wife prays, Hogg inserts a passage illustrative of the strange humorous edge he adds to his macabre tale, noting that the laird began "to sound a nasal bugle of no ordinary calibre—the notes being little inferior to those of a military trumpet."

The symbolically named Rev. Robert Wringhim, a Calvinist bigot himself, enjoys long conversations with Mrs. Cowan, whose weak mind he can easily confuse. Eventually she bears her husband an heir, whom they christen George, and Lord Dalcastle prizes his son above all his possessions. The conflict between Dalcastle and Rev. Wringhim escalates, particularly after Mrs. Cowan has a second son, which Dalcastle believes to be the reverend's offspring. He agrees to materially support the boy but refuses to associate with him, and Wringhim takes him in, naming him after himself. The young Robert Wringhim matures to become the novel's villain, eventually meeting and then stalking George, shadowing his every move. Mixed in with the escalation of tension between the brothers are scenes emphasizing the political and social unrest characteristic of that era.

When George is stabbed in the back, Dalcastle is filled with grief over the loss of his "only hope." The old man dies, accusing the forces of "faith in absolute predestination" as having ruined his house. His companion, Miss Logan, thereafter calling herself Mrs. Logan, assumes that the Wringhims and Dalcastle's wife plotted to destroy George and, by extension, Lord Dalcastle. Robert Wringhim Colwan, now the young laird, is testified against by Mrs. Logan and her friend, but when authorities arrive, "It was in vain that they overturned beds, raised floors, and broke open closets: Robert Wringhim Colwan was lost once and for ever. His mother also was lost; and strong suspicions attached to some of the farmers and house servants to whom she was obnoxious, relating to her disappearance."

In a macabre turn, the second portion of the book is composed of a memoir retrieved one hundred years later from the younger Wringhim's grave, a literal voice from the past. In eerie psychologically disturbing detail, of interest to PSYCHOANALYTIC CRITICS and revealing the troubled mind that led Wringhim to suicide, Wringhim reveals he was a serial killer. He first murdered his supposed father, the Rev. Wringhim, then his brother and his mother, all at the bidding of a supposed stranger. The stranger represents the evil side of Wringhim's nature, through which he convinces himself that he was acting as God's servant, killing evil beings in exchange for eternal glory. That Rev. Wringhim and Mrs. Cowan, declared devotees of evangelicalism are murdered by their own deranged offspring, who is convinced that he commits the crimes in God's name, proves highly ironic. At the memoir's conclusion, Wringhim discovers the so-called stranger, in reality his delusional alter-ego, to be Satan. Physical evidence at the grave, including a perfectly preserved corpse with a skull that has sprouted horns, suggests the devil in the end claimed Wringhim's soul.

Although the work did not receive the attention it deserved until the 20th century, it is now available in print and electronic form.

BIBLIOGRAPHY

Simpson, Louis Aston Marantz. *James Hogg: A Critical Study.* New York: St. Martin's Press, 1962.

PROFESSOR, THE CHARLOTTE BRONTË

(1857) Although written in 1846, Charlotte BRONTË's first novel, *The Professor,* would not be published until after her 1855 death. Clearly autobiographical, it served as a model for her later, more fully developed version of her experiences in Brussels as a young woman in *VILLETTE* (1853). While focusing on the romantic experiences of its protagonist and first-person point-of-view narrator, William Crimsworth, a character some critics feel represented a disguised woman, it also stresses themes including the poor working conditions of England's industrial force and the few choices available to women who wished to work.

An orphan who attended Eton and did not get on well with other members of his family, Crimsworth abandons his unpromising position as a Yorkshire mill clerk for a career as a teacher, a profession in which he hopes to advance his natural talents. The reader understands his attitude toward women when he speaks of studying his sister-in-law's face in search of finding a spark of intelligence in its pretty, blank countenance, a search that fails. The fact that her husband, Crimsworth's brother Edward, enjoys success as a businessman suggests that an ideology of materialism may not be conducive to an intellectual and superior life.

Crimsworth takes a position in Brussels and becomes enamored of Frances Henri, an intelligent Anglo-Swiss Protestant fellow teacher and lace-mender.

She first impresses Crimsworth as having "at least two good points—mainly, perseverance and a sense of duty." Their relationship is complicated by the presence of the egotistical and manipulative headmistress, the Catholic Zoraïde Reuter, to whom Crimsworth is clearly physically attracted, despite his protestation that he is not moved by a woman's physical beauty. Crimsworth marries Frances and lives hopefully with their son Victor, whose name suggests Crimsworth's accomplishment of his modest plans for a future. In the closing lines of the novel, he learns from his fellow former-worker at the mill, Hunsden, of his brother's burgeoning fortune and news of his "first flame, Zoraïde," who apparently has gained a good deal of weight. Because the news is delivered by a man neither Crimsworth nor Frances views as completely desirable, the reader understands that the couple need feel no jealousy over their former rivals.

The quiet novel remains important as an example of the developing approach toward REALISM in fiction during the mid-19th century. While Brontë's best-known novel, *JANE EYRE* (1847), was not well received due to what contemporary critics viewed as its immoral and unchristian themes, Elizabeth GASKELL's *The Life of Charlotte Brontë,* published a few months before the release of *The Professor,* had softened the public's attitude toward the author. The intrigue it raised over Brontë's life likely affected the gentle critical reception of the posthumously published novel. Considered by many as representing a flawed narrative approach, the novel later gained interest as study of the Brontë sisters increased.

BIBLIOGRAPHY

Gaskell, Elizabeth. *The Life of Charlotte Brontë. Edited by Charles Lemon. London: Routledge/Thoemmes Press,* 1997.
Malone, Catherine. "'We have learnt to love her more than her books': The Critical Reception of Brontë's *Professor.*" *The Review of English Studies* 47 (May 1996): 175–188.

PROVOST, THE JOHN GALT (1822) John

GALT had written four Scottish regional stories for William Blackwood's *BLACKWOOD'S EDINBURGH MAGAZINE* before he published his fifth, *The Provost,* in that journal. The series boosted Galt's reputation beyond that of a writer of biographies, articles, travel books, and academic texts; he had become a novelist of note. In March of 1822, the journal announced that *The Provost* would appear in early May. As Blackwood read the sections forwarded to him by Galt, he was said to have been so delighted that he refrained from his usual editing.

The novel's 2,000 copies sold in a fortnight that May, as reported in the June edition of *Blackwood's,* with a second edition printing already selling out. The poet Samuel Coleridge had a copy, as did many other notables. Coleridge wrote that he knew of "no equal in Literature" to Galt's depiction in the egoistic narrator Mr. Pawkie of the "Irony of Self-delusion." Pawkie opens explaining his plan to win election. He became "jocund," even with the beggars, in order to ingratiate himself with others and gain their support, as he "had a part to play in the public world." He modestly admits, "I became, both by habit and repute, a man of popularity in the town, in so much that it was a shrewd saying of old James Alpha, the bookseller, that 'mair gude jokes were cracked ilka day in James Pawkie's shop, than in Thomas Curl, the barber's, on a Saturday night." In another example fraught with the irony noted by Coleridge, Pawkie describes how he managed to soothe an agitated acquaintance who was jealous over the choice of another to lead a volunteer brigade. The pompous self-assurance is laced with a curious sympathy that enriched Galt's ironic tone: "Mr. Dinton, who was a proud man, and an offset from one of the county families, I could see, was not overly pleased at the preferment over him given to Mr. Pipe, so that I was in a manner constrained to loot a sort a-jee ["bend a bit sideways"], and to wile him into good-humour with all the ability in my power . . . and I winknit to Mr. Pipe, as I said this, and he could with a difficulty keep his countenance at hearing how I so beguiled Mr. Dinton into a spirit of loyalty." Critics later compared Galt's style to that of Daniel DEFOE, with its sharpness of detail rendering scenes as clear as a series of photographs.

Laced with rich humor and an obvious grasp of the Scots vernacular, the novel focused on Mr. Pawkie's three rounds of service in the office of provost, or mayor, of his town. Pawkie allows insight into Scotland and its people as he relates how he entered and progressed through a political life, contrasting his provincial experiences with the sophistication of the outside world. His setting of Gudetown reflected precisely many details of Galt's hometown of Irvine. Critics later hailed the novel as a perfect meld of the pre–INDUSTRIAL REVOLUTION local Scottish scene with the political sphere. Manipulative of a forgiving political system, Mr. Pawkie stands as the ultimate self-aggrandizer, pleasant and kind, but thorough in serving his own needs before those of others.

The Bodleian Library has a first edition, and printed and electronic versions remain readily available.

BIBLIOGRAPHY
Ashley, A. J. "Coleridge on Galt." *Times Literary Supplement* (September 25, 1930): 757. Scott, P. H. *John Galt.* Scottish Academic Press, 1985.

PSYCHOANALYTIC CRITICISM   Originally psychoanalytic criticism utilized Freud's psychoanalysis techniques to analyze literature, gaining it the name Freudianism. However, as Freud's theories fell out of favor, and additional schools of psychoanalysis developed, the title changed to psychoanalytic criticism, denoting a dependence on various psychological theories. With no pure aesthetic theory of its own, but rather a focus on human behavior as its tool, psychoanalytic criticism has been adopted by other schools of criticism, including FEMINIST CRITICISM and MARXIST CRITICISM, for use in their analysis of literature.

Freud's belief in the neurosis of all artists forms the basis for psychoanalytic criticism. The artist avoids mental illness through his creative projects. Because a literary text results from an artist's dream, it can be interpreted as a dream can, with the assumption that the dream is actually a secret desire. One analyzes literature for meaning as one would a dream.

Another critical approach based its methods on the practices and beliefs of Freud's most famous student, Carl Jung. Jung believed in the collective unconscious, a seat in the mind of all cumulative human experience and knowledge in response to certain myths shared by all mankind that grow from ancient archetypes. Those archetypes are images or figures that represent repeated experience, such as the seasons and life and death. Recurrent story plots and character types, such as those of the QUEST and the ROMANCE hero, deeply affect the reader, awakening images in the collective unconscious.

An application of Jung's methods to literature is called archetypal criticism, as practiced by the Canadian critic Northrup Frye. Frye diagrammed a circle he labeled a Monomyth, with the four seasons placed at the north and south poles, as well as the east and west sides. They each represented separate phases corresponding to specific human experiences, such as summer relating to the romance phase, telling a story of independence, joy and celebration, and winter to the anti-romance phase, telling a story of imprisonment and fear. At first, psychoanalytic criticism focused on determining motivations of the author, and later on the author's characters and their motivations. Eventually, the manner by which readers interpret the characters also became important to this critical approach.

BIBLIOGRAPHY
Bressler, Charles E. *Literary Criticism: An Introduction to Theory and Practice*. Englewood Cliffs, N.J.: Prentice Hall, 1994.

Frye, Northrup. *Anatomy of Criticism*. Princeton, N.J.: Princeton University Press, 1957.

Klein, George. *Psychoanalytic Theory: An Exploration of Essentials*. New York: International Universities Press, 1976.

Wright, Elizabeth. *Psychoanalytic Criticism: Theory in Practice*. London: Methuen, 1984.

PUNCH'S PRIZE NOVELISTS WILLIAM MAKEPEACE THACKERAY (1847)   *Punch's Prize Novelists* is a collection of PARODY pieces spoofing his contemporary novelists by William Makepeace THACKERAY. Thackeray took aim at the style and format of such popular British and American writers as Edward BULWER-LYTTON, James Fenimore Cooper, G. P. R. James, Charles LEVER, and Benjamin DISRAELI. He focused on themes such as heroism that became important to his own novel written during the same time frame, *VANITY FAIR* (1848). The collection first appeared in the periodical *Punch*, to be later issued in volume form, titled *Novels by Eminent Hands*. Later critics considered brilliant Thackeray's ability to suggest his personal ideal of the novel form by reflecting the deficiencies in the practice of his contemporaries.

QUARTERLY REVIEW, THE Founded in 1809 by John Murray of the powerful publishing house of the same name, as a Tory rival to the Whig periodical the *Edinburgh Review,* the *Quarterly Review* was distinguished through association with Sir Walter SCOTT, among others. Many readers felt the tone of the *Edinburgh Review* had grown too pompous, ignoring good taste and offending readers in its articles on national affairs. Thus, the conservative *Quarterly Review* debuted with much support and fanfare. While clearly Tory in nature, it inherited a devotion to literature and the arts from publications such as the *European* during its last decade of print, which critically proclaimed that the new *Quarterly Review* advocated "every antiquated system of government." Murray received a letter declaring that the *Edinburgh Review* had lost is "proper character and usefulness," spurring him to found a competitor. Centuries later, despite criticism against its contents, the critical work produced by the *Quarterly Review* stood the test of time as to its quality. However, in its early years, it gained a reputation for heaping unmerited criticism on some artists, in an attempt to counter Whig opinion. One of its nastiest reviews focused on the poet John Keat's famous work, *Endymion,* in 1818, and supposedly contributed to his early death.

Scott himself had been an important reviewer for the *Edinburgh Review* until he also became disgusted with it. Taking interest in the rival venture, he helped develop the focus of *Quarterly Review,* which would carry work by him, Robert Southey, Samuel Rogers, Prime Minister Gladstone, William Makepeace THACKERAY, and Edward BULWER-LYTTON. Scott's letters indicate he was the single most important force during the periodical's first years. Until he felt confident that the new venture would succeed, he proved its leading editorial spirit. The first public praise of Jane AUSTEN, in a review of her novel *EMMA* (1814) by Scott, appeared in *Quarterly Review,* as did Scott's review of his own works, *Tales of My Landlord.* The periodical had a long chain of general editors, some of whom decreased its emphasis on literary criticism. By 1895, when editor Arthur R. D. Elliot took over the editorship, its once high standings had diminished. It regained them again and became one of the longest-published quality periodicals, contributing significantly to the development of literary criticism. With its rival *Edinburgh Review,* it dominated 19th-century letters and continued to be read through 1967.

BIBLIOGRAPHY
Graham, Walter. *English Literary Periodicals.* New York: Octagon Books, 1966.

QUENTIN DURWARD SIR WALTER SCOTT **(1823)** Sir Walter SCOTT's *Quentin Durward* was one of three novels Scott issued in 1823. The first edition was printed in 10,000 copies, the sheets carried in bales by steamship to London on May 16, 1823, where binders worked the night through. Hurst, Robinson & Co. had purchased 8,180 books for £7600, and by 11 A.M. on May 17, the novels arrived in three volumes to booksellers, with additional sets sent into the country.

The novel features Scott's trademark interest in history, focusing on 15th-century France during the reign of King Louis XI. At that time, the monarch was feuding with Charles the Bold, Duke of Burgundy, whose ambitions included taking over the throne and acquiring more territory. William de la Marck, whose nickname, the Wild Boar of the Ardennes, threateningly foreshadows problems to come, supports Louis's cause by agreeing to create a rebellion against Burgundy's forces in Liège. At this point, the novel's protagonist, Quentin Durward, is introduced as a young Scottish Archer, a guard serving Louis whose responsibility becomes to provide safe escort for the Burgundian heiress, Isabelle de Croye. She is traveling to Liège seeking the protection of its bishop, Louis of Bourbon, to avoid an arranged marriage to Count Campo-Basso, an Italian who serves Burgundy. Scott laces the QUEST with various anticipated dangers from Burgundy, but adds interest by indicting William de la Marck's activities as irresponsible. His wild nature, of course, is what recommended him to Louis, but Scott makes clear the double-edged sword such a rebel may represent. He balances la Marck's irresponsible proclivities with Durward's level-headed approach, inserting detail regarding his hero's nature: "With more than his wonted care, [he had] seen that every thing was prepared for the day's journey. Girths and bridles, the horse furniture, and the shoes of the horses themselves, were carefully inspected with his own eyes, that there might be as little chance as possible of the occurrence of any of those casualties, which, petty as they seem, often interrupt or disconcert traveling." Thus Scott emphasizes that erring on the side of caution, as Shakespeare had suggested in his history plays, is often the preferred approach.

Durward's characterization as "the Scot," a frequent reference, who brings much needed steadfastness in a volatile situation, would interest NEW HISTORICIST CRITICS, considering the popular views of Scots as perhaps too staid at times. Later Scott proves Durward's prowess in a scene of attack upon the bishop, writing that whoever had witnessed Durward's seemingly frantic activity, not understanding its motivation, might have labeled him "a raging madman." However, "whoever had appreciated his motives, had ranked him nothing beneath a hero of romance." He also tempers praise of Durward's heritage to emphasize that the value of the individual, not of any particular group, remains crucial. When Isabelle hopes to flee to Scotland for safety, Durward truthfully confesses, "I scarce know that my blood flows in the veins of an individual who now lives in my native land." He goes on to explain that clans continue to battle one another, "for little more than the pleasure of revenge and the lust of bloodshed," and would readily attack a representative of the French king. Durward does later meet up with his uncle, Le Balafré, and their respectful and affectionate interaction assures readers that family connections may supersede all political ties. Scott does not wander too far from his traditional support of his forbearers, as another character, Lord Crawford, declares of Durward, "My dear boy—my own lad! . . . Ye think like a Scot, every joint of you!"

When La Marck murders the bishop, Isabelle is physically and emotionally threatened, as are Louis's plans for control of Burgundy and his forces. However, the loyal guard Durward well fulfills his duties. He eventually confronts la Marck in a scene in which they are described as "the wolf and the wolf-dog." In a move that 21st-century readers would find amusing, Durward requests that his enemy wait for a few minutes while he helps Isabelle escape danger. Le Balafré takes over the fight with his two-handed sword and appears a short time later dangling La Marck's severed head. The novel concludes with Durward awarded Isabelle as the comely treasure that ends his quest, after Lord Crawford makes clear to King Louis that Durward is descended from Allan Durward, High Steward of Scotland. FEMINIST CRITICS find little to admire in the mostly passive characterization of Isabelle, who must play the trophy damsel-in-distress to Durward's hero.

Scott feels obliged to explain any deviations from historical accounts in his story, and he inserts various footnotes to that end. For example, he footnotes the murder of the bishop of Liège, Louis de Bourbon, to advise readers that he has collapsed history in the service of fiction, allowing the death to occur some 14 years previous to the true murder date of 1482, adding that a rumor of the bishop's murder had circulated during the year Scott chooses for that deed, 1468. Such painstaking attempts to be faithful to reality, in addition to Scott's usual healthy infusion of detail, did help educate his audience regarding events crucial to England's future, due to its relationships with France.

This popular tale was transformed into a stage play and an opera and remains eminently readable for romance-novel aficionados. While not Scott's most successful book, it remained respectably popular; the original manuscript of 224 leaves is housed in the National Library of Scotland.

BIBLIOGRAPHY

Alexander, J. H., and G. A. M. Wood, eds. "Essay on the Text." *Quentin Durward* by Sir Walter Scott. Edinburgh: Edinburgh University Press, 2001, 403–446.

Bird, Elizabeth. *The Sources and the Literary Character of Scott's Quentin Durward.* Champaign/Urbana: University of Illinois Press, 1933.

Duncan, Ian. *Modern Romance and Transformations of the Novel: The Gothic, Scott and Dickens.* Boston: Cambridge University Press, 1992.

QUEST   The quest story has existed for centuries, Homer's *The Odyssey* serving as the prototypical example. Also known as the hero's journey, plot aspects of the quest often appear in the modern English language ROMANCE NOVEL and may be identified in international literature. In a classical quest, the male hero completes a journey focused on "winning" a prize through the application of wits and daring. As the plot developed, females also became hero figures and, beginning in the latter half of the 19th century, the quest could focus on an internal, or psychological, journey toward self-realization or actualization, generally signaled by an epiphany on part of the protagonist. Closely related is the Arthurian romance legend, later used in the service of English nationalism, as well as the religious myth of the pursuit of the Holy Grail.

The journey itself must be understood as a series of steps, labeled and analyzed by critics and philosophers such as the 20th-century's American expert on mythology Joseph Campbell. His *The Hero with a Thousand Faces* (1949) and *The Power of Myth* (1988) use an approach based on the psychoanalytic theories of Carl Gustav Jung, who used the theory of the collective unconscious to explain the similarities in the hero story across cultures, which lack any knowledge of one another's existence. Jung believed that such an unconscious dwells in the depths of the psyche, housing the cumulative knowledge, experience, and imagery of the entire human race. From that accumulation emerged, in literature, recurrent plot patterns, images, and characters, referred to as archetypes, that can arouse emotions, due to each individual's collective unconscious. His archetype theory can be applied to an understanding of traditional SYMBOLS, such as the seasons, colors, water, and other objects representing human ideas and emotions, many of which occur in the quest. Canadian critic Northrup Frye gained fame using archetypes to develop a codification of symbols, seen in his famous work *The Secular Scripture: A Study of the Structure of Romance.*

The initial stage of the hero's journey may be referred to as "Of the Ordinary World," featuring the man/woman who acts as protagonist of the story tending to everyday matters. The second stage, called "Departure," depicts substages such as "A Call to Adventure," when a particular occurrence stirs conflict in the hero over whether to depart a comfortable routine to accept a challenge to seek a reward outside his normal sphere. That call may be met with "Refusal," when the protagonist for a time declares he will not embark on the journey. He immediately suffers a loss, of someone or something dear, and then comes to understand the importance of the task he has been given. He is then observed "Crossing the Threshold," indicating he physically departs his familiar world to enter a new one. The journey from home undertaken by countless young male protagonists in countless novels who leave to "seek their fortunes" represents this stage. While Odysseus traveled over water, the journey may be cross-country, through outer space, or through the subconscious.

In the "Initiation" stage, the hero must meet, and prove his valor or intelligence in, a number of challenges, which may be physical, spiritual, or psychological. He may have help from a guide figure, as Athena helped Odysseus, or Obi-Wan Kenobi and Yoda help Luke Skywalker in the popular *Star Wars* movie trilogy. With this guidance, the hero may fight monsters, deal with shape shifters, witches, or other enchanted beings, see and interpret visions, be caught up in disorienting magical spells, and learn new skills affording him new powers. The hero will also suffer a loss during the journey, often of the guide, which may plunge him into depression or cause him to feel he cannot complete the journey. This necessitates a renewal of purpose, moving the hero into the next stage, labeled "Descent." He may undertake a literal descent; Odysseus descended into Hades to consult with past heroes, collecting their wisdom. Hades may be represented by any number of dark locations, generally reached by a movement downward, whether into a cave, a tunnel, dark woods at the bottom of a hill, or a concrete bunker. An example of these stages may be clearly identified in the biblical story of Jonah and the whale. Jonah is ordered to make a journey, he refuses, attempts to hide, and loses his independence when he is swallowed by a whale. The belly of the whale represents an archetypical symbol, a dark, forbidden, frightening, sometimes deadly location, into which the hero descends. The colloquial phrase "in the belly of the whale" or "in the belly of the fish" indicates a threatening retreat from the real world where a person may be tested.

Once the hero gains the necessary knowledge, he emerges, moving literally upward or outward from the low ground, reemerging with renewed strength and confidence. While he may be further challenged, he will successfully reach his goal, procure his treasure, and begin the final stage, "The Return Home." The hero may at first refuse or resist, necessitating an event to convince him, or the return may become a lengthy quest on its own, as was that of Odysseus; it may also be completed quickly and without event.

An additional stage might involve a responsibility on the hero's part to share what they have learned, through storytelling and writing, as in the German version of an INITIATION story that traces the development of a writer, called a *Künstlerroman*. The BILDUNGSROMAN, which features the development of a young person into maturity, may feature many aspects of the quest. Examples are legion, and include romance-genre novels by Sir Walter SCOTT, Charles DICKENS, Gothic-genre novels by the BRONTË sisters, Henry FIELDING, seafaring tales by Frederick MARRYAT, and adventure/survival tales by Robert Louis STEVENSON and Sir Henry Rider HAGGARD. Modern darker versions of the quest may be designed to question what constitutes success, or may exist as ironic quests, in which no reward is gained by the protagonist, or the protagonist even loses his/her life or a grasp on the meaning of life or self-identity. Works by Thomas HARDY offer excellent examples, as do works incorporating the supernatural or science fiction, such as Mary SHELLEY's *FRANKENSTEIN*.

BIBLIOGRAPHY

Campbell, Joseph. *The Hero with a Thousand Faces*. 1949. Reprint, Princeton, N.J.: Princeton University Press, 1968.

———. *The Power of Myth*. Edited by Betty Sue Flowers. New York: Doubleday, 1988.

Fraser, Robert. *Victorian Quest Romance: Stevenson, Haggard, Kipling and Conan Doyle*. Jackson, Miss.: University Press of Mississippi, 1998.

Frye, Northrup. *The Secular Scripture: A Study of the Structure of Romance*. Harvard University Press, 1976.

Luttrell, Claude. *The Creation of the First Arthurian Romance: A Quest*. Chicago: Northwestern University Press, 1974.

Schechter, Harold, and Jonna Gormely Semeiks, eds. *Discoveries: 50 Stories of the Quest*. Indianapolis: Bobbs-Merrill Educational Publishers, 1983.

QUILLER-COUCH, SIR ARTHUR (1863–1944)

Anthony Quiller-Couch, later affectionately known by his audience as simply "Q," was born in Bodmin in Cornwall. He was educated at Newton Abbott, Clifton and Trinity Colleges, where he distinguished himself. He then worked as a journalist and book reviewer before publishing his first novel, *DEAD MAN'S ROCK* (1887) at age 24. In that work, as well as many to follow, he incorporated his knowledge of Cornwall in their settings and wrote with a style later critics described as more "charming" than that of contemporaries. They included other followers of Robert Louis STEVENSON and his anti-realism approach, such as Henry Rider HAGGARD and Stanley J. Weyman, all of whom wrote ROMANTIC NOVELS often featuring QUEST plots. Quiller-Couch would later complete a romance of a Napoleonic prisoner in Scotland left unfinished by Stevenson upon his death in 1894 titled *St. Ives* (1898). He followed Stevenson's exhortation to write works that readers would find "absorbing and voluptuous," incorporating much adventure and detail into his fiction.

Q moved back to Cornwall in 1892, where he remained for 20 years. Additional novels included *Troy Town* (1888), *The Splendid Spur* (1889), and *The Ship of Stars* (1899), and his poetry volumes were *Verses and Parodies* (1893), *Poems and Ballads* (1896), and *The Vigil of Venus* (1912); he also published various short stories, still anthologized. Quiller-Couch enjoyed a brilliant career writing and editing for the Oxford University Press, editing in 1900 the first of several anthologies, the *Oxford Book of English Verse,* which he continued to edit in further printings. Also well known for his liberal political views, in 1910 he was knighted for services and two years later became the first King Edward VII Professor of English Literature at Cambridge. His popularity grew with the successful publication of collections of his learned lectures, *On the Art of Writing* (1916) and *On the Art of Reading* (1920). In the first, he urged his students to strive in all their writing, as Cambridge graduates, for accuracy, perspicuity, persuasiveness, and appropriateness. The lectures are readily accessible in electronic form. Q left a body of work enjoyed by scholars as well as fans of the romance and quest genres.

BIBLIOGRAPHY
Brittain, Frederick. *Arthur Quiller-Couch, a Biographical Study of Q.* New York, Macmillan, 1948.

R

RADCLIFFE, ANN (1764–1823)

Ann Radcliffe had a mixed social heritage. Her father came from a wealthy background, the Ward family being populated by physicians and bishops, while her mother's family included plumbers and glaziers. As a child, Ann spent much time with an uncle named Thomas Bentley. A convivial intelligent partner to Josiah Wedgwood of china-goods fame, Bentley lived in a mansion at Turnham Green, where Ann was exposed to various notables of the day. Bentley had business connections with the *GENTLEMAN'S MAGAZINE* as well as the *Monthly Review,* and would later encourage Radcliffe's publication. In 1722, the Ward family relocated from Holborn to Bath, where her father managed the Wedgwood and Bentley china displays. Ann matured in Bath, making friends with Harriet and Sophia Lee, well-known sister schoolmistresses. She married William Radcliffe in 1786 and began to write to entertain herself as William worked. A journalist himself as well as an attorney, Radcliffe encouraged his shy wife's writing. Her first novel, *The Castles of Athlin and Dunbayne,* appeared in 1789 at the time of the French Revolution. It was important in shaping her approach to the popular GOTHIC genre, of which she would become the undisputed queen. While the *Monthly Review* might have criticized an overabundance of dungeons and dark passages, Radcliffe's send-up of Shakespeare's *Macbeth* enjoyed popularity.

Radcliffe published *Sicilian Romance* (1790) to a better critical reception; it proved important due to its emphasis on a mysterious captive, a plot aspect widely imitated, for instance, in the character of Bertha from Charlotte BRONTË'S *JANE EYRE* (1847). She followed with the highly successful *The Romance of the Forest* (1791), but her reputation was made with her seminal Gothic *The MYSTERIES OF UDOLPHO* (1794), followed by the equally popular *The Italian* (1797), her response to M. G. LEWIS'S *The MONK* (1796). Sir Walter SCOTT found her work intriguing if not engaging, labeling it the "explained supernatural." He implied that Radcliffe proved singularly capable of explaining the mystical aspects of her work, not a compliment regarding her approach. Both parents died within two years, leaving Radcliffe a comfortable inheritance. She retired from writing after an astonishingly successful seven years and published no additional work, enjoying a quiet life of travel while nursing chronic mild asthma until her death in 1823. Her husband then published some of her poetry, along with a historical romance.

FEMINIST CRITICS find interesting Radcliffe's shaping of a feminine BILDUNGSROMAN in much of her fiction, incorporating a high degree of sexual threat against her heroines. PSYCHOANALYTIC CRITICS find Gothics intriguing in their emphasis on dark, damp, mysterious womblike passages and dreamlike sequences. Radcliffe's works remain readily available in print and electronic text, and serve as the focus of literary and critical study.

BIBLIOGRAPHY

Sage, Lorna. "Radcliffe, Ann." *The Cambridge Guide to Women's Writing in English.* Cambridge: Cambridge University Press, 1999, 518.

Showalter, Elaine. *A Literature of Their Own: British Women Novelists from Brontë to Lessing.* Princeton, N.J.: Princeton University Press, 1999.

Spender, Dale. *Mothers of the Novel: 100 Good Women Writers Before Jane Austen.* New York: Pandora, 1986.

RAMÉE, MARIE LOUISE DE LA   See OUIDA.

RASSELAS, PRINCE OF ABYSSINIA, THE HISTORY OF SAMUEL JOHNSON (1759)

Most critics note that Samuel JOHNSON's *History of Rasselas, Prince of Abyssinia,* is as much essay, parable, and cautionary tale as novel. Johnson sought to counter the popular optimistic philosophy supported by the French Rousseau and German Leibnitz, which held that introspection remains all-important, with emotion championing action. Johnson believed such focus on thought as solution would lead to no solutions at all. One must gather evidence, make a decision, and take action. Johnson was not alone in his protest, as the Frenchman Voltaire published *Candide,* his counter to the current belief, at almost exactly the same time. As a parable, *Rasselas* does not reflect realistic writing, its moral points overriding character and plot development. Johnson intended the action merely as basis for his argument. Supposedly he wrote the book in spare evening moments without revision in order to pay his mother's funeral expenses. He sent it to a publisher and received an immediate £100. The foreign setting appealed to readers, as did Johnson's detail, the result of knowledge he gained in part from translating *A Voyage to Abyssinia* by Father Jerome Lobo, although he did not strive particularly for a realistic setting, choosing an exotic locale.

The three sections of the book encompass the journey of Rasselas, an emperor's son who, like the Buddha, decides to leave his luxurious environment to become familiar with the real world. He slips away from his happy valley accompanied by his sister,

Nekayah, and Imlac, an aged philosopher. In Egypt, Rasselas's idealism regarding the outer world is challenged by its reality. Rasselas discovers that literature, love, philosophy, and science all promote false hope, grasped in moments of conflict by otherwise rational human beings. Through his various encounters, Johnson shapes philosophical discussions with a gently humorous style, inserting the aphorisms for which he became well known. In expounding on "The Dangerous Prevalence of Imagination," he makes clear the danger of immersion into thought, when man "must conceive himself what he is not; for who is pleased with what he is?" He continues regarding the results, which include "boundless futurity," as he, "amuses his desires with impossible enjoyments, and confers upon his pride unattainable dominion."

Johnson does leaves unresolved some important issues, emphasizing the value of discussion, as he deflates pastoral idealism in favor of more realistic action. The fact that Rasselas cannot resolve certain issues, discovering that sympathy for the ills of others offers no solution, allows Johnson to emphasize that wisdom without action proves useless.

In 1750, Johnson had written an essay for *The Rambler* which reminded writers of what he labeled "the comedy of romance," seen in Henry FIELDING's *TOM JONES* (1749), of their responsibility to the reading public not to draw their characters too realistically and not to romanticize criminal acts. He believed that "that observation which is called knowledge of the world will be found much more frequently to make men cunning than good," his statement prefiguring his own later work, designed to counter the philosophy of optimism. While Johnson's simplistic, enjoyable style recommends the book, it remains important mainly for establishing the novel as a vehicle for intellectual theory.

BIBLIOGRAPHY

Damrosch, Leopold. *Samuel Johnson and the Tragic Sense.* Princeton, N.J.: Princeton University Press, 1972.

Green, Donald, ed. *Samuel Johnson: The Major Works.* Oxford: Oxford University Press, 2000.

Phelps, Gilbert. *An Introduction to Fifty British Novels 1600–1900.* London: Pan Books, 1979.

RAVENSHOE HENRY KINGSLEY (1861)

Henry KINGSLEY has long been considered a "lesser novelist," one who failed to fulfill the destiny achieved by his famous brother, Charles KINGSLEY. However, of his novels *Ravenshoe* is considered his best, a fine example of his trademark quirky reality. His academic background at Worcester College, Oxford, informs his novels, many of which he peppers with scenes of athletic prowess on the part of young men likely to be intoxicated and described with adjectives such as "frantic," completing a portrait of "madmen."

As a wartime novel, set partially during the Crimean War, *Ravenshoe* features a wealthy Catholic protagonist named Charles Ravenshoe. Ravenshoe desires to disappear from England in an attempt to avoid accusations regarding his birth and true family, so he elects to fight in Crimea. Kingsley himself had traveled to Australia as a young man to make his fortune, only to suffer extreme isolation and privation, cut off from his supportive family for five years. He eventually became what was known as a "sundowner," a beggar who would turn up at day's end at way stations, asking for food and a place to sleep. Likewise, Ravenshoe's experiences prove emotionally disastrous, partly due to earlier confusion caused by his Jesuit confessor, and his betrayal by Lord Welter, a man he believed to be his friend. When Ravenshoe eventually returns to England, his will has been destroyed, echoing Kingsley's own return home following a disastrous stint in the Australian Mounted Police, where he experienced and took part in unspeakable brutalities. He returned having failed at everything he tried, dejected and disillusioned, but his brother took him in, and Kingsley again enjoyed a pleasant existence. Like Kingsley, Ravenshoe would enjoy the aid of close friends at home, helping him eventually to discover the true facts of his birth, allowing the novel to conclude on a positive note. Kingsley's stint as a war reporter during the Franco-Prussian war supplied him with the brutal detail and inhumanity that haunts the war scenes of *Ravenshoe*. While not a BILDUNGSROMAN, which mirrors its author's life, as does Charles DICKENS's *DAVID COPPERFIELD*, it yet contains several autobiographical aspects.

With questionable details and plot contrivances that challenge the reader's belief, such as an unrealistic switch of newborns, false charges of illegitimacy, convenient coincidence, and religious subterfuge, the novel nevertheless exudes a charm and presents in Charles Ravenshoe Kingsley's best-realized character. Although a hero subjected to the normal ideology of the melodrama, Ravenshoe remains flawed and complex. He learns the importance of humility, but at no time does Kingsley subjugate the adventure of romance to DIDACTICISM. He clearly writes to entertain, embroidering his exciting plot with an obvious sympathy for what one reviewer in the *Edinburgh Review*, October 1924, referred to as "splendour in decay . . . the forlorn present of a noble past."

BIBLIOGRAPHY

Scheuerle, William H. Introduction to *Ravenshoe* by Henry Kingsley. Lincoln, Neb.: University of Nebraska Press, 1967, vii–xxv.

READE, CHARLES (1814–1884)

Charles Reade, the son of a Tory squire, was born at Ispen House in Oxfordshire, where he matured with nine siblings. His father's comfortable income allowed him to be educated at private schools before he attended Magdalen College at Oxford, where he qualified as a barrister. Deciding against making a living at law, he moved to Edinburgh to learn medicine but found he did not have the constitution for that profession, either. Ironically, his knowledge of contractual law and copyright caused him to print most of his works privately, making exact dating of their production a challenge. He also constantly revised his works, converting them from drama to fiction and vice versa.

Reade served as bursar at Magdalen following an 1844 election and later held additional offices, but he spent most of his time at Birkenhead. His fascination with musical instruments, particularly the violin, caused him to search Europe for specific models. He took up management for a time in London but in 1851 began his career writing for the stage with a dramatization of Tobias SMOLLETT's well-known novel, *SIR PEREGRINE PICKLE*. After becoming vice president of Magdalen, he wrote his first successful drama, *Masks and Faces* (1852), collaborating with Tom Taylor. Deciding to devote himself to the stage, he began management of the Strand Theatre in 1852. Shortly thereafter another play of his, *Gold,* was performed. When he turned his hand to fiction writing, he published *Peg Woffington,* converting *Masks and Faces* into narrative. He followed a family interest in fishing to write CHRISTIE JOHNSTONE, a novel with autobiographical elements that focused on a Scottish fishing village. By 1854, he had moved on to St. James's Theatre, which he managed with an actress named Laura Seymour, who would become his lifelong companion. He continued to write a series of plays, some again with Tom Taylor. They included *The King's Rival, Honour before Titles (or Nobs and Snobs), The Courier of Lyons* (later as *The Lyons Mail*), and the *Peregrine Pickle* adaptation.

Reade's first successful novel, IT IS NEVER TOO LATE TO MEND (1856), focused on prison abuse and made clear his reformist passions. Other novels followed in rapid order: *The Course of True Love Never Did Run Smooth* (1857), *Jack of All Trades* (1858), *The Autobiography of a Thief* (1858), *Love Me Little, Love Me Long* (1859), and *White Lies* (1860). His experience as a dramatist remained evident in the stagelike dialogue in most of his novels. His best novel was *The* CLOISTER AND THE HEARTH (1861), which showcases the talents that made him as popular as Charles DICKENS and George ELIOT in his day. It told the imagined story of Gerard, the father of Erasmus. Reade continued his reformist bent with HARD CASH (1863), which focused on problems in insane asylums. That novel was followed by *Foul Play* (1868), an exposé about abuse of sailors, dramatized that same year by Irish playwright Dion Boucicault; *Put Yourself in His Place* (1870), an indictment of trade union–closed shops, dramatized later that year as *Free Labour;* and *A Woman-Hater* (1877), which presented the negative side of village life. Reade prided himself on his attention to detail and research, which he had to show more than once to defend himself against charges of misstatement or exaggeration.

Reade's 1866 work GRIFFITH GAUNT proved his personal favorite, a book considered daring in its consideration of marital problems due to religious differences. He dramatized the novel with the help of Boucicault. He managed the Adelphi Theatre in 1870, publishing another novel the following year, *A* TERRIBLE TEMPTATION: *A* STORY OF THE DAY, another attack against insane asylum abuses. In 1871, he serialized *A Simpleton* and published *The Wandering Heir,* based on the well-known Tichborne case involving disputed identity; Reade dramatized and produced the work in 1872. He wrote additional, lesser-known novels and, after suffering confinement due to bronchitis, began writing short stories. The death of Seymour in 1879 left him despondent, and his health deteriorated. After his death, a completed novel titled *A Perilous Secret* was found with instructions that his research, meticulous as always, be available for public scrutiny for two years.

BIBLIOGRAPHY

Phillips, Walter Clarke. *Dickens, Reade, and Collins: Sensation Novelists; a Study in the Conditions and Theories of Novel Writing in Victorian England.* New York: Russell & Russell, 1962.

Smith, Elton Edward. *Charles Reade.* Boston: Twayne, 1976.

READER-RESPONSE CRITICISM   One approach to gaining meaning from a story is by the application of literary criticism. Matthew Arnold, 19th-century literary critic, offered a definition of literary criticism that remained in favor as "a disinterested endeavor to learn and propagate the best that is known and thought in the world" (Bresslar 3). Within that disciplined activity, which analyzes literature, several different critical approaches have arisen; reader response criticism is one. Reader response theory views the reader as essential to the existence of a meaningful text. Until the 1800s the reader was believed to be passive and received little attention; only the text itself bore importance, a fact still adhered to by critics practicing FORMALISM/NEW CRITICISM. But with the arrival of the romantic writers in the 19th century, the author or poet assumed a new importance. Focus shifted from the text to include information about the writer's life and era as important analysis tools. This would lead to the development of NEW HISTORICISM. In the early 20th century, the text again became an autonomous object, complete unto itself, with the arrival of new criticism. Then one of its founders, I. A. Richards, turned his

interest to the reading process, recognizing that the reader brings to the text a host of experiences and assumptions that will guide her or his understanding. Finally, by the 1930s, Louise Rosenblatt shifted focus away from the text alone to emphasize the importance of interaction between the text and reader.

Reader-response critics believe that only in the context of reading can a text assume meaning. They take three approaches. In one, the reader brings assumptions and a background of certain signs to a text, and meaning emerges according to the discovery of such signs within the text. In a second method, supported by Rosenblatt, the reader enjoys a transactional experience while reading, so that the reader and the text have equal importance in gaining meaning. Finally, a third group emphasizes the reader's thoughts, beliefs, and experiences above the text itself as crucial to shaping that text's meaning. While reading, an individual is reminded of personal experiences that may overshadow the text.

BIBLIOGRAPHY

Bleich, David. *Subjective Criticism.* Baltimore: Johns Hopkins University Press, 1978.

Bressler, Charles E. *Literary Criticism: An Introduction to Theory and Practice.* Englewood Cliffs, N.J.: Prentice Hall, 1994.

Davis, Todd F, and Kenneth Wommack. *Formalist Criticism and Reader Response Theory.* New York: Palgrave, 2002.

Tompkins, Jane O. *Reader-Response Criticism: From Formalism to Post-Structuralism.* Baltimore: Johns Hopkins University Press, 1980.

REALISM   The term *realism* was first used in 1850s France to describe works that represented the world as it appears, rather than as an ideal. Containing a preponderance of authentic detailed description and using the rhetoric of everyday speech, realistic works reproduced environments objectively, observing colloquial life and language and focusing on characters from every social stratum. Realist writers focused on life events previously considered unimportant by the world of art, adopting human suffering as a topic eschewed by those with delicate tastes. It grew dominant in 19th-century Continental works as well as in the works of English writers. Important early examples include George ELIOT's *MIDDLEMARCH* and *The MILL ON THE FLOSS,* often termed DOMESTIC REALISM, Elizabeth GASKELL's *MARY BARTON,* George MACDONALD's works for children, George MEREDITH's *RHODA FLEMING,* Charles READE's *HARD CASH,* and H. G. WELLS's *Tono-Bungay,* to name a few.

BIBLIOGRAPHY

Levine, George. *The Realistic Imagination.* Chicago: University of Chicago Press, 1981.

REBEL OF THE FAMILY, THE   ELIZA LYNN LINTON (1880)   First serialized in *Temple Bar* in 1880, Eliza Lynn LINTON's *The Rebel of the Family* has enjoyed renewed interest in the 21st century due to the efforts of FEMINIST CRITICS who have focused on the novel's several controversial issues. While Linton gained reputation as an anti-feminist, her fiction portrays a sympathetic view of what her era called "the New Woman," an individual interested in intellectual and sexual freedoms not previously experienced by females, and likely to dye her hair, don outrageous fashions, and behave in a "vulgar" manner. Linton's contemporaries wondered in print in various reviews of the book whether the author intended her sympathetic voice to be taken as ironic, or whether her somewhat autobiographical protagonist, Perdita Winstanley, is meant to gain the admiration of readers.

Perdita remains out of step with the rigid cadences of her highly patriarchal society. She espouses social equity, work for women, and freedom to choose a marriage partner free from economic restraints. Linton peppers her novel with additional, related controversial themes, including lesbianism and the importance of an intellectual life for young females. As the lone plain, bookish democrat in a family of beautiful, vacuous, genteelly impoverished aristocrats, Perdita finds herself at odds with her sisters due to her rebellious behavior. Thomasina is described as having a "style and a perfect smile," while "Eva's blush-rose face took the heart out of men and made the wise like unto fools." The narrator adds, "So it has been ever since the sons of God lost their heaven for woman's eyes; and so it will be till the end of time—or the beginning of the

Emancipated Woman's supremacy." Perdita aspires to be that emancipated woman, embarrassing her mother and sisters by professing "extraordinary opinions," thereby "spoiling" her sisters' chances of a harmonious social life. Linton plays on stereotypical representations of women and society's double message regarding an attractive female, who was given the unenviable assignment of remaining simultaneously desirable to men while chaste and pure. Otherwise, she was in danger of becoming a wicked seductress. The narrator says of the lovely Eva (obviously a version of the name Eve), "she had the power of a veritable witch," and describes Eva as exhibiting "harmless little sensualities," such as the manner by which her "red ripe lips closed over bonbons, and the white sharp little teeth buried themselves in the fleshy pulp of fruit," actions reflecting "the naive innocence of evil."

As "unconventional" in her dress as in her opinions, Perdita calls attention to herself by proclaiming that middle-class women be permitted to work. She accepts the position in the Post Office savings bank offered to her through the influence of Thomasina's suitor to act on her ideology. When she befriends, and later becomes romantically involved with, a druggist, she engages in the social mixing her sisters decry, and most dismays them by taking part in the West Hill Society for Women's Rights. There she forms a questionable relationship with the organization's president, Bell Blount. While Perdita will eventually denounce feminists as hypocrites and conform through marriage to Leslie Crawford, freeing her sisters to also form solid matches, her experiences make problematic her abrupt reversal of feelings. While Bell is at last revealed to be, in critic Deborah Meem's words, "a vampire on the prowl," Linton has also made clear the character's magnetic personality, revealing Linton's own awareness of a type of lesbian culture that in her own age grew along with increasing opportunities for women.

Like George ELIOT, Elizabeth Linton wrote of subjects said to cause readers "repulsion," gaining her the criticism of contemporaries like Charles DICKENS. However, her effect on the writing community materialized in later fiction, including Henry JAMES's *The Bostonians* (1886). While James could as a male writer deal with themes such as lesbianism and not fall victim to charges of moral turpitude, a female writer could not. *The Rebel of the Family* adds to the development of a narrative persona on Linton's part that continues to fascinate those who wonder whether it resembled the "real" Elizabeth Linton, or simply promoted robust sale of her fiction.

BIBLIOGRAPHY

Meem, Deborah T. Introduction to *The Rebel of the Family,* by Elizabeth Linton. Peterborough, Ontario, Canada: Broadview Press, Ltd., 2002, 9–16.

REDGAUNTLET SIR WALTER SCOTT (1824)

Sir Walter SCOTT has long been acknowledged as the first writer of HISTORICAL FICTION, and when he chose Scotland as a setting, he generally produced his best work. He introduced this approach in his first novel, *WAVERLEY* (1814), when he sent his English hero into Scotland during the 1745–64 Jacobite rebellion, the second of its type in Scotland. Some in Scotland remained loyal to the exiled Stewart prince, Charles Edward, who wished to regain the throne for his father, James Francis, son of the banished James. James's dual titles, VII for England and II for Scotland, helped set the framework for Scott's later theme of questioned identity in *Redgauntlet*. He again sends an Englishman, Darsie Latimer, into Scotland, this time some 20 years following the second attempt to overthrow the English Hanoverian monarchy in favor of the Stewart line. While Scott's additional novel, *ROB ROY* (1817), had focused on the also factual original Stewart uprising of 1715, *Redgauntlet* proposes a fictional third revolution by Prince Charles Edward, thus challenging Scott in a new manner. He had few facts on which to base his fiction, other than the dreams of a nation to form a new identity.

When Darsie enters Scotland, a man who bears no "certain name," Edward Hugh Redgauntlet, also dubbed the Laird of the Lakes and Herries of Birrenswork, kidnaps him. Redgauntlet holds Latimer hostage in hopes of promoting the prince's cause in England, revealing to Darsie that he is actually his nephew, properly Sir Arthur Darsie Redgauntlet, a new identity he gains when crossing into a kind of no-man's-land geographically located between England

and Scotland, called the Solway. As a tourist, Darsie enters Solway without taking seriously its history. He has also recently eschewed the practice of law, an act that will prove ironic. He soon suffers an odd suspension between reality and fantasy, when even his own identity is questioned. Redgauntlet is not the only individual in the novel with multiple names, and Darsie's split identity as Englishman and Scotsman symbolizes Scotland's struggle for a national identity separate from that of England, which has, in a real sense, had a new nationalism forced upon it by its Hanoverian rulers.

When Darsie's friend, Alan Fairford, arrives to rescue him, the two men discover that even representatives of the law in the Solway suffer from split allegiances. On the one hand, they are bound to the Hanoverian system, while on the other, history dictates loyalty to Sir Hugh. As for Redgauntlet, he holds a tyrannical view of life, believing that only fate can dictate a man's situation. Questions of identity become paramount. Even the book's title somewhat concerned Scott's publisher, who felt readers might expect the novel to be a tale of chivalry, when instead its focus on family history and connections took precedent over any single life gallantly lived.

Much has been made of the autobiographical elements in this particular novel. According to critic Kathryn Sutherland, in an 1806 letter Scott confessed that "I became a valiant Jacobite at the age of ten years old; and, ever since reason & reading came to my assistance, I have never quite got rid of the impression which the gallantry of Prince Charles made on my imagination." As Sutherland discusses, Darsie represents several of Scott's early acquaintances and even Scott himself, in his indulgence in romance fancy. Fairford acts as a foil to Darsie and symbolizes Scott's alter ego, one more grounded in logic, while his relationship with the character Saunders, a man whose overbearing manner suffocates Fairford, has been said to be similar to Scott's strained dealings with his own father. In addition, the beautiful woman labeling herself "Green Mantle," who later turns out to be Darsie's own sister Lilias, may have represented an early love for Scott that proved to be another traumatic relationship.

Various schools of criticism find much of interest in the novel. When Fairford eventually marries Lilias, he weds a feminine version of his best friend, Darsie, of interest to PSYCHOANALYTIC CRITICS, who also investigate the various self-identity crises in the story. Scott's telescoping of time and history attracts NEW HISTORICIST critical comment, and the "Green Mantle" label for Lilias, suggesting fertility as well as an assumption of a leadership role, might interest FEMINIST CRITICS, who often find little to investigate in the flat characterizations of women populating most of Scott's novels.

Darsie's firsthand report of his captivity reflects often on the act of writing itself as a method by which he managed to focus his energies and claim independence from his captor. Almost an EPISTOLARY NOVEL in the tradition of Samuel RICHARDSON's *PAMELA* (1740), Scott's work, like Richardson's, focuses on a protagonist under the control of a representative of the law whose only recourse to freedom is that of self-expression. *Redgauntlet* represents one of the few occasions on which Scott utilizes a first-person point of view through letter and journal writing, a narrative structure that had gone out of fashion in the previous century. Furthermore, as with his predecessor Tobias SMOLLETT, Scott shapes a tale made up of multiple adventures with no overriding directed plot, perhaps in order to reflect more of what humans experience, although transformed from the everyday into a more imaginative world under the influence of Darsie's imagination. The novel was not well received, perhaps due to its self-reflective nature and lack of a clearly defined hero, as Scott contemplated questions of self-identity, supported by multiple references to other fictions, such as Cervantes's *Don Quixote*.

Ultimately judged a novel of social REALISM, *Redgauntlet* presents a view of a new society, which, while flawed, allowed figures such as Alan Fairford to achieve a social status his father could not. The manuscript, missing two leaves, survives in the National Library of Scotland, while the novel remains readily available to students and readers.

BIBLIOGRAPHY

Robertson, Fiona. *Legitimate Histories: Scott, Gothic, and the Authorities of Fiction.* Oxford: Oxford University Press, 1994.

Sutherland, Kathryn. Introduction to *Redgauntlet,* by Sir
Walter Scott. New York: Oxford University Press, 1985,
vii–xxiii.

REEVE, CLARA (1729–1807)

Born at Ipswich in Suffolk, Clara Reeve grew up as a rector's daughter in a genteel family. While her first publications included poetry and translations, she gained fame with her contributions to the development of the GOTHIC genre. With *The Champion Virtue: A Gothic Story* (1777), published later in revised form as *The Old English Baron,* she made her reputation. Acknowledging Horace Walpole and his *The CASTLE OF OTRANTO* (1764) as her predecessor, she criticized his work as too dependent upon the supernatural, purposely toning down such effects in her own highly DIDACTIC fiction. She followed her first success with *The Two Mentors* (1783) and a third Gothic titled *The Exiles* (1788) featuring, in the French style, taboo subjects such as bigamy. She departed from fiction to write *The Progress of Romance* (1785), important for its seminal consideration of the differences separating the romance from the novel, noting that the romance held women in high esteem, while the novel denigrated them through elevated emotion, using as an example work by Samuel RICHARDSON, Sarah FIELDING, and Charlotte Lennox, all of whom envisioned fiction as a possible instrument of morality. Reeve depicts her characters in a lively debate between Hortensius, Sophronia, and Euphrasia. Euphrasia acts as spokesperson for women and, thus, for Reeve, defending female authority. *The School for Widows* (1791) was later labeled, among others of her books, DOMESTIC FICTION, while she wrote *The Memoirs of Sir Roger Clarendon* (1793) in order to compare medieval ideas of chivalry to modern ideas regarding the efficacy of revolution. Additional works included *Plans of Education* (1792) and *Destination* (1799). Considered an important writer and critic, Reeve influenced many later female writers, including Ann RADCLIFFE. Her works are available in print and electronic texts.

BIBLIOGRAPHY

Clery, E. J. *Women's Gothic: From Clara Reeve to Mary Shelley.*
Tavistock, U.K.: North Cote House, 2000.

Sage, Lorna, ed. *Women's Writing in English.* Cambridge:
Cambridge University Press, 1999, 526.

RETURN OF THE NATIVE, THE THOMAS HARDY (1878)

Thomas HARDY's *The Return of the Native* moves at a slow pace that drives some readers to distraction. His narrative pace mirrors that of country life, very much a topic in his novel, featured in his setting of Egdon Heath. Natives of Egdon for the most part appreciate its laconic lifestyle; some, however, such as Eustacia Vye, do not. Eustacia revolts against a life that lacks romance and adventure, risking all to escape that existence, with tragic results. Hardy uses landscape as symbol, causing later critics to proclaim Egdon Heath as the novel's most important character. He adopted his native region as the setting for many novels, using its historic label of Wessex, adding to an illusion of reality in his fiction.

As the novel opens, readers enjoy a description of the heath with no humans present. Imagery suggests an enormous living entity, unaffected by time's passing. The novel's plot spans exactly one year and one day, adjusted to the growing cycle of the heath with its suggestions of life and death. The land offers no placid surface beneath which dangers lie. Nothing is hidden, except to those individuals who refuse to acknowledge life's harsh potential. In strong foreshadowing, the narrator warns early on that the Heath is not "friendly to women."

Hardy introduces his traditional large cast of characters with multiple love interests as his subject. The appropriately named innkeeper, Damon Wildeve, has returned to the heath to operate The Quiet Woman following a failed attempt to leave the heath that he hates. Not an evil man, he will nevertheless cause multiple problems. He is engaged to Thomasin Yeobright, whose surname identifies her with the work ethic employed by those yoked to the earth for their sustenance. A gentle creature, she eventually marries Wildeve, although he has enjoyed a sexual affair with Eustacia Vye. Eustacia detests her surroundings and, in the scene in which she is introduced, listens to the November wind across the heath, described in further foreshadowing as resembling "the ruins of human song."

Living with her grandfather, Eustacia desires nothing more than a wild romance but is deceived by Wildeve, who declares that his reason for marrying

Thomasin is to drive Eustacia to distraction. Thomasin's cousin, Clym Yeobright, another native who has lived abroad as a jeweler in Paris, returns to his roots where he hopes to teach, but immediately falls in love with Eustacia, although others warn him of potential danger. Eustacia assumes that as Clym's wife, she will enjoy the delights of Paris, and the two marry. At that point Hardy allows fate to intervene, striking Clym blind, forcing him to change his plans. He must cut furze in order to support his family, and Eustacia is driven nearly insane with her lot in life. Foreshadowing of a grim climax includes the melting of a wax doll representing Eustacia, symbolic of the universal practice of assigning a black magic curse.

Eustacia renews a relationship with Wildeve and accidentally helps cause the death of Mrs. Yeobright, mother of Clym and Thomasin. When Mrs. Yeobright arrives at their cottage in an effort to end the conflict in the family, Eustacia mistakenly believes that Clym hears her knock and will admit his mother. When no one opens the door, Mrs. Yeobright sits down to wait outside next to a poisonous snake, that traditional symbol of temptation and discord, which ends her life. The coincidental presence of a boy to witness the scene leads Clym to believe that Eustacia ignored her mother-in-law.

Eustacia quarrels with Clym, leaves home, and drowns in Shadwater Weir. Ironically, Hardy employs a traditional symbol of rebirth, water, as one of death, further emphasized when Wildeve also drowns in an attempt to rescue Eustacia. Eustacia represents the folly of human struggle against fate, demonstrating that such resistance leads to disaster not only for the individual who challenges destiny, but for others as well. The use of water as the instrument of death serves to mock the traditional religious ceremony of baptism, while also emphasizing the power of nature and its elements. Critics have suggested plot weakness in Eustacia's death following so closely the melting of her wax model. However, Hardy's belief in the power of coincidence made this an acceptable event. Clym will eventually become a preacher, adopting religion simply as an escape from grief, allowing Hardy to emphasize the futility of spirituality to improve the human lot, but also the inner strength inherent to a stoic acceptance of fate. The widowed Thomasin abandons all hope for love but still believes in the ritual of marriage, as she takes the strange but loyal Diggory Venn as her second husband. Her compliant acceptance of her fate is rewarded with a modicum of happiness.

The novel remains popular, is available in electronic and print versions, and was made into at least one film version, a vehicle for a young Catherine Zeta-Jones and that also starred Joan Plowright. It continues as a subject for critical study, with Hardy's characterization of women always interesting to FEMINIST CRITICS, his heavy-handed use of symbolism to practitioners of FORMALISM, its use as a vehicle for Hardy's personal philosophy to NEW HISTORICIST critics, and its implied sexuality to PSYCHOANALYTIC CRITICS.

BIBLIOGRAPHY

Mallet, Phillip V., and Ronald P. Draper, eds. *A Spacious Vision: Essays on Hardy.* Newmill: Patton, 1994.
Malton, Sara A. "'The Woman Shall Bear her Iniquity'": (1) Death as Social Discipline in Hardy's *The Return of the Native.*" *Studies in the Novel* 32, no. 2 (Summer 2002): 147. *Expanded Academic ASAP.* Infotrac. Triton Col Library. Available online. URL: http://web4.infotrac.galegroup.com. Downloaded March 14, 2003.

REVIEW, THE   Author Daniel DEFOE founded *The Review* in February 1704. Although he received some help from Robert Harley, earl of Oxford, the publication was without question Defoe's own. His journalism background is credited for his creation of detail so realistic in his later prose ROMANCE *ROBINSON CRUSOE* (1719) that readers believed the story to be true. First titled *A Weekly Review of the Affairs of France, Purged from the Errors and Partiality of News-Writers and Petty-Statesmen, of All Sides,* the periodical adopted the shortened title in 1713, also the year Defoe ceased its publication. As indicated by its title, the publication brought readers' opinions on European affairs as well as English society and offered the first examples of the literary essay. Defoe was often absent, serving Harley as a spy in travels throughout England and Scotland, making remarkable the thrice-weekly appearances of the periodical. He became the first English journalist, halting publication of *The Review* only due to his second imprisonment. A devout dissenter, his early years writing political propaganda pamphlets honed the journalistic skills that made *The Review* so appealing.

BIBLIOGRAPHY

Backscheider, Paula. *Daniel Defoe: His Life.* Baltimore: Johns Hopkins University Press, 1989.

Bloom, Harold, ed. *Daniel Defoe.* New York: Chelsea House, 1987.

RHODA FLEMING GEORGE MEREDITH

(1865) George MEREDITH's fourth novel, *Rhoda Fleming* dealt with a familiar theme, the pressure society places on both genders, but especially women, to conform to unrealistic expectations. That his culture governed love relationships with laws, such as those relating to marriage and divorce, greatly concerned Meredith. His own experiences supported his concerns, and autobiographical aspects may be found in many of his novels. Written over a three-year period while Meredith also worked on *SANDRA BELLONI* (originally *Emilia in England*) (1864) and its sequel, *Vittoria,* the novel was meant to be a one-volume straightforward moral tale. However, it stretched to two volumes in order for Meredith to fulfill publisher expectations of stringing readers along as long as possible. Such expectations during that time period account for an abundance of melodramatic detail and slow plot twists that bore contemporary readers, greatly reducing the popularity of once-successful novels.

The title character is one of two daughters, who lives with her widowed Kent farmer father, William. Her sister Dahlia serves as company for their London uncle, Anthony Hackbut, who works at Boyne's Bank. Both girls find city life intriguing, and Rhoda visits London, where she discovers that Edward Blancove has seduced her sister. Blancove, son of the bank's head, Sir William Blancove, and his brother Algernon, the squire of Wrexby, a village in the Fleming farm area, will play a major part in the emotional and physical maturity of the sisters. Algernon forms one part of a love triangle with Rhoda and Robert Eccles, an ex-soldier and farm assistant to Fleming. Rhoda cannot focus on her own romantic fulfillment, due to her concerns about Dahlia, whose name serves as symbol of her innocence as well as her fate. She joins Meredith's other heroines in her blond, beautiful naiveté, designed to provoke erotic reactions from unprincipled males.

When Dahlia travels through Italy for several months with Edward, she ruins the reputation that society holds sacrosanct. Although she tells Rhoda and her father that Edward has married her, they doubt the truth of her statement. They look for her at a London address that she gave them and find that she has moved, leaving no clue as to where to find her. Predictably, Edward has tired of his dalliance and plans on leaving Dahlia alone while he participates in a Christmas house party at Fairly Hall, Hampshire. Before he departs, he escorts Dahlia and Algernon to the theater, where Rhoda and her father see her. They mistakenly believe that Algernon has seduced Dahlia when they glimpse the two together.

At the house party, Edward and Algernon are both drawn to the charming widow, Mrs. Margaret Lovell, who is revealed through Robert's connections to have had an affair with Major Waring while in India. Waring, Robert's friend, still loves her. Seeking to punish Algernon for his perceived seduction of Dahlia, Robert pulls him from horseback and attacks him. Edward plans revenge by hiring a local thug named Nicodemus Segett to beat Robert, while Margaret discovers Dahlia's address and passes it on to Robert. When Robert finds the address, Dahlia has again disappeared. In the meantime, Margaret has developed a plan to dissolve Edward's entanglement with Dahlia. She convinces Edward to bribe the dastardly Sedgett with £1,000 to marry Dahlia. Edward visits Algernon in Paris, giving him the note to hand over to Sedgett after he has completed the plan. Because Dahlia is in poor health after having lived on the streets, when her uncle discovers her, she agrees to the marriage plan. Although humiliated and repulsed by Sedgett, she does not share her fears with Rhoda, who knows nothing of the bribe and believes the marriage proposal to be legitimate. In her opinion, it offers the perfect escape from the problems Dahlia faces as a ruined woman, cast off by "legitimate" society.

Unfortunately, Algernon has spent the bribe money to pay his debts. Circumstances seem to change for the better when Edward realizes that he really loves

Dahlia. He returns to England to discuss the situation with his wealthy father, however, who explains that his marriage to this ruined woman would destroy his own reputation. Readers cannot miss the irony in such a statement. Sir William urges Edward to emigrate, but his love for Dahlia proves strong, and he rushes to her lodgings, only to be intercepted by Rhoda, who mistakenly believes that her sister will do well by marrying Sedgett. She turns Edward away and only learns of the marriage scheme later from Robert, after Sedgett abandons his wife, Dahlia, when he does not receive the bribe money. In a subplot centering on their uncle, Anthony Hackbut, Rhoda finds him roaming London with a bag of gold he was to deliver; he has become mentally unstable and pours the contents of the bag into Rhoda's lap. His act would interest PSYCHOANALYTIC CRITICS, who might apply a Freudian interpretation of the act as symbolically sexual, emphasizing women as commodities to be bought and sold.

Rhoda, Dahlia, and Robert take Anthony with them to the Fleming farm, where Sedgett appears, demanding money and that Dahlia accompany him. Her father, another conformist traditional figure, orders her to leave with her husband, although Rhoda explains the disaster awaiting her sister, should she comply. Suddenly Major Waring resurfaces. He has investigated Sedgett and determined he was already married to a woman he sent to America, but who Waring encountered when she came onshore at Warbeach. Sedgett escapes, and the action continues as Edward arrives to declare his love for Dahlia, who has attempted suicide by drinking poison. Although she does not physically die, she suffers an emotional death that prevents her from reuniting with Edward.

Algernon takes the position as squire, following his father's death, and Fleming urges Rhoda to marry him and make an admirable financial match. While Rhoda finds the strength to revolt against her father's expectations and marries Robert for love, Major Waring is disappointed when Margaret makes a money match with Sir William Blancove. Edward also pays for his early sins, never finding a wife and living a lonely existence. Dahlia finds temporary ease living with Rhoda, Robert, and their children, but survives only seven years.

Although a dark tale with a sober message, *Rhoda Fleming* offers comic relief through Meredith's trademark humor, found in characterizations such as Master Gammon, Mrs. Sumfit and Mrs. Boulby. Not caricatures like comic figures created by Charles DICKENS, they also offer balance to the grasping, greedy antagonists through their honesty and loyalty.

BIBLIOGRAPHY

Jones, Mervyn. *The Amazing Victorian: A Life of George Meredith.* London: Constable, 1999.

RICHARDSON, SAMUEL (1689–1761)

Born in Derbyshire, Samuel Richardson matured in London, where his father worked as a joiner. In school he earned the nicknames "Serious" and "Gravity" and entertained the other students by telling tales. By age 13, his imaginative and writing skills were such that he wrote love letters on the part of servant girls. In 1706 he began an apprenticeship with a printer and married his master's daughter, Allington Wilde, in 1721. That same year, he established his own printing business and began a family that would include five sons and one daughter. While his business flourished and he eventually owned multiple homes, his family life did not. All his children died, as did their mother, and Richardson married again, to Elizabeth Leake. She produced five girls and a boy; four of the girls survived.

In 1733, Richardson published *The Apprentice's Vade Mecum,* a DIDACTIC book preaching the values of self-denial, followed by another preachy volume of *Aesop's Fables.* Among other early endeavors, he finished Daniel DEFOE's *A Tour Through The Whole Island of Great Britain,* published anonymously. Elected Master of the Stationers' Company in 1754, he continued his industrious approach to life, becoming, although vain by nature, a highly successful man. The first of his three books, a collection of fictional epistles, later labeled an EPISTOLARY NOVEL, called *PAMELA* (1740), made an invaluable contribution to the development of the novel by focusing on what he considered everyday life, even though it featured a wealthy antagonist. He followed that popular work with *CLARISSA* (1747–48), which created a stir among readers over the anticipated death of its main characters; many wrote to Richardson and begged him to allow the antagonist Lovelace a change of heart. Richardson did not change his plot, but confessed to a friend that he himself had been shocked by the appalling development of Lovelace's character. He spent five years producing his next novel, *The HISTORY OF SIR CHARLES GRANDISON* (1753–54), also epistolary in form. He wanted to prove that he could write with an aristocratic man, rather than a working-class woman, as protagonist. Seeking to correct the evil nature of his previous male characters in his title character, Richardson made Grandison so good that the work lacked the tension and impact of his previous books.

Imitation is always an important measure of the effect of a work, and Henry FIELDING's PARODY *Shamela* (1741) took to task what Fielding viewed as the revolting sentimentality of *Pamela*. Seeking to increase his SATIRE by writing a book about Shamela's brother in *JOSEPH ANDREWS* (1742), Fielding instead discovered his calling as a writer, producing a remarkably unified piece that further advanced the novel's development. Richardson's popularity had waned by the century's end, but his books are still studied for their immeasurable contribution to development of the novel form.

BIBLIOGRAPHY

Doody, Margaret Anne. *A Natural Passion: A Study of the Novels of Samuel Richardson.* Oxford: Clarendon Press, 1974.

Eaves, T. C. Duncan, and Ben D. Kimpel. *Samuel Richardson: A Biography.* Oxford: Clarendon Press, 1971.

RIENZI: THE LAST OF THE TRIBUNES
EDWARD BULWER-LYTTON (1835)

An author with an avid interest in history, especially that of Italy, Edward BULWER-LYTTON focused his HISTORICAL FICTION, *Rienzi: the Last of the Tribunes,* on a real-life figure named Cola di Rienzo. He proves an idealist who brings peace to various contentious forces in 14th-century Rome. More important, he succeeds in establishing a republic, which he serves as tribune. Displeased with his utopian ideas, Rome's citizens revolt against his forced government, a fact that Rienzi refuses to accept. As he explains to his son-in-law, Adrian, "the People love me, the Barons have fled from Rome, the Pontiff approves" and "never since the days

of the old Republic, did Roman dream a purer and a brighter aspiration . . . Peace restored—law established—arts, letters, intellect, dawning upon the night of time . . . the People ennobled from a mob, brave to protect, enlightened to guide, themselves. Then, not by the violence of arms, but by the majesty of her moral power, shall the Mother of Nations claim the obedience of her children." His words prove particularly ironic in light of the grisly end he meets at the hands of unhappy citizens following the entry into Rome of Montreal, the Knight of St. John. Although Rienzi proves victorious over Montreal, supervising his public execution by beheading, the Tribune will not survive such fractiousness. The crowd burns his home, driving Adrian with Rienzi's daughter Irene to escape, and leaving the senator's loving wife, Nina, to die in the flames as their home collapses. As for Rienzi, a crazed crowd in the streets of Rome dismembers him.

The novel supposedly served as a message to politicians of Bulwer-Lytton's own day. He warned against forcing freedoms upon people not yet ready or willing to accept the responsibilities accompanying independence. In an appendix to the novel, the author notes that Rienzi did not "fall from his own faults," was not killed by his excesses or "the vulgar moral of ambition," but rather he "fell from the vices of the People." In the end, a small group of 150 soldiers led by the Count of Minorbino entered Rome, forced Rienzi to abdicate, and met no resistance from the people as the soldiers "overthrew their liberties, and restored their tyrants."

As he did in his earlier novel *The LAST DAYS OF POMPEII* (1834), Bulwer-Lytton incorporated details gathered during his travels to Italy. He explains in his preface that he put aside *Rienzi* for a time to complete work on *Pompeii*, but that thoughts of the tribune haunted him as he delayed finishing the second novel. He wrote that he felt a "duty" to complete his novel about a "very remarkable man" who he felt had been "superficially judged, and a very important period crudely examined." He adds that while his plot is definitely a "Romance," he adheres with great "fidelity" to "all the leading events of the public life of the Roman Tribune." The novel has been reproduced in various dramatic forms, including an 1842 Richard Wagner opera, dedicated to Frederick August II, king of Saxony. Of interest to fans of historical fiction, the novel continues to be read in both print and electronic form, particularly by those who enjoy Bulwer-Lytton.

BIBLIOGRAPHY

Christensen, Allan Conrad. *Edward Bulwer-Lytton: The Fiction of New Regions*. Athens: University of Georgia Press, 1976.

RITCHIE, ANNE (ISABELLA) THACKERAY, LADY (1837–1919)

Born into a distinguished writing family, Anne Thackeray was the eldest daughter of celebrated British writer William Makepeace THACKERAY. Her mother had to be placed in a mental asylum, and Anne spent most of her childhood years with her grandparents in France. She served as secretary for her father as a teenager and published her first novel, *The Story of Elizabeth* (1862), in his magazine, *The CORNHILL MAGAZINE*. She based the French setting on her own experiences as a child. Her DOMESTIC FICTION made her famous and included *The Village on the Green* (1867) and *Old Kensington* (1873), probably her best-remembered work. She found love at age 40 with a much-younger cousin named Richmond Ritchie, a civil servant stationed in India. Despite the 17-year age difference, they married in 1877, and she had two children. Ritchie then focused on writing memoirs, biographies, and essays, and she later penned introductions to the 13-volume posthumous "biographical edition" of Thackeray's works (1894–98).

Ritchie also wrote the introduction to works by Maria EDGEWORTH and compiled journals and correspondence later published for their insight into writing of her era. Her sister Minnie was the first wife of Leslie Stephen. Although Minnie died young, Anne later played aunt to Stephen's children by his second wife, one of whom was famous novelist and critic Virginia Stephen Woolf. Woolf based her character Mrs. Hilbery in *Night and Day* (1919) on Anne Thackeray Ritchie. Woolf wrote Ritchie's obituary, noting the realistic sketches of her aunt's characters. She remains best known for her biographies, replete with firsthand details regarding individuals she had been fortunate enough to know due to family connections. Such works included *Records of Tennyson, Ruskin and Robert and Elizabeth Browning* (1892) and chapters from *Some Memoirs* (1894).

BIBLIOGRAPHY

Bloom, Abigail Burnham, and John Maynard, eds. *Anne Thackeray Ritchie: Journals And Letters*. Columbus: Ohio State University Press, 1994.
Mackay, Carol Hanbery. *Creative Negativity: Four Victorian Exemplars of the Female Quest*. Stanford, Calif.: Stanford University Press, 2001.
Sage, Lorna, ed. *Women's Writing in English*. Cambridge: Cambridge University Press, 1999, 535–36.

ROBERT ELSMERE MRS. HUMPHRY WARD (1888)

Mrs. Humphry (Mary Augusta) WARD became famous with the publication of her controversial novel *Robert Elsmere,* in which her protagonist undergoes a crisis of faith similar to her own. Just as she reacted to the decline in Christianity among the English populace in the latter part of the 19th century, Elsmere finds he can no longer adhere to the Articles of Faith of the Anglican Church, based on a literal interpretation of the Bible.

During his early training to become an Anglican parson, Robert Elsmere willingly accepts the church's teaching, although he learns of two schools of thought that counter the acceptance of the Bible as truth. One Oxford movement that countered orthodoxy was that of Edward Langham, an approach resulting in a spiritual immobility, and the other, based on the philosophy of the German philosopher Hegel, held that man must reject the tyrannical teachings of old to achieve a liberation of the mind; he may achieve a spiritual unity with God without following the theology of the punishment of sins by an angry deity. Elsmere marries a pious Anglican woman and moves to a country living where he pursues historical studies and his scientific interests while engaging in a life of service. When Squire Roger Wendover invites Elsmere to read from his immense library, Elsmere encounters philosophical works, which, combined with the rationalist commentary of the squire, lead the young man to doubt his faith. As his studies continue, he gradually moves from blind engagement with biblical teachings and the miracles of Christ to accept the Bible as symbolic, with

Christ representing a divine spirit at large, promoting humanity.

Elsmere leaves the Anglican Church to seek a new approach to expression of his nontraditional spirituality. His journey culminates in his founding a new order, The New Brotherhood of Christianity, a slum school in London. Elsmere's emotional anguish adds tension to a plot that lacks traditional action, with his spiritual pilgrimage replacing the more common physical journey. Although some of the novel's tenets fell more closely in line with mid-19th-century thought than that occurring at the century's close, the novel gained a wide audience and high popularity. An article expressing concern regarding its challenge to Anglicanism written by the politician William Gladstone in the *Nineteenth Century* further advanced its sales.

BIBLIOGRAPHY

Walters, J. Stuart. *Mrs. Humphry Ward: Her Work and Influence.* London: K. Paul, Trench, Trübner & Co., Ltd., 1912.

ROBINSON CRUSOE DANIEL DEFOE (1719)

Arguably the first English novel, Daniel DEFOE's prose ROMANCE *Robinson Crusoe* recounts the fictional adventures of the title character, an ambitious Englishman, through Crusoe's first-person autobiographical narrative. In the formally titled *The Life and Strange Surprising Adventures of Robinson Crusoe, of York, Mariner. Written by Himself,* Crusoe describes in realistic detail his adventures, his struggles to survive, his religious quandaries, and his strivings for economic advancement, from his headstrong youth into his relative old age. The majority of the book, and the part most popularly familiar, consists of Crusoe's description of his experiences stranded for 28 years on an uninhabited island off the coast of South America.

Written when Defoe was nearly 60, *Robinson Crusoe* was the first of a number of novels he wrote late in life after an earlier career as a prolific essayist and pamphleteer. *Robinson Crusoe* was probably inspired by the popularly reported, real-life adventures of Alexander Selkirk, a British sailor rescued in 1709 from Juan Fernandez, a desolate island off the coast of Chile, where he had lived alone for more than four years.

Although the young Crusoe of the first part of the novel sneaks off to sea against his father's wishes, he nevertheless impresses with his industry and hard work, building a successful plantation in South America after only several years away. Crusoe is a self-made man well on his way to economic success when, prodded by ambition, he sets sail to obtain plantation slave labor for himself and neighboring plantation holders. Crusoe's subsequent adventures with pirates, his capture, and eventual escape, shipwreck, and his strivings for survival largely alone on his island, coupled with the book's descriptions of exotic places, scenes, and wildlife, undoubtedly appealed to contemporary readers with whom travel and adventure books were very popular.

After the shipwreck, Defoe provides a detailed account of Crusoe's industry and self-reliance in his use of wreck-salvaged material first to provide for his own survival and later to build a comfortable home alone on his island. The virtues of hard work are clearly stressed, and later critics felt Defoe clearly embraced his culture's enthusiasm for mercantilist endeavors.

Crusoe's self-reflective and self-critical remarks form the basis for a Puritan message on obedience and duty, despite his headstrong behavior and failure to heed his father's advice to accept and pursue the "middle station" in life. Thus, his physical struggles for survival mirror his ethical struggles on religion and duty. While Crusoe periodically returns to his ethical reflections, he reaches a pivotal point when, alone and sick on the island, he repents and vows to be a better, more obedient servant of God. His epiphany is foreshadowed as he thinks to himself after having spent some time on the island, "I never felt so earnest, so strong a desire, after the society of my fellow-creatures, or so deep a regret at the want of it." The fever of his illness, symbolic of his spiritual disease, breaks with his repentance and new resolve.

His interactions and adventures with two characters, Xury and later the more famous Friday, further underscore the Puritan religious message. Unlike Crusoe, who has to learn to accept his station in life, the "savages" willingly accept theirs as subjects to Crusoe. The subjugation of Xury and Friday is just another part of

God's order, additionally justified by their resulting education in Christianity and European deportment. They are also, in effect, cheap labor for Crusoe. The book's secular Puritanism extols acquisition and the accumulation of wealth as the natural result of hard work, a Puritan value, and thus virtually a religious duty. As Crusoe instructs Friday, he strengthens his own beliefs and proves the value of proselytizing, musing that "in laying things open to him, I really informed and instructed myself in many things that I either did not know or had not fully considered before."

Modern readers may find the emphasis on Puritan Christianity, laissez-faire economics, middle-class economic individualism, and the white man's Christian burden as a justification for slavery farcically outdated. Even though the views expressed on these issues, especially Crusoe's treatment of Xury and Friday, seem offensive now, they most probably simply reflect the views of Defoe's time and place. As such, *Robinson Crusoe* can be read as a period piece indicative of 18th-century English political and racial views as well as a Puritan religious fable and adventure tale.

This first-person novel is written so convincingly, and with such realistic detail, even to the point of detailed accountings of Crusoe's assets, that it easily captures readers' imaginations. The book's autobiographical format underscores its individualist hue while also providing details that add to *Crusoe*'s REALISM. Although *Crusoe* was not well received by refined readers, it sold very well to the general public, going through several printings. Its success encouraged Defoe to follow it with *The Farther Adventures of Robinson Crusoe* (1719) and *The Serious Reflections . . . of Robinson Crusoe* (1720), neither of which proved nearly as popular as the original novel.

Robinson Crusoe is a moral tale, extolling the virtues of a secular Puritanism, wrapped up in an appealing, realistic adventure story. It also appealed to contemporary readers because of its novelty. Robinson Crusoe represents a middle-class character, neither the classical figure nor the stereotype typically used in earlier works. The original plot and Defoe's strong rendering of an ordinary man, his island milieu, and his adventures in striking realistic detail continues its appeal. The use of realism and a common-man protagonist in

a vivid and convincingly detailed plot such that readers identify with Crusoe and his plight separates the novel from preceding books.

Critic Ian Watt argues that these qualities are important to the development of the novel as a literary form. He also argues as essential the growth of a protagonist's sense of identity over the course of a book, a quality that many argue is lacking in *Crusoe*. But while some argue that Crusoe does not fully evolve as a character and lacks the psychological development that marks the protagonist in a fully developed novel, Defoe clearly takes the written word in new and important directions. *Robinson Crusoe* remains available in print, as well as in various media forms, and continues to be widely studied and enjoyed.

BIBLIOGRAPHY

Hunter, J. Paul. "The Conclusion of *Robinson Crusoe*." *Daniel Defoe: A Collection of Critical Essays.* Edited by Max Byrd. Upper Saddle River, N.J.: Prentice-Hall, 1976.

———. *The Reluctant Pilgrim: Defoe's Emblematic Method and Quest for Form in Robinson Crusoe.* Baltimore: Johns Hopkins University Press, 1966.

Novak, Maximillian E. "Robinson Crusoe's Original Sin." *Daniel Defoe: A Collection of Critical Essays.* Edited by Max Byrd. Upper Saddle River, N.J.: Prentice Hall, 1976.

Starr, George A. "Robinson Crusoe's Conversion." *Daniel Defoe: A Collection of Critical Essays.* Edited by Max Byrd. Upper Saddle River, N.J.: Prentice-Hall, 1976.

Watt, Ian. *The Rise of the Novel.* Berkeley: University of California Press, 1974.

ROB ROY SIR WALTER SCOTT (1817) A Robin Hood figure, the factual individual named Rob Roy formed the basis for Sir Walter SCOTT's HISTORICAL FICTION *Rob Roy*. The real Rob Roy (literally Red Robert, for his red hair) was a drover who became an outlaw, leading his clan in powerful support of England's Jacobites (Roman Catholics) in the 18th century. A dangerous man, he nevertheless gained a reputation for helping those in need, both the politically and economically oppressed. He eventually enjoyed the duke of Argyle's protection and adopted his mother's maiden name of Campbell. In Scott's traditional introduction, presenting the facts used to create his fiction, he wrote that a man who knew the outlaw described him as "a benevolent and humane man 'in his own way,'" adding that "his ideas of morality were those of an Arab chief, being such as naturally arose out of his wild education."

True to history, the novel's setting is the north of early 18th-century England and Scotland. Scott employs a device he had used before, that of an English visitor to Scotland unknowingly becoming involved in an uprising. Despite its title, the novel features as protagonist young Francis Osbaldistone, an untried Englishman driven from his homeland by his father, a merchant who believes his son needs to mend his obstinate ways. The plot opens when Osbaldistone is an old man, recording his story from the vantage point of decades. Scott comments on his own methodology when Osbaldistone writes in his memoir that a tale between friends "loses half its charms when committed to paper." Osbaldistone reveals aspects of his character when he adds that, rather than a portrait of himself, he bequeaths to his friend "a faithful transcript of my thoughts and feelings, of my virtues and my failings."

Osbaldistone arrives as a young adventurer at the house of his uncle, Sir Hildebrand. There he meets the novel's antagonist and his cousin, the dastardly Rashleigh, who has designs on another cousin, Diana Vernon, a character critics agree is likely reminiscent of a Scottish woman that Scott loved and lost in his youth. She represented a departure for Scott from his traditional sweet, innocent, and often completely passive heroines. Intelligent, active, and brave, she forms a perfect match for Osbaldistone, who will mature in the novel from a brash, too-conventional figure into a thoughtful, mature man of keen judgment. As a Protestant Whig, he will be forced to reconsider his beliefs in light of Diana's Jacobite and Roman Catholic sentiments. Diana's obvious attraction to Osbaldistone arouses the thieving, treacherous Rashleigh's ire, and he decides to destroy not only his cousin but Osbaldistone's father as well.

Diana urges Osbaldistone to seek assistance from Rob Roy MacGregor against Rashleigh. Osbaldistone searches for the outlaw with the help of Bailie Nicol Jarvie, whose MacGregor roots will help the travelers'

acceptance by the outlaw clan. Scott's use of the first-person narrator allows Osbaldistone to reflect his maturation as he witnesses a battle between the clansmen and the men's troops, which endanger Rob Roy. Helen MacGregor offers Scott an additional strong female character, whose ferocity in defending her family, both immediate and extended, proves memorable. The reader meets her as seen through Osbaldistone's eyes: "I have seldom seen a finer or more commanding form than this woman . . . [who] had a countenance which must once have been of a masculine cast of beauty though . . . by the wasting influence of grief and passion, its features were only strong, harsh and expressive." Obaldistone later refers to the awe-inspiring figure as an "Amazon" and is astounded by her ferocity as a clan leader. As the only individual who will not only stand up to her husband but also argue convincingly with him, she contributes to the development of Rob Roy as a real human, subverting his mythological image. Both of the novel's women offer personalities of interest to FEMINIST CRITICS in their assumption of male characteristics.

Rob Roy escapes and aids Osbaldistone and Diana, who surprises her cousin on the road in "masculine dress," ready to aid him in revealing the treachery of Rashleigh. Rashleigh proves one of Scott's most effective villains, due to his complete inhumanity. As suggested by his surname, his impatience overcomes his cleverness. When his part in embezzling from the elder Osbaldistone is revealed, Francis Osbaldistone returns to London and brings various lawsuits against his cousin. As he explains, Rashleigh proves a difficult opponent, as "the information he had given to the government was critically well-timed . . . and the artful manner in which he contrived to assume both merit and influence, had, to a certain extent, procured him patrons among ministers." While in London, he cannot stand thinking of Diana, assuming she has married an aristocrat.

Osbaldistone further infuriates Rashleigh by assuming his place in Sir Hildebrand's will, although Rashleigh does assume his father's title, his older brothers having all died in ways for which his father blamed him. Sir Hildebrand also bequeaths to Diana, now, Osbaldistone learns, Lady Diana Vernon Beauchamp, diamonds and a silver ewer engraved with the arms of the Vernon Osbaldistone family. Osbaldistone learns, upon his return to Osbaldistone Hall to procure his property, that Diana's father, Sir Frederick Vernon, an enemy of the English Crown, had been masquerading as the man he had known as Father Vaughan. Had Diana crossed Rashleigh, who learned their secret, her father would have paid a heavy price, possibly with his life. However, she has refused to marry her cousin, a fact over which Osbaldistone rejoices.

Rashleigh betrays his cousins and Sir Frederick, leading supporters of King George to the Hall. His efforts are foiled by Rob Roy, who suddenly appears, stabbing his nemesis only after Rashleigh refuses to apologize for his treachery. He dies a slow and painful death, remaining despicable to the end, telling Osbaldistone "that the pangs of death do not alter one iota of my feelings toward you. I hate you!" Although Diana and her father escape to France, Osbaldistone follows and marries her. They have enjoyed many years as man and wife by the time he relates this history.

The novel's major characters receive support from a host of minor comic characters, all contributing to the book's continued success. *Rob Roy* is one of the novels that prompted modern critics to reconsider Scott's work as important in the early consideration of inequality in economic and social development within the United Kingdom, increasing interest by NEW HISTORICIST critics. Whatever the reader's motivation for reading, it remains one of Scott's most revered works, still widely read and converted to various media forms.

BIBLIOGRAPHY

Duncan, Ian. "Primitive Inventions: 'Rob Roy,' Nation, and World System." *Eighteenth-Century Fiction* 15, no. 1 (October 2002): 81–102.

Lincoln, Andrew. "Scott and Empire: The Case of *Rob Roy.*" *Studies in the Novel* 34, no. 1 (Spring 2002): 43–59.

RODERICK HUDSON HENRY JAMES (1875)

Roderick Hudson was Henry JAMES's first extensive novel, appearing as installments in 1875 in *The Atlantic Monthly*. James chose as protagonist an amateur American sculptor, placing him in Europe with a wealthy patron named Rowland Mallet. Critics agreed that this novel ended a writing apprenticeship for James, advancing him into his serious work. He used for the first time a dislocated American in a scenario that he would often repeat, focusing on an individual who must learn to cope within a foreign community. James's own experience as an American who chose to spend much of his life in Europe contributed the necessary background and familiarity with conflict that allowed his characters lifelike attributes; he wrote most of the novel while in Florence. While completing the book in America, he made the decision to return to Europe with the intention of remaining for a protracted period.

Roderick Hudson becomes a part of Rome's social art circle, sparking criticism of his talent by a French sculptor named Gloriani. Lured from his art by the ironically named Christina Light, whose father is an expatriate American, Hudson disconnects from his passion. Hudson will sacrifice talent to indulge passion, a fatal decision.

In hopes of bringing Hudson back to sculpting, Mallet asks the artist's mother and fiancée, Mary Garland, to travel to Rome from their New England home. Roderick realizes his folly and returns to work, sculpting first a bust of his mother. He becomes known for his enormous sculptures and his exploits in the Coliseum, allowing James to comment on the possibility that what appears to be artistic genius may dissolve simply into grandiosity. Roderick's revolt against demands such as those inflicted on him by the studio world mark his immaturity and self-centered nature. Still enthralled with Christina, he is again distracted from work when her mother urges him to marry Prince Casamassima, who will appear as a character in a future James novel, *The PRINCESS CASAMASSIMA* (1885–86). Clearly Hudson lacks both the self-discipline and focus necessary to a successful artist.

Hoping that a change of environment will move Hudson to work again, Mallet plans for the group to visit Switzerland, but when they run into Christina there, Hudson sinks so low as to ask Mary for funds so that he may trail Christina. Mallet censors Hudson and his ego for such an act, and the sculptor leaves to walk in the mountains, where an unexpected storm arises.

When Hudson's body is discovered, some believe he committed suicide rather than be separated from Christina and continue to live a life of disgrace.

James deals with his traditional themes of the consequence of choice and the necessity for individual responsibility in accepting those consequences. As did his contemporaries William Makepeace THACKERAY and George MEREDITH, James chose to write about well-read and well-spoken members of the upper class who have the freedom to travel. He contrasts that individual with an unsuspecting American who does not share the class values, setting the foreigner at odds with a social code he cannot understand. James's focus on the mind of his characters created psychological profiles that had never before been seen in fiction. While he remained intrigued by moral dilemma, his work rarely assumed the tone of DIDACTIC FICTION. He sought instead to encourage the reader in believing that he had on his own analyzed the situation at hand. This proved mostly true in *Roderick Hudson,* where he moralizes to a greater extent than in his more mature work. While not as commonly read as James's other work, the novel remains important to demonstrating the development of his approach.

BIBLIOGRAPHY

Cargill, Oscar. *The Novels of Henry James.* New York: Macmillan, 1961.

Dupee, F. W. *Henry James.* New York: William Morrow, 1974.

Stevenson, Elizabeth. *Henry James: the Crooked Corridor.* New Brunswick, N.J.: Transaction Publishers, 2000.

RODERICK RANDOM TOBIAS SMOLLETT (1748)

Tobias SMOLLETT's first novel reflected both the reading interests of the day and Smollett's own attitude toward fiction. As a PICARESQUE with first-person narration, the novel offered readers an action-centered story with a rogue main character, but Roderick Random could hardly be termed the traditional picaro developed in a humorous vein. Framed with images that reflected Smollett's fixation on human filth, and caught up in incidents focused on violence and destruction, the novel's actors appear as flat caricatures with names describing their personalities, such as

Squire Gawky and Mr. Snarly; some represented vices, in the tradition of medieval and Renaissance drama. Smollett's fixation on decay and brutality grew from his own horrifying experiences as a surgeon's mate on a British ship that saw action in an ill-fated 1741 expedition against Cartagena. An author who dealt with life's disappointing experiences by shaping his real-life enemies into savage book characters, Smollett embraced the picaresque, showing his devotion by translating novels by Alain-René Lesage and Miguel de Cervantes. He demonstrated his admiration by mentioning *Gil Blas of Santillane* and *Don Quixote de la Mancha* in *Roderick Random*'s preface. However, he took issue with Le Sage's method of exciting "mirth" rather "than compassion," and moving readers too quickly "from distress to happiness." In Smollett's opinion, that left the reader no time to pity the character "nor himself to be acquainted with affliction." When translated and published in France in 1748, the anonymous work was attributed to Henry FIELDING, causing Smollett to travel to Paris, where he corrected that impression.

The child of Scottish parents, Random has a miserable childhood. His father has been disinherited for making a poor marriage, and the family barely subsists. Before her son's birth, Random's mother dreams that "she was delivered of a tennis-ball." Satan, serving as her midwife, takes a racket to the ball and strikes it "so forcibly" that it disappears from view. Her vision foreshadows the fact that Random will be propelled by a force beyond his control through many adventures. Like Smollett himself, Random will experience bitter disappointment in life, and Smollett's preface states that the novel will expose mankind's "selfishness, envy, malice and base indifference." His chapter titles, such as that of Chapter XXI, Volume I, make clear this attempt at exposure: "Squire Gawky comes to lodge with my master—is involved in a troublesome affair, out of which he is extricated by me—he marries my master's daughter—they conspire against me—I am found guilty of theft—discharged—deserted by my friends—I hire a room in St. Gile's—where by accident I find the lady to whom I made my addresses, in a miserable condition—I relieve her."

The debilitating effects of poverty kill Random's mother, and, unable to bear his grief, Random's father deserts his son, leaving him with an embittered grand-father. Trapped in an unloving home, Random gains an education through the help of his uncle, Tom Bowling, a naval officer later forced out of the navy following a disagreement with his captain. Although he loses touch with his uncle, Random secures a lifelong friend-ship with his devoted companion, Strap. Random trav-els with Strap to London and begins the series of adventures that mark the novel as rogue fiction; how-ever, Random does not mete out the chicanery, but instead becomes its mark. He is denied happiness, even discovering his betrothed in bed with another man, and considers suicide several times, at one point climbing atop a chair to hang himself while in jail. Other prisoners alert the authorities, and he receives "thirty stripes," or lashes, as punishment. Because he lacks the appropriate bribe money, his attempt to enter the navy as a surgeon's mate is foiled. Instead, he works as an assistant to a French apothecary, but is pressed into navy service after all. Finding himself tired of Strap's company, Random encourages him to leave, then later bitterly regrets his shallow act. Managing eventually to become a surgeon's mate, he witnesses the carnage at Cartegena, is eventually shipwrecked, robbed, and stripped on the shore by a gang of marauders, then taken on as a footman by a woman poet. He falls in love with her niece, Narcissa, who has wealthier suitors that her family finds more suitable.

Many more harrowing adventures follow, including Random's kidnapping to France, but there he reunites with his uncle, Tom Bowling. After fighting in the French army, he meets up with Strap, who has trans-formed himself through good fortunes into Monsieur d'Estrapes. With the help of his old friend, Random scores his own financial success and courts an heiress after he and Strap return to London. His efforts prove unsuccessful, and he meets up at Bath with Narcissa, but again fails to win her hand. A disagreement with Narcissa's brother drives Random back to London. Distraught over his lack of love and fulfillment, he gambles away his funds and ends up in debtor's prison. Once again, Tom Bowling appears and gains Random's release from prison and his entrance into the navy.

On the next adventure, Random travels to South America and meets a mysterious trader, Don Roderigo.

In the picaresque tradition of disguise and question-able identity, Don Roderigo turns out to be Random's long-lost father. The two men return to Scotland, pro-cure the family's property, and Random marries Nar-cissa, while Strap marries her servant.

Smollett wrote in a 1747 letter to Alexander Carlyle that the novel is a SATIRE, and he used the book to lam-baste all individuals who had ever caused him harm, including those who rejected a play he tried for years to publish in London. Smollett also hoped to correct negative English attitudes toward Scots, growing from England's IMPERIALISM regarding Scotland. Smollett himself felt he had suffered for those attitudes. The positive presentation of Random in the face of contin-uous harsh treatment is a part of Smollett's revisionist efforts. Mrs. Random's dream also supports the positive view of Scotland, as it concludes with the tennis ball's return to the land of its birth, where it "immediately sprung up a goodly tree covered with blossoms, the scent of which operated so strongly on her nerves that she awoke." While critics have wondered over the value of this particular novel in the picaresque tradi-tion, Smollett played a crucial role in the extension of realism into novels, and influenced the later modified picaresque works by Charles DICKENS.

BIBLIOGRAPHY

Lutz, Alfred. "Representing Scotland in Roderick Random and Humphry Clinker: Smollett's Development as a Nov-elist." Studies in the Novel 33.1 (Spring 2001): 1–18.

Phelps, Gilbert. "Tobias Smollett: The Adventures of Roderick Random." An Introduction to Fifty British Novels: 1600–1900. London: Pan Books, 1979, 89–95.

ROMAN À CLEF   Roman à clef refers to a novel "bearing a key," which identifies the real persons rep-resented by characters in the novel. The French term roman, meaning "novel," refers to the ROMANCE tradi-tion in both French and English literature in which writers explored the development of their main char-acter through his reactions to conflicts and challenges, while clef may be translated as "keystone," or in music as the "tuning-key." Although the characters would generally be recognizable without the key, it is part of the satiric approach of the form. Examples are Thomas

Love PEACOCK's *MELINCOURT* and *NIGHTMARE ABBEY* and Aphra BEHN's *LOVE LETTERS BETWEEN A NOBLEMAN AND HIS SISTER.*

ROMAN À THÈSE   See THESIS NOVEL.

ROMANCE NOVEL

The term *romance* for centuries denoted a composition written in any of the several Romance languages. During the Middle Ages, the term came to mean a work of popular verse or prose focusing on legendary subjects and characters, often involving supernatural happenstance and featuring elements of love. Early romances generally featured aristocrats and knights engaged in activities of derring-do. All plots find roots in Christian and/or pagan mythology, narratives that include the supernatural in an attempt to explain the origin of the earth and the many forces that affect it; examples include Dante Alighieri's *The Divine Comedy* (14th century) and John Milton's *Paradise Lost* (1667). Mythology focuses on the human condition, which also includes a desire for love. While popular as early as the 12th century, romances lost their appeal during the 16th century. At that point, traditional ideas regarding chivalry and religious observances no longer were as meaningful to most communities. Ironically, not until the Spanish writer Miguel de Cervantes satirized the classical romance in his *Don Quixote* (1605) did the romance regain favor. By the 18th century, the romance convention was placed in a different context, and the more modern idea of romance as a genre focused on adventure with romantic love an important theme. That approach is evident in the wildly popular GOTHIC FICTION of that century, introduced most notably by Horace Walpole in *The CASTLE OF OTRANTO,* and expanded through works by Ann RADCLIFFE and M. G. "Monk" LEWIS, among others. Thus, much fiction came to be labeled romance, and subgenres mixed, producing, for instance, a HORROR romance or a SCIENCE FICTION romance; both descriptions could apply to Mary SHELLEY's *FRANKENSTEIN* (1818). Shelley's work renewed interest in the English romance, which had waned due to the Gothic's typical use of hyperbole and sentimentalism. She focused on the interior life of her characters, while incorporating many of the external elements common to romance. Romance elements came to be used in an ironic or subversive manner, as in William Makepeace THACKERAY's *VANITY FAIR* (1848), which bears the subtitle *A Novel without a Hero.* The 19th-century romance also transferred the hero role to women, evident in Jane AUSTEN's many novels, as well as those by the BRONTË sisters and Henry JAMES's *PORTRAIT OF A LADY* (1881).

When the term is applied to contemporary literature, it assumes a different meaning than that of the earlier romance tradition. It emphasizes, according to critic Angus Easson, "alternatives to realism's determinism. Realism stresses a mimetic representation, in content and style, whereas romance offers representational possibilities." Those possibilities may be presented through characters' dreams, which may introduce alternative idealistic or terrifying worlds or states, or illnesses, during which time characters may imagine a world different from their own. Romance elements also appear through the stylistic use of symbols and allusion, suggesting meanings different from the literal. For instance, while Charles DICKENS introduced the realistic theme of prostitution through the character Nancy in his novel *OLIVER TWIST* (1838), he romanticized her through her loving actions toward the child Oliver; the only true sign of her profession was her red boots. He also indulged in pure romance by arranging for Oliver a positive fate that was most unlikely in view of all the hardships and abuse the child had suffered.

BIBLIOGRAPHY

de Rougemont, Denis. *Love in the Western World.* Princeton: Princeton University Press, 1983.

Duncan, Ian. *Modern Romance and Transformations of the Novel: The Gothic, Scott, and Dickens.* Boston: Cambridge University Press, 1992.

Easson, Angus. Introduction to *Ruth,* by Elizabeth Gaskell. New York: Penguin, 1997, vii–xxiv.

Frye, Northrup. *The Secular Scripture: A Study of the Structure of Romance.* Cambridge: Harvard University Press, 1976.

ROMAN-FLEUVE

Any sequence of novels sharing characters in common may be labeled a roman-fleuve. The French term *roman,* meaning "novel," refers to the ROMANCE tradition in both French and English literature in which writers explored the development of their main character through his reactions to conflicts and challenges, while *fleuve* means literally "river," current, or torrent, as in the phrase *Fleuve de la vie,* or "the current of one's life." The approach flourished during the 18th and 19th centuries, including most notably Sir Walter SCOTT's first, second, and third Tales of My Landlord series and Anthony TROLLOPE's Chronicles of Barsetshire series and Palliser series.

ROOKWOOD WILLIAM HARRISON AINSWORTH (1834)

When William Harrison AINSWORTH wrote *Rookwood,* he was struggling against a recent bankruptcy of the business he shared with his father-in-law. Returning to the practice of law in 1830 and anticipating the birth of his third daughter, according to biographer Stephen James Carver, Ainsworth wrote to a friend asking whether he knew of any gypsy stories and any accounts of "authentic middle-age speeches delivered over the dead." His interests signal that he had begun work on the manuscript that would propel him to long-lasting fame. For a public mourning the recent death of Sir Walter SCOTT and still years away from recognizing the great talent that would be Charles DICKENS, Ainsworth's blend of GOTHIC and ROMANCE was heartily welcomed.

The novel's gruesome tale begins with the legend that a branch falling from an old lime tree on the ground of Rookwood Place always precedes a death. As predicted, the lord, Sir Piers Rookwood, dies and leaves behind one legitimate son, Ranulph, and one illegitimate son, Luke, to battle for the family fortune. Into their conflict come the mad Sexton Peter Bradley, actually Sir Piers's long-lost brother, Alan, and Lady Maud Rookwood, Ranulph's mother. They pit the brothers against one another in romance, as both fall in love with beautiful Eleanor Mowbray. As Ranulph's cousin and heir to a family fortune, Eleanor seems to be the key to a second prophecy that distant branches of the family will marry and then gain control over a powerful family empire. One of several incantations and songs in the book, the prophecy reads, "When the stray Rook shall perch on the topmost bough, / There shall be clamour and screaming, I trow; / But of right,

and of rule, of the ancient nest, / The Rook that with Rook mates shall hold him possest."

Eleanor loves Ranulph but falls victim to Luke's apparent obsession with her; he is urged to pursue his passion by Bradley. Luke rejects his Gypsy lover, Sybil Lovel, and asks for help in winning Eleanor from the famous highwayman Dick Turpin. Instead of gaining Eleanor, Luke marries Sybil by mistake, as Eleanor has been drugged and kidnapped, hidden in a Gypsy camp. Sybil liberates Eleanor and then kills herself, causing her grandmother to send Luke a poisoned lock of Sybil's hair, which leads to his death. As Lady Maud and Bradley, now revealed to be Alan Rookwood, fight in a tomb, it mysteriously seals itself, leading to two more grisly deaths. Lady Rookwood is crushed inside a sarcophagus, while Alan waits in vain for Luke to rescue him, not knowing of Luke's death. Ainsworth indulges in further melodrama as he describes Alan's terror with the emotional hyperbole that characterizes the entire novel: "The dead, he fancied, were bursting from their coffins, and he peopled the darkness with grisly phantoms. They were around about him on each side, whirling and rustling, gibbering, groaning, shrieking, laughing, and lamenting . . . . The air seemed to grow suffocating, pestilential; the wild laughter was redoubled; the horrible troop assailed him." His knuckles grow bloody and his nails "were torn off by the roots." While Ranulph and Eleanor are left to marry and realize their love, it is the novel's horror, rather than its romance, that enthralled readers for decades.

BIBLIOGRAPHY
Carver, Stephen James. *The Life and Works of the Lancashire Novelist William Harrison Ainsworth, 1805–1882.* Lewiston, N.Y.: The Edwin Mellen Press, 2003.

ROXANA, OR THE FORTUNATE MISTRESS DANIEL DEFOE (1724)

Daniel DEFOE claims in his preface to the novel fully titled *The Fortunate Mistress; or, a History of the Life and Vast Variety of Fortunes of Mademoiselle de Beleau, Afterwards Call'd the Countess de Wintselshiem, in Germany. Being the Person Known by the Name of the Lady Roxana, in the Time of King Charles II,* that it represents an autobiography. He claims that the account differs from "most of the modern performances" of its kind in that its "foundation . . . is laid in truth of fact; and so the work is not a story, but a history." In the traditional 18th-century approach, Defoe seeks to validate the novel form, which had not yet achieved full acceptance as a valid approach to writing, by claiming for it a logistical truth, rather than the applicable human truth, which became sufficient to readers in later centuries. A call to identify with the protagonist and to empathize with her conflict signals the defining of fiction's purpose, shared with all literature, which is to study the human condition. Defoe also tactfully uses rhetoric to avoid censure for any material readers might find salacious, by employing an argument to be echoed almost two centuries later by Oscar WILDE: "If the reader makes wrong use of the figures, the wickedness is his own."

The beautiful Roxana is born to Huguenot refugees in England with ambitions that rise beyond what her husband can afford. A London brewer, he soon loses all his money, prompting Roxana to depart in search of a better life, abandoning not only her husband but their five children as well. She moves from England to Holland and on to France, supported by lovers whom she chooses to term "protectors." She encounters various adventures along the way, early on having a premonition of the death of her jeweler lover, who has set her up in a high-class home. When robbers kill him, Roxana is the one who makes out like a bandit, procuring the jewels, cash and other valuables he left behind. Although inconsolable, she finds her wits to wonder how "his relations, or his wife's friends," might behave and sends a message to her loyal maid, Amy, who proved "so dextrous, and did her work so nimbly, that she gutted the house." Roxana proves herself equal to most situations in which she finds herself caught up, gaining her nickname because she danced like Alexander the Great's widow.

When Roxana's children learn of her identity, however, her fortunes begin to turn. She has married a wealthy Dutch merchant, but in a narrative turn representative of several such throughout the novel, Roxana explains to the reader the guilt she felt, thus arousing reader sympathy: "I know than ever Belshazzar did at the handwriting on the wall, and the occasion was every way as just. Unhappy wretch, said I to myself, shall my ill-got wealth, the product of prosperous lust, and of a vile and vicious life of whoredom and adultery, be intermingled with the honest well-gotten estate of this innocent gentleman?"

Having charged Amy to find her children when she, now a countess, and her husband move back to London, Amy mistakenly reveals the identity of the countess who has been contributing toward the children's well-being and eventually employed them as her own servants. Amy's solution is to murder one especially troublesome daughter, but Roxana becomes angry with her maid for the first time in her life, then excuses her with the knowledge that only her "excess of affection and fidelity" caused her to suggest such a thing. Eventually Roxana concluded the original 1724 version with the summary statement that after "flourishing" for some years in "happy circumstances," she and Amy suffered a reversal of fortune thanks to the efforts of her unrelentingly curious daughter and "was brought low again." A continuation of Roxana's life was published in 1745 containing a lengthy explanation as to who had authored it. While historians cannot claim absolutely that Defoe wrote the addendum, its style bears close resemblance to his own.

In a plot that runs on too long and, as critics later observed, becomes fragmented, tedious, and anticlimactic, Amy disappears for a time, Roxana believes her daughter murdered, finds the daughter is not dead after all, Amy returns, and Roxana's husband learns of her identity thanks to the efforts of her own children, labeling her "an abandoned wretch," with "a fair countenance, joined to a false unrelenting heart." He dies shortly thereafter, leaving her only a small income. Remorseful and poor, Roxana must live the remainder of her life paying for her sins.

Claiming to write a true history, supporting the illusion of reality with varied and accurate external facts, Defoe sacrifices characterization in his early novel. As critic Lionel Stevenson notes, Defoe "is a chronicler of phenomena, not an interpreter of them," and none of his works can be considered major novels. *Roxana's* importance lies in its place on the continuum of the novel's development. Drawing from works that likely included those by Aphra BEHN and Mary Delarivière

MANLEY, Defoe helped advance an approach that separated itself from the hyperbole of ROMANCE fiction, presented in a simple and straightforward style that allowed focus on the quotidian, or events of everyday life. Thus, readers could better identify with the characters in his more realistic presentations, although they proved so objective in his striving for resemblance to "truth" that they could not represent the complex aspects of life that the novel would eventually supply.

BIBLIOGRAPHY

Novak, Maximillian E. *Daniel Defoe: Master of Fictions: His Life and Ideas.* New York: Oxford University Press, 2001.

Stevenson, Lionel. *The English Novel: A Panorama.* Boston: Houghton Mifflin, 1960.

Zimmerman, Everett A. *Defoe and the Novel.* Berkeley: University of California Press, 1975.

RUTH ELIZABETH GASKELL (1853)

Elizabeth GASKELL's second novel, *Ruth,* focused, as had her first, MARY BARTON (1848), on a young working-class woman. However, in *Ruth* she makes a heroine of an unlikely figure in a seamstress who bears an illegitimate child. While other novels of her era featured unmarried pregnant women, the characters generally died, often by violence, as if they committed social suicide through their pregnancies. Dedicated to social reform, Gaskell used her novels to comment on British society and its failure to care for its marginalized segments. When Henry Bellingham, a member of a higher class, seduces Ruth and abandons her, Gaskell clearly illustrates his lack of responsibility, both personal and social.

Ruth first meets Bellingham as she serves ladies at a ball. Innocent of the possible consequences, she accompanies him to Wales, where he falls ill, necessitating the arrival of his mother, who summarily dismisses the pregnant Ruth with a £50 payoff. While Ruth would gladly accept death, Thurstan Benson, an English clergyman on vacation in Wales, and his sister, the aptly named Faith, rescue her. Gaskell suggests the power of faith to overcome civil judgments, but does not overtly emphasize organized religion. Rather, she emphasizes the power of the spirit willing to be in touch with something greater than itself, as suggested in the romantic theories of the British poet William Wordsworth. Romantic influences are also evident in the awakening that Ruth undergoes when exposed to the wonders of nature.

In the Bensons' Eccleston home, Ruth assumes the identity of a widowed relation named Mrs. Denbigh and raises her son, Leonard. The community welcomes her, and she eventually acts as governess to the wealthy Bradshaw family. When Bellingham, calling himself Donne, reappears, he proposes marriage to Ruth, but she declines, believing he would be a poor role model for Leonard. Although Bellingham has renamed himself, he has gained no new self-understanding or identity improving his values.

A crisis occurs when the Bradshaws learn of Ruth's past and dismiss her, resulting in the rejection by the community of the entire Benson family and also provoking Leonard's horror over discovering the truth about his birth. The persistent Ruth later works in a medical ward during a cholera epidemic, her heroic and selfless actions winning her and the Bensons a new place in the community. A physician named Dr. Davis offers to support Leonard's education as a doctor, promising a happy ending to Ruth's story. However, Bellingham/Donne again falls ill, and Ruth feels she must nurse him, then catches his disease and dies as he recovers. The community mourns her loss and clearly values her humanity far more than they judge her past errors.

Because in each of her first two novels Gaskell wrote of topics about which she had little firsthand knowledge, they were not received well critically, although both proved popular. Still, her characterizations are praised and her sympathy with Ruth as a victim of the social injustice she so abhorred remains pronounced. She employs Mr. Bradshaw as a representative of those who practice a strict moral code, but one directed by law, rather than spirit. While Bradshaw himself is a devoted Christian, resisting temptations such as those offered by the theater, he makes his own son a hypocrite, forcing him to lie about his theater attendance. That parent/son relationship offers a contrast to the much more understanding one shared by Ruth and Leonard.

Bellingham/Donne also offers a contrast to Ruth in his ego-centered behavior. While Ruth undergoes an epiphany in Wales regarding the beauty of the world and her own inner beauty, Bellingham is blind to such elements. He goes to Wales primarily to promote his secret alliance with the innocent Ruth. Ruth's admirable development of self-awareness, rather than egotism, allows her to recognize her own weaknesses and to change her behavior as a result, something impossible for her seducer. Her total absence of guile is well represented in a scene where she is so moved by Benson's sermon, Faith must cling to her limp hand, "helpless on a cushion," as Ruth "sat on the ground, bowed down and crushed in her sorrow, till all was ended." Ruth retains a dignity that gains the admiration even of Bradshaw, her onetime accuser. In the closing scene following her death, after he visits the graveyard to plan a monument for Ruth's grave, Bradshaw leads the grieving Leonard into the Benson house, choked with sympathy, and eyes filled with tears. Only Bellingham/Donne learns nothing from Ruth, refusing to kiss her on her deathbed, and leaving his son in Benson's care, offering money to help atone for his "youthful folly." In a satisfying response, Benson, only then realizing that Donne is Leonard's father, rejects his money in Leonard's name, telling him sternly, "Men may call such actions as yours, youthful follies! There is another name for them with God, Sir!"

While Gaskell's craftsmanship in her two early novels may pale in contrast to that evident in her far better work CRANFORD (1853), they remain important examples of the "problem novel" of her era. Both continue to be studied and read for pleasure, and will likely never go out of print.

BIBLIOGRAPHY

Easson, Angus. Introduction to *Ruth,* by Elizabeth Gaskell. New York: Penguin, 1997, vii–xxiv.

RUTHERFORD, MARK   See WHITE, WILLIAM HALE.

S

ST. RONAN'S WELL SIR WALTER SCOTT

(1824) While not considered a major novel, *St. Ronan's Well* remains important in demonstrating a change of topic for its author, Sir Walter SCOTT. Scott, who basically invented HISTORICAL FICTION, varies from his traditional approach to employ as setting a fashionable 19th-century Scottish spa that frames a love-triangle plot. In his introduction, Scott explained he wanted to "*celebrare domestica facta*—to give an imitation of the shifting manners of our own time, and paint scenes the originals of which are daily passing round us, so that a minute's observation may compare the copies with the originals." In so writing, Scott interrogates an age-old argument as to whether art had a duty to imitate life. His historical fiction claimed to be based in the truth of history, but for this novel, he had only his own observations as basis. Many of the character contrivances remain familiar to readers of ROMANCE and of Scott's other novels. The heroine, Clara Mowbray, cannot stand on her own but must instead be related to power; she is the daughter of a Scottish laird, in this case laird of St. Ronan's. Blood relations play an equal consideration in the male characters as the two men who battle for Clara's favor are half-brothers, both sons of the dead Earl of Etherington.

As the novel opens, Scott introduces the best-drawn character in the book in the form of Meg Dods, landlady of St. Ronan's inn and the land around it. Her unusual position as a landowner came about due to the energy of her parents in taking over the crumbling mansion of St. Ronan's and converting it into a public house. The laird so approved of their venture, that he gave them the property to bequeath to their daughter, and Meg does not hesitate to remind visitors of her landed position. Her characterization as an independent and active female overshadows that of Clara Mowbray, who, while considered a free spirit as she roams the area unescorted on her pony, remains burdened by her past relationship with the brothers. She tells her own brother, John, in a statement that clearly foreshadows her fate, "Do not trust to Fortune . . . she has never been a friend to our family—not at least for many a day," marking her as burdened by melancholy.

When Clara meets one of the brothers, the artist Frank Tyrell, their conversation lets readers understand that a bitter past has left Clara disappointed by love. Her name symbolizes clarity of vision and thought, neither of which helps her enjoy life. Her later expressions of "excited imagination" and belief she has seen "an empty shadow" from her past when the present earl of Etherington, Frank's half-brother, visits her at her estate marks her clearly as a romantic heroine. As the earl reveals to Clara's father that Frank is the bastard son of his father, ineligible to inherit title or property, many of the elements of romance fall into place, with questions of identity and class offered as barriers to the fulfillment of love. As readers suspect, the man claiming to be the earl will be unmasked by

Clara's brother as an impostor with the ironic name of Valentine Bulmer, but the knowledge will be discovered too late to save Clara from tragedy. Clara's sharing of Shakespeare's Ophelia's fate may have surprised some readers, but it was part of the melodrama that fascinated Scott, who could not focus all his energies on jealousy at a country spa. He had to include a pretend marriage, deathbed confessions, and other trappings for sheer entertainment value.

BIBLIOGRAPHY

Allen, Walter Ernst. *Six Great Novelists: Defoe, Fielding, Scott, Dickens, Stevenson, Conrad.* Folcroft, Pa.: Folcroft Library Editions, 1971.

Rigney, Ann. *Imperfect Histories: The Elusive Past and the Legacy of Romantic Historicism.* Ithaca: Cornell University Press, 2001.

SANDITON JANE AUSTEN (unfinished)

Begun in 1817, when Jane AUSTEN had become ill with what researchers believe to be Addison's disease, *Sanditon* remains incomplete. It promised to resemble Austen's previous novels in its focus on the relationships of the fashionable. However, it also promised some differences, one of those being a focus on health, as three of her characters were hypochondriacs. Austen wrote with a comic tone about illness, as she herself was dying. While she commented to her niece Fanny on March 23 that the writing was not going well, the activity provided satisfaction for Austen. Some critics feel she may have been trying to cheer herself by making fun of those who imagined themselves ill, others that the subject was simply so much on her mind that she naturally incorporated it into her work. That those ill would travel to Bath for "the cure" did not signal a new practice. Seawater cures were common as early as 1750, and Austen had written to her sister Cassandra of her enjoyment of "bathing."

Featuring healthy protagonist Charlotte Heywood, the plot was to turn on Charlotte's visit to the seaside village Sanditon to stay with the Parkers and their offspring, the lazy Arthur and his bored, imaginative sisters, Diana and Susan. Upon her arrival, she meets Lady Denham, her niece Miss Denham, and her nephew, Sir Edward. Diana, Susan, Sir Edward, and Lady Denham all seem caricatures, while Charlotte lacks humor, to the point of being annoyingly prim. Thus, Austen's focus veers from complicated relationships and the strong characterizations exhibited in her other novels. It shifts to setting, bringing Sanditon and social conventions of the day to life, including fashion.

Living at Bath as she wrote, Austen had noticed that men had begun to carry umbrellas, which proved practical in that rainy town, but not everyone had accepted this new accessory as masculine. Austen demonstrates this minor conflict in *Sanditon,* as Mrs. Parker plans to buy her daughter a parasol in order to make her feel more mature and womanly, but Mr. Parker declares that his son should lead a more "robust" existence by playing in the sun. The narrative is framed in irony, for Arthur Parker, said to be too "delicate" to enter the water, is actually overweight and inert with no intention of exerting himself in any manner. Her characters indulge in the baubles offered everywhere, as does Charlotte Heywood, who goes to the library to purchase gloves and brooches. Mr. Parker takes great pride in his blue shoes and nankin boots, but Mr. Heywood remarks on the problems fashionable seaside retreats may cause the economy, raising prices and making "the poor good for nothing." Austen does not make fun of those who indulge in the material, for they are not bad people. Conversely, Lady Denham is not sympathetically drawn; she is mean and old-world, completely unaccepting of those not of her own social level. Austen also stressed one of her favorite subjects, the bleak future suffered by females who lacked wealth, expressed crudely by Lady Denham: "Young ladies that have no money are very much to be pitied."

No one knows the turn the plot would have taken. Austen's unusually hard SATIRE, likely explained by her severe illness, differs so much from her traditional approach that any attempt to complete *Sanditon* could not depend on familiarity with Austen's other novels. Such attempts have been made, including Julia Barrett's *Jane Austen's Charlotte* (2000).

BIBLIOGRAPHY

Barrett, Julia. *Jane Austen's Charlotte.* New York: M. Evans and Co., 2000.

Drabble, Margaret. Introduction to Jane Austen's *Lady Susan, The Watsons, Sanditon.* Middlesex, U.K.: Penguin Books, 1974.

SANDRA BELLONI (EMILIA IN ENGLAND) GEORGE MEREDITH (1864)

George MEREDITH first published his third novel, *Sandra Belloni,* under the title *Emilia in England.* The title character is a singer, discovered while singing in the woods by the three Pole daughters, Arabella, Cornelia, Adela, and their brother Wilfrid, an army officer without merit recently returned from India. Their party also includes Mr. Pericles, a Greek merchant who partners with Samuel Pole, the girls' father and a great music aficionado. Excited by his discovery, Pericles wants to train Emilia to become an opera singer. After inquiries, Wilfrid discovers she is Emilia Sandra Belloni, daughter of a violinist in a London orchestra who has been exiled from Italy. The Pole sisters move Emilia to London and introduce her to the social scene. At one gathering, she meets the Welshman Merthyr Powys, an Italian sympathizer, and also Captain Gambier, a socialite who once tried to pick up Sandra in a park and with whom Adela has struck up a flirtation. All admire Emilia's talent, and then she departs to keep a promised singing engagement at a village club. When she is caught up in a dispute between men of different villages, Wilfrid rescues her, causing Emilia to fall in love with him.

Love triangles develop between Mr. Pole's children and their various suitors and love interests, causing intense conflict. Two of the would-be matches are ordered by Pole himself, allowing Meredith his traditional commentary lambasting society's requirements of women and men of position for "good" marriages, often not based on love. Wilfrid is loved by, and sometimes loves, both Emilia and his father's choice as his wife, Lady Charlotte Chillingworth. Cornelia, in love with the disinherited son of a baronet, Purcell Barrett, is destined, according to Pole, to marry instead the middle-aged member of Parliament Sir Twickenham Pryme. Arabella does not feel strongly enough about either of her suitors, Edward Buxley and Freshfield Sumner, to express a preference. As for the widower Pole, he romances an Irish widow named Martha Chump, whom his daughters despise for her brogue and her commonness.

The setting for much of the novel is the Pole home in Surrey, Brookfield, where Pole invites Martha to visit. He engages in speculation with Martha's money to finance a much grander home in a higher status area called Besworth, a move that Wilfrid assumes will improve his chances of marrying the well-placed Lady Charlotte. In a regrettable move, Emilia pursues Wilfrid to Stornley, Lady Charlotte's mansion, pestering him to marry her, offering to sacrifice her opportunity to train in Milan at the renowned Conservatorio. This infuriates Pericles, who has plans for her future.

Wilfrid tells Emilia that he would like to marry her but cannot, due to his father's plans for him to marry Charlotte. Pole has suffered a financial disaster and depends more than ever on Wilfrid making a wealthy match, a recurring theme in fiction of the day. Recovering from a stroke, Pole escorts Emilia to a theater where she sees her father performing, causing her conflict, and leading her to attack Pole for turning Wilfrid against her. A short time later, Charlotte hears a rumor from Pole that Wilfrid has "compromised" Emilia, provoking Charlotte to meet with Emilia to persuade her to stop pressuring Wilfrid. Charlotte later agrees to marry Wilfrid even should he lose his fortune, when he attempts to break his engagement with her in order to marry Emilia, displaying his weak will.

Emilia has in the meantime developed three additional romantic interests. The symbolic meaning of character names holds true with the poet Tracy Runningbrook and one of Pole's clerks, Braintop; Merthyr also pursues Emilia. Charlotte invites Emilia to eavesdrop on a planned conversation with Wilfrid, in which he denies loving Emilia, a plot contrivance that hearkens back to Shakespeare's dramas and beyond. Convinced at last of Wilfrid's worthlessness, Emilia decides to train for the opera after all, but when she attempts to sing formally for Pericles, her voice deserts her. FEMINIST CRITICS find interesting her self-silencing at this point in her career, as silence traditionally was inflicted on women by society. Meredith emphasizes the arbitrary value placed on humans, and particularly women, as commodities when Pericles no longer has use for Emilia, who contemplates suicide, equating her value with her capacity to perform.

As Emilia wanders London, alone and hungry, Merthyr, her one true love, finds and rescues her. She learns as she recovers that Wilfrid has plans to depart England for a commission in the Austrian army, a fact Merthyr and his half-sister Georgianna try to distract Emilia from considering by taking her to a ball at Penarvon Castle. Wilfrid surfaces there, appealing to Emilia as she sits in her carriage. Merthyr, ever vigilant for Emilia's well-being, dissuades her from accompanying Wilfrid, and then departs to fight for freedom in Italy. Wilfrid begs for Emilia's hand and she refuses, but bargains to stay in England if he will not go to Austria.

While all this conflict is disconcerting, tragedy occurs through a misunderstanding with Cornelia's love, Barrett. He has become a baronet after all following his father's death and travels to Brookfield to deliver the good news. While there, another eavesdropping scene occurs when he overhears discussion of a pending marriage, believes incorrectly that Cornelia is to marry Pryme, and kills himself. Meredith again emphasizes the terrible consequences possible when parents force partners on their offspring, as well as the manner by which money is used to manipulate others; Pericles uses it to control Emilia's fate, and Pole takes advantage of a widow in attempts to restore his fortune.

The novel seems to come full circle when Emilia regains her voice, travels to Italy after all and is again heard singing in the woods by Pericles and Wilfrid, who are on this occasion accompanied by Charlotte. The imagery suggests the traditional female symbol of a bird in nature, as Emilia's art is identified with independence and the natural order. Pericles becomes excited again about Emilia's future career and agrees to support her training at the Conservatorio. Again vacillating between affections, Wilfrid declares his love for Emilia, but she cannot be deterred from her studies. Charlotte at last cuts Wilfrid lose, determining him of irredeemable character, and he loses her support in obtaining a diplomatic post. Upon the wounded Merthyr's return to England following the crushed Italian uprising, Pole has been rescued from his debts by Pericles, who takes Emilia to Milan. She corresponds with Merthyr and writes that she belongs in Italy but will always remember England; learns from Merthyr that Wilfrid has completed his plan to join the Austrian army. Merthyr anticipates Emilia's eventual return to England, at which time he hopes they may marry. Their relationship would act as the focus for Meredith's later novel *Vittoria* (1867). In that novel, many of the characters reappear to play roles in one of Meredith's most directly political works, in which Emilia, who has renamed herself Vittoria, marries an Italian revolutionary.

Sandra Belloni was praised by critics for its presentation of a strong, shrewd female protagonist, rather that the stereotypically helpless nonintellectual being of most popular literature.

BIBLIOGRAPHY

Jones, Mervyn. *The Amazing Victorian: A Life of George Meredith*. London: Constable, 1999.

SATIRE   Satire may be defined as literature in which wit and irony are employed to mock views expressed by another. While its effect may be entertainment, satire traditionally intended to provoke change in the form of social or political reform. Because not all readers may agree with the author's desire for reform, the author must retain the reader's interest through skill and an intelligent revelation of his/her opinions. Satire may be categorized as Juvenalian, the type that attacks wickedness with open indignation, or Horatian, the type that takes a suave approach to attacking folly. In the 18th century, satirists viewed satire as laying the lash to the backs of foolish authors. In English literature, early examples of satire in fiction included Aphra BEHN's *The City Heiress* (1682), which attacked the folly of London high society, while her *The Luck Chance* (1686) satirized arranged marriages. Jonathan SWIFT's *GULLIVER'S TRAVELS* (1726) took to task moral weaknesses in the human race; Henry FIELDING satirized Samuel RICHARDSON's style and theme in *PAMELA, OR VIRTUE REWARDED* (1740), in his PARODY of that work, *Shamela* (1741), as well as in *JOSEPH ANDREWS* (1742), in which Andrews is a brother to Richardson's fictional Pamela. Charles DICKENS employed satire to attack social ills, including poverty and abuse of women and children in several novels, including OLIVER TWIST (1837–39) and DAVID COPPERFIELD (1849–50), while William Makepeace THACKERAY used more subtlety and less sentimentality than Dickens in his VANITY FAIR (1847–48), satirizing social inequity and human frailty. Lewis CARROLL employed satire to criticize children's education through CHILDREN'S LITERATURE in his ALICE IN WONDERLAND (1862), and Samuel BUTLER's EREWHON (1872) created a utopian community to attack the moral hypocrisy he found in England, particularly in its attitude toward crime, religion, and treatment of children. Anthony TROLLOPE satirized English religious dissent between the high and low churches as well as England's political scene in a number of novels, including his chronicles of Barsetshire. Trollope's popular The WAY WE LIVE NOW (1875) brazenly satirized what he comprehended as the decaying ethical structure of British life. Satire's heavy-handed approach became less popular in the 20th century when readers desired more subtlety and less DIDACTICISM in novels of reform.

BIBLIOGRAPHY

Nilson, Don Lee Fred. Humor in Eighteenth- and Nineteenth-Century British Literature: A Reference Guide. Westport, Conn.: Greenwood, 1998.

Ogborn, Jane, and Peter Buckroyd. Satire. Cambridge: Cambridge University Press, 2001.

Rawson, C. J. Satire and Sentiment, 1660–1830. New Haven: Yale University Press, 1994.

SATURDAY REVIEW, THE

The Saturday Review was published from 1855 to 1930. Reviews of fiction were supervised by L. P. Hartly, but the magazine featured articles of general interest and those of miscellany. Before 1860, contributors included Edward Shanks, Robert Lynd, and Humbert Wolfe. By 1860, literary reviews received the uppermost priority. In the 1880s, the journal gained in literary value with the contributions of John St. Loe Strachey, who regarded literature as a fine art. By 1893, the journal had decreased its number of reviews. Sectional headings included "Letters to the Editor," "Acrostics," "Literary Competitions," and "The City."

From 1894 to 1930, seven men ascended to editorship, including Frank Harris, editor from 1894 to 1898, who "discovered" H. G. WELLS, Bernard Shaw, Aubrey Beardsley, and Max Beerbohm. Excellence in theater, art, and poetry criticism was maintained by Ivor Brown, Walter Bayes, and Gerald Bullet, respectively. Thomas HARDY, Hugh Walpole, and Hillaire Belloc also wrote for the journal. In 1930, the publication's name was changed to Week End Review.

BIBLIOGRAPHY

Graham, Walter. English Literary Periodicals. New York: Octagon Books, Inc., 1966.

SAVAGE, MARMION (1803–1872)

Anglo-Irish writer Marmion Savage produced six novels, with the best known being FALCON FAMILY (1845), a SATIRE of the Young Ireland party, with one character remarking that in Ireland, "your poets are politicians and your politicians poets." His humorous approach emphasized his theory that the conflict between England and Ireland could be solved through the application of moderation. He also served as fourth editor for the Examiner. A talented Dubliner, he has been mostly neglected in critical circles, overshadowed by later, more nationalistic authors.

BIBLIOGRAPHY

Norman, Paralee. "A Neglected Irish Novelist: Marmion W. Savage." Books at Iowa 35. Available online. URL: http://www.lib.uiowa.edu/spec-coll/Bai/norman.htm. Updated May 25, 1999.

SCHREINER, OLIVE (1855–1920)

A precocious girl born sixth of 12 children into a missionary family in Basutoland, South Africa, Olive Schreiner was raised at various mission stations by her rule-bound English mother, Rebecca Lyndall, and strict German father, Gottlab Schreiner. Brought up in an atmosphere of Evangelical conservatism, her interest in social causes developed early. Profoundly affected by an acute awareness of suffering before she became a teen, Schreiner rejected organized Christianity at age nine. A crucial component in her questioning of her parents' beliefs was likely the death of a beloved sister.

Already teaching school by the age of 15, Schreiner found her agnosticism supported in work by Herbert Spencer, who anticipated Charles DARWIN's evolutionary theory and insisted on individualism as crucial to a free ethical society. His *First Principles* (1862) seemed to validate her beliefs and feed her intellect. She began her writing career in 1873, featuring in her fiction the distinctive South African setting and populating her works with women who demonstrated social inequality. While she was not born in England, she was raised British, and her writing proved important to the development of the British novel.

Schreiner served as a governess between 1874 and 1881, her position considered little higher than that of a household servant. That experience strengthened her empathy for working individuals, and she took a great interest in those marginalized, from streetwalkers to piecemeal workers. She moved to England in hopes of finding a publisher in 1881, succeeding with the acceptance of *The STORY OF AN AFRICAN FARM* (1883) at Chapman & Hall by English poet, editor, and novelist, George MEREDITH. Her novel contrasted the bleak farm, bereft of any spiritual sustenance, with that of its promising surrounding landscapes, countering romantic images of the frontier and emphasizing concerns of women. It proved seminal in the development of colonial literature.

During a return to South Africa in 1889, Schreiner embarked on an effort to oppose racism and IMPERIALISM, always envisioning herself more an individual endeavoring to reform society than a popular writer. That vision is apparent in *Dreams* (1891) and *Dream Life and Real Life* (1893), in which one topic is sexual equality. In 1894, she married Samuel Cronwright, later a politician, and continued to champion those victimized by an unjust society in *A South African's View of the Situation* (1898). Women's rights offered her focus in *Woman and Labour* (1911). Two additional important works were published posthumously, *From Man to Man* (1926), an experimental work that leaves unresolved the tensions between two sisters, an artist and a "fallen woman," and *Undine* (1929). A memorable pacifist radical, Schreiner wrote works of great interest to FEMINIST CRITICS that continue to be studied as seminal in the advance of literary feminism as well as South African anglophone literature; most are available as electronic texts.

BIBLIOGRAPHY

Barsby, Tina. *Olive Schreiner: An Introduction.* Grahamstown, South Africa: National English Literary Museum, 1995.

Berkman, Joyce Avrech. *The Healing Imagination of Olive Schreiner: Beyond South African Colonialism.* Amherst: University of Massachusetts Press, 1989.

Krebs, Paula M. "Olive Schreiner's Racialization of South Africa." *Victorian Studies* 40, no. 3 (Spring 1997): 427–34.

Sanders, Mark. "Towards a Genealogy of Intellectual Life: Olive Schreiner's *The Story of an African Farm.*" *Novel* (Fall 2000): 77–97.

SCIENCE FICTION   Science fiction incorporates elements of other genres and subgenres, including FANTASY and ROMANCE. Plots turn on logical developments that might occur in technology beyond those available in the author's era. That could include the use of inanimate figures, such as robots, powered by technology to serve man, or the use of electric power to animate (from the term *anima,* literally "breath" or "soul") the dead. Developments might also include advances allowing humans to ignore natural laws like gravity, or the confinements of time or space. Humans might also discover a way to assume animal powers, such as flight, speed, or strength, by ingesting potions or through the discovery of an unknown source of energy. The stories may be cautionary in nature, allowing readers a glimpse of a terrifying future or alternative existence that may promise advancement but that should ultimately be avoided. Some science fiction creates what seems an ideal world as UTOPIAN FICTION, only to reveal its conflicts and sometimes horrors. The power necessary to execute the types of advancement depicted by science fiction often corrupt those who may begin to use that power with the best of intentions, supplying a moral statement about man's tendency toward depravity. Developments at first thought to advance and improve the plight of mankind may become its scourge instead, resulting in disease, famine, war, pollution, chaos, or other aspects of doom, cautioning readers against unbridled enthusiasm over new concepts. Although few representatives of science fiction in its purest sense appeared during the 18th century, Robert PALTOCK's *The LIFE AND ADVENTURES OF PETER WILKINS* (1751) qualifies as an early form. More examples of the developing subgenre appeared in the 19th century, due to the nascent condition of technology and scientific advancement. They include works such as Mary SHELLEY's *FRANKENSTEIN* (1818) and Robert Louis STEVENSON's *The STRANGE CASE OF DR. JEKYLL AND MR. HYDE* (1886), both of which also qualify as HORROR FICTION; Edward BULWER-LYTTON's *The COMING RACE OR THE NEW UTOPIA* (1871), which also qualifies as SATIRE; Samuel BUTLER's *EREWHON* (1872); and H. G. WELLS's *The TIME MACHINE* (1895).

BIBLIOGRAPHY

Bainbridge, William Sims. *Dimensions of Science Fiction.* Cambridge: Harvard University Press, 1986.

Clute, John, and Peter Nichols, eds. *The Encyclopedia of Science Fiction.* London: Orbit, 1993.

Golden, Kenneth L. *Science Fiction, Myth, and Jungian Psychology.* Lewiston, N.Y.: Edwin Mellen Press, 1995.

SCOTT, SIR WALTER (1771–1832)

Born the ninth child among 12 to a Scottish Writer to the Signet, Walter Scott would overcome early illness to complete education at Edinburgh High School and study law at Edinburgh University. A lover of the written and spoken word, he consumed books and studied with delight ballads and Scottish history. His interest in the supernatural led him to contribute to Matthew Gregory (Monk) LEWIS's "hobgoblin repast," also known as *Tales of Wonder.* A poet early in his career, Scott also published an edition of poetry by John Dryden, a monumental edition on Jonathan SWIFT, and translated German GOTHIC tales. He first gained attention in 1805 with *The Lay of the Last Minstrel,* which he followed with many lengthy poems, including *Marmion* (1808), *The Lady of the Lake* (1810), *The Vision of Don Roderick* (1811), and *The Bridal of Triermain* (1813). His original ballads gained him fame, but he felt poetry better served by his contemporary, George Gordon, Lord Byron, and turned to writing novels. The change was partly a practical one, as Scott needed to increase his income, although he hesitated at first, considering fiction a lower order of literature.

Scott remains crucial to the development of the novel, gaining credit for the popularity of what would later be labeled HISTORICAL FICTION. His effect on other writers proved immense, as his incorporation of ROMANCE and QUEST elements, as well as detailed focus on a particular locality, would influence American writer James Fenimore Cooper and English writers with as diverse approaches as Charles DICKENS, William Makepeace THACKERAY, and Jane AUSTEN. A lifelong correspondence with another Scottish novelist, Maria EDGEWORTH, began in 1814, culminating in her visiting Scott in 1823. He described to friends the day of her visit as one of the happiest of his life, emphasizing his friendly and outgoing nature.

Scott produced an amazing 20-plus novels between 1814 and 1828 featuring individuals dealing with conflicting cultures and reflecting the 18th-century influence of the Enlightenment. His three different Tales of My Landlord series stressed his belief in the necessity of progress built on tradition and included an astounding output: *WAVERLEY* (1814), *GUY MANNERING* (1815), and *The ANTIQUARY* (1816) were followed by the first Tales series, *The Black Dwarf* and *OLD MORTALITY* (both 1816). The second series included *ROB ROY* (1817) and *The HEART OF MIDLOTHIAN* (1818), with the third including *The BRIDE OF LAMMERMOOR* and *The LEGEND OF MONTROSE* (both 1819). Additional novels included *IVANHOE* (1819), *The MONASTERY,* and *The ABBOTT* (both 1820), *KENILWORTH* and *The Pirate* (both 1821), *The Fortunes of Nigel* (1822), *Peveril of the Peak, QUENTIN DURWARD,* and *ST. RONAN'S WELL* (all 1823), *REDGAUNTLET* (1824), *Tales of the Crusaders,* including *The Betrothed* and *The TALISMAN* (1825) and *WOODSTOCK* (1826).

Scott's success allowed him to build a baronial mansion in Scotland, which he named Abbotsford, and he became a baronet in 1820. However, Scott's amiable nature allowed others to take advantage of him, and financial investment in a failed firm left him more than £100,000 in debt. He spent the rest of his life in an honorable attempt to pay his debts, continuing editing and writing large volumes of literary criticism, as well as corresponding with other writers. From 1820 through 1825, he published Chronicles of the Canongate, which included *The Two Drovers, The Highland*

Widow, and *The Surgeon's Daughter* in the first series of 1827, *St. Valentine's Day, or The Fair Maid of Perth* in the second series, and the fourth series in the Landlord group, *Anne of Geierstein* (1829), *Count Robert of Paris,* and *Castle Dangerous* (both in 1832). Too weakened to sustain such a pace, he left Italy, where he had been writing, to return to Abbotsford, where he died in September of 1832.

Not only was Scott a literary force, he actually affected British culture as well, boosting Scotland's reputation following its 1745 rebellion against England. While some later critics judged his characters shallow and one-dimensional and his plots thin, his focus on history and on cultural development through political and social change has always been praised. The enormous source material on Scott demonstrates the huge effect he had on literature, and especially on fiction. Important contributions include his journal, edited by W. E. K. Anderson (1972); his letters, edited by Sir H. J. C. Grierson (12 vol., 1932–37); biographies by his son-in-law, J. G. Lockhart (10 vol., 1902) and E. Johnson (2 vol., 1970); and studies by A. O. J. Cockshut (1969), R. Mayhead (1973), J. Millgate (1984), J. Wilt (1986), J. Kerr (1989), and A. N. Wilson (1989). His works will be studied and enjoyed forever; many have been transformed into dramatic presentations for the stage and film, and several are available in electronic as well as print versions. At least one novel, *The Abbot,* inspired a painting, *The Abdication of Mary Queen of Scots at Lochleven Castle* by W. B. C. Fyfe (1860).

BIBLIOGRAPHY

Allen, Walter Ernst. *Six Great Novelists: Defoe, Fielding, Scott, Dickens, Stevenson, Conrad.* Folcroft, Pa.: Folcroft Library Editions, 1971.

Hayden, John O., ed. *Scott: The Critical Heritage.* London: Routledge & Kegan Paul, 1970.

Rigney, Ann. *Imperfect Histories: The Elusive Past and the Legacy of Romantic Historicism.* Ithaca, N.Y.: Cornell University Press, 2001.

Rubenstein, Jill. *Sir Walter Scott: An Annotated Bibliography of Scholarship and Criticism, 1975–1990.* Aberdeen: Association for Scottish Literary Studies, 1994.

Sutherland, John. *The Life of Walter Scott: A Critical Biography.* Cambridge: Blackwell, 1995.

SCOTTISH CHIEFS, THE JANE PORTER (1810)

Jane PORTER's *The Scottish Chiefs* predated by four years, and proved second only to, Sir Walter SCOTT's novel WAVERLEY (1814) in arousing the reading public's interest in Scotland and its history. An enormously ambitious work in terms of both length and researched material, it chronicles the feats of the two Scottish war heroes, William Wallace and Robert the Bruce, in their revolutions against the tyranny of England over Scotland during the reign of Edward II. While both men are touted as seminal in Scotland's revolutionary history, Wallace receives the most attention.

Porter did not spare the reader from scenes of gruesome violence, beginning with perhaps the most unsettling of the death scenes in the murder of Lady Marion Wallace by Heselrigge, the dastardly English governor of Lanark. When she will not reveal her husband's hiding place, declaring, "I kneel to heaven alone; and may it ever preserve my Wallace from the fangs of Edward and his tyrants!" Heselrigge becomes so incensed, he plunges his sword through her body, killing her unborn child as well Lady Marion. The murder of innocents galvanizes the Scots against Heselrigge, who is deserted by some of his own followers, so appalled at his act of cruelty that their personal sense of honor demands their withdrawal of support.

The setting of Stirling Castle provides a backdrop for hundreds of bloody deaths. While Porter does not support war, she does distinguish between those men who act within its artificially imposed boundaries of behavior with valor and those who act with duplicity, betraying and lying to men whose trust they have gained. Wallace is depicted as an angel of vengeance, adhering to popular belief of the day; comparisons to Gideon and also to Ulysses help support the myth-building. Even so, Wallace is not drawn as a bloodthirsty warrior. His stance as a willing leader but unwilling participant in war is clear, for example, when he reacts to a fellow soldier's call for Loch Lomond to run red with English blood: "To hail the field of blood with the fierceness of a hatred eager for the slaughter of its victim—to know any joy in combat but that each contest might render another less necessary—did not enter into the imagination of Wallace." All 89 chapters of the novel are available online at The Celebration of Women Writers Web site.

BIBLIOGRAPHY

Dennis, Ian. *Nationalism and Desire in Early Historical Fiction.* New York: St. Martin's Press, 1997.

Sage, Lorna. "Porter, Jane." *The Cambridge Guide to Women's Writing in English.* Cambridge: Cambridge University Press, 1999, 505.

SECRET HISTORY OF QUEEN ZARAH AND THE ZARAZIANS, THE MARY DELARIVIÈRE MANLEY (1705)

The Secret History of Queen Zarah and the Zarazians proved to be Mary Delarivière MANLEY's first success, following the unimpressive productions of two of her dramas. Her story proved popular enough to follow with a sequel, also in 1705. A political piece published during parliamentary elections, it delighted readers with SATIRE aimed at members of the Whig Party, including Sarah and John Churchill, the Duke and Duchess of Marlborough, and Sidney, Earl of Godolphin. Like many members of the more conservative Tory Party, Manley despised Queen Anne, who had risen to the throne in 1702 after her brother-in-law, William III, died. Gossip spread that the Churchills maintained undue influence over the weak queen, manipulating her from the time she was a princess at odds with the king. Both Churchills achieved high appointments at court and appeared to dominate Anne.

In the tale of sexual and political intrigue, Zarah represents Sarah Jenyns, later Sarah Churchill. The narrative describes her as a woman "whom fortune had cut out purely for the service of her own interest, without any regard to the strict rules of honor or virtue." As she seeks to ingratiate herself with the princess Albania (Princess Anne) and plots to endanger the life of Mulgarvius (John Sheffield, Duke of Buckingham), Zarah's actions are described as "a treacherous part as was ever acted by woman filled with love and ambition, for though she was resolved to gain the last, she was one who left no stone unturned to secure to herself the first, which has always made her life one continued scene of politic intrigue." Readers would later gain a key identifying each character with a real-life person, offering an example of the ROMAN À CLEF, a French approach to satire.

Almost as interesting as the story itself was Manley's introduction, a vastly important statement that discussed changes in the fiction genre. It was considered a crucial statement regarding English literature until scholars discovered the introduction to be a translation of a French essay from a 1702 French courtesy book. Manley writes of the story, "little histories of this kind have taken place of romances," explaining that "these little pieces which have banished romances are much more agreeable to the brisk and impetuous humor of the English." She also discusses proper subject matter, noting that to aid reader understanding the topic should not be from the too-distant past, and suggests regarding style that "names of persons ought to have a sweetness in them, for a barbarous name disturbs the imagination." Her discourse regarding truth brings up points still arguable, such as whether a character may indulge in improbable actions and still demonstrate realism. She also holds that fear and pity in romance and tragedy are what capture reader sympathy. She suggests that stories conclude with a moral "which may engage virtue," as history's end is "to instruct and inspire into men the love of virtue and abhorrence of vice by the examples proposed to them." All of Manley's writings became important during the revival of interest in early women writers inspired through FEMINIST CRITICISM in the mid-20th century.

BIBLIOGRAPHY

Backscheider, Paula R., and John J. Richetti. *Popular Fiction by Women 1660–1730, An Anthology.* Oxford: Clarendon Press, 1996.

SELF CONTROL: A NOVEL MARY BRUNTON (1811)

Had her short life not ended tragically by death in childbirth, Mary BRUNTON might have greatly expanded her volume of work, which influenced writers as important as Jane AUSTEN. Austen praised Brunton's first novel, *Self Control*, wondering in print whether she might ever reach its excellence with her own writing. With Brunton's additional two novels, *DISCIPLINE* (1815) and *Emmeline* (1819, posthumous), *Self Control* takes its place in the group of works deemed crucial to a women's writing tradition and valued by FEMINIST CRITICS. While all her writing is laced with moral passages, Brunton's pace remains lively with a tone that edges on SATIRE.

A clergyman's wife, Brunton used fiction to assemble cautionary tales. In *Self Control* she focuses on Laura Montreville, a Scottish innocent who throughout the lengthy novel must resist seduction. The reader learns from the first page that Laura will meet the challenge when the narrative notes that she possesses "an active mind, a strong sense of duty, and the habit of meeting and of overcoming adverse circumstances." That she will be victorious is of little doubt, despite the many pages of conflict ahead of her. They began with her contentious mother, who "had no principles and her heart was a mere 'pulsation on the left side.'" However, Laura's father, Captain Montreville, adores her. When Laura is 17 her mother dies, and romance becomes important, entering her life in the form of the dastardly Colonel Hargrave, later described as having been "the spoiled child of a weak mother." He holds little interest for Laura, who has fantasized about the perfect man, next to whom Hargrave pales. To escape Hargrave, she moves in with her friends the Douglases, in their country cottage. Her father eventually joins her, and they relocate to England as she continues to hope for her hero. In an amusing conversation, a friend asks Laura whether she might like a lover like Tom Jones, title character of Henry FIELDING's novel. Laura makes clear her opinion by saying, "I could not admire in a lover qualities which would be odious in a husband," declaring that the public tolerates Tom only because he compares so positively with the novel's horrid antagonist Blifil. Laura declares that her favored heroes are from works by Jane PORTER, allowing Brunton to emphasize female writers and the importance of creativity to women, also evident in Laura's painting.

When Montreville falls ill, Laura must sell some jewelry to help support herself and her father and accidentally encounters Hargrave, who is overjoyed to have found her following a three-month search. Unfortunately the toll of her recent concerns overcomes her and she faints, caught up by Hargrave, who feels she has especially chosen him to support her. As Hargrave renews his acquaintance with the ill Montreville, he convinces the older man that his union with Laura would be in her best interest. Laura grows wan and

pale, as a good ROMANCE heroine should, bravely attempting to hold up under the pressure to marry a man she does not love. Her continued pursuit of her art emphasizes the value of the release of passion such creation involves.

The novel presents an excellent example of the overblown language of the period and the popular romance novel when Laura protests her father's attempts to persuade her to accept Hargrave's offer: "How can a father urge his child to join to pollution this temple, (and she laid her hand emphatically on her breast) which my great master has offered to hallow as his own abode? No! The express command of heaven forbids the sacrilege." Following her father's death, Laura falls on predictable hard times, yet manages to escape Hargrave, her virtue and stamina rewarded by an eventual loving union with the virtuous Montague de Courcy.

While many early critics stressed Laura's more obvious characteristics (her religious piety, moral superiority to many around her, natural sense of self-worth and dignity, modesty and passivity), later feminist critics noted that through Laura's actions, Brunton clearly supports a woman's right to creative work and to the income made possible by that work. And while Laura fantasizes about a certain man, she never waits passively to be rescued by one. Instead, she is an active heroine who disengages herself from threatening situations. Brunton's work may hold little aesthetic appeal for readers centuries after its writing, but it remains of great interest to those seeking to understand the development of women's writing, and as an example of work by an ordinary woman of a middle class that would soon be heard in its demand for social reform.

BIBLIOGRAPHY

Maitland, Sara. Introduction to *Self Control: A Novel*, by
  Mary Brunton. New York: Pandora, 1986, ix–xi.
Spender, Dale. *Mothers of the Novel: 100 Good Women Writers
  Before Jane Austen*. New York: Pandora, 1988.

SENSATION FICTION   Wilkie COLLINS wrote in the preface to his novel *Basil: A Story of Modern Life* (1852) that the extraordinary, such as themes and events found in French drama of the day, yielded just as legitimate a subject matter as did ordinary daily events, lending itself well to fiction. His admiration of the approach of those sensational plays led to his production of the first true sensation fiction in his *Hide and Seek* (1854). He borrowed freely from Charles DICKENS's *BLEAK HOUSE* (1853), in which questions regarding the parentage of an illegitimate child form the basis of the plot. His mixture in that novel of tranquil aspects with sensational ones did not yield success. However, he had honed his approach by the time *The WOMAN IN WHITE* (1860) appeared, and it proved hugely popular. Similar to the approach of GOTHIC FICTION, in which authors attempted to produce fear and an overabundance of curiosity in the reader through abundant sordid detail, sensation fiction focused on crime and mystery, with their resultant tone of suspense and overstimulation to excite readers. This Victorian genre sold many novels, both in a pure sensation form and as a blended approach with other styles, including Charles READE's *Peg Woffington* and *CHRISTIE JOHNSTONE* (both 1853), *IT IS NEVER TOO LATE TO MEND* (1856), his most popular work, *The CLOISTER AND THE HEARTH* (1861), and *HARD CASH* (1868). In addition, Mary Elizabeth BRADDON's *LADY AUDLEY'S SECRET* (1862), Charles DICKENS's uncompleted *The MYSTERY OF EDWIN DROOD* (1870), and Thomas HARDY's first novel, *Desperate Remedies* (1871), represent only a few examples of the sensation approach.

BIBLIOGRAPHY

Bachman, Maria K., and Don Richard Cox, eds. *Reality's Dark Light: The Sensational Wilkie Collins*. Knoxville: University of Tennessee Press, 2003.

Phillips, Walter Clarke. *Dickens, Reade, and Collins: Sensation Novelists; a Study in the Conditions and Theories of Novel Writing in Victorian England*. New York: Russell & Russell, 1962.

Van Sant, Ann Jessie. *Eighteenth-century Sensibility and the Novel: The Senses in Social Context*. Cambridge: Cambridge University Press, 1993.

SENSE AND SENSIBILITY JANE AUSTEN

(1811) Begun in 1795 with the early title of *Marianne and Elinor,* Jane AUSTEN's second published novel, *Sense and Sensibility,* would become one of her most famous. Austen signed the novel "by a Lady" and had to publish it at her own expense. Begun in the 18th century, the novel reflects the views of that age and Austen's own resistance to new ideas and expression of emotion. Firmly a member of the social class best described as minor social gentry, Austen remained unaffected by the ambition for material goods of the working class and resistant toward the self-indulgences of the aristocratic class. She rarely traveled outside of southwestern England, spending most of her time in small villages or resort areas immune from the INDUSTRIAL REVOLUTION, and most of her friendships were with those of her own age or the elderly. Thus, she focused on the concerns of those groups, which were basically proper etiquette and social behavior and romantic relationships, specifically marriage. But within that romance theme, she focused on specific details, not emotions. Her title notes her dominant themes, with sense proving superior to sensibility, culminating in a judgment against the recent wildly popular SENTIMENTAL FICTION.

Marianne Dashwood represents sensibility, with her high spirits, public displays of enthusiasm, and adoration of poetry, while her older sister, Elinor, represents sense, approaching situations with logic and determination, and remaining ever mindful of social conventions. When their father dies, the Dashwood sisters and their mother must abandon the family home in Sussex, when it passes to Mr. Dashwood's son by a first marriage, John Dashwood. Although Mr. Dashwood had asked John to care generously for the women, John's selfish nature is supported by those of his wife and mother-in-law, Mrs. Ferrars, prompting him to remove the family to a Devonshire cottage. There Elinor meets and forms an affection for Edward Ferrars but later discovers he has promised himself to Lucy Steele. Because Edward had not shared that information with her himself, Elinor feels betrayed, but her self-control allows her to continue to function in her normal manner.

Another character, Colonel Brandon, a man who had suffered due to a lost love when young, becomes interested in the Dashwoods, especially Marianne, whose high spirits he admires. In the meantime, Marianne has fallen passionately in love with John Willoughby, and he seems to return her passion. However, he suddenly departs for London with little explanation, which greatly upsets Marianne. Colonel Brandon is not surprised by this behavior, as he had known Willoughby to behave in a dishonorable way in the past. While Elinor handles her separation from Edward with quiet grace, Marianne, never one to keep her emotions secret, pursues Willoughby when the sisters visit their London friend, Mrs. Jennings. Willoughby behaves coldly toward Marianne, further distressing her, and she at last learns he is engaged, an engagement he pursues to please a relative whose fortune he hopes to inherit. Marianne falls ill, and Colonel Brandon plays a crucial part in her recovery, during which time she realizes that steady love is far more important than a momentary passion. As for Elinor's happiness, Edward's mother has disowned him for his honorable agreement to keep his engagement to Lucy, and she assigns the family fortune to his brother Robert with whom Lucy then elopes. That frees Edward to propose to Elinor. He accepts the offer from Colonel Brandon of a pastorship at a church that will allow the couple to remain close to the rest of the Dashwood family.

As do all Austen's novels, this one ends happily, with all misunderstandings settled. Because of her chosen subject matter, a happy ending necessarily equated to the marriage of all eligible female characters. Austen often emphasized the limited choices available to women of her own class, who remained dependent on husbands, fathers, or brothers, as she herself did, supported by her brother when she failed to marry. For that reason, FEMINIST CRITICS remain interested in Austen's fiction, despite its lack of overt emphasis on female independence. Austen's quiet approach well makes the point that Britain's property entailment system was flawed, always following the male line and sacrificing to circumstance innocent and deserving women.

Sense and Sensibility has never been out of print, remaining popular with the general reading public as well as academic programs. Its production in a 1995 movie version brought it renewed attention.

BIBLIOGRAPHY

Ross, Josephine. *Jane Austen: A Companion.* New Brunswick: Rutgers University Press, 2003.

SENTIMENTAL FICTION   Sentimental fiction grew from a tradition of belief, like that espoused by French philosopher Jean-Jacques Rousseau, that human emotions were pure and good, growing from a natural state. By the 1850s, the theory of original sin attracted fewer believers, as many followed Rousseau's suggestion that civilization proved a corrupter of humans, not honest feelings. They also hoped to tap the strength from sentimentality once furnished by religion. Long believed to be the first English novel, Samuel RICHARDSON's *PAMELA* (1740) represented the first sentimental fiction as well, and Richardson's next novel, *CLARISSA* (1747–48), continued the trend. Taking a high moral tone, Richardson produced work based on the method of French drama, shaped to appeal to a mostly female and sentimental readership. His plot of a poor young woman who succeeds in moving up in life was a common one, appearing in broadside ballads and scandalous chronicle sheets of the day. It proved so popular that readers would flaunt copies in public, fans were printed with scenes from the work, and the famous actor David Garrick appeared in a stage version. Told in a hyperbolic first-person narration, via the use of letters from various characters as the full text of the novel, both plots were buoyed by sentiment and emotion that many readers enjoyed, but many other abhorred, including Henry FIELDING, who would write *Shamela* (1741) as a PARODY of the form and a particular rebuff of Richardson's work. Unlike those who saw Pamela as filled with virtue and innocence, Fielding agreed with others that she represented nothing more than an opportunistic hypocrite.

Readers of sentimental fiction could anticipate main characters that were cloyingly good, set apart from a hostile world in which they often could not survive. Examples include Henry MACKENZIE's novel *The MAN OF FEELING* (1771) and Oliver GOLDSMITH's *The VICAR OF WAKEFIELD* (1776). As the century closed, authors began rebelling against the demands of such predictable storytelling. Jane AUSTEN mocked the approach in her novels *SENSE AND SENSIBILITY* (1811) and *NORTHANGER ABBEY* (1818), the latter also a parody of GOTHIC FICTION, another approach utilizing pronounced tension and sustained unrealistic emotion in its style. Elizabeth GASKELL added a large dollop of sentimentality to her DIDACTIC yet appealing tales of the trials of young workingwomen, *MARY BARTON* (1848) and *RUTH* (1853). Later, such fiction became synonymous to moralists with sex tales, as indeed *Pamela* was, in its focus on the attempted seduction of a servant girl by her master. Young women were discouraged from reading tales to prevent heightened passion and overwrought temperaments. Yet even astute readers such as Samuel JOHNSON preferred Richardson's work in his day, and he once wrote of that novelist, "you must read him for the sentiment." Mrs. Eliza HAYWOOD adhered to Richardson's pattern in her *The History of Pompey the Little* and *The History of Miss Betsy Thoughtless,* didactic works of mediocrity.

BIBLIOGRAPHY

Ellis, Markman. *The Politics of Sensibility: Race, Gender, and Commerce in the Sentimental Novel.* New York: Cambridge University Press, 1996.

Lenard, Mary. *Preaching Pity: Dickens, Gaskell, and Sentimentalism in Victorian Culture.* New York: Peter Lang, 1999.

Rawson, C. J. *Satire and Sentiment, 1660–1830: Stress Points in the English Augustan Tradition.* New Haven, Conn.: Yale University Press, 2000.

SENTIMENTAL JOURNEY, A LAURENCE STERNE (1768)

Published only a few weeks before Laurence STERNE's death, *A Sentimental Journey Through France and Italy by Mr. Yorick* featured a parson character made famous in Sterne's first novel, *The Life and Opinions of Tristram Shandy,* the title later shortened through familiarity to simply *TRISTRAM SHANDY.* Although Sterne did not complete. *A Sentimental Journey,* and Yorick spent most of his time in France, it became popular due to some extent to the author's close identification with his character. Sterne based Yorick's experiences on his own, including much detail from his travels. More to the point, he had to some extent traded personas with his fictional character, referring to himself as Yorick and Tristram and inserting one of his own sermons into *Tristram Shandy* for Yorick's delivery before his congregation. The conflation of character with author proved so successful that Yorick's actions in *Tristram Shandy* elicited anger against Sterne himself. One critic expressed outraged, as Parson

Yorick's wearing of a harlequin coat to deliver a sermon amounted to Sterne's satirizing the Anglican Church and his own pledge of sobriety in all actions as a church representative. Sterne must have delighted in resurrecting his alter-ego to wander through France and Italy.

Later critics question much of Yorick's behavior in *A Sentimental Journey* as to its motivation. He supposedly acted as suggested by the novel's title in treating those he met along his journey with sentiment, or sympathy. As Paul Goring explains, the term *sentiment* had multiple meanings in Sterne's era, its first recorded use seen in a letter written by Lady Bradshaight to Samuel RICHARDSON in 1749. She asked the famous novelist what he believed to be the meaning of the fashionable term, often overheard in conversation. Generally it represented an idea expressed with some emotion, but it also related to the intellectual idea of sympathy, as in Adam Smith's expression in *Theory of Moral Sentiments* (1759), when he argued that society could not engage in proper conduct without exercising sympathy for all its members. Richardson had used the approach to strong effect, eliciting sympathy for the protagonist of his novel *PAMELA* (1740) by arousing reader emotion through overuse of hyperbole and repetition. The SENTIMENTAL NOVEL gained immediate popularity, its formulaic nature prompting SATIRE and PARODY on the part of artists who declared it opportunistic fiction. However, Sterne's use of the term was based on its original sense as the capacity of human nature to feel sympathy toward others, prompting actions that would help relieve their suffering. Thus, his obvious use of irony in undercutting Yorick's so-called selflessness have caused critics, particularly PSYCHOANALYTIC CRITICS, to question whether Sterne was conscious of Yorick's egoism and even what might been seen as repressed hostility.

For example, the chapter "Montriul" concludes with Yorick meeting a group of unfortunates he determines to help. He decides at first to present each one with a single sou, a French coin of low value, an insulting amount in exchange for the travails of the individuals; one traveler had lost a hand in war, while one woman suffered a dislocated hip. In addition, he repeatedly calls attention to his own sacrifice in a patronistic tone, writing, "I gave one simply *pour l'amour de Dieu*" (for the love of God), and in the next chapter refers to his acts as "little matters." When he later donates to a young girl and describes his reaction to her expressions of gratitude by stating "it was a small tribute . . . which I could not avoid paying to virtue," Yorick seems to refer to his own virtue. His penchant for placing monetary value on human suffering also suggests a worldly nature, and Yorick seems obsessed in commodifying human experience. This may be a conscious effort on Sterne's part, representing his sly attitude toward his subject and readers. Yorick is, after all, a creation of Shakespeare, based on the skull discovered in *Hamlet,* a fact of which readers are reminded by Monsieur Le Count de B****. While Yorick the narrator takes some pains to separate himself in the minds of his characters and readers from the original Yorick, he clearly lacks humility in laying claim to the greatest writer in the English language as his father creator. On the other hand, his self-consciousness may reflect Sterne's determination to satirize the popular genre of travel literature, specifically that of Tobias SMOLLETT; he clearly suggests Smollett's title, *Travels through France and Italy,* with his own. Sterne judged most examples of the genre as dull and boring in their generalized descriptions of geography and the practices of local inhabitants. Thus, he focuses on individual characters during his travels, in order to add interest and color and emphasizes Yorick's reactions to those characters to set his work apart.

Based on Sterne's general attitudes toward life and his other writings, *A Sentimental Journey* offers a fitting finale to his work. Regardless of his motives and sincerity, he shapes a humorous witty tale supported by the truths of his own experience that continues to be enjoyed as a subject of study. Yorick best expresses Sterne's ability when he comments on the joy of reading Shakespeare's *Much Ado about Nothing,* allowing his comment to represent the universal effect of all fine literature: "Sweet pliability of man's spirit, that can at once surrender itself to illusions, which cheat expectation and sorrow of their weary moments."

BIBLIOGRAPHY

Battestin, Martin C. "*A Sentimental Journey* and the Syntax of Things." *Augustan Worlds: Essay in Honour of A. R. Humphreys.* Edited by J. C. Hilson, M. M. B. Jones, and J. R. Watson. Leicester: Leicester University Press, 1978, 223–29.

Goring, Paul. Introduction to *A Sentimental Journey,* by Laurence Sterne. New York: Penguin, 2001, xi–xxxii.

Loveridge, Mark. *Laurence Sterne and the Argument About Design.* London: Macmillan, 1982.

SEWELL, ANNA (1820–1878)

Born in Great Yarmouth, Norfolk, Anna Sewell was destined to write only one book, which would become a children's classic. Her Quaker upbringing and home education, along with a permanent ankle injury, combined to keep her at home during much of her childhood and adolescence. Exacerbating her lameness was a debilitative condition, later suggested to be depression, causing her to visit various health spas seeking relief. Except for an occasional visit to relatives, she lived with her parents and was especially close to her mother. Mary Sewell began to write late in life, publishing moral verses for the middle classes, and Anna edited her work. Anna also taught in their self-organized evening gatherings, the Working Men's Evening Institute, and pursued with her mother various causes, including temperance. She followed Mary Sewell's lead in practicing a religious life, although she occasionally questioned Quakerism and studied other approaches to spirituality. Later in life confined to a sofa, Sewell revealed her compassion when she wrote BLACK BEAUTY (1877), an enduring classic of CHILDREN'S LITERATURE, the first novel to formally decry cruelty to animals. Published within the last year of Sewell's life, the book became instrumental in motivating the establishment of a Society Against Cruelty to Animals, its popularity garnering that movement much support.

BIBLIOGRAPHY

Chitty, Susan, Lady. *The Woman Who Wrote Black Beauty: A Life of Anna Sewell.* London: Hodder and Stoughton, 1971.

Sage, Lorna, ed. *Women's Writing in English.* Cambridge: Cambridge University Press, 1999, 569–570.

SHARP, WILLIAM (1855–1905)

William Sharp was born in Paisley, Scotland, and attended Glasgow University, although he did not earn a degree.

He chose to live for a time in Australia, blaming his heritage of Scandinavian "wander blood" for the urge to travel. Sharp would later visit America, France, and Greece, and travel to Italy multiple times, eventually dying in Sicily. He became secretly engaged to his cousin Elizabeth in 1875 but, with little financial resources to support a wife, did not marry. The two spent a season together in Scotland in 1876, but the death of Sharp's father proved a shock to Sharp's health, and he was "ordered a voyage to Australia," according to Elizabeth.

When Sharp returned from Australia to London in 1878, his interests involved work by Dante Gabriel Rosetti, with whom he corresponded; his wife later published copies of their letters. While working at jobs including one bank appointment, he continued to dabble in poetry, but was advised by poet and playwright Robert Buchanan, whose work he admired, "not to dream of literature as a career." Elizabeth noted that previous to their marriage, Sharp underwent a struggle between his public identity and "the sensitive, delicate, feminine side of him that he buried carefully out of sight." He would later publish under the name "Fiona Macleod," but according to Elizabeth, that aspect of his personality offered no inspiration during his early career.

Sharp was heartbroken over Rosetti's death but was jubilant when asked to write the painter's biography. It was later judged hack work, and Sharp seemed to agree in an 1890 diary entry, in which he described the book as "my first serious effort in prose, my honest and enthusiastic, and indeed serviceable, but badly written, 'Life of Rosetti.'" He later became so depressed over his poverty (he owned only a revolver) and lack of financial prospects that he determined to join the service. According to his wife's account, the receipt from *Harper's* of a £40 check for his poetry "Transcripts from Nature," along with a sudden windfall of £200 from a friend of a friend, convinced him to continue writing. He traveled to Italy for five months, where he met OUIDA, who arranged introductions to other artists.

After nine years of engagement, Sharp and Elizabeth married on October 31, 1884, and were entertained by notables including Oscar WILDE and Walter Pater. Over his lifetime, Sharp published a large volume of work,

most of it pronounced second-rate. Publications included biographies on poets Percy Bysshe Shelley (1887), husband of novelist Mary SHELLEY, and Robert Browning (1890), husband to poet Elizabeth Barrett BROWNING. Those biographies were not considered scholarly, nor was the criticism and introductions to volumes of popular poetry that he wrote. He published the novels *The SPORT OF CHANCE* (1888) and *The Children of Tomorrow* (1889), as well as volumes of poetry including *The Human Inheritance, The New Hope, Motherhood and Other Poems* (1882), *Earth's Voices* (1884), *Romantic Ballads and Poems of Phantasy* (1888), and *Sospiri di Roma* (1891). His later verse and prose romances were published under the pseudonym Fiona Macleod, including *Pharais* (1894), *The Mountain Lovers* (1895), *The Sin Eater and Other Tales* (1895), *The WASHER OF THE FORD* (1895), and a collection of short nonfiction prose, *The Winged Destiny* (1904).

BIBLIOGRAPHY
Sharp, Elizabeth A. *William Sharp (Fiona Macleod), A Memoir Compiled by His Wife.* New York: Duffield & Co., 1910.

SHE: A HISTORY OF ADVENTURE
HENRY RIDER HAGGARD (1887)   Like Henry Rider HAGGARD's other ROMANCE NOVELS set in Africa, including *KING SOLOMON'S MINES* (1885) and *ALLAN QUATERMAIN* (1887), *She: A History of Adventure* is based in part on Haggard's experience in that country. As assistant to Sir Henry Bulwer, lieutenant-governor of Natal, a British colony, Haggard hoped to rise in the ranks of British colonial representatives. However, the unrest in Africa, particularly the Boer Wars, both disillusioned and endangered Haggard when he brought his new wife, Louisa Margitson, to a newly established ostrich farm in Natal. The couple later had to abandon the project, and Haggard settled down in England to practice law and write romances that expressed his fantasies not only about Africa but also about women.

Separated from his first and true love, Lilith Jackson, by his determined father, Haggard would project her as his ideal into many of his stories in the form of his fictional women. However, in the figure of Ayesha, or she-who-must-be-obeyed, a light-skinned ruler of an undesirable African tribe who has discovered the secret to mortality, Haggard went far beyond his ideal of woman to describe every man's terror. FEMINIST CRITICS especially would later point out the danger to males represented by Ayesha's power and her symbolic role as the "eternal feminine." Her use of uninhibited sexuality to control employs language of interest to PSYCHOANALYTIC CRITICS, as when she speaks of her enduring beauty, inviting the novel's narrator not to blame her "if passion mount thy reason." NEW HISTORICIST critics note Haggard's focus on British IMPERIALISM and his shared belief that the British were the most superior of all members of the white race and bore the burden to enlighten "noble savages." Those included members of the Zulu tribe, a group always represented in his fiction as heroic, although also of questionable ability to be educated. In addition, Haggard had long believed that the Boers, although white, were ignorant detestables who had somehow not developed in the same way as the British, reflecting his post-DARWINian belief in all humans as a member of the same species but with enormous biological and cultural differences. While he found certain aspects of the "gentleman" in the Zulus, he found no such aspects in the Boers or those whose brown skin color suggested a mixing of light and dark races.

She is narrated by Horace Holly, a proclaimed misogynist with ugly, near apelike features who acts as guardian to Leo Vincey, the novel's young adventurer protagonist. While Leo's Christian name suggests the aristocratic position of king, his surname suggests the conflicting idea that he remains "vincible," or defeatable. In a later scene when a crocodile, representative of Africa and Ayesha, fights a lion in a graphically violent struggle that leaves both dead, readers will recognize foreshadowing.

Vincey discovers a family history suggesting his duty in life is to seek revenge, and that the ancestor he should revenge first was named Kallidrates, meaning the-beautiful-in-strength, who was killed by a mysterious woman. When Holly and Vincey travel to Africa, they are almost killed by a brown-skinned tribe of cannibals, the Amahaggar tribe, who torture their victims by placing hot pots on their heads. Their tribal name suggests that of the biblical figure Hagar, the Arab woman with whom the father of all Jewish tribes,

Abraham, fathered Ishmael, supposedly the progenitor of the Arab tribes. Because Hagar was cast off by Abraham upon the birth of the wife's son Isaac, Christian-Judaic tradition suggests the brown-skinned Arab's inferiority. Haggard practices a neat character twist in both the simian Holly and the Arab character of Mahomed, subverting the negative connotations readers would bring to an understanding of both characters. When Vincey and another white man, Job, suffer enormous swelling due to the attack of mosquitoes, Holly tells the reader that he had come off best, likely owing to his darker skin and his abundant body hair, while he notes that in Mahomed the mosquitoes recognized "the taste of a true believer" and would not touch him. He adds, "how often, I wonder, during the next week or so did we wish that we were flavoured like an Arab!"

The Amahaggar's dwelling of Kôr is ruled by the light-skinned Ayesha, a fearsome queen who controls through her sexuality and magic abilities. She saves Vincey from a fatal illness and discovers he is the reincarnation of Kallikrates, whom she had murdered centuries earlier because he refused her love. In true QUEST fashion, the group descends into the feared Place of Life, a cave where Ayesha urges the two white men to walk through the Fire of Life to become immortal. Haggard adopts the traditional symbol of fire as representative of new life and cleansing. However, the men refuse, and Ayesha herself enters the fire, only to be seemingly destroyed, undergoing a Darwinian transformation into an ancient, monkeylike figure that asks the men to remember her beauty before she dies. Like all quest heroes, the men ascend from the depths, burdened by a new wisdom, both horrified and awed by what they have observed. They hope to rediscover Ayesha, who will, indeed, be resurrected by Haggard in his later novels *She-Ayesha* (1905) and *Wisdom's Daughters* (1923).

The novel has never been out of print, and Ayesha has been represented in multiple film and stage versions. Not only the plot but also Haggard's employment of traditional quest and ROMANCE aspects continue to interest FORMALIST critics. He incorporates the quest plot evident in the most traditional of all such tales, Homer's *Odyssey*, even adopting some of

Homer's imagery. Where Homer repeatedly references the "rosy-fingered dawn," Haggard begins the sixth chapter of *She* with the phrase "Next morning, at the earliest blush of dawn." He also incorporates traditionally patriarchal references to females as evil temptresses, as when the woman-hating Holly refers to Ayesha's perfect body as having a "serpent-like" grace, draped in a white robe with a belt "fastened by a double-headed snake of solid gold." Ayesha also only shows weakness when considering her long-dead love, Kallidrates.

BIBLIOGRAPHY

Brantlinger, Patrick. Introduction to *She: A History of Adventure* by Henry Rider Haggard. New York: Penguin Books, 2001, vii–xxvii.

Katz, Wendy R. *Rider Haggard and the Fiction of Empire: A Critical Study of British Imperial Fiction.* Cambridge: Cambridge University Press, 1987.

McClintock, Anne. *Imperial Leather: Race, Gender and Sexuality in the Colonial Contest.* New York: Routledge, 1995.

SHELLEY, MARY WOLLSTONECRAFT

(1797–1851)   Mary Wollstonecraft Shelley was born into a family of influential writers. Her mother, Mary WOLLSTONECRAFT, had distinguished herself as one of the earliest feminist writers, while her father, William GODWIN, was a well-known philosopher and novelist. Wollstonecraft died due to complications in child delivery a few days after Mary's birth, leaving Godwin to raise not only Mary, but also Wollstonecraft's illegitimate daughter, Fanny Imlay. He remarried when Mary was four years old to the widowed Jane Clairmont, who brought an additional two children, Charles and Jane, into the family. The new Mrs. Godwin naturally favored her own children, and Mary developed an independent and willful nature, adoring her scholarly father, although he proved emotionally distant and overly protective. Ironically, his vigilance over Mary contradicted the individual freedoms he supported in his writing, most particularly his anti-marriage stance, one that had also been supported by Wollstonecraft. Mary's romance with the already-married 22-year-old aristocratic poet Percy Bysshe Shelley, a Godwin devotee, did not please Godwin. His

attitude helped prompt the 16-year-old Mary in 1814 to run away to France and Switzerland with Shelley, living with him for a time unmarried. Shelley left behind one child and a pregnant wife, marking the beginning of an unrelenting personal conflict that would haunt Mary; both her life and work would be continually marked by what critics Sandra Gilbert and Susan Gubar term "emotional extremes." By age 17 she had lost her first child, a daughter born prematurely. Within less than one year of her baby's death, both her half-sister Fanny Imlay and Shelley's wife committed suicide. Percy Shelley began a protracted battle to adopt his two children but would never succeed.

Mary Shelley remains best known for her cross between SCIENCE FICTION, HORROR FICTION, and ROMANTIC FICTION, *FRANKENSTEIN, OR THE MODERN PROMETHEUS* (1818), which grew from a challenge. The Shelleys and their friend, romantic poet George Gordon, Lord Byron, and his friend Polidori had wondered which of them could write the best horror tale while they shared a cabin on Lake Geneva in the summer of 1816. Critics believe the novel to be influenced by Mary's first pregnancy, based on her written statements desiring that the dead child have its life restored.

While the Shelleys occasionally returned to England to visit family, they settled in Italy in 1818 and remained there until Percy Shelley's death by drowning in 1822. They had several additional children, but only one son, Percy Florence, survived. Mary Shelley devoted herself entirely to his welfare, moving back in 1823 to England, where she pursued a writing career. While her later writings never seemed to equal *Frankenstein* in originality, strength of plot, or style, she did publish *Lodore* (1835) and *Faulkner* (1837). Those two works remain of interest to FEMINIST CRITICS, but represent a cross between SENSATION FICTION and SENTIMENTAL FICTION, no longer palatable to a reading public newly exposed to the REALISM of authors such as Charles DICKENS. She later produced the first authorized edition of Percy Shelley's work, and published short stories and some biography.

Mary Shelley's life formed the basis for a later unfinished fiction titled *Mathilde,* begun in 1819 but not published until 1959. Its reflection of her relationships with the romantic poets made it of great

interest to 20th-century feminist critics and NEW HIS-
TORICIST CRITICS. Her focus on 14th-century Italian
political ambition and intrigue in *Valperga* (1823) and
on the end of man in a futuristic FANTASY FICTION set
in the 21st century, *The Last Man* (1826), are also of
interest and continue to be studied in academic settings. Only the latter compares favorably with
Frankenstein and seems to express Mary's feeling of
isolation and despair over having survived so many of
the people she loved. In her own lifetime, a final trav-
elogue, *Rambles in Germany and Italy, in 1840, 1842
and 1843* (1844), proved popular.

   Frankenstein has been reproduced in various dramatic media. In its foreword, Mary Shelley famously
wrote that she had tried to conceive a story "which
would speak to the mysterious fears of our nature, and
awaken thrilling horror—one to make the reader dread
to look round, to curdle the blood, and quicken the
beatings of the heart." Critics and fans agree that she
achieved her goal.

BIBLIOGRAPHY

Gilbert, Sandra M., and Susan Gubar, eds. "Mary Shelley."
   *The Norton Anthology of Literature by Women: The Traditions
   in English.* 2nd ed. New York: W.W. Norton, 1996,
   353–356.
Seymour, Miranda. *Mary Shelley.* London: John Murray,
   2000.
Shelley, Mary. *Frankenstein: Complete, Authoritative text with
   Biographical, Historical, and Cultural Contexts, Critical His-
   tory, and Essays from Contemporary Critical Perspectives.*
   Edited by Johanna M. Smith. Boston: Bedford/St. Martin's
   Press, 2000.
Spark, Muriel. *Child of Light: Mary Shelley.* New York: Wel-
   come Rain, 2002.
Williams, John. *Mary Shelley, a Literary Life.* New York: St.
   Martin's Press, 2000.

SHERIDAN, FRANCES (1724–1766) Born
in Dublin, Frances Chamberlain depended on her
brothers for a secret education, as her father disapproved of study for women. She wrote her first work, a
ROMANCE named *Eugenia and Adelaide,* in her teens, but
it remained unpublished. Her next endeavor was to
write a pamphlet defending the Dublin Theater's

actor/manager Thomas Sheridan. When she later met
Sheridan, they fell in love and married, and Frances
gave birth to Richard Brinsley Sheridan, destined to
become one of Ireland's most famous playwrights. She
later spent much effort in entertaining her volatile husband's friends, having to write in secret. Despite difficult
creative conditions, she published a verse fable in 1746
but became best known after relocating from Dublin to
London and publishing *The MEMOIRS OF MISS SIDNEY
BIDULPH* (1761), an EPISTOLARY NOVEL she had developed
over many years. A popular work quickly translated
into both French and German, it caused Dr. Samuel
JOHNSON consternation over the suffering inflicted on its
readers due to the loss of the heroine's morality. Sheridan also wrote plays, and her *The Discovery* (1763)
proved a hit, featuring her own husband along with
other players. She followed that drama with *The Dupe*
(1763) and *A Journey to Bath,* produced at Drury Lane,
but unpublished until 1902, neither of which proved
successful. Her dramas most certainly influenced her
son's work and helped to support the family, whose
finances suffered from her husband's imprudent investments and the burden of caring for her father in his later
years. After settling later in France, Sheridan wrote *Sidney Bidulph* (1767), a sequel to her first novel, and *The
History of Nourjahad* (1767, posthumous), an Asian
fable. Her husband later discovered her first novel and
published it posthumously in 1791. In 1824, Sheridan's
daughter, Alicia Lefanu, wrote Sheridan's biography, in
which she touted her mother as strongly domestic in
addition to being a writer.

BIBLIOGRAPHY

Lefanu, Alicia. *Memoirs of the Life and Writings of Mrs.
   Frances Sheridan.* London: G. and W.B. Whittaker, 1824.
Sage, Lorna, ed. *Women's Writing in English.* Cambridge:
   Cambridge University Press, 1999, 573.

SHERWOOD, MARY MARTHA (1775–
1851) Daughter of an English clergyman, Reverend
George Butt, Mary Sherwood was born near Worcester and educated partially at the Abbey School at
Bath, also attended by Jane AUSTEN and her sister,
Cassandra. She wrote from an early age, and recorded
facts of her upbringing, including the wearing of an

iron collar for punishment, an experience that likely affected her later harsh depictions of punishments for children's misbehavior. She matured to become a stern but compassionate Evangelical Christian, consumed by religious fervor following her father's 1795 death. Her first work of note, *History of Susan Gray* (1802), she wrote with her sister. A highly moral tale ending in the sordid death of its protagonist, it foreshadowed her later works, which, although highly moralistic and with mature themes, fell into the category of CHILDREN'S LITERATURE.

In 1803, Mary married British officer Henry Sherwood and, during his service in colonial India beginning in 1803, focused on the condition of the English children forced to live there. They often spent their days in barracks-rooms or with Indian nurses where they gained scant education. A deeply religious woman, Sherwood reacted by founding army post schools where children learned from a Bible-based curriculum. As part of the teaching materials, she contributed DIDACTIC literature in the form of cautionary stories, vehicles for the Evangelical messages of punishment and redemption through belief in Jesus Christ. *The History of Little Henry and His Bearer* (1814) became wildly popular in England, where readers viewed India as an exotic world, offering an appealing setting for Sherwood's tales. Before the publication in 1818 of her most successful novel/sermon and prayer booklet, *The History of the Fairchild Family, Part I,* she had read it aloud and circulated the manuscript version, publishing it shortly after her return to England from India. She followed with *Part II* in 1842 and *Part III* in 1847, but the first release remained the most popular. Subtitled *The Child's Manual: Being a Collection of Stories Calculated to Shew the Importance and Effects of a Religious Education,* the book, according to Barry Westburg, reflects "the author's special genius for producing an almost perfect concatenation of religious aim and narrative plan." Difficult for the modern reading palate to tolerate, Sherwood's books provided almost every middle- and upper-class British household a springboard into teaching morality to its children. Over her 50 writing years, Sherwood wrote almost 400 tracts, tales, and novels. Her many works were seldom enjoyed after the 19th century, due to their Evangelical tone and Victorian moral excesses.

BIBLIOGRAPHY

Westburg, Barry. Preface to *The History of the Fairchild Family* by Mary Sherwood. New York: Garland Publishing, 1977.

SHIPS THAT PASS IN THE NIGHT BEATRICE HARRADEN (1893)

Suffragist Beatrice HARRADEN had written short stories and one novel before publishing *Ships That Pass in the Night,* but that work brought her fame as a writer. An example of SENTIMENTAL FICTION, it depicts the doomed love of two patients suffering from tuberculosis. The setting is a "consumptive" patient winter resort, the Kurhaus at Petershof, where 250 gather, hoping for a cure. In heavy foreshadowing in the opening pages, a character identified perfunctorily as the Disagreeable Man tells the protagonist, Bernardine Holme, that she will not recover, as "I know your type well; you burn yourselves out quickly. And—my God—how I envy you!" Her uncle, in a typical sentimental fashion, next describes Bernardine as "thin and drawn" with eyes that "seemed to be burning themselves away." Within six pages the appearance of two references to a burning fire, symbol of destruction, but also renewal and rebirth, signal the reader that Bernardine is not long for this world. However, both references also connote envy or wistfulness on the part of the observers, suggesting that Bernardine will not die without passion. When the narrator describes her childhood as one "which even the fairies have failed to touch with the warm glow of affection," Bernardine's part as a sentimental heroine has been made clear.

Once a woman of interest and ambition, "a diligent scholar" and "self-reliant," a "modern product," Bernardine has come to a standstill due to illness. However, only through this weakness will she experience love, which she encounters at the clinic. This fact proves important to FEMINIST CRITICS, who understand that even though a staunch supporter of women's rights, Harraden had to employ a traditional aspect of sentimental fiction, the invalid female, in order to make her work acceptable to readers of the day. Other conventional approaches used in shaping Bernardine include the diminutive nicknames bestowed on her, such as "Little Brick." When the Disagreeable Man, Robert Allitsen, becomes her love, he refers to her as "You little thing," and she even refers to herself as a "little playmate." However, she also makes wise pronouncements, including "we realize that we stand practically alone, out of any one's reach for help or comfort," allowing clear delivery of Harraden's subversive message regarding the isolation forced upon independent females who may be misunderstood as cold and without emotion. She seems, however, to counter her own message as Bernardine returns to a life of books, realizing love had made her become "probably more human, and probably less self-confident. She had lived in a world of books, and she had burst through that bondage and come out into a wider and a freer land." While Harraden seems to suggest that women must have love to achieve self-realization, and that education may prevent that love, the scene may instead by interpreted as one with the message that a woman is allowed to reach her full potential only when separated from vocation, a declaration against society's defined confining roles for women.

When Bernardine learns of the death of Allitsen's wife she begins writing a book, and he suddenly reappears in her life, with the promise of future happiness for both himself and Bernardine. However, the novel supplies the expected tragic conclusion with Bernardine dying in an accident, without realizing a life of love. Knocked down in the street by a wagon, she is taken to a hospital, where a doctor pronounces, "she will not recover . . . poor little thing."

Harraden loved America and in a preface to the first authorized American edition of her novel explained that the title came from American poet Henry Wadsworth Longfellow's poem "Tales of a Wayside Inn." The phrase "ships that pass in the night" would come to connote star-crossed lovers. In an edition that followed the original by seven years, Harraden added a preface describing the unexpected effects of the novel's popularity in its bringing the "best gifts" of life: "generous appreciation, good-fellowship, friendship, and love, and a genial freemasonry with all sorts of conditions of men and women in many parts of the world." That the novel created opportunities for Harraden to spread her ideas regarding the condition of women

may be its most important achievement. While little read or studied, it remains readily available in print form and is an excellent example of sentimental fiction that profits from a revisionist reading.

SHIRLEY CHARLOTTE BRONTË (1849)

Charlotte BRONTË's second novel, *Shirley,* is set in Yorkshire during the Luddite riots of 1848, sparked in part by changes that had occurred since the INDUSTRIAL REVOLUTION and echoed by riots throughout the continent. NEW HISTORICIST CRITICS believe that Brontë based her depiction on her father's experience as a clergyman near Dewsbury and Rawfold's Mill, where a riot led to the execution of 14 men. The owner of the mill in her story, Robert Moore, may be based on William Cartwright, who helped defend Rawfold's Mill, while the title character, Shirley Keeldar, may be based on Brontë's sister Emily BRONTË. By focusing on the deplorable working conditions of those who manned England's factories, Brontë's novel takes its place among many others by novelists including Elizabeth GASKELL, Charles DICKENS, Benjamin DISRAELI, George ELIOT, and Charles KINGSLEY, often termed THESIS NOVELS, which sought social reform. *Shirley* also focused on the subject of "good" marriages, in which material advancement is deemed more important than love, and the often-limited choices for support available to women.

When the novel opens, Robert Moore owns a mill where he hopes to place new machinery, although his workers protest the move, as the machines will replace humans. They first try unsuccessfully to destroy the mill, ironic in that they would destroy their own means of support, and later plot to murder Moore. The plot also focuses on Moore's brother Louis, who tutors children in the wealthy Keeldar family. Charlotte Brontë could base her depiction of the tutoring life on her own experience as a governess.

Robert loves a rector's niece named Caroline Helstone, but feels he must try to marry into money to assure a stable future, seemingly unattainable on his own due to the economic depression that occurred at the end of the Napoleonic war. For that reason he attempts to court the independent Shirley Keeldar, but she rejects him in her outspoken way, knowing that he does not love her. The scorn she shows the proposal may echo that felt by Brontë herself, who, although shy and described as "drab," rejected two proposals of marriage before the age of 25.

Strongly influenced by William Makepeace THACKERAY'S VANITY FAIR (1848), Brontë developed two heroines for the novel, not using Caroline and Shirley as foils, but more as representatives of different levels of society. When the war concludes, Robert may follow his heart and marry Caroline. While critics suggest his character is simply a different type of BYRONIC HERO for a new age, he ultimately conforms to the realistic demands of society. Shirley is not left without love, as she becomes attracted to Louis. The novel suggests that the social system in England might change, allowing lovers to marry outside their social class, although that hope would not reach fruition for some time. Brontë varies from her approach in JANE EYRE (1847), debating women's-rights issues at length, rather than simply suggesting their importance.

Although the novel's narrative shows support for those who follow their instinctive passions, rather than society's dictates, Brontë warns her readers not to expect "sentiment, and poetry, and reverie . . . passion, and stimulus, and melodrama," informing them that instead, "something real, cool, and solid lies before you; something unromantic as Monday morning." While critics agree that the social consciousness of the novel threatens to overshadow its plot, the novel stands as part of the vitally important oeuvre of the Brontë sisters, the most gifted, according to Lionel Stevenson, of all new novelists emerging between 1847 and 1848.

BIBLIOGRAPHY

Lloyd Evans, Barbara, and Gareth Lloyd Evans. *The Scribner Companion to the Brontës.* New York: Scribner, 1982.

Stevenson, Lionel. *The English Novel: a Panorama.* Boston: Houghton Mifflin, 1960.

Winnifrith, Tom, and Edward Chitham. *Charlotte and Emily Brontë: Literary Lives.* Houndmills, Basingstoke, Hampshire U.K.: Macmillan, 1989.

SHORTHOUSE, JOSEPH HENRY (1834–1903)

Joseph Henry Shorthouse was born into a Quaker family in Birmingham, maturing to become a chemist who worked with his father. He turned away from the Quaker beliefs, experiencing a difficult conversion at age 27 to the Anglican faith, and later became interested in the OXFORD MOVEMENT, which had cast a light on conflicts between Anglicans and Catholics. His novel JOHN INGLESANT (1881) remains his major work, representing the problem novel, a type of work examining characters challenged to make a decision based on personal creeds. George ELIOT made the approach popular, and others followed, showcasing controversies over various religious and moral questions and social situations, such as the status of women in British society. That type of book became popular following the decline of the SENSATION NOVEL and DOMESTIC FICTION. Based on Shorthouse's conversion experience, *John Inglesant* focused on a Jesuit-trained aristocrat during the era of Charles I who must learn forgiveness toward his brother's murderer. Quotations from the work, including "All creeds and opinions are nothing but the mere result of chance and temperament," appear in the popular reference book *Bartlett's Familiar Quotations.* Shorthouse worked on the novel for 10 years before publishing it privately. It sold to Macmillan & Company, who issued it in 1881 to much critical and popular praise. Shorthouse published additional novels and edited 17th-century poet and priest George Herbert's collection *The Temple* (1882).

BIBLIOGRAPHY

Bartlett, John. *Familiar Quotations: A Collection of Passages, Phrases and Proverbs Traced to Their Sources in Ancient and Modern Literature.* 10th ed. Boston: Little, Brown and Co., 1919.

SIGN OF FOUR, THE ARTHUR CONAN DOYLE (1890)

Sir Arthur Conan DOYLE published the second Sherlock Holmes novel, *The Sign of Four,* to little fanfare. *A Study in Scarlet,* Doyle's first novel to feature the superdetective and his friend and chronicler, Dr. Watson, appeared in the 1887. However, the characters only became popular when featured in a series of short stories Doyle published in *The STRAND MAGAZINE,* a periodical later to be forever identified with Doyle and Holmes.

The Sign of Four begins with a chapter titled "The Science of Deduction," which introduces several important Holmes trademarks. As indicated, it outlines Holmes's approach to crime solving, as well as describing his dwelling at 221b Baker Street, where he lives under the watchful eye of his housekeeper, Mrs. Hudson. In addition, readers observed Holmes using cocaine, a habit he indulged when bored, as well as Dr. Watson's vehement opposition to drug use. Doyle's own background in medicine surfaces in Watson's admonition to "Count the cost! Your brain may, as you say, be roused and excited, but it is a pathological and morbid process, which involves increased tissue-change, and may at last leave a permanent weakness." The topic was a timely one, as increased drug use in London during the late 19th century had given rise to infamous opium dens, places Doyle also later featured in his series. Holmes speaks of his monographs on various topics and uses his trademark pipe and deer-stalker hat. Dr. Watson's enduring fondnesses for pretty young women, as well as his experiences as an army surgeon, are also important topics. Finally, Watson's first-person-narrator voice, one with which millions of readers would become acquainted over the following century, frames the tale.

The plot begins when the lovely Miss Morstan employs Holmes to investigate a recent mysterious note, seemingly connected to the disappearance 10 years earlier of her father, Captain Morstan. Morstan was to have taken a year's leave from the navy, which he planned to spend with his daughter following a visit to a Mr. Sholto, but he never arrived to meet his daughter. Miss Morstan explains that the annual delivery of a single perfect pearl to her place of employment with a Mrs. Cecil Forrester began a few years following her father's disappearance. On the day of her visit to Holmes, she had received a letter asking her to bring two friends to "the third pillar from the left outside Lyceum Theatre tonight," and Holmes and Watson agree to play the part of the friends. Holmes has found the mystery he needed to substitute for his cocaine use. It will involve exotic men from the Orient; the bald-headed Sholto twins, sons of the original Mr. Sholto who first befriended, then betrayed, Captain Morstan; the mysterious phrase "the sign of the four"; murder; and a treasure chest filled with jewels. Holmes and Watson eventually work with Inspector Athelney Jones

to discover that Captain Morstan had been involved with a group of men who planned to recover the treasure stolen by one of them during a revolt in India. However, Sholto betrayed the group, and a scheme of vengeance was hatched by one group member, Mr. Small. In the end, the mystery of the sign of four is solved, and Small is discovered as a murderer. While his pursuers dream of wealth, he throws the treasure into the Thames rather than letting anyone else have it. However, Watson discovers a real treasure when he falls in love with Mary Morstan and takes her as his bride. The plot itself offers nothing remarkable. Rather, Holmes's methodology captures the reader's imagination. Cool, detached, logical to a fault, he sees clues where others see nothing, following the trail they form to the mystery's answer.

Sherlock Holmes set the standard for the modern detective, his name becoming an integral part of popular culture. He has appeared countless times in various media forms since Doyle's death, including a popular television series filmed by the BBC starring the late Jeremy Brett in the title role.

BIBLIOGRAPHY

Liebman, Arthur. *The Biographical Sherlock Holmes: An Anthology/Handbook: His Career from 1881 to 1914.* New York: Rosen Publishing Group, 1984.

SILAS MARNER GEORGE ELIOT (1861)

Generations of readers continue to enjoy the appealing story of an old miser who regains his humanity through the love of a lost child in George ELIOT's *Silas Marner*. In typical Eliot fashion, the novel reveals the tensions in a small English community, much of which turns upon the theme of wealth, both of a material and a spiritual kind.

The novel begins with a fairy-tale air, suggested by the opening phrase "In the days when," and introduces the reader to certain "undersized men" who resemble "remnants of a disinherited race." It foreshadows Eliot's emphasis on inheritance, in both a literal and figurative sense, as she features family relationships and fortunes lost and regained. The protagonist Silas Marner has been unjustly condemned as a thief and thus has lived apart from his dissenting community for 15 years. His vocation as a linen weaver suggests the act of creation and indirectly reflects on the metaphoric weaving of Eliot's tale, while the linen fabric suggests both finery and a death shroud. Marner's proximity to a deserted stone pit emphasizes his isolation but also ties him to the basic element of the earth, albeit a rocky earth where little could grow. The imagery Eliot uses to surround Marner includes "lingering echoes of the old demonworship" and "a shadowy conception of power" as the shape "most easily taken by the sense of the Invisible in the minds of men . . . pressed close by primitive wants." Marner's primitive desire will begin as one for material goods as he accumulates a large hidden sum of money, but will later be for love and companionship.

In the village of Raveloe reside Squire Cass and his two sons, Godfrey and Dunstan (Dunsey). Godfrey proves driven by base passion, secretly marrying and impregnating the opium-addicted Molly Farren, while also pursuing the lovely Nancy Lammeter. The evil Dunstan discovers his brother's secret and blackmails him. He then steals Marner's fortune and disappears, and Molly attempts to cross snow-covered fields with her toddler daughter, Eppie, to tell the squire of her marriage to his son. She dies close to Marner's cottage, and he discovers Eppie, taking her in as a solution to his loneliness. He proves a surprisingly excellent parent, allowing Eliot to contrast him with Squire Cass. The book fast-forwards 16 years, and Eppie has become a lovely young woman, devoted to Marner as they survive on the income from his weaving. He has long realized her value to be superior to that of the gold Dunstan stole from him, an epiphany that changes his life. When Dunstan's remains and Marner's gold are discovered ironically close to Marner in the stone pit, Godfrey confesses his earlier marriage to Nancy, now his wife. They have no children and set out to adopt Eppie, but even though they tempt her with their wealth, she refuses to leave Marner. She eventually marries Aaron Winthrop, and Marner shares their home, inheriting a full family after regaining his fortune.

Although Eliot's style suggests a cautionary tale, *Silas Marner* cannot be reduced to a simple moralistic presentation. In her traditional manner, she reveals through painstaking detail the complicity of characters that could never be mistaken for flat fairy-tale contrivances. Nancy's romantic nature is played off against that of her sister, the "good-natured" and commonsensical Priscilla. While Nancy indulges in "inward drama," vowing never to marry a man "whose conduct showed him careless of his character," she will learn that such character is not always clearly revealed, even among those highly born. The discussions between Aaron Winthrop's mother, Dolly, and Marner about the proper way to raise a child introduce a gently ironic emphasis on the morality that common folk assume their "betters" possess. She instructs Marner, "You must bring her up like christened folks's children, and take her to church, and let her learn her catechize," adding that no one could die and rest peacefully "if they hadn't done their part by the helpless children as come wi'out their own asking." Eliot examines that native innocence that all humans possess at birth, demonstrating that community and family guidance remains imperative if they are to retain that guileless state. Her continued emphasis on the fact that guilt of the conscience can prove a more powerful force than the guilt awarded an individual by a civic court supports her favored theme of ethics and the sense of duty and personal responsibility that should be practiced by all. Clearly, Marner is rewarded for acting on that sense, while Godfrey is punished through rejection by his daughter for delaying his action. His fate proves infinitely more desirable than that of Dunstan, who had never developed the sense at all.

Silas Marner remains a satisfying read more than a century after its publication. Its moral sense readers of any age can relate to, and Eliot's details about country life ring satisfyingly true. Both television and movie versions have been produced.

BIBLIOGRAPHY

Pangallo, Karen L., ed. *The Critical Response to George Eliot.* Westport, Conn.: Greenwood Press, 1994.

Perkin, J. Russell. *A Reception-History of George Eliot's Fiction.* Rochester, N.Y.: University of Rochester Press, 1990.

Rignall, John, ed. *Oxford Reader's Companion to George Eliot.* Oxford: Oxford University Press, 2000.

Semmel, Bernard. *George Eliot and the Politics of National Inheritance.* New York: Oxford University Press, 1994.

SILVER-FORK/FASHIONABLE FICTION

Before the 1840s, novels had almost exclusively portrayed the "high life" of the wealthy, thus gaining the label "silver-fork" or "fashionable" fiction. One story credits the label to a comment in the November 18, 1827, edition of the *Examiner* by William Hazlitt accusing Theodore HOOK of a preoccupation with "silver forks" in his novels. Another explanation holds that *FRASER'S MAGAZINE* accused Edward BULWER-LYTTON of being a "silver polisher." Most writers of ROMANCE produced silver-fork fiction, including Frances TROLLOPE, Benjamin DISRAELI, Lady Blessington, and Mrs. Catherine Grace GORE. Said to allow the middle class to vicariously enjoy the lives of aristocrats, the silver-fork form would later be mocked by authors including Charles DICKENS.

The silver-fork subgenre enjoyed a relatively short life, replaced by the emphasis on REALISM in novels. In an 1845 edition of *BLACKWOOD'S EDINBURGH MAGAZINE*, the editor asked, "Where now are all the novels portraying fashionable life with which the shops of publishers teemed, and the shelves of circulating libraries groaned, not ten years ago? Buried in the vault of all the Capulets." In April of 1849 a *Fraser's Magazine* reviewer gave the opinion that the fashionable novel had become "most un-fashionable . . . aping the tone of a school and system of society which really died once and for ever . . . on the 10th of April last," the date being that of the CHARTIST petition. Thanks in great part to *Fraser's* unrelenting attacks, new novels of that form had all but disappeared by 1840.

BIBLIOGRAPHY

Rosa, Matthew Whiting. *The Silver-Fork School: Novels of Fashion Preceding Vanity Fair.* New York: Columbia University Press, 1936.

Tillotson, Kathleen. *Novels of the Eighteen-forties.* Oxford: Clarendon Press, 1954.

SIMPLE STORY, A ELIZABETH INCHBALD

(1791)   In Elizabeth INCHBALD'S traditional story of forbidden love, a Catholic priest named Dorriforth loves his Protestant ward, Miss Milner, a character who in her youth had been indulged "to the extreme of folly." Inchbald's career as an actress informs the melodrama in the novel, which is DIDACTIC fiction, as does her lifelong devotion to Catholicism. The novel can be considered the first Catholic novel, not because she dwells on questions of faith, but rather because most of its characters are among England's Catholic minority. She models the character of Dorriforth on her own lover, the great actor John Philip Kemble. According to editor J. M. S. Tompkins, Inchbald's contemporary, novelist Maria EDGEWORTH, wrote to her that unlike any other novel, hers "possessed me with the belief in the real existence of all the people it represents." Edgeworth believed that was due to the fact that Inchbald left "more than most other writers do to the imagination." Inchbald used her dramatic training to accomplish that feat through, for example, the description of her characters' body language. Like Henry FIELDING did, she used the experience of the dramatist, but she had the added advantage of having been an actor herself.

Although the Miss Milner character is flirtatious, she is also somewhat sophisticated, so she does not attempt to act on her feelings, understanding Dorriforth's vow of chastity. She enjoys the attention of several suitors, and is accustomed to being "too frequently told" the "high value" of her beauty. Their situation changes when Dorriforth becomes Lord Elmwood due to inheritance and leaves the priesthood. Inchbald did not design Dorriforth as a priest without dedication, although she shows him involved in only one major religious duty, private prayer. She may have feared the reaction against her story of a mainly non-Catholic readership had she included further detail regarding his duties, or gone beyond suggesting the importance of maintaining the Catholic nobility. That importance, as well as Dorriforth's dedication to his vows, prompt his actions.

At that point, Dorriforth, now Lord Elmwood, can marry Miss Milner. However, the story is one of a mutual attraction between people who by nature remain incompatible, and their marriage cannot last. As Lady Elmwood, Miss Milner becomes involved in an affair with Sir Frederick Lawnley, despite the fact that Elmwood loves her and they have a young daughter, Matilda. Elmwood orders her to leave with the child. When she later dies, never having received forgiveness from Elmwood, Lady Matilda is left alone and is in danger. Only after Matilda is kidnapped does Elmwood realize his loss, helped by his replacement as spiritual adviser, Father Sandford. He finds her abductor and brings her home as his heir.

Biographers suggest Inchbald based Dorriforth on Kemble, an attractive and impressive scholarly fellow Catholic who originally intended to enter the priesthood. Inchbald's characterization received later critical praise, even that of her minor characters. Mrs. Horton's slightly comic tone provides relief from extended tension, while Sandford's fear of the former pupil he once goaded to love the exquisite Miss Fenton, because "to resemble her, I believe, is above your ability," adds irony. In addition, Matilda's displays of temper add dimension to a characterization that could have simply dissolved into a victim stereotype. Inchbald excused the scenes of passion and the theme of infidelity by claiming in a note to her readers to be an invalid who only wrote because she had to. Critics later praised her simple style, and the book remained in print through 1908. It returned to print with the rising interest in women's writing in the mid-20th century, supported by FEMINIST CRITICISM.

BIBLIOGRAPHY

Jenkins, Annabelle. *I'll Tell You What: The Life of Elizabeth Inchbald*. Lexington: University Press of Kentucky, 2002.

Tompkins, J. M. S. Introduction to *A Simple Story*, by Elizabeth Inchbald. New York: Oxford University Press, 1967, vii–xvi.

SIN EATER AND OTHER TALES, THE

See *WASHER OF THE FORD, THE AND SIN EATER AND OTHER TALES, THE*.

SIREN, A THOMAS ADOLPHUS TROLLOPE

(1870) Anthony TROLLOPE's less famous novelist brother, Thomas Adolphus TROLLOPE, proved a minor novelist, his writing notable mainly for much inclusion of detail about Italy, where he lived for a number of years. *A Siren* is no exception, providing an example of an overused, overwritten mystery plot. The story turns around the murder of a young female Venetian artist, Paolina Foscarelli, sent to Ravenna at Carnival time to copy for an English patron some famous artwork there. She lives in the care of the Marchesino Ludovico Castlemare, nephew to the wealthy and influential bachelor Marchese Lamberto. Trollope begins inserting stock

ROMANCE contrivances, making Paolina an orphan, and having her fall in love with the womanizing Ludovico, who is enthralled with an opera diva, Bianca Lalli, brought by his uncle the marchese to entertain the people of Ravenna. An additional love triangle is established when the Conte Leandro Lombardoni, a pretentious, overweight, self-styled Don Juan type, hopes to marry Bianca. When he learns of a clandestine meeting and trip into the nearby woods planned during the Ash Wednesday celebration by Ludovico and Bianca for the following day, he informs the marchese. Unbeknownst to anyone else, the marchese has also set his sights on Bianca, and shares his plans with his lawyer, Signor Fortini, who attempts to talk him out of marrying the young performer. When Paolina sees Ludovico and Bianca enter the woods in a carriage, she runs to follow them. Fortini meets the upset Ludovico returning to the town without Bianca, who he fears is lost. He left her napping in the forest, but when he returned, she was gone. When Fortini accompanies Ludovico back into the forest to search for her, they meet several men carrying a covered body on a door. Ludovico is horrified, fearing it is Bianca, but he pulls back the sheet to expose the body of what the readers suppose is Paolina, although they cannot be sure, as Ludovico, the only person present who can identify the victim, faints.

Trollope then engages in a lengthy flashback, filling hundreds of pages in the three-volume work. He supplies detail about each character, including the fact that Ludovico had pledged his love to Paolina and engaged in eight months of clandestine meetings with her, which concerns the marchese, who had planned for his nephew to marry the niece of his friend, the cardinal legate. Bianca had also schemed with her adopted father, the singing master Quinto Lalli, to marry a wealthy man, considering either the marchese or Ludovico acceptable. A woman of various past affairs, she had much experience in tempting men. Not until Chapter I, Book V, Volume II does the reader discover that the body at the city gate was that of Bianca Lalli. The murder mystery at last begins, far too late to hold the interest of most readers, especially when the expected occurs, and Ludovico is accused, then acquitted, with Paolina substituted in his place. As the romance tradition demands, all will end well with

Ludovico and Paolina marrying, assuming the titles of marchese and marchesa.

Trollope populates his novel with stock characters, thus providing no one with complexity about whom the reader may care.

BIBLIOGRAPHY
Glendinning, Victoria. *Anthony Trollope.* New York: Knopf, 1993.

SIR HARRY HOTSPUR OF HUMBLE-THWAITE ANTHONY TROLLOPE (1871)

First published as a serial in MACMILLAN'S MAGAZINE between May and December 1870, Anthony TROLLOPE'S *Sir Harry Hotspur of Humblethwaite* differs from much of his fiction. Rather than constructing a large number of "portraits" as he normally did, Trollope sought to focus on "some pathetic incident in life," describing the novel to the founder and editor of *Macmillan's Magazine* as a common love story with a sad conclusion. The protagonist is Emily Hotspur, daughter to Sir Harry Hotspur. A wealthy man who lost his son two years earlier, Sir Harry must consider passing on his estate to a cousin named George Hotspur. While George possesses wit and charm, his reputation as a gambler causes Sir Harry to reject him as heir. Instead, he takes the unusual step of settling the estate on Emily and hoping that whoever she marries will choose to adopt the name Hotspur. Because he is a just man, Sir Harry bestows on George £5,000 and a promise that he will inherit double that amount upon Sir Harry's death. While Sir Harry and his wife, Lady Elizabeth, choose a suitable prospect in Lord Alfred Gesley, son of Harry's old friend the Marquis of Milnthrop, Emily does not care for him. Instead, she falls in love with George, who has not accepted Sir Harry's money with the grace and understanding for which Harry had hoped. Instead, he does his best to attract Emily, understanding the fortune she will bring to a marriage.

Despite her father's warnings and evidence that George leads an improvident life, Emily cannot resist his charms. She feels that she can change George and promises not to marry him unless Sir Harry approves, which he does not. George continues his racetrack gambling, lying about it to Emily. Lady Elizabeth is horrified when she asks Emily what she would do if George had done "the wickedest things in the world," and her daughter replies, "I might break my heart in thinking of it, but I should never give him up." Trollope does paint a sympathetic mother figure when he has Elizabeth also succumb to George, "not knowing why, but feeling that she herself became bright, amusing, and happy when talking to him." When George is pressed by creditors and in danger of criminal charges, he accepts Sir Harry's payment of his debts and promise of a yearly income if he will stay away from Emily. The Hotspurs take the miserable young woman to Italy, where she will later die, ostensibly of a broken heart, leaving behind grieving parents.

In describing Hotspur in the opening sentences as "a mighty person in Cumberland, and one who well understood . . . what sort the magnificence, which his position as a great English commoner required of him," Trollope prepares readers for a fall from grace that will be all the greater due to Hotspur's position and wealth. The fact that he was "a proud man" hints at the stubbornness that will lead him to sacrifice his daughter to his own ideals. That the sacrifice will be made becomes clear as foreshadowing when Emily tells her mother, "George will always be to me the dearest thing in the whole world—dearer than my own soul." While Trollope rarely sketched true villains in his novels, George Hotspur comes close. He has no redeeming qualities, and as a drinker, womanizer, and gambler, he fails to accept responsibility for his own actions, anathema to Trollope. Trollope did not lack understanding regarding moneylenders; he had had experience with them in his own youth. However, he had never stooped to lying and theft, and when George does so, his social designation as "gentleman" assumes the emptiness of a mere label.

The book opened to mixed reviews but remains important as an unusual Victorian indictment of the narrow-mindedness often accompanying ancestral pride. It is readily available.

BIBLIOGRAPHY
Bradbury, Sue. Introduction to *Sir Harry Hotspur of Humblethwaite,* by Anthony Trollope. London: The Trollope Society, 1992, vii–xvii.
Kincaid, James. *The Novels of Anthony Trollope.* Oxford: Oxford University Press, 1977.

SMALL HOUSE AT ALLINGTON, THE
ANTHONY TROLLOPE (1864)   The fifth novel in Anthony TROLLOPE's Barsetshire sequence, *The Small House at Allington* introduced Lily Dale, the protagonist who would become his readers' favorite. It is a sad tale, for which Trollope makes no excuse, although he acts more tenderly toward Lily in her loss of love, leaving her to survive a spinster, than he did with the heroine of his SIR HARRY HOTSPUR OF HUMBLETHWAITE (1871), who dies from her broken heart. The novel reflects many of the elements common to the sequence, including multiple plots, with the subplots supporting themes of the major action. It also incorporates humor, often in the form of skillful irony, despite its sadness. In addition, it contains characters recognizable to avid Trollope readers from his other work, Septimus Harding and Plantagnet Palliser, the latter in a subplot romance of Griselda Dumbello that emphasizes the male assumption that women will conform to their wishes.

Trollope assumes a narrative approach that he seemed to favor, telling his story from the point of view, or perspective, of a female character. Lily and her sister Bell live with their widowed mother at the title residence, the Small House at Allington, where they enjoy the patronage of Mrs. Dale's late husband's brother, Squire Dale. The squire remains unmarried, living in his great house, removed from life but sympathetic toward his extended family. A London civil servant, Adolphus Crosbie, captures Lily's heart, fascinated by her naiveté and the arcadian innocence suggested by her name, but too jaded to recognize her spiritual value. Adolphus's focus on materialism becomes clear in an interview with Squire Dale when the squire questions his ability to support Lily "with all those comforts to which she has been accustomed." Endeavoring to get some promise of income from the wily squire, Crosbie nobly states, "As a matter of course, I would not take a shilling from her," and is surprised by the squire's return, "Then that settles it." While Lily cannot recognize an opportunist, the squire certainly does.

Crosbie rejects Lily for the wealthy Lady Alexandrina Decourcy of Courcy Castle. The two make an unhappy marriage that ends with their separation. Despite courtship by the admirable Johnny Eames, Lily cannot overcome her passion for the out-of-reach Adolphus, and she rejects Eames's attentions. Her name remains a symbol of death, but it is the death of hope rather than a physical death Lily will endure, later explained when she states that she feels married to the man to whom she gave herself and in whose love she "rejoiced." Trollope emphasizes his often-used theme of the capricious nature of love, portraying without DIDACTICISM the fickle nature of passion. Eames's lonely existence in London is emphasized along with the financial problems that grow from his isolation. His observations add a dark humor as well as some balance to the innocence of the rural life enjoyed by the Dales, whose surname suggests their surroundings. Episodes in Eames's life include drunken husbands, obvious duplicity on the part of scheming women who trap inexperienced men, and all the farce expected in a boarding house that acts as the setting for a raw burlesque. Eames serves as a reflection of Crosbie, a young man not born to wealth yet corrupted by the city in the same way Crosbie was corrupted, by compromising his ideals in order to become successful. He eventually fights and defeats Crosbie, an act finding favor with the Dales but producing small satisfaction for the brokenhearted Lily. The various heartbreaks are relieved by Bell's romance with and marriage to Dr. Crofts, a local physician she chooses over her uncle's wish that she marry her well-placed cousin, Bernard Dale. Crofts remains the only male in the story that respects the wishes of women, thus acting as a foil to the other men.

In addition to a poignant love tale, the novel might be seen as a comment on the selfish concerns of aristocracy, the pride of family name, or an elevation of country life over the more duplicitous life of the city. Trollope revisits his enduring belief that a woman should never be forced into an arranged marriage, his famously stated idea in his autobiography. His writing a story about men who err in judging more correct women might be considered a socially subversive approach during his Victorian era. He includes a sharp reflection on his own trade when Mrs. Dale observes about Plantagenet, "The quick seeing of the meaning must depend a little on the reader, must it not?"

BIBLIOGRAPHY

Kincaid, James. *The Novels of Anthony Trollope*. Oxford: Oxford University Press, 1977.

Markwick, Margaret. Introduction to *The Small House at Allington*, by Anthony Trollope. London: The Trollope Society, 1997, xi–xvii.

SMITH, CHARLOTTE (1749–1806)

Born in London, Charlotte Turner lost her mother at age three and lived with an aunt. She attended school and at age 14 was married to 21-year-old Benjamin Smith, handsome son of a West India merchant. Smith was extravagant and unfaithful, and the couple's home, in which Charlotte had to care for her demanding invalid mother-in-law, proved unhappy. Her husband entered debtors prison in 1783, enduring a seven-month sentence Charlotte was forced to share. By that time, the family included eight children, and she began to publish in order to support them. Her first collection of poetry was titled *Elegiac Sonnets and other Essays* (1784), making her the first English woman to publish sonnets. Her investment in that work turned her a profit, with 11 editions of her poetry appearing in rapid sequence. Forced to live in near-poverty in France, she began to work on translations, eventually gaining a divorce from her husband, although she agreed to continue supporting him. She could do so thanks to a successful novelist career. Her first work, *EMMELINE, OR THE ORPHAN OF THE CASTLE* (1788) gained praise from several critics, including Sir Walter SCOTT. A novel with a heroine whom NEW HISTORICIST CRITICS recognize as reflecting Smith herself, including her reading as a type of salvation, it became quite popular. Additional work included *Ethelinde* (1789), *Celestina* (1791), *Desmond* (1792), and, considered her best work, *The Old Manor House* (1793). She continued to publish quick adventure plots characterized by witty dialogue, issuing a novel each year through 1799. She also wrote for children and published additional poetry.

BIBLIOGRAPHY

Sage, Lorna. "Smith, Charlotte." *The Cambridge Guide to Women's Writing in English*. Cambridge: Cambridge University Press, 1999, 584.

SMITH, GEORGE (1824–1901)

George Smith remains important to the development of the British novel due to his publishing through the business he took over from his father, Smith & Elder, of authors who made enormous contributions to the development of the British novel. He not only discovered the BRONTË sisters, he also published works by William Makepeace THACKERAY, Elizabeth GASKELL, Wilkie COLLINS, Charles READE, George MEREDITH, Charles DARWIN, and Mrs. Humphry WARD. In addition, he founded *The CORNHILL MAGAZINE,* edited first by Thackeray and later Leslie Stephen, father to Virginia Stephen Woolf. In addition to work by authors named above, *The Cornhill* published fiction by Anthony TROLLOPE, Charles LEVER, George ELIOT, Edward BULWER-LYTTON and Thomas HARDY.

BIBLIOGRAPHY

Graham, Walter. *English Literary Periodicals*. New York: Octagon Books, 1966.

SMITH, TOBIAS (1721–1771)

Tobias Smollett was a Scotsman from a village near Loch Lomond. As a boy, he wrote and dedicated poetry to the Scottish hero William Wallace and by 18 years of age had written a tragedy titled *The Regicide,* about King James I and Queen Anne. Educated at Glasgow University, he desired a military career but instead studied Greek, mathematics, and philosophy, leaving school with no degree. He also served an apprenticeship with a physician qualifying him to perform surgery. Smollett decided to move to London at age 19 and became a surgeon's mate, serving in the navy. He saw action at the 1741 siege of Carthagena in the Caribbean, witnessing the tragic British loss. His experiences hardened him to death, as well as to the horrid physical conditions present on the ship, including lack of food and sanitation, harsh corporal punishment of crewmembers, uncomfortable climate conditions, and surgery in the most basic surroundings. In Jamaica he fell in love with a planter's daughter. A wealthy woman, she brought to their marriage the financial support Smollett needed to leave the service. He then returned to London to establish his own medical practice.

After failing to convince anyone to produce his drama, Smollett became embittered and published SATIRE in verse considering contemporary literature and politics. The subjects suited well his proud and sometimes belligerent nature. His early poems, "Advice" (1746), "Reproof" (1747), and "The Tears of Scotland" (1747), gained him some attention, the latter focusing on reprisals against Scotland by the Duke of Cumberland following the 1745 rebellion.

When Smollett was 26, he began a full-length novel titled *The Adventures of* RODERICK RANDOM, published anonymously in January 1748. He relied heavily on his own experiences and included characters representative of real individuals. He featured a Scottish surgeon's apprentice who relocates to London and enjoys many adventures, some on the sea, including the Carthagena expedition, where he romances a native. He eventually returns to England and through happenstance finds his once-lost father, becomes wealthy, and marries well. In its autobiographical approach and action in foreign lands, it followed the lead of Daniel DEFOE, but differed greatly in its REALISM and in the insertion of some humorous episodes. He took care to offer a disclaimer, writing that he simply reproduced scenes already familiar to the general reader, applying an "amusing point of view."

Smollett next wrote an opera titled *Aleste,* setting it to music by Handel. It was not staged, but Handel adapted the music for poet John Dryden's "Song for St. Cecilia's Day." Continually frustrated at not finding a producer for his drama, Smollett at last published it in 1749; its sales were by subscription, and he added a typical harangue against untrustworthy theater managers. After publishing another novel, *Sir Peregrine Pickle* (1751), he became a degreed physician and began practice in Bath, where he published a single professional piece.

Smollett did not practice medicine for long, relocating to Chelsea and writing prefaces and other piecework for pay, but this would not support the spending habits of his wife, Anne. His next novel was *The Adventures of Ferdinand Count Fathom* (1753), followed by a translation of *Don Quixote* (1755), not well received, due to his poor knowledge of Spanish. His comedy, *The Reprisal, or, The Tars of Old England,* enjoyed a run

at Drury Lane, and from 1756 to 1763, Smollett edited the *Critical Review or Annals of Literature,* engaging in criticism that led to a suit for libel, gaining him three months' imprisonment. He used the time to write another novel, *The Life and Adventures of Sir Launcelot Greaves,* first published in *The British Magazine,* which he edited for a time. His fortunes had at last shifted when he published *Complete History of England Deduced from the Defeat of Julius Caesar to the Treaty of Aiz-la-Chapelle, 1748* (1758), as it would earn him the huge sum of £2,000. Smollett published a weekly journal named *The Briton* beginning in 1762, later defending the questionable actions of the earl of Bute, First Lord of the Treasury, leading to the earl's resignation.

Following time spent in France and Italy in 1764, Smollett wrote *Travels through France and Italy* (1766) and was later satirized by Laurence STERNE in his *A SENTIMENTAL JOURNEY THROUGH FRANCE AND ITALY* (1768). In poor health, he published another satire, *Adventures of an Atom* (1748), with politics as his target. A move to Edinburgh in 1770 for his health's sake allowed him to live into 1771, the year he published *The Expedition of* HUMPHRY CLINKER. Smollett's writing remains an excellent example of the satire of his age and is available in both print and electronic versions.

BIBLIOGRAPHY
Hannay, David. *Life of Tobias George Smollett.* Port Washington, N.Y.: Kennikat Press, 1972.

SPIRITUAL QUIXOTE, OR THE SUMMER'S RAMBLE OF MR. GEOFFRY WILDGOOSE, THE: A COMIC ROMANCE

RICHARD GRAVES (1772)   *The Spiritual Quixote* represents Richard GRAVES's most important and best work, popular enough in its own time to require a second edition. Graves supposedly wrote the book while in a "pique" following an experience with an itinerant preacher who moved into his parish and succeeded in stealing much of Graves's congregation. The book does not have an angry tone, however, and Graves himself describes it not as SATIRE but rather as a "comic ROMANCE." Some disagree, labeling his characterization of Methodism as a movement promoted by overzealous showmen as deserving of the satiric label. His title includes the novel within the tradition of Miguel Cervantes's great *Don Quixote,* and the similarities between the two books are many, although Cervantes's work is unquestionably superior.

As Don Quixote did, the comically named Geoffry Wildgoose takes to the road, leaving his life of luxury behind to preach Methodism in hopes of meeting his idol, George Whitefield. While Graves respected the leader of the movement, John Wesley, he believed Whitefield to be a charlatan and a hypocrite, and that view clearly comes across in the book. As do Don Quixote and Sancho Panza, the two main characters of Graves's novel, Geoffry and his cobbler companion, Jerry Tugwell, experience many adventures in their pursuit of a goal. Most critics agree that the descriptions of the 18th-century social scene and details about the individuals the travelers meet represent the true value of the tale. Graves also incorporates erudite humor in his description of Geoffry's excitement following their first sunrise; he was so inspired that he broke into quotations from John Milton.

NEW HISTORICIST CRITICS can point to various autobiographical aspects of the book, including the fact that Geoffry is likely based on Graves's brother, who converted to Methodism, while Tugwell represents a true rustic type common to Graves's era. The antics of Mr. Graham and Mr. Rivers are based on Graves's own innocent youthful activities. Other characters in addition to Whitefield so resembled real people that W. J. Croker in 1831 produced a "key" identifying the figures, aligning the work with the ROMAN À CLEF tradition. Influences include Henry FIELDING's comic prose epic narrative, as well as Laurence STERNE's abundant use of multiple obscure quotations, many of which in Graves's novel come from minor writers of his era.

Graves retains his good humor throughout, remaining always respectful of men who do their duty, regardless of their faith, and admitting that genuine piety may exist even within Methodism; it is just not practiced by Whitefield. He was particularly critical of Whitefield's manipulation of crowds into what he termed hysteria, and also of what Graves claimed was Methodism's reintroduction of certain superstitions that had been absent from the High Church for some time. Modern readers living in a world of televangelists and charismatic leaders that prey on the naive in hopes of reaping material benefit can still enjoy the novel, well understanding Graves's outrage.

BIBLIOGRAPHY

Ellis, Haveloc, "Richard Graves and *The Spiritual Quixote.*" *Nineteenth Century.* 77 (1915): 848–860.

Hill, Charles Jarvis. *The Literary Career of Richard Graves.* Northampton, Mass.: Smith College, 1935.

Tracy, Clarence. Introduction to *The Spiritual Quixote,* by Richard Graves. London: Oxford University Press, 1967, xv–xxiii.

SPORT OF CHANCE, THE WILLIAM SHARP (1888)

First published serially in *The People's Friend* as "A Deathless Hate" in 1887, William SHARP's three-volume SENSATION FICTION *The Sport of Chance* was based in part on time he spent in Australia. An attack of typhoid prompted him to move temporarily to Australia for recovery, and Australia and Scotland formed the setting of the novel. He would not publish it until several years after its writing, as he mentions in a letter dated November 1887 to Edward Dowden: "Have just issued a 3 vol. novel *The Sport of Chance* written 3 or 4 yrs ago, & been running serially." The novel remains a predictable ROMANCE, which features a lovely endangered young heroine, Mona Cameron Armitage, delusional from "brain fever"; the Cameron family with a disgraced son; a kindly physician, Dr. Sterne; a long journey on the part of the protagonist, Hew Armitage, to reclaim his runaway bride and missing child; mistaken identity; mysterious visitors, including the wicked Charles Leith; and the aid of strong fearless helpers, in particular the Cornwall fisherman Garth Trendall.

While not a remarkable tale, *The Sport of Chance* offers an excellent subject for analysis by various critical schools. FEMINIST CRITICS will find predictable Mona's helpless state. The invalid female, driven mad following childbirth, was a stock figure of hysteria in Victorian fiction. Her manipulation by strong males makes her an unwilling party to forgery and theft, but her child/woman personality assures readers of her innocence, despite her husband's doubts. The various delusions and visions she suffers in which she and her infant daughter fall victim to a male stalker interest PSYCHOANALYTIC CRITICS as well as feminists. In addition, abundant imagery of snakes, long considered phallic symbols, and of those snakes pursuing and even consuming Mona, may combine with some of the novel's other elements to tempt critics to psychoanalyze Sharp himself. A childless man, he eventually published secretly as Fiona Macleod. His wife's later comments about this alter ego suggested that Fiona might have been a manifestation of the child that the couple never had. In addition to the symbolism mentioned above, additional symbolic imagery would be easily analyzed by FORMALIST critics. The opening storm, accompanying comet, and flashes of dark and light all signal a cleansing through destruction of the old, making possible a new beginning, an idea further emphasized in the birth imagery of a naked man's body delivered from the sea following a shipwreck. The detailed scene of a shoat stalking and killing a hare clearly suggests the victimized Mona pursued by Leith. Students recognize Armitage staring at his reflection in a mirror as a strong suggestion of themes of self-identity. Characterization remains shallow, with the novel's characters acting as type, adding unintentional humor to the NARRATIVE for many 21st-century readers who prove more sophisticated and judgmental than readers of previous centuries. Sharp's rendition of setting proves his major accomplishment, his familiarity with the rugged geography that he describes producing faithful renditions of surroundings so important to the story, that they almost become characters themselves.

BIBLIOGRAPHY

Hallorhan, William F., ed. "The Letters of William Sharp, 'Fiona Macleod.'" The Institute of English Studies, University of London School of Advanced Studies. Available online. URL: http://www.sas.ac.uk/. Downloaded on July 7, 2004.

STERNE, LAURENCE (1713–1768)

Laurence Sterne was born on November 24, 1713, at Clonmel, in Tipperary, Ireland. His father Roger was an ensign in the infantry; his death in 1731 left Sterne in financial straits, but through the help of an uncle, Richard Sterne, he was able to continue his education. In 1737, he graduated with a B.A. from Jesus College, Cambridge, was ordained, and became the vicar of Sutton in 1738. He received his M.A. in 1740. It was during this period that Sterne suffered a hemorrhage in his lungs, which led to incurable tuberculosis.

Family was a source of pain and conflict for Sterne. In 1741, he began writing for his uncle Dr. Jacques Sterne's newspaper, but he stopped in 1742. This caused a rift between the two, and Jacques had Sterne's mother thrown in prison just to embarrass him. The year 1741 also saw his marriage to Elizabeth Lumley. The Sternes' only child to survive into adulthood, Lydia, was born in 1747. The marriage was an unhappy one; in 1758 Elizabeth had a breakdown. In the meantime, Sterne had become famous for his numerous extramarital affairs. The most significant of these liaisons (just a year before Sterne's death) was to Elizabeth Draper, the wife of an East Indian Company official, to whom Sterne wrote *Journal to Eliza*. Like Sterne's sermons and other nonfictional writings, the journal is generally only available in complete collections of his works. For fairly obvious reasons, it was not published in Sterne's lifetime.

The vicar Laurence Sterne, known as a wit, an eccentric, and a practical joker whose behavior was often shocking for a man of the cloth, occasionally published in the early years of his career, including some sermons and *The History of a Warm Coat* (1759), a political SATIRE on church politics, which was burned by church members. However, there is nothing in the basic facts of Sterne's pre-1760 life that would prepare one for the publication of TRISTRAM SHANDY. By this time, Sterne had settled in Yorkshire. R. & J. Dodsley of London published the novel's first two volumes on January 1, 1760. Like all succeeding volumes, they were extremely popular. Volumes three through six were published the following year. Unfortunately, Sterne's health again failed him, and he spent several years traveling in France and Italy in search of a more favorable climate.

While Sterne was not Tristram, there is little doubt that this experience changed the mood of the novel and indeed directly influenced its later content. Volumes seven and eight were published in 1765. The ninth and final volume was published in 1767 and was followed by a short and comparatively minor novel, *A SENTIMENTAL JOURNEY* (*through France and Italy*). Much of this later writing shows the influence of Sterne's travels in his later years, as well as a feeling of melancholy brought on by his failing health.

The same year (1767) that Tristram "ran out of pages," Sterne wrote and published *A Sentimental Journey,* a novel that brought back Yorick, this time as the supposed narrator. However, as the novel follows an Englishman through France and Italy, makes direct reference to a woman named Eliza, and is written in a voice far more similar to Volume VII of *Tristram Shandy* than to Yorick's, one may suspect that this travel book is somewhat autobiographical, and that Yorick's profession may well be the reason that he was selected to be Sterne's voice. As critic A. Alvarez has noted, "perhaps it gave him a soothing illusion of immortality to identify so completely with a character in his own work."

In April, Eliza had returned to India. Sterne left his wife and daughter in Paris (they visited him later in the year) and returned to England, where he worked on *A Sentimental Journey* and *Journal to Eliza.* Throughout this period, his health continued to deteriorate. He died in his lodgings at Bond Street on 18 March 1768.

BIBLIOGRAPHY

Cash, Arthur H. *Laurence Sterne: The Early and Middle Years.* London: Methuen, 1975.

———. *Laurence Sterne: The Later Years.* London: Methuen, 1986.

Piper, William Bowman. *Laurence Sterne.* New York: Twayne, 1965.

Watt, Ian. *The Rise of the Novel.* Los Angeles: University of California, 1957.

STEVENSON, ROBERT LOUIS (1850–1894)

Robert Louis Stevenson was born in Edinburgh, where, despite a childhood marred by fragile health, he attended Edinburgh University in 1867. His mother Margaret was a religious person, her father having been a Church of Scotland minister, while Stevenson's father, Thomas, worked as a respected lighthouse and harbor engineer. Both were devoted to their son and worried over his delicate health. Suffering from frequent bouts of fever, he at times spent weeks in bed, often worrying during sleepless nights about the devil and hell, concepts learned in the church. He later said that those days of terror honed his imaginative skills.

Stevenson first studied engineering but changed his major to law, a subject more to his liking. He would join others in rebelling against Victorian conventions in the later half of the 19th century. His respect for his parents conflicted with his desire to investigate new ideas, but he overcame his hesitation to pursue his own interests. By 1875 he gained his advocacy and considered a career in writing, beginning with contributions to the university magazine. His health continued to challenge his adventurous spirit, but he overcame his problem to embark on a tour of France and Belgium by canoe. His original account of that experience, *An Inland Voyage* (1878), was followed by a sequel, *Travels with a Donkey in Cevennes* in 1879, the same year he visited the United States. While in California, Stevenson met and later returned to marry Mrs. Fanny Osbourne after her divorce became final. It was for his stepson Lloyd that he supposedly wrote his enduring juvenile ROMANCE *TREASURE ISLAND* (1883). Travel pieces followed, and his publishing success convinced him to continue writing for a living. Considered a brilliant conversationalist, he enthralled others with his enthusiasm and love of storytelling. Critic Jenni Calder notes that in one letter to his mother, Stevenson wrote, "I wish that life were an opera. I should like to *live* in one."

Stevenson's work appeared in *The CORNHILL MAGAZINE,* and its editor, Leslie Stephen, father of Virginia Woolf, nurtured Stevenson's writing ambitions. But his famous essay "A Humble Remonstrance," written in response to Henry JAMES's "The Art of Fiction," was published in *Longman's Magazine* in 1884. Best known for his novels, which included *Prince Otto* (1885), *The STRANGE CASE OF DR. JEKYLL AND MR. HYDE* (1886), *KIDNAPPED* (1886), *Catriona* (1893), *The Black Arrow* (1888) and *The MASTER OF BALLANTRAE* (1889), Stevenson published many volumes of short stories, including *Virginibus Puerisque* (1881), *Familiar Studies of Men and Books* (1882), *New Arabian Nights* (1882), *The Merry Men* (1887), *Memories and Portraits* (1887), *Across the Plains* (1892), and *Island Nights' Entertain-*

ments (1893). While his work contained sensational-ism in the vein of SENSATIONAL FICTION, reflecting the influence of Wilkie COLLINS, his graceful style miti-gated against the vulgarity and horror that marked Collins's work. Stevenson left unfinished WEIR OF HEMISTON (1896) and *St. Ives* (1897 and 1898), com-pleted by Sir Arthur QUILLER-COUCH. He also wrote poetry and drama that never achieved the success of his fiction, with the exception of his still-popular *A Child's Garden of Verses* (1885).

Stevenson's poor health drove him from England for good in 1888, with his subsequent experiences in the Pacific Islands and Samoa inspiring later works. With Fanny he set up a farm called Vailima, and the couple worked to become self-sufficient, although their efforts were not as successful as they wished. His interest in Polynesian culture and firm belief that Europe exploited the islands led him to write letters of protest and the books *In The South Seas* (1896) and *A Footnote to History* (1892). The latter focused on the struggle between Germany, America, and Britain to assume power in Samoa, their efforts damaging its culture. His two novellas, *The Beach of Falesá* (1893) and *The Ebb-Tide* (1894), continued his theme of protest against colonization. His Calvinist background contributed to his concern for injustice and his feeling a responsibil-ity toward those marginalized by society. While he enjoyed Lloyd and his stepdaughter Belle and her son Austin living with them for a time, Belle's husband, Joe Strong, proved an embarrassment to the family. That problem eased following the couple's separation, but then Fanny became ill and grappled with poor mental health. Stevenson's writing helped him escape the depression that threatened his own well-being.

While in Samoa, Stevenson enjoyed much improved health for a time, yet he died from a sudden cerebral hemorrhage on December 3, 1894, at the age of 44, leaving behind a reputation as a local storyteller and champion for the island ways. According to Calder, Henry JAMES wrote of "this ghastly extinction of the beloved R.L.S.," while during Stevenson's lifetime, Edmund Gosse said he was "the most entrancing per-sonality" he had ever known. His influence as a romance writer was great, touching in addition to Quiller-Couch, Stanley J. Weyman, Arthur Conan DOYLE, and Rudyard

KIPLING. Stevenson's classics will long be enjoyed in both written form and in various dramatic media.

BIBLIOGRAPHY

Allen, Walter Ernst. *Six Great Novelists: Defoe, Fielding, Scott, Dickens, Stevenson, Conrad.* Folcroft, Pa.: Folcroft Library Editions, 1971.

Calder, Jenni, ed. *Robert Louis Stevenson: A Critical Celebra-tion.* Totowa, N.J.: Barnes & Noble, 1980.

Hammond, J. R. *A Robert Louis Stevenson Companion.* Lon-don: Macmillan Press, 1984.

STOKER, BRAM (1847–1912)

Born in Dublin as Abraham Stoker, the third of seven children, Bram Stoker suffered a childhood illness that kept him bedridden during the first years of his life. He fully recovered to engage in sports and attend school in his hometown and then matriculated to Trinity College in 1866. He later worked as a civil servant and wrote as drama critic of *The Dublin Mail* while also editing *The Penny Press.* He published FANTASY and a HORROR FICTION titled "The Chain of Destiny," which appeared in *The Shamrock* in 1875. In 1878, Stoker moved to London and served as a manager at Lyceum Theater for Sir Henry Irving, a famous and celebrated actor-manager, affording him a more creative environment. He married Florence Balcome, and they had one son, named Noel.

While working with Sir Henry for 27 years, Stoker published *The Duties of Clerks of Petty Sessions in Ireland* (1879), written during his earlier stint at service in Dublin. He followed with more than a dozen books, the first a collection of scary CHILDREN'S LITERATURE titled *Under the Sunset* (1882), and his first novel, *The Snake's Pass* (1890). In 1897, Stoker published DRAC-ULA, one of the most enduring examples of horror fic-tion in English. Its success was due in part to the use of a documentary narrative, which included dated diaries, letters, and journal entries, to add REALISM to the plot, a ploy he borrowed from Wilkie COLLINS. His statement preceding the story explained that the "papers" were "placed in sequence" and that "a history almost at variance with the possibilities of later-day belief may stand forth as simple fact." *Dracula,* while dealing solely with the subject of vampires, is con-structed in the GOTHIC NOVEL tradition, with debts to

Horace WALPOLE's *The CASTLE OF OTRANTO* (1764) and Anne RADCLIFFE's *The MYSTERIES OF UDOLPHO* (1794). Stoker never again matched the success of that novel. His final publication was the nonfiction *Personal Reminiscences of Henry Irving* (1906).

BIBLIOGRAPHY

Belford, Barbara. *Bram Stoker: A Biography of the Author of Dracula.* Cambridge: Da Capo Press, 2002.

Farson, Daniel. *The Man Who Wrote Dracula: A Biography of Bram Stoker.* New York: St. Martin's Press, 1976.

STORY OF AN AFRICAN FARM, THE

OLIVE SCHREINER (1883)   While Olive SCHREINER was born and lived for years in South Africa, she remains important to the British writing tradition as the first colonial novelist held important by British readers. She brought a manuscript with her when, at age 26, she moved to England, where she searched for a publisher. Her novel, *The Story of an African Farm,* became important to later FEMINIST CRITICS in its development of a strong independent female protagonist, exhausted by the demands of the land. The farm itself, an unremittingly bleak landscape, serves as a symbol to counter the romantic traditional version of the frontier. It focuses on two sisters, one of whom dies delivering her lover's child. It also offered readers a cross-dressing male character with the ironic surname of Rose. The workers' suffering indicts the imperialistic attitudes of those "civilizing" Africa, as did the violence that characterized IMPERIALISM, and she galvanized feminist issues in the first work by a colonial writer to garner acclaim. Critics were appalled by her promotion of a "free union" in the place of marriage, and she was roundly taken to task for her revolutionary attitude on the pages of publications including *Punch* and *Progress*. It also proves of interest to MARXIST critics, and socialist Edward B. Aveling, while not praising her style, wrote that Schreiner was "pointing the eyes" of her audience toward a "great socialist revolution" that he judged imminent. Schreiner published adopting the name Ralph Iron, and her protagonist voices many of the author's own views, such as "I regard marriage as other people regard death." She

later received credit for anticipating what would be labeled the New Woman fiction in the next decade.

Schreiner's condition as a governess writing of her observations adds to the importance of her achievement. Her style omits all sentimentality as she adopts a tone of frank hostility, sketching the unpleasant reality of the lack of women's rights, the spiritual struggles caused by isolation and sexual harassment. The narrative includes some polemic material in Part II delivered by the novel's protagonist, Lyndall, focusing on women's rights. In addition, two sections resemble ALLEGORY; in those sections, Schreiner imitates, in order to subvert, biblical diction. She avoids sensationalizing scenes involving sex, by suggesting the action.

In addition to the first-person point-of-view narrator, Lyndall, who will die following the death of her three-hour-old child, the plot follows a number of additional characters. They include the evil Bonaparte Blenkins, an Irish shyster who brings ruin to the farm; Tant' Sannie, who believes Blenkins's lies and prospers due to her material nature; Sannie's wealthy niece, Trana, whom Blenkins hopes to marry; Em, Lyndall's sister and a young woman of low self-esteem who marries out of loneliness a man she had once rejected, the gentle naive German farmer, Otto, who will die due to Blenkins's duplicity; and Otto's son Waldo, who becomes an agnostic and dies an early death.

Readers understand that those honorable characters that seek an ethical life will not survive in an environment where material gain alone is admired. Tant' Sannie represents the most practical of the characters. Twice widowed and placed in charge of Em and Lyndall by their dying father, she finds freedom when Em turns 16 years old and inherits the farm. Released from control over the property and the girls, Sannie at age 30 makes a marriage of convenience to a 19-year-old albino named Piet Vander Walt, a widower. Those individuals who develop relationships share a sense of humanity, and they will lose everything in a land made barren more by the lack of compassion and by inequity than by nature. Even the spiritual bond that develops between foils Lyndall and Waldo will not save them. Death haunts this group, and no relief comes from religion. Waldo questions his family's faith as a result of the inexplicable suffering he witnesses. He suffers for every death that occurs, not only in his own environment but the world over. His compassion is such that when Blenkins pleads with him at the conclusion of Part I for food and water, Waldo supplies his needs, despite Blenkins's persecution of the farms' inhabitants. Such a sensitive nature as Waldo's cannot survive on Schreiner's African farm.

Critics compared Schreiner's rendition of Lyndall's lot as a governess to that constructed by Charlotte BRONTË through the title heroine of her novel JANE EYRE (1847). At the time Bronte's novel was published, the public stood unprepared for the stark facts laid out by the diminutive Jane. When Schreiner's novel arrived almost 40 years later, social revolutionaries of a new generation welcomed her as their champion.

BIBLIOGRAPHY

Aveling, Edward B. "A Notable Book." *Progress: A Monthly Magazine of Annotated Thought.* 1 (1883):162.
Berkman, Joyce Avrech. *The Healing Imagination of Olive Schreiner: Beyond South African Colonialism.* Amherst: University of Massachusetts Press, 1989.
Bristow, Joseph. Introduction to *The Story of an African Farm,* by Olive Schreiner. New York: Oxford University Press, 1992, vii–xxix.

STRAND, THE

The Strand was founded in 1891 by Mr. (later Sir) George Newnes, an experienced publisher and editor who had made his name with a magazine called *Tit-Bits,* while also editing several other publications. Newnes hoped to compete with the American magazines imported to Great Britain, which he labeled "smarter" and "brighter" than the stodgy British publications. *The Strand* featured fiction by notables including P. G. Wodehouse, H. G. WELLS, Rudyard KIPLING, and Somerset Maugham, and is perhaps best known for Arthur Conan DOYLE's tales featuring the enduring detective Sherlock Holmes. It appeared at a time when such periodicals no longer required a polemic bent, a revolutionary change for magazines; the expanding middle class desired simply entertainment with no political message. *The Strand* and other popular publications were nicknamed "railway magazines," indicating their attraction for railroad passengers. *The Strand's* glossy pages and beautiful

illustrations, featured in imaginative layouts, supported its reputation for high quality. Readers could buy single issues or bound versions of six months' worth of magazines, with a choice of half-leather or blue-cloth binding. *The Strand* retained its popularity for decades, not ceasing publication until 1950.

BIBLIOGRAPHY

Pound, Reginald. *The Strand Magazine.* London: Heinemann, 1966.
"The Story of the Strand Magazine." Golante So. Available online. URL: http://www.jhenry.demon.co.uk/strand2.htm. Downloaded on May 27, 2004.

STRANGE CASE OF DR. JEKYLL AND MR. HYDE, THE ROBERT LOUIS STEVENSON (1886)

A study of man's duality, Robert Louis STEVENSON's *The Strange Case of Dr. Jekyll and Mr. Hyde* vies with his TREASURE ISLAND (1883) for his most popular work. He wrote the piece while recovering from a hemorrhage, a nightmare having inspired its plot. When his wife, Fanny, heard it in its original version as a traditional HORROR tale, she suggested it might be better as an ALLEGORY. After a furious rewriting of only three days, Stevenson produced his enduring tale of a man who could alter his own character, both physically and emotionally. It was published to enthusiastic reviews praising Stevenson's capacity for sustained tension and entertaining terror, masterfully crafted.

Told through narration by Mr. Engeild, Mr. Utterson, Dr. Lanyon, Poole the butler, and Dr. Jekyll himself, the tale reveals Dr. Jekyll's desire to separate his positive aspects from his evil ones, recognizing that human nature places both into the same body. A respected man, Dr. Jekyll develops a formula, which he drinks, releasing the odious figure, Mr. Hyde. As he continues the transformations, he finds increasingly difficult his return to his "true" self. Stevenson's use of an unemotional tone in relaying detail helps build tension and heightens the reader's sense of perception, increasing the horror of each moment. Hyde's propensity to violate laws both civic and moral leads to his committing murder. Terrified that he might permanently become Mr. Hyde when his formula is gone, Dr.

Jekyll commits suicide. The body discovered belongs to Hyde, but a note written by Dr. Jekyll confirms the dual identities of one being. The note represents the first expression from the doctor's point of view, his confession answering points previously unclear in other accounts, thus bringing the story to a unified conclusion. His obvious agony as he realizes his decline and eventually his inability to escape Hyde's hold contrasts satisfactorily with the nonjudgmental, rational tone of the previous narrators.

Critics feel both Charles DICKENS and American author Edgar Allan Poe influenced the novel, which relies on the German myth of the doppelgänger to appeal to readers' trust in the story's veracity. PSYCHO-ANALYTIC CRITICS also see Jekyll and Hyde not as equal personalities, but Hyde as a suppressed version of Jekyll, undercutting Jekyll's idea that separation of the two personalities may be achieved. While most praise Stevenson's narrative skill, many find weakness in the description of the physical conversion of the physically normal Dr. Jekyll into the ugly and disgusting form of Mr. Hyde. The criticism has not hindered continued enjoyment of the tale, both in book form and in various film and stage presentations.

BIBLIOGRAPHY

Hammond, J. R. *A Robert Louis Stevenson Companion.* London: Macmillan Press, 1984.

STUDY IN SCARLET, A SIR ARTHUR CONAN DOYLE (1887)

While the reading world took little note at the time, the appearance of Arthur Conan DOYLE's *A Study in Scarlet* in the 1887 *Beeton's Christmas Annual* marked a momentous occasion. The first in the tales of investigation by the soon-to-be-legendary Sherlock Holmes and his friend Dr. John Watson set the tone not only for additional Holmes's mysteries to follow but also for mystery writing in general. While the "Scarlet" mentioned in the title refers to the many references to blood and passion in the novel, it might also, in hindsight, be seen as symbolic for the royal carpet on which Holmes, the undisputed king among fictional detectives, would walk for decades to come.

Doyle's first Holmes story would be viewed as a treasure to later readers eager to discover the background to the celebrated Holmes/Watson relationship. In a meeting arranged by an acquaintance of both men who knew of their need to share living quarters, the long-lasting partnership was formed. When Watson quotes Alexander Pope to the acquaintance, "The proper study of mankind is man," the friend replies, "You must study him then," referring to Holmes, and he adds, "You'll find him a knotty problem. . . . I'll wager he learns more about you than you about him." The brief scene sets the tone for the two men's relationship.

As Holmes's chronicler, Watson would spend his life studying the detective as he gained famed for his approach to solving crime. Thus, Watson fills Holmes's need for someone to remedy the problem Holmes expresses early on when explaining to Watson that he often helped the two inspectors, Lastrade and Gregson, but never received any credit in the press for his assistance: "Whatever they do, they will have followers." In an ironic turn, Watson will gain for Holmes a much more appreciative following. Readers will encounter in the novel for the first time many oft-repeated elements throughout the series of tales, including the phrases "I have written a monograph upon the subject" and "the plot thickens"; figures such as the inspectors and the Baker Street irregulars; Holmes's tendency to play nothing at all on his violin while deep in thought; and his sensitivity, as Watson explains, "to flattery on the score of his art," meaning his deductive talents, "as any girl could be of her beauty."

Readers also encounter Doyle's frequent use of timely political and ethical/moral topics in his stories. For example, Holmes refers to Charles DARWIN's theory about music and also compares the first murder victim's appearance to that of an ape, a fitting unflattering depiction, as the victim turns out to be an immoral hypocritical religious fanatic of the worst type and a murderer in his own right. Doyle also includes excerpts from press clippings of the day, such as one newspaper's comment "upon the fact that lawless outrages . . . usually occurred under a Liberal administration," then demonstrates that the murders have no relation to politics of the day, but rather to human nature. Doyle even comments upon literature, both classic, as the reference to Pope and another to Boccaccio's *Decameron* demonstrate, and popular. In a neat self-reference to his own genre and subject matter, he includes a brief discussion between Watson and Holmes of Edgar Alan Poe's popular investigator Dupin, the first such figure to appear in fiction. Watson's comment to Holmes that he reminds him of Dupin causes the retort that Holmes finds Dupin "a very inferior fellow . . . he was by no means such a phenomenon as Poe appeared to imagine."

The plot of the story is based on revenge for an act that allows Doyle to comment on another topic, his disdain for all organized religion, although readers do not encounter that aspect of the plot until midway through the book. A murder of the American Joseph Stangerson and later of his partner, E. J. Drebber, allow Holmes to practice his clue-gathering skills. The capture of the murderer, Jefferson Hope, begins the lengthy flashback that explains his actions. Hope had fallen in love with Lucy Ferrier, the adopted daughter of John Ferrier, both lone survivors of an attempt by a group to settle in the wilds of the western United States. Their rescue by members of the Mormon faith requires that they practice that faith, an edict to which Ferrier conforms, though in outward actions only. When Lucy matures, the stranger, Jefferson Hope, rescues her from possible death in a cattle drive and the two fall in love. He is traveling to the California silver mines and must continue his journey with plans to return to marry her. Ferrier, long desiring to remove his beloved Lucy from the oppressive lifestyle, agrees. Simultaneously two members of the Mormon community, Stangerson and Drebber, desire to add Lucy to their multiple wives and demand that Ferrier allow her to choose one of them. Filled with trepidation due to the rumored mystical happenings associated with the Mormons and their leader Brigham Young, Ferrier grows anxious that Hope will not return in time to rescue Lucy from the cult that Ferrier loathes. Doyle even describes a frightening visit from Young to Ferrier to emphasize his low view of such groups. While Hope returns in time to flee with the Ferriers, Stangerson and Drebber pursue the group, murder Ferrier, and kidnap Lucy, forcing her to marry Drebber. She survives only one month before dying of grief. For the

next 20 years, Hope pursues the two Mormons, although both have left the religious group, and he at last exacts his revenge. Hope's heart is first broken symbolically by Lucy's fate and later literally when an aortic aneurysm bursts and kills him, allowing his escape from British civic justice.

The story closes with Holmes explaining to Watson his famous analytical approach. He notes that most people could predict a possible result when supplied the events leading up to an end. However, when told the result first, few "would be able to evolve from their own inner consciousness what the steps were which led up to that result. This power is what I mean when I talk of reasoning backward, or analytically." Readers would come to admire that power as much as did Watson. *A Study in Scarlet* was later produced in various dramatic forms and remains readily available in print.

BIBLIOGRAPHY

Liebman, Arthur. *The Biographical Sherlock Holmes: An Anthology/Handbook: His Career from 1881 to 1914.* New York: Rosen Publishing Group, 1984.

SUFFRAGE MOVEMENT   Almost since its inception, fiction has focused on social problems, including the rights of women. By its nature, art reflects its era, and much fiction proved to be political, supporting the rights of women and other marginalized groups, either overtly or more covertly through suggested themes. From the 18th century onward, written fiction and nonfiction by both women and men began to examine social causes. By the mid-19th century, the suffrage movement focused on gaining various rights for women and gathered strength in both the United States and in England, its aims naturally incorporated into the literature of both countries. The suffrage movement focused not only on gaining women the vote so they might have a right to help shape their own destinies through law, it also supported votes for African Americans in the United States, a woman's right to custody of her children, a woman's right to own property, and also temperance, as male alcoholism contributed to the abuse and the annual murders of hundreds of women and children.

Mary WOLLSTONECRAFT, mother of novelist Mary Wollstonecraft SHELLEY, was one of the earliest women writers to protest the legal restrictions placed on women in her seminal nonfiction treatise *A Vindication of the Rights of Woman* (1792). In the first justification of women's rights, Wollstonecraft constructed an elaborate critique of 18th-century misogyny, claiming that men projected a view of women as weak creatures in order to control them politically, economically, and socially. Other publications, including Catharine Macaulay's *Letters on Education* (1790), had argued for certain rights for women, but *A Vindication* represented the first claim that existing legal "protection" of women in fact transformed them into an inferior class. Not only did she lambaste writers such as John Milton, Alexander Pope, and Jacques Rousseau for promoting imagery of weak women, she took female readers to task for their fondness for ROMANCE, a genre that continued to depict women as passive, ignorant beings. Wollstonecraft's novel, *Mary, A Fiction* (1788), an autobiographical account of the horrendous struggle for survival thrust upon a woman protagonist, countered those images. She also began shortly before her death following childbirth a fictionalized version of *A Vindication* titled *The Wrongs of Woman: Or, Maria,* demonstrating a man's power to commit his wife to an insane asylum with no real proof of insanity, a theme that would become an enduring one in women's literature and of special importance to FEMINIST CRITICS. Wollstonecraft's contemporaries, Hannah More and Fanny BURNEY, also wrote in support of women's rights. They battled 17th-century beliefs that a woman's womb would wander about her body when she was emotionally upset, and that reading and learning would cause a woman's womb to shrink, thereby endangering her capacity to give birth to male heirs. Wollstonecraft affected a new generation of writers, including George ELIOT, with her visionary ideas.

By 1800, despite the American and French Revolutions' bid for human rights, women remained as confined to what became known as the domestic sphere than ever. While few authors focused overtly on women's rights in their fiction, feminist critics later offered a feminist reading of the enduring *FRANKENSTEIN* (1818), a novel by Wollstonecraft's daughter, Mary SHELLEY. Some critics consider the monster as representing women, marginalized and controlled by the book's male protagonist. His developing intellectual and physical independence as he moves outside the restrictions of law suggests the fate of nonconformist women. Even Frankenstein's monstrous form reflects a male vision of women who fail to bend to the wishes of men, becoming monstrous anomalies. Another early-19th-century writer, Jane AUSTEN, fashioned a number of novels in which she emphasized women's lack of rights to inherit property, which would become a major focus of the suffrage movement.

Movements to gain rights for workers, most famously the CHARTIST revolutions, included many working women, and in 1831, the *Westminster Review* included an anonymous article supporting suffrage for females, support that would spread to the Parliament as early as 1832. Chartist causes would later become a topic for several popular socially conscious novels, including Charles KINGSLEY's *ALTON LOCKE* (1850). By 1839, Parliament supported Lady Caroline Norton's famous bid to regain custody of her children lost in divorce, causing her to publish several pamphlets, such as *The Natural Right of a Mother to the Custody of Her Child* (1837), leading to the Custody Act of 1839. In America, anti-slavery efforts would later become part of the suffrage movement, spurred on by London's 1840 World Anti-Slavery Convention. From that meeting grew a strong suffrage push in America, lead by Lucretia Mott and Elizabeth Cady Stanton, later to be joined by Lucy Stone and Susan B. Anthony. In England comparable figures arose, including Barbara Leigh Smith (later Barbara Bodichon), whose 1855 petition supporting a Married Women's Property Act brought her to the forefront of the movement. She helped found a feminist newspaper in 1857 called *The Englishwoman's Journal,* later becoming a leader in women's suffrage and helping to form England's first Women's Suffrage Committee. Among writers supporting the cause was Harriet Taylor, who reported for the *Westminster Review* about the first Worcester Women's Rights convention held in 1851 in Massachusetts, the United States. She would later marry philosopher John Stuart Mill, whose 1869 *The Subjection of Women* was informed by his wife's vision and became seminal in advancing rights for women the world over. When he was elected to the House of Commons, he helped bring about the first debate on women's suffrage in Parliament. While English women would not gain the vote until after World War I, the movement never weakened until their vision was achieved. The process leading to that achievement is mirrored in British fiction of the 19th century.

An ideology of conforming women prompted an early vision of a weak being prone to hysteria (from the Greek word *hyster* for "womb"), still present in Victorian times. Acceptable female stock characters in literature included the whore, the angel of the house, and the invalid. Ironically, some women writers promoted such imagery in conduct books, designed to educate young women in proper behavior. Mrs. Sarah Ellis in 1844 suggested in her conduct book that women's very existence, or self-identity, depended on their serving others. In such an atmosphere of the feminine ideal, the concept of women voting for their own rights amused many. Some believed that civic activity would bring on fainting, emotionally overpowering hysteria-prone women. They were expected to appear fragile, prompting many women to engage in ridiculous fads, including drinking vinegar to bring on a frail complexion. William Makepeace THACKERAY created an independent, active woman in the heroine of *VANITY FAIR* (1848), Becky Sharp, depicted as an immoral, improvident, manipulating shrew. He contrasted her with Amelia Smedley, an angelic, impossibly good heroine. While Thackeray satirized both these women as caricatures, they were based on an awful truth of the Victorian perception of women.

Novelists began to counter female stereotypes in the 1840s THESIS NOVELS, designed to emphasize the mistreatment of marginalized groups, such as factory workers, including women. Examples included Benjamin DISRAELI's *SYBIL, OR THE TWO NATIONS* (1845) and Mrs. Elizabeth GASKELL's *MARY BARTON* (1848), as well as many of Charles DICKENS's novels. In Dickens's *OLIVER TWIST* (1838), he had protested the treatment of working-class children and also included Nancy, a prostitute cast in an unusually heroic light. Even such attempts to improve visions of women sometimes promoted stereotypes, as did Nancy in her representation of the one-dimensional and totally unrealistic "whore with a heart of gold" that would continue to appear in popular literature. Already victimized by a patriarchal society, Nancy's goodness leads her to brutal murder by a man, in a scene representing the large amount of violence enacted on women in popular literature. Later critics suggested that some readers would see Nancy's murder as justice for her scandalous lifestyle, rather than as the culmination of the social injustice that forced women into self-support through the use of sex. Gaskell departed from her early socially conscious novels in *CRANFORD* (1853), largely proclaimed her best work, which promotes a distinctly feminine point of view. She features a community of women forced to practice what she euphemistically refers to as "elegant economy" in the absence of supportive males. It skillfully depicts the lifestyle of a vanishing group, marginalized by the encroaching mechanization and dehumanization of British culture.

Women writers attempting to make statements against the disempowerment of women sometimes instead advanced the cause for control with double messages in their literature. Charlotte BRONTE's *JANE EYRE* (1847), celebrated for emphasizing the deplorable treatment of female governesses, was autobiographical, based on the author's own poor treatment in that condition. Hers was a timely topic; in 1840 the Governesses' Benevolent Institution had been founded to help "ladies in temporary distress" and was immediately overwhelmed by the application for aid. The founders of that group hosted a series of lectures, which evolved into Queens College for women in 1848. As pertinent to women's needs as Bronte's novel proved, it also contained a monstrous woman in the character of Bertha Mason Rochester, the madwoman contained by her husband in the attic without any legal recourse. Similarly, Elizabeth Barrett BROWNING, in her verse novel, *AURORA LEIGH* (1857), celebrated the artistic nature of her noble protagonist but pitted her against an independent-minded and monstrous Lady Waldemat. Both those works had the intention of advancing women's freedoms, yet worked against their own efforts by including romanticized stereotypical female images.

Other authors, such as George ELIOT, transformed ideas about women and their problems into fiction, although she did not write specifically for that purpose. In ADAM BEDE (1859), she highlighted cruel attitudes toward women pregnant out of wedlock that led to infanticide, while her later MIDDLEMARCH: A STUDY OF PROVINCIAL LIFE (1871–72 and 1874–76) focused on a bright female protagonist who, guided by her culture, chooses to subjugate her own intellectual needs to those of her husband. In her final novel, DANIEL DERONDA (1876), she suggests that women lead lives limited by the goodwill of male relatives. Like the Brontë sisters, Eliot adopted a male pseudonym in order to publish; Jane Austen had published anonymously, in order to avoid resistance to the female voice in literature. For decades, those women would remain among the few acceptable in the English language canon for reading within educational institutions. Only in the mid-20th century would women find their voice in popular literature with the onset of the feminist movement. Due to the interests of NEW HISTORICISM, MARXIST CRITICISM, and especially feminist criticism, women writers would take their rightful place in the canon and newly distinguished representatives of color would also appear. All would agree with Browning's character Aurora Leigh that "every creature, female as the male, / Stands single in responsible act and thought."

BIBLIOGRAPHY

Eustance, Claire, Joan Ryan, and Laura Ugolini, eds. Charting Directions in British Suffrage History. New York : Leicester University Press, 2000.

Gilbert, Sandra M., and Susan Gubar, eds. The Norton Anthology of Literature by Women: Traditions in English. 2nd ed. New York: W. W. Norton, 1996.

Holton, Sandra Stanley. Suffrage Days: Stories from the Women's Suffrage Movement. New York: Routledge, 1996.

Perkin, J. Russell. A Reception-History of George Eliot's Fiction. Rochester, N.Y.: University of Rochester Press, 1990.

Tillotson, Kathleen. Novels of the Eighteen-forties. Oxford: Clarendon Press, 1954.

Todd, Janet. Mary Wollstonecraft: A Revolutionary Life. New York: Columbia University Press, 2000.

SURTEES, R(OBERT) S(MITH) (1805–1864)

Born in County Durham, R. S. Surtees passed his childhood on his father's English country estate named Hamsterley Hall, later attending Durham School. He matriculated to Newcastle and London in a study of law, for which he passed qualifying exams in 1828 to become a barrister. A sporting man at heart, he worked much more vigorously at chasing the hounds than law. He exploited an interest about which no one else was writing to launch a career, sharing a major characteristic of fiction in the 1830s; authors took advantage of personal experiences, hobbies, and interests, converting them into stories. The result for Surtees was fiction with strong characterizations and realistic details regarding the hunt.

Surtees began contributing in 1831 to Sporting Magazine, later becoming cofounder and editor of the New Sporting Magazine, finding that occupation far more satisfying than practice of law. His participation in various hunting events gave him material from which he developed his later satirical protagonist, Mr. Jorrocks. Surtees devoted himself to full-time writing in 1835, inheriting the family estate in 1838. He married, raised a family, and during the remainder of his life, he spent much time hunting. He published several novels, all anonymously, eventually becoming High Sheriff of Durham in 1856 after occupying several offices. A man with a fine sense of humor, he included comical characters in his novels representing all his earned and elected titles.

Surtees's best-known works included the officially titled The Jaunts and Jollities of that Renowned Sporting Citizen, Mr. John Jorrocks, but familiarly called Jorrock's Jaunts and Jollities (1838, with an expanded posthumous edition in 1869). It lacked a unified plot, consisting of a collection of events in the life of Jorrocks, a character who would reappear in later novels. Other works were HANDLEY CROSS (1843, expanded in 1854); HILLINGDON HALL (1845); and Mr. Sponge's Sporting Tour (1853), the latter widely acclaimed for its antihero protagonist, Soapey Sponge, described by Lionel Stevenson as a male version of William Makepeace THACKERAY's manipulative Becky Sharp. It joined the group of 1850s novels that focused on social hypocrisy and conflict, including works by Charles DICKENS,

Thackeray, Charles KINGSLEY, and Elizabeth GASKELL. Surtees also published *Ask Mamma* (1858) and *Plain or Ringlets?* (1860). Critics praised his depiction of England's traditional country life, with a tone similar to that of Thomas Love PEACOCK, both of whom held the modern world of commerce in contempt. When Surtees died, he was at work on *Mr. Facey Romford's Hounds,* which later appeared in book form in 1865. Although little read in the 21st century, Surtees's books are readily available and the subject of study in literary programs.

BIBLIOGRAPHY

Neuman, Bonnie Rayford. *Robert Smith Surtees.* Boston: Twayne Publishers, 1978.

Stevenson, Lionel. *The English Novel: A Panorama.* Boston: Houghton Mifflin, 1960.

Welcome, John. *The Sporting World of R. S. Surtees.* New York: Oxford University Press, 1982.

SYBIL, OR THE TWO NATIONS BENJAMIN DISRAELI (1845)

The two nations to which Benjamin DISRAELI referred in his *Sybil, or the Two Nations,* did not relate to governments. It referred rather to the wealthy class and the working class, the rich and the poor. His interest in the social conditions of England were highly visible in the measures he introduced in Parliament, which focused on child-labor and sanitary reform, as well as support for the CHARTIST movement. Disraeli always felt empowered by his writing, and the novel acted as a means of analysis, the testing of possible future policy. While his novels represented the ideal side of politics, they helped him relish the realism of public service. The novel supports Disraeli's attitude that England's youth were the trustees of its posterity, and they would set the atmosphere necessary for reform. In a famous speech in 1844 at the opening of the Manchester Athenaum, Disraeli stated, "It is not so much to the action of laws as to the influence of manners that we must look."

The novel's title character is the daughter of Walter Gerard, a man of great faith who represents the labor class and is the true heir to the Mowbray Estates. He works with the editor-reformist Stephen Morley tirelessly fighting social injustice. They are balanced by, first, the affluent, cold, spurious Marneys, whose ancestors obtained a dukedom following the revolution, by appropriating the local abbey lands. A second representative of heartless greed, the Mowbray family holds property rightfully belonging to Walter Gerard. They are descended from an 18th-century waiter who became the right hand of a wealthy nabob and was given stolen property. Both the Mowbrays and Marneys are fairly new to the aristocracy and feel no compunction to fulfill any traditional social responsibility. Disraeli showed readers misery that existed in industrial towns and the working mines, hoping to gain the sympathy that had to precede reform.

A devoted Catholic, Sybil plans to become a nun but instead marries the book's male hero, aristocrat Charles Egremont from the Marney family, after he embraces the cause of the oppressed workers. She first meets Egremont with her father and Stephen Morley after an argument with his brother in the ruined abbey, symbol of the destructive forces at work in English society. The two young people encounter irate mobs and the storming of a local business, as the independent Sybil seeks to convert Egremont to her point of view, and he attempts to convince her that hope exists for the two sides to reach some agreement based on their shared humanity. Multiple minor characters representing the upper class and various egregious acts against the workers, from neglect to direct abuse, include the Fitz-Waren daughters, Lady Marney, Alfred Mountchesney, Cocky Graves, Captain Grouse, Lady St. Julians, Sarah Lady Jersey, and the mean-spirited Lady Firebrace. They find balance in the rebel Devilsdust, the ill and tragic Warner, and the factory workers Harriet, Caroline, and Julia.

Later critics found narrative excess in the novel and an overblown use of language, leading to unintended humor. However, most agree that Sybil represents Disraeli's most powerful heroine and is an apt representative of her class and times.

BIBLIOGRAPHY

Maurois, André. *Disraeli.* New York: Time Life Books, 1965.

Sichel, Walter. Introduction to *Sybil* by Benjamin Disraeli. New York: Oxford University Press, 1970, v–xii.

T

TALE OF TWO CITIES, A CHARLES DICKENS (1859)

Among the great Charles DICKENS's final novels, *A Tale of Two Cities* well represents his maturity as a novelist. Like his previous works, this novel investigates man's capacity for inhumanity. However, its emphasis on the cause for the abuses men heap on one another as an unwillingness to learn from history is something new. While not his most critically praised work, *A Tale of Two Cities* is Dickens's most widely read, continuing its obvious popularity at the time of its printing. It ran in serial installments in the newly created periodical ALL THE YEAR ROUND from April through November 1859. The first issue of the new publication sold 120,000 copies, with subsequent issues selling around 100,000. It has remained a best-seller into the 21st century. Accounting for that fact may be in part NEW HISTORICISM's theory that all historical fiction is ultimately about the era in which the writer writes, an idea that could be expanded to include, according to critic Jane Smiley, about the era in which it is read. When art mirrors reality, audiences find it irresistible.

Dickens had long been interested in the French Revolution, not unusual in light of his constant emphasis on the importance of social revolution. He repeatedly read Thomas Carlyle's *History of the French Revolution,* even carrying the work with him. Carlyle had met Dickens, knew of his high regard, and sent the author boxes of research when he learned of the project. Not only did Dickens value the idea of revolution in general, he particularly valued the French, having visited France many times, becoming fluent in the language. In addition, a relationship with the 18-year-old Ellen Ternan, following Dickens's bitter and well-publicized divorce, may have affected Dickens's desire to create a feminine character mirroring Ellen's sweetness, possibly accomplished with Lucie Manette. For whatever reason, Dickens developed in *A Tale of Two Cities* more in-depth female characters than ever before. The passion of Madame Defarge, who can reply to Lucie's appeal for mercy on the basis that they were both women and mothers with "Is it likely that the trouble of one wife and mother would be much to us now?" provides evidence of her devotion to covert revolutionary activity delegated previously to male Dickens characters.

Both London and Paris at the beginning of the French Revolution provide the setting, allowing a consideration of the conflict in two distinct cultures. Dr. Manette seeks refuge in London with his daughter, Lucie, following his release from 18 years of imprisonment in the Bastille, due to his innocent relationship with the aristocratic Evrémonde family. Dickens seems to emphasize the peril in associating with those involved in what others may judge criminal activity, whether or not it is so judged by civil authorities. The Madame Defarges and the Vengeances of the world exist as society's conscience, although jaded by in-depth suffering that leads to a desire for revenge. Lucie is in love with Charles Darnay, a descendent of the despicable Evrémondes but an honest and decent citizen, allowing Dickens to enforce the idea that choice for change remains open to every individual.

In one of literature's most famous love triangles, Lucie is loved by Sydney Carton, who will become the unwilling hero of the novel. Carton's similar physical appearance to that of Darnay helps achieve Darnay's release from unfounded charges, foreshadowing Carton's later crucial role in saving Darnay's life. When Darnay returns to France to help free a servant unjustly accused by the revolutionaries, he himself is imprisoned, freed on the basis of Manette's intercession. Although Darnay should immediately return to England, his wife, and their daughter, little Lucie, he lingers in France, determined to make right his ancestors' wrongs, a doomed undertaking. He is again arrested and condemned to death on the basis of Manette's own written words again the Evrémondes. Dickens hints at the power of words, particularly when placed in powerful hands, which can employ them to ironic ends. Prior to Darnay's execution, Carton travels to France to support Lucie's unsuccessful efforts to free her husband. When those efforts fail, he decides to replace Darnay in prison, their physical similarities again allowing the mistaken identity, and the Darnays escape to England. A friendship with an also doomed young woman allows redemption of the once-drunken Carton, in a way that his love for the pure figure of Lucie could not. His closing statement regarding "the far better" thing represented in his execution has become an immediately recognizable metaphor for the value of self-sacrifice.

Dickens did not, however, believe Carton's act should be evaluated as sacrifice. Carton remains the only one of the novel's characters not metaphorically imprisoned by history. The past does not paralyze him into inactivity, or doom him to repeat actions already proven improvident, as it does the Mannettes and Darnay. The execution experience provides his sole spiritual connection with another human being, the young servant girl, and as is evident in Dickens's quotation of the biblical passage that includes the phrase "whosoever liveth in me shall never die," Carton views his substitution for Darnay as his one opportunity to live on in the memories of his acquaintances. He does not give into the temptation to flee, and Dickens stresses that bowing to temptation can lead to chaos. Although one can understand Darnay's temptation to rectify the past, and the revolutionaries' desire to reduce their attempts to correct society to a force for revenge on personal enemies, the choices of such paths inevitably lead to self-destruction. Carton also ignored the temptation for self-aggrandizement in his final action, choosing instead to die with a dignity and purpose that allowed him to gain through his actions.

The novel remains often taught, studied, and reproduced in various media forms. The application of its themes to any era will support its continued popularity.

BIBLIOGRAPHY

Hawes, Donald. *Who's Who in Dickens.* London: Routledge, 2001.

Jordan, John O., ed. *The Cambridge Companion to Charles Dickens.* Cambridge: Cambridge University Press, 2001.

Sanders, Andrew. *Companion to a Tale of Two Cities.* Boston: Unwin Hyman, 1988.

Smiley, Jane. *Charles Dickens.* New York: Penguin Putnam, 2002.

TALISMAN, THE SIR WALTER SCOTT (1825)

Sir Walter SCOTT introduces *The Talisman,* second in his group of books comprising his *Tales of the Crusade,* explaining how he selected the topic for his novel. *The Talisman,* as indicated by the title, focuses on a charm or amulet called the Lee-penny that Scotsman Sir Simon Lockhart, famous for exploits with Robert the Bruce, procured during the Crusade led by James, the Good Lord Douglas. While ransoming a prisoner to his mother, Sir Simon noticed her care to scoop up a coin with a pebble in the middle, "some say of the Lower Empire," which fell from her purse. He demands the amulet as part of her son's ransom, and she explains its peculiar powers, including healing powers derived from its having been dipped in holy water. Each leader of the Lockharts of the Lee bequeathed the talisman to the next generation, and the hero in possession of the amulet in the novel is Kenneth, the Knight of the Couching Leopard. He travels in service to King Richard the Lion Hearted (Richard I) in an attempt to reclaim the Holy Land, and his adventures made the book extremely popular. The accusations of treason against Kenneth, his near death at the hands of Richard, and his salvation through the efforts of the Saracen Saladin, are enhanced by the jousts Scott's medieval-setting novels always contain.

Scott explains that the Richard he sketches in the novel will differ from he who appeared in his earlier work. He bases his characterization on the reports that the monarch respected for observing the code of chivalry in his homeland "showed all the cruelty and violence of an Eastern sultan" during the invasion, while the sultan in the novel, Saladin, "on the other hand displayed the deep policy and prudence of a European sovereign."

Although not the case in later times, in Scott's own day, The Talisman proved even more popular than what later readers know as the author's classic, IVANHOE (1819). Scott struggled in deciding upon which aspect of the Orient to focus, explaining in his introduction that most of his knowledge of the area came from his reading of "Arabian Nights' Entertainments." He admitted he lacked insights into the present-day Orient of the author of ANASTASIUS (1819, Thomas HOPE) and HAJJI BABA (ADVENTURES OF HAJJI BABA OF ISPAHAN, 1824, James MORIER), leading him to focus on medieval times, with history as his guide. Removal of Scott's trademark local color present in his earlier series to focus on the exotic setting of the medieval Crusades advanced Scott's popularity on the Continent. There, readers found thrilling the circumstances that pitted Christian against Muslim.

Like Scott's other works, this novel provided an excellent example of a QUEST, with elements borrowed from the GOTHIC and ROMANCE, such as dreams/visions; mysterious figures including hermits and dwarfs; the foreboding setting of Syria, compared to "brimstone and salt"; and the constant threat of bodily harm. It also advanced the development of HISTORICAL FICTION. In addition, The Talisman exhibits the author's trademark vision of great events in terms of the human beings they involved, handled with compassion and insight into human nature, although many of his characters lack true complexity. Scott emphasizes the burden of choice shared by all humans, and how such choice converts some men into heroes and others into scoundrels. More important than battlefield heroism was the achievement involved in survival of day-to-day conflict and its pressures. Clear in The Talisman is that after 1820, Scott emphasized romance elements over realistic detail. While some critics took offense at his loose play with fact, Scott clearly stated he was writing romance, not history, a fact that NEW HISTORICISM critics appreciate.

BIBLIOGRAPHY
Allen, Walter Ernst. Six Great Novelists: Defoe, Fielding, Scott, Dickens, Stevenson, Conrad. Folcroft, Pa.: Folcroft Library Editions, 1971.

Rigney, Ann. Imperfect Histories: The Elusive Past and the Legacy of Romantic Historicism. Ithaca, N.Y.: Cornell University Press, 2001.

TANCRED, OR THE NEW CRUSADE
BENJAMIN DISRAELI (1847)   With Conigsby, or the New Generation (1844), and SYBIL, OR THE TWO NATIONS (1845), Benjamin DISRAELI's Tancred, or the New Crusade made up his most successful and famous trilogy of works. All deal with individuals caught in the conflict of different communities—religious, social, and/or political—neither of which they fit into comfortably. Tancred draws its title both from the protagonist's name and the QUEST on his part to retrace his ancestors' journey to Jerusalem during the times of the Crusade in defense of Christianity. Disraeli's personal conflicts surface, as he examines the value of the preservation of his own Jewish culture, a culture he could never fully accept.

Disraeli reintroduces characters from his two previous novels, most particularly Sidonia, the proudly Jewish character from Conigsby who rejected a life in politics, where his religion would be questioned. In Tancred, Sidonia serves as a negotiator, involved when the book's protagonist, Tancred, Lord Montacute, is abducted in Jerusalem, but through the negative experience becomes part of a community that holds the Greek gods as their deities. Having traveled to Jerusalem's Holy Sepulchre in search of understanding "The Asian mystery," he will discover the importance of belief in the divine, regardless of the name given to its representative deity. Disraeli wrote the book to develop his own theories regarding religion, one of which was the importance of spiritualism.

Tancred becomes enthralled with the daughter of a Jewish financier named Eva Besso. Eva, whose name suggests Eve, the first woman of biblical fame, teaches Tancred about the history of the area's civilization. She tells him that communities around the Mediterranean were accomplished long before those in Europe. When Tancred declares his love and desire to marry Eva, she rejects him as his parents arrive to take him back to Europe.

Disraeli's biographers make much of the fact that he wrote the mystical ROMANCE at the very time he should have been assuring his fellow members of Parliament of his "normalcy." Referred to often as "an Oriental," Disraeli actually proved the most English of men, far removed from the Jewish lands of his ancestors. However, he did hold the Eastern outlook, made clear in his novel, on material goods as desirable but ultimately dissatisfying.

The novel shocked many of Disraeli's contemporaries. Historian and philosopher Robert Carlyle detested Disraeli and his book, referring to him as a monkey. Many more of his peers did not much read, and so Disraeli did not come under attack in Parliament due to the novel. He would, however, expound on his ideas in Parliament when the Jewish Lionel de Rothschild was elected but could not assume his seat, as he was required to swear on the Christian faith. In a speech that left the House of Commons silent, Disraeli declared that Christ's church had itself made the Jewish religion famous, and that as a Christian, he could not exclude from the legislature men who were of Christ's original religion. Like the novel, his speech won him few supporters. His novel serves as a fine example of the expression of private sentiment in fiction.

BIBLIOGRAPHY

Maurois, André. *Disraeli*. New York: Time Life Books, 1965.

TAPESTRY ROOM, THE MRS. MARY LOUISA MOLESWORTH (1879)

Popular works of 19th-century CHILDREN'S LITERATURE included several by Mrs. MOLESWORTH, *The Tapestry Room* among them. With the subtitle, *A Child's Romance,* readers know to expect to find in the story elements of magic, a journey, examples of heroism, disguise, and some threat of danger, although it will occur on a scale appropriate to young readers.

The novel follows the FANTASY adventure of two cousins, the French Jeanne and the orphan Hugh, who come to live with Jeanne's family. They are accompanied by anthropomorphological animals through a tapestry that acts as gateway to an enchanted land. Led by a wise old raven with a crooked leg, Dudu, the children are able to glimpse their family's past, as Dudu has lived close to their family for centuries. They also enjoy a tale within a tale, entertained by the story of a princess who carries magical balls of light and breaks the spell of an evil fairy that transformed a prince into a monstrous bull. Molesworth's imagery is strong as she constructs a land unlike any the children have seen. For example, the children enjoy a boat ride in a craft pulled by frogs: "Each frog threw over several threads which he seemed to unwind from his body; these threads were caught by something invisible down below, and twisted round and round several times." Each frog grasps the cables they made with their front legs and "to the children's great delight, they felt the boat beginning to move." As they advance down the river, "the pass between the hills was dark and gloomy," foreshadowing that their journey will not be an entirely smooth one. In the DIDACTIC tradition of her age, Molesworth stresses the power of love, which has a magic of its own. Her books proved popular, many with drawings by the well-known illustrator Walter Crane.

BIBLIOGRAPHY

Laski, Marghanita. *Mrs. Ewing, Mrs. Molesworth, and Mrs. Hodgson Burnett.* New York: Oxford University Press, 1951.

Showalter, Elaine. *A Literature of Their Own: British Women Novelists from Brontë to Lessing.* Princeton, N.J.: Princeton University Press, 1999.

TENANT OF WILDFELL HALL, THE ANNE BRONTË (1848)

As Anne BRONTË worked on her second novel, *The Tenant of Wildfell Hall,* she had in mind the terrible ravages alcohol had inflicted on her brother, Branwell. When her sister Charlotte took exception to her portrayal due to its uncomfortable association with their brother, Anne defended it, believing the topic was just as appropriate to fiction as her sister's favored topic of social equality.

The novel's protagonist is its first-person point-of-view narrator, the farmer Gilbert Markham. He loves Helen Graham, who is the title's tenant of Wildfell Hall, but knows little about her other than the beauty and grace she possesses. While most believe her to be a widow, Markham does not know the truth, but he defends her against negative gossip that arises as others question her past and the propriety of her circumstances. When he observes her affectionate interaction with her landlord, Frederick Lawrence, Markham becomes incensed, understanding that such actions verge on social scandal. As the two appear to become intimate, Markham attacks Lawrence in a jealous rage.

Brontë then employs the flashback technique, a narrative approach new to her. Helen notes her love for Markham in a diary, but also records details of her past, moving readers through time. She writes of her doomed marriage to an alcoholic named Arthur Huntingdon, who ultimately abused and humiliated her when she attempted to reform him. Her sharp portrait of Huntingdon's dissipation mirrored the real dissipation of Branwell, who would die from drug and alcohol abuse only three months following the novel's publication. That detail, in addition to Brontë's scenes of Helen's locking her door against her husband, and drunken men invading their wives' bedrooms, succeeded in shocking readers to consider the negative effects of alcohol, precisely Brontë's intent.

Markham learns that Helen had left her husband to live with Lawrence, who is actually her brother. She returns to care for the ill Huntingdon, who mercifully dies. Now Helen is free to marry Markham, but he is at first put off by her sudden wealth, brought about through inheritance. In an interesting reversal on the traditional situation of a man wondering whether he should marry beneath his station, Brontë emphasizes the folly of class separation. Ironically, Markham's mother does not approve of the marriage, due to the past rumors regarding Helen; she also does not want Markham to leave the farm to live at Helen's estate. Markham also must win the approval of Helen's aunt

and her son, Arthur. He does so and, eight months after Huntingdon's death and with everyone's support, leaves the family farm in the hands of his brother Fergus and marries Helen. The last pages describe their life together following their wedding.

Brontë was assailed so vigorously by complaints about the novel and criticism as to its inappropriate subject matter that she appended a famous foreword to its second edition, defending her presentation. She maintained it better to present vicious characters in reality rather than as she wished they might be, adding, "I wished to tell the truth, for truth always conveys its own moral." Her defense of this new approach to fiction enlarged the already considerable contributions of the Brontë sisters to the novel's development. Despite protests, the novel proved popular and was a financial success; it is frequently studied and readily available.

BIBLIOGRAPHY

Lloyd Evans, Barbara, and Gareth Lloyd Evans. *The Scribner Companion to the Brontës*. New York: Scribner, 1982.

TERRIBLE TEMPTATION, A: A STORY OF THE DAY CHARLES READE (1871)   Like

his contemporaries Charles DICKENS and Charles KINGSELY, Charles READE wrote SENSATION FICTION, in which fear played a prominent part. In *A Terrible Temptation,* he returns to a favorite frightening topic, the insane asylum, first featured in *HARD CASH* (1863). Like that novel, *A Terrible Temptation* deals with the inheritance of money and the lengths to which individuals will go to obtain funds they believe they rightfully deserve. Such is the situation with Richard Bassett, who feels his cousin Sir Charles Bassett stole his inheritance from him. The plot centers on that family feud, in which Sir Charles also "steals" the woman Richard loves.

Although details about the asylum disturbed readers, they were more scandalized by Reade's depiction of heartless intrigue within the upper class as well as its immorality. His intimate details regarding Rhoda Somerset, the mistress of Sir Charles, brought back the accusations of salaciousness lodged against Reade's *GRIFFIN GAUNT* (1866). A writer for *The Times* suggested that mothers might want to hide the first volume of the novel from their daughters, prompting a furious retort from Reade, who stated he found his subject matter in *The Times* itself. According to Walter Phillips, Reade wrote that "no mother need forbid my book to her daughter; at all events until she has forbidden her daughter to enter Hyde Park, and *The Times* to enter her drawing room, and has locked up every Bible on her premises." Reade includes an autobiographical character in Mr. Rolfe, who mirrors Reade's social consciousness and his research technique of using filing cards. Rolfe is deemed the only individual who can rescue Bassett when his cousin imprisons him in an asylum, emphasizing Reade's inflated self-view. However Reade envisioned himself, he rarely allowed his penchant for melodrama and hyperbole to mask his theme. Identity is put right at the novel's conclusion, when Lady Bella Bassett must admit that she has masqueraded the child of another as her own, correcting the mistaken impression Reade purposely gives readers that Bella engaged in an affair. The children of the feuding cousins fall in love, and balance is regained.

BIBLIOGRAPHY

Phillips, Walter C. *Dickens, Reade, and Collins: Sensation Novelists.* New York: Russell & Russell, 1962.

TESS OF THE D'URBERVILLES THOMAS HARDY (1891)

Thomas HARDY's novel *Tess of the d'Urbervilles,* originally subtitled *A Pure Woman,* is about Tess d'Urberville's tragic dilemma between her seducer, Alec, and her named husband, Angel, both of whom intrude into her life. In epic form Hardy describes Tess's life from about the time she is 16 or 17 to about 21. The plot centers solely on the female protagonist. The reader not only observes her actions but also understands her motivations, her continual struggles, and her efforts to overcome circumstances and events caused by providence and fate.

In *Tess* Hardy addresses Victorian beliefs about class, morals, patriarchal society, conventionality, and the influence of fate or chance in individuals' lives. The novel begins with Tess's father learning of his lineage in the d'Urberville family and thus feeling that work is beneath him. It is fate that Tess is the first born of her family, creating feelings of responsibility for its members. Blaming herself for the loss of the family's livelihood, Tess's guilt causes her to acquiesce to parental pressure to seek help from the rich Mrs. d'Urberville, her supposed relation. Fate intervenes and Tess meets the son, Alec d'Urberville, before she meets his mother, and consequently Alec presents her as just a servant. Ironically, Alec's family isn't aristocratic; they only purchased the name because no one claimed it. It allows them to disassociate themselves from their past. Meeting Alec first proves paramount in directing Tess's future. Alec seduces and rapes her; she returns home disgraced, pregnant, and unmarried. The child fathered by Alec dies, and Tess flees to a place where her past is unknown to try to find happiness.

Working as a dairymaid at Talbothays Dairy, Tess encounters Angel Clare. Angel is ironically named, as he proves to be no guardian to Tess and also because he claims to have rejected religion. Angel is there to become a dairyman after deciding not to follow his father into the clergy. Tess and Angel fall in love and decide to marry even though Tess is concerned about her past and worries about confessing all to Angel. On the eve of their wedding, Tess slides a letter of confession under his door, but as fate would have it the letter slips under the carpet and Angel never receives it. Realizing Angel didn't read her letter, Tess convinces him to exchange confessions on their wedding night. Angel tells of a previous indiscretion and is forgiven by Tess, but when she reveals her past victimization, Angel rejects her, an act of power interesting to FEMINIST CRITICS. Angel's actions show that he is a product of Victorian convention, hypocrisy, and double standards. His sensibilities are offended because Tess isn't the "pure and virginal woman" he believed her to be.

The story continues with Angel in South America. Tess, dependent on herself to make a living, is working under deplorable conditions at another farm. Finally, in desperation, she sets out to appeal to Angel's parents for help; fatefully, she overhears Angel's brothers discussing his marriage and tragically misjudges the character of Angel's parents by the negative comments of his brothers, causing her to abandon her plan. On her return trip, fate once more intervenes and Tess encounters Alec, who convinces her that Angel will never return. He pleads with her to come with him; she refuses, but as her circumstances and those of her family worsen, she eventually succumbs to his pressure. At long last, but not until after Tess has joined Alec, Angel returns to Tess, who tells him he is too late. In anger and frustration, Tess kills Alec for once again destroying her life and her only chance at happiness. She spends a few blissful days in hiding with Angel, but the novel ends tragically: Tess hangs for her crime.

Hardy employs numerous GOTHIC elements in his work through omens, symbols, and biblical references. A sign painter appears throughout the novel, painting signs with biblical warnings and foreshadowing events to follow. The day Angel proposes to Tess, he sees the "red interior of her mouth as if it had been a snake," symbolizing impending evil. A cock crows in the afternoon on their wedding day, which also signifies betrayal and denial, as Peter denied Christ before his crucifixion. Angel's fateful decision to spend their wedding night at the old d'Urberville mansion proves to be unfortunate. The two life-size portraits of her ancestors upset Tess and symbolize the treachery that will follow. These portraits also keep Angel from entering the room later to reconcile with Tess. Perhaps the most prophetic is the scene in which Angel tells Tess that her situation might be different if "the man were dead," pointing out the effect her past would have on their children, and foreshadowing the ultimate demise of Alec.

Hardy reveals the double standards and hypocrisies of his time. He addressed Tess's sexuality and presented her as a sensual protagonist, thus redefining the role of women. As an independent and passionate woman, Tess represented a new characterization of woman, threatening the accepted Victorian model of women in society, but these characteristics resulted in her isolation and execution. Hypocritical Victorian values play a vital role in the heroine's loss of innocence and death. When Tess stabs Alec in the heart, her action symbolizes retribution and rebellion against a system that had already judged her guilty, though she had committed no crime. Subsequently she ends up in the hands of the authorities and becomes victim to another hypocritical value of the Victorians, that one must pay for their sins.

Fate or providence proved true in Tess's case. She was destined to die with the d'Urberville curse. Defeated by an unaccepting society, she took the law into her own hands. While Alec's payment for his sins seemed fair, Tess's only crime was that of being a woman caught in a hypocritical value system. The reader feels her death is unjustified.

BIBLIOGRAPHY

Anonby, John A. "Hardy's Handling of Biblical Allusions in His Portrayal of Tess in *Tess of the D'Urbervilles*." *Christianity and Literature* 30, no. 3 (1981): 13–26.

Hardy, Thomas. *Tess of the D'Urbervilles. A Complete, Authoritative Text with Biographical, Historical, and Cultural Contexts, Critical History, and Essays from Contemporary Critical Perspectives.* Edited by John Paul Riquelme. New York: Bedford Books, 1998.

Harris, Nicola. "An Impure Woman: The Tragic Paradox and Tess as Totem." *Thomas Hardy Yearbook* 26 (1998): 18–21.

THACKERAY, WILLIAM MAKEPEACE (1811–1863)

William Makepeace Thackeray was born in India, where his father, who died when Thackeray was six years old, served in the East India Company. Upon his mother's remarriage, he was sent home to England to the preparatory school Charterhouse, where he had a thoroughly miserable experience. He moved on to Trinity College, Cambridge, for two years but took no degree, wasting money at gambling. He later traveled throughout Europe, living for a time in France and also Germany, where he met the great writer Goethe, who would appear in his later novel *VANITY FAIR* as the character Pumpernickel. He read law, studied art, and wrote for the *National Standard* newspaper.

Thackeray lost most of his money in the 1833 failure of the Bank of India, and the newspaper went out of business in 1834. Often destitute and without many friends, Thackeray began drawing caricatures and published cartoons featuring ballet dancers in 1836 in a book titled *Flore et Zéphyr.* He worked as correspondent for another short-lived paper, *The Constitutional,* and married a young Irish woman named Isabella Shawe, a union that would prove disastrous due to her mental instability. They returned to London and began a family that included a daughter, later famous as a novelist, Anne Thackeray Ritchie, and another who later married Leslie Stephen, father of Virginia Woolf (by a second wife), Minnie Thackeray Stephen. His early struggles for self-identity and success combined with his miserable marital experience to make Thackeray a bitter man. His childhood feeling of isolation and rejection by his mother, adult financial difficulties, and an unusually tall build, which exacerbated his self-consciousness, all helped shape his satirical tone. A friendly man, he felt especially hurt by those who abandoned him during his financial distress but developed deep attachments to the loyal few who did not desert him.

While contributing pieces including reviews, PARODIES, and SATIRES to several publications, primarily FRASER'S MAGAZINE and Punch, Thackeray often used alter-egos such as James Yellowplush, a near-illiterate Cockney whose phonetic spellings reproduced the Cockney speech, and Major Goliah Gahagan, who had served in India and delivered exaggerated reports of his service. As Michael Angelo Titmarsh, he wrote art criticism for Fraser's; the public never suspected one man stood behind the various voices. Pen names were common with writers, and they helped Thackeray to create more interesting material than he felt he could under his own name.

As a book reviewer of many works he viewed as poorly executed, Thackeray developed a dislike for melodrama and hyperbole, which disregarded the REALISM to which he as a journalist was dedicated. He attacked such shoddy writing through a parody of popular NEWGATE FICTION in a piece titled Catherine, by Ikey Solomons, Jr., published serially in Fraser's. He stopped the series after six entries, as his characters began to develop a humanity that, ironically, converted them to sympathetic beings. As he struggled to make a living with mixed success, the Thackerays lost one daughter when she was eight months old, and Isabella's mental instability worsened. By 1840, he institutionalized her. He based his next fiction, The History of Samuel Titmarsh and the Great Hoggarty Diamond, published in Fraser's, on his own experiences, but the melancholy work did not catch readers' imagination.

At last gaining a permanent writing position on the periodical Punch, Thackeray improved his writing of short pieces and also wrote travel books: The Paris Sketch Book (1840), The Irish Sketch Book (1843), and Notes of a Journey from Cornhill to Grand Cairo (1846). His first full novel, The MEMOIRS OF BARRY LYNDON (1852) appeared as a serial titled The Luck of Barry Lyndon in Fraser's in 1844. He varied his normal narrative approach, adopting a first-person point-of-view narrator, producing a far more subtle character study than in his previous works; however, readers did not warm to the tale written by one George Savage Fitzboodle. With his series of satirical portraits titled the Snobs of England, Thackeray at last began to shape his novelist identity as a social satirist. The term snob in his age meant townspeople, and readers of Thackeray's piece parlayed it into slang indicating a member of the pretentious bourgeoise. A second parody, his self-illustrated PUNCH'S PRIZE NOVELISTS (1847) criticized what he viewed as mundane popular writers: G. P. R. James, Benjamin DISRAELI, Catherine Grace GORE, and Charles James LEVER.

Thackeray's greatest achievement, Vanity Fair (1848), appeared first in monthly installments, 1847–48. While writing the novel, he had fallen in love with Jane Brookfield, who was married to a good friend. The frustration he felt on never being able to act on that love has been credited by some critics with his development of the character of Amelia, who worships an undeserving husband rather than returning the love of her husband's far more deserving friend. He followed that hugely popular success with another well-received work, The HISTORY OF PENDENNIS (1850), also first published in monthly installments between 1848 and 1850. It served as a mostly autobiographical BILDUNGSROMAN, reflecting a theme of melancholy love, one he extended into The HISTORY OF HENRY ESMOND (1852), set during the age of Queen Anne. He confessed that novel was the only one he had planned well before writing, and it was the only one of his works to appear in the traditional three-volume format. His 1815 lectures on The English Humorists of the Eighteenth Century were published in 1853, later forming the basis of his first lecture tour to the United States. A panoramic work featuring English society during the first part of the 19th century, *The Newcomes* (1853–55) was followed by *The Rose and the Ring* (1855), the last of six books based on Christmas. Thackeray returned to the United States from 1855 to 1856 to lecture on *The Four Georges* (1860), and he published another historical novel featuring the Esmond family, *The Virginians,* in monthly installments, 1857–59. It focused on the American grandsons of Henry Esmond and their involvement in the War of Independence. He had met with two American novelists while in the States, John Esten Cooke and John Pendleton Kennedy, to ensure accurate facts. Many critics point to this work as representing Thackeray's deterioration as a writer, mainly due to his lack of any new material.

Thackeray served as the initial editor of George SMITH's *The CORNHILL MAGAZINE,* a successful venture begun in 1859. He would have to resign three years later due to poor health but continued to contribute fiction to the periodical, including *Lovel the Widower* (1860) and *The Adventures of Phillip* (1861–62). When he died in 1863, he was working on a novel titled *Denis Duval* (1864).

Thackeray's influence on fiction proved immense, directly affecting the work of Henry JAMES, Robert Louis STEVENSON, George du Maurier, and many other writers who practiced social satire or used high society and its abuses as themes. His works remain widely studied and read, have been converted into various dramatic forms, and many are available as electronic texts.

BIBLIOGRAPHY

Peters, Catharine. *Thackeray: A Writer's Life.* Stroud, Gloucestershire: Sutton Pub., 1999.

Shillingsburg, Peter L. *William Makepeace Thackeray: A Literary Life.* New York: Palgrave, 2001.

Taylor, D. J. *Thackeray: The Life of a Literary Man.* New York: Carroll & Graf, 2001.

Tillotson, Kathleen. *Novels of the Eighteen-forties.* Oxford: Clarendon Press, 1954.

THESIS NOVEL
The thesis novel, also known as the *roman à thèse,* became popular with socially conscious writers at the end of the 1840s, when the troubling conditions for laborers that followed the INDUSTRIAL REVOLUTION became clear. Efforts at social reform on the part of novelists paralleled a number of government probes into labor problems and poverty that resulted in formal Commissions of Enquiry. The movement in literature to alert the general public to such issues began in the 1830s with works such as Charles DICKENS's *OLIVER TWIST* (1837–38) and continued into the next decade with Frances TROLLOPE's *Michael Armstrong* (1840). Benjamin DISRAELI's *SYBIL, OR THE TWO NATIONS* (1845) focused on CLASS STRUCTURE and the wide disparity between the rich and the poor, with Mrs. Elizabeth GASKELL's *MARY BARTON* (1848) expanding that theme by demonstrating the violence that can erupt over such disparity. Dickens continued his attack against society's disgraceful tolerance of the ravages of poverty in *Barnaby Rudge* (1841) and in *HARD TIMES* (1854), a novel born out of Dickens's investigative journalism into the factory conditions suffered by cotton workers that precipitated a strike. A November 1850 *FRASER's* review of Charles KINGSLEY's *ALTON LOCKE* (1850), a novel revealing the terrible working conditions for tailors, along with other novels, noted the growing tendency for "political pamphlets, ethical treatises, and social dissertations" to be published "in the guise of novels." How painful, the editor wrote, to expect pleasure when opening a novel but to be greeted instead by "an essay upon labour and capital," an experience "by no means agreeable." The thesis novel indicated the expansion of the concerns of literature, described in the same article as fiction's bold invasion of "those realms of politics and economy, upon the confines of which she has hitherto stopped short with hesitating tread and averted eyes. It is growing up into a kind of ambition amongst authors of all creeds, colours and capabilities, to write books 'with a purpose in them.'"

BIBLIOGRAPHY

Cripps, Elizabeth. Introduction. *Alton Locke.* New York: Oxford University Press, 1983.

"Review." *Fraser's Magazine* 42 (November 1850): 574.

Tillotson, Kathleen. *Novels of the Eighteen-forties.* Oxford: Clarendon Press, 1954.

THREE CLERKS, THE ANTHONY TROLLOPE (1858)

By the time Anthony TROLLOPE published his autobiographical *The Three Clerks,* he had established himself as a novelist who resisted the DIDACTIC fiction on which his mother, Frances TROLLOPE, had made her name. He did not shy away from tales with moral dilemmas; rather, he did not comment on those conflicts faced by his characters, choosing, instead, to reserve judgment on their realistic actions. He had proven this approach in *BARCHESTER TOWERS* (1857), published three months before he completed work on *The Three Clerks.* Due to the subject matter of *The Three Clerks,* however, Trollope slipped into an accusatory tone and a heavy-handed characterization that qualified as caricature of the public-service men who controlled the fate of the clerks he depicted.

Trollope had worked unhappily as a postal clerk for several years before moving to Ireland, where he became more independent and finally proved himself a success. In those early years, he suffered at the hands of his superiors, who adhered to a promotion system with which Trollope did not agree. In the novel, Harry Norman suffers from the discrimination that Trollope experienced throughout the flawed civil-service system. He describes various levels on which one might take a post as a civil servant, including the fictional Internal Navigation Office, considered higher than the Post Office.

Harry Norman works with Alaric Tudor at the Weights and Measures Office and, along with Alaric's cousin Charley Tudor, visits often Mrs. Woodward and her three daughters. The Woodward family composition of a widowed mother with three attractive daughters became a staple in Trollope's fiction, a tribute to the real-life Grant family, who played a large role in his life as a young man. When Harry falls in love with the eldest daughter, Gertrude, he is bested by Alaric, who receives a promotion following a successful scoring on the civil service exam. Alaric proves by nature more competitive, aggressive and ambitious, attributes valued by his superiors more than the good character of Harry. Gertrude agrees to marry Alaric, but financial problems arise due to his foolish investments. With this plot turn, Trollope suggests that high test scores do not always represent intelligence, a rationalization of his own poor showing on the job in his early years. He reproduces early in the novel his experience on an entry exam, when he had misspelled and blotted words from a passage he was asked to copy from the *Times* newspaper and embarrassed himself due to his lack of math skills. Trollope later opposed such testing, arguing that exams could be passed simply through a cramming technique that in no way reflected one's honesty or sense of responsibility.

Far worse than simple bad investments is Alaric's panicked embezzlement of company funds to pay his debts. He is caught and sent to prison, serving a sentence that may seem to readers more a result of his betraying his friendship with Harry than of his illegal activities. Thus, Alaric's ambition suggests a character flaw leading to immorality. Trollope offers a metaphor of the political games that proved Alaric's downfall with his depiction of the hunting of badgers by dogs, an activity that he had regularly observed as a child on the Hampshire downs. He suggests that members of the House of Commons routinely play both roles, depending on which party was in power.

Charley represents a foil for his cousin, working diligently to repay his debt and overcome a youthful weakness that threatened to leave him broke and trapped in an imprudent relationship with a common barmaid named Norah Geraghty. His situation suggests Trollope's own prior to his transfer to Ireland. Trollope writes in his autobiography of the selling of his £12 debt to a professional moneylender, which caused his debt to grow. A collector embarrassed him at work, a scene reproduced in *The Three Clerks,* but characterized as far more horrible. While Trollope suffered pursuit by a presentable elderly man, the horrible character Mr. Jabez M'Ruen, whose dirty room near Mecklenburgh Square Charley is forced to visit, haunts poor Charley.

Simultaneously Harry marries the second of the Woodward daughters, Linda, and becomes a country squire. After championing his problems, Charley takes the third daughter, Katie, as a wife, having proven himself literally a hero by rescuing her from drowning in the Thames. Charley is promoted into the Weights and Measures office, with a far more promising future there than either Alaric or Harry had enjoyed. Readers cannot miss the heavy-handed symbolism in the setting, where a man's honor is weighed and measured according to his propensity for advancement on the job. Charley and Harry prosper, while Alaric and his family become outcasts, immigrating to Australia to settle there with many other English convicts.

While the civil service did eventually undergo necessary reforms, Trollope's book did not promote those reforms. Rather, it acted as a type of revenge for him against an early miserable working experience that silenced and threatened to rob him of a strong self-identity. Having gained a public voice and the accompanying audience, he offered his readers a firsthand view into a corrupt system while enjoying a catharsis in its production.

BIBLIOGRAPHY

Glendinning, Victoria. *Anthony Trollope.* New York: Knopf, 1993.

Super, R. H. *Trollope in the Post Office.* Ann Arbor: University of Michigan Press, 1981.

Trollope, Anthony. *An Autobiography.* London: Blackwood, 1883.

THROUGH THE LOOKING-GLASS AND WHAT ALICE FOUND THERE LEWIS CARROLL (1871)

Lewis CARROLL wrote the sequel to *ALICE'S ADVENTURES IN WONDERLAND* (1865) and continued to alter forever CHILDREN'S LITERATURE by omitting any moralizing from *Through the Looking-glass and What Alice Found There,* just as he had in the original Alice book. He well realized his goal of writing stories for the pure amusement of their readers that lacked the traditional preachy nature of DIDACTIC literature, a common narrative approach with books for the young.

Alice is again caught up in an absurd FANTASY world where its inhabitants seem not to adhere to the same rules that govern Alice's world. In reality, the fantasy world represents a chess game, a logical outgrowth of Carroll's love for math and puzzles. That very fact allows Carroll's emphasis on the absurdity of humans, or their representatives in this instance, adhering to rules controlling their movements, when they understand neither the rules or know the identity of the force making them move. It proved a brilliant concept, one

that speaks to adult readers just as clearly as absurdist writings by later philosophers Franz Kafka and John Paul Sartre.

The story makes simple fodder for critics of all schools. PSYCHOANALYTIC CRITICS examine various sexual references, such as that suggested by the unicorn, particularly from a Freudian perspective. In addition, Carroll's shaping of the Red Queen as cruel and heartless and the White King as a more kindly being, characterizations that appear to reflect on his fondness for his father and his dislike of his mother, may be reversed in the looking-glass world to suggest an Oedipus complex on Carroll's part. One more of many interesting psychological aspects is the fact that the entire incident occurs as Alice's dream. FEMINIST CRITICS find of interest Alice's logical approach to problem solving, which counters stereotypes of females who depend on intuition to guide their actions, as well as the querulous natures of the two most powerful females, the queens. MARXIST CRITICS find the Queen and King's rule over their subjects in the interest of material gain pertinent, as well as the fact that Alice seeks a crown in hopes of changing her commoner status through the donning of a traditional class symbol. NEW HISTORICISTS may posit that the abundant use of red and white suggests the War of the Roses, an interpretation also applied to the first Alice story. They may share the interest of psychoanalytic critics in Carroll's interest in girl children and how that preference surfaces in the Alice tales. Deconstructionists could examine Carroll's use of puns and the language as controlled by the chess game in progress, applying their theory that language developed through its own internal system of sounds that act as signifiers, suggesting concepts, which are what is signified.

While not as successful in later centuries as Carroll's first Alice book, *Through the Looking Glass* proved quite popular in its own day with both young and adult readers. For children removed by time and geography from Victorian England, the book became a challenge, as many cultural references proved confounding. It remains popular with aficionados of Victorian literature, of children's literature, and of humorous literature, a supremely constructed jest to those who understand that Carroll's story is not at all random, but instead achieves a unity based on mathematical principles unique before Carroll.

BIBLIOGRAPHY

Carroll, Lewis. *The Annotated Alice: Alice's Adventures in Wonderland & Through the Looking-glass.* New York: Norton, 2000.

Jones, Jo Elwyn, and J. Francis Gladstone. *The Alice Companion: A Guide to Lewis Carroll's Alice Books.* New York: New York University Press, 1998.

Oates, Joyce Carol. "Personal Best: *Alice in Wonderland* and *Alice Through the Looking-glass.*" *Salon.* Available online. URL: http://www.salon.com/weekly/carroll960930.html. Downloaded July 17, 2002.

Reichertz, Ronald. *The Making of the Alice Books: Lewis Carroll's Uses of Earlier Children's Literature.* Montreal: McGill-Queen's University Press, 1997.

TIME MACHINE, THE H. G. WELLS (1895)

H. G. WELLS had written the basis for his brief novel *The Time Machine* in a series of stories published in *The Science Schools Journal* in 1888. Labeled a dystopia by some critics, the story acts as a warning to readers that man's future may not be a positive one. Wells wrote in the tradition of Edward BULWER-LYTTON's *The COMING RACE* (1871), the extremely popular cautionary futuristic tale of a threatening underworld.

The nameless characters in *The Time Machine* meet together in the home of a man called simply the Time Traveller on a Thursday in late-Victorian England. Guests include representatives from important vocations: a mayor, a doctor, an editor, and a psychologist, all men. The Traveller introduces his guests to a machine, described in detail by the narrator, that will allow him to travel through time. As they observe him, he sits in the saddle of his metal two-levered machine, pulls the levers, and disappears. The men follow his written instructions to return one week later when they will learn of his discoveries.

When the Traveller arrives, his appearance is disheveled, pale, and bloody. As critic Harry Geduld suggests, he falls into a tradition of scientists not taken seriously, such as Victor Frankenstein in Mary SHELLEY's *FRANKENSTEIN* (1818) and Dr. Jekyll in Robert Louis STEVENSON's *The STRANGE CASE OF DR. JEKYLL AND MR. HYDE* (1886). After cleaning himself up, the Traveller tells a tale of arrival in London in the year A.D. 802,701. Two distinct groups populate the land, the first being the small, robed Eloi, who move with an aristocratic bearing and seem to have the perfect society. Then the Traveller learns of the smelly cannibalistic subterranean Morlocks, supposedly descendants of the working class, who leave their caves at night in the dark to attack the Eloi. Biographers suggest that the dark imagery associated with the Morlocks grew from Wells's childhood in a house with its kitchen completely underground. He recorded memories of strange dark men marching through the kitchen in order to store bags of coal under the staircase. He had also nursed an irrational fear and dislike of working men, a strange attitude for a boy whose own father practiced a trade.

In typical QUEST fashion, the Traveller meets with a guide, whose life he first saves, a female named Weena. His home base is a museum filled with artifacts, some of which he recognizes, some he does not. He worries over the disappearance of his time machine, which he had disabled by removing its levers, fearful of never being able to return to his own time. He eventually avoids an attack by the Morlocks by threatening them with fire. However, Weena disappears, leaving the Traveller lonely. Wells himself had admitted his debt to Jonathan Swift's prose SATIRE *GULLIVER'S TRAVELS* (1726). The story of the lone traveler threatened by inhabitants of an alien land had haunted Wells in the manner Swift intended for it to haunt his readers, as reflecting the disinterested attitude of a civilization in jeopardy of losing its humanity.

The Traveller at last discovers his machine and departs as the Morlocks surround him. Before returning to his own time, he moves forward, landing on a deserted shore where he sees only giant crabs, suggesting a mutation of life. Through eight different versions of the story, many published in various venues, Wells varied details, describing evolved beings some critics determined too gruesome. In a version printed in the *New Review,* Wells described creatures resembling rabbits that represented further evolved Eloi, hunted and eaten by the evolved Morlocks in the form of centipede-like monsters.

The Traveller moves further forward, viewing the earth 30 million years into the future in its last decline as a deserted sterile landscape. His guests remain skeptical about the Traveller's report, and some critics suggest this as the novel's goal. Wells hoped to depict men blindly complacent in the face of a grim evolutionary future. As the Traveller again departs, he leaves behind a flower of unknown species, the only hard evidence of his travel.

Wells stressed how important the time he spent with Thomas Henry Huxley, a great proponent of the theories of Charles DARWIN, proved to his writing. He sent a copy of the book to Huxley with a note reminding him that Wells had been his student, asking him to accept the novel with "the central idea—of degeneration following security," which "was the outcome of a certain amount of biological study." He added as a partial excuse for what could be considered a presumptuous act, "The book is a very little one." Wells's tale has been retold a number of times, taking various dramatic and written forms. Most suggest his original warning, that if humans do not learn to co-exist peacefully, all civilization will disappear.

BIBLIOGRAPHY

Connes, G. A. *A Dictionary of the Characters and Scenes in the Novels, Romances, and Short Stories of H.G. Wells.* Folcroft, Pa.: Folcroft Press, 1969.

Firchow, Peter. "H. G. Wells's Time Machine: In Search of Time Future and Time Past." *The Midwest Quarterly* 25, no. 2 (Winter 2004): 123–136.

Geduld, Harry M., ed. *The Definitive Time Machine: A Critical Edition of H. G. Wells's Scientific Romance with Introduction and Notes.* Bloomington: Indiana University Press, 1987.

Gill, Stephen M. *Scientific Romances of H.G. Wells: A Critical Study.* Cornwall, Ontario: Vesta Publications, 1975.

TOM BROWN'S SCHOOL DAYS THOMAS HUGHES (1857)

In *Tom Brown's School Days,* Thomas HUGHES established a long-lasting model for stories about the education of the young. The novel is highly autobiographical, demonstrating how much Hughes enjoyed and benefited from his years attending Rugby, made famous by the great educator and historian Thomas Arnold. Mainly due to Arnold, Rugby became the epitome of education, both of an intellectual and a spiritual and emotional type, for middle-class parents. The school promised a thorough program of training that included a religious and sports emphasis, as well as an academic one. Tom Brown's boarding school does the same, and even features Arnold as Tom's tutor. Hughes's association with THESIS NOVEL writers including Charles KINGSLEY in their campaigns supporting education of the working-class male and Christian socialism also is reflected in the novel's themes.

The novel introduces a character approach that would be repeated in such "hale and hearty" tales, shaping a protagonist accompanied by friends who represent foils in personality; one is shy, idealistic to a fault, and mannered, while the other is outspoken, practical, and physically adept. Tom's friends deserving of such description are the gentle Arthur and the irreverent East. Each helps Tom in various ways. For instance, Arthur is ever ready with words of wisdom and encouragement, while East helps Tom defend weaker boys at the school against bullies, stressing the importance of equality and charging readers to protect those not as strong as they. Termed muscular Christianity, Tom's practice of leadership, spirituality, and sportsmanship was deemed more important than mere academics. The tone is decidedly DIDACTIC and idealistic, as an intrusive narrator calls to England's youth, "O young England! young England! . . . why don't you know more of your own birthplace," attaching a patriotic bent to the tale.

Burdened with stereotypes of women as weak and passive, detected in reductive phrases such as "The little governess" and in scenes where girls are commanded to kiss boys as rewards for their astounding physical performances, frequent authorial intervention, too many "plucky" feats by the title character, and the use of war terminology applied to boys' activities, the novel may offend more sophisticated modern readers. However, those same elements offer excellent examples of what popular reading audiences craved in the mid-19th century—the promise of a bright future for boys properly trained. Still, the book offers opportunities for universal identification when bullies with unlikely names such as Flashman and Slogger meet

satisfying consequences for their actions, rugby victories are celebrated, and the boys mourn the death of
one of their own. Hughes wrote a sequel titled *Tom
Brown at Oxford* (1861) that did not prove nearly as
successful as his first published work.

BIBLIOGRAPHY
Mack, Edward Clarence. *Thomas Hughes: The life of the
author of* Tom Brown's Schooldays. London: Benn, 1952.

TOM JONES, A FOUNDLING, THE HIS-
TORY OF HENRY FIELDING (1749)   One of
fiction's more irreverent and likable characters, the title
character of Henry FIELDING's *Tom Jones* has entertained
readers and viewers of the multiple dramatic forms he
later assumed for centuries. What has become familiar
to 21st-century readers proved an entirely new
approach for those of the 18th, as Fielding wrote whole
chapters to introduce each of the novel's 18 books. He
used those introductions to explain the purpose of fiction and suggest for readers the way they might judge
the narrative, touching on the moral purpose that
Fielding's contemporaries believed literature should
have. As Tom himself proves a most immoral protagonist, that Fielding could convince his readers proved a
delightful feat. Fielding's readers recognized in Tom the
18th-century ideal of a natural goodness in man that
could, with encouragement, be revealed even in the
most mischievous human. He represents a prototype of
the playboy hero that would appear in later fiction.
Much of the novel's enduring success is due not only to
Tom's likability as a flawed hero but to the shaping of
the heroine, Sophia Western, free of stereotype, as well
as of the detestable Blifil, Tom's antagonist and a disreputable aristocrat that readers loved to hate. The
well-drawn characters and dramatic tension counter
the sometimes-contrived coincidence and mistaken
identity on which much early drama and fiction
turned, an inheritance from classic ROMANCE.

As suggested by the novel's subtitle, Tom is literally
found as an infant, discovered by the good and wealthy
Mr. Allworthy, whose name is only one of several symbolic names in the story. He elects to raise Tom along
with his nephew and heir, the detestable Blifil, already
a spoiled, self-centered brat who lives to torture Tom

with the help of their tutor, the aptly named
Thwackum and the so-called philosopher Mr. Square.
While Tom prefers keeping company with common
folk, including poachers on Mr. Allworthy's property,
Blifil is too good to mingle with the ordinary man. The
gamekeeper's daughter, Molly Seagrim, likes Tom, but
he loves Squire Western's daughter Sophia, who has
already been pledged to Blifil. Sophia first feels affection for Tom when he attempts to help her with a bird,
symbolic of Sophia herself, a creature Blifil simply
wants to kill. She first voices that Tom possesses a
noble character, assuring readers that nobility will triumph in the end. Tom can get into enough trouble on
his own, without being framed by Blifil, but the conflict between the two escalates until they become
young men. Tom's first sign of honor occurs when
Molly announces she is pregnant, and he agrees to take
responsibility for his actions and marry her. He is freed
of that commitment when he learns that she has slept
with several men and there is no way to know the
identity of the father. However, Blifil ensures that Tom's
reputation is ruined with Mr. Allworthy, who sorrow-
fully ejects him from his home. Tom plans to join the
army and travels with a teacher companion named
Partridge.

Tom is surprised to encounter Sophia traveling with
her maid, Mrs. Honour. She is fleeing to London to
escape the arranged marriage with Blifil, a fact that
thrills Tom. When he discovers her lost pocket book,
he vows to deliver it to her in London, but has several
adventurers along the way in the tradition of the classic
ROMANCE. Each proves his honorable intentions, some
of which are lost in mischief and the passion of the
moment. He engages in a sexual affair in London with
Lady Bellaston in return for her support. Sophia again
enters the plot when Lady Bellaston plans a meeting for
her with her friend Lord Fellamar, leading the horrified
Sophia to discover Tom's illicit relationship with his
mistress. All hope for establishing a relationship with
Sophia seems lost, and after Tom's participation in a
duel in which he believes he has killed his opponent,
Bellaston and Fellamar have him arrested for murder.
Although he spends a stint in prison, he has not actually killed anyone, and so is released. Despite Tom's best
attempts, his actions continue to be misunderstood and

misjudged. Even so, Sophia continues to pursue Tom, even when she understands he has taken yet another lover in Mrs. Waters; she leaves her hand muff on his bed with her name pinned to it, informing Tom of her continued interest. That Sophia remains on Tom's mind is evident when he refuses the attentions of yet another possible conquest, the Widow Hunt, choosing to commune with the muff, and by extension Sophia, instead.

Tom's fortunes return when Mrs. Waters explains to Mr. Allworthy that Tom had "rescued" her from the hands of a "villain." She testifies, "he is the worthiest of men. No young gentleman of his age is, I believe, freer from vice and few have the twentieth part of his virtues; nay, whatever vices he hath had, I am firmly persuaded he hath now taken a resolution to abandon them." After being proclaimed a gentleman, Tom is proved one when Allworthy learns from Mr. Dowling that Blifil had hidden a letter intended for him that revealed Tom's true identity as the son of Allworthy's sister Bridget, and thus his nephew. Following this revelation, Blifil earns his just desserts. Tom becomes heir to Allworthy's fortune and recipient of his blessings, and he at last is worthy of Sophia, who is in love with him.

All schools of criticism find much to study in Fielding's novel. FEMINIST CRITICS are interested in Sophia's stance as the novel's moral center and also in Fielding's sexual allusions, as in his vulgar implications in discussions of Sophia's muff and the control it exerts over Tom, one of several inferences in the novel that also interest PSYCHOANALYTIC CRITICS; NEW HISTORICIST CRITICS find of interest Fielding's stance on issues of the day such as copyright, and the definitions of history and truth, as they pertain to writing; and FORMALISTS look to this early novel for development of narrative and unified plot. Modern readers enjoy Tom's rebellious personality and the fact that he is rewarded for his ultimate honesty, although Fielding commented that the quality of one's inner being is worth little without actions that support it. Despite that statement, only when Tom is proved a member of the wealthy class does he earn his reward, a condition totally acceptable to readers of Fielding's age, when fiction that featured the commoner as protagonist had not yet developed.

BIBLIOGRAPHY

Allen, Walter Ernst. *Six Great Novelists: Defoe, Fielding, Scott, Dickens, Stevenson, Conrad.* Folcroft, Pa.: Folcroft Library Editions, 1971.

Bissell, Frederick Olds. *Fielding's Theory of the Novel.* New York: Cooper Squares, 1969.

Hipchen, Emily A. "Fielding's Tom Jones." *The Explicator* 53, no. 9 (Fall 1994): 16–18.

Lawrence, Frederick. *The Life of Henry Fielding with Notices of His Writings, his Times, and His Contemporaries.* 1855. Folcroft, Pa.: Folcroft Library Editions, 1976.

TRAGIC COMEDIANS, THE GEORGE MEREDITH (1880)

George MEREDITH based his novel *The Tragic Comedians* on an account of a love affair that became famous in social circles of his day. In the opinion of later critics, his use of the true account stifled the ingenuity apparent in his previous novel, *The EGOIST* (1879). In the 1892 edition, an introductory note about the historic Ferdinand Lassalle was added to the novel, in which an effort is made to sort fact from myth. The book's NARRATIVE derives from Helene von Donnige's remembrance of her relationship with Ferdinand Lassalle, a notorious German socialist. Helene was a young woman of 19, betrothed to an Italian 28 years her elder, when she first met Lassalle. Their dramatic meeting produced love at first sight, and the two could not dream of parting. They would part, however, and regardless of whether her version were entirely true, Lassalle did die a tragic death following imprisonment for an incident in which he claimed innocence, when he fought and died with the Turks in the Crimean war.

In the novel the Lassalle figure is named Alvan, while von Donnige is Clothilde, a young woman easily manipulated by her high-society family. She commits to marry Alvan, although she suspects her aristocratic family will never agree to the match. In the name of honor, Alvan sends her to her family to gain their blessing on the union. Clothilde's family insists she marry their chosen match, Marko Romaris, and they eventually trick her into committing to him. Meredith suggests she is rendered incapable of action in one scene in which she wishes to appeal to Alvan's friend, Dr. Storchel, but the sight of the family friend,

Colonel von Tresten, "had *frozen* her," so she "stood petrified" before the doctor, "as if affected by some wicked spell." Enraged at the family's refusal of him, Alvan insults Clothilde's father, an aging general, and challenges him. Clothilde's mind is further muddled by "the collision of ideas driven together by Alvan and a duel . . . Alvan, the contemner of the senseless appeal to arms for the settlement of personal disputes!" As Marko leaves to confront Alvan in the general's place, Clothilde exclaims "'I am a prisoner!'" and knows the horror of being "dragged to her happiness through a river of blood," as she feels confident that Alvan will kill Marko. However, Marko shoots Alvan, who dies three days later. Giving in to her fate, Clothilde proceeds with the wedding to Marko. Meredith remarks on Alvan's acting against character in a final statement regarding the way the world should view such men. Of Alvan, he writes, "he perished of this weakness, but it was a strong man that fell. If his end was unheroic, the bolt does not overshadow his life . . . a stormy blood made wreck of a splendid intelligence." In doing so, he suggests that Alvan and Clothilde must share the blame for Alvan's death, as two egotistical sentimentalists.

Meredith provides the context for understanding his title by writing of Alvan, "he was neither fool nor madman, nor man to be adored: his last temptation caught him in the season before he had subdued his blood, and amid the multitudinously simple of this world, stamped him a tragic comedian: that is, a grand pretender, a self-deceiver." He thus incorporates into fiction his theory shared in 1877 in a lecture on "The Idea of Comedy and the Uses of the Comic Spirit," in which he held, according to Lionel Stevenson, that "perfect comedy is neither satire nor burlesque, but a dispassionate and clear-sighted perception of folly, sentimentality, and conceit."

BIBLIOGRAPHY

Lindsay, Jack. *George Meredith: His Life and Work.* 1956. Reprint, Millwood, N.Y.: Kraus, 1980.

Moffat, James. *George Meredith: A Primer to the Novels.* Port Washington, N.Y., Kennikat Press 1969.

Stevenson, Lionel. *The English Novel: A Panorama.* Boston: Houghton Mifflin, 1960.

TREASURE ISLAND ROBERT LOUIS STEVENSON (1883)   First published as a serial in the magazine *Young Folks* between October 1881 and January 1882, Robert Louis STEVENSON's *Treasure Island* would be labeled a masterpiece of storytelling by notables including author Henry JAMES. Stevenson began the story in 1881 while on vacation with his stepson, Lloyd Osbourne. As Lloyd played with a paint box, Stevenson began sketching an island, later writing that the idea for a book appeared to spring from the woods he imagined there, along with "brown faces and bright weapons." First titled *The Sea Cook,* the tale developed at an astounding speed as Stevenson wrote a chapter each day for 15 days. He entertained his family by reading each chapter in the evenings. When he returned from vacation, his inspiration again carried him through two frantic weeks of writing to produce a complete manuscript. While the book's success as a children's story caused critics to disregard it as serious literature until the 20th century, they eventually reassessed its format, from its frame as a child's narrative to its well-drawn multidimensional characters, valuing *Treasure Island* for its literary qualities.

Stevenson's knack at capturing a child's true voice resulted from his own boyhood memories. As his protagonist, Jim Hawkins, describes bad dreams, Stevenson drew on his own experience as a youth, often ill and bedridden, haunted by vivid nightmares. The description also reflects his influence by Charles DICKENS, who reproduced nightmares for his David in *DAVID COPPERFIELD* (1850) and Pip from *GREAT EXPECTATIONS* (1861). Always adept at ROMANCE NOVELS, Stevenson includes all the elements of adventure, verging on fantasy, expected from that genre. With a call to adventure based on an alluring map, an ocean voyage, Jim's adult guide figure in the person of the not-altogether-admirable Long John Silver, a treasure, and a sudden maturing on Jim's part, the book uses the QUEST format to frame a BILDUNGSROMAN and an INITIATION/COMING-OF-AGE tale.

Stevenson goes beyond the plot-driven formula to produce strong characterizations, particularly in his rendering of Long John Silver. At once beastly and caring, shrewd and protective, treacherous and trustworthy, the pirate embodies the idea of conflict present in many humans. Stevenson's fascination with human nature's opposing capabilities, one for good, one for evil, would be more thoroughly investigated in his equally popular *The Strange Case of Dr. Jekyll and Mr. Hyde* (1886). Some critics feel that Silver represents Dr. Jekyll in an early form. While Silver's relationship with Jim changes according to which side of his personality he exercises, Jim does respect him, evidenced by the fact that when he has occasion to escape, he refuses to do so, as he has given Silver his word that he would not. Although undoubtedly a scoundrel, the one-legged Silver remains sympathetic and liked by readers. Readers' fondness for the pirate is likely why he escapes execution in the story's conclusion. The realistic relationship between boy and man, along with the lively descriptions of setting Stevenson rendered with the help of his knowledge from early studies of engineering and surveying, raise the novel above the traditional melodrama often inherent to romance. Vivid scenes that reproduce the island's topography in minute detail support Stevenson's study of human nature and man's ethical ambiguity. Painful decisions, such as abandoning mutineers on the island, must be made for pragmatic reasons, so that what may at first seem immoral is accounted for by logic.

In his writing of *Treasure Island*, Stevenson produced his first novel, used as a vehicle for his imaginative consideration of the human instinct for survival beyond mere existence. He demands that his characters survive for an ideal higher than themselves, even if, as with Long John Silver, it remains a fleeting experience. The novel continues to enthrall readers of all ages and has been converted multiple times to screen, film, and stage versions.

BIBLIOGRAPHY

Hammond, J. R. *A Robert Louis Stevenson Companion.* London: MacMillan Press, 1984.

TRISTRAM SHANDY LAURENCE STERNE (1760–1767)

Dr. Samuel Johnson once claimed that "nothing odd can last." As an example, he cited Laurence Sterne's novel *The Life and Opinions of Tristram Shandy,* which had temporarily fallen from favor. Over two centuries later, that same novel may well be one of the best examples of something odd lasting amazingly well. While even contemporary readers are often confused or at least surprised by the often-digressive narrative technique used by Sterne in his masterpiece, *Tristram Shandy* continues to find an audience. Furthermore, unlike the works of his major near-contemporaries, Daniel Defoe, Samuel Richardson, and Henry Fielding, Sterne's novel is, on the surface at least, not an obvious product of its time. This does not necessarily mean that the novel is *ahead* of its time, despite the playful technique that may remind readers of modernist and post-modernist experimentation in its lack of a traditional beginning, middle section, or conclusion. It is perhaps more accurate to say that *Tristram Shandy* is in its own time, particularly as time is one of the novel's most important aspects.

Sterne vowed to continue writing the novel until his death and produced volumes one to nine from 1760 until 1767. He filled his rendition of a life with multiple digressions and authorial interference, producing a remarkably personal account of a protagonist that mirrors much of his own life and ideas. Highly influenced by the satire of Jonathan Swift in works such as *Gulliver's Travels* (1726), Sterne modeled his tale to gain momentum from its themes, rather than its plot. While a proponent of sentimentalism, Sterne tempered his sentiment with a sharp wit and a keen sense of humor. He peppered his volumes with characters representative of both his enemies and his friends, with Parson Yorick closely resembling himself, a resemblance he would perpetuate by inserting one of his own sermons into Yorick's mouth and by publicly referring to himself as Yorick and his home as "Shandy Hall."

In the more optimistic early volumes, Tristram supposedly relates his "life and opinions" to his reader, yet he gives the reader nothing resembling a life history as he waits in the womb for his birth. Indeed, readers learn more about several of the other characters than about Tristram. Walter Shandy, Tristram's father, is a would-be scientist in constant conflict with his wife. Tristram's Uncle Toby was a soldier, wounded in the groin, whose hobbyhorse is to re-create battle scenes assisted by his friend Corporal Trim. The corporal spends volume five producing a running commentary on morality, his own hobbyhorse. Sterne suggests that such hobbyhorses stifle true communication, as the speakers become so immersed in their own passions that they end all successful verbal communication with those around them. However, they do remain united by sentimentality, or love. Those characters reflect some aspects of the failed military career of Sterne's father and his unwise marriage to the widow of a captain, possibly because he owed her father money. After his father's death from malaria, Sterne lived with a disinherited uncle who resembled Uncle Toby.

It is not until the third volume that Tristram is born, his nose crushed by the appropriately named Dr. Slop (an incident that, somewhat surprisingly, is not a major part of the novel) who makes clear his hobbyhorse is Catholic doctrine. Walter Shandy feels responsible for the baby's injury, blaming it on his habit of winding his clock on the first day of each month, one of multiple references to time. Tristram continues after his birth to stretch time. In volume four he announces: "I am this month one whole year older than I was this time twelve-month; and having got, as you perceive, almost into the middle of my fourth volume—and no farther than my first day's life—. . ."

As many critics have pointed out, Sterne comments on the digressive and discursive manner of the act of writing as he engages in that act. Demonstrating the arbitrary nature of plotting, Yorick reappears in the novel following his supposed death, and Sterne's next novel, *A SENTIMENTAL JOURNEY* (1768), would have Yorick participating in travels to France and Italy, although he had already died. Various pages contain wiggly lines, brackets, asterisks, Gothic printing, and other freakish insertions, with much of the punctuation including dashes and an occasional set of dots. Chapter lengths vary greatly, and some appear out of order. Readers eventually follow Tristram as he attempts to closely examine short isolated and unconnected moments in his life, and in this way attempts to stop time, only to find in the end that time outside the page has continued and (as with Sterne) his death will soon come. The disconnections in Tristram's narrative emphasize the difficulty in telling anyone's life, due to the labyrinthine nature of human existence.

Sterne did not publish volumes seven and eight until 1765, while the ninth and final volume did not appear until 1767. Much of this writing reflects the influence of Sterne's travels in his later years, as well as a feeling of melancholy brought on by his failing health. For example, in volume seven Tristram finally faces the passing of time by moving away from the moment of birth and writing of the current time—when he is facing death. Tristram promises to write until the end of his days, and Sterne did exactly that. When Tristram had described the death of Yorick (supposedly a descendent of Shakespeare's Yorick and, like Sterne, a parson) as a sort of tribute to the character, he presented readers with a black page. His own death will not be represented by a black page but by a lack of pages.

Sterne's disgressions and colloquialisms are influenced by his favorite authors, Rabelais, Cervantes, and Robert Burton. He also borrowed from, and ridiculed, ideas contained in John Locke's famous An *Essay Concerning Human Understanding*. Locke theorized that multiple ideas or impressions that occur at the same time in an individual's mind would forever remain associated for that individual. According to critic Lionel Stevenson, *Tristram Shandy* on the one hand seems to agree with Locke's theory, demonstrating that "the workings of every individual brain are controlled by a different pattern of irrelevant associations and personal quirks." However, Locke believed his "associative theory" to be an important move toward human communication, while Sterne makes clear that such association of ideas in the individual mind will prevent that communication.

In volume eight, Tristram again attempts to prolong time: He now goes back to the time before his birth. It is in this chapter that we are told of the "amours" of his eccentric Uncle Toby, perhaps Sterne's greatest comic creation. But as he acknowledges in the final volume, every "adieu" and "every absence which follows it, are preludes to that eternal separation which we are shortly to make." The novel ends in a fairly unambiguous fashion. Having again gone back in time, Sterne gives Parson Yorick, now alive, the novel's appropriate final words. When asked by Tristram's mother "what is all this story about?" he replies, "A COCK and a BULL, . . . "—And one of the best I ever heard."

While no one can say whether Sterne might have added further volumes to *Tristram Shandy* had time allowed, it is difficult to imagine a more appropriate ending. Tristram's tales may indeed be a lot of "cock and bull," yet through all of the strangeness, through all of the tall tales, few stories have lasted any better than *Tristram Shandy*.

BIBLIOGRAPHY

Bloom, Harold Bloom, ed. *Modern Critical Interpretations: Laurence Sterne's Tristram Shandy*. New York: Chelsea House, 1987.

Stevenson, Lionel. *The English Novel: A Panorama*. Boston: Houghton Mifflin, 1960.

Watt, Ian. Introduction to *Tristram Shandy*, by Laurence Sterne. Boston: Houghton Mifflin, 1965, vii–xxxv.

TROLLOPE, ANTHONY (1815–1882)

Anthony Trollope was born in London, the youngest of four sons and one of six children; he was considered the least bright of the group. His father was a barrister who unsuccessfully tried his hand at farming, leaving his family in poverty. Anthony spent his school days embarrassed over the family's financial problems, being bullied by his older brother Thomas Aldolphus TROLLOPE. When he left school after a dull career, always at the bottom of his class, he had no idea of what to do with his future and gained a job in the Post Office thanks only to his mother's influence. Frances TROLLOPE had rescued the family's finances when she traveled to the United States, leaving Anthony behind in school, in an attempt to open a business, her husband's idea. While the business did not flourish, she began a successful writing career when more than 50 years old, beginning with the highly popular *Domestic Manners of the Americans* (1832), based on her time in the States. Anthony would also become a successful writer at the late age of 40, partly due to his mother's fame and reputation.

Trollope remained uninspired and unhappy with few friends, a situation he would later feature in his fiction. Out of boredom he played pranks that irritated his superiors, ran up debts and often neglected his assignments. He decided to change his surroundings following a serious bout with illness in 1840 and moved a year later to Ireland to assist a surveyor. He seemed to find a niche, organizing the postal service

and romancing Rose Hesel, the English girl he married in 1844. Part of his amazing transformation included taking up hunting and, most important, producing the first of many novels, *The Macdermots of Ballycloran* (1847). It focused on the personal decay of an Irish family during a period of national miserable poverty. He had begun that work in 1843, concluded it in 1845, and then held it for two years before submitting it for publication. He had enjoyed the Irish novels of Maria EDGEWORTH and Lady Sydney MORGAN, but did not find them faithful to the country he had come to revere. His novel set out to correct that problem.

After a decade in Ireland, Trollope returned briefly to London, then moved back to Ireland, then finally returned permanently to England in 1859. His second novel, *The Kellys and the O'Kellys* (1848), also featured Irish life, while his next, *La Vendée,* reflected Trollope's interest in the French Revolution. Rather than an exciting story of revolution, Trollope produced a political overview that readers found dull; the book proved as little read as had his two Irish novels. He at last achieved his first success with *The WARDEN* (1855), a novel whose idea he developed while strolling around Salisbury Cathedral. The plot focused on an elderly clergyman, Septimus Harding, whose salary is suddenly revealed by an investigative reporter to be out of line with his work, and the resultant ethical dilemma. Trollope included petty wars among members of the diocese, demonstrating that the church is often motivated by forces that do not include the welfare of parishioners or figures low in the hierarchy. He created an investigation of human behavior that would become his trademark approach to fiction.

From that first story, Trollope developed his famous Barsetshire series with familiar characters that delighted readers by reappearing throughout the collection. That extremely popular series defined Trollope for his public and eventually included *BARCHESTER TOWERS* (1857); *DOCTOR THORNE* (1858); *FRAMLEY PARSONAGE* (1860); *The SMALL HOUSE AT ALLINGTON* (1862–64); and *The LAST CHRONICLE OF BARSET* (1866–67). Trollope's gentle character development and focus on the minutiae of everyday life for his cathedral-town inhabitants entertained Victorian readers for years. It marked a striking departure from the robust adventure novel and from SENSATION FICTION. He resisted the DIDACTIC approach of his mother, who tended to shape her novels as strident social critiques. He did break his vow not to intrude into his narrative with THE THREE CLERKS (1858). While it presented an interesting view of his miserable early work experience, his bitter tone and vituperative caricatures of superiors reduced the novel's quality. Trollope would become known for his accurate reproduction of everyday conversation and his gentle acceptance of human nature in its many forms, not for the judgmental approach projected in this novel.

Trollope created a second masterful series called the Palliser novels, which differed from the Barsetshire sequence in their focus on politics. That group focused on the character Plantagenet Palliser, whom readers knew from *The Small House at Allington*. He and his wife, the independent and admirable Glencora, appeared in most of the books, which included *CAN YOU FORGIVE HER?* (1864–65); *PHINEAS FINN* (1867–69); *The EUSTACE DIAMONDS* (1871–73); *PHINEAS REDUX* (1873–74); *The PRIME MINISTER* (1876); and finally, *The DUKE'S CHILDREN* (1879–80). Their tone regarding the state of English politics was not always positive, growing partly from Trollope's own disappointment in running for office and not being elected. However, he continued to separate himself from the heavy-handed moralizing of his contemporary writers, even including caricatures of Charles DICKENS and Thomas CARLYLE in his fiction. Trollope believed that the Pallisers and Mr. Crawley from *The Last Chronicle of Barset* were his greatest character achievements and the ones the public would the longest remember. Additional fine work outside the two series included *Orley Farm* (1861–62); *The Claverings* (1866–67); *HE KNEW HE WAS RIGHT* (1868–69); *SIR HARRY HOTSPUR OF HUMBLEWAITE* (1870), and *Dr. Wortle's School* (1880).

After what had evolved into a distinguished career with the Post Office, Trollope retired in 1867, having left his mark on the system by inventing the pillar-box. His unsuccessful bid for Beverley as a Liberal came in 1868 and resulted in the constituency losing its organization due to a bribery conviction of the opposing Conservative candidate. Trollope's novel *Ralph the Heir* (1870–71) focused closely on that experience. He turned his full-time energies to literature and became part of a circle that included novelist George ELIOT among others. He worked as editor of *St. Paul's Magazine* between 1867 and 1870, but published another novel, *The WAY WE LIVE NOW* (1874–75) with a skeptical view of society that eschewed man's contempt for his fellow man as material gain was privileged over family and personal honor. That example of social SATIRE endured in popularity, transformed into various media forms in the next century. Trollope also wrote several travel books and his famous autobiography, while maintaining a large correspondence with other writers, including his brother Thomas, who also became a novelist. In a series titled English Men of Letters, he wrote the volume featuring William Makepeace THACKERAY, adding to his enormous volume of published material. His production of 47 novels caused him to repeat some plot lines and many themes, but the quality of the work never varied, nor did Trollope's consummate consideration of human nature as his major focus. Critics place him within the tradition of DOMESTIC FICTION such as that by Charlotte YONGE, as his work lacked the irony and skill of his idol Thackeray. However, Lionel Stevenson has judged Trollope the "third great realist in English fiction, in succession to [Daniel] DEFOE and [Jane] AUSTEN." His tremendous contribution to the quiet novel's realistic characterization is evident in the work of many writers who would follow.

BIBLIOGRAPHY

Bell, Arnold Craig. *A Guide to Trollope*. Braunton, Devon, England: Merlin, 1989.

Glendinning, Victoria. *Anthony Trollope*. New York: Knopf, 1993.

Macdonald, Susan Peck. *Anthony Trollope*. Boston: Twayne, 1987.

Mullen, Richard. *Anthony Trollope: A Victorian in His World*. London: Duckworth, 1990.

Nardin, Jane. *He Knew She Was Right: The Independent Woman in the Novels of Anthony Trollope*. Carbondale: Southern Illinois University Press, 1989.

Stevenson, Lionel. *The English Novel: A Panorama*. Boston: Houghton Mifflin, 1960.

Tingay, Lance O. *The Trollope Student: An Annotated List of Full Length Studies and a Check List of the Writings of Anthony Trollope and Other Members of the Trollope Family (1743–1909)*. London: Silverbridge, 1990.

TROLLOPE, FRANCES (MILTON) (1779–1863)

Mother of famous novelist Anthony TROLLOPE, Frances (Fanny) Milton matured in a clergyman's family in Hampshire. She married Thomas Anthony Trollope in 1809, following her move to London in 1803, and they had six children. Anthony failed in attempts as a barrister and a farmer, and Frances traveled to America in an attempt to regain a steady income. Accompanied by three of her children and her future illustrator, Auguste Hervieu, she joined a utopian community in Tennessee, and then moved on to Cincinnati, where her husband hoped she might establish an emporium. She put into motion a scheme involving the development of a flamboyant bazaar containing a ballroom, art gallery, bar, and coffeehouse, among other social establishments. The bazaar failed, leaving the family more deeply in debt than ever. She decided to try writing and produced a travel book about her American experiences, *Domestic Manner of the Americans* (1832), an immediately successful endeavor. She wrote of being bored in a culture that encouraged women to simply "mix puddings and cakes" in the morning and "watch them baking" in the afternoon, angering her American audience but entertaining her English readers. She employed the generous profits from her book to continue in a writing career that produced additional travel books, all of which sold well. Her novels also reflected her experiences abroad and included comedy, such as that in *The Widow Barnaby* (1839); GOTHIC, *The Abess* (1833); anti-Catholicism, *Father Eustace, a Tale of the Jesuits* (1847); and SATIRE, *The VICAR OF WREXHILL* (1837), one of her most enduring works. She also wrote social-problem novels, *Michael Armstrong, the Factory Boy* (1839), one of the first "industrial" novels of the Victorian Age; and *Jessie Phillips* (1843). Although occasionally ill, she continued to work at writing that often incited much criticism due to her social themes. Despite the attention drawn at their time of publishing, much of her work was ignored by 1883, when her son

Anthony's biography praised her industry and inspiration to him and his novelist brother, Thomas Adolphus TROLLOPE.

BIBLIOGRAPHY

Heineman, Helen. *Frances Trollope*. Boston: Twayne, 1984.
———. *Mrs Trollope: The Triumphant Feminine in the Nineteenth Century*. Athens, Ohio: Ohio University Press, 1979.
Sage, Lorna. "Trollope, Frances." *The Cambridge Guide to Women's Writing in English*. Cambridge: Cambridge University Press, 1999. 634.
Tingay, Lance O. *The Trollope Student: An Annotated List of Full Length Studies and a Check List of the Writings of Anthony Trollope and Other Members of the Trollope Family (1743–1909)*. London: Silverbridge, 1990.

TROLLOPE, THOMAS ADOLPHUS (1810–1892)

Born the eldest son of writer Frances TROLLOPE and older brother of novelist Anthony TROLLOPE, Thomas Adolphus Trollope remains important mainly due to those relationships. Though he delivered regular thrashings to Anthony as a child, Thomas, called Tom by the family, became his good friend as an adult. Following an education at Harrow and Winchester and a stint in America, Trollope took a degree from Magdalen Hall, Oxford, in 1835. He had a reputation as a great walker, regularly having walked the 47 miles between Harrow and home when in school, and walking great distances through London with Anthony in tow. He would later adopt Anthony's favorite saying from Alexander Pope's *Essay on Man,* "Whatever is, is right," incorporating it into his family crest as a motto.

Trollope taught at King Edward's School, Birmingham, then traveled with his mother, later settling in Florence, where he married Theodosia Garrow in 1848; they had a daughter named Bice. Their home, Villino Trollope, attracted many expatriate writers to its beautiful grounds, containing a garden and orchards of orange and lemon trees, funded by Theodosia's inheritance. Following Theodosia's death, Trollope married Frances Eleanor Ternan. They moved to Rome, where Trollope wrote for the London *Standard* and completed 60 volumes of fiction, history, and travel writing, the latter being the type of writing that had brought his mother fame. He was grief-stricken over his brother's death in 1882, providing through his letters the most detailed account of Anthony Trollope's condition following his stroke. Thomas Trollope's fiction is little read; his *A Siren* is briefly discussed in this volume. More important is his *What I Remember* (1887–89), an autobiography in which he recalls his years in Italy and many writers crucial to the development of the novel, including Charles Dickens, Elizabeth Barrett Browning (verse novel), and George Eliot.

BIBLIOGRAPHY

Glendinning, Victoria. *Anthony Trollope*. New York: Knopf, 1993.

Tingay, Lance O. *The Trollope Student: An Annotated List of Full Length Studies and a Check List of the Writings of Anthony Trollope and Other Members of the Trollope Family (1743–1909)*. London: Silverbridge, 1990.

Trollope, Thomas Adolphus. *What I Remember*. 1887. London: Kimber, 1973.

TROY TOWN, THE ASTONISHING HISTORY OF SIR ARTHUR QUILLER-COUCH (1888)

Although works by Sir Arthur Quiller-Couch faded from the public's favor soon after his death in 1944, they had been extremely popular in the author's day. When his publishers Messrs J. M. Dent chose to mark the centenary of "Q," they did so by reissuing his 1888 novel, *The Astonishing History of Troy Town*. Q. referred to the novel in a preface to a later edition as "this indiscretion of my youth," then explained his total devotion to Fowey in Cornwall, the model for Troy, the town he "pokes fun at" in the book. While the book was not Q's favorite, its humorous tone, imaginative scenes, and what Professor Basil Willey describes fondly as an "irresponsible story," seemed to fit the celebratory occasion designed by the publishers. Its protagonist, Mr. Fogo, offered some gravity to the plot, mainly through a tongue-in-cheek irony, but it is his attendant, the boatman Caleb Trotter, for which the novel is known. His misuse of language in the tradition of Richard Sheridan's celebrated character Mrs. Malaprop and rustic temperament celebrate an Arcadian innocence that Q's contemporaries found endearing. Although not representative of the larger body of Quiller-Couch's more

seriously toned work, it well captures his fondness for place and for country life.

The cast populating Troy includes the blustery Admiral Buzza and his wife, Emily; Miss Priscilla Limpenny; the portly antique vicar; blind Sam Hockin and his Mrs.; Bathsheba Merryfield; the wooden-legged Cobbledick; Mr. Moggridge; the poet, Caleb Trotter; the twins Peter and Paul Dearlove; and their sister Tamsin, who live upriver from Troy, where they operate an inn called Kit's House. Into this mix wanders Mr. Philip Fogo, a man seeking peace and quiet in Troy, who is bewildered to be met by a marching band playing "The Conquering Hero." The town will not listen to his protests until finally he is allowed to explain to the insulted admiral that they must have made a mistake in their welcome. When the admiral discovers he is not the Honourable Frederic Goodwyn-Sandys who is arriving to inhabit the villa known as "The Bower," he must suffer the townspeople's laughter as the crowd "cast its April folly, as a garment, upon the Admiral's shoulders." When the celebrated Goodwyn-Sandys does arrive, he is accompanied by his beautiful young temptress wife, Gertrude, and the foolish intrigue begins.

The town members rush to supply the Goodwyn-Sanders with everything needed, even though they never pay their bills. They eventually discover what readers have already learned, that the refined couple are actually revolutionaries who use Troy as a place to store dynamite. They plan to use the explosives to blow up St. Paul's in London, a scheme the good folk of Troy do not discover for some time. Gertrude even convinces Moggridge and Sam to unwittingly aid in the plan by unloading the dynamite, stored in tea canisters, from Sam's schooner. The alluring Gertrude tempts each by confessing she hates her husband, promising to marry them. Fogo becomes the hero the town had sought in Goodwyn-Sanders, although his heroism is accidental. While seeking to sample the tea, he creates an explosion that destroys a good deal of the dynamite on the schooner. This causes him to lapse into a fever through which the good Tamsin nurses him, and they fall in love and marry. With the truth about Mr. and Mrs. Goodwyn-Sanders revealed, the townspeople rush The Bower to recover all the goods and furnishings they had "sold" their distinguished visitors, both of whom disappeared, never to be found. Lest the story grow too serious on Fogo's account, it concludes with his most ungraceful toss by the twins into a train car filled with clay on his wedding day, when he almost misses the train where Tamsin awaits him.

BIBLIOGRAPHY

Willey, Basil. Introduction to *The Astonishing History of Troy Town,* by Sir Arthur Quiller-Couch. London: Dent, 1963, v–xi.

TRUMPET-MAJOR, THE THOMAS HARDY (1880)

Judged the most romantic book written by Thomas HARDY, *The Trumpet-Major* ran first as a serial in the publication *Good Words* from January to December in 1880. While the character referred to by the title does not find romance, several other characters in the novel do, making it an exception among Hardy's works. The female love interest is Anne Garland, daughter of a painter, who lives with her widowed mother in the Overcombe Mill, a highly symbolic name as love will overcome all its inhabitants. Miller Loveday, whose family also bears a symbolic name, lives in half the mill with his two sons. Robert (Bob) Loveday is a sailor, while John Loveday serves as trumpet-major of a dragoon regiment that may see action during the Napoleonic Wars. John nurtures an unrequited love for Anne, asking her to allow him "to court" her. She refuses him by arguing that the life of a soldier's wife is a trial, although she hesitates to dismiss "a man who has all the natural and moral qualities she would desire, and only fails in the social." But she does not love John; she loves Bob. Critics of the novel have pointed out the inconsistency in Hardy's dealing with the differences in the social classes. As daughter and wife of a painter, neither Anne nor Mrs. Garland should take any interest in a miller and his sons. Hardy deserves such criticism, as the overwhelming majority of his fiction deals pointedly with such social inequalities.

A third male character named Festus Derriman provides a comic touch for the novel in his clownish actions, as does his elderly uncle Benjy, a semi-hermit to whom Anne kindly reads the newspaper. Festus is enthralled with Anne, who cannot abide his presence.

While Bob is away, he narrowly escapes two threats, first a kidnapping attempt by the press-gang, which is intent on dragging him into service, and second, the attentions of a tainted woman named Matilda Johnson. The two become engaged until John selflessly acts to break them up, regardless of the effect it will have on him. Anne becomes peevish over his interaction with Matilda, and her annoyance grows when he begs her not to carry a "wrong notion" regarding his character. As much as Anne wants to express her affection, she scolds him, saying, "You are too easily impressed by new faces and that gives me a *bad opinion* of you: yes, a *bad opinion*." Bob joins the British navy of his own volition, while John comes home to beat Festus so he will leave Anne alone. Anne and Bob end the novel together, as do Anne's mother and Miller Loveday. Poor John, however, departs alone to take up another battle, going "off to blow his trumpet till silenced for ever upon one of the bloody battle-fields of Spain."

Hardy includes his traditional sharp eye for detail concerning those who live in the countryside. Minor characters such as Benji Derriman's worker, Cripplestraw, and Mrs. Garland bring life to the landscape, as do details about King George III's "bucolic" arrival at nearby Gloucester Lodge and the working of a mill where Anne meets Bob. Despite the novel's serious and realistic ending, Hardy includes much farce as he traces the characters' various adventures. Along with only one later additional of his works, TWO ON A TOWER (1882), Hardy would officially classify *The Trumpet-Major* under the heading "Romance and Fantasies." Critics took issue with the classification, viewing the book as more HISTORICAL FICTION, claiming the humor Hardy does include is undercut by the sadness and death of his topic of war. Others argue it cannot be historical fiction because the characters in no way represent their era's social practices or any of the historical forces at work in the novel.

BIBLIOGRAPHY

May, C. E. *Thomas Hardy: An Agnostic and a Romantic.* Lawrenceville, Va.: Brunswick Pub. Corp., 1992.

Nemesvari, Richard. Introduction to *The Trumpet-Major,* by Thomas Hardy. New York: Oxford University Press, 1991, xi–xxii.

TURN OF THE SCREW, THE HENRY JAMES (1898)

One of Henry JAMES's shortest novels, *The Turn of the Screw* first appeared in *Collier's Weekly*. When published in a volume titled *The Two Magics*, it appeared with another story titled *Covering End*. Although brief, it captured readers' imagination and became important to the mystery genre as well as the ghost genre, due to unanswered questions regarding its first-person point-of-view narrator.

When an unnamed young woman becomes governess for the children Flora and Miles at Bly, England, their uncle gives her orders not to bother him with any information about the children and their activities. Bly is an isolated estate with little contact with the outside world. The governess at first finds the children obedient and cooperative and enjoys their company. However, their secretive behavior soon clues her in to possible conflict. When she sees the ghosts of Peter Quint and Miss Jessel, a former steward and governess at Bly, she makes inquiries about them and learns they have died. While the governess feels certain the children witnessed the ghostly forms, they avoid directly answering her questions about the scene. She later discovers that Quint, who had been in charge of Miles, and Jessel, who had care of Flora, had been lovers and were evil. James's characterization of the governess allows him to exercise his lifelong interest in the psychology of his characters, rather than in the events caused by their internal conflicts. Readers are allowed access to the governess's vision, with no judgment as to the "truth" of her perception burdening the tale. All the readers see is the children react to an apparent influence; no description of the horror inflicted upon them is supplied.

Whether due to her own mounting paranoia or the children's increasing duplicity, the governess feels a demonic force she determines to shatter possesses them. Flora becomes hysterical when the governess directly confronts her, leading to an unexplained illness. When she confronts Miles, Quint's ghost returns to the window. In an attempt to protect Miles from Quint's evil force, the governess steps between the apparition and the child. However, Miles becomes hysterical as Flora did, and dies in her arms, evidently driven to his death by the struggle between two worlds to possess him.

While somewhat unsatisfying in its never reaching a conclusion regarding the plot events, the book remains a good example of the questionable character of a first-person narrator. One critical camp has posed that James intended the tale to be ironic, with the source of evil in the governess projected onto the characters of Quint and Jessel. Another counters that nothing else James wrote suggested this interpretation of the governess as merely imagining the scenario. The story remains popular and has appeared in film versions.

BIBLIOGRAPHY

Edel, Leon, ed. *The Ghostly Tales of Henry James.* New Brunswick, N.J.: Rutgers University Press, 1948.

———, ed. *The Letters of Henry James.* 4 vols. Cambridge: Belknap Press, 1974–1984.

———. *The Life of Henry James.* New York: Penguin Books, 1977.

TWO ON A TOWER THOMAS HARDY (1882)

First appearing as a serial in *The Atlantic Monthly* between May and December of 1882, Thomas HARDY's *Two on a Tower* has been considered an extreme example of Hardy's employing enormous settings, in this case the universe, to minimalize the importance of human suffering. Hardy had long expressed an interest in astronomy, including multiple references to the heavens in his poetry. His family had owned a telescope and Hardy as a teen had read voraciously from *The Popular Educator*, which carried much information about astronomy. In addition, his was an era with a great interest in science. Hardy remarked, as recorded by editor Michael Millhouse, that he and his wife saw "the new comet from the conservatory" of their house in east Dorset, that comet being Tebbutt's Comet, which excited the public.

The novel focuses on the astronomer Swithin St. Cleeve, who pursues with a stellar backdrop a doomed love affair with Lady Viviette Constantine. The tower of the title refers to a monument standing between their houses, which seems to point to the stars. Challenging the taboo of Viviette being 10 years his senior, Swithin engages in clandestine meetings with her at his observatory, Rings-Hill Speer. The observatory is located on the property of Viviette's husband, Sir Blount. The

Constantines share an unhappy marriage, and the news of Sir Blount's disappearance and presumed death while hunting in Africa does not grieve Viviette.

Hardy makes use of a traditional ROMANCE plot in which a deserted wealthy woman falls in love with a poor earnest suitor. However, he subverts some traditional elements, making the woman the older member of the couple, and she is also the aggressor in this relationship, playing a male role. In addition, Swithin takes on a traditionally female role when he falls ill, assuming a prone position due to emotional distress over a disappointment.

Viviette secretly weds Swithin, even though he could collect an inheritance if he adhered to a provision that he not marry until age 25; he ignores the potential fortune in favor of his love of Viviette and the wealth she already possesses. Viviette insists on a secret marriage, hoping to preserve the appearance of propriety, but also, Hardy implies, because she enjoys her role as lady of the manor. Hardy inserts a storm, a destructive hurricane that serves as a symbol that the couple have inverted the natural order. The partial destruction of the observatory and Swithin's home; his receiving letters of import the day before their wedding that are ignored by both lovers; and, finally, the black tie that Swithin dons for the ceremony all act to foreshadow a negative future.

In his usual twist of fate, Hardy plots that Sir Blount had remained alive for six weeks following the marriage, rendering the marriage illegal. At Viviette's urging, Swithin claims his inheritance, moving to South Africa to continue his study of astronomy. Viviette then discovers she is pregnant and marries at the urging of her scheming brother Louis, the bishop of Melchester, to bring legitimacy to the baby. She does so due to her obsession over the 10 years that separate her in age from Swithin. She cannot visualize a future for them, fearing that by the time he returned she would be at least 35 years old with fading beauty. The "frost" she feels at that thought begins to immediately kill their love before it can reach maturity.

Having begun the novel apparently a nontraditionalist, Viviette falls right in line with society's expectations and fate's determination to inhibit any development of self-awareness outside those expectations succeeds. The proper completion of social and religious activities replace her interest in the stars, symbolic of a boundless existence, shortly following her marriage to Swithin. She never again finds the passion that they had shared.

Viviette's marriage to the bishop scandalized many readers who condemned the novel as immoral fiction as well as subversive literature, categorized as SATIRE against the Church of England. Melchester dies, and when Swithin returns a few years later, he finds Viviette to again propose marriage. In true Hardy form, Viviette dies of joy, never experiencing a legitimate love.

The novel is not Hardy's most widely read work, although it remains important in his oeuvre. He categorized *Two on a Tower,* along with only one other novel, *The* TRUMPET-MAJOR (1880), under the heading "Romance and Fantasies."

BIBLIOGRAPHY

Ahmad, Suleiman M. Introduction to *Two on a Tower,* by Thomas Hardy. New York: Oxford University Press, 1993. xi–xxii.

May, C. E. *Thomas Hardy: an Agnostic and a Romantic.* Lawrenceville, Va.: Brunswick Pub. Corp., 1992.

Millhouse, Michael, ed. *The Life and Work of Thomas Hardy.* London: Macmillan, 1985.

UNCLE SILAS: A TALE OF BARTRAM-HAUGH SHERIDAN LE FANU (1864)

According-ing to Sheridan LE FANU, he had published a shorter form of his novel *Uncle Silas: A Tale of Bartram-Haugh* under the title "A Passage in the Secret History of an Irish Countess"; reports as to where the story appeared vary. He explained the story's publication in the "Preliminary Word" that prefaced the novel, ostensibly to be relieved of charges of plagiarism of his own work. Such a charge would likely never have been leveled, as he adopted as basis for his plot a familiar sequence: an evil older relative schemes to obtain the rightful inheritance of a young and helpless woman placed into his or her care. In this instance, the relative is Uncle Silas, whose brother, Austin Ruthyn of Knowl, at his death places his only daughter, Maud, in his care. He does this even though Silas had been years before accused of murdering his wife; Ruthyn believes in his brother's innocence. Maud, quite literally, becomes a pawn and even has foreknowledge of the fact that her father plans to use her to regain the family's honor. He calculates that his action may convince an unbelieving world of Silas's unjust censure by society, a commentary on the importance of family reputation in Ireland.

The first half of the book takes place at Maud's home, in order to reinforce that Silas and Austin are foils. Where the widower Austin is the respected, although seldom seen, head of an ancient and traditional family, the widower Silas has two children he cares little for, his wife having died and he having been accused of her murder. Whereas Austin practices a social religion, following the teachings of Swedenborg with the guidance of his director, Dr. Bryerly, Silas has no spiritual beliefs. Even their places of abode greatly contrast. At her home of Knowl, Maud suffers isolation, must practice formalities and adhere to many rules, while at Silas's home, Bartram-Haugh, she is allowed to run wild in the woods on the grounds with her cousin Milly.

Although the change of environment at first seems for Maud's betterment, heavy foreshadowing signals it will not be so. As Maud approaches her new home at night, with only a "filmy disc of the moon" as light, she cannot clearly make out its appearance. With the moon a traditional symbol of the female, readers understand that Maud, as the female protagonist, will be unable to cast light on the mystery she will find there. As her party passes a group of Gypsies, she notes "a couple of dark, withered crones, veritable witches," signaling that forces beyond her understanding may control her fate, an idea confirmed when she purchases from one wild-looking girl a special brass pin designed to save her from "a malevolent spirit."

At first, Maud enjoys her stay, exulting in the company of a young woman of her own age. Even Uncle Silas is not the threat she had anticipated, and she is able to ignore Milly's annoying brother, Dudley. But as the plot progresses, readers understand the threat to

Maud through contrivances similar to those found in GOTHIC FICTION, although mysticism is simply suggested and no true magic is involved. Le Fanu builds terror by forcing readers, like Maud, to wait for an inevitable tragedy to occur.

Eventually Milly is sent to France, and Dudley begins pressing Maud to marry him. Dr. Byerly reappears to reverse Maud's original impression of him as a man to be feared. Instead, she needs to fear the new governess, a woman her own father had refused to hire. When Uncle Silas employs Madame de la Rougierre, ostensibly as a companion in Milly's absence, Maud fears for her future. The plot advances as Maud discovers Dudley was already married when his wife seeks him out. Now Maud understands that Silas and Dudley intend to take her fortune in any way possible. They kidnap her, spreading the word that she has traveled to France to be with Milly, and she assumes that she will die, then witnesses in a chilling scene the murder of the governess by Dudley, who mistakes her for Maud. Le Fanu skillfully describes the murder, which is actually only heard by Maud.

Maud remains a typically passive ROMANCE heroine, attempting to escape her fate by running blindly, with no particular escape plan. She sees Tom Brice approach, a person she felt had betrayed her, and tells the reader, "So it was vain: I was trapped, and all was over." As it turns out, she had, with the reader, once again misjudged a character's motives, and Brice is actually her protector. He has been sent by a devoted servant who learned of the plot against Maud and proves her salvation. Safely swept from danger by Brice, she returns home to testify against her family. Uncle Silas commits suicide, and Dudley is later identified living in secret in debauched surroundings. Maud closes her first-person narrative describing a scene with her daughter and husband, along with a reminder to readers of the brief nature of life, which should be celebrated daily.

Le Fanu has never received the attention that contemporaries such as Wilkie COLLINS and other writers of SENSATION FICTION enjoyed. He actually wrote that he feared dismissal of his novel due to misclassification as sensation fiction, deemed a work that depended on jarring reader's emotions, rather than challenging their intellect. However, later critics agree that it should be so labeled, and that such labeling does not detract from his skillful tension building. He did so using psychological terror, an approach later readers appreciated, avoiding graphic violence, dismemberment, and the overt sex scenes often used to titillate readers. The novel remains readily available in both print and electronic forms and was adapted to film in 1947.

BIBLIOGRAPHY

Peterson, Audrey. *Victorian Masters of Mystery: From Wilkie Collins to Conan Doyle.* New York: F. Ungar Publication, 1984.

Sage, Victor. *Le Fanu's Gothic: The Rhetoric of Darkness.* New York : Palgrave Macmillan, 2004.

Sullivan, Jack. *Elegant Nightmares: The English Ghost Story from Le Fanu to Blackwood.* Athens: Ohio University Press, 1978.

UNDER DRAKE'S FLAG: A TALE OF THE SPANISH MAIN G. A. HENTY (1883)

G. A. HENTY's works today remain useful as examples of 19th-century CHILDREN'S LITERATURE for boys of a chauvinistic bent. Overbearingly patriotic, the novels prove bombastic to modern readers. However, in Henty's day, novels such as *Under Drake's Flag* captured the imagination of their young readers. It features feats by Sir Francis Drake in 16th-century England, opening with his organization while still a captain of an expedition composed of volunteers from Devon County, as it was "ahead of all England in its enterprise and its seamanship." The promise of treasure and adventure draws young men into a typical QUEST, where their courage will be tried at a time when peace was upheld with Spain in English waters but not on the Spanish main of the West Indies. The storm that rises in the first pages symbolizes and foreshadows the conflict the men will face, including one Ned Hearne, nicknamed "the Otter," who convinces his reluctant schoolmaster father to allow him to join Drake's group.

Readers learn that the sailors look "upon their mission as a crusade. In those days England had a horror of Popery, and Spain was the mainstay and supporter of this religion." The sailors regard Spaniards as enemies of their country, church and humanity. Ned will rescue a young woman, the daughter of a wealthy Spaniard at Nombre de Dios, from drowning as his first "plunder." True to the ROMANCE tradition, all the adventurers treat her with respect until she can be returned to her father. The captain's brother, John Drake, is killed in battle, as are many of the crew, and the ship eventually wrecks, casting Ned and a young crewmate named Gerald into the sea. When they swim to shore, they meet up through the coincidence so common to romance with the same young woman, Donna Anna, Ned had previously rescued. She aids the young travelers in gratitude for Ned's having saved her life.

The plot continues in a predictable manner, with Ned making new friends as he travels to America, eventually returning home victorious to reunite with Drake. Drake is knighted by the queen, becoming Sir Francis Drake, while Queen Elizabeth herself receives Ned and his companions. The book concludes with the defeat of the Spanish Armada and the aging of Ned, now Sir Edward Hearne and married to Gerald's sister, and his companions. They regularly gather with their children and grandchildren to celebrate their past victories and tell their tales of conquest.

UNDER THE GREENWOOD TREE, OR THE MELLSTOCK QUIRE; A RURAL PAINTING OF THE DUTCH SCHOOL

THOMAS HARDY (1872)   Thomas HARDY at last attracted public notice as a novelist with his tale of pastoral simplicity, *Under the Greenwood Tree, or the Mellstock Quire*. It was his third novel. He had destroyed the first and written a second, *Desperate Memories* (1871), a mystery of which he was later embarrassed, at the suggestion of George MEREDITH. Working as a reader for Chapman & Hall, Meredith told Hardy his first manuscript, "The Poor Man and the Lady," would not succeed, and told him to write a novel with "a purely aesthetic purpose" with a more complex plot. In *Under the Greenwood Tree,* Hardy produced a love story, but also focused on loss of ritual and dreams. Some felt the title had come from a Shakespeare song included in his play, *As You Like It,* but Hardy took the line from a ballad of the same title. The ballad features couples at play under a greenwood tree and was designed to be

accompanied by choir pipe. While never considered one of Hardy's great works, it remains important for advancing his career as a novelist.

Dick Dewey's name calls to mind a damp pasture in spring, or the tears sentimentality calls to one's eyes. He is described as having "an ordinary-shaped nose, an ordinary chin, an ordinary neck, and ordinary shoulders," emphasizing his lack of any special attribute to recommend him. Even his occupation as a tranter, a man who takes on additional work using his horse and cart, does not distinguish him. He loves the fickle Fancy Day, whose symbolic name leads readers to understand her attraction for the opposite sex. She is described at her first appearance in a line with the local ladies as "a flower among vegetables." Fancy's charm touches several men, as she begins her teaching job at the parish school. But strong foreshadowing alerts readers that she and Dick will end up together, as they are paired in a dance, moving down a row of other dancers, "like two persons tripping down a lane to be married."

Another plot aspect involves Fancy's plan to become organist at Mellstock and the modernization of the church with the introduction of a cabinet-organ to replace the traditional traveling bands of musicians. Biographers point to Hardy's love and appreciation for church music, gained partially through his father's memories of choirs and orchestras, which performed in local churches. They had practiced in the Hardys' home, served refreshments, and in turn provided welcome fellowship. That tradition ended when Hardy was still an infant, and his narrative captures his father's longing for those times. An early discussion between members of one such group includes the remark "People don't care much about us now! I've been thinking we must be almost the last left in the county of the old string players? [sic]."

Fancy does love Dick, but is courted also by Farmer Shiner and Parson Maybold. Although she agrees to marry the parson, she later changes her mind and avoids her own personal tragedy by ending their engagement, leaving her free to marry Dick. The parson, a good man, is left with a broken heart and a new order, through the new music, inhabits the church. Both conditions add a tone of longing and regret to the novel, although Hardy's brilliant presentation of Wessex as the setting makes the tone appropriate. He would later return to that setting for many of his tragic novels. As for structure, the plot is completed over a full turn of all four seasons beginning with winter, then spring, summer, and fall, symbolic of death, birth, youthful exuberance, and a decrease of life forces. The fact that Fancy misrepresents her agreement with Maybold to Dick, although the parson suggested "Tell him everything; it is best. He will forgive you," also takes away from the traditional happy ending. Fancy's duplicity suggest possible future problems for the simple tranter.

Later readers complained about Hardy's treatment of the peasants in *Under the Greenwood Tree*. His characterizations verge on stereotypes, rendering Dick and others low bred with little irony. This later bothered Hardy, and biographers feel his own maturation as member of a lower social level contributed to his discomfort. As Geoffrey Grigson reports, in later preparation for publication of FAR FROM THE MADDING CROWD (1874), Hardy wrote to Leslie Stephen, editor of *The CORNHILL MAGAZINE,* where the novel was first serialized, that "he hoped 'that the rustics, although quaint, may be made to appear intelligent, and not boorish at all.'"

UTOPIAN FICTION   Utopian fiction presents an ideal world, fully imagined by the author as a type of paradise. Such literature has a long tradition, with early representatives including the most honored of the genre, the Greek Plato's *Republic* (third century); the Italian Dante Aligheri's epic poem *Paradiso,* one of three parts of his 14,233 line *Divina Commedia* (1320), an example of a biblically based perfect world; Englishman Thomas More's political perfection *Utopia* (1516); and Englishman John Milton's epic religious poem *Paradise Lost* (1667). Such mythic worlds inhabited the first spoken fiction, the earliest scriptures, folk and fairy tales, ROMANCE FICTION, and various ALLEGORIES, both religious

and secular, and contain aspects of the subgenres FANTASY and SCIENCE FICTION. As a balance, dystopian fiction also arose, mainly in reaction to the World Wars and technological advancements, in which a world presumed by some to be perfect contains other individuals who suffer at the hands of the ideal technology or government. Twentieth-century examples of dystopia include George Orwell's *Animal Farm* (1945) and *1984* (1949), Aldous Huxley's *Brave New World* (1932), Ayn Rand's *Anthem* (1937), Ray Bradbury's *Fahrenheit 451* (1953), William Golding's *Lord of the Flies* (1954), and Margaret Atwood's *The Handmaid's Tale* (1986). These works built on a tradition of 18th- and 19th-century British middle-road novels, in which aspects of dystopia, based more on an anti-political than anti-technological message, appear. Those novels present a seemingly perfect world visited by human outsiders who discover its weaknesses and often seek escape. Examples include Samuel JOHNSON's RASSELAS, PRINCE OF ABISSINIA (1759), a poem/novel in which a young Oriental prince leaves his perfect aristocratic world to discover human suffering outside the palace walls; Edward BULWER-LYTTON's *The COMING RACE OR THE NEW UTOPIA* (1871), a satiric look at a subterranean culture in which humanlike beings have wings and gain super power from a force labeled *vril;* as well as Samuel BUTLER's satire of More's *Utopia,* EREWHON (1872), in which the title spelled backward equates roughly to the term "nowhere"; and H. G. WELLS's *The TIME MACHINE* (1895), a novella of social allegory focusing on the dehumanization of the human race. Within the island-perfection fantasy that inspired Golding's reactionary *Lord of the Flies* is Daniel DEFOE's ROBINSON CRUSOE (1719), which stresses the important them of man's relation to God and nature. Robert Louis STEVENSON's collection of poetry, *A Child's Garden of Verses* (1885), offers readers an escape from reality into the fantasy of the gentle garden world, retreating even into dreams in one selection from that collection, "The Land of Nod."

V

VANITY FAIR: A NOVEL WITHOUT A HERO WILLIAM MAKEPEACE THACKERAY
(1848) William Makepeace THACKERAY first published his novel *Vanity Fair* as a serial between January 1847 and July 1848. He subtitled the book "A Novel without a Hero," signaling a new type of novel. Having suffered bitterly himself due to what he considered societal constraints, he constructed a SATIRE to blast those groups he had felt wronged him. He introduces the reader to a carnival filled with individuals deserving of scorn before launching into a plot that incorporates one of the most independent, and unlikable, women in fiction, Becky Sharp, whose surname is entirely appropriate. As he countered the traditional biographical narrative established by Daniel DEFOE, Thackeray featured details from lives of several characters, all meant to represent various recognizably personality types. While not an ALLEGORY, *Vanity Fair* suggests one, beginning with its title derived from John Bunyan's famous allegory, *The PILGRIM'S PROGRESS* (1678 and 1684). Some characters also represented recognizable real figures, such as Lord Hertford (Lord Steyne) or members of Thackeray's own family, including his own grandmother (Miss Sedley) his wife, Isabella Thackeray, and Amelia Sedley, while Captain Dobbin may have represented Thackeray himself.

Thackeray's book caused much excitement, drawing criticism for various reasons. His cynical tone dismayed many; others complained that his most intelligent characters also proved duplicitous and untrustworthy, sometimes even vicious, while those characters with virtue proved dull, stupid, and unequal to the task. Yet another group charged Thackeray was a sentimentalist who spent too much effort in attempts to reveal something important about common people. While he suggested all sorts of vice, he seemed deliberately, and unrealistically, to avoid sex, and when it was present, the narrative voice, ostensibly another character in the story but identifiably that of Thackeray, intervened to intrude into and fracture the action.

The orphaned but incredibly ambitious lowly born Becky Sharp moves in with her school friend, Amelia Sedley, established as Becky's foil. Where Becky is ever mindful of her own needs, Amelia is sickeningly self-sacrificing. Where Becky proves a con artist of extraordinary skill and resources, Amelia functions totally without guile but not in an admirable way. When Becky fails at trapping Amelia's brother, the overweight Jos Sedley, into marriage, she departs to serve as governess in Hampshire to the Crawleys. There she sets her sights on the elderly and gullible Sir Pitt Crawley's son Rawdon. The smitten Pitt wastes no time following his wife's death to propose to Becky and becomes incensed to learn that she is already secretly married to his son. That news also greatly offends Rawdon's wealthy aunt, a source of funds on which the couple had depended, and they must depart the comfortable lifestyle to live on their own. Meanwhile, the Sedleys fall on hard times as Mr. Sedley loses his fortune when the Napoleonic Wars, which would culminate in Waterloo, threaten England. Amelia faces additional conflict with the disapproving father of her love George Osborne, a silly and vain but handsome young man whose best friend, William Dobbin, convinces him to marry Amelia despite Mr. Osborne's attitude. The three form a sad love triangle, with the penniless disinherited Dobbin in love with Amelia.

Becky and Rawdon have borrowed and schemed in a desperate attempt to support themselves. Rawdon joins the army, as does Dobbin and Osborne, and they are joined in Brussels by Becky and Amelia. Becky flirts with Osborne, who is later killed. Dobbin escorts the grieving and pregnant Amelia back to the Sedley home, where her son Georgy is born. She remains so consumed by her passion for her dead husband and the baby as his extension that she cannot acknowledge Dobbin's love for her. While Georgy receives all the attention one child can stand, the Crawleys have a son who Becky completely ignores, although Rawdon loves him. This characteristic somewhat redeems Rawdon, who, however manipulated by Becky, supports her various schemes and demands. Becky continues to deceive others and gamble away what money the Crawleys have, then forms a questionable alliance with Lord Steyne, who gladly fulfills all her material desires. The naive Rawdon at last finds his wife too revolting to tolerate when he discovers her in the early stages of making love with Lord Steyne. He elects to leave her and moves to India, where he tries unsuccessfully to gain custody of his son.

Becky has finally pushed a society accepting of some degree of scandal too far. Ostracized by all, she must move to the Continent, where she hopes to elude her creditors. There she accidentally meets Amelia, who has, again in contrast to Becky, regained most of her fortune through the return from India of Dobbin and Jos, as well as through the adoption of Georgy by his grandfather Osborne, who overcame his estrangement from Amelia. Dobbin warns Amelia away from the disreputable Becky to no avail, until Amelia learns that her husband had plotted to run away with Becky while the families were in Brussels. Totally disillusioned, Amelia at last can put her worship of George's memory

aside to accept Dobbin's marriage proposal. However, Jos does not escape Becky's tentacles and dies mysteriously while they cohabitate. When Rawdon also dies in India, his son inherits his estate and refuses to ever see his mother again, although he grants her a pension. With her usual resolve and tenacity, Becky adopts a new identity as a grieving widow, devoted to the good of the misfortunate.

One of the great novels of the English language, *Vanity Fair* reflects the influence of various subgenres of fiction, including SILVER-FORK FICTION and the PICARESQUE. Its wide reception by the public was incomparable to that of any other novel of the day. Those who found work by Thackeray's great rival Charles DICKENS vulgar or too sentimental for all but the most common taste appreciated Thackeray's graceful style and its implication of social cultivation. At the same time, middle- and lower-class readers identified with the bawdy Becky Sharp as a poor girl who took advantage of the wealthy, a "have not" who swindles the "haves." The novel has never been out of print and has been converted to various dramatic media.

BIBLIOGRAPHY

Allen, Brooke. "Sadness Balancing Wit: Thackeray's Life & Works." *New Criterion* 19.5 (Jan 2001): 19–28.

Bruce, Donald. "Thackeray the Sentimental Sceptic." *Contemporary Review* (June 1993): 313–321.

Peters, Catharine. *Thackeray's Universe: Shifting Worlds of Imagination and Reality.* New York: Oxford University Press, 1997.

Tillotson, Kathleen. *Novels of the Eighteen-forties.* Oxford: Clarendon Press, 1954.

VICAR OF WAKEFIELD, THE OLIVER GOLDSMITH (1766)

Though written between 1761 and 1762, Oliver GOLDSMITH's single novel, *The Vicar of Wakefield,* was not published until several years following its completion. As the story goes, Goldsmith, a hack writer ever in peril of imprisonment due to debts, pleaded with Samuel JOHNSON to look through his work and choose something publishable. Johnson selected the manuscript from a pile and thrilled Goldsmith by placing it with a publisher in return for £60. The publisher reconsidered and held the novel for a time, due to its lack of resemblance to the day's popular fiction of horror and prejudice. Once distributed, it represented the only quality work between the publication of works by Laurence STERNE and Jane AUSTEN and remained the most widely read novel from the 18th century for more than a century after its publication. It proved shorter than most books and its protagonist, the kindly and stoic Vicar Dr. Primrose, suffered no melodramatic situations, although he did face conflict from many sources. Unlike most fiction of its era, the novel lacked satire, it was neither obscene nor propagandistic, and it offered themes including the value of family and Christian faith. While trials and tribulations existed, they were not exploitive of readers' emotions, and Goldsmith championed no contemporary ideology. That meant the novel would never be time-bound, allowing it to continue enormously popular for decades. Goldsmith warned readers about the vicar in his preface: "Such as mistake ribaldry for humor, will find no wit in his harmless conversation; and such as have been taught to deride religion, will laugh at one whose chief stores of comfort are drawn from futurity."

The aptly named Dr. Primrose narrates the tale concerning himself, his social-climber wife, Deborah, and his six children. His practical personality maintains balance in his family until the bankruptcy of a firm in which he had invested. Nearly destitute, he nevertheless expresses his generosity in aiding a gentleman of questionable character named Mr. Burchell. Burchell suggests that Mrs. Primrose be cautious in making matches for her daughters, advice the good lady rejects. Primrose takes a position through the goodwill of Squire Thornhill, whose surname foreshadows his villainy. He tricks Olivia Primrose into a faked wedding and leaves her to be reclaimed by her father and brought home. When the Primrose house burns down and Thornhill calls for a payoff of the vicar's debts, Primrose must serve time in debtors' prison. His son George challenges Thornhill to a duel but is overpowered by the squire's hired thugs and thrown in prison. Primrose's grief increases when he learns that his daughter Sophia has been kidnapped and Olivia supposedly has died of a broken heart. He manages to suffer nobly, retaining his faith. Luckily, Burchell appears and rescues Sophia, later revealing his true identity as the evil Thornhill's uncle, Sir William Thornhill. He proves that the squire had abducted Sophia, that Olivia's marriage had been legal, and that she still lives. Primrose is released from prison, as is George, who marries his true love. The vicar regains his lost fortune when the swindler Ephraim Jenkinson is brought to justice.

While not without weaknesses, such as some hasty plotting that appears to have missing episodes, *The Vicar of Wakefield* deserved its fame due to its bright characterizations, vivid expression, and its protagonist's fortitude and right nature. The novel appeared at the conclusion of an era of experimentation in fictional form, taking its place as the first "normal" novel of its age. It owed a debt to Samuel RICHARDSON's *PAMELA* (1740) and *CLARISSA* (1747–48), as well as Henry FIELDING's *Amelia* (1751).

BIBLIOGRAPHY

Murray, David Aaron. "From Patrimony to Paternity in *The Vicar of Wakefield*." *Eighteenth-Century Fiction* 9 (April 1997): 327–336.

Rutledge, Archibald. Introduction to *The Vicar of Wakefield* by Oliver Goldsmith. Boston: Gin and Co., 1923.

Sells, A. Lytton. *Oliver Goldsmith: His Life and Works.* New York: Barnes & Nobles Books, 1974.

VICAR OF WREXHILL, THE FRANCES TROLLOPE (1837)

Frances TROLLOPE wrote many novels, but most critics agree *The Vicar of Wrexhill* is her best. Framed in her normally intrusive, authorial DIDACTIC voice, the novel focuses on corruption in the Church of England. Her combined themes of religious and gender conflict would later serve her son Anthony TROLLOPE as well as they had her, although he would learn to abandon the judgmental voice for which his mother was well known. For that reason, his novels generally offered stronger appeal for later generations. *The Vicar of Wrexhill* is also noted for one characteristic of its narrative structure. In the first 200 pages of the three-volume work, 11 epistles appear. While not an EPISTOLARY NOVEL, its feature of this mode, introduced in English work by Samuel RICHARDSON a century before, adds interest for the various voices they represent, both female and male.

Readers are introduced to a family with the symbolic surname of Freeman in the early pages. The narrator's description of the Freeman's alehouse, the Mowbray Arms, leaves little doubt regarding Trollope's staunch belief in the Protestant work ethic: "Industry, neatness, and their fitting accompaniment and reward, comfort, were legible throughout the small domain." Of the "decent peasant-boy" hired to help the Freemans, the narrator remarks, "and happy was the cottager whose son got the appointment, for both in morals and manners the horseboy at the Mowbray Arms might have set an example to his betters." The description of the Mowbray family continues the idyllic tone, with the young Master Mowbray preparing to celebrate his coming of age. However, disaster strikes with the death of Charles Mowbray, Sr., a matter of much grief for his family, which includes, in addition to Charles, Jr., Mrs. Clara Mowbray, Charles's older sister Helen, and their younger sister, 16-year-old Fanny. Their circle also includes the orphan Rosalind Torrington, whose mother had been "high born," but was cut off by a family dismayed over her choice of a husband, an Irish Protestant clergyman. The Mowbrays love Rosalind and treat her as one of their own.

Into the Mowbray's grief appears a dastardly antagonist in the form of William Jacob Cartwright, Vicar of Wrexhill. He begins to insinuate himself into the Mowbray family, proving to be one of the more calculating, loathsome, and cruel men of the cloth in fiction. According to information from George Mason University's Ellen Moody, one reviewer in *The Athenaeum* described the Vicar of Wrexhill as "handsome, silkly spoken, with his black eyes and caressing hands, which make such sad havoc among the bevy of admiring village ladies. He glides on his way, like a serpent— glossy, silent and poisonous—throwing out hints here, innuendos there; blighting with the language of brotherly love, and under the mask of Scriptural sanctity, creeping steadily upwards towards wealth and power. His is a fearful character." Trollope's use of the snake/serpent imagery usually reserved for women results in a neat reversal of tradition and associates Cartwright with temptation of a sexual nature. His first wriggling into the Mowbray space involves his calling on the family following their bereavement, after which Rosalind declares her frank dislike of his too-smooth personality.

Cartwright returns to hear the reading of Mr. Mowbray's will, attended traditionally only by males, and learns along with Charles, Jr., and his friend and supporter, Sir Gilbert Harrington, that Clara Mowbray received all her husband's estate. Charles steps outside to spend a moment with Sir Gilbert, returning to find Rosalind upset and accusatory, scolding him for not presenting the facts of the will to his mother herself. The confused Charles learns that the vicar has superseded him in speaking with his mother, a fact that incenses Rosalind, although she is relieved that Charles had not purposely ignored his mother. Not only has the vicar shared information that was not his to share, he presented it in such a way that Mrs. Mowbray believed her son to be unhappy about the will's provisions, which he is not in the least.

As the lengthy plot develops, other locals enter the fray, including Cartwright's son Jacob and daughter Henrietta; the widowed Mrs. Simpson, who occasionally ignores her eight-year-old daughter, distracted by fashions; the widow Mrs. Richardson, devoted to her husband's memory and left with three daughters to raise; the gentle Mrs. Williams; and the dashing Colonel Harrington, Sir Gilbert's son. Some of the local women will be caught in Cartwright's trap, too naive to realize his advances and attentions are inappropriate.

Eventually Cartwright convinces Mrs. Mowbray to marry him and gains through her wealth even greater power in the community, as he oversees her writing of a will leaving all her possessions to him. He even withholds power from Rosalind to take possession of the inheritance that she receives from her father's repentant family. And the consequences almost prove disastrous to Helen Mowbray, pursued by Cartwright's weasly cousin, Mr. Stephen Corbold—all this while Charles is absent at school. While Helen proves intelligent enough to escape Corbold's advances, and Colonel Harrington literally horsewhips him for his insolence, Cartwright's own daughter cannot be rescued from the loss of faith she experiences due to her father and her subsequent alienation from him. Her deathbed scene allows Trollope to deliver one of the more didactic speeches in the novel, this one on the subject of truth.

When Cartwright turn away from his own daughter's plea for assurance of God's existence, saying, "You have lived a scoffing infidel,—and a scoffing infidel will you die," he reveals his true villainy.

The novel satisfactorily concludes, as it began, with a will, written by Clara Cartwright, who died soon after delivering Cartwright's son, who also died. A codicil drawn up secretly with the help of Sir Gilbert left everything to the Mowbray children, with not one penny left to the dastardly Cartwright. Cartwright Park returns to Mowbray Park, and the vicar disappears. The colonel and Helen marry, as do Charles and Rosalind, and the village "once more became happy and gay, and the memory of their serious epidemic rendered its inhabitants the most orderly, peaceable, and orthodox population in the whole country."

In Trollope's day her novel was widely read, mentioned in a SATIRE by William Makepeace THACKERAY's "Roundabout Papers" titled "On a Lazy Idle Boy," in which he pondered whether novelists read many novels. He theorized that they did not, as too much fiction proves "cloying," and asks whether "the author of the 'Vicar of Wrexhill' laugh[s] over the 'Warden' and the 'The Three Clerks'?" His question proved ironic on two fronts, of course, as neither book mentioned is meant to be humorous and both were written by Trollope's son Anthony.

BIBLIOGRAPHY

Moody, Ellen. Personal Web site. Available online. URL: http://www.jimandellen.org/trollope/warden.show.html. Downloaded July 17, 2004.

Thackeray, William Makepeace. "Roundabout Papers." Project Gutenberg Etext. Available online. URL: http://www.gutenberg.net/. Downloaded July 19, 2004.

VILLETTE CHARLOTTE BRONTË (1853)

Charlotte BRONTË called on her own experience in writing her third novel, *Villette*. Like her other novels, this one contains various autobiographical aspects. Brontë had taught for a time in Brussels at the school of Monsieur and Madame Heger. She transforms Brussels into Villette, offering one of the most accurate and detailed portrayals of Belgian life in print. While she had published JANE EYRE (1847) and SHIRLEY (1849) successfully, another novel, titled *The PROFESSOR*, had been rejected, although it would be published posthumously, and she based much of *Villette* on that manuscript.

The first-person narrator, Lucy Snowe, begins the novel in relative luxury, spending six months with her godmother, Mrs. Bretton, her son Graham Bretton, later called John, and a young boarder, Pauline (Polly) Home, whose father has temporarily left her in Mrs. Bretton's care as he travels to America. When he later sends for Polly to join him, Lucy returns home following a six-month absence. She falls on hard times there and loses contact with the Brettons, who she learns had some ill fortune of their own. Lucy represents many young women of Brontë's era who, having been born to comfort, eventually found themselves in need of employment. Few opportunities for self-support existed for women, one of which was serving older women as companions, and Lucy chooses this route, going into the employ of the wealthy invalid Miss Marchmont. Lucy describes her world as "two hot, close rooms" and "a crippled old woman, my mistress, my friend, my all. Her service was my duty." Thinking she might waste her life in this way for 20 years, she hears a howling wind one evening reminiscent of a banshee and recalls she has heard that wind prior to every great tragic change in her life. In a bittersweet death scene, Miss Marchmont reveals something of her love for her dead husband to Lucy and then leaves Lucy alone once again. Before relocating to London, Lucy overhears a friend from her past mention that many young women live abroad, and she stores away that information.

From London, Lucy travels by boat to Villette in the kingdom of Labassecour, meeting a passenger named Ginevra Fanshawe. Beautiful and egotistical, Ginevra is a student at a girls' school in Villette operated by the headmistress Madame Beck. With Ginevra's reluctant support, Lucy eventually wins Madame Beck's favor, serving her children as a governess and later becoming a teacher in the school. There she meets again the son of her godmother, who she had known years before, Dr. John Bretton, as well as Paulina Home, who has returned from America. While Lucy develops feelings for John, he develops a crush on Ginevra. Keeping secret her own emotions, she can only hope he eventually realizes Ginevra's shortcomings. While John does reject Ginevra due to her vanity, he falls in love with his childhood friend Paulina.

Lucy once again faces isolation but slowly comes to appreciate a professor, Paul Emmanuel, whose fussy critical personality had at first dismayed her. He is a cousin to Madame Beck, who does her best to prevent any relationship from developing, feeling Lucy beneath Paul's social status. Once again Brontë emphasizes society's misuse of vulnerable young women. Love triumphs, however, although Paul must depart at the novel's conclusion for the West Indies, promising to return in three years and marry Lucy. Readers wonder whether the marriage ever occurs, as Brontë concludes her plot three years later with Paul's return imminent.

However, when Lucy again hears the keening of the wind, that seems to foreshadow disaster, particularly when she describes the aftermath of the seven-day storm: "the Atlantic was strewn with wrecks."

While not widely read, *Villette* is studied in academic programs as an excellent example of Charlotte Brontë's superb sense of place and atmosphere.

BIBLIOGRAPHY

Lloyd Evans, Barbara, and Gareth Lloyd Evans. *The Scribner Companion to the Brontës.* New York: Charles Scribner's Sons, 1982.

Winnifrith, Tom, and Edward Chitham. *Charlotte and Emily Brontë: Literary Lives.* Houndmills, Basingstoke, Hampshire, U.K.: Macmillan, 1989.

W

WARD, MARY AUGUSTA (1851–1920)
Mary Arnold was born in Hobart, Tasmania, to Thomas Arnold, brother of the famous philosopher Matthew Arnold. Arnold worked as a school inspector, but resigned when he converted to Catholicism in 1856. The family returned to England, where, two years later in 1858, Mary began attending private school. Her father worked in Dublin and Birmingham in Catholic education, and Mary did not rejoin her family until 1867. Her father reconverted to Anglicanism and began a teaching post at Oxford. In 1872, Mary married Thomas Humphry Ward, an Oxford don who would later serve as art critic for the *Times.* Thomas Arnold's next reconversion, back to Catholicism, occurred in 1876, and the family again relocated, but Mary remained with her husband in Oxford.

Obviously affected by her father's continued spiritual journey, she developed her own academic and spiritual interests in such illustrious company as that of J. R. Green, Walter Pater, and Benjamin Jowett, who encouraged her study and writing. Pater's work in aestheticism and Jowett's in challenging the authority of the Bible informed her future writing. Adopting the publication name of Mrs. Humphry Ward, she first published in the *Dictionary of Christian Biography* on the early Spanish ecclesiastics, then took the first secretary of Somerville College post in 1879. Her next work as a pamphleteer and novelist focused on man's need for freedom to reject the theory that the Bible represented historical truth. Her unorthodox approach to spirituality resembled that of Matthew Arnold in supporting the application of Christianity to practical humanitarian work, rather than scholarly biblical study. Her novel ROBERT ELSMERE (1888) reflects such ideas in its study of the spiritual development of a young man whose intellectual and emotional growth mirrored her own. Her hero is influenced by a skepticism that causes him as a young clergyman to reject the Church's Thirty-nine Articles of faith. While Elsmere attempts to establish a new brotherhood in London's slums, his wife supports him even as she clings to her Anglican faith. The novel created a flurry of criticism and debate regarding the future of the Anglican Church. The 1911 sequel, titled *The Case of Richard Meynell,* proved a disappointment but sparked a SATIRE by her nephew, famous novelist Aldous Huxley, of her jingoistic tone in his own work *The Farcical History of Richard Greenow* (1920).

In 1881 she and her husband relocated to London, where she worked reviewing and editing the writing of others while continuing a career that resulted in 25 novels. Taking a deep interest in the Passmore Edwards Settlement in Bloomsbury in 1897, she oversaw children's recreational programs and instituted education for the handicapped. Contradicting her interest in individual freedom and her campaigning for her son's political career, she did not support suffrage. She disapproved so strongly of the idea of women voting that she became President of the Women's Anti-Suffrage League in 1908. Paradoxically she came to represent what some considered to be the worst of the negative stereotypes regarding Victorian conservatism. The quality of her writing suffered when she published a series of popular works with society themes to help alleviate her debts, including *Daphne* (1909), about divorce, and *Delia Blanchflower* (1913), focusing on the suffrage movement.

Ward regained her reputation when American president Theodore Roosevelt requested that she write a series of articles and letters about the Allied war effort, later published under the titles *England's Effort* (1916), *Towards the Goal* (1917), and *Field of Victory* (1919). In 1920 she enjoyed an appointment as one of the first seven female magistrates, dying a short time later. Additional notable works included *A Writer's Recollections* (1918), in which she described her interactions with famous figures including George ELIOT and Henry JAMES, as well as details regarding Oxford's intellectual scene during the early years of her marriage. She translated the *Journal Intime* of Swiss mystic Henri Amiel (1885), regarded as the seminal work in that area for decades.

BIBLIOGRAPHY

Jones, Enid Huws. *Mrs. Humphry Ward*. London: Heinemann, 1973.

Sage, Lorna. "Ward, [née Arnold], Mrs. Humphry (Mary)." *The Cambridge Guide to Women's Writing in English.* Cambridge: Cambridge University Press, 1999, 651.

Smith, Esther Marian Greenwell. *Mrs. Humphry Ward*. Boston: Twayne Publishers, 1980.

Sutherland, John. *Mrs. Humphry Ward: Eminent Victorian, Pre-eminent Edwardian.* New York: Oxford University Press, 1990.

WARDEN, THE ANTHONY TROLLOPE (1855)

Anthony TROLLOPE's first installment in his Barsetshire sequence, *The Warden*, is a quiet novel. Its story of the Reverend Septimus Harding and his struggle with conscience is masterfully presented, without need for grandiose action. When Harding's income as warden of Hiram's Hospital, which cares for 12 elderly men through a medieval charity fund, comes under scrutiny, more is involved than the funds themselves. Trollope convinces readers that Harding had simply never considered the disparity between his own weekly income, furnished by the Bishop of Barchester, and the paltry sum received by the inhabitants of the almshouse hospital. The conflict occurs over who made public that discrepancy. The reformer is the symbolically named John Bold, a writer for the *Jupiter* newspaper who denounces the issue as an instance of abuse by the church. Because Bold loves Mr. Harding's youngest daughter, Eleanor, the tension caused by his investigation and accusation of abuse makes life uncomfortable for all involved. While Eleanor convinces Bold to halt his investigation, other reformers pick up the battle and take on the conservative clerical party and its head, Archdeacon Grantly, who happens to be Mr. Harding's son-in-law. Harding eventually resigns and moves to Barchester, and Eleanor marries Bold.

In addition to its skillful rendering, *The Warden* is interesting for several reasons. It represents Trollope's first entry in a series allowing him to explore his interest in cathedral towns like Winchester, where he lived as a boy. It also reflects his belief system, particularly regarding the type of writing he wanted to do and the themes he hoped to consider. This is obvious in his characterizations of philosopher Thomas Carlyle as Dr. Pessimist Anticant, and of fellow novelist Charles DICKENS as Mr. Popular Sentiment. Trollope saw both as reformers who privileged moral imperialism in the cause of an abstract justice over specific individual honor and conscience, something he could not abide. He also had a rather low opinion of reporters such as Bold, seeking sensationalism at the cost of another's reputation, and intended the *Jupiter* to represent *The Times,* whose investigation of scandals provided source material.

Articles about inflated incomes granted to church officials bothered Trollope, but his autobiography revealed he was just as bothered by the use of innocent men as scapegoats, as they were hardly "the chief sinners in the matter." One such scandal, that of St. Cross, revealed a misappropriation of church funds leading to the demotion of its master, Francis North, later the earl of Guilford, who had been appointed by his father, the bishop of Winchester. The nepotism in that case made a defense of the recipient difficult, but no such nepotism existed with Mr. Harding. Trollope obviously admires a man with a conscience, clearly demonstrated in the scene in which Harding testifies before Sir Abraham and states he has joined others in beginning to question the justice of his income and announces he will resign his post, following which Sir Abraham asks him to sleep on that decision. Harding replies, "I have done more than sleep on it . . . I have laid awake upon it, and that night after night. I found I could not sleep upon it; now I hope to do so."

Like most of Trollope's work, the novel is available as electronic text.

BIBLIOGRAPHY

Gilmour, Robin. Introduction to *The Warden* by Anthony Trollope. London: Penguin Classics, 1987, vii–xxvi.

Kincaid, James. *The Novels of Anthony Trollope.* Oxford: Clarendon Press, 1977.

Smalley, ed. *Trollope: The Critical Heritage.* London: Routledge & Kegan Paul, 1969.

Trollope, Anthony. *Anthony Trollope: An Autobiography.* 1883. Oxford: Oxford Paperbacks, 1999.

WAR OF THE WORLDS H. G. WELLS (1898)

H. G. WELLS's SCIENCE FICTION masterpiece, *The War of the Worlds,* first appeared in *Pearson's Magazine* in 1897 as a serial. The prototype for later alien-invasion fiction, it details an attack on London by aliens from Mars in its first section. Humans cannot defend themselves, suggesting that the Martians are superior beings with greater technological knowledge, allowing them to develop armor and weapons with crushing power. In the second part of the novel, the humans who survive have moved underground, where they have two leaders, one a member of the clergy and the other a military expert. Wells suggests the dichotomy of faith versus scientific knowledge in its technical manifestation. Unable to develop a true plan to defend themselves, the people must listen to the one-time military leader engage in fantasy about defeating the Martians with new and fearsome weapons. However, defeat comes from nature when bacteria invade the Martians, destroying them, whereby Wells introduces a nicely ironic statement regarding the value of the natural over man's contrivances. Critics praise Wells's use of detail and comment on his mixed tone, at once somewhat gleeful regarding society's destruction but also wise in considering the extent of the catastrophe. The tale became famous worldwide when a Howard Koch adaptation for radio, broadcast from New York City on October 30, 1938, by actor Orson Welles, convinced listeners that an invasion was really taking place, causing panic in some areas of the United States.

BIBLIOGRAPHY

Connes, G. A. *A Dictionary of the Characters and Scenes in the Novels, Romances, and Short Stories of H. G. Wells.* Folcroft, Pa.: Folcroft Press, 1969.

Gill, Stephen M. *Scientific Romances of H. G. Wells: A Critical Study.* Cornwall, Ontario: Vesta Publications, 1975.

Holmsten, Brian, and Alex Lubertozzi, eds. *The Complete War of the Worlds: Mars' Invasion of Earth from H. G. Wells to Orson Welles.* Naperville, Il.: Sourcebooks, 2001.

WASHER OF THE FORD, THE, and SIN EATER AND OTHER TALES, THE FIONA MACLEOD (WILLIAM SHARP) (1895)

William SHARP wrote several books adopting the persona of Fiona Macleod. While more collections of loosely linked tales than novels, two worth considering include *The Washer of the Ford* and *The Sin Eater and Other Tales,* both published in 1895. They strongly represent stories of place, where setting becomes a work's crucial element. Macleod dedicates *The Sin Eater and Other Tales* to George MEREDITH, noting, "because he is Prince of Celtdom." He goes on to explain in a lengthy introductory letter to Meredith "from Iona," name of the community around which the tales congregate, the importance of retaining Celtic traditions, his ROMANCE collection being a prime example of such attempts. He notes that the "Cornishman has lost his language," leaving no link between himself and his predecessors; "the Manxman has ever been the mere yeoman of the Celtic chivalry," and his "rude dialect" is fading; the Welsh preserve their traditions, while in Ireland, "a supreme tradition fades through sunset-hued horizons to the edge o' dark"; and in Celtic Scotland, "a despairing love and longing narrows yearly before a bastard utilitarianism," which he blames partly on an invasion of the "curse" of Calvinism.

What follows are a series of folktales presenting a mix of religion and superstition. Readers understand that as romances, the stories will contain various references to mysticism and also journeys and change, both physical and emotional. For example, in the title story, "The Sin Eater," locals believe that the living can ingest the sins of the dead, in order that the deceased may seek some comfort in the afterlife. When Adam Blair dies, his son convinces a tramp named Neil Ross to participate for money in the ceremony that will allow him to take on Blair's sins. Later, Ross learns that Blair showed signs of life while being carried to his grave, but the local wise woman and "deid watcher," Maisie Macdonald, poured salt into his eyes and made sure the coffin tipped enough to severely rattle the body. Ross begins to feel he had actually become the "Scapegoat" that others label him and eventually believes he has become Judas, lashing himself to a cross and allowing the sea to carry him out. The overriding imagery for all the tales is that of the sea, and Macleod sprinkles throughout a good deal of the local dialect, which he translates for readers.

The Washer of the Ford continues the approach of *The Sin Eater,* with an even more pronounced emphasis on religion in tales listed in its table of contents under the heading "Legendary Moralities" with titles such as "The Fisher of Men," and "The Last Supper." In the title story, a harpist named Torcall Dall has been struck blind as he awaits death. When his sight returns the narrative relates a mystical moment, one of many that might interest FEMINIST CRITICS, as it features a powerful female figure: "at the ford he saw a woman stooping and washing shroud after shroud of woven moonbeams; washing them there in the flowing water." The moon as a symbol of woman and water as a symbol of baptism/new life are two of multiple references allowing FORMALIST critics access to the text's meaning.

The works are little read, due to a heavy-handed sentimentality and simplistic consideration of death. They do include some provocative imagery, including "the breath of the Death-Weaver at the Pole," and

death's description in metaphors: "it is more than a reed, it is more than a wild doe on the hills, it is more than a swallow lifting her wing against the coming of the shadow, it is more than a swan drunken with the savour of the blue wine of the waves." However, little is original, and the stories remain most appealing to scholars of Macleod/Sharp.

WASHINGTON SQUARE HENRY JAMES (1881)

One of Henry JAMES's shorter novels, *Washington Square* ran first as a serial in *The CORNHILL MAGAZINE* in 1880. James considers his trademark-displaced protagonist in the form of Catherine Sloper, daughter of a wealthy New York physician. While the New York setting is well drawn and adds interest, the story of an individual made to feel an outsider by her own family could occur anywhere. With no mother to look after her social needs, and only an old-world aunt available for guidance, the plain Catherine matures lonely and isolated from others, allowing James to emphasize a favorite belief in the vital importance of shared experience. Lack of such sharing proves harmful to the emotional and spiritual well-being of all individuals. Catherine's models fail her; her widowed Aunt Penniman mourns a dead husband, while Dr. Sloper mourns a dead wife. Their narrow-minded sorrow causes them to regard Catherine with near-contempt. As she leaves for a ball in one scene dressed in a decidedly unattractive red dress, her father inanely compliments the dress, paying no heed to Catherine herself. In a painful irony, he never actually sees his own daughter as a real person. Had he done so, he would have recognized how completely out of place Catherine would be at the society event.

At last romance appears in the form of poverty-stricken Morris Townsend, whose invitation to marry thrills Catherine. Although she accepts and anticipates escaping her father's inattention with a new husband, Dr. Sloper suddenly becomes active in her life to forbid her marriage, recognizing Townsend as an opportunist. Dr. Sloper's views appear outdated to Catherine, who is desperate for the comfort of human interaction. She assumes a more realistic stance, believing the fact that she will bring the money to the marriage unimportant. Complicating matters is Mrs. Penniman's strange and inappropriate attraction to Townsend. Catherine does not mind that her betrothed is a fortune hunter and remains devoted to their relationship during the year in Europe that her father enforces upon her. However, when Townsend understands Sloper will disinherit Catherine should she marry him, he ends their engagement.

While James's protagonists generally find themselves navigating a foreign path as Americans abroad, Catherine feels a foreigner in her native surroundings. James makes the point that isolation and rejection is no easier to bear when guised in the misplaced concern Sloper feels can, not toward Catherine as a human, but rather toward his own pride. He could not bear the idea of his daughter having so little pride as to marry beneath her social level, humiliating him. James thus emphasizes his traditional conflict of individuality versus social expectations, but he reserves a triumph for Catherine in the plot's conclusion. According to James's journals, a near-identical incident to that featured in his novel occurred in England, which he followed with great curiosity. He depended purely on his imagination to calculate what might happen to those involved many years into the future as he concludes his novel.

Almost 20 years later, following Dr. Sloper's death, Morris contacts Catherine, hopeful of renewing their relationship. At that point, having accepted her life as a spinster, Catherine exercises her independence from men at long last by rejecting his renewed attentions. Although she had to wait many years to gain comfort from her identity separate from others, she does at least achieve a balance and grace with conditions not of her own design. Surrounded by the monumental egos of her father, aunt, and Morris, and without much sense of self-identity, even the unintelligent Catherine can act out of a basic sense of self-preservation.

The novel remains popular as a well-written piece, although James had not yet fully discovered his original voice. He seems to adopt American writer Nathaniel Hawthorne's figure of pride in Dr. Sloper, while Mrs. Penniman resembles some of Charles DICKENS's sadly humorous characters. *Washington Square* has remained constantly in print and been converted to various media versions.

BIBLIOGRAPHY

Bell, Milicent. *Meaning in Henry James*. Cambridge: Harvard University Press, 1991.

Dupee, F. W. *Henry James*. New York: William Morrow & Company, 1974.

WATER BABIES, THE: A FAIRY TALE FOR A LAND BABY CHARLES KINGSLEY (1863)

Charles KINGSLEY had already contributed to CHILDREN'S LITERATURE when he published his FANTASY *The Water-Babies: A Fairy Tale for a Land Baby,* first read as a serial in MACMILLAN'S MAGAZINE between 1862 and 1863. His juvenile novel *The Heroes* had been written for his older children, while his youngest child is the land baby mentioned in the title of *The Water Babies.* Published two years prior to Lewis CARROLL'S ALICE'S ADVENTURES IN WONDERLAND, the book was not free from moralizing, as would be Carroll's popular works. It remained in the tradition of instructional literature for young readers and was actually aimed at the adult audience that would read it aloud for children. Its content suggested SATIRE and contained symbolism that escaped young readers but appeared obvious to adults. Its protagonist is a victimized working-class child named Tom who must elude an abusive employer. Tom's brutal occupation of chimney sweep had been made infamous in the poetry of William Blake. Social movements had decried practices such as forcing naked children to fit into the tight chimneys where they contracted often-fatal lung diseases. Mostly orphans, many died from starvation, overexposure to the elements and various infections that easily ravaged bodies without natural defenses.

Tom lives and toils in "the North country," where he suffers constant hunger, filth, and beatings, does not read, write, or bathe, but occasionally plays with his mates and fantasizes about a successful future. During a visit to work at Harthover Hall, he enters the room of a sleeping "little white lady," where he sees reflected in a mirror "a little ugly, black, ragged figure, with bleared eyes and grinning white teeth." Incensed that such a "monkey" would enter the room of such a perfect girl, he realizes with dismay it is his own reflection. When the girl awakes and screams, he is chased away to the edge of a river.

Tom falls into the water, enjoying a symbolic rebirth, water traditionally suggesting baptism and the birth waters of the womb. There he undergoes transformation and a literal rebirth as a water baby in a FANTASY world free of care. The freedom is both spiritual and emotional, as he undergoes internal and external "cleansing," his tired limbs freed of all literal and figurative weight by the water. Tom "had been sadly overworked in the land-world; and so now, to make up for that, he had nothing but holidays in the water-world for a long, long time to come." He joins a large group of "water-babies in the thousands," all rescued from abusive situations. Tom indulges his boyish propensity to tease and bother, learning he will receive his just reward for such actions by "Mrs. Bedonebyasyoudid," among others. When he regains land, the lessons he has learned serve him well. He finds friendship and a career as "a great man of science" before Kinglsey appends a section titled "Moral," explaining to his readers what they should learn from his "parable." The story remains popular and has appeared in various media forms.

BIBLIOGRAPHY

Hartley, Alan J. *The Novels of Charles Kingsley: A Christian Social Interpretation.* Folkestone, England: Hour-Glass Press, 1977.

Hunt, Peter, ed. *The International Companion Encyclopedia of Children's Literature.* New York: Routledge, 1996.

WAVERLEY, OR 'TIS SIXTY YEARS SINCE   SIR WALTER SCOTT (1814)

Sir Walter SCOTT wrote his first novel, *Waverley,* over several years, having completed a romance begun by Joseph Strutt in 1808. He rediscovered the manuscript two years later and shared its seven chapters with his publisher, who discouraged him from altering the course Scott had set for himself as a poet. Labeled the best poet of his era after the publishing of *The Lady of the Lake,* by 1813 he nevertheless needed a new source of income and again turned back to the novel. Although the thought of moving from poetry to fiction seemed humiliating, as prose was seen as a lower calling, Scott decided to finally publish *Waverley* anonymously. His novel resembled no others of the time. He employed what would become his trademark interest in the past to produce HISTORICAL FICTION, focusing on the 1745 Jacobite uprising. Scott avoided GOTHIC excesses, using his natural sense of humor to enrich his narrative in lieu of gruesome detail. *Waverley* proved so popular that four editions sold in its first 12 months in print.

The novel's protagonist, Edward Waverley, is devoted to his uncle, the Jacobite sympathizer Sir Edward Digby. Edward joins the army, becoming active in a Scottish regiment. In Scotland he visits with his uncle's friend Bradwardine, also a Jacobite. Equally important, he is drawn to Rose Bradwardine, a simple Lowland girl. These various plot elements allowed Scott to indulge his affinity for ROMANCE, while also including much realistic detail. Not only did the Jacobites hope to place the Stuarts back on the throne, the rebellion that forms the novel's setting represented Scotland's last attempt to gain equality with England. It also framed a struggle between the Scottish Highland clans, which represented the old feudal ways, and the inhabitants of the modern Lowland regions. Although not a Catholic himself and strongly supportive of the House of Hanover, Scott saw the dramatic and sentimental appeal in a story of a lost cause.

Eager for adventure, Edward Waverley travels to the Highlands to find Donald Bean Lean and meets two additional devoted Jacobite supporters, Fergus Mac-Ivor and his sister, the lovely and sophisticated Flora. While not precisely a foil for Rose, Flora's attitude helps reflect the difference between the Highland and Lowland groups. Edward learns the danger of guilt by association and is accused by his colonel of plotting a mutiny; only Rose is able to keep him from going to prison. By this time convinced to adopt the Jacobite cause, Edward meets the Pretender to the throne. Edward's transition allows Scott to emphasize the sincerity felt by members of both sides of the conflict. By viewing the struggle through the lives of specific individuals, he helps readers identify with humans supporting a cause they feel will result in a better way of life. Some readers found themselves sympathizing along with Edward with the Catholic Jacobite view, coming to better understand the Scots. Edward fights in the Battle of Prestonpans, where the Jacobites are dispersed. His heroism in rescuing Colonel Talbot secures his pardon. Fergus does not fare so well, is convicted, and eventually executed, driving Flora into a convent. Although Edward had loved Flora, her refusal of his marriage proposal helps him realize that she could not be happy without her cause. He eventually regains his feelings for Rose and marries her.

Thanks to Scott's attention to historical detail, the novel appealed to intellectual readers as well as to the more common reader who loved an adventure tale. It remains a popular novel, readily available in print and electronic text.

WAY WE LIVE NOW, THE ANTHONY TROLLOPE (1875)

Anthony TROLLOPE wrote *The Way We Live Now* to study what he termed "the commercial profligacy of the age," and he succeeded in publishing the most savage attack on human nature since William Makepeace THACKERAY's *VANITY FAIR* (1848). He viewed his era as guided by greed resulting in the most immoral cheaters of all time. His novel has as its center Lady Carbury, who represents the frailties of human nature, although Trollope goes to lengths to demonstrate her own victimization. With divorced parents, she entered an abusive marriage at 18, producing a profligate son, Felix, who has already spent his own inheritance and demands that of his mother as well as his sister Henrietta (Hetta). Lady Carbury, a hack writer, nurtures her career at all cost. Trollope may have based her character on popular author Margaret Oliphant or, in some respects, even on his own mother, Frances TROLLOPE.

Lady Carbury and her children consult often with the Carbury family head, Roger. At age 40, Roger Carbury still lives alone at Carbury Hall and represents traditional values in the novel. He loves Hetta, but gives way to his friend and rival for her affections, Paul Montague. Montague is a decent man, but in his past in America had formed an alliance with Mrs. Hurtle, which will soon return to haunt him.

The handsome but wicked Felix Carbury seeks a solution to his eternal need for money from Marie Melmotte. Her father, Augustus Melmotte, has an obscure past that does not discourage admirers drawn to his reportedly enormous wealth. A supposed financier, he tempts others by promises of sharing in his wealth through investment in an American railroad. Ostensibly persuaded to do so by a corrupt American friend of Paul Montague named Hamilton Fisker, Melmotte is drawn into a scheme far more fraudulent than he understood. In fact, the railroad does not exist, but Melmotte continues the ruse as he receives attention usually reserved for royalty, activity that includes entertaining the Emperor of China at his Grosvenor Square mansion. Investors rush to hand him their money, because "money was the very breath of Melmotte's nostrils, and therefore his breath was taken for money." He eventually comes to believe in his own myth and advances to elected office as a member of Parliament. Pulled into the impending disaster is Melmotte's daughter Marie, who is regularly slapped and beaten by Melmotte. She loves the ne'er-do-well Sir Felix, envisioning him as her key to freedom.

Lady Carbury has suffered financial setbacks and hopes to regain her good standing through the marriage of Felix to Marie. When Sir Felix disgraces himself by gambling away at the Beargarden Club the money Marie gives him to finance their elopment, the wedding plans are destroyed. Poor Marie knows nothing of the change in plans and is already on a train, receiving a telegram at Liverpool with the message for her to return home. Humiliated and heartbroken, the bewildered girl remains in love with Felix. An outsider in her father's newfound society, she is so desperate for companionship that she turns a blind eye to Felix's abundant faults.

Trollope emphasizes anti-Semitism in the regard of Miss Goldsheiner by Lord Nidderdale as worthy only if "the money's really there." Georgiana Longstaffe, having searched for a husband for 12 long years, accepts, to the horror of her father, the Jewish Brehgert's proposal, who comments that he is a nice person but "absolutely a Jew." She is later outraged when he breaks the engagement with her due to her obvious disappointment over his financial losses, caused by her own father. Trollope also satirizes the marriage market through Nidderdale, who laments the lack of a published statement revealing the worth of all eligible women, most of whom engaged in trickery themselves, wearing false hair and strategically padding certain body parts.

Roger Carbury argues for rationality and also for proof that the American railway is advancing, somewhat alienating Hetta. Into the mix Trollope adds the American Mrs. Hurtle, who has come to England in pursuit of her previous lover, Paul Montague. Montague loves Hetta, not the scandalous Mrs. Hurtle. Unwilling to cede Montague to Hetta, Mrs. Hurtle threatens to blackmail him with the information of their previous affair. Felix is sought by Ruby Ruggles, a country girl whom Felix has compromised. Although he does not care for her, Ruby loves Felix and refuses to marry her fiancé, the corpulent miller John Crumb.

Felix becomes angered at his sister Hetta for her scolding of him regarding his heartless treatment of Marie Melmotte. He retaliates by divulging Montague's attachment to Mrs. Hurtle, causing her to break their engagement. Eventually Hetta accepts Montague, while a desperate Mr. Longstaffe in need of his funds discovers Melmotte's role in cheating the railroad investors. Rumors spread regarding his financial situation, and many important members of London high society refuse to attend his dinner for the Chinese emperor. Deserted by his one-time friends, Melmotte faces prosecution. Suffering under the pressure, his false sense of identity collapses, and he attends Parliament drunk. He is ousted and then commits suicide. Melmotte's death and the loneliness of Mrs. Hurtle and Carbury lend a sad tone to the novel's conclusion, although some satisfaction may be derived from the beating Felix receives over Ruby by Crumb.

As with all Trollope's novels, *The Way We Live Now* contains autobiographical aspects, some mentioned above. In addition, one of its positive characters, the Bishop of Elmham, he based on Dr. Longley, the headmaster of Harrow when Trollope attended in 1830 as a charity boy. He commented that Dr. Longley never let pass one angry word; Longley later became archbishop of Canterbury. Melmotte was based in part on Charles Bianconi, an Irish mayor with Italian ancestry who ran fleets of horse-drawn "long cars" with the mail around Ireland until the railroads destroyed his business. Trollope's own father-in-law, Edward Heseltine, had been involved in scandals including one at a bank that involved a railway swindle. Others involved left the country, while Heseltine died a short time

later, and one John Sadleir, a crooked politician as well as banker, committed suicide. Trollope had written in his story "The New Zealander," "It is not of swindlers and liars that we need to live in fear, but of the fact that swindling and lying are gradually becoming not abhorrent to our minds." He wondered in writing later whether Sadleir would have perished if those around him had not been so accepting of his unethical behavior. Trollope long held that when a community perceived individual dishonesty as success, it had a widespread corrupting effect on that community.

Critics of Trollope's day viewed his indictment of various aspects of society as misanthropy and did not evaluate the novel positively. Not only did he savage the world of gambling and speculation, but he also took on corruption in the world of publishing and the Church of England, city frauds, and the materialistic approach to love and marriage. The novel would outlive their criticism, to be declared a great achievement in the 21st century, when a television version would be produced. Its critics observed how timely Trollope's plot appeared, more than a century after its first publication. Trollope biographer Victoria Glendinning goes so far as to claim that had Trollope written no other novel, *The Way We Live Now* would have assured him eternal fame.

BIBLIOGRAPHY

Bell, Arnold Craig. *A Guide to Trollope.* Braunton, Devon, U.K.: Merlin, 1989.

Glendinning, Victoria. *Anthony Trollope.* New York: Knopf, 1993.

WEIR OF HERMISTON ROBERT LOUIS STEVENSON (1896) Although Robert Louis STEVENSON died in Samoa before completing his final novel, *Weir of Hermiston,* the fragment did appear posthumously. Because he had also written out plans for the balance of the novel, the full story is known. Even in its incomplete form, the novel is judged to be of high quality.

The Weir referenced in the title is the widower Lord Justice-Clerk Adam Weir, Lord Hermiston. Not from the moorland parish, he marries a local woman,

Jeannie Rutherford, a colorless but devoted wife who dotes on their only child and dies early. A hard man known for handing down merciless courtroom sentences, Weir proves just as hard on his son Archie. Archie tells a friend that he does not love his father, explaining, "He has never spoken to me, never smiled upon me; I do not think he has ever touched me." Archie and Weir disagree on Weir's courtroom conduct, and Archie publicly insults his father. Incensed, Weir banishes Archie to the village of Hermiston and forbids his study of the law. Archie lives an isolated existence, where his only company is his housekeeper Kirstie Elliott, a distant cousin of Jeannie Weir, who idolizes the boy.

Kirstie's four nephews Robert, Gilbert, Clement, and Andrew are commonly known as the "Four Black Brothers of Cauldstaneslap," because they had hunted and captured their father's murderer. Their sister, Christina, and Archie fall in love, a fact they try to keep a secret. Christina is an admirable young woman, a free spirit, made clear in Stevenson's description: "She was in love with herself, her destiny, the air of the hills, the benediction of the sun." When Archie's supposed friend Frank Innes arrives for a visit, he decides he wants Christina for himself. He manipulates Archie into ending his relationship with her. Stevenson's plot plans indicate that he intended for Frank to seduce Christina, leading to an argument with Archie in which Archie kills Frank. Archie's own father hands down a sentence of capital punishment, but he will be rescued from prison by the nephews. They reunite Archie with Christina, and the couple escapes to the United States. Weir suffers guilt over having sentenced his son to death and dies from the shock of realizing exactly what he had done in the name of pride.

The fragment form of *Weir of Hermiston* is available in both print and electronic text.

BIBLIOGRAPHY

Hammond, J. R. *A Robert Louis Stevenson Companion: A Guide to the Novels, Essays and Short Stories.* New York: Macmillan, 1984.

Miller, Karl. Introduction to *Weir of Hermiston,* by Robert Louis Stevenson. New York: Penguin Books, 1996, vii–xxxiv.

WELLS, H(ERBERT) G(EORGE) (1866–1946)

Later to become probably the best-known SCIENCE FICTION writer in the English language, Herbert George Wells was born at Bromley, Kent. He matured in an environment of deprivation, due to his father's various unsuccessful ventures. Originally a gardener, Mr. Wells also played cricket professionally until an injury ended his career, and he operated a failing china-and-glassware shop. Mrs. Wells worked as a housekeeper, and Bertie, as Wells was known as a child, became apprenticed to a draper at age 13. His early life resembled that of Charles DICKENS, with the characters in novels of both men reflecting their own unhappy childhoods and unfortunate parents. Wells became determined to escape his poverty and at 16 began work at the local Midhurst Grammar School as an assistant master. A scholarship in 1884 allowed him to attend the Normal School of Science (later Imperial College), where guidance by T. H. Huxley, well-known believer in the theories of Charles DARWIN, in comparative anatomy proved crucial to Wells's development. He also greatly benefited from astronomy instruction by Norman Lockyear, becoming a supporter of scientific advancement as a panacea to society's ills. He began his writing career, contributing to a magazine he founded and edited. He continued teaching at private schools while earning his bachelor's degree at London University, where he published a biology textbook and cowrote a text on physiology (sources differ on the subject matter of the second text, some listing it as geography). When he had to leave teaching due to a ruptured vein affecting his kidneys at age 28, he turned to article writing, inspired by novelist and playwright J. M. Barrie's book *When a Man's Single*. He married his cousin Isabel in 1891, a union that proved unhappy and led to divorce. His second marriage in 1895 to Amy Catherine Robbins proved more fortunate; he would refer to her as Jane throughout their long life together.

In the same year as his second marriage, Wells published four books, one of SATIRE, but the others in the new fiction genre introduced by novelist Jules Verne, a French writer of SCIENCE FICTION. Unlike Verne's stories, Wells's novels were supported by his knowledge of science and therefore more ingenious in their seeming reality. Underpinned by his strong social consciousness, his first novel, *The Time Machine,* became one of his most enduringly popular tales. It grew from a serialized story, "The Cosmic Argonauts," published in the *Science Schools Journal.*

Wells also published *The Wonderful Visit* (1895), in which an angel is shot to earth by a preacher ornithologist; *The Island of Dr. Moreau* (1896), a cautionary tale of science run amok; *The Invisible Man* (1897), a psychological study of a physicist who discovers the key to a special power; *The War of the Worlds* (1898), a tale of an earthly invasion by beings from Mars; *When the Sleeper Wakes* (1899), an adaptation of the Rip Van Winkle tale; *The First Men in the Moon* (1901), and *The War in the Air* (1908). He departed from science fiction to publish *The Wheels of Chance* (1896), a farce based on his experience as a draper's apprentice.

Wells's early works were highly influenced by the ROMANCE adventure fiction of Robert Louis STEVENSON, Henry Rider HAGGARD, and the suspense incorporated into the Sherlock Holmes stories by Sir Arthur Conan DOYLE, and all his writings containing social themes reflect the influence of Rudyard KIPLING, Joseph CONRAD, and Henry JAMES. Some of the novels, including *Dr. Moreau,* included elements of HORROR FICTION and reflected back on the traditional GOTHIC FICTION and works such as Mary SHELLEY's *FRANKENSTEIN* (1818). His DIDACTIC fiction, biased toward themes of social equality, drew heavily on his experience in poverty and included *Love and Mr. Lewisham* (1900); *Kipps: The Story of a Simple Soul* (1905); *Tono-Bungay,* judged a highly ambitious work, and *Ann Veronica,* judged scandalous for its focus on an independent woman (both in 1909); *The History of Mr. Polly* (1910), in which the title character is based on Wells's father; and *Boon* (1915). Books promoting his post-Victorian philosophy included *Anticipations* (1901); *Mankind in the Making* (1903); *The Food of the Gods* (1904); *A Modern Utopia* (1905) and *The New Machiavelli* (1911). The author's reputation was damaged by his belief in sexual freedom and his acting on that belief in a long-standing relationship with writer Rebecca West that caused him to live apart from Jane in Essex from 1912 until she died in 1927. *Mr Britling Sees It Through* (1916) reflects on his Essex life. Later in life, he supported in 1919 formation of The League of Nations and published much antiwar nonfiction and additional autobiographical books, including *Outline of History* (1920); *Men like Gods* (1923); *The Open Conspiracy: Blue Prints for a World Revolution* (1928); *The Science of Life* (1931); *The Work, Wealth, and Happiness* (1932); *The Shape of Things to Come* (1933); *Experiment in Autobiography* (1934); *Apropos of Dolores* (1938), and *Mind at the End of Its Tether* (1945).

Wells's works had a tremendous effect on the development of science fiction, converted into multiple media and stage presentations, they remain extremely popular.

BIBLIOGRAPHY

Smith, David C. *H. G. Wells: Desperately Mortal: A Biography.* New Haven, Conn.: Yale University Press, 1996.

WESTMINSTER REVIEW, THE   Founded and published by James Mill and Jeremy Bentham, *The Westminster Review* appeared as a quarterly from 1824 to 1887 and until 1914 was a monthly publication. Bentham, along with John Bowring, Henry Southern, and Colonel T. Perronet Thompson, were among the early editors. As editor from 1836 to 1840, John Stuart Mill renamed the publication *London and Westminster Review.* In 1846, editor John Chapman changed the name to *Westminster and Foreign Quarterly Review* but returned the magazine to its original name in 1852. George ELIOT served as an editor from 1852 to 1854, and the wife of John Chapman assumed editorship from 1895 to 1914.

Formed to disseminate utilitarian ideals, the publication affected social thought in Victorian England. Rivaling the Whig *Edinburgh Review* and the Tory *QUARTERLY REVIEW,* its combative tone sought to strengthen the middle class while weakening the two main parties. Affecting parliamentary reforms was a major goal. Early on, the response of the founders to literature was not impressive. It tolerated poetry and fiction only when these writings were either useful or harmless. After 1836, John Stuart Mill included more distinguished literary reviews: William Makepeace THACKERAY on Charles DICKENS, Carlyle on Sir Walter SCOTT, Mill on Coleridge. Social and economic essays were of a more broad and humanistic Victorianism during this period.

BIBLIOGRAPHY

Fader, Daniel, and George Bornstein. *British Periodicals of the 18th and 19th Centuries*. University Microfilms, Ann Arbor, Michigan 48106. 1974, 67–68.

WESTWARD HO! CHARLES KINGSLEY (1855)

Charles KINGSLEY wrote his most popular work, the patriotic *Westward Ho!*, for adults, although it quickly fell into the category of CHILDREN'S LITERATURE. While Kingsley had long been a political radical, the onset of the Crimean War, which many British protested, converted him to a conservative. IMPERIALISM is an overt theme in the novel, and he made clear his support of old-fashioned heroism and ardent devotion to England, at a time when the Manchester school countered the war for reasons economic and humanitarian. A far-reaching historical novel, *Westward Ho!* celebrated England's victory over Spain in the days of well-known figures that appear as characters in the novel, including Sir Francis Drake, Sir Walter Raleigh, and the poet Edmund Spenser, celebrator of Queen Elizabeth I. It proved a great adventure story, affecting British children for decades with its ROMANCE notions of the country and its real-life heroes.

Kingsley incorporated his affection for the North Devon coast into the setting, his appreciation for physical prowess into the plot, and his enduring admiration of courage in the face of danger into the shaping of his characters. Religion was also a theme, as Kingsley reveals his prejudice against Catholics in his focus on the Inquisition and the suffering it caused. His bias toward Protestantism remains realistic for the era and is featured in the novel when Jesuits inflict gruesome torture on prisoners, roasting them alive. Protestant heroes correct such injustices, battling what appear to readers as the dark forces of evil. To those who protested that Kingsley made his protagonist, Amyas Leigh, and his brother Frank, who in the novel serves with Sir Philip Sidney, too exaggerated to prove acceptable, supporters of the novel reminded readers to recall the "high types" that lived in England in 1588. As an example, the character Sir Richard Grenville tells his godson Amyas early on, "To conquer our own fancies, Amyas, and our own lusts, and our ambition in the sacred name of duty; this it is to be truly brave, and truly strong; for he who cannot rule himself, how can he rule his crew or his fortunes?" Readers know what follows will highlight men who live by those rules.

To be expected, the narrative includes broad stereotypes, especially of women, with both Rose Salterne, the wealthy mayor's daughter, and the young "beautiful vision," half-English and half-Spanish Ayacanora, as examples. Rose serves as the focus of a band of young men who label themselves the Brotherhood of the Rose, vowing to forever serve her and one another, as knights did for the wives of their lords in feudal days. Rose remains dedicated to her Christian faith. Along with Frank, Rose will be burned in the Inquisition, providing sacrificial icons around which Amyas will rally, swearing revenge against the Spaniards.

Ayacanora falls in love with Amyas, but in the romance tradition, he ignores all passion except for vengeance. At the novel's conclusion, when Amyas returns from upholding his nation's honor, Ayacanora begs him to "let me fetch and carry for you, tend you, feed you, lead you, like your slave, your dog!" Amyas agrees, and a symbolic peace, represented by Ayacanora's mixed blood, also represents the literal peace the Amyas Leigh, now a captain, feels. Once joined to Amyas in marriage in a country temporarily free of strife, Ayacanora's ability to sing returns, and her voice soars "as on a skylark's wings, into the highest heaven." Kingsley's hyperbole is not unexpected, as he writes in the style of medieval romance, clearly indicated in the novel's complete title: *Westward Ho! or The Voyages and Adventures of Sir Amyas Leigh, Knight of Burrough, in the County of Devon, in the Reign of Her Most Glorious Majesty Queen Elizabeth, Rendered into Modern English by Charles Kingsley*. Kingsley supports well his ruse of paraphrasing a true medieval tale by including all those elements of a heroic legendary past, which he so valued.

BIBLIOGRAPHY

Hartley, Alan J. *The Novels of Charles Kingsley: A Christian Social Interpretation*. Folkestone, U.K.: Hour-Glass Press, 1977.

WHAT MAISIE KNEW HENRY JAMES (1898)

When Henry JAMES produced *What Maisie Knew* late in his career, he had to employ a transcriber to write as he dictated, due to hand pain that may have been caused by arthritis. Some critics attribute to that mechanical challenge the change from James's traditional style to a more elliptical approach that resulted in reduced clarity. However, his more elaborate style may have well complemented the subject matter of this novel, as the plot suggested more than it revealed about Maisie Farange. Because James never reveals what the title references as to what his young protagonist knew, his covert style suits the topic. First published in *The Chap Book* between January and August 1897, the novel would next run as a serial in the *New Review* in 1898 before publication as a separate volume. Although not James's most highly acclaimed novel, the book would continue to resonate with readers due to its topic of a child caught up in the conflicted relationships of an adult world. As divorce and subsequent child custody issues became all too common in the 20th century, a reading audience could better relate to Maisie's situation.

Had Maisie suffered through only the divorce of her parents Beale and Ida Farange, neither of whom are particularly interested in her, the situation would have contained challenge enough. However, after her father marries her former governess, Miss Overmore, and her mother marries Sir Claude, the confusion over who will be responsible for Maisie only begins. The immature and decidedly unlikable Ida continues her sexual affairs, while Miss Overmore and Beale do not get along. They all realize they have made bad marriages too late. The former Miss Overmore, now Mrs. Farange, and Sir Claude form an ironic partnership in their shared concern for Maisie, cared for primarily by Mrs. Wix, Maisie's new governess. As the girl is passed about among the caretaker adults, she is unable to find a true caregiver. Eventually the second marriages for her birth parents dissolve, at which point Sir Claude and the former Miss Overmore marry. Readers may hope that Maisie will find at last a loving home with that step-couple, as they both share a genuine fondness for the girl. However, because Miss Overmore Farange, now married to Sir Claude, cannot get along with Mrs. Wix, Maisie will not find a home with the couple to whom she seems best suited. She prefers the prickly Mrs. Wix because she is unshakably dependable. Even in her bad habits she remains predictable, something the other parents in Maisie's life do not.

The novel is told from Maisie's naive point of view, and early on she contemplates her parents' view of her as a stupid individual. Once she had absorbed that label, "she had a new feeling, the feeling of danger; on which a new remedy rose to meet it, the idea of an inner self or, in other words, of concealment." Perhaps what Maisie knew grows from this feeling of separateness that all humans must eventually perceive in a painful epiphany during childhood. She knew the moment at which she had become her own person, and from that moment on, she could never again count on anyone, most especially those supposedly competent authority figures who surrounded her.

BIBLIOGRAPHY

Johnson, Diane. Introduction to *What Maisie Knew* by Henry James. New York: The Modern Library, 2002, xi–xvii.

WHITE, WILLIAM HALE (1831–1913)

William Hale White was born in Bedford, where his politically active father worked as a printer and bookseller, serving later in life as a doorman at the House of Commons. The elder William White passed on his interest in politics to his son, as well as his writing talent, evident in his entertaining sketches of Parliament. The younger White attended Bedford Modern School, experienced a spiritual awakening, and moved on to the Countess of Huntingdon's college at Cheshunt. His meeting with the Reverend Caleb Morris, an Independent minister, would later have a great effect on his spiritual attitudes. Expected to study the ministry, White moved next in 1850 to New College of London, St. John's Wood, but was expelled after only one year for criticizing accepted biblical doctrine. He joined Chapman Publishers to work on the *WESTMINSTER REVIEW* and preached in Unitarian chapels during the 1850s. In 1856, he married the first of his two wives, Harriett Arthur.

White's work at Chapman proved crucial, as he met novelist George ELIOT there, who would influence his later writing. In 1858, he began work as a clerk in the Registrar-General's Office in Somerset House. He would work there until 1892, retiring as Assistant Director of Contracts at the Admiralty. He first visited Germany in 1860, where he developed a lifelong appreciation for its philosophy and music. From 1861 to 1863, he wrote articles about House of Commons debates for publication in local newspapers and in 1866 published *An Argument for the Extension of the Franchise,* supporting a reform bill. Acting as a correspondent for *The Scotsman,* White wrote many articles that focused on politics and literature. He became absorbed by the work of Walt Whitman and began publishing fiction under the name Mark Rutherford. White would prove extremely protective of his identity, even denying having written the works bearing Rutherford's name, including his *The Autobiography of Mark Rutherford* (1881). He developed an intense interest in the romantic poets, particularly Wordsworth and Coleridge, both subjects of his later publications. During the 20 years before the publication of the *Autobiography,* White experienced an enormous spiritual change, moving from Unitarianism through theism, then becoming an agnostic, and finally finding more peace in a resignation and acceptance of life without a deity. Wordsworth's observance of the spiritual nature of the natural environment proved crucial to his own belief, or lack thereof. His nonfiction is marked by an admiration of the truth, producing what he termed serious writings. *Mark Rutherford's Deliverance* (1885) continued his account of his intellectual and spiritual journey, and in 1889, he added a study of astronomy to his activities, purchasing a telescope.

White's wife died in 1891, and the next year upon his retirement he received a £500 annual pension. He brought out his first novel, CATHERINE FURZE, in 1893, and a new edition of his original 1883 translation of Spinoza appeared with a new lengthy introduction in 1894. His second novel, *Clara Hopgood* (1896), was criticized for immorality, a charge that would seem ironic to later generations in light of White's puritanical devotion to the truth, a devotion forming the basis of the intellectual conflict his characters experience. Additional important publications included *An Examination of the Charge of Apostasy Against Wordsworth* (1898); *Coleridge's Poems, a Facsimile Reproduction of the Proofs and MSS. of Some of the Poems* (1899); "George Eliot as I Knew Her," in *The Bookman* (1902); edited excerpts from correspondence of Dorothy Wordsworth, published in *The Athenaeum* (1904); *John Bunyan* (1905); and *Selections from Dr. Johnson's "Rambler"* and Carlyles's *The Life of John Sterling,* a reprint with a new Introduction by White, both in 1907.

For one who suffered frequent bouts of melancholy and self-questioning, White remained amazingly active into his later years. In 1907, at age 76, he began a romance with 31-year-old Dorothy Vernon Horace Smith, who would describe him as still bounding into carriages with excitement over new projects or discoveries. They married in 1911. He died on March 14, 1913, the year he published *The Early Life of Mark Rutherford.* Posthumous publications included *Last Pages from a Journal* (1915), *Letters to Three Friends* (1924), and Dorothy Vernon White's *The Groombridge Diary* (1924), which related her experiences with White.

White/Rutherford gained the attention of critics later in the 20th century who supported the need for an increased and closer reading of his works. According to biographer and critic Stephen Merton, White's novels "remain indeed the single clear echo of an extremely powerful and rather small segment of English culture—the Calvinistic minority that reached back to Oliver Cromwell and to John Bunyan and that had, one suspects, a determining influence on the Victorian mileu." His influence on later writers, including Joseph CONRAD, Stephen Crane, D. H. Lawrence, and André Gide, proved strong. Critic Lionel Trilling sees White's books as "exemplifying for us the natural passage from the Victorian period to the modern period."

BIBLIOGRAPHY

Merton, Stephen. *Mark Rutherford (William Hale White).* New York: Twayne Publishers, 1967.

Stock, Irvin. *William Hale White (Mark Rutherford).* 1950. Freeport, N.Y.: Twayne Publishers, 1970.

Trilling, Lionel. Foreward. *William Hale White (Mark Rutherford).* 1950. Freeport, N.Y.: Twayne Publishers, 1970, v–x.

WILDE, OSCAR (FINGAL O'FLAHERTIE WILLS) (1854–1900)

Born in Dublin into aristocracy, Oscar Wilde was the son of Sir William Wilde and Lady Jane Francesca Wilde. His mother was a poet, publishing revolution pieces under the pen name Speranza. He had an older brother, Willie, and a sister named Emily, who died when she was 10 years old, leaving a grieving family. During his early schooling, Oscar excelled at classics, registering the highest scores in his class. He later attended Trinity College in Dublin, where he won the Berkeley gold medal for Greek studies and received a scholarship to Magdalen College, Oxford.

Considered an accomplished student with a brilliant mind, in 1878 Wilde wrote the poem "Ravenna," for which he won the Newdigate Prize. Wilde developed a reputation for ostentation and witty repartee, rejecting the athletics used by many young aristocrats to distinguish themselves for the life of an aesthete. A self-labeled follower of Walter Pater, he supported the Aesthetic Movement and enjoyed collecting items such as blue china. In 1881 he published a volume of poetry receiving mixed critical reviews and drew attention with his outrageous costumes, which often included velvet knee-britches. He also supported less restrictive fashions for women, speaking against the wearing of corsets and tight clothing. An advocate of artistic freedom, he fashioned himself a socialist, but politics held no true attraction. Wilde constantly drew attention to himself, particularly on an 1882 tour of the United States, where crowds were at once repelled and fascinated by him. Wilde's aggression and exhibitionism proved similar to that displayed by fellow Irish writer George MOORE. His play *Vera* was staged in New York in 1883, but it proved unsuccessful. He was said to have left before the end of the performance, declaring his boredom with his own work.

In 1884 he married Constance Lloyd, a bright multilingual woman, despite the wide rumors of his homosexuality. His publishing career began in earnest in 1888 with *The Happy Prince and Other Tales,* stories that grew from his interaction with his two sons, Cyril and Vyvyan. The title story would become a Christmas classic. He published his enduring FANTASY/HORROR FICTION, *The PICTURE OF DORIAN GRAY* in 1890, which represented an important contribution to British fiction. He adopted Robert Louis STEVENSON's dichotomy of man's conflicting natures made famous in *The STRANGE CASE OF DR. JEKYLL AND MR. HYDE* (1886).

More fairy tales followed, with *A House of Pomegranates* and *Lord Arthur Savile's Crime and Other Stories.* Wilde's second play, *The Duchess of Padua,* also proved unsuccessful, but he soon corrected his past luck with the more inspired *Lady Windermere's Fan* (1892), *A Woman of No Importance* (1893), *An Ideal Husband* (1895), and his best-known play, *The Importance of Being Earnest* (1895); all were light romantic comedies that were caricatures of British high society. In 1891, he had met Lord Alfred (Bruce) Douglas, the third son of the Marquis of Queensbury and an Oxford student, and the two became lovers. He wrote his next drama, *Salome,* in French, and it was published in 1894 following translation by Douglas.

In 1895, Lord Douglas's father publicly accused Wilde of homosexuality for his relationship with Alfred; Wilde sued for libel, but lost his case when during the trial he dismayed a jury that had been entertained by his wit up to that point by making light of the act of having sex with children. That taboo could not be tolerated, and Wilde spent several years in prison, following the 1895 prosecution for gross indecency. The trial created a furor, with citizens attacking the negative effects of art general in their anger over Wilde's sexual exploits. Wilde almost succeeded in single-handedly ruining the new avant-garde publication *The YELLOW BOOK* by holding what appeared to be a copy of the periodical under his arm as he left the courtroom. In reality, he had picked up a yellow-cover French novel, but the damage to the magazine had been done. Constance moved with the boys to Switzerland, adopting a family name, Holland. Wilde wrote a letter to Lord Alfred published in 1905 with the title *De Profundis,* but the public soon lost interest in him.

When released, Wilde moved to France under the name Sebastian Melmoth, adopting the protagonist's name from *MELMOTH THE WANDERER* (1820), a GOTHIC novel by Charles MATURIN. He published *The Ballad of Reading Gaol* (1898) to little notice and died in Paris following complications from an ear infection. His novel and plays remain quite popular, the plays continuing to be performed and adapted to the screen, and his life inspiring various fictional works, the best known being Robert HICHENS's *The GREEN CARNATION* (1894).

BIBLIOGRAPHY

Murray, Isobel, ed. *Oscar Wilde: The Major Works.* New York: Oxford University Press, 2000.

Pearce, Joseph. *The Unmasking of Oscar Wilde.* London: HarperCollins, 2000.

Pritchard, David. *Oscar Wilde.* New Lanark, Scotland: Geddes & Grossett, 2001.

Sloane, John. *Oscar Wilde.* New York: Oxford Press, 2003.

WILD IRISH GIRL, THE SYDNEY OWENSON (1806)

Like other works by Sydney OWENSON, Lady Morgan, *The Wild Irish Girl* unabashedly celebrates all things Irish. An EPISTOLARY NOVEL, it uses traditional ROMANCE devices in plotting a tale focusing on an Anglo-Irish law student named Horatio M. He is ordered out of England and into Ireland by his wealthy father, a landowner who hopes to distance Horatio from London's temptations. However, Horatio will also find temptation in Ireland, falling in love with Glorvina, a proud blond musician skillful at the harp. While her father is supposedly an Irish prince, she lives with him in poverty, inhabiting a dilapidated old castle on the rocky shoreline of Inismore. The castle stands on land belonging to Horatio's father, although Glorvina and her father remain unaware of Horatio's identity, and that setting becomes a major element in the novel. The Bay of Dublin is described as "one of the most splendid spectacles" Horatio had ever seen, with the use of the term *spectacle* emphasizing its fluid nature. When he tells the prince that he has come to Ireland to "seize some of the finest features" of the landscape, he actually intends to seize the land away from the prince. However, his love for Glorvina conflates with his growing love for the landscape, and he decides to become part of the region, rather than taking physical possession of it. It begins to possess him, and Owenson hints that this is a common occurrence among those who first experience Ireland.

Owenson's view of the Atlantic shoreline as symbolic of Irish independence supports the novel's praise of Ireland's proud history, much of which Horatio learns from a local priest, Father John. He bears a sensibility that Horatio admires and decides to adopt as his own, celebrating the idea of independence from corrupting social institutions, and the errors that often result from an irrational dedication to edict. Irish chauvinism is pronounced, and Owenson, who played the harp, soon became identified by the reading public with her fictional character, Glorvina, as she fed the 19th-century Anglo desire for Gaelic history. Her novel touches on all aspects of Irish culture, from its music to its politics, from its religion to its secular mythology. The book proved so influential that novelist Charles Robert Maturin satirized the acceptance of such jingoism by certain members of the aristocracy in his 1808 book, *The Wild Irish Boy*.

BIBLIOGRAPHY

Tessone, Natasha. "Displaying Ireland: Sydney Owenson and the Politics of Spectacular Antiquarianism." *Eire-Ireland: A Journal of Irish Studies.* (Fall–Winter 2002): 169–188.

WIVES AND DAUGHTERS ELIZABETH GASKELL (1866)

Elizabeth GASKELL never completed her final novel, *Wives and Daughters,* due to her early death in 1865. It appeared serially in *The CORNHILL MAGAZINE* between August 1864 and January 1866. Her last work is considered her best, representing the pinnacle of her achievements and the evidence of a style much improved since her early THESIS NOVELS *MARY BARTON* (1848) and *RUTH* (1853). However, she continues to pursue a favorite theme, the restrictions individuals suffer within a culture intent on categorizing humans according to the social strata they occupy.

The novel's protagonist, Molly Gibson, matures from a young girl, her life touched by many additional characters. The daughter of a Hollinford doctor, Molly enjoys her existence in the small town until her father marries the odious widow Clare Kirkpatrick. Clare had served Lord and Lady Cumnor as governess and schoolmistress and adopted some of their Whig attitudes. This causes conflict for Molly, whose second home is Hamley Hall with Tory landowner Squire Hamley and his sons Roger and Osborne. Clare's lovely daughter Cynthia moves into the community, and Molly develops a fondness for her intelligence, despite her flirtatious nature. The two become foils, allowing bright contrast in characterization.

Cynthia had committed to marry a Mr. Preston, a crass employee of the Cumnors, but she enters an engagement with Roger Hamley. While Roger finds Cynthia amusing, he does not love her. After a time, he moves on to study science, while Cynthia weds Henderson, a London barrister. Molly tries to assist the various characters in their pursuits, even helping Cynthia shed Preston. Gaskell skillfully introduces irony in her handling of the everyday activity that represents the characters' existence. Unlike the strident narrative of her early social-problem novels, *Wives and Daughters* displays a quiet indulgent and nonjudgmental attitude toward its characters, which has been compared to those of Anthony TROLLOPE.

Molly will eventually wed Roger and learn to deal with the annoying Clare. One sad note occurs when Roger's brother Osborne secretly marries a French girl who does not match the social status of his own family and dies apart from those he loves. The difference in their social standing, in that of Molly and Roger, of Cynthia and the land agent Preston, and of Clare and the doctor, offer an opportunity for Gaskell to reflect on the foolish divisions such observances of class create. In a clever and crafty manner, she lightens the sometimes-serious tone with the introduction of comic minor characters, including Lady Harriet and Mr. Coxe. While her character study lacks the uncontrolled passion in the characters of her friend, Charlotte BRONTË, Gaskell produces a masterpiece in *Wives and Daughters*. She writes of matters to which her personal experience adds weight and realism.

BIBLIOGRAPHY

Duthie, Enid Lowry. *The Themes of Elizabeth Gaskell*. London: Macmillan, 1980.

WOLLSTONECRAFT, MARY (1759–1797)

Mary Wollstonecraft was born in Spitalfields, London, to a father who wasted much of his family fortune in unsuccessful farming schemes. He moved his family to various farms in England and Wales, causing his children to lack steady education. Like most females of her day, Mary was self-taught, although she did enjoy some day-school instruction between the ages of nine and 15. At age 16 she formed an important friendship with Fanny Blood, whose family poverty did not squelch her intelligence. The two planned to live together later while managing a school, but in the meantime, Mary worked as a companion to a Bath widow from 1778 to 1781, an experience that engendered her scorn for the wealthy. When her mother fell ill, she returned to England to care for her, taking control of her younger siblings upon her mother's death. Shortly thereafter, she moved in with Fanny and her mother and joined their seamstress activities. She and Fanny later helped remove one of Wollstonecraft's younger sisters from an abusive marriage following the birth of a baby, which later died.

With Fanny and her siblings, Wollstonecraft opened a school at Newington Green and began associating with various social and religious dissenters. Fanny later became pregnant and left the country; Wollstonecraft joined her in Lisbon to help with the delivery. Devastated following Fanny's death and the failure of the school, Wollstonecraft began her writing career with *Thoughts on the Education of Daughters* (1787). Working in Ireland as a governess for Lord Kingsborough, she began an account of her own childhood and relationship with Fanny titled *MARY: A FICTION* (1788), published a year following her dismissal from service. Determined to support herself with her writing, she worked as a translator, reviewer, and, eventually, an editorial assistant for Joseph Johnson on his liberal journal, *Analytical Review*. Her relationship with the admiring Johnson allowed her to meet Thomas Paine, the artist Henry Fuseli, poet and engraver William Blake, and William GODWIN. During 1787–90 her two children's books, *Original Stories from Real Life; with Conversations Calculated to Regulate the Affections, and Form the Mind to Truth and Goodness* and *The Female Reader*, continued to promote her belief in the importance of equality for women. A supporter of the French Revolution, she rebutted Edmund Burke's anti-revolution polemic, *Reflections on the Revolution in France* with her strongest statements thus far in *A Vindication of the Rights of Men* (1790), her personal narrative supporting individual rights. She staunchly defended reformist movements, claimed brotherhood with enlightenment movements of Europe, and took the British propertied class to task for trivializing women and exploiting the working class. Although her work was overshadowed by Tom Paine's *The Rights of Man* (1791–92), it was well received, and she quickly wrote and published a companion piece, *A Vindication of the Rights of Woman* (1792). She joined the ranks of women including Hannah More and Fanny BURNEY, both professional writers, arguing for women's rights. In that work she argued that women must be educated in order to be good citizens and properly support necessary revolutions; it became a cornerstone for feminist causes in the following centuries.

Following an affair with Fusali that began a lifelong conflict between Wollstonecraft's publicly declared belief in female independence and the personal torment she would suffer due to her disastrous romantic relationships, she visited France in 1792, producing *History and Moral View of the Origin and Progress of the French Revolution* in 1794. While interacting with various political and social figures, she fell in love with an American ex-officer in the revolutionary army, Gilbert Imlay, and gave birth to their daughter, Fanny, in 1794. While he declared Wollstonecraft his wife to gain her the benefits of American citizenship, Imlay's interest in his family waned, and his attitude provoked Wollstonecraft's return to England in 1795. She had refused the legal relationship of marriage to Imlay and attempted suicide upon learning of his multiple affairs. In an unusual move, she agreed to represent Imlay in business during a trip to Scandinavia, producing an intriguing history of that time in *Letters Written during a Short Residence in Sweden, Norway and Denmark* (1796). She again attempted suicide by jumping from Putney Bridge into the Thames River, and then formed a close friendship with William Godwin that brought much needed stability to balance Wollstonecraft's often-destructive passion.

Godwin encouraged her continued writing, and she began *The Wrongs of Woman: Or, Maria,* fictionalizing her previous *A Vindication of the Rights of Women.* In this novel, the protagonist Maria is committed to an insane asylum by her physically and emotionally abusive husband, stressing the lack of rights on the part of women. Maria believes he killed her baby daughter by grabbing

hold of her as Maria ran from her house. While imprisoned, she tells the story of Jemima, working as a warden, also a prostitute suffering unbearable poverty, one of several characters that allows Wollstonecraft to emphasize the oppression of women and the legal theft of their labor and property. Maria develops a love relationship with Darnford, which Wollstonecraft makes clear is based on the romantic, irrational visions of Rousseau, and engages in activities allowing the emphasis on free sexuality for women by Wollstonecraft, a fact that would bring heightened criticism upon the work's publication.

Wollstonecraft became pregnant and married Godwin, although she did not live with him. Their relationship, and Wollstonecraft herself, proved the basis for Amelia OPIE's later novel *ADELINE MOWBRAY* (1802). Eleven days following the August 1797 birth of their daughter Mary, who would write *FRANKENSTEIN* (1818) and marry poet Percy Bysshe Shelley, Wollstonecraft died from infection. The distraught Godwin published his *Memoirs* of his wife, along with her posthumous writings, including her final novel, letters to her former lover, Imlay, and a fragment of autobiographical fiction titled "Cave of Fancy" a year later. His 1799 novel, *St. Leon,* contains a character based on Wollstonecraft who was attacked during growing British conservatism as an unsexed, promiscuous, and immoral woman. She was labeled a "hyena in petticoats" and a "wanton," her vital philosophy publicly ridiculed. Although later women writers, including George ELIOT, found her fascinating, not until the 20th century would Mary Wollstonecraft gain her inarguable position as one of early feminism's most vital and respected figures.

BIBLIOGRAPHY

Jacobs, Diane. *Her Own Woman: The Life of Mary Wollstonecraft.* New York: Simon and Schuster, 2001.

Todd, Janet. *Mary Wollstonecraft: A Revolutionary Life.* New York: Columbia University Press, 2000.

WOMAN IN WHITE, THE WILKIE COLLINS (1860)

Wilkie COLLINS first published *The Woman in White* as a serial in *All the Year Round* between November 1859 and August 1860. Collins was praised by critics for the care he took with both plotting and character development. When the mystery came out in volume form, Collins attached a preface, first reassuring readers that all legal detail was true, as he had carefully consulted "a solicitor of great experience" to ensure realism. Second, he explained his belief that "the primary object of a work of fiction should be to tell a story," and if that requirement were met, an author was in no danger of "neglecting the delineation of character." He had the idea for both plot and character from reading information about some French trials, which focused on mistaken identity, also long an important element of much ROMANCE fiction. A letter from someone he did not even know mentioned the possibility that an individual might be mistakenly held in an insane asylum, powerless to object to the admission by a second party. He developed the first-person-narrative approach to the novel from the fact that witnesses testify singly in courtroom proceedings. This also allowed him to withhold knowledge from the reader, as it would be revealed a bit at a time. His approach captivated his audience, which found small details frightening simply because they were without explanation, drawing them further into the story. His attraction to frightening his readers placed his work firmly within the tradition of SENSATION FICTION.

The plot features two sisters who act as foils. While Laura Fairlie, as her name suggests, is pretty and fair, her half-sister, Marian Halcombe, is unattractive and dark, but also extremely intelligent. That dichotomy suggests the traditional fairy tale, in which the blond beautiful heroine is also passive and sometimes dense, while the undesirable female in the form of a step-relative often proves the most active and bright. Walter Hartright, another character with a symbolic surname, tutors the sisters in drawing and falls in love with Laura, but she is engaged to marry Sir Percival Glyde, whose surname suggests a smooth, and perhaps tricky, personality. A mysterious woman dressed in white is introduced named Anne Catherick, who is already known by Walter. She has managed to escape from a lunatic asylum to which Sir Percival had her committed, apparently due to some damning information she possesses about Percival. Her circumstances interest FEMINIST CRITICS, as women had frequently been "committed" by controlling males for refusing to remain

silent or to behave as a patriarchal society deemed correct. Laura is not moved by the possibility of trouble and chooses to marry Sir Percival, causing Walter to take his leave. However, Marian is intrigued and chooses to pursue Anne's claims, prompting Percival to seek aid in the form of the Italian count Fosco. When Anne dies, Percival and Fosco kidnap Laura, taking advantage of her resemblance to Anne to lock her up in the asylum in Anne's place, while they bury Anne under Laura's name. The determined Marian uncovers the scheme, discovering her sister in the asylum and helping her escape. Although Laura began as the story's heroine, that position is co-opted by the brilliant and dogged Marian, who remarks "Nothing, in my opinion, sets the odious selfishness of mankind in such a repulsively vivid light as the treatment, in all Classes of society, which the Single people receive at the hands of the Married people."

The women and Walter then find a parish registry that reveals Sir Percival is actually illegitimate and not heir to an aristocratic title or property. Percival reacts by attempting to burn the records, lets the fire get out of hand, and is destroyed along with the church by the flames. The fire symbolizes a new beginning through purification, and Walter gains that new beginning for Laura by forcing Count Fosco to admit to her true identity, freeing her both physically and emotionally so she may marry Walter. He concludes from reading Laura's journals and overheard remarks that Fosco was actually a spy. A further satisfaction occurs when Fosco is murdered by a secret Italian society, the Brotherhood, in revenge for his past betrayals. The book closes focused on Laura and Walter's son, to whom Marian served as godmother. She receives the credit she deserves as Walter completes his part of the tale by writing "Marian was the good angel of our lives."

The Woman in White proved of great importance to the development of crime and DETECTIVE FICTION, offering a new type of villain in Fosco, because he is suave, but also fat. In addition, within the serious narrative Collins inserts much irreverent humor, which helps to delineate his characters. In Walter's early testimony he describes Professor Pesca sharing information about a family to whom he teaches Italian: "A Mamma, fair and fat; three young Misses, fair and fat;

two young Misters, fair and fat; and a Papa, the fairest and the fattest of all, who is a mighty merchant . . . a fine man once, but seeing that he has got a naked head and two chins, fine no longer at the present time." In another amusing testimony, the girls' guardian laments his condition as a single person, of whom all the married people in the world take advantage. The novel remains popular and has appeared in various stage and film versions.

BIBLIOGRAPHY

Bachman, Maria K., and Don Richard Cox, eds. *Reality's Dark Light: The Sensational Wilkie Collins.* Knoxville: University of Tennessee Press, 2003.

Peterson, Audrey. *Victorian Masters of Mystery: from Wilkie Collins to Conan Doyle.* New York: Ungar, 1984.

Phillips, Walter Clarke. *Dickens, Reade, and Collins: Sensation Novelists; a Study in the Conditions and Theories of Novel Writing in Victorian England.* New York: Russell & Russell, 1962.

WOOD, ELLEN PRICE (MRS. HENRY) (1814–1887)

Ellen Price was born in Worcester and matured in a wealthy family, which enjoyed life due to her father's successful glove-manufacturing business. She suffered health problems, including a hunched back, but married Henry Wood at age 22, then moved to France and began publishing her short fiction in 1855. In 1860, her novel about the evils of alcohol, *Danesbury House,* won a prize from the Scottish Temperance League; she claimed to have written it in one month's time. EAST LYNNE (1861) was the novel that gained her fame, becoming a best-seller.

Wood wrote an additional 15 novels, all in the subgenre of SENSATION FICTION. Her overly melodramatic style did not prove universally popular, but it did capture the imagination of enough readers to support her prolific career. Her output included the somewhat autobiographical *Mrs. Halliburton's Troubles* (1862), *The Channings* (1862), *Verner's Pride* (1862–63), and her personal favorite, *The Shadow of Ashlydat* (1863), all four also judged her best by later critics. Additional novels were *Lord Oakburn's Daughters* (1864), *Anne Hereford* (1868), *Roland Yorke* (1869), *Bessy Rane* (1870), *Dene Hollows* (1871), *Within the Maze* (1872),

The Master of Greylands (1873), *Parkwater* (1875), *Edina* (1876), *Pomeroy Abbey* (1878), *Court Netherleigh* (1881), and *Lady Grace* (1887). Many of the later novels appeared first in a periodical Wood purchased, *The Argosy,* after its publisher abandoned it in the wake of the uproar following his publication of Charles READE'S *GRIFFITH GAUNT* (1866) with its theme of bigamy. Wood managed to avoid the scandal evoked by fellow sensation fictionalists Reade and Wilkie COLLINS through maintenance of the strict morality that informed her personal beliefs. Her moral code supported tales with themes of adultery and additional taboo subjects that might otherwise have been rejected by readers. She competed with Mary BRADDON, a much younger and less morally focused writer, for the public's support of her fiction. Wood's excessive style provoked a loathing in writers including George MEREDITH, a reader for the firm Chapman & Hall, who reacted by producing fiction that supported his feeling that oversentimentality had become a prime vice of the public. Her son Charles published a memoir in 1894.

BIBLIOGRAPHY

Wood, Charles W. *Memorials of Mrs. Henry Wood.* London: R. Bentley, 1895.

WOODLANDERS, THE THOMAS HARDY (1887)

Thomas HARDY first published *The Woodlanders* as a serial in MACMILLAN'S MAGAZINE between May 1886 and April 1887. It emphasizes themes of marriage and adultery, faith and duplicity, and, a favorite element for Hardy, unrequited love and the human propensity to love anyone other than the one who loves us. *The Woodlanders* has never received the attention given to Hardy's other works, although he felt that in some ways, the novel was his best work.

The woods become a symbol of a particular way of life, one more innocent and dictated by tradition than that of the impersonal industrial city. That emphasis on setting calls attention to the fact that when the woodlanders engage in actions that go against their traditions, they defy their heritage and tempt fate to cause them to fail. George Melbury represents an individual who disregards his culture's ritual. He has remained diligent in obtaining for his daughter Grace the best education, in hopes that she can leave wood-lander traditions behind. He wants her to move up the social scale by marrying above the family's "place," but she has already been promised to a rustic named Giles Winterbourne who is completely devoted to her. Melbury plots to extricate Grace from the engagement by cruelly using Giles's financial problems against him. In a subplot, a common worker named Marty South is fiercely in love with Winterbourne, but he is fixated on Grace.

Free from her promise to Giles, Grace may instead marry Dr. Edred Fitzpiers, member of a family once particularly well thought of but who has fallen on hard times. Fitzpiers conducts himself in a manner beneath his good breeding, and Grace resists the match, knowing that he has had an affair with a local loose woman named Suke Damson. Because her father pushes her, she completes the marriage, after which Fitzpiers takes up with the recently returned from the Continent Felice Charmond, his former lover. As one who owns land but spends little time on it, Felice represents a foreigner in her own home. Her movements in and out of the community help promote the symmetry of plot for which Hardy was well known. Another example is the appearance at both the beginning and the end of the novel of the barber, Mr. Percomb. Percomb represents an evil force that descends on the woods people. His main role is to convince poor Marty, who thinks Percomb resembles the devil, to sell her beautiful hair in order to make a wig for Felice. The false hair helps Felice in the deception that contributes to her temptation of Fitzpiers.

Melbury understands his mistake too late and personally attacks Fitzpiers as he visits Felice at her home, Hintock Manor House. Felice takes Fitzpiers into her care and they escape to the Continent but have a disagreement that ends their tenuous relationship. In typical Hardy irony, it is the false hair that brought the two together that also ends up separating them. In a tragic turn, a past American lover of Felice murders her out of jealousy. That unexpected event allows Hardy to emphasize that all must assume responsibility for their actions, and that our past always stays with us. His abundant detail accumulates to promote an overall effect of repeated patterns. In those patterns, readers may see parallels between characters and events. His

ability to cause each detail to function as a part of a whole made him much more a modernist writer than a Victorian, according to critic David Lodge.

Melbury again interferes, encouraging Grace to obtain a divorce and to begin anew her relationship with Winterbourne. She had always had feelings for Winterbourne and does not need much urging. However, when she arrives at his home, a storm dictates that she must remain there overnight. As a foil to Fitzpiers, Winterbourne does not take advantage of the situation but moves outside into a flimsy shelter. Exposure to the elements sickens Winterbourne, who dies and is mourned by the brokenhearted Marty. Fitzpiers returns to Grace, and the novel concludes with no character realizing his or her true desire.

Lodge ventures the reason that the novel remains little known is because within Hardy's collection of "Novels of Character and Environment," it "belongs to the genre of pastoral elegy rather than tragedy." He explains that no heroism exists, the death of Giles draws from its readers "pathos" rather than "pity and fear," and the violent murder of Felice Charmond is too distant for readers to relate to. Giles's death actually represents the death of a way of life, which is regrettable but, in the tradition of REALISM, inevitable.

BIBLIOGRAPHY

Lodge, David. Introduction to *The Woodlanders,* by Thomas Hardy. London: Macmillan, 1974, 13–32.

WOODSTOCK, OR THE CAVALIER, A TALE OF THE YEAR 1651 SIR WALTER SCOTT (1826)

Sir Walter SCOTT published his 17th-century-setting ROMANCE *Woodstock, or the Cavalier, a Tale of the Year 1651* using his traditional approach to HISTORICAL FICTION. He identified an era that caught his interest for political and/or social movements, creating a heroic figure to best represent that age. *Woodstock* helped fill a gap left by his previous fiction of the years of conflict between Royalists and Parliamentarians, or Roundheads, loyal to Cromwell. It features an aging Scottish Cavalier named Sir Henry Lee, an elderly man "bent more by sorrow and infirmity than by the weight of years," who works as a ranger at the royal lodge of Woodstock in Scotland. Romance enters the tale in the form of Lee's daughter Alice, "a slight and sylphlike form," who loves Colonel Markham Everard, a cousin whom her father dislikes due to his allegiance to Cromwell. Everard had loved Alice at first as a younger sister but develops a romantic interest in her.

Cromwell allows Everard to intervene on the Lees' behalf when Parliamentary agents attempt to take Woodstock. To receive Cromwell's support, Everard sends another old Cavalier friend, Wildrake, with a message. Wildrake would like to take Cromwell into "a field of battle, where he could have had the pleasure to exchange pistol-shots with him." Cromwell is described as a "remarkable man" who "had acquired that influence over the minds of his enemies which constant success is so apt to inspire—they dreaded while they hated him."

Cromwell's action on the Lees' behalf does not reflect any affection for Everard. Rather, he understands the Lees' commitment to the crown and hopes to trap the dethroned Prince Charles at Woodstock. When Charles does arrive in disguise as a page to Alice's brother Colonel Albert Lee, he becomes enamored of Alice, raising Everard's ire. The prince confesses his true identity, stating "Master Everard must be pleased in finding only a fugitive prince in the person in whom he thought he had discovered a successful rival," and Everard swears to remain loyal to him.

Shortly thereafter, Cromwell's forces arrive and order Everard arrested, at which point Albert plays the part of Charles, allowing the prince to sneak away covertly from Woodstock. In Cromwell's anger, he orders execution of the Lees but later relents. The prince has left behind a message for the Lees, explaining Everard's innocence in the situation, and Sir Henry accepts the young man as a future son-in-law. In the final scene, Lee dies after having taken the hand of King Charles, who greatly pleased onlookers when "with his own hand" he waved away "the feeble attempts of the old man to rise and to do him homage."

The year before publishing *Woodstock,* Scott had lost £130,000 in a disastrous investment with the Ballantine publishing firm. The novel would represent the first fiction he published, although begun years earlier, in an attempt to repay the debt, as his already phenomenal output of writing increased. In addition to shouldering the burden of the debt, Scott lost his wife and discovered the grandson upon whom he doted had a terminal illness. His style suffered somewhat, prompting his editor, Andrew Lang, to write in an introduction to the novel, "Henceforth we see the Magician turned journeyman." The novel achieved decent sales and has remained available.

WORKERS IN THE DAWN GEORGE GISSING (1880)   Often referred to as George GISSING's first novel, *Workers in the Dawn* is actually his first published novel, one Gissing himself supported with a £150 investment. Not at all popular with reviewers, who criticized its excessive pessimism, attacks on organized religion, and SATIRE on the lifestyle of the wealthy, the novel languished for decades, at last revived later in the 20th century with a renewed interest in Gissing. With the effects of fate and the dissipation caused by alcohol as prominent themes, the plot relates the story of Arthur and Carrie, who share an unloving marriage fated to fail from the beginning. The characters are based on Gissing and his first wife, Marianne Helen Harrison, called Nell. Like Arthur, Gissing was easily attracted to pretty female faces, and he could not resist Nell, despite her obvious "low breeding" and eventually fatal alcoholism. As the two novel characters suffer through disagreements and disappointments, fated by Carrie's flawed heredity and Arthur's poor judgment to fail, so did Gissing and Nell experience the raw reality that followed his flight of fantasy regarding his ability to "raise" his wife to his own level. Carrie's conduct grows from that of Nell, as does her incorrect manner of speaking, her duplicity toward her husband, and her habit of spending time with other women like herself. Arthur also suffers from hereditary problems, on his part a nervous fragility that counteracts his natural intelligence and desire to succeed. He ends up a failure, despite an heroic struggle against inevitable defeat. Arthur does have a love interest in Helen, a woman who follows the philosophy of Schopenhauer, as did Gissing, but she exhausts herself trying to teach illiterate adults to read and eventually contracts consumption and dies.

The novel may be viewed as a BILDUNGSROMAN and is one of the few Gissing works in which a child, in this case Arthur as a youth, receives a considerable amount of attention. It includes an entire INITIATION/COMING-OF-AGE STORY prior to its consideration of Arthur as an adult. Reviewers note similarities between the boy Arthur and Charles DICKENS's characters, such as Oliver Twist and Pip. While he belongs in a high social class, he does not fit there, and outside forces intervene to block his reentry. Gissing basically focuses on failures in this first published of 32 novels—the failure of society as well as individuals. In one early passage, the kindly Mr. Tollady discusses the burning of martyrs with Arthur, arguing against admiring them simply because their bodies suffered. He explains, "I esteem all alike as involuntary agents in the hands of a great power which most call Providence, but which I prefer to call the inexplicable spirit of the world." He also has an answer for the younger man's question as to why one does not just sit still and watch the world go by, if the world pursues a "certain path which has been fore-ordained." Tollady answers that we do not sit still and watch "because we *cannot!*" We cannot choose what we do, but we can choose how we do it. That philosophy sums Gissing's own.

BIBLIOGRAPHY

Coustillas, Pierre. Introduction to *Workers in the Dawn,* by George Gissing. Brighton Sussex, England: The Harvester Press, 1985, ix–xxxii.
———, and Colin Partridge, eds. *Gissing: The Critical Heritage.* London: Routledge & Keagan Paul, 1972.

WUTHERING HEIGHTS EMILY BRONTË (1847)

Emily BRONTË would never know the extent of fame she achieved with her only novel, *Wuthering Heights,* as she died a year after its publication. Required reading in many modern literature programs, the novel proved a sensation, although not popular, when published. As a ghost story in its truest sense, its dark tone and BYRONIC HERO Heathcliff prove both literally and figuratively haunting. Brontë chose an unusual narrative structure, furnishing a story within a story, as the first-person point-of-view narrator, Mr. Lockwood, hears the history of Cathy and Heathcliff from Mrs. Nelly Dean, told in third-person point of view with the use of flashback technique. Mrs. Dean

has spent her life at the Heights and Thrushcross Grange on the moors, the novel's setting.

Lockwood is the new tenant at the Grange and discovers on his first night there names scratched in the wall of his bedroom: "Catherine Earnshaw," "Catherine Heathcliff" and "Catherine Linton," foreshadowing the multiple representations of the initial female protagonist throughout the novel. In the book's opening, Wuthering Heights belongs to Mr. Heathcliff. While readers could anticipate much of the GOTHIC content of the novel, including a mysterious male protagonist, a woman in distress, an environment haunted by its past, and themes of love and betrayal, Brontë goes beyond the traditional suggestion of mystical elements to convert Catherine Earnshaw Linton into a literal ghost, her spirit commanded by Heathcliff's strength of passion to remain on earth following her death.

Heathcliff was a foundling, brought to live at Wuthering Heights by Catherine's father, Mr. Earnshaw. He existed as a worker in an uneasy relationship with Cathy's brother Hindley, an animalistic man with none of the gentleman's sensibility his breeding should have provided. Cathy and Heathcliff inappropriately love one another despite their difference in social status, growing up together on the moors with Heathcliff's wild personality mirroring the surroundings. When Cathy begins to spend time with her wealthy neighbors the Lintons at Thrushcross Grange, Heathcliff becomes irrationally jealous, observing through a window her interaction with Edgar and Isabella Linton during a five-week stay following an ankle injury. Edgar falls in love with Cathy and proposes to her. She makes an offhand remark, overheard by Heathcliff, to Nelly that Edgar will be her husband. Morosely wretched, Heathcliff leaves before hearing Cathy's additional statement that no mortal creature could ever separate her from Heathcliff. While Brontë established Edgar and Heathcliff as foils early on, their contrasts become even greater later in the novel.

Heartbroken over Heathcliff's disappearance, Cathy marries Edgar, and several years pass before Heathcliff suddenly reappears. Having made a fortune in America, he seeks retribution against Cathy, Hindley, and Edgar, all the people who had caused his misery. Hardly recognizable in his clean, gentlemanly state,

Heathcliff has not changed emotionally. Neither Cathy, still in love with Heathcliff, nor Edgar, a gentle soul, are prepared to battle Heathcliff, who romances and weds Isabella Linton simply to hurt Cathy and Edgar. Cathy remains miserable, unable to enjoy her relationship with Edgar and literally cursed by Heathcliff for breaking their bond. She dies giving birth to a daughter, also named Catherine, as Heathcliff waits outside, pacing like an animal. An abusive husband, he later chases a pregnant Isabella away from his estate and plots to take possession of Wuthering Heights and Thrushcross Grange. Isabella gives birth to a weakling son named Linton who returns to live with his neglectful father after her death.

Hindley Earnshaw unwittingly mortgages the Heights to Heathcliff and drinks himself to death, leaving behind a wild son named Hareton who comes under Heathcliff's care. Still bent on revenge, Heathcliff mistreats Hareton as he does his own sickly son. However, Hareton's independent spirit and wild nature cause Heathcliff to develop a brooding affection for the boy. When Catherine, now a young woman, learns her cousin lives at Wuthering Heights, she visits with Nelly as an escort, against her ill father's wishes; Edgar has suffered from poor health since losing Cathy. Heathcliff shares with Nelly the final piece to complete his plan of revenge: he will force Catherine to marry Linton. When Nelly tells Heathcliff that Catherine will then inherit all from his fragile son who will obviously soon die, he tells her of the plans he has made to guarantee that if they marry, he retains possession of his son's, and future daughter-in-law's, property. That means that when Edgar dies, Heathcliff will also own the Grange.

Although all happens as Heathcliff anticipates, he enjoys no satisfaction or peace. Even the bond that develops between Hareton and Catherine Linton Heathcliff, a widow following Linton's predicted death, does not bother him. He lives only to die and join Cathy, who has remained his soul mate for all those years. At the story's conclusion, the first-person narration resumes, and Lockwood observes the courage of Catherine and Hareton, who he feels will be able to successfully confront the forces that victimized Heathcliff and Cathy.

Published under the pseudonym of Ellis Bell, *Wuthering Heights* caused readers to object to its dark nature; Heathcliff's brutality, which made his feelings of love and hate resemble one and the same passion; and a problematic structure. Later critics found those very weaknesses to be strengths in a work unique for its era. Within Brontë's supposed plot-structure problems hides a master plan. In order to diminish the confusion accompanying a switch in the middle of the book from one heroine to another who share the same name, Brontë's flashback technique worked well. In addition, Mr. Lockwood's position as a stranger to the area mimics that of the reader. His interview technique of Nelly allows tension to build as she respond to his questions.

Among the most popular English-language books ever written, *Wuthering Heights* has remained in print and has been converted to multiple screen versions.

BIBLIOGRAPHY

Peterson, Linda H., ed. *Wuthering Heights: Complete, Authoritative Text with Biographical and Historical Contexts, Critical History, and Essays from Five Contemporary Critical Perspectives.* Boston: St. Martin's Press, 1992.

Y

YEAST: A PROBLEM CHARLES KINGSLEY

(1850) Charles KINGSLEY'S THESIS NOVEL *Yeast: A Problem* first ran serialized in *FRASER'S MAGAZINE* in 1848. Kingsley incorporates vivid and distressing detail of poverty among England's rural population to emphasize his themes of anti-Catholicism and sanitary reform. He also suggests that the sewage that ends up in rivers should be used as fertilizer for crops, stressing society's lax attitude toward the environment that all must share. In his preface to the first edition, he wrote with concern, "the more thoughtful are wandering either towards Rome, towards sheer materialism, or towards an unchristian and unphilosophic spiritualism." He judged "Epicureanism" the most evil ill, because "it looks at first sight most like an angel of light."

The novel's protagonist, Lancelot Smith, is a member of the upper class who has "read Byron and Shelley" and devoured "BULWER[-LYTTON]," whom he left "for old ballads and romances, and Mr. Carlyle's reviews; was next alternatively chivalry-mad, and Germany-mad; was now reading hard at physical science," all in the hopes of becoming a great man. Kingsley stresses the irony of Lancelot's consumption of the best written, which leads to no change in his ideals, or lack thereof. As the plot progresses, Lancelot's master teacher turns out to be Paul Tregarva, an uneducated Dissenter who possesses a sharp intelligence. Lancelot will eventually learn that while "it was a fine thing to be 'superior,' gentleman-like," his class will itself suffer

for having ignored the suffering of the lower classes, as the physical filth they long ignore will spread disease and death among them. Of one such victim, Honoria Lavington, the narrator notes she is "beautiful no more; the victim of some mysterious and agonizing disease, about which the physicians agree on one point only— that it is hopeless."

Lancelot at first has admiration only for men like Lord Minchampstead, who has no alms for the poor, takes advantage of the workers, enforces all Poor Laws, and hires London workers instead of locals, although he does establish an industrial school. Lancelot will finally turn away from his "morbid vanity" only through love for Argemone. She is tricked into a nunnery, however, due to "the rickety old windmill of sham-Popery which" she had "taken for a real giant," dashing Lancelot's hopes for marriage. He is later convinced he must change, destroying his possessions and vowing to touch no money that comes "from a system of which I cannot approve." The detailed scenes of death and degradation sickened many readers, and Argemone's own death makes her a sad victim of a romantic and naive outlook on life. Kingsley leaves "Lancelot's history unfinished," suggesting he represents the future of England.

Like many authors of his day, Kingsley produced novels of conscience, all designed to bolster various reform movements. In his preface to the fourth edition of *Yeast,* he expressed his approval of improved conditions, noting, "the labourers, during the last ten years, are altogether better off" and "more and more" he finds "swearing banished from the hunting-field, foul songs from the universities, drunkenness and gambling from the barracks." Young men have learned to do "their duty as Englishmen," have altered their "tone toward the middle classes" and learned to use the term "snob" in its true sense, "(thanks very much to Mr. Thackeray)." While heavily overwritten with hyperbole perhaps offensive to 21st-century readers, *Yeast: A Problem* remains pure Kingsley material.

YELLOW BOOK, THE   Titled after its bright cover, the periodical called *The Yellow Book* appeared to much fanfare in March 1894. It would soon gain notoriety, due to its connection with decadent British writers and artists of the day. Published by John Lane, already known as a leader of the *avant garde,* it was to have departed "as far as may be from the bad old traditions of periodical literature." It satisfied that goal early on, as its first edition, although containing fiction by popular authors including Henry JAMES, carried illustrations by the outrageous Aubrey Beardsley, previously linked with Oscar WILDE, and a controversial essay by Max Beerbohm titled "A Defence of Cosmetics." Critics attacked Beardsley, dubbing him "Weirdlsey Daubery" and "Awfully Weirdly," while they labeled Beerbohm "Max Mereboom." Rather than being issued from the Bodley Head, SATIRIC attacks had its distribution point as "The Bogey Head." When in 1895 Wilde, in actuality not a fan of the publication, left court following his failed libel case against the marquis of Queensbury and stuck what appeared to be a copy of *The Yellow Book* under his arm, it seemed doomed. Guilt by association took over in the public's mind, and Mrs. Humphrey WARD and other moralists publicly demanded Beardsley's dismissal from the *The Yellow Book* staff. Crowds stoned the Bodley Head, and Lane, on a boat bound for America, received a copy of Wilde's photo when he arrived. After some hesitation, he ordered the upcoming edition recalled from the printers and all trace of Beardsley removed. Ironically, Wilde had not even been holding a copy of the periodical, but instead had grabbed a French novel in yellow cover titled *Aphrodite*. The public did not want to hear the truth of the matter, so intent was it on sanitizing the threatening publication.

The Yellow Book continued its run through 1897, eventually printing work by many well-known writers, including George GISSING, H. G. WELLS, Arnold Bennett, and W. B. Yeats. It became part of the aesthetics debate of the 1890s and was satirized in musicals by W. S. Gilbert. Most issues from its three-year run remain readily available.

BIBLIOGRAPHY
Harrison, Fraser, ed. *The Yellow Book.* Suffolk, U.K.: The Boydell Press, 1982.

YONGE, CHARLOTTE M(ARY) (1823–1901)   Born the daughter of a country gentleman who undertook her education, Charlotte Mary Yonge spent her entire life in her home village of Otterbourne. Deeply devout from a young age, she was strongly affected by the vicar of neighboring Hursley, John Keble, a leading figure in the OXFORD MOVEMENT and professor of poetry at that institution early in his career. Keble observed her talents of expression even while she was a small child teaching Sunday school at the age of seven. He encouraged her writing, and she expressed many of his ideas in her prolific works, which would number 160 books for children and adults.

Yonge's first published book was *Abbey-church, or, Self-control and Self-conceit* (1844), but she made her reputation with the wildly popular HEIR OF REDCLYFFE (1853). Like all her works, that novel preached redemption through self-sacrifice. Her beloved father had firmly informed her that women published for either self-aggrandizement, to accumulate wealth, or in order to promote good works, and that he would only tolerate her career if she employed didacticism and donated all publication income. According to Ethel Romanes's account, Yonge never dared to challenge her father, "the hero of heroes," whose approval was her "bliss," and whose anger her "misery." A lovely young woman once photographed by Lewis CARROLL, she impressed most who met her as reserved and quiet to the point of being haughty. Her good friend, Elizabeth Wordsworth, reported that impression as erroneous; Yonge admitted herself cursed with a self-consciousness that made others at times mistake her timidity for rudeness. In the presence of friends, she could talk incessantly and impressed them with her strength and forceful expression. A conservative like her father and grandfather, she supported Benjamin DISRAELI's Tory views and often expressed her political stance.

Yonge followed with several volumes that traced the May family, the first being *The Daisy Chain* (1856), the proceeds from which went to support missionaries in Melanesia. It promoted her belief in the weak will of females and their set roles as helpmates to other family members. According to critic Elaine Showalter, Yonge once held that, while the BRONTË sisters suffered dastardly effects due to their drug-addicted brother Branwell, such sibling gender relationships were normal and expected. However, some of her biographers were surprised to learn of her great interest in the male-centered activity of war; she loved to discuss military strategy. Like other traditional women writers, she had to study such topics in order to write from the male point of view for her characters. FEMINIST CRITICS such as Showalter suggest that even the most compliant women enjoyed identifying with the "power and privilege of the male world." Influenced by Charlotte Brontë's heroine Jane Eyre in the novel of the same name, Yonge did shape heroines with stronger intellects and senses of self-identity than did contemporary male novelists, such as William Makepeace THACKERAY and Edward BULWER-LYTTON.

Yonge's didacticism held that men should be educated in order to earn their fortunes, while women made theirs through "good" marriages. Her most brilliant and creative heroines consistently sacrificed their own opportunities to the needs of others. In addition to publishing novels, for 39 years she devoted herself to editing the *Monthly Packet,* preaching the precepts of the Oxford Movement to young readers. All her works provide excellent detail regarding the Victorian home, representing DOMESTIC FICTION, but with far more traditional and predictable Christian-based plotting than other members of that genre. Additional important works were *The Clever Woman of the Family* (1865), *The Pillars of the House* (1873) and, of her children's works, *The Little Duke* (1854), which told the story of the

great-grandfather to William the Conqueror. Christabel Coleridge wrote a hagiographic biography of Yonge, committing a disservice to scholars who followed by destroying many of the primary documents used in her research.

BIBLIOGRAPHY
Coleridge, Cristabel R. *Charlotte Mary Yonge: Her Life and Letters.* 1903. Detroit: Gale Research, 1969.
Dennis, Barbara. *Charlotte Yonge: Novelist of the Oxford Movement: A Literature of Victorian Culture and Society.* Lewiston, N.Y.: E. Mellen Press, 1992.
Romanes, Ethel. *Charlotte Mary Yonge, an Appreciation.* Oxford: A. R. Mowbray & Co., 1908.
Showalter, Elaine. *A Literature of Their Own: Women Novelists from Brontë to Lessing.* Princeton, N.J.: Princeton University Press, 1999.

YOUTH AND MANHOOD OF CYRIL THORNTON, THE THOMAS HAMILTON (1827)

While not as well written as military fiction by Frederick MARRYAT, *The Youth and Manhood of Cyril Thornton* allowed Scottish author Thomas HAMILTON to take advantage of his military experience by using it as background for fiction. Hamilton had been wounded in the thigh while serving in Spain, and this would be his only fiction based on that era of his life. After retiring from the service, his friendship with publisher William Blackwood and residence as a neighbor to Sir Walter SCOTT encouraged his writing. He first sent "a few sheets of Cyril Thornton" to Blackwood on January 20, 1826, and continued to send progress reports, including the statement, "the ending is melancholy, and I am not quite sure that the cause is fully adequate to the effect, but I think it is out of the common run and that, in these days of imitation, is in itself something." Hamilton wanted to kill Cyril during his participation of the storming of St. Sebastian, concluding with a "description of his grave in a grove of cork trees." However, he eventually capitulated with Blackwood's request for a "happy ending," correctly judging it would reduce the novel's quality but increase its sales. While some initial reviews remained equivocal, *Edinburgh Review* in October 1830 noted that the novel had been published three years previously, and "we should not have noticed it now, if we had not thought that it deserved to be remembered much longer. It is one of the best of its class." Also published in America, the book remained in print through 1880.

Divided into three sections, the novel's first portion focuses on Cyril Thornton's studies at Glasgow, where Hamilton had also studied. Cyril carries guilt for having accidentally killed his brother in a shooting accident, which succeeded in alienating him from his family, particularly his father. He spends time with his uncle David Spreull, a merchant in Glasgow who has as his crusty companion a man named Girzy. Some critics note that the various characters, including the provost, his wife, Archie Shortridge, and Miss Spreulls, represent stereotypical stock figures of Scottish fiction. They do, however, praise the REALISM of Hamilton's depiction of Glasgow trade and his easy readable style. Cyril joins the army, and his military experiences occupy the novel's second section. Critic Maurice Lindsay notes that no writer in a productive period that included Sir Walter SCOTT, John GALT, Jane AUSTEN, and Susan FERRIER captured "the sense of war's utter confusion, misunderstanding, cruelty, chaos and strategic chance" as did Hamilton. By the third section, which brings Thornton back into society, Hamilton's

approach weakens. The loquacious characterizations of his upper-class figures, realistic or not, add tedium to the narrative, and he miscues his readers into believing the character of Laura Willoughby will become Thornton's love interest. Instead, he chooses the daughter of Lord Amersham, Lady Melicent, whose character remains inconsistent. Although clear about her distaste for war veterans and their messy wounds, she warmly embraces the wounded Thornton, an individual far below her class, then casts him aside to marry a wealthy man her social equal. While Hamilton had originally planned for Thornton to return to the service of his country and die in battle, he satisfied Blackwood by recalling the figure of Laura Willoughby and settling the love-triangle conflict in traditional 19th-century fiction fashion.

Burdened with a style sometimes classified as "clumsy," *The Youth and Manhood of Cyril Thornton* is yet recommended as eminently readable, in great part due to its sincere tone and realistic setting.

BIBLIOGRAPHY

Lindsay, Maurice. Introduction to *The Youth and Manhood of Cyril Thornton,* by Thomas Hamilton. Aberdeen: The Association for Scottish Literary Studies, 1990, vii–xviii.

Z

ZANONI EDWARD BULWER-LYTTON (1842)

Edward BULWER-LYTTON wrote a FANTASY/SCIENCE FICTION piece in his novel *Zanoni*. The novel's protagonist, labeled by those familiar with him in Italy "the rich *Zanoni* . . . his wealth is incalculable!," possesses special powers of the occult that give him control over his own mortality. He finds the key to eternal life is the sacrifice of all compassion toward humans and exists for 5,000 years feeling nothing toward his fellow man. As the Spanish Inquisition winds down, France's Reign of Terror begins, and in that setting, Zanoni finds that the power of love trumps his own dark powers.

While watching an opera in Naples, Zanoni sees Viola Pisani, daughter of the composer, on stage. "The little singer of San Carlo" so moves him that he leads the crowd in applause for her performance. She sees him close to the stage and "could not withdraw her gaze from that face." Zanoni is veiled in mystery that forms the basis of local gossip concerning "strange reports" that the same individual had appeared "in the same splendour" in Milan, where a man recalled having seen him "sixty years before in Sweden."

Bulwer-Lytton's placing of an internal struggle in an environment filled with external conflict helps emphasize the extreme reaction Zanoni undergoes; others choose to die for war, while he chooses to die for love. In a discussion with Mejnour, a stranger who the reader discerns is somehow responsible for Zanoni's immortality, Zanoni explains, "the transport and the sorrow, so wildly blended, which have at intervals diversified my doom, are better than the calm and bloodless tenor of the solitary way. Thou . . . lovest nothing, hatest nothing, feelest nothing; and walkest the world with the noiseless and joyless footsteps of a dream!" His love for Viola leads to marriage and his sacrifice of his superhuman state. Clarence Glyndon later warns Viola following the birth of her child about the powers that have affected Zanoni, describing "in words that froze the blood of his listener" the phantom with eyes "that seared the brain and congealed the marrow of those who beheld." Although Viola is frightened at the thought of her husband captivated by such a phantom, she need not be. As the novel moves into Book the Seventh with a first chapter titled "The Reign of Terror," Zanoni now prefers the brighter spiritual powers that passion allows. In the face of Robespierre's fury, he gives up not only a chance at immortality, but also his literal life as he takes the place of his wife when she is sentenced to death on the guillotine. In his thin morality fable, Bulwer presses an argument already long won in literature, that love conquers all other desires and forces.

Bulwer-Lytton considered *Zanoni* his greatest work, and despite his generous inclusion of hyperbole and tendency toward cliché, the tone echoes Bulwer's honest belief in his theme. In the novel's dedicatory epistle to a sculptor named John Gibson, Bulwer-Lytton writes that his novel, "this well-loved work of my matured manhood," is not meant for the masses that cannot appreciate it. He adds, "I love it not the more, because it has found enthusiastic favourers amongst the Few. My affection for my work is rooted in the solemn and pure delight which it gave me to conceive and to perform." The novel projects his feeling that artists fare better on the Continent than in his own country. A character called Mervale, "a downright honest man," comments to Clarence that anyone in England would believe a wealthy Englishman who married a singer had "been lamentably taken in." When Clarence comments, "Artists have been friends of princes," Mervale replies, "Very rarely so, I fancy, in sober England. There in the great center of political aristocracy, what men respect is the practical, not the ideal."

BIBLIOGRAPHY

Wolff, Robert Lee. *Strange Stories and Other Explorations in Victorian Fiction.* Boston: Gambit, 1971.

ZOE: THE HISTORY OF TWO LIVES
GERALDINE JEWSBURY (1849)   Geraldine JEWSBURY's first novel, *Zoe: The History of Two Lives,* was one of the first Victorian novels to interrogate religious skepticism. Jewsbury could not rush through such an important topic, as she explained to her lifelong friend and correspondent Jane Welsh Carlyle in a letter dated October 19, 1846: "I am writing away at my book, and have got two or three more chapters done, but I cannot get on fast; I must go through a certain process, and cannot make haste." She had been thinking of the topic for some time before she published her book in three volumes, as evidenced in her letter of August 12, 1848. She asks Carlyle whether she has read Daniel DEFOE's "Religious Courtship," assuring her friend that she would like it, adding, "The thing that has struck me lately in the course of my reading is, though we are terrible unbelievers in this age, without a rag of a creed to cover us, yet we have a much deeper reverence for religion, a more religious sentiment is spread abroad, than was general in Defoe's days." In a letter of January 17, 1850, she continues in this vein, remarking, "I am in such a state of reaction against all moral complications that I don't believe that I will meddle with the metaphysics of

the Ten Commandments any time this side of the Millennium. I am bothered to death with that kind of thing in real life enough just now." She knew that others might not understand her attitude, writing that spring that "the Rectory people . . . are really nice, and Mrs.___ actually read 'Zoe,' and made some extracts from it, in spite of being so dreadfully shocked."

The dreadful shock received by Jewsbury's readers derived from her plot in which the Zoe of her title begins her life in scandal as the bastard daughter of an English serviceman named George Clifford and a beautiful Greek woman, also named Zoe, and ends it in love with an ex-priest named Everhard. That double taboo surprisingly did not land the novel among those labeled SENSATION FICTION, partly due to Jewsbury's high moral tone throughout. While mildly DIDACTIC, due to detailed scenes describing Everhard's conflict over faith, the novel remains entertaining. It might appeal especially to FEMINIST CRITICS in its characterization of Zoe and her stepdaughter, Clothilde, as well as to PSYCHOANALYTIC CRITICS, in its suggestions about sex and gender-related power in the 19th century, as well as the obvious symbolism of Everhard's name and additional sexually charged elements, however unconsciously they may have been formed by Jewsbury.

Zoe Clifford does not appear until after 100 pages of the first volume, as the initial portion reviews the youth of two brothers, Everhard and Louis Burrows, sons of an English man and a French woman. Everhard has been dedicated to the Catholic Church, a reason his quickly widowed mother employs basically to ignore him, resulting in his miserable childhood. He will eventually spend time with his uncle in Paris, then move on to Rome and enter the church. Later he meets Zoe, who, while eventually legitimized as a toddler when her father at last married her mother, nevertheless remained on the fringes of the best society due to the details of her birth. Unable to make a traditional marriage to the squire's son, who requests her hand despite the protest of his family, she marries instead a 50-year-old widower with a pockmarked face named Gifford. They produce two children and Gifford dies, leaving Zoe to raise their sons and his daughter by his first wife, Clothilde. Clothilde matures to enter a convent, gaining the extreme respect and devotion of a man she eventually orders to conduct himself according to his social level; he goes on to become a leader in his church and his government, marrying Zoe's best friend, Lady Clara.

Zoe will meet and fall in love with Everhard, who leaves the church following a crisis of faith, but Zoe understands his vow of chastity as lifelong. Their love will never be realized. She also falls in love with the somewhat unscrupulous Frenchman Count Mirabeau, but she rejects his proposal due to her conflict over her feelings for Everhard. In the final chapter, Zoe receives a letter Everhard wrote to her on his deathbed, proclaiming his love and devotion.

Part of the approach known as feminist criticism is to "reclaim" female-written text by revealing subtexts buried beneath the surface meaning of those works. In this novel, such critics would immediately note what seems to be an underlying message regarding powerful, active women, that they must live as something other than traditional women in order to claim that power. Zoe's uncle, to whose care she is entrusted when orphaned, decides to educate her as a man, figuratively transforming her from female to male, ostensibly because her birth out of wedlock causes her peculiarly independent personality. The suggestion that "normal" women, those complying with society's moral mold, cannot be educated as men, suggests that the taboo relationship of Zoe's parents (the absence of a legal father) liberates her mind. In addition, she remains single for the greater part of the book, having married basically in order to procreate dutifully; her mothering instincts remain firmly in place, and she is able to mother not only her own two sons, but also Clothilde.

As a widow, Zoe commands the admiration of all society and the close devotion of two men. One is a libertine who functions outside polite society's acceptable boundaries, but due to his maleness is excused for his actions and will be made acceptable by marriage to a respectable woman. The other man whose devotion Zoe claims is a priest, protected by the boundary of celibacy. Both are extremely desirable and bright men with Everhard an acknowledged author and philosopher of sorts. Their positions remain unthreatened, as their behavior fits into one or more of the many roles allowed men. However, Zoe, had she been born a "normal" woman, would remain confined by her culture's

expectations. In a passage illustrating Jewsbury's ability to move beyond mere stereotype, Mirabeau tells Zoe as he anticipates her rejection, "remorse is the only hell a noble-minded man can dread. Women feel nothing, but the hell of consequences; understand nothing, beyond the blame of the world, and the loss of reputation." As if those "nothings" were not a heavy enough load, Zoe assumes yet another. She disagrees with him, explaining, "Some women can fear the reality of doing wrong, more than the blame attached to it." That is a different sort of woman, indeed, than the one society anticipates. Although Zoe participates in the marriage ritual, she never achieves the type of normality expected of the majority of women, which actually works to her advantage.

Clothilde, on the other hand, does comply with the limited roles available to a woman, although she selects one preferable to a minority of females. Clothilde chooses servitude, as did traditional wives, but servitude to another patriarchal institution, the church. The nunnery even adopts the traditional feminine labels, calling nuns "wives" of Christ or of the Church, and using the term "mother" as a title of high status, indicating a leader of nuns. In her protected position, the quiet Clothilde wields enormous power over men as well as women. Freed from the confines of a sexual relationship and all its expectation, Clothilde may function as an adviser to important men. Because of her life in a community of women and professed elevation through an enriched otherworldly existence, she becomes imbued with special talents and is utterably desirable but not as a sexual object.

Jewsbury's works deserve more attention than they have received; many are not available outside rare-book collections. Fortunately, *Zoe* was selected as one in a collection of 121 novels by professor Robert Lee Wolff of Harvard University to become part of a Garland Publishing series titled "Victorian Fiction: Novels of Faith and Doubt." This happy circumstance makes it easy to find.

BIBLIOGRAPHY

Ireland, Mrs. Alexander, ed. *Selections from the Letters of Geraldine Endsor Jewsbury to Jane Welsh Carlyle.* London: Longmans, Green and Co., 1892.

GLOSSARY
The Elements of Fiction

antagonist   character that causes conflict for the PROTAGONIST; the antagonist may be a ROUND CHARACTER, but seldom experiences an EPIPHANY.

character   person who operates within fiction's plot. Any number of characters may appear in fiction, either as major or minor characters. Characters may be either FLAT or ROUND.

denouement   a French term that literally means "unknotting." In the denouement, revelations solving questionable identities and unidentified character motivation important to concluding the plot occur. Thus, by the story's end, all tension should reach a resolution (not to be confused with a solution).

dialect   an author may choose as a part of style to include dialect in the characters' speech, to emphasize elements such as geographic location, era, or level of education of the characters.

dialogue   the words of characters.

dramatic irony   a condition in which a character acts in a way inappropriate to the situation, out of ignorance of circumstances to which the reader may or may not be privy.

epiphany   the moment of realization that motivates a major change in a character. The term *epiphany* was borrowed from religion; James Joyce is widely credited as the first to apply it to literature.

exposition   description of actions that occurred before the plot began, which provide background for the story. Narration, character thought, and character DIALOGUE supply the exposition.

external conflict   conflict observable by those who interact with the PROTAGONIST and may be either of two types, human versus human or human versus environment. The first type generally occurs between the protagonist and the ANTAGONIST. The second may be further divided into two elements, which include nature, or the natural environment, and culture, or the social environment, either of which may cause problems for the protagonist.

falling action   the few events that follow the climax, leading to the story's conclusion. Within the climax and falling action is contained the DENOUEMENT.

first-person point of view   a point of view in which the narrative voice belongs to a character involved in the story, who appears as an actor within the plot; it will contain the self-reference "I." Because the

---

*Terms set in small capital letters have their own entry in the glossary.

narrator is privy only to his or her thoughts, this approach limits access to information regarding other characters, which must be gained through their actions and DIALOGUE. The first-person narrator may be untrustworthy or naive, limiting reader understanding of the world the narrator observes.

flat character a one-dimensional character, as opposed to a ROUND CHARACTER

foil a character designed for comparison and contrast to the PROTAGONIST, to aid in reader understanding of the protagonist.

foreshadowing a verbal or dramatic clue, implanted in a NARRATION or DIALOGUE, regarding future events or circumstances.

internal conflict conflict involving crises of conscience or struggle regarding a decision on the part of the PROTAGONIST, often invisible to the outside world. Such conflict is commonly labeled "man versus self."

irony an author's presentation of ideas, objects, or people that are not as they seem. There are two major types of irony: DRAMATIC IRONY and VERBAL IRONY.

limited point of view a point of view in which the third-person narrator describes actions, feelings, and thought from a single character's understanding.

minor characters characters who may be crucial, but who do not change throughout the story, do not appear as often as the PROTAGONIST and ANTAGONIST, and often remain FLAT, or one-dimensional, characters.

narration the manner in which the plot is revealed; the telling of the story.

omniscient point of view a point of view in which the THIRD-PERSON narrator describes actions, feelings, and thoughts from all characters' understandings; often generally seen in novel-length works.

plot the action or events of a story, which focus on conflict between characters or within the mind of the main character.

point of view the voice that tells the story or presents the narrative. The author's choice of point of view will naturally affect the amount of information to which the reader remains privy and can greatly affect the reader's comprehension of PLOT, THEME, and CHARACTER. Point of view may be first person or

third person, and if third person, either limited or omniscient. Occasionally, both first person and third person points of view will be used in a novel, such as in Henry James's novella, *Daisy Miller* (1879; see entry in text).

protagonist the main character, identified by having the most page space dedicated to him or her and, usually, as the only character who will experience a major change. That change makes him or her a dynamic character. That change generally occurs in reaction to conflict and causes the protagonist to alter his or her approach to the future.

rising action the accumulation of actions in the plot and the escalation of tension between characters or within the main CHARACTER. Rising action may be composed of any number of events, all leading to the major action when the tension peaks, called the climax.

round character a character whom the reader comes to know in a way that adds multiple dimensions to the character's personality. The PROTAGONIST generally is a round character.

setting the background against which the PLOT unfolds. It may include three elements: era/time period, geographic location, and culture. The NARRATION may not always include specific information about setting but will furnish clues for the reader through information describing clothing and transportation, climate, indigenous plants and animals, work habits of the characters, and the social ideals and values that motivate the local population's actions. Setting occasionally becomes so crucial that it may be perceived as the ANTAGONIST to a PROTAGONIST.

style the vocabulary or word choice of the author and the effect of those choices on readers.

symbols objects or people that are important for their literal meaning in a story, but which also represent an additional meaning, chosen by the author. Some symbols are traditional, used consistently over centuries to represent the same abstract concept, regardless of context, i.e., a rose symbolizes love, and water symbolizes rebirth or renewal. Symbols may also be literary, symbolic only in a particular story due to its particular context.

theme   the meaning or message of a story. Not merely a "moral," the theme acts as a unifying idea for all of fiction's elements and is generally an abstract concept that grows from the interaction of CHARACTER and PLOT.

third-person point of view   a point of view in which the narrative voice is outside the action, not belonging to a CHARACTER involved in the story.

tone   the author's attitude toward subject matter and/or the reader is revealed through tone, which may be positive, i.e. joyful, hopeful, celebratory, or negative, i.e. sarcastic, bitter, rebellious.

verbal irony   a condition in which a CHARACTER means the opposite of what he or she says, or has a hidden meaning to his or her speech.

SELECTED BIBLIOGRAPHY

Ackroyd, Peter. *Introduction to Dickens*. New York: Ballantine Books, 1992.

Bennett, Betty T., ed. *Lives of the Great Romantics III: Godwin, Wollstonecraff & Mary Shelley by Their Contemporaries*. Brookfield, Vt.: Pickering & Chatto, Publishers, 1999.

Bloom, Harold, ed. *Eighteenth-century British Fiction*. New York: Chelsea House, 1988.

British Writers and Their Work. Lincoln, Nb.: University of Nebraska Press, 1965.

The Cambridge Guide to English Literature. Compiled by Michael Stapleton. New York: Cambridge University Press, 1983.

Chesterton, G. K. *The Victorian Age in Literature*. Notre Dame: University of Notre Dame Press, 1963.

Copeland, Edward. *Women Writing about Money: Women's Fiction in England, 1790–1820*. New York: Cambridge University Press, 1995.

Doody, Margaret Anne. *A Natural Passion: A Study of the Novels of Samuel Richardson*. Oxford: Clarendon Press, 1974.

Feldman, Paula R., and Diana Scott-Kilvert, eds. *The Journals of Mary Shelley: 1814–1844*. New York: Oxford University Press, 1987.

Fergus, Jan. *Jane Austen: A Literary Life*. New York: St. Martin's Press, 1994.

Fido, Martin. *The World of Charles Dickens: The Life, Times and Work of the Great Victorian Novelist*. London: Carlton Books, 1997.

Gilbert, Pamela K. *Disease, Desire, and the Body in Victorian Women's Popular Novels*. New York: Cambridge University Press, 1997.

Goldfarb, Sheldon. *William Makepeace Thackeray: An Annotated Bibliography, 1976–1987*. New York: Garland, 1989.

Hahn, H. George, and Carl Behm III, eds. *The Eighteenth-Century British Novel and Its Background: An Annotated Bibliography and Guide to Topics*. Metuchen, N.J.: Scarecrow Press, 1985.

Hutchings, Bill, and Malcolm Hicks. *Literary Criticism: A Practical Guide for Students*. N.Y.: Routledge, Chapman and Hall, 1989.

Kincaid, James R. *The Novels of Anthony Trollope*. New York: Oxford University Press, 1977.

Kitzan, Laurence. *Victorian Writers and the Image of Empire: The Rose-Colored Vision*. Westport, Conn.: Greenwood Press, 2001.

Lenard, Mary. *Preaching Pity: Dickens, Gaskell, and Sentimentalism in Victorian Culture*. New York: Peter Lang, 1999.

Le Faye, Deirdre. *Jane Austen, the World of Her Novels*. New York: Abrams, 2002.

Miller, Lucasta. *The Brontë Myth*. New York: Knopf, 2003.

Mullen, Richard, and James Munson, eds. *The Penguin Companion to Trollope*. New York: Penguin, 1996.

Neville-Sington, Pamela. *Fanny Trollope: The Life and Adventures of a Clever Woman*. New York: Viking, 1998.

The Novel: A Guide to the Novel from Its Origins to the Present Day. Edited by Andrew Michael Roberts. London: Bloomsbury, 1993.

Rawlins, Jack P. *Thackeray's Novels: A Fiction that Is True*. Berkeley: University of California Press, 1974.

Sage, Victor, ed. *The Gothic Novel: A Casebook*. New York: Macmillan, 1990.

Schellinger, Paul, ed. *Encyclopedia of the Novel*. Chicago: Fitzroy Dearborn, 1998.

Selby, Keith. *How to Study a Charles Dickens Novel*. Basingstoke: Macmillan Education, 1989.

Shattock, Joanne. *The Oxford Guide to British Women Writers*. New York: Oxford University Press, 1993.

Skinner, Gillian. *Sensibility and Economics in the Novel, 1740–1800: The Price of a Tear*. New York: St. Martin's Press, 1999.

Smith, Grahame. *The Novel & Society: Defoe to George Eliot*. London: Batsford, 1984.

Stevenson, Lionel. *The English Novel: A Panorama*. Boston: Houghton Mifflin, 1960.

Sutherland, James. *Daniel Defoe: A Critical Study*. Cambridge, Mass.: Harvard University Press, 1971.

Trollope, Anthony. *Thackeray*. 1887. Reprint, New York: AMS Press, 1968.

Varney, Andrew. *Eighteenth-century Writers in their World: A Mighty Maze*. New York, N.Y: St. Martin's Press, 1999.

West, Richard. *Daniel Defoe: The Life and Strange, Surprising Adventures*. New York: Carroll & Graf Publishers, Inc., 1998.

Women, Writing, and the Public Sphere: 1700–1830. Edited by Elizabeth Eger, et al. New York: Cambridge University Press, 2001.

Wynne, Deborah. *The Sensation Novel and the Victorian Family Magazine*. New York: Palgrave, 2001.

Zlotnick, Susan. *Women, Writing, and the Industrial Revolution*. Baltimore, Md.: The Johns Hopkins University Press, 2001.

INDEX

O

Oates, Joyce Carol 15
O'Connell, Daniel 257
O'Connor, Feargus 68
Odd Women, The (Gissing) 159, **323–324**
O'Donohue, The (Lever) 260
Odyssey, The (Homer) 38, 346, 361, 362, 404–405
Of Population (Godwin) 160–161
Old Curiosity Shop, The (Dickens) 103, **324–325**
Old English Baron, The (Reeve) 372
Old Kensington (Ritchie) 377
Old Manor House, The (Smith) 416
Old Mortality (Scott) 186, **325–326**, 395
Old Saint Paul's (Ainsworth) 13
Oliphant, Margaret 257
Oliver Twist, or The Parish Boy's Progress (Dickens) **326–327**
    in *Bentley's Miscellany* 37, 326, 345
    Bulwer-Lytton's (Edward) influence on 52
    female character in 427
    as Newgate fiction 315, 327
    Nicholas Nickleby (Dickens) compared to 318
    The Old Curiosity Shop (Dickens) compared to 324
    popularity of 103
    romantic elements in 384
    as satire 327, 393
    as thesis novel 327, 427, 439
omniscient point of view 500
Once a Week (periodical) 77, **328**
"On Comedy and the Uses of the Comic Spirit" (Meredith) 292
One of Our Conquerors (Meredith) 266, 292, **328–329**
On the Art of Reading (Quiller-Couch) 363
On the Art of Writing (Quiller-Couch) 363
On the Origin of Species (Darwin) 93, 176, 184
ontological criticism. *See* formalism/formalist criticism
"On Women" (Juvenal) 313
Open Country (Hewlett) 195
Opie, Amelia **329–330**
    Adeline Mowbray, or The Mother and Daughter **5–6**, 330, 483
    in anti-slavery movement 6, 330
    Holcroft (Thomas) influencing 204
opium use 302, 303, 410
oral tradition xi
Ordeal of Richard Feveral, The (Meredith) 123, 291
Oroonoko, or The Royal Slave (Behn) xii, 26, 35, 36, 219, **330–331**
Ouida **331**
    Ainsworth (William Harrison) and 331
    Black (William) compared to 352

    Lawrence (George Alfred) influencing 172
    Moths **306–307**, 331
    and Sharp (William) 403
Our Mess. Jack Hinton, the Guardsman (Lever) 260
Our Mutual Friend (Dickens) **331–332**
"Our Village" (Mitford) 296
Outcast of the Islands, An (Conrad) 82
Outcry, The (James) 231
Owen, Robert 50, 51, 99
Owenson, Sydney, Lady Morgan **332–333**
    Maturin (Charles Robert) influenced by 481
    Trollope (Anthony) influenced by 449
    The Wild Irish Girl 332, **481**
Oxford Book of English Verse (Quiller-Couch) 363
Oxford Movement **333–334**
    in *Robert Elsmere* (Ward) 377
    Shorthouse (Joseph Henry) in 409
    Yonge (Charlotte M.) in 334, 492, 493

P

Pagan Poems (Moore) 303
Paine, Thomas 204, 483
Painters of Japan, The (Morrison) 305
Pair of Blue Eyes, A (Hardy) 240
Palliser series (A. Trollope) 60–61, 116, 135, 341, 343, 350, 351, 450
Pall Mall, The (periodical) 266
Paltock, Robert **335**
    The Life and Adventures of Peter Wilkins **261–262**, 335, 395
Pamela, or Virtue Rewarded (Richardson) **335–337**
    Clarissa (Richardson) compared to 74
    as epistolary novel xii, 74, 129, 335, 375
    The History of Sir Charles Grandison (Richardson) compared to 200
    parody of 147, 186–187, 336, 337, 376, 392, 400
    Redgauntlet (Scott) compared to 371
    as sentimental fiction 400, 401
    Sheridan (Frances) influenced by 289
Pankhurst, Emmeline 185
Parent's Assistant, The (Edgeworth) 121
Paris Sketch Book, The (Thackeray) 438
Parliament 75–76
parody **337**. *See also* burlesque; satire
    of Bulwer-Lytton (Edward) by Thackeray (William Makepeace) 357

    of Disraeli (Benjamin) by Thackeray (William Makepeace) 108, 357, 438
    of Fielding (Henry) by Smollett (Tobias) 213
    of Gore (Catherine Grace) by Thackeray (William Makepeace) 162, 308, 438
    of Gothic fiction, by Austen (Jane) 29, 163, 321, 400
    Handy Andy: A Tale of Irish Life (Lover) 180
    of James (George) by Thackeray (William Makepeace) 229
    of Lever (Charles) by Thackeray (William Makepeace) 260, 357, 438
    of *The London Magazine* 265
    Nightmare Abbey (Peacock) 320, 400
    Pride and Prejudice (Austen) 350
    Punch's Prize Novelists (Thackeray) 357
    of Richardson (Samuel) by Fielding (Henry) xii, 75, 147, 187, 336, 337, 376, 392, 400
    of Richardson (Samuel) by Haywood (Eliza) 186–187
    Sense and Sensibility (Austen) 399, 400
    of sentimental fiction, by Austen (Jane) 28, 399, 400
    A Sentimental Journey (Sterne) 401, 417
    of silver-fork fiction 412
    of Smollett (Tobias) by Sterne (Laurence) 402, 417
"Passage in the Secret History of an Irish Countess, A" (Le Fanu) 457
Passionate Pilgrim and Other Tales, A (James) 230
Pater, Walter 230, 480
Paterson, Robert 326
Pathways of the Gods (Caird) 58
Patmore, Coventry 146
Patronage (Edgeworth) 121–122
Paul Clifford (Bulwer-Lytton) 52, 315
Paul Ferroll (Clive) **337–338**
Peacock, Thomas Love **338–339**
    character based on 123, 339
    Headlong Hall **187–188**, 288, 320, 338
    Melincourt, or Sir Oran Haut-ton **288–289**, 320, 338
    Meredith (George) and 291
    The Misfortunes of Elphin **295–296**, 339
    Nightmare Abbey **320–321**, 338
    Smollett (Tobias) compared to 188
    Surtees (R. S.) compared to 429
Pearson's Magazine 469
Peel, Robert 85, 107, 108
Peg Woffington (Reade) 368

Pelham, or The Adventures of a Gentleman (Bulwer-Lytton) 51, **339–340**
People's Charter to Parliament (1837) 68
People's Friend, The (periodical) 418
Percy, Bishop 295
Peregrine Pickle (Smollett) 33, 367
Persian life 8–10, 304
Personal History, Experience and Observations of David Copperfield the Younger, of Blunderstone Rookery, Which He Never Meant to Be Published on Any Account (Dickens). *See* David Copperfield
Persuasion (Austen) 29, **340–341**
Peter Pan (Barrie) 243
Peter Simple (Marryat) 280
Phantastes (MacDonald) 273
Phillips, Walter 436
Phineas Finn: The Irish Member (A. Trollope) 191, **341–343**, 351, 450
Phineas Redux (A. Trollope) 342, **343–344**, 351, 450
picaresque 203, **344**
    The Adventures of Hajji Baba of Ispahan (Morier) 8, 304, 344
    Anastasius, or Memoirs of a Greek (T. Hope) 23
    The Cloister and the Hearth (Reade) 77
    Humphry Clinker, The Expedition of (Smollett) 213
    origin of word 344
    Roderick Random (Smollett) 382, 383
    Vanity Fair: A Novel Without a Hero (Thackeray) 462
Pickwick Papers, The (Dickens) 103, **345**
Picture of Dorian Gray, The (Wilde) 167, 209, **345–346**, 480
Pictures from Italy (Dickens) 104
Pilgrim's Progress, The: From This World to That Which Is to Come (Bunyan) xii, 17, 70, 105, **346–347**, 461
Pillars of the House, or Under Wode Under Rode (Yonge) 334
plague 239–240
Plain Tales from the Hills (Kipling) 251
Plays of William Shakespeare, The (Johnson) 238
plot 500
Pocket Magazine 12
Poe, Edgar Allan 100, 260, 424, 425
Poems (Browning) 48
Poems (Meredith) 291
Poems Before Congress (Browning) 49
point of view
    definition of 500
    first-person 499–500
    limited 500
    omniscient 500
    third-person 500, 501